Orkney
Islands

155

Shetland
Islands

155

Outer
Hebrides

Stornoway

154

Thurso
148 149 150 151 Wick

Ullapool
144 145 146 147

Banff
Portree 136 137 138 139 140 141 Peterhead
Inverness 142 143

Aberdeen
128 129 130 131 132 133 134 135

Coll and
Tiree
Fort
William Pitlochry
120 121 122 123 124 125 126 127
Oban Perth Dundee

Edinburgh
112 113 114 115 116 117 118 119
Largs Glasgow Berwick

Peebles
104 105 106 107 108 109 110 111
Campbeltown Ayr

Dumfries
100 101 102 103
Newcastle
98 99 upon Tyne
96 97
Stranraer

Londonderry 92 93 94 95 Middlesbrough
156 157 Workington
Belfast Scarborough
Kendal 86 87 88 89 90 91
Isle of Lancaster
Man 153
Douglas York
Blackpool Hull
80 81 82 Leeds 84 85
83
Liverpool Grimsby
78
Dublin Manchester Sheffield
79 74 75 76 77
68 69 70 71 Lincoln
Caernarfon Chester
Stoke
72 73
Nottingham
Limerick 56 57 62 63 King's Lynn 66 67
Shrewsbury 64 65 Norwich
58 59 Leicester Great
Peterborough Yarmouth
158 159 42 Aberystwyth 60 61
Waterford 43 Birmingham 50 51
Coventry
44 45 46 47 Northampton 52 53 54 55
Cork Worcester 48 49 Cambridge
Hereford Felixstowe
38 39
Fishguard Gloucester Chelmsford
30 31 Carmarthen Oxford 40 41
Pembroke Swansea 34 35 36 37 LONDON
32 33 Reading 26 27
Cardiff Bristol Maidstone
24 25 Guildford 28 29
Barnstaple 20 21 22 23 14 15 16 17 Dover
18 19 Salisbury Brighton Folkestone
Taunton Southampton Newhaven
10 11 12 13
8 Exeter 9 Weymouth Bournemouth
4 5 6 7
2 Truro 3 Plymouth

Scilly
Isles 2

The Channel
Islands 152

AA GREAT BRITAIN ROAD ATLAS 1993

1 : 200,000
Approximately 3 miles to 1 inch

7th edition September 1992
6th edition September 1991
5th edition September 1990
4th edition September 1989
3rd edition October 1988
2nd edition October 1987
Reprinted April 1988
1st edition October 1986

© The Automobile Association 1992

Produced by the Publishing Division of The Automobile Association

Mapping produced by the Cartographic Department of The Automobile
Association. This atlas has been compiled and produced from the Automaps
database utilising electronic and computer technology.

Published by The Automobile Association, Fanum House, Basingstoke,
Hampshire RG21 2EA
ISBN 0 7495 0605 9, ISBN 0 7495 0608 3

Printed by L.E.G.O. SpA, Vicenza, Italy.

The contents of this atlas are believed correct at the time of printing, although
the publishers cannot accept any responsibility for errors or omissions, or for
changes in the details given. They would welcome information to help keep this
atlas up to date; please write to the Cartographic Editor, Publishing Division,
The Automobile Association, Fanum House, Basingstoke, Hampshire RG21 2EA.

A CIP catalogue record for this book is available from the British Library.

Information on National Parks provided by the Countryside Commission for England and Wales.

*Information on National Scenic Areas - Scotland provided by the Countryside Commission for
Scotland.*

Information on Forest Parks provided by the Forestry Commission.

The RSPB sites shown are a selection chosen by the Royal Society for the Protection of Birds.

Picnic sites are those inspected by the AA and are located on or near A and B roads.

*National Trust properties shown are those open to the public as indicated in the handbooks of
the National Trusts of England, Wales and Northern Ireland, and Scotland.*

•Contents

•Using this atlas

ROUTE PLANNING

Pages VIII – XVII contain specially designed route-planning maps. These clearly show the basic road network – motorways, primary routes and most A-roads – and enable you to plan your long-distance journey both quickly and easily.

A road   Motorway

Primary routes

THE ATLAS

Clear and easy-to-read mapping helps you plan more detailed journeys, and provides a whole host of information for the motorist. All motorways, primary routes, A-roads, B-roads and unclassified roads are shown. The atlas also identifies those roads outside urban areas which are under construction. Additional features include rivers, lakes and reservoirs, railway-lines, places to visit, picnic sites and tourist information centres. To assist you in estimating the length of your journey distances (in miles) are shown between blue marker symbols.

Unclassified road   Primary destination   B road   Railway   Motorways and junctions   Road under construction

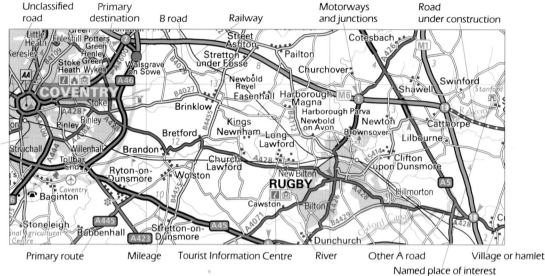

Urban area

Primary route   Mileage   Tourist Information Centre   River   Other A road   Village or hamlet   Named place of interest

FERRY AND RAIL ROUTES

Coastal stretches of mapping provide basic offshore information including ferry routes within Great Britain and to the Continent, to assist you with planning an overseas journey. Throughout the atlas, railway lines, stations and level crossings are marked in order to assist with general navigation or with rail travel requirements.

AA Port Shop

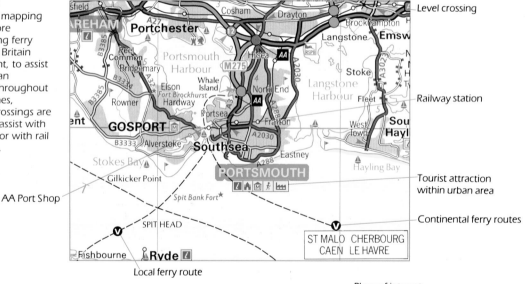

Level crossing

Railway station

Tourist attraction within urban area

Continental ferry routes

Local ferry route

TOURISM AND LEISURE

Red pictorial symbols and red type highlight numerous places of interest, catering for every taste. Red symbols within yellow boxes show tourist attractions within towns. These can be used to plan days out, or to choose where to visit on holiday. In order to avoid disappointment, you should always remember to check opening times before you set out.

Tourist Information Centre

Heritage coast   Place of interest located and named

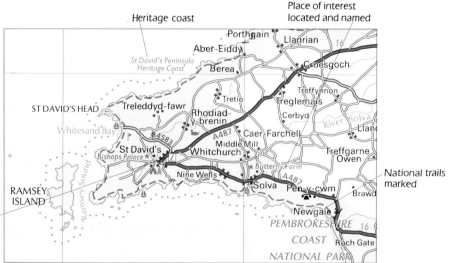

National trails marked

IV

•Using this atlas

PORTS AND AIRPORTS

Maps show the major Channel and east coast ports, as well as detailed maps of the main airports in Britain, giving approach roads and car-parking facilities. In addition there is information about garages, hotels and public transport services. The map on page 182 locates all major British ports and airports.

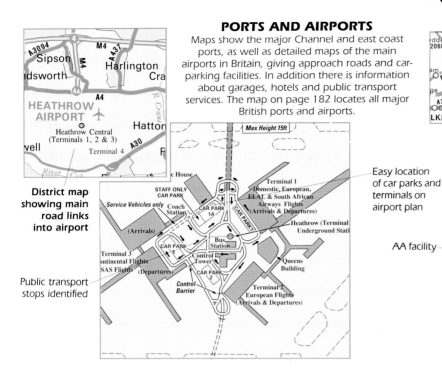

District map showing main road links into airport

Public transport stops identified

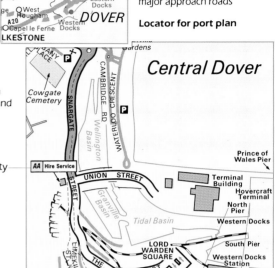

District map showing main road links

Road number for major approach roads

Locator for port plan

Easy location of car parks and terminals on airport plan

AA facility

Local approach road named

Ship piers, ferry and hovercraft terminals and railway station clearly shown

TOWN PLANS

Up-to-date, fully indexed town plans show AA recommended roads and other practical information such as one way streets, car parks and restricted roads, making navigation much easier. Area plans show major road networks into and out of the region.

Area map showing main road links and neighbouring towns

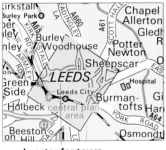

Locator for town plan

Pedestrian areas located

Churches located

Town parking facilities

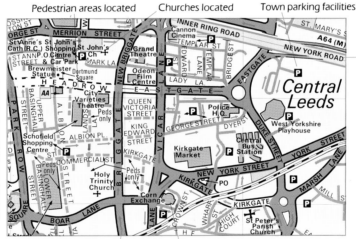

One way streets shown

Major buildings and places of interest highlighted and named

AA recommended throughroutes clearly identified

Street index with every plan

Leeds

Aire Street	C3
Albion Place	D4
Albion Street	D3-D4-D5
Archery Road	C7-C8
Argyle Road	F5
Back Hyde Terr	A6
Back Row	C1
Barrack Road	E8-F8
Barrack Street	E8
Bath Road	B1-B2
Bedford Street	C4

LONDON

Easy-to-read, fully indexed street maps of Inner London provide a simple guide to finding your way around the city.

Underground railway stations located and named

Major places of tourist interest shown

Open spaces and parks highlighted

Garage parking identified

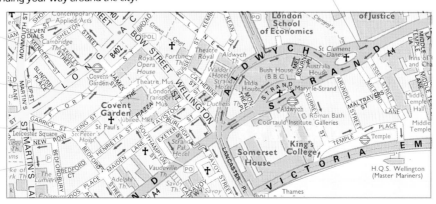

One way systems clearly shown

AA recommended routes for easier navigation

Alphabetical street index

Ludgate Broadway EC4	165	D2
Pilgrim Street		
Ludgate Circus EC4	165	D2
Luke Street EC2	165	F3
Lukin Street E1	171	D3
Lumley Street W1	163	E1
Brown Hart Garden		
Lupus Street SW1	167	F1
Luton Street NW8	162	C3
Luxborough Street W1	163	E3

•Journey planning

Are you fit to drive? Food, tiredness, drink and drugs all affect your driving.

Fit to drive
Many accidents are caused by one or more of the drivers involved being unfit to drive when the accident occurred. The most obvious reason for such accidents is alcohol; even the smallest quantity can affect driving performance. The only safe advice is; if you drive, don't drink — and if you drink, don't drive. However, alcohol is just one of a number of factors that can make someone unfit to drive.

Tiredness
People vary in their susceptibility to tiredness, but the following are sensible guidelines which you should aim to keep: for every three hours on the road, you should rest for 20 minutes; always share the driving if at all possible; limit yourself to no more than eight hours behind the wheel in any one day; and try to avoid driving at any time when you are normally asleep or resting. Additionally, you should avoid driving after strenuous exercise, a large meal and, of course, after consuming alcohol.

Other factors which can contribute to tiredness are temperature inside the car and medication; a warm, stuffy atmosphere — and some drugs, including those bought *without* a prescription— can induce drowsiness. If you are on such medication, check with your medical practitioner whether or not you should be driving at all. One final point; making sure that you are not on the road during peak hours keeps delays to a minimum, reduces frustration and minimises journey time.

Always plan your route carefully — doing so will save time in the long run.

How to get there
Special route-planning maps enable you easily to plan a basic route, while referring to the main pages of the atlas allows you to arrange a more detailed route. It is probably a good idea to make a note of the road numbers, towns and other general directions, since this should mean you will not need to stop and consult the atlas on the journey.

Road classification
London is the hub for the spokes of roads numbered A1 to A6, Edinburgh the hub for the A7, A8 and A9. Beginning with the A1, running north from London, the roads radiate clockwise from the capital; the A2 runs roughly east, the A3 south-west, and so forth. This system has made the numbering of other roads very simple; generally, the lower the subsequent number, the closer the road's starting point to London (or Edinburgh). Motorways roughly approximate to this plan as well.

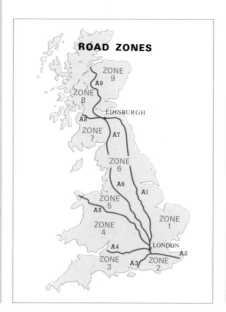

ROAD ZONES

Call AA Roadwatch or listen to local radio to avoid delays on your journey.

Delays and hold-ups
Motorways are — despite ever increasing traffic — the quickest means of getting from A to B. Nevertheless, a hold-up on a motorway can easily delay you for hours. There are several ways of gleaning information on the stretches of motorway to avoid; by phone, radio and newspaper.

AA Roadwatch
If you need as much information as possible about your journey before you set out, you can call AA Roadwatch. Updated every 15 minutes, this service provides details of major roadworks and weather conditions for the whole country, and can be used as part of your basic journey-planning. (See route-planning pages for more information.) AA Roadwatch also supplies information on current roadworks to many daily newspapers.

Radio
Frequent radio bulletins are issued by both the BBC and by independent local radio stations on road and weather conditions, likely hold-ups, etc — and these can be of great assistance. By tuning into the local radio stations as you pass through the area, you can avoid delays and prepare to make changes to your route. However, local radio does not yet cover the entire country; consult the regional route-planning pages for radio frequencies. (Some local radio stations also offer flight information from and to nearby airports.)

Carry out regular checks to make sure that you and your car arrive safely.

Daily Checks

Before you start every journey, you should always ensure that:

✓ you check the dashboard warning lights both before and after starting the engine

✓ there are no unusual noises once the engine is running

✓ all the lights are both clean and working

✓ the windscreen and all other windows are clean

✓ you have sufficient petrol for your journey

Weekly checks

Every week — or before you set out on a long journey — you should also ensure that:

✓ the engine oil level is correct, looking for obvious signs of leakage

✓ the coolant level is correct, checking the anti-freeze before the onset of winter

✓ the battery connections and terminals are clean and free from corrosion

✓ the brake (and clutch, if hydraulic) fluid is correct

✓ the tyres (including the spare) are properly inflated and not damaged

✓ the tyres are changed if the tread falls below 2mm

✓ the fan belt is not worn or damaged and that the tension is correct

✓ the windscreen wipers are clean and that the screen wash reservoir is topped up with a mixture of water, non-smear and freezing inhibitor additive

Where exactly are you going? You can find on the map any place listed in the index of this atlas by using the National Grid, explained in simple terms below...

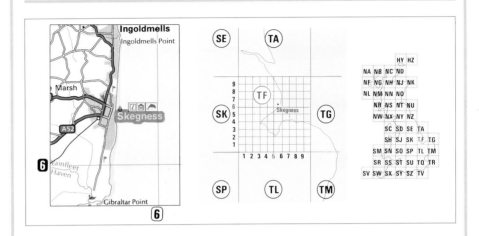

Finding your place

One of the unique features of AA mapping is the use of the National Grid system.

It covers Britain with an imaginary network of squares, using blue horizontal lines called northings and vertical lines called eastings.

On the atlas pages these lines are numbered along the bottom and the left hand side.

The Index

Each entry in the index is followed by a page number, two letters denoting an area on the map and a 4-figure grid reference. You will not need to use the two letters for simple navigation, but they come in useful if you want to use your map in relation to the rest of the country and other map series.

Quick reference

For quick reference, the four figures of the grid reference in the index are arranged so that the 1st and 3rd are in bolder type than the 2nd and 4th.

The 1st figure shows which number along the bottom to locate, and the 3rd figure, which number up the left hand side. These will indicate the square in which you will find the place name.

Pinpoint accuracy

However to pinpoint a place more accurately, you use the 2nd and 4th numbers also. The 2nd will tell you how many imaginary tenths along the bottom line to go from the first number, and the 4th will tell you many tenths up the line to go from the 3rd number.

Where these two lines intersect, you will locate your place. Eg Skegness 77TF5663. Skegness is located on page 77, within grid square 56 in National Grid square TF. Its exact location is 5663.

Remember

If you find you get the numbers confused, it might help if you can imagine entering a house, walking in the door and along a corridor first, and then going up the stairs, then you will remember how to get them in the correct order.

•The South West and South Wales

The maps and charts at the beginning of this atlas are designed to help you plan your journey with ease and economy.

The following Route Planning Maps indicate the page grids and page numbers for easy reference to the atlas. In addition, you will find regional radio frequencies on the relevant pages and AA Roadwatch numbers on the South, East Anglia and East Midlands pages.

Finding it

Look for the place name you want in the index section at the back of the atlas. The name is followed by a page number and a National Grid reference. Turn to the atlas page indicated and use the National Grid reference to pinpoint the place.

The National Grid and how to use are explained on page VII.

Getting there

Having found your destination in the main atlas, find the nearest large town. This will be shown on the following Route Planning Maps, pages VIII-XVII. These maps show the principal routes throughout Britain and a basic route can be planned from them. A special feature of these maps is that a key to the atlas pages is superimposed — making place location much easier. A more detailed route can then be worked out from the main atlas. Taking a note of road numbers and directions reduces the need to stop and consult the atlas on the way

How far?

The length of the journey is a fundamental consideration when a journey is being planned. The mileage chart on the inside back cover gives the distance between main towns and can be used to make a rough calculation of the total journey length. You should then be able to estimate the time needed for the journey

Which road?

Motorways are quicker and more economical than other routes because you can maintain a consistent speed and avoid traffic delays.

Primary routes should be considered where you cannot use motorways. These are marked in green on the maps and sign-posted in green on the roads. The shortest route is not always the quickest, and primary routes tend to take you round towns rather than through their centres, thus avoiding delays caused by traffic lights, one-way systems etc.

Traffic Information

Frequent bulletins on road conditions, local hold ups, the weather etc are issued both by national and local radio stations, and also the AA Roadwatch telephone service, these can be of great assistance to the driver.

Local and regional radio frequencies and AA Roadwatch telephone numbers are shown on the pages of the Route Planning Maps. The names of radio stations are in **bold type** and are followed by the FM frequency (MHz), then the MW frequency (KHz) eg **RADIO SCOTLAND** 92.5-94.7 810. In some cases stations do not broadcast on medium wave (MW).

Isles of Scilly

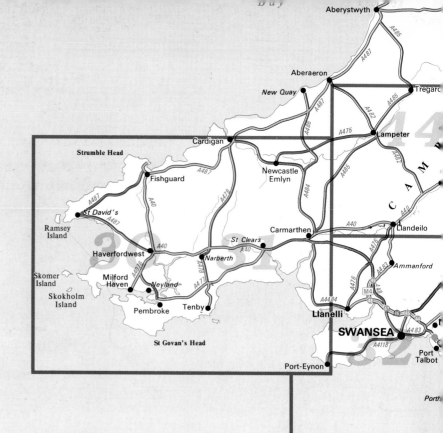

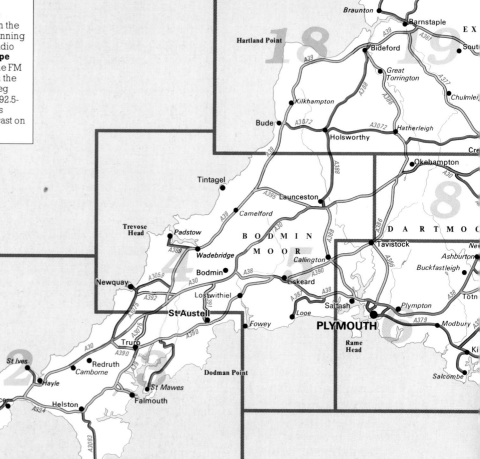

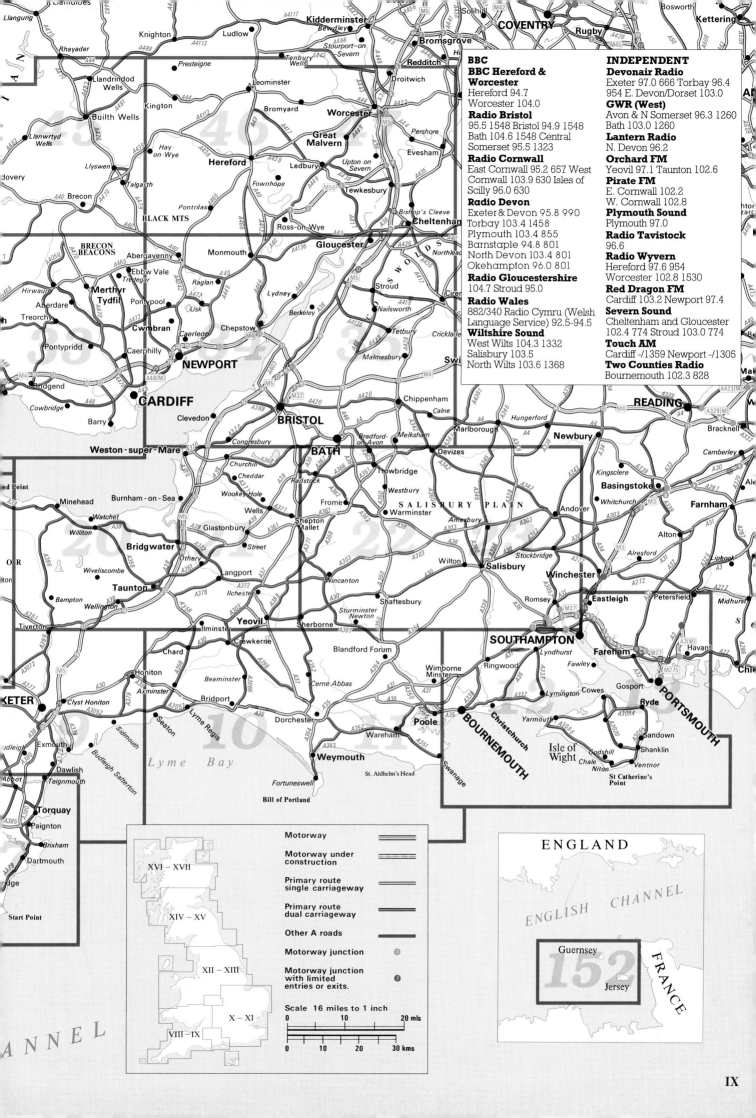

BBC

**BBC Hereford &
Worcester**
Hereford 94.7
Worcester 104.0
Radio Bristol
95.5 1548 Bristol 94.9 1548
Bath 104.6 1548 Central
Somerset 95.5 1323
Radio Cornwall
East Cornwall 95.2 657 West
Cornwall 103.9 630 Isles of
Scilly 96.0 630
Radio Devon
Exeter & Devon 95.8 990
Torbay 103.4 1458
Plymouth 103.4 855
Barnstaple 94.8 801
North Devon 103.4 801
Okehampton 96.0 801
Radio Gloucestershire
104.7 Stroud 95.0
Radio Wales
882/340 Radio Cymru (Welsh
Language Service) 92.5–94.5
Wiltshire Sound
West Wilts 104.3 1332
Salisbury 103.5
North Wilts 103.6 1368

INDEPENDENT

Devonair Radio
Exeter 97.0 666 Torbay 96.4
954 E. Devon/Dorset 103.0
GWR (West)
Avon & N Somerset 96.3 1260
Bath 103.0 1260
Lantern Radio
N. Devon 96.2
Orchard FM
Yeovil 97.1 Taunton 102.6
Pirate FM
E. Cornwall 102.2
W. Cornwall 102.8
Plymouth Sound
Plymouth 97.0
Radio Tavistock
96.6
Radio Wyvern
Hereford 97.6 954
Worcester 102.8 1530
Red Dragon FM
Cardiff 103.2 Newport 97.4
Severn Sound
Cheltenham and Gloucester
102.4 774 Stroud 103.0 774
Touch AM
Cardiff -/1359 Newport -/1305
Two Counties Radio
Bournemouth 102.3 828

Motorway	
Motorway under construction	
Primary route single carriageway	
Primary route dual carriageway	
Other A roads	
Motorway junction	
Motorway junction with limited entries or exits.	

Scale 16 miles to 1 inch

0   10   20 mls

0   10   20   30 kms

ENGLAND

ENGLISH CHANNEL

152

Guernsey

Jersey

FRANCE

IX

The South, East Anglia and East Midlands

BBC

BBC CWR (Coventry & Warwick)
Coventry 94.8 Warwickshire 103.7

BBC Essex
103.5 765 NE Essex 103.5 729 SE Essex 95.3 1530

Greater London Radio
94.9 1458

Radio Bedfordshire
95.5 630 Bedford 95.5 1161 Luton & Dunstable 103.8 630 Bletchley 104.5 630

Radio Berkshire
104.1 Henley 94.6 Reading 104.6 Windsor 95.4

Radio Cambridgeshire
96.0 1026 Peterborough & W Cambs 95.7 1449

Radio Derby
104.5 1116 Derby 94.2 1116 Bakewell & Matlock 95.3

Radio Kent
96.7 1035 Tunbridge Wells 96.7 1602 East Kent 104.2 774

Radio Leicester
104.9 837

Radio Norfolk
East Norfolk 95.1 855 West Norfolk 104.4 873

Radio Northampton
104.2 Corby 103.6

Radio Nottingham
103.8 Central Notts. 95.5

Radio Oxford
95.2

Radio Solent
96.1 999 Bournemouth 96.1 1359

Radio Suffolk
Bury St Edmunds 104.6 Ipswich 103.9 Lowestoft 95.5

Radio Surrey
104.6

Radio Sussex
Brighton & Worthing 95.3 1485 East Sussex & part of West Sussex 104.5 1161 Crawley & Horsham 95.1 1368 Newhaven 95.0 1485 Reigate 104.0 1368

INDEPENDENT

BRMB FM
Birmingham 96.4

Breeze AM
Chelmsford -/1359, Southend -/1431

Capital Radio
95.8 1548

Chiltern Radio
Bedford 96.9 792 Luton 97.6 828

CN FM
Cambridge & Newmarket 103.0

County Sound AM
Surrey & NE Hants -/1476 Crawley & W. Sussex -/1521

Essex Radio
Chelmsford 102.6 Southend 96.3

Fox FM
Oxford 102.6 Banbury 97.4

Gem AM
Leicester -/1260 Nottingham -/999 Derby -/945

GWR (East)
Swindon 97.2 West Wilts 102.2 Marlborough 96.5

Hereward Radio
Peterborough 102.7 133.2

Horizon Radio
Milton Keynes 103.3

Invicta FM
Kent 103.1 1242 Canterbury 102.8 603 Thanet 95.9 603 Dover/Folkestone 97.0 603 Ashford 96.1 603

Kings Lynn FM
96.7

LBC
London 97.3

Leicester Sound
Leicester 103.2

London Talkback Radio
-/1152

Melody Radio
London 104.9

Mellow AM
NE Essex -/1557

Mercia FM
Coventry 97.0 Leamington Spa 102.9

Northants Radio
96.6 1557

Ocean Sound
Southampton 103.2 Winchester 96.7 Portsmouth, Chichester 97.5

Radio 210
Thames Valley 97.0 1431 Basingstoke, Andover 102.9 1431

Radio Broadland
Gt Yarmouth & Norwich 102.4 1152

Radio Mercury
Crawley/Reigate 102.7 Horsham 97.5 Guildford 96.4

Radio Orwell
Ipswich 97.1 1170

Saxon Radio
Bury St. Edmunds 96.4 1251

South Coast Radio
Portsmouth, Chichester -/1170 Southampton -/1557 Brighton -/1323

Southern Sound
Brighton 103.5 Eastbourne 102 Hastings 97.5 Newhaven 96.9

Spire FM
Salisbury 102

Xtra AM
Birmingham -/1152 Coventry -/1359

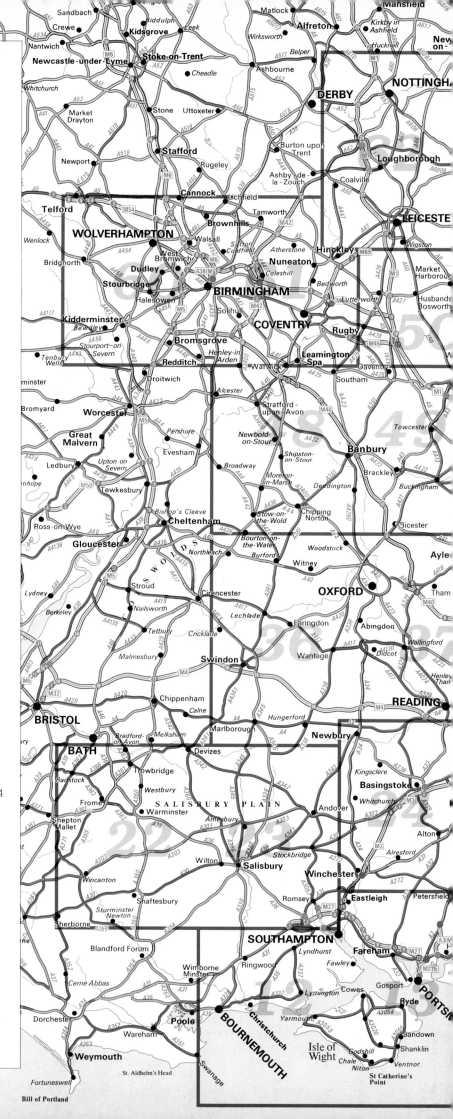

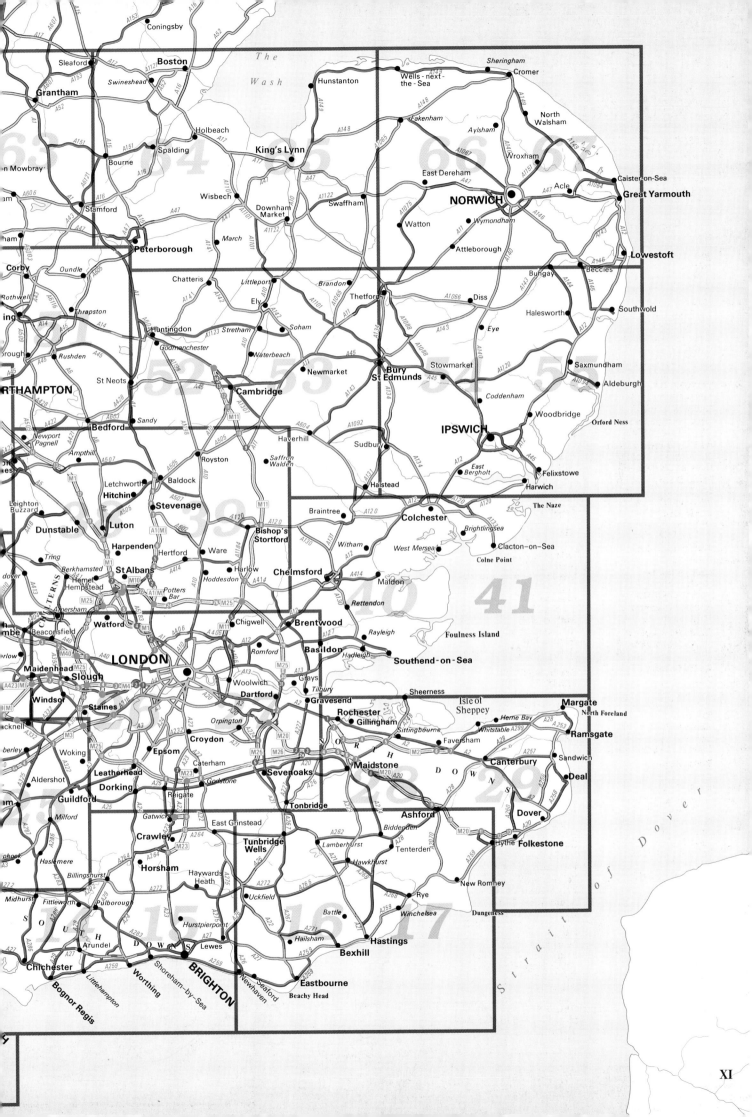

XI

North Wales, West Midlands and the North

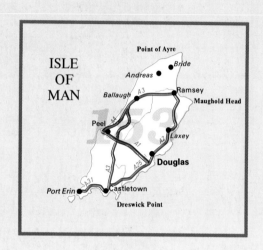

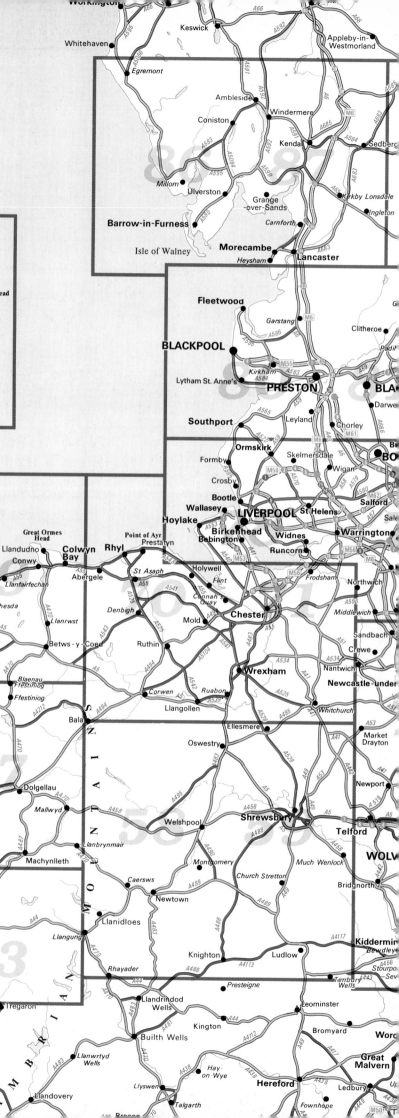

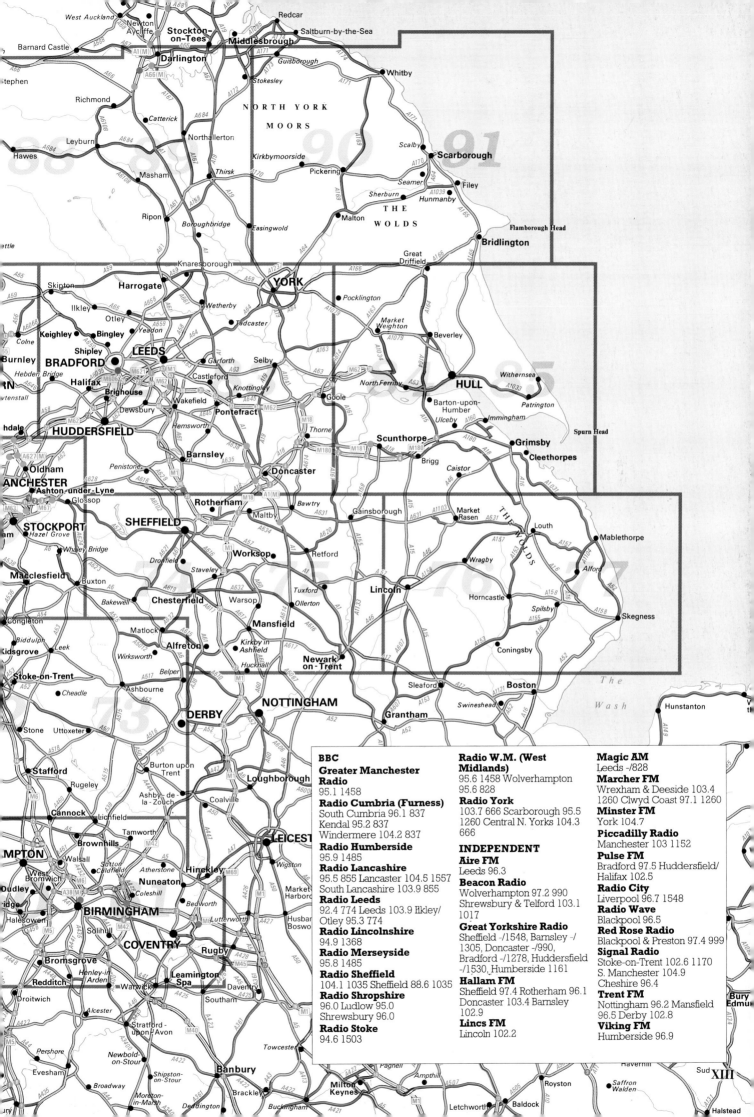

BBC

Greater Manchester Radio
95.1 1458

Radio Cumbria (Furness)
South Cumbria 96.1 837
Kendal 95.2 837
Windermere 104.2 837

Radio Humberside
95.9 1485

Radio Lancashire
95.5 855 Lancaster 104.5 1557
South Lancashire 103.9 855

Radio Leeds
92.4 774 Leeds 103.9 Ilkley/
Otley 95.3 774

Radio Lincolnshire
94.9 1368

Radio Merseyside
95.8 1485

Radio Sheffield
104.1 1035 Sheffield 88.6 1035

Radio Shropshire
96.0 Ludlow 95.0
Shrewsbury 96.0

Radio Stoke
94.6 1503

Radio W.M. (West Midlands)
95.6 1458 Wolverhampton
95.6 828

Radio York
103.7 666 Scarborough 95.5
1260 Central N. Yorks 104.3
666

INDEPENDENT

Aire FM
Leeds 96.3

Beacon Radio
Wolverhampton 97.2 990
Shrewsbury & Telford 103.1
1017

Great Yorkshire Radio
Sheffield -/1548, Barnsley -/
1305, Doncaster -/990,
Bradford -/1278, Huddersfield
-/1530, Humberside 1161

Hallam FM
Sheffield 97.4 Rotherham 96.1
Doncaster 103.4 Barnsley
102.9

Lincs FM
Lincoln 102.2

Magic AM
Leeds -/828

Marcher FM
Wrexham & Deeside 103.4
1260 Clwyd Coast 97.1 1260

Minster FM
York 104.7

Piccadilly Radio
Manchester 103 1152

Pulse FM
Bradford 97.5 Huddersfield/
Halifax 102.5

Radio City
Liverpool 96.7 1548

Radio Wave
Blackpool 96.5

Red Rose Radio
Blackpool & Preston 97.4 999

Signal Radio
Stoke-on-Trent 102.6 1170
S. Manchester 104.9
Cheshire 96.4

Trent FM
Nottingham 96.2 Mansfield
96.5 Derby 102.8

Viking FM
Humberside 96.9

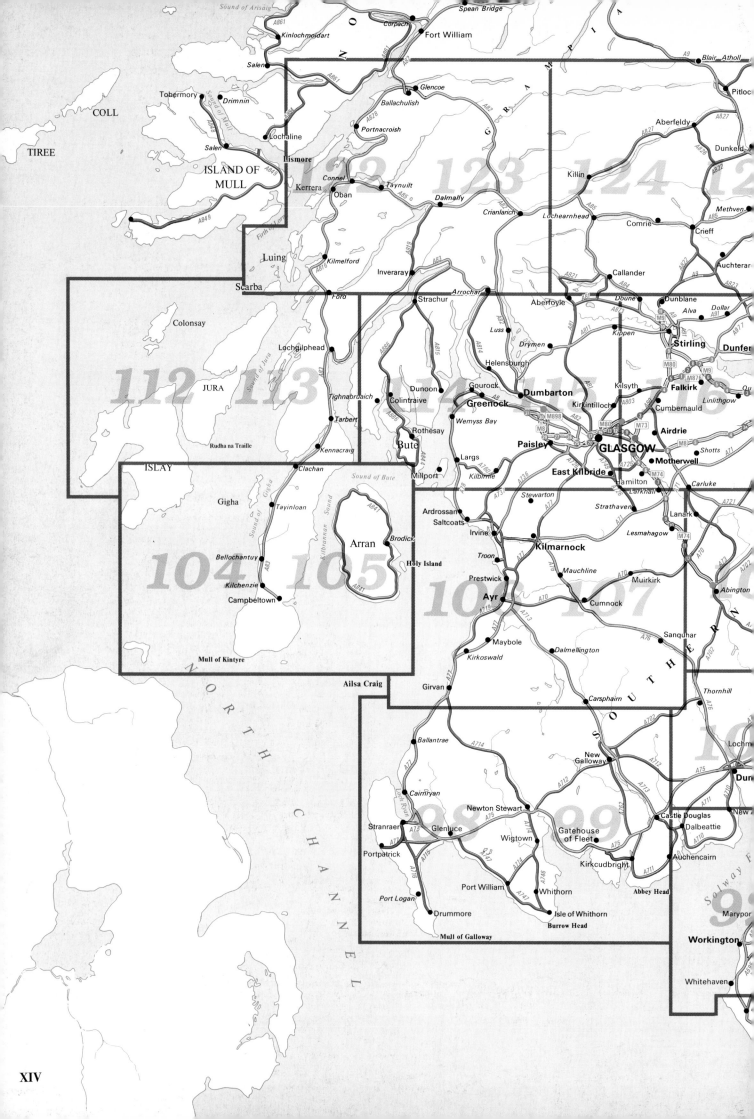

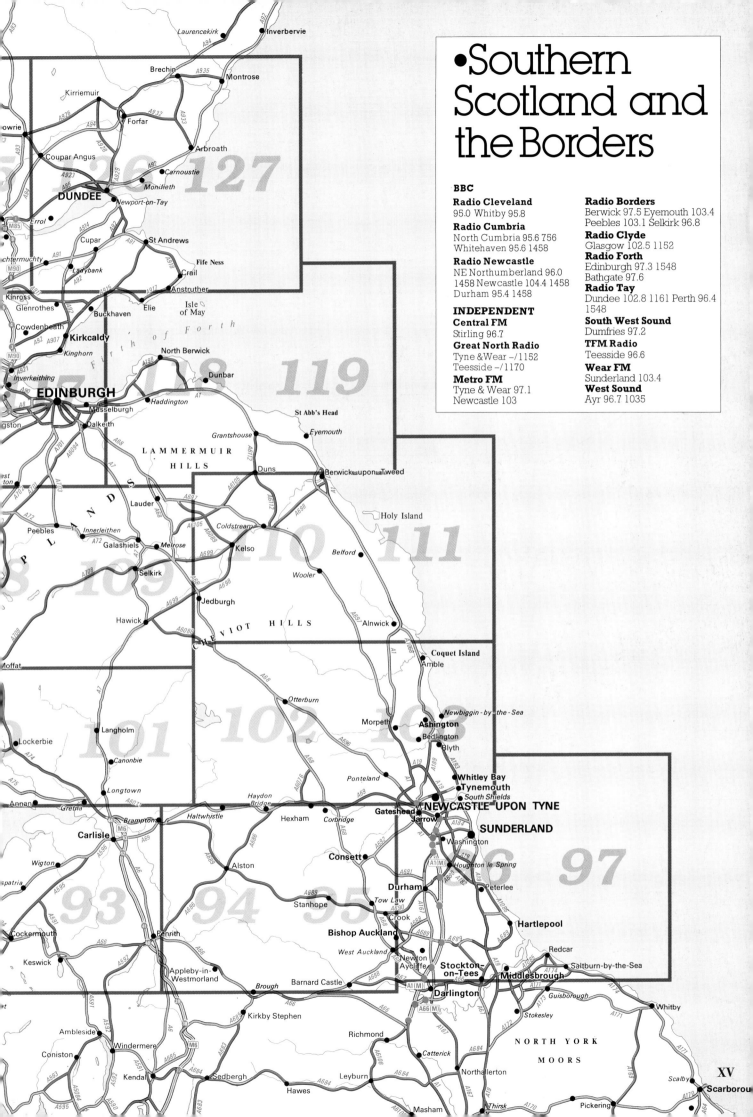

•Southern Scotland and the Borders

BBC

Radio Cleveland
95.0 Whitby 95.8

Radio Cumbria
North Cumbria 95.6 756
Whitehaven 95.6 1458

Radio Newcastle
NE Northumberland 96.0
1458 Newcastle 104.4 1458
Durham 95.4 1458

INDEPENDENT
Central FM
Stirling 96.7
Great North Radio
Tyne &Wear –/1152
Teesside –/1170
Metro FM
Tyne & Wear 97.1
Newcastle 103

Radio Borders
Berwick 97.5 Eyemouth 103.4
Peebles 103.1 Selkirk 96.8
Radio Clyde
Glasgow 102.5 1152
Radio Forth
Edinburgh 97.3 1548
Bathgate 97.6
Radio Tay
Dundee 102.8 1161 Perth 96.4
1548
South West Sound
Dumfries 97.2
TFM Radio
Teesside 96.6
Wear FM
Sunderland 103.4
West Sound
Ayr 96.7 1035

XV

•Northern Scotland

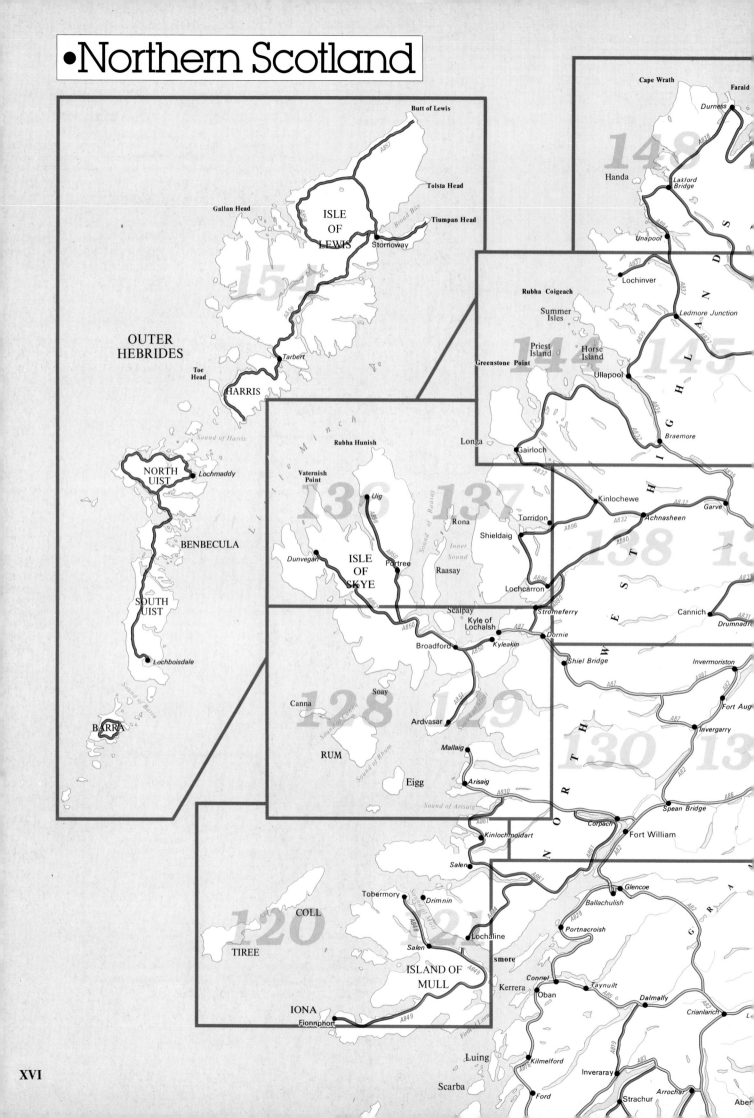

Cape Wrath
Faraid
Durness
148
Handa
Laxford Bridge
Unapool
Rubha Coigeach
Lochinver
A837
Ledmore Junction
Summer Isles
145
Priest Island
Horse Island
144
Greenstone Point
Ullapool
HIGHLAND
Butt of Lewis
A857
ISLE OF LEWIS
Tolsta Head
Gallan Head
A858
Broad Bay
Tiumpan Head
Stornoway
154
Longa
Braemore
A832
OUTER HEBRIDES
Gairloch
A832
Garve
Tarbert
Kinlochewe
A832
Toe Head
HARRIS
137
Torridon
Achnasheen
A896
A890
Rona
Shieldaig
128
Sound of Harris
136
Rubha Hunish
WEST
NORTH UIST
Lochmaddy
Vaternish Point
Uig
A866
Sound of Raasay
Lochcarron
A896
Cannich
A831
Stromeferry
Drumnadr
Dunvegan
ISLE OF SKYE
Portree
A850
Raasay
Inner Sound
BENBECULA
Scalpay
A87
Dornie
Little Minch
A850
Kyle of Lochalsh
Invermoriston
A863
Shiel Bridge
A87
SOUTH UIST
Lochboisdale
128
Soay
Broadford
A850
Kyleakin
A87
A867
Fort Aug
Canna
Ardvasar
A851
129
Invergarry
Sound of Barra
Sound of Canna
RUM
Mallaig
130
13
BARRA
Eigg
Arisaig
A86
Sound of Rhum
A830
Spean Bridge
Sound of Arisaig
NORTH
A82
Corpach
Fort William
A861
Kinlochmoidart
N
A861
Salen
GRA
Glencoe
A82
Tobermory
Drimnin
Ballachulish
120
COLL
Sound of Mull
A884
Portnacroish
A828
TIREE
Lochaline
121
Salen
Connel
A849
smore
Kerrera
Taynuilt
ISLAND OF MULL
Oban
A85
Dalmally
A819
A816
Crianlarich
IONA
A849
Fionnphort
Luing
Kilmelford
Inveraray
A83
Scarba
Ford
Strachur
Arrochar
Aber

XVI

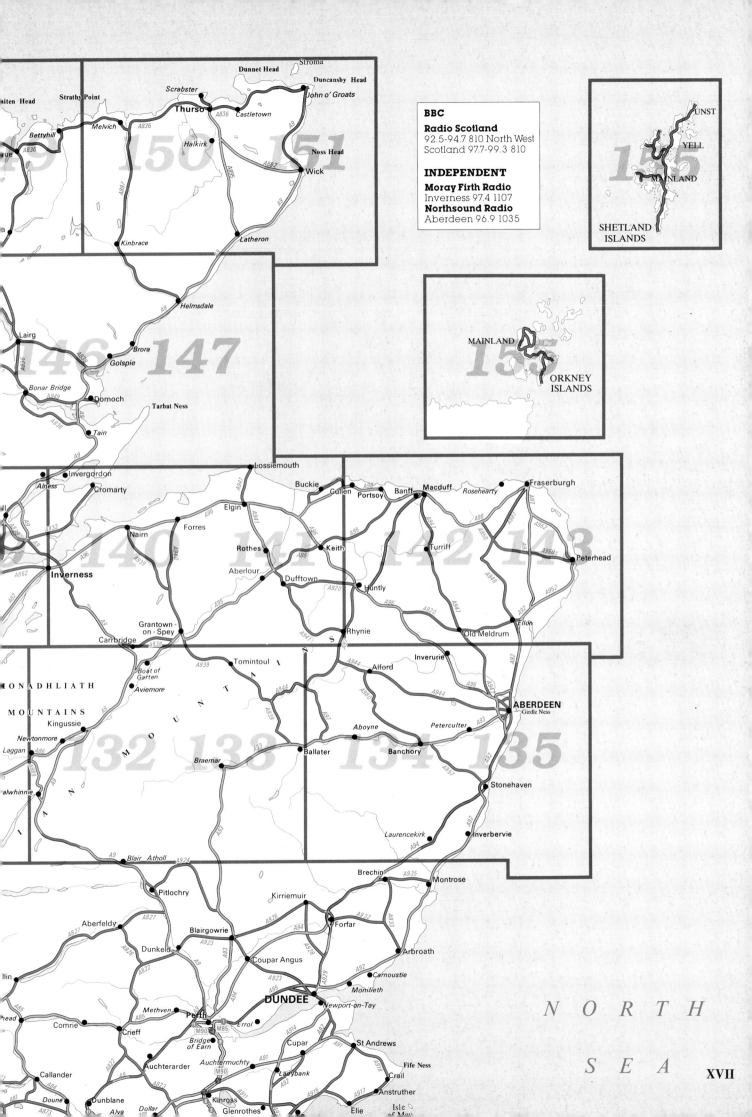

149 150 151

146 147

148 140 141 142 143

132 133 134 135

155 SHETLAND ISLANDS

155 MAINLAND ORKNEY ISLANDS

BBC
Radio Scotland
92.5-94.7 810 North West
Scotland 97.7-99.3 810

INDEPENDENT
Moray Firth Radio
Inverness 97.4 1107
Northsound Radio
Aberdeen 96.9 1035

Stroma
Dunnet Head
Scrabster
John o' Groats
Duncansby Head
Thurso
Castletown
Halkirk
Strathy Point
aiten Head
Melvich
A836
A836
Bettyhill
A836
Noss Head
A897
A882
Wick
Kinbrace
A9
Latheron

Helmsdale
A9
Lairg
Brora
A839
Golspie
Bonar Bridge
A949
Dornoch
Tarbat Ness
A836
Tain
A9

Lossiemouth
Invergordon
Buckie
A941
Cullen
Banff Macduff
Fraserburgh
Rosehearty
A98
A97
A98
A952
Alness
Cromarty
Elgin
A96
Portsoy
A95
Nairn
Forres
A947
Turriff
A950
Peterhead
A96
A939
A940
Rothes
Keith
A95
A920
A947
Inverness
A862
Aberlour
Dufftown
Huntly
A948
Ellon
A96
A970
Old Meldrum
A92
Grantown-on-Spey
Rhynie
A941
A97
Inverurie
Carrbridge
A938
A93
Tomintoul
A944
Alford
Boat of Garten
A939
A980
A944
MONADHLIATH
Aviemore
A939
A96
A93
MOUNTAINS
Kingussie
A97
Aboyne
Peterculter
ABERDEEN
Girdle Ness
Newtonmore
A944
Laggan
A86
Braemar
A93
Ballater
Banchory
alwhinnie
A957
Stonehaven

Laurencekirk
Inverbervie
A94
A92

Blair Atholl
A924
Brechin
A935
Montrose
A9
Pitlochry
Kirriemuir
Aberfeldy
A827
A926
Forfar
A932
A933
A827
Blairgowrie
A94
Arbroath
A826
A923
Dunkeld
A822
Coupar Angus
A92
A923
A928
Carnoustie
Methven
A85
A929
Monifieth
Comrie
A85
DUNDEE
Newport-on-Tay
Perth
A914
Crieff
Errol
St Andrews
M90 M85
Cupar
A91
A918
head
Bridge of Earn
A92
Fife Ness
Callander
A822
Auchterarder
Auchtermuchty
A915
Crail
A84
M90
Ladybank
A917
Doune
A873
Dollar
Kinross
A911
Anstruther
Dunblane
Alva
Glenrothes
Elie
Isle

NORTH

SEA XVII

•The Channel Tunnel

All you need to know about the Channel Tunnel, now due to open in the autumn of 1993

A Colossal Undertaking

Napoleon dreamt of invading England through a tunnel underneath the Channel, but the size of the undertaking deterred all would-be civil engineers until 1986. The scale of the project is vast. One of the most immense schemes to be planned, it is *the largest* privately funded construction ever to see the light of day. Hardly surprisingly, there were delays in the initial stages, but on 1 December 1990, just over four years after the monstrous boring machines began to devour their way toward each other through the chalk marl, breakthrough was made. For the first time since the Ice Age, there was a dry route from Folkestone to Calais!

The link is not so much one tunnel as three, two 'running tunnels' 25 feet (7.6m) in diameter and a service tunnel in between, joined by a passage every 410 yards (375m). Their total length, from Folkestone to Sangatte, near Calais, is 30.7 miles (49km), of which 23.6 miles (38km) are beneath the sea. For most of their length the tunnels are between 80 and 130 feet (25 and 40m) below the sea bed.

Services To The Continent

The trains that will run through the tunnel are of four different types:

1. passenger vehicle shuttles (for cars, coaches, motorcycles and bicycles)
2. lorry shuttles
3. through passenger trains
4. through freight trains.

The first two are run by Eurotunnel and simply connect the new terminals at Folkestone and Calais. They allow passengers either to continue their journey by the road network or to join a different branch of the public transport network on the other side of the Channel. The other two types of train will be run by the rail companies (usually British Rail or SNCF — French railways) and will enable passengers to board a train in London or Glasgow and disembark in Paris or Bonn without leaving the comfort of the train. Freight trains will operate similarly. Cars, coaches, motorcycles and bicycles are carried in special trains, which will run 24 hours a day, 365 days a year. Up to 185 cars or 25 lorries can be carried on each shuttle, although these are not combined on the same journey.

Up To 20,000 Vehicles A Day

By the year 2008 it is hoped that as many as 20,000 vehicles will be using the tunnel every day. Indeed the tunnel's capacity is immense; during peak times passenger vehicle shuttles will depart every 15 minutes, with a minimum service of one shuttle every hour right through the night. It is intended that when at full capacity as many as 600 trains will run in each direction every day. Considerable modernisation of the road networks on both sides of the Channel has been proceeding in recent years and will allow easy access to and from the new terminals. Some miles before you reach the terminal you can tune in to Radio Eurotunnel to discover whether there are any delays. If there are none, turning off the M20 at Junction 11a takes you straight to the Folkestone terminal.

Booking, Payment And Boarding The Trains

As soon as you reach the terminal you will need to pay at a toll booth — or present a pre-paid ticket. (No advance booking is required since the tunnel is run in much the same way as a toll road.) Using the shuttle will cost roughly the same as a ferry crossing. After you have bought your ticket you have the choice of using the facilities at the terminal (duty-free and other shops, cafés, toilets, bureaux de change and restaurants) or going straight to France. Once through the frontier controls — even in the Single Market you will, at least initially, need a passport — you will be told to drive your car to a particular lane. Next, a message board tells you to load on a particular platform. Follow the signs to the platform, down a ramp and in through a wide door in the side of the train. It is as straightforward as that.

Under The Channel In Under An Hour

Loading should take no more than eight minutes — and then the journey begins. Just 35 minutes later the shuttle draws to a halt in Sangatte; eight more minutes' unloading and you are on the Continental roads.

•Regional roadworks and bottlenecks

20 Wisley Interchange
A3 at junction with M25
Morning rush hour
northbound — congestion
due to volume of traffic.

21 Reigate
M25 junctions 7-8
Clockwise, peak periods —
congestion due to slow
moving lorries.

22 Maidstone
M20 junctions 5-8 —
widening work.

23 Uxbridge
M25 junctions 15-16
Anti-clockwise morning
rush hour; clockwise
evening rush hour —
congestion due to
volume of traffic.

24 St Albans-Luton
M1 junctions 6-10
Southbound, Monday to
Friday, morning rush
hour; northbound, Friday
evening rush hour —
congestion due to
volume of traffic.

25 Camberley-Chertsey
M3 junctions 2-4
Eastbound, morning rush
hour — congestion due to
volume of traffic.

26 Winchester Bypass
A33 and B3335
Peak periods, especially
summer weekends —
congestion due to
volume of traffic.

13 Newport
M4 junctions 25-26
Peak times — heavy
congestion due to
volume of traffic and
road construction.

14 Severn Bridge
M4
Peak times — heavy
congestion due to
volume of traffic.

15 Bristol
M5 junctions 14-20
Summer Saturdays —
southbound congestion
due to volume of traffic.

16 Penmaenmawr
A55
Peak periods, especially
summer weekends —
congestion due to
volume of traffic and
road construction.

17 Porthmadog
A487
Summer weekends —
congestion at toll gate
due to volume of traffic
and toll collection.

18 Tamar Bridge
A38
Peak periods, especially
summer weekends —
heavy congestion due to
volume of traffic.

19 Indian Queens and Fraddon
A30 and A39
Summer Saturdays —
congestion due to
volume of traffic.

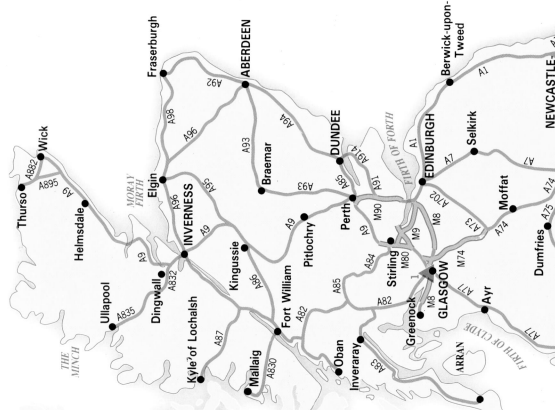

BOTTLENECKS

Roadworks and the sheer volume of traffic in an area can cause major delays and disruption to your journey if you come across them unawares. Knowing where they are likely to occur means you can alter your route to avoid them or allow more time for travelling. This list and its accompanying map highlight the major bottlenecks on motorways and primary routes. These are caused by traffic congestion or long-term roadworks, as predicted by the AA for 1993. Information on problems within major towns and cities is not included.

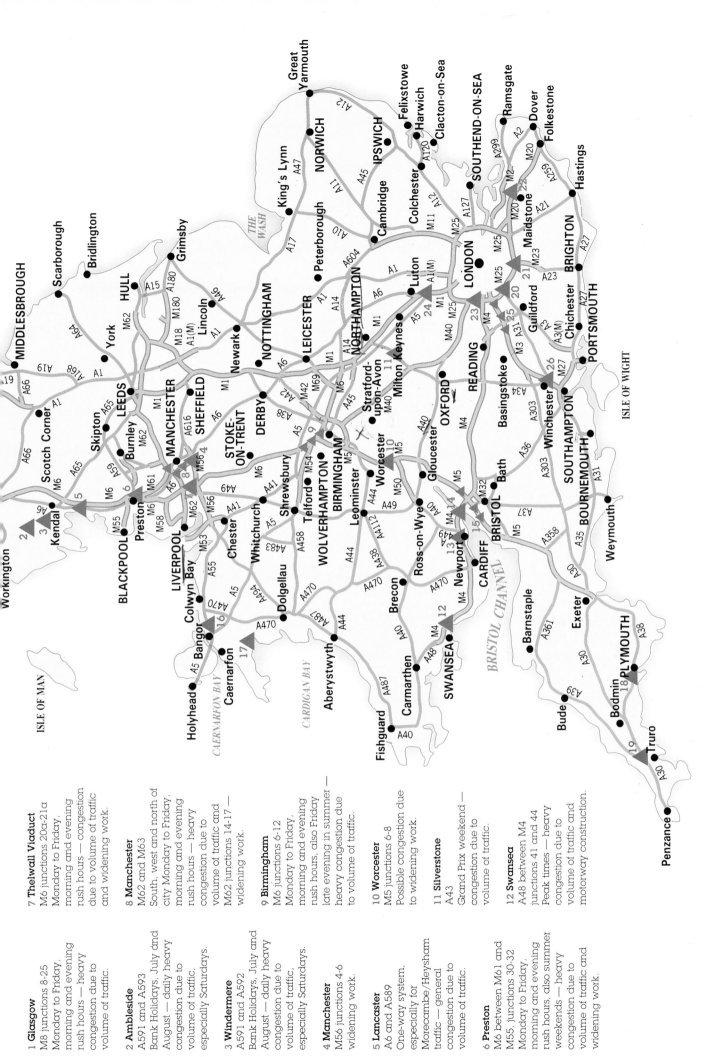

1 Glasgow
M8 junctions 8-25
Monday to Friday,
morning and evening
rush hours — heavy
congestion due to
volume of traffic.

2 Ambleside
A591 and A593
Bank Holidays, July and
August — daily heavy
congestion due to
volume of traffic,
especially Saturdays.

3 Windermere
A591 and A592
Bank Holidays, July and
August — daily heavy
congestion due to
volume of traffic,
especially Saturdays.

4 Manchester
M56 junctions 4-6
widening work.

5 Lancaster
A6 and A589
One-way system,
especially for
Morecambe/Heysham
traffic — general
congestion due to
volume of traffic.

6 Preston
M6 between M61 and
M55, junctions 30-32
Monday to Friday,
morning and evening
rush hours, also summer
weekends — heavy
congestion due to
volume of traffic and
widening work.

7 Thelwall Viaduct
M6 junctions 20a-21a
Monday to Friday,
morning and evening
rush hours — congestion
due to volume of traffic
and widening work.

8 Manchester
M62 and M63
South, west and north of
city Monday to Friday,
morning and evening
rush hours — heavy
congestion due to
volume of traffic and
M62 junctions 14-17 —
widening work.

9 Birmingham
M6 junctions 6-12
Monday to Friday,
morning and evening
rush hours, also Friday
late evening in summer —
heavy congestion due
to volume of traffic.

10 Worcester
M5 junctions 6-8
Possible congestion due
to widening work.

11 Silverstone
A43
Grand Prix weekend —
congestion due to
volume of traffic.

12 Swansea
A48 between M4
junctions 41 and 44
Peak times — heavy
congestion due to
volume of traffic and
motorway construction.

•Motorway
and primary route
service areas

This map shows, in diagrammatic form, service areas on the motorways and primary routes.

The companies running them are shown after the name of the service area. They cater for the needs of long-distance travellers, including the disabled—up to 2 hours free parking, refreshments, toilets, telephones and fuel 24 hours a day. Many include additional facilities such as shops, breakdown and repair services, picnic areas, business and banking facilities, overnight parking for caravans and special changing areas for babies, plus accommodation.

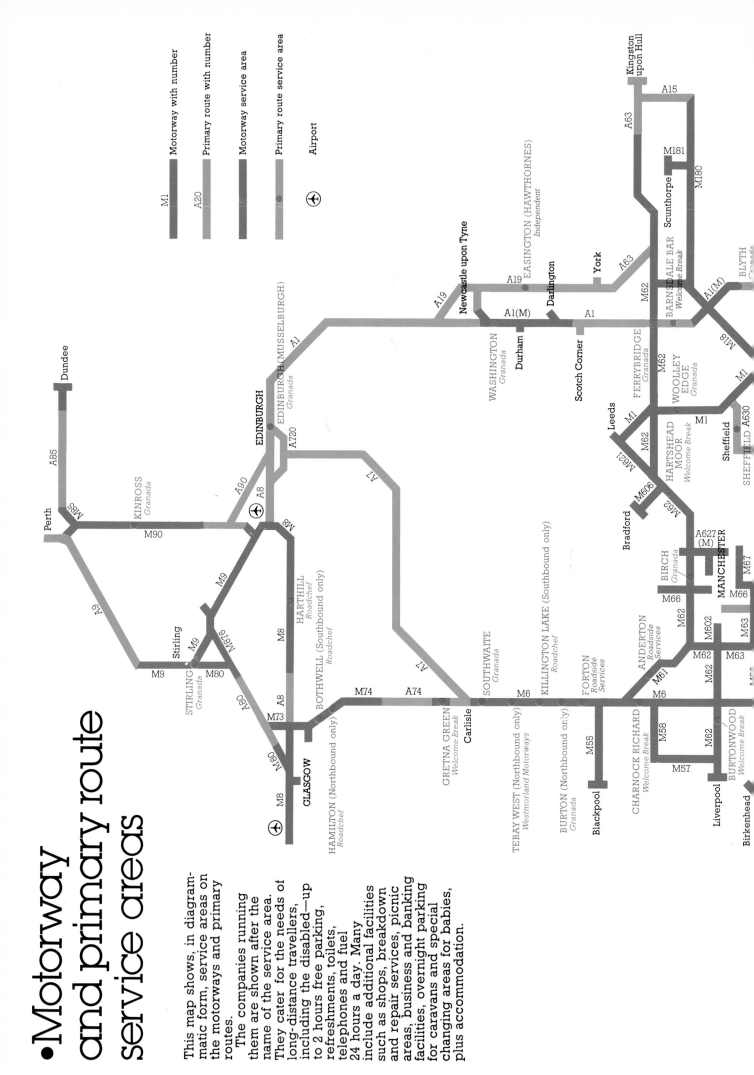

M1 — Motorway with number
A20 — Primary route with number
— Motorway service area
— Primary route service area
✈ Airport

Dundee
A85
Perth
M85
M90
KINROSS
Granada
A9
Stirling
M9
M80
M9
STIRLING
Granada
M73
M80
M876
A80
A8
M8
GLASGOW
✈
A8
M9
M876
A90
A8
✈
A720
EDINBURGH
EDINBURGH (MUSSELBURGH)
Granada
HARTHILL
Roadchef
BOTHWELL (Southbound only)
Roadchef
HAMILTON (Northbound only)
Roadchef
M74
A74
GRETNA GREEN
Welcome Break
Carlisle
A1
A1
SOUTHWAITE
Granada
M6
TEBAY WEST (Northbound only)
Westmorland Motorways
KILLINGTON LAKE (Southbound only)
Roadchef
BURTON (Northbound only)
Granada
FORTON
Roadside Services
M6
Blackpool
M55
CHARNOCK RICHARD
Welcome Break
M61
ANDERTON
Roadside Services
BURTONWOOD
Welcome Break
M58
M62
M57
Liverpool
Birkenhead
BIRCH
Granada
A627 (M)
MANCHESTER
M66
M66
M602
M62
M62
M63
M63
M67
A1
Newcastle upon Tyne
A19
A19
A19
EASINGTON (HAWTHORNES)
Independent
WASHINGTON
Granada
A1(M)
Durham
Darlington
A1
Scotch Corner
York
A1
Leeds
M1
Bradford
M606
M621
M62
M62
HARTSHEAD MOOR
Welcome Break
M1
Sheffield
SHEFFIELD A630
SHEFFIELD
A63
Kingston upon Hull
A15
A63
M181
M180
Scunthorpe
BARNSDALE BAR
Welcome Break
A1(M)
BLYTH
M62
FERRYBRIDGE
Granada
M62
WOOLLEY EDGE
Granada
M1
M18
M1
A1(M)

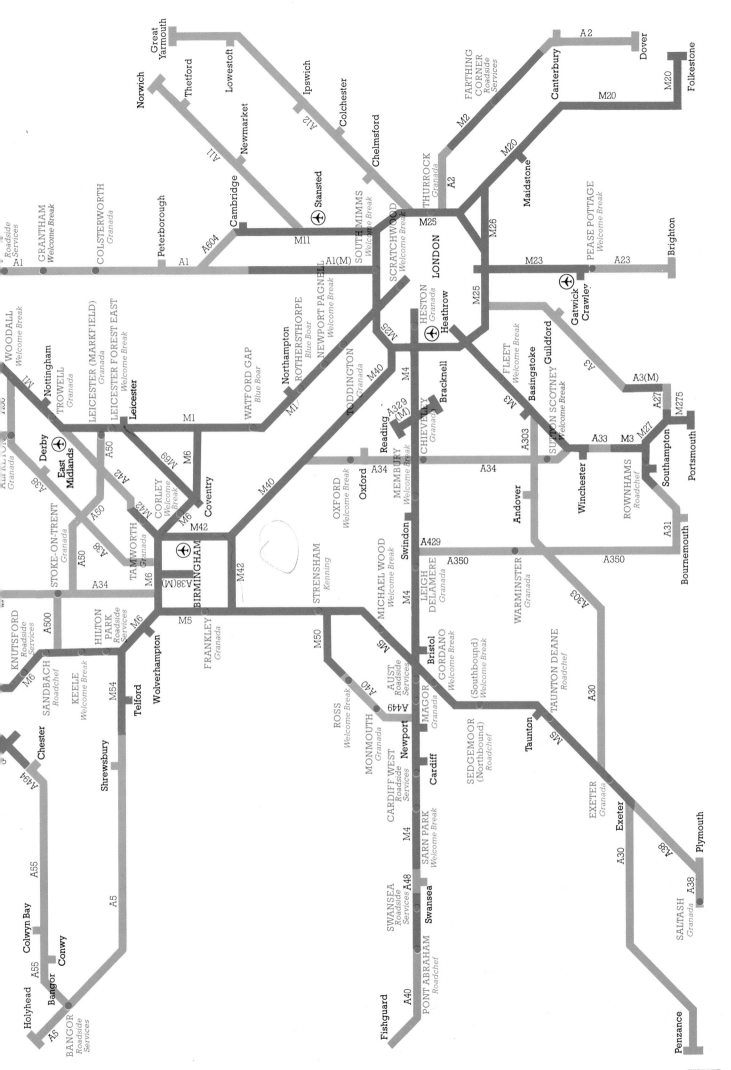

•Map pages

•Map symbols

MOTORING INFORMATION

Symbol	Description
M4	Motorway with number
11	Motorway junction with and without number
3	Motorway junction with limited access
S	Motorway service area
	Motorway and junction under construction
A4	Primary route single/dual carriageway
S	Primary route service area
BATH	Primary destination
A1123	Other A road single/dual carriageway
B2070	B road single/dual carriageway
	Unclassified road single/dual carriageway
	Road under construction
	Narrow primary, other A or B road with passing places (Scotland)
	Road tunnel
	Steep gradient (arrows point downhill)
Toll	Road toll
5	Distance in miles between symbols

Symbol	Description
V	Vehicle ferry – Great Britain
CHERBOURG V	Vehicle ferry – Continental
H	Hovercraft ferry
✈	Airport
H	Heliport
	Railway line/in tunnel
X	Railway station and level crossing
+++++++	Tourist railway
AA	AA Shop – full services
AA	AA Roadside Shop – limited services
AA	AA Port Shop open as season demands
☎	AA telephone
☎	BT telephone in isolated places
	Urban area/village
628	Spot height in metres
	River, canal, lake
	Sandy beach
	County/Regional boundary
	National boundary
88	Page overlap and number

TOURIST INFORMATION

Symbol	Description
i	Tourist Information Centre
i	Tourist Information Centre (seasonal)
⋔	Abbey, cathedral or priory
⋔	Ruined abbey, cathedral or priory
♜	Castle
	Historic house
M	Museum or art gallery
	Industrial interest
❀	Garden
♣	Arboretum
	Country park
	Agricultural showground
	Theme park
	Zoo
	Wildlife collection – mammals
	Wildlife collection – birds
	Aquarium
	Nature reserve
RSPB	RSPB site
	Nature trail
.....	Forest drive
---	National trail
☼	Viewpoint
	Picnic site

Symbol	Description
	Hill fort
	Roman antiquity
	Prehistoric monument
X 1066	Battle site with year
	Steam centre (railway)
	Cave
	Windmill
	Golf course
	County cricket ground
	Rugby Union national ground
	International athletics stadium
	Horse racing
	Show jumping/equestrian circuit
	Motor racing circuit
	Coastal launching site
	Ski slope – natural
	Ski slope – artificial
NT	National Trust property
★	Other places of interest
	Boxed symbols indicate attractions within urban areas
	National Park (England & Wales)
	National Scenic Area (Scotland)
	Forest Park
	Heritage Coast

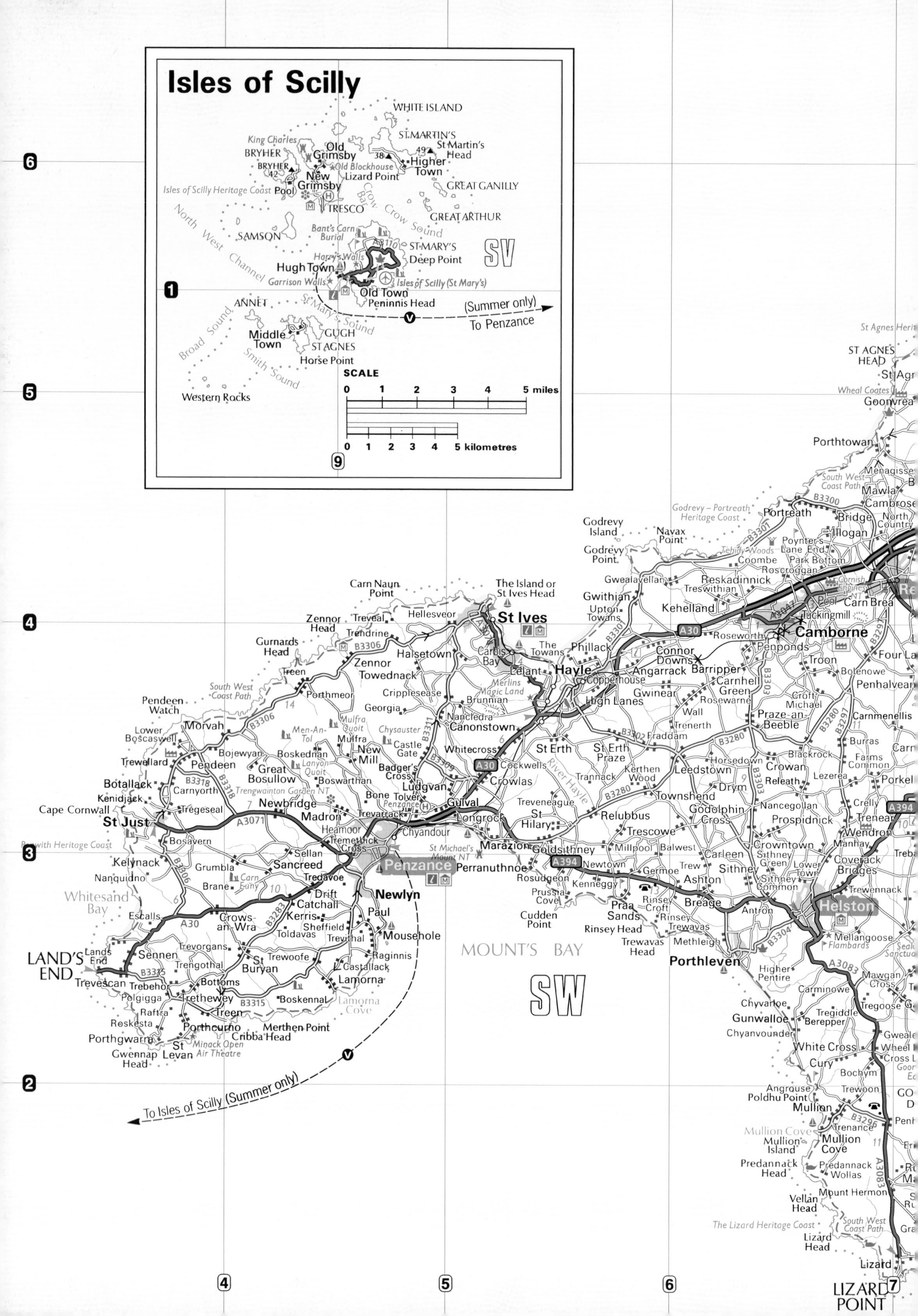

Isles of Scilly

WHITE ISLAND

King Charles
ST. MARTIN'S
St Martin's Head
BRYHER
Old Grimsby
38
49
Higher Town
BRYHER
42
Old Blockhouse
New Grimsby
Lizard Point
Pool
GREAT GANILLY
Isles of Scilly Heritage Coast
TRESCO
GREAT ARTHUR

North West Channel

Crow Sound

Bant's Carn Burial
SAMSON
SV
ST. MARY'S
Deep Point
Harry's Walls
170
Hugh Town
Isles of Scilly (St Mary's)
Garrison Walls
Old Town
ANNET
Peninnis Head
(Summer only)
To Penzance
St Mary's Sound
Middle Town
GUGH
ST AGNES
Horse Point

Broad Sound

Smith Sound

Western Rocks

SCALE

0 1 2 3 4 5 miles

0 1 2 3 4 5 kilometres

9

St Agnes Heri
ST AGNES HEAD
St Agr
Wheal Coates
Goonvrea
Porthtowan
Menagisse
B3300
Mawla
Cambrose
North Country
Godrevy Island
Godrevy Point
Navax Point
Portreath
Bridge
Tuckingmill
Re
B3301
Poynter's Lane End
Park Bottom
Coombe
Roscroggan
Tehidy Woods
NT
Cornish Engines NT
Pool
Carn Brea
Gwealavellan
Treswithian
Reskadinnick
Upton Towans
Gwithian
Kehelland
Roseworthy
Penponds
A30
Camborne
Carn Naun Point
Treveal
The Island or St Ives Head
Phillack
Connor Downs
Barripper
Troon
Bolenowe
Penhalvear
Zennor Head
Trendrine
Helleswor
St Ives
Carbis Bay
The Towans
Hayle
Angarrack
Carnhell Green
Rosewarne
Croft Michael
Carnmenellis
Gurnards Head
B3306
Halsetown
Copperhouse
Wall
Trenerth
Praze-an-Beeble
Burras
Treen
Zennor Towednack
Merlins Magic Land
High Lanes
Gwinear
Leedstown
B3280
B3297
Carr
South West Coast Path
Porthmeor
Brunnian
Fraddam
B3302
Drym
Crowan
Farms Common
Blackrock
Pendeen Watch
14
Cripplesease
Georgia
Nancledra
Canonstown
St Erth
St Erth Praze
Kerthen Wood
Releath
Lezerea
Porkel
Lower Boscaswell
Morvah
B3306
Men-An-Tol
Mulfra Quoit
Whitecross
A30
Cockwells
Townshend
Godolphin Cross
Nancegollan
Crelly
Trewellard
Bojewyan
Great Bosullow
Lanyon Quoit
New Mill
Castle Gate
River Hayle
Horsedown Cross
Trannack
Prospidnick
Treneer
A394
Pendeen
Boskednan
Badger's Cross
Trevaskis
B3280
Relubbus
Crowntown
Manhay
Botallack
Carnyorth
Boswarthan
Ludgvan
Gulval
St Hilary
Trescowe
Sithney Green
Trewennack
Kenidjack
B3318
7
Newbridge
Bone Tolver
Penzance H
Longrock
Treveneague
Millpool
Balwest
Carleen
Lower Sithney
Treb
Cape Cornwall
B3318
Tregeseal
Madron
Trevartack
St Michael's Mount NT
Goldsithney
Ashton
Coverack Bridges
St Just
A3071
Heamoor
Chyandour
Marazion
A394
Newtown
Germoe
Sithney Common
Helston
Penwith Heritage Coast
Tremethick Cross
Perranuthnoe
Rosudgeon
Kenneggy
Trew
B3304
Mellangoose
Kelynack
Sancreed
Penzance
Rosudgeon
Prussia Cove
Breage
Flambards
Seal Sanctu
Nanquidno
Grumbla
Tredavoe
Newlyn
Praa Sands
Rinsey Croft
Rinsey
Trewavas
Antron
A3083
Brane
Carn Euny
10
Drift
Catchall
Paul
Cudden Point
Rinsey Head
Methleigh
Higher Pentire
Mawgan Cross
Whitesand Bay
Escalls
A30
Crows-an-Wra
Kerris
Sheffield
Mousehole
Rinsey Head
Trewavas Head
Porthleven
Carminowe
Tregoose Cro
6
B3283
Toldavas
Trevithal
Raginnis
MOUNT'S BAY
Chyvarloe
Tregiddle
Berepper
LAND'S END
Lands End
Sennen
Trevorgans
St Buryan
Trewoofe
Castallack
Lamorna
SW
Gunwalloe
Chyanvounder
White Cross
Gweale
Wheal Cross
Trevescan
Trebehor
Bottoms
Trengothal
Trethewey
Treen
B3315
Boskennal
Lamorna Cove
Cury
Bochym
Polgigga
Raftra
Merthen Point
Angrouse
Trewoon
GO
Resketa
Porthcurno
Cribba Head
Poldhu Point
Mullion
Pen
Porthgwarra
St Levan
Minack Open Air Theatre
Mullion Cove
Trenance
B3296
Gwennap Head
Mullion Island
Mullion Cove
M
11
To Isles of Scilly (Summer only)
Predannack Head
Predannack Wollas
R
Vellan Head
Mount Hermon
South West Coast Path
Seal
The Lizard Heritage Coast
Lizard Head
Gra
LIZARD POINT
Lizard
7

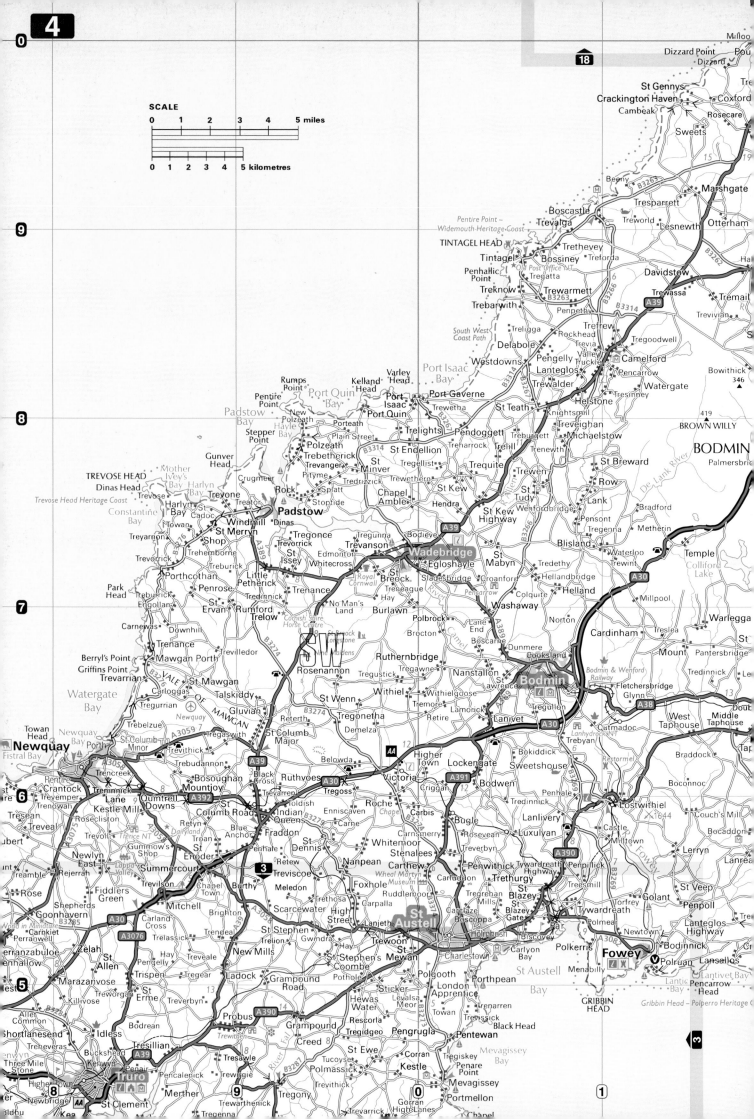

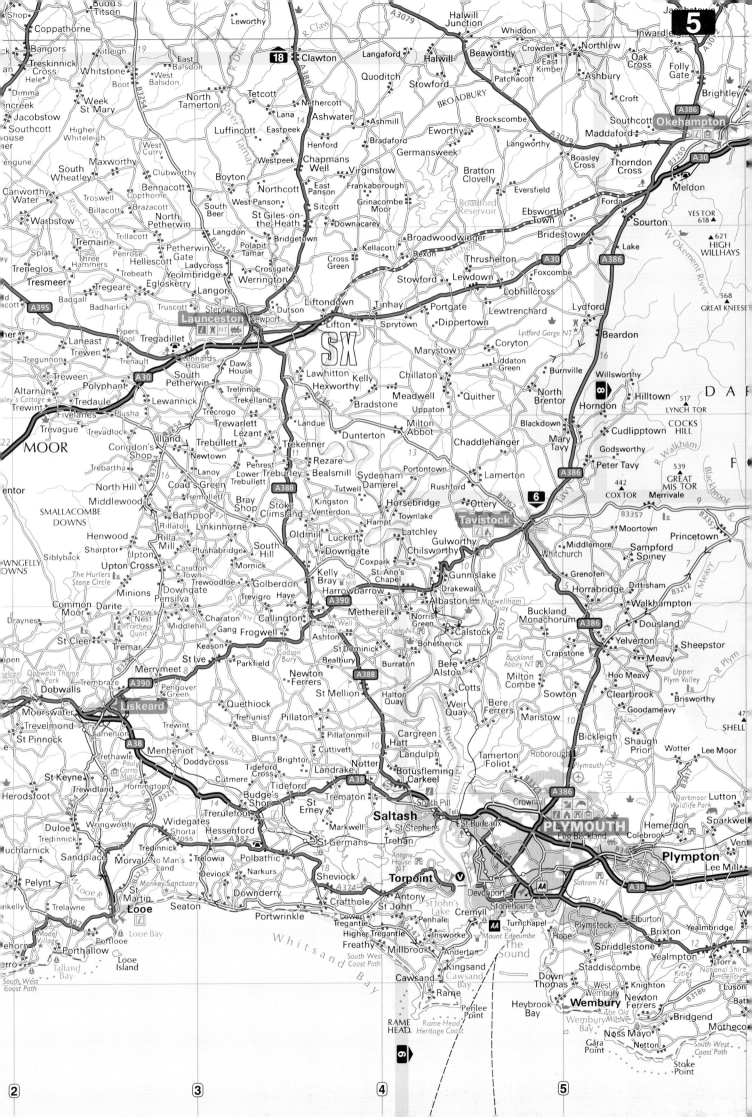

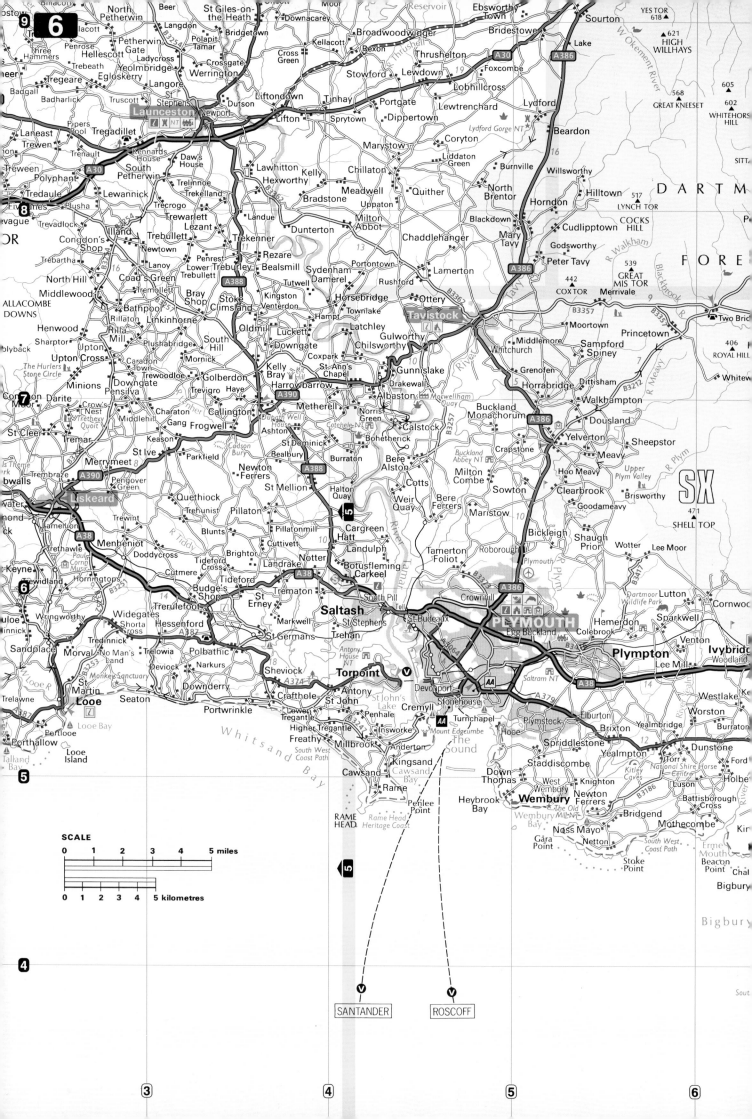

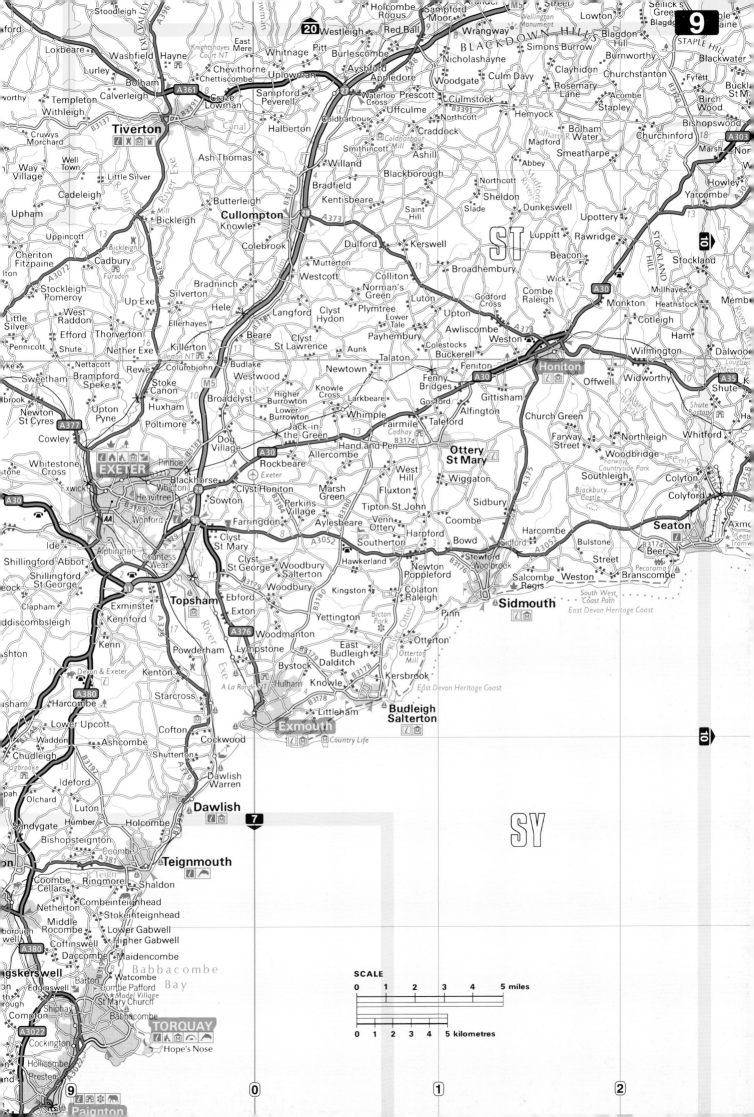

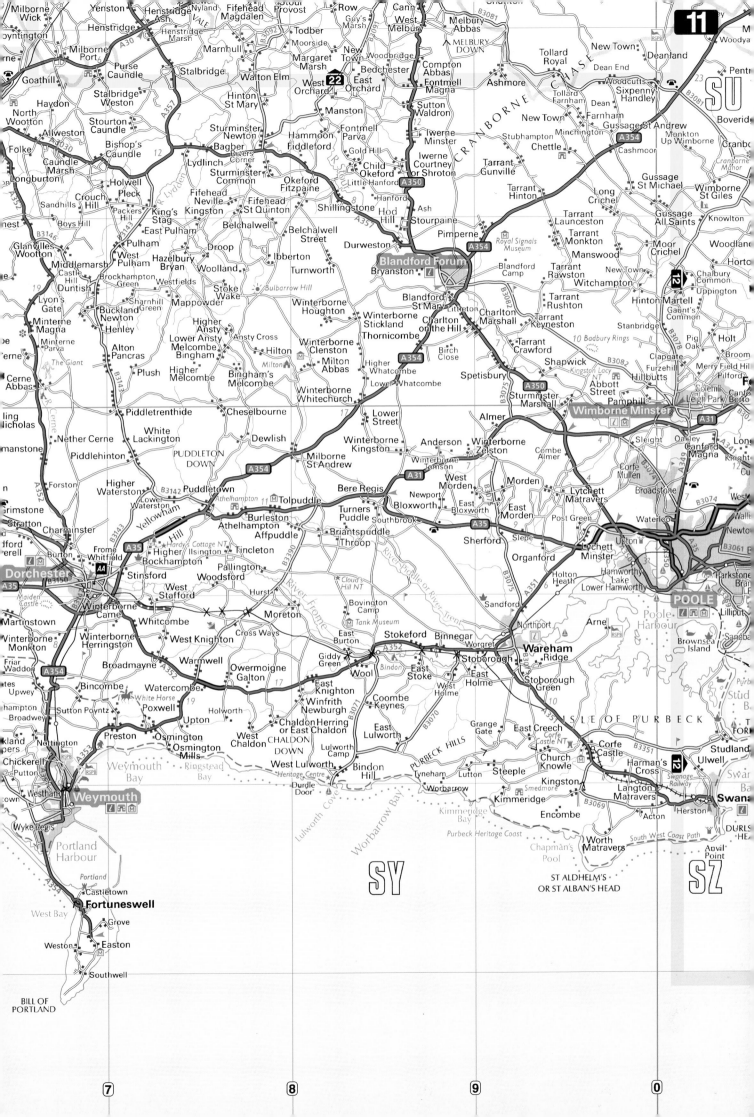

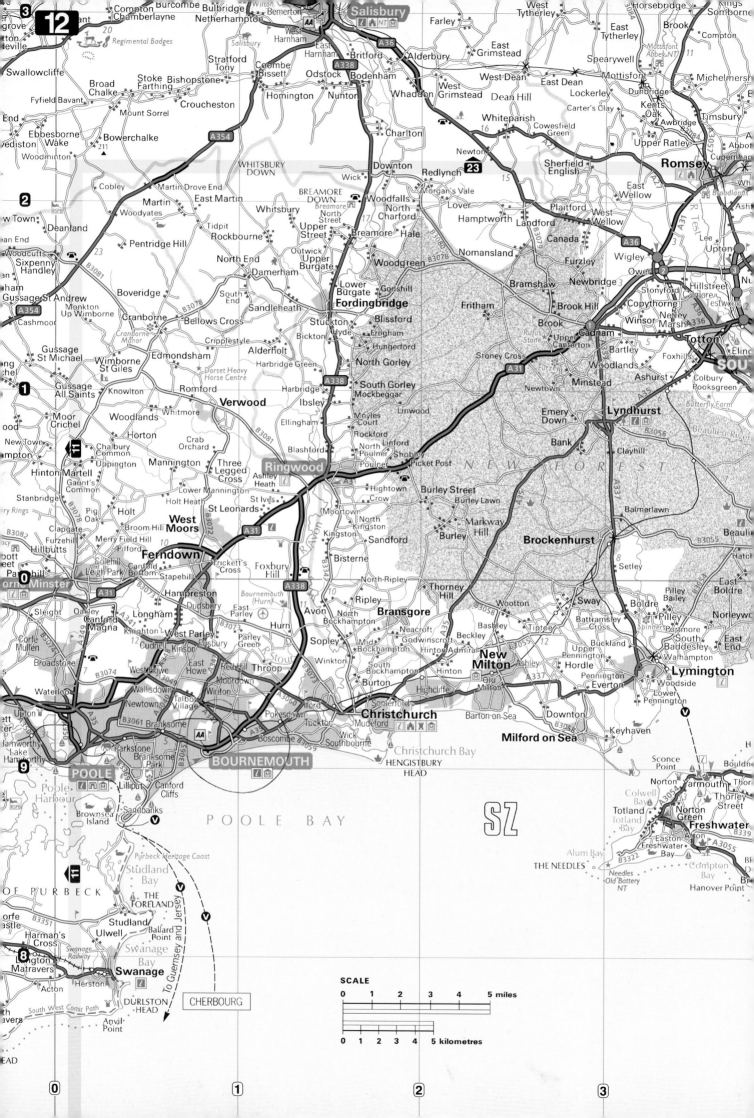

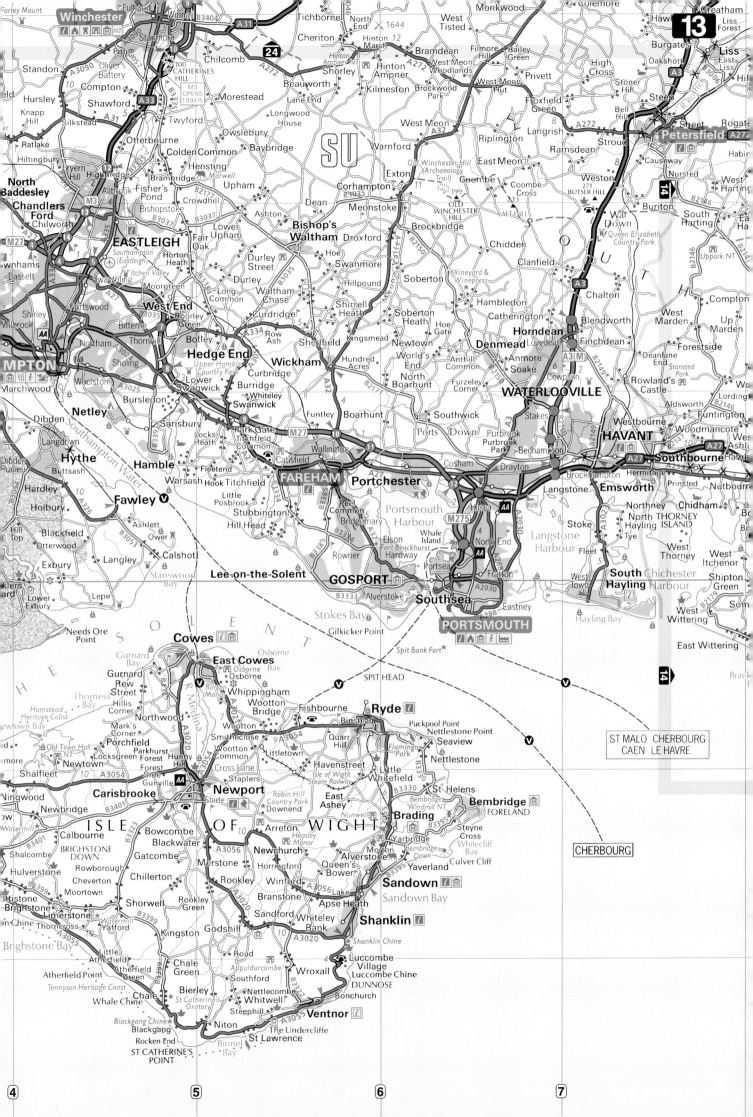

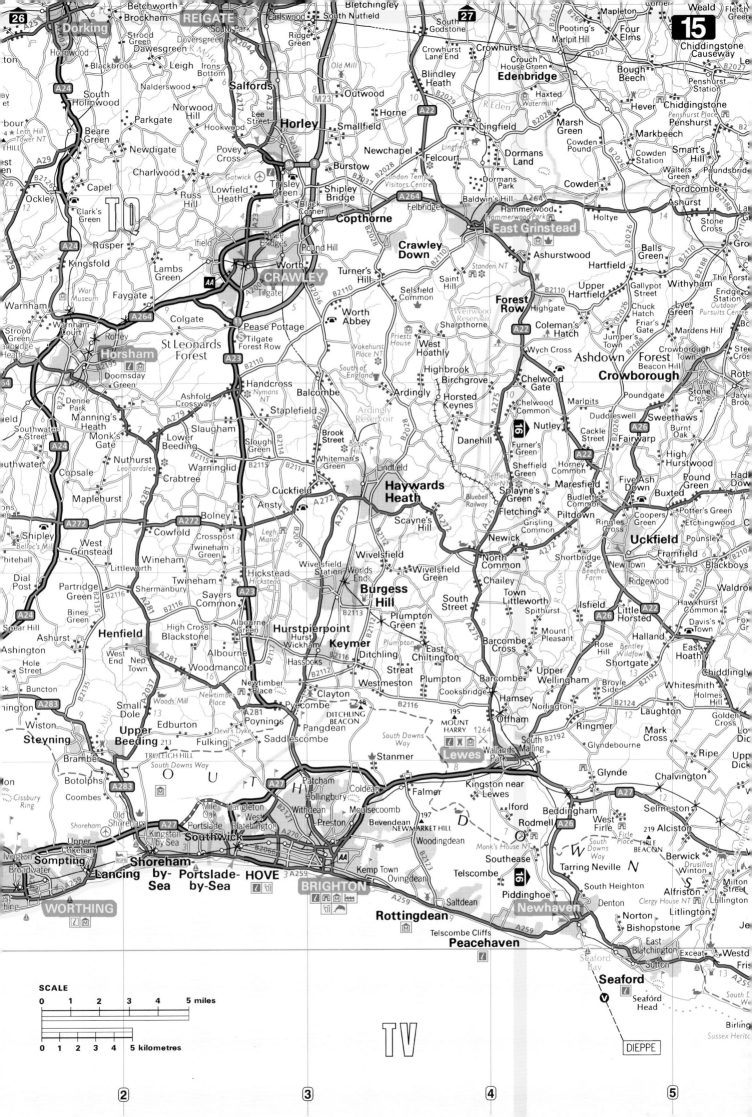

North West
Point
Lundy
Heritage Coast
LUNDY
▲142
Marisco
Surf Point

SCALE
0   1   2   3   4   5 miles

0 1 2 3 4   5 kilometres

Bull Point
Rockham
Bay
Lee
Bay
Morte Point
Mortehoe
Woolacombe
Morte Bay
Pickwell
Baggy Point   Putsborough
Croyde Bay
Georgeha
Croyde Bay
Croyde
Darracott
Knowl
Saunton
Lobb

BARNSTAPLE

OR

BIDEFORD BAY

Bull Point

Appledore
Northam
Westward Ho!
Eastleigh
Pillh
Bideford
A386

HARTLAND
POINT   Shipload
Bay
Titchberry
Dameho le
Point
South West
Coast Path
Brownsham
Clovelly
Court
Clovelly
Abbotsham
Fairy
Cross
Ford
Hartland
Heritage Coast
Yeo
Vale
Landcross
Hartland Quay
Stoke
Hartland
Velly
Slerra
Buck's
Mills
Horns
Cross
A39
Woodtown
Littleham
Spekes Mill
Mouth
Milford
Philham
A39
Milky Way
Buck's
Cross
Dyke
Goldworthy
Parkham
Saltrens
W
Gi
Elmscott
Cranford
Parkham
Ash
Cabbacott
Buckland
Brewer
Monkleigh
Hardisworthy
Woolfardisworthy
Melbury
Frithelstock
South
Hole
Frithelstock
Stone
Taddiport
Welcombe
Darracott
Meddon
Ashmansworthy
Thornehillhead
Southcott
A388
Mead
Woolley
18
Gooseham
Eastcott
16
East
Youlstone
Dinworthy
West
Putford
East Putford
Langtree
Lang
Week
Morwenstow
Higher Sharpnose
Point
West
Youlstone
Bradworthy
Colscott
Haytown
Bulkworthy
Stibb
Cross
Berry
Cross
Pe
Ma
Shop
Kimworthy
Lower Sharpnose
Point
Tamar Lakes
Darracott
Alfardisworthy
Sutcombe
Abbots
Bickington
Newton
St Petrock
Steeple
Point
Kilkhampton
Sutcombemill
Venngreen
Milton Damerel
Sandy
Mouth
Thurdon
Soldon
Soldon
Cross
River Waldon
Stibb
A39
B3254
Dunsden
Holsworthy
Beacon
Thornbury
Shebbear
Buckland
Filleigh
Northcott
Mouth
Maer
Poughill
Hersham
Venn
A388
Little
Lashbrook
Bradford
Priestacott
Bude
Flexbury
Bush
Grimscott
Lana
Brendon
Cookbury
Hole
Dippermill
Bude
Bay
Bude
Stratton
Launcells
Launcells
Cross
Kingford
Chilsworthy
Cookbury
Wick
Holemoor
Lashbrook
Black
Torringt
Lynstone
10
Pancrasweek
Holsworthy
Anvil
Corner
A3072
Brandis
Corner
13
Upton
A3072
Derril
Derriton
Whimble
Odham
Helebridge
Marhamchurch
Bridgerule
Pyworthy
Chasty
Hollacombe
Chilla
Widemouth
Bay
Box's Shop
Budd's
Titson
R Claw
Leworthy
A3079
Halwill
Junction
Whiddon
Mullook
Dizzard Point
Poundstock
Coppathorne
Bangors
Kitleigh
19
Clawton
5
Langaford
Halwill
Beaworthy
Crow
Dizzard
Penlean
Treskinnick
Cross
Hele
West
Balsdon
East
Balsdon
A388
Quoditch
Stowford
Patchacott
St Gennys
4
ackington Haven
1
Tregole
imma
Trencreek
Whitstone
Boot
B3254
th
Tamerton
R Deer
Tetcott
Nethercott
4
BROADBURY
Cambeak
Coxford
2
Week
St Mary
3
Lana
Ashwater
Brockscombe
Rosecare
Jacobstow

SS

EXMOOR FOREST

EXMOOR NATIONAL PARK

Exmoor Heritage Coast

Foreland Point
Lynmouth Bay
Countisbury Cove
Hurtstone Point
Porlock Bay
Bossington
Lynton
Lynbridge
Lynmouth
Countisbury
Brendon
Culbone
West Porlock
Porlock Weir
Porlock
Horner
Luccombe
Woody Bay
Martinhoe
Trentishoe
Woody Bay
Dean
West
Barbrook
Wilsham
Rockford
Malmsmead
Oare
Tippacott
Lucott
Elwill Bay
Kemacott
Heale
Killington
West Ilkerton
East Ilkerton
Cheriton
Furzehill
Woolhanger
Hoaroak Hill 474
Dry Hill
Dunkery Hill
Combe Martin Bay
Water Mouth
Watermouth
Hele Bay
Hele
Hele Mill
Combe Martin
Sterridge
Berrynarbor
Ruggaton
Bodstone Barton Farm Park
Two Pots
Mullacott Cross
West Down
Bittadon
Berry Down Cross
East Down
Churchill
Patchole
Kentisbury
Kentisbury Ford
Arlington Beccott
Stowford
Barton Town
Challacombe
Swincombe
Arlington
Exmoor Bird Gardens
Arlington Court NT
Knightacott
Loxhore
Loxhore Cott
Lower Loxhore
Leworthy
Fullaford
Lydcott
Simonsbath
Newland
Blackland
Edgcott
Exford
Luckwell Bridge
Withypool
Winsford
Halsinger
Higher Muddiford
Milltown
Muddiford
Upcott
Shirwell
Shirwell Cross
Bratton Fleming
Benton
Stoke Rivers
Whitefield
Span Head 493
Kinsford Water
Worth Hill
Knaplock
Liscombe
Tarr
Tarr Steps
Hawkridge
Winsham
Marwood
Guineaford
Kingsheanton
Heanton Punchardon
Ashford
Bradford Pilton
Northleigh
Goodleigh
Willesleigh
Gunn
Bradninch
Accott
Whitsford
Stoodleigh
Charles
Brayford
High Bray
Bentwichen
North Radworthy
North Heasley
South Radworthy
Molland
Slade
West Anstey
East Anstey
Dulverton
Barnstaple
Newport
Lake
Landkey Town
Bishop's Tawton
Swimbridge Newland
West Buckland
Yarnacott
Elwell
East Buckland
Heasley Mill
Upcott
North Molton
Newtown
Twitchen
Knowstone
Nightcott
Bickington
Landkey
Hannaford
Kerscott
Swimbridge
Bremridge
South Molton
Aller
Bish Mill
Ash Mill
Oldways End
Sowerhill
Exe
St John's Chapel
Horsacott
Tawstock
Herner
Cobbaton
Traveller's Rest
East Stowford
Filleigh
Quince Honey Farm
Newtown
Crooked Oak
East Knowstone
Roachill
Oakfordbridge
Harracott
Week
Ensis
Hiscott
Chapelton
Chittlehampton
Umberleigh
Clapworthy
George Nympton
Radley
Bishop's Nympton
Knowstone
Oakford
Westcott
Delley
Yarnscombe
Atherington
Warkleigh
Satterleigh
Alswear
Mariansleigh
Yard
Rose Ash
Newton Tracey
Langridge Ford
Huntshaw Cross
Chittlehamholt
Romansleigh
Meshaw
Creacombe
Rackenford
High Bullen
Dodscott
High Bickington
King's Nympton
Cadbury Barton
Week
Queen Dart
Loxbeare
Great Torrington
St Giles in the Wood
Rosemoor
Kingscott
Roborough
Burrington
Elstone
Colleton Mills
Chulmleigh
Worlington
Witheridge
Edgeworthy
Templeton
Witheligh
Beaford
Little Potheridge
Riddlecombe
Ashreigney
Bridge Reeve
Chawleigh
Cheldon
Drayford
Nomansland
Cruwys Morchard
Great Potheridge
Dolton
Chittlehampton
Ashley
Eggesford
Filleigh
Hele Lane
Littleborough
Washford Pyne
Pennymoor
Puddington
Way Village
Merton
Huish
Dowland
Hollocombe
Wembworthy
Moor End
Nymet Rowland
Lapford
Eastington
Black Dog
Woolfardisworthy
Poughill
Upham
Cadeleigh
Petrockstow
Ash
Meeth
Iddesleigh
Winkleigh
Brushford Barton
Coldridge
Morchard Bishop
Kennerleigh
Stockleigh English
East Village
Cheriton Fitzpaine
Barwick
Ingleigh Green
West Leigh
East Leigh
Weeke
Chilton
Upton Hellions
Uppincott
Monkokehampton
Splatt
Broadwood Kelly
Bondleigh
Zeal Monachorum
Loosebeare
Down St Mary
Sutton
Newbuildings
Sandford
East Village
Stockleigh Pomeroy
West Raddon
Fishleigh
Hatherleigh
Honeychurch
North Tawton
Barons Wood
Weeke
Clannaborough
Woolsgrove
West Sandford
Lower Creedy
Little Silver
Efford
Pennicott
Jacobstowe
Exbourne
Sampford Courtenay
Lowton
Bow
Nymet Tracey
Coleford
Knowle
Penstone
Colebrooke
Creedy Park
Shobrooke
Northlew
Oak Cross
Folly Gate
Brightley
Corscombe
Chichacott
Taw Green
Spreyton
Itton
Highfield
Woodland Head
Spestos
Hillerton
Crediton
Fordton
Uton
Hookway
Smallbrook
Sweetham
Inwardleigh
Trecott
Broadnymett
Hittisleigh
Colebrooke
Yeoford
Neopardy
Venny Tedburn
Oldridge
Newton St Cyres
Cowley
Rowden

SK
6
7
8
9

20

A39
A361
A377
A386
A3072
A3123
A3230
B3226
B3227
B3358
B3223
B3224
B3096
B3042
B3137
B3220
B3217
B3219
B3215
B3216

River Exe
River Barle
Winsford Hill
R Bray
River Mole
River Taw
R Dalch
R Torridge
R Okement
R Creedy
R Yeo
Little Dart River
River Troney
Castle Hill
Watersmeet House NT
Chambercombe Manor
Marwood Hill

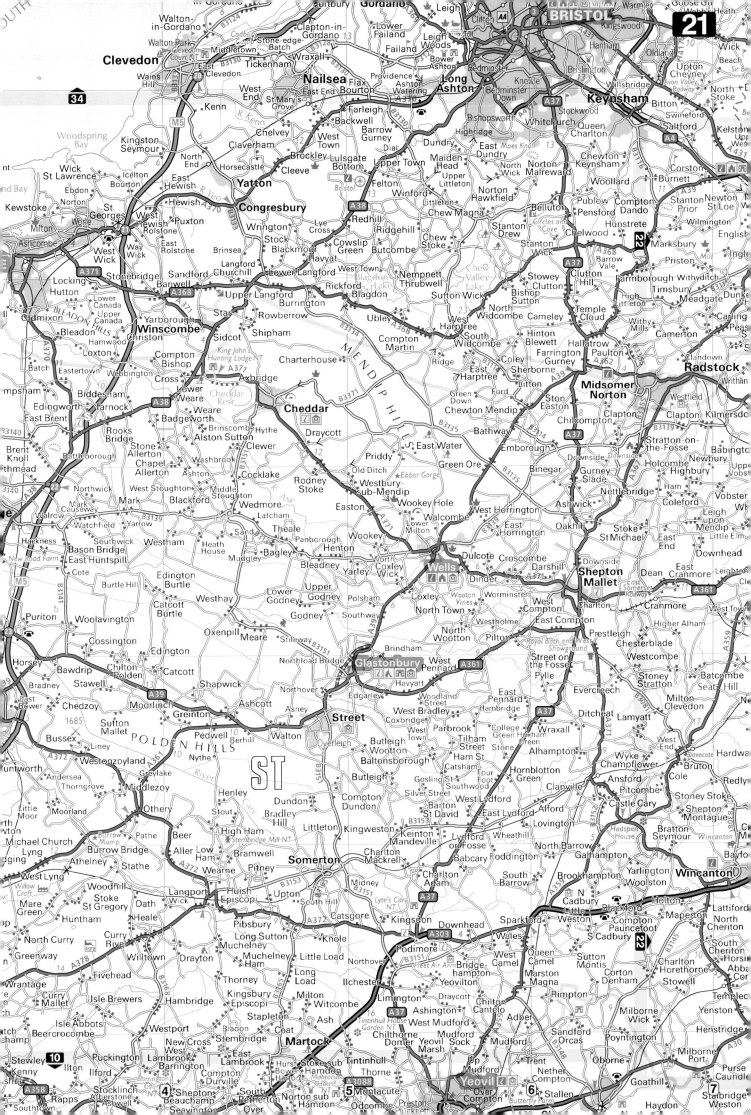

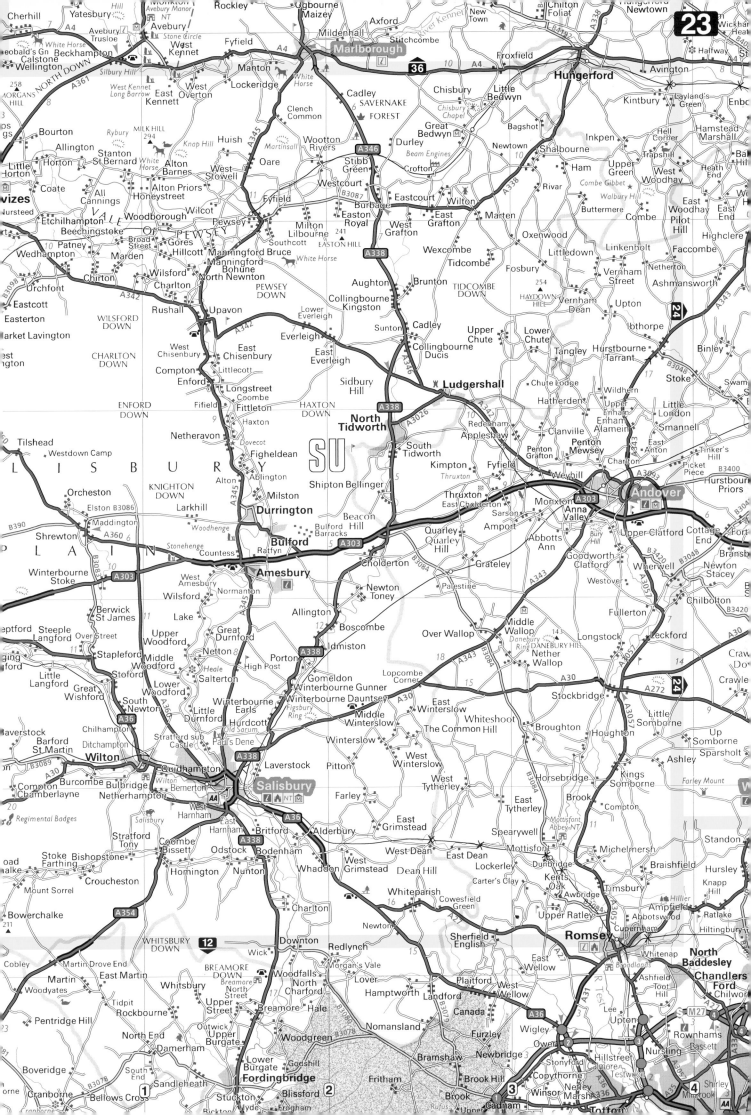

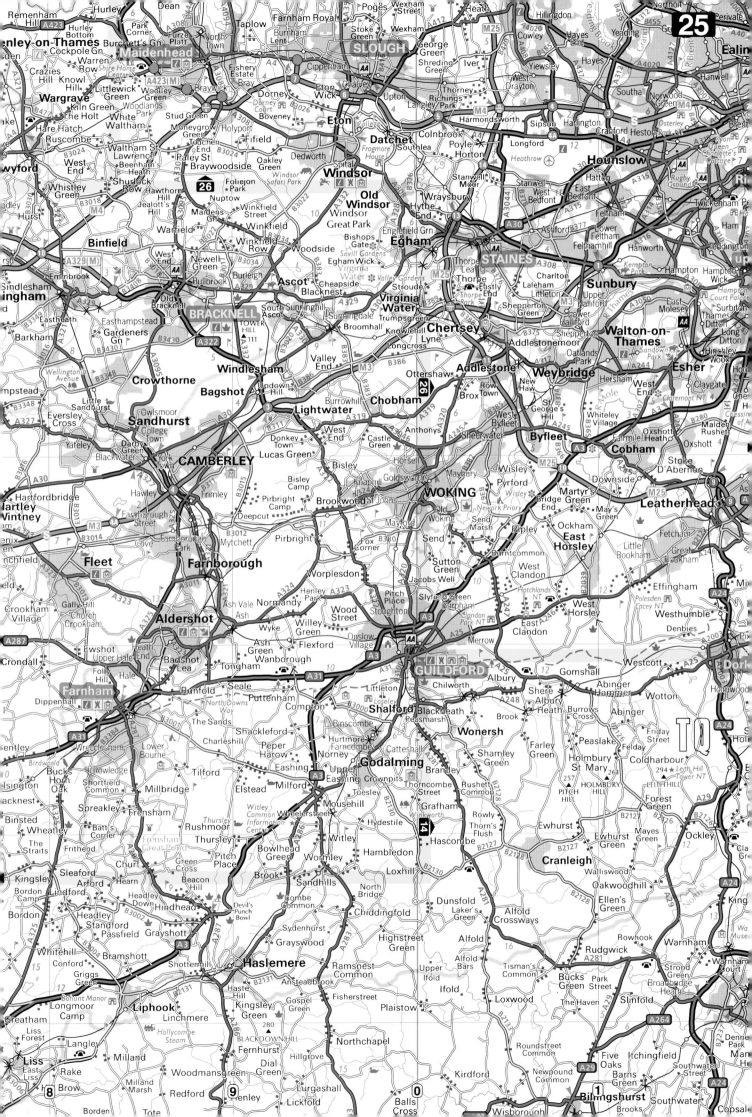

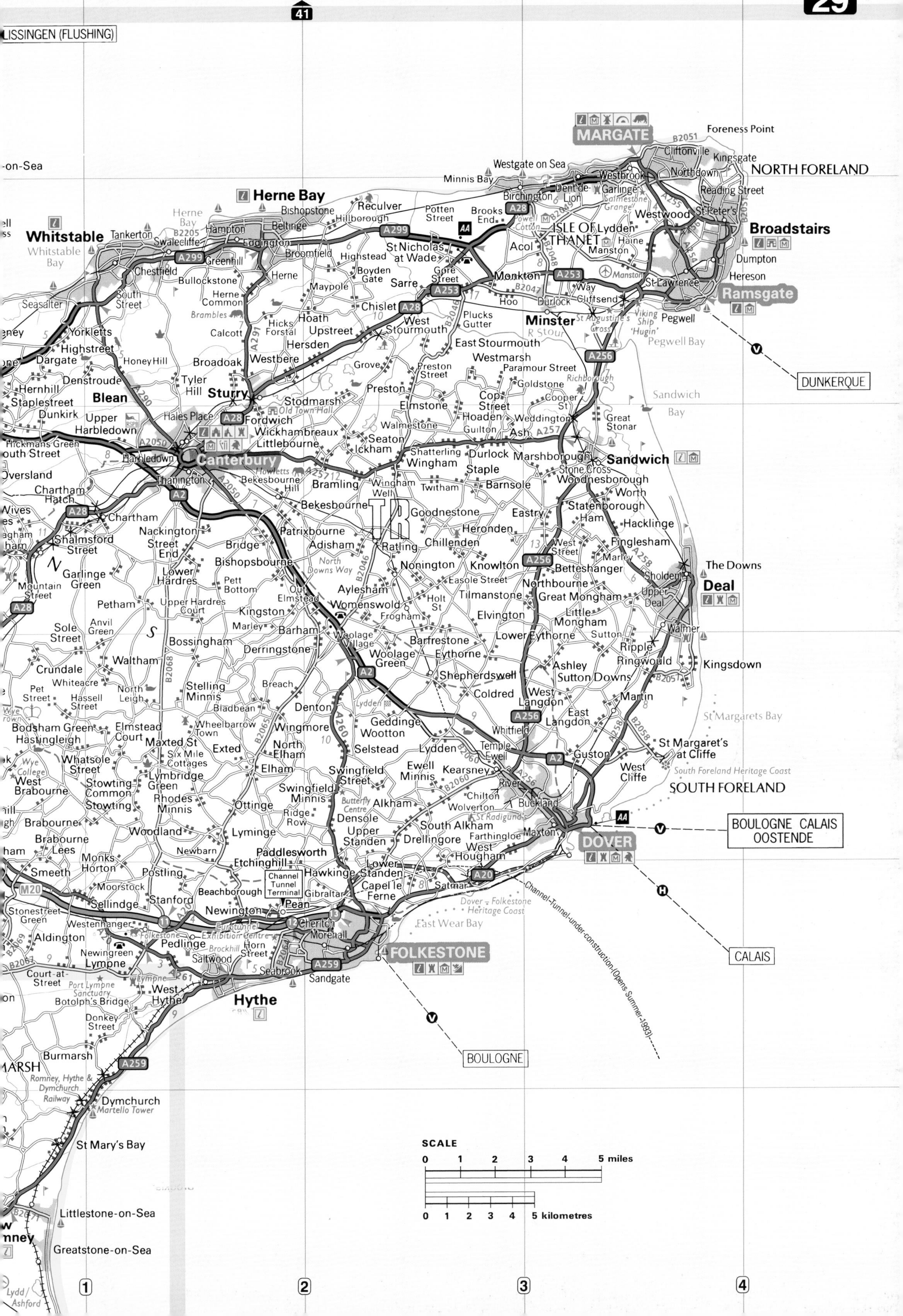

VLISSINGEN (FLUSHING)

MARGATE
Foreness Point
Cliftonville Kingsgate
Westgate on Sea Westbrook Northdown
Minnis Bay Birchington Dent de Garlinge Reading Street **NORTH FORELAND**
on-Sea Lion Salmestone
Bishopstone Reculver Potten Brooks Grange Westwood
Herne Bay Hillborough Street End Powell St Peter's
Beltinge Cotton ISLE OF Lydden **Broadstairs**
Hampton St Nicholas THANET Manston
Whitstable Tankerton Swalecliffe Edington at Wade Acol Haine Dumpton
Whitstable Greenhill Broomfield Highstead Gore St Monkton Manston Way
Bay Chestfield Herne Boyden Street Sarre Hoo Durlock St Lawrence **Ramsgate**
South Bullockstone Gate Maypole Chislet West Minster Cliffsend Viking Pegwell
Street Herne Hoath Upstreet Stourmouth St Augustine's Ship
Seasalter Common Calcott Hersden East Stourmouth Westmarsh Cross 'Hugin' Pegwell Bay
Yorkletts Highstreet Brambles Tyler Broadoak Westbere Grove Preston Paramour Street Richborough Sandwich
Dargate Honey Hill Hill Preston Street Goldstone Bay
Denstroude Sturry Stodmarsh Elmstone Cop Cooper St DUNKERQUE
Hernhill Staplestreet Upper Fordwich Wickhambreaux Seaton Street Hoaden Great Stonar
Blean Harbledown Littlebourne Ickham Walmestone Guilton Weddington Ash Sandwich
Hickmans Green Hales Place Shatterling Durlock Marshborough
South Street Harbledown **Canterbury** Wingham Staple Stone Cross Woodnesborough
Oversland Thanington Howletts Bekesbourne Bramling Twitham Barnsole Worth
Chartham Hill Bekesbourne Wingham Statenborough
Hatch Nackington Bridge Well Goodnestone Eastry Ham Hacklinge
Chartham Street End Patrixbourne Adisham Ratling Heronden Finglesham
Wives Bishopsbourne Chillenden West Marley The Downs
Garlinge Lower Pett Out Nonington Knowlton Street Betteshanger **Deal**
Mountain Green Hardres Bottom Elmstead Aylesham Easole Street Northbourne Sholden
Street Petham Upper Hardres Kingston Womenswold Holt St Tilmanstone Great Mongham Upper
Anvil Court Marley Frogham Elvington Little Deal
Sole Green Barham Barfrestone Lower Eythorne Mongham Walmer
Street Bossingham Derringstone Woolage Eythorne Ashley Sutton Ripple
Waltham Village Woolage Shepherdswell West Downs Ringwould
Crundale Stelling Green Coldred Langdon Martin Kingsdown
Whiteacre Minnis Breach Denton Wingmore Wotton Selstead Lydden Whitfield East
North Bladbean Langdon St Margarets Bay
Pet Leigh Wheelbarrow Town North Lydden Temple St Margaret's
Street Hassell Elmstead Maxted St Elham Swingfield Ewell Ewell Guston at Cliffe
Bodsham Green Court Six Mile Exted Street Minnis Kearsney West
Hastingleigh Whatsole Stowting Cottages Swingfield Alkham Chilton River Cliffe SOUTH FORELAND
Street Common Lymbridge Minnis Wolverton Buckland South Foreland Heritage Coast
West Stowting Green Rhodes Ottinge Ridge St Radigunds West
Brabourne Woodland Minnis Lyminge Row Densole Upper South Alkham Maxton Cliffe
Brabourne Newbarn Standen Drellingore Farthingloe **DOVER** BOULOGNE CALAIS
Lees Monks Paddlesworth West OOSTENDE
Smeeth Horton Postling Etchinghill Hawkinge Lower Hougham
Moorstock Beachborough Standen Capel le
Stonestreet Sellindge Stanford Channel Tunnel Gibraltar Ferne Satmar Dover Folkestone CALAIS
Green Terminal Pean Heritage Coast
Westenhanger Newington Cheriton East Wear Bay
Aldington Eurotunnel Morehall
Newingreen Pedling Exhibition Centre Channel Tunnel under construction (Opens Summer 1993)
Lympne Brockhill Horn **FOLKESTONE**
Court-at- West Saltwood Street
Street Port Lympne Hythe Seabrook Sandgate
Sanctuary
Botolph's Bridge **Hythe**

Donkey
Street

BOULOGNE

Burmarsh

Romney, Hythe &
Dymchurch
Railway Dymchurch
Martello Tower

MARSH

St Mary's Bay

SCALE
0 1 2 3 4 5 miles

0 1 2 3 4 5 kilometres

Littlestone-on-Sea

Greatstone-on-Sea

Lydd
Ashford

1 2 3 4

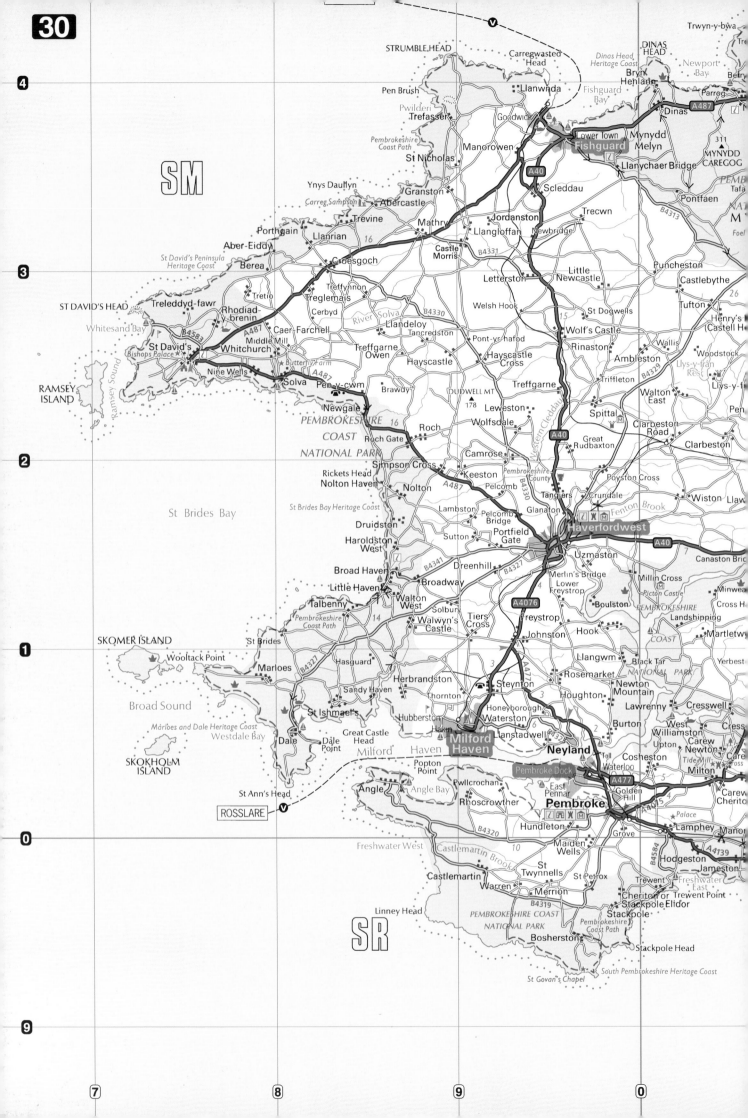

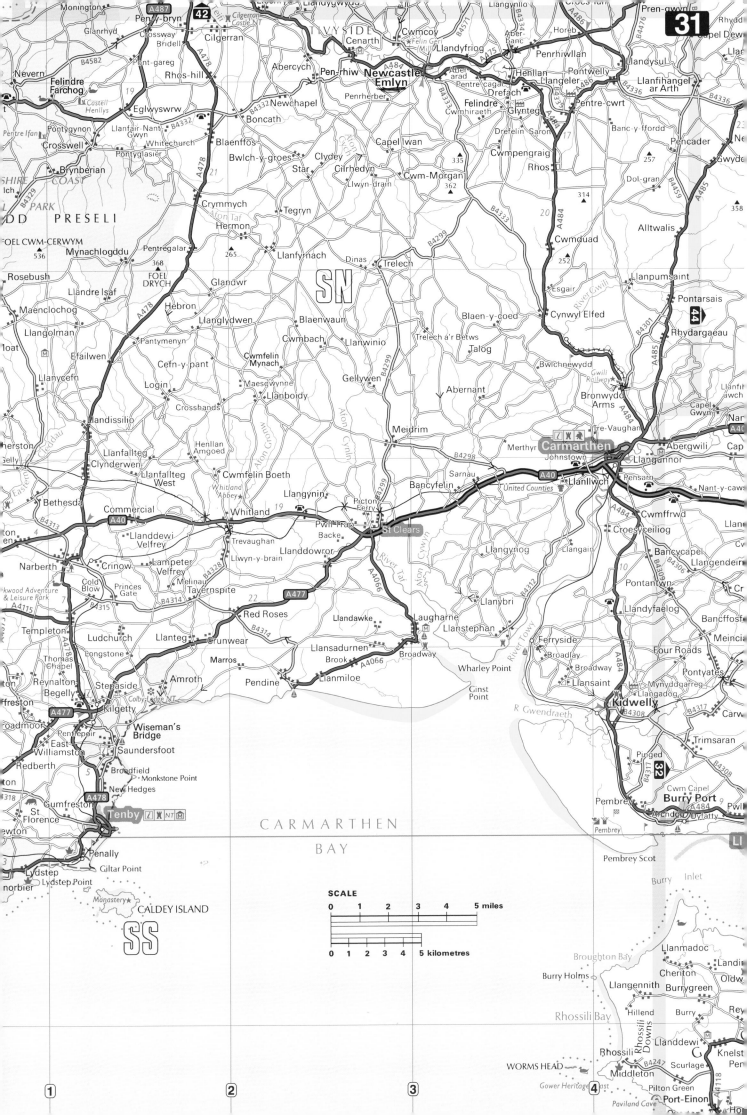

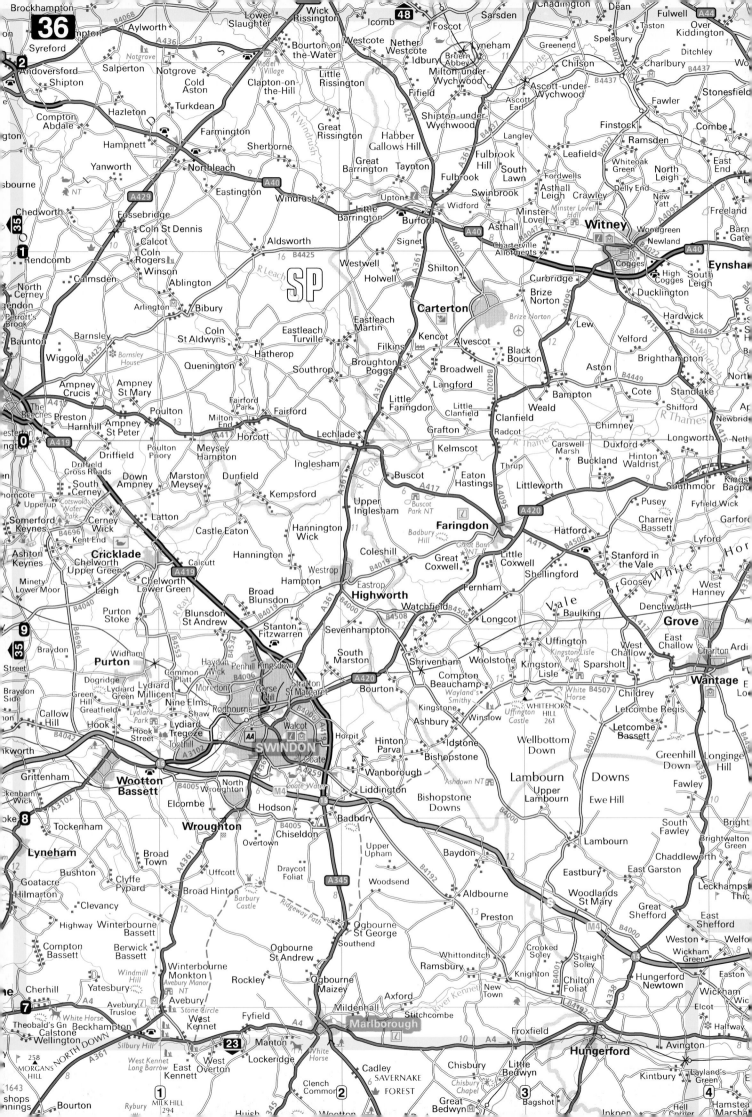

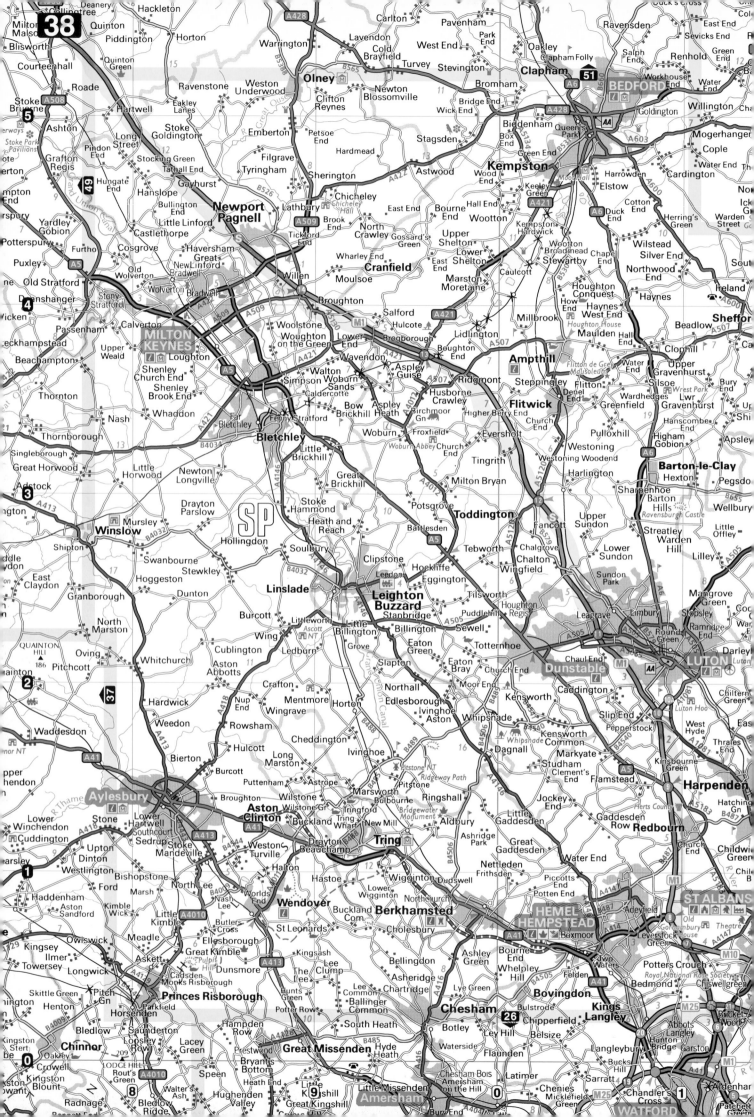

Felixstowe

Boxted
Langham
Dedham
Cattawade
Holbrook Bay
Gate
Parkeston
Quay
Parkeston
55
AA
Harwich
Harbour
Landguard Fort

Horkesley
Green
Boxted Cross
Dedham
Heath
Manningtree
New Mistley
River Stour
Wrabness
Bath
Side
The Redoubt
Landguard
Point

reat
Heath
Langham
Wick
Castle House
Lawford
Mistley
Ramsey
A120
Upper
Dovercourt
Harwich
ZEEBRUGGE

kesley
eath
Langham
Moor
Ardleigh
Heath
B1035
Mistley
Heath
Bradfield
Bradfield Heath
B1352
Dovercourt

Vest
rgholt
A12
Ardleigh
Horsleycross
Street
Wix
Little
Oakley
B1414
ESBJERG GOTEBORG
HAMBURG
HOEK VAN HOLLAND

8
Fox
Street
Burnt
Heath
Horsley
Cross
19
Goose
Green
Wix
Green
Great
Oakley
Pennyhole
Bay

Mile
End
A1232
Crockleford
Heath
A120
Bromley
Cross
Great
Bromley
A120
Tendring
Green
Tendring
Green
Stones
Green
17
Horsey
Island

A12
A604
Parson's
Heath
A120
Elmstead
Market
Little
Bentley
Goose
Green
Beaumont
Horsey
Island
The Naze

exden
4
COLCHESTER
Hare
Green
Tendring
B1035
Thorpe
Green
Thorpe-le-
Soken
Kirby-le-
Soken
1034

AA
Greenstead
A133
New
Quay
Beth Chatto
Frating
Green
16
Weeley
A133
B1033
B1033
Kirby
Cross
Walton on
the Naze

hrub
End
B1026
Old
Heath
Wivenhoe
Cross
Elmstead
Heath
Frating
Elmstead Row
Great
Bentley
Weeley
Heath
B1441
Great
Holland
Frinton-on-sea

Blackheath
Rowhedge
Wivenhoe
Alresford
Aingers
Green
Little
Clacton
B1032

Malting
Green
Fingringhoe
High Park
Corner
Tenpenny
Heath
Cook's
Green
Great
Holland
TM

Abberton
South Green
Thorrington
Samson's
Corner
Great
Clacton
Holland-on-Sea

Langenhoe
R Colne
Hurst
Green
B1027
B1027
A133
Rush
Green

Abberton
Reservoir
Peldon
Brightlingsea
St Osyth
CLACTON-ON-SEA

Great
Wigborough
B1025
MERSEA
ISLAND
Point Clear
Jaywick

West
Mersea
East
Mersea
Colne Point

Shinglehead
Point

Sales Point
Bradwell
Waterside

B1021
Bradwell-on-Sea

rence
Tillingham

rence
Dengie

Asheldham

uthminster

eyhills

Holliwell Point
nham-on-
Crouch

Foulness Point

llasea
land
Courtsend

Churchend

FOULNESS
ISLAND

SCALE

0	1	2	3	4	5 miles

0	1	2	3	4	5 kilometres

TR

0
VLISSINGEN (FLUSHING)
1
2
3

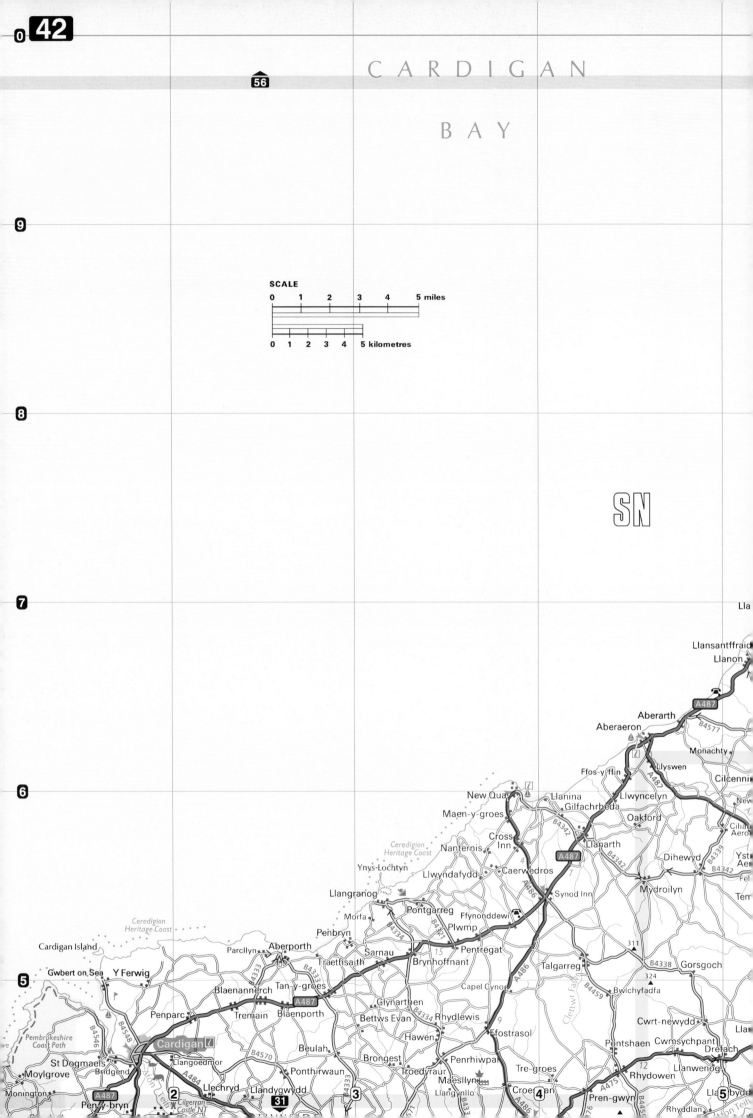

56

C A R D I G A N

B A Y

9

SCALE

| 0 | 1 | 2 | 3 | 4 | 5 miles |

| 0 | 1 | 2 | 3 | 4 | 5 kilometres |

8

SN

7

Lla

Llansantffrai
Llanon

Aberarth
A487
Aberaeron
B4577

Monachty

Ffos-y-ffin
Llyswen
Cilcenni

6
New Quay
Llanina
Gilfachrheda
Llwyncelyn
New

Maen-y-groes
B4342
Oakford

Cross
Inn
Llanarth
Ceredigion
Heritage Coast
Nanternis
Dihewyd
Yst
A487
Ael

Ynys-Lochtyn
Caerwedros
B4342
Fel

Llwyndafydd
A486
Mydroilyn
Tem

Llangranog
Synod Inn

Pontgarreg

Morfa
Ffynonddewi

Penbryn
Plwmp
311

Ceredigion
Heritage Coast
B4334
Pentregat
A486
Gorsgoch

Cardigan Island
Parcllyn
Aberporth
Sarnau
B4338
324

Gwbert on Sea
Y Ferwig
Traethsaith
Brynhoffnant
Talgarreg
Bwlchyfadfa
B4459

5
Blaenannerch
Tan-y-groes
Capel Cynon

A487
Glynarthen
Cwrt-newydd
Penparc
Tremain
Blaenporth
Bettws Evan
B4334
Rhydlewis

St Dogmaels
Cardigan
Beulah
Hawen
Efostrasol
Pontshaen
Cwmsychpant
Drefach

Moylgrove
Bridgend
Llangoedmor
Ponthirwaun
Brongest
Penrhiwpa
Tre-groes
Rhydowen
Llanwenog

Pembrokeshire
Coast Path
B4570
Troedyraur
Maesllyn
Llanwenog
Lla

Monington
A487
Llechryd
Llandygwydd
Croesan
Pren-gwyn
Lla

Pen-y-bryn
A484
B4333
Llangynllo
Rhyddlan

31
Cilgerran
Castle NT
2
3
4
5

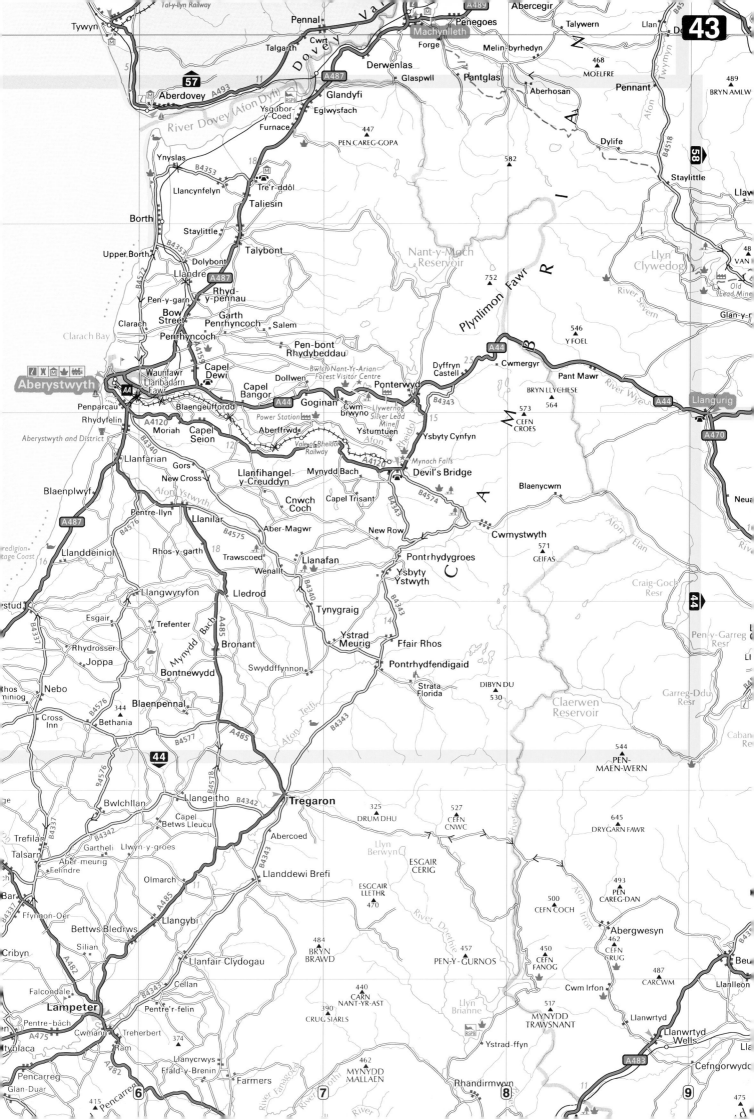

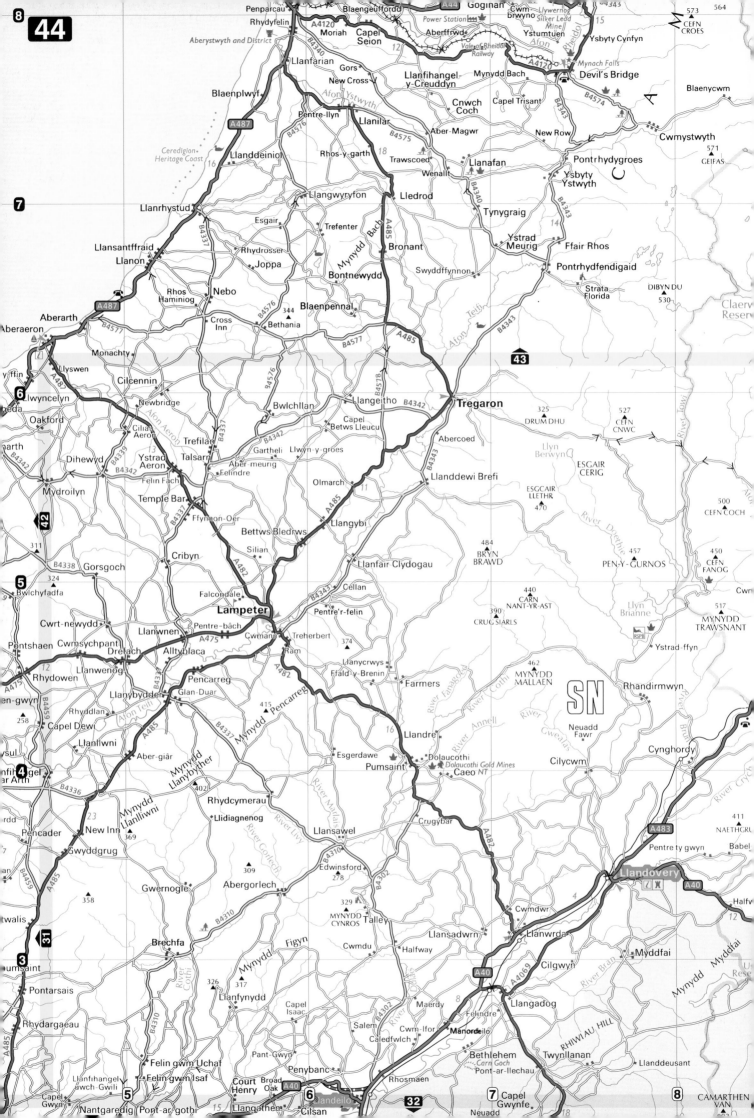

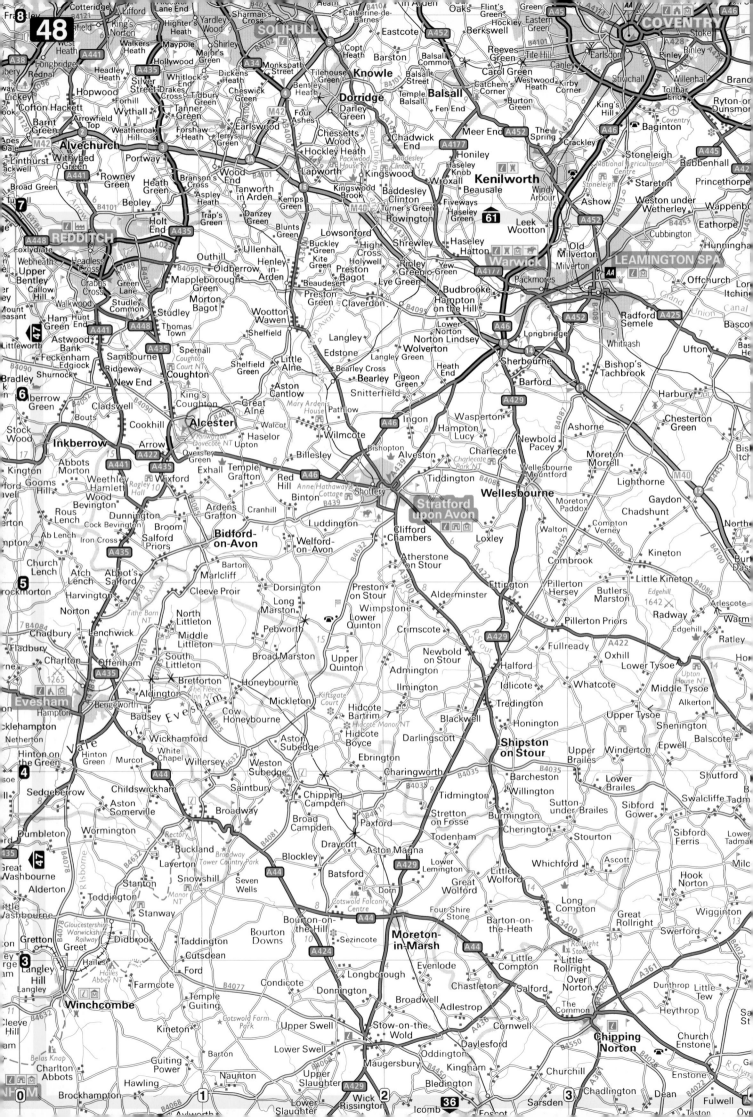

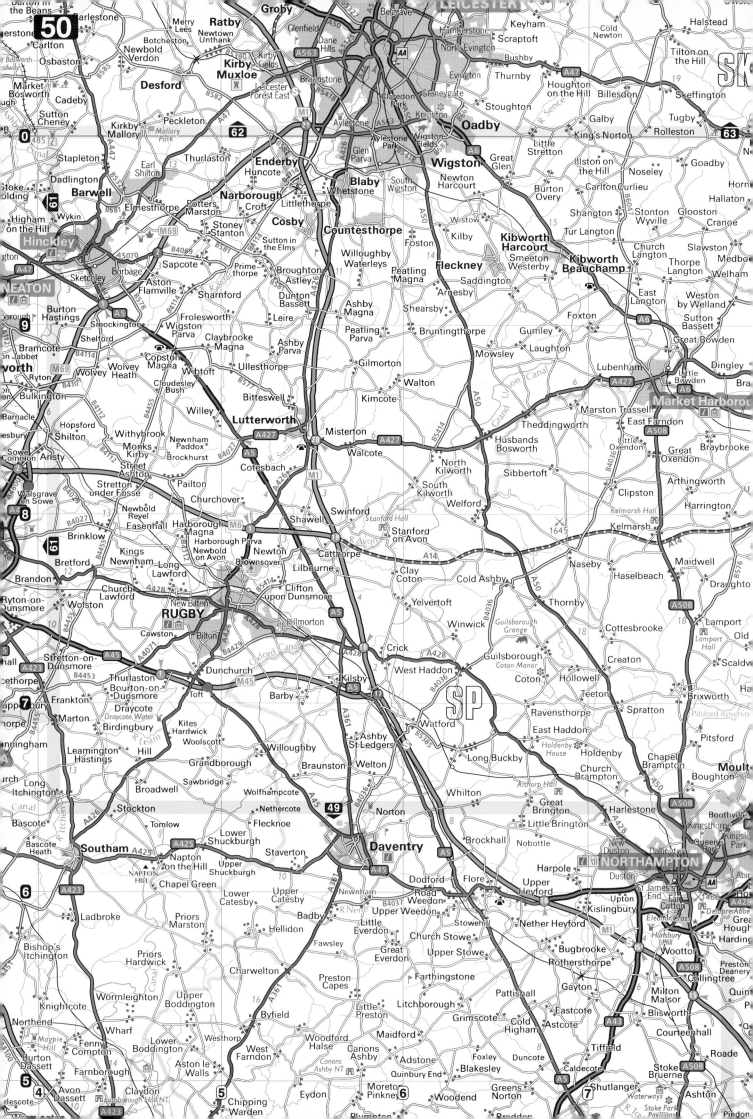

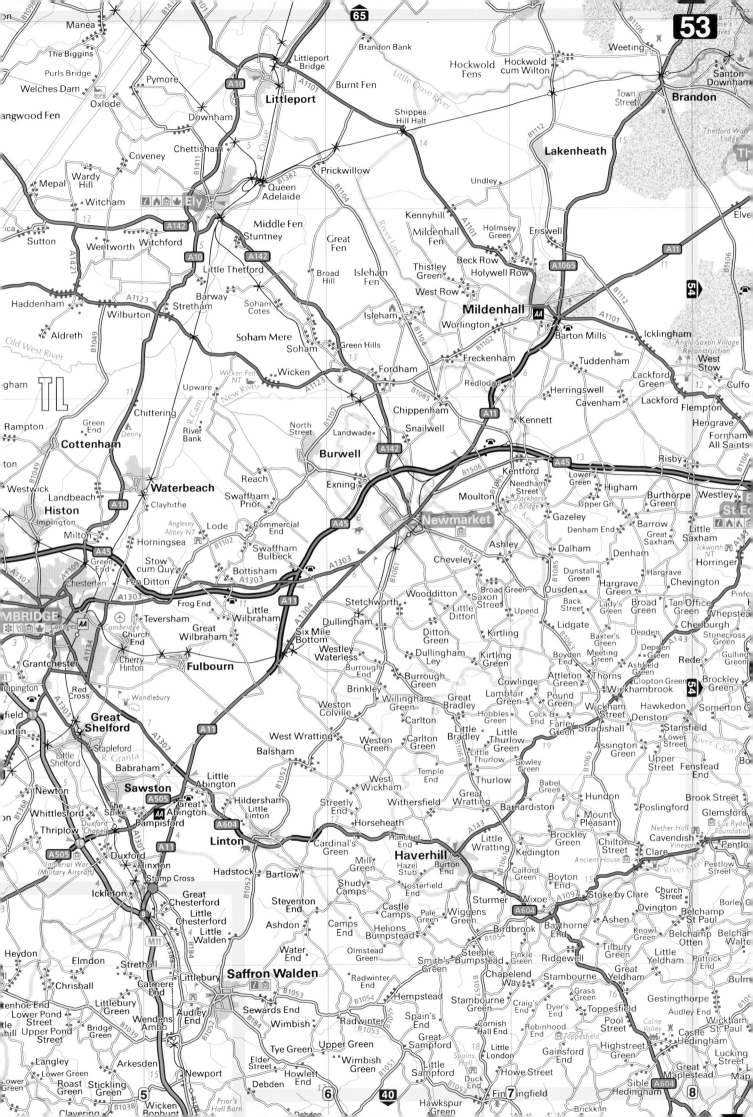

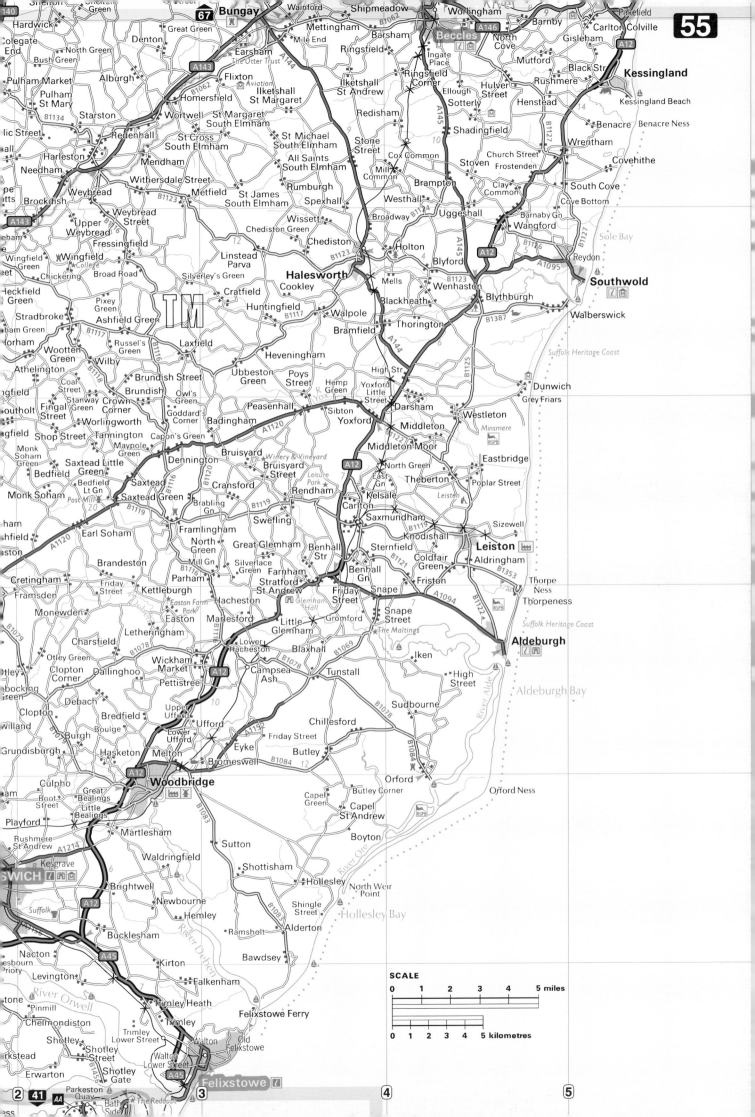

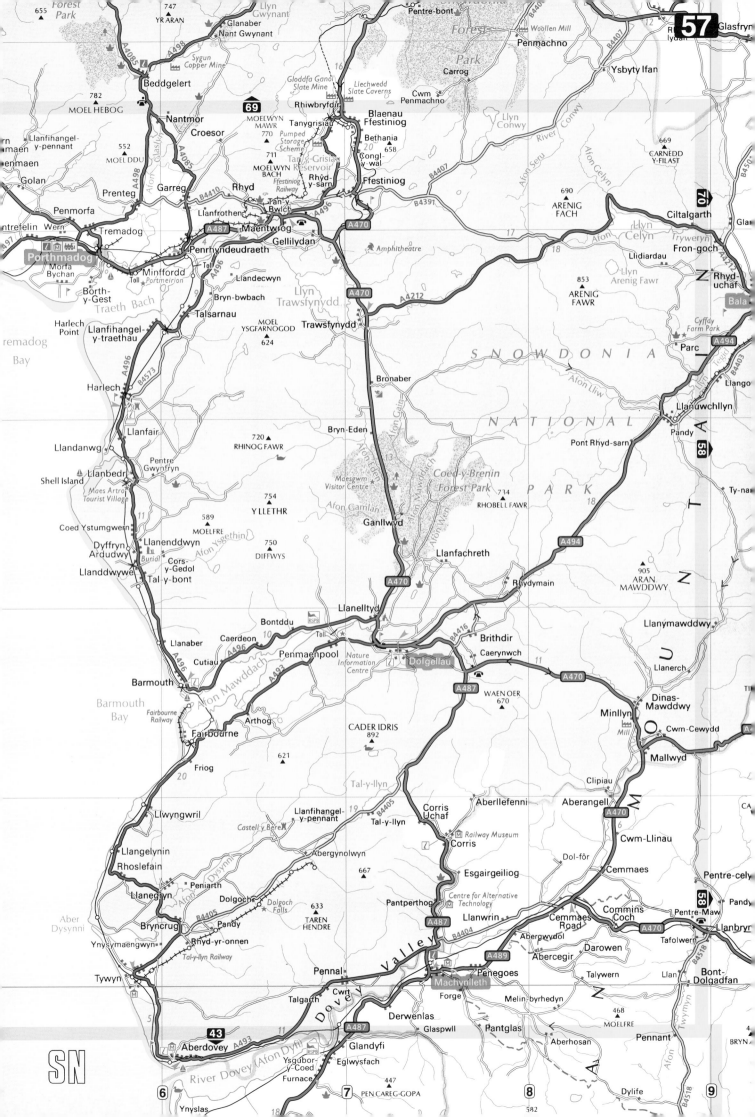

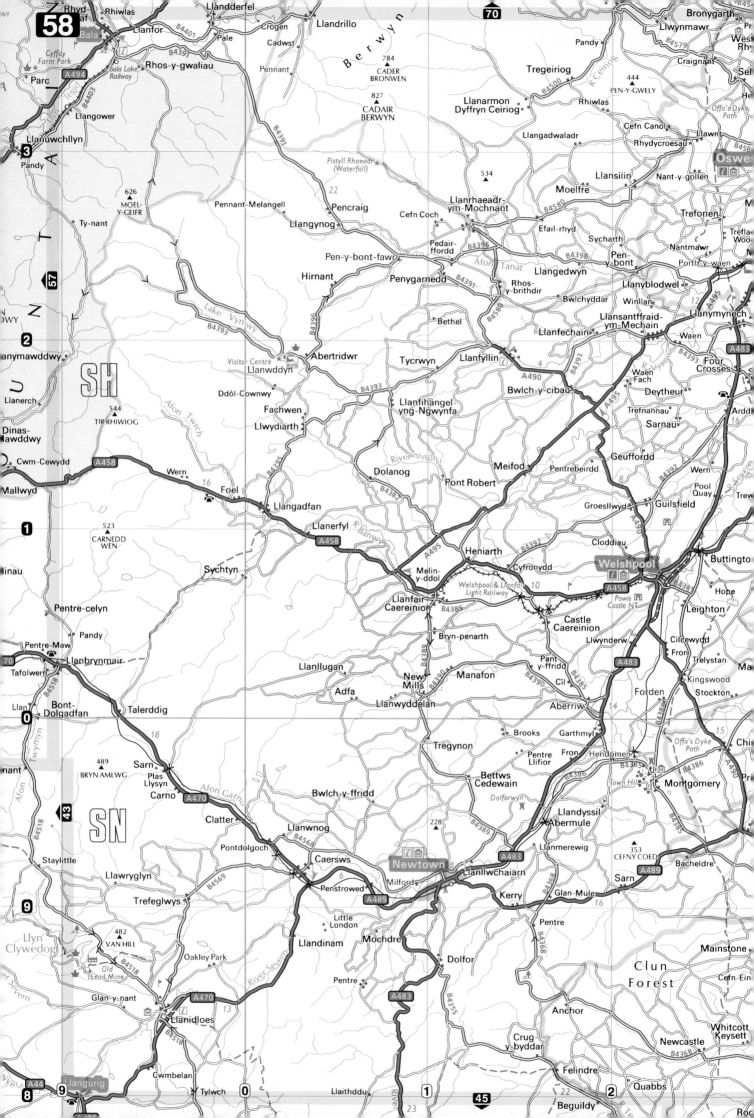

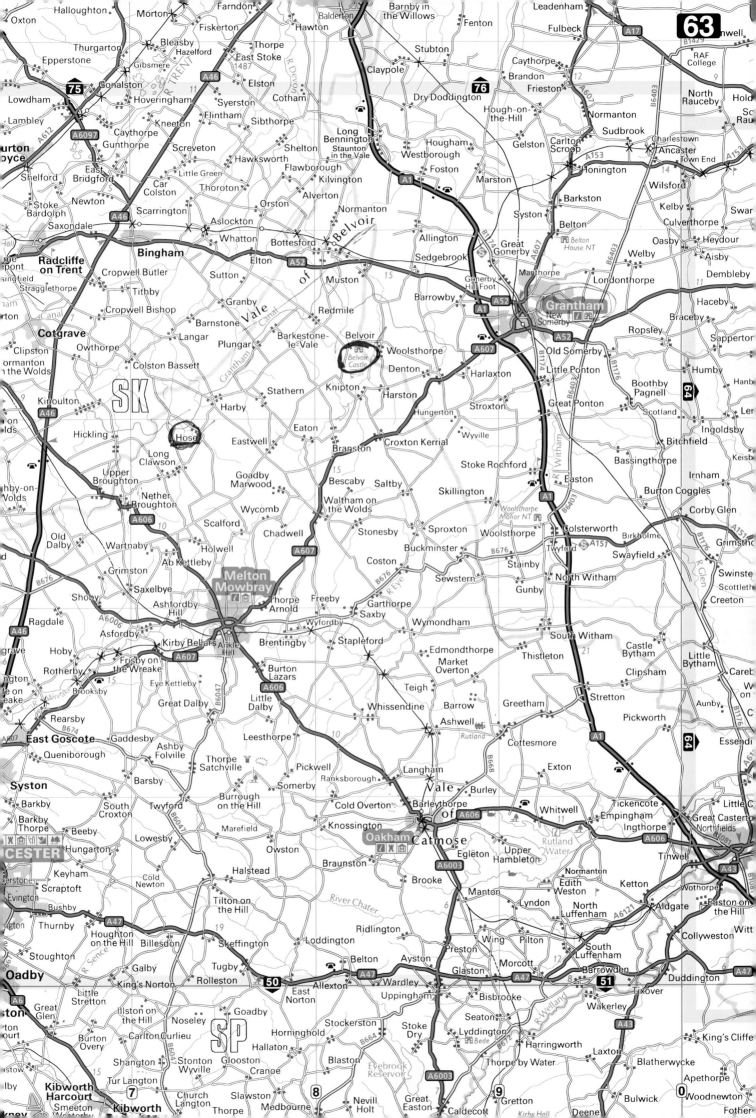

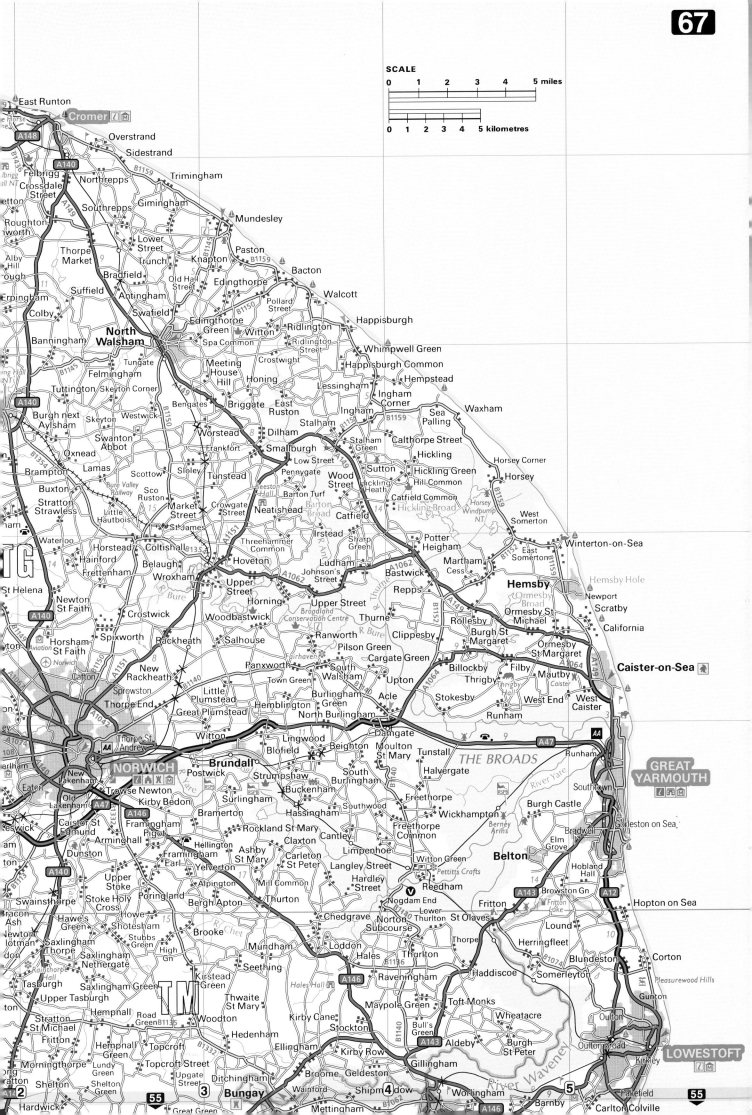

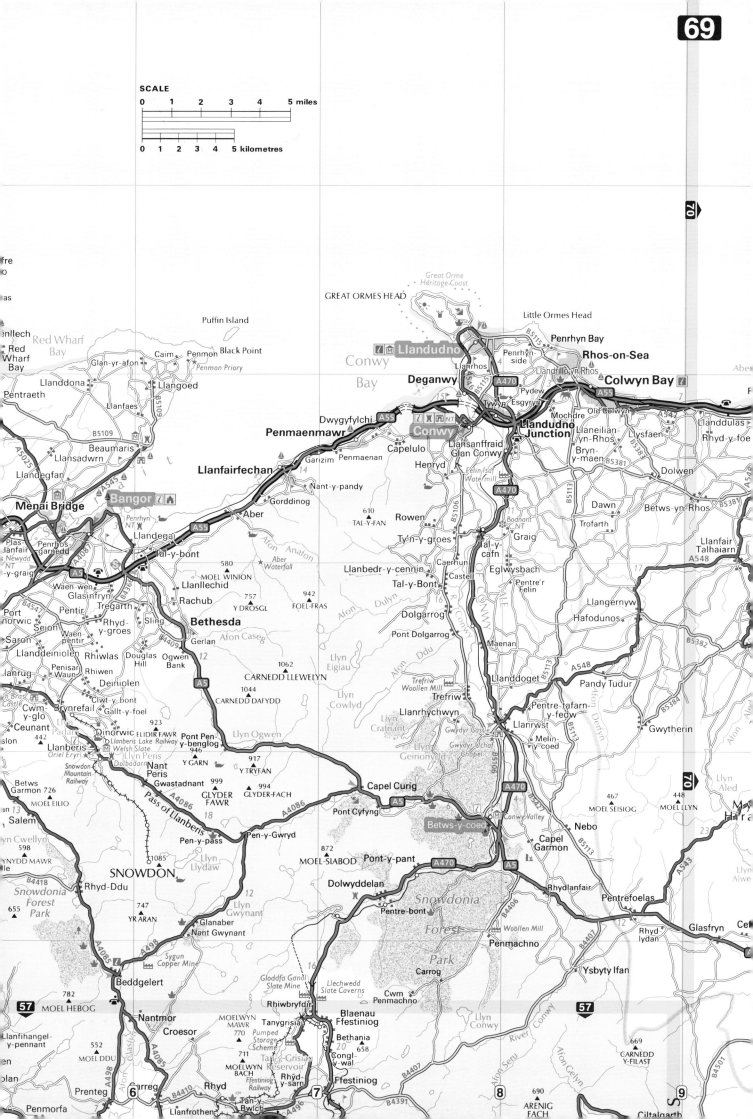

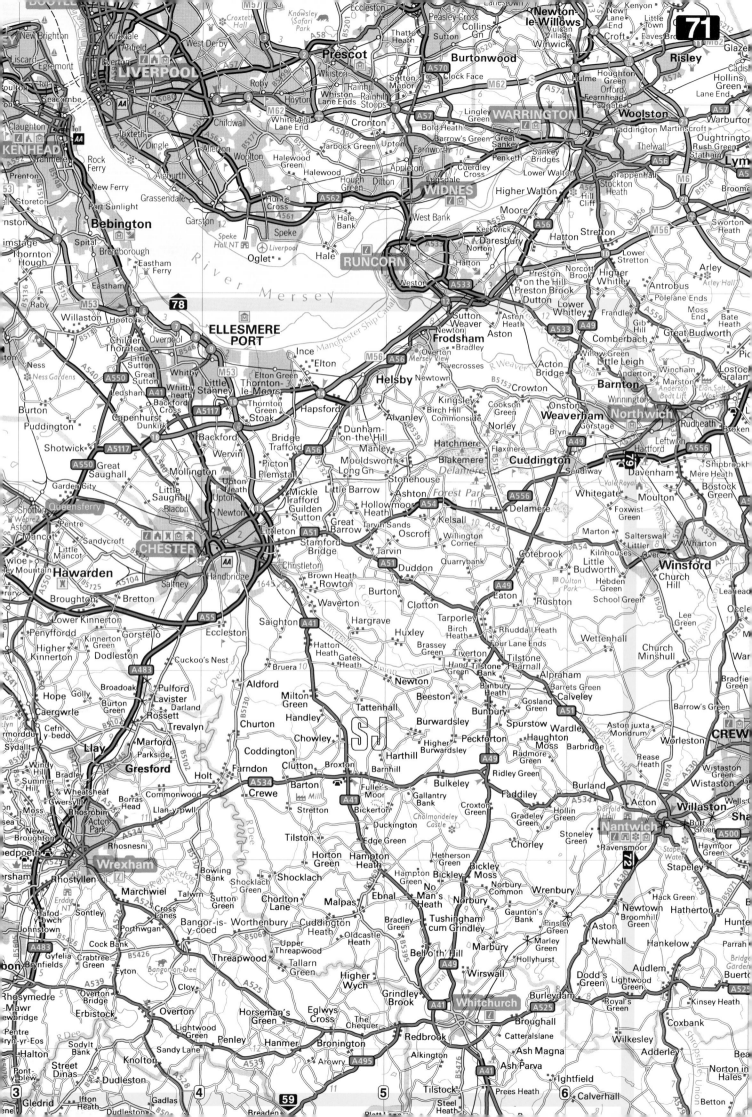

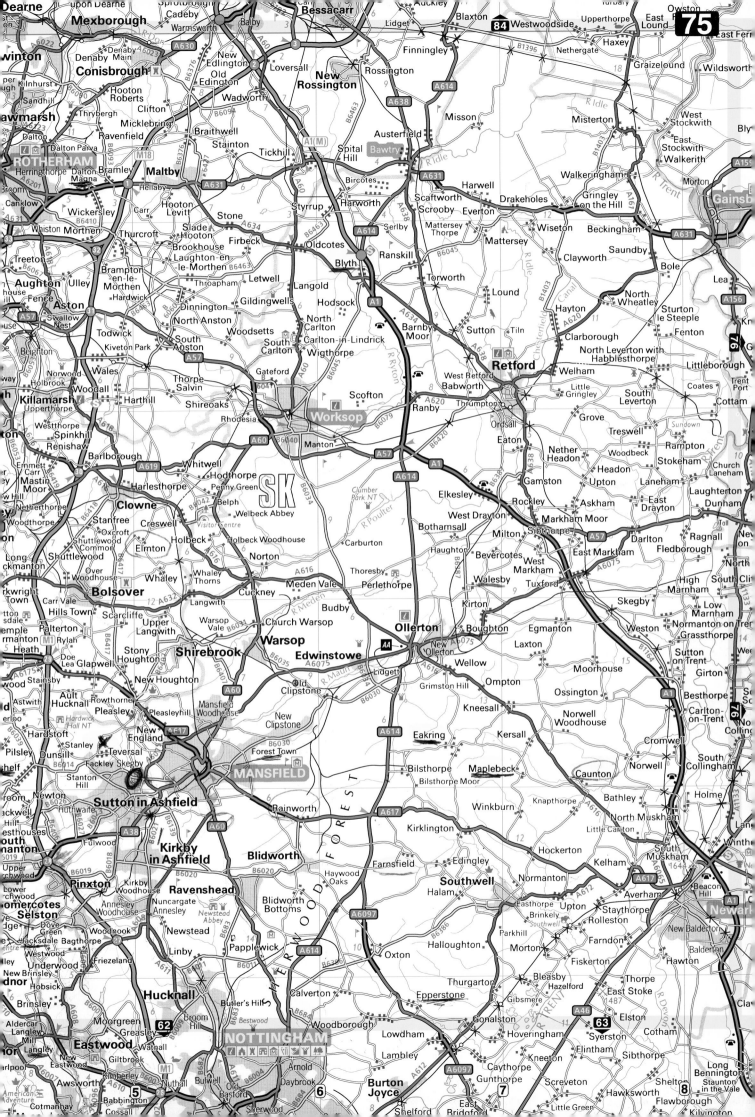

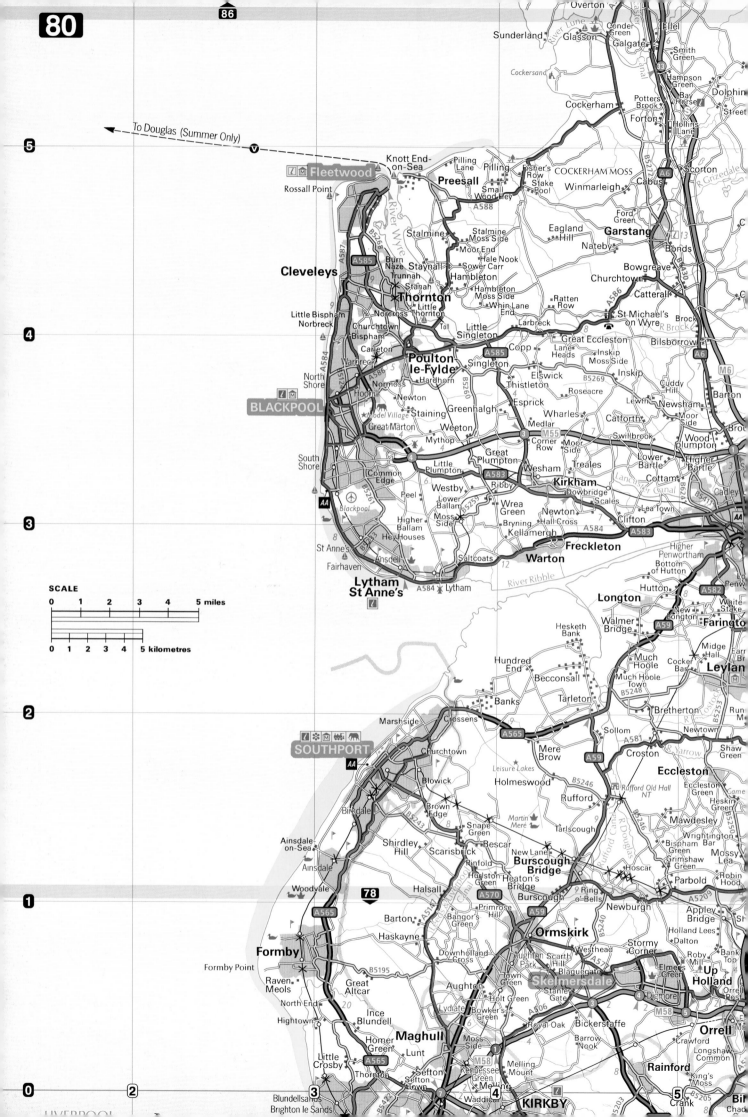

86

To Douglas (Summer Only)

5

Sunderland · Glasson · Conder Green · Ellel · Galgate · Smith Green
River Lune · Cockersand · Hampson Green
Cockerham · Potters Brook · Forton · Hollins Lane · Bay Horse · Dolphin Street
A6

Fleetwood · Knott End-on-Sea · Pilling Lane · Pilling · Fisher's Row · Stake Pool · COCKERHAM MOSS · Cabus · Scorton
Rossall Point · Preesall · Small Wood Hey · Winmarleigh · Ford Green
A588 · Eagland Hill · Nateby · Garstang · Bonds
Stalmine · Stalmine Moss Side · Moor End · Hale Nook · Sower Carr · B5430 · Bowgreave · Catterall
Burn Naze · Staynall · Hambleton · Churchtown
Cleveleys · Trunnah · Stanah · Hambleton Moss Side · Ratten Row · A586 · St Michael's on Wyre · Brock
Thornton · Little Thornton · Whin Lane End · Larbreck · R Brock · Bilsborrow · A6
Little Bispham · Noreross · Churchtown Bispham · Toll · Little Singleton · Great Eccleston · Lane Heads · Inskip Moss Side · Inskip · Cuddy Hill · Barton · M6
Norbreck · Carleton · Copp · Elswick · Roseacre · Newsham · Moor Side
4 · Warbreck · A585 · Singleton · Thistleton · Lewth · Wood- plumpton · Higher Bartle
North Shore · Hoohill · Normoss · Hardhorn · B5260 · Staining · Greenhalgh · Medlar · Wharles · Catforth · Swillbrook · Lower Bartle · Cottam · B5411 · Cadley
BLACKPOOL · Model Village · Newton · Weeton · M55 · Corner Row · Moor Side · Treales
Great Marton · Mythop · 3 · M55 · Clifton · Lea Town · AA
South Shore · 4 · Little Plumpton · Great Plumpton · Wesham · Kirkham · Dowbridge · Scales
Common Edge · Westby · A583 · Ribby · A583
Peel · Lower Ballam · Wrea Green · Newton · Lancaster Canal
Blackpool · Higher Ballam · Moss Side · Bryning · Hall Cross · A584 · A583 · Higher Penwortham
3 · Hey Houses · Kellamergh · Freckleton · Bottom of Hutton
St Anne's · Ansdell · Saltcoats · Warton · Hutton · A582 · Penw
Fairhaven · Lytham · River Ribble · Longton · New Longton · White Stake · Faringto
Lytham St Anne's · A584 · Lytham · Walmer Bridge · A59
Hesketh Bank · Midge Hall · Leylan
SCALE · Hundred End · Much Hoole · Cocker Bar · Earn Br
0 1 2 3 4 5 miles · Becconsall · Much Hoole Town · B5248
0 1 2 3 4 5 kilometres · Banks · Tarleton · Bretherton · B5253 · Run M
Marshside · Crossens · 9 · A565 · Sollom · A581 · Newtown
2 · Churchtown · Mere Brow · A59 · Croston · R Yarrow · Shaw Green
SOUTHPORT · Leisure Lakes · Holmeswood · B5246 · Rufford · Eccleston · Ga
AA · Blowick · Rufford Old Hall NT · Eccleston Green · Heskin Green
Birkdale · Brown Edge · Snape Green · Martin Mere · Tarlscough · Mawdesley · Wrightington · Bispham Green · Mossy Lea
Ainsdale-on-Sea · Shirdley Hill · Scarisbrick · Bescar · New Lane · Burscough Bridge · Hoscar · Grimshaw Green · Parbold · Robin Hood
Ainsdale · Rinfold · Hulston Green · Burscough · 9 Ring o' Bells · Appley Bridge
Woodvale · 78 · Halsall · Heaton's Bridge · A570 · Newburgh · Holland Lees · Dalton
1 · A565 · Barton · Bangor's Green · Primrose Hill · A59 · Ormskirk · B5240 · Stormy Corner · Roby Mill · Bank Top
Formby · Haskayne · Downholland Cross · Aughton Park · Scarth Hill · Westhead · A5 · Elmers Green · Up Holland · Orrell
Formby Point · B5195 · Bangor's Green · Town Green · Blaguegate · SKELMERSDALE · Digmore · M58
Raven Meols · Great Altcar · Aughton · Holt Green · Bowker's Green · Stanley Gate · 3 · 4 · Crawford · Longshaw Common
North End · Ince Blundell · Lydiate · A506 · Royal Oak · Bickerstaffe · Barrow Nook · M58 · Rainford · King's Moss
Hightown · Homer Green · Lunt · Moss Side · Melling Mount · Chad
0 · 2 · Little Crosby · Thornton · Sefton · Nettleson Green · Melling · 5 · Crank · Bi
LIVERPOOL · Blundellsands · Brighton le Sands · 3 · Ford · Waddicar · 4 · KIRKBY · Rainford

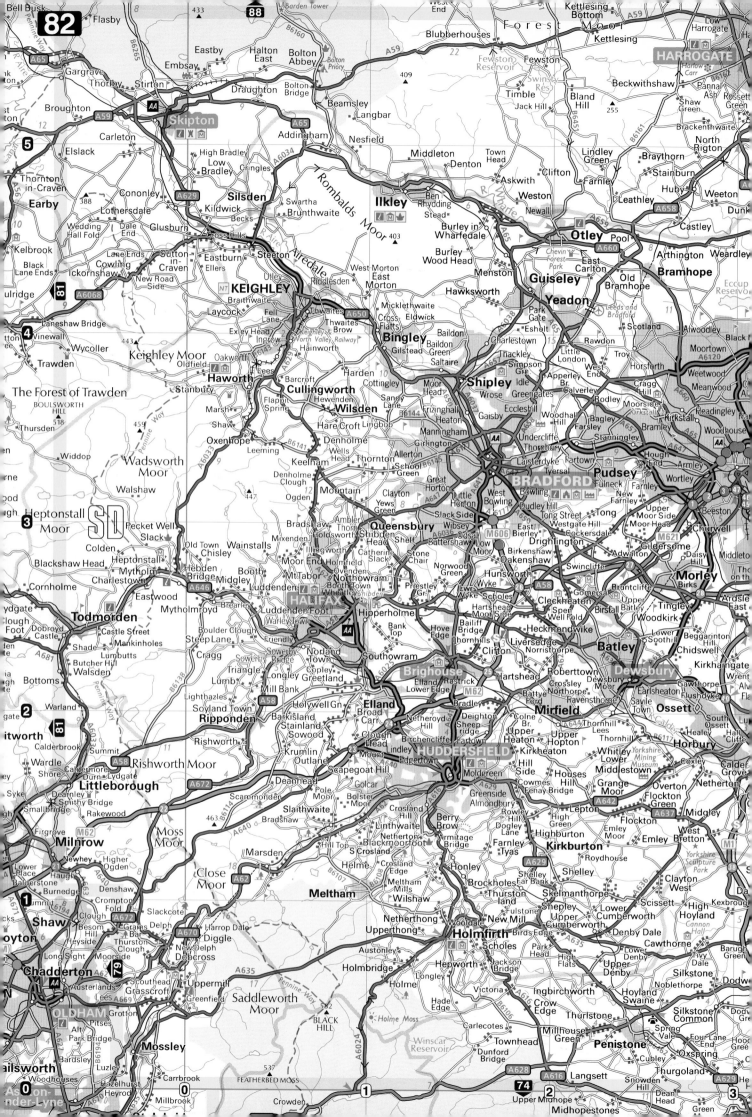

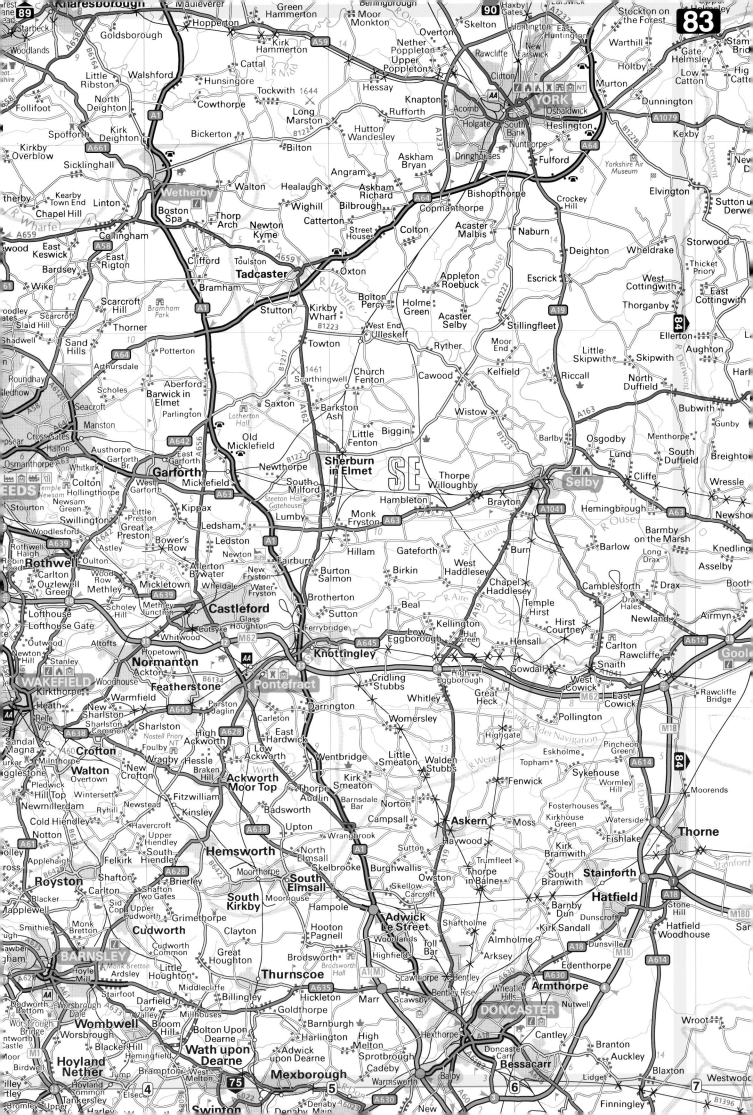

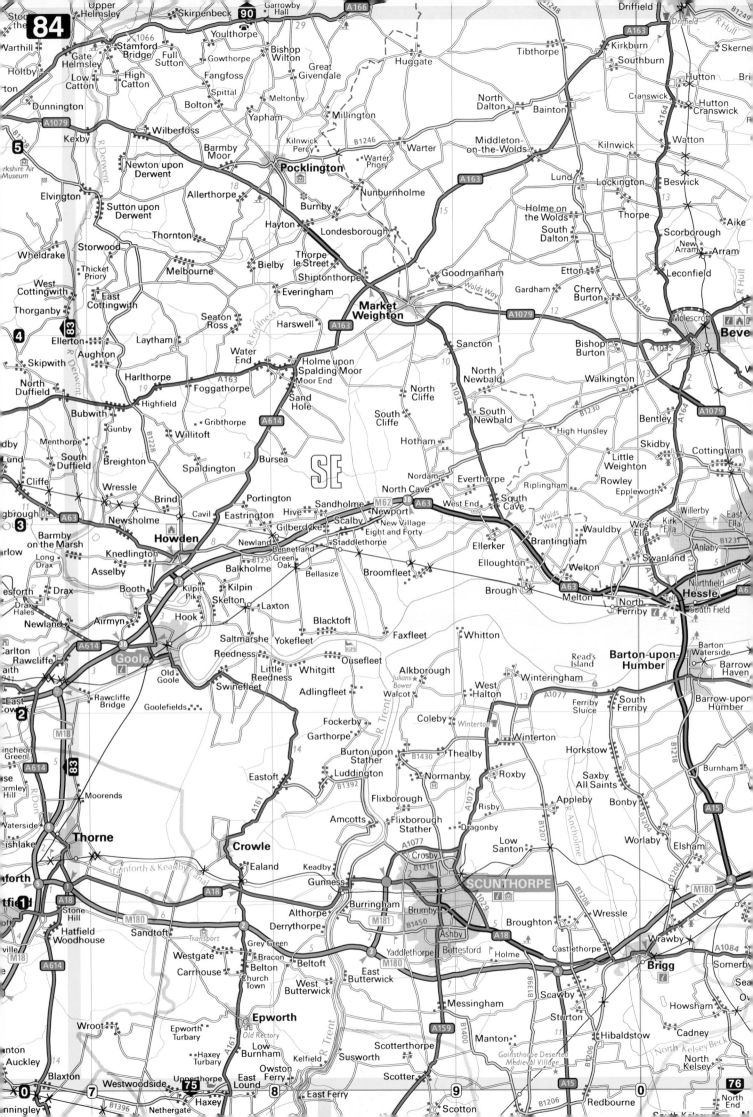

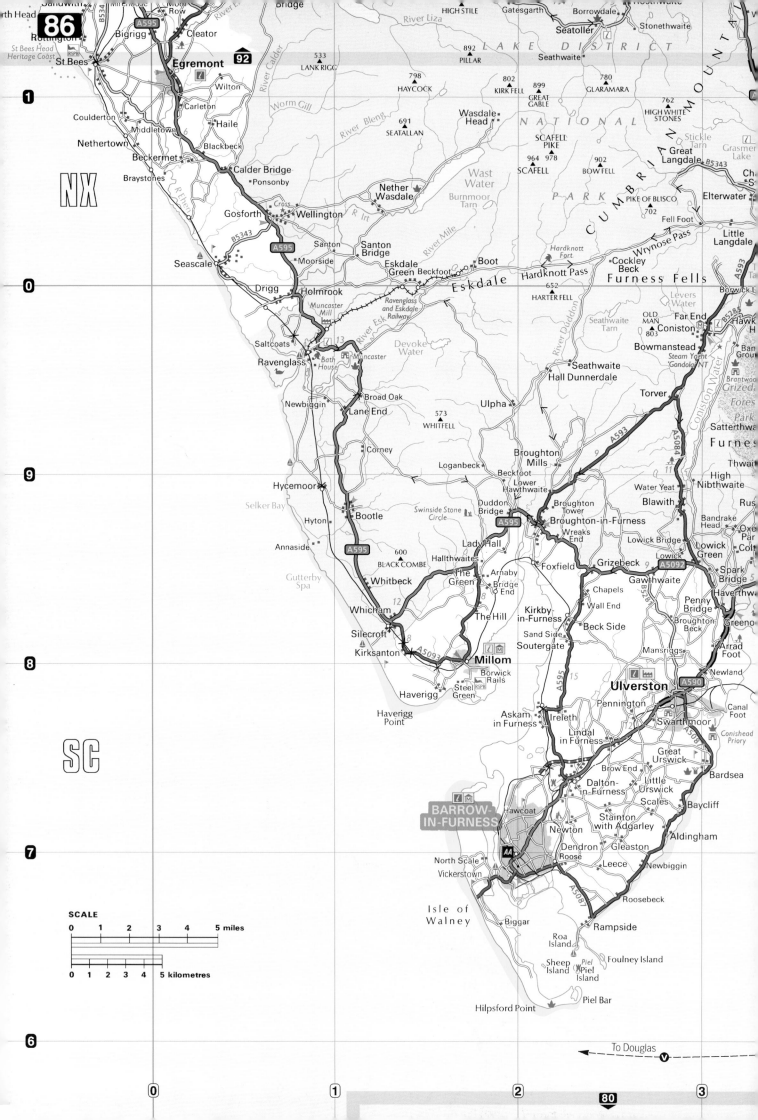

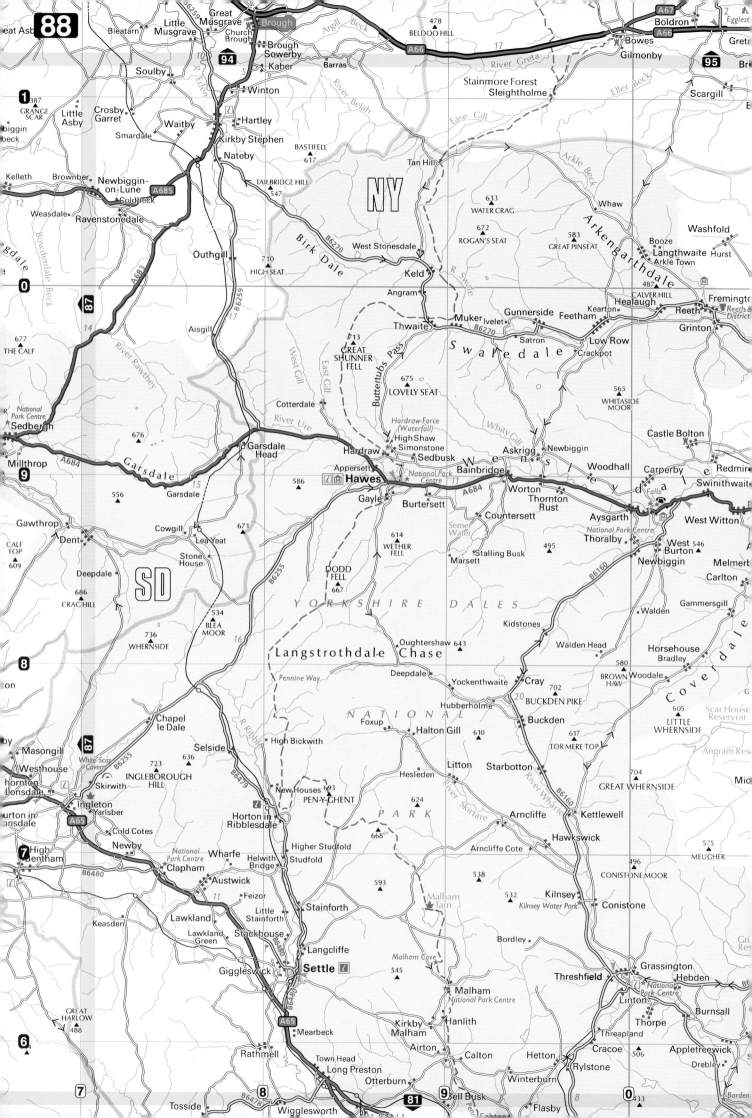

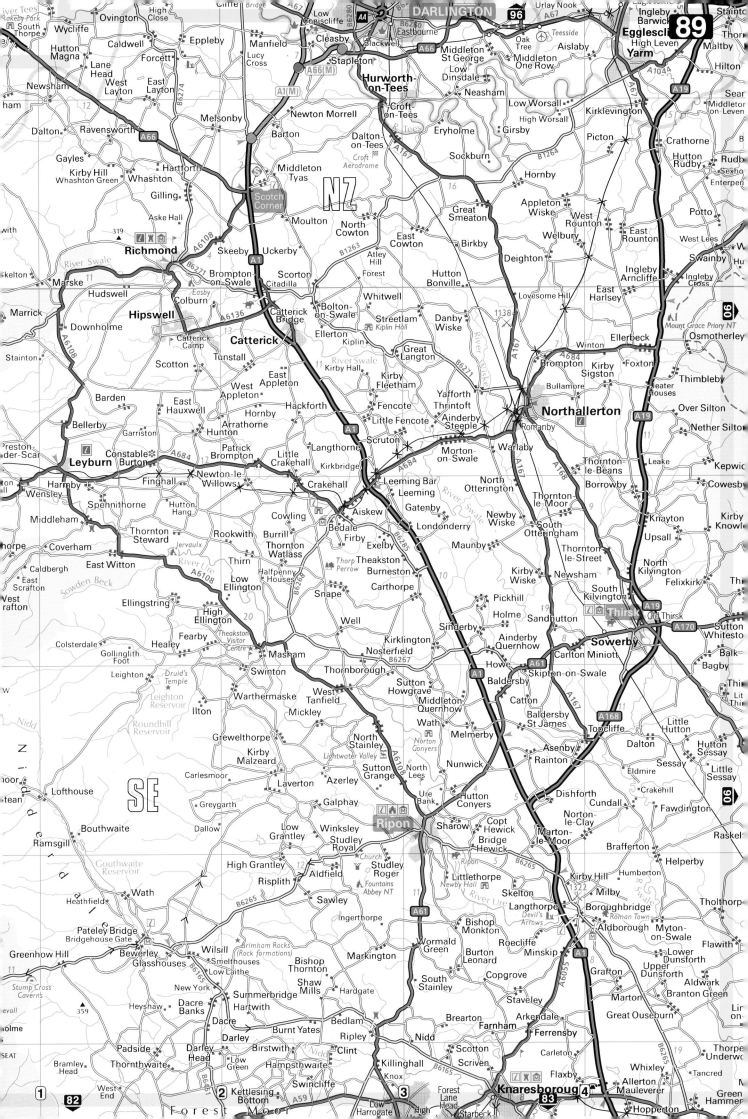

SCALE

0 1 2 3 4 5 miles

0 1 2 3 4 5 kilometres

Whitby
Saltwick Bay
Stainsacre
High Hawsker
Sneaton
Ilebranby
Low Hawsker
Sneatonthorpe
Raw
Ness Point or North Cheek
Robin Hood's Bay
Fylingthorpe
Robin Hood's Bay
Old Peak or South Cheek
Ravenscar
A171
20
Staintondale
Hayburn Wyke
Harwood Dale
Cloughton Newlands
Cloughton Wyke
Cloughton
Burniston
Cromer Point
Bickley
Silpho
Broxa
Cleveland Way
Langdale End
Hackness
Suffield
Newby
A165
Wrench Green
Everley
Scalby
ng Forest Park
River Derwent
Falsgrave
Scarborough
Sea Cut
Oliver's Mount
A170
East Ayton
West Ayton
AA A165
Sawdon
Hutton Buscel
Irton
Osgodby
Eastfield
Cayton Bay
TA
Ebberston
Ruston
Wykeham
Seamer
B1261
High Killerby
The Wyke
A170
Brompton
Cayton
Lebberston
Snainton
A64
Gristhorpe
Filey Brigg
R Hertford
Folkton
Muston
A1039
Filey
Yedingham
Willerby
Flixton
West Flotmanby
A1039
Staxton
s
Filey Bay
Sherburn
A64
Ganton
Hunmanby
16
Potter Brompton
A165
East Heslerton
B1249
Fordon
Reighton
West Heslerton
Speeton
ntringham
Foxholes
Wold Newton
B1229
Butterwick
Burton Fleming
Buckton
Thornwick Bay
Weaverthorpe
RSPB
Bempton
'Flamborough Headland Heritage Coast
Helperthorpe
Octon
Grindale
North Landing
West Lutton
East Lutton
Thwing
Selwicks Bay
FLAMBOROUGH HEAD
Kirby Grindalythe
B1253
Boynton
Flamborough
Low Mowthorpe
14
Langtoft
Rudston
Monolith
B1255
Sewerby
BRIDLINGTON
Sledmere
Cottam
Kilham
Bessingby
Portminion Model Village
Bridlington
Towthorpe
B1251
B1252
Carnaby
Haisthorpe
Hilderthorpe
BAY
Ruston Parva
12
Burton Agnes
Carnaby
Thornholme
A165
Lowthorpe
Harpham
Norman Manor House
Fraisthorpe
Garton-on-the-Wolds
A166
Nafferton
Gransmoor
thorpe
Wetwang
A166
Elmswell
Little Kelk
Great Kelk
Lissett
Barmston
9
Driffield
B1248
Little Driffield
B1249
R.H.
Wansford
Gembling
85
B1242
Ulrome
0
1
2
Easton

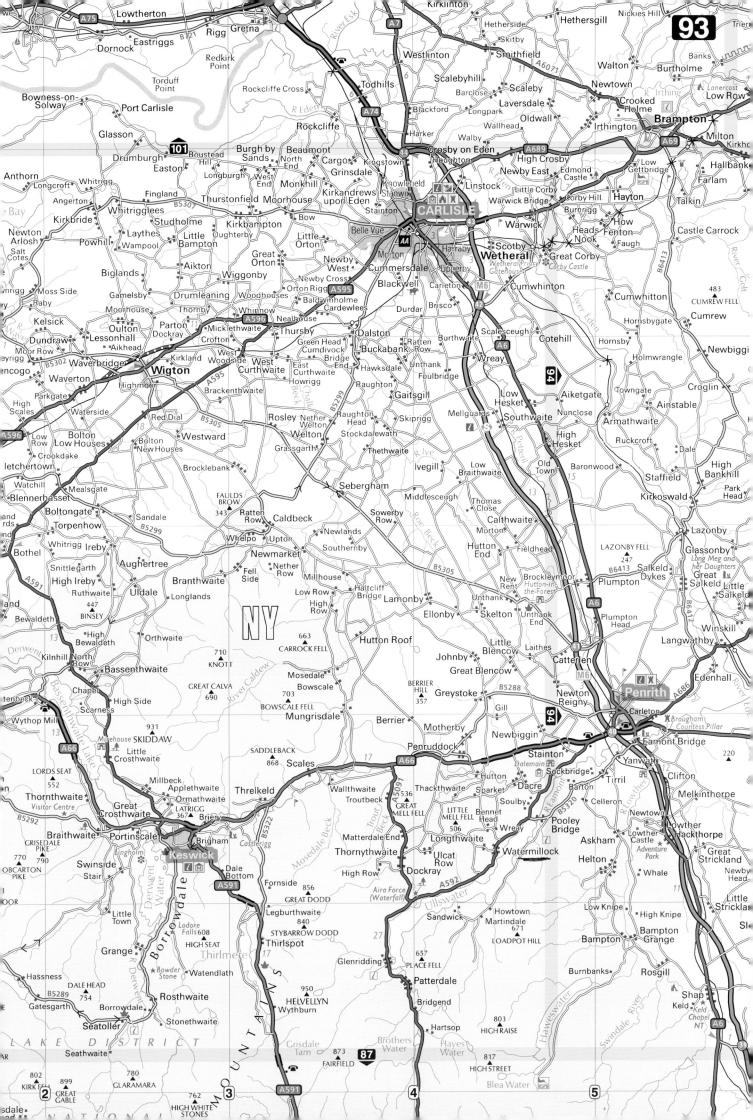

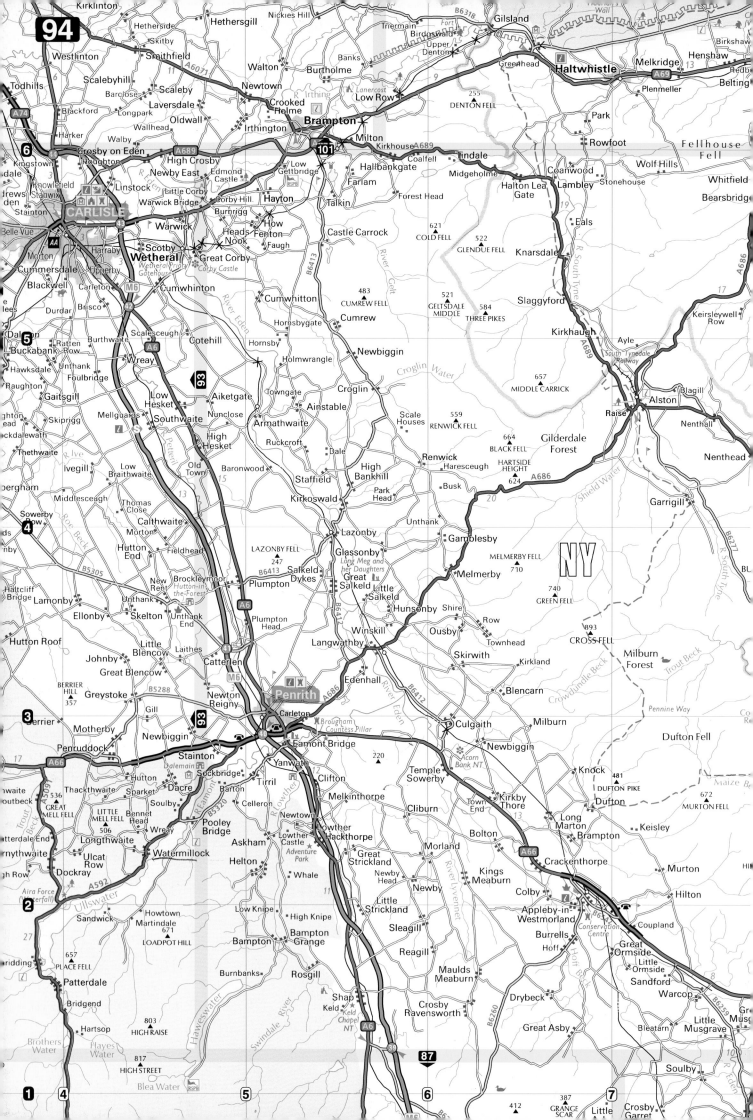

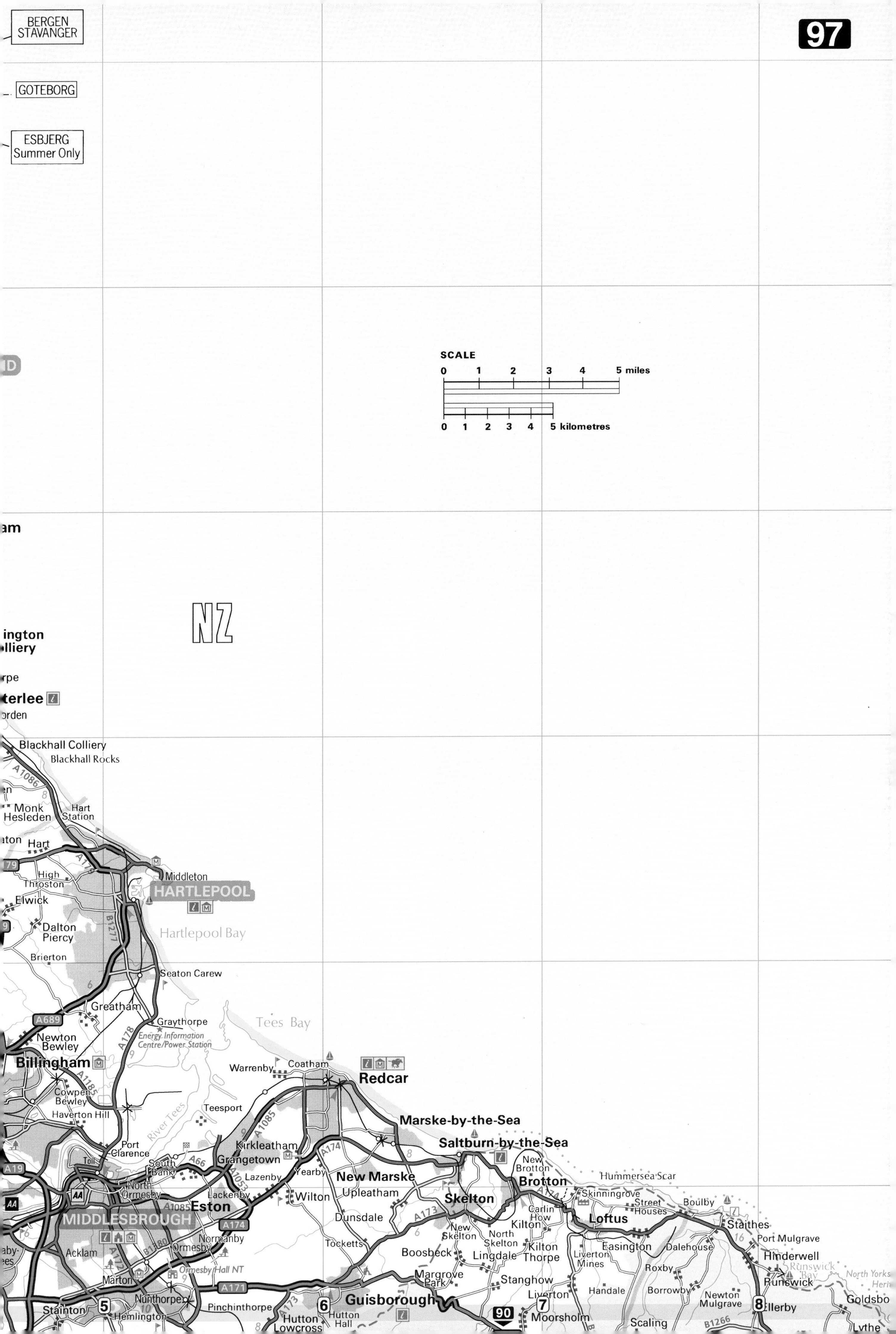

SCALE

0	1	2	3	4	5 miles

0	1	2	3	4	5 kilometres

ID

am

NZ

ington
lliery

rpe

terlee ℹ
orden

Blackhall Colliery
Blackhall Rocks

A1086

en
8

Monk
Hesleden

Hart
Station

ton   Hart

79

High
Throston

Elwick

Middleton

Ⓜ

HARTLEPOOL
ℹ Ⓜ

9

Dalton
Piercy

Hartlepool Bay

Brierton

Seaton Carew

A689

Greatham

6

Newton
Bewley

Graythorpe

A178

Energy Information
Centre/Power Station

Tees Bay

Billingham   Ⓜ

A1185

Cowpen
Bewley

Warrenby   Coatham   ℹ Ⓜ 🐎

Haverton Hill

River Tees

Teesport

Redcar

A19

Port
Clarence

Toll

South
Bank

A66

Marske-by-the-Sea

Kirkleatham

A1085

A174

Saltburn-by-the-Sea

North
Ormesby

Lazenby

Grangetown
Ⓜ

Yearby

8

New
Brotton

Hummersea Scar

AA

Lackenby   A1053

Wilton

New Marske

Brotton

Skinningrove   Boulby

MIDDLESBROUGH
ℹ Ⓜ

Eston

A174

Upleatham

Skelton

Carlin
How

Street
Houses

by-s

Normanby

Dunsdale

Ormesby

B1380

Tocketts

New
Skelton   Kilton

North
Skelton   Kilton
Thorpe

Loftus

Staithes

Acklam

Ormesby Hall NT

Boosbeck

Lingdale

Easington   Dalehouse

Port Mulgrave

Marton

A171

Margrove
Park

Stanghow   Handale   Borrowby

Newton
Mulgrave

Hinderwell

Runswick

Roxby

Runswick
Bay

North Yorks
Heri

5
Stainton

Nunthorpe

A173

Pinchinthorpe

6
Guisborough

Hutton
Lowcross   Hutton
Hall

Liverton

90
Moorsholm

7

Liverton
Mines

Scaling

B1266

Ⓜ

8
Ellerby

Goldsbo

Lythe

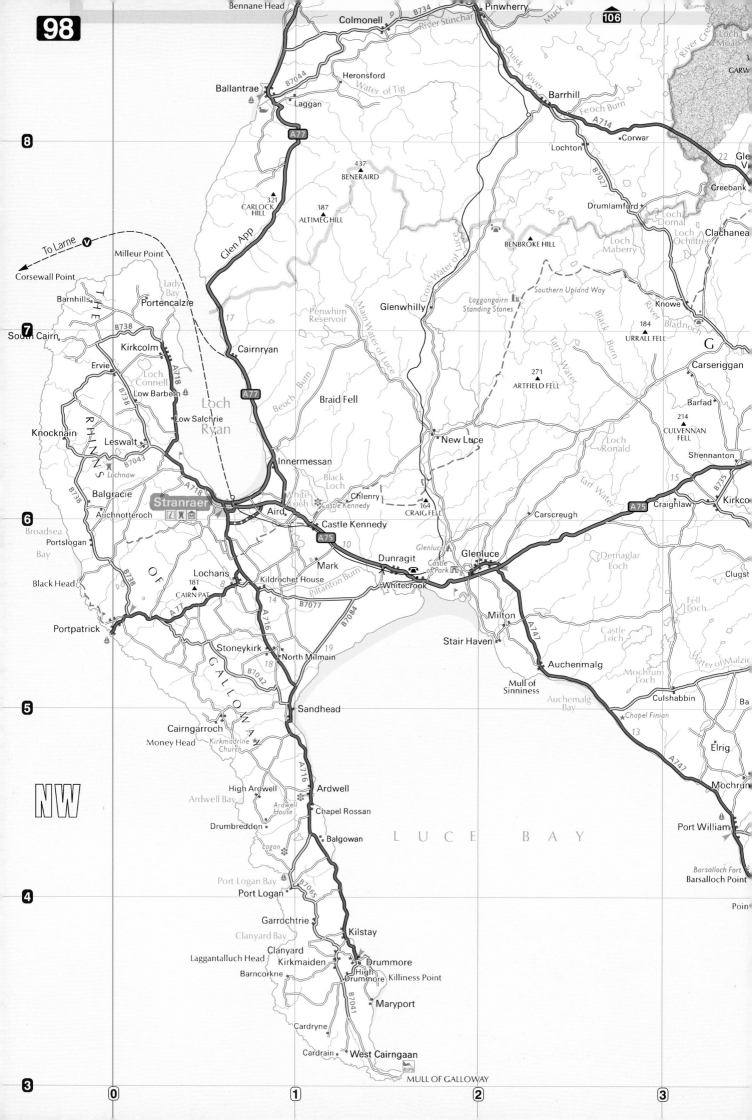

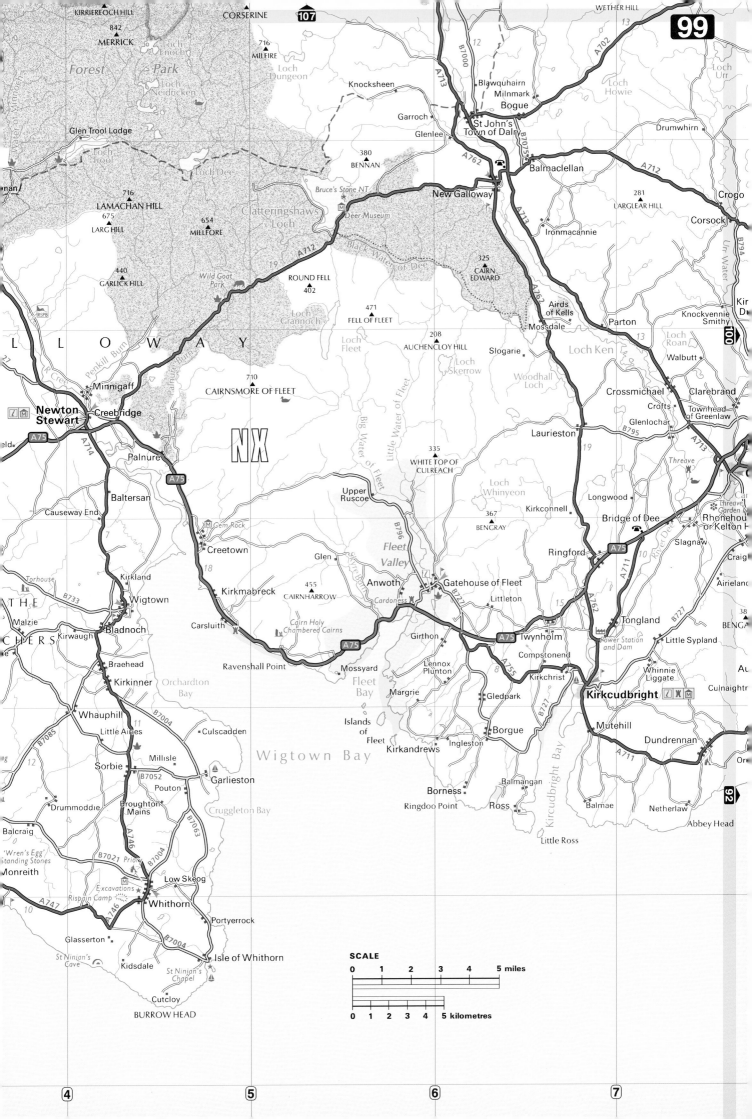

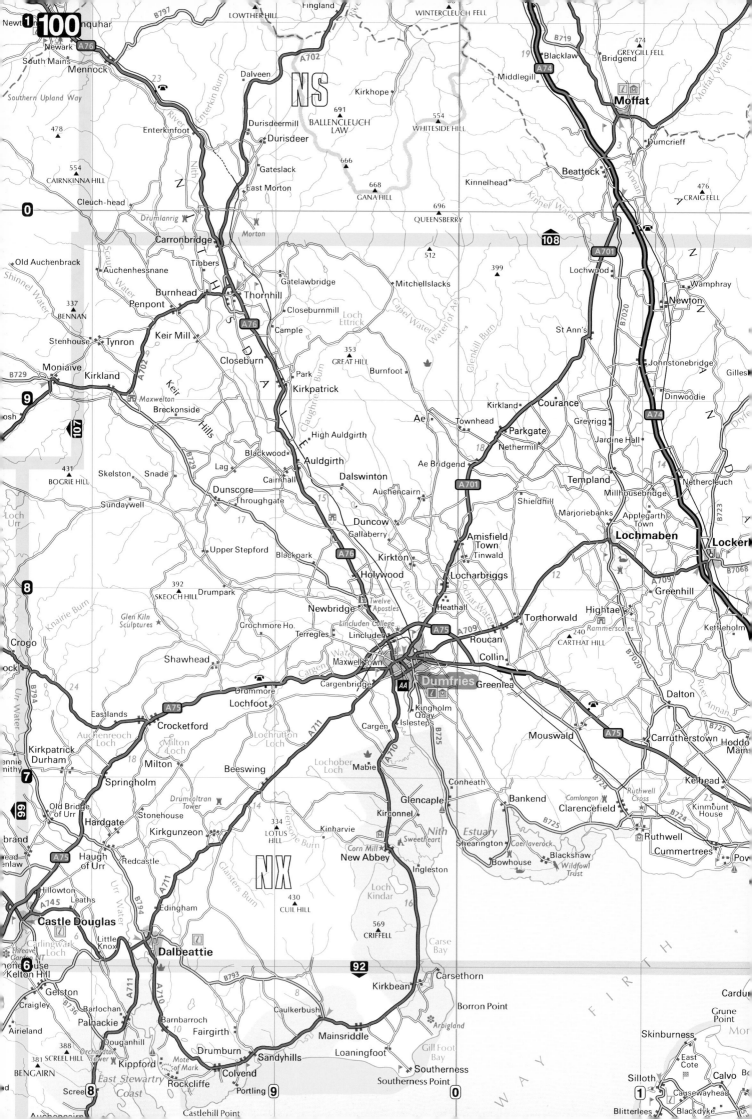

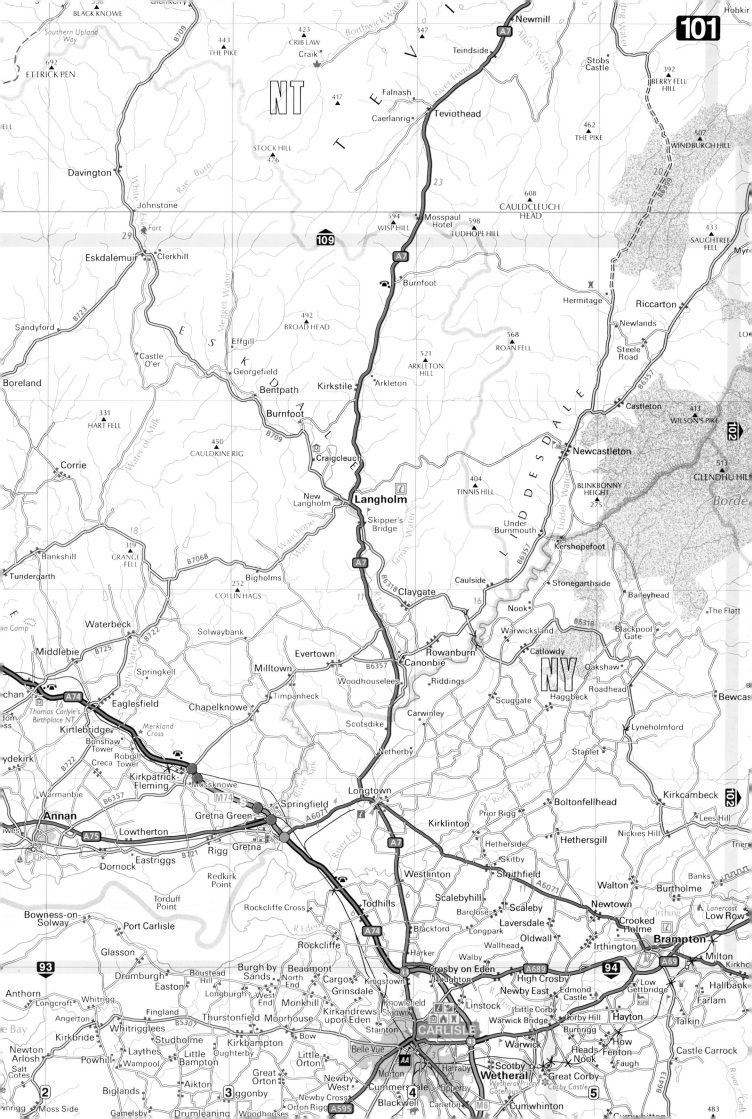

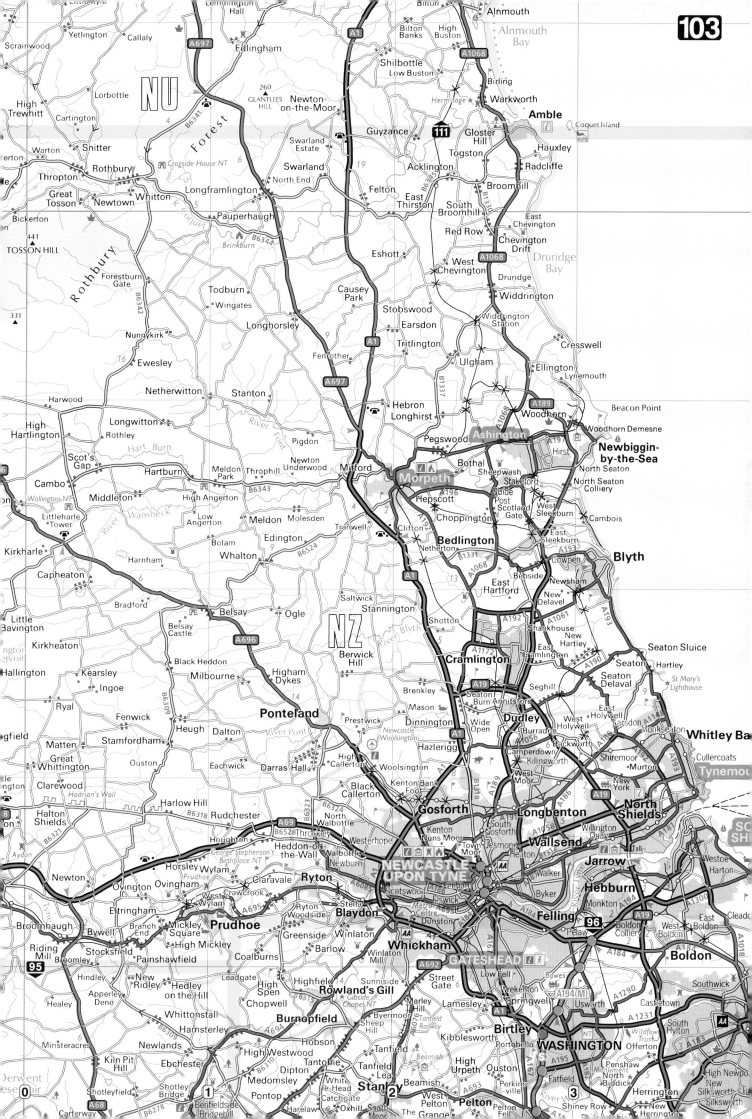

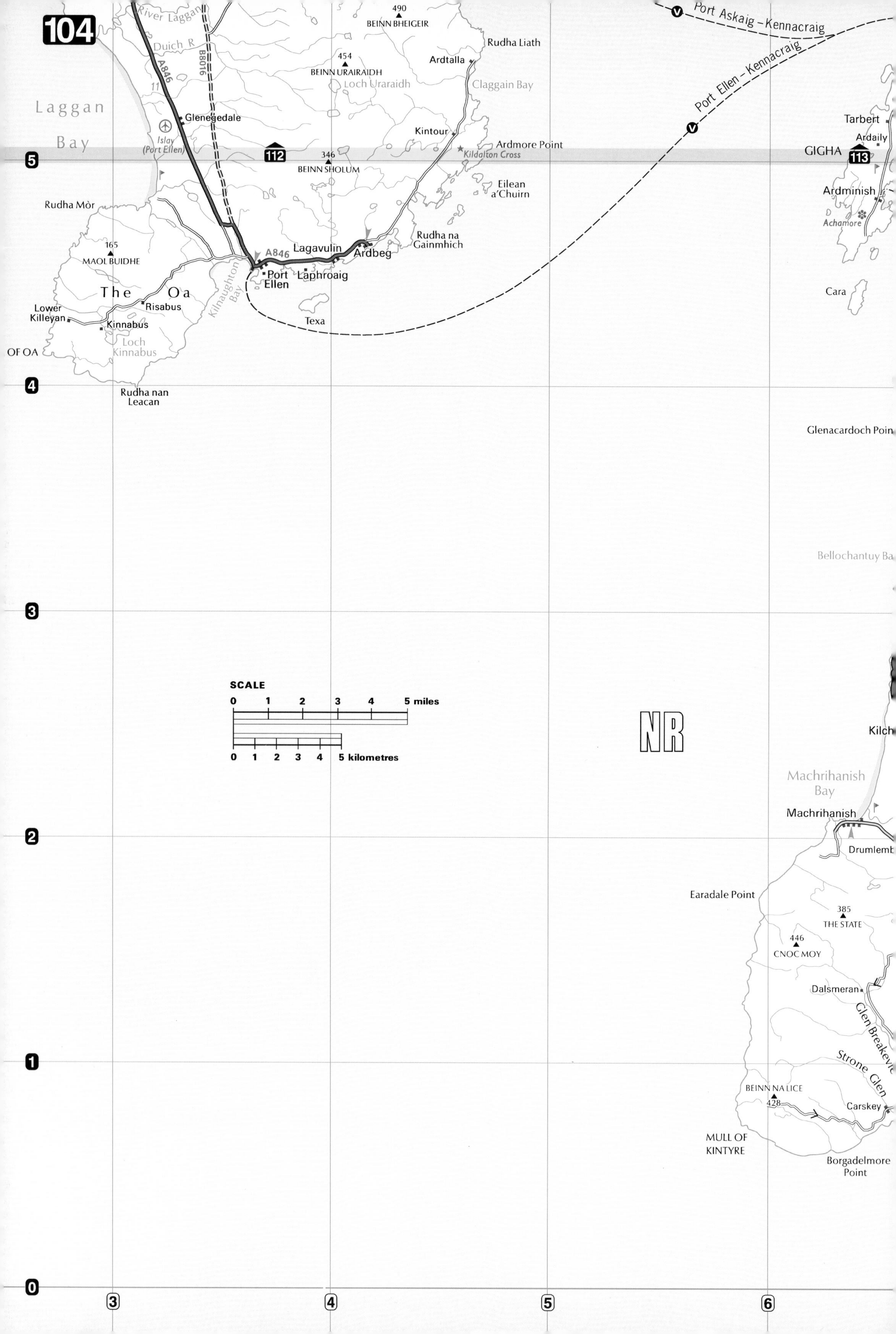
River Laggan
Duich R
A846
B8016
490
BEINN BHEIGEIR
454
BEINN URAIRAIDH
Loch Uraraidh
Rudha Liath
Ardtalla
Claggain Bay
Port Askaig – Kennacraig
Port Ellen – Kennacraig
Laggan
Bay
Glenegedale
Islay (Port Ellen)
112
346
BEINN SHOLUM
Kintour
Ardmore Point
Kildalton Cross
Eilean a'Chuirn
Tarbert
Ardaily
GIGHA
113
Ardminish
Achamore
Rudha Mòr
165
MAOL BUIDHE
Lagavulin
Ardbeg
Rudha na Gainmhich
Port Ellen
Laphroaig
Kilnaughton Bay
The Oa
Risabus
Lower Killeyan
Kinnabus
Loch Kinnabus
OF OA
Texa
Cara
Rudha nan Leacan
Glenacardoch Poin
Bellochantuy Ba
SCALE
0 1 2 3 4 5 miles
0 1 2 3 4 5 kilometres
NR
Kilch
Machrihanish Bay
Machrihanish
Drumlemt
Earadale Point
385
THE STATE
446
CNOC MOY
Dalsmeran
Glen Breakevie
Strone Glen
BEINN NA LICE
428
Carskey
MULL OF KINTYRE
Borgadelmore Point
5
4
3
2
1
0
3
4
5
6

Bay

Sound of Bute

Skipness Point

Cock of Arran

Claonaig

Ronachan
Point
Clachan
A83
Ronachan
Loch
Ciaran
Ballochroy

Crossaig

Cour Bay
Cour

247
CRUACH
MHIC GOUGAIN
264
CNOC-AN
T-SAMHLAIDH

38
Rhunahaorine

Tayinloan

B842

Loch
Garasdale

Grogport
Barmollack

Penrioch
Pirnmill

Lochranza
Catacol
114
A841
Glen Chalmadale
8

Glen Catacol

North Arran

834
CAISTEAL ABHAIL
Mid Sannox

Whitefarland
715
BEINN BHARRAIN
Loch
Tanna

Corrie
874
GOATFELL
A841

Imachar

Balliekine
792
BEINN NUIS

Merkland Point
106

Dougarie
Glen Rosa
Brodick NT

ARRAN
Brodick
Strathwhillan
Corrygills

Stone Circle
Auchagallon
Machrie
Bay
Machrie
Farm
Glenloig
11
512
A'CHRUACH
B880

Clauchland
Margnaheglish
Lamlash
Holy Is

Tormore
Machrie Moor
503
BEINN BHREAC
Lamlash
Bay
Cordon

Moss Farm Road
Stone Circle
Ballymichael

Torbeg
Shiskine
Birchburn
North Feorline
Blackwaterfoot
South Feorline

A841
4
Auchencairn
Kingscross

Knockenkelly
Whiting Bay
Whiting Bay
Drumadoon
Bay
Kilpatrick
Kilpatrick Dun
Glen Scorrodale

Brown Head
Largymore

Largybeg
Dippin
Dippin Head

Corriecravie
Glen Ashdale

Torr a' Chaisteal
Fort
Sliddery
Lagg Kilmory
Levencorroch
Kildonan
16
Cairn
Torrylin
Bennan

Bennan Head
Pladda

West

Loch Gigha

R

Belloch

Arnicle
354
CRUACH NAN GABHAR

Carradale
Dippen
B879
Carradale House

Glenbarr
454
BEINN AN TUIRC
Torrisdale
Square
Carradale
Point
Carradale
Bay

leongart
319

408
BÒRD MOR

Saddell

Saddell Bay

lochantuy
Z

396
SGREADAN HILL
Ugadale

angy Loch
Ballachgair

I
Glen Lussa
Peninver
Ardnacross
Bay

Kilmichael
A83
Drumore

Campbeltown

Island Davaar

6
B842

43
K

Kildalloig
352
BEINN
GHUILEAN
Achinhoan

10

Ru Stafnish

Conie Glen
B842
Glen Kerran

ale
Macharioch
Polliwilline
Bay
Southend
Dunaverty

Sanda Sound
Sheep Island

Sanda Island

NS

106

Ailsa Craig

Y

KILBRANNAN SOUND

SOUND OF KILBRANNAN

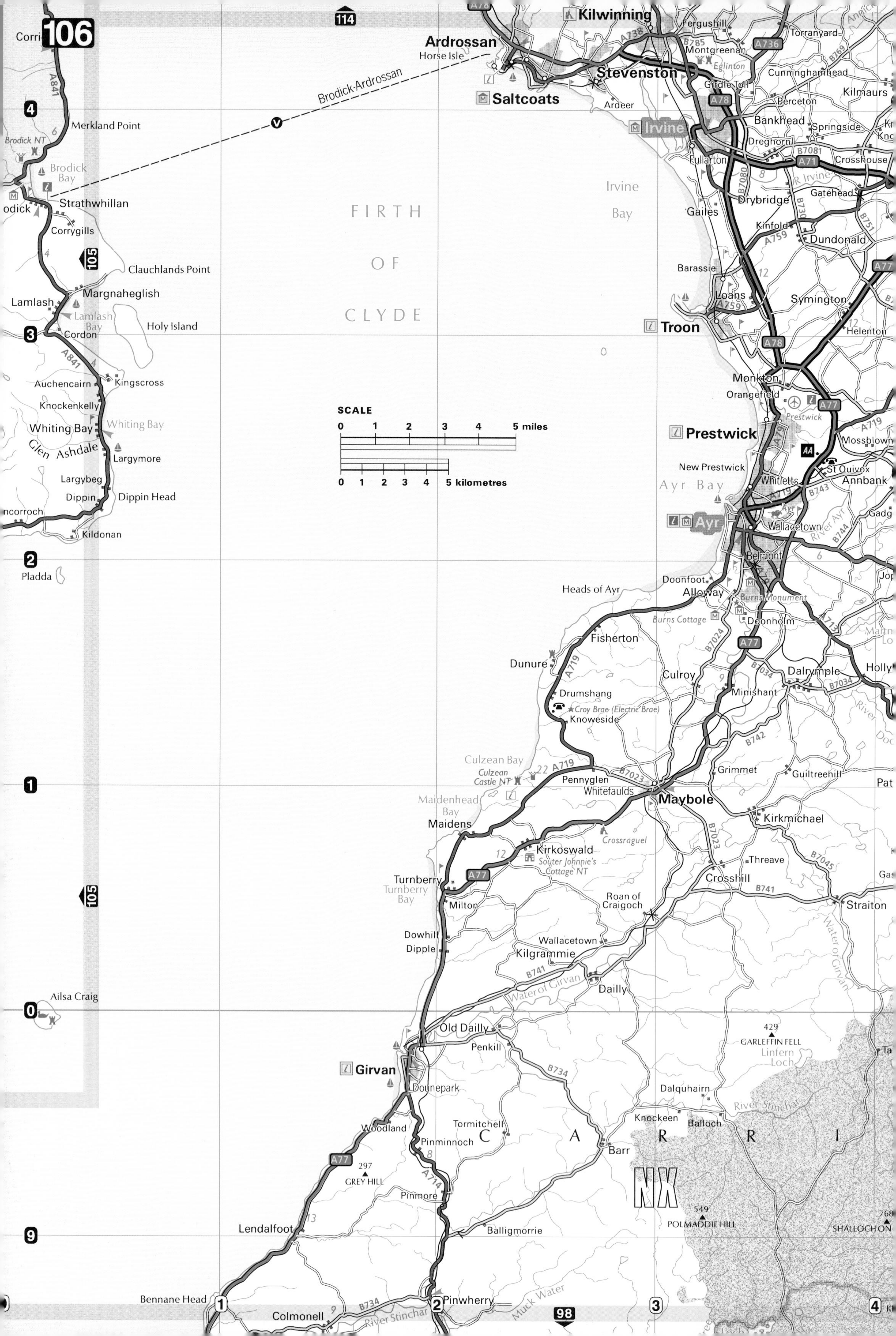

114

Kilwinning

Ardrossan
Horse Isle
Brodick-Ardrossan
V
Saltcoats

4
Merkland Point

Brodick NT

Brodick
Bay

Strathwhillan

Corrygills

105

Clauchlands Point

Margnaheglish

Lamlash
Lamlash
Bay
Holy Island

3
Cordon

Auchencairn
Kingscross
Knockenkelly
Whiting Bay
Whiting Bay
Glen Ashdale
Largymore
Largybeg
Dippin
Dippin Head
ncorroch
Kildonan

2
Pladda

Fergushill
Torranyard
Montgreenan
Eglinton
Cunninghamhead
Kilmaurs
Stevenson
Girdle Toll
Perceton
Springside
Ardeer
Bankhead
Knc
Irvine
Dreghorn
Crosshouse
Fullarton
Gatehead
Drybridge
Gailes
Kinfold
Dundonald
Barassie
Loans
Symington
Helenton
Troon
Monkton
Orangefield
Prestwick
Prestwick
Mossblown
New Prestwick
St Quivox
Annbank
Ayr Bay
Whitletts
Gadg
Ayr
Wallacetown
Jo
Belmont
Heads of Ayr
Doonfoot
Alloway
Burns Monument
Burns Cottage
Deonholm
Fisherton
Dunure
Culroy
Dalrymple
Holly
Drumshang
Croy Brae (Electric Brae)
Minishant
Knoweside
Grimmet
Guiltreehill
Culzean Bay
Culzean
Castle NT
Pennyglen
Whitefaulds
Maybole
Pat
Maidenhead
Bay
Maidens
Kirkmichael
Crossraguel
Kirkoswald
Souter Johnnie's
Cottage NT
Threave
Turnberry
Turnberry
Bay
Milton
Roan of
Craigoch
Crosshill
Dowhill
Dipple
Wallacetown
Kilgrammie
Straiton
Water of Girvan
Dailly
Gas
Ailsa Craig
Old Dailly
Penkill
429
GARLEFFIN FELL
Linfern
Loch
Girvan
Dounepark
Dalquhairn
Woodland
Tormitchell
C
A
R
R
I
Knockeen
Balloch
Pinminnoch
Barr
NX
297
GREY HILL
A714
Pinmore
549
Ta
POLMADDIE HILL
SHALLOCH ON
Lendalfoot
Balligmorrie
Bennane Head
Colmonell
Pinwherry
98
River Stinchar
Muck Water

FIRTH

OF

CLYDE

Irvine
Bay

SCALE
0   1   2   3   4   5 miles

0 1 2 3 4   5 kilometres

1

105

0

9

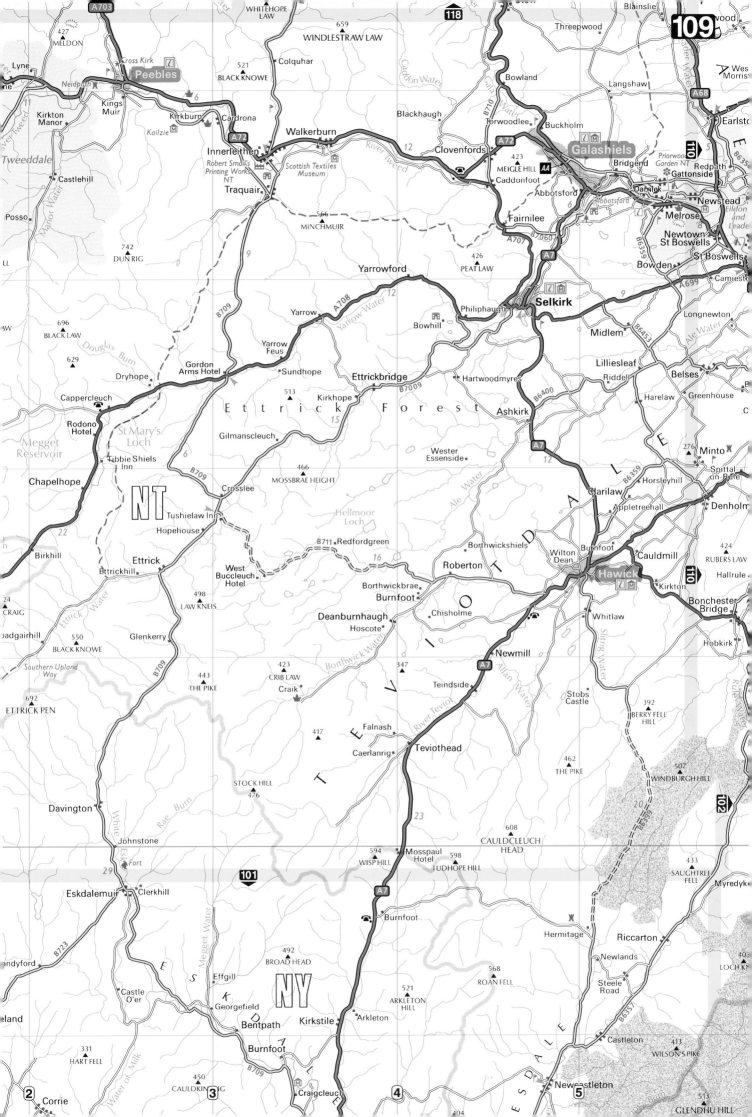

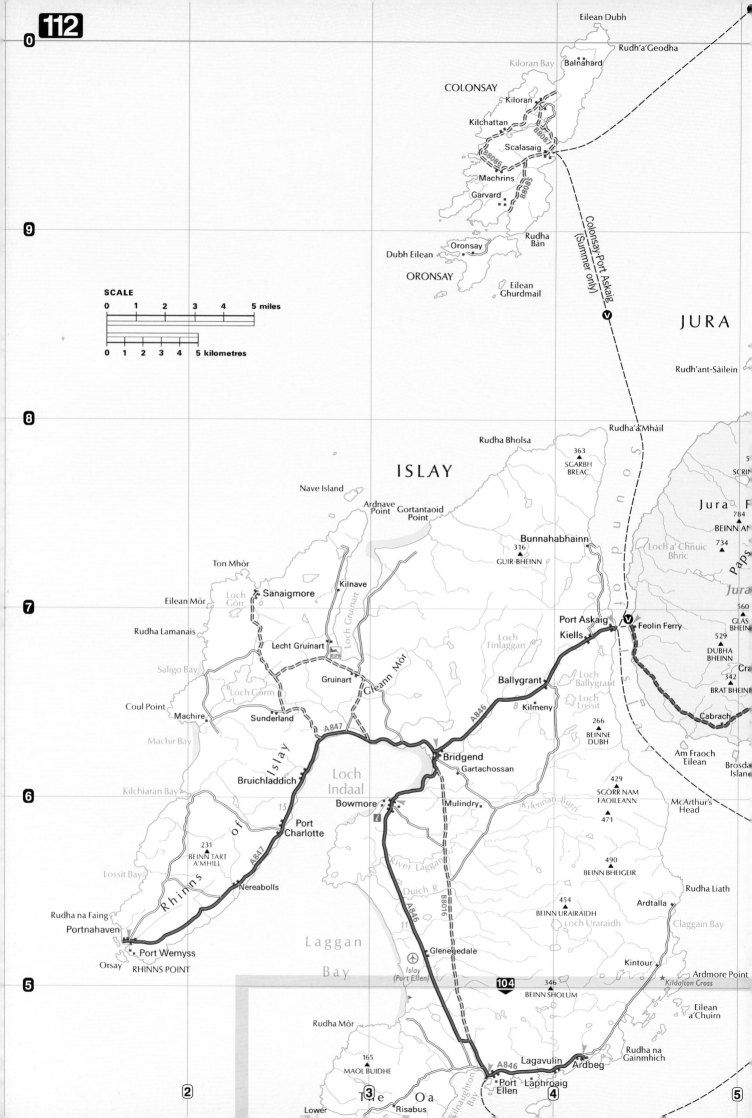

SCALE

0 1 2 3 4 5 miles

0 1 2 3 4 5 kilometres

Eilean Dubh

Rudh'a'Geodha

Kiloran Bay

Balnahard

COLONSAY

Kiloran

Kilchattan

B8087

Scalasaig

B8086

Machrins

B8085

Garvard

Colonsay-Port Askaig
(Summer only)

J U R A

Oronsay

Rudha Bàn

Dubh Eilean

ORONSAY

Eilean Ghurdmail

Rudh'ant-Sàilein

Rudha Bholsa

Rudha'a'Mhàil

363 ▲
SGARBH
BREAC

ISLAY

SCRIN

Jura F

784 ▲
BEINN AN

Nave Island

Ardnave
Point

Gortantaoid
Point

Loch a' Chnuic
Bhric

734 ▲

Bunnahabhainn

316 ▲
GUIR-BHEINN

Ton Mhòr

Kilnave

560 ▲

Jura

Eilean Mòr

Sanaigmore

Loch
Gorr

Loch Gruinart

Port Askaig

Kiells

Feolin Ferry

GLAS
BHEINN

Rudha Lamanais

Lecht Gruinart

RSPB

Gruinart

Gleann Mòr

Loch
Finlaggan

Ballygrant

Loch
Ballygrant

529 ▲

DUBHA
BHEINN

342 ▲
BRAT BHEINN

Cra

Saligo Bay

Loch Gorm

Kilmeny

Loch
Lossit

Coul Point

Machire

Sunderland

A847

266 ▲
BEINNE
DUBH

Am Fraoch
Eilean

Cabrach

Machir Bay

Bridgend

Gartachossan

Brosda
Islan

Bruichladdich

Loch
Indaal

429 ▲
SGÒRR NAM
FAOILEANN

McArthur's
Head

Kilchiaran Bay

15

Bowmore

Mulindry

Kilennan Burn

471 ▲

Port
Charlotte

A847

231 ▲
BEINN TART
A'MHILL

River Laggan

490 ▲
BEINN BHEIGEIR

Lossit Bay

Nereabolls

Duich R.

454 ▲
BEINN URAIRAIDH

Rudha Liath

Ardtalla

Loch Uraraidh

Claggain Bay

Rudha na Faing

Portnahaven

A846

B8016

Rhinns of Islay

Glenegedale

Kintour

Port Wemyss

Orsay

RHINNS POINT

Islay
(Port Ellen)

104

346 ▲
BEINN SHOLUM

Ardmore Point

Kildalton Cross

Rudha Mòr

Eilean
a'Chuirn

Laggan

Bay

Lagavulin

Ardbeg

Rudha na
Gainmhich

165 ▲
MAOL BUIDHE

A846

Laphroaig

Port
Ellen

2

3

The Oa

4

5

Lower

Risabus

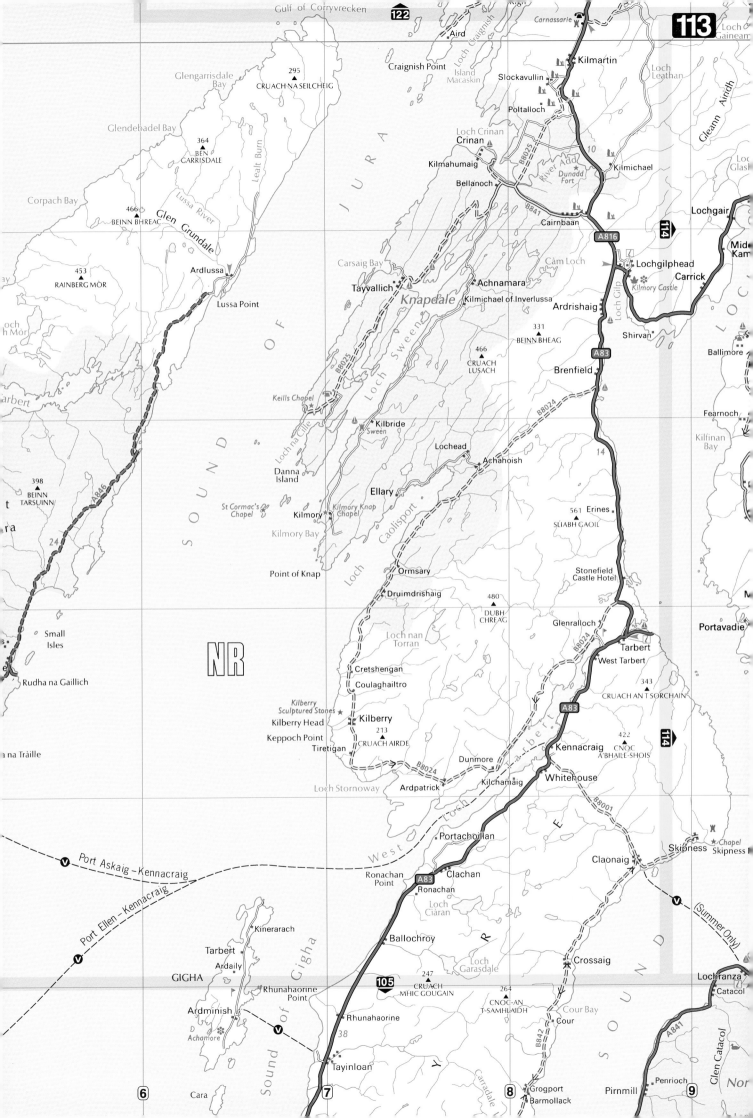

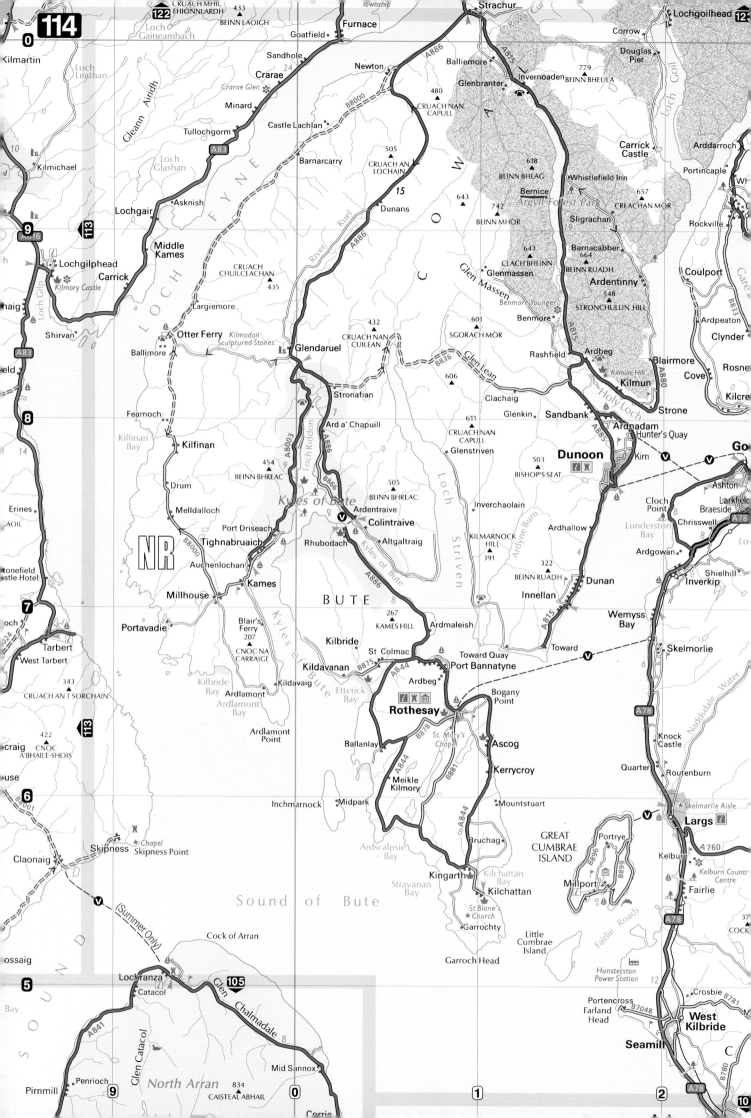

128

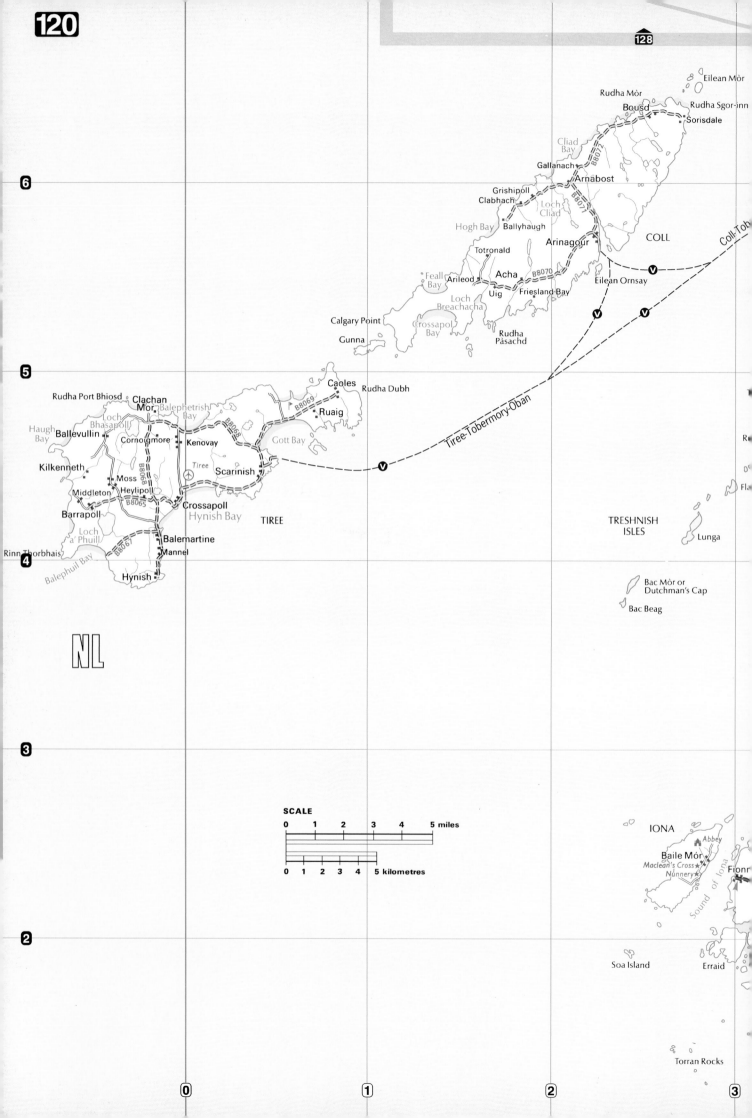

Eilean Mòr

Rudha Mòr

Bousd

Rudha Sgor-inn

Sorisdale

Cliad
Bay

Gallanach

Arnabost

Coll-Tob

Grishipoll

Clabhach

Loch
Cliad

B8071

Hogh Bay

Ballyhaugh

COLL

Totronald

Arinagour

Feall
Bay

Arileod

Acha

B8070

Uig

Friesland Bay

Eilean Ornsay

Loch
Breachacha

V

Calgary Point

Crossapol
Bay

Gunna

Rudha
Pàsachd

V

V

Caoles

Rudha Dubh

Rudha Port Bhiosd

**Clachan
Mor**

Balephetrish
Bay

B8069

Tiree-Tobermory-Oban

Ruaig

Loch
Bhasapoll

B8068

Haugh
Bay

Ballevullin

Cornaigmore

Kenovay

Gott Bay

Kilkenneth

B8068

Tiree

Scarinish

V

Moss

Middleton

Heylipoll

TRESHNISH
ISLES

B8065

Crossapoll

Lunga

Barrapoll

Hynish Bay

TIREE

Loch
a' Phuill

Balemartine

Mannel

Bac Mòr or
Dutchman's Cap

Rinn Thorbhais

B8067

Bac Beag

Balephuil Bay

Hynish

NL

SCALE

0   1   2   3   4   5 miles

IONA

0   1   2   3   4   5 kilometres

Abbey

Baile Mór

Maclean's Cross
Nunnery

Fionr

Soa Island

Erraid

Torran Rocks

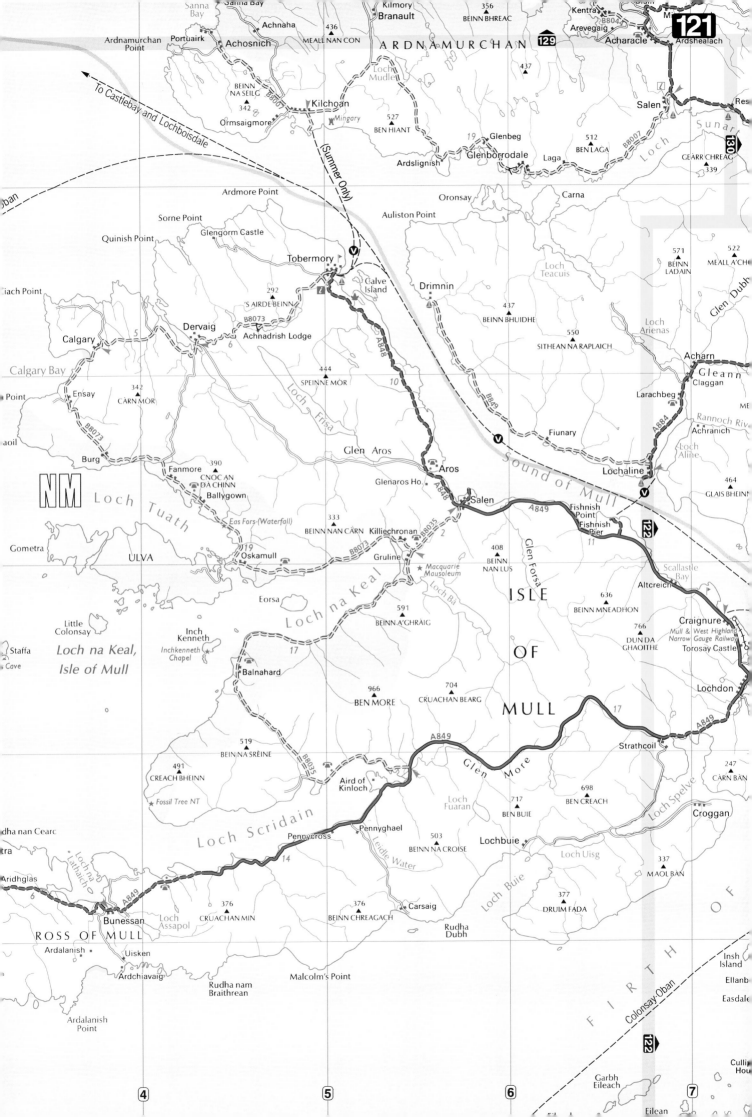

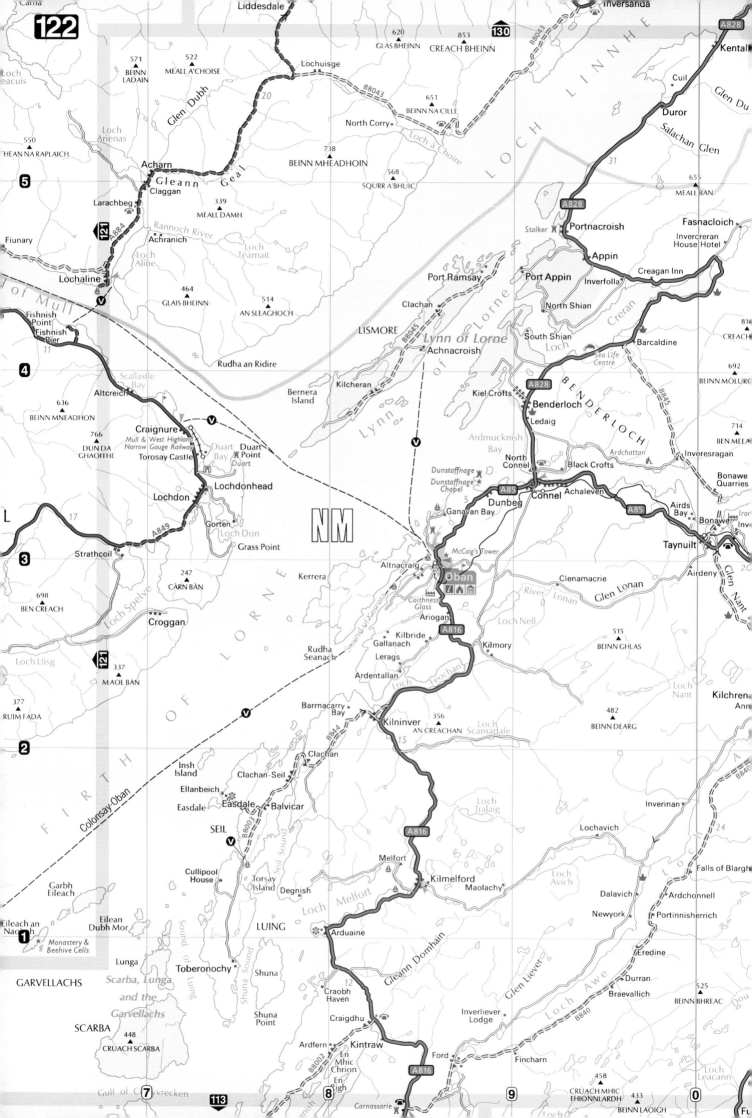

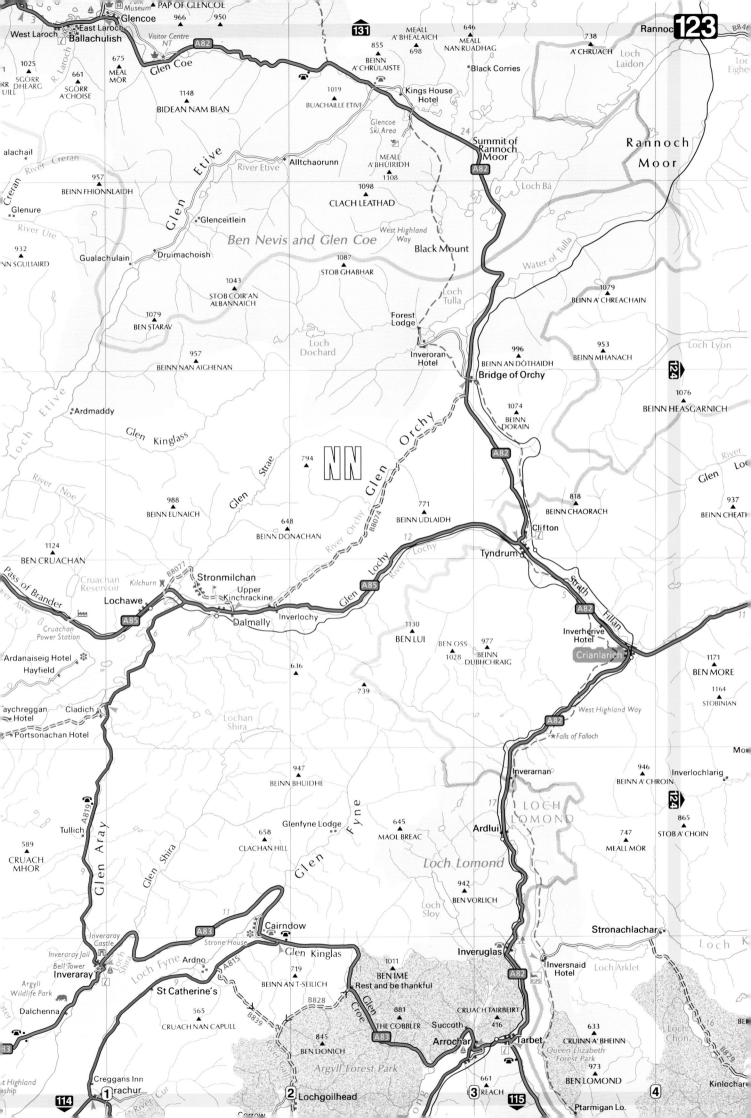

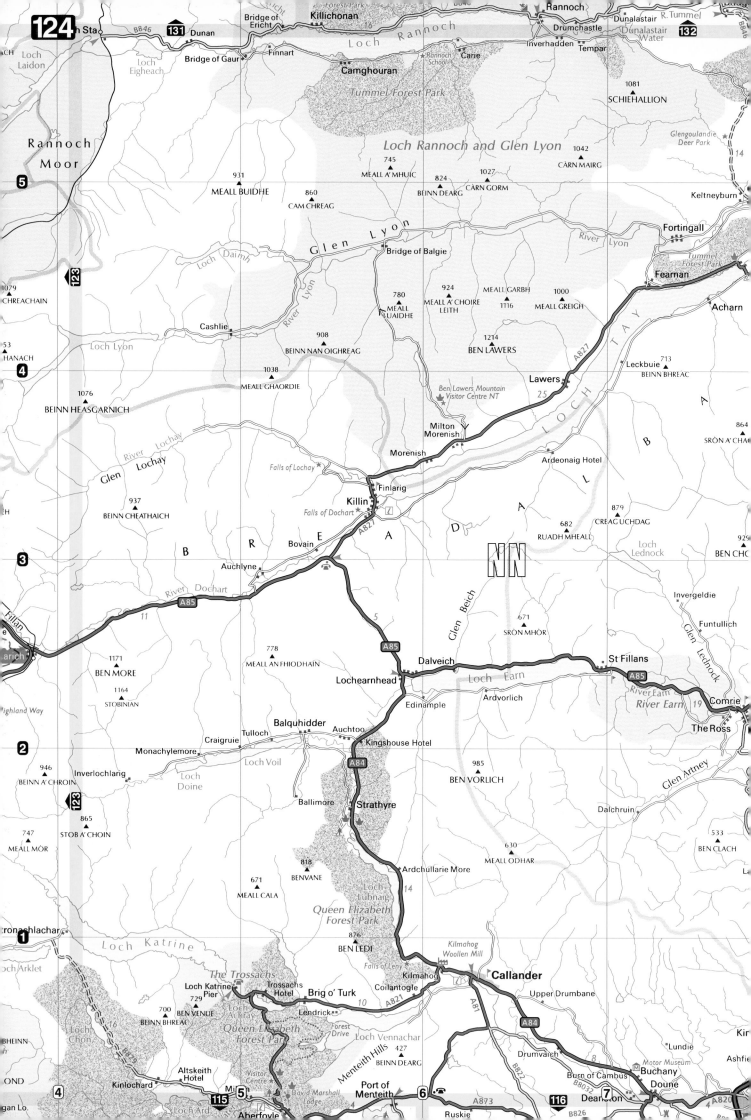

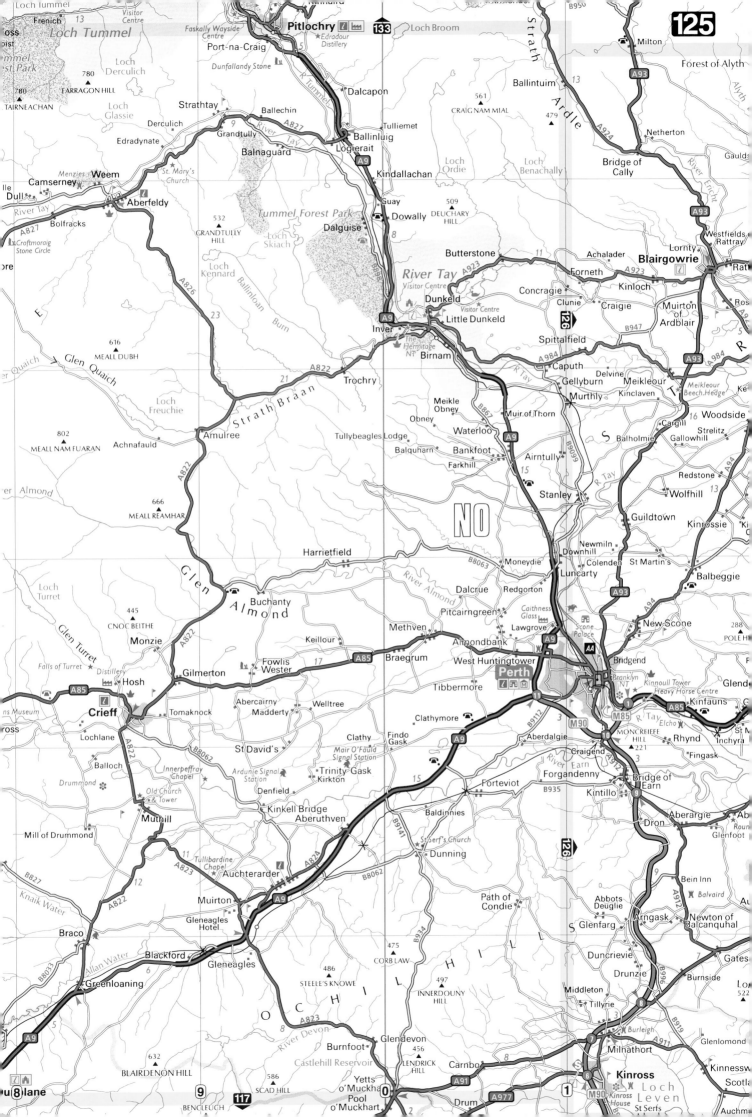

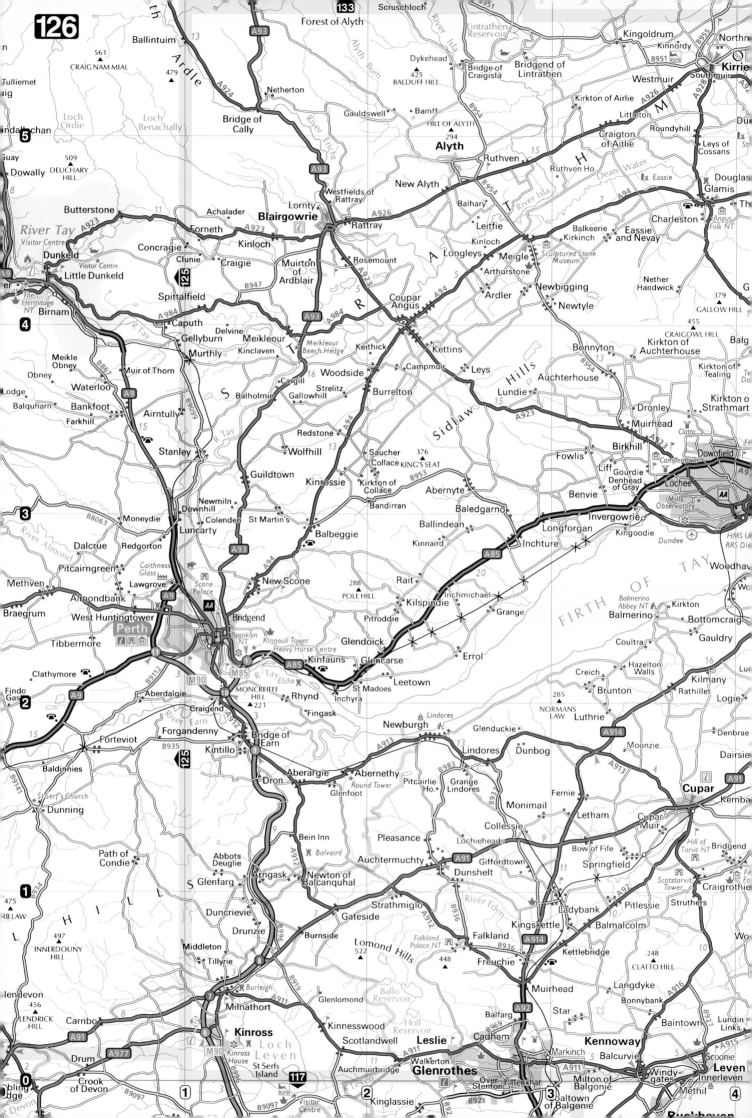

B134 Oathlaw
Battledykes
R
Finavon
Crosston
A94 Carse Gray
shoe
Lunanhead
ram
Clochtow
Kemp's Castle
Restenneth Priory
Forfar
Forfar Loch
Kingsmuir
Dunnichen
Bowriefauld
Craichie
Inverarity
B9127
Whigstreet
Kirkbuddo
Hatton
uld
14
Petterden
Todhills
CARROT HILL
259
Newbigging
Bucklerheads
urnside of
Duntrune
Murroes
ouglas
d Angus
B961
Baldovie
A92
A930
Barnhill
Broughty Ferry
OUNDEE
Scotscraig
Newport
on-Tay
A92
A919
13
Balmullo
13
Guardbridge
Kincaple
River Eden
A91
Strathkinness
B939
lebocraigs
itscottie
Baldinnie
B940
m
Peat Inn
Radernie
Lathones
Largoward
Colinsburgh
B941
Drumeldrie
Abercrombie
Kilconquhar
B942
pper
argo
B118
ARGO
BAY
Earlsferry
Elie

Aberlemno
Pitkennedy
Melgund Castle
B9134
B9113
Reswallie
Balgavies
A932
Guthrie
Burnside
Letham
Pitmuies
Balmuir
Idvies
Redford
Greystone
B961
Hayhillock
Carmyllie
B978
Crombie
Monikie
Affleck
Kirkton of Monikie
Monikie
Craigton
Wellbank
Newbigging
B9128
17
Muirdrum
Upper Victoria
Barry
11
Buddon
Monifieth

Finavon Castle
Farnell
A934
11
Bolshan
WUDDY LAW
132
A933
17
Glasterlaw
Kinnell
Boysack
Friockheim
Leysmill
Chapelton
B965
Colliston
6
A933
Letham Grange
Marywell
A92
St Vigeans
Elliot Water
B9127
Bonnington
Arbirlot
Arbroath
East Haven
Panbride
West Haven
Carnoustie
BUDDON NESS

135
Maryton
A933
Westerton
Craig
A92
Ferryden
Usan
Boddin Point
Braehead
Lunan
Inverkeilor
LUNAN BAY
Red Head
13
Cauldcots
Auchmithie
Carlingheugh Bay
The Deil's Head
Scurdie Ness

ST ANDREWS BAY
Leuchars
Earlshall
NO
Tayport

Botanic Gardens
St Andrews
Brownhills
Boarhills
Craigtoun
Denhead
Cameron Reservoir
A915
Stravithie
B9131
Dunino
Kingsbarns
A917
10
Balcomie Links
FIFE NESS
Kingsmuir
B940
Lochty
B9171
Crail
Carnbee
Easter Pitkierie
A917
Kellie Castle NT
Wester Pitkierie
B9131
Kilrenny
Arncroach
Anstruther Easter
Fisheries Museum
Anstruther
Colinsburgh
Pittenweem
St Monans

SCALE
0   1   2   3   4   5 miles
0 1 2 3 4   5 kilometres

5
6
Isle of May
7
B119
8

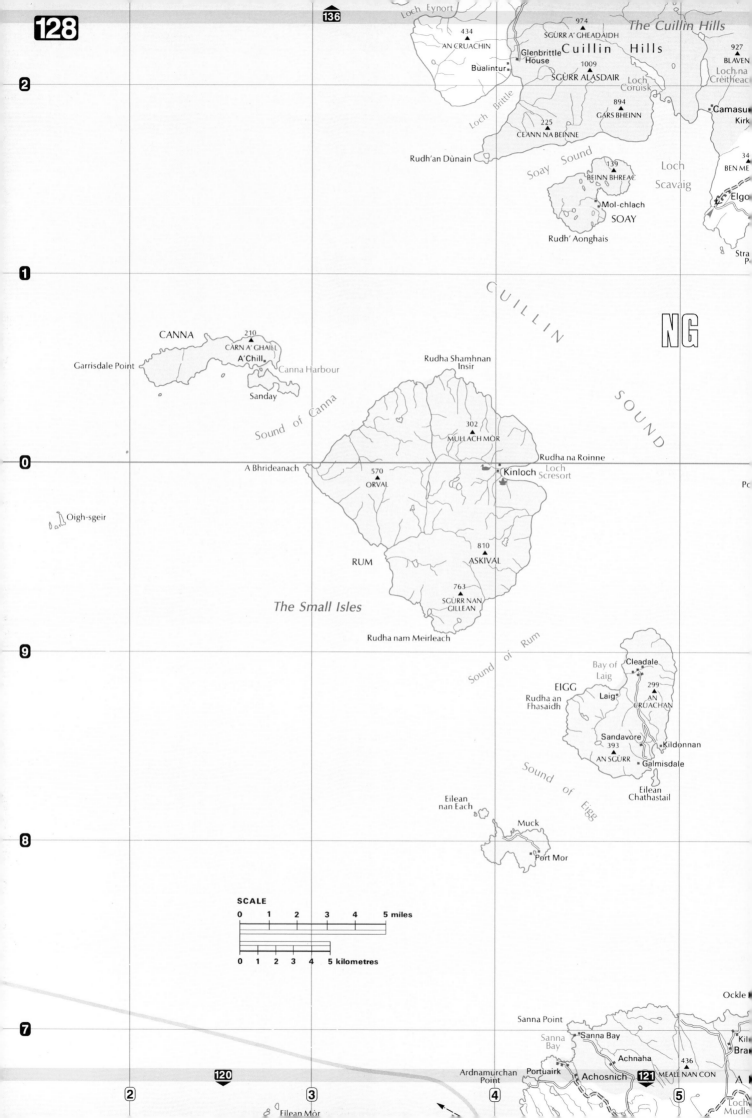

The Cuillin Hills

974
SGÙRR A' GHEADAIDH

927
BLAVEN
Loch na
Créitheach

434
AN CRUACHIN

Glenbrittle
House
Bualintur

Cuillin Hills

1009
SGÙRR ALASDAIR
Loch
Coruisk

Camasu
Kirk

894
GARS BHEINN

225
CEANN NA BEINNE

Rudh'an Dùnain

Soay Sound

34
BEN ME

Loch
Scavaig

139
BEINN BHREAC

Elgo

Mol-chlach

SOAY

Stra
P

Rudh' Aonghais

136

2

CANNA

210
CÀRN A' GHAILL
A'Chill

CUILLIN SOUND

NG

Garrisdale Point

Canna Harbour

Rudha Shamhnan
Insir

1

Sanday

Sound of Canna

Oigh-sgeir

A Bhrideanach

302
MULLACH MÒR

570
ORVAL

Rudha na Roinne

Kinloch
Loch
Scresort

Po

0

RUM

810
ASKIVAL

The Small Isles

763
SGÙRR NAN
GILLEAN

Rudha nam Meirleach

Sound of Rum

Bay of
Laig

Cleadale

9

EIGG

299
AN
CRUACHAN

Rudha an
Fhasaidh

Laig

Sandavore

393
AN SGÙRR

Kildonnan

Galmisdale

Eilean
nan Each

Eilean
Chathastail

Sound of Eigg

Muck

Port Mor

8

SCALE

0   1   2   3   4   5 miles

0   1   2   3   4   5 kilometres

Ockle

7

Sanna Point

Sanna
Bay
Sanna Bay

Achnaha

Kil
Bra

Ardnamurchan
Point

Portuairk

Achosnich

436
MEALL NAN CON

A

Loch
Mudle

120

121

2

3

4

5

Eilean Mòr

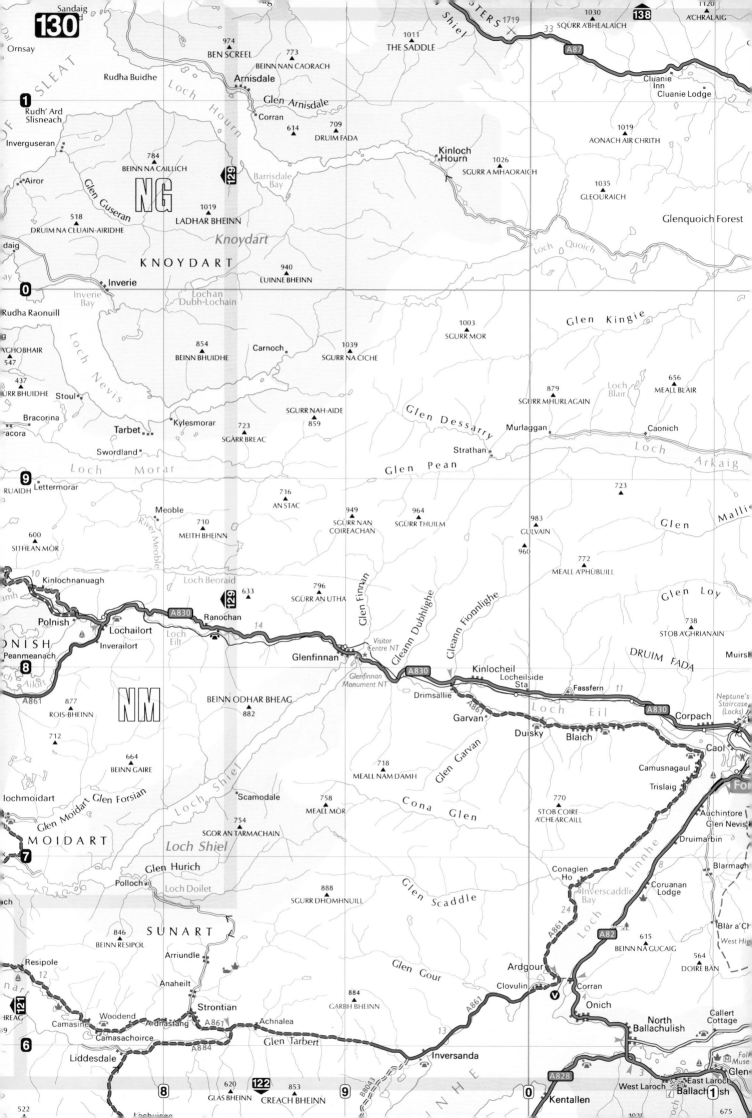

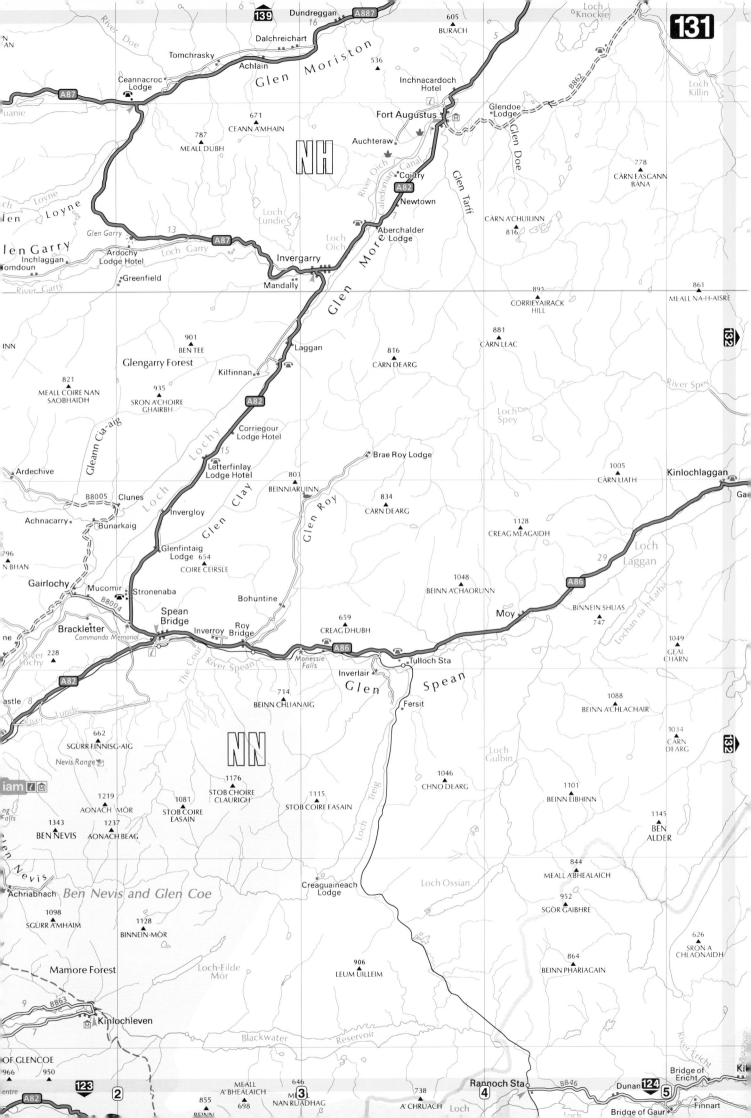

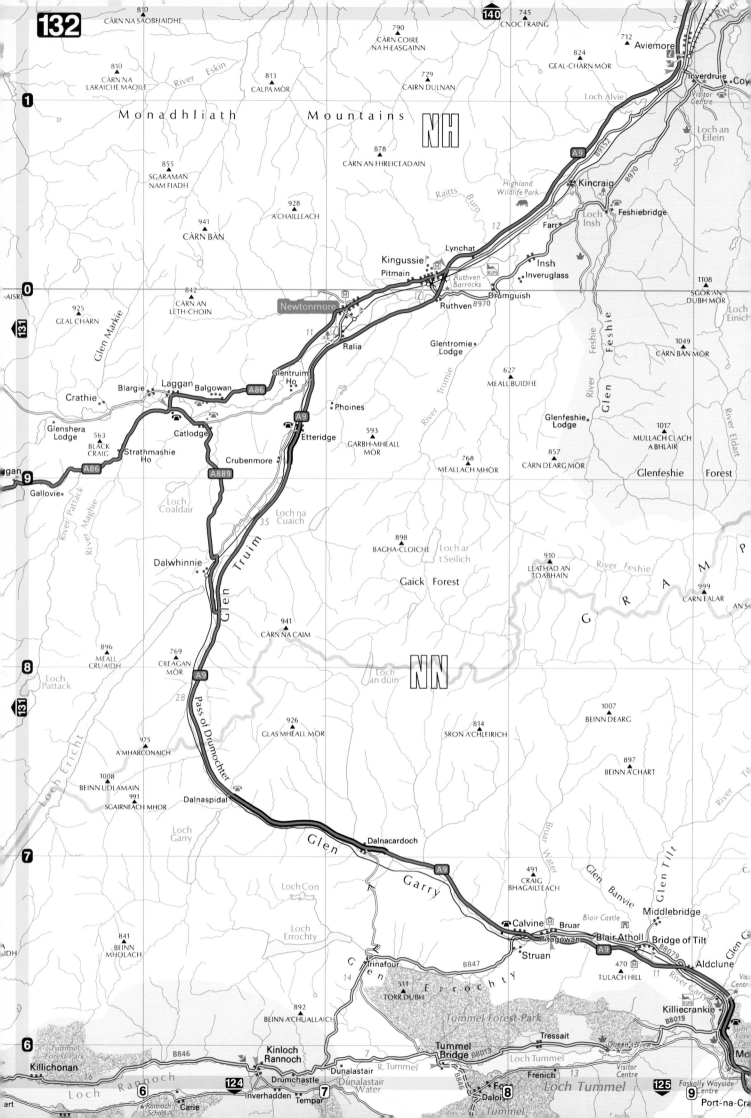

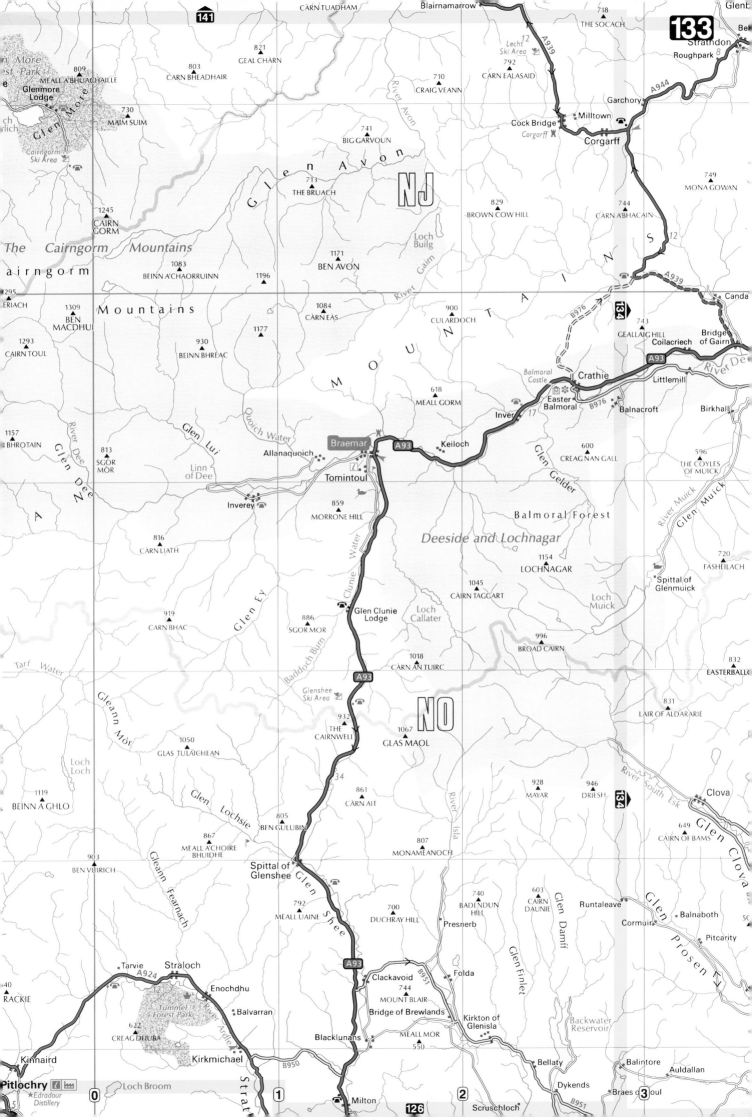

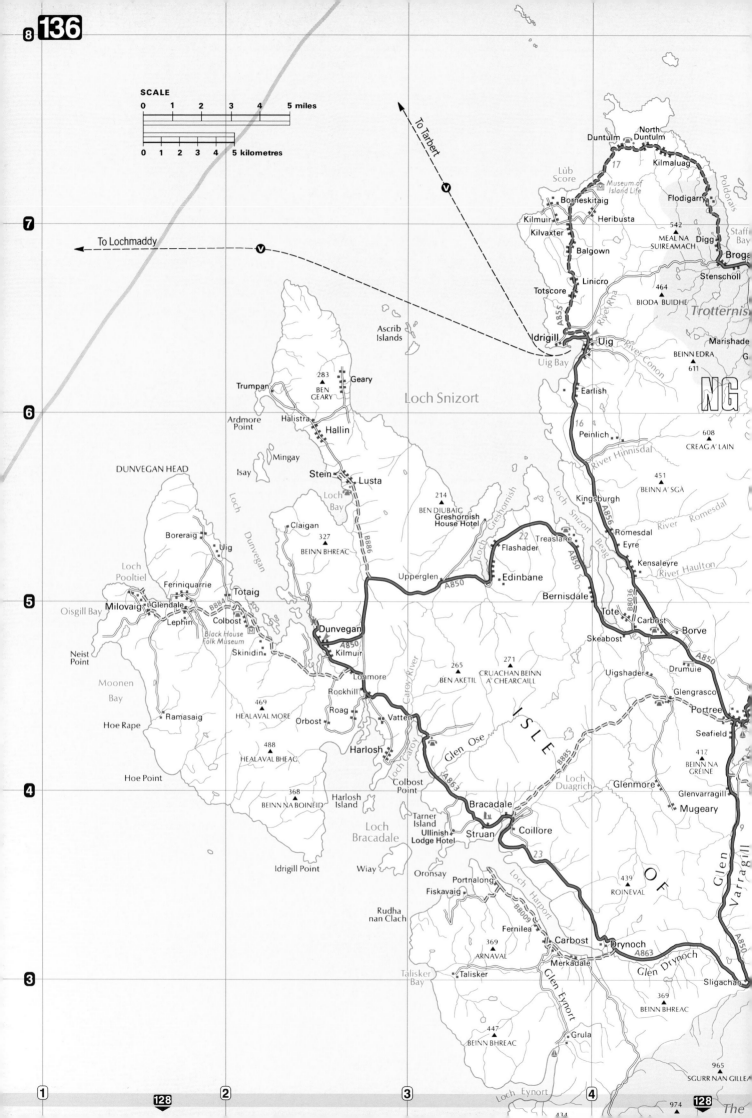

SCALE

0 1 2 3 4 5 miles

0 1 2 3 4 5 kilometres

To Tarbert

To Lochmaddy

Duntulm
North Duntulm
Kilmaluag
Lùb Score
Museum of Island Life
Borneskitaig
Flodigarry
Kilmuir
Heribusta
Kilvaxter
542
MEAL NA SUIREAMACH
Digg
Poldorais
Balgown
Broga
Linicro
Stenscholl
Staffin Bay
Totscore
464
BIODA BUIDHE
Trotternis
A855
River Rha
River Conon
Ascrib Islands
Loch Snizort
Idrigill
Uig
Marishade
BEINN EDRA
611
G
Uig Bay
Earlish
NG
Trumpan
283
BEN GEARY
Geary
Ardmore Point
Halistra
Hallin
16
Peinlich
608
CREAG A' LAIN
River Hinnisdal
DUNVEGAN HEAD
Mingay
Isay
Stein
Lusta
451
BEINN A' SGÀ
Loch Bay
214
BEN DIUBAIG
Greshornish House Hotel
Kingsburgh
River Romesdal
Claigan
327
BEINN BHREAC
B886
Loch Greshornish
22
Treaslane
Romesdal
Eyre
Boreraig
Uig
Loch Snizort Beag
Flashader
A856
Upperglen
A850
Edinbane
Kensaleyre
River Haulton
Loch Pooltiel
Feriniquarrie
Totaig
Bernisdale
B8036
Oisgill Bay
Milovaig
Glendale
B8884
Colbost
Dunvegan
Tote
Carbost
Borve
Lephin
Black House Folk Museum
Kilmuir
Skeabost
A850
Neist Point
Skinidin
Caroy River
265
BEN AKETIL
271
CRUACHAN BEINN A' CHEARCAILL
Uigshader
Drumuie
Lonmore
Glengrasco
Moonen Bay
Rockhill
469
HEALAVAL MORE
Roag
ISLE
Portree
Ramasaig
Orbost
Vatten
Seafield
Hoe Rape
488
HEALAVAL BHEAG
Harlosh
Loch Caroy
Glen Ose
B885
Loch Duagrich
Glenmore
417
BEINN NA GRÈINE
Hoe Point
368
BEINN NA BOINEID
Harlosh Island
Colbost Point
A863
Bracadale
Glenvarragill
Mugeary
Loch Bracadale
Tarner Island
Ullinish Lodge Hotel
Struan
Coillore
OF
Idrigill Point
Wiay
Oronsay
23
439
ROINEVAL
Glen Varragill
Portnalong
Loch Harport
Fiskavaig
B8009
Rudha nan Clach
Fernilea
A850
369
ARNAVAL
Carbost
Drynoch
A863
Glen Drynoch
Talisker Bay
Talisker
Merkadale
369
BEINN BHREAC
Glen Eynort
Sligachan
447
BEINN BHREAC
Grula
965
SGURR NAN GILLEA
Loch Eynort
974
The
434

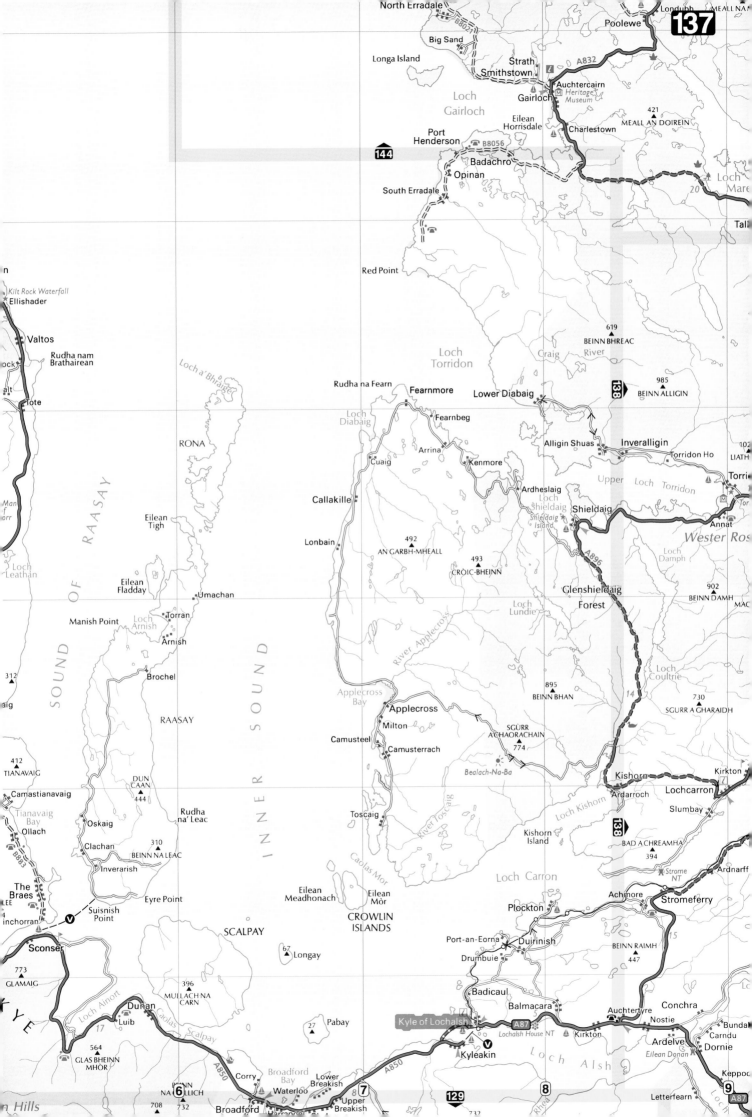

North Erradale
Londubh   MEALL NA
Poolewe
B8021
Big Sand
Longa Island
Strath
Smithstown
Auchtercairn
Gairloch   Heritage
Museum
A832
Loch
Gairloch
421
Eilean
Horrisdale   Charlestown
MEALL AN DOIREIN
Port
Henderson   B8056
Badachro   Loch
Mare
Opinan
20
South Erradale
Tal

Red Point

Kilt Rock Waterfall
Ellishader
619
BEINN BHREAC
Craig
River
Loch
Torridon
Valtos
Rudha nam
Brathairean
Loch a' Bhraige
Rudha na Fearn
Fearnmore   Lower Diabaig
985
BEINN ALLIGIN
Tote
Fearnbeg
Loch
Diabaig   Alligin Shuas   Inveralligin
102
RONA   Arrina   Torridon Ho   LIATH
Cuaig   Kenmore
Man
f
orr   Callakille   Ardheslaig   Upper Loch Torridon   Torri
Loch
Shieldaig   Shieldaig
Loch
Leathan   Eilean
Tigh   Shieldaig
Island   Annat
492   West er Ros
Lonbain   AN GARBH-MHEALL
Eilean
Fladday   Umachan   493
CROIC-BHEINN   Glenshieldaig
Forest   902
BEINN DAMH   MAC
312   Manish Point   Loch
Arnish   Torran   Loch
Lundie   A896
aig   Arnish   Loch
Damph
Brochel   Loch
Coultrie
RAASAY   895
BEINN BHAN   730
SGURR A GHARAIDH
412   Applecross
Bay   14
TIANAVAIG   Applecross
DUN
CAAN   Milton   SGURR
A'CHAORACHAIN
774   Kirkton
Camastianavaig   444   Camusteel
Camusterrach
Tianavaig
Bay   Rudha
na' Leac   Bealach-Na-Ba   Kishorn   Kirkton
Ollach   310   Ardarroch   Lochcarron
Oskaig   BEINN NA LEAC   Toscaig   Slumbay
Clachan   Loch Kishorn
Inverarish   Kishorn
Island   BAD A CHREAMHA
394
The
Braes   Eyre Point
LEE   Caolas Mor   Loch Carron   Strome
NT   Ardnarff
4   Suisnish
Point   Eilean
Meadhonach   Eilean
Mòr   Achmore
inchorran   V   Plockton
Port-an-Eorna   Stromeferry
SCALPAY   CROWLIN
ISLANDS   Duirinish   15
Sconser   67 Longay   Drumbuie   BEINN RAIMH
447
773   396
GLAMAIG   MULLACH NA
CARN   Badicaul
Balmacara   Auchtertyre   Conchra
KYE   Dunan   27 Pabay   Kyle of Lochalsh   Lochalsh House NT   Nostie   Bunda
Luib   Kirkton   Ardelve   Carndu
Loch Ainort   A850   Kyleakin   Eilean Donan   Dornie
17   Conchra
564   Corry   Broadford
Bay   Lower
Breakish   Keppoc
GLAS BHEINN
MHÒR   A850   Loch Alsh   2
BEINN   Waterloo   Rhea
NA CAILLICH   Upper
Breakish   Letterfearn   A87
708 732   Broadford   732   Keppoc
n Hills

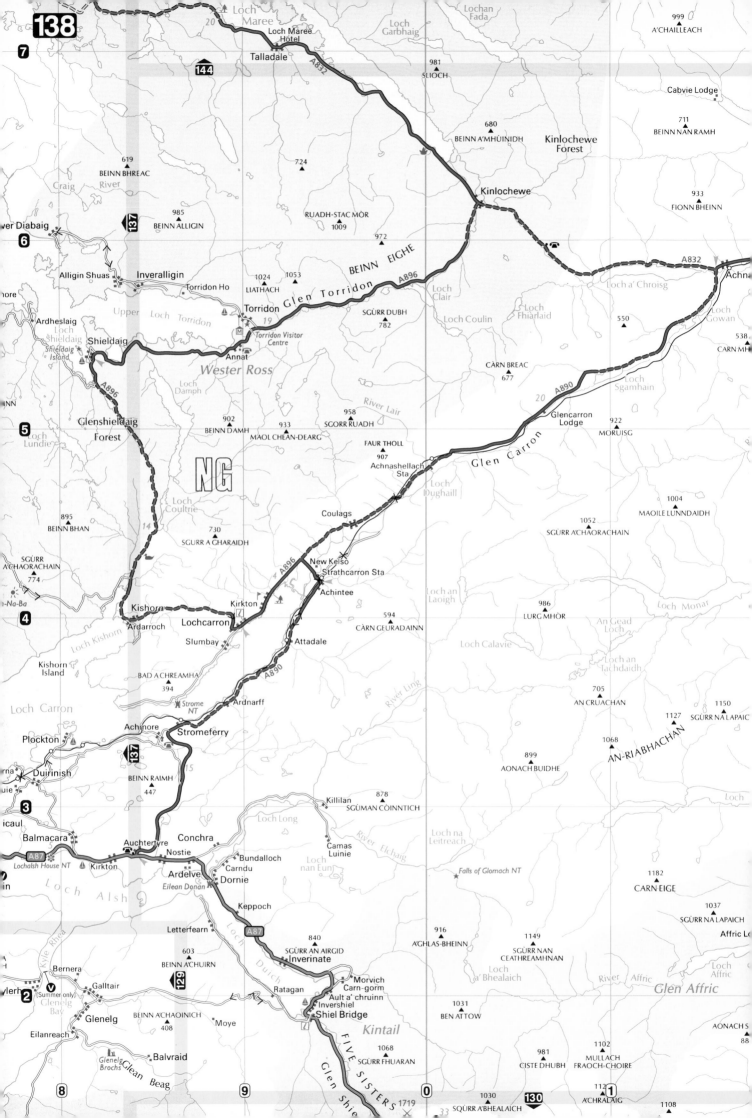

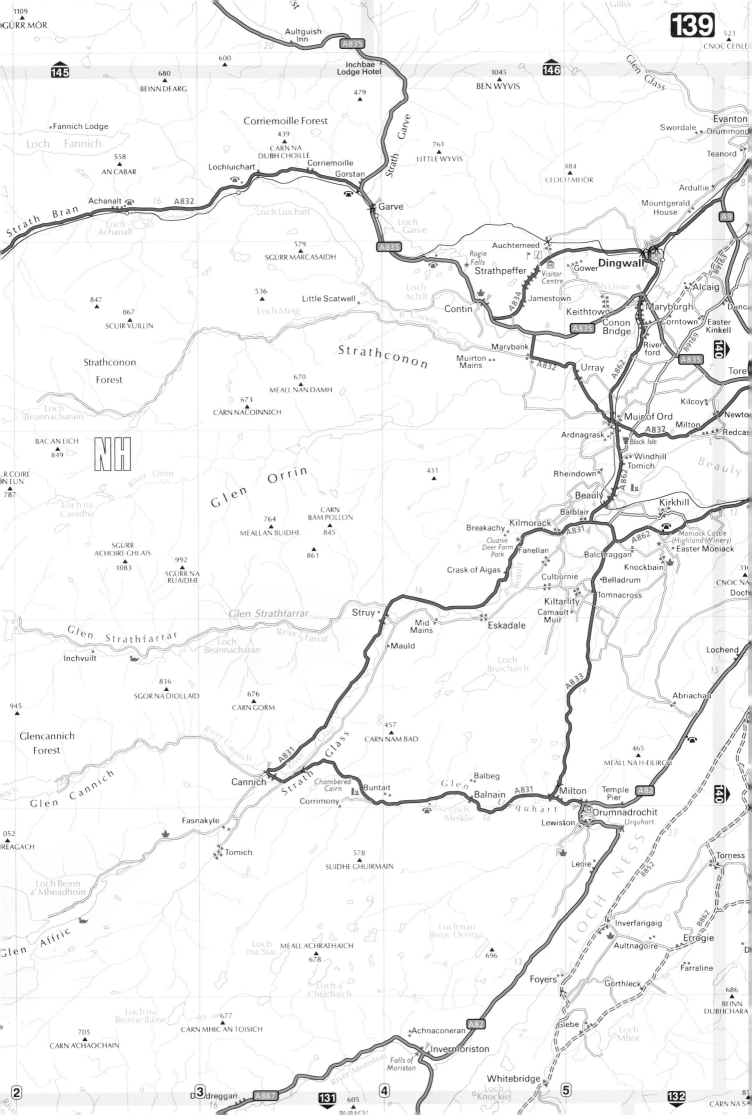

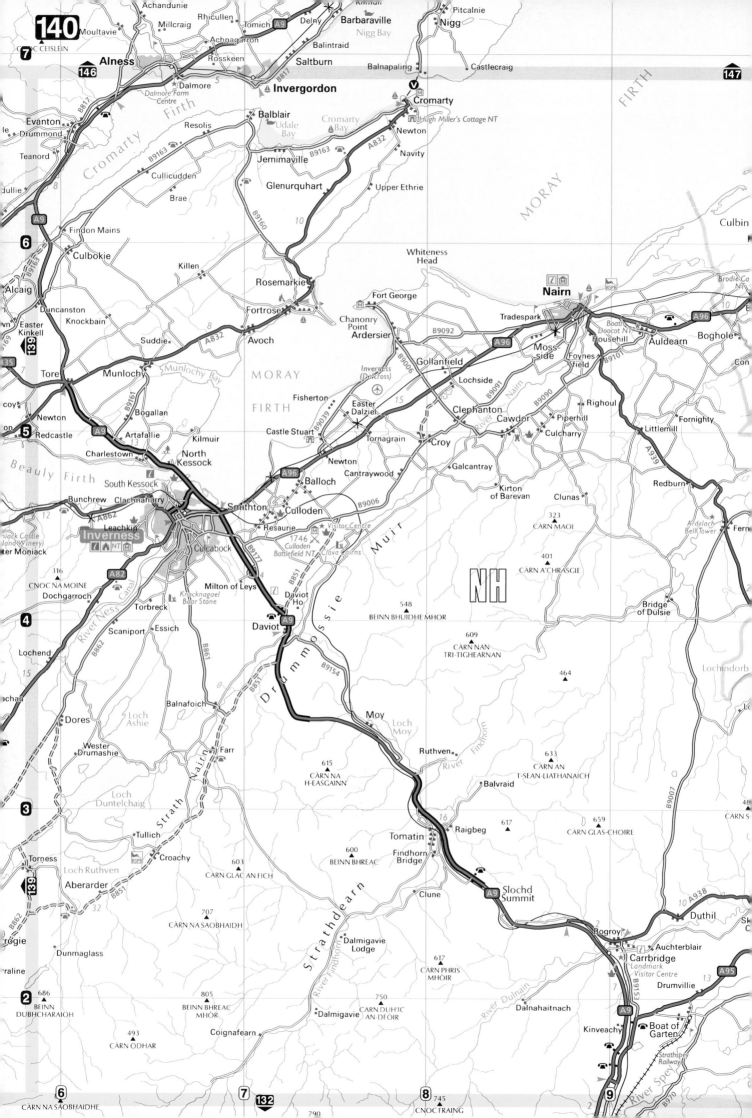

Troup Head

Rosehearty
Sandhaven
Kinnaird
Fraserburgh
Pittulie
Peathill
Craigiefold
Percyhorner
Fraserburgh Bay
Cairnbulg
Crovie
Pennan
Pitblae
Kirktown
Whitelink Bay
Inverallochy
Protstonhill
New Aberdour
Aberdour Bay
Coburby
Mid Ardlaw
B9031
St Combs
Netherbrae
Boyndlie
B9032
Memsie
B9033
A92
Bracklamore Hill 221
A98
Rathen
Crofts of Savoch
Newburgh
Lonmay
Crimonmogate
Loch of Strathbeg
Rattray Head
New Pitsligo
Waughton Hill 234
A981
Strichen
Crimond
Blackhill 18
A952
New Byth
Bonnykelly
B9030
New Leeds
Denhead
Leys
Backfolds
Kirktown
St Fergus
Garmond
Oldwhat
A950
B9093
Fetterangus
Rora
River Ugie
minestown 13
A981
B9106
Deer Abbey
Dunshillock
Mintlaw
A92
Inverugie
Buchanhaven
A952
Peterhead
New Deer
Maud
Old Deer
Aden Visitor Centre
Longside
A950
Hillhead of Cocklaw
Peterhead Bay
B9170
B9029
Inverquhomery
Maryhill
Slacks of Cairnbanno
Blackhill of Clackriach
Bulwark
Stuartfield
Millbreck
Nether Kinmundy
Little Dens
Burnhaven
Millbrex
A948
Drymuir
Nethermuir
Clola
Blackhill
Boddam
Buchan Ness
Kirkton
B9170
Knaven
B9030
Kinnadie
Stirling
Lendrum Terrace
Cottown
Cairnorrie
Brownhill
Inkhorn
Auchnagatt 12
Kinknockie
Blackhill
Coldwells
Lethenty
B9005
oodhead
Haddo
Methlick
Coldwells
Muirtack 14
Hatton
Auchiries
Bullers of Buchan
A952
Barthol Chapel
Haddo House NT
R. Ythan
B9005
Arthrath
North Haven
Cruden Bay
Earlsford
A915
Tulloch
Auchedly
Wedderlairs
Birness
Bogbrae
Chapel Hill
Bay of Cruden
The Skares
Medieval Tomb
Ythsie
Whinnyfold
Tarves
Kinharrachie
Artrochie
Craigdam
Tolquhon
A948
Ellon
eldrum
Pitmedden Garden NT
Esslemont
Kirkton of Logie Buchan
Collieston
Kirktown of Slains
A920
Carnbrogie
Pitmedden
B9000
Kirktown of Bourtie
Udny Green
Housieside
32
A92
Whiterashes
Woodland
Pettymuk
Cultercullen
Newburgh
Foveran
Nether Crimond
A947
Tillygreig
Staloch
Delfrigs
rurie
B993
Reisque
Causeyend
Balmedie
17
Kinmuck
Newmachar
Balmedie
kell Church
B979
Whitecairns
Belhelvie
Kinmundy
B977
Hatton of Fintray
R. Don
Dyce Symbol Stones
Parkhill
Potterton
B979
Overton
B997
B999
Blackdog
8
135
9
Dyce
Aberdeen
0
1

NK

SCALE
0 1 2 3 4 5 miles
0 1 2 3 4 5 kilometres

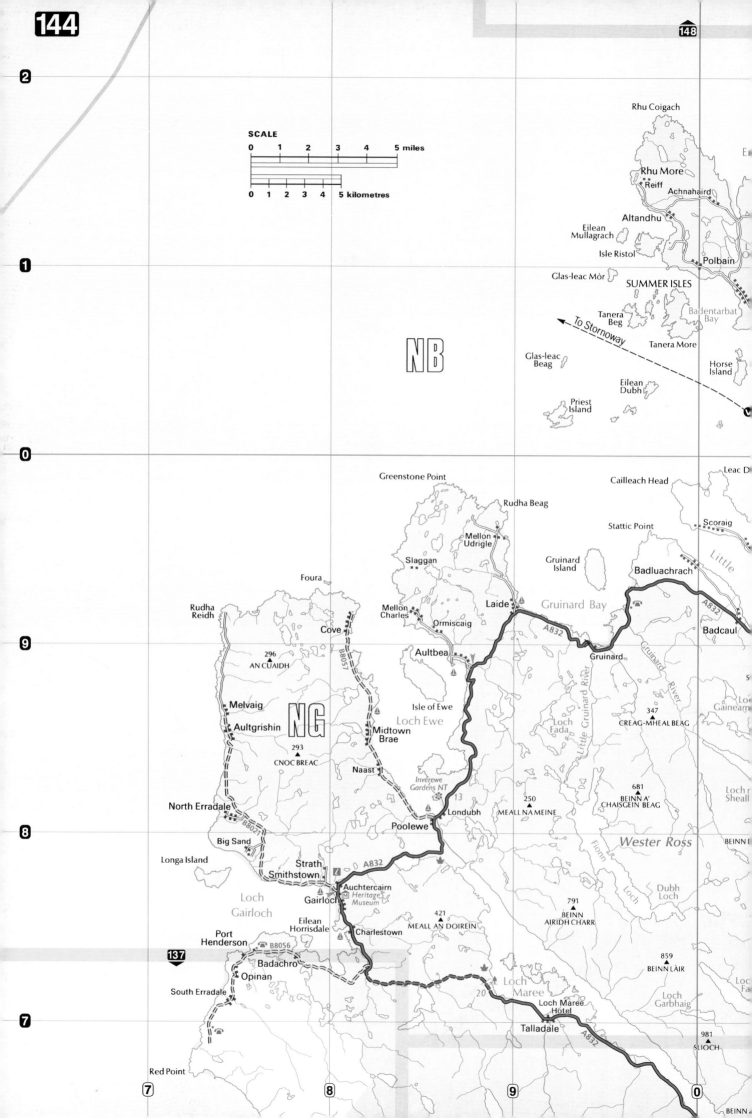

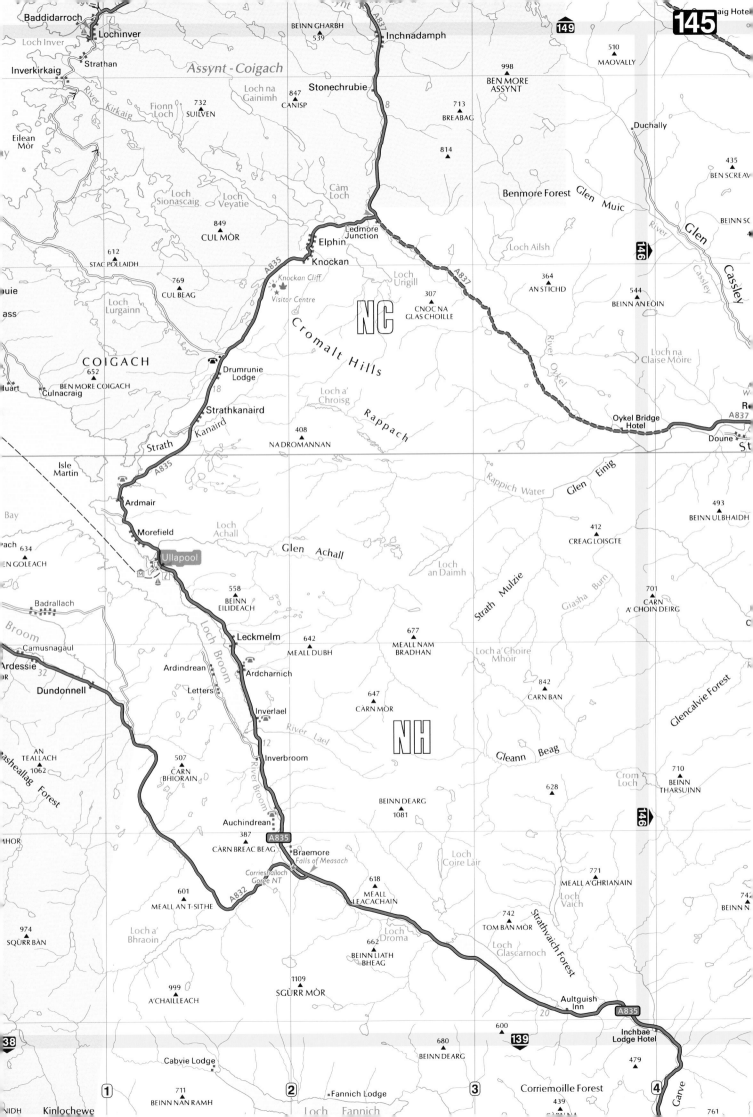

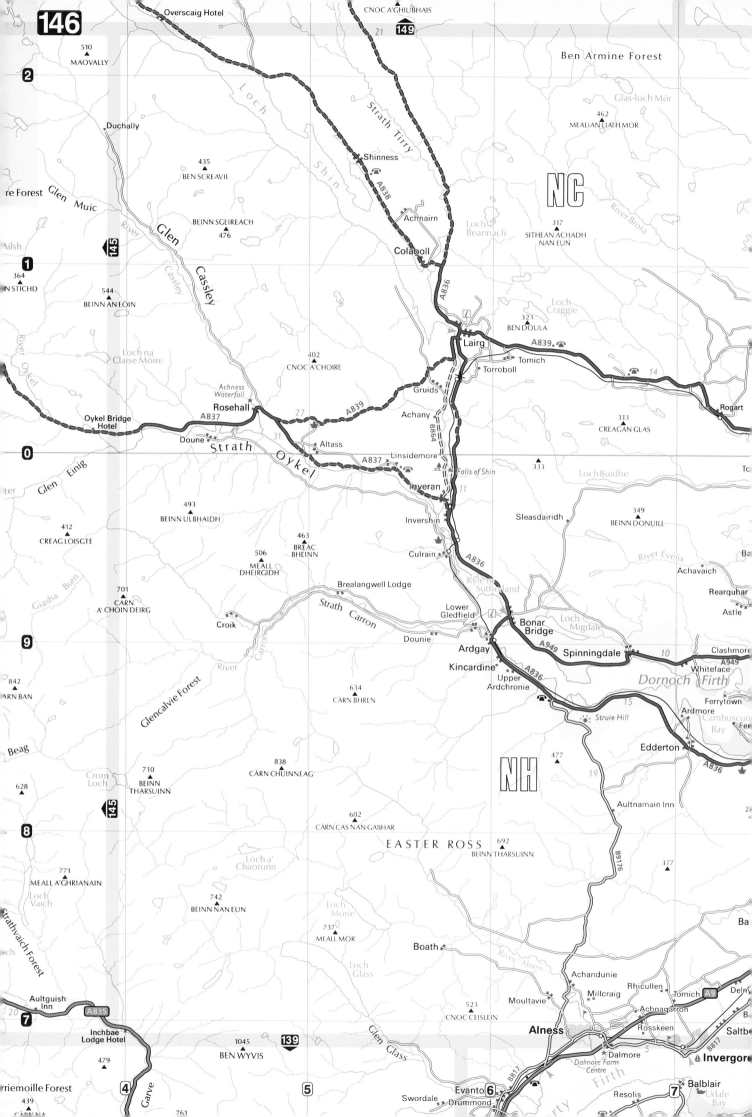

BREUN-CHOILLE

CREAG NAM FIADH

& Stone Circle

CREAG SCALABSDALE

Langwell Ho.

Kildonan
Lodge

Kildonan 416
BEINN DUBHAIN

Strath of Kildonan

401
CNOC NA MAOILE

River Helmsdale

17

Torrish

A897

404

Ord of Caithness

A9

ND

Strath Skinsdale

337
CNOC NA
H-INNSE MOIRE

421
CNOC NAN
CRUBAG MÓR

624
BEINN DHORAIN

591
BEINN NA MÈILICH

West
Helmsdale

Navidale House
Hotel

East Helmsdale

Helmsdale

Gartymore

Portgower

Glen Loth

Black Water

Balnacoil Lodge

Strath Brora

539
COL-BHEINN

Lothmore

CHD

River Brora

Loch
Brora

Lothbeg

A9

21

lreavoch Lodge

520
BEN HORN

Loch
Horn

378
CAGAR FEOSAIG

Dalchalm

Brora

Golspie Burn

446
BEINN LUNDIE

Backies

Doll

Cairn Liath

Rhives

Dunrobin Castle

Golspie

A9

Loch
Fleet

avie
orm

Skelbo

Skelbo Street

Fourpenny

Embo

richin

B9168

Embo Street

Pitgrudy

elix

A949

3

Camore

Dornoch

uthill

Dornoch Firth

Innis Mhor

Tarbat Ness

Brucefield

Wilkhaven

NJ

Portmahomack

Rockfield

Tain

Inver

Arboll

B9165

Toulvaddie

Loch
Eye

Rhynie

A9

11

B9165

Fearn

Newfield

Hill of Fearn

Balmuchy

Hilton of Cadboll Chapel

Tullich

B9166

Hilton of
Cadboll

B9175

Balintore

gan

Shandwick Bay

Milton

Ankerville

Shandwick

Kilmuir

Pitcalnie

rbaraville

Nigg

Nigg Bay

Balnapaling

140

Castlecraig

141

Burghead

Hopeman

Burghead Well

Cummingston

FIRTH

Burghead
Bay

Roseisle

V M

Cromarty

8

Miller's Cottage NT

9

0

1

College of

A832

Newton

B9013

SCALE

0   1   2   3   4   5 miles

0   1   2   3   4   5 kilometres

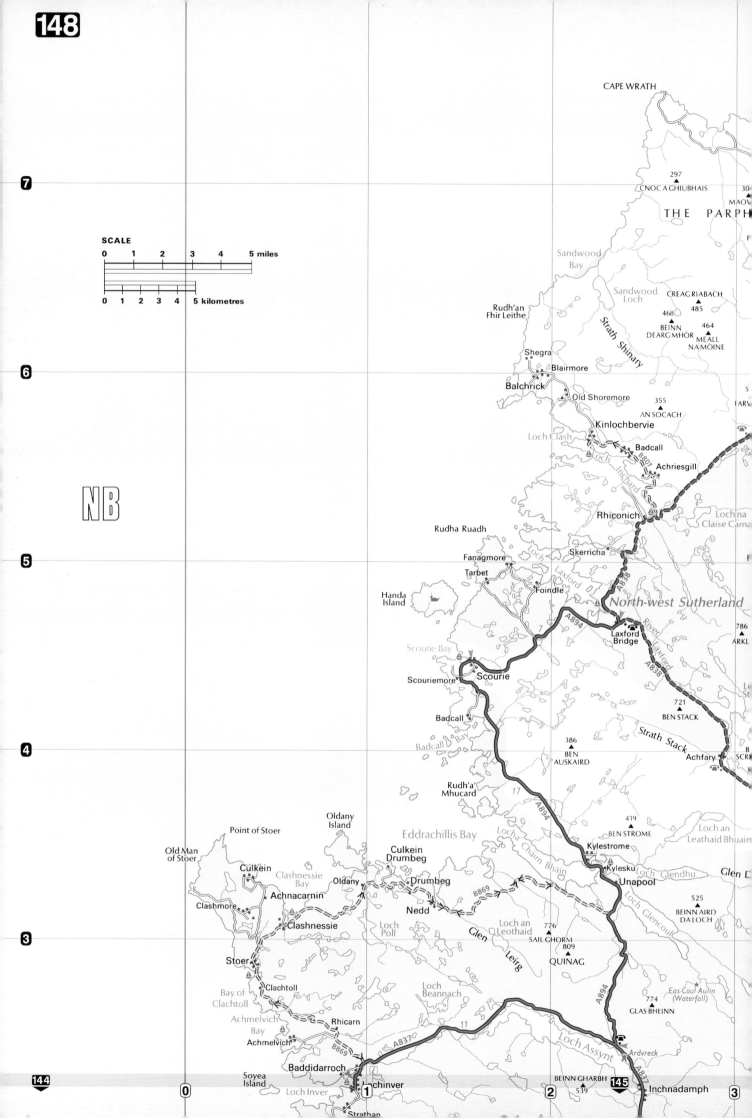

NB

SCALE

0 1 2 3 4 5 miles

0 1 2 3 4 5 kilometres

CAPE WRATH

THE PARPH

297
CNOC A GHIUBHAIS

MAOV

Sandwood
Bay

Sandwood
Loch

CREAG RIABACH
485

Rudh'an
Fhir Leithe

468
BEINN
DEARG MHOR
464
MEALL
NA MOINE

Strath Shinary

Shegra
Blairmore
Balchrick
Old Shoremore
355
AN SOCACH

FARW

Kinlochbervie

Loch Clash
Badcall

Loch Inchard
B801
Achriesgill

Rhiconich

Loch na
Claise Carna

Rudha Ruadh

Skerricha

Fanagmore
Tarbet
Foindle

Loch Laxford

A838

North-west Sutherland

Handa
Island

786
ARKL

Laxford
Bridge

River Laxford

A838

Scourie Bay

7
A894

Scouriemore
Scourie

721
BEN STACK

Strath Stack

Badcall

Badcall Bay

386
BEN
AUSKAIRD

Achfary
SCRI

Rudh'a'
Mhucard

17
A894

419
BEN STROME

Loch an
Leathaid Bhuain

Point of Stoer

Oldany
Island

Eddrachillis Bay

Locha Chàirn Bhàin

Kylestrome

Glen Glendhu

Glen D

Old Man
of Stoer

Culkein
Drumbeg

Kylesku
Unapool

Culkein

Clashnessie
Bay

Oldany
Drumbeg

B869

Loch Glencoul

525
BEINN AIRD
DA LOCH

Achnacarnin

Nedd

Clashmore

Clashnessie

Loch
Poll

Glen
Leirg

Loch an
Leothaid
776
SAIL GHORM
809
QUINAG

Eas Coul Aulin
(Waterfall)

Stoer

Clachtoll

Loch
Beannach

774
GLAS BHEINN

Bay of
Clachtoll

A894

Achmelvich
Bay

Rhicarn

11

Loch Assynt

Achmelvich

B869

A837

Ardvreck

Baddidarroch

Soyea
Island

Lochinver

BEINN GHARBH
539

A837

Inchnadamph

Loch Inver

Strathan

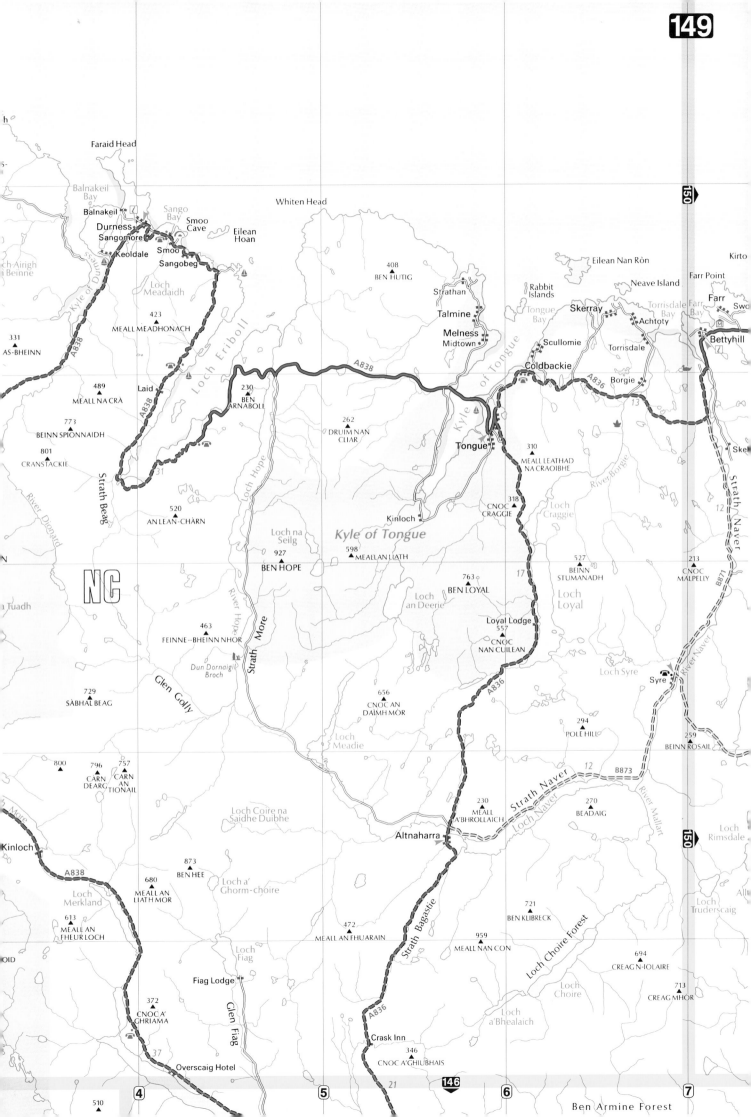

Faraid Head

Balnakeil
Bay

Balnakeil
Durness
Sangomore
Keoldale
Smoo
Sangobeg

Sango
Bay
Smoo
Cave

Eilean
Hoan

Whiten Head

408
BEN HUTIG

Strathan

Talmine

Melness
Midtown

Eilean Nan Ròn

Neave Island

Rabbit
Islands

Skerray

Tongue
Bay

Scullomie

Torrisdale
Bay

Farr Point

Farr

Achtoty

Torrisdale

Borgie

Kirto

Swo

Bettyhill

Loch
Meadaidh

A838

423
MEALL MEADHONACH

331
AS-BHEINN

489
MEALL NA CRÀ

Laid

773
BEINN SPIONNAIDH

801
CRANSTACKIE

ch-Airigh
i Beinne

Kyle of Durness

A838

Strath Beag

31

Loch Eriboll

230
BEN
ARNABOLL

262
DRUIM NAN
CLIAR

A838

Kyle of Tongue

Coldbackie

A836

13

Tongue

310
MEALL LEATHAD
NA CRAOIBHE

Strath Naver

12

Skel

River Dionard

520
AN LEAN-CHÀRN

Loch Hope

Loch na
Seilg

927
BEN HOPE

Kinloch

Kyle of Tongue

318
CNOC
CRAGGIE

Loch
Craggie

B871

a Tuadh

N

NC

598
MEAELAN LIATH

763
BEN LOYAL

Loch
an Deerie

17

527
BEINN
STUMANADH

213
CNOC
MALPELLY

River Borgie

River Naver

463
FEINNE--BHEINN NHOR

River Hope

Strath More

Loyal Lodge

557
CNOC
NAN CUILEAN

Loch
Loyal

Dun Dornaigil
Broch

729
SÀBHAL BEAG

Glen Golly

656
CNOC AN
DAIMH MÒR

294
POLE HILL

Loch Syre

Syre

259
BEINN ROSAIL

Loch
Meadie

800

796
CARN
DEARG

757
CARN
AN
TIONAIL

Loch Coire na
Saidhe Duibhe

230
MEALL
A'BHROLLAICH

Altnaharra

Strath Naver

Loch Naver

270
BEADAIG

12

B873

River Mallart

150

Loch
Rimsdale

Kinloch

A838

Loch
Merkland

873
BEN HEE

680
MEALL AN
LIATH MOR

Loch a'
Ghorm-chòire

721
BEN KLIBRECK

Loch Choire Forest

Loch
Truderscaig

All

613
MEALL AN
FHEUR LOCH

472
MEALL AN FHUARAIN

959
MEALL NAN CON

694
CREAG N-IOLAIRE

OID

Loch Fiag

Fiag Lodge

Strath Bagastie

Loch
Choire

713
CREAG MHOR

372
CNOC A'
GHRIAMA

Glen Fiag

A836

Loch
a'Bhealaich

37

Overscaig Hotel

Crask Inn

346
CNOC A'GHIUBHAIS

510

21

Ben Armine Forest

More

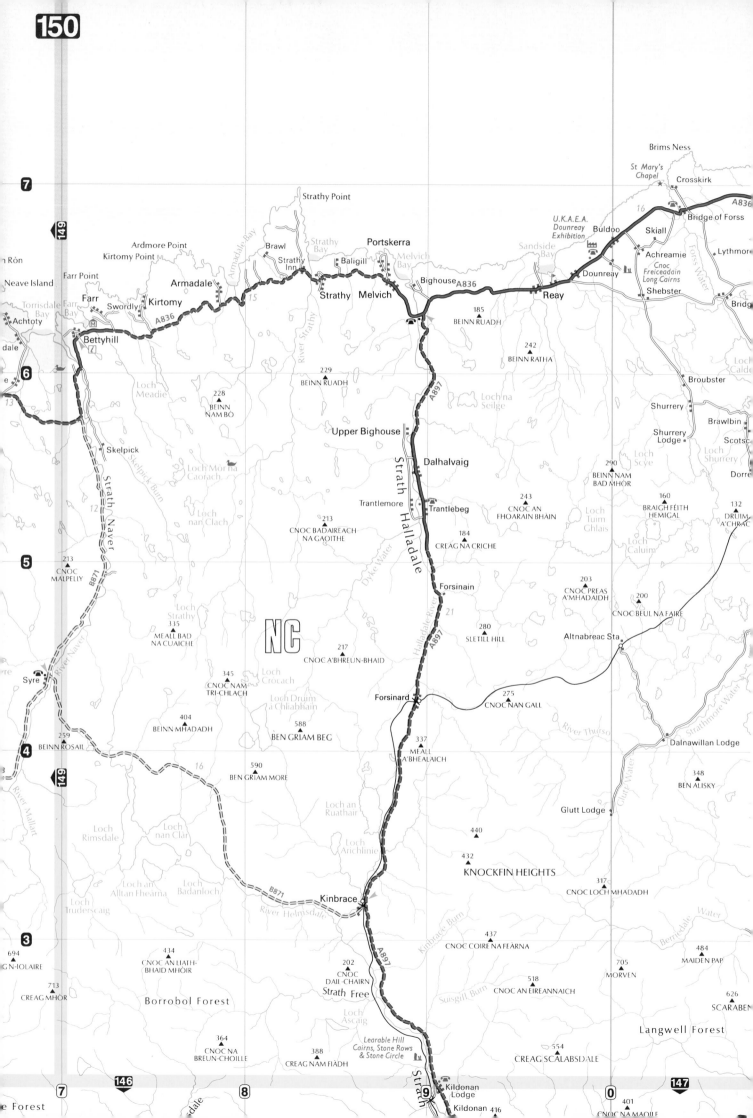

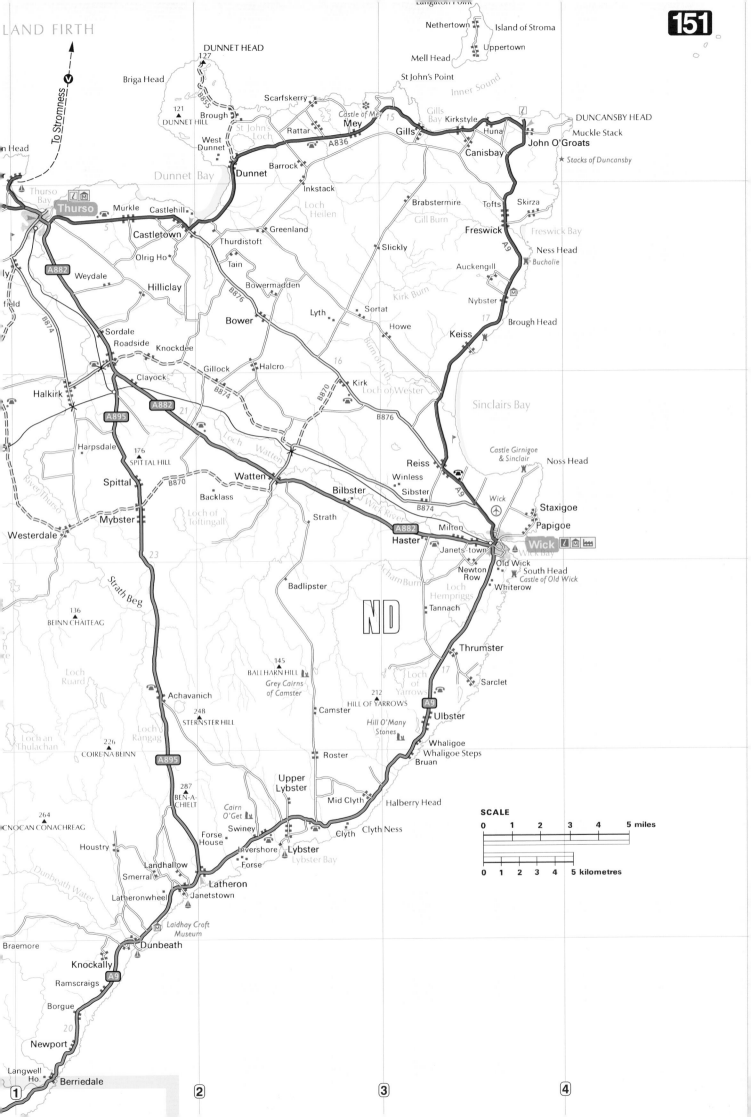

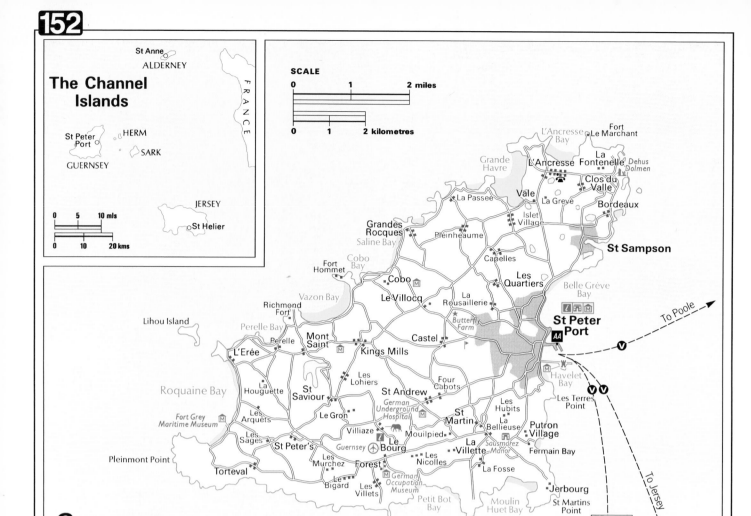

The Channel Islands

St Anne
ALDERNEY

FRANCE

St Peter Port
HERM
SARK
GUERNSEY

JERSEY
St Helier

SCALE
0   1   2 miles
0   1   2 kilometres

0   5   10 mls
0   10   20 kms

L'Ancresse Bay
Fort Le Marchant
La Fontenelle
Dehus Dolmen
Grande Havre
L'Ancresse
Clos du Valle
Vale
La Grève
Bordeaux
La Passee
Islet Village
Grandes Rocques
Pleinheaume
St Sampson
Saline Bay
Capelles
Les Quartiers
Belle Grève Bay
Fort Hommet
Cobo Bay
Cobo
Le Villocq
La Rousaillerie
St Peter Port
To Poole
Vazon Bay
Butterfly Farm
AA
Richmond Fort
Perelle Bay
Mont Saint
Castel
Havelet Bay
Lihou Island
Perelle
Kings Mills
Four Cabots
L'Erée
Les Lohiers
Les Terres Point
Roquaine Bay
La Houguette
St Saviour
St Andrew
German Underground Hospital
Les Hubits
To Jersey
Le Gron
St Martin
La Bellieuse
Putron Village
Fort Grey Maritime Museum
Les Arquets
Villiaze
Mouilpied
Fermain Bay
Les Sages
St Peter's
Guernsey
Le Bourg
Les Nicolles
La Villette
Sausmarez Manor
Pleinmont Point
Les Murchez
Forest
La Fosse
Torteval
Le Bigard
Les Villets
German Occupation Museum
Jerbourg
St Martins Point
Petit Bot Bay
Moulin Huet Bay
Point de la Moye
Icart Point
ST MALO

Guernsey

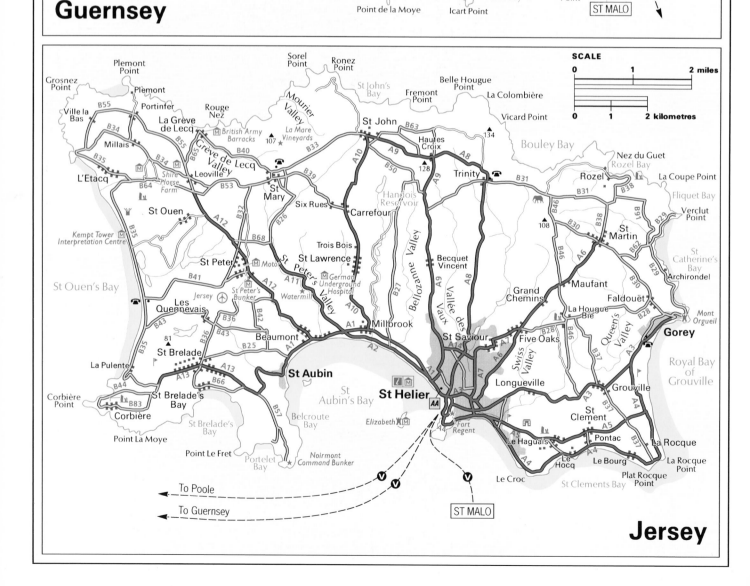

SCALE
0   1   2 miles
0   1   2 kilometres

Plemont Point
Sorel Point
Ronez Point
Belle Hougue Point
La Colombière
Grosnez Point
Plemont
St John's Bay
Fremont Point
Vicard Point
Ville la Bas
B55
Portinfer
Rouge Nez
Mourier Valley
St John
B63
Bouley Bay
Millais
B34
La Grève de Lecq
British Army Barracks
107
La Mare Vineyards
B33
Hautes Croix
A8
Nez du Guet
Rozel Bay
L'Etacq
B35
Grève de Lecq Valley
B39
A10
A9
B50
128
Trinity
B31
Rozel
La Coupe Point
B40
B65
Leoville
B53
St Mary
Six Rues
Carrefour
Handois Reservoir
134
B46
B31
Fliquet Bay
B64
Shire Horse Farm
B32
B26
Trois Bois
Bellozanne Valley
108
B30
St Martin
Verclut Point
St Ouen
A12
B68
St Lawrence
Becquet Vincent
B46
A6
B62
B29
St Catherine's Bay
Kempt Tower Interpretation Centre
B35
German Underground Hospital
A9
A8
Vallée des Vaux
Grand Chemins
Archirondel
St Peter
A11
St Peter's Valley
Watermill
Maufant
B30
B28
Mont Orgueil
St Ouen's Bay
B41
Jersey
St Peter's Bunker
A10
St Saviour
La Hougue Bie
Faldouët
Les Quennevais
B36
B42
A1
Millbrook
A14
Five Oaks
B46
Queen's Valley
Gorey
La Pulente
B43
B36
B43
Beaumont
B25
A1
A2
A6
A7
A3
B37
Royal Bay of Grouville
81
St Brelade
Swiss Valley
A3
A4
Corbière Point
B44
St Aubin
A1
Longueville
Grouville
B83
Corbière
A13
B66
St Aubin's Bay
A4
St Clement
A5
Point La Moye
B57
Belcroute Bay
Elizabeth
A3
La Hougue
Pontac
La Rocque
Point Le Fret
St Brelade's Bay
Fort Regent
A4
Le Hocq
Le Bourg
La Rocque Point
Portelet Bay
Noirmont Command Bunker
To Poole
St Helier
AA
Le Croc
St Clements Bay
Plat Rocque Point
To Guernsey
ST MALO

Jersey

Isle of Man

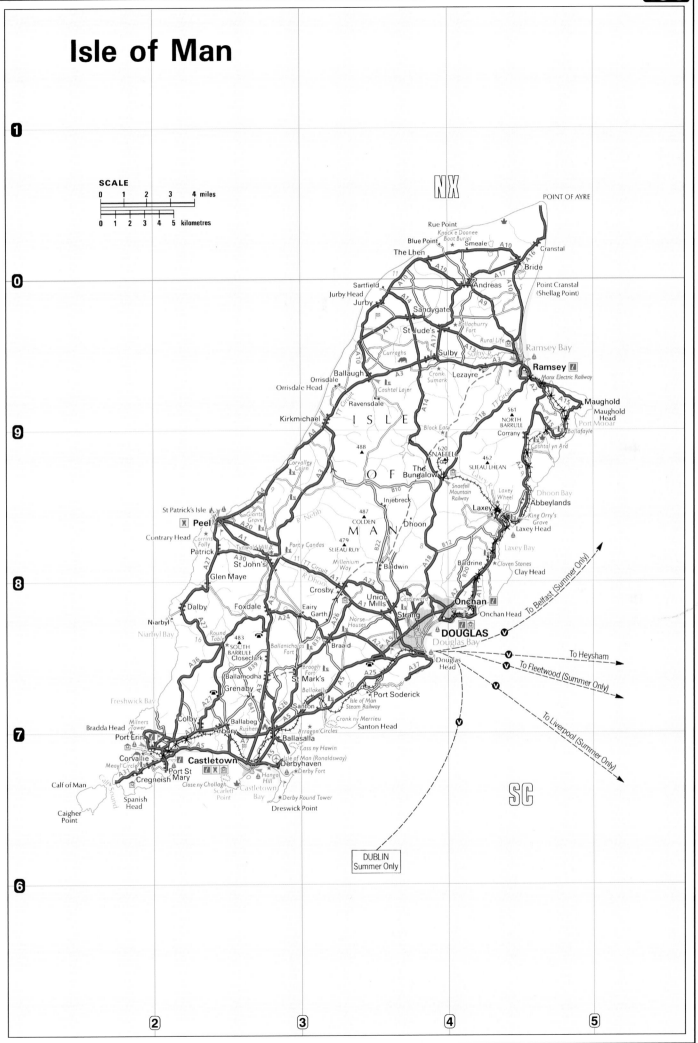

SCALE

0 1 2 3 4 miles

0 1 2 3 4 5 kilometres

NX

POINT OF AYRE

Rue Point
Knock e Doonee
Boat Burial
Blue Point
Smeale
Cranstal
The Lhen
Bride
A10

Sartfield
Andreas
Point Cranstal
(Shellag Point)
Jurby Head
Jurby
Sandygate
St Jude's
Ballachurry
Fort
Rural Life
Ramsey Bay
Sulby
Sulby R.
Ramsey
Curraghs
Cronk
Sumark
Lezayre
Manx Electric Railway
Ballaugh
Maughold
Orrisdale
Cashtal Lajer
Maughold
Head
Orrisdale Head
Ravensdale
Port Mooar
Ballafayle
Kirkmichael
I S L E
Block Eary
Cashtal yn Ard
488
561
NORTH
BARRULE
SNAEFELL
620
Corvallgy
Cojen
O F
Fort
SLIEAU LHEAN
462
The
Bungalow
Dhoon Bay
B10
Snaefell
Mountain
Railway
Abbeylands
Injebreck
Laxey
Wheel
St Patrick's Isle
Giants
Grave
487
Laxey
King Orry's
Grave
Peel
M A N
COLDEN
Dhoon
Laxey Head
Contrary Head
Corrins
Folly
R. Neb
479
SLIEAU RUY
Laxey Bay
B12
Patrick
Tynwald Hill
Port y Candas
Millenium
Way
Baldrine
Glen Maye
St John's
R. Dhoo
Baldwin
Cloven Stones
Clay Head
Crosby
Dalby
Foxdale
Union
Mills
Castleward
Onchan
To Belfast (Summer Only)
Eairy
Garth
Strang
Niarbyl
Norse
Houses
Onchan Head
Niarbyl Bay
Round
Table
483
SOUTH
BARRULE
Braaid
DOUGLAS
To Heysham
Closeclark
Ballanicholas
Fort
Douglas Bay
To Fleetwood (Summer Only)
Brough
Fort
Douglas
Head
Ballamodha
St Mark's
Freshwick Bay
Grenaby
Ballakellig
Port Soderick
Isle of Man
Steam Railway
To Liverpool (Summer Only)
Bradda Head
Milners
Tower
Colby
Ballabeg
Rushen
Santon
Cronk ny Merrieu
Arragon Circles
Santon Head
Port Erin
Arbory
Ballasalla
Cass ny Hawin
SC
Corvalie
Meayl Circle
Castletown
Derbyhaven
Cregneish
Port St
Mary
Isle of Man (Ronaldsway)
Derby Fort
Calf of Man
Close ny Chollagh
Scarlett
Point
Castletown
Bay
Spanish
Head
Hango
Hill
Derby Round Tower
Caigher
Point
Dreswick Point

DUBLIN
Summer Only

The Western Isles

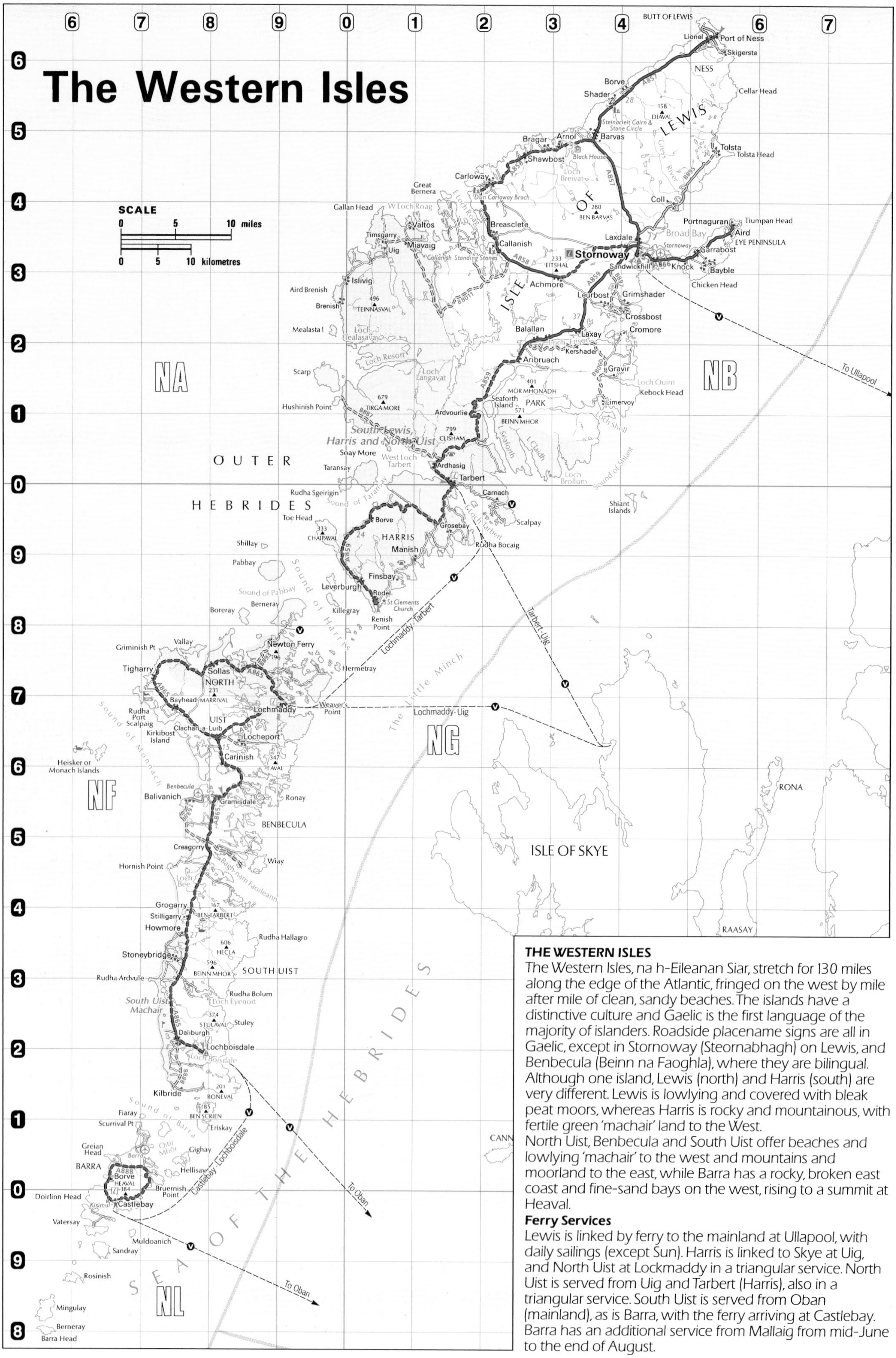

THE WESTERN ISLES

The Western Isles, na h-Eileanan Siar, stretch for 130 miles along the edge of the Atlantic, fringed on the west by mile after mile of clean, sandy beaches. The islands have a distinctive culture and Gaelic is the first language of the majority of islanders. Roadside placename signs are all in Gaelic, except in Stornoway (Steornabhagh) on Lewis, and Benbecula (Beinn na Faoghla), where they are bilingual. Although one island, Lewis (north) and Harris (south) are very different. Lewis is lowlying and covered with bleak peat moors, whereas Harris is rocky and mountainous, with fertile green 'machair' land to the West.

North Uist, Benbecula and South Uist offer beaches and lowlying 'machair' to the west and mountains and moorland to the east, while Barra has a rocky, broken east coast and fine-sand bays on the west, rising to a summit at Heaval.

Ferry Services

Lewis is linked by ferry to the mainland at Ullapool, with daily sailings (except Sun). Harris is linked to Skye at Uig, and North Uist at Lockmaddy in a triangular service. North Uist is served from Uig and Tarbert (Harris), also in a triangular service. South Uist is served from Oban (mainland), as is Barra, with the ferry arriving at Castlebay. Barra has an additional service from Mallaig from mid-June to the end of August.

Scottish Islands

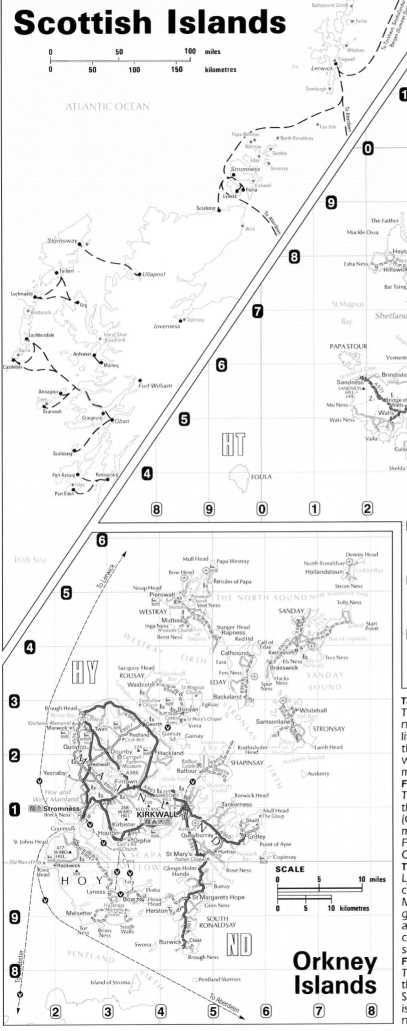

ATLANTIC OCEAN

Irish Sea

Orkney Islands

HY

ND

SCALE
0   5   10 miles
0   5   10 kilometres

Shetland Islands

HP

HU

SCALE
0   5   10 miles
0   5   10 kilometres

TÓRSHAVN
SEYDISFJORDUR
BERGEN
Summer Only

OUT SKERRIES

THE SHETLAND ISLANDS

The most northerly of all Britain's islands, this group numbers 100, though only 15 are inhabited. Most people live on the largest island, Mainland, on which Lerwick is the only town of importance. The scenery is magnificent, with unspoiled views, and the islands' northerly position means summer days have little or no darkness.

Ferry Services

The main service from the mainland is from Aberdeen to the island port of Lerwick. A service from Stromness (Orkney) to Lerwick is also available. During the summer months there are also services linking Shetland with Faroe, Iceland, Norway and Denmark. Shetland Islands Council operates an inter-island service.

THE ORKNEY ISLANDS

Lying 20 miles north of the Scottish mainland, Orkney comprises 70 islands, of which 18 are inhabited, Mainland being the largest. Apart from Hoy, Orkney is generally green and flat, with few trees. The islands abound with prehistoric antiquities and rare bird life. The climate is one of even temperatures and 'twilight' summer nights but with violent winds at times.

Ferry Services

The main service is from Scrabster on Caithness coast to the island port of Stromness. A service from Aberdeen to Stromness provides a link to Shetland at Lerwick. Inter-island services are also operated (advance reservations necessary).

Abbeydorney G2
Abbeyfeale G2
Abbeyleix G4
Adamstown G4
Adare G2
Adrigole H2
Ahascragh F3
Ahoghill D5
Allihies H1
Anascaul H1
Annalong E5
Annestown H4
Antrim D5
Ardagh G2
Ardara D3
Ardcath F5
Ardee E4
Ardfert G2
Ardfinnan G3
Ardglass E5
Ardgroom H1
Arklow G5
Arless G4
Armagh D4
Armoy C5
Arthurstown H4
Arvagh E4
Ashbourne F4
Ashford F5
Askeaton G2
Athboy E4
Athea G2
Athenry F3
Athleague F3
Athlone F3
Athy F4
Augher D4
Aughnacloy D4
Aughrim G5
Avoca G5

Bailieborough E4
Balbriggan F5
Balla F2
Ballacolla G4
Ballaghaderreen E3
Ballina G3
Ballina G3
Ballinafad E3
Ballinagh E4
Ballinakill G4
Ballinalee E3
Ballinamallard D4
Ballinamore F3
Ballinamore F3
Ballinascarty H2
Ballinasloe F3
Ballindine E2
Ballineen H2
Ballingarry G3
Ballingarry G2
Ballingeary H2
(Beal Atha an Ghaorfthaidh)
Ballinhassig H3
Ballinlough E3
Ballinrobe E2
Ballinspittle H2
Ballintober E3
Ballintra D3
Ballivor F4
Ballon G4
Ballybay F3
Ballybofey D3
Ballybunion G2
Ballycanew G5
Ballycarry D5
Ballycastle D2
Ballycastle C5
Ballyclare D5
Ballyconneely F1

Ballycotton H3
Ballycumber F3
Ballydehob J2
Ballydesmond H2
Ballyduff H3
Ballyduff G2
Ballyfarnan E3
Ballygalley D5
Ballygar F3
Ballygawley D4
Ballygowan D5
Ballyhaise E4
Ballyhale G4
Ballyhaunis E3
Ballyhean E2
Ballyheige G1
Ballyjamesduff E4
Ballylanders G3
Ballykeeran F3
Ballylongford G2
Ballylooby G3
Ballylynan G4
Ballymahon F3
Ballymakeery H2
Ballymaloe H3
Ballymena D5
Ballymoe E3
Ballymoney C4
Ballymore F3
Ballymore Eustace F4
Ballymote E3
Ballynahinch D5
Ballynure D5
Ballyragget G4
Ballyronan D4
Ballyronan E3
Ballysadare E3
Ballyshannon D3
Ballyvaughan F2
Ballywalter D5
Balrothery F5
Baltimore J2
Baltinglass G4
Banagher F3
Banbridge D5
Bandon H2
Bangor D5
Bangor Erris E2
Bansha G3
Banteer H2
Bantry H2
Barryporeen H3
Beaufort H2
Belcoo D3
Belfast D5
Belgooly H3
Bellaghy D4
Belleek D3
Belmullet D2
(Beal an Muirhead)
Belturbet E4
Benburb D4
Bennettsbridge G4
Beragh D4
Birr F3
Blacklion D3
Blackwater G5
Blarney H3
Blessington F4
Boherbue H2
Borris G4
Borris-in-Ossory G3
Borrisokane G3
Borrisoleigh G3
Boyle E3
Bracknagh F4
Bray F5
Bridgetown H4
Brittas F4
Broadford G3
Broadford G2

Broughshane D5
Bruff G3
Bruree G3
Bunclody G4
Buncrana C4
Bundoran D3
Bunnahowen D2
Bunnyconnellan E2
Bushmills C4
Butler's Bridge E4
Buttevant H2

Cadamstown F3
Caherconlish G3
Caherdaniel H1
Cahir G3
Cahirciveen H1
Caledon D4
Callan G4
Caltra F3
Camolin G4
Camp G1
Cappagh White G3
Cappamore G3
Cappoquin H3
Carlanstown E4
Calingford E5
Carlow G4
Carndonagh C4
Carnew G4
Carnlough C5
Carracastle E3
Carrick D3
(An Charraig)
Carrickfergus D5
Carrickmacross E4
Carrickmore D4
Carrick-on-Shannon E3
Carrick -on-Suir G4
Carrigahorig F3
Carrigaline H3
Carrigallen E3
Carriganimmy H2
Carrigans C4
Carrigtohill H3
Carrowkeel C4
Carryduff D5
Cashel G3
Castlebar E2
Castlebellingham E4
Castleblayney E4
Castlebridge G4
Castlecomer G4
Castleconnell G3
Castledermot G4
Castleisland G2
Castlemaine H2
Castlemartyr H3
Castleplunkett E3
Castlepollard E4
Castlerea E3
Castlerock C4
Castleshane E4
Castletown F4
Castletownbere H1
Castletownroche H3
Castletownshend J2
Castlewellan E5
Causeway G2
Cavan E4
Ceananus Mor (Kells) E4
Celbridge F4
Charlestown E3
Clady D4
Clane F4
Clara F3
Clarecastle G2
Claremorris E2
Clarinbridge F2
Clashmore H3

Claudy C4
Cliffony D3
Cloghan F3
Clogh G4
Clogheen H3
Clogher D4
Clohamon G4
Clonakilty H2
Clonard F4
Clonaslee F4
Clonbulloge F4
Clonbur (An Fhairche) E2
Clondalkin F4
Clones E4
Clonmany C4
Clonmel G3
Clonmellon E4
Clonmore G3
Clonony F3
Clonoulty G3
Clonroche G4
Clontibret E4
Cloonbannin H2
Cloondara E3
Cloonkeen H2
Cloonlara G3
Clough D5
Cloughjordan F3
Cloyne H3
Coagh D4
Coalisland D4
Cobh H3
Coleraine C4
Collinstown E4
Collon E4
Collooney E3
Comber D5
Conna H3
Cookstown D4
Coole E4
Cooraclare G2
Cootehill E4
Cork H3
Cork Airport H3
Cornamona F2
Corofin F2
Courtmacsherry H2
Courtown Harbour G5
Craigaven D5
Craughwell F3
Creggs E3
Cresslough C3
Croagh G2
Crolly (Croithli) C3
Crookedwood E4
Crookhaven J1
Crookstown H2
Croom G2
Crossakeel E4
Cross Barry H2
Crosshaven H3
Crossmaglen E4
Crossmolina E2
Crumlin D5
Crusheen F2
Culdaff C4
Culleybackey D5
Curracloe G4
Curraghboy F3
Curry E3

Daingean F4
Delvin E4
Derrygonnelly D3
Derrylin E4
Dervock C4
Dingle (An Daingean) H1
Doagh D5
Donaghadee D5
Donaghmore G3
Donegal D3

Doneraile H3
Doonbeg G2
Douglas H3
Downpatrick D5
Dowra E3
Draperstown D4
Drimoleague H2
Dripsey H2
Drogheda E5
Droichead Nua F4
(Newbridge)
Dromahair D3
Dromcolliher G2
Dromore D5
Dromore D4
Dromore West D2
Drum D3
Drumconrath E4
Drumkeeran E3
Drumlish E3
Drumod E3
Drumquin D4
Drumshanbo E3
Drumsna E3
Duagh G2
Dublin F5
Duleek E4
Dunboyne F4
Duncormick H4
Dundalk E5
Dunderrow H2
Dundrum E5
Dunfanaghy C3
Dungannon D4
Dungarvan H3
Dungarvan G4
Dungiven C4
Dungloe C3
Dungourney H3
Dunkineely D3
Dun Laoghaire F5
Dunlavin F4
Dunleer E4
Dunloy C5
Dunmanway H2
Dunmore E3
Dunmore East H4
Dunmurry D5
Dunshauglin F4
Durrow G4
Durrus H2

Eaky D2
Edenderry F4
Edgeworthstown E3
Eglinton C4
Elphin E3
Emyvale D4
Enfield F4
Ennis G2
Enniscorthy G4
Enniscrone D2
Enniskean H2
Enniskillen D4
Ennistymon F2
Eyrecourt F3

Farnaght E3
Farranfore H2
Feakle F3
Fenagh E3
Fermoy H3
Ferns G4
Fethard H4
Fethard G3
Finnea E4
Fintona D4
Fivemiletown D4
Fontstown F4
Foulkesmills G4
Foxford E2

Foynes G2
Freemount G2
Frenchpark E3
Freshford G4
Fuerty E3

Galbally G3
Galway F2
Garrison D3
Garvagh C4
Geashill F4
Gilford D5
Glandore J2
Glanmire H3
Glanworth H3
Glaslough D4
Glassan F3
Glenamaddy E3
Glenarm C5
Glenavy D5
Glenbeigh H1
Glencolumbkille D3
(Gleann Cholm Cille)
Glendalough F5
Glenealy G5
Glenfarne D3
Glengarriff H2
Glenmore G4
Glenties D3
Glenville H3
Glin G2
Glinsk F2
(Glinsce)
Golden G3
Goleen J1
Goresbridge G4
Gorey G5
Gort F2
Gortin D4
Gowran G4
Graiguenamanagh G4
Grallagh G3
Granard E4
Grange E3
Greencastle E5
Greyabbey D5
Greystones F5
Gulladuff D4

Hacketstown G4
Headford F2
Herbertstown G3
Hillsborough D5
Hilltown E5
Hospital G3
Holycross G3
Holywood D5
Howth F5

Inch H1
Inchigeelagh H2
Inishannon H2

Johnstown G3

Kanturk H2
Keadue E3
Keady E4
Keel G1
Keenagh E3
Kells D5
Kenmare H2
Kesh D3
Kilbeggan F4
Kilberry E4
Kilbrittain H2
Kilcar D3
(Cill Charthaigh)
Kilcock F4
Kilcolgan F2
Kilconnell F3

Kilconnell F2
Kilcoole F5
Kilcormac F3
Kilcullen F4
Kilcurry E4
Kildare F4
Kildavin G4
Kildorrery H3
Kildress D4
Kilfenora F2
Kilfinnane G3
Kilgarvan H2
Kilkee G2
Kilkeel E5
Kilkelly E2
Kilkenny G4
Kilkieran F2
(Cill Ciarain)
Kilkinlea G2
Kill H4
Killadysert G2
Killala D2
Killaloe G3
Killarney H2
Killashandra E3
Killashee E3
Killeagh H3
Killeigh F4
Killenaule G3
Killimer G2
Killimor F3
Killiney F5
Killinick H4
Killorglin H1
Killough E5
Killucan F4
Killybegs D3
Killyleagh D5
Kilmacanoge F5
Kilmacrenan C3
Kilmacthomas H4
Kilmaganny G4
Kilmaine E2
Kilmallock G3
Kilmanagh G4
Kilmanahan G3
Kilmeaden H4
Kilmeage F4
Kilmeedy G2
Kilmichael H2
Kilmore Quay H4
Kilnaleck E4
Kilrea C4
Kilrush G2
Kilsheelan G3
Kiltealy G4
Kiltegan G4
Kiltimagh E2
Kiltoom F3
Kingscourt E4
Kinlough D3
Kinnegad F4
Kinnitty F3
Kinsale H3
Kinvarra F2
Kircubbin D5
Knock E2
Knockcroghery E3
Knocklofty G3
Knockmahon H4
Knocktopher G4

Lahinch F2
Lanesborough E3
Laragh F5
Lauragh H1
Laurencetown F3
Leap J2
Leenene E2
Leighlinbridge G4
Leitrim E3

Leixlip F4
Lemybrien H3
Letterfrack E2
Letterkenny C3
Lifford D4
Limavady C4
Limerick G3
Lisbellaw D4
Lisburn D5
Liscarroll G3
Lisdoonvarna F2
Lismore H3
Lisnaskea D4
Lisryan E4
Listowel G2
Loghill G2
Londonderry C4
Longford E3
Loughbrickland D5
Loughgall D4
Loughgilin E3
Loughrea F3
Louisburgh E2
Lucan F4
Lurgan D5
Lusk F5

Macroom H2
Maghera E5
Maghera D4
Magherafelt D4
Maguiresbridge D4
Malahide F5
Malin C4
Malin More D3
Mallow H3
Manorhamilton D3
Markethill D4
Maynooth F4
Maze D5
Middletown D4
Midleton H3
Milford C4
Millstreet H2
Milltown H2
Milltown Malbay G2
Mitchelstown H3
Moate F3
Mohill E3
Molls Cap H1
Monaghan E4
Monasterevin F4
Moneygall G3
Moneymore D4
Monivea F3
Mooncoin H4
Moorfields D5
Mount Bellew F3
Mount Charles D3
Mountmellick F4
Mountrath F4
Mountshannon F3
Mourne Abbey H3

Moville C4
Moy D4
Moylett E4
Moynalty E4
Moyvore F3
Muckross H2
Muff C4
Muine Bheag G4
Mullabohy E4
Mullagh F4
Mullinavat G4
Mullingar F4
Myshall G4

Naas F4
Nad H2
Naul F5
Navan E4
Neale G3
Nenagh G3
Newbliss E4
Newcastle E5
Newcastle West G2
Newinn G3
Newmarket H2
Newmarket-on-Fergus G2
Newport D3
Newport E2
New Ross G4
Newry E5
Newtown G4
Newtownabbey D5
Newtownards D5
Newtown Butler E4
Newtown Forbes E3
Newtownhamilton E4
Newtown Mount Kennedy F5
Newtownstewart D4
Nobber E4

Oilgate G4
Oldcastle E4
Omagh D4

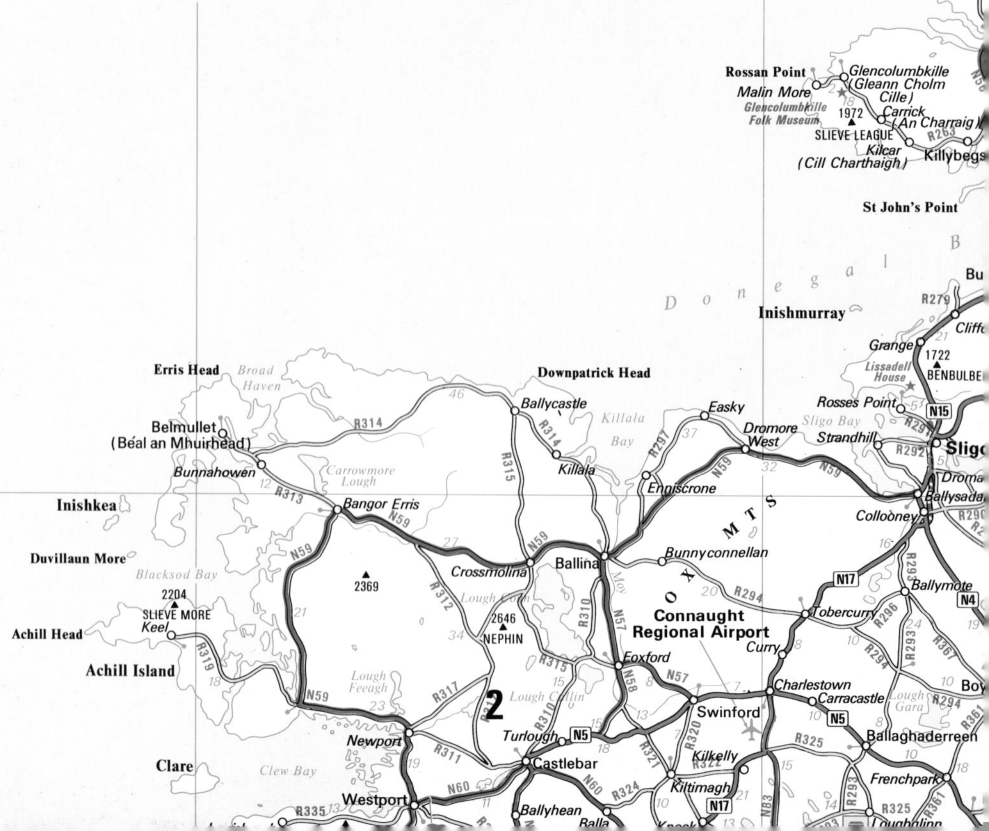

C
D
E

1   2

Map labels:
Aran Island
Blo
Gweebarra B
Rossan Point
Malin More
Glencolumbkille (Gleann Cholm Cille)
Glencolumbkille Folk Museum
1972
SLIEVE LEAGUE
Carrick (An Charraig)
Kilcar (Cill Charthaigh)
Killybegs
St John's Point
Donegal B
Bu
Inishmurray
Grange
1722
BENBULBE
Lissadell House
Rosses Point
N15
Cliffo
Erris Head
Broad Haven
Downpatrick Head
Ballycastle
Killala Bay
Easky
Dromore West
Strandhill
Sligo
Belmullet (Béal an Mhuirhead)
R314
46
Killala
Sligo Bay
Bunnahowen
R313
12
Carrowmore Lough
R315
Enniscrone
R292
Inishkea
Bangor Erris
N59
Bunnyconnellan
N17
Ballysada
Droma
Colloon
Duvillaun More
Blacksod Bay
2204 SLIEVE MORE
Keel
Achill Head
R319
Achill Island
Lough Feeagh
R317
2369
R312
2646 NEPHIN
Crossmolina
Ballina
Connaught Regional Airport
Tobercurry
R293
Ballymote
N4
Foxford
Curry
Charlestown
Carracastle
N5
Ballaghaderreen
Clare
Clew Bay
Newport
R311
Turlough
N5
Swinford
Kiltimagh
N17
Frenchpark
R325
Westport
Castlebar
N60
Ballyhean
Balla
Mox Mts

th **E5**
G3
more **F2**
terard **F2**
s **H2**
green **G3**
aasilla **H1**
y **E2**
age East **H4**
age West **H3**
kswell **G2**
town **G4**
go **D3**
bridge **D4**
eroy **D4**
adown **D4**
aferry **D5**
arlington **F4**
vogie **D5**
alenone **D4**
arnock **F5**
ane **F6**
oe **G3**
rush **C4**
stewart **C4**
umna **F3•**
etzpass **D5**

arney **F4**
alstown **D5**
arkin **C4**
angen **F4**
coole **F4**
cormack **H3**
downey **H2**
drum **G5**
friland **E5**
keale **G2**
Luric **G2**
rleville) **G2**
melton **C4**

Rathmolyon **F4**
Rathmore **H2**
Rathmullan **C4**
Rathnew **F5**
Rathowen **E4**
Rathvilly **G4**
Ratoath **F4**
Ray **C4**
Ring **H3**
(An Rinn)
Ringaskiddy **H3**
Riverstown **F3**
Rockcorry **E4**
Roosky **E3**
Rosapenna **C3**
Rosebercon **G4**
Roscommon **E3**
Roscrea **F3**
Ross Carberry **J2**
Rosscor **F3**
Rosses Point **D3**
Rosslare Harbour **H4**
Rosslea **E4**
Rostrevor **E5**
Roundstone **F2**
Roundwood **F5**
Rush **F5**

St Johnstown **C4**
Saintfield **D5**
Sallins **F4**
Scarriff **G3**
Scartaglen **H2**
Scarva **D5**
Schull **J2**
Scramoge **E3**
Scribbagh **D3**
Seskinore **D4**
Shanagolden **G2**
Shannon Airport **G2**
Shannonbridge **F3**
Shercock **E4**
Shillelagh **G4**

Shinrone **F3**
Shrule **F2**
Silvermines **G3**
Sion Mills **D4**
Sixmilebridge **G2**
Skerries **F5**
Skibbereen **J2**
Slane **C4**
Sligo **D3**
Smithborough **E4**
Sneem **H1**
Spiddal **F2**
(An Spideal)
Sporthouse Cross Roads **H4**
Stewartstown **D4**
Stonyford **G4**
Strabane **D4**
Stradbally **F4**
Stradone **E4**
Strandhill **D3**
Strangford **D5**
Stranorlar **D3**
Stratford **F4**
Strokestown **E3**
Summerhill **F4**
Swanlinbar **E3**
Swatragh **D4**
Swinford **E2**
Swords **F5**

Taghmon **G4**
Tagoat **H4**
Tahilla **H1**
Tallaght **F5**
Tallow **H3**
Tallowbridge **H3**
Tandragee **D5**
Tang **F3**
Tarbert **G2**
Templemore **F3**
Templepatrick **D5**
Templetouhy **G3**
Termonfeckin **E5**

Thomas Street **F3**
Thomastown **G4**
Thurles **G3**
Timahoe **F4**
Timoleague **G2**
Tinahely **G4**
Tipperary **G3**
Tobercurry **E3**
Tobermore **D4**
Togher **F3**
Toomyvara **G3**
Toomore **J1**
Tralee **G2**
Tramore **H4**
Trim **F4**
Tuam **F2**
Tuamgraney **G3**
Tulla **G2**
Tullamore **F4**
Tullow **G4**
Tulsk **E3**
Turlough **F3**
Tyholland **D4**
Tyrrellspass **F4**

Urlingford **G3**

Virginia **E4**
Waddington **H4**
Warrenpoint **E5**
Waterford **H4**
Watergrasshill **H3**
Waterville **H1**
Westport **E2**
Wexford **G4**
Whitegate **H3**
Whitehead **D5**
Wicklow **F5**
Woodenbridge **G5**
Woodford **F3**

Youghal **H3**

M1	Motorway
N17	National Primary Route
N54	National Secondary Route } Republic of Ireland
R182	Regional Road
A4	Primary Route
A21	A Road } Northern Ireland
B75	B Road

Road under construction
5 Distance in miles between symbols
International Boundary
Frontier Posts

Scale: 16 miles to 1 inch (approx)

0   10   20   30 miles
0 10 20 30 40 kilometres

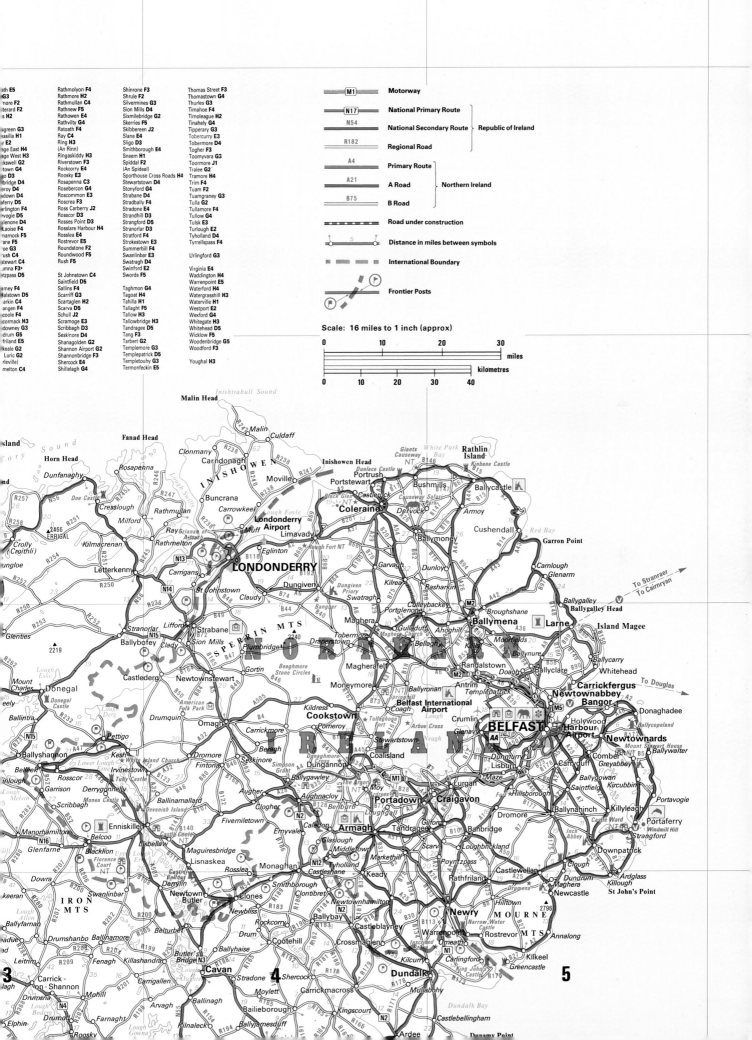

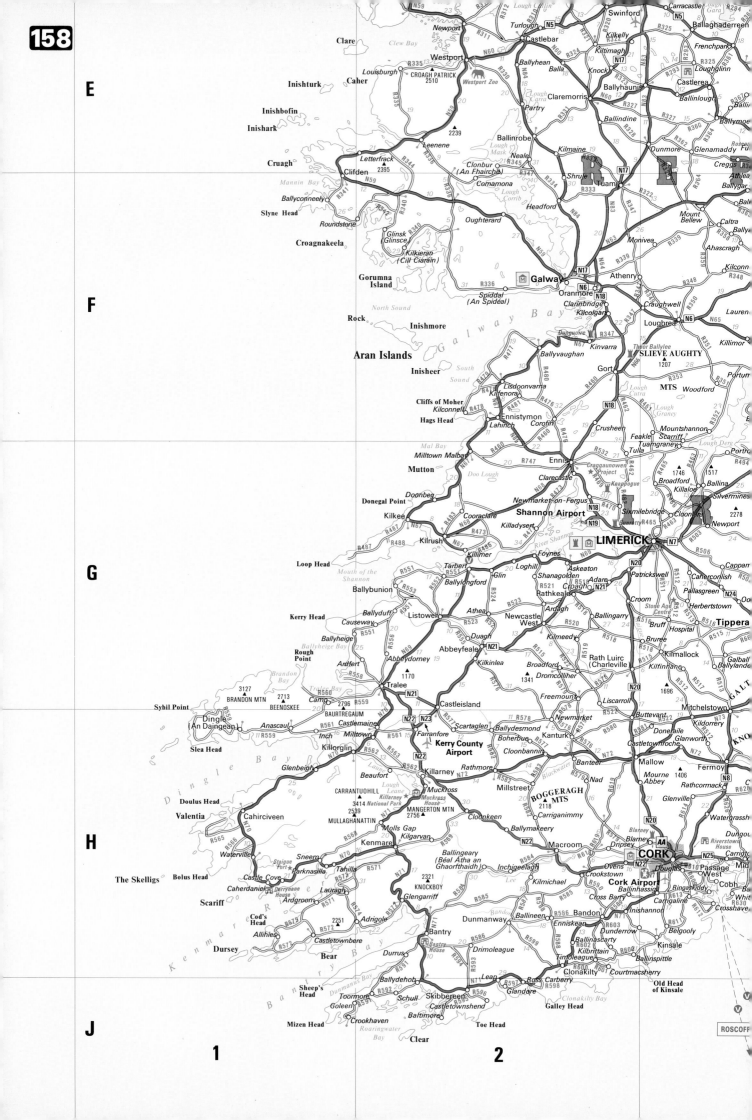

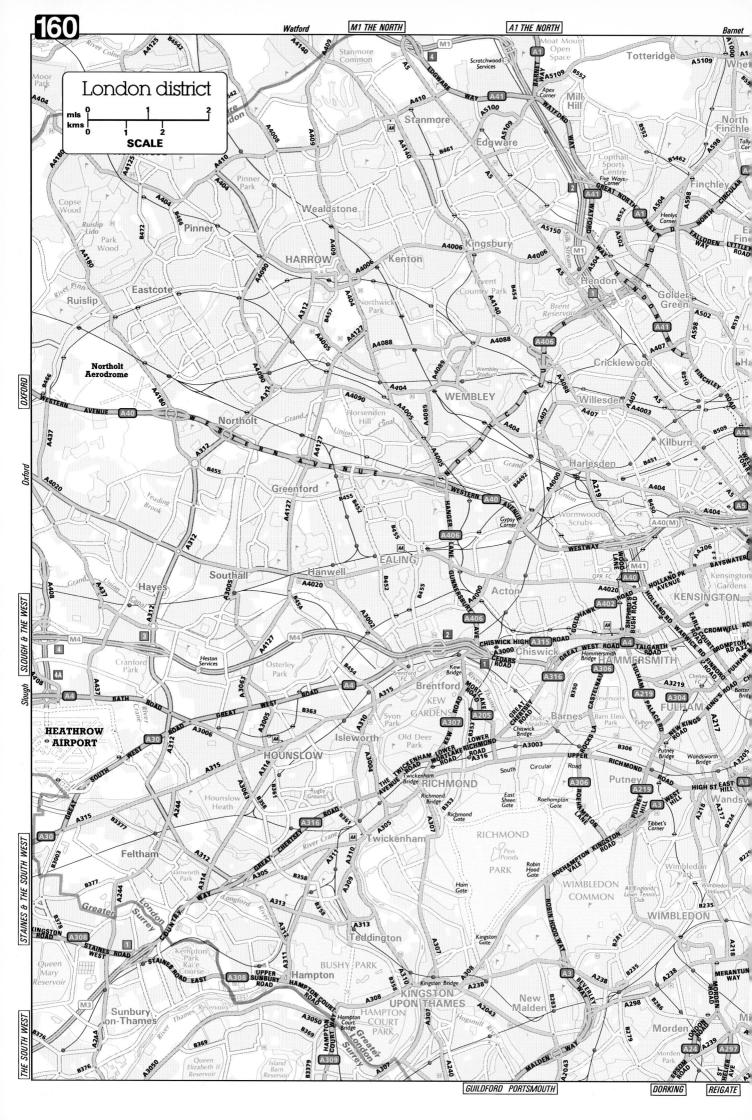

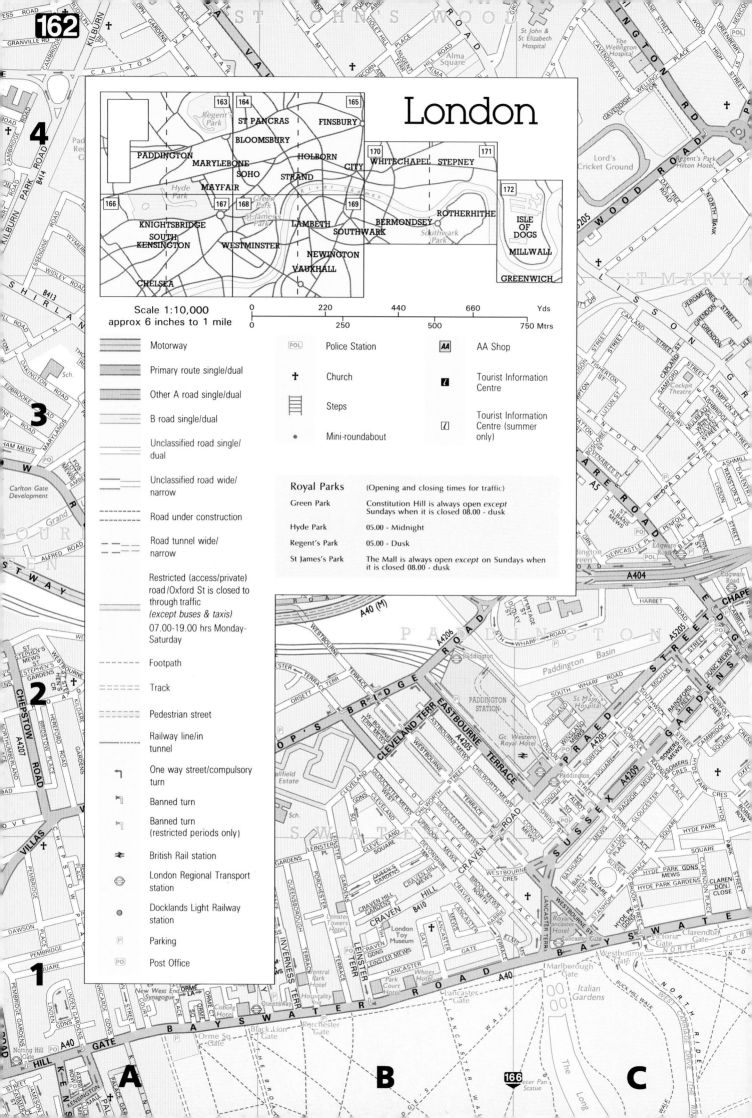

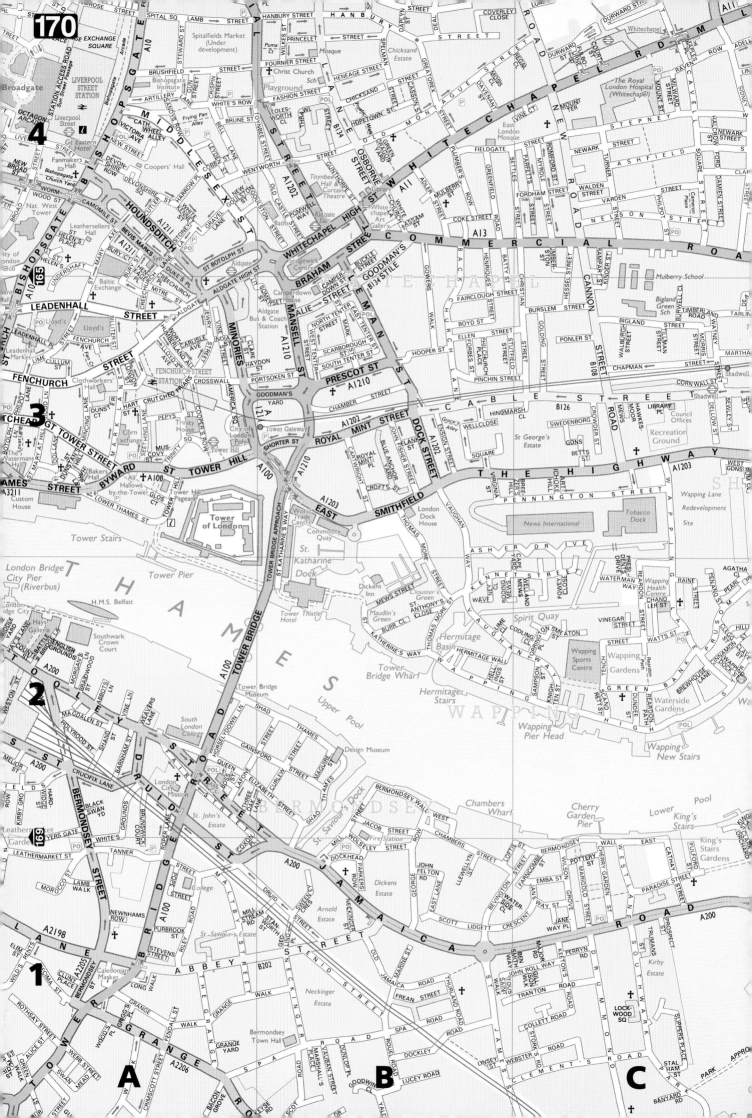

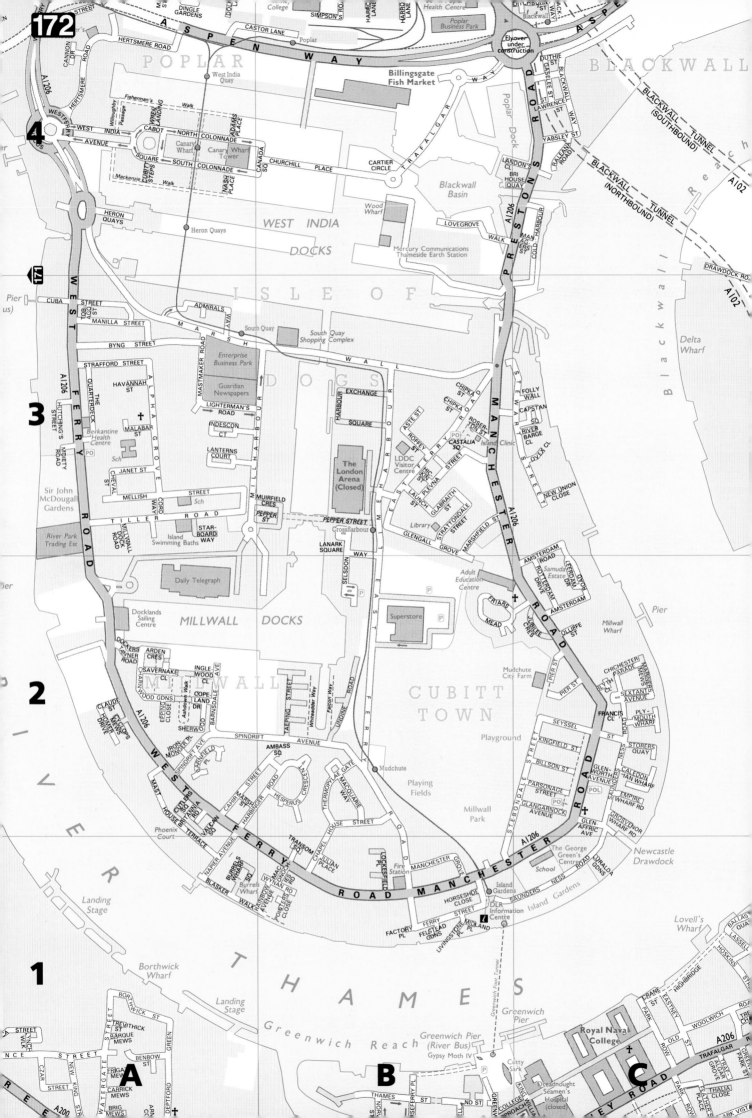

•London street index

In the index, the street names are listed in alphabetical order and written in full, but may be abbreviated on the map. Postal codes are listed where information is available. Each entry is followed by its map page number in bold type and an arbitrary letter and figure grid reference eg Exhibition Road SW7 **166** C3. Turn to page '166'. The letter 'C' refers to the grid square located at the bottom of the page. The figure '3' refers to the grid square located at the lefthand side of the page. Exhibition Road is found within the intersecting square. SW7 refers to the postcode. A proportion of street names and their references are also followed by the name of another street in italics. These entries do not appear on the map due to insufficient space but can be located adjacent to the name of the road in italics.

173

Lamlash Street Northampton Road

Lamlash Street SE11 169 D2
Lanark Square E14 172 B3
Lancaster Gate W2 162 B1
Lancaster Mews W2 162 B1
Lancaster Place WC2 167 D3
Lancaster Street SE1 169 D3
Lancaster Terrace W2 162 C1
Lancaster Walk W2 162 B1
Lancelot Place SW7 167 D3
Lancing Street NW1 164 A4
Langdale Close SE17 169 E1
Langham Place W1 163 F2
Langham Street W1 163 F2
Langley Lane SW8 168 B1
Langley Street WC2 164 B1
Langton Close WC1 164 C3
Lansdowne Row W1 163 F1
Lansdowne Terrace WC1 164 B3
Lant Street SE1 169 E3
Larcom Street SE17 169 E2
Launcelot Street SE1 168 C3
Lower Marsh
Launceston Place W8 166 B3
Laurence Pountney Lane EC4 165 F1
Lavender Close SW3 166 C1
Lavender Road SE16 171 E2
Laverton Place SW5 166 A2
Lavington Street SE1 169 E4
Law Street SE1 169 F3
Lawn Lane SW8 168 B1
Lawrence Lane EC2 165 E2
Trump Street
Lawrence Street SW3 166 C1
Laxton Place NW1 163 F3
Laystall Street EC1 164 C3
Leadenhall Place EC3 165 F1
Leadenhall Street EC3 165 F2
Leake Street SE1 168 C3
Leather Lane EC1 165 D3
Leathermarket Street SE1 169 F3
Lecky Terrace SW7 166 C1
Lees Place W1 163 E1
Leicester Court WC2 164 B1
Cranbourn Street
Leicester Place WC2 164 A1
Lisle Street
Leicester Square WC2 164 B1
Leicester Street WC2 164 B1
Leigh Hunt Street SE1 169 E3
Leigh Street WC1 164 B4
Leinster Gardens W2 162 B1
Leinster Mews W2 162 B1
Leinster Place W2 162 B1
Leinster Terrace W2 162 B1
Leman Street E1 170 B3
Lennox Gardens Mews SW1 167 D2
Lennox Gardens SW1 167 D2
Leonard Street EC2 165 F3
Leopold Street E3 171 F4
Leroy Street SE1 169 F2
Lever Street EC1 165 E4
Leverett Street SW3 167 D2
Mossop Street
Lewisham Street SW1 168 B3
Lexham Gardens W8 166 A2
Lexham Mews W8 166 A2
Lexington Street W1 164 A1
Leyden Street E1 170 A4
Leydon Close SE16 171 E2
Library Place E1 170 C3
Library Street SE1 169 D3
Lilestone Street NW8 162 C3
Lillie Yard SW6 166 A1
Lime Close E1 170 B2
Lime Street EC3 165 F1
Limehouse Causeway E14 171 F3
Limerston Street SW10 166 B1
Lincoln Street SW3 167 D2
Lincoln's Inn Fields WC2 164 C2
Linden Gardens W2 162 A1
Lindley Street E1 170 C4
Lindsay Square SW1 168 B2
Lindsey Street EC1 165 E3
Linhope Street NW1 162 D3
Linsey Street SE16 170 B1
Lion Street E1 164 C2
Lipton Road E1 171 D3
Lisle Street W1 164 A1
Lisson Grove NW1 & NW8 162 C3
Lisson Street NW1 162 C3
Litchfield Street WC2 164 B1
Little Albany Street NW1 163 F4
Little Argyle Street W1 168 A2
Regent Street
Little Britain EC1 165 E2
Little Chester Street SW1 167 E3
Little College Street SW1 168 B3
Little Dorrit Close SE1 169 E4
Little Edward Street NW1 163 F4
Little George Street SW1 168 B3
Great George Street
Little Malborough Street W1 163 F1
Kingly Street
Little New Street EC4 165 D2
New Street Square
Little Newport Street WC2 164 B1
Little Portland Street W1 163 F2
Little Russell Street WC1 164 B2
Little Sanctuary SW1 168 B3
Broad Sanctuary
Little Smith Street SW1 168 B3
Little Somerset Street E1 168 A3
Little St James's Street SW1 168 A4
Little Titchfield Street W1 163 F2
Little Trinity Lane EC4 165 E1
Liverpool Grove SE17 169 E1
Liverpool Street EC2 165 F2
Livonia Street W2 164 A2
Lizard Street EC1 165 E4
Llewellyn Street SE16 170 B1
Lloyd Baker Street WC1 164 C4
Lloyd Square WC1 164 C4
Lloyd Street WC1 164 C4
Lloyd's Avenue EC3 170 A3
Lloyd's Row EC1 165 D4
Lockesfield Place E14 172 B1
Locksley Street E14 171 F4
Lockwood Square SE16 170 C1
Lodge Road NW8 162 C4
Loftie Street SE16 170 B1
Lolesworth Close E1 170 B4
Lollard Street SE11 168 C2
Loman Street SE1 169 E4
Lomas Street E1 170 C4
Lombard Lane EC4 165 A2
Temple Lane
London Bridge EC4 & SE1 165 F1
London Bridge Street SE1 169 F4
London Road SE1 169 D3
London Street EC3 170 A3
London Street W2 162 C2
London Wall EC2 165 E2
Long Acre WC2 164 B1
Long Lane EC1 165 E2
Long Lane SE1 169 F3
Long Walk SE1 170 A1
Long Yard WC1 164 C3
Longford Street NW1 163 F3
Longmoore Street SW1 167 F2
Longville Road SE11 169 D2
Lord North Street SW1 168 B3
Lordship Place SW3 166 C1
Lawrence Street
Lorenzo Street WC1 164 C4
Lorrimore Road SE7 169 E1
Lorrimore Square SE17 169 E1
Lothbury EC2 165 F2
Loughborough Street SE11 168 C1
Lovat Lane EC3 165 F1
Love Lane EC2 165 E2
Lovell Place SE16 171 E1
Lovers' Walk W1 167 E4
Lowell Street E14 171 E4
Lower Belgrave Street SW1 167 E3
Lower Grosvenor Place SW1 167 F3
Lower James Street W1 164 A1
Lower John Street W1 164 A1
Lower Marsh SE1 168 C3
Lower Road SE8 & SE16 171 D1
Lower Sloane Street SW1 167 E1
Lower Thames Street EC3 165 F1
Lowndes Place SW1 167 E3
Lowndes Square SW1 167 D3
Lowndes Street SW1 167 E3
Lowood Street E1 170 C3
Bewley Street
Loxham Street WC1 164 B3
Cromer Street
Lucan Place SW3 166 C2
Lucerne Mews W8 166 A4
Lucey Road SE16 170 B1
Ludgate Broadway EC4 165 D2
Pilgrim Street
Ludgate Circus EC4 165 D2
Luke Street EC2 165 F3
Lukin Street E1 171 D3
Lumley Street W1 163 E1
Brown Hart Garden
Lupus Street SW1 167 F1
Luton Street NW8 162 C3
Luxborough Street W1 163 E3
Lyall Street SW1 167 E3
Lygon Place SW1 167 F3
Lytham Street SE17 169 F1

Mabledon Place WC1 164 B4
Macclesfield Road EC1 165 E4
Mackenzie Walk E14 172 A4
Macklin Street WC2 164 B2
Mackworth Street NW1 163 F4
Macleod Street SE17 169 E1
Maddox Street W1 163 F1
Magdalen Street SE1 170 A2
Magee Street SE11 169 D1
Maguire Street SE1 170 B2
Mahognay Close SE16 171 E2
Maiden Lane WC2 164 B1
Maiden Lane SE1 169 E4
Major Road SE16 170 C1
Makins Street SW3 170 D2
Malet Street WC1 164 A3
Mallord Street SW3 166 C1
Mallory Street NW8 162 C3
Mallow Street EC1 165 F3
Malta Street EC1 165 D3
Maltby Street SE1 170 A1
Maltravers Street WC2 164 C1
Manchester Square W1 163 E2
Manchester Street W1 163 E2
Manciple Street SE1 169 F3
Mandarin Street E14 171 F3
Mandeville Place W1 163 E2
Manette Street W1 164 B2
Manningford Close EC1 165 D4
Manningtree Strwwt E1 170 B4
Commercial Road
Manor Place SE17 169 E1
Manresa Road SW3 166 C1
Mansell Street E1 170 B3
Mansfield Mews W1 163 F2
Mansfield Street
Mansfield Street W1 163 F2
Mansion House Place EC4 165 A1
St Swithun's Lane
Manson Mews SW7 166 B2
Manson Place SW7 166 C2
Maple Leaf Square SE16 171 E2
Maple Street W1 163 F3
Maples Place E1 170 C4
Marble Arch W1 163 D1
Marchmont Street WC1 164 B3
Margaret Court W1 163 F2
Margaret Street
Margaret Street W1 163 F2
Margaretta Terrace SW3 166 C1
Margery Street WC1 164 C4
Marigold Street SE16 170 C1
Marjorie Mews E1 171 D4
Mark Lane EC3 170 A3
Market Court W1 163 E1
Oxford Street
Market Mews W1 167 E4
Market Place W1 163 F2
Markham Square SW3 167 D2
Markham Street SW3 167 D2
Marlborough Close SE17 169 E2
Marlborough Road SW1 168 A4
Marlborough Street SW3 166 C2
Marloes Road W8 166 A3
Marlow Way SE16 171 D2
Marne Street W10 170 B1
Maroon Street E14 171 E4
Marsh Wall E14 172 A3
Marshall Street W1 164 A1
Marshall's Place SE16 170 B1
Marshalsea Road SE1 169 E4
Marsham Street SW1 168 B3
Marsland Close SE17 169 E1
Martha Street E1 170 C3
Martin Lane EC4 165 F1
Martin's Street WC2 164 B1
Martlett Court WC2 164 B2
Bow Street
Marylebone High Street W1 163 E3
Marylebone Lane W1 163 E2
Marylebone Mews W1 163 E2
Marylebone Road NW1 163 D3
Marylebone Street W1 163 E2
Marylee Way SE11 168 C2
Mason Street SE17 169 F2
Mason's Arms Mews W1 163 F1
Maddox Street
Mason's Place EC1 165 E4
Mason's Yard SW1 163 E2
Duke Street St James's
Massinger Street SE17 169 F2
Mast House Terrace E14 172 A2
Master's Street E1 171 E4
Matlock Street E14 171 E4
Matthew Parker Street SW1 168 B3
Maunsel Street SW1 168 A2
Mayfair Place W1 167 F4
Mayflower Street SE16 171 D1
May's Court WC2 164 B1
St Martin's Lane
McAuley Close SE1 168 C3
McCleod's Mews SW7 166 B2
Mead Row SE1 169 D3
Meadcroft Road SE11 169 D1
Meadow Row SE1 169 E2
Meard Street W1 164 A2
Mecklenburgh Place WC1 164 C3
Mecklenburgh Square
Mecklenburgh Square WC1 164 C3
Mecklenburgh Street WC1 164 C3
Medway Street SW1 168 A2
Melbury Terrace NW1 163 D3
Melcombe Place NW1 163 D3
Melcombe Street NW1 163 D3
Melior Place SE1 169 F4
Snowsfields
Melton Street NW1 164 A4
Melon Place W8 166 A4
Memel Court EC1 165 E3
Baltic Street
Mepham Street SE1 168 C4
Mercer Street WC2 164 B1
Meredith Street EC1 165 D4
Merlin Street WC1 165 D4
Mermaid Court SE1 169 F4
Mermaid Row SE1 169 F3
Merrick Square SE1 169 E3
Merrington Road SW6 166 A1
Merrow Street SE17 169 E1
Methley Street SE11 169 D1
Mews Street E1 170 B2
Meymott Street SE1 169 D4
Micawber Street N1 165 E4
Midford Place W1 164 A3
Tottenham Court Road
Middle Street EC1 165 E2
Middle Temple Lane EC4 164 C2
Middle Yard SE1 169 F4
Middlesex Street E1 170 A4
Middleton Drive SE16 171 E2
Midhope Street WC1 164 B4
Midland Road NW1 164 B4
Midship Close SE16 171 E2
Milborne Grove SW10 166 B1
Milcote Street SE1 169 D3
Mile End Road E1 170 C4
Miles Street SW8 168 B1
Milford Lane WC2 164 C1
Milk Street EC2 165 E2
Milk Yard E1 171 D3
Mill Place E14 171 F3
Mill Street SE1 170 B1
Mill Street W1 163 F1
Millbank SW1 168 B2
Milligan Street E14 171 F3
Millman Street WC1 164 C3
Millstream Road SE1 170 A1
Milner Street SW3 167 D2
Milton Court EC2 165 F3
Milton Street EC2 165 F3
Milverton Street SE11 169 D1
Milward Street E1 170 C4
Mincing Lane EC3 170 A3
Minera Mews SW1 167 E2
Minories EC3 170 A3
Mint Street SE1 169 E3
Mitchell Street EC1 165 E3
Mitre Road SE1 169 D3
Mitre Street EC3 170 A3
Moiety Road E14 171 F1
Molyneux Street W1 163 D2
Monck Street SW1 168 B3
Moncorvo Close SW7 166 C3
Monkton Street SE11 169 D2
Monkwell Square EC2 165 E2
Monmouth Street WC2 164 B1
Montagu Mansions W1 163 D3
Montagu Mews North W1 163 D2
Montagu Mews South W1 163 D2
Montagu Mews West W1 163 D2
Montagu Place W1 163 D2
Montagu Row W1 163 D2
Montagu Square W1 163 D2
Montagu Street W1 163 D2
Montague Close SE1 169 F4
Montague Place WC1 164 D3
Montague Street WC1 164 B3
Montague Street EC1 165 E2
Montford Place SE11 168 C1
Montpelier Mews SW7 167 D3
Montpelier Place SW7 167 D3
Montpelier Square SW7 167 D3
Montpelier Street SW7 167 D3
Montpelier Walk SW7 167 D3
Montreal Place WC2 164 C1
Montrose Court SW7 166 C3
Montrose Place SW1 167 E3
Monument Street EC3 165 F1
Monza Street E1 171 D3
Moodkee Street SE16 171 D1
Moor Lane EC2 165 F2
Moore Street SW3 164 A1
Old Compton Street
Moorfields EC2 165 F2
Moorgate EC2 165 F2
Mora Street EC1 165 E4
Morecambe Close E1 171 D4
Morecambe Street SE17 169 E2
Moreland Street EC1 165 E4
Moreton Place SW1 168 A2
Moreton Street SW1 168 A2
Moreton Terrace SW1 168 A1
Morgan's Lane SE1 170 A2
Morley Street SE1 169 D3
Morocco Street SE1 169 F3
Morpeth Terrace SW1 167 F2
Morris Street E1 170 C3
Mortimer Market WC1 164 A3
Capper Street
Mortimer Street W1 163 F2
Morwell Street WC1 164 A2
Moss Close E1 170 B4
Mossop Street SW3 167 D2
Motcomb Street SW1 167 E3
Mount Pleasant WC1 164 C3
Mount Row W1 163 E1
Mount Street E1 170 C4
Mount Street W1 163 E1
Mount Terrace E1 170 C4
Moxon Street W1 163 E2
Mozart Terrace SW1 167 E2
Muirfield Crescent E14 172 B3
Mulberry Street E1 170 B4
Mulberry Walk SW3 166 C1
Mulready Street NW8 162 C3
Mulvaney Way SE1 169 F3
Mumford Court EC2 165 E2
Milk Street
Mundy Street N1 165 F4
Munster Square NW1 163 F4
Munton Road SE17 169 E2
Murphy Street SE1 168 C3
Murray Grove N1 165 E4
Musbury Street E1 171 D4
Muscovy Street EC3 170 A3
Museum Street WC1 164 B2
Myddelton Passage EC1 165 D4
Myddelton Square EC1 165 D4
Myddelton Street EC1 165 D4
Mylne Street EC1 165 D4
Myrdle Street E1 170 C4
Myrtle Walk N1 165 F4

Narrow Street E14 171 E3
Nash Place E14 172 A4
Nash Street NW1 163 F4
Nassau Street W1 163 F2
Nathanial Close E1 170 B4
Thrawl Street
Neal Street WC2 164 B2
Neathouse Place SW1 167 F2
Wilton Road
Nebraska Street SE1 169 E3
Neckinger SE1 170 B1
Neckinger Street SE1 170 B1
Nelson Passage EC1 165 E4
Mora Street
Nelson Place N1 165 E4
Nelson Square SE1 169 D4
Nelson Street E1 170 C4
Nelson Terrace N1 165 D4
Nelson Walk SE16 171 E2
Neptune Street SE16 171 D1
Neston Street SE16 171 D2
Netherton Grove SW10 166 B1
Netley Street NW1 163 F4
Nevern Place SW5 166 A2
Nevern Square SW5 166 A2
Neville Street SW7 166 C2
Neville Terrace SW7 166 C1
New Bond Street W1 163 F1
New Burlington Mews W1 170 A3
Hart Street
New Bridge Street EC4 165 D2
New Broad Street EC2 165 F2
New Burlington Place W1 163 F1
New Burlington Street W1 163 F1
New Cavendish Street W1 163 E2
New Change EC4 165 E2
New Compton Street WC2 164 B2
New Fetter Lane EC4 165 D2
New Goulston Street E1 170 A4
New Kent Road SE1 169 E2
New North Place EC2 165 F3
New North Road N1 165 F4
New North Street WC1 164 C3
New Oxford Street WC1 164 B2
New Quebec Street W1 163 D2
New Ride SW7 166 C3
New Road E1 170 C4
New Row WC2 164 B1
New Spring Gardens Walk SE11 168 B1
Goding Street
New Square WC2 164 C2
New Street EC2 170 A4
New Street Square EC4 165 D2
New Turnstile WC1 164 B2
High Holborn
Newark Street E1 170 C4
Newburgh Street W1 164 F1
Foubert's Place
Newburn Street SE11 168 C1
Newbury Street EC1 165 E2
Newcastle Place W2 162 C3
Newcomen Street SE1 169 F4
Newell Street E14 171 F3
Newgate Street EC1 165 D2
Newington Butts SE1 & SE11 169 D2
Newington Causeway SE1 169 E3
Newlands Quay E1 171 D3
Newman Street W1 164 A2
Newman's Row WC2 164 C2
Lincoln's Inn Fields
Newnham Terrace SE1 168 C3
Newnhams Row SE1 170 A1
Newport Place WC2 164 B1
Newport Street SE11 168 C2
Newton Street WC2 164 B2
Nicholas Lane EC4 165 F1
Nicholson Street SE1 169 D4
Nile Street N1 165 E4
Nine Elms Lane SW8 168 A1
Noble Street EC2 165 E2
Noel Street W1 164 A2
Norbiton Road E14 171 F4
Norfolk Crescent W2 162 C2
Norfolk Place W2 162 C2
Norfolk Square W2 162 C2
Norman Street EC1 165 E4
Norris Street SW1 164 A1
North Audley Street W1 163 E1
North Bank NW8 162 C4
North Colonnade E14 172 A4
North Crescent WC1 164 A3
North Flockton Street SE16 170 B1
Chambers Street
North Gower Street NW1 164 A4
North Mews WC1 164 C3
North Ride W2 162 C1
North Row W1 163 E1
North Tenter Street E1 170 B3
North Terrace SW3 166 C2
North Wharf Road W2 162 B2
Northampton Road EC1 165 D3

Northampton Row Russia Dock Road

Northampton Row EC1 **165** D3
Exmouth Market
Northampton Square EC1 **165** D4
Northburgh Street EC1 **165** D3
Northchurch SE17 **169** F2
Northdown Street N1 **164** C4
Northington Street WC1 **164** C3
Northumberland Alley EC3 **170** A3
Northumberland Avenue WC2 **168** B4
Northumberland Street WC2 **168** B4
Northy Street E14 **171** E3
Norway Gate SE16 **171** E1
Norway Place E14 **171** F3
Norwich Street EC4 **165** D2
Notting Hill Gate W11 **162** A1
Nottingham Place W1 **163** E3
Nottingham Street W1 **163** E3

O'leary Square E1 **171** D4
O'meara Street SE1 **169** E4
Oak Lane E14 **171** F3
Oak Tree Road NW8 **162** C4
Oakden Street SE11 **169** D2
Oakfield Street SW10 **166** B1
Oakley Crescent EC1 **165** E4
Oakley Gardens SW3 **167** D1
Oakley Street SW3 **166** C1
Oat Lane EC2 **165** E2
Observatory Gardens W8 **166** A4
Occupation Road SE17 **169** E1
Ocean Street E1 **171** E4
Octagon Arcade EC2 **165** F2
Odessa Street SE16 **171** F1
Ogle Street W1 **163** F2
Old Bailey EC4 **165** D2
Old Bond Street W1 **163** F1
Old Broad Street EC2 **165** F2
Old Brompton Road SW5 & SW7 **166** A1
Old Burlington Street W1 **163** F1
Old Castle Street E1 **170** B4
Old Cavendish Street W1 **163** F2
Old Church Road E1 **171** D4
Old Church Street SW3 **166** C1
Old Compton Street W1 **164** A1
Old Court Place W8 **166** A3
Old Gloucester Street WC1 **164** B3
Old Jamaica Road SE16 **170** B1
Old Jewry EC2 **165** F2
Old Marylebone Road NW1 **163** D2
Old Mitre Court EC4 **165** D2
Fleet Street
Old Montagu Street E1 **170** B4
Old North Street WC1 **164** C3
Theobalds Road
Old Palace Yard SW1 **168** B3
Old Paradise Street SE11 **168** C2
Old Park Lane W1 **167** E4
Old Pye Street SW1 **168** A3
Old Quebec Street W1 **163** D2
Old Queen Street SW1 **168** A3
Old Square WC2 **164** C2
Old Street EC1 **165** E3
Oldbury Place W1 **163** E3
Olivers Yard EC1 **165** F3
Olney Road SE7 **169** E1
Olympia Mews W2 **162** B1
Onega Gate SE16 **171** E1
Ongar Road SW6 **166** A1
Onslow Gardens SW7 **166** B2
Onslow Mews SW7 **166** C2
Onslow Square SW7 **166** C2
Onslow Street EC1 **165** D3
Saffron Street
Ontario Street SE1 **169** E3
Opal Street SE11 **169** D2
Orange Place SE16 **171** D1
Orange Street WC2 **164** B1
Orb Street SE17 **169** F2
Orchard Street W1 **163** E2
Orchardson Street NW8 **162** C3
Orde Hall Street WC1 **164** C3
Orme Court W2 **162** A1
Orme Lane W2 **162** A1
Orme Square W2 **162** A1
Ormond Yard SW1 **164** A1
Ormonde Gate SW3 **167** D1
Orsett Street SE11 **168** C2
Orsett Terrace W2 **162** B2
Orton Street E1 **170** B2
Wapping High Street
Osbert Street SW1 **168** A2
Osborne Street E1 **170** B4
Oslo Square SE16 **171** E1
Osnaburgh Street NW1 **163** F3
Osnaburgh Terrace NW1 **163** F4
Albany Street
Ossington Buildings W1 **163** E2
Moxon Street
Ossington Street W2 **162** A1
Ossulston Street NW1 **164** A4
Osten Mews SW7 **166** B2
Oswin Street SE11 **169** D2
Othello Close SE1 **169** D2
Otto Street SE17 **169** D1
Oval Way SE11 **168** C1
Ovington Gardens SW3 **167** D3
Ovington Square SW3 **167** D3
Ovington Street SW3 **167** D2
Oxendon Street SW1 **164** A1
Coventry Street
Owen Street EC1 **165** D4
Oxford Square W2 **162** C2
Oxford Street W1 **163** E1

Paddington Green W2 **162** C3
Paddington Street W1 **163** E3
Page Street SW1 **168** B2
Paget Street EC1 **165** D4
Pakenham Street WC1 **164** C3
Palace Avenue W8 **166** A4
Palace Court W2 **162** A1
Palace Gardens Mews W8 **166** A4
Palace Gardens Terrace W8 **166** A4
Palace Gate W8 **166** B3
Palace Street SW1 **167** F3
Pall Mall East SW1 **164** B1
Pall Mall SW1 **168** A4
Palmer Street SW1 **168** A3
Pancras Lane EC4 **165** E2
Panton Street SW1 **164** A1
Paradise Street SE16 **170** C1
Paradise Walk SW3 **167** D1
Paragon Mews SE1 **169** F2
Searles Road
Pardoner Street SE1 **169** F3
Parfetts Street E1 **170** C4
Paris Garden SE1 **169** D4
Park Approach SE16 **170** C1
Park Crescent Mews East W1 **163** F3
Park Crescent Mews West W1 **163** E3
Park Crescent W1 **163** E3
Park Lane W1 **163** E1
Park Place SW1 **167** F4
Park Road NW1 & NW8 **163** D4
Park Square East NW1 **163** F3
Park Square Mews W1 **163** E3
Harley Street
Park Square West NW1 **163** E3
Park Street SE1 **169** D4
Park Street W1 **163** E1
Park Walk SW10 **166** B1
Park West Place W2 **163** D2
Parker Street WC2 **164** B2
Parkers Row SE1 **170** B1
Parliament Square SW1 **168** B3
Parliament Street SW1 **168** B4
Parnham Street E14 **171** E4
Parry Street SW8 **168** B1
Pasley Close SE17 **169** E1
Passmore Street SW1 **167** E2
Pastor Street SE11 **169** D2
Pater Street W8 **166** A3
Paternoster Row EC4 **165** E2
Paternoster Square EC4 **165** E2
Paul Street EC2 **165** F3
Paultons Square SW3 **166** C1
Paveley Street NW8 **162** C4
Pavilion Road SW1 **167** D2
Pavilion Street SW1 **167** D3
Peabody Avenue SW1 **167** F1
Peacock Street SE17 **169** E2
Pear Tree Court EC1 **165** D3
Pear Tree Street EC1 **165** E3
Pearl Street E1 **170** C2
Pearman Street SE1 **169** D3
Peartree Lane E1 **171** D3
Peerless Street EC1 **165** E4
Pelham Crescent SW7 **166** C2
Pelham Place SW7 **166** C2
Pelham Street SW7 **166** C2
Pelier Street SE17 **169** E1
Pelling Street E14 **171** F4
Pemberton Row EC4 **165** D2
Pembridge Gardens W2 **162** A1
Pembridge Road W11 **162** A1
Pembridge Square W2 **162** A1
Pembroke Mews W8 **166** A2
Earls Court Road
Penang Street E1 **170** C2
Penfold Place NW1 **162** C3
Penfold Street NW1 & NW8 **162** C3
Pennant Mews W8 **166** A2
Pennington Street E1 **170** C3
Penrose Grove SE17 **169** E1
Penrose Street SE17 **169** E1
Penryn Street NW1 **166** A2
Penton Place SE17 **169** D2
Penton Rise WC1 **164** C4
Pentonville Road N1 **164** C4
Pepper Street SE1 **169** E4
Pepper Street E14 **172** B3
Pepys Street EC3 **170** A3
Percival Street EC1 **165** D3
Percy Circus WC1 **164** C4
Percy Street W1 **164** A2
Perkin's Rents SW1 **168** A3
Perkins Square SE1 **169** E4
Perryn Road SE16 **170** C1
Peter Street W1 **164** A1
Peter's Hill EC4 **165** E2
Carter Lane
Peter's Lane EC1 **165** D3
Petersham Lane SW7 **166** B3
Petersham Mews SW7 **166** B3
Petersham Place SW7 **166** B3
Peto Place NW1 **163** F3
Petty France SW1 **168** A3
Petyward SW3 **167** D2
Phelp Street SE17 **169** F1
Phene Street SW3 **167** D1
Philchurch Place E1 **170** B3
Phillimore Walk W8 **166** A3
Philpot Lane EC3 **165** F1
Philpot Street E1 **170** C4
Phipp Street EC2 **165** F3
Phoenix Place WC1 **164** C3
Phoenix Road NW1 **164** A4
Phoenix Street WC2 **164** B2
Charing Cross Road
Piccadilly W1 **167** F4
Pickard Street EC1 **165** E4
Pickwick Street SE1 **169** E3
Picton Place W1 **163** E2
Piggot Street E14 **171** F3
Pilgrim Street EC4 **165** D2
Pilgrimage Street SE1 **169** F3
Pimlico Road SW1 **167** E2
Pinchin Street E1 **170** B3
Pindar Street EC2 **165** F3
Pine Street EC1 **165** D3
Pitfield Street N1 **165** F4
Pitsea Place E1 **171** E3
Pitsea Street E1 **171** E3
Pitt Street W8 **166** A3
Pitt's Head Mews W1 **167** E4
Pixley Street E14 **171** F4
Platina Street EC2 **165** F3
Playhouse Yard EC4 **165** D1
Pleydell Street EC4 **165** D1
Bouverie Street
Plough Place EC4 **165** D2
Fetter Lane
Plover Way SE16 **171** E1
Plumber's Row E1 **171** B4
Plumtree Court EC4 **165** D2
Plympton Place NW8 **162** C3
Plympton Street
Plympton Street NW8 **162** C3
Pocock Street SE1 **169** D3
Poland Street W1 **164** A2
Pollitt Drive NW8 **162** C3
Polygon Road NW1 **164** A4
Pomwell Way E1 **170** B4
Pond Place SW3 **166** C2
Ponler Street E1 **170** C3
Ponsonby Place SW1 **168** B2
Ponsonby Terrace SW1 **168** B2
Pont Street Mews SW1 **167** D3
Pont Street SW1 **167** D3
Poolmans Street SE16 **171** D2
Poonah Street E1 **171** D3
Pope Street SE1 **170** A1
Fleet Street
Poppins Court EC4 **165** D2
Porchester Place W2 **163** D2
Porchester Square W2 **162** B2
Porchester Terrace W2 **162** B1
Porchester Terrace W2 **162** B2
Porlock Street SE1 **169** F3
Porter Street W1 **163** E3
Porter Street SE1 **169** E4
Portland Place W1 **163** F2
Portland Street SE17 **169** F1
Portman Close W1 **163** E2
Portman Mews South W1 **163** E2
Portman Square W1 **163** E2
Portman Street W1 **163** E2
Portpool Lane EC1 **164** C3
Portsea Place W2 **163** D2
Portsmouth Street WC2 **164** C2
Portugal Street
Portsoken Street EC3 **170** B3
Portugal Street WC2 **164** C2
Potier Street SE1 **169** F3
Pottery Street SE16 **170** C1
Poultry EC2 **165** E2
Praed Street W2 **162** C2
Pratt Walk SE11 **168** C2
Prescot Street E1 **170** B3
President Street EC1 **165** E4
Central Street
Presidents Drive E1 **170** C2
Prestwood Street N1 **165** E4
Wenlock Road
Price's Street SE1 **169** D4
Prideaux Place WC1 **164** C4
Primrose Hill EC4 **165** D1
Hutton Street
Primrose Street EC2 **170** A4
Prince Albert Road NW1 & NW1 **162** C4
Prince Consort Road SW7 **166** C3
Prince of Wales Terrace W8 **166** B1
Kensington Road
Prince's Gardens SW7 **166** C3
Prince's Gate Mews SW7 **166** C3
Prince's Gate SW7 **166** C3
Princelet Street E1 **170** B4
Princes Circus WC2 **164** B2
Princes Street EC2 **165** F2
Princes Street W1 **163** F2
Princess Street SE1 **169** D3
Princeton Street WC1 **164** C2
Printer Street EC4 **165** D2
Prioress Street SE1 **169** F3
Priory Walk SW10 **166** B1
Procter Street WC1 **164** C2
Prospect Place E1 **171** D2
Prospect Street SE16 **170** C1
Providence Court W1 **163** E1
Provost Street N1 **165** F4
Prusom Street E1 **170** C2
Pudding Lane EC3 **165** F1
Puddle Dock EC4 **164** D1
Pullen Street W1 **163** F1
Puma Court E1 **170** B4
Purbrook Street SE1 **170** A1

Quarley Way SE15 **163** D2
New Quebec Street
Quebec Way SE16 **171** E1
Queen Anne Mews W1 **163** F2
Chandos Street
Queen Anne Street W1 **163** E2
Queen Anne's Gate SW1 **168** A3
Queen Elizabeth Street SE1 **170** A2
Queen Square WC1 **164** B3
Queen Street EC4 **165** E1
Queen Street Place EC4 **165** E1
Queen Street W1 **165** F4
Queen Victoria Street EC4 **165** D1
Queen's Gardens SW1 **167** F3
Queen's Gardens W2 **162** B1
Queen's Gate Gardens SW7 **166** B2
Queen's Gate Mews SW7 **166** B3
Queen's Gate Place Mews SW7 **166** B2
Queen's Gate Place SW7 **166** B3
Queen's Gate SW7 **166** B3
Queen's Gate Terrace SW7 **166** B3
Queen's Row SE17 **169** E1
Queen's Walk SW1 **167** F4
Queenhithe EC4 **165** E1
Queensberry Mews West SW7 **166** B2
Queensberry Place SW7 **163** F4
Harrington Street
Queensborough Terrace W2 **162** B1
Queensway W2 **162** A1
Quick Street N1 **165** D4

Rabbit Row W8 **166** A4
Radcot Street SE11 **169** D1
Radley Court SE16 **171** E2
Radley Mews W8 **166** A2
Radnor Mews W2 **162** C2
Radnor Place W2 **162** C2
Radnor Street EC1 **165** D3
Radnor Walk SW3 **167** D1
Railway Approach SE1 **169** F4
Railway Avenue SE16 **171** D2
Raine Street E1 **170** C2
Rainsford Street W2 **162** C2
Ralston Street SW3 **167** D1
Ramillies Place W1 **163** F2
Ramillies Street W1 **164** A2
Rampart Street E1 **170** C4
Rampayne Street SW1 **168** A2
Randall Road SE11 **168** C2
Randall Row SE11 **168** C2
Ranelagh Bridge W2 **162** B2
Ranelagh Grove SW1 **167** E2
Ranelagh Road SW1 **168** A1
Ranston Street NW1 **162** C3
Raphael Street SW7 **167** D3
Ratcliff Grove EC1 **165** E4
Ratcliffe Cross Street E1 **171** E3
Ratcliffe Lane E14 **171** E3
Rathbone Place W1 **164** A2
Raven Row E1 **170** C4
Ravensdon Street SE11 **169** D1
Ravent Road SE11 **168** C2
Ravey Street EC2 **165** F3
Rawlings Street SW3 **167** D2
Rawstorne Place EC1 **165** D4
Rawstorne Street
Rawstorne Street EC1 **165** D4
Ray Street EC1 **165** D3
Reardon Path E1 **170** C2
Reardon Street E1 **170** C2
Rebecca Terrace SE16 **171** D1
Rectory Square E1 **171** E4
Red Lion Row SE17 **169** E1
Red Lion Square WC1 **164** C2
Red Lion Street WC1 **164** C2
Redburn Street SW3 **167** D1
Redcastle Close E1 **171** D3
Redcliffe Gardens SW10 & SW5 **166** A1
Redcliffe Mews SW10 **166** B1
Redcliffe Place SW10 **166** B1
Redcliffe Road SW10 **166** B1
Redcliffe Square SW10 **166** A1
Redcliffe Street SW10 **166** A1
Redcross Way SE1 **169** E4
Redesdale Street SW3 **167** D1
Redfield Lane SW5 **166** A2
Redhill Street NW1 **163** F4
Redman's Road E1 **171** D4
Redmead Lane E1 **170** B2
Wapping High Street
Redriff Road SE16 **171** E1
Redwood Close SE16 **171** E2
Reece Mews SW7 **166** C1
Reedworth Street SE11 **169** D2
Reeves Mews W1 **163** E1
Regal Close E1 **170** C4
Regan Way N1 **165** F4
Regency Street SW1 **168** A2
Regent Square WC1 **164** B4
Regent Street W1 & SW1 **163** F2
Regnart Buildings NW1 **164** A4
Euston Street
Relton Mews SW7 **167** D3
Remington Street N1 **165** E4
Remnant Street WC2 **164** C2
Kingsway
Renforth Street SE16 **171** D1
Renfrew Road SE11 **169** D2
Rennie Street SE1 **165** E1
Rephidim Street SE1 **169** F3
Repton Street E14 **171** E4
Reston Place SW7 **166** B3
Reveley Close SE16 **171** E1
Rex Place W1 **163** E1
Rhodeswell Road E14 **171** F4
Rich Lane SW5 **166** A1
Rich Street E14 **171** F3
Richard's Place SW3 **167** D2
Richbell Place WC1 **164** C3
Emerald Street
Richmond Buildings W1 **164** A2
Dean Street
Richmond Mews W1 **164** A2
Richmond Terrace SW1 **168** B4
Rickett Street SW6 **166** A1
Ridgmount Gardens WC1 **164** A3
Ridgmount Street WC1 **164** A3
Riding House Street W1 **163** F2
Riley Road SE1 **170** A1
Risborough Street SE1 **169** E4
Risdon Street SE16 **171** D1
River Street EC1 **165** D4
Riverside Walk SE1 **168** C4
Rivington Street EC2 **165** F3
Robert Adam Street W1 **163** E2
Robert Dashwood Way SE17 **169** E2
Robert Street NW1 **163** F4
Robert Street WC2 **164** B1
Robinson Street SW3 **167** D1
Flood Street
Rochester Row SW1 **168** A2
Rochester Street SW1 **168** A2
Rockingham Street SE1 **169** E3
Rocliffe Street N1 **165** E4
Roding Mews E1 **170** B2
Rodmarton Street W1 **163** D2
Rodney Place SE17 **169** E2
Rodney Road SE17 **169** E2
Roger Street WC1 **164** C3
Roland Gardens SW7 **166** B1
Roland Way SE17 **169** F1
Roland Way SW7 **166** B1
Rolls Buildings EC4 **165** D2
Rolls Passage EC4 **164** C2
Romford Street E1 **170** C4
Romilly Street W1 **164** A1
Romney Street SW1 **168** B2
Ronald Street E1 **171** D3
Rood Lane EC3 **165** F1
Rope Street SE16 **171** E1
Ropemaker Road SE16 **171** E1
Ropemaker Street EC2 **165** F3
Ropemaker's Fields E14 **171** F3
Roper Lane SE1 **170** A1
Rosary Gardens SW7 **166** B2
Roscoe Street EC1 **165** E3
Rose Alley SE1 **169** E4
Rosebery Avenue EC1 **167** D3
Rosemoor Street SW3 **167** D2
Rosoman Place EC1 **165** D4
Rosoman Street
Rosoman Street EC1 **165** D4
Rossmore Road NW1 **163** D3
Rotary Street SE1 **169** D3
Rotherhithe Street SE16 **171** D2
Rotherhithe Tunnel Approach E3 **171** E3
Rotherhithe Tunnel Approach SE16 **171** F1
Rothsay Street SE1 **169** F3
Rotten Row SW7 & SW1 **166** C4
Rouel Road SE16 **170** B1
Roupell Street SE1 **169** D4
Roxby Place SW6 **166** A1
Roy Square E14 **171** F3
Royal Avenue SW3 **167** D1
Royal Exchange Buildings EC3 **165** F2
Cornhill
Royal Hospital Road SW3 **167** D1
Royal Mint Place E1 **170** B3
Royal Mint Street E1 **170** B3
Royal Opera Arcade SW1 **168** A4
Royal Road SE17 **169** D1
Royal Street SE1 **168** C3
Rudolf Place SW8 **168** B1
Rufus Street N1 **165** F4
Rugby Street WC1 **164** C3
Rugg Street E14 **171** F3
Rum Close E1 **170** C3
Rupack Street SE16 **171** D1
Rupert Street W1 **164** A1
Rushworth Street SE1 **169** D3
Russell Square WC1 **164** B3
Russell Street WC2 **164** C1
Russia Dock Road SE16 **171** E2

•M25 London orbital motorway

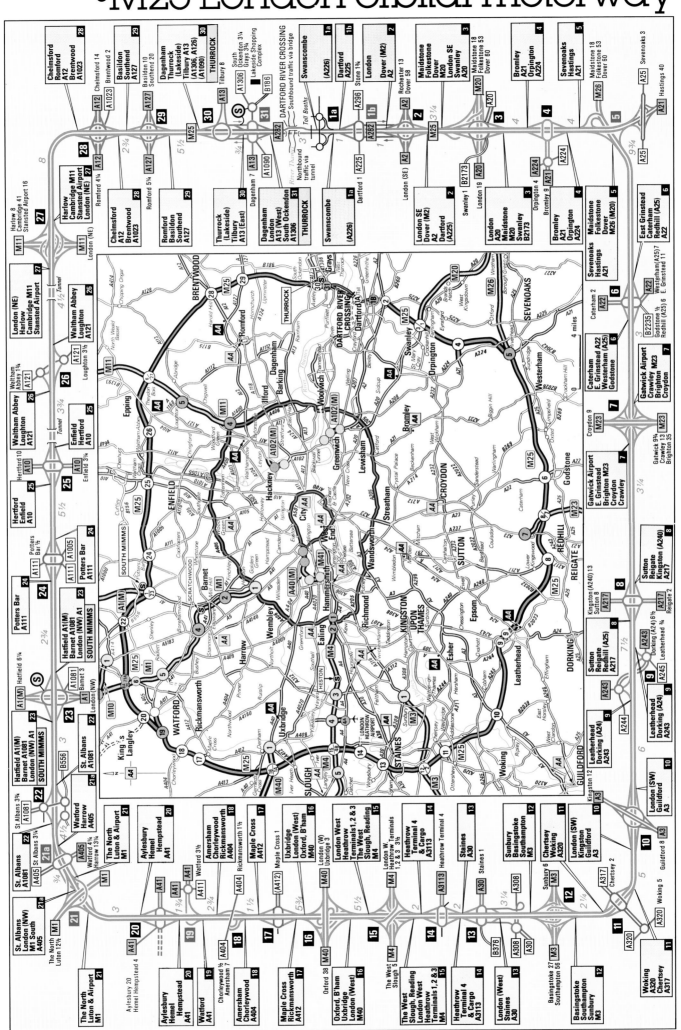

•Ports and airports

Most people who leave Britain by air or sea use the airports and seaports detailed in these pages. The maps indicate the approach roads into each complex with information on parking and telephone numbers through which details on costs and other travel information can be obtained. The hotels listed are AA-appointed, and the garages have been selected because they provide adequate long term parking facilities.

International airports

Other airports with scheduled services abroad

Smaller airports

Major ports

Ports with summer services only

Military airfields are not shown on this map. Ports and airports on the Channel Islands are located within the main atlas section.

AIRPORT PLANS		PORT PLANS	
Birmingham	Page 185	Dover	Page 188
Edinburgh	187	Felixstowe	188
Gatwick	184	Harwich	188
Glasgow	187	Newhaven	188
Heathrow	183		
Luton	185		
Manchester	185		
Stansted	186		

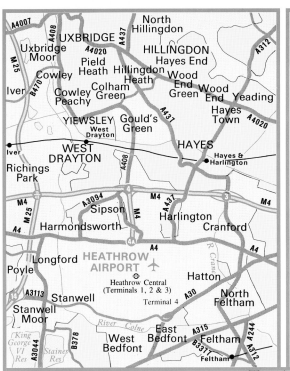

HEATHROW AIRPORT tel: 081 759 4321

Heathrow, one of the world's busiest international airports lies 16 miles west of London. Terminals 1, 2 and 3 are situated in the central area of Heathrow and Terminal 4 is situated at the south-east of the perimeter road.

The London Underground (Piccadilly Line) has two stations, at Terminals 1-3 and at Terminal 4. Regular bus and coach services operate to and from the airport with direct coach links to and from Gatwick and Stansted airports. Short-term multi-storey car parking is available at Terminals 1, 2, 3 and 4 tel: 081 745 7906 for charges.

Long-term car parking for all terminals is available off the Eastern Perimeter Road tel: 081 745 5677 for charges. A courtesy bus takes passengers to and from the terminals.

There are numerous commercial garages within easy reach of the airport offering long-term parking facilities.

There are several 4-star and 3-star hotels within easy reach of the airport and car hire facilities are available:

Avis	tel: 071 235 3235	Europcar	tel: 081 897 0811
Budget	tel: 081 759 2216	Hertz	tel: 071 485 4585
Euro Dollar	tel: 081 397 3232	Kenning	tel: 081 890 1167
(Terminals 1, 2 and 3)		Woods	tel: 081 759 9400
Euro Dollar	tel: 081 751 6466		
(Terminal 4)			

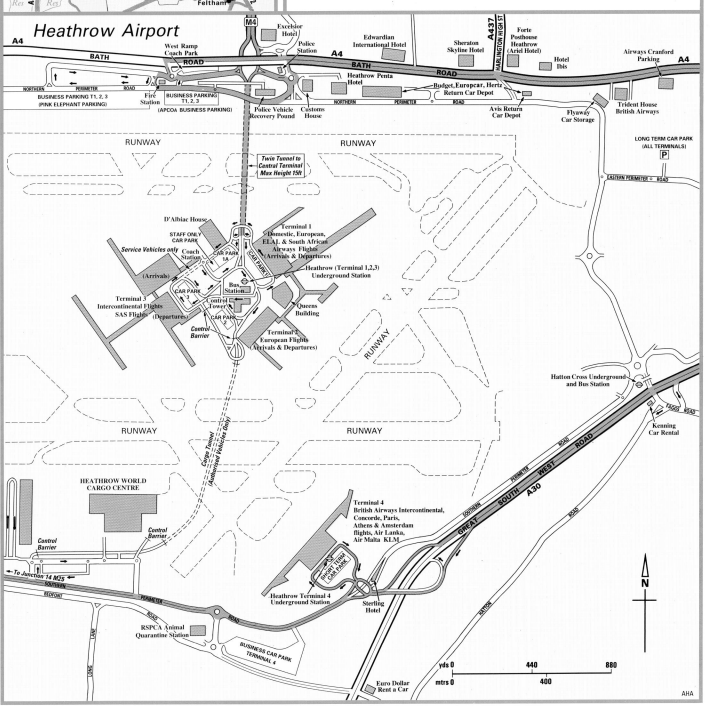

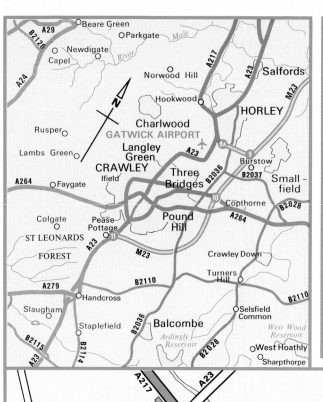

GATWICK AIRPORT tel: 0293 535353
London's second airport is served by regular bus and coach services. The Gatwick Express rail service linking London (Victoria) with the airport operates every 15 minutes during the day and hourly at night.

Parking: ample multi-storey and open-air car parking available. For latest charges tel: 0293 502737 (North Terminal) or 0293 502896 (South Terminal).

MANCHESTER AIRPORT tel: 061 489 3000
Situated nine miles south of the city. Manchester Airport provides regular scheduled services for many of the leading airlines. A spacious concourse, restaurants and parking facilities are available for passengers. For parking enquiries tel: 061-489 3723/3000 ext 4635/2021.

LUTON AIRPORT tel: 0582 405100
Used mainly for package holiday tour operators, the airport has ample open-air parking. Covered garage space is available from Central Car Storage tel: 0582 26189 for a booking form.

BIRMINGHAM AIRPORT tel: 021 767 5511 (Main Terminal)
tel: 021 767 7502 (Eurohub terminal)
A three-storey terminal building gives access from the first floor to the Maglev transit system which offers a 90 second shuttle service to Birmingham International Railway Station. Multi-storey parking for 2000 cars and surface parking for 4700 cars. tel: 021 767 7861.

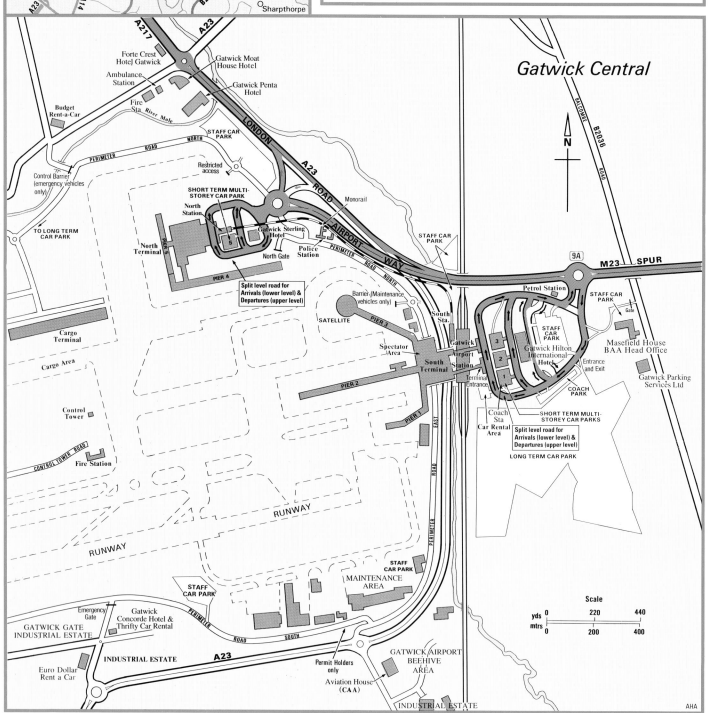

Gatwick Central

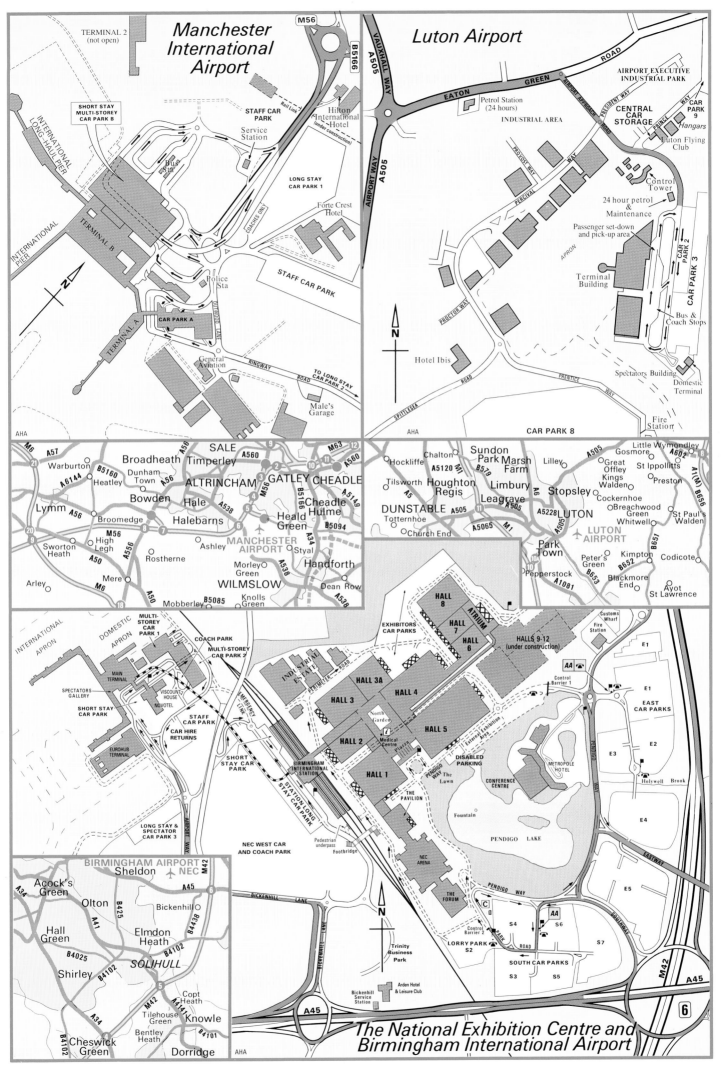

Manchester International Airport

TERMINAL 2 (not open)

M56
B5166
A505

SHORT STAY MULTI-STOREY CAR PARK B

INTERNATIONAL LONG-HAUL PIER

STAFF CAR PARK

Rail Link

Hilton International Hotel (under construction)

Service Station

Bus Sta

LONG STAY CAR PARK 1

Forte Crest Hotel

TERMINAL B

COACHES ONLY

INTERNATIONAL PIER

N

TERMINAL A

Police Sta

CAR PARK A

OUTWOOD LANE

STAFF CAR PARK

General Aviation

TO LONG STAY CAR PARK 2

RINGWAY ROAD

Male's Garage

AHA

Luton Airport

EATON GREEN ROAD

VAUXHALL WAY

AIRPORT APPROACH

PRESIDENT WAY

AIRPORT EXECUTIVE INDUSTRIAL PARK

CAR PARK 9

Petrol Station (24 hours)

INDUSTRIAL AREA

CENTRAL CAR STORAGE

PRINCE WAY

Hangars

Luton Flying Club

PROVOST WAY

PERCIVAL WAY

Control Tower

24 hour petrol & Maintenance

Passenger set-down and pick-up area

APRON

PROCTOR WAY

N

CAR PARK 2

CAR PARK 3

Terminal Building

Bus & Coach Stops

Hotel Ibis

PRENTICE WAY

Spectators Building

Domestic Terminal

SPITTLESEA ROAD

CAR PARK 8

Fire Station

AHA

M6
A57
A560
SALE
M63
12

21
Warburton
B5160
A6144
Heatley
Dunham Town
A56
Broadheath
Timperley
ALTRINCHAM
A560
2
9
10
11
GATLEY CHEADLE
A560
8

Lymm
A56
Bowden
Hale
A538
3
M56
B5166
B5149
Cheadle Hulme

Broomedge
Halebarns
4
Heald Green
B5094

20
9
M56
8
7
5
6
MANCHESTER AIRPORT
A34

Sworton Heath
High Legh
A556
Ashley
Styal

Arley
Mere
Rostherne
Morley Green
A538
Handforth

M6
18
A50
Mobberley
B5085
Knolls Green
A538
Dean Row

WILMSLOW

Hockliffe
Chalton
Sundon Park
Marsh Farm
Lilley
A505
Little Wymondley
Gosmore
A602
8

A5120
M1
B579
Great Offley
Kings Walden
St Ippollitts
A1(M)
B656

Tilsworth
Houghton Regis
A5
Limbury
Leagrave
A6
Stopsley
Cockernhoe
Preston

DUNSTABLE
A505
11
A505
LUTON
Breachwood Green
St Paul's Walden

Totternhoe
A5228
A5065
M1
LUTON AIRPORT
Whitwell

Church End
A5065
Park Town
Peter's Green
Kimpton
B651
Codicote

10
A1081
Pepperstock
B652
Blackmore End
Ayot St Lawrence
B653

INTERNATIONAL APRON
DOMESTIC APRON
MULTI-STOREY CAR PARK 1
COACH PARK
MULTI-STOREY CAR PARK 2

MAIN TERMINAL
SPECTATORS GALLERY
VISCOUNT HOUSE
NOVOTEL
SHORT STAY CAR PARK
STAFF CAR PARK
CAR HIRE RETURNS
EUROHUB TERMINAL
SHORT STAY CAR PARK
EMERGENCY LINK
PERIMETER ROAD

INDUSTRIAL ESTATE

HALL 8
ATRIUM
HALL 7
HALL 6
HALLS 9-12 (under construction)
Customs Wharf
Fire Station
E1

EXHIBITORS CAR PARKS
HALL 3A
HALL 4
AA
E1
Control Barrier 1
EAST CAR PARKS

HALL 3
North Garden
HALL 5
E2

HALL 2
Medical Centre
Plaza
External Exhibition Area
E3

BIRMINGHAM INTERNATIONAL STATION
STATION LONG STAY CAR PARK

HALL 1
DISABLED PARKING
Metropole Hotel
PENDIGO WAY
The Lawn
CONFERENCE CENTRE
Holywell Brook

THE PAVILION
E4

LONG STAY & SPECTATOR CAR PARK 3
AIRPORT WAY

NEC WEST CAR AND COACH PARK
Pedestrian underpass
Footbridge
Fountain
PENDIGO LAKE

NEC ARENA
PENDIGO WAY
E5

PENDRIGO WAY
EASTWAY
SOUTHWAY
M42

BIRMINGHAM AIRPORT
Sheldon
NEC
M42

Acock's Green
A34
Olton
B425
Bickenhill
A45
6

Hall Green
A41
Elmdon Heath
B4438

B4025
Shirley
B4102
SOLIHULL
B4102

5
Copt Heath
M42
B4101
Tilehouse Green
Knowle
A34
Bentley Heath

B4102
Cheswick Green
Dorridge

BICKENHILL LANE
BICKENHILL LANE
N

THE FORUM
C
AA
S4
S6

Control Barrier 2
LORRY PARK S2
SOUTH CAR PARKS
S7

Trinity Business Park
A45
S3
S5
ROAD

Bickenhill Service Station
Arden Hotel & Leisure Club
6
A45

AHA

The National Exhibition Centre and Birmingham International Airport

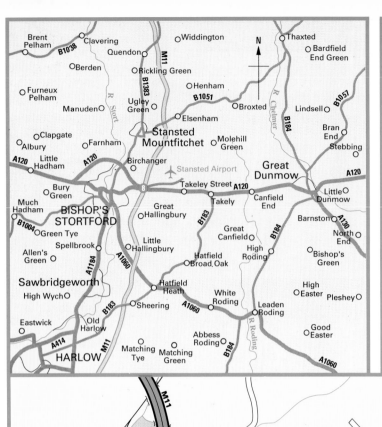

STANSTED AIRPORT tel: 0279 680500

London's third airport is situated 30 miles to the north-east of London with direct access from Junction 8, M11. A new modern airport on a single level with scheduled flights to many European destinations.

Regular bus and coach services operate to the surrounding towns and central London. There is also a direct rail link to central London, 'The Stansted Express'.

Open-air parking is available for 7760 cars tel: 0279 662373 for charges.

The information desk is situated in the International Arrivals concourse tel: 0279 662379/662520.

At the airport is one 3-star hotel and several top class hotels are within easy reach of the airport.

Car hire facilities are available.

Avis	tel: 0279 663030
Budget Rent-a-car	tel: 0279 681194
Europcar	tel: 0279 680240
Hertz	tel: 0279 680154/5

Stansted Airport Cars operate a 24-hour taxi service
tel: 0279 662444

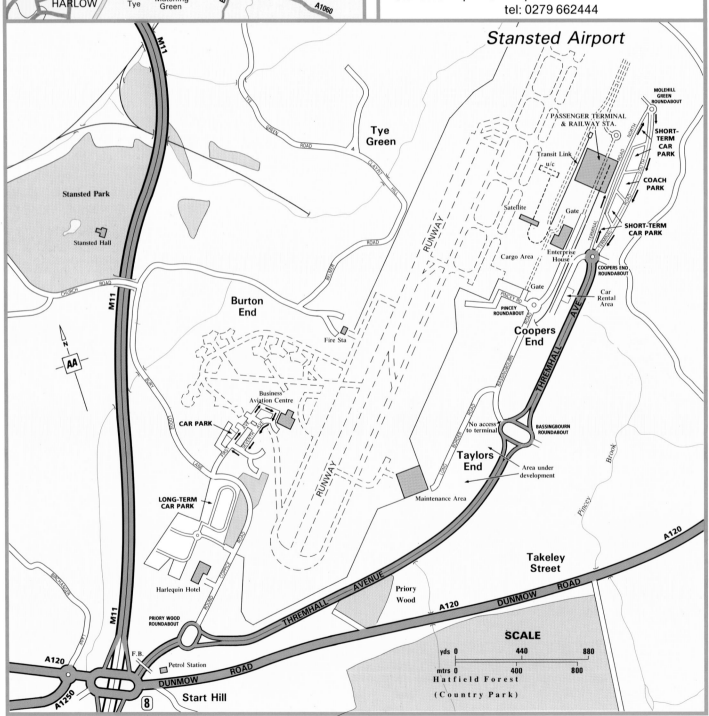

Stansted Airport

SCALE

| yds 0 | | 440 | | 880 |
| mtrs 0 | 400 | | 800 | |

Hatfield Forest
(Country Park)

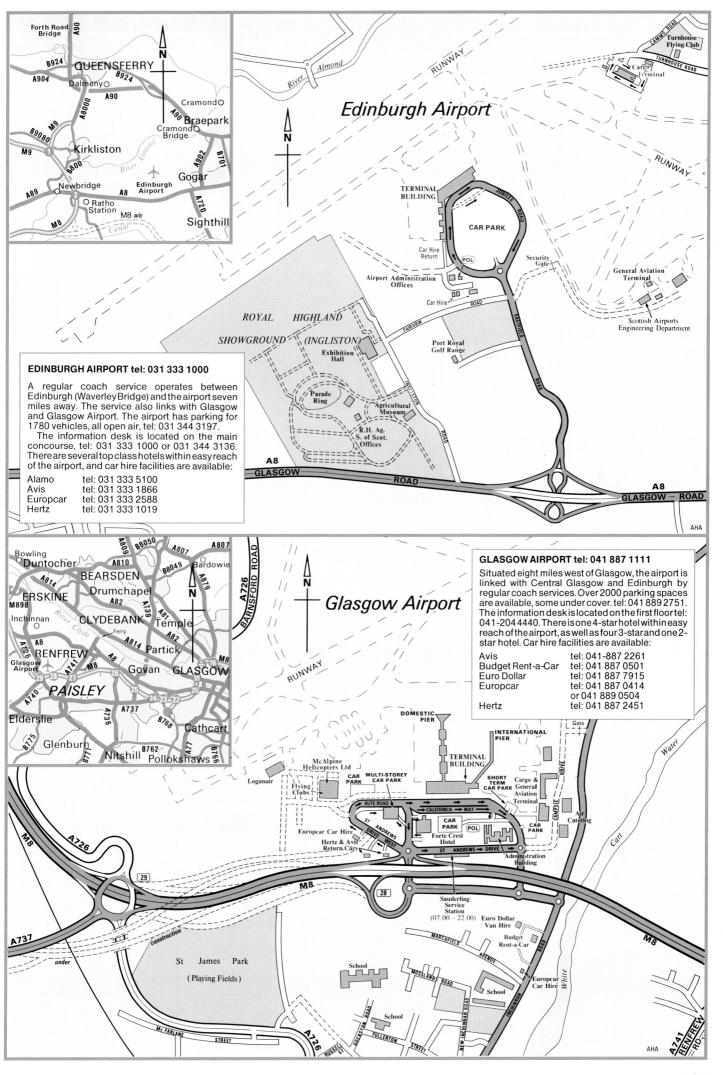

Edinburgh Airport

Forth Road Bridge
QUEENSFERRY
B924
A904
A90
Dalmeny
B924
Cramond
Braepark
A8000
A90
Cramond Bridge
B9080 M9
B800
Kirkliston
Gogar
M9
A89 Newbridge
A8
Ratho Station
Edinburgh Airport
A720
M8 u/c
Canal
Sighthill
A902
B701

RUNWAY
River Almond
Cammo Road
Turnhouse Flying Club
Turnhouse Road
Cargo Terminal
RUNWAY

TERMINAL BUILDING
CAR PARK
JUBILEE ROAD
General Aviation Terminal
Car Hire Return
POL
Security Gate
Scottish Airports Engineering Department
Airport Administration Offices
Car Hire
EASTFIELD ROAD
FAIRVIEW ROAD
INGLISTON ROAD
Port Royal Golf Range

ROYAL HIGHLAND SHOWGROUND (INGLISTON)
Exhibition Hall
Parade Ring
Agricultural Museum
R.H. Ag. S. of Scot. Offices

EDINBURGH AIRPORT tel: 031 333 1000

A regular coach service operates between Edinburgh (Waverley Bridge) and the airport seven miles away. The service also links with Glasgow and Glasgow Airport. The airport has parking for 1780 vehicles, all open air, tel: 031 344 3197.

The information desk is located on the main concourse, tel: 031 333 1000 or 031 344 3136. There are several top class hotels within easy reach of the airport, and car hire facilities are available:

Alamo	tel: 031 333 5100
Avis	tel: 031 333 1866
Europcar	tel: 031 333 2588
Hertz	tel: 031 333 1019

A8 GLASGOW ROAD
A8 GLASGOW ROAD
AHA

Glasgow Airport

Bowling
Duntocher
A809 B8050
A807 A807
BEARSDEN
A810
B8049
Bardowie
A814
Drumchapel
ERSKINE
A82
A739
M898
A81
Inchinnan
CLYDEBANK
Temple
A82
River Clyde
Ferry
A814
Partick
A125
RENFREW
A8
Govan
GLASGOW
A741
Glasgow Airport
M8
29 28 27 26 25 24 23 22 21 20 19 18 16 17
M8
PAISLEY
A740
A736
A737
B768
Cathcart
Elderslie
B775
A77
B762
B766
Glenburn
B711
Nitshill
Pollokshaws

BARNSFORD ROAD
A726
RUNWAY

GLASGOW AIRPORT tel: 041 887 1111

Situated eight miles west of Glasgow, the airport is linked with Central Glasgow and Edinburgh by regular coach services. Over 2000 parking spaces are available, some under cover. tel: 041 889 2751. The information desk is located on the first floor tel: 041-204 4440. There is one 4-star hotel within easy reach of the airport, as well as four 3-star and one 2-star hotel. Car hire facilities are available:

Avis	tel: 041-887 2261
Budget Rent-a-Car	tel: 041 887 0501
Euro Dollar	tel: 041 887 7915
Europcar	tel: 041 887 0414
	or 041 889 0504
Hertz	tel: 041 887 2451

DOMESTIC PIER
INTERNATIONAL PIER
Gate
TERMINAL BUILDING
McAlpine Helicopters Ltd
CAR PARK
MULTI-STOREY CAR PARK
SHORT TERM CAR PARK
Cargo & General Aviation Terminal
Loganair
Flying Clubs
BUTE ROAD
CALEDONIA WAY
CAR PARK
POL
CAMPSIE DRIVE
Air Catering
CAR PARK
Europcar Car Hire
ST ANDREWS DRIVE WEST
Forte Crest Hotel
Hertz & Avis Return Cars
ST ANDREWS DRIVE
Administration Building
Cart Water
M8
A726
29
28
Sauderling Service Station (07.00 - 22.00)
Euro Dollar Van Hire
Budget Rent-a-Car
Europcar Car Hire
A737
construction under
St James Park (Playing Fields)
School
MARCHFIELD AVENUE
MOSSLANDS ROAD
School
INCHINNAN ROAD
NEW INCHINNAN ROAD
White Cart
M8
School
McFARLANE STREET
RUSSELL ST
ECKFORD ROAD
FULLERTON STREET
A726
A741 RENFREW RD
AHA

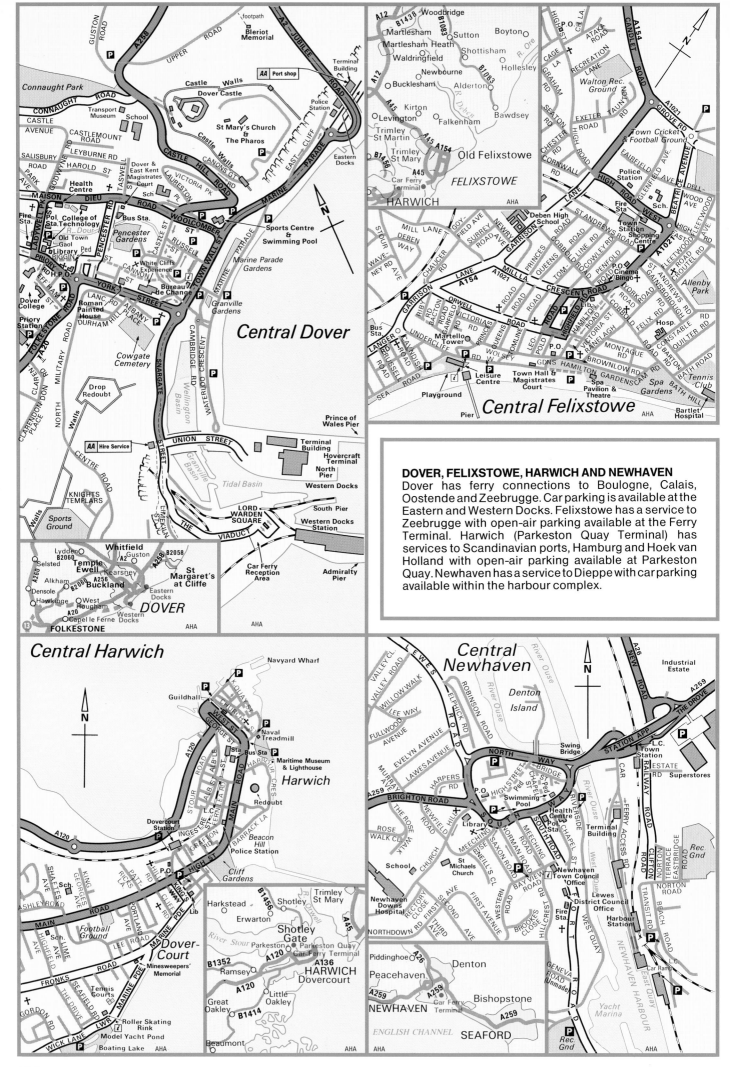

Central Dover

Connaught Park
Castle Walls
Dover Castle
AA Port shop
Terminal Building
Police Station
St Mary's Church & The Pharos
Eastern Docks
Bleriot Memorial
footpath
GUSTON ROAD
A258
A2 JUBILEE ROAD
UPPER ROAD
CASTLE HILL ROAD
EAST CLIFF
MARINE PARADE
CONNAUGHT ROAD
CASTLE AVENUE
Transport Museum
School
CASTLEMOUNT ROAD
FLEYBURNE RD
SALISBURY ROAD
PARK AVE
GODWYNE
HAROLD ST
TASWELL ST
CANONS GT
VICTORIA PK
LAURESTON RD
Health Centre
MAISON DIEU
Dover & East Kent Magistrates Court
Sch
WOOLCOMBER ST
Bus Sta.
Sports Centre & Swimming Pool
Fire Sta.
Pol. College of Sta.Technology
R. Dour
Old Town Gaol
BIGGIN
Ped
PENCESTER ROAD
Pencester Gardens
CASTLE ST
RUSSELL ST
Marine Parade Gardens
LADYWELL
Library
P.O.
White Cliffs Experience
CANNON ST
TOWN WALL ST
MARINE PARADE
PRIORY RD
EFFINGHAM CR
YORK STREET
LANC RD
ALBANY PLACE
Bureau de Change
Granville Gardens
Dover College
Roman Painted House
DURHAM HILL
Central Dover
Priory Station
FOLKESTONE ROAD
A20
CLARENDON PLACE
Cowgate Cemetery
CAMBRIDGE RD
SNARGATE
WATERLOO CRESCENT
Wellington Basin
Drop Redoubt
Walls
NORTH MILITARY ROAD
CENTRE ROAD
KNIGHTS TEMPLARS
Walls
Sports Ground
STREET
UNION STREET
Granville Basin
LIMEKILN STREET
THE VIADUCT
Tidal Basin
LORD WARDEN SQUARE
AA Hire Service
Prince of Wales Pier
Terminal Building
Hovercraft Terminal
North Pier
Western Docks
South Pier
Western Docks Station
Car Ferry Reception Area
Admiralty Pier

DOVER
Lydden
B2060
Selsted
A260
Alkham
Densole
Hawkinge
A20
Capel le Ferne
Whitfield
Guston
Temple Ewell
Kearsney
B2060
A256
Buckland
West Hougham
A2
A258
B2058
St Margaret's at Cliffe
Eastern Docks
Western Docks
DOVER
13
FOLKESTONE
AHA

Central Felixstowe

A12
B1438
Woodbridge
B1083
Martlesham
Sutton
Boyton
Martlesham Heath
Shottisham
Waldringfield
R. Ore
Hollesley
A12
Newbourne
B1083
Bucklesham
Alderton
A45
Kirton
R. Deben
Bawdsey
Levington
Falkenham
A45 A154
Trimley St Martin
Old Felixstowe
Trimley St Mary
B1456
FELIXSTOWE
A45
HARWICH
Car Ferry Terminal
AHA

N
A12
B1438
Deben High School
MILL LANE T
Surrey ROAD
GOY
FIELD AVE
NEWRY AVE
GARRISON
St ANDREWS ROAD
Town Station
STOUR AVE
DEBEN WAY
Princes ROAD
CHAUCER
QUEENS ROAD
COBBOLD ROAD
COWLEY RD
PENFOLD ROAD
P.O
Police Station
Fire Sta
Shopping Centre
A1021
FLEETWOOD RD
GLENFIELD AVE
Sch
BEATRICE AVE
DELL-
FLEETWOOD RD
ST ANDREWS RD
GAINSBOROUGH RD
Allenby Park
A154
A1021
GARRISON LANE
RIBY
ORWELL
BACTON
GARFIELD
VICTORIA S
Lib
CRESCENT ROAD
HIGHFIELD
HAMILTON RD
COBBOLD
FELIX ROUTEL RD
RANELAGH
Hosp.
CONSTABLE RD
QUILTER RD
Bus Sta.
Martello Tower
Princes
LEO-
POLD
RD
P.O
VICTORIA ST
MONTAGUE RD
CAM RD
BATH RD
LANGER ROAD
UNDERCLIFF RD W.
CANDLET RD
WOLSEY
GDNS
HAMILTON GARDENS
BROWNLOW RD
Spa Gardens
Spa Bath Hill
Tennis Club
SEA ROAD
Leisure Centre
Playground
Town Hall & Magistrates Court
Spa Pavilion & Theatre
Bartlet Hospital
Pier
Central Felixstowe
AHA

DOVER, FELIXSTOWE, HARWICH AND NEWHAVEN
Dover has ferry connections to Boulogne, Calais, Oostende and Zeebrugge. Car parking is available at the Eastern and Western Docks. Felixstowe has a service to Zeebrugge with open-air parking available at the Ferry Terminal. Harwich (Parkeston Quay Terminal) has services to Scandinavian ports, Hamburg and Hoek van Holland with open-air parking available at Parkeston Quay. Newhaven has a service to Dieppe with car parking available within the harbour complex.

Central Harwich

N
Navyard Wharf
Guildhall
KING'S QUAY ST
CHURCH ST
WEST ST
GEORGE ST
A120
STOUR ROAD
Sta.
Bus Sta
ALBION ST
MAIN ROAD
Naval Treadmill
Maritime Museum & Lighthouse
Harwich
HARBOUR CRES
Redoubt
INGESTRE ST
WEST ST
L.C.
Dovercourt Station
GRAFTON RD
EASTERN ESPLANADE
BARRACK LA
Beacon Hill Police Station
Cliff Gardens
A120
HIGH ST
P.O.
KING'S RD
CLIFF RD
Lib
A120
SHAFTESBURY AVE
KING GEORGES AVE
KINGS ROAD
PORTLAND AVE
PATRICKS LA
Sch.
Football Ground
MARINE PDE
LEE RD
Dover-Court
MAIN ROAD
ASHLEY ROAD
Sch.
LIME AVE
HIGHFIELD AVE
GORDON RD
FRONKS ROAD
SEAFIELD RD
Tennis Courts
THE DRIVE
WICK LANE
LWR MARINE PDE
Minesweepers' Memorial
i
Roller Skating Rink
Model Yacht Pond
Boating Lake
AHA

Harkstead
B1456
Shotley
Trimley St Mary
Erwarton
R. Orwell
A45
River Stour
Shotley Gate
Parkeston
Parkeston Quay Car Ferry Terminal
B1352
Ramsey
A120
HARWICH
Dovercourt
Great Oakley
Little Oakley
B1414
A136
Beaumont
AHA

Central Newhaven

N
River Ouse
Denton Island
Industrial Estate
A26
NEW ROAD
THE DROVE
A259
VALLEY CL.
VALLEY ROAD
LEWES ROAD
WILLOW WALK
LEE WAY
FULLWOOD AVENUE
ELPHICK RD
ROBINSON ROAD
Swing Bridge
L.C.
Town Station
ESTATE RD
Superstores
EVELYN AVENUE
LAWES AVENUE
NORTH WAY
BRIDGE ST
STATION APP.
Car
RAILWAY RD
A259
MURRAY RD
HARPERS RD
HIGH STREET
Ped
CHAPEL ST
Swimming Pool
River Ouse
FERRY ACCESS RD
CLIFTON ROAD
TERRACE
EASTBRIDGE
NORTON ROAD
Rec. Gnd
BRIGHTON ROAD
A259
P.O.
Library
SOUTH ROAD
Health Centre
Post Sta.
Terminal Building
BEACH ROAD
ROSE WALK CL.
NEWFIELD RD
NORMAN RD
MEECHING ROAD
SAXON RD
BINELL'S CL.
BAY VIEW ROAD
Newhaven Town Council Office
Lewes District Council Office
Fire Sta.
West Quay
Harbour Station
School
St Michaels Church
RECTORY CLOSE
CHURCH HILL
FIRST AVE
SECOND AVE
THIRD AVE
WESTERN ROAD
BROOKES CLOSE
HILLCREST RD
GENEVA ROAD (Unmade)
WEST QUAY
Newhaven Downs Hospital
NORTHDOWN RD
Newhaven Harbour
Car Ramp
L.C.
Yacht Marina
Rec Gnd

Piddinghoe
A26
Denton
Peacehaven
A259
Car Ferry Terminal
Bishopstone
NEWHAVEN
A259
SEAFORD
ENGLISH CHANNEL
AHA

•Town plans

189

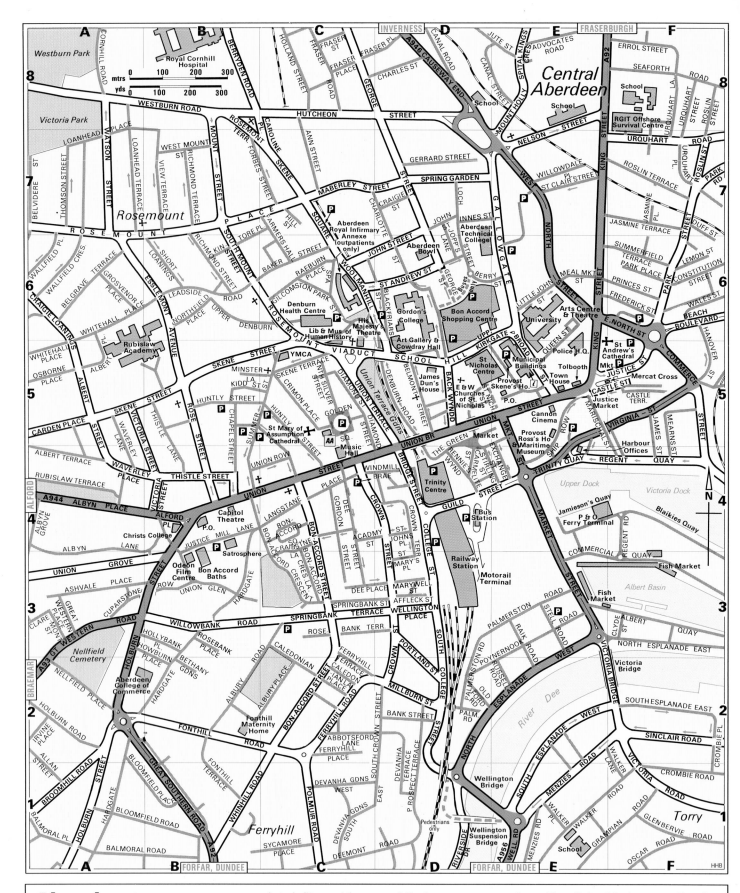

Aberdeen

Granite gives Aberdeen its especial character; but this is not to say that the city is a grim or a grey place, the granites used are of many hues – white, blue, pink and grey. Although the most imposing buildings date from the 19th century, granite has been used to dramatic effect since at least as early as the 15th century. From that time dates St Machar's Cathedral, originally founded in AD580, but rebuilt several times, especially after a devasting fire started on the orders of Edward III of England in 1336. St Machar's is in Old Aberdeen, traditionally the ecclesiastical and educational hub of the city, while 'New' Aberdeen (actually no newer) has always been the commercial centre. Even that definition is deceptive, for although Old Aberdeen has King's College, founded in 1494, New Aberdeen has Marischal College, founded almost exactly a century later (but rebuilt in 1844) and every bit as distinguished as a seat of learning. Both establishments functioned as independent universities until they were merged in 1860 to form Aberdeen University. The North Sea oil boom has brought many changes to the city, some of which threatened its character. But even though high-rise buildings are now common, the stately façades, towers and pillars of granite still reign supreme and Union Street remains one of the best thoroughfares in Britain.

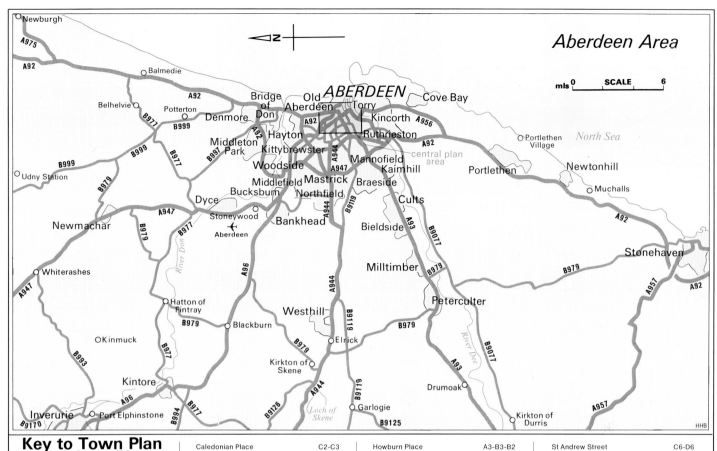

Aberdeen Area

SCALE mls 0 ___ 6

North Sea

Key to Town Plan and Area Plan

Town Plan
A A Recommended roads
Other roads
Restricted roads
Buildings of interest — Cinema
Car Parks — P
Parks and open spaces
One Way Streets
Churches — +

Area Plan
A roads
B roads
Locations — Hattoncrook
Urban area

Street Index with Grid Reference

Aberdeen

Abbotsford Lane	C2-D2
Academy Street	C4-D4
Advocates Road	E8
Affleck Street	D3
Albert Quay	E3-F3
Albert Place	A5-A6
Albert Street	A4-A5
Albert Terrace	A4-A5
Albury Place	B2-C2
Albury Road	B2-C2-C3
Albyn Grove	A4
Albyn Lane	A4-A3-B3-B4
Albyn Place	A4-B4
Alford Place	B4
Allan Street	A1-A2
Ann Street	C7-C8
Ashvale Place	A3-B3
Back Wyndd	D5
Baker Street	B6-C6
Balmoral Place	A1
Balmoral Road	A1-B1
Bank Street	D2
Beach Boulevard	F6
Belgrave Terrace	A6
Belmont Street	D5
Belvidere Street	A7
Berryden Road	B8-C8
Bethany Gardens	B2
Blackfriars Street	D6
Bloomfield Place	A2-A1-B1
Bloomfield Road	A1-B1
Bon-Accord Crescent	B4-C4-C3
Bon-Accord Crescent Lane	C3-C4
Bon-Accord Square	C4
Bon-Accord Street	C2-C3-C4
Bridge Place	D4
Broad Street	E5-E6
Broomhill Road	A1-A2
Caledonian Lane	C2

Caledonian Place	C2-C3
Canal Road	D8
Canal Street	D8-E8
Carden Place	A5
Carmelite Street	D4
Caroline Place	B8-B7-C7-C8
Castle Street	E5-F5
Castle Terrace	F5
Causeway End	D8
Chapel Street	B4-B5
Charles Street	C8-D8
Charlotte Street	C7-D7-D6
Claremont Street	A3
Clyde Street	F3
College Street	D3-D4
Commerce Street	F4-F5
Commercial Quay	E3-F3
Constitution Street	F6
Cornhill Road	A8
Craibstone Lane	C3-C4
Craigie Loanings	A5-A6
Craigie Street	D7
Crimon Street	C5
Crombie Place	F1-F2
Crombie Road	F1
Crown Street	D2-D3-D4-C4
Crown Terrace	D3-D4
Cuparstone Row	A3-B3
Dee Place	C3-D3
Dee Street	C3-C4
Deemont road	C1-D1
Denburn Road	D5
Devanha Gardens East	C1
Devanha Gardesn West	F1-F2
Devanha Terrace	D1-D2
Diamond Street	C4-D4-C5
Duff Street	F6-F7
East North Street	E6-F6
Errol Street	F8
Esslemont Avenue	A6-B6-B5
Exchange Street	E4-E5
Farmers Hill	C6-C7
Ferryhill Place	C2
Ferryhill Road	C2-D2
Ferryhill Terrace	C2-D2
Fonthill Road	A2-B2-C2
Fonthill Terrace	B1-B2
Forbes Street	B7-C7
Fraser Place	C8-D8
Fraser Road	C8
Fraser Street	C8
Frederick Street	E6-F6
Gallowgate	D7-E7-E6
George Street	C8-D8-D7-D6-D5
Gerrard Street	D7
Gilcomston Park	C6
Glenbervie Road	F1
Golden Square	C5
Gordon Street	C3-C4
Grampian Road	E1-F1
Great Southern Road	A1-B2-B1
Great Western Place	A3
Great Western Road	A2-A3
Grosvenor Place	A6
Guild Street	D4-E4
Hanover Street	F5-F6
Hardgate	A1-A2-B2-B3-B4
Hill Street	C7
Holburn Road	A2
Holburn Street	A1-A2-A3-B3-B4
Holland Street	C8
Hollybank Place	A3-B3

Howburn Place	A3-B3-B2
Huntly Street	B5-C5-C4
Hutcheon Street	B8-C8-D8
Innes Street	D7-E7
Irvine Place	A2
James Street	F4-F5
Jasmine Place	F7
Jasmine Terrace	E7-F7
John Street	C6-D6-D7
Jopp's Lane	D6-D7
Justice Street	E5-F5-F6
Justice Mill Lane	B3-B4
Jute Street	D8-E8
Kidd Street	B5-C5
King Street	E5-E6-E7-E8-F8
Kintore Place	B6-B7-C7
Langstone Place	C4
Leadside Road	B6
Lemon Street	F6
Little John Street	E6
Loanhead Place	A7-A8-B8
Loanhead Terrace	A7
Loch Street	D6-D7
Maberley Street	C7-D7
Marischal Street	E5-F5-F4
Market Street	E3-E4-E5
Marywell Street	D3
Meal Market Street	E6
Mearns Street	F4-F5
Menzies Road	E1-E2-F2
Millburn Street	D2
Minster Holly	B5-C5
Mount Holly	E7-E8
Mount Street	B7-B8
Nellfield Place	A2
Nelson Street	E7-E8
North Esplanade East	E3-F3
North Esplanade West	D1-D2-E2-E3
North Silver Street	C5
Northfield Place	B6
Old Ford Road	D2
Osborne Place	A5
Oscar Road	F1
Palmerston Place	D2
Palmerston Road	D2-D3-E3
Park Place	F6
Park Road	F7
Park Street	F6-F7
Polmuir Road	C1-C2
Portland Street	D2-D3
Poynernook Road	D2-E2-E3
Princes Street	E6-F6
Prospect Terrace	D1-D2
Queen Street	E5-E6
Raeburn Place	C6
Raik Road	E2-E3
Regent Road	F3-F4
Regent Quay	E5-F5
Rennies Wyndd	D4
Richmond Street	B6-B7
Richmond Terrace	B7
Riverside Drive	D1
Rose Street	B4-B5
Rosebank Place	B5
Rosebank Terrace	C3-D3
Rosemount Place	A7-A6-B6-B7-C7
Rosemount Terrace	B7-B8
Rosemount Viaduct	B6-C6-C5
Roslin Street	F7-F8
Roslin Terrace	E7-F7
Rubislaw Terrace	A4
Russell Road	E2

St Andrew Street	C6-D6
St Clair Street	E7
St John's Place	D4
St Mary's Place	D3
St Nicholas Street	D5-E5
School Hill	D5
Seaforth Road	F8
Ship Row	E4-E5
Short Loanings	B6
Sinclair Road	F2
Skene Square	C6-C7
Skene Street	A5-B5-C5
Skene Terrace	C5
South College Street	D2-D3
South Crown Street	C1-D1-D2
South Esplanade East	F2
South Esplanade West	E1-E2
South Mount Street	B6-B7
Spa Street	C6
Spital Kings Crescent	E8
Spring Garden	D7
Spring Bank Street	C3-D3
Spring Bank Terrace	C3-D3
Stell Road	E3
Stirling Street	D4-E4
Summer Street	B4-B5
Summerfield Terrace	E6-F6
Sycamore Place	B1-C1
The Green	D4-D5
Thistle Lane	B4-B5
Thistle Street	B4
Thomson Street	A7
Trinity Quay	E4
Upper Denburn	B6-C6
Upper Kirkgate	D5-D6-E5-E6
Urquhart Lane	F7-F8
Urquhart Place	F7
Urquhart Road	F7
Urquhart Street	F7-F8
Union Bridge	D4-D5
Union Glen	B3
Union Grove	A3-B3
Union Row	B4-C4
Union Street	B4-C4-D4-D5-E5
Union Terrace	C5-D5
Victoria Bridge	E3-E2-F2
Victoria Road	F1-F2
Victoria Street	A5-B4-B5
View Terrace	B7
Virginia Street	E5-F5
Wales Street	F6
Walker Lane	F1-F2
Walker Place	E1
Walker Road	E1-F1
Wallfield Crescent	A6
Wallfield Place	A6-A7
Watson Street	A7-A8
Waverley Lane	A4-A5
Waverley Place	A4-B4
Wellington Place	D3
Wellington Road	E1
West Mount Street	B7
West North Street	E6-E7-E8
Westburn Road	A8-B8
Whinhill Road	B1-C1-C2
Whitehall Place	A5-A6-B6
Willow Bank Road	B3-C3
Willowdale Place	E7
Windmill Brae	C4-D4
Woolmanhill	C6-D6-D5

191

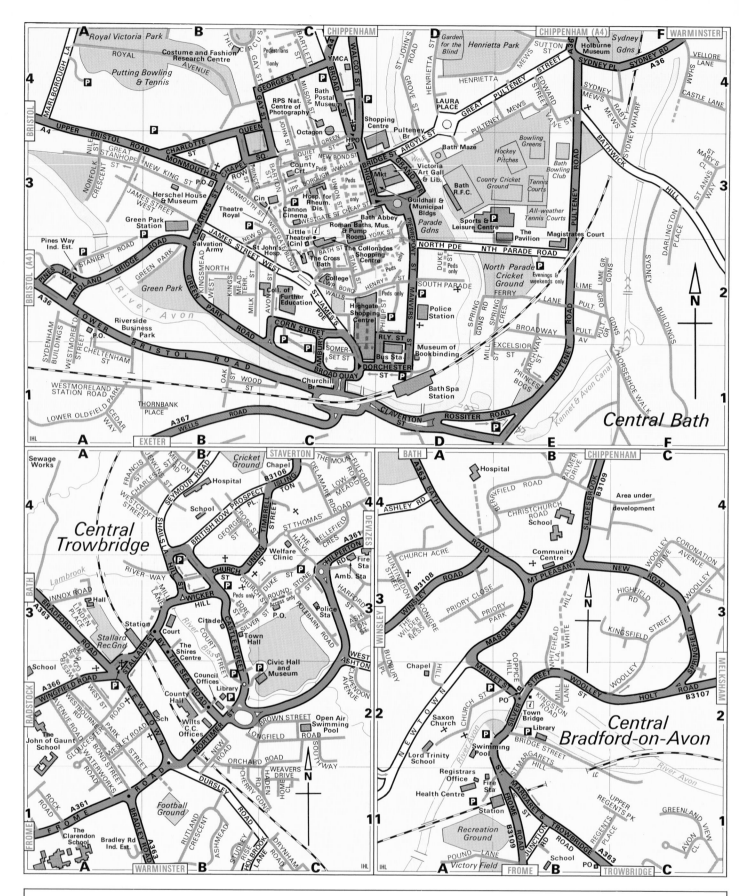

Bath

This unique city combines Britain's most impressive collection of Roman relics with the country's finest Georgian townscape. Its attraction to Romans and fashionable 18th-century society alike was its mineral springs, which are still seen by thousands of tourists who visit the Roman Baths every year. They are now the centre-piece of a Roman museum, where exhibits give a vivid impression of life 2000 years ago. The adjacent Pump Room to which the waters were piped for drinking was a focal point of social life in 18th-and 19th-century Bath.

The Georgian age of elegance also saw the building of Bath's perfectly proportioned streets, terraces and crescents. The finest examples are Queen Square, the Circus, and Royal Crescent, all built of golden local stone. Overlooking the Avon from the west is the great tower of Bath Abbey - sometimes called the "Lantern of the West"

because of its large and numerous windows.

Bath has much to delight the museum-lover. The Holburne Museum in Great Pulteney Street houses collections of silver, porcelain, paintings, furniture and glass of all periods.

The Assembly Rooms in Bennett Street, very much a part of the social scene in Georgian Bath, are now the home of the Museum of Costume with displays illustrating fashion through the ages.

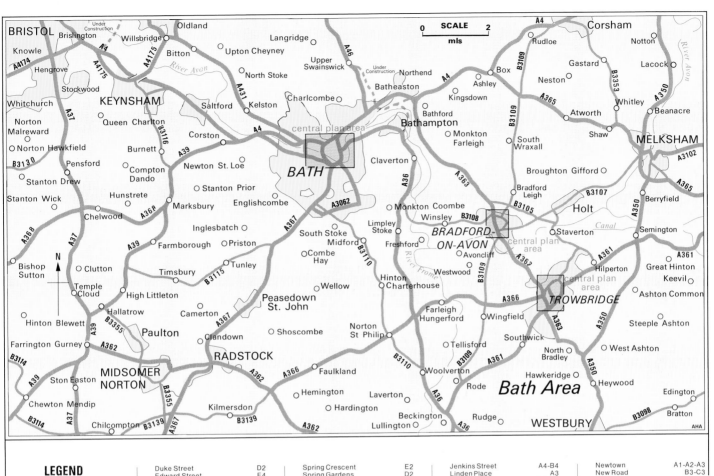

LEGEND

Town Plan

AA Recommended roads
Other roads
Restricted roads
Buildings of interest — Museum
Churches — +
Car parks — P
Parks and open spaces
One way streets

Area Plan

A roads
B roads
Locations — Oldland ○
Urban area

Street Index with Grid Reference

Central Bath

Ambury	C1-C2
Archway Street	E1-E2
Argyle Street	D3-D4
Avon Street	C2
Bartlett Street	C4
Barton Street	C3
Bath Street	C2
Bathwick Hill	E3-F3
Bridge Street	C3-D3
Broadway	E2
Broad Street	C3-C4
Broad Quay	C1
Chapel Row	D3
Charles Street	B2-B3
Charlotte Street	B3-B4
Cheap Street	C3
Cheltenham Street	A1
Claverton Street	C1-D1
Corn Street	C2
Darlington Place	F2-F3
Dorchester Street	C1-D1
Duke Street	D2
Edward Street	E4
Excelsior Street	E1
Ferry Lane	D2-E2
Gay Street	B4-C4-C3
George Street	B4-C4
Grand Parade	D3
Great Pulteney Street	D4-E4
Green Park	A2-B2
Green Park Road	B1-B2-C2-C1
Green Street	C3
Grove Street	D3-D4
Henrietta Mews	D4-E4
Henrietta Street	D4
Henry Street	C2-D2
High Street	C3
Horseshoe Walk	F1
James Street West	A3-B3-B2-C2
John Street	C3-C4
Kingsmead North	B2
Kingsmead Terrace	B2
Kingsmead West	B2
Laura Place	D3-D4
Lime Grove	E2-F2-F1
Lime Grove Gardens	F2
Lower Bristol Road	A2-A1-B1-C1
Lower Borough Walls	C2
Lower Oldfield Park	A1
Manvers Street	D1-D2
Marlborough Lane	A4
Midland Bridge Road	A2-B2-B3
Milk Street	B2
Mill Street	D1
Milsom Street	C3-C4
Monmouth Place	B3
Monmouth Street	B3-C3
New Street	B2-B3-C3
New Bond Street	C3
New King Street	A3-B3
Nile Street	A3
Norfolk Crescent	A3
North Parade	D2
North Parade Road	D2-E2
Oak Street	B1
Philip Street	C1-C2-D2
Pierrepont Street	E1
Pines Way	A2
Princes Buildings	E1
Princes Street	B3
Pulteney Avenue	E2
Pulteney Gardens	E2
Pulteney Grove	E2
Pulteney Mews	E4
Pulteney Road	E1-E2-E3-E4
Queen Square	B3-B4-C4-C3
Quiet Street	C3
Raby Mews	E4-F4
Railway Street	D2
Rossiter Road	D1-E1
Royal Avenue	A4-B4
St Ann's Way	F3
St James's Parade	C2
St John's Road	D4r
St Mary's Close	F3
Sham Castle Lane	F4
Somerset Street	C1
Southgate	C1-C2
South Parade	D2
Spring Crescent	E2
Spring Gardens	D2
Stall Street	C2-C3
Stanhope Street	A3
Stanier Road	A2
Sutton Street	E4
Sydenham Buildings	A1-A2
Sydney Buildings	F1-F2-F3
Sydney Mews	E4-F4
Sydney Place	E4-F4
Sydney Road	F4
Sydney Wharf	F3-F4
The Circus	B4
Thornbank Place	B1
Union Street	C3
Upper Borough Walls	C3
Upper Bristol Road	A4-A3-B3
Vane Street	E4
Vellore Lane	F4
Walcot Street	C3-C4
Wells Road	A1-B1-C1
Westgate Buildings	C2-C3
Westgate Street	C3
Westmoreland Station Road	A1
Westmoreland Street	A1
Wood Street	B1
York Street	C2-D2-D3

Trowbridge

Ashmead	D1
Ashton Street	C3
Avenue Road	A2
Bellefield Crescent	C4
Bond Street	A1-A2
Bradford Road	A2-A3
Bradley Road	A1-B1
British Row	B4
Brown Street	B2-C2
Bythesea Road	B2-B3
Castle Street	B2-B3
Charles Street	A4-B4
Cherry Gardens	B1-C1
Church Street	B3-C3
Clapendon Avenue	C2
Court Street	B2-B3
Cross Street	B4-C4
Delamare Road	C4
Dynham Road	C1
Duke Street	C3-C4
Dursley Road	B1-C1
Fore Street	B3
Francis Street	A4-B4
Frome Road	A1-B1
Fulford Road	C4
George Street	B4
Gloucester Road	A2
Haden Road	C1
Harford Street	C3
Hill Street	B3
Hilperton Road	C3-C4
Holbrook Lane	B1-C1
Home Close	C1
Innox Road	A3
Islington	C4
Jenkins Street	A4-B4
Linden Place	A3
Longfield Road	B2-C2
Lowmead	C4
Melton Road	B4
Mill Lane	B3
Mortimer Street	B2
New Road	B1-B2
Newtown	A2-B2
Orchard Road	B1-B2-C2-C1
Park Street	A2-A1-B1
Polebarn Road	C3
Prospect Place	D4-C4
River Way	A3-B3
Rock Road	A1
Roundstone Street	C3
Rutland Crescent	B1
St Thomas' Road	C4
Seymour Road	B4
Shails Lane	B3-B4
Silver Street	B3-C3
Southway	C2
Stallard Street	A2-A3-B3
Studley Rise	B1
The Halve	C4
The Mount	C4
Timbrell Street	C4
Union Street	B3-B4-C4-C3
Waterworks Road	A1-A2
Weavers Drive	C1
Wesley Road	A2-B2
West Street	A2
West Ashton	C2-C3
Westbourne Gardens	A2-A3
Westbourne Road	A2
Westcroft Street	A4-B4
Wicker Hill	B3
Wingfield Road	A2

Bradford -upon-Avon

Ashley Road	A4
Avon Close	C1
Bath Road	A3-A4-B4-B3
Berryfield Road	A4-B4
Bridge Street	B2
Christchurch Road	B4
Christchurch Road	B4
Church Acre	A4
Church Street	A2-B2
Conigre Hill	A2-A3
Coppice Hill	B2-B3
Coronation Avenue	C3-C4
Frome Road	B1
Greenland View	C1
Highfield Road	C3
Holt Road	B2-C2
Huntingdon Street	A3
Kingston Road	B2
Junction Road	B1
Market Street	A2-B2
Masons Lane	A3-B3
Mill Lane	B2
Mount Pleasant	B3
Newtown	A1-A2-A3
New Road	B3-C3
Palmer Drive	B4
Pound Lane	A1-B1
Priory Close	A3-B3
Priory Park	A3-B3
Regents Place	B1-C1
Rome Road	B1
St Margaret's Place	B1-B2
St Margaret's Street	B1-C2
Silver Street	B2
Sladesbrook	B3-B4
Springfield	C2-C3
The Wilderness	A3
Trowbridge Road	B1
Upper Regents Park	B1-C1
White Hill	B2-B3
Whitehead Lane	B2-B3
Winsley Road	A3-A4
Woolley Drive	C3-C4
Woolley Street	C2-C3

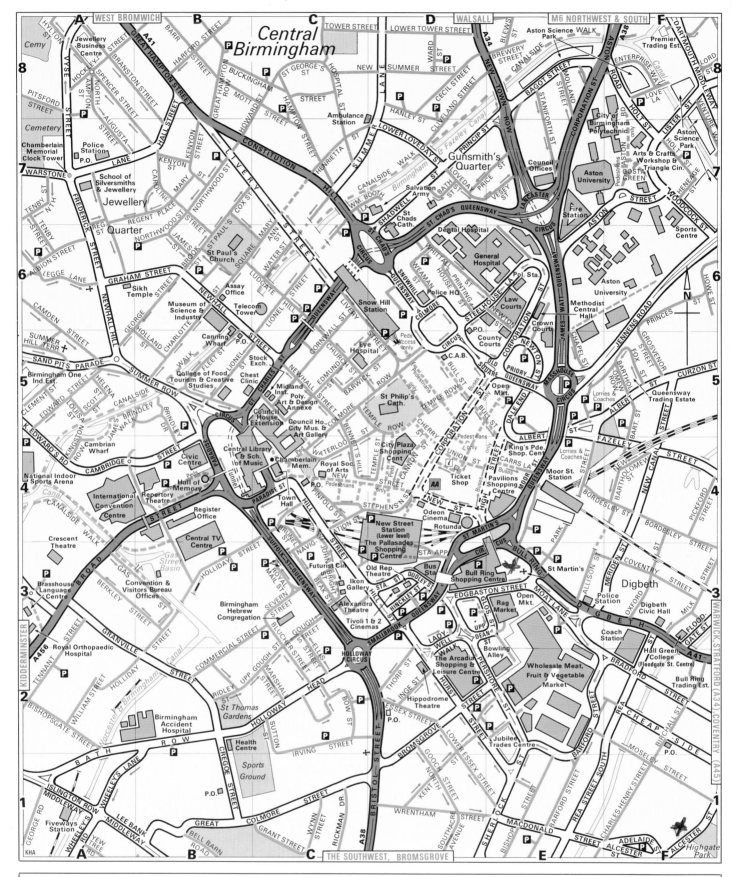

Birmingham

When the Romans were in Britain, Birmingham was little more than a staging post on Icknield Street. Throughout medieval times it was a minor agricultural centre in the middle of a heavily-forested region. Timbered houses clustered together round a green that was eventually to be called the Bull Ring. But by the 16th century, although still a tiny and unimportant village by today's standards, it had begun to gain a reputation as a manufacturing centre. Tens of thousands of sword blades were made here during the Civil War. Throughout the 18th century more and more land was built on. In 1770 the Birmingham Canal was completed, making trade very much easier and increasing the town's development dramatically. All of that pales into near insignificance compared with what happened in the 19th century. Birmingham was not represented in Parliament until 1832 and had no town council until 1838. Yet by 1889 it had already been made a city, and after only another 20 years it had become the second largest city in England. Many of Birmingham's most imposing public buildings date from the 19th century, when the city was growing rapidly. The International Convention Centre and National Indoor Sports Arena are two of the most recent developments. Surprisingly, the city has more miles of waterway than Venice.

194

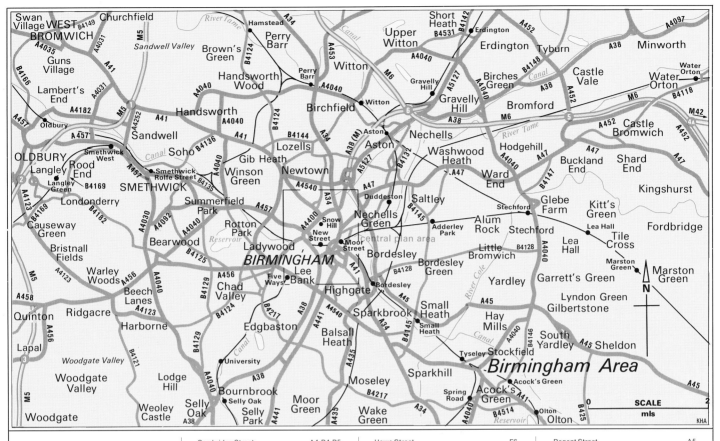

LEGEND

Town Plan

AA Recommended roads	
Other roads	
Restricted roads	
One-way streets	
AA shop/Insurance	AA
Buildings of interest	▪
Churches	†
Car parks	P
Parks and open spaces	

Area Plan

Motorways	
A roads	
B roads	
Railway station	●

INDEX

Birmingham

Adelaide Street	F1
Albert Street	E4-E5-F5
Albion Street	A6
Alcester Street	F1
Allison Street	E3
Aston Road	F8-E8-F8-F7
Aston Street	E6-E7-F7
Augusta Street	A7-A8
Bagot Street	E8
Barford Street	E1-E2-F2
Barr Street	B8
Bartholomew Row	F5
Bartholomew Street	F4-F5
Barwick Street	C5-D5
Bath Row	A1-A2-B2
Bath Street	D7
Beak Street	C3
Bell Barn Road	B1
Bennett's Hill	C4-C5
Berkley Street	A3-B3
Birchall Street	F1-F2
Bishop Street	E1
Bishopsgate Street	A2
Blews Street	E8
Blucher Street	C2-C3
Bordesley Street	E4-F4-F3
Bow Street	C2
Bradford Street	E3-E2-F2
Branston Street	A8-B8-B7
Brewery Street	E8
Bristol Street	C1-D1-D2-C2
Broad Street	A2-A3-A4-B4-B5
Bromsgrove Street	D1-D2-E2
Brook Street	B6
Brunel Street	C3-C4
Buckingham Street	B8-C8-B7
Bull Ring	E3
Bull Street	D5-E5-E4

Cambridge Street	A4-B4-B5
Camden Street	A5-A6
Cannon Street	D4
Caroline Street	B6-B7
Carrs Lane	E4
Cecil Street	D8
Chapel Street	E5-E6
Charles Henry Street	F1
Charlotte Street	B5-B6
Cheapside	F1-F2
Cherry Street	D4-D5
Church Street	C6-C5-D5
Clement Street	A5
Cliveland Street	D7-D8-E8
Colmore Circus	D5-D6
Colmore Row	C4-C5-D5
Commercial Street	B2-B3-C3
Constitution Hill	B7-C7
Cornwall Street	C5-C6
Corporation Street	D4-D5-E5-E6-E7-E8-F8
Coventry Street	E3-F3
Cregoe Street	B1-B2
Cumberland Street	A3
Curzon Street	F5
Dale End	E4-E5
Dartmouth Middleway	F7-F8
Digbeth	E3-F3
Dudley Street	D3
Edgbaston Street	D3-E3
Edmund Street	C5-D5
Edward Street	A5
Ellis Street	C2-C3
Enterprise Way	F7-F8
Essex Street	D2
Fazeley Street	E5-E4-F4
Fleet Street	B5
Floodgate Street	F3
Fox Street	F5
Frederick Street	A6-A7
Gas Street	A3-B3
George Road	A1
George Street	A5-B5-B6
Gloucester Street	D3-E3
Gooch Street North	D1-D2
Gosta Green	F7
Gough Street	C3
Graham Street	A6-B6
Grant Street	C1
Granville Street	A3-A2-B2
Great Charles St Queensway	B5-C5-C6
Great Colmore Street	B1-C1-D1
Great Hampton Row	B8
Great Hampton Street	A8-B8-B7
Grosvenor Street	F5-F6
Hall Street	B7-B8
Hampton Street	C7-C8
Harford Street	B8
Hanley Street	D7-D8
Helena Street	A5
Heneage Street	F7
Henrietta Street	C7-D7
High Street	D4-E4
Hill Street	C4-C3-D3
Hinckley Street	D3
Hockley Street	A8-B8
Holland Street	B5
Holliday Street	A2-B2-B3-C3-C4
Holloway Circus	C2-C3-D3-D2
Holloway Head	B2-C2
Holt Street	F7-F8
Hospital Street	C7-C8
Howard Street	B7-C7-C8

Howe Street	F6
Hurst Street	D3-D2-E2-E1
Hylton Street	A8
Inge Street	D2
Irving Street	C2-D2
Islington Row Middleway	A1
James Brindley Walk	A5-B5
James Street	B6
James Watt Queensway	E5-E6
Jennens Road	E5-F5-F6
John Bright Street	C3-C4
Kent Street	D1-D2
Kenyon Street	B7
King Edward's Road	A4-A5
Kingston Row	A4
Ladywell Walk	D2-D3
Lancaster Circus	E6-E7
Lee Bank Middleway	A1-B1
Legge Lane	A6
Lionel Street	B5-C5-C6
Lister Street	F7-F8
Livery Street	B7-C7-C6-D6-D5
Louisa Street	A5
Love Lane	F8
Loveday Street	D7
Lord Street	F8
Lower Essex Street	D2-D1-E1
Lower Loveday Street	D7
Lower Tower Street	D8
Ludgate Hill	B6-C6
Macdonald Street	E1-F1
Marshall Street	C2
Mary Street	B7
Mary Ann Street	C6-C7
Masshouse Circus	E5
Meriden Street	E3-F3
Milk Street	F3
Moat Lane	E3
Molland Street	D4
Moor Street Queensway	E4-E5
Moseley Street	E2-F2-F1
Mott Street	B8-C8-C7
Navigation Street	C3-C4
New Street	C4-D4
New Bartholomew Street	F4
New Canal Street	F4-F5
Newhall Hill	A5-A6
Newhall Street	B6-B5-C5
New Summer Street	C8-D8
Newton Street	E5
New Town Row	D8-E8-E7
Northampton Street	A8
Northwood Street	B6-B7
Old Square	D5-E5
Oozells Street	A3-A4
Oozells Street North	A3-A4
Oxford Street	F3-F4
Paradise Circus	B4-B5
Paradise Street	C4
Park Street	E3-E4
Pershore Street	D3-D2-E2
Pickford Street	F4
Pinfold Street	C4
Pitsford Street	A8
Price Street	D7-E7
Princes Street	F6
Princip Street	D7-E7-E8
Printing House Street	D6
Priory Queensway	E5
Rea Street	E2-F2-F3
Rea Street South	E1-F1-F2
Regent Place	A7-B7

Regent Street	A5
Rickman Drive	C1
Ripley Street	B2
Royal Mail Street	C3
St Chad's Circus	C7-C6-D6
St Chad's Queensway	D6-D7-E7
St George's Street	C8
St Martin's Circus	D3-D4-E4-E3
St Paul's Square	B7-B6-C6
Sand Pits Parade	A5
Scotland Street	A5
Severn Street	C3
Shadwell Street	D6-D7
Sheepcote Street	A3
Sherlock Street	D1-E1-E2
Smallbrook Queensway	C3-D3
Snow Hill Queensway	D6
Spencer Street	A8-A7-B7
Staniforth Street	E7-E8
Station Approach	D3
Station Street	D3
Steelhouse Lane	D6-E6
Stephenson Street	C4-D4
South Acre Street	D1
Suffolk Street Queensway	B4-C4-C3
Summer Hill Terrace	A5
Summer Row	A5-B5
Summer Lane	C7-D7-D8
Sutton Street	C2
Temple Row	C5-D5
Temple Street	D4-D5
Tenby Street	A6-A7
Tenby Street North	A7
Tennant Street	A2-A3
Thorp Street	D2-D3
Tower Street	C8-D8
Union Street	D4
Upper Dean Street	D3-E3
Upper Gough Street	B2-C2-C3
Venture Way	F7-F8
Vesey Street	D7-E7
Vittoria Street	A6-A7
Vyse Street	A7-A8
Ward Street	D8
Warstone Lane	A7-B7
Water Street	C6
Waterloo Street	C4-C5-D5
Weaman Street	D6
Wheeley's Lane	A1-B1-B2
Wheeley's Road	A1
Whittall Street	D6-E6
William Booth Lane	C7-D7
William Street	A2
Woodcock Street	F6-F7
Wrentham Street	D1-E1
Wynn Street	C1
Yew Tree Road	A1
AA shop, 134 New Street	
Birmingham B2 4NP	
Tel: 021-643 2321	D4

195

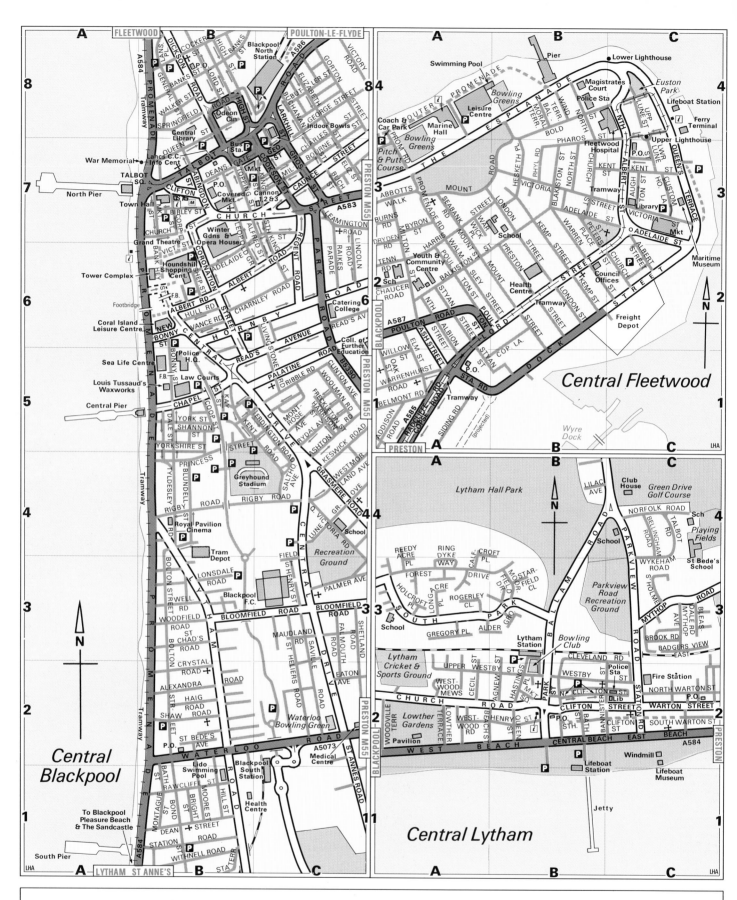

Blackpool

No seaside resort is regarded with greater affection than Blackpool. It is still the place where millions of North Country folk spend their holidays; its famous illuminations draw visitors from all over the world. It provides every conceivable kind of traditional holiday entertainment, and in greater abundance than any other seaside resort in Britain. The famous tower – built in the 1890s as a replica of the Eiffel

Tower – the three piers, seven miles of promenade, five miles of illuminations, countless guesthouses, huge numbers of pubs, shops, restaurants and cafes play host to eight million visitors a year.

At the base of the tower is a huge entertainment complex that includes a ballroom and an aquarium. Other 19th-century landmarks are North Pier and Central Pier, the great Winter Gardens and Opera House and the famous trams that still run along the promenade – the last traditional urban tramway system still

operating in Britain. The most glittering part of modern Blackpool is the famous Golden Mile, packed with amusements, novelty shops and snack stalls. Every autumn it becomes part of the country's most extravagant light show – the illuminations – when the promenade is ablaze with neon representations of anything and everything from moon rockets to the Muppets. Autumn is also the time when Blackpool is a traditional venue for political party conferences.

Blackpool Area

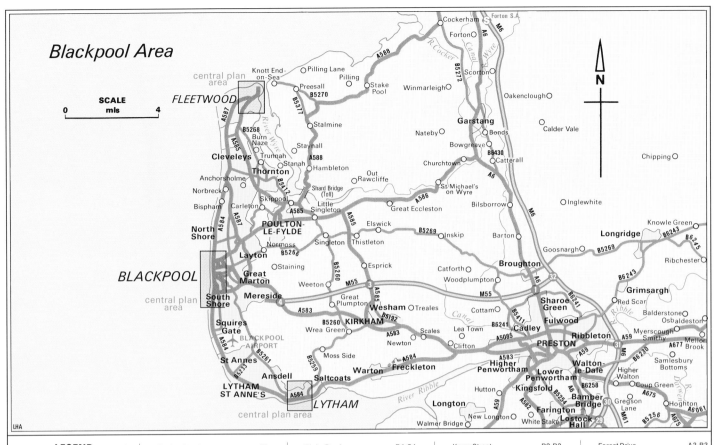

SCALE
0 mls 4

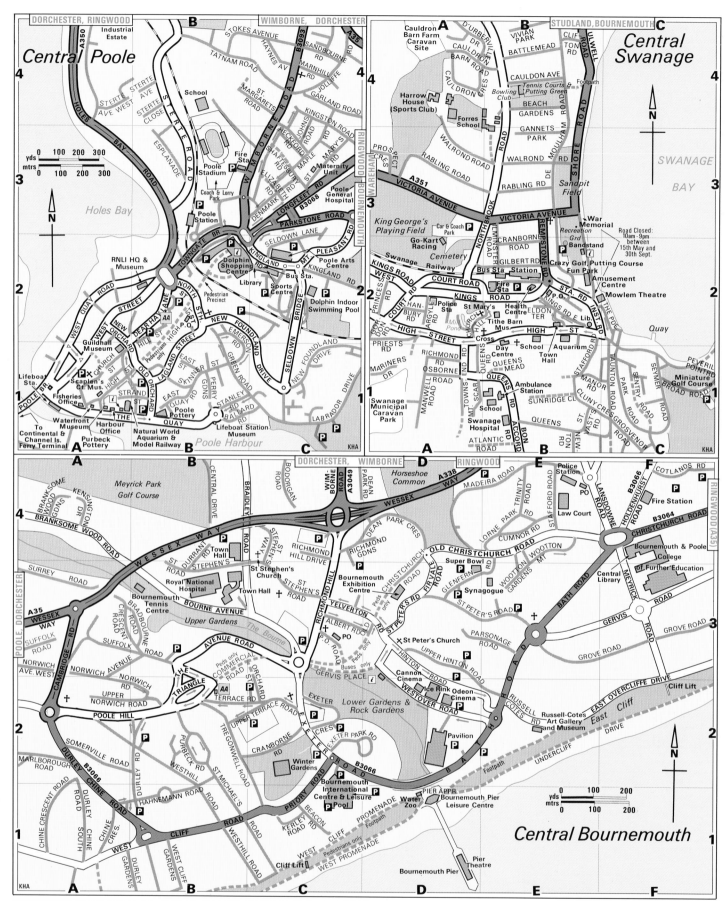

Bournemouth

Until the beginning of the 19th-century the landscape was open heath. Bournemouth's rise began in Victorian times when the idea of seaside holidays was very new. In the next 50 years it had become a major resort. Holidaymakers today enjoy miles of sandy beaches, a mild climate and beautiful setting, along with a tremendous variety of amenities, including some of the best shopping in the south. Entertainments range from variety shows and cinemas to opera and the world famous Bournemouth Symphony Orchestra. Major features of interest are the Exhibition Centre, containing the Turin Shroud and Chinese Terracotta Warriors exhibitions, and at nearby Canford Cliffs the magnificent Compton Acres Gardens overlooking Poole Harbour.

Poole is famous for the large natural harbour and the old town around the Quay with its unique historical interest. The waterfront Maritime Museum illustrates the town's associations with the sea since prehistoric times and the famous Poole Pottery offers guided tours of its workshops. Among other places to be seen are Scaplen's Court, the Guildhall Museum and the RNLI Headquarters Museum.

Swanage, one of Dorset's most popular holiday resorts still retains much of its Victorian character. Dramatic coastal scenery with cliff top walks and many places of interest are within easy reach. A major attraction is the Swanage Railway which operates steam-hauled trains to Harman's Cross and, in the near future, Corfe Castle.

198

LEGEND

Town Plan

AA Recommended roads	
Other roads	
Restricted roads	
One-way streets	
AA Shop/Insurance	AA
Buildings of interest	Hall □
Churches	†
Car parks	P
Parks and open spaces	

Street Index with Grid Reference

Bournemouth

Albert Road	C3-D3
Avenue Road	B3-C3
Bath Road	D2-E2-E3-E4-F4
Beacon Road	C1
Bodorgan Road	C4
Bourne Avenue	B3-C3
Bradbourne Road	B3
Braidley Road	B3-B4
Branksome Wood Gardens	A4
Branksome Wood Road	A4
Cambridge Road	A2-A3
Central Drive	B4
Chine Crescent	A1
Chine Crescent Road	A1-A2
Christchurch Road	F4
Commercial Road	B2
Cotlands Road	F4
Cranbourne Road	B2-C2
Crescent Road	A3-B3
Cumnor Road	E4
Dean Park Crescent	C4-D4
Dean Park Road	C4
Durley Chine Road	A1-A2
Durley Chine Road South	A1
Durley Gardens	A1-A2
Durley Road	A1-A2-B1
Durrant Road	B4
East Overcliff Drive	E2-F2-F3
Exeter Crescent	C2
Exeter Park Road	C2-D2
Exeter Road	C2-D2
Fir Vale Road	D3-D4

Gervis Place	C3-D3
Gervis Road	E3-F3
Glenfern Road	D3-E3-E4
Grove Road	E3-F3
Hahnemann Road	A1-B1-B2
Hinton Road	D2-D3-E2
Holdenhurst Road	F4
Kensington Drive	A4
Kerley Road	C1
Lansdowne Road	E4-F4
Lorne Park Road	E4
Madeira Road	D4-E4
Marlborough Road	A2
Meyrick Road	F3-F4
Norwich Avenue	A2
Norwich Avenue West	A3
Norwich Road	A2-B2
Old Christchurch Road	D3-D4-E4-F4
Orchard Street	C2-C3
Parsonage Road	D3-E3
Poole Hill	A2-B2
Poole Road	A2
Post Office Road	C3
Priory Road	C1-C2
Purbeck Road	B2
Richmond Gardens	C4
Richmond Hill	C3-C4
Richmond Hill Drive	C4
Russell Cotes Road	E2
Somerville Road	A2
St Michael's Road	B2-B1-C1
St Peter's Road	D3-E3
St Stephen's Road	B3-B4-C4-C3
St Stephen's Way	C4
Stafford Road	E4
Suffolk Road	A3-B3
Surrey Road	A3
Terrace Road	B2-C2
The Triangle	B2-B3
Tregonwell Road	B2-C2-C1
Trinity Road	E4
Undercliffe Drive	D1-D2-E1-E2-F2
Upper Hinton Road	D2-D3-E2
Upper Norwich Road	A2-B2
Upper Terrace Road	B2-C2
Wessex Way	A3-A4-B4-C4-D4-E4
West Cliff Gardens	B1
West Cliff Promenade	B1-C1-D1-C1
West Cliff Road	A1-B1
Westhill Road	A2-B2-B1
Westover Road	D2-D3
West Promenade	C1-D1
Wimborne Road	C4
Wootton Gardens	E3-E4
Wootton Mount	E4
Yelverton Road	C3-D3
AA Shop, 96 Commercial Road Bournemouth, Dorset BH2 5LR Tel: 0202 293241	B2

Poole

Ballard Road	B1-C1
Church Street	A1
Dear Hay Lane	A2-B2
Denmark Road	C3
East Quay Road	B1

East Street	B1
Elizabeth Road	C3
Emerson Road	B1-B2
Esplanade	B3
Garland Road	C4
Green Road	B2-B1-C1
Haynes Avenue	C4
Heckford Road	C3-C4
High Street	A1-B1-B2
Hill Street	B2
Holes Bay Road	A4-B3
Johns Road	C3-C4
Jolliffe Road	C4
Kingland Road	B2-C2
Kingston Road	C3-C4
Labrador Drive	C1
Lagland Street	B1-B2
Longfleet Road	C3
Maple Road	C3-C4
Marnhill Road	C4
Mount Pleasant Road	C2-C3
Newfoundland Drive	C1
New Orchard	A1-A2
North Street	B2
Old Orchard	B1
Parkstone Road	C1-C2
Perry Gardens	B1
Poole Bridge	A1
Sandbourne Road	C4
St Margarets Road	B4-C4
St Mary's Road	C3
Seldown Bridge	C1-C2
Seldown Lane	C2-C3
Shaftesbury Road	C3
Skinner Street	B1
South Road	B2
Stanley Road	B1
Sterte Avenue	B4
Sterte Avenue West	A4
Sterte Close	B4
Sterte Road	B2-B3-B4
Stokes Avenue	B4-C4
Strand Street	A1-B1
Tatnam Road	B4-C4
The Quay	A1-B1
Towngate Bridge	B2-B3
West Quay Road	A1-A2-B2
West Street	A1-A2-B2
Wimborne Road	B3-C3-C4

Swanage

Argyle Road	A2
Atlantic Road	A1-B1
Battlemead	B4
Beach Gardens	B4
Bon Accord Road	B1
Broad Road	C1
Cauldron Avenue	B4
Cauldron Barn Road	A4-B4
Cauldron Crescent	A4
Church Hill	A2
Clifton Road	B4
Cluny Crescent	B1-C1
Court Road	A2
Cranborne Road	B2
De Moulham Road	B3-B4

D'uberville Drive	A4-B4
Eldon Terrace	B2
Exeter Road	B1-C1
Gannets Park	B3
Gilbert Road	A2-B2
Gordon Road	B1
Grosvenor Road	C1
Hanbury Road	A2
High Street	A2-B3
Ilminster Road	B2-B3
Institute Road	B2-B2
Kings Road	A2-B2
Kings Road East	B2
Kings Road West	A2
Manor Road	B1-C1
Manwell Road	A1
Mariners Drive	A1
Mountscar	A1
Newton Road	B1
Northbrook Road	A2-A3-B3-B4
Osborne Road	A1
Park Road	C1
Princess Road	A2
Prospect Crescent	A3
Peveril Point Road	C1
Priests Road	C1
Queens Mead	B1
Queens Road	A1-B1-C1
Rabling Road	A3-B3
Rempstone Road	B2-B3
Richmond Road	A1
St Vast's Road	B1
Sentry Road	C1
Seymer Road	C1
Shore Road	B3-B4
Stafford Road	B1-B2
Station Road	B2
Sunridge Close	B1
Taunton Road	C1
The Parade	C2
Ulwell Road	B4
Victoria Avenue	A3-B3
Vivian Park	B4
Walrond Road	A3-B3

BOURNEMOUTH
The pier, safe sea-bathing, golden sands facing south and sheltered by steep cliffs, and plenty of amenities for the holiday maker make Bournemouth one of the most popular resorts on the south coast of England.

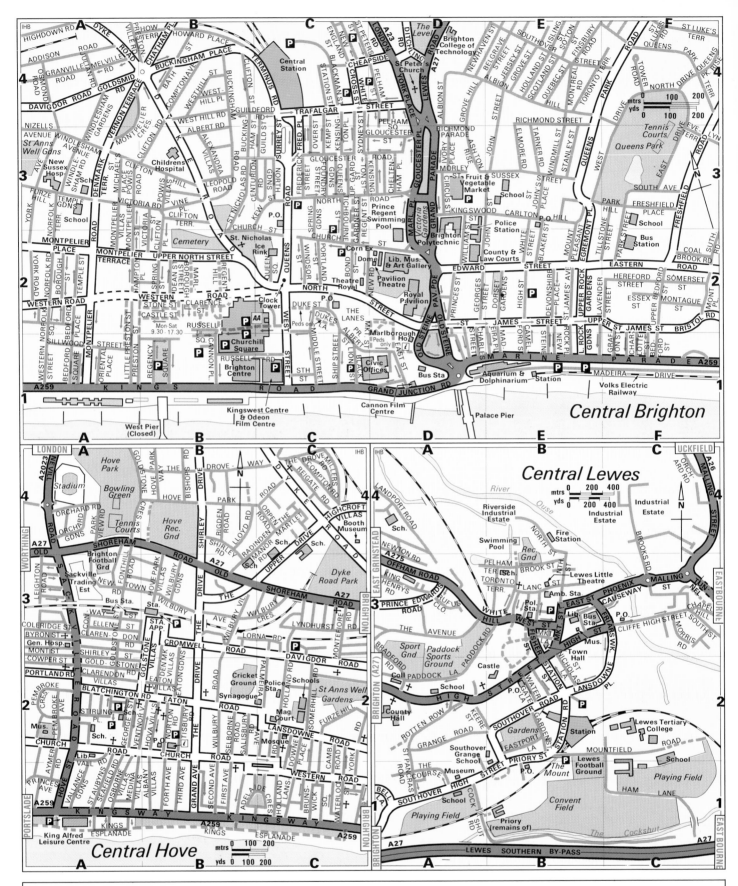

Central Brighton

Central Lewes

Central Hove

Brighton

Dr Richard Russell, from nearby Lewes, created the resort of Brighton almost singlehandedly. And he did it not by building houses or hotels, but by writing a book. His book, which praised the health-giving properties of sea-bathing and sea air, soon came to the attention of George, then Prince Regent and one day to become King George IV. He stayed at Brighthelmstone – as it was then known –

in 1783 and again in 1784. In 1786 the Prince rented a villa on the Steine – a modest house that was eventually transformed into the astonishing Pavilion. By 1800 – its popularity assured by royal patronage – the resort was described in a contemporary directory as 'the most frequented and without exception one of the most fashionable towns in the kingdom'.

Perhaps the description does not quite fit today, but Brighton is a perennially popular seaside

resort, as well as a shopping centre, university town and cultural venue. The Pavilion still draws most crowds, of course. Its beginnings as a villa are entirely hidden in a riot of Near Eastern architectural motifs, largely the creation of John Nash. Brighton's great days as a Regency resort *par excellence* are preserved in the sweeping crescents and elegant terraces, buildings which help to make it one of the finest townscapes in the whole of Europe.

STREET INDEX WITH GRID REFERENCE

BRIGHTON

Addison Road A4
Albert Road B3
Albion Hill D4-E4-F4-F3
Albion Street D4
Alexandra Villas B3
Ashton Rise D3
Bath Street B4
Bedford Place A1-A1
Bedford Square A1
Bedford Street A1-A2
Bedford Square F1-F2
Belgrave Street D4-E4
Black Lion Street C1
Blackman Street C4
Blaker Street E2-E3
Bond Street C2
Borough Street A2
Bread Street C2-C3
Bristol Road F2
Buckingham Place B4
Buckingham Road B3-B4
Buckingham Street B3-B4
Camelford Street E1-E2
Cannon Place B1-B2
Carlton Hill E3
Castle Street B2
Centurion Road B3
Charles Street D1-D2
Charlotte Street F1-F2
Chatham Place B4
Cheapside C4-D4
Cheltenham Place D3
Church Street B2-C2-D2
Circus Street D3
Clarence Street B2
Clifton Hill A3-B3
Clifton Place B2-B3
Clifton Road B3-B4
Clifton Street B4
Clifton Terrace B3
Coalbrook Road F2
Compton Avenue B4
Davigdor Road A4
Denmark Terrace A3
Devonshire Place E2
Ditchling Road D4
Dorset Gardens E2
Duke Street C2
Dukes Lane C2
Dyke Road A4-B4-B3-B2-C2
East Drive F3-F4
East Street D1-D2
Eastern Road E2-F2
Edward Street D2-E2
Egremont Place E2-E3
Elmon Road E3
Essex Street F2
Finsbury Road E4
Foundry Street C3
Frederick Place C3-C4
Frederick Street C3
Freshfield Place F3
Freshfield Road F2-F3-F4
Furze Hill A3
Gardner Street C2-C3
George Street D2
Gloucester Place D3
Gloucester Road C3-D3
Gloucester Street C3-D3
Goldsmid Road A4-B4
Grafton Street F1-F2
Grand Junction Road D1
Grand Parade D2-D3
Granville Road A4
Grove Hill D4
Grove Street E4
Guildford Road B4-C4
Guildford Street C3-C4
Hampton Place A2
Hereford Street F2
High Street E2
Highdown Road A4
Holland Street E4
Howard Place B4
Howard Terrace B4
Islingword Street E4
Ivory Place D3
Jersey Street E4
John Street D2-D3-E3-E4
Julian Road A4
Kemp Street C3-C4
Kensington Place C3-C4
Kensington Street C3
Kew Street C2-C3
King's Road A1-B1-C1
Kingswood Street D3
Lavender Street E2-F2
Leopold Road B3
Little Preston Street A1-A2
Lewes Road D4
London Road D4
Lower Rock Gardens E1-E2
Madeira Drive D1-E1-F1
Madeira Place E1-E2
Marine Parade D1-E1-F1
Market Street C2-D2-D1
Marlborough Place D2-D3
Marlborough Street B2
Melville Road A4
Middle Street C1-C2
Montague Place F2
Montague Street F2
Montpelier Crescent A3-B3-B4
Montpelier Place A2
Montpelier Road A1-A2-A3
Montpelier Street A2-A3
Montpelier Terrace A2-B2
Montpelier Villas A2-A3
Montreal Road E4
Morley Street D3
Mount Pleasant E2-E3
New England Street C4
New Road C2
New Steine E1-E2
Newhaven Street D4-E4
Nizells Avenue A3
Norfolk Road A2
Norfolk Square A1-A2
Norfolk Terrace A2-A3
North Drive F4
North Gardens C3
North Road C3-D3
North Street C2-D2
Old Steine D1-D2
Oriental Place A1
Osmond Road A4
Over Street C3-C4
Park Hill E3-F3
Park Street F2-F3
Pavilion Parade D2
Pelham Square D4
Portland Street C2
Powis Road A3-B3
Powis Villas B3
Preston Street B1-B2
Prestonville Road A4-B4
Prince Albert Street C1-C2
Princes Street D2
Quebec Street E4
Queen Square C2
Queens Gardens C3
Queens Park Rise F4
Queens Park Road E3-E4-F4
Queens Park Terrace F4
Queens Road C2-C3-C4
Regency Square B1
Regent Hill B2
Regent Street C3
Richmond Parade D3
Richmond Street E3-E4
Rock Gardens E1-E2
Rock Place E1-E2
Russell Road B1-C1
Russell Square B2
St James' Avenue E2
St James Street D2-E2
St John's Place E3
St Luke's Road F4
St Luke's Terrace F4
St Michael's Place A3
St Nicholas Road B2-B3
St Peters Street C4
Scotland Street E4
Ship Street C1-C2
Sillwood Road A1-A2
Sillwood Street A1
Somerset Street F2
South Avenue F3
South Street C1
Southampton Street E4
Southover Street E4-F4
Spring Gardens C2-C3
Spring Street B2
Stanley Street E3
Station Street C4
Stone Street B2
Surrey Street C3-C4
Sussex Street E3
Sutherland Road F2
Sydney Street C3-C4
The Lanes C2
Tarner Road E3
Temple Gardens A3
Temple Street A2
Terminus Road B4-C4
Tichbourne Street C2-C3
Tilstone Street E2-F2-F3
Trafalgar Street C4-D4
Toronto Terrace E4-F4
Tower Road F4
Upper Bedford Street F2
Upper North Street B2
Upper Rock Gardens E2
Upper St James Street E2-F2
Vernon Terrace A3-A4-B4
Victoria Road A3-B3
Victoria Street B2-B3
Vine Place B3
West Drive E3-F3-F4
West Hill Place B4
West Hill Road B4
West Hill Street B4
West Street C1-C2
Western Road A2-B2-C2
Western Street A1
White Street E2-E3
William Street D2-D3
Windlesham Avenue A3
Windlesham Gardens A3-A4
Windlesham Road A3
Windmill Street E3
Windsor Street C2
York Avenue A2-A3
York Place D3-D4
York Road A2

HOVE

Adelaide Crescent B1-C1
Albany Villas B1
Aymer Road A1-A2
Blatchington Road A2-B2
Bishops Road B4
Brunswick Square C1
Byron Street B3
Cambridge Road C1-C2
Church Road A2-B2-B1
Clarendon Road A3-B3
Clarendon Villas A2
Coleridge Street A3
Compton Road C4
Conway Street A3-B3
Cowper Street A2
Cromwell Road B3-C3-C2
Davigdor Road C2-C3
Denmark Villas B2-B3
Dyke Road C3-C4
Eaton Gardens B2
Eaton Road B2
Eaton Villas B2
Ellen Street A3-B3
First Avenue B1
Fonthill Road A3-A4
Fourth Avenue B1
Furze Hill C2
George Street A2
Goldstone Crescent A4-B4-A4
Goldstone Road A2
Goldstone Street A2-A3
Goldstone Villas B2-B3
Grand Avenue B1
Highcroft Villas C4
Holland Road C1-C2
Hova Villas B2
Hove Park Road B4-C4
Hove Park Villas B3
Hove Park Way B4
Hove Street A1-A2
Kings Esplanade A1-B1-C1
Kingsway A1-B1-C1
Lansdowne Place C1-C2
Lansdowne Road C2
Leighton Road A3
Lloyd Road B4
Lorna Road B3-C3
Lyndhurst Road C3
Medha Villas A1
Millers Road C4
Montefiore Road C3
Montgomery Street A3
Nevill Road C4
Newton Road A3-B3
Norton Road B2
Old Shoreham Road A4-C3
Orchard Gardens A4
Orchard Road A4
Orpen Road C4
Osborne Villas A1-A2
Palmeira Avenue C2
Park View Road A4
Pembroke Avenue A2
Pembroke Crescent A2
Portland Road A2
Princess Avenue A1
Radinden Manor Road B3-C4
Reigate Road C4
Rigden Road B4
Sackville Road A2-A3
St Aubyns A1-A2
Salisbury Road B2
Seafield Road A1-A2
Second Avenue B1
Selborne Road B2
Shirley Drive B4
Shirley Road B3-B4
Shirley Street A2-A3
Somerhill Road C2
Station Approach B3
Stirling Place A2
The Drive B2-B3
The Drove C4
The Droveway B4-C4
The Martlet C4
The Upper Drive B3-C3-C4
Third Avenue B1
Tilsbury Road B2
Vallance Gardens A1
Vallance Road A1-A2
Ventnor Villas B2
Waterloo Street C1
Wilbury Avenue B3
Wilbury Gardens B3, B3-C3
Wilbury Road B2-B3
Wilbury Villas B3
York Road C1-C2

LEWES

Bell Lane A1
Bradford Road A2-A3
Brook Street B3
Brooks Road C3-C4
Chapel Hill C3
Cliffe High Street C3
Cockshut Road A1-B1
Eastport Lane B2
Fisher Street B3
Friars Walk C3
Garden Street B2
Grange Road A2-B2
Ham Lane B2-B1-C1-C2
High Street A2-B2-B3-C3
Keere Street A2-B2
King Henrys Road A3
Lancaster Street B3
Landport Road A4
Lansdowne Place B2-C2
Lewes Southern By-Pass A1-B1-C1
Little East Street B3
Malling Street C3-C4
Market Lane B3
Market Street B3
Morris Road C3
Mountfield Road B2-C2
Newton Road A3-A4
North Street B3-B4
Offham Road A3
Orchard Road C4
Paddock Lane A2
Paddock Road A2-A3-B3
Pelham Terrace A3-B3
Phoenix Causeway B3-C3
Prince Edwards Road A3
Priory Street B1-B2
Rotten Row A2
Rufus Close A3
St Nicholas Lane B2-B3
St Pancras Road A1-A2
School Hill B3-C3
South Street C3
Southover Road B2
Southover High Street A1-B1
Station Road B2
Station Street B2
The Avenue A3
The Course A1
Toronto Terrace A3-B3
Tunnel C3
Watergate Lane B2
West Street B3
White Hill A3-B3

HAYWARDS HEATH

Amberley Close A2
Augustines Way C2
Burrell Road A4
Bentswood Road C2-C3
Boltro Road A2-A3
Bramber Close A2
Caxton Way B1-C1-C2
Church Avenue B4
Church Road A2-B2
Clair Road B4
Climping Close A1
Courtlands B1
Culross Avenue A3-A4
Eastern Road C1
Fairbanks B2
Fairford Close B3-C3
Farlington Avenue C3-C4
Farlington Close B3-C3
Fields End Close C2
Franklynn Road B1-C1
Greenways C4
Gordon Road B4
Gower Road B1
Hazelgrove Road B1-B2
Harlands Road A4
Haywards Road B1-B2
Heath Road B3
Highland Court B2
Hightrees B2-B3
Kents Road C1
Lucasters Avenue A3
Market Place A4-B4
Mayflower Road C2
Mill Green Road B4
Mitton Road A4
Muster Green South A2
New England Road B2-C2-C3
Oathall Avenue C4
Oathall Road B2-B3-C3-C4
Oaklands Road A3
Oakwood Road A2
Paddockhall Road A2-A3
Park Road A1-B1
Pasture Hill Road A4
Perrymount Road B3-B4
Pineham Close C2
Priory Way C1-C2
Queens Road B4-C4
Ryecroft A1-B1
Sergison Road A3
Sharrow Close B2-B3
South Road A2-B2-B1
Sunnywood Drive A1
Sussex Road B1
Sussex Square B1
Sydney Road B4-C4
Syresham Gardens C1-C2
The Broadway A4-B4
Triangle Road B1-C1
Turners Mill Road A4
Wealden Way A1-A2
Western Road C1-C2
Windermere Road C2
Winnals Park A3-A4
Woodlands Road A2
Wood Ride A1
Wychperry Road A3

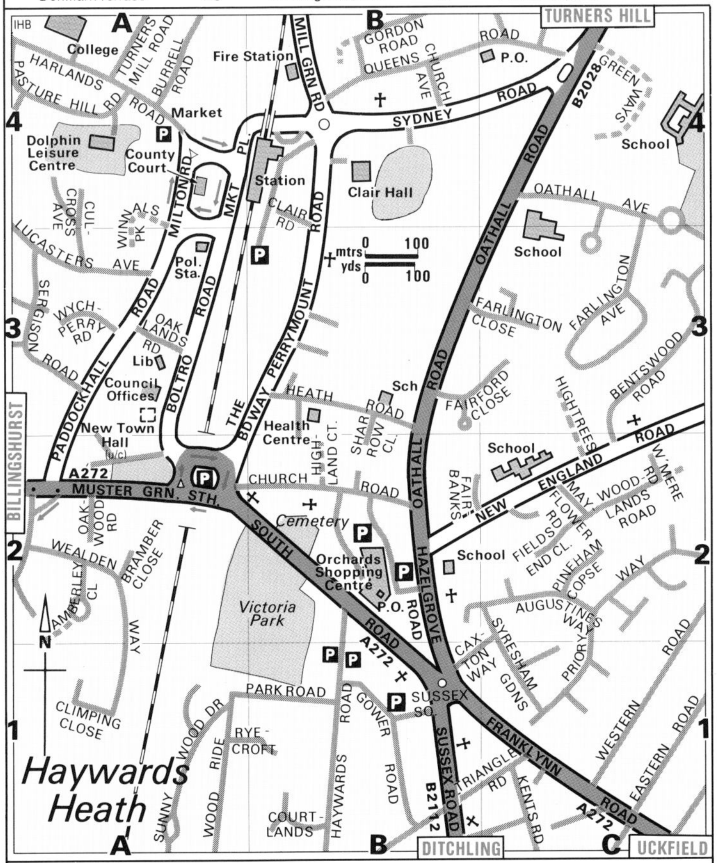

LEGEND

AA Recommended roads
Other roads
Restricted roads
One Way Streets
Buildings of interest
Churches
Car Parks
Parks and open spaces

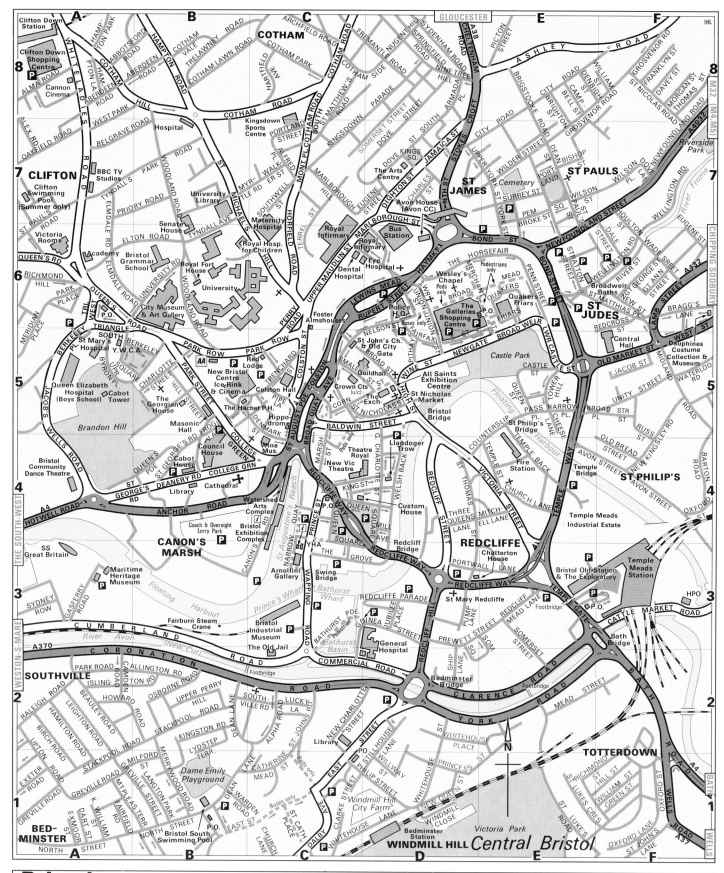

Bristol

One of Britain's most historic seaports, Bristol retains many of its visible links with the past, despite terrible damage inflicted during bombing raids in World War II. Most imposing is the cathedral, founded as an abbey church in 1140. Perhaps even more famous than the cathedral is the Church of St Mary Redcliffe. Ranking among the finest churches in the country, it owes much of its splendour to 14th- and 15th-century merchants who bestowed huge sums of money on it.

The merchant families brought wealth to the whole of Bristol, and their trading links with the world are continued in today's modern aerospace and technological industries. Much of the best of Bristol can be seen in the area of the Floating Harbour. Several of the old warehouses have been converted into museums, galleries and exhibition centres. Among them are genuinely picturesque old pubs, the best known which is the Llandoger Trow. It is a timbered 17th-century house, the finest of its kind in Bristol. Further up the same street - King Street - is the Theatre Royal, built in 1766 and the oldest theatre in the country. In Corn Street, the heart of the business area, is a magnificent 18th-century corn exchange. In front of it are the four pillars known as the 'nails', on which merchants used to make cash transactions, hence to 'pay on the nail';

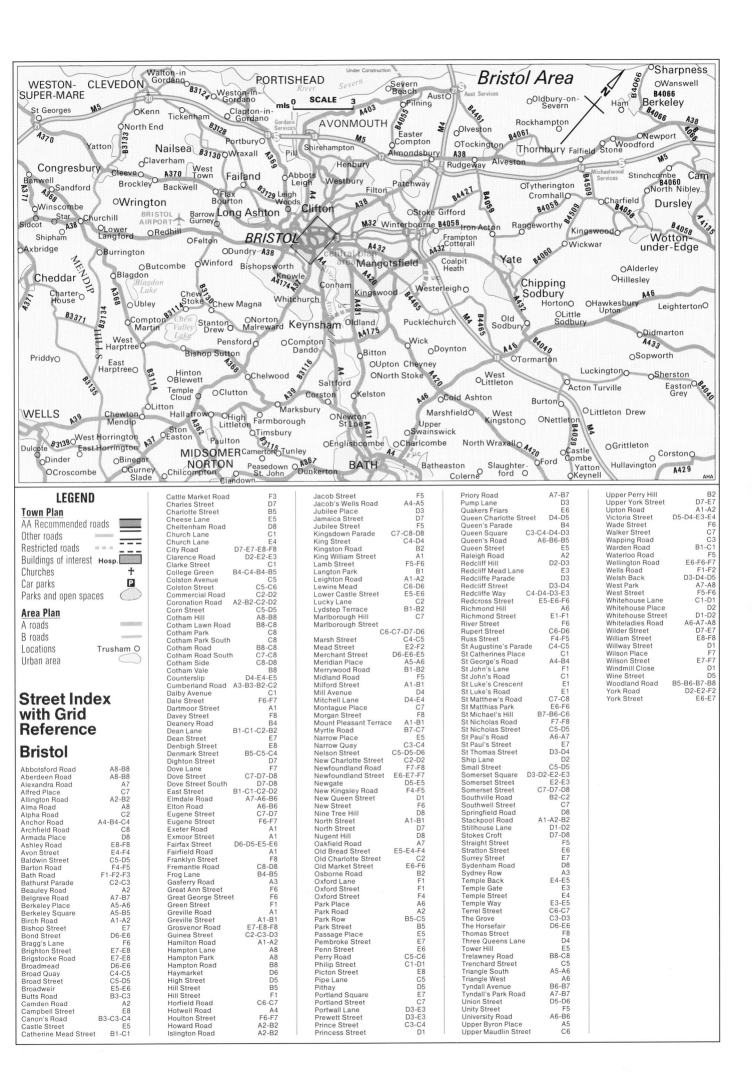

LEGEND

Town Plan

AA Recommended roads
Other roads
Restricted roads
Buildings of interest   Hosp.
Churches   +
Car parks   P
Parks and open spaces

Area Plan

A roads
B roads
Locations   Trusham O
Urban area

Street Index with Grid Reference

Bristol

Abbotsford Road	A8-B8
Aberdeen Road	A8-B8
Alexandra Road	A7
Alfred Place	C7
Allington Road	A2-B2
Alma Road	A8
Alpha Road	C2
Anchor Road	A4-B4-C4
Archfield Road	C8
Armada Place	D8
Ashley Road	E8-F8
Avon Street	E4-F4
Baldwin Street	C5-D5
Barton Road	F4-F5
Bath Road	F1-F2-F3
Bathurst Parade	C2-C3
Beauley Road	A2
Belgrave Road	A7-B7
Berkeley Place	A5-A6
Berkeley Square	A5-B5
Birch Road	A1-A2
Bishop Street	E7
Bond Street	D6-E6
Bragg's Lane	F6
Brighton Street	E7-E8
Brigstocke Road	E7-E8
Broadmead	D6-E6
Broad Quay	C4-C5
Broad Street	C5-D5
Broadweir	E5-E6
Butts Road	B3-C3
Camden Road	A2
Campbell Street	E8
Canon's Road	B3-C3-C4
Castle Street	E5
Catherine Mead Street	B1-C1
Cattle Market Road	F3
Charles Street	D7
Charlotte Street	B5
Cheese Lane	E5
Cheltenham Road	D8
Church Lane	C1
Church Lane	C1
City Road	D7-E7-E8-F8
Clarence Road	D2-E2-E3
Clarke Street	C1
College Green	B4-C4-B4-B5
Colston Avenue	C5
Colston Street	C5-C6
Commercial Road	C2-D2
Coronation Road	A2-B2-C2-D2
Corn Street	C5-D5
Cotham Hill	A8-B8
Cotham Lawn Road	B8-C8
Cotham Park	C8
Cotham Park South	C8
Cotham Road	B8-C8
Cotham Road South	C7-C8
Cotham Side	C8-D8
Cotham Vale	B8
Countership	D4-E4-E5
Cumberland Road	A3-B3-B2-C2
Dalby Avenue	C1
Dale Street	F6-F7
Dartmoor Street	A1
Davey Street	F8
Deanery Road	B4
Dean Lane	B1-C1-C2-B2
Dean Street	E7
Denbigh Street	E8
Denmark Street	B5-C5-C4
Dighton Street	D7
Dove Lane	E4
Dove Street	C7-D7-D8
Dove Street South	D7-D8
East Street	B1-C1-C2-D2
Elmdale Road	A7-A6-B6
Elton Road	A6-B6
Eugene Street	C7-D7
Eugene Street	F6-F7
Exeter Road	A1
Exmoor Street	A1
Fairfax Street	D6-D5-E5-E6
Fairfield Road	A1
Franklyn Street	F8
Fremantle Road	C8-D8
Frog Lane	B4-B5
Gasferry Road	A3
Great Ann Street	F6
Great George Street	F6
Green Street	A1
Greville Road	A1
Greville Road	A1-B1
Grosvenor Road	E7-E8-F8
Guinea Street	C2-C3-D3
Hamilton Road	A1-A2
Hampton Lane	A8
Hampton Park	A8
Hampton Road	B8
Haymarket	D6
High Street	D5
Hill Street	B5
Hill Street	B7
Horfield Road	C6-C7
Hotwell Road	A4
Houlton Street	F6-F7
Howard Road	A2-B2
Islington Road	A2-B2
Jacob Street	F5
Jacob's Wells Road	A4-A5
Jubilee Place	D3
Jamaica Street	D7
Jubilee Street	F5
Kingsdown Parade	C7-C8-D8
King Street	C4-D4
Kingston Road	B2
King William Street	A1
Lamb Street	F5-F6
Langton Park	B1
Leighton Road	A1-A2
Lewins Mead	C6-D6
Lower Castle Street	E5-E6
Lucky Lane	C2
Lydstep Terrace	B1-B2
Marlborough Hill	C7
Marlborough Street	C6-C7-D7-D6
Marsh Street	C4-C5
Mead Street	E2-F2
Merchant Street	D6-E6-E5
Meridian Place	A5-A6
Merrywood Road	B1-B2
Midland Road	F5
Milford Street	A1-B1
Mill Avenue	D4
Mitchell Lane	D4-E4
Montague Place	C7
Morgan Street	F8
Mount Pleasant Terrace	A1-B1
Myrtle Road	B7-C7
Narrow Place	E5
Narrow Quay	C3-C4
Nelson Street	C5-D5-D6
New Charlotte Street	C2-D2
Newfoundland Road	F7-F8
Newfoundland Street	E6-E7-F7
Newgate	D5-E5
New Kingsley Road	F4-F5
New Queen Street	D1
New Street	F6
Nine Tree Hill	D8
North Street	A1-B1
North Street	D7
Nugent Hill	D8
Oakfield Road	A7
Old Bread Street	E5-E4-F4
Old Charlotte Street	C2
Old Market Street	E6-F6
Osborne Road	B2
Oxford Lane	F1
Oxford Street	F1
Oxford Street	F4
Park Place	A6
Park Road	A2
Park Row	B5-C5
Park Street	B5
Passage Place	E5
Pembroke Street	E7
Penn Street	E6
Perry Road	C5-C6
Philip Street	C1-D1
Picton Street	E8
Pipe Lane	C5
Pithay	D5
Portland Square	E7
Portland Street	C7
Portwall Lane	D3-E3
Prewett Street	D3-E3
Prince Street	C3-C4
Princess Street	D1
Priory Road	A7-B7
Pump Lane	D3
Quakers Friars	E6
Queen Charlotte Street	D4-D5
Queen's Parade	B4
Queen Square	C3-C4-D4-D3
Queen's Road	A6-B6-B5
Queen Street	E5
Raleigh Road	A2
Redcliff Hill	D2-D3
Redcliff Mead Lane	E3
Redcliffe Parade	D3
Redcliff Street	D3-D4
Redcliffe Way	C4-D4-D3-E3
Redcross Street	E5-E6-F6
Richmond Hill	A6
Richmond Street	E1-F1
River Street	F6
Rupert Street	C6-D6
Russ Street	F4-F5
St Augustine's Parade	C4-C5
St Catherines Place	C1
St George's Road	A4-B4
St John's Lane	F1
St John's Road	C1
St Luke's Crescent	E1
St Luke's Road	E1
St Matthew's Lane	C7-C8
St Matthias Park	E6-F6
St Michael's Hill	B7-B6-C6
St Nicholas Road	F7-F8
St Nicholas Street	C5-D5
St Paul's Road	A6-A7
St Paul's Street	E7
St Thomas Street	D3-D4
Ship Lane	D2
Small Street	C5-D5
Somerset Square	D3-D2-E2-E3
Somerset Street	E2-E3
Somerset Street	C7-D7-D8
Southville Road	B2-C2
Southwell Street	C7
Springfield Road	D8
Stackpool Road	A1-A2-B2
Stillhouse Lane	D1-D2
Stokes Croft	D7-D8
Straight Street	F5
Stratton Street	E6
Surrey Street	E7
Sydenham Road	D8
Sydney Row	A3
Temple Back	E4-E5
Temple Gate	E3
Temple Street	E4
Temple Way	E3-E4
Terrel Street	C6-C7
The Grove	C3-D3
The Horsefair	D6-E6
Thomas Street	F8
Three Queens Lane	D4
Tower Hill	E5
Trelawney Road	B8-C8
Trenchard Street	C5
Triangle South	A5-A6
Triangle West	A6
Tyndall Avenue	B6-B7
Tyndall's Park Road	A7-B7
Union Street	D5-D6
Unity Street	F5
University Road	A6-B6
Upper Byron Place	A5
Upper Maudlin Street	C6
Upper Perry Hill	B2
Upper York Street	D7-E7
Upton Road	A1-A2
Victoria Street	D5-D4-E3-E4
Wade Street	F6
Walker Street	C7
Wapping Road	C3
Warden Road	B1-C1
Waterloo Road	F5
Wellington Road	E6-F6-F7
Wells Road	F1-F2
Welsh Back	D3-D4-D5
West Park	A7-A8
West Street	F5-F6
Whitehouse Lane	C1-D1
Whitehouse Place	D2
Whitehouse Street	D1-D2
Whiteladies Road	A6-A7-A8
Wilder Street	D7-E7
William Street	E8-F8
Willway Street	D1
Wilson Place	F7
Wilson Street	E7-F7
Windmill Close	D1
Wine Street	D5
Woodland Road	B5-B6-B7-B8
York Road	D2-E2-F2
York Street	E6-E7

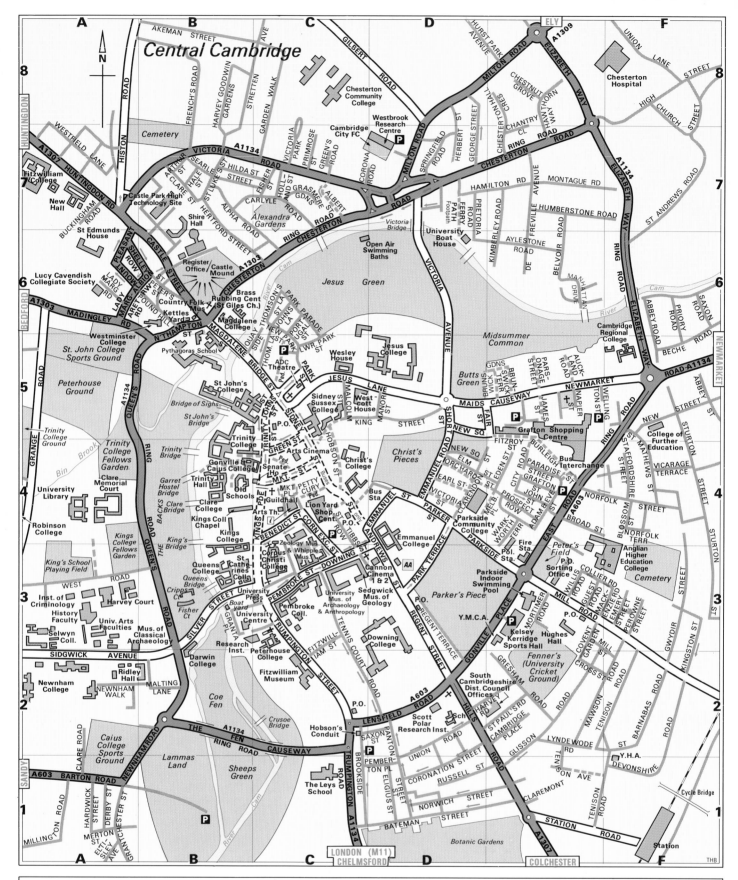

Cambridge

Few views in England, perhaps even in Europe, are as memorable as that from Cambridge's Backs towards the colleges. Dominating the scene, in every sense, is King's College Chapel. One of the finest Gothic buildings anywhere, it was built in three stages from 1446 to 1515.

No one would dispute that the chapel is Cambridge's masterpiece, but there are dozens of buildings here that would be the finest in any other town or city. Most are colleges, or are attached to colleges, and it is the university which permeates every aspect of Cambridge's landscape and life. In all there are 33 university colleges in the city, and nearly all have buildings and features of great interest. Guided tours of the colleges are available.

Cambridge can provide a complete history of English architecture. The oldest surviving building is the tower of St Benet's Church dating back to before the Norman Conquest, and its most famous church is the Church of the Holy Sepulchre, one of only four round churches of its kind.

Of the many notable museums in Cambridge, the Fitzwilliam Museum contains some of the best collections of ceramics, paintings, coins, medals and Egyptian, Greek and Roman antiquities outside London.

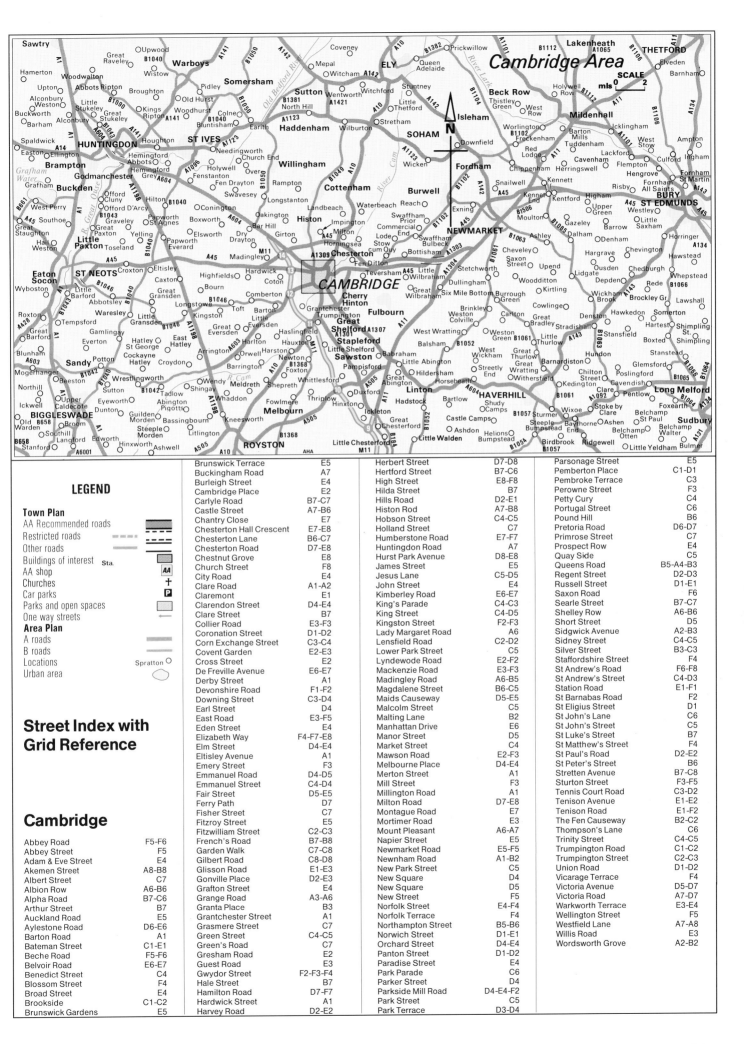

LEGEND

Town Plan

AA Recommended roads	
Restricted roads	
Other roads	
Buildings of interest	Sta.
AA shop	AA
Churches	†
Car parks	P
Parks and open spaces	
One way streets	←

Area Plan

A roads	
B roads	
Locations	Spratton
Urban area	

Street Index with Grid Reference

Cambridge

Abbey Road	F5-F6
Abbey Street	F5
Adam & Eve Street	E4
Akemen Street	A8-B8
Albert Street	C7
Albion Row	A6-B6
Alpha Road	B7-C6
Arthur Street	B7
Auckland Road	E5
Aylestone Road	D6-E6
Barton Road	A1
Bateman Street	C1-E1
Beche Road	F5-F6
Belvoir Road	E6-E7
Benedict Street	C4
Blossom Street	F4
Broad Street	E4
Brookside	C1-C2
Brunswick Gardens	E5

Brunswick Terrace	E5
Buckingham Road	A7
Burleigh Street	E4
Cambridge Place	E2
Carlyle Road	B7-C7
Castle Street	A7-B6
Chantry Close	E7
Chesterton Hall Crescent	E7-E8
Chesterton Lane	B6-C7
Chesterton Road	D7-E8
Chestnut Grove	E8
Church Street	F8
City Road	E4
Clare Road	A1-A2
Claremont	E1
Clarendon Street	D4-E4
Clare Street	B7
Collier Road	E3-F3
Coronation Street	D1-D2
Corn Exchange Street	C3-C4
Covent Garden	E2-E3
Cross Street	E2
De Freville Avenue	E6-E7
Derby Street	A1
Devonshire Road	F1-F2
Downing Street	C3-D4
Earl Street	D4
East Road	E3-F5
Eden Street	E4
Elizabeth Way	F4-F7-E8
Elm Street	D4-E4
Eltisley Avenue	A1
Emery Street	F3
Emmanuel Road	D4-D5
Emmanuel Street	C4-D4
Fair Street	D5-E5
Ferry Path	D7
Fisher Street	C7
Fitzroy Street	E5
Fitzwilliam Street	C2-C3
French's Road	B7-B8
Garden Walk	C7-C8
Gilbert Road	C8-D8
Glisson Road	E1-E3
Gonville Place	D2-E3
Grafton Street	E4
Grange Road	A3-A6
Granta Place	B3
Grantchester Street	A1
Grasmere Street	C7
Green Street	C4-C5
Green's Road	C7
Gresham Road	E2
Guest Road	E3
Gwydor Street	F2-F3-F4
Hale Street	B7
Hamilton Road	D7-F7
Hardwick Street	A1
Harvey Road	D2-E2

Herbert Street	D7-D8
Hertford Street	B7-C6
High Street	E8-F8
Hilda Street	B7
Hills Road	D2-E1
Histon Rod	A7-B8
Hobson Street	C4-C5
Holland Street	C7
Humberstone Road	E7-F7
Huntingdon Road	A7
Hurst Park Avenue	D8-E8
James Street	E5
Jesus Lane	C5-D5
John Street	E4
Kimberley Road	E6-E7
King's Parade	C4-C3
King Street	C4-D5
Kingston Street	F2-F3
Lady Margaret Road	A6
Lensfield Road	C2-D2
Lower Park Street	C5
Lyndewode Road	E2-F2
Mackenzie Road	E3-F3
Madingley Road	A6-B5
Magdalene Street	B6-C5
Maids Causeway	D5-E5
Malcolm Street	C5
Malting Lane	B2
Manhattan Drive	E6
Manor Street	D5
Market Street	C4
Mawson Road	E2-F3
Melbourne Place	D4-E4
Merton Street	A1
Mill Street	F3
Millington Road	A1
Milton Road	D7-E8
Montague Road	E7
Mortimer Road	E3
Mount Pleasant	A6-A7
Napier Street	E5
Newmarket Road	E5-F5
Newnham Road	A1-B2
New Park Street	C5
New Square	D4
New Square	D5
New Street	F5
Norfolk Street	E4-F4
Norfolk Terrace	F4
Northampton Street	B5-B6
Norwich Street	D1-E1
Orchard Street	D4-E4
Panton Street	D1-D2
Paradise Street	E4
Park Parade	C6
Parker Street	D4
Parkside Mill Road	D4-E4-F2
Park Street	C5
Park Terrace	D3-D4

Parsonage Street	E5
Pemberton Place	C1-D1
Pembroke Terrace	C3
Perowne Street	F3
Petty Cury	C4
Portugal Street	C6
Pound Hill	B6
Pretoria Road	D6-D7
Primrose Street	C7
Prospect Row	E4
Quay Side	C5
Queens Road	B5-A4-B3
Regent Street	D2-D3
Russell Street	D1-E1
Saxon Road	F6
Searle Street	B7-C7
Shelley Row	A6-B6
Short Street	D5
Sidgwick Avenue	A2-B3
Sidney Street	C4-C5
Silver Street	B3-C3
Staffordshire Street	F4
St Andrew's Road	F6-F8
St Andrew's Street	C4-D3
Station Road	E1-F1
St Barnabas Road	F2
St Eligius Street	D1
St John's Lane	C6
St John's Street	C5
St Luke's Street	B7
St Matthew's Street	F4
St Paul's Road	D2-E2
St Peter's Street	B6
Stretten Avenue	B7-C8
Sturton Street	F3-F5
Tennis Court Road	C3-D2
Tenison Avenue	E1-E2
Tenison Road	E1-F2
The Fen Causeway	B2-C2
Thompson's Lane	C6
Trinity Street	C4-C5
Trumpington Road	C1-C2
Trumpington Street	C2-C3
Union Road	D1-D2
Vicarage Terrace	F4
Victoria Avenue	D5-D7
Victoria Road	A7-D7
Warkworth Terrace	E3-E4
Wellington Street	F5
Westfield Lane	A7-A8
Willis Road	E3
Wordsworth Grove	A2-B2

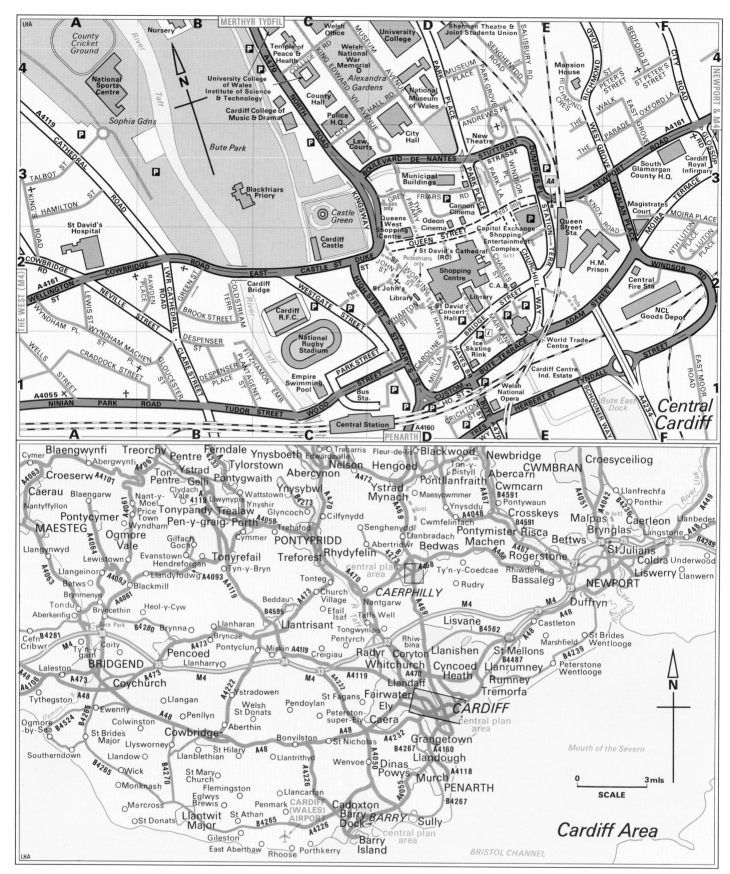

Cardiff

Once strategically important to both Romans and Normans, Cardiff declined to the level of a market town until transformed by the Industrial Revolution. Through the coal-mining and iron-making industries of the valleys it became a major export centre and by the end of the 19th-century was the world's largest coal-exporting port. Today it is a modern commercial, administrative and tourist centre, with new shopping precincts and a fine concert hall. Close to the famous castle, which contains features from the Roman period to the last century, is the Civic Centre, a fine range of early 20th-century buildings among which is the National Museum of Wales. In the docklands, an area of considerable redevelopment, is the Welsh Industrial and Maritime Museum, and at Llandaf the 13th-century cathedral contains the magnificent work "Christ in Majesty" by Epstein. Cardiff is also the home of Welsh rugby, with the National Stadium at Cardiff Arms Park while nearby is the Empire Swimming Pool.

Barry Like Cardiff, Barry grew as a result of the demands for coal and iron but now its dock complex is involved in the petro-chemical and oil industries. Nearby Barry Island, for decades a popular seaside resort for day-trippers, has a sandy beach, entertainment arcades and fun-fairs.

Caerphilly is famous for two things – its castle and cheese. The cheese is no longer made here but the massive 13th-century castle – slighted by Cromwell – still looms above its moat. No castle in Britain, with the exception of Windsor, is larger.

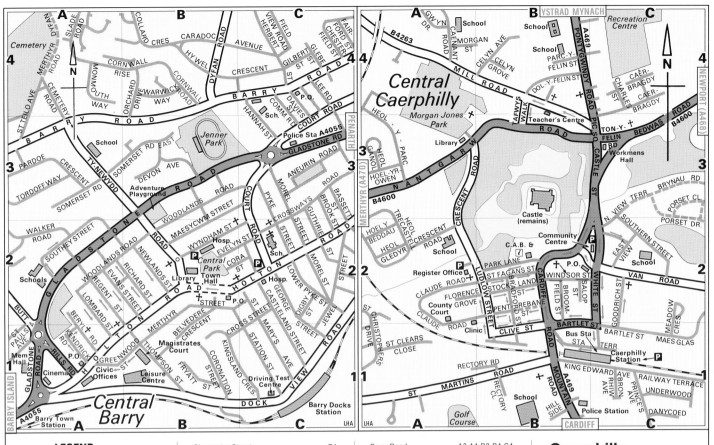

LEGEND

Town Plan

AA recommended route
Restricted roads
Other roads
Buildings of interest   Cinema 🔲
Car parks   🅿
Parks and open spaces
One way streets

Area Plan

A roads
B roads
Locations   Glyncoch ⭘
Urban area

Street Index with Grid Reference

Cardiff

Adam Street	E1-E2-F2
Bedford Street	F4
Boulevard de Nantes	C3-D3
Bridge Street	D1-D2-E2
Brook Street	B2
Bute Street	D1-E1
Bute Terrace	D1-E1
Caroline Street	D1
Castle Street	C2
Cathedral Street	A4-A3-B3-B2-A2
Charles Street	D2-E2
Churchill Way	E2-E3
City Hall Road	C3-C4-D4
City Road	F4
Clare Street	B1
Coldstream Terrace	B2
College Road	C4
Cowbridge Road	A2
Cowbridge Road East	A2-B2-C2
Craddock Street	A1-B1
Crichton Street	D1
Customhouse Street	D1
Despenser Place	B1
Despenser Street	B1
Duke Street	C2-D2
Dumfries Place	E3
East Grove	F4-F3
East Moor Road	F1
Fitzalan Place	F3-F2
Fitzhamon Embankment	B1-C1
Glossop Road	F3

Gloucester Street	B1
Green Street	B2
Greyfriars Road	D3
Hamilton Street	A3
Hayes Bridge Road	D1
Herbert Street	E1
High Street	C2-D2
King Edward VII Avenue	C4-D4-D3-C3
King's Road	A2-A3
Kingsway	C3-D3-D2
Knox Road	E3-F3-F2
Lewis Street	A2
Lower Cathedral Road	B1-B2
Machen Place	A1-B1
Mary Ann Street	E1-E2
Mill Lane	D1
Moira Place	F3
Moira Terrace	F2-F3
Museum Avenue	C4-D4
Museum Place	D4
Neville Street	A2-B2-B1
Newport Road	E3-F3-F4
Ninian Park Road	A1-B1
North Luton Place	F2-F3
North Road	B4-C4-C3
Oxford Lane	F4
Park Grove	D4-E4
Park Lane	D3-E3
Park Place	D4-D3-E3
Park Street	C1-D1
Plantagenet Street	B1-C1
Queen Street	D2-D3
Rawden Place	B2
Richmond Crescent	E4
Richmond Road	E4
St Andrew's Place	D4-E4
St John Street	D2
St Mary's Street	D1-D2
St Peter's Street	E4-F4
Salisbury Road	E4
Schooner Way	E1-F1
Senghenydd Road	D4-E4
South Luton Place	F2-F3
Station Terrace	E2-E3
Stuttgart Strasse	D3-E3
The Friary	D2-D3
The Hayes	D1-D2
The Parade	E3-F3-F4
The Walk	E3-E4-F4
Talbot Street	A3
Tresillian Way	D1
Tudor Street	B1-C1
Tyndall Street	E1-F1
Wellington Street	A2
Wells Street	A1
Westgate Street	C2-D2-D1
West Grove	E4-E3-F3
Wharton Street	D2
Windsor Place	E3
Windsor Road	F2
Wood Street	C1-D1
Working Street	D2
Wyndham Place	A2
Wyndham Street	A1-A2

Barry

Aneurin Road	C3
Barry Road	A3-A4-B3-B4-C4
Bassett Street	C2-C3
Belvedere Crescent	B1-B2
Beryl Road	A1-A2
Brook Street	C2-C3
Buttrills Road	A1-A2
Caradoc Avenue	B4-C4
Castleland Street	C1-C2
Cemetery Road	A3-A4
Chesterfield Street	C4
Collard Crescent	B4
Commercial Road	C3-C4
Cora Street	B2-C2
Cornwall Rise	A3-A4
Cornwall Road	B4
Coronation Street	B1
Cross Street	B1-C1-C2
Crossways Street	C2-C3
Court Road	C2-C3-C4
Davies Street	C3-C4
Devon Avenue	B3
Digby Street	C2
Dock View Road	B1-C1-C2
Dyfan Road	B4
Evans Street	A2-B2
Evelyn Street	B2-C2
Fairford Street	C4
Field View Road	C4
Fryatt Street	B1
George Street	C1-C2
Gilbert Street	C4
Gladstone Road	A1-A2-B2-B3-C3
Glebe Street	C4
Greenwood Street	A1-B1
Guthrie Street	C3-C2
Hannah Street	C4-C3
Herbert Street	C4
Holton Road	A1-B1-B2-C2
Hywell Crescent	B4-C4
Jewel Street	C1-C2
Kendrick Road	A1
Kingsland Crescent	B1-C1
Lee Road	C4
Lombard Street	A1-A2
Lower Pyke Street	C2
Maesycwm Street	B2-B3-C3
Merthyr Dyfan Road	A4
Merthyr Street	B1-B2-C2
Monmouth Way	A4
Morel Street	C2-C3
Newlands Street	B2
Orchard Drive	B3-B4
Pardoe Crescent	A3
Pyke Street	C3-C2
Regent Street	A2-B2
Richard Street	A2-B2
St Mary's Avenue	C1-C2
St Pauls Avenue	A1
St Teilo Avenue	A3-A4
Slade Road	A4
Somerset Road	A3
Somerset Road East	A3-B3
Southey Street	A2-A3
Station Street	C1
Thompson Street	B1
Tordoff Way	A3
Ty-Newydd Road	A3-B3-B2
Walker Road	A2
Warwick Way	B4
Woodlands Road	A2-B2-B3-C3
Wyndham Street	B2-C2

Caerphilly

Bartlet Street	B2-B1-C1
Bedwas Road	C3-C4
Bradford Street	B1-B2
Broomfield Street	B2
Bronrhiw Avenue	C1
Brynau Road	C3
Caenant Road	A4
Caer Bragdy	C4
Cardiff Road	B1-B2
Castle Street	C3
Celyn Avenue	B4
Celyn Grove	B4
Charles Street	C4
Claude Road	A1-A2-B2
Clive Street	B1-B2
Crescent Rod	A2-A3-B3
Danycoed	C1
Dol-y-Felen Street	B4
East View	C2
Florence Grove	A2-B2
Goodrich Street	C1-C2
Gwyn Drive	A4
Heol Ganol	A3
Heol Gledyr	A2
Heol-y-Beddau	A2
Hillside	B1
Heol	A2
Heol-yr-Owen	A3
King Edward Avenue	B1-C1
Ludlow Street	A2-B2-B1
Maes Glas	C1
Meadow Crescent	C1-C2
Mill Road	A4-B4-B3
Morgan Street	A4-B4
Mountain Road	B1
Nantgarw Road	A3-B3
North View Terrace	C2-C3
Parc-y-Felin Street	B4
Park Lane	B2
Pentrebone Street	B2
Piccadilly Square	C3
Pontygwindy Road	B4-C4
Porset Close	C3
Porset Drive	C2-C3
Prince's Avenue	C1
Railway Terrace	C1
Rectory Road	A1-B1
Rectory Close	B1
St Christopher's Drive	A1-A2
St Clears Close	A1
St Fagans Street	B2
St Martins Road	A1-B1
Salop Street	B2
Southern Street	C2-C3
Station Terrace	B1-C1
Stockland Street	B2
Tafwy Walk	B3-B4
Ton-y-Felin Road	C3
Underwood	C1
Van Road	C2
White Street	C2
Windsor Street	B2

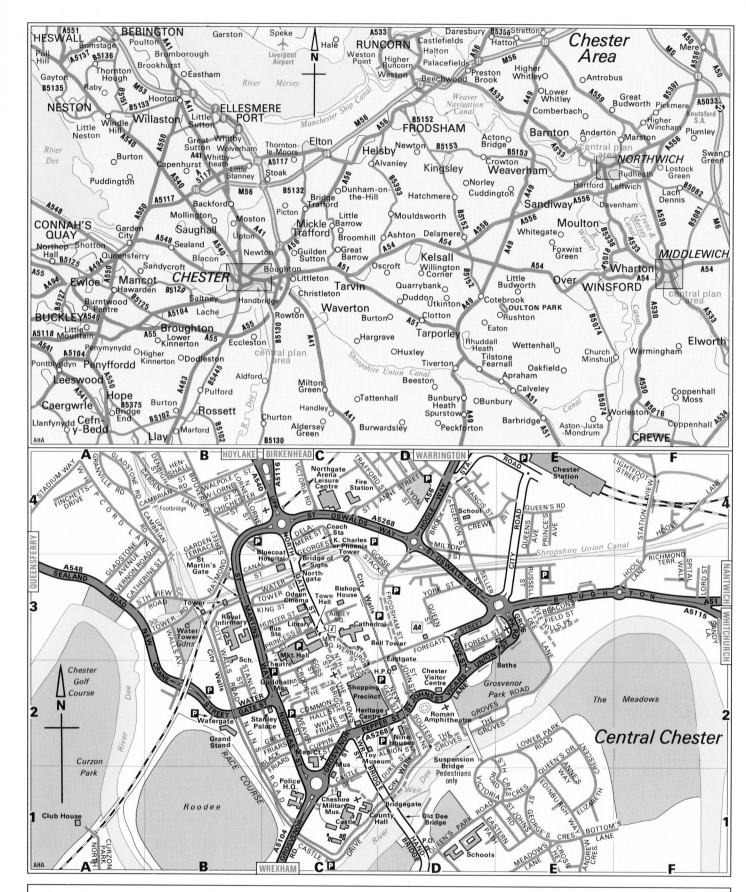

Chester

Chester is the only English city to have preserved the complete circuit of its Roman and medieval walls. On the west side, the top of the walls is now at pavement level, but on the other three sides the walk along the ramparts is remarkable. Two of the old watchtowers contain small museums: the Water Tower, built to protect the old river port, displays relics of medieval Chester; King Charles's

Tower, from which Charles I watched the defeat of the Royalist army at the Battle of Rowton Moor in 1645, portrays Chester's role in the Civil War.

Looking down from the top of the Eastgate, crowned with the ornate and gaily-coloured Jubilee Clock erected in 1897, the view down the main street, the old Roman *Via Principalis*, reveals a dazzling display of the black-and-white timbered buildings for which Chester is famous. One of these, Providence House, bears the inscription

'God's Providence is Mine Inheritance', carved in thanks for sparing the survivors of the plague of 1647 that ravaged the city.

On either side of Eastgate, Watergate and Bridge Street are the Rows, a feature unique to Chester, and dating back at least to the 13th century. These covered galleries of shops, raised up at first-floor level, protected pedestrians from weather and traffic. Chester's magnificent cathedral has beautifully carved choir stalls.

208

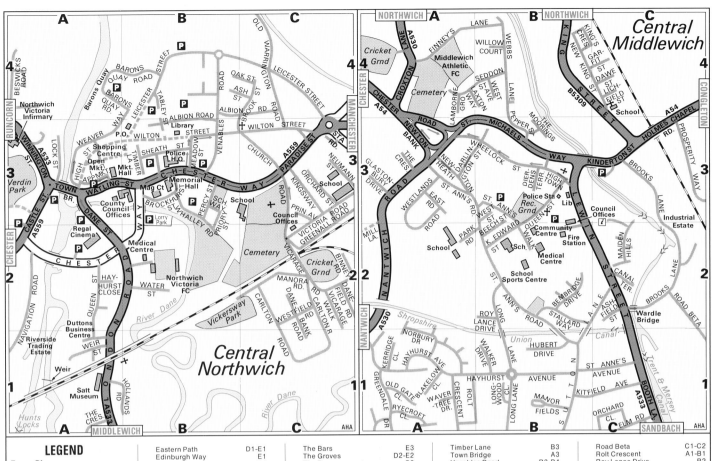

LEGEND

Town Plan

AA Recommended roads
Other roads
Restricted roads
Buildings of interest   Hall
Churches   †
Car parks   P
Parks and open spaces
One way streets   ←

Area Plan

A roads
B roads
Locations   Palacefields ○
Urban area

Street Index with Grid Reference

Chester

Abbey Square	C3
Albion Street	D2
Andrews Crescent	E1
Anne's Way	E2-E1
Beaconsfield Street	E3
Black Friars	C1-C2
Bottom's Lane	E1-F1
Boughton	E3-F3
Bouverie Street	B4
Bridge Street	C2
Brook Street	D4
Cambrian Road	A4-B4
Canal Street	B3-C3
Castle Drive	C1
Castle Street	C1
Catherine Street	A3-B3
Chichester Street	B4-C4
City Road	E3-E4
City Walls Road	B3-B2
Commonhall Street	C2
Crewe Street	D4-E4
Crook Street	C2
Cross Heys	E1
Cuppin Street	C2
Curzon Park North	A1
Dee Hills Park	E3
Dee Lane	E3
Delamere Street	C4
Denbigh Street	B4
Duke Street	D1-D2
Eastern Path	D1-E1
Edinburgh Way	E1
Egerton Street	D4
Elizabeth Crescent	E1-E2
Finchetts Drive	A4
Foregate Street	D3
Forest Street	D3-E3
Francis Street	D4
Frodsham Street	D3
Garden Lane	A4-B4
Garden Terrace	B3-B4
George Street	C3-C4
Gladstone Avenue	A3-A4
Gladstone Road	A4
Gorse Stacks	C4-C3-D3
Goss Street	C2
Granville Road	A4
Grey Friars	C2
Grosvenor Park Road	E3
Grosvenor Road	C1
Grosvenor Street	C1-C2
Groves Road	D2-E2
Handbridge	D1
Henshall Street	B4
Hoole Lane	F3-F4
Hoole Way	D4
Hunter Street	B3-C3
King Street	B3-C3
Lightfoot Street	E4-F4
Lord Street	F3
Lorne Street	D4
Lower Bridge Street	C2-C1-D1
Lower Park Road	D2-E2
Love Street	D3
Lyon Street	D4
Meadows Lane	E1
Milton Street	D4
New Crane Street	A3-B3-B2
Newgate Street	D2
Nicholas Street	C2-C1
Northgate Street	C3-C2
North Lorne Street	B4
Nuns Road	B2-B1-C1
Pepper Street	C2-C1
Princess Street	C3
Prince's Avenue	E4
Queens Avenue	E4
Queen's Drive	E1-E2
Queen's Park Road	D1-E1
Queen's Road	E4
Queen Street	D3
Raymond Street	B3-B4
Richmond Terrace	F4
Russell Street	E3
St Anne Street	C4-D4
St Georges Crescent	E1
St Johns Road	E1
St Johns Street	D2
St John Street	D3-D2
St Martins Way	B4-B3-C3-B2-C2
St Oswalds Way	C4-D4-D3
St Werburgh Street	C3
Sealand Road	A3
Sellier Street	D3
Souters Lane	D2
South Crescent Road	D2-E2-E1
South View Road	A3-B3
Spittal Walk	F4-F3
Stadium Way	A4
Stanley Street	B2
Station Road	D4-E4
Station View	F4

The Bars	E3
The Groves	D2-E2
The Rows	C2
Tower Road	B3
Trafford Street	C4-D4
Union Street	D2-D3-E3
Upper Cambrian Road	A4-B4-B3
Upper Northgate Street	
	B4-C4-C3
Vernon Road	A3-B3-B4
Vicars Lane	D2
Victoria Crescent	D1-E1
Victoria Path	D1-E1
Victoria's Road	C4
Walls Avenue	B3-B2
Walpole Street	B4
Watergate Street	B2-C2
Water Tower Street	B3-C3
Weaver Street	C2
West Lorne Street	B4
White Friars	C2
Whipcord Lane	A4-B4
York Street	D3

Northwich

Albion Road	B3
Apple Market	A3
Ash Street	B4-C4
Barons Quay Road	A4-B4
Beswicks Road	A4
Binney Road	C2
Brockhurst Street	B3
Brook Street	B3-C3-C4
Carlton Road	C2-C1
Castle Street	A2-A3
Chester Way	A2-B2-B3-C3
Church Road	C3
Danebank Road	C2-C1
Danefield Road	C2
Dane Street	A3-A2
Greenall Road	C2-C3
Hayhurst Close	A2
High Street	A3
Hollands Road	A1-B1
Kingsway	C3
Leicester Street	B3-B4
Lock Street	A3
London Road	A1-A2-B2
Manora Road	C2
Meadow Street	B3
Navigation Road	A1-A2
Neumann Street	C3
Oak Street	B4-C4
Old Warrington Road	C4-C3
Orchard Street	C3
Paradise Street	C3
Percy Street	B3
Post Office Place	C3
Princes Avenue	C3
Priory Street	B2-B3
Queen Street	A2
School Way	B3
Sheath Street	B3
Station Road	C3
The Crescent	A1
Tabley Street	B4-B3

Timber Lane	B3
Town Bridge	A3
Venables Road	B3-B4
Vicarage Road	C2
Vicarage Walk	C2
Victoria Road	C2-C3
Water Street	B2
Watling Street	A3-B3
Weaver Way	A3-B3-B4
Weir Street	A1
Wesley Place	C3
Westfield Road	C2
Whalley Road	B3-B2
Winnington Street	A3
Witton Street	B3-C3

Middlewich

Ashfield Street	C2
Beech Street	B2-B3
Bembridge Drive	B2
Beta Road	C2-C1
Blakelow Close	A1
Booth Lane	C1
Brooks Lane	C3-C2
Canal Terrace	C2
Chester Road	A4-A3
Croxton Lane	A4
Darlington Street	A3-B3
Dawe Street	C4
Dierdene Terrace	B3
East Road	A3
Elm Road	C1
Finney's Lane	A4-B4
Garfit Street	B4-C4
Greendale Drive	A1
Glastonbury Drive	A3
Hauhurst Avenue	A1-B1
High Town	B3
Holmes Chapel Road	C3-C4
Hubert Drive	B1
Kerridge Close	A1
Kinderton Street	B3-C3
King Edward Street	B2
King's Crescent	B4-C4
King Street	B4-C4
Kittfield Avenue	B1-C1
Lamborne Grove	A4
Laxton Way	A4
Lewin Street	B3-B2-C2-C1
Lichfield Street	C4
Long Lane	B1
Longwood Close	B2
Maidon-Hills	C2
Manor Fields	B1
Mill Lane	A2
Nantwich Road	A1-A2-A3
New King Street	B4-C4
Newton Bank	A4-A3
Newton Heath	A3
Norbury Drive	A1-A2
Old Gate Close	A1
Orchard Close	C1
Park Road	A2-B2
Pepper Street	B4-B3
Prosperity Way	C3
Queen Street	B2-B3

Road Beta	C1-C2
Rolt Crescent	A1-B1
Roy Lance Drive	B2
Ryecroft Close	A1
St Anne's Avenue	B1-C1
St Ann's Road	A3-B3-B2-B1
St Ann's Walk	B2-B3
St Michaels Way	A3-B3
Seddon Street	B4
Southway	B3
Stallard Way	B2
Sutton Lane	B1-B2-C2
The Crescent	A3
The Moorings	B3
Walker Drive	B1
Wavertree Drive	A1
Webbs Lane	B4
West Avenue	B4
Westlands Road	A3-A2
West Street	B3
Wheelock Street	A3-B3
Willow Court	B4
Wych House Lane	B3-C3

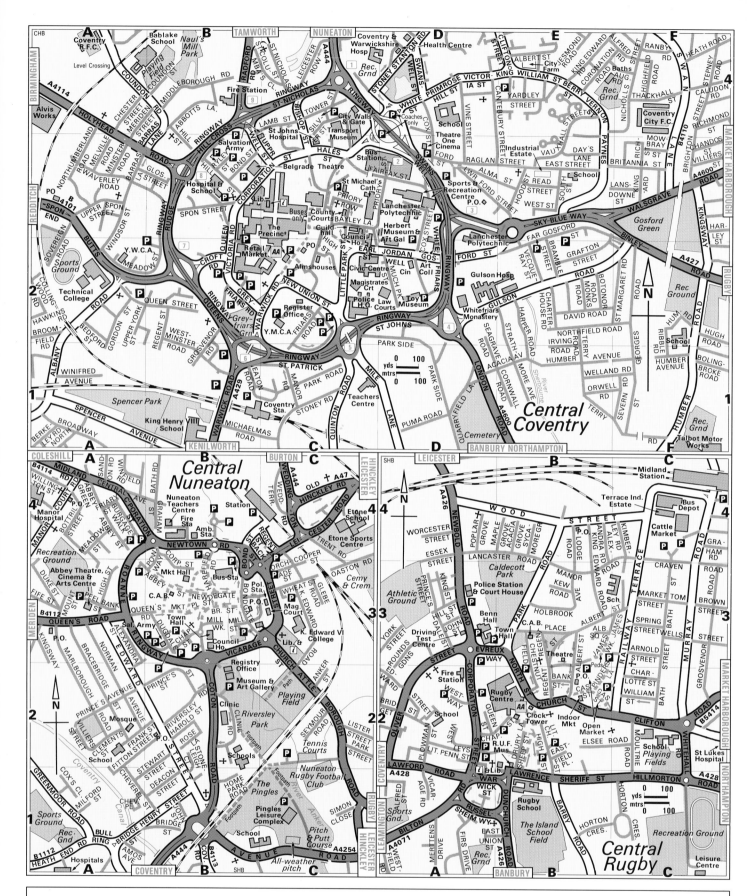

Coventry

Few British towns were as battered by the Blitz as Coventry. A raid in November 1940 flattened most of the city and left the lovely cathedral church a gaunt shell with only the tower and spire still standing. Rebuilding started almost immediately. Symbolising the creation of the new from the ashes of the old is Sir Basil Spence's cathedral, completed in 1962 beside the bombed ruins.

A few medieval buildings have survived intact in the city. St Mary's Guildhall is a finely restored 14th-century building with an attractive minstrels' gallery. Whitefriars Monastery now serves as a local museum. The Herbert Art Gallery and Museum has several collections. Coventry is an important manufacturing centre – most notably for cars – and it is also a university city with the fine campus of the University of Warwick some four miles from the centre.

Nuneaton is an industrial town to the north of Coventry with two distinguished old churches – St Nicholas' and St Mary's. Like Coventry it was badly damaged in the war and its centre has been rebuilt.

Rugby was no more than a sleepy market town until the arrival of the railway. Of course it did have the famous Rugby School, founded in 1567 and one of the country's foremost educational establishments. The railway brought industry – still the town's mainstay.

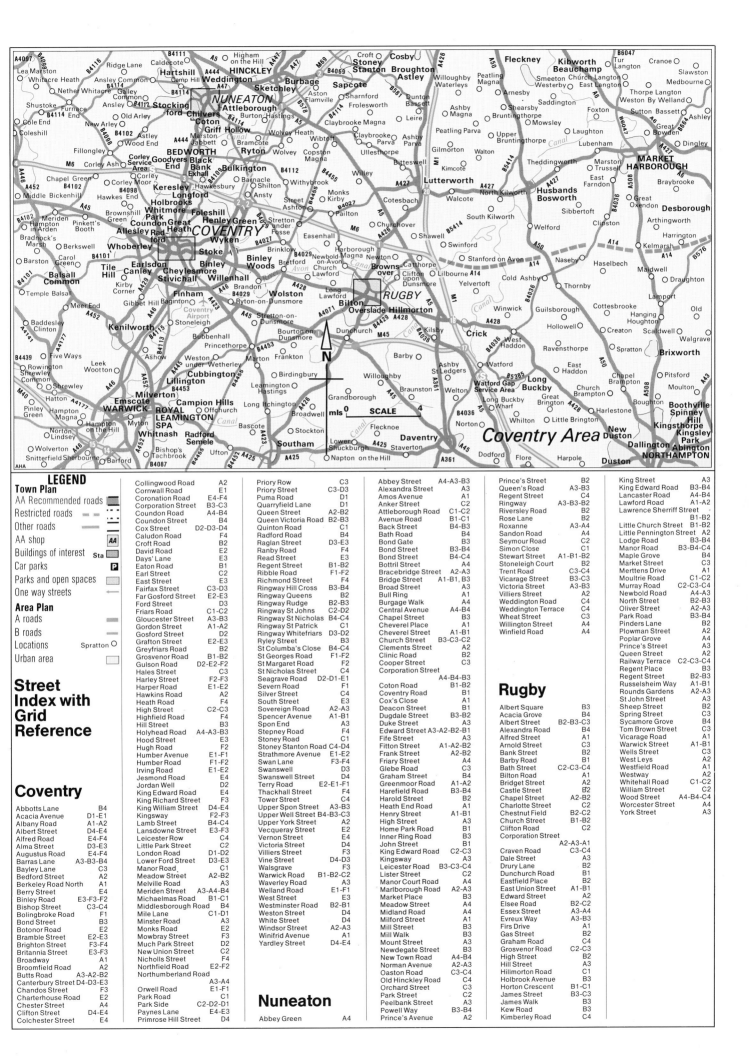

LEGEND

Town Plan
AA Recommended roads
Restricted roads
Other roads
AA shop **AA**
Buildings of interest **Sta**
Car parks **P**
Parks and open spaces
One way streets

Area Plan
A roads
B roads
Locations Spratton ○
Urban area

Street Index with Grid Reference

Coventry

Abbotts Lane	B4
Acacia Avenue	D1-E1
Albany Road	A1-A2
Albert Street	D4-E4
Alfred Road	E4-F4
Alma Street	D3-E3
Augustus Road	E4-F4
Barras Lane	A3-B3-B4
Bayley Lane	C3
Bedford Street	A2
Berkeley Road North	A1
Berry Street	E4
Binley Road	E3-F3-F2
Bishop Street	C3-C4
Bolingbroke Road	F1
Bond Street	B3
Botonor Road	E2
Bramble Street	E2-E3
Brighton Street	F3-F4
Britannia Street	E3-F3
Broadway	A1
Broomfield Road	A2
Butts Road	A3-A2-B2
Canterbury Street	D4-D3-E3
Chandos Street	F3
Charterhouse Road	E2
Chester Street	A4
Clifton Street	D4-E4
Colchester Street	E4
Collingwood Road	A2
Cornwall Road	E1
Coronation Road	E4-F4
Corporation Street	B3-C3
Coundon Road	A4-B4
Coundon Street	B4
Cox Street	D2-D3-D4
Caludon Road	F4
Croft Road	B2
David Road	E2
Days' Lane	E3
Eaton Road	B1
Earl Street	C2
East Street	E3
Fairfax Street	C3-D3
Far Gosford Street	E2-E3
Ford Street	D3
Friars Road	C1-C2
Gloucester Street	A3-B3
Gordon Street	A1-A2
Gosford Street	D2
Grafton Street	E2-E3
Greyfriars Road	B2
Grosvenor Road	B1-B2
Gulson Road	D2-E2-F2
Hales Street	C3
Harley Street	F2-F3
Harper Road	E1-E2
Hawkins Road	A2
Heath Road	F4
High Street	C2-C3
Highfield Road	F4
Hill Street	B4
Holyhead Road	A4-A3-B3
Hood Street	E3
Hugh Road	F2
Humber Avenue	E1-F1
Humber Road	F1-F2
Irving Road	E1-E2
Jesmond Road	E4
Jordan Well	D2
King Edward Road	E4
King Richard Street	F3
King William Street	D4-E4
Kingsway	F2-F3
Lamb Street	B4-C4
Lansdowne Street	E3-F3
Leicester Row	C4
Little Park Street	C2
London Road	D1-D2
Lower Ford Street	D3-E3
Manor Road	C1
Meadow Street	A2-B2
Melville Road	A3
Meriden Street	A3-A4-B4
Michaelmas Road	B1-C1
Middlesborough Road	B4
Mile Lane	C1-D1
Minster Road	A4
Monks Road	E2
Mowbray Street	F3
Much Park Street	D2
New Union Street	C2
Nicholls Street	F4
Northfield Road	E2-F2
Northumberland Road	A3-A4
Orwell Road	E1-F1
Park Road	C1
Park Side	C2-D2-D1
Paynes Lane	E4-E3
Primrose Hill Street	D4
Priory Row	C3
Priory Street	C3-D3
Puma Road	D1
Quarryfield Lane	D1
Queen Street	A2-B2
Queen Victoria Road	B2-B3
Quinton Road	C1
Radford Road	B4
Raglan Street	D3-E3
Ranby Road	F4
Read Street	E3
Regent Street	B1-B2
Ribble Road	F1-F2
Richmond Street	F4
Ringway Hill Cross	B3-B4
Ringway Queens	B2
Ringway Rudge	B2-B3
Ringway St Johns	C2-D2
Ringway St Nicholas	B4-C4
Ringway St Patrick	C1
Ringway Whitefriars	D3-D2
Ryley Street	B3
St Columba's Close	B4-C4
St Georges Road	F1-F2
St Margaret Road	F2
St Nicholas Street	C4
Seagrave Road	D2-D1-E1
Severn Road	F1
Silver Street	C4
South Street	E3
Sovereign Road	A2-A3
Spencer Avenue	A1-B1
Spon End	A3
Stepney Road	E3
Stoney Road	C1
Stoney Stanton Road	C4-D4
Strathmore Avenue	E1-E2
Swan Lane	F3-F4
Swanswell	D3
Swanswell Street	C4
Terry Road	E2-E1-F1
Thackhall Street	E4
Tower Street	C4
Upper Spon Street	A3-B3
Upper Well Street	B4-B3-C3
Upper York Street	A3
Vecqueray Street	E2
Vernon Street	E4
Victoria Street	D4
Villiers Street	F3
Vine Street	D4-D3
Walsgrave	F3
Warwick Road	B1-B2-C2
Waverley Road	A3
Welland Road	E1-F1
West Street	E3
Westminster Road	B2-B1
Weston Street	D4
White Street	D4
Windsor Street	A2-A3
Winifred Avenue	A1
Yardley Street	D4-E4

Nuneaton

Abbey Green	A4
Abbey Street	A4-A3-B3
Alexandra Street	A3
Amos Avenue	A1
Anker Street	C2
Attleborough Road	C1-C2
Avenue Road	B1-C1
Back Street	B4-B3
Bath Road	B4
Bond Gate	B3
Bond Street	B3-B4
Bond Street	B4-C4
Bottril Street	A4
Bracebridge Street	A2-A3
Bridge Street	A1-B1, B3
Broad Street	A3
Bull Ring	A1
Burgage Walk	A4
Central Avenue	A4-B4
Chapel Street	B3
Cheverel Place	A1
Cheverel Street	A1-B1
Church Street	B3-C3-C2
Clements Street	A2
Clinic Road	B2
Cooper Street	C3
Corporation Street	A4-B4-B3
Coton Road	B1-B2
Coventry Road	B1
Cox's Close	A1
Deacon Street	B1
Dugdale Street	B3-B2
Duke Street	A3
Edward Street	A3-A2-B2-B1
Fife Street	A1-A2-B2
Fitton Street	A1-A2-B2
Frank Street	A2-B2
Friary Street	A4
Glebe Road	C3
Graham Street	B4
Greenmoor Road	A1-A2
Harefield Road	B3-B4
Harold Street	B2
Heath End Road	A1
Henry Street	A1-B1
High Street	A3
Home Park Road	B1
Inner Ring Road	B3
John Street	B1
King Edward Road	C2-C3
Kingsway	A3
Leicester Road	B3-C3-C4
Lister Street	C2
Manor Court Road	A4
Marlborough Road	A2-A3
Market Place	B3
Meadow Street	A4
Midland Road	A4
Milford Street	A3
Mill Street	B3
Mill Walk	B3
Mount Street	A3
Newdegate Street	A3
New Town Road	A4-B4
Norman Avenue	A2-A3
Oaston Road	C3-C4
Old Hinckley Road	C4
Orchard Street	C3
Park Street	C2
Peelbank Street	C2
Powell Way	B3-B4
Prince's Avenue	A2
Prince's Street	B2
Queen's Road	A3-B3
Regent Street	C4
Ringway	A3-B3-B2
Riversley Road	B2
Rose Lane	B2
Roxanne	A3-A4
Sandon Road	A4
Seymour Road	C2
Simon Close	C1
Stewart Street	A1-B1-B2
Stoneleigh Court	B2
Trent Road	C3-C4
Vicarage Street	B3-C3
Victoria Street	A3-B3
Villiers Street	A2
Weddington Road	C4
Weddington Terrace	C4
Wheat Street	C3
Willington Street	A4
Winfield Road	A4

Rugby

Albert Square	B3
Acacia Grove	B4
Albert Street	B2-B3-C3
Alexandra Road	B4
Alfred Street	A1
Arnold Street	C3
Bank Street	B2
Barby Road	B1
Bath Street	C2-C3-C4
Bilton Road	A1
Bridget Street	A2
Castle Street	B2
Chapel Street	A2-B2
Charlotte Street	C2
Chestnut Field	B2-C2
Church Street	B1-B2
Clifton Road	C2
Corporation Street	A2-A3-A1
Craven Road	C3-C4
Dale Street	A3
Drury Lane	B2
Dunchurch Road	B1
Eastfield Place	B2
East Union Street	A1-B1
Edward Street	A2
Elsee Road	B2-C2
Essex Street	A3-A4
Evreux Way	A3-B3
Firs Drive	A1
Gas Street	B2
Graham Road	C4
Grosvenor Road	C2-C3
High Street	B2
Hill Street	A3
Hillmorton Road	C1
Holbrook Avenue	B3
Horton Crescent	B1-C1
James Street	B3-C3
James Walk	B3
Kew Road	B3
Kimberley Road	C4
King Street	A3
King Edward Road	B3-B4
Lancaster Road	A4-B4
Lawford Road	A1-A2
Lawrence Sherriff Street	B1-B2
Little Church Street	B1-B2
Little Pennington Street	A2
Lodge Road	B3-B4
Manor Road	B3-B4-C4
Maple Grove	B4
Market Street	C3
Merttens Drive	A1
Moultrie Road	C1-C2
Murray Road	C2-C3-C4
Newbold Road	A4-A3
North Street	B2-B3
Oliver Street	A2-A3
Park Road	B3-B4
Pinders Lane	B2
Plowman Street	A2
Poplar Grove	A4
Prince's Street	A3
Queen Street	B2
Railway Terrace	C2-C3-C4
Regent Place	B3
Regent Street	B2-B3
Russelsheim Way	A1-B1
Rounds Gardens	A2-A3
St John Street	A3
Sheep Street	B2
Spring Street	C3
Sycamore Grove	B4
Tom Brown Street	C3
Vicarage Road	A1
Warwick Street	A1-B1
Wells Street	C3
West Leys	A2
Westfield Road	A1
Westway	A2
Whitehall Road	C1-C2
William Street	C2
Wood Street	A4-B4-C4
Worcester Street	A4
York Street	A3

211

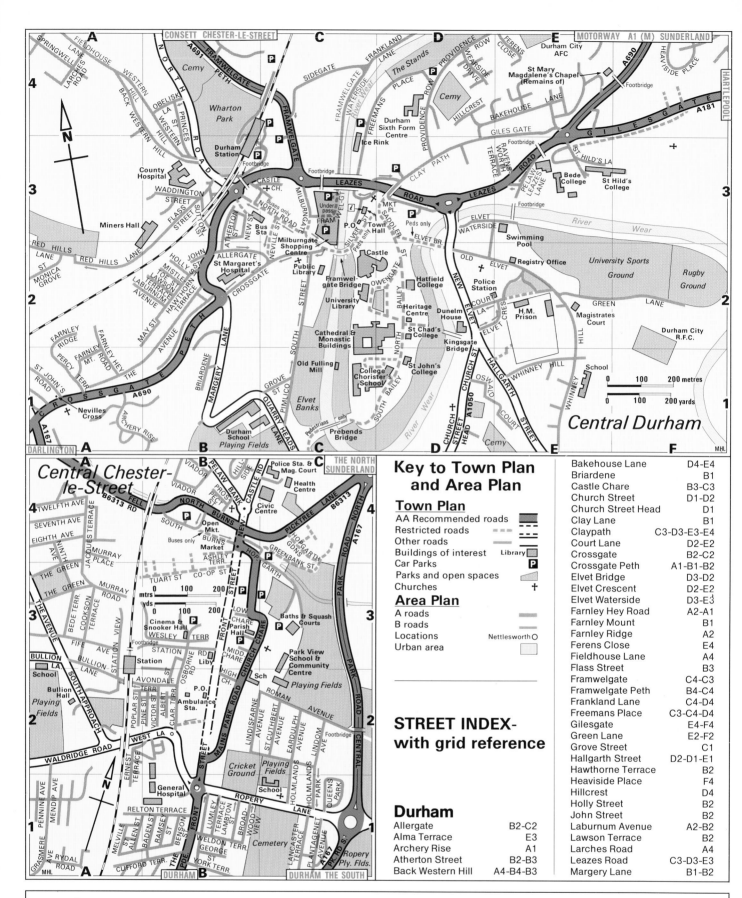

Key to Town Plan and Area Plan

Town Plan

AA Recommended roads	
Restricted roads	
Other roads	
Buildings of interest	Library
Car Parks	P
Parks and open spaces	
Churches	+

Area Plan

A roads	
B roads	
Locations	Nettlesworth ○
Urban area	

STREET INDEX- with grid reference

Durham

Durham

The castle and the cathedral stand side by side high above the city like sentinels, dramatically symbolising the military and religious power Durham wielded in the past. Its origins date from about 995 when the remains of St Cuthbert arrived from Lindisfarne and his shrine was a popular centre of pilgrimage. Soon after that early fortifications were built, later replaced by a stone castle which became the residence of the Prince-Bishops of Durham – powerful feudal rulers appointed by the King. Today the city's university, the oldest in England after Oxford and Cambridge, occupies the castle and most of the buildings around peaceful, secluded Palace Green. The splendid Norman cathedral, sited on the other side of the Green, is considered to be one of the finest in Europe. Its combination of strength and size, tempered with grace and beauty, is awe-inspiring.

Under the shadow of these giants the old city streets, known as vennels, ramble down the bluff past the 17th-century Bishop Cosin's House and the old grammar school, to the thickly-wooded banks of the Wear. Here three historic bridges link the city's heart with the pleasant Georgian suburbs on the other side of the river.

Although Durham is not an industrial city, it has become the venue for the North-East miners' annual Gala Day in July.

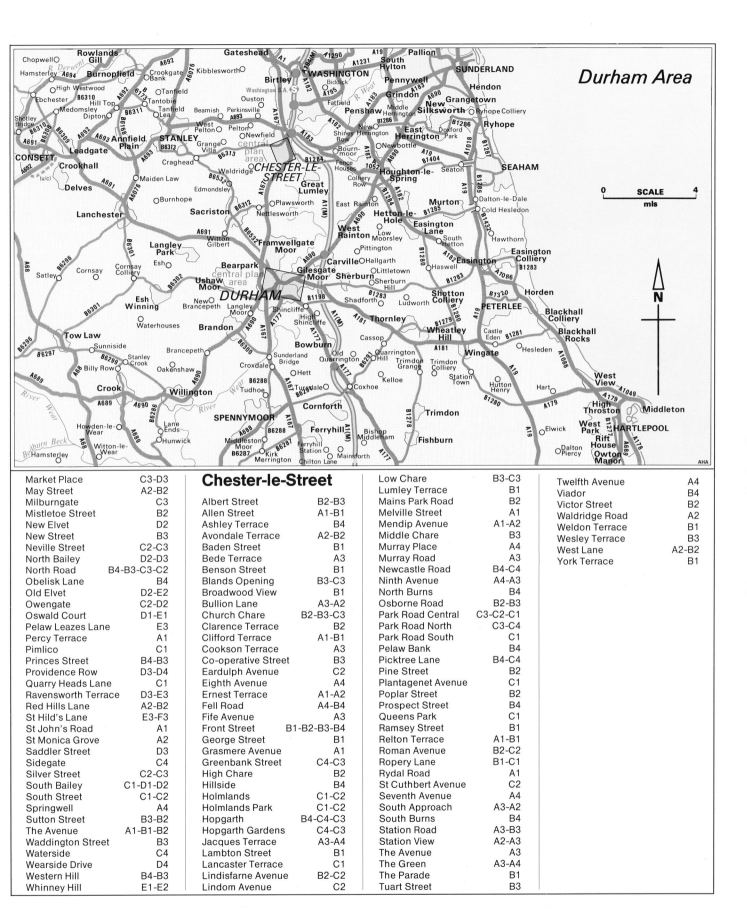

Durham Area

SCALE 0 — 4 mls

Chester-le-Street

Market Place	C3-D3
May Street	A2-B2
Milburngate	C3
Mistletoe Street	B2
New Elvet	D2
New Street	B3
Neville Street	C2-C3
North Bailey	D2-D3
North Road	B4-B3-C3-C2
Obelisk Lane	B4
Old Elvet	D2-E2
Owengate	C2-D2
Oswald Court	D1-E1
Pelaw Leazes Lane	E3
Percy Terrace	A1
Pimlico	C1
Princes Street	B4-B3
Providence Row	D3-D4
Quarry Heads Lane	C1
Ravensworth Terrace	D3-E3
Red Hills Lane	A2-B2
St Hild's Lane	E3-F3
St John's Road	A1
St Monica Grove	A2
Saddler Street	D3
Sidegate	C4
Silver Street	C2-C3
South Bailey	C1-D1-D2
South Street	C1-C2
Springwell	A4
Sutton Street	B3-B2
The Avenue	A1-B1-B2
Waddington Street	B3
Waterside	C4
Wearside Drive	D4
Western Hill	B4-B3
Whinney Hill	E1-E2

Albert Street	B2-B3
Allen Street	A1-B1
Ashley Terrace	B4
Avondale Terrace	A2-B2
Baden Street	B1
Bede Terrace	A3
Benson Street	B1
Blands Opening	B3-C3
Broadwood View	B1
Bullion Lane	A3-A2
Church Chare	B2-B3-C3
Clarence Terrace	B2
Clifford Terrace	A1-B1
Cookson Terrace	A3
Co-operative Street	B3
Eardulph Avenue	C2
Eighth Avenue	A4
Ernest Terrace	A1-A2
Fell Road	A4-B4
Fife Avenue	A3
Front Street	B1-B2-B3-B4
George Street	B1
Grasmere Avenue	A1
Greenbank Street	C4-C3
High Chare	B2
Hillside	B4
Holmlands	C1-C2
Holmlands Park	C1-C2
Hopgarth	B4-C4-C3
Hopgarth Gardens	C4-C3
Jacques Terrace	A3-A4
Lambton Street	B1
Lancaster Terrace	C1
Lindisfarne Avenue	B2-C2
Lindom Avenue	C2

Low Chare	B3-C3
Lumley Terrace	B1
Mains Park Road	B2
Melville Street	A1
Mendip Avenue	A1-A2
Middle Chare	B3
Murray Place	A4
Murray Road	A3
Newcastle Road	B4-C4
Ninth Avenue	A4-A3
North Burns	B4
Osborne Road	B2-B3
Park Road Central	C3-C2-C1
Park Road North	C3-C4
Park Road South	C1
Pelaw Bank	B4
Picktree Lane	B4-C4
Pine Street	B2
Plantagenet Avenue	C1
Poplar Street	B2
Prospect Street	B4
Queens Park	C1
Ramsey Street	B1
Relton Terrace	A1-B1
Roman Avenue	B2-C2
Ropery Lane	B1-C1
Rydal Road	A1
St Cuthbert Avenue	C2
Seventh Avenue	A4
South Approach	A3-A2
South Burns	B4
Station Road	A3-B3
Station View	A2-A3
The Avenue	A3
The Green	A3-A4
The Parade	B1
Tuart Street	B3

Twelfth Avenue	A4
Viador	B4
Victor Street	B2
Waldridge Road	A2
Weldon Terrace	B1
Wesley Terrace	B3
West Lane	A2-B2
York Terrace	B1

DURHAM
High above the wooded banks of the River Wear, Durham's castle and cathedral crown the steep hill on which the city is built. They share the site with several of the university's attractive old buildings.

213

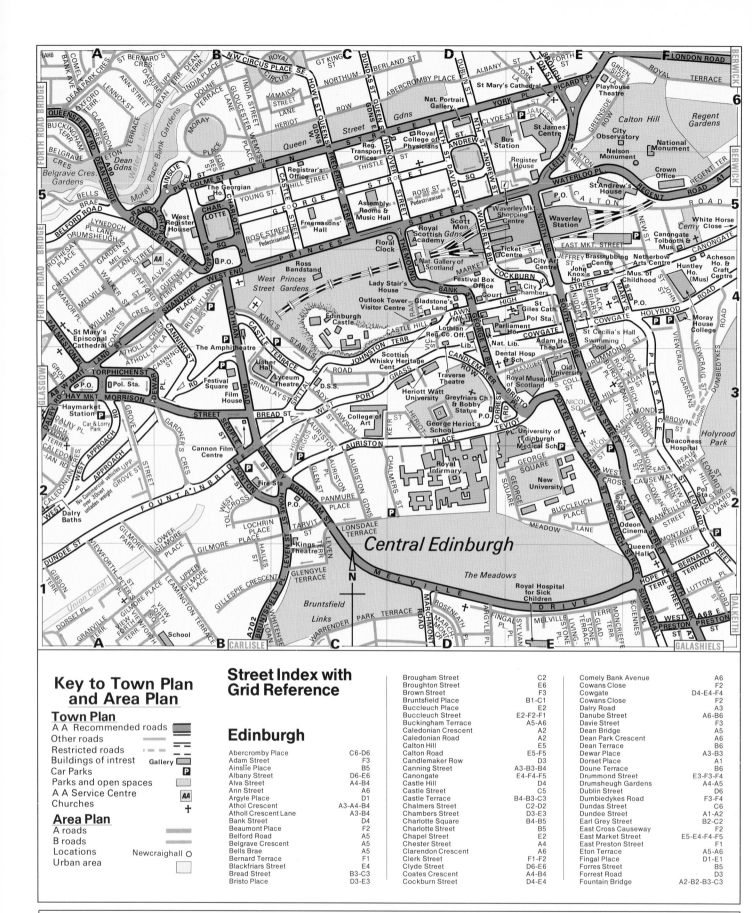

Key to Town Plan and Area Plan

Town Plan

A A Recommended roads
Other roads
Restricted roads
Buildings of intrest   Gallery ▣
Car Parks   ℙ
Parks and open spaces
A A Service Centre   AA
Churches   ✝

Area Plan

A roads
B roads
Locations   Newcraighall ○
Urban area

Street Index with Grid Reference

Edinburgh

Abercromby Place	C6-D6
Adam Street	F3
Ainslie Place	B5
Albany Street	D6-E6
Alva Street	A4-B4
Ann Street	D1
Argyle Place	D1
Athol Crescent	A3-A4-B4
Atholl Crescent Lane	A3-B4
Bank Street	D4
Beaumont Place	F2
Belford Road	A5
Belgrave Crescent	A5
Bells Brae	A5
Bernard Terrace	F1
Blackfriars Street	E4
Bread Street	B3-C3
Bristo Place	D3-E3

Brougham Street	C2
Broughton Street	E6
Brown Street	F3
Bruntsfield Place	B1-C1
Buccleuch Place	E2
Buccleuch Street	E2-F2-F1
Buckingham Terrace	A5-A6
Caledonian Crescent	A2
Caledonian Road	A2
Calton Hill	E5
Calton Road	E5-F5
Candlemaker Row	D3
Canning Street	A3-B3-B4
Canongate	E4-F4-F5
Castle Hill	D4
Castle Street	C5
Castle Terrace	B4-B3-C3
Chalmers Street	C2-D2
Chambers Street	D3-E3
Charlotte Square	B4-B5
Charlotte Street	B5
Chapel Street	E2
Chester Street	A4
Clarendon Crescent	A6
Clerk Street	F1-F2
Clyde Street	D6-E6
Coates Crescent	A4-B4
Cockburn Street	D4-E4

Comely Bank Avenue	A6
Cowans Close	F2
Cowgate	D4-E4-F4
Cowans Close	F2
Dalry Road	A3
Danube Street	A6-B6
Davie Street	F3
Dean Bridge	A5
Dean Park Crescent	A6
Dean Terrace	B6
Dewar Place	A3-B3
Dorset Place	A1
Doune Terrace	B6
Drummond Street	E3-F3-F4
Drumsheugh Gardens	A4-A5
Dublin Street	D6
Dumbiedykes Road	F3-F4
Dundas Street	C6
Dundee Street	A1-A2
Earl Grey Street	B2-C2
East Cross Causeway	F2
East Market Street	E5-E4-F4-F5
East Preston Street	F1
Eton Terrace	A5-A6
Fingal Place	D1-E1
Forres Street	B5
Forrest Road	D3
Fountain Bridge	A2-B2-B3-C3

Edinburgh

Scotland's ancient capital, dubbed the "Athens of the North", is one of the most splendid cities in the whole of Europe. Its buildings, its history and its cultural life give it an international importance which is celebrated every year in its world-famous festival. The whole city is overshadowed by the craggy castle which seems to grow out of the rock itself. There has been a fortress here since the 7th century and most of the great figures of Scottish history have been associated with it. The old town grew up around the base of Castle Rock within the boundaries of the defensive King's Wall and, unable to spread outwards, grew upwards in a maze of tenements. However, during the 18th century new prosperity from the shipping trade resulted in the building of the New Town and the regular, spacious layout of the Georgian development makes a striking contrast with the old hotch-potch of streets. Princes Street is the main east-west thoroughfare with excellent shops on one side and Princes Street Gardens with their famous floral clock on the south side.

As befits such a splendid capital city there are numerous museums and art galleries packed with priceless treasures. Among these are the famous picture gallery in 16th-century Holyroodhouse, the present Royal Palace, and the fascinating and unusual Museum of Childhood.

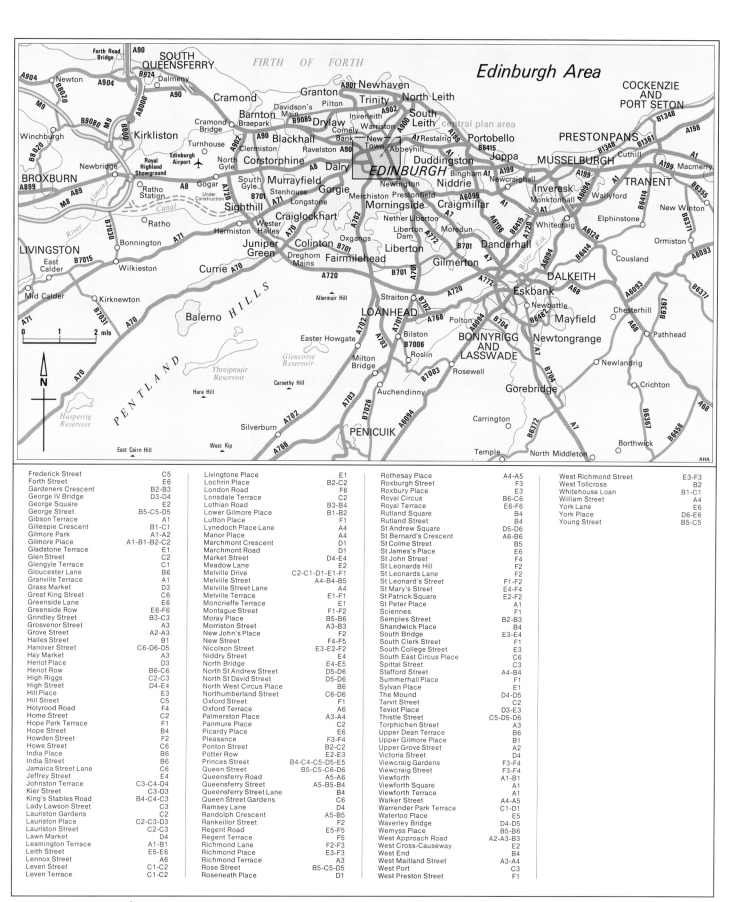

Edinburgh Area

Frederick Street	C5	Livingtone Place	E1	Rothesay Place
Forth Street	E6	Lochrin Place	B2-C2	Roxburgh Street

EDINBURGH
Holyrood Palace orginated as a guest house for the Abbey of Holyrood in the 16th century, but most of the present building was built for Charles II. Mary Queen of Scots was one of its most famous inhabitants.

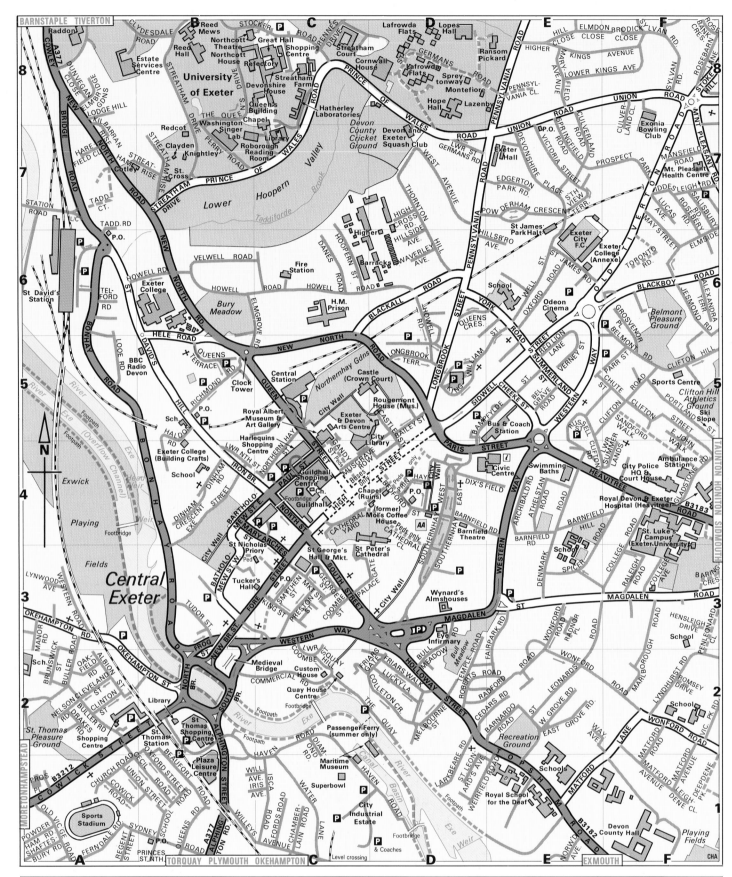

Exeter

The cathedral is Exeter's greatest treasure. Founded in 1050, but rebuilt by the Normans during the 12th-century and again at the end of the 13th-century, it has many beautiful and outstanding features - especially the exquisite rib-vaulting of the nave. Most remarkable, perhaps, is the fact that it still stood after much around it was flattened during the bombing raids in World War II.

There are still plenty of reminders of Old Exeter; Roman and medieval walls circle parts of the city;

14th-century underground passages can be explored; the Guildhall is 15th-century; and Sir Francis Drake is said to have met his explorer companions at Mol's Coffee House. Of the city's ancient churches the most interesting are St Mary Steps, St Mary Arches and St Martin's. The extensive Maritime Museum has over 100 boats from all over the world. Other museums include the Rougemont House, the Devonshire Regiment and the Royal Albert Memorial Museum and Art Gallery.

Exmouth has a near-perfect position at the

mouth of the Exe estuary. On one side it has expanses of sandy beach, on another a wide estuary alive with wildfowl and small boats, while inland is beautiful Devon countryside.

Honiton is famous for traditional hand-made lace and pottery which can still be bought in the busy town.

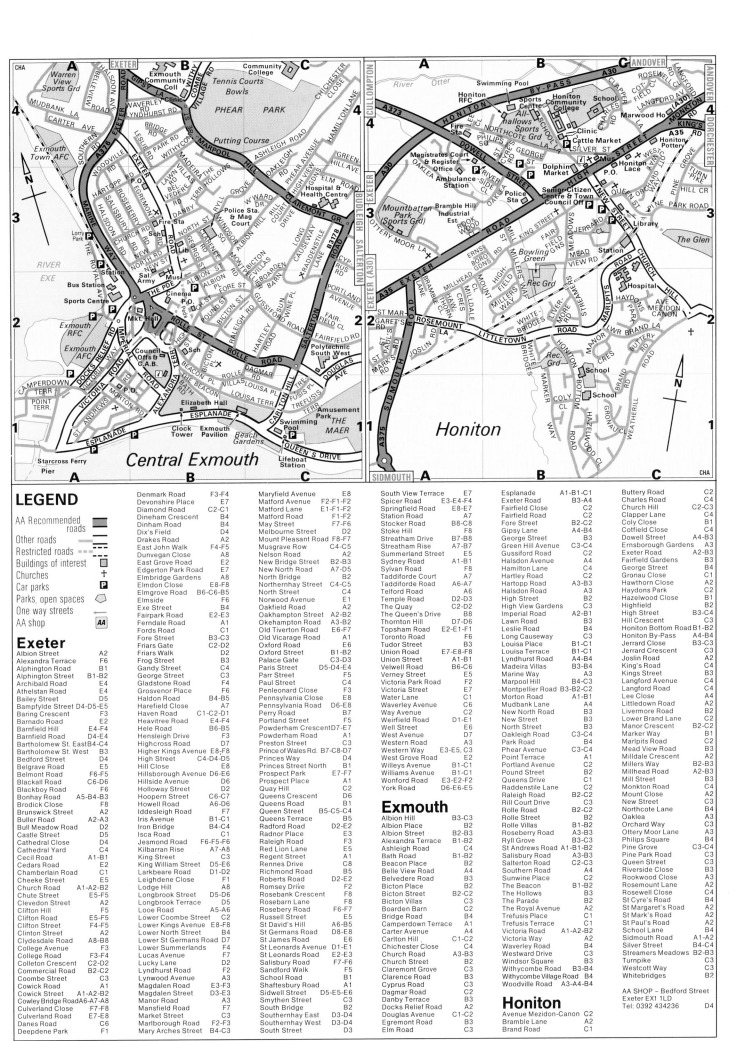

Central Exmouth

Honiton

LEGEND

AA Recommended roads
Other roads
Restricted roads
Buildings of interest
Churches ✝
Car parks 🅿
Parks, open spaces
One way streets ←
AA shop 🆎

Exeter

Albion Street	A2	Denmark Road	F3-F4	Maryfield Avenue	E8
Alexandra Terrace	F6	Devonshire Place	E7	Matford Avenue	F2-F1-F2
Alphington Road	B1	Diamond Road	C2-C1	Matford Lane	E1-F1-F2
Alphington Street	B1-B2	Dineham Crescent	B4	Matford Road	F1-F2
Archibald Road	E4	Dinham Road	B4	May Street	F7-F6
Athelstan Road	E4	Dix's Field	D4	Melbourne Street	D2
Bailey Street	D5	Drakes Road	A2	Mount Pleasant Road	F8-F7
Bampfylde Street	D4-D5-E5	East John Walk	F4-F5	Musgrave Row	C4-C5
Baring Crescent	F3	Dunvegan Close	A8	Nelson Road	A2
Barnado Road	E2	East Grove Road	E2	New Bridge Street	B2-B3
Barnfield Hill	E4-F4	Edgerton Park Road	E7	New North Road	A7-D5
Barnfield Road	D4-E4	Elmbridge Gardens	A8	North Bridge	B2
Bartholomew St. East	B4-C4	Elmdon Close	E8-F8	North Street	C4
Bartholomew St. West	B3	Elmgrove Road	B6-C6-B5	Northernhay Street	C4-C5
Bedford Street	D4	Elmside	F6	Norwood Avenue	E1
Belgrave Road	E5	Exe Street	B4	Oakfield Road	A2
Belmont Road	F6-F5	Fairpark Road	E2-E3	Oakhampton Street	A2-B2
Blackall Road	C6-D6	Ferndale Road	A1	Okehampton Road	A3-B2
Blackboy Road	F6	Fords Road	C1	Old Tiverton Road	E6-F7
Brodick Road	F8	Fore Street	B3-C3	Old Vicarage Road	A1
Brunswick Street	A2	Friars Gate	C2-D2	Oxford Road	E6
Buller Road	A2-A3	Friars Walk	D2	Oxford Street	B1-B2
Bull Meadow Road	D2	Frog Street	B3	Palace Gate	C3-D3
Castle Street	D5	Gandy Street	C4	Paris Street	D5-D4-E4
Cathedral Close	D4	George Street	C3	Parr Street	F5
Cathedral Yard	C4	Gladstone Road	F4	Paul Street	C4
Cecil Road	A1-B1	Grosvenor Place	F4	Penleonard Close	F3
Cedars Road	E2	Haldon Road	B4-B5	Pennsylvania Close	E8
Chamberlain Road	C1	Harefield Close	A8	Pennsylvania Road	D6-E8
Cheeke Street	E5	Haven Road	C1-C2-D1	Perry Road	B7
Church Road	A1-A2-B2	Heavitree Road	E4-F4	Portland Street	F5
Chute Street	E5-F5	Hele Road	B6-B5	Powderham Crescent	D7-E7
Clevedon Street	A2	Hensleigh Drive	F3	Powderham Road	A1
Clifton Hill	F5	Highcross Road	D7	Preston Street	C3
Clifton Road	E5-F5	Higher Kings Avenue	E8-F8	Prince of Wales Rd.	B7-C8-D7
Clifton Street	F4-F5	High Street	C4-D4-D5	Princes Way	D4
Clinton Street	A2	Hill Close	D6	Princes Street North	B1
Clydesdale Road	A8-B8	Hillsborough Avenue	D6-E6	Prospect Park	E7-F7
College Avenue	F3	Hillside Avenue	D6	Prospect Place	A1
College Road	F3-F4	Holloway Street	D2	Quay Hill	C2
Colleton Crescent	C2-D2	Hoopern Street	C6-C7	Queens Crescent	D6
Commercial Road	B2-C2	Howell Road	A6-D6	Queens Road	B1
Coombe Street	C3	Iddesleigh Road	F7	Queen Street	B5-C5-C4
Cowick Road	A1	Iris Avenue	B1-C1	Queens Terrace	B5
Cowick Street	A1-A2-B2	Iron Bridge	B4-C4	Radford Road	D2-E2
Cowley Bridge Road	A6-A7-A8	Isca Road	C1	Radnor Place	E3
Culverland Close	F7-F8	Jesmond Road	F6-F5-F6	Raleigh Road	F3
Culverland Road	E7-E8	Kilbarran Rise	A7-A8	Red Lion Lane	E5
Danes Road	C6	King Street	C3	Regent Street	A1
Deepdene Park	F1	King William Street	D5-E6	Rennes Drive	C8
		Larkbeare Road	D1-D2	Richmond Road	B5
		Leighdene Close	F1	Roberts Road	D2-E2
		Lodge Hill	A8	Romsey Drive	F2
		Longbrook Street	D5-D6	Rosebank Crescent	F8
		Longbrook Terrace	D5-D6	Rosebarn Lane	F8
		Looe Road	A5-A6	Rosebery Road	F6-F7
		Lower Coombe Street	C2	Russell Street	B3
		Lower Kings Avenue	E8-F8	St David's Hill	A6-B5
		Lower North Street	B4	St Germans Road	D8-E8
		Lower St Germans Road	D7	St James Road	E6
		Lower Summerlands	F4	St Leonards Avenue	D1-E1
		Lucas Avenue	F7	St Leonards Road	E2-E3
		Lucky Lane	D2	Salisbury Road	F7-F6
		Lyndhurst Road	F2	Sandford Walk	F5
		Lynwood Avenue	A3	School Road	B1
		Magdalen Road	E3-F3	Shaftesbury Road	A1
		Magdalen Street	D3-E3	Sidwell Street	D5-E5-E6
		Manor Road	A3	Smythen Street	C3
		Mansfield Road	F7	South Bridge	B2
		Market Street	C3	Southernhay East	D3-D4
		Marlborough Road	F2-F3	Southernhay West	D3-D4
		Mary Arches Street	B4-C3	South Street	D3

South View Terrace	E7
Spicer Road	E3-E4-F4
Springfield Road	E8-E7
Station Road	A7
Stocker Road	B8-C8
Stoke Hill	F8
Streatham Drive	B7-B8
Streatham Rise	A7-B7
Summerland Street	E5
Sydney Road	A1-B1
Sylvan Road	F8
Taddiforde Court	A7
Taddiforde Road	A6-A7
Telford Road	A6
Temple Road	D2-D3
The Quay	C2-D2
The Queen's Drive	B8
Thornton Hill	D7-D6
Topsham Road	E2-E1-F1
Toronto Road	F6
Tudor Street	B3
Union Road	E7-E8-F8
Union Street	A1-B1
Velwell Road	B6-C6
Verney Street	E5
Victoria Park Road	F2
Victoria Street	E7
Water Lane	C1
Waverley Avenue	C6
Way Avenue	C2
Weirfield Road	D1-E1
Well Street	E6
West Avenue	D7
Western Road	A3
Western Way	E3-E5, C3
West Grove Road	E2
Willeys Avenue	B1-C1
Williams Avenue	B1-C1
Wonford Road	E3-E2-F2
York Road	D6-E6-E5

Exmouth

Albion Hill	B3-C3
Albion Place	B2
Albion Street	B2-B3
Alexandra Terrace	B1-B2
Ashleigh Road	C4
Bath Road	B1-B2
Beacon Place	B2
Belle View Road	A4
Belvedere Road	B3
Bicton Place	B2
Bicton Street	B2-C2
Bicton Villas	C3
Boarden Barn	C2
Bridge Road	B4
Camperdown Terrace	A1
Carter Avenue	A4
Carlton Hill	C1-C2
Chichester Close	C4
Church Road	A3-B3
Church Street	B2
Claremont Grove	C3
Clarence Road	B3
Cyprus Road	C3
Dagmar Road	C2
Danby Terrace	B3
Docks Relief Road	A2
Douglas Avenue	C1-C2
Egremont Road	B3
Elm Road	C3

Esplanade	A1-B1-C1
Exeter Road	B3-A4
Fairfield Close	C2
Fairfield Road	C2
Fore Street	B2-C2
Gipsy Lane	A4-B4
George Street	B3
Green Hill Avenue	C3-C4
Gussiford Road	C2
Halsdon Avenue	A4
Hamilton Lane	C4
Hartley Road	C2
Hartopp Road	A3-B3
Halsdon Road	A3
High Street	B2
High View Gardens	C3
Imperial Road	A2-B1
Lawn Road	B3
Leslie Road	B4
Long Causeway	C1
Louisa Place	B1-C1
Louisa Terrace	B1-C1
Lyndhurst Road	A4-B4
Madeira Villas	B3-B4
Marine Way	A3
Marpool Hill	B4-C3
Montpellier Road	B3-B2-C2
Morton Road	A1-B1
Mudbank Lane	A4
New North Road	B3
New Street	B3
North Street	B3
Oakleigh Road	C3-C4
Park Road	B4
Phear Avenue	C3-C4
Point Terrace	A1
Portland Avenue	C2
Pound Street	B2
Queens Drive	C1
Raddenstile Lane	C2
Raleigh Road	B2-C2
Rill Court Drive	C3
Rolle Road	B2-C2
Rolle Street	B2
Rolle Villas	B1-B2
Roseberry Road	A3-B3
Ryll Grove	B3-C3
St Andrews Road	A1-B1-B2
Salisbury Road	A3-B3
Salterton Road	C2-C3
Southern Road	A4
Sunwine Place	C2
The Beacon	B1-B2
The Hollows	B3
The Parade	B2
The Royal Avenue	A2
Trefusis Close	C1
Trefusis Terrace	C1
Victoria Road	A1-A2-B2
Victoria Way	A2
Waverley Road	B4
Westward Drive	C3
Windsor Square	B3
Withycombe Road	B3-B4
Withycombe Village Road	B4
Woodville Road	A3-A4-B4

Honiton

Avenue Mezidon-Canon	C2
Bramble Lane	A2
Brand Road	C1

Buttery Road	C2
Charles Road	C4
Church Hill	C2-C3
Clapper Lane	C4
Coly Close	B1
Cotfield Close	C4
Dowell Street	A4-B3
Ernsborough Gardens	A3
Exeter Road	A2-B3
Fairfield Gardens	B3
George Street	B4
Gronau Close	C1
Hawthorn Close	A2
Haydons Park	C2
Hazelwood Close	B1
Highfield	B2
High Street	B3-C4
Hill Crescent	C3
Honiton Bottom Road	B1-B2
Honiton By-Pass	B4-B4
Jerrard Close	B3-C3
Jerrard Crescent	A3
Joslin Road	A2
King's Road	C4
Kings Street	B3
Langford Avenue	C4
Langford Road	C4
Lee Close	A4
Littledown Road	A2
Livermore Road	B2
Lower Brand Lane	C2
Manor Crescent	B2-C2
Marker Way	B2
Marlpits Road	C2
Mead View Road	B3
Milldale Crescent	A2
Millers Way	B2-B3
Millhead Road	A2-B3
Mill Street	B3
Monkton Road	C4
Mount Close	A2
New Street	C3
Northcote Lane	B4
Oaklea	A3
Orchard Way	C3
Ottery Moor Lane	A3
Philips Square	B4
Pine Grove	C3-C4
Pine Park Road	C3
Queen Street	C3
Riverside Close	B3
Rookwood Close	A3
Rosemount Lane	A2
Rosewell Close	C4
St Cyre's Road	B4
St Margaret's Road	A2
St Mark's Road	A2
St Paul's Road	A2
School Lane	B4
Sidmouth Road	A1-A2
Silver Street	B4-C4
Streamers Meadows	B2-B3
Turnpike	C3
Westcott Way	C4
Whitebridges	B2

AA SHOP – Bedford Street
Exeter EX1 1LD
Tel: 0392 434236   D4

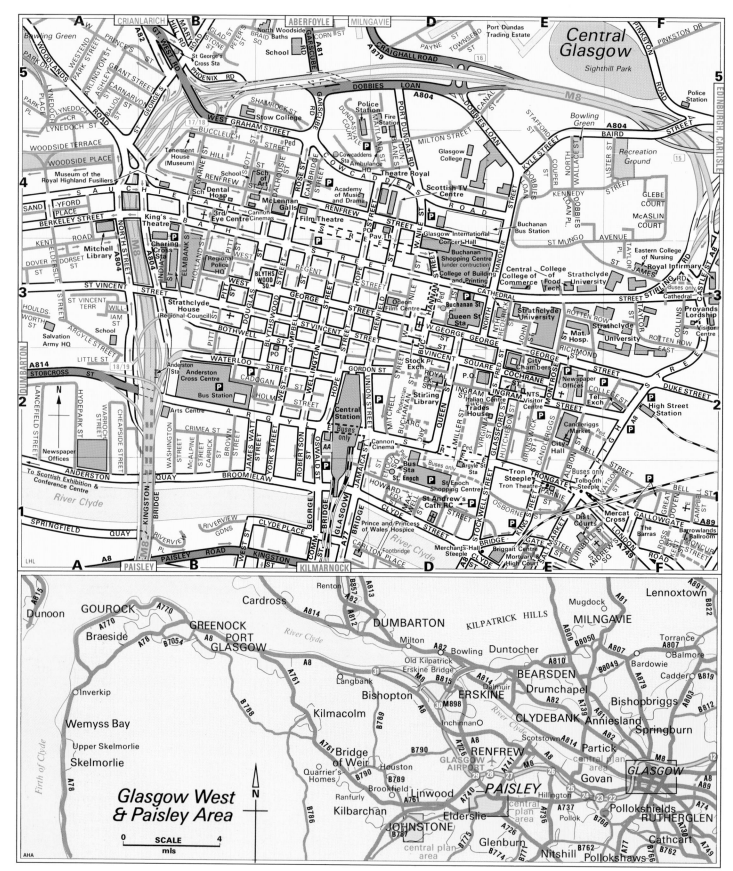

Glasgow

Although much of Glasgow is distinctly Victorian in character, its roots go back very many centuries. It's best link with the past is the Cathedral, in High Street. Founded in the 6th-century, it has features from many succeeding centuries, including an exceptional 13th-century crypt. Nearby is Provand's Lordship, the city's oldest house. It dates from 1471 and is now a museum. Two much larger museums are to be found a little out of the centre the Art Gallery and Museum contains one of the

finest collections of paintings in Britain, while the Hunterian Museum, attached to the University, covers geology, archaeology, ethnography and more general subjects. On Glasgow Green is People's Palace - a museum of city life. Most imposing of the Victorian buildings are the City Chambers and City Hall which was built in 1841 as a concert hall. A new International Concert Hall has now been built.

Paisley is famous for the lovely fabric pattern to which it gives its name. It was taken from

fabrics brought from the Near East in the early 19th-century, and its manufacture, along with the production of thread, is still important. Coats Observatory is one of the best equipped in the country.

Johnstone grew rapidly as a planned industrial town in the 19th-century, but suffered from the effects of the Industrial Revolution. Today, engineering is the main industry.

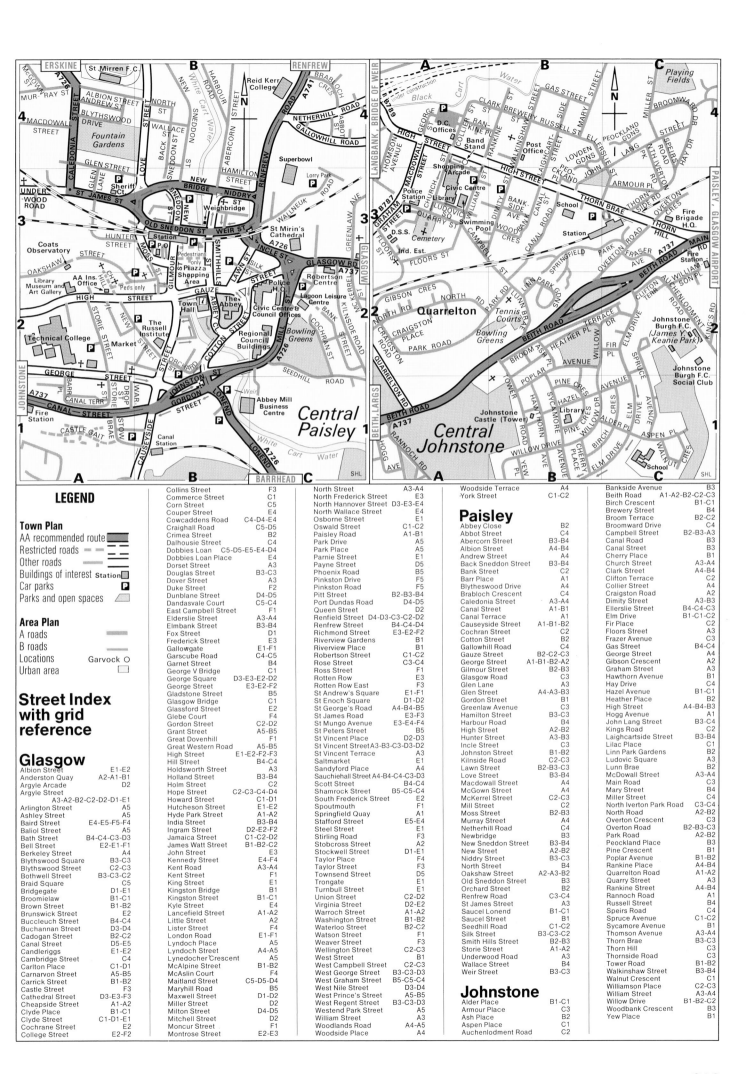

LEGEND

Town Plan

AA recommended route
Restricted roads
Other roads
Buildings of interest   Station ▣
Car parks   🅿
Parks and open spaces

Area Plan

A roads
B roads
Locations   Garvock ○
Urban area

Street Index with grid reference

Glasgow

Albion Street	E1-E2
Anderston Quay	A2-A1-B1
Argyle Arcade	D2
Argyle Street	A3-A2-B2-C2-D2-D1-E1
Arlington Street	A5
Ashley Street	A5
Baird Street	E4-E5-F5-F4
Baliol Street	A5
Bath Street	B4-C4-C3-D3
Bell Street	E2-E1-F1
Berkeley Street	A4
Blythswood Square	B3-C3
Blythswood Street	C2-C3
Bothwell Street	B3-C3-C2
Braid Square	C5
Bridgegate	D1-E1
Broomielaw	B1-C1
Brown Street	B1-B2
Brunswick Street	E2
Buccleuch Street	B4-C4
Buchanan Street	D3-D4
Cadogan Street	B2-C2
Canal Street	D5-E5
Candleriggs	E1-E2
Cambridge Street	C4
Carlton Place	C1-D1
Carnarvon Street	A5-B5
Carrick Street	B1-B2
Castle Street	F3
Cathedral Street	D3-E3-F3
Cheapside Street	A1-A2
Clyde Place	B1-C1
Clyde Street	C1-D1-E1
Cochrane Street	E2-F2
College Street	E2-F2
Collins Street	F3
Commerce Street	C1
Corn Street	C5
Couper Street	E4
Cowcaddens Road	C4-D4-E4
Craighall Road	C5-D5
Crimea Street	B2
Dalhousie Street	C4
Dobbies Loan	C5-D5-E5-E4-D4
Dobbies Loan Place	E4
Dorset Street	A3
Douglas Street	B3-C3
Dover Street	A3
Duke Street	F2
Dunblane Street	D4-D5
Dandasvale Court	C5-C4
East Campbell Street	F1
Elderslie Street	A3-A4
Elmbank Street	B3-B4
Fox Street	D1
Frederick Street	E3
Gallowgate	E1-F1
Garscube Road	C4-C5
Garnet Street	B4
George V Bridge	C1
George Square	D3-E3-E2-D2
George Street	E3-E2-F2
Gladstone Street	B5
Glasgow Bridge	C1
Glassford Street	E2
Glebe Court	F4
Gordon Street	C2-D2
Grant Street	A5-B5
Great Dovenhill	F1
Great Western Road	A5-B5
High Street	E1-E2-F2-F3
Hill Street	B4-C4
Holdsworth Street	A3
Holland Street	B3-B4
Holm Street	C2
Hope Street	C2-C3-C4-D4
Howard Street	C1-D1
Hutcheson Street	E1-E2
Hyde Park Street	A1-A2
India Street	B3-B4
Ingram Street	D2-E2-F2
Jamaica Street	C1-C2-D2
James Watt Street	B1-B2-C2
John Street	E3
Kennedy Street	E4-F4
Kent Road	A3-A4
Kent Street	F1
King Street	E1
Kingston Bridge	B1
Kingston Street	B1-C1
Kyle Street	E4
Lancefield Street	A1-A2
Little Street	A2
Lister Street	F4
London Road	E1-F1
Lyndoch Place	A5
Lyndoch Street	A4-A5
Lynedoch Crescent	A5
McAlpine Street	B1-B2
McAslin Court	F4
Maitland Street	C5-D5-D4
Maryhill Road	B5
Maxwell Street	D1-D2
Miller Street	D2
Milton Street	D4-D5
Mitchell Street	D2
Moncur Street	F1
Montrose Street	E2-E3
North Street	A3-A4
North Frederick Street	E3
North Hannover Street	D3-E3-E4
North Wallace Street	E4
Osborne Street	E1
Oswald Street	C1-C2
Paisley Road	A1-B1
Park Drive	A5
Park Place	A5
Parnie Street	E1
Payne Street	D5
Phoenix Road	B5
Pinkston Drive	F5
Pinkston Road	F5
Pitt Street	B2-B3-B4
Port Dundas Road	D4-D5
Queen Street	D2
Renfield Street	D4-D3-C3-C2-D2
Renfrew Street	B4-C4-D4
Richmond Street	E3-E2-F2
Riverview Gardens	B1
Riverview Place	B1
Robertson Street	C1-C2
Rose Street	C3-C4
Ross Street	F1
Rotten Row	E3
Rotten Row East	F3
St Andrew's Square	E1-F1
St Enoch Square	D1-D2
St George's Road	A4-B4-B5
St James Road	E3-F3
St Mungo Avenue	E3-E4-F4
St Peters Street	B5
St Vincent Place	D2-D3
St Vincent Street	A3-B3-C3-D3-D2
St Vincent Terrace	A3
Saltmarket	E1
Sandyford Place	A4
Sauchiehall Street	A4-B4-C4-C3-D3
Scott Street	B4-C4
Shamrock Street	B5-C5-C4
South Frederick Street	E2
Spoutmouth	F1
Springfield Quay	A1
Stafford Street	E5-E4
Steel Street	E1
Stirling Road	F3
Stobcross Street	A2
Stockwell Street	D1-E1
Taylor Place	F4
Taylor Street	F3
Townsend Street	D5
Trongate	E1
Turnbull Street	E1
Union Street	C2-D2
Virginia Street	D2-E2
Warroch Street	A1-A2
Washington Street	B1-B2
Waterloo Street	B2-C2
Watson Street	F1
Weaver Street	F3
Wellington Street	C2-C3
West Street	B1
West Campbell Street	C2-C3
West George Street	B3-C3-D3
West Graham Street	B5-C5-C4
West Nile Street	D3-D4
West Prince's Street	A5-B5
West Regent Street	B3-C3-D3
Westend Park Street	A5
William Street	A3
Woodlands Road	A4-A5
Woodside Place	A4
Woodside Terrace	A4
York Street	C1-C2

Paisley

Abbey Close	B2
Abbot Street	C4
Abercorn Street	B3-B4
Albion Street	A4-B4
Andrew Street	A4
Back Sneddon Street	B3-B4
Bank Street	C2
Barr Place	A1
Blytheswood Drive	A4
Brabloch Crescent	C4
Caledonia Street	A3-A4
Canal Street	A1-B1
Canal Terrace	A1
Causeyside Street	A1-B1-B2
Cochran Street	C2
Cotton Street	B2
Gallowhill Road	C4
Gauze Street	B2-C2-C3
George Street	A1-B1-B2-A2
Gilmour Street	B2-B3
Glasgow Road	C3
Glen Lane	A3
Glen Street	A4-A3-B3
Gordon Street	B1
Greenlaw Avenue	C3
Hamilton Street	B3-C3
Harbour Road	B4
High Street	A2-B2
Hunter Street	A3-B3
Incle Street	C3
Johnston Street	B1-B2
Kilnside Road	C2-C3
Lawn Street	B2-B3-C3
Love Street	B3-B4
Macdowall Street	A4
McGown Street	A4
McKerrel Street	C2-C3
Mill Street	C2
Moss Street	B2-B3
Murray Street	A4
Netherhill Road	C4
Newbridge	B3
New Sneddon Street	B3-B4
New Street	A2-B2
Niddry Street	B3-C3
North Street	B4
Oakshaw Street	A2-A3-B2
Old Sneddon Street	B3
Orchard Street	B2
Renfrew Road	C3-C4
St James Street	A3
Saucel Lonend	B1-C1
Saucel Street	B1
Seedhill Road	C1-C2
Silk Street	B3-C3-C2
Smith Hills Street	B2-B3
Storie Street	A1-A2
Underwood Road	A3
Wallace Street	B4
Weir Street	B3-C3

Johnstone

Alder Place	B1-C1
Armour Place	C3
Ash Place	B2
Aspen Place	C1
Auchenlodment Road	C2
Bankside Avenue	B3
Beith Road	A1-A2-B2-C2-C3
Birch Crescent	B1-C1
Brewery Street	B4
Broom Terrace	B2-C2
Broomward Drive	C4
Campbell Street	B2-B3-A3
Canal Road	B3
Canal Street	B3
Cherry Place	B2
Church Street	A3-A4
Clark Street	A4-B4
Clifton Terrace	C2
Collier Street	A4
Craigston Road	A2
Dimity Street	A3-B3
Elm Drive	B1-C1-C2
Fir Place	C2
Floors Street	A3
Frazer Avenue	C3
Gas Street	B4-C4
George Street	A4
Gibson Crescent	A2
Graham Street	A3
Hawthorn Avenue	B1
Hay Drive	C4
Hazel Avenue	B1-C1
Heather Place	B2
High Street	A4-B4-B3
Hogg Avenue	A1
John Lang Street	B3-C3
Kings Road	C2
Laighcartside Street	B3-B4
Lilac Place	C1
Linn Park Gardens	B2
Ludovic Square	A3
Lunn Brae	B2
McDowall Street	A3-A4
Main Road	C3
Mary Street	B4
Miller Street	C4
North Iverton Park Road	C3-C4
North Road	A2-B2
Overton Crescent	C3
Overton Road	B2-B3-C3
Park Road	A2-B2
Peockland Place	B3
Pine Crescent	B2
Poplar Avenue	B1-B2
Rankine Place	A4-B4
Quarrelton Road	A1-A2
Quarry Street	A3
Rankine Street	A4-B4
Rannoch Road	A1
Russell Street	B4
Speirs Road	C4
Spruce Avenue	C1-C2
Sycamore Avenue	B1
Thomson Avenue	A3-A4
Thorn Brae	B3-C3
Thorn Hill	C3
Thornside Road	C3
Tower Road	B1-B2
Walkinshaw Street	B3-B4
Walnut Crescent	C1
Williamson Place	C2-C3
William Street	A3-A4
Willow Drive	B1-B2-C2
Woodbank Crescent	B3
Yew Place	B1

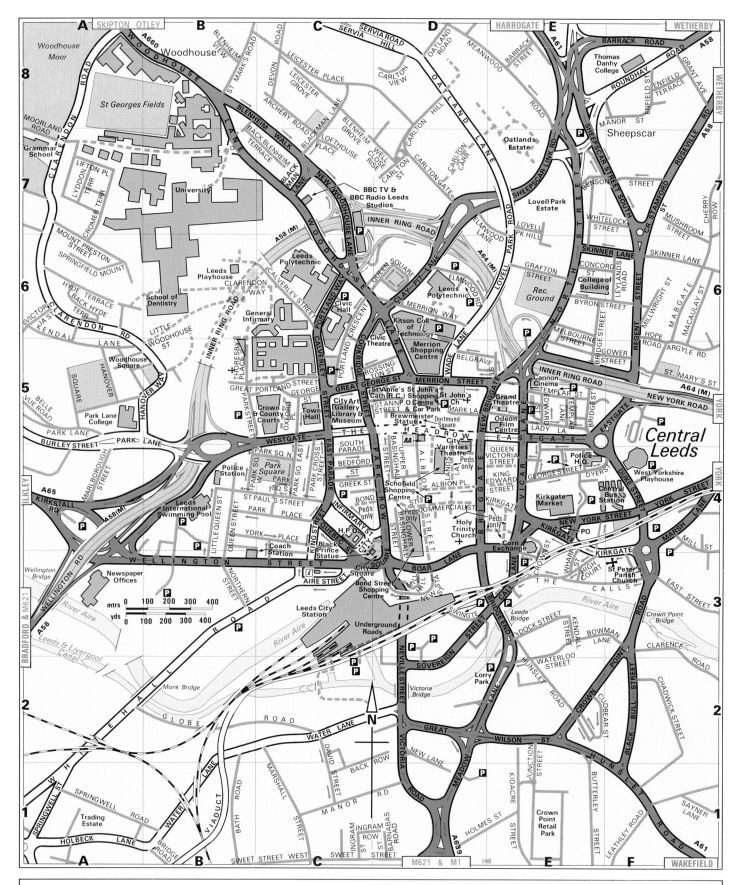

Leeds

In the centre of Leeds is its town hall – a monumental piece of architecture with a 225ft clock-tower. It was opened by Queen Victoria in 1858, and has been a kind of mascot for the city ever since. It exudes civic pride; such buildings could only have been created in the heyday of Victorian prosperity and confidence. Leeds' staple industry has always been the wool trade, but it only became a boom town towards the end of the 18th century, when textile mills were introduced. Today, the wool trade and ready-made clothing (Mr Hepworth and Mr Burton began their work here) are still important, though industries like paper, leather, furniture and electrical equipment are prominent.

Across Calverley Street from the town hall is the City Art Gallery, Library and Museum. Its collections include sculpture by Henry Moore, who was a student at Leeds School of Art. Nearby is the Headrow, Leeds' foremost shopping thoroughfare. On it is the City Varieties Theatre, venue for many years of the famous television programme 'The Good Old Days'. Off the Headrow are several shopping arcades, of which Leeds has many handsome examples. Leeds has a good number of interesting churches; perhaps the finest is St John's, unusual in that it dates from 1634, a time when few churches were built.

220

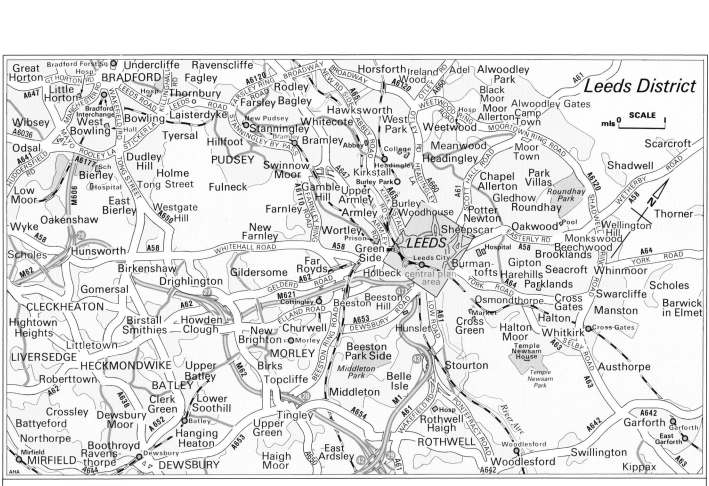

Leeds District

SCALE
mls 0 | 1

LEGEND

Town Plan

AA Recommended roads
Other roads
Restricted roads
Buildings of interset — Museum
AA Shop — AA
Parks and open spaces
Car Parks — P
Churches — †
One way streets — ←

District Plan

A roads
B roads
Stations — Kirkgate O
Urban area
Buildings of interest — Hospital

Street Index with Grid Reference

Aire Street	C3
Albion Place	D4
Albion Street	D3-D4-D5
Archery Road	C7-C8
Argyle Road	F5
Back Hyde Terr	A6
Back Row	C1
Barrack Road	E8-F8
Barrack Street	E8
Bath Road	B1-B2
Bedford Street	C4
Belgrave Street	D5-E5
Belle Vue Road	A5
Benson Street	E7-F7
Black Blenheim Terr	C7
Black Bull Street	F1-F2-F3
Black Man Lane	C7
Blenheim Grove	C8-C7-D7
Blenheim View	B8
Blenheim Walk	B8-C8-C7
Boar Lane	D3-D4
Bond Street	C4-D4
Bowman Lane	E3-F3
Bridge End	D3-E3
Bridge Road	B1
Bridge Street	E5-E6
Briggate	D3-D4-D5
Burley Street	A4-A5
Butterley Street	E1-E2
Byron Street	E6-F6
Call Lane	E3
Calverley Street	C5-C6

Carlton Carr	D7
Carlton Gate	D7
Carlton St	D7
Chadwick Street	F2
Chapeltown Road	E8
Cherry Row	F7
City Square	C3-C4-D4-D3
Clarence Road	F2-F3
Clarendon Road	A8-A7-A6-A5-B5
Clay Pit Lane	D6
Cloberry Street	A7
Commercial Street	D4
Cookridge Street	C5-C6-D6
Cromer Terr	A7
Cross Stamford Street	F6-F7
Crown Street	E3-E4
Crown Point Road	E2-F2-F3
Cudbear St	E2
David Street	C1-C2
Devon Road	C8
Dock Street	E3
Dyer Street	E4-F4
East Parade	C4-C5
East Street	F3
Eastgate	E5-F5
Edward Street	F5
Elmwood Lane	D7
Elmwood Road	D6
Enfield Street	F8
Enfield Terrace	F8
George Street	C5
George Street	E4
Globe Road	A2-B2-C2
Gower Street	E5-F5
Grafton Street	E6
Grant Ave	F7
Great George Street	C5-D5
Great Portland Street	B5-C5
Great Wilson Street	D2-E2
Greek Street	C4-D4
Hanover Square	A5
Hanover Way	A5-B5
High Court	E3
Holbeck Lane	A1-B1
Holmes Street	D1-E1
Hope Road	F5-F6
Hunslett Road	E3-E2-E1-F1-F2
Hyde Street	A6
Hyde Terrace	A6
Infirmary Street	C4-D4
Ingram Row	C1
Ingram Street	C1
Inner Ring Road	B5-B6-C6-C7-D7-D6-E6-E5-F5
Junction Street	E1-E2
Kendal Lane	A5-A6
Kendal Street	E3
Kidacre Street	E1
King Street	C3-C4

King Edward Street	D4-E4
Kirkgate	E4-E3-F3-F4
Kirkstall Road	A4
Lady Lane	E5
Lands Lane	D4-D5
Leathley Road	F1
Leicester Grove	C8
Leicester Place	C8
Leylands Road	F6
Lifton Place	A7
Lisbon Street	B3-B4
Little Queen Street	B3-B4
Little Woodhouse Street	B6
Lofthouse Place	C7-D7
Lovell Park Hill	E7
Lovell Park Road	D6-E6-E7
Lower Basinghall Street	D3-D4
Mabgate	F6
Manor Road	C1-D1
Manor Street	ED8-F8
Mark Lane	D5
Malborough Street	A4
Marsh Lane	F4
Marshall Street	C1-C2
Meadow Lane	D1-D2-E2-E3
Meanwood Road	D8-E8
Melbourne Street	E6
Merrion Street	D5-E5
Merrion Way	D6
Mill Hill	D3
Mill Street	F4
Moorland Road	A7-A8
Mount Preston Street	A6-A7
Mushroom Street	F6-F7
Neville Street	D2-D3
New Briggate	D5-E5
New Lane	D2
New Station Street	D3
New Woodhouse Lane	C6-C7
New York Road	F5
New York Street	E4-F4
North Street	E5-E6-E7
Northern Street	B3
Oatland Lane	D8-D7-E7
Oatland Road	D8
Oxford Place	C5
Park Cross Street	C4-C5
Park Lane	A5-B5-B4
Park Place	B4-C4
Park Row	C4-C5-D5-D4
Park Square East	C4
Park Square North	B4-C4
Park Square South	C4
Park Square West	B4
Park Street	B5-C5
Portland Crescent	C5-C6
Portland Way	C6
Quebec Street	C3-C4
Queen Street	B3-B4

Queen Square	C6-D6
Queen Victoria Street	D4-E4
Regent Street	F5-F6
Roseville Road	F7-F8
Rossington Street	C5-D5
Roundhay Road	E8-F8
St Ann Street	C5-D5
St Barnabas Rd	D1
St Mark's Spur	B8-C8
St Paul's Street	B4-C4
St Peter's Street	E4-F4
Sayner Lane	F1
Servia Hill	C8-D8
Servia Road	C8-D8
Sheepscar Link Road	E7-E8
Sheepscar Street North	E8
Sheepscar Street South	E8-E7-F7
Skinner Lane	E6-F6
South Parade	C4
Sovereign Street	D2-D3-E3
Springfield Mount	A6
Springwell Road	A1-B1
Springwell Street	A1
Sweet Street	C1-D1
Sweet Street West	B1-C1
Swinegate	D3
The Calls	E3-F3
The Headrow	C5-D5
Templar Lane	E5
Templar Street	E5
Thoresby Place	B5-B6
Trinity Street	D4
Upper Basinghall Street	D4-D5
Vicar Lane	E4-E5
Victoria Road	D1-D2
Victoria St	A6
Wade Lane	D5-D6
Water Lane	B1-B2-C2-D2
Waterloo Street	E2-E3
Well Close Rise	D7
Well Close View	D8
Wellington Road	A3
Wellington Street	A3-B3-C3
Westgate	B4-B5-C5-C4
Wharf Street	E3-E4
Whitehall Road	A1-A2-B2-B3-C3
Whitelock Street	E7-F7
Woodhouse Lane	A8-B8-B7-C7-C6-D6-D5
York Place	B4-C4
York Street	F4

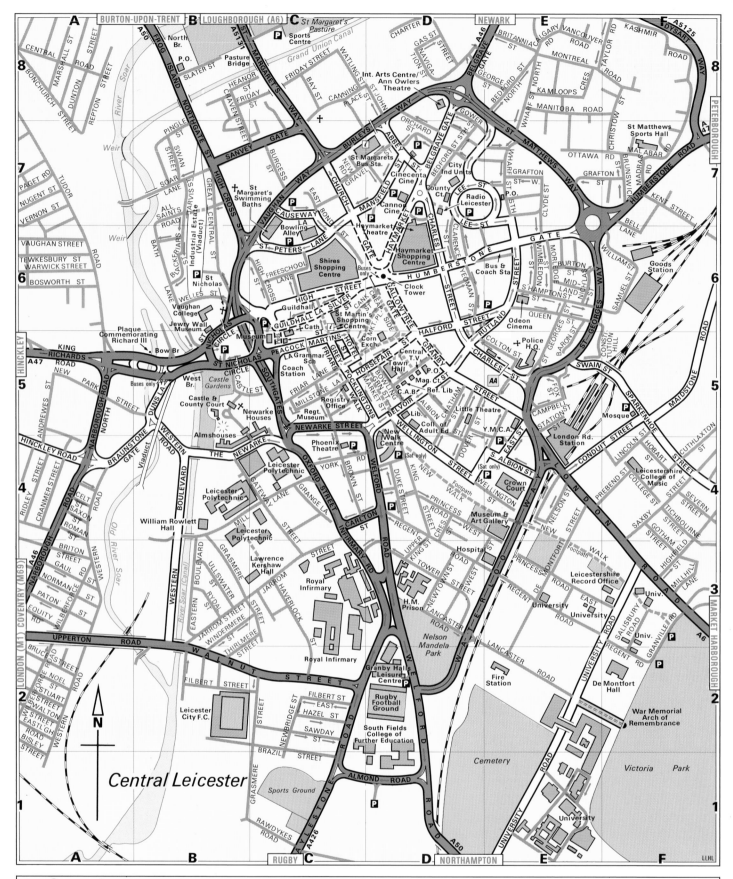

Leicester

A regional capital in Roman times, Leicester has retained many buildings from its eventful and distinguished past. Today the city is a thriving contrast of heritage and modern amenities, including the modern Shires shopping mall, and one of Europe's largest permanent open-air markets. Among the most outstanding monuments from the past is the Jewry Wall, a great bastion of

Roman masonry. Close by are remains of the Roman baths and several other contemporary buildings. Attached is a musuem covering all periods from prehistoric times to 1500. Nine museums include the Wygston's House Museum of Costume, Newarke House, showing changing social conditions in Leicester through four hundred years; and Leicestershire Museum and Art Gallery, with collections of drawings, paintings, ceramics, geology and natural history.

The medieval Guildhall has many features of interest, including a great hall, library and police cells. Leicester's castle, although remodelled in the 17th century, retains a 12th-century great hall. The Church of St Mary de Castro, across the road from the castle, has features going back at least as far as Norman times; while St Nicholas's Church is even older, with Roman and Saxon foundations. St Martin's Cathedral dates mainly from the 13th- to 15th-centuries and has a notable Bishop's throne.

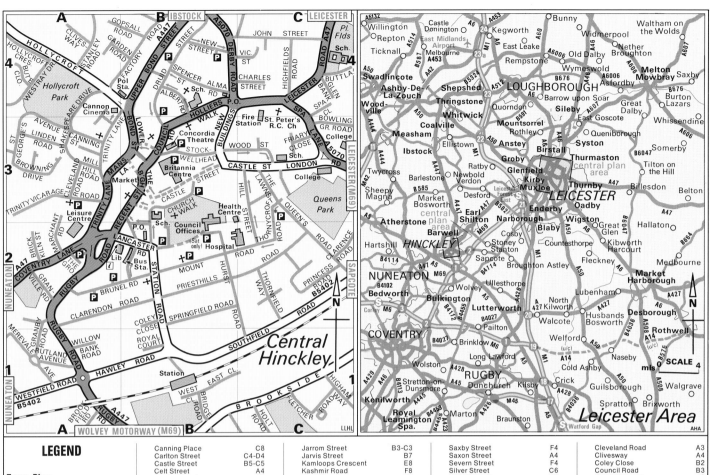

LEGEND

Town Plan

AA Recommended route	▬▬▬
Restricted roads	═══
Other roads	═══
Buildings of interest	▭
Car parks	**P**
Parks and open spaces	▱

Area Plan

A roads	▬
B roads	▬
Locations	Creaton○
Urban area	▱

Street Index with Grid Reference

Leicester

Abbey Road	D7
Albion Street	D4-D5
All Saints Road	B7
Almond Road	C1-D1
Andrewes Street	A4-A5
Aylestone Road	C1-C2
Baron Street	E5-E6
Bath Lane	B5-B6
Bay Street	C8
Bedford Street North	E8
Bedford Street South	D7
Belgrave Gate	D7-D8-E8
Bell Lane	F6-F7
Belvoir Street	D5
Bisley Street	A1-A2
Blackfriars Street	B6
Bonchurch Street	A7-A8
Bosworth Street	A6
Bowling Green Street	D5
Braunstone Gate	A4-B4-B5
Brazil Street	C1-C2
Britannia Street	E8
Briton Street	A3
Brown Street	C4
Bruce Street	A2
Brunswick Street	F7
Burgess Street	C7-D7-D8
Burleys Way	C7-D7-D8
Burton Street	E6
Calgary Road	E8
Campbell Street	E5
Cank Street	C6-D6
Canning Place	C8
Carlton Street	C4-D4
Castle Street	B5-C5
Celt Street	A4
Central Road	A8
Charles Street	D7-D6-D5-E5
Charter Street	D8
Chatham Street	D4-D5
Cheapside	D5-D6
Christow Street	F7-F8
Church Gate	C7-C6-D6
Clarence Street	D6-D7
Clyde Street	E6-E7
College Street	F4
Colton Street	D5-E5
Conduit Street	E4-F4-F5
Constitution Hill	E5-F5
Crafton Street	E7-F7
Cranmer Street	A4
Craven Street	B7-B8
Crescent Street	D4
Cuthlaxton Street	F4-F5
De Montfort Street	E3-E4
Dover Street	D4-D5
Duke Street	D4
Duns Lane	B5
Dunton Street	A8
Dysart Way	F7-F8
East Bond Street	C6-C7-D6
East Street	E4-E5
Eastern Boulevard	B3-B4
Eastleigh Road	A2
Equity Road	A3
Filbert Street	B2-C2
Filbert Street East	C2
Fox Street	E5
Freeschool Lane	C6
Friar Lane	C5
Friday Street	B8-C8
Frog Island	B8
Gallowtree Gate	D6
Gas Street	D8
Gateway Street	B4-C4-C3
Gaul Street	A3
George Street	D8-E8
Gotham Street	F3-F4
Grafton Street West	E7
Granby Street	D5-E5
Grange Lane	C4
Granville Road	F2-F3
Grasmere Street	B4-B3-C3-C2-C1-B1
Gravel Street	C7-D7
Great Central Street	B6-B7
Greyfriars	C5
Guildhall Lane	C6
Halford Street	D5-D6-E6
Haverlock Street	C2-C3
Haymarket	D6-D7
Hazel Street	C2
Heanor Street	B8-C8
High Cross Street	B7-B6-C6
Highfield Street	F3
High Street	C6-D6
Hinckley Road	A4
Hobart Street	F4
Horsefair Street	C5-D5
Hotel Street	C5
Humberstone Gate	D6-E6
Humberstone Road	F7
Infirmary Road	C4-C3-D3
Jarrom Street	B3-C3
Jarvis Street	B7
Kamloops Crescent	E8
Kashmir Road	F8
Kent Street	F7
King Richards Road	A5
King Street	D4-D5
Lancaster Road	D3-E3-E2
Lee Street	D6-D7-E7
Lincoln Street	F4-F5
London Road	E5-E4-F4-F3
Madras Road	F7
Maidstone Road	F5-F6
Malabar Road	F7
Manitoba Road	E8-F8
Mansfield Street	D6
Market Place	C5-C6-D6
Market Street	D5
Marshall Street	A8
Midland Street	E6
Mill Hill Lane	F3
Mill Lane	B4-C4
Millstone Lane	C5
Morledge Street	E6
Montreal Road	E8-F8
Narborough Road	A3-A4
Narborough Road North	A4-A5
Navigation Street	D8
Nelson Street	E4
Newarke Street	C5
Newbridge Street	C2
New Park Street	A5-B5
New Road	C7
Newtown Street	D3
New Walk	D4-E4-E3-F3
Nicholas Street	E6
Noel Street	A2
Northgate Street	B7-B8
Norman Street	A3
Nugent Street	A7
Orchard Street	D7-D8
Ottawa Road	E7-F7
Oxford Street	C4
Paget Road	A7
Paton Street	A3
Peacock Lane	C5
Pingle Street	B7
Pocklingtons Walk	C5-D5
Prebend Street	E4-F4
Princess Road East	E3-F3
Princess Road West	D4-E4
Queen Street	E6
Rawdykes Road	B1-C1
Regent Road	D4-D3-E3-F3-F2
Repton Street	A7-A8
Ridley Street	A4
Roman Street	A4
Rutland Street	D5-E5-E6
Rydal Street	B3
St George Street	E5-E6
St Georges Way	E6-F6
St John Street	D8
St Margaret's Way	B8-C8-C7
St Martins	C5
St Mathews Way	E7
St Nicholas Circle	B6-B5-C5
St Peters Lane	C6
Salisbury Road	F2-F3
Samuel Stuart	F6
Sanvey Gate	B7-C7
Sawday Street	C2
Saxby Street	F4
Saxon Street	A4
Severn Street	F4
Silver Street	C6
Slater Street	B8
Soar Lane	B7
South Albion Street	E4
Southampton Street	E6
Southgates	C5
Sparkenhoe Street	F4-F5
Station Street	E5
Stuart Street	A2
Swain Street	E5-F5
Swan Street	B7
The Newarke	B4-C4
Taylor Road	E8-F8
Tewkesbury Street	A6
Thirlemere Street	B2-B3-C3
Tichbourne Street	F3-F4
Tower Street	D3
Tudor Road	A5-A6-A7-A8
Ullswater Street	B3
Union Street	C6
University Road	E1-E2-E3-F3
Upper King Street	D3-D4
Upperton Road	A3-B3-B2
Vancouver Road	E8
Vaughan Way	C6-C7
Vaughan Street	A6
Vernon Street	A6-A7
Walnut Street	B3-B2-C2
Walton Street	A2
Warwick Street	A6
Waterloo Way	D2-D3-E3-E4
Watling Street	C8
Welford Road	D1-D2-D3-D4
Welles Street	B6
Wellington Street	D4-E4-D5
Western Boulevard	B3-B4
Western Road	A1-A2-A3-A4-B4-B5
West Street	D3-E3-E4
Wharf Street North	E7-E8
Wharf Street South	E7
Wilberforce Road	A2-A3
William Street	F6
Wimbledon Street	E6
Windermere Street	B2-B3-C3
Yeoman Street	D6
York Road	C4

Hinckley

Albert Road	B4
Alma Road	B4
Bowling Green Road	C3
Brick Kiln Street	A2
Bridge Road	B1
Brookfield Road	A1
Brookside	B1-C1
Browning Drive	A3
Brunel Road	A2-B2
Bute Close	A4
Butt Lane	C4
Canning Street	A3
Castle Street	B3-C3
Charles Street	C4
Church Walk	B3
Clarence Road	C2
Clarendon Road	A2-B2
Cleveland Road	A3
Clivesway	A4
Coley Close	B2
Council Road	B3
Coventry Lane	A2
Derby Road	B4
Druid Street	B3-B4
East Close	B1-C1
Factory Road	A4-B4
Fletcher Road	C1
Friary Close	C3
Garden Road	A4-B4
Glen Bank	C4
Gopsall Road	B4
Granby Road	A1-A2
Granville Road	A2
Hawley Road	A1-B1
Higham Way	C1
Highfields Road	C4
Hill Street	C2-C3
Holliers Walk	B3-B4
Hollycroft	A4
Hollycroft Crescent	A4
Holt Road	C1
Hurst Road	B2-C1-C2
John Street	C4
Lancaster Road	A2-B2
Leicester Road	C4
Linden Lane	A3
London Road	C3
Lower Bond Street	B3-B4
Mansion Lane	A3-B3
Marchant Road	A2-A3
Merevale Avenue	A1
Mill Hill Road	A3
Mount Road	B2-C2
New Buildings	B3-B4
New Street	B4
Priesthills Road	B2-C2
Princess Road	C2
Queens Road	C2-C3
Regent Street	A2-B2-A3-A3
Royal Court	B1
Rugby Road	A2-A1-B1
Rutland Avenue	A1
St George's Avenue	A3-A4
Shakespeare Drive	A3-A4
Southfield Road	B1-C1-C2
Spa Close	C4
Spa Lane	C3-C4
Spencer Street	B4
Springfield Road	B2
Stanley Road	A4
Station Road	B1-B2
Stockwellhead	B3
The Borough	B3
The Grove	A2
The Lawns	C3
Thornfield Way	C2
Thornycroft Road	C2-C3
Trinity Lane	A2-A3-A4-B4
Trinity Vicarage Road	A3
Upper Bond Street	B4
Victoria Road	C4
West Close	B1
Westray Drive	A4
Westfield Road	A1
Willow Bank Road	A1
Wood Street	B3-C3

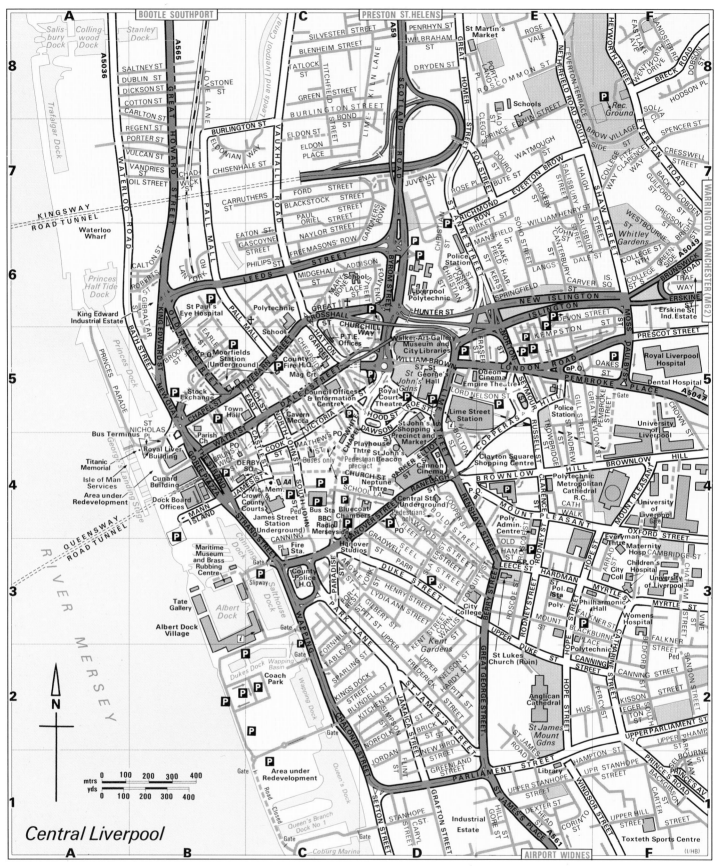

Liverpool

Although its dock area has been much reduced, Liverpool was at one time second only to London in pre-eminence as a port. Formerly the centrepiece of the docks area are three monumental buildings - the Dock Board Offices, built in 1907 with a huge copper-covered dome; the Cunard Building, dating from 1912 and decorated with an abundance of ornamental carving; and best-known of all, the world-famous Royal Liver Building, with the two 'liver birds' crowning its twin cupolas.

Some of the city's best industrial buildings have fallen into disuse in recent years, but some have been preserved as monuments of the idustrial age. One has become a maritime museum housing full-sized craft and a workshop where maritime crafts are demonstrated. Other museums and galleries include the Walker Art Gallery, with excellent collections of European painting and sculpture; Liverpool City Libraries, one of the oldest and largest public libraries in Britain, with a vast collection of books and manuscripts; and Bluecoat

Chambers, a Queen Anne building now used as a gallery and concert hall. Liverpool has two outstanding cathedrals: the Roman Catholic, completed in 1967 in an uncompromising controversial style; and the Protestant, constructed in the great tradition of Gothic architecture, but begun in 1904 and only recently completed.

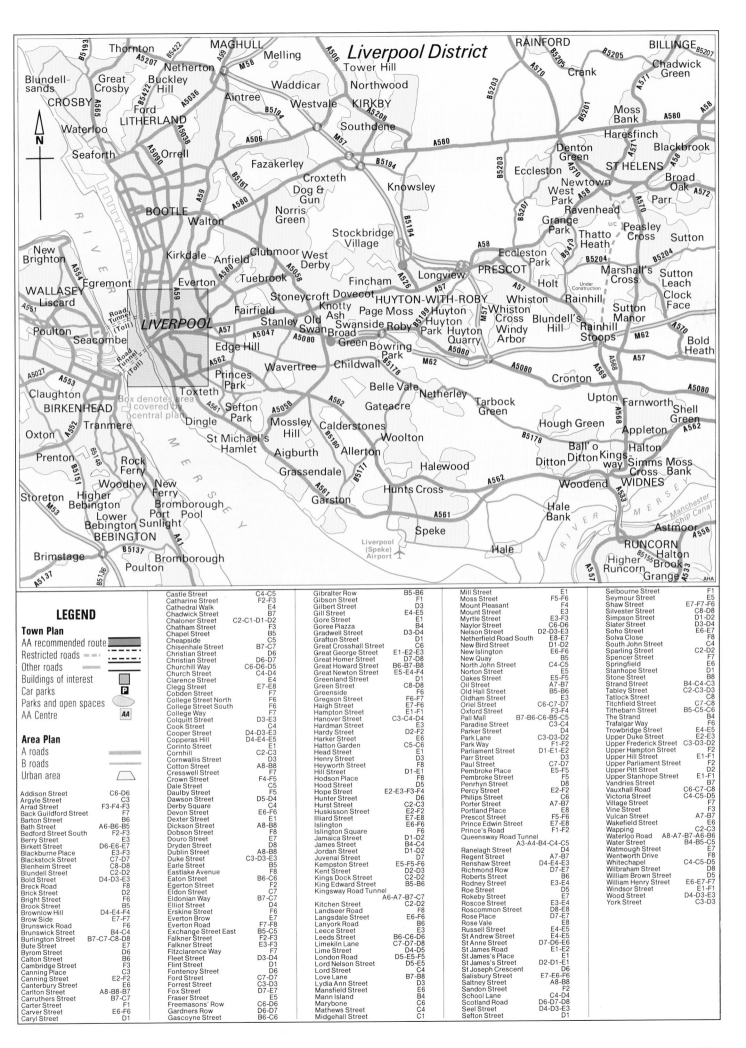

Liverpool District

LEGEND

Town Plan
AA recommended route
Restricted roads
Other roads
Buildings of interest
Car parks P
Parks and open spaces
AA Centre AA

Area Plan
A roads
B roads
Urban area

Addison Street	C6-D6
Argyle Street	C3
Arrad Street	F3-F4-F3
Back Guildford Street	F7
Barton Street	B6
Bath Street	A6-B6-B5
Bedford Street South	F2-F3
Berry Street	E3
Birkett Street	D6-E6-E7
Blackburne Place	E3-F3
Blackstock Street	C7-D7
Blenheim Street	C8-D8
Blundell Street	C2-D2
Bold Street	D4-D3-E3
Breck Road	F8
Brick Street	D2
Bright Street	F6
Brook Street	B5
Brownlow Hill	D4-E4-F4
Brow Side	E7-F7
Brunswick Road	F6
Brunswick Street	B4-C4
Burlington Street	B7-C7-C8-D8
Bute Street	E7
Byrom Street	D6
Calton Street	B6
Cambridge Street	F3
Canning Place	C3
Canning Street	E2-F2
Canterbury Street	E6
Carlton Street	A8-B8-B7
Carruthers Street	B7-C7
Carter Street	E5
Carver Street	E6-F6
Caryl Street	D1

Castle Street	C4-C5
Catharine Street	F2-F3
Cathedral Walk	E4
Chadwick Street	B7
Chaloner Street	C2-C1-D1-D2
Chatham Street	F3
Chapel Street	B5
Cheapside	C5
Chisenhale Street	B7-C7
Christian Street	D6
Christian Street	D6-D7
Churchill Way	C6-D6-D5
Church Street	C4-D4
Clarence Street	E4
Clegg Street	E7-E8
Cobden Street	F7
College Street North	F6
College Street South	F6
College Way	F7
Colquitt Street	D3-E3
Cook Street	C4
Cooper Street	D4-D3-E3
Copperas Hill	D4-E4-E5
Corinto Street	E1
Cornhill	C2-C3
Cornwallis Street	D3
Cotton Street	A8-B8
Cresswell Street	F7
Crown Street	F4-F5
Dale Street	C5
Daulby Street	F5
Dawson Street	D5-D4
Derby Square	C4
Devon Street	E6-F6
Dexter Street	E1
Dickson Street	A8-B8
Dobson Street	F8
Douro Street	E7
Dryden Street	D8
Dublin Street	A8-B8
Duke Street	C3-D3-E3
Earle Street	B5
Eastlake Avenue	F8
Eaton Street	B6-C6
Egerton Street	F2
Eldon Street	C7
Eldonian Way	B7-C7
Elliot Street	D4
Erskine Street	F6
Everton Brow	E7
Everton Road	F7-F8
Exchange Street East	B5-C5
Falkner Street	F2-F3
Falkner Street	E3-F3
Fitzclarence Way	F7
Fleet Street	D3-D4
Flint Street	D1
Fontenoy Street	D6
Ford Street	C7-D7
Forrest Street	C3-D3
Fox Street	D7-E7
Fraser Street	E5
Freemasons' Row	C6-D6
Gardners Row	D6-D7
Gascoyne Street	B6-C6

Gibralter Row	B5-B6
Gibson Street	F1
Gilbert Street	D3
Gill Street	E4-E5
Gore Street	E1
Goree Piazza	B4
Gradwell Street	D3-D4
Grafton Street	D1
Great Crosshall Street	C6
Great George Street	E1-E2-E3
Great Homer Street	D7-D8
Great Howard Street	B6-B7-B8
Great Newton Street	E5-E4-F4
Greenland Street	D1
Green Street	C8-D8
Greenside	F6
Gregson Street	F6-F7
Haigh Street	E7-F6
Hampton Street	E1-F1
Hanover Street	C3-C4-D4
Hardman Street	F3
Hardy Street	D2-F2
Harker Street	E6
Hatton Garden	C5-C6
Head Street	E1
Henry Street	D3
Heyworth Street	F8
Hill Street	D1-E1
Hodson Place	F8
Hood Street	D5
Hope Street	E2-E3-F3-F4
Hunter Street	D6
Hurst Street	C2-C3
Huskisson Street	E2-F2
Illiard Street	E7-E8
Islington	E6-F6
Islington Square	F6
Jamaica Street	D1-D2
James Street	B4-C4
Jordan Street	D1-D2
Juvenal Street	D7
Kempston Street	E5-F5-F6
Kent Street	D2-D3
Kings Dock Street	C2-D2
King Edward Street	B5-B6
Kingsway Road Tunnel	A6-A7-B7-C7
Kitchen Street	C2-D2
Landseer Road	F8
Langsdale Street	E6-F6
Lanyork Road	B6
Leece Street	E3
Leeds Street	B6-C6-D6
Limekiln Lane	C7-D7-D8
Lime Street	D4-D5
London Road	D5-E5-F5
Lord Nelson Street	D5-E5
Lord Street	C4
Love Lane	B7-B8
Lydia Ann Street	D3
Mansfield Street	E6
Mann Island	B4
Marybone	C6
Mathews Street	C4
Midgehall Street	C1

Mill Street	E1
Moss Street	F5-F6
Mount Pleasant	F4
Mount Street	E3
Myrtle Street	E3-F3
Naylor Street	C6-D6
Nelson Street	D2-D3-E3
Netherfield Road South	E8-E7
New Bird Street	D1-D2
New Islington	E6-F6
New Quay	B5
North John Street	C4-C5
Norton Street	E5
Oakes Street	E5-F5
Oil Street	A7-B7
Old Hall Street	B5-B6
Oldham Street	E3
Oriel Street	C6-C7-D7
Oxford Street	F3-F4
Pall Mall	B7-B6-C6-B5-C5
Paradise Street	C3-C4
Parker Street	D4
Park Lane	C3-D3-D2
Park Way	F1-F2
Parliament Street	D1-E1-E2
Parr Street	D3
Paul Street	C7-D7
Pembroke Place	E5-F5
Pembroke Street	F5
Penrhyn Street	D8
Percy Street	E2-F2
Philips Street	C6
Porter Street	A7-B7
Portland Place	E8
Prescot Street	F5-F6
Prince Edwin Street	E7-E8
Prince's Road	F1-F2
Queensway Road Tunnel	A3-A4-B4-C4-C5
Ranelagh Street	D4
Regent Street	A7-B7
Renshaw Street	D4-E4-E3
Richmond Row	D7-E7
Roberts Street	B6
Rodney Street	E3-E4
Roe Street	D5
Rokeby Street	E7
Roscoe Street	E3-E4
Roscommon Street	D8-E8
Rose Place	D7-E7
Rose Vale	E8
Russell Street	E4-E5
St Andrew Street	E4-E5
St Anne Street	D7-D6-E6
St James Road	E1-E2
St James's Place	E1
St James's Street	D2-D1-E1
St Joseph Crescent	D6
Salisbury Street	E7-E6-F6
Saltney Street	A8-B8
Sandon Street	F2
School Lane	C4-D4
Scotland Road	D6-D7-D8
Seel Street	D4-D3-E3
Sefton Street	D1

Selbourne Street	F1
Seymour Street	E5
Shaw Street	E7-F7-F6
Silvester Street	C8-D8
Simpson Street	D1-D2
Slater Street	D3-D4
Soho Street	E6-E7
Solva Close	E7
South John Street	C4
Sparling Street	C2-D2
Spencer Street	E6
Springfield	E6
Stanhope Street	D1
Stone Street	B8
Strand Street	B4-C4-C3
Tabley Street	C2-C3-D3
Tatlock Street	C8
Titchfield Street	C7-C8
Tithebarn Street	B5-C5-C6
The Strand	B4
Trafalgar Way	E4-E5
Trowbridge Street	E4-E5
Upper Duke Street	E2-E3
Upper Frederick Street	C3-D3-D2
Upper Hampton Street	F2
Upper Hill Street	E1-F1
Upper Parliament Street	F2
Upper Pitt Street	D2
Upper Stanhope Street	E1-F1
Vandries Street	B7
Vauxhall Road	C6-C7-C8
Victoria Street	C4-C5-D5
Village Street	F3
Vine Street	F3
Vulcan Street	A7-B7
Wakefield Street	E6
Wapping	C2-C3
Waterloo Road	A8-A7-B7-A6-B6
Water Street	B4-B5-C5
Watmough Street	E7
Wentworth Drive	F8
Whitechapel	C4-C5-D5
Wilbraham Street	D8
William Brown Street	D5
William Henry Street	E6-E7-F7
Windsor Street	E1-F1
Wood Street	D4-D3-E3
York Street	C3-D3

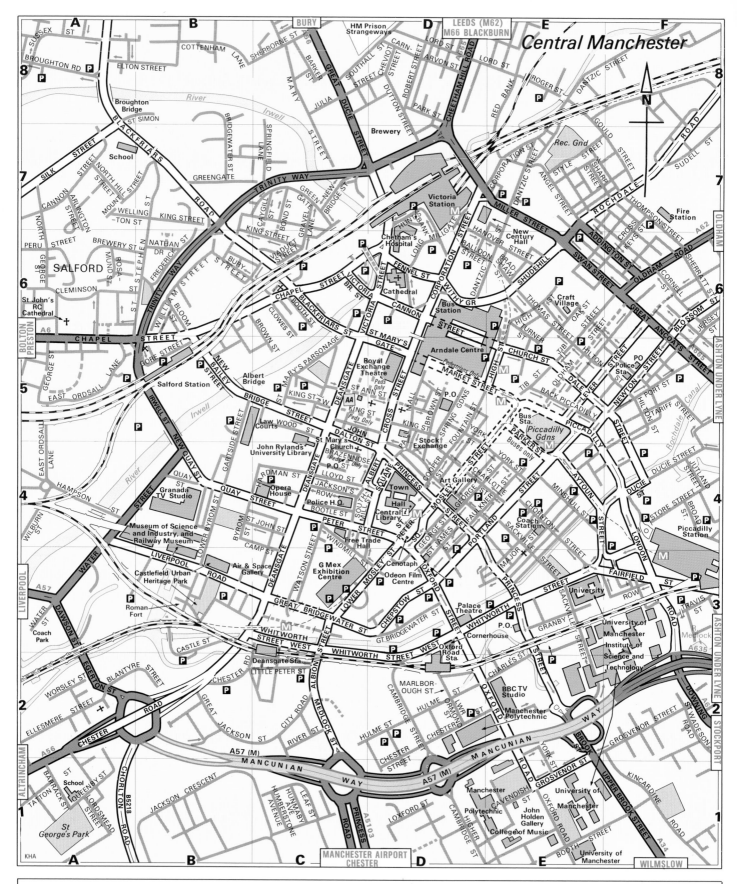

Manchester

Manchester is the regional centre for North-west England with a population of over half a million. Commerce and industry are vital aspects of the city's character, but it is also an important cultural centre – the Halle Orchestra has its home at the Free Trade Hall (a venue for many concerts besides classical music), there are several theatres, the John Rylands Library which houses one of the most important collections of books in the world, and a

number of museums and galleries, including the Whitworth Gallery with its lovely watercolours.

Like many great cities it suffered badly during World War II, but some older buildings remain including the massive Gothic-style town hall of 1877.

Manchester Cathedral dates mainly from the 15th century and is noted for its fine tower and outstanding carved woodwork. Nearby is Chetham's Hospital, also 15th-century and new housing has taken place, and more is planned. The massive Arndale Shopping Centre caters for the vast population, and there are

huge international-standard hotels. The Museum of Science and Industry in the Castlefield Urban Heritage Park contains exhibits from the Industrial Revolution to the Space Age and includes the world's first passenger railway station. Nearby are the Granada Television Studios where visitors can walk through the various film sets including the famous 'Coronation Street', and the impressive G-Mex exhibition centre. Manchester is also the first city in Britain to re-instate an on-street tramway system.

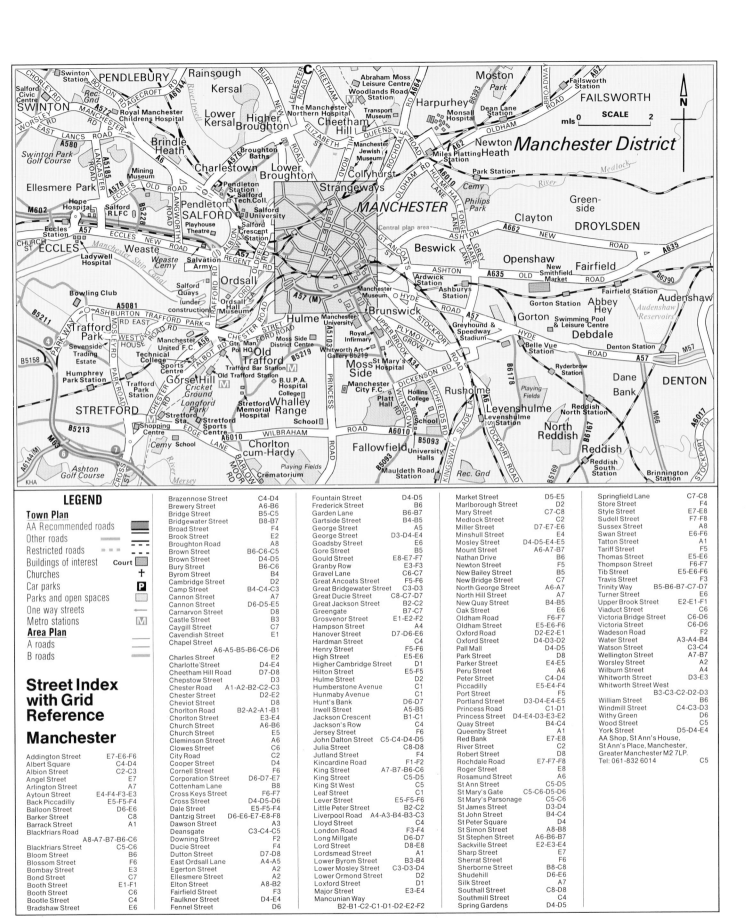

LEGEND

Town Plan

AA Recommended roads
Other roads
Restricted roads
Buildings of interest   Court
Churches   †
Car parks   P
Parks and open spaces
One way streets   ←
Metro stations   M

Area Plan

A roads
B roads

Street Index with Grid Reference

Manchester

Addington Street	E7-E6-F6
Albert Square	C4-D4
Albion Street	C2-C3
Angel Street	E7
Arlington Street	A7
Aytoun Street	E4-F4-F3-E3
Back Piccadilly	E5-F5-F4
Balloon Street	D6-E6
Barker Street	C8
Barrack Street	A1
Blackfriars Road	A8-A7-B7-B6-C6
Blackfriars Street	C5-C6
Bloom Street	B6
Blossom Street	F6
Bombay Street	E3
Bond Street	C7
Booth Street	E1-F1
Booth Street	C6
Bootle Street	C4
Bradshaw Street	E6
Brazennose Street	C4-D4
Brewery Street	A6-B6-B6
Bridge Street	B5-C5
Bridgewater Street	B8-B7
Broad Street	F4
Brook Street	E2
Broughton Road	A8
Brown Street	B6-C6-C5
Brown Street	D4-D5
Bury Street	B6-C6
Byrom Street	B4
Cambridge Street	D2
Camp Street	B4-C4-C3
Cannon Street	A7
Cannon Street	D6-D5-E5
Carnarvon Street	D8
Castle Street	B3
Caygill Street	C7
Cavendish Street	E1
Chapel Street	A6-A5-B5-B6-C6-D6
Charles Street	E2
Charlotte Street	D4-E4
Cheetham Hill Road	D7-D8
Chepstow Street	D3
Chester Road	A1-A2-B2-C2-C3
Chester Street	D2-E2
Cheviot Street	D8
Chorlton Road	B2-A2-A1-B1
Chorlton Street	E3-E4
Church Street	A6-B6
Church Street	E5
Cleminson Street	A6
Clowes Street	C6
City Road	C2
Cooper Street	D4
Cornell Street	F6
Corporation Street	D6-D7-E7
Cottenham Lane	B8
Cross Keys Street	F6-F7
Cross Street	D4-D5-D6
Dale Street	E5-F5-F4
Dantzig Street	D6-E6-E7-E8-F8
Dawson Street	A3
Deansgate	C3-C4-C5
Downing Street	F2
Ducie Street	F4
Dutton Street	D7-D8
East Ordsall Lane	A4-A5
Egerton Street	A2
Ellesmere Street	A2
Elton Street	A8-B2
Fairfield Street	F3
Faulkner Street	D4-E4
Fennel Street	D6

Fountain Street	D4-D5
Frederick Street	B6
Garden Lane	B6-B7
Gartside Street	B4-B5
George Street	A5
George Street	D3-D4-E4
Goadsby Street	E6
Gore Street	B5
Gould Street	E8-E7-F7
Granby Row	E3-F3
Gravel Lane	C6-C7
Great Ancoats Street	F5-F6
Great Bridgewater Street	C3-D3
Great Ducie Street	C8-C7-D7
Great Jackson Street	B2-C2
Greengate	B7-C7
Grosvenor Street	E1-E2-F2
Hampson Street	A4
Hanover Street	D7-D6-E6
Hardman Street	C4
Henry Street	F5-F6
High Street	E5-E6
Higher Cambridge Street	D1
Hilton Street	E5-F5
Hulme Street	D2
Humberstone Avenue	C1
Hunmaby Avenue	C1
Hunt's Bank	D6-D7
Irwell Street	A5-B5
Jackson Crescent	B1-C1
Jackson's Row	C4
Jersey Street	F6
John Dalton Street	C5-C4-D4-D5
Julia Street	C8-D8
Jutland Street	F4
Kincardine Road	F1-F2
King Street	A7-B7-B6-C6
King Street	C5-D5
King St West	C5
Leaf Street	C1
Lever Street	E5-F5-F6
Little Peter Street	B2-C2
Liverpool Road	A4-A3-B4-B3-C3
Lloyd Street	C4
London Road	F3-F4
Long Millgate	D6-D7
Lord Street	D8-E8
Lordsmead Street	A1
Lower Byrom Street	B3-B4
Lower Mosley Street	C3-D3-D4
Lower Ormond Street	D2
Loxford Street	D1
Major Street	E3-E4
Mancunian Way	B2-B1-C2-C1-D1-D2-E2-F2

Market Street	D5-E5
Marlborough Street	D2
Mary Street	C7-C8
Medlock Street	C2
Miller Street	D7-E7-E6
Minshull Street	E4
Mosley Street	D4-D5-E4-E5
Mount Street	A6-A7-B7
Nathan Drive	B6
Newton Street	F5
New Bailey Street	B5
New Bridge Street	C7
North George Street	A6-A7
North Hill Street	A7
New Quay Street	B4-B5
Oak Street	E6
Oldham Road	F6-F7
Oldham Street	E5-E6-F6
Oxford Road	D2-E2-E1
Oxford Street	D4-D3-D2
Pall Mall	D4-D5
Park Street	D8
Parker Street	E4-E5
Peru Street	A6
Peter Street	C4-D4
Piccadilly	E5-E4-F4
Port Street	F5
Portland Street	D3-D4-E4-E5
Princess Road	C1-D1
Princess Street	D4-E4-D3-E3-E2
Quay Street	B4-C4
Queenby Street	A1
Red Bank	E7-E8
River Street	C2
Robert Street	D8
Rochdale Road	E7-F7-F8
Roger Street	A6
Rosamund Street	A6
St Ann Street	C5-D5
St Mary's Gate	C5-C6-D5-D6
St Mary's Parsonage	C5-C6
St James Street	D3-D4
St John Street	B4-C4
St Peter Square	D4
St Simon Street	A8-B8
St Stephen Street	A6-B6-B7
Sackville Street	E2-E3-E4
Sharp Street	E7
Sherrat Street	F6
Sherborne Street	B8-B6-B2
Shudehill	D6-E6
Silk Street	A7
Southall Street	C8-D8
Southmill Street	C4
Spring Gardens	D4-D5

Springfield Lane	C7-C8
Store Street	F4
Style Street	E7-E8
Sudell Street	F7-F8
Sussex Street	A8
Swan Street	E6-F6
Tatton Street	A1
Tariff Street	F5
Thomas Street	E5-E6
Thompson Street	F6-F7
Tib Street	E5-E6-F6
Travis Street	F3
Trinity Way	B5-B6-B7-C7-D7
Turner Street	E6
Upper Brook Street	E2-E1-F1
Viaduct Street	C6
Victoria Bridge Street	C6-D6
Victoria Street	C6-D6
Wadeson Road	F2
Water Street	A3-A4-B4
Watson Street	C3-C4
Wellington Street	A7-B7
Whitworth Street	D3-E3
Whitworth Street West	B3-C3-C2-D2-D3
William Street	B6
Windmill Street	C4-C3-D3
Withy Green	D6
Wood Street	C5
York Street	D5-D4-E4

AA Shop, St Ann's House,
St Ann's Place, Manchester,
Greater Manchester M2 7LP.
Tel: 061-832 6014   C5

MANCHESTER
The Barton Swing Bridge carries the Bridgewater Canal over the Manchester Ship Canal, which links Manchester with the sea nearly 40 miles away. Completed in 1894, the canal is navigable by vessels up to 15,000 tons.

227

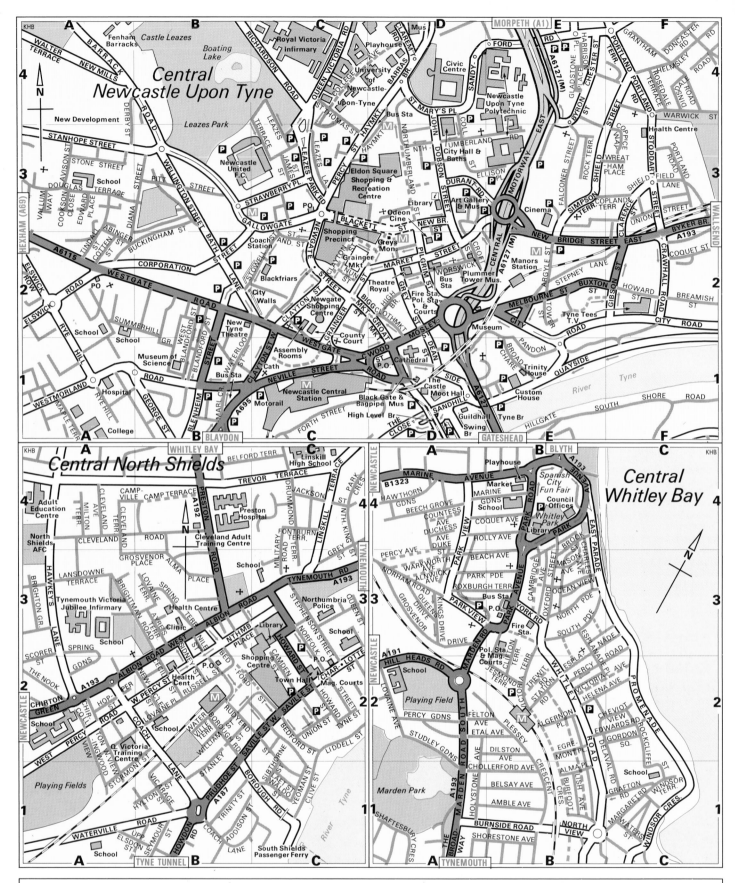

Newcastle

Six bridges span the Tyne at Newcastle; they all help to create a striking scene, but the most impressive is the High Level Bridge, built by Robert Stephenson in 1845-49 and consisting of two levels, one for the railway and one for the road. It is from the river that some of the best views of the city can be obtained. Grey Street is Newcastle's most handsome thoroughfare. It dates from the time, between 1835 and 1840, when much of this part of the city was replanned and rebuilt. Elegant façades curve up to Grey's Monument. Close to the Monument is the Eldon Centre, combining sports facilities and shopping centre to form an integrated complex which is one of the largest of its kind in Europe. Newcastle has many museums. The industrial background of the city is traced in the Museum of Science and Engineering, while the Laing Art Gallery and Museum covers painting, costumes and local domestic history. The Hancock Museum has an exceptional natural history collection and the John George Joicey Museum has period displays in a 17th-century almshouse. In Black Gate is one of Britain's most unusual museums – a collection of over 100 sets of bagpipes. Within the University precincts are three further museums. Of the city's open spaces, Town Moor is the largest. At nearly 1,000 acres it is big enough to feel genuinely wild.

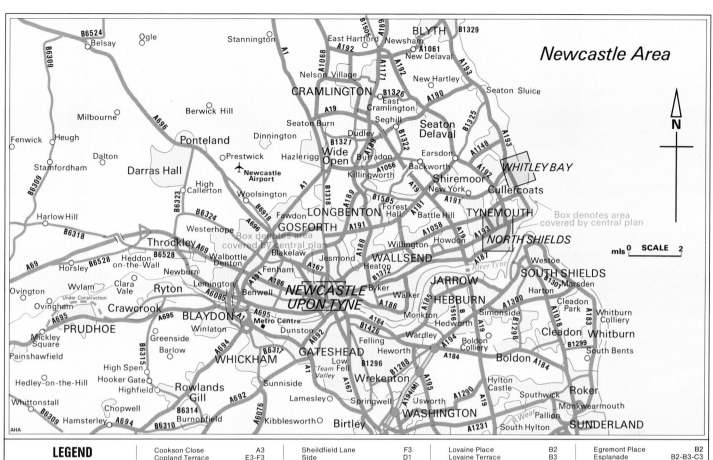

Newcastle Area

N

Box denotes area covered by central plan

Box denotes area covered by central plan

mls 0 SCALE 2

AHA

LEGEND

Town Plan

AA recommended route
Restricted roads
Other roads
Buildings of interest Library
Car parks P
Parks and open spaces
Metro stations M
One way streets ←
Churches †

Area Plan

A roads
B roads
Locations Dudley ○
Urban area

Street Index with Grid Reference

Newcastle

Abinger Street	A2
Argyle Street	E2
Avison Street	A3
Barrack Road	A4-B4-B3
Barras Bridge	D4
Bath Lane	B2-C2
Bigg Market Street	C2-D2
Blackett Street	C3-D3-D2
Blandford Street	B1-B2
Blenheim Street	B1-B2
Breamish Street	F2
Broad Chare	E1
Buckingham Street	A2-B2-B3
Buxton Street	E2
Byker Bridge	F2-F3
Byran Street	E3-E4
Central Motorway	E1-D1-D2-E2-E3-E4
Chester Street	E4
City Road	E1-E2-F2
Clarance Street	F2-F3
Claremont Road	D4
Clayton Street	C2
Clayton Street West	B1-C1-C2
Clothmarket	D2
College Avenue	C4-D4
College Street	D3-D4
Collingwood Street	C1-D1
Cookson Close	A3
Copland Terrace	E3-F3
Coppice Way	F3
Coquet Street	F2
Corporation Street	B2-B3
Cotten Street	A2
Crawhill Road	F2
Croft Street	D2
Dean Street	D1-D2
Derby Street	A3-A4
Diana Street	A2-A3-B3
Dinsdale Road	F4
Doncaster Road	F4
Douglas Terrace	A3-B3
Durant Road	D3
Edward Place	A3
Ellison Place	D3-E3
Elswick Road	A2
Elswick Row	A2
Falconer Street	E3
Forth Street	C1-D1
Gallowgate	B3-C3
George Street	A1-B1
Gibson Street	F2
Gladstone Place	E4
Grainger Street	C1-C2-D2
Grantham Road	F4
Grey Street	D2
Great Market	D1-D2
Harrison Place	E4
Haymarket	D3-D4
Helmsley Road	F4
High Bridge	D2
Hillgate	E1
Howard Street	F2
John Dobson Street	D3-D4
Leazes Lane	C3
Leazes Park Road	C3-C4
Leazes Terrace	C3-C4
Maple Terrace	A1
Market Street	D2
Marlborough Crescent	B1
Melbourne Street	E2-F2
Moseley Street	D1-D2
Neville Street	C1
New Bridge Road	F2-F3
New Bridge Street	D3-E3-E2-F2
New Bridge Street East	E2-F2
Newgate Street	C2-C3
New Mills	A4
Northumberland Street	D4-D3-D4
Nun Street	C2
Oakes Place	A2-B2-B3
Pandon	E1
Percy Street	C3-D3-D4
Pilgrim Street	D2
Pitt Street	B3
Portland Road	F3-F4
Portland Terrace	F4
Quayside	D1-E1-F1-F2
Queen Victoria Road	C4
Rock Terrace	E3
Rosedale Terrace	F4
Rye Hill	A1-A2
St Andrews Street	C2
St James Street	C3
St Mary's Place	D4
St Nicholas Square	D1-D2
St Thomas Street	C3-C4
Sandyford Road	D4-E4
Sandhill	D1
Shield Street	E3-F3-F4

Sheildfield Lane	F3
Side	D1
Simpson Terrace	E3
South Shore Road	E1-F1
Stanhope Street	A3-B3
Stepney Lane	E2-F2
Stoddart Street	F3
Stone Street	A3
Stowell Street	B2-C2
Strawberry Place	B3-C3
Summerhill Grove	A2-B2-B1
The Close	D1
Tindall Street	A2
Tower Street	E2
Union Street	F3
Vallum Way	A3
Victoria Square	E4
Walter Terrace	A4
Warwick Street	F4
Waterloo Street	B1-B2-C2
Wellington Street	B3
Westgate Road	A2-B2-C2-C1-D1
Westmorland Road	A1-B1
West Blandford Street	B1-B2
Worswick Street	D2
Wreatham Place	E3-F3

North Shields

Addison Street	B1
Albion Road	B3-C3
Albion Road West	A2-B2-B3
Alma Place	B3
Ayre's Terrace	B3
Bedford Street	B3-B2-C2
Belford Terrace	B4-C4
Borough Road	B2-B1-C1
Brightman Road	A3-B3
Brighton Grove	A3
Camden Street	C2-C3
Camp Terrace	B4
Campville	A4-B4
Cecil Street	B2
Charlotte Street	C2-C3
Chirton Green	A2
Chirton West View	A1-A2
Cleveland Avenue	A4
Cleveland Road	A4-B4
Cleveland Terrace	A3-A4
Clive Street	C1-C2
Coach Lane	A2-B2-B1
Collingwood View	A1-A2
Drummond Terrace	C3-C4
Fontbarn Terrace	C4
Grey Street	C3-C4
Grosvenor Place	A3-B3
Hawkey's Lane	A2-A3-A4
Hopper Street	A2
Howard Street	C2-C3
Howdon Road	B1
Hylton Street	A1-B1
Jackson Street	C4
Laet Street	C1
Lansdowne Terrace	A3
Liddell Street	C2
Linskill Terrace	C3-C4

Lovaine Place	B2
Lovaine Terrace	B3
Military Road	C3-C4
Milton Terrace	A4
Nile Street	B3
Norfolk Street	C2-C3
North King Street	C3-C4
Northumberland Place	B3-C3
Park Crescent	C4
Preston Road	B3-B4
Prudhoe Street	B1-B2
Queen Street	C3
Rudyard Street	B2-C2-C1
Russell Street	B2
Sackville Street West	B2-C2
Saville Street	C2
Scorer Street	A2-A3
Seymour Street	B1
Sibthorne Street	C1-C2
Sidney Street	B2-B3
Spring Gardens	A2-A3
Spring Terrace	A3
Stanley Street	B1-B2
Stephenson Street	C2-C3
Stormont Street	A1-A2-B2
The Nook	A2
Trevor Terrace	B4-C4
Trinity Street	B1
Tyne Street	C2
Tynemouth Road	C3
Union Street	C2
Upper Elsdon Street	A1-B1
Vicarage Street	B1
Waldo Street	C1
Waterville Road	A1-B1
Waterville Terrace	B2
West Percy Road	A1-A2
West Percy Street	A2-B2-B3
William Street	B2-C2
Yeoman Street	C1-C2

Whitley Bay

Algernon Place	B2
Alma Place	B1
Alnwick Avenue	A3
Amble Avenue	A1-B1
Beach Avenue	A3-B3-B4
Beech Grove	A4
Belsay Avenue	A1-B1
Brook Street	B3-B4
Burfoot Crescent	B1
Burnside Road	A1-B1
Cambridge Avenue	B3-B4
Charles Avenue	B3-B4
Cheviot View	B2-C2
Chollerford Avenue	A1-B1
Clifton Terrace	B2-B3
Coquet Avenue	A4-B4
Countess Avenue	A4
Delaval Road	B2-C2-C1
Dilston Avenue	A2-B2
Duchess Avenue	A4
Duke Street	A4
East Parade	B3-B4
Edwards Road	B2-C2

Egremont Place	B2
Esplanade	B2-B3-C3
Esplanade Place	B3-B2-C2
Etal Avenue	A2-B2
Felton Avenue	A2-B2
Gordon Square	C2
Grafton Road	C1
Grosvenor Drive	A3
Hawthorne Gardens	A4
Helena Avenue	B2-C2
Hill Heads Road	A2-A3-A2
Holly Avenue	A4-B4
Holystone Avenue	A1-A2
Jesmond Terrace	A2-B2
Kings Drive	A3
Lish Avenue	B1
Lovaine Avenue	A2
Marden Road	A2-A3-B3
Marden Road South	A1-A2
Margaret Road	C1
Marine Avenue	A4-B4
Marine Gardens	A4-B4
Mason Avenue	B3
Norham Road	A3
North Parade	B3
North View	B1
Ocean View	B3
Oxford Street	B3-B4
Park Avenue	B3-B4
Park Parade	A3-B3
Park Road	B4
Park View	A3-A4
Percy Avenue	A3-A4
Percy Gardens	A2
Percy Road	B2-C2-C3
Plessey Crescent	A2-B2-B1
Promenade	C1-C2-C3
Queens Drive	A3
Rockcliffe Street	C1-C2
Roxburgh Terrace	A3-B3
Shaftesbury Crescent	A1
Shorestone Avenue	A1-B1
South Parade	B3
Station Road	B2
Studley Gardens	A1-A2
The Broadway	A1
Trewit Road	B2
Victoria Avenue	B2-C2
Victoria Terrace	B2-B3
Warkworth Avenue	A3
Waters Street	C1
Whitley Road	B1-B2-B3
Windsor Crescent	C1
Windsor Terrace	C1
York Road	B3

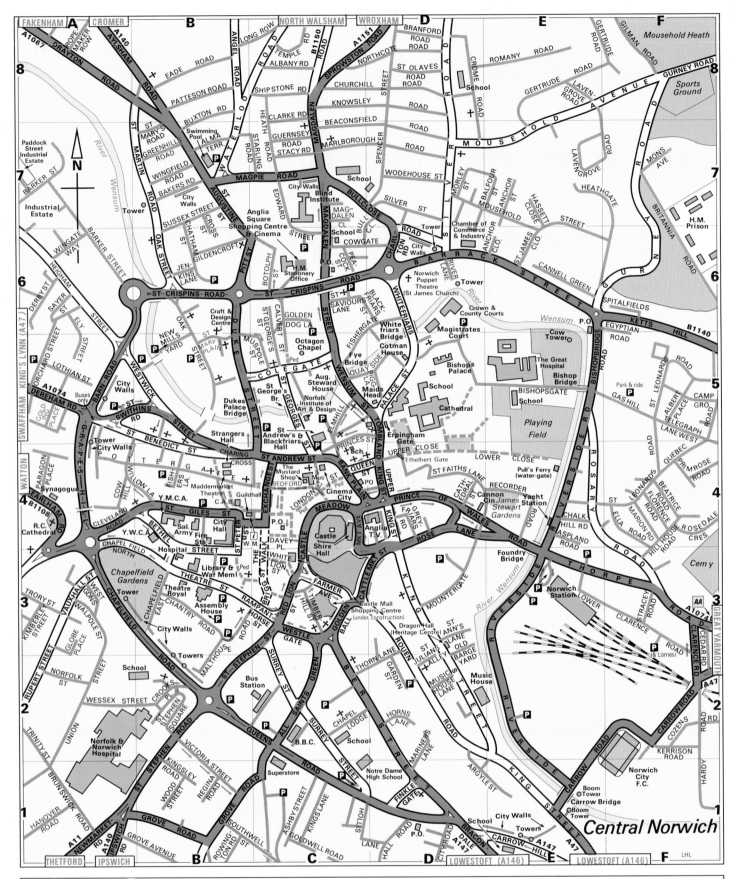

Norwich

Fortunately the heart has not been ripped out of Norwich to make way for some bland precinct, so its ancient character has been preserved. Narrow alleys run between the streets – sometimes opening out into quiet courtyards, sometimes into thoroughfares packed with people, sometimes into lanes which seem quite deserted. It is a unique place, with something of interest on every corner.

The cathedral was founded in 1096 by the city's first bishop, Herbert de Losinga. Among its most notable features are the nave, with its huge pillars, the bishop's throne (a Saxon survival unique in Europe) and the cloisters with their matchless collection of roof bosses. Across the city is the great stone keep of the castle, set on a mound and dominating all around it. It dates from Norman times, but was refaced in 1834. The keep now forms part of Norwich Castle Museum – an extensive and fascinating collection. Other museums are Bridewell Museum – collections relating to local crafts and industries within a 14th-century building – and Strangers' Hall, a genuinely 'old world' house, rambling and full of surprises, both in its tumble of rooms and in the things which they contain. Especially picturesque parts of the city are Elm Hill – a street of ancient houses; Tombland – with two gateways into the Cathedral Close; and Pull's Ferry – a watergate by the river.

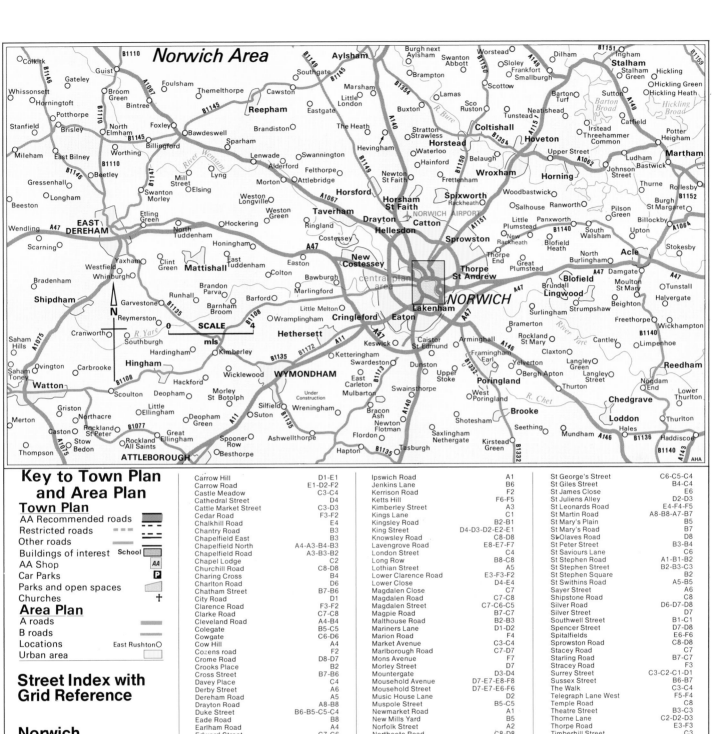

Key to Town Plan and Area Plan

Town Plan

AA Recommended roads	
Restricted roads	
Other roads	
Buildings of interest	School
AA Shop	AA
Car Parks	P
Parks and open spaces	
Churches	+

Area Plan

A roads	
B roads	
Locations	East Rushton ○
Urban area	

Street Index with Grid Reference

Norwich

Albany Road	C8	Carrow Hill	D1-E1	Ipswich Road	A1	St George's Street	C6-C5-C4
Albert Place	F5	Carrow Road	E1-D2-F2	Jenkins Lane	B6	St Giles Street	B4-C4
All Saints Green	C2-C3	Castle Meadow	C3-C4	Kerrison Road	F2	St James Close	E6
Alma Terrace	B7	Cathedral Street	D4	Ketts Hill	F6-F5	St Juliens Alley	D2-D3
Anchor Close	E6	Cattle Market Street	C3-D3	Kimberley Street	A3	St Leonards Road	E4-F4-F5
Anchor Street	E7	Cedar Road	F3-F2	Kings Lane	C1	St Martin Road	A8-B8-A7-B7
Angel Road	B8	Chalkhill Road	E4	Kingsley Road	B2-B1	St Mary's Plain	B5
Argyle Street	D1-E1	Chantry Road	B3	King Street	D4-D3-D2-E2-E1	St Mary's Road	B7
Ashby Street	C1	Chapelfield East	B3	Knowsley Road	C8-D8	St Olaves Road	D8
Aspland Road	E4	Chapelfield North	A4-A3-B4-B3	Lavengrove Road	E8-E7-F7	St Peter Street	B3-B4
Aylsham Road	A8-B8	Chapelfield Road	A3-B3-B2	London Street	C4	St Saviours Lane	C6
Bakers Road	B7	Chapel Lodge	C2	Long Row	B8-C8	St Stephen Road	A1-B1-B2
Balfour Street	E7	Churchill Road	C8-D8	Lothian Street	A5	St Stephen Street	B2-B3-C3
Bank Plain	C4	Charing Cross	B4	Lower Clarence Road	E3-F3-F2	St Stephen Square	B2
Barker Street	A7-A6	Charlton Road	D6	Lower Close	D4-E4	St Swithins Road	A5-B5
Barn Road	A5	Chatham Street	B7-B6	Magdalen Close	C7	Sayer Street	A6
Barrack Street	D6-E6	City Road	D1	Magdalen Road	C7-C8	Shipstone Road	C8
Beaconsfield Road	C7-D7	Clarence Road	F3-F2	Magdalen Street	C7-C6-C5	Silver Road	D6-D7-D8
Beatrice Road	F4	Clarke Road	C7-C8	Magpie Road	B7-C7	Silver Street	D7
Bedford Street	C4	Cleveland Road	A4-B4	Malthouse Road	B2-B3	Southwell Street	B1-C1
Ber Street	C3-C2-D2-D1	Colegate	B5-C5	Mariners Lane	D1-D2	Spencer Street	D7-D8
Bethel Street	B4-B3	Cowgate	C6-D6	Marion Road	F4	Spitalfields	E6-F6
Bishopsbridge Road	E5-E6	Cow Hill	A4	Market Avenue	C3-C4	Sprowston Road	C8-D8
Bishopsgate	D5-E5	Cozens road	F2	Marlborough Road	C7-D7	Stacey Road	C7
Blackfriars Street	C6-D6	Crome Road	D8-D7	Mons Avenue	F7	Starling Road	B7-C7
Boltolph Street	C6	Crooks Place	B2	Morley Street	D7	Stracey Road	F3
Bracondale	D1-E1	Cross Street	B7-B6	Mountergate	D3-D4	Surrey Street	C3-C2-C1-D1
Branford Road	D8	Davey Place	C4	Mousehold Avenue	D7-E7-E8-F8	Sussex Street	B6-B7
Brigg Street	C3	Derby Street	A6	Mousehold Street	D7-E7-E6-F6	The Walk	C3-C4
Britannia road	F7-F6	Dereham Road	A5	Music House Lane	D2	Telegraph Lane West	F5-F4
Brunswick Road	A1	Drayton Road	A8-B8	Muspole Street	B5-C5	Temple Road	C8
Bull Close	C6-C7-C7	Duke Street	B6-B5-C5-C4	Newmarket Road	A1	Theatre Street	B3-C3
Bull Close Road	C7-D7-D6	Eade Road	B8	New Mills Yard	B5	Thorne Lane	C2-D2-D3
Buxton Road	B7-B8	Earlham Road	A4	Norfolk Street	A2	Thorpe Road	E3-F3
Calvert Street	C5-C6	Edward Street	C7-C6	Northcote Road	C8-D8	Timberhill Street	C3
Camp Grove	F5	Egyptian Road	E6-F6-F5	Oak Street	B6-B5	Tombland	D5-D4
Cannel Green	E6	Ella Road	F4-F3	Old Barge Yard	D2-D3	Trinity Street	A2-A1
		Elmhill	C5	Orchard Street	A5-A6	Trory Street	A3
		Ely Street	A5-A6	Palace Street	D5	Union Street	A1-A2-A3
		Exchange Street	C4	Paragon Place	A4	Upper Close	D4
		Farmer Avenue	C3	Patterson Road	B8	Upper King Street	D4
		Finklegate	D1	Peacock Street	C6	Vauxhall Street	A3
		Fishergate	C5-C6-D6	Pigg Lane	D5	Victoria Street	B2-B1
		Fishers Lane	B4	Pitt Street	B6-C6	Walpole Street	A3
		Florence Road	F4	Pottergate	A4-B4	Waterloo Road	B7-B8-C8
		Garden Street	D2	Prince of Wales Road	D4-E4-E3	Whitefriars	D6-D5
		Gas Hill	E5-F5	Primrose Road	F4	White Lion Street	C3
		Getrude Road	E8-E7	Princes Street	C4-C5-D5	Willow Lane	A4-B4
		Gildencroft	B6	Quay Side	C5-D5	Wingfield Road	B7
		Gilman Road	F8	Quebec Road	F4-F5	Wensum Street	C5-D5
		Globe Place	A3	Queens Road	B2-C2-C1	Wessex Street	A2-B2
		Golden Ball	C3	Queens Street	C4-D4	West Gardens	A3
		Golden Dog Lane	C6	Record Road	E4	Westle Gate	C3
		Golding Place	A5	Red Lion Street	C3	Westwick Street	A5-B5-B4
		Goldwell Road	C1	Regina Road	B1	Woodhouse Street	D7
		Grapes Hill	A5-A4	River Lane	D6	Wood Street	B1
		Greenhills Road	B7	Riverside	E3-E2-E1		
		Greyfriars Road	D4	Riverside Road	E3-E4-E5		
		Grove Avenue	A1-B1	Romany Road	D8-E8		
		Grove Road	A1-B1-C1-C2	Ropemaker Row	A8		
		Gurney Road	E6-F6-F7-F8	Rosary Road	E5-E4-F4-F3		
		Guernsey Road	C7	Rosedale Crescent	F4		
		Hall Road	D1	Rose Lane	D3-D4-E4		
		Hanover Road	A1	Rouen Road	C3-D3-D2		
		Hardy Road	F1-F2	Rowington Street	B1		
		Hassett Close	E7	Rupert Street	A2-A3		
		Heathgate	E7-F7	St Andrew Street	C4		
		Heath Road	C8-C7	St Ann's Lane	D3		
		Heigham Street	A6-A5	St Augustine Street	B7-B6		
		Hill House Road	F3-F4	St Benedict Street	A5-B5-B4		
		Hollis Lane	C1-D1	St Crispins Road	B6-C6-D6		
		Horns Lane	D2	St Faiths Lane	D4		

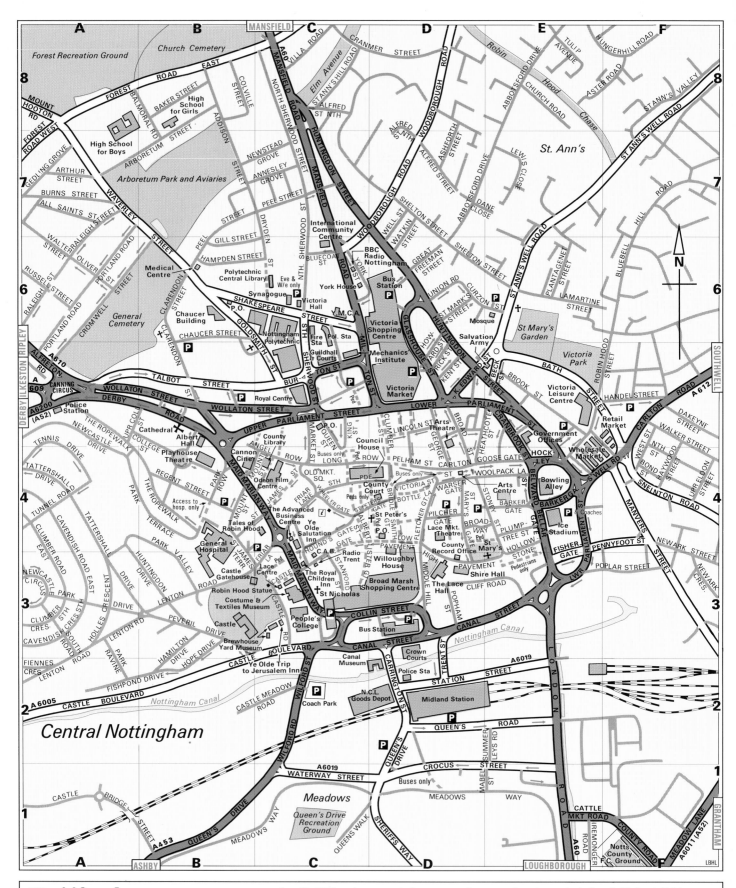

Nottingham

Hosiery and lace were the foundations upon which Nottingham's prosperity was built. The stockings came first – a knitting machine for these had been invented by a Nottinghamshire man as early as 1589 – but a machine called a 'tickler', which enabled simple patterns to be created in the stocking fabric, prompted the development of machine-made lace. The earliest fabric was produced in 1768, and an example from not much later than that is kept in the city's Castlegate Costume and Textile Museum. In fact, the entire history of lacemaking is beautifully explained in this converted row of Georgian terraces. The Industrial Museum at Wollaton Park has many other machines and exhibits tracing the development of the knitting industry, as well as displays on the other industries which have brought wealth to the city – tobacco, pharmaceuticals, engineering and printing. At Wollaton Hall is a natural history museum, while nearer the centre are the Canal Museum and the Brewhouse Yard Museum, a marvellous collection which shows items from daily life in the city up to the present day. Nottingham is not complete without mention of Robin Hood, the partly mythical figure whose statue is in the castle grounds. Although the castle itself has Norman foundations, the present structure is largely Victorian. It is now a museum.

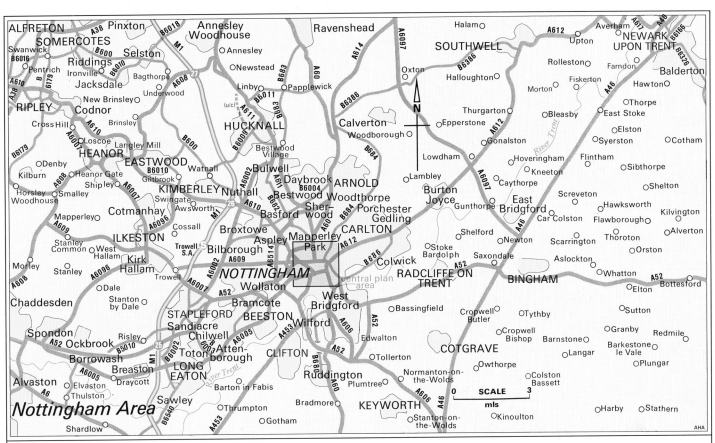

Nottingham Area

Key to Town Plan and Area Plan
Town Plan
AA Recommended roads
Restricted roads
Other roads
Buildings of interest   Theatre
Car Parks   P
Parks and open spaces
Churches   +
One Way Streets

Area Plan
A roads
B roads
Locations   BagthorpeO
Urban area

Street Index with Grid Reference

Nottingham

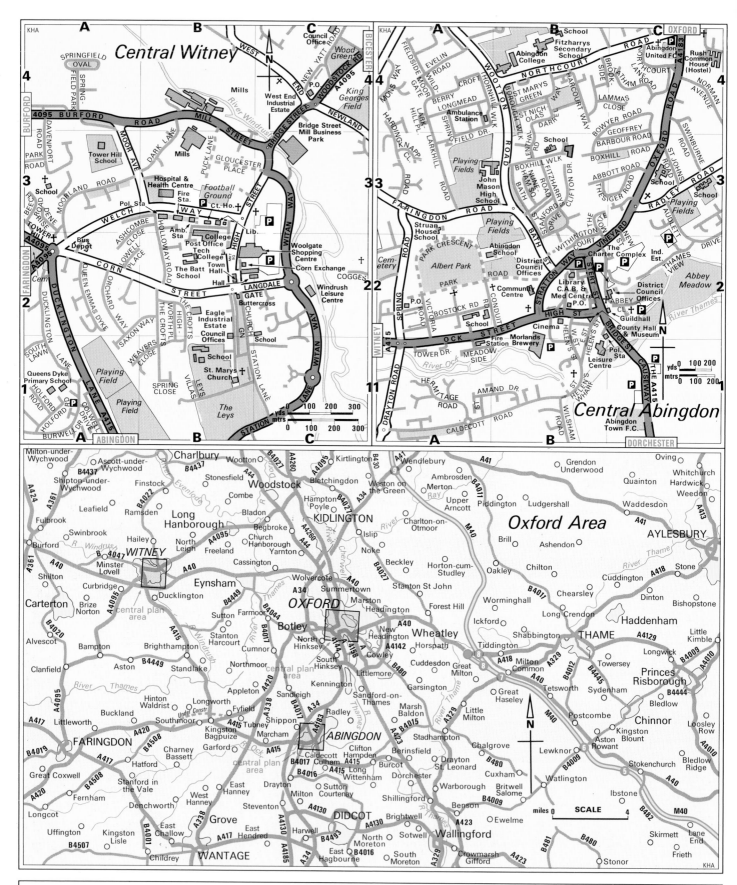

Oxford

From Carfax (at the centre of the city) round to Magdalen Bridge stretches High Street, one of England's best and most interesting thoroughfares. Shops rub shoulders with churches and colleges, alleyways lead to ancient inns and to a large covered market, and little streets lead to views of some of the finest architecture to be seen anywhere. Catte Street, beside St Mary's Church (whose lovely tower gives a panoramic view of Oxford), opens out into Radcliffe Square, dominated by the Radcliffe Camera, a great round structure built in 1749. Close by is the Bodleian Library, one of the finest collections of books and manuscripts in the world. All around are ancient college buildings. Close to Magdalen Bridge is Magdalen College, founded in 1448 and certainly not to be missed. Across the High Street are the Botanical Gardens, founded in 1621 and the oldest such foundation in England. Footpaths lead through Christ Church Meadow to Christ Church College and the cathedral. Tom Tower is the college's most notable feature; the cathedral is actually its chapel and is the smallest cathedral in England. Among much else not to be missed in Oxford is the Ashmolean Museum, whose vast collections of precious and beautiful objects from all over the world repay many hours of study; perhaps the loveliest treasure is the 9th-century Alfred Jewel.

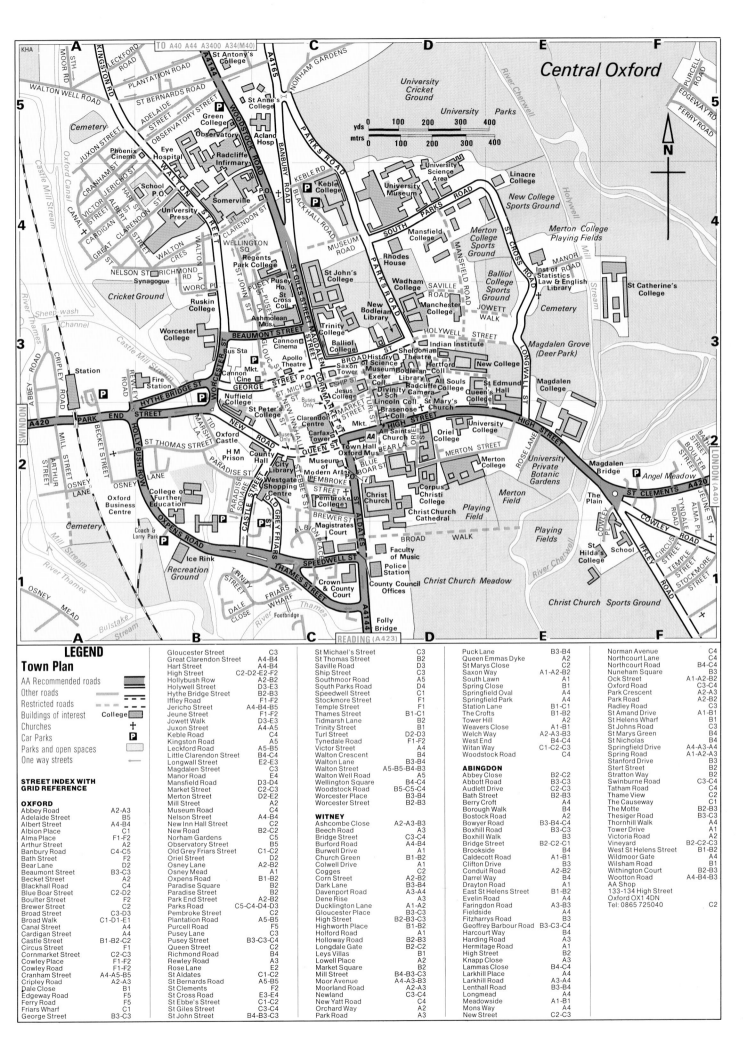

Central Oxford

STREET INDEX WITH GRID REFERENCE

OXFORD

Abbey Road	A2-A3
Adelaide Street	B5
Albert Street	A4-B4
Albion Place	C1
Alma Place	F1-F2
Arthur Street	A2
Banbury Road	C4-C5
Bath Street	F2
Bear Lane	D2
Beaumont Street	B3-C3
Becket Street	A2
Blackhall Road	C4
Blue Boar Street	C2-D2
Boulter Street	F2
Brewer Street	C2
Broad Street	D3-D3
Broad Walk	C1-D1-E1
Canal Street	A4
Cardigan Street	A4
Castle Street	B1-B2-C2
Circus Street	F1
Cornmarket Street	C2-C3
Cowley Place	F1-F2
Cowley Road	F1-F2
Cranham Street	A4-A5-B5
Cripley Road	A2-A3
Dale Close	B1
Edgeway Road	F5
Ferry Road	F5
Friars Wharf	C1
George Street	B3-C3

Gloucester Street	C3
Great Clarendon Street	A4-B4
Hart Street	A4-B4
High Street	C2-D2-E2-F2
Hollybush Row	D3-E3
Holywell Street	B2-B3
Hythe Bridge Street	B2-B3
Iffley Road	F1-F2
Jericho Street	A4-B4-B5
Jeune Street	F1-F2
Jowett Walk	D3-E3
Juxon Street	A4-A5
Keble Road	C4
Kingston Road	A5
Leckford Road	A5-B5
Little Clarendon Street	B4-C4
Longwall Street	E2-E3
Magdalen Street	C3
Manor Road	E4
Mansfield Road	D3-D4
Market Street	C2-C3
Merton Street	D2-E2
Mill Street	A2
Museum Road	C4
Nelson Street	A4-B4
New Inn Hall Street	C2
New Road	B2-C2
Norham Gardens	C5
Observatory Street	B5
Old Grey Friars Street	C1-C2
Oriel Street	D2
Osney Lane	A2-B2
Osney Mead	A1
Oxpens Road	B1-B2
Paradise Square	B2
Paradise Street	B2
Park End Street	A2-B2
Parks Road	C5-C4-D4-D3
Pembroke Street	C2
Plantation Road	A5-B5
Purcell Road	F5
Pusey Lane	C3
Pusey Street	B3-C3-C4
Queen Street	C2
Richmond Road	B4
Rewley Road	A3
Rose Lane	E2
St Aldates	C1-C2
St Bernards Road	A5-B5
St Clements	F2
St Cross Road	E3-E4
St Ebbe's Street	C1-C2
St Giles Street	C3-C4
St John Street	B4-B3-C3

St Michael's Street	C3
St Thomas Street	B2
Saville Road	D3
Ship Street	C3
Southmoor Road	A5
South Parks Road	D4
Speedwell Street	C1
Stockmore Street	F1
Temple Street	F1
Thames Street	B1-C1
Tidmarsh Lane	B2
Trinity Street	B1
Turl Street	D2-D3
Tynedale Road	F1-F2
Victor Street	A4
Walton Crescent	B4
Walton Lane	B4
Walton Street	A5-B5-B4-B3
Walton Well Road	A5
Wellington Square	B4-C4
Woodstock Road	B5-C5-C4
Worcester Place	B3-B4
Worcester Street	B2-B3

WITNEY

Ashcombe Close	A2-A3-B3
Beech Road	A3
Bridge Street	C3-C4
Burford Road	A4-B4
Burwell Drive	A1
Church Green	B1-B2
Colwell Drive	C1
Cogges	C2
Corn Street	A2-B2
Dark Lane	B3-B4
Davenport Road	A3-A4
Dene Rise	A3
Ducklington Lane	A1-A2
Gloucester Place	B3
High Street	B2-B3-C3
Highworth Place	B1-B2
Holford Road	A1
Holloway Road	B2-B3
Longdale Gate	B2-C2
Leys Villas	B1
Lowell Place	A2
Market Square	B2
Mill Street	B4-B3-C3
Moor Avenue	A4-A3-B3
Moorland Road	A2-A3
Newland	C3-C4
New Yatt Road	C4
Orchard Way	A2
Park Road	A3

Puck Lane	B3-B4
Queen Emmas Dyke	A2
St Marys Close	C2
Saxon Way	A1-A2-B2
South Lawn	A1
Spring Close	B1
Springfield Oval	A4
Springfield Park	A4
Station Lane	B1-C1
The Crofts	B1-B2
Tower Hill	A2
Weavers Close	A1-B1
Welch Way	A2-A3-B3
West End	B4-C4
Witan Way	C1-C2-C3
Woodstock Road	C4

ABINGDON

Abbey Close	B2-C2
Abbott Road	B3-C3
Audlett Drive	C2-C3
Bath Street	B2-B3
Berry Croft	A4
Borough Walk	B4
Bostock Road	A2
Bowyer Road	B3-B4-C4
Boxhill Road	B3-C3
Boxhill Walk	B3
Bridge Street	B2-C2-C1
Brookside	B4
Caldecott Road	A1-B1
Clifton Drive	B3
Conduit Road	A2-B2
Darrel Way	B4
Drayton Road	A1
East St Helens Street	B1-B2
Evelin Road	A4
Faringdon Road	A3-B3
Fieldside	A4
Fitzharrys Road	B3
Geoffrey Barbour Road	B3-C3-C4
Harcourt Way	B4
Harding Road	A3
Hermitage Road	A1
High Street	B2
Knapp Close	A4
Lammas Close	B4-C4
Larkhill Place	A4
Larkhill Road	A3-A4
Lenthal Road	B3-B4
Longmead	A4
Meadowside	A1-B1
Mons Way	A4
New Street	C2-C3

Norman Avenue	C4
Northcourt Lane	C4
Northcourt Road	B4-C4
Nuneham Square	B3
Ock Street	A1-A2-B2
Oxford Road	C3-C4
Park Crescent	A2-A3
Park Road	A2-B2
Radley Road	A1
St Amand Drive	A1-B1
St Helens Wharf	B1
St Johns Road	C3
St Marys Green	B4
St Nicholas	A4-A3-A4
Springfield Drive	A4
Spring Road	A1-A2-A3
Stanford Drive	B3
Stert Street	B2
Stratton Way	B2
Swinburne Road	C3-C4
Tatham Road	B4
Thame View	C2
The Causeway	C1
The Motte	B2-B3
Thesiger Road	B3-C3
Thornhill Walk	A4
Tower Drive	A2
Victoria Road	A1
Vineyard	B2-C2-C3
West St Helens Street	B1-B2
Wildmoor Gate	A4
Wilsham Road	B1
Withington Court	B2-B3
Wootton Road	A4-B4-B3

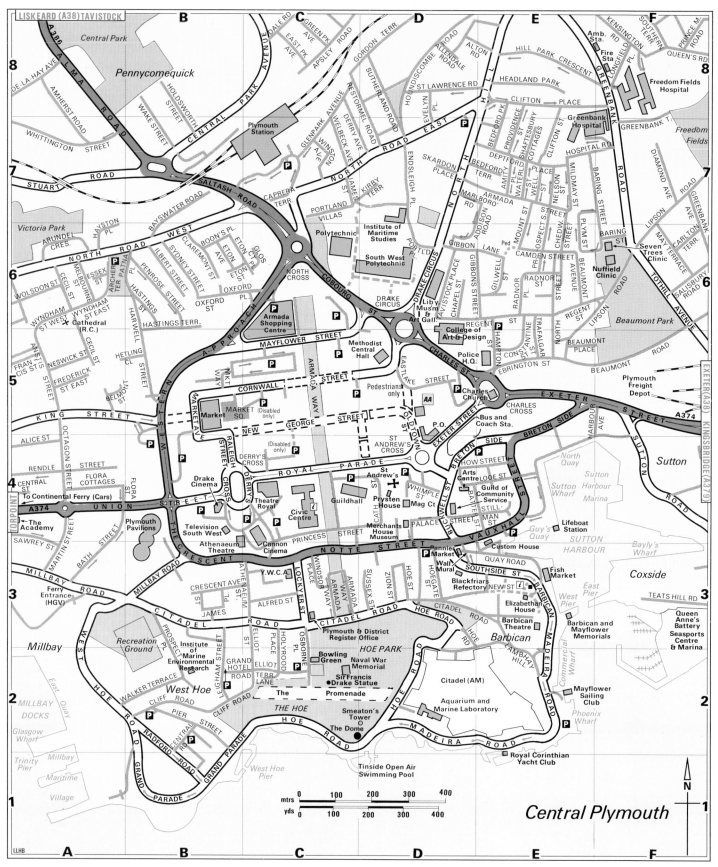

Plymouth

Ships, sailors and the sea permeate every aspect of Plymouth's life and history. Its superb natural harbour - Plymouth Sound - has ensured its importance as a port, yachting centre and naval base (latterly at Devonport) over many centuries. Sir Francis Drake is undoubtedly the city's most famous sailor. His statue stands on the Hoe - where he really did play bowls before tackling the Spanish Armada. Also on the Hoe are Smeaton's Tower, which once formed the upper part of the third Eddystone Lighthouse, and the impressive Royal Naval War Memorial. Just east of the Hoe is the Royal Citidel, an imposing fortress built in 1666 by order of Charles II. North is Sutton Harbour, perhaps the most atmospheric part of Plymouth. Here fishing boats bob up and down in a harbour whose quays are lined with attractive old houses, inns and warehouses. One of the memorials on Mayflower Quay just outside the harbour commemorates the sailing of the *Mayflower* from here in 1620. Plymouth's shopping centre was built after the old centre was badly damaged in World War II. Nearby is the 200ft-high tower of the impressive modern Civic Centre. Some buildings escaped destruction, including the Elizabethan House and the 500-year-old Prysten House. Next door is St Andrew's Church, with stained glass by John Piper.

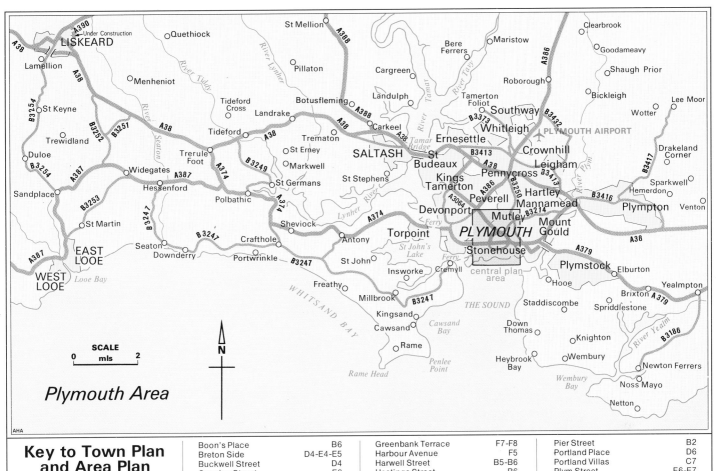

Plymouth Area

SCALE
0 — mls — 2

N

AHA

Key to Town Plan and Area Plan

Town Plan

AA Recommended roads
Other roads
Restricted roads
Buildings of interest
Car Parks — P
Parks and open spaces
AA Shop — AA

Area Plan

A roads
B roads
Locations — Sandplace O
Urban area

Street Index with Grid Reference

Plymouth

Addison Road	D6-D7-E7
Alfred Street	C3
Alice Street	A4
Allendale Road	D8
Alma Road	A8-A7-B7
Alton Road	D8-E8
Amherst Road	A7-A8
Amity Place	E7
Anstis Street	A5-A6
Apsley Road	C8
Archer Terrace	A6
Armada Street	D7-E7-F7
Armada Way	C3-C4-C5-C6
Arundel Crescent	A6
Athenaeum Street	C3
Barbican	E3
Baring Street	E7-F7-F6
Bath Street	A3-A4
Batter Street	D4-E4
Bayswater Road	B6-B7
Beaumont Avenue	E6
Beaumont Place	E5-F5
Beaumont Road	E5-F5-F6
Bedford Park	E7-E8
Bedford Terrace	D7-E7
Belmont Street	A5
Blenheim Road	D6

Boon's Place	B6
Breton Side	D4-E4-E5
Buckwell Street	D4
Camden Street	E6
Caprera Terrace	C7
Carlton Terrace	F6
Catherine Street	D4
Cecil Street	A6
Central Road	B2
Central Street	A4
Central Park Avenue	B7-B8-C8
Chapel Street	D6
Charles Street	D5
Chedworth Street	E6-E7
Citadel Road	B3-C3-D3-E3
Claremont Street	B6
Cliff Road	B2-C2
Clifton Place	E8-F8
Clifton Street	E7-E8
Cobourg Street	C6-D6
Constantine Street	E5-E6
Cornwall Street	B5-C5-D5
Crescent Avenue	B3-C3
Dale Road	C8
De-la-Hay-Avenue	A8
Deptford Place	D7-E7
Derry Avenue	C8-C7-D7
Derry's Cross	B4-C4
Diamond Avenue	F7
Drake Circus	D6
East Park Avenue	C8
Eastlake Street	D5
Ebrington Street	E5
Elliot Street	C2-C3
Elliot Terrace Lane	C2
Endsleigh Place	D7
Essex Street	A6
Eton Avenue	B6
Eton Place	B6-C6
Eton Street	B6-C6
Evelyn Place	D7-D8
Exeter Street	D4-D5-E5-F5
Flora Cottages	A4
Flora Street	A4
Francis Street	A5
Frederick Street East	A5
Gibbons Lane	D6-E6
Gibbon Street	E6
Gilwell Street	E6
Glanville Street	C6-D6
Glenpark Avenue	C7-C8
Gloucester Court	C6
Gordon Terrace	C8-D8
Grand Hotel Road	B2-C2
Grand Parade	B1-B2-C2
Green Park Avenue	C8
Greenbank Avenue	F6-F7
Greenbank Road	F6-F7-F8-E8

Greenbank Terrace	F7-F8
Harbour Avenue	F5
Harwell Street	B5-B6
Hastings Street	B6
Hastings Terrace	B5-B6
Hayston Place	A6
Headland Park	E8
Hetling Close	B5
Hill Park Crescent	E8-F8
Hoe Road	C2-D2-D3
Hoe Street	D3
Hoegate Street	D3
Holdsworth Street	B7-B8
Holyrood Place	C2-C3
Hospital Road	E7-F7
Houndiscombe Road	D7-D8
How Street	D4-E4
Ilbert Street	B6
James Street	C6-C7
Kensington Road	F8
King Street	A5-B5
Kirby Terrace	C7-D7
Lambhay Street	E3
Leigham Street	B2-B3
Lipson Road	E5-E6-F6-F7
Lockyer Street	C3
Longfield Place	F8
Looe Street	D4-E4
Madeira Road	D2-E2-E3
Marlborough Road	D7-E7
Market Avenue	B4-B5
Market Square	B5-C5
Market Way	B5
Martin Street	A3-A4
May Terrace	F6
Mayflower Street	B5-C5-C6-D5-D6
Melbourne Street	A6
Mildmay Street	E7
Millbay Road	A3-B3
Mount Street	E6-E7
Nelson Street	E7
Neswick Street	A6
New Street	D3-E3
New George Street	B4-B5-C5-D5
North Cross	C6
North Hill	D6-D7-E7-E8
North Road East	C7-D7-D8-E8
North Road West	A6-B6-B7-C7
North Street	E5-E6
Notte Street	C3-D3-D4
Octagon Street	A4-A5
Old Town Street	D4-D5
Osborne Place	C2-C3
Oxford Place	B6-C6
Oxford Street	B6
Palace Street	D4
Patna Place	B6
Penrose Street	B6

Pier Street	B2
Portland Place	D6
Portland Villas	C7
Plym Street	E6-E7
Prince Maurice Road	F8
Princess Street	C3-C4-D4
Prospect Place	B2-B3
Prospect Street	E6-E7
Providence Street	E7-E8
Quay Road	D3-E3
Queen's Road	F8
Radford Road	B1-B2
Radnor Place	E6
Radnor Street	E6
Raleigh Street	B4
Regent Street	D6-E6-F6
Rendle Street	A4
Restormel Road	C8-D8-D7
Royal Parade	C4-D4
Stillman Street	E4
St James Place	B3
St Lawrence Road	D8-E8
Salisbury Road	F6
Saltash Road	B7-C7-C6
Sawrey Street	A3-A4
Shaftesbury Cottages	E7
Skardon Place	D7
Southern Terrace	F8
Southside Street	D3-E3
Stuart Road	A7-B7
Sussex Street	D3
Sutherland Road	D7-D8
Sutton Road	F4-F5
Sydney Street	B6
Tavistock Place	D6
Teats Hill Road	F3
The Crescent	B4-B3-C3
Tothill Avenue	F5-F6
Trafalgar Street	E5-E6
Union Street	A4-B4
Vauxhall Street	D3-D4-E4
Wake Street	B7-B8
Walker Terrace	A2-B2
Waterloo Street	E7
Welbeck Avenue	C7
Wellington Street	E7
West Hoe Road	A3-A2-B2
Western Approach	B4-B5-B6-C6
Whimple Street	D4
Whittington Street	A7
Windsor Place	C3
Winston Avenue	C7
Wolsdon Street	A6
Wyndham Street East	A6
Wyndham Street West	A6
Zion Street	D3

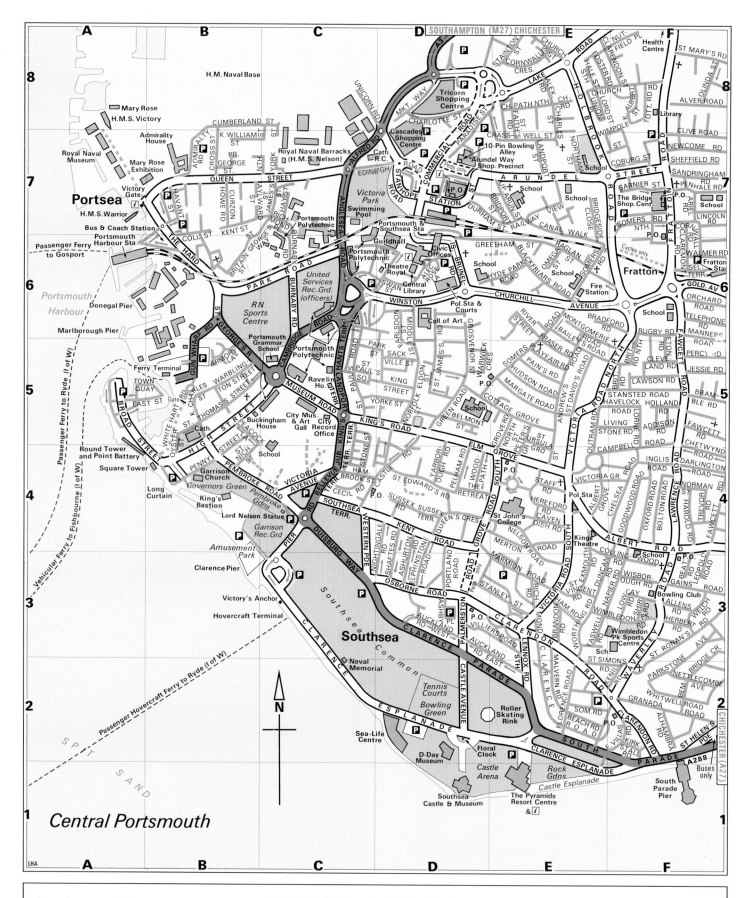

Portsmouth

Richard the Lionheart recognised the strategic importance of Portsea Island and ordered the first docks, and later the town to be built. Succeeding monarchs improved the defences and extended the docks which now cover some 300 acres – as befits Britain's premier naval base. Of the defensive fortifications, Fort Widley and the Round Tower are the best preserved remains. Three famous ships rest in Portsmouth; HMS Victory, the Mary Rose and

HMS Warrior. The former; Lord Nelson's flagship, has been fully restored and the adjacent Royal Navy museum houses numerous relics of Trafalgar. The Mary Rose, built by Henry VIII, lay on the sea bed off Southsea until she was spectacularly raised in 1982. She has now been put on display and there is an exhibition of artefacts that have been recovered from her. HMS Warrior is the world's first iron hulled warship.

Portsmouth suffered greatly from bombing in World War II and the centre has been almost completely

rebuilt. However, the old town clustered around the harbour mouth, escaped severe damage and, now restored, forms an attractive and fashionable area.

Southsea developed in the 19th century as an elegant seaside resort with fine houses and terraces, an esplanade and an extensive seafront common where the Sea-Life Centre, Southsea Castle & Museum, the D-Day Museum and the Pyramids Leisure Centre are to be found. Off shore, the restored Spit Bank Fort is worth a visit.

238

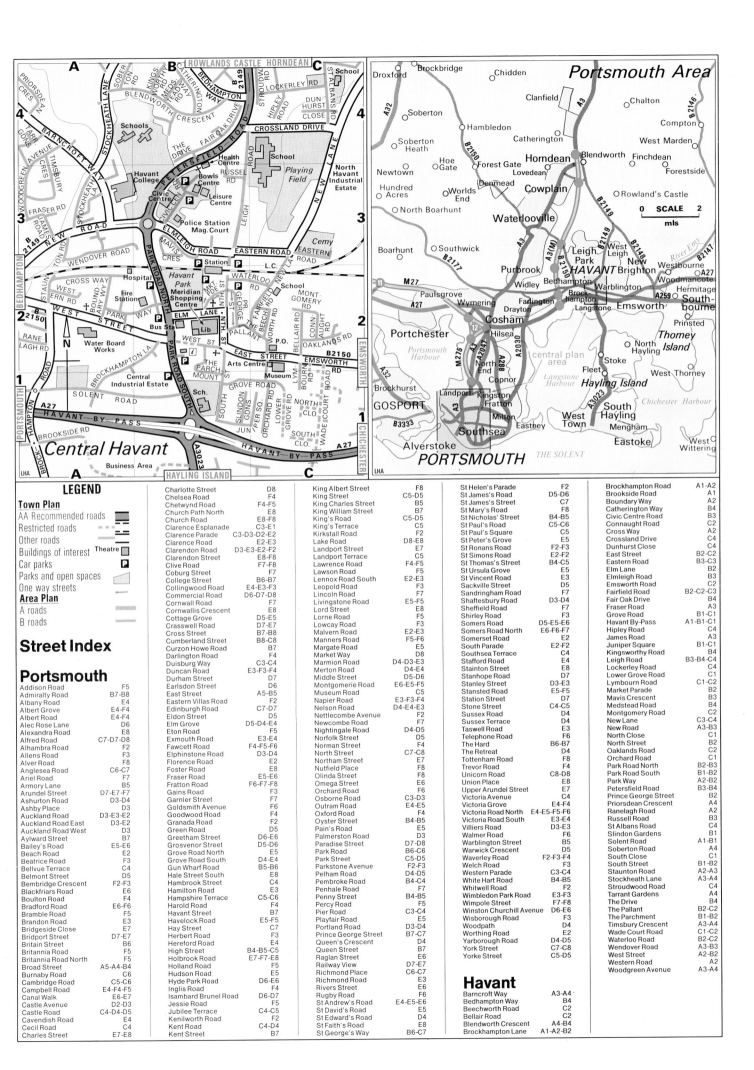

LEGEND

Town Plan
- AA Recommended roads
- Restricted roads
- Other roads
- Buildings of interest — Theatre
- Car parks
- Parks and open spaces
- One way streets

Area Plan
- A roads
- B roads

Street Index

Portsmouth

Addison Road	F5
Admiralty Road	B7-B8
Albany Road	E4
Albert Grove	E4-F4
Albert Road	E4-F4
Alec Rose Lane	D6
Alexandra Road	E8
Alfred Road	C7-D7-D8
Alhambra Road	F2
Allens Road	F3
Alver Road	F8
Anglesea Road	C6-C7
Ariel Road	F7
Armory Lane	B5
Arundel Street	D7-E7-F7
Ashurton Road	D3-D4
Ashby Place	D3
Auckland Road	D3-E3-E2
Auckland Road East	D2-E2
Auckland Road West	D3
Aylward Street	B7
Bailey's Road	E5-E6
Beach Road	E2
Beatrice Road	F3
Bellvue Terrace	C4
Belmont Street	D5
Bembridge Crescent	F2-F3
Blackfriars Road	E6
Boulton Road	F4
Bradford Road	E6-F6
Bramble Road	F5
Brandon Road	E3
Bridgeside Close	E7
Bridport Street	D7-E7
Britain Street	B6
Britannia Road	F5
Britannia Road North	F5
Broad Street	A5-A4-B4
Burnaby Road	C6
Cambridge Road	C5-C6
Campbell Road	E4-F4-F5
Canal Walk	E6-E7
Castle Avenue	D2-D3
Castle Road	C4-D4-D5
Cavendish Road	E4
Cecil Road	C6
Charles Street	E7-E8

Charlotte Street	D8
Chelsea Road	F4
Chetwynd Road	F4-F5
Church Path North	E8
Church Road	E8-F8
Clarence Esplanade	C3-E1
Clarence Parade	C3-D3-D2-E2
Clarence Road	E2-E3
Clarendon Road	D3-E3-E2-F2
Clarendon Street	E8-F8
Clive Road	F7-F8
Coburg Street	F7
College Street	B6-B7
Collingwood Road	E4-E3-F3
Commercial Road	D6-D7-D8
Cornwall Road	F7
Cornwallis Crescent	E8
Cottage Grove	D5-E5
Crasswell Road	D7-E7
Cross Street	B7-B8
Cumberland Street	B8-C8
Curzon Howe Road	B7
Darlington Road	F4
Duisburg Way	C3-C4
Duncan Road	E3-F3-F4
Durham Street	D7
Earlsdon Street	D6
East Street	A5-B5
Eastern Villas Road	F2
Edinburgh Road	C7-D7
Eldon Street	D5
Elm Grove	D5-D4-E4
Eton Road	F5
Exmouth Road	E3-E4
Fawcett Road	F4-F5-F6
Florence Road	E2
Foster Road	E8
Fraser Road	E5-E6
Fratton Road	F6-F7-F8
Gains Road	F3
Garnler Street	F7
Goldsmith Avenue	F6
Goodwood Road	F4
Granada Road	F2
Green Road	D5
Greetham Street	D6-E6
Grosvenor Street	D5-D6
Grove Road North	E5
Grove Road South	D4-E4
Gun Wharf Road	B5-B6
Hale Street South	E8
Hambrook Street	C4
Hamilton Road	E3
Hampshire Terrace	C5-C6
Harold Road	F4
Havant Street	B7
Havelock Road	E5-F5
Hay Street	C7
Herbert Road	F3
Hereford Road	E4
High Street	B4-B5-C5
Holbrook Road	E7-F7-F8
Holland Road	F5
Hudson Road	E5
Hyde Park Road	D6-E6
Inglis Road	F4
Isambard Brunel Road	D6-D7
Jessie Road	F5
Jubilee Terrace	C4-C5
Kenilworth Road	F2
Kent Road	C4-D4
Kent Street	B7

King Albert Street	F8
King Street	C5-D5
King Charles Street	B5
King William Street	B7
King's Road	C5-D5
King's Terrace	C5
Kirkstall Road	F2
Lake Road	D8-E8
Landport Street	E7
Landport Terrace	C5
Lawrence Road	F4-F5
Lawson Road	F5
Lennox Road South	E2-E3
Leopold Road	F3
Lincoln Road	E7
Livingstone Road	E5-F5
Lord Street	E8
Lorne Road	F5
Lowcay Road	F3
Malvern Road	E2-E3
Manners Road	F5-F6
Margate Road	E5
Market Way	D8
Marmion Road	D4-D3-E3
Merton Road	D4-E4
Middle Street	D5-D6
Montgomerie Road	E6-E5-F5
Museum Road	C5
Napier Road	E3-F3-F4
Nelson Road	D4-E4-E3
Nettlecombe Avenue	F2
Newcombe Road	F7
Nightingale Road	D4-D5
Norfolk Street	D5
Norman Street	F4
North Street	C7-C8
Northam Street	E7
Nutfield Place	F8
Olinda Street	F8
Omega Street	E6
Orchard Road	F6
Osborne Road	C3-D3
Outram Road	E4-E5
Oxford Road	F4
Oyster Street	B4-B5
Pain's Road	E5
Palmerston Road	D3
Paradise Street	D7-D8
Park Road	B6-C6
Park Street	C5-D5
Parkstone Avenue	F2-F3
Pelham Road	D4-D5
Pembroke Road	B4-C4
Penhale Road	F7
Penny Street	B4-B5
Percy Road	F5
Pier Road	C3-C4
Playfair Road	E5
Portland Road	D3-D4
Prince George Street	B7-C7
Queen's Crescent	D4
Queen Street	B7
Raglan Street	E6
Railway View	D7-E7
Richmond Place	C6-C7
Richmond Road	E3
Rivers Street	E6
Rugby Road	F6
St Andrew's Road	E4-E5-E6
St David's Road	E5
St Edward's Road	D4
St Faith's Road	E8
St George's Way	B6-C7

St Helen's Parade	F2
St James's Road	D5-D6
St James's Street	C7
St Mary's Road	F8
St Nicholas' Street	B4-B5
St Paul's Road	C5-C6
St Paul's Square	C5
St Peter's Grove	E5
St Ronans Road	F2-F3
St Simons Road	E2-F2
St Thomas's Street	B4-C5
St Ursula Grove	E5
St Vincent Road	E3
Sackville Street	D5
Sandringham Road	F7
Shaftesbury Road	D3-D4
Sheffield Road	F7
Shirley Road	F3
Somers Road	D5-E5-E6
Somers Road North	E6-F6-F7
Somerset Road	E2
South Parade	E2-F2
Southsea Terrace	C4
Stafford Road	E4
Stainton Street	E8
Stanhope Road	D7
Stanley Street	D3-E3
Stansted Road	E5-F5
Station Street	D7
Stone Street	C4-C5
Sussex Road	D4
Sussex Terrace	D4
Taswell Road	E3
Telephone Road	F6
The Hard	B6-B7
The Retreat	D4
Tottenham Road	F8
Trevor Road	F4
Unicorn Road	C8-D8
Union Place	E8
Upper Arundel Street	E7
Victoria Avenue	C4
Victoria Grove	E4-F4
Victoria Road North	E4-E5-F5-F6
Victoria Road South	E3-E4
Villiers Road	D3-E3
Walmer Road	F6
Warblington Street	B5
Warwick Crescent	D5
Waverley Road	F2-F3-F4
Welch Road	F3
Western Parade	C3-C4
White Hart Road	B4-B5
Whitwell Road	F5
Wimbledon Park Road	E3-F3
Wimpole Street	F7-F8
Winston Churchill Avenue	D6-E6
Wisborough Road	F3
Woodpath	D4
Worthing Road	E2
Yarborough Road	D4-D5
York Street	C7-C8
Yorke Street	C5-D5

Havant

Barncroft Way	A3-A4
Bedhampton Way	B4
Beechworth Road	C2
Bellair Road	C2
Blendworth Crescent	A4-B4
Brockhampton Lane	A1-A2-B2

Brockhampton Road	A1-A2
Brookside Road	A1
Boundary Way	A2
Catherington Way	B4
Civic Centre Road	B3
Connaught Road	C2
Cross Way	A2
Crossland Drive	C4
Dunhurst Close	C4
East Street	B2-C2
Eastern Road	B3-C3
Elm Lane	B2
Elmleigh Road	B3
Emsworth Road	C2
Fairfield Road	B2-C2-C3
Fair Oak Drive	B4
Fraser Road	A3
Grove Road	B1-C1
Havant By-Pass	A1-B1-C1
Hipley Road	C4
James Road	A3
Juniper Square	B1-C1
Kingsworthy Road	B4
Leigh Road	B3-B4-C4
Lockerley Road	C4
Lower Grove Road	C1
Lymbourn Road	C1-C2
Market Parade	B2
Mavis Crescent	B3
Medstead Road	B4
Montgomery Road	C2
New Lane	C3-C4
New Road	A3-B3
North Close	C1
North Street	B2
Oaklands Road	C2
Orchard Road	C1
Park Road North	B2-B3
Park Road South	B1-B2
Park Way	A2-B2
Petersfield Road	B3-B4
Prince George Street	B2
Priorsdean Crescent	A4
Ranelagh Road	A2
Russell Road	B3
St Albans Road	C4
Slindon Gardens	B1
Solent Road	A1-B1
Soberton Road	A4
South Close	C1
South Street	B1-B2
Staunton Road	A2-A3
Stockheath Lane	A3-A4
Stroudwood Road	A4
Tarrant Gardens	A4
The Drive	B4
The Pallant	B2-C2
The Parchment	B1-B2
Timsbury Crescent	A3-A4
Wade Court Road	C1-C2
Waterloo Road	B2-C2
Wendover Road	A3-B3
West Street	A2-B2
Western Road	A2
Woodgreen Avenue	A3-A4

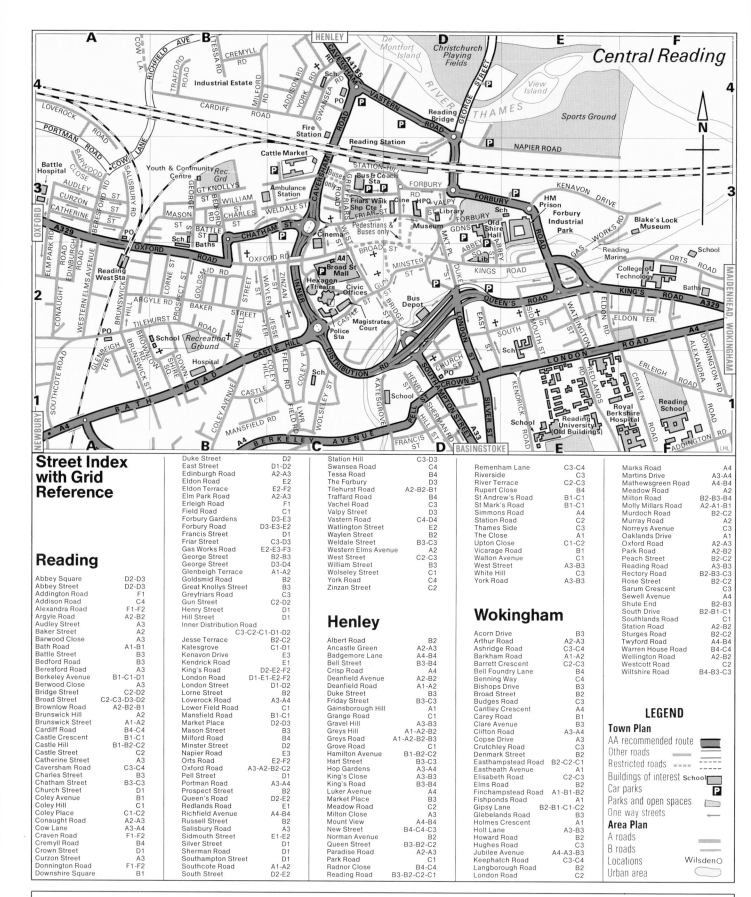

Street Index with Grid Reference

Reading

Abbey Square	D2-D3
Abbey Street	D2-D3
Addington Road	F1
Addison Road	C4
Alexandra Road	F1-F2
Argyle Road	A2-B2
Audley Street	A3
Baker Street	A2
Barwood Close	A3
Bath Road	A1-B1
Battle Street	B3
Bedford Road	B3
Beresford Road	A3
Berkeley Avenue	B1-C1-D1
Berwood Close	A3
Bridge Street	C2-D2
Broad Street	C2-C3-D3-D2
Brownlow Road	A2-B2-B1
Brunswick Hill	A2
Brunswick Street	A1-A2
Cardiff Road	B4-C4
Castle Crescent	B1-C1
Castle Hill	B1-B2-C2
Castle Street	C2
Catherine Street	A3
Caversham Road	C3-C4
Charles Street	B3
Chatham Street	B3-C3
Church Street	D1
Coley Avenue	B1
Coley Hill	C1
Coley Place	C1-C2
Conaught Road	A2-A3
Cow Lane	A3-A4
Craven Road	F1-F2
Cremyll Road	B4
Crown Street	D1
Curzon Street	A3
Donnington Road	F1-F2
Downshire Square	B1

Duke Street	D2
East Street	D1-D2
Edinburgh Road	A2-A3
Eldon Road	E2
Eldon Terrace	E2-F2
Elm Park Road	A2-A3
Erleigh Road	F1
Field Road	C1
Forbury Gardens	D3-E3
Forbury Road	D3-E3-E2
Francis Street	D1
Friar Street	C3-D3
Gas Works Road	E2-E3-F3
George Street	B2-B3
George Street	D3-D4
Glenbeigh Terrace	A1-A2
Goldsmid Road	B2
Great Knollys Street	B3
Greyfriars Road	C3
Gun Street	C2-D2
Henry Street	D1
Hill Street	D1
Inner Distribution Road	
	C3-C2-C1-D1-D2
Jesse Terrace	B2-C2
Katesgrove	C1-D1
Kenavon Drive	E3
Kendrick Road	E1
King's Road	D2-E2-F2
London Road	D1-E1-E2-F2
London Street	D1-D2
Lorne Street	B2
Loverock Road	A3-A4
Lower Field Road	C1
Mansfield Road	B1-C1
Market Place	D2-D3
Mason Street	B3
Milford Road	B4
Minster Street	D2
Napier Road	E3
Orts Road	E2-F2
Oxford Road	A3-A2-B2-C2
Pell Street	D1
Portman Road	A3-A4
Prospect Street	B2
Queen's Road	D2-E2
Redlands Road	E1
Richfield Avenue	A4-B4
Russell Street	B2
Salisbury Road	A3
Sidmouth Street	E1-E2
Silver Street	D1
Sherman Road	D1
Southampton Street	D1
Southcote Road	A1-A2
South Street	D2-E2

Station Hill	C3-D3
Swansea Road	C4
Tessa Road	B4
The Forbury	D3
Tilehurst Road	A2-B2-B1
Traffard Road	B4
Vachel Road	C3
Valpy Street	D3
Vastern Road	C4-D4
Watlington Street	E2
Waylen Street	B2
Weldale Street	B3-C3
Western Elms Avenue	A2
West Street	C2-C3
William Street	B3
Wolseley Street	C1
York Road	C4
Zinzan Street	C2

Henley

Albert Road	B2
Ancastle Green	A2-A3
Badgemore Lane	A4-B4-B3
Bell Street	B3-B4
Crisp Road	A4
Deanfield Avenue	A2-B2
Deanfield Road	A1-A2
Duke Street	B3
Friday Street	B3-C3
Gainsborough Hill	A1
Grange Road	C1
Gravel Hill	A3-B3
Greys Hill	A1-A2-B2
Greys Road	A1-A2-B2-B3
Grove Road	C1
Hamilton Avenue	B1-B2-C2
Hart Street	B3-C3
Hop Gardens	A3-A4
King's Close	A3-B3
King's Road	B3-B4
Luker Avenue	A4
Market Place	B3
Meadow Road	C2
Milton Close	A3
Mount View	A4-B4
New Street	B4-C4-C3
Norman Avenue	C1
Queen Street	B3-B2-C2
Paradise Road	A2-A3
Park Road	C1
Radnor Close	B4-C4
Reading Road	B3-B2-C2-C1

Remenham Lane	C3-C4
Riverside	C3
River Terrace	C2-C3
Rupert Close	B4
St Andrew's Road	B1-C1
St Mark's Road	B1-C1
Simmons Road	A4
Station Road	C2
Thames Side	C3
The Close	A1
Upton Close	C1-C2
Vicarage Road	B1
Walton Avenue	C1
West Street	A3-B3
White Hill	C3
York Road	A3-B3

Wokingham

Acorn Drive	B3
Arthur Road	A2-A3
Ashridge Road	C3-C4
Barkham Road	A1-A2
Barrett Crescent	C2-C3
Bell Foundry Lane	B4
Benning Way	C4
Bishops Drive	B3
Broad Street	B2
Budges Road	C3
Cantley Crescent	A4
Carey Road	B1
Clare Avenue	B3
Clifton Road	A3-A4
Copse Drive	A3
Crutchley Road	C3
Denmark Street	B2
Easthampstead Road	B2-C2-C1
Eastheath Avenue	A1
Elisabeth Road	C2-C3
Elms Road	B2
Finchampstead Road	A1-B1-B2
Fishponds Road	A1
Gipsy Lane	B2-B1-C1-C2
Glebelands Road	B3
Holmes Crescent	A1
Holt Lane	A3-B3
Howard Road	B2
Hughes Road	C3
Jubilee Avenue	A4-A3-B3
Keephatch Road	C3-C4
Langborough Road	B2
London Road	C2

Marks Road	A4
Martins Drive	A3-A4
Mathewsgreen Road	A4-B4
Meadow Road	A2
Milton Road	B2-B3-B4
Molly Millars Road	A2-A1-B1
Murdoch Road	B2-C2
Murray Road	A2
Norreys Avenue	C3
Oaklands Drive	A1
Oxford Road	A2-A3
Park Road	A2-B2
Peach Street	B2-C2
Reading Road	B2-B3-C3
Rectory Road	B2-B3-C3
Rose Street	B2-C2
Sarum Crescent	C3
Sewell Avenue	A4
Shute End	B2-B3
South Drive	B2-B1-C1
Southlands Road	C1
Station Road	A2-B2
Sturges Road	B2-C2
Twyford Road	A4-B4
Warren House Road	B4-C4
Wellington Road	A2-B2
Westcott Road	A3
Wiltshire Road	B4-B3-C3

LEGEND

Town Plan

AA recommended route
Other roads
Restricted roads
Buildings of interest — School
Car parks — P
Parks and open spaces
One way streets

Area Plan

A roads
B roads
Locations — Wilsden O
Urban area

Reading

Shopping and light industry first spring to mind when thinking of Reading, but the town actually has a long and important history. Its rise to significance began in 1121 when Henry I founded an abbey here which became the third most important in England. However, after the Dissolution of the Monasteries, only a few ruins were left. Reading also used to be one of the major centres of the medieval cloth trade, but, already declining in the early 17th century, this source of income was reduced still further as a result of Civil War disturbances.

A fascinating collection of all types of farm implements and domestic equipment can be found in the extremely comprehensive Museum of English Rural Life, situated in the University Campus at Whiteknights Park. The town's own museum has major displays about nearby Silchester – the powerful Roman town of *Calleva*.

Henley-on-Thames, famous for its annual rowing regatta, is a lovely old town, well-provided with old coaching inns, Georgian façades and numerous listed buildings.

Wokingham has been a market town for centuries and over the years has been known for its silk industry and its bell-foundry. Half-timbered gabled houses can be seen in the town centre, although modern development surrounds it.

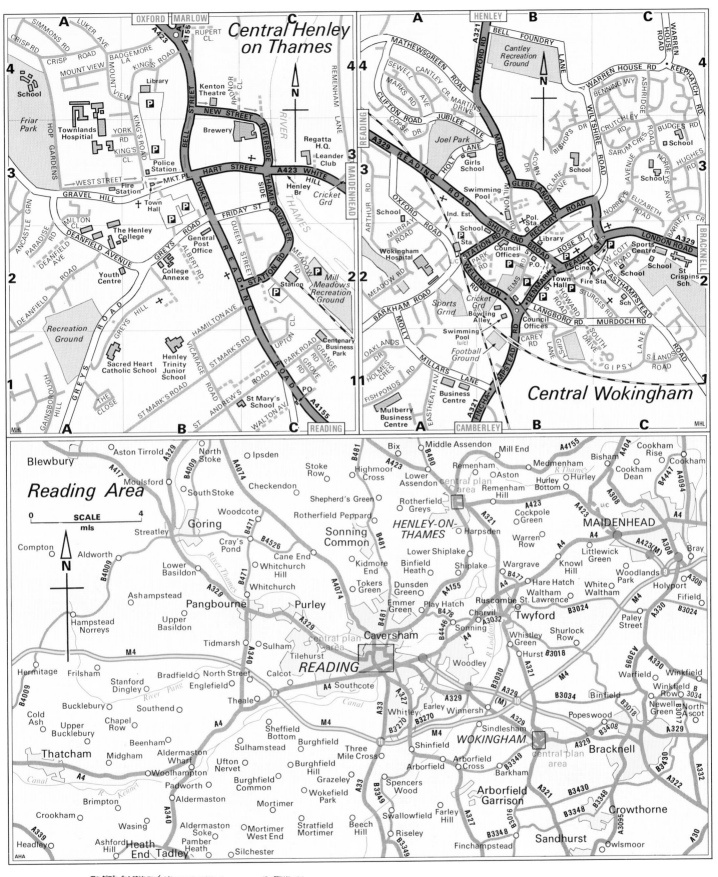

Central Henley on Thames

A Simmons Rd, Luker Ave, Crisp Rd, Crisp Road, Mount View, Badgemore La, King's Road, Mount View, School, Friar Park, Hop Gardens, Townlands Hospital, York Rd, King's Cl., Library

B/C OXFORD, MARLOW, A423, A4155, Rupert Cl., Kenton Theatre, Radnor Cl., New Street, Brewery, Bell Street, Riverside, RIVER, Regatta H.Q., Leander Club, Remenham Lane

4/3 West Street, Gravel Hill, Police Station, Fire Station, MKT. PL., Town Hall, Hart Street, Duke St, White Hill, Henley Br, Cricket Grd, THAMES, A423, HENLEY

Milton Cl., The Henley College, Greys Road, General Post Office, College Annexe, Albert Rd, Deanfield Ave, Deanfield Avenue, Paradise Rd, Ancastle Grn, Youth Centre, Friday St, Queen St, Station Rd, Thames Side, Meadow, Mill Meadows Recreation Ground, Station

2/1 Gainsborough Rd, Greys Hill, THE CLOSE, Recreation Ground, Sacred Heart Catholic School, Henley Trinity Junior School, Hamilton Ave, St Mark's Road, Vicarage Road, St Andrew's Road, Walton Ave, St Mary's School, St Mark's Rd, Upton Cl., Grange Rd, Grove Rd, Park Road, Reading Road, A4155, Centenary Business Park, PO

MAIDENHEAD, READING

Central Wokingham

A HENLEY, A321, Twyford Rd, Mathewsgreen Road, Sewell Ave, Marks Rd, Cantley Cr, Clifton Road, Copse Dr, Martins Drive, Jubilee Ave, Reading, A329, Reading Road, Arthur Rd, Oxford Road, Murray Road, School, Ind. Est., Wokingham Hospital, Barkham Road, Meadow Rd, Molly Rd, Oaklands Dr, Holmes Cres, Millars Lane, Fishponds Rd, Eastheath Av, Finchampstead, Mulberry Business Centre, Business Centre, CAMBERLEY

B BELL FOUNDRY LANE, Cantley Recreation Ground, N, Joel Park, Holt Lane, Girls School, Milton Rd, Glebeland Rd, Swimming Pool, Sta., Station Rd, Park Rd, Council Offices, Wellington Rd, Denmark St, Broad St, Rose St, Town Hall, Fire Sta, Sports Grnd, Cricket Grd, Bowling Alley, Swimming Pool (u/c), Football Ground, Langboro Rd, Council Offices, Murdoch Rd, Carey Rd, Gipsy Lane, Gipsy, A321

C WARREN HOUSE ROAD, KEEPHATCH RD, Warren House Rd, Benning Wy, Ashridge Rd, Crutchley Rd, Budges Rd, Sarum Cres, School, Norreys Ave, Hughes Rd, Schools, Elizabeth Road, Barrett Cr, London Road, A329, BRACKNELL, Sports Centre, School, School, St Crispins Sch, Easthampstead Rd, Sch, Sturges Rd, Howard Rd, South Drive, S. Lands Road, S. Landson Road

Reading Area

Blewbury, Aston Tirrold, A329, North Stoke, Ipsden, Bix, Middle Assendon, Mill End, A4155, A404, Cookham Rise, Cookham, Moulsford, B4009, A4074, Stoke Row, Highmoor Cross, B481, A423, A480, Remenham, Medmenham, Bisham, Cookham Dean, B4447, A4094, Reading Area, South Stoke, Checkendon, Shepherd's Green, Lower Assendon, central plan area, Aston, Hurley, Hurley Bottom, R Thames, A4, Compton, Aldworth, Goring, B471, Woodcote, Rotherfield Peppard, Sonning Common, B481, Rotherfield Greys, HENLEY-ON-THAMES, Harpsden, Remenham Hill, Warren Row, A423, Cockpole Green, A321, U/C, MAIDENHEAD, A308, A4, A423(M), A308, A4, Streatley, Cray's Pond, B4526, Cane End, Kidmore End, Lower Shiplake, Wargrave, A4, Littlewick Green, Bray, Lower Basildon, Whitchurch Hill, Whitchurch, Tokers Green, Binfield Heath, Shiplake, B477, Knowl Hill, Hare Hatch, White Waltham, Woodlands Park, Holyport, A330, B3024, B3024, Fifield, Ashampstead, Pangbourne, A329, Purley, A4074, Dunsden Green, Emmer Green, A4155, Play Hatch, Ruscombe, St. Lawrence, Twyford, B3024, Paley Street, A330, A308, A4, Hampstead Norreys, Upper Basildon, Tidmarsh, Sulham, Tilehurst, central plan area, Caversham, B478, Charvil, A3032, Sonning, Whistley Green, Hurst, B3018, Shurlock Row, Winkfield, A330, A309, B3095, Hermitage, Frilsham, Bradfield, North Street, Englefield, Calcot, A4, Southcote, READING, Woodley, A321, B3030, A329, (M), Warfield, Winkfield Row, B3034, B3018, B3017, North Ascot, Stanford Dingley, Theale, 12, A33, Whitley, Earley, B3270, A329(M), A329, B3034, Binfield, Newell Green, Popeswood, B3408, A329, Bracknell, B4009, Cold Ash, Buckleury, Southend, Sheffield Bottom, M4, Burghfield, Shinfield, Winnersh, A329, Sindlesham, B3408, central plan area, A329, A3430, A322, A332, Upper Bucklebury, Chapel Row, Beenham, Sulhamstead, Three Mile Cross, Arborfield, WOKINGHAM, Arborfield Cross, Barkham, A321, B3430, B3348, Thatcham, Midgham, Aldermaston Wharf, Ufton Nervet, Burghfield Hill, Grazeley, Spencers Wood, B3349, Arborfield Garrison, B3348, Crowthorne, A3095, Canal, A4, R Kennet, Woolhampton, Padworth, Burghfield Common, Wokefield Park, Mortimer, Farley Hill, A327, B3016, Sandhurst, Brimpton, Aldermaston, Mortimer West End, Stratfield Mortimer, Beech Hill, Swallowfield, B3349, Riseley, Finchampstead, B3348, Owlsmoor, Crookham, A339, Wasing, A340, Aldermaston Soke, Pamber Heath, Silchester, A30, Headley, Ashford Hill, Heath End, Tadley, Mortimer Common

SCALE 0 — 4 mls, N, M4, AHA, MHL

READING
Whiteknights, which consists of 300 acres of landscaped parkland, provides Reading's modern university with an incomparable campus setting and includes a conservation area and a biological reserve for research purposes.

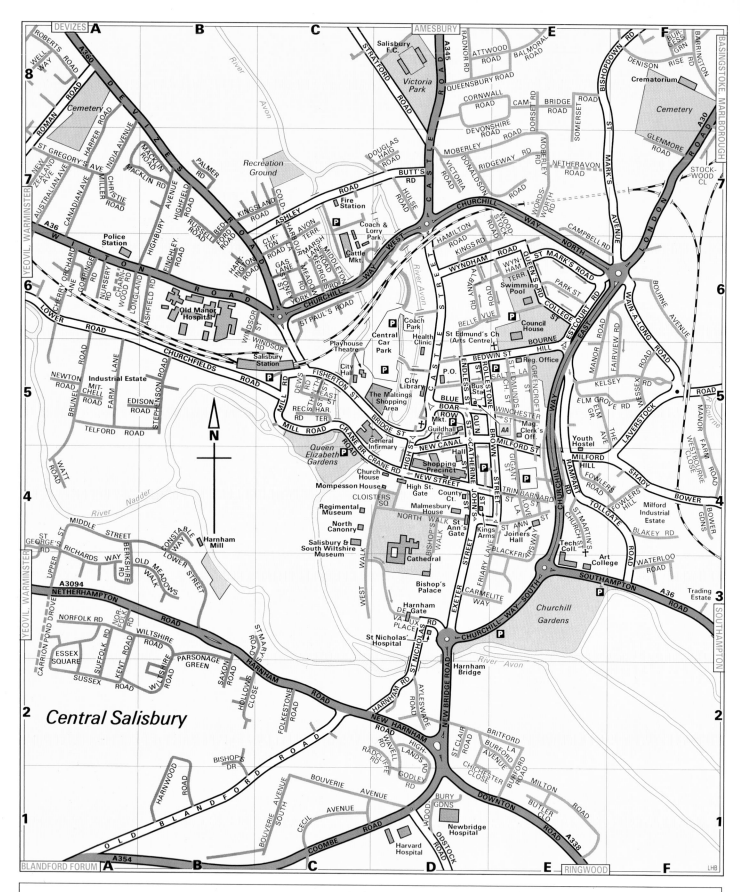

Salisbury

Its attractive site where the waters of the Avon and Nadder meet, its beautiful cathedral and its unspoilt centre put Salisbury among England's finest cities. In 1220 the people of the original settlement at Old Sarum, two miles to the north, moved down to the plain and laid the first stone of the cathedral.

Within 38 years it was completed and the result

is a superb example of Early English architecture. The cloisters are the largest in England and the spire the tallest in Britain. All the houses within the Cathedral Close were built for cathedral functionaries, and although many have Georgian facades, most date back to the 13th century. Mompesson House is one of the handsome mansions here and as it belongs to the National Trust, its equally fine interior can be seen. Another building houses the Museum of the Duke of Edinburgh's Royal Regiment, At one time, relations

between the clergy and the citizens of Salisbury were not always harmonious, so the former built a protective wall around the Close.

The streets of the modern city follow the medieval grid pattern of squares, or 'chequers', and the tightly-packed houses provide a very pleasing townscape. Salisbury was granted its first charter in 1227 and flourished as a market and wool centre; there is still a twice-weekly market in the spacious square.

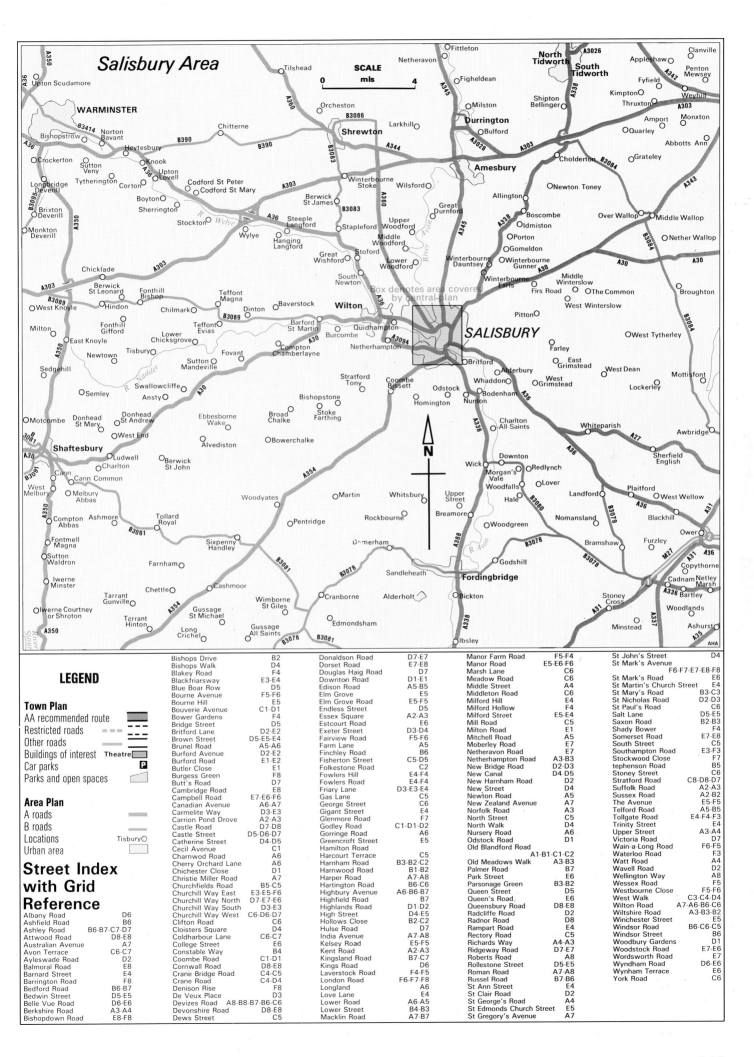

Salisbury Area

SCALE

0 mls 4

WARMINSTER

Durrington
Amesbury
Shrewton
Wilton
SALISBURY
Shaftesbury
Fordingbridge
North Tidworth
South Tidworth

Box denotes area covered by central-plan

N

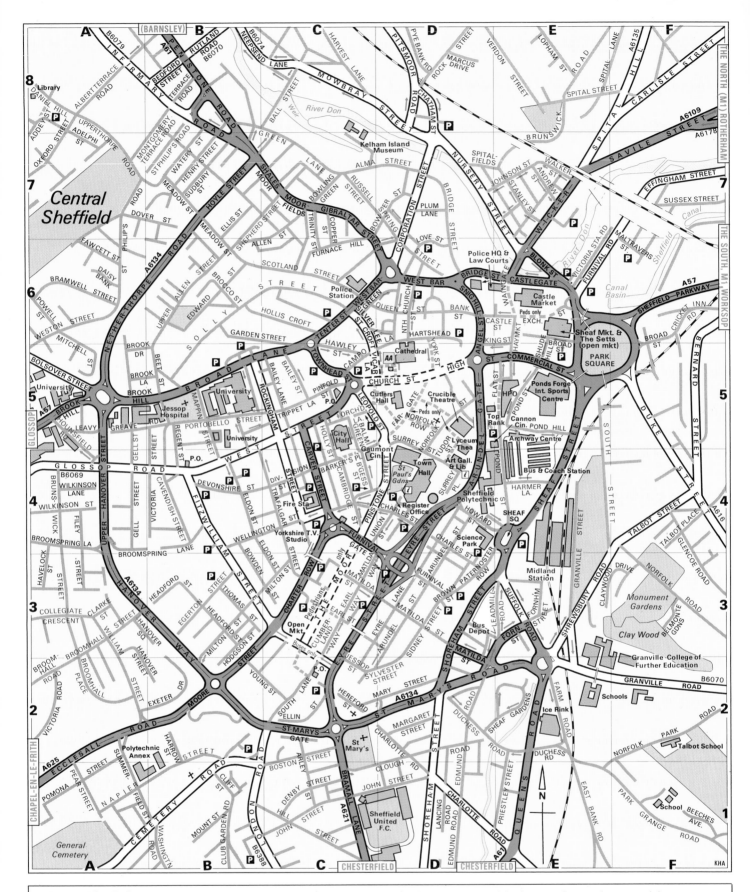

Sheffield

Cutlery – which has made the name of Sheffield famous throughout the world – has been manufactured here since at least as early as the time of Chaucer. The god of blacksmiths, Vulcan, is the symbol of the city's industry, and he crowns the town hall, which was opened in 1897 by Queen Victoria. At the centre of the industry, however, is Cutler's Hall, the headquarters of the Company of Cutlers. This society was founded in 1624 and has the right to grant trade marks to articles of a sufficiently high standard. In the hall is the company's collection of silver, with examples of craftsmanship dating back every year to 1773. A really large collection of cutlery is kept in the city museum. Steel production, a vital component of the industry, was greatly improved when the crucible process was invented here in 1740. At Abbeydale Industrial Hamlet, 3½ miles south-west of the city centre, is a complete restored site open as a museum and showing 18th-century methods of steel production. Sheffield's centre, transformed since World War II, is one of the finest and most modern in Europe. Modern developments include the Ponds Forge International Sports Centre and a few miles to the north east the Meadowhall Shopping Centre. Many parks are set in and around the city, and the Pennines are within easy reach.

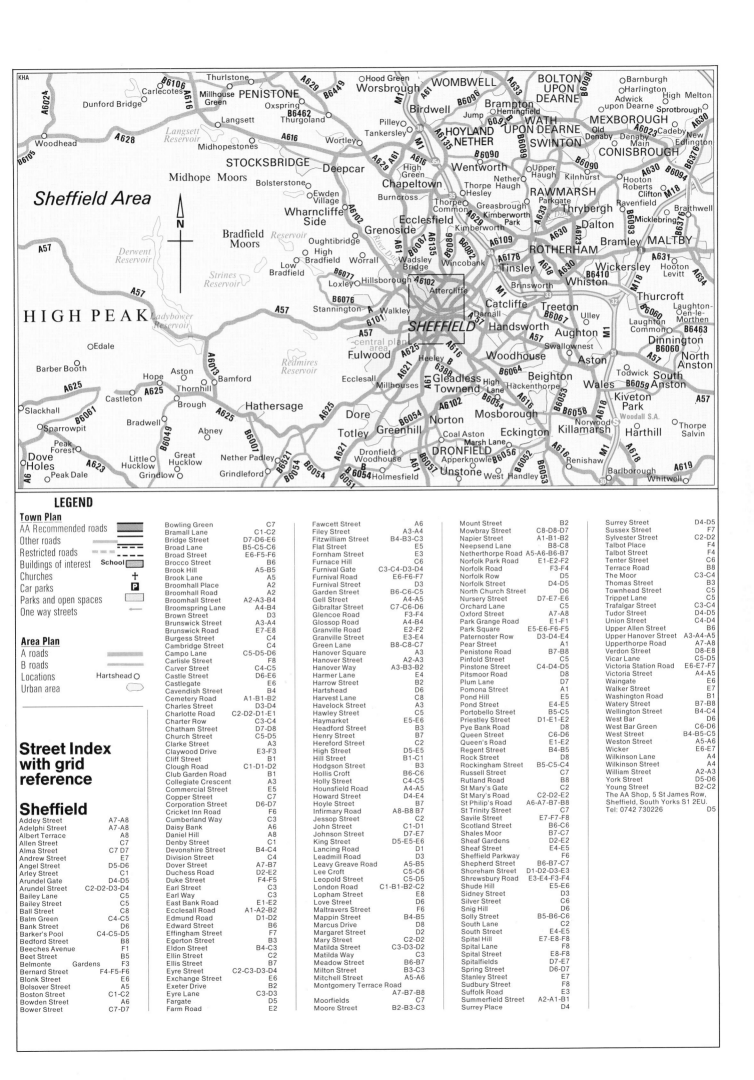

LEGEND

Town Plan
- AA Recommended roads
- Other roads
- Restricted roads
- Buildings of interest — School
- Churches
- Car parks
- Parks and open spaces
- One way streets

Area Plan
- A roads
- B roads
- Locations — Hartshead
- Urban area

Street Index with grid reference

Sheffield

Addey Street	A7-A8
Adelphi Street	A7-A8
Albert Terrace	A8
Allen Street	C7
Alma Street	C7 D7
Andrew Street	E7
Angel Street	D5-D6
Arley Street	C1
Arundel Gate	D4-D5
Arundel Street	C2-D2-D3-D4
Bailey Lane	C5
Bailey Street	C5
Ball Street	C8
Balm Green	C4-C5
Bank Street	D6
Barker's Pool	C4-C5-D5
Bedford Street	B8
Beeches Avenue	F1
Beet Street	B5
Belmonte Gardens	F3
Bernard Street	F4-F5-F6
Blonk Street	E6
Bolsover Street	A5
Boston Street	C1-C2
Bowden Street	A6
Bower Street	C7-D7
Bowling Green	C7
Bramall Lane	C1-C2
Bridge Street	D7-D6-E6
Broad Lane	B5-C5-C6
Broad Street	E6-F5-F6
Brocco Street	B6
Brook Hill	A5-B5
Brook Lane	A5
Broomhall Place	A2
Broomhall Road	A2
Broomhall Street	A2-A3-B4
Broomspring Lane	A4-B4
Brown Street	D3
Brunswick Street	A3-A4
Brunswick Road	E7-E8
Burgess Street	C4
Cambridge Street	C4
Campo Lane	C5-D5-D6
Carlisle Street	F8
Carver Street	C4-C5
Castle Street	D6-E6
Castlegate	E6
Cavendish Street	B4
Cemetery Road	A1-B1-B2
Charles Street	D3-D4
Charlotte Road	C2-D2-D1-E1
Charter Row	C3-C4
Chatham Street	D7-D8
Church Street	C5-D5
Clarke Street	A3
Claywood Drive	E3-F3
Cliff Street	B1
Clough Road	C1-D1-D2
Club Garden Road	B1
Collegiate Crescent	A3
Commercial Street	E5
Copper Street	C7
Corporation Street	D6-D7
Cricket Inn Road	F6
Cumberland Way	C3
Daisy Bank	A6
Daniel Hill	A8
Denby Street	C1
Devonshire Street	B4-C4
Division Street	C4
Dover Street	A7-B7
Duchess Road	D2-E2
Duke Street	F4-F5
Earl Street	C3
Earl Way	C3
East Bank Road	E1-E2
Ecclesall Road	A1-A2-B2
Edmund Road	D1-D2
Edward Street	B6
Effingham Street	F7
Egerton Street	B3
Eldon Street	B4-C3
Ellin Street	C2
Ellis Street	B7
Eyre Street	C2-C3-D3-D4
Exchange Street	E6
Exeter Drive	B2
Eyre Lane	C3-D3
Fargate	D5
Farm Road	E2

Fawcett Street	A6
Filey Street	A3-A4
Fitzwilliam Street	B4-B3-C3
Flat Street	E5
Fornham Street	E3
Furnace Hill	C6
Furnival Gate	C3-C4-D3-D4
Furnival Road	E6-F6-F7
Furnival Street	D3
Garden Street	B6-C6-C5
Gell Street	A4-A5
Gibraltar Street	C7-C6-D6
Glencoe Road	F3-F4
Glossop Road	A4-B4
Granville Road	E2-F2
Granville Street	E3-E4
Green Lane	B8-C8-C7
Hanover Square	A3
Hanover Street	A2-A3
Hanover Way	A3-B3-B2
Harmer Lane	E4
Harrow Street	B2
Hartshead	D6
Harvest Lane	C8
Havelock Street	A3
Hawley Street	C5
Haymarket	E5-E6
Headford Street	B3
Henry Street	B7
Hereford Street	C2
High Street	D5-E5
Hill Street	B1-C1
Hodgson Street	B3
Hollis Croft	B6-C6
Holly Street	C4-C5
Hounsfield Road	A4-A5
Howard Street	D4-E4
Hoyle Street	B7
Infirmary Road	A8-B8 B7
Jessop Street	C2
John Street	C1-D1
Johnson Street	D7-E7
King Street	D5-E5-E6
Lancing Road	D1
Leadmill Road	D3
Leavy Greave Road	A5-B5
Lee Croft	C5-C6
Leopold Street	C5-D5
London Road	C1-B1-B2-C2
Lopham Street	E8
Love Street	D6
Maltravers Street	F6
Mappin Street	B4-B5
Marcus Drive	D8
Margaret Street	D2
Mary Street	C2-D2
Matilda Street	C3-D3-D2
Matilda Way	C3
Meadow Street	B6-B7
Milton Street	B3-C3
Mitchell Street	A5-A6
Montgomery Terrace Road	A7-B7-B8
Moorfields	C7
Moore Street	B2-B3-C3

Mount Street	B2
Mowbray Street	C8-D8-D7
Napier Street	A1-B1-B2
Neepsend Lane	B8-C8
Netherthorpe Road	A5-A6-B6-B7
Norfolk Park Road	E1-E2-F2
Norfolk Road	F3-F4
Norfolk Row	D5
Norfolk Street	D4-D5
North Church Street	D6
Nursery Street	D7-E7-E6
Orchard Lane	C5
Oxford Street	A7-A8
Park Grange Road	E1-F1
Park Square	E5-E6-F6-F5
Paternoster Row	D3-D4-E4
Pear Street	A1
Penistone Road	B7-B8
Pinfold Street	C5
Pinstone Street	C4-D4-D5
Pitsmoor Road	D8
Plum Lane	D7
Pomona Street	A1
Pond Hill	E5
Pond Street	E4-E5
Portobello Street	B5-C5
Priestley Street	D1-E1-E2
Pye Bank Road	D8
Queen Street	C6-D6
Queen's Road	E1-E2
Regent Street	B4-B5
Rock Street	D8
Rockingham Street	B5-C5-C4
Russell Street	C7
Rutland Road	B8
St Mary's Gate	C2
St Mary's Road	C2-D2-E2
St Philip's Road	A6-A7-B7-B8
St Trinity Street	C7
Savile Street	E7-F7-F8
Scotland Street	B6-C6
Shales Moor	B7-C7
Sheaf Gardens	D2-E2
Sheaf Street	E4-E5
Sheffield Parkway	F6
Shepherd Street	B6-B7-C7
Shoreham Street	D1-D2-D3-E3
Shrewsbury Road	E3-E4-F3-F4
Shude Hill	E5-E6
Sidney Street	D3
Silver Street	C6
Snig Hill	D6
Solly Street	B5-B6-C6
South Lane	C2
South Street	E4-E5
Spital Hill	E7-E8-F8
Spital Lane	F8
Spital Street	E8-F8
Spitalfields	D7-E7
Spring Street	D6-D7
Stanley Street	E7
Sudbury Street	F8
Suffolk Road	E3
Summerfield Street	A2-A1-B1
Surrey Place	D4

Surrey Street	D4-D5
Sussex Street	F7
Sylvester Street	C2-D2
Talbot Place	F4
Talbot Street	F4
Tenter Street	C6
Terrace Road	B8
The Moor	C3-C4
Thomas Street	B3
Townhead Street	C5
Trippet Lane	C5
Trafalgar Street	C3-C4
Tudor Street	D4-D5
Union Street	C4-D4
Upper Allen Street	B6
Upper Hanover Street	A3-A4-A5
Upperthorpe Road	A7-A8
Verdon Street	D8-E8
Vicar Lane	C5-D5
Victoria Station Road	E6-E7-F7
Victoria Street	A4-A5
Waingate	E6
Walker Street	E7
Washington Road	B1
Watery Street	B7-B8
Wellington Street	B4-C4
West Bar	D6
West Bar Green	C6-D6
West Street	B4-B5-C5
Weston Street	A5-A6
Wicker	E6-E7
Wilkinson Lane	A4
Wilkinson Street	A4
William Street	A2-A3
York Street	D5-D6
Young Street	B2-C2

The AA Shop, 5 St James Row, Sheffield, South Yorks S1 2EU.
Tel: 0742 730226 D5

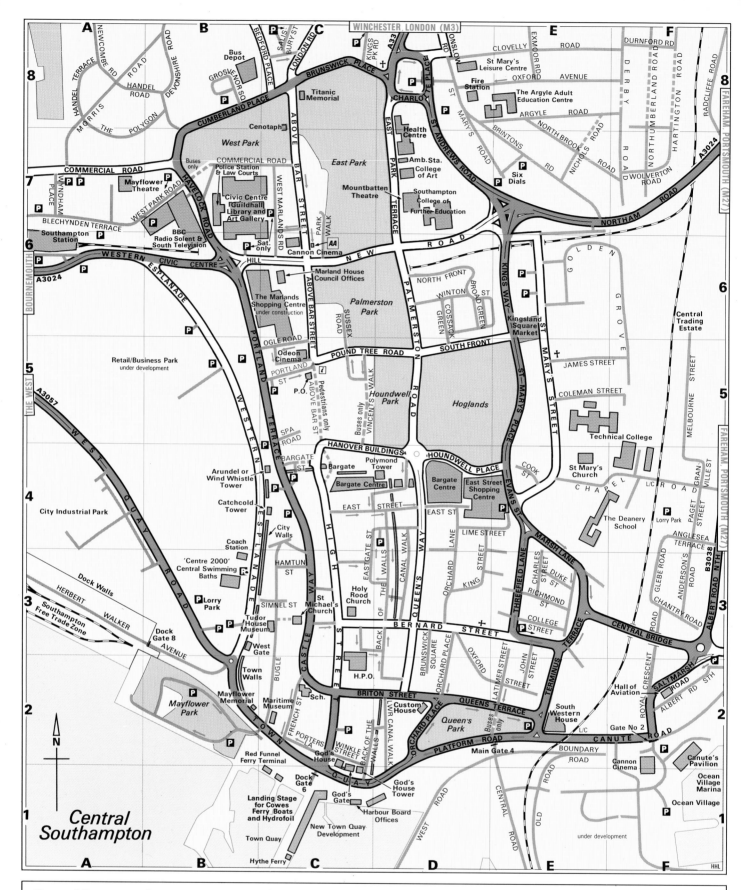

Southampton

In the days of the great ocean-going liners, Southampton was Britain's premier passenger port. Today container traffic is more important, but cruise liners still berth there. A unique double tide caused by the Solent waters, and protection from the open sea by the Isle of Wight, has meant that Southampton has always been a superb and important port. Like many great cities it was devastated by bombing raids during World War II. However, enough survives to make the city a fascinating place to explore. Outstanding are the town walls, which stand to their original height in some places, especially along Western Esplanade. The main landward entrance to the walled town was the Bargate – a superb medieval gateway with a Guildhall (now a museum) on its upper floor. The best place to appreciate old Southampton is in and around St Michael's Square. Here is St Michael's Church, oldest in the city and founded in 1070. Opposite is Tudor House Museum, a lovely gabled building housing much of interest. Down Bugle Street are old houses, with the town walls, pierced by the 13th-century West Gate, away to the right. At the corner of Bugle Street is the Wool House Maritime Museum, contained in a 14th-century warehouse. On the quayside is God's House Tower, part of the town's defences and now an archaeological museum.

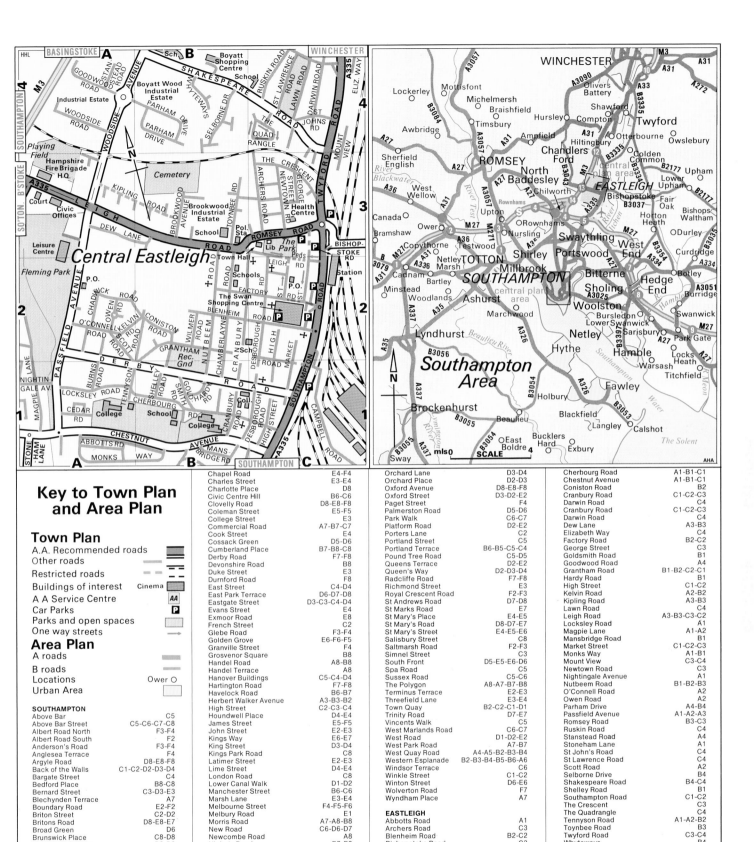

Key to Town Plan and Area Plan

Town Plan

A.A. Recommended roads	
Other roads	
Restricted roads	
Buildings of interest	Cinema
A A Service Centre	AA
Car Parks	P
Parks and open spaces	
One way streets	→

Area Plan

A roads	
B roads	
Locations	Ower O
Urban Area	

SOUTHAMPTON

Above Bar	C5
Above Bar Street	C5-C6-C7-C8
Albert Road North	F3-F4
Albert Road South	F2
Anderson's Road	F3-F4
Anglesea Terrace	F4
Argyle Road	D8-E8-F8
Back of the Walls	C1-C2-D2-D3-D4
Bargate Street	C4
Bedford Place	B8-C8
Bernard Street	C3-D3-E3
Blechynden Terrace	A7
Boundary Road	E2-F2
Briton Street	C2-D2
Britons Road	D8-E8-E7
Broad Green	D6
Brunswick Place	C8-D8
Brunswick Square	D2-D3
Bugle Street	C2-C3
Canal Walk	D3-D4
Canute Road	E2-F2
Castle Way	C2-C3-C4
Central Bridge	E3-F3
Central Road	E1-E2
Chantry Road	F3

Chapel Road	E4-F4
Charles Street	E3-E4
Charlotte Place	D8
Civic Centre Hill	B6-C6
Clovelly Road	D8-E8-F8
Coleman Street	E5-F5
College Street	E3
Commercial Road	A7-B7-C7
Cook Street	E4
Cossack Green	D5-D6
Cumberland Place	B7-B8-C8
Derby Road	F7-F8
Devonshire Road	B8
Duke Street	E3
Durnford Road	F8
East Street	C4-D4
East Park Terrace	D6-D7-D8
Eastgate Street	D3-C3-C4-D4
Evans Street	E4
Exmoor Road	E8
French Street	C2
Glebe Road	F3-F4
Golden Grove	E6-F6-F5
Granville Street	F4
Grosvenor Square	B8
Handel Road	A8-B8
Handel Terrace	A8
Hanover Buildings	C5-C4-D4
Hartington Road	F7-F8
Havelock Road	B6-B7
Herbert Walker Avenue	A3-B3-B2
High Street	C2-C3-C4
Houndwell Place	D4-E4
James Street	E5-F5
John Street	E2-E3
Kings Way	E6-E7
King Street	D3-D4
Kings Park Road	C8
Latimer Street	E2-E3
Lime Street	D4-E4
London Road	C8
Lower Canal Walk	D1-D2
Manchester Street	B6-C6
Marsh Lane	E3-E4
Melbourne Street	F4-F5-F6
Melbury Road	E1
Morris Road	A7-A8-B8
New Road	C6-D6-D7
Newcombe Road	A8
Nichols Road	E7-E8
North Brook Road	E8-E7-F7
North Front	D6
Northam Road	E6-E7-F7
Northumberland Road	F7-F8
Ogle Road	C5
Old Road	E1-E2
Onslow Road	D8

Orchard Lane	D3-D4
Orchard Place	D2-D3
Oxford Avenue	D8-E8-F8
Oxford Street	D3-D2-E2
Paget Street	F4
Palmerston Road	D5-D6
Park Walk	C6-C7
Platform Road	D2-E2
Porters Lane	C2
Portland Street	C5
Portland Terrace	B6-B5-C5-C4
Pound Tree Road	C5-D5
Queens Terrace	D2-E2
Queen's Way	D2-D3-D4
Radcliffe Road	F7-F8
Richmond Street	E3
Royal Crescent Road	F2-F3
St Andrews Road	D7-D8
St Marks Road	E7
St Mary's Place	E4-E5
St Mary's Road	D8-D7-E7
St Mary's Street	E4-E5-E6
Salisbury Street	C8
Saltmarsh Road	F2-F3
Simnel Street	C3
South Front	D5-E5-E6-D6
Spa Road	C5
Sussex Road	C5-C6
The Polygon	A8-A7-B7-B8
Terminus Terrace	E2-E3
Threefield Lane	E3-E4
Town Quay	B2-C2-C1-D1
Trinity Road	D7-E7
Vincents Walk	C5
West Marlands Road	C6-C7
West Road	D1-D2-E2
West Park Road	A7-B7
West Quay Road	A4-A5-B2-B3-B4
Western Esplanade	B2-B3-B4-B5-B6-A6
Windsor Terrace	C6
Winkle Street	C1-C2
Winton Street	D6-E6
Wolverton Road	F7
Wyndham Place	A7

EASTLEIGH

Abbotts Road	A1
Archers Road	C3
Blenheim Road	B2-C2
Bishopstoke Road	C3
Brookwood Avenue	B3
Burns Road	A1
Campbell Road	C1
Cedar Road	A1
Chadwick Road	A2-B2
Chamberlayne Road	B1-B2-B3
Chandlers Ford By-pass	A4

Cherbourg Road	A1-B1-C1
Chestnut Avenue	A1-B1-C1
Coniston Road	B2
Cranbury Road	C1-C2-C3
Darwin Road	C4
Cranbury Road	C1-C2-C3
Darwin Road	C4
Dew Lane	A3-B3
Elizabeth Way	C4
Factory Road	B2-C2
George Street	C3
Goldsmith Road	B1
Goodwood Road	A4
Grantham Road	B1-B2-C2-C1
Hardy Road	B1
High Street	C1-C2
Kelvin Road	A2-B2
Kipling Road	A3-B3
Lawn Road	C4
Leigh Road	A3-B3-C3-C2
Locksley Road	A1
Magpie Lane	A1-A2
Mansbridge Road	B1
Market Street	C1-C2-C3
Monks Way	A1-B1
Mount View	C3-C4
Newtown Road	C3
Nightingale Avenue	A1
Nutbeem Road	B1-B2-B3
O'Connell Road	A2
Owen Road	A2
Parham Drive	A4-B4
Passfield Avenue	A1-A2-A3
Romsey Road	B3-C3
Ruskin Road	C4
Stanstead Road	A4
Stoneham Lane	A1
St John's Road	C4
St Lawrence Road	C4
Scott Road	A2
Selborne Drive	B4
Shakespeare Road	B4-C4
Shelley Road	B1
Southampton Road	C1-C2
The Crescent	C3
The Quadrangle	C4
Tennyson Road	A1-A2-B2
Toynbee Road	B3
Twyford Road	C3-C4
Whyteways	B4
Wilmer Road	B2
Woodside Avenue	A3-A4-B4
Woodside Road	A4

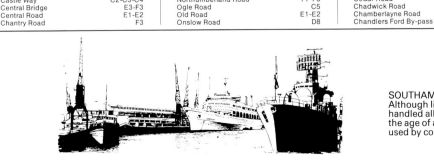

SOUTHAMPTON
Although liners still use Southampton's docks which handled all the great ocean-going passenger ships before the age of air travel replaced sea travel, the port is chiefly used by commercial traffic today.

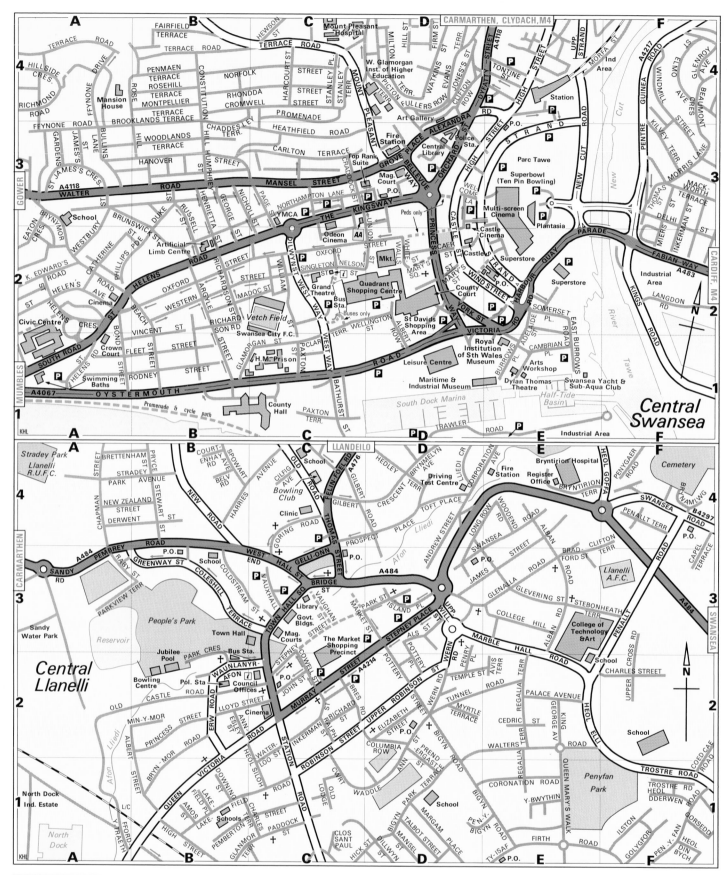

Swansea

Like nearly all towns in the valleys and along the coast of Glamorgan, Swansea grew at an amazing speed during the Industrial Revolution. Ironworks, non-ferrous metal smelting works and mills and factories of every kind were built to produce the goods which were exported from the city's docks. There had been a settlement here from very early times - the city's name is derived from Sweyn's Ea - Ea means Island, and Sweyn was a Viking pirate who had a base here.

Heavy industry is still pre-eminent in the area, but commerce is of increasing importance and the university exerts a strong influence. Hundreds of acres of parkland and open space lie in and around the city, and just to the west is the Gower, one of the most beautiful areas of Wales. The history of Swansea is traced in the Maritime and Industrial Museum and Royal Institution of South Wales Museum, while the Glynn Vivian Art Gallery contains notable paintings and porcelain.

Llanelli is the largest town in southeast Dyfed. Originally a market centre, its rapid growth began with the 19th-century introduction of ironworks and continued with the exploitation of its coal resources which in turn gave way to the modern steelworks.

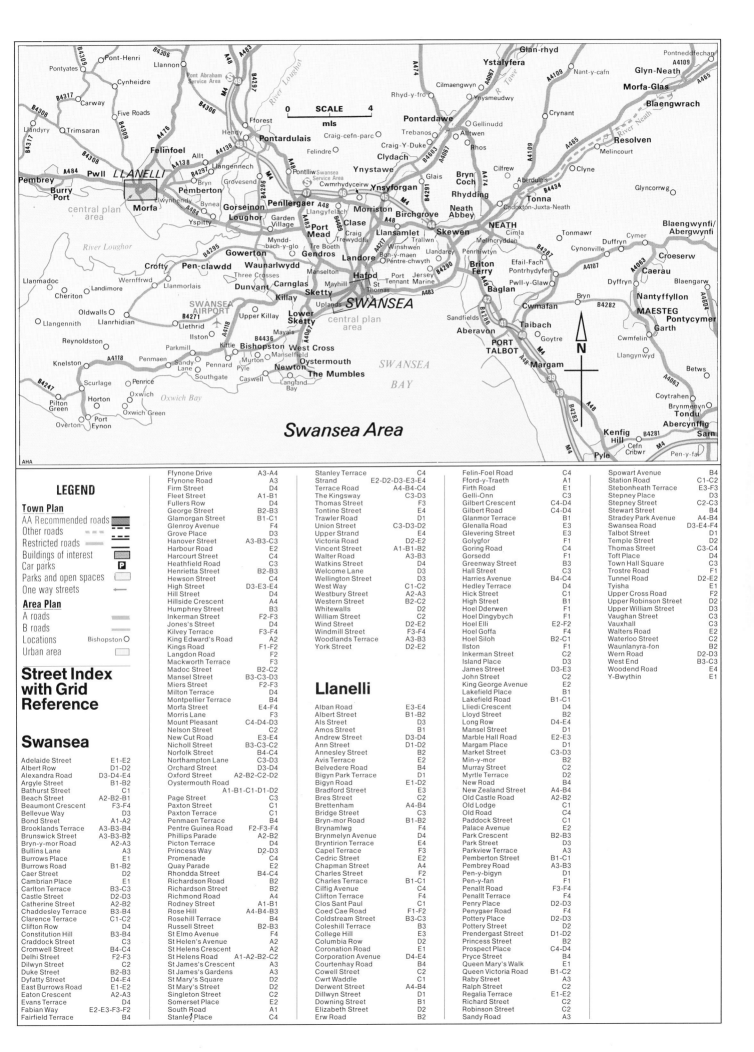

Swansea Area

LEGEND

Town Plan

AA Recommended roads
Other roads
Restricted roads
Buildings of interest
Car parks   P
Parks and open spaces
One way streets

Area Plan

A roads
B roads
Locations   Bishopston ○
Urban area

Street Index with Grid Reference

Swansea

Adelaide Street	E1-E2
Albert Row	D1-D2
Alexandra Road	D3-D4-E4
Argyle Street	B1-B2
Bathurst Street	C1
Beach Street	A2-B2-B1
Beaumont Crescent	F3-F4
Bellevue Way	D3
Bond Street	A1-A2
Brooklands Terrace	A3-B3-B4
Brunswick Street	A3-B3-B2
Bryn-y-mor Road	A2-A3
Bullins Lane	A3
Burrows Place	E1
Burrows Road	B1-B2
Caer Street	D2
Cambrian Place	E1
Carlton Terrace	B3-C3
Castle Street	D2-D3
Catherine Street	A2-B2
Chaddesley Terrace	B3-B4
Clarence Terrace	C1-C2
Clifton Row	D4
Constitution Hill	B3-B4
Craddock Street	C3
Cromwell Street	B4-C4
Delhi Street	F2-F3
Dilwyn Street	C2
Duke Street	B2-B3
Dyfatty Street	D4-E4
East Burrows Road	E1-E2
Eaton Crescent	A2-A3
Evans Terrace	D4
Fabian Way	E2-E3-F3-F2
Fairfield Terrace	B4
Ffynone Drive	A3-A4
Ffynone Road	A3
Firm Street	D4
Fleet Street	A1-B1
Fullers Row	D4
George Street	B2-B3
Glamorgan Street	B1-C1
Glenroy Avenue	F4
Grove Place	D3
Hanover Street	A3-B3-C3
Harbour Road	E2
Harcourt Street	C4
Heathfield Road	C3
Henrietta Street	B2-B3
Hewson Street	C4
High Street	D3-E3-E4
Hill Street	D4
Hillside Crescent	A4
Humphrey Street	B3
Inkerman Street	F2-F3
Jones's Street	D4
Kilvey Terrace	F3-F4
King Edward's Road	A2
Kings Road	F1-F2
Langdon Road	F2
Mackworth Terrace	F3
Madoc Street	B2-C2
Mansel Street	B3-C3-D3
Miers Street	F2-F3
Milton Terrace	D4
Montpellier Terrace	B4
Morfa Street	E4-F4
Morris Lane	F3
Mount Pleasant	C4-D4-D3
Nelson Street	C2
New Cut Road	E3-E4
Nicholl Street	B3-C3-C2
Norfolk Street	B4-C4
Northampton Lane	C3-D3
Orchard Street	D3-D4
Oxford Street	A2-B2-C2-D2
Oystermouth Road	A1-B1-C1-D1-D2
Page Street	C3
Paxton Street	C1
Paxton Terrace	C1
Penmaen Terrace	B4
Pentre Guinea Road	F2-F3-F4
Phillips Parade	A2-B2
Picton Terrace	C4
Princess Way	D2-D3
Promenade	C4
Quay Parade	E2
Rhondda Street	B4-C4
Richardson Road	B2
Richardson Street	B2
Richmond Road	A4
Rodney Street	A1-B1
Rose Hill	A4-B4-B3
Rosehill Terrace	B4
Russell Street	B2-B3
St Elmo Avenue	F4
St Helen's Avenue	A2
St Helens Crescent	A2
St Helens Road	A1-A2-B2-C2
St James's Crescent	A3
St James's Gardens	A3
St Mary's Square	D2
St Mary's Street	D2
Singleton Street	C2
Somerset Place	E2
South Road	A1
Stanley Place	C4
Stanley Terrace	C4
Strand	E2-D2-D3-E3-E4
Terrace Road	A4-B4-C4
The Kingsway	C3-D3
Thomas Street	F3
Tontine Street	E4
Trawler Road	D1
Union Street	C3-D3-D2
Upper Strand	E4
Victoria Road	D2-E2
Vincent Street	A1-B1-B2
Walter Road	A3-B3
Watkins Street	D4
Welcome Lane	D3
Wellington Street	D3
West Way	C1-C2
Westbury Street	A2-A3
Western Street	B2-C2
Whitewalls	D2
William Street	C2
Wind Street	D2-E2
Windmill Street	F3-F4
Woodlands Terrace	A3-B3
York Street	D2-E2

Llanelli

Alban Road	E3-E4
Albert Street	B1-B2
Als Street	D3
Amos Street	B1
Andrew Street	D3-D4
Ann Street	D1-D2
Annesley Street	B2
Avis Terrace	E2
Belvedere Road	B4
Bigyn Park Terrace	D1
Bigyn Road	E1-D2
Bradford Street	E3
Bres Street	C2
Brettenham	A4-B4
Bridge Street	C3
Bryn-mor Road	B1-B2
Brynamlwg	F4
Brynmelyn Avenue	D4
Bryntirion Terrace	E4
Capel Terrace	F3
Cedric Street	E2
Charles Street	D4
Charles Terrace	B1-C1
Cilfig Avenue	C4
Clifton Terrace	F4
Clos Sant Paul	C1
Coed Cae Road	F1-F2
Coldstream Street	B3-C3
Coleshill Terrace	B3
College Hill	E3
Columbia Row	D2
Coronation Road	E1
Corporation Avenue	D4-E4
Courtenhay Road	B4
Cowell Street	C2
Cwrt Waddle	C1
Derwent Street	A4-B4
Dillwyn Street	D1
Downing Street	B1
Elizabeth Street	D2
Erw Road	B2
Felin-Foel Road	C4
Fford-y-Traeth	A1
Firth Road	E1
Gelli-Onn	C3
Gilbert Crescent	C4-D4
Gilbert Road	C4-D4
Glanmor Terrace	B1
Glenalla Road	E3
Glevering Street	E3
Golygfor	F1
Goring Road	C4
Gorsedd	F1
Greenway Street	B3
Hall Street	C3
Harries Avenue	B4-C4
Hedley Terrace	D4
Hick Street	C1
High Street	B1
Hoel Dderwen	F1
Hoel Dingybych	F1
Hoel Elli	E2-F2
Hoel Goffa	F4
Hoel Siloh	B2-C1
Ilston	F1
Inkerman Street	C2
Island Place	D3
James Street	D3-E3
John Street	C2
King George Avenue	E2
Lakefield Place	B1
Lakefield Road	B1-C1
Lliedi Crescent	D4
Lloyd Street	B2
Long Row	D4-E4
Mansel Street	D1
Marble Hall Road	E2-E3
Margam Place	D1
Market Street	C3-D3
Min-y-mor	B2
Murray Street	C2
Myrtle Terrace	D2
New Road	B4
New Zealand Street	A4-B4
Old Castle Road	A2-B2
Old Lodge	C1
Old Road	C4
Paddock Street	C1
Palace Avenue	E2
Park Crescent	B2-B3
Park Street	D3
Parkview Terrace	A3
Pemberton Street	B1-C1
Pembrey Road	A3-B3
Pen-y-bigyn	D1
Pen-y-fan	F1
Penallt Road	F3-F4
Penallt Terrace	F4
Penry Place	D2-D3
Penygaer Road	F4
Pottery Place	D2-D3
Pottery Street	D2
Prendergast Street	D1-D2
Princess Street	B2
Prospect Place	C4-D4
Pryce Street	B4
Queen Mary's Walk	E1
Queen Victoria Road	B1-C2
Raby Street	A3
Ralph Street	C2
Regalia Terrace	E1-E2
Richard Street	C2
Robinson Street	C2
Sandy Road	A3
Spowart Avenue	B4
Station Road	C1-C2
Stebonheath Terrace	E3-F3
Stepney Place	D3
Stepney Street	C2-C3
Stewart Street	B4
Stradey Park Avenue	A4-B4
Swansea Road	D3-E4-F4
Talbot Street	D1
Temple Street	D2
Thomas Street	C3-C4
Toft Place	D4
Town Hall Square	C3
Trostre Road	F1
Tunnel Road	D2-E2
Tyisha	E1
Upper Cross Road	F2
Upper Robinson Street	D2
Upper William Street	D3
Vaughan Street	C3
Vauxhall	C3
Walters Road	E2
Waterloo Street	C2
Waunlanyra-fon	B2
Wern Road	D2-D3
West End	B3-C3
Woodend Road	E4
Y-Bwythin	E1

249

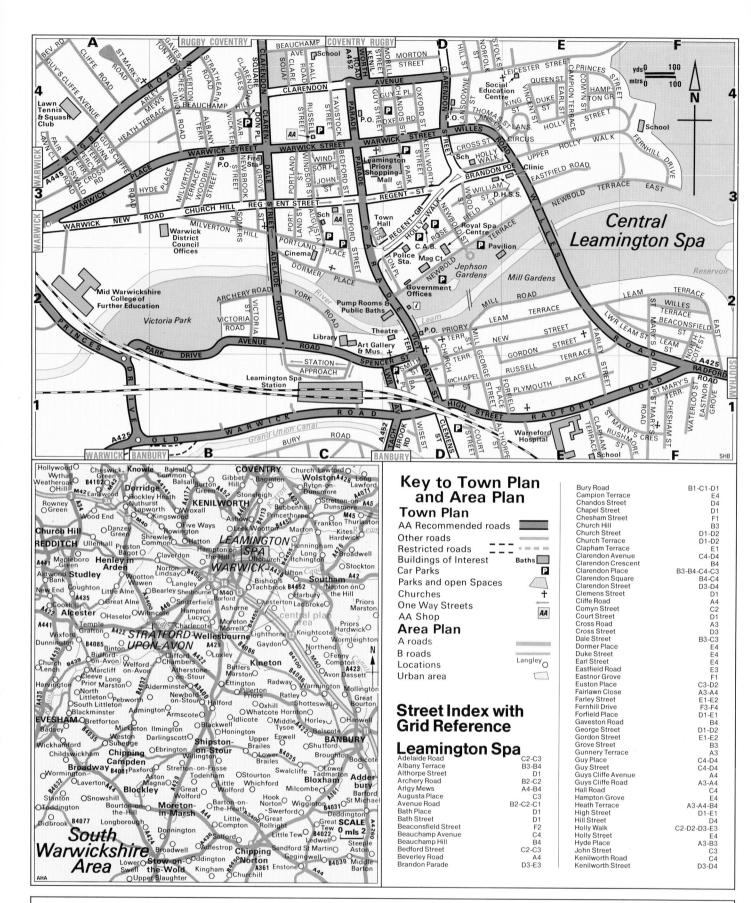

Key to Town Plan and Area Plan

Town Plan

AA Recommended roads	▬▬
Other roads	▬ ▬
Restricted roads	– – –
Buildings of Interest	Baths ▭
Car Parks	P
Parks and open Spaces	◣
Churches	+
One Way Streets	→
AA Shop	AA

Area Plan

A roads	▬
B roads	▬
Locations	Langley ○
Urban area	◢

Street Index with Grid Reference

Leamington Spa

Adelaide Road	C2-C3
Albany Terrace	B3-B4
Althorpe Street	D1
Archery Road	B2-C2
Arlgy Mews	A4-B4
Augusta Place	C3
Avenue Road	B2-C2-C1
Bath Place	D1
Bath Street	D1
Beaconsfield Street	F2
Beauchamp Avenue	C4
Beauchamp Hill	B4
Bedford Street	C2-C3
Beverley Road	A4
Brandon Parade	D3-E3
Bury Road	B1-C1-D1
Campion Terrace	E4
Chandos Street	D4
Chapel Street	D1
Chesham Street	F1
Church Hill	B3
Church Street	D1-D2
Church Terrace	D1-D2
Clapham Terrace	E1
Clarendon Avenue	C4-D4
Clarendon Crescent	B4
Clarendon Place	B3-B4-C4-C3
Clarendon Square	B4-C4
Clarendon Street	D3-D4
Clemens Street	D1
Cliffe Road	A4
Comyn Street	C2
Court Street	D1
Cross Road	A3
Cross Street	D3
Dale Street	B3-C3
Dormer Place	E4
Duke Street	E4
Earl Street	E4
Eastfield Road	E3
Eastnor Grove	F1
Euston Place	C3-D2
Fairlawn Close	A3-A4
Farley Street	E1-E2
Fernhill Drive	F3-F4
Forfield Place	D1-E1
Gaveston Road	B4
George Street	D1-D2
Gordon Street	E1-E2
Grove Street	B3
Gunnery Terrace	A3
Guy Place	C4-D4
Guy Street	C4-D4
Guys Cliffe Avenue	A4
Guys Cliffe Road	A3-A4
Hall Road	C4
Hampton Grove	E4
Heath Terrace	A3-A4-B4
High Street	D1-E1
Hill Street	D4
Holly Walk	C2-D2-D3-E3
Holly Street	E4
Hyde Place	A3-B3
John Street	D1
Kenilworth Road	C4
Kenilworth Street	D3-D4

Warwick

The old county town of the shire, Warwick lies in the shadow of its massive, historic castle which occupies the rocky ridge above the River Avon. Thomas Beauchamp and his son built the huge towers and curtain walls in the 14th century, but it was the Jacobean holders of the earldom, the Grevilles, who transformed the medieval stronghold into a nobleman's residence. In 1694,

the heart of the town was almost completely destroyed by fire and the few medieval buildings that survived lie on the outskirts of the present 18th-century centre. Of these Oken House, now a doll museum, and Lord Leycester's Hospital, almshouses dating back to the 14th century, are particularly striking.

Stratford-upon-Avon, as the birthplace of William Shakespeare, England's most famous poet and playwright, is second only to London as a

tourist attraction. This charming old market town is a living memorial to him; his plays are performed in the Royal Shakespeare Theatre which dominates the river bank, a waxwork museum specialises in scenes from his works, and his childhood home in Henley Street is a museum.

Leamington Spa, an inland spa on the River Leam, gained the prefix 'Royal' after Queen Victoria had visited it in 1838, and the town has been a fashionable health resort ever since.

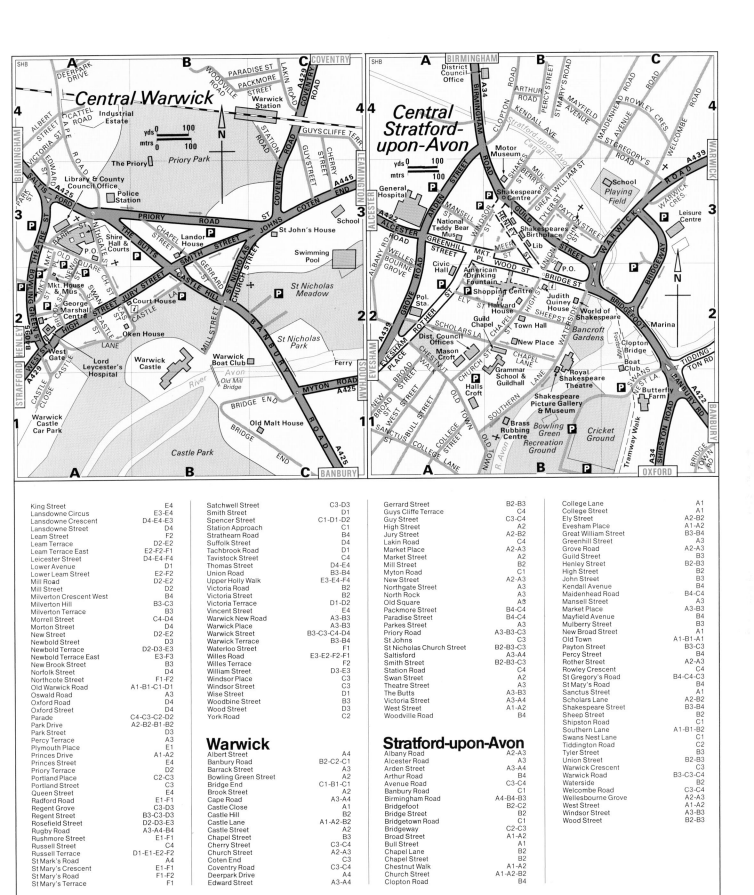

King Street	E4	Satchwell Street	C3-D3
Lansdowne Circus	E3-E4	Smith Street	D1
Lansdowne Crescent	D4-E4-E3	Spencer Street	C1-D1-D2
Lansdowne Street	D4	Station Approach	C1
Leam Street	F2	Strathearn Road	B4
Leam Terrace	D2-E2	Suffolk Street	D4
Leam Terrace East	E2-F2-F1	Tachbrook Road	D1
Leicester Street	D4-E4-F4	Tavistock Street	C4
Lower Avenue	D1	Thomas Street	D4-E4
Lower Leam Street	E2-F2	Union Road	B3-B4
Mill Road	D2-E2	Upper Holly Walk	E3-E4-F4
Mill Street	D2	Victoria Road	B2
Milverton Crescent West	B4	Victoria Street	B2
Milverton Hill	B3-C3	Victoria Terrace	D1-D2
Milverton Terrace	B3	Vincent Street	E4
Morrell Street	C4-D4	Warwick New Road	A3-B3
Morton Street	D4	Warwick Place	A3-B3
New Street	D2-E2	Warwick Street	B3-C3-C4-D4
Newbold Street	D3	Warwick Terrace	B3-B4
Newbold Terrace	D2-D3-E3	Waterloo Street	F1
Newbold Terrace East	E3-F3	Willes Road	E3-E2-F2-F1
New Brook Street	B3	Willes Terrace	F2
Norfolk Street	D4	William Street	D3-E3
Northcote Street	F1-F2	Windsor Place	C3
Old Warwick Road	A1-B1-C1-D1	Windsor Street	C3
Oswald Road	A3	Wise Street	D1
Oxford Road	D4	Woodbine Street	B3
Oxford Street	D4	Wood Street	D3
Parade	C4-C3-C2-D2	York Road	C2
Park Drive	A2-B2-B1-B2		
Park Street	D3		
Percy Terrace	A3		
Plymouth Place	E1		
Princes Drive	A1-A2		
Princes Street	E4		
Priory Terrace	D2		
Portland Place	C2-C3		
Portland Street	C3		
Queen Street	E4		
Radford Road	E1-F1		
Regent Grove	C3-D3		
Regent Street	B3-C3-D3		
Rosefield Street	D2-D3-E3		
Rugby Road	A3-A4-B4		
Rushmore Street	E1-F1		
Russell Street	C4		
Russell Terrace	D1-E1-E2-F2		
St Mark's Road	A4		
St Mary's Crescent	E1-F1		
St Mary's Road	F1-F2		
St Mary's Terrace	F1		

Warwick

Albert Street	A4	Gerrard Street	B2-B3
Banbury Road	B2-C2-C1	Guys Cliffe Terrace	C4
Barrack Street	A3	Guy Street	C3-C4
Bowling Green Street	A2	High Street	A2
Bridge End	C1-B1-C1	Jury Street	A2-B2
Brook Street	A2	Lakin Road	C4
Cape Road	A3-A4	Market Place	A2-A3
Castle Close	A1	Market Street	A2
Castle Hill	B2	Mill Street	B2
Castle Lane	A1-A2-B2	Myton Road	C1
Castle Street	B2	New Street	A2-A3
Chapel Street	B3	Northgate Street	A3
Cherry Street	C3-C4	North Rock	A3
Church Street	A2-A3	Old Square	A3
Coten End	C3	Packmore Street	B4-C4
Coventry Road	C3-C4	Paradise Street	B4-C4
Deerpark Drive	A4	Parkes Street	A3
Edward Street	A3-A4	Priory Road	A3-B3-C3
		St Johns	C3
		St Nicholas Church Street	B2-B3-C3
		Saltisford	A3-A4
		Smith Street	B2-B3-C3
		Station Road	C4
		Swan Street	A2
		Theatre Street	A3
		The Butts	A3-B3
		Victoria Street	A3-A4
		West Street	A1-A2
		Woodville Road	B4

Stratford-upon-Avon

Albany Road	A2-A3	College Lane	A1
Alcester Road	A3	College Street	A1
Arden Street	A3-A4	Ely Street	A2-B2
Arthur Road	B4	Evesham Place	A1-A2
Avenue Road	C3-C4	Great William Street	B3-B4
Banbury Road	C1	Greenhill Street	A3
Birmingham Road	A4-B4-B3	Grove Road	A2-A3
Bridgefoot	B2-C2	Guild Street	B3
Bridge Street	B2	Henley Street	B2-B3
Bridgetown Road	C1	High Street	B2
Bridgeway	C2-C3	John Street	B3
Broad Street	A1-A2	Kendall Avenue	B4
Bull Street	A1	Maidenhead Road	B4-C4
Chapel Lane	B2	Mansell Street	A3
Chapel Street	B2	Market Place	A3-B3
Chestnut Walk	A1-A2	Mayfield Avenue	B4
Church Street	A1-A2-B2	Mulberry Street	B3
Clopton Road	B4	New Broad Street	A1
		Old Town	A1-B1-A1
		Payton Street	B3-C3
		Percy Street	B4
		Rother Street	A2-A3
		Rowley Crescent	C4
		St Gregory's Road	B4-C4-C3
		St Mary's Road	B4
		Sanctus Street	A1
		Scholars Lane	A2-B2
		Shakespeare Street	B3-B4
		Sheep Street	B2
		Shipston Road	C1
		Southern Lane	A1-B1-B2
		Swans Nest Lane	C1
		Tiddington Road	C2
		Tyler Street	B3
		Union Street	B2-B3
		Warwick Crescent	C3
		Warwick Road	B3-C3-C4
		Waterside	B2
		Welcombe Road	C3-C4
		Wellesbourne Grove	A2-A3
		West Street	A1-A2
		Windsor Street	A3-B3
		Wood Street	B2-B3

WARWICK
These pretty brick and timbered cottages standing in the
shadow of the great medieval towers of Warwick Castle are
among the few buildings in the town that survived a
devastating fire in the late 17th century.

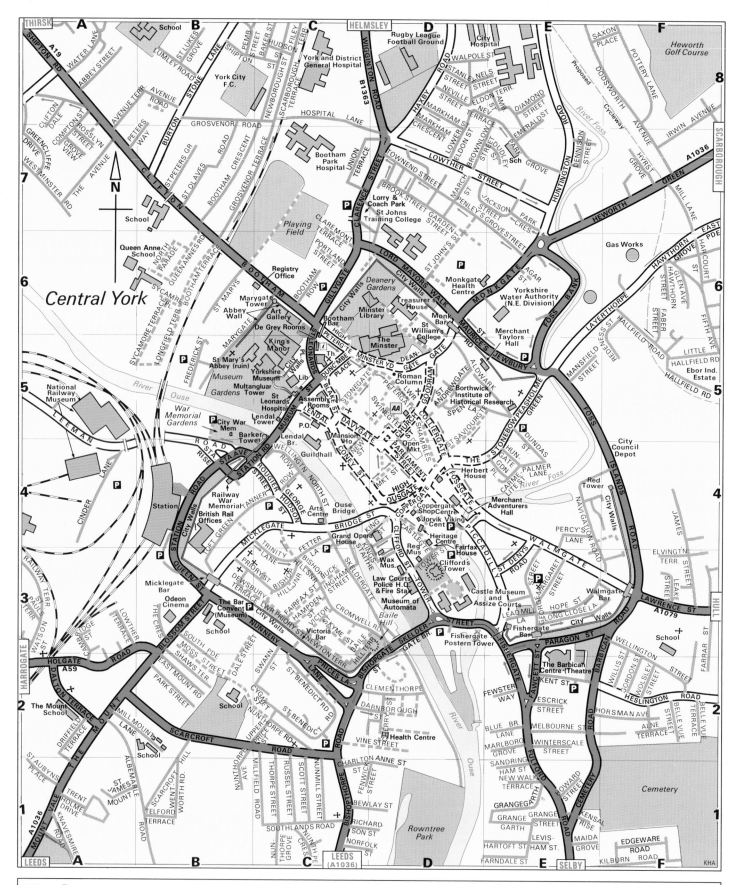

York

York Minster, unquestionably the city's outstanding glory, is considered to be one of the greatest cathedral churches in Europe. It is especially famous for its lovely windows which contain more than half the medieval stained glass in England.

Great medieval walls enclose the historic city centre and their three-mile circuit offers magnificent views of the Minster, York's numerous fine buildings, churches and the River Ouse. The ancient streets consist of a maze of alleys and lanes, some of them so narrow that the overhanging upper storeys of the houses almost touch. The most famous of these picturesque streets is The Shambles, formerly the butchers' quarter of the city, but now colonised by antique and tourist shops. York flourished throughout Tudor, Georgian and Victorian times and handsome buildings from these periods also feature throughout the city.

The Castle Museum gives a fascinating picture of York as it used to be and the Heritage Centre interprets the social and architectural history of the city. Other places of exceptional note in this city of riches include the Merchant Adventurer's Hall; the Treasurer's House, now owned by the National Trust and filled with fine paintings and furniture; the Jorvik Viking Centre, where there is an exciting restoration of the original Viking settlement at York, and the National Railway Museum.

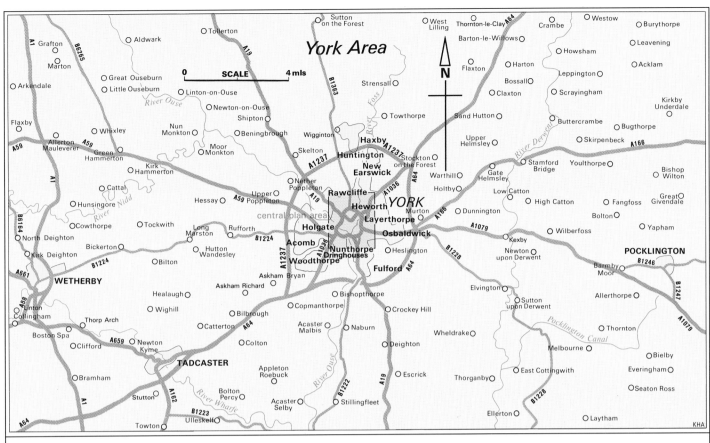

Key to Town Plan and Area Plan

Town Plan

AA Recommended roads
Other roads
Restricted roads
Buildings of interest   Station
Churches
Car Parks
Parks and open spaces
AA Service Centre
One Way Streets

Area Plan

A roads
B roads
Locations   Fangfoss O
Urban area

Street Index with Grid Reference

York

Abbey Street	A8
Agar Street	E6
Albemarle Road	A2-A1-B1
Aldwark	D5-E5
Alne Terrace	F2
Amber Street	E8
Anne Street	D1
Avenue Road	B8
Avenue Terrace	A7-A8-B8
Baile Hill Terrace	C2-C3-D3
Baker Street	C8
Barbican Road	E2-F2-F3-E3
Belle Vue Street	F2
Belle Vue Terrace	F2
Bewlay Street	C1-D1
Bishopgate Street	C2-D2-D3
Bishophill Junior	C3
Bishophill Senior	C3
Bishopthorpe Road	C1-C2
Blake Street	C5
Blossom Street	B2-B3
Blue Bridge Lane	E2
Bootham	B6-C6
Bootham Crescent	B7-C7-C8
Bootham Row	C6
Bootham Terrace	B6
Bridge Street	C4-D4
Brook Street	D7
Brownlow Street	D7-E7-E8
Buckingham Street	C3
Burton Stone Lane	B7-B8
Cambridge Street	A2-A3
Carmelite Street	D4-E4
Castlegate	D3-D4
Cemetery Road	E1-E2
Charlton Street	C1-D1
Cherry Street	D2
Church Street	D5
Cinder Lane	C6-C7
Claremont Terrace	C6-C7
Clarence Street	C6-C7-D7
Clementhorpe	C2-D2
Clifford Street	D3-D4
Clifton	A8-A7-B7
Clifton Dale	A7-A8
Colliergate	D4-D5
Compton Street	A7-A8
Coppergate	D4
Cromwell Road	C3-D3
Cygnet Street	C2
Dale Street	B2-B3
Dalton Terrace	A2
Darnborough Street	C2-D2
Davygate	C5-C4-D4-D5
Deangate	D5
Dennison Street	E7
Dewsbury Terrace	B3-C3
Diamond Street	E8
Dodsworth Avenue	E8-F8-F7
Driffield Terrace	A2
Dudley Street	D7-E7
Duncombe Place	C5
Dundas Street	E4-E5
East Parade	F6-F7
East Mount Road	B2
Ebor Street	C2-D2
Edgeware Road	F1
Eldon Terrace	D8-E8
Elvington Terrace	F3
Emerald Street	E7-E8
Escrick Street	E2
Faber Street	F6
Fairfax Street	C3
Farndale Street	E1
Farrar Street	F2-F3
Fawcett Street	E2-E3
Fenwick Street	C1-D1
Fetter Lane	C3-C4
Fewster Way	E2
Fifth Avenue	F5-F6
Filey Terrace	C8
Fishergate	E2-E3
Foss Bank	E5-E6
Fossgate	D4
Foss Islands Road	E4-E5-F5-F4
Frederick Street	B5
Fulford Road	E1-E2
Garden Street	D7
George Hudson Street	C4
George Street	E3-E4
Gillygate	C6
Glen Avenue	F6
Goodramgate	D5-D6
Gordon Street	F2
Grange Garth	E1

Grange Street	E1
Greencliffe Drive	A7-A8
Grosvenor Road	B6
Grosvenor Terrace	B6-B7-C7-C8
Grove View	A7
Hallfield Road	F5-F6
Hampden Street	C3
Harcourt Street	F6
Harloft Street	E1
Hawthorn Grove	F6
Hawthorne Street	F6
Haxby Road	D7-D8
Heslington Road	E2-F2
Heworth Green	E6-E7-F7
High Ousegate	D4
High Petergate	C5-C6
Holgate Road	A2-A3-B3
Hope Street	E3
Horsman Avenue	E2-F2
Hospital Lane	C8
Howard Street	E1
Hudson Street	C8
Hungate	D4
Huntington Road	E6-E7-E8
Hyrst Grove	F7
Irwin Avenue	F7-F8
Jackson Street	D7-E7
James Street	F3-F4
Jewbury	E5
Kensal Rise	E1
Kent Street	E2
Kilburn Road	E1-F1
Kings Staithe	C4-D4-D3
King Street	C4-D4
Knavesmire Road	A1
Kyme Street	C3
Lawrence Street	F3
Layerthorpe	E5-E6-F6
Lead Mill Lane	E3
Leake Street	F3
Leeman Road	A5-A4-B5-B4
Lendal Coney Street	C5-C4-D4
Levisham Street	E2
Little Hallfield Road	F5
Long Close Lane	E3-F3
Longfield Terrace	B5-B6
Lord Mayors Walk	C6-D6
Love Lane	A1-A2
Lower Eldon Street	D7
Lower Petergate	D5
Lower Priory Street	C3
Lowther Street	D7-E7
Lowther Terrace	A3
Maida Grove	E1
Mansfield Street	E5
March Street	D7
Margaret Street	E3
Market Street	D4
Markham Crescent	D7-D8
Markham Street	D7-D8
Marlborough Grove	E2
Marygate	B5-B6-C6
Melbourne Street	E2
Micklegate	B3-B4-C4
Millfield Road	C1-C2
Mill Lane	F7
Mill Mount Lane	A2-B2
Minster Yard	C5-D5
Monkgate	D6-E6

Moss Street	B2-B3
Mount Vale	A1
Museum Street	C5
Navigation Road	E4-E3-F3
Nelson Street	D8-E8
Neville Street	D8
Neville Terrace	D8-E8
Newborough Street	C8
New Street	C4-C5
Newton Terrace	C2-C3
New Walk Terrace	E1
Norfolk Street	C1-D1
North Parade	B6
North Street	C4
Nunmill Street	C1-C2
Nunnery Lane	B3-C3-C2
Nunthorpe Avenue	B1-B2
Nunthorpe Grove	C1
Nunthorpe Road	B2-C2
Palmer Lane	E4
Paragon Street	E3-F3
Park Crescent	E7
Park Grove	E7-E8
Park Street	B2
Parliament Street	D4-D5
Peasholme Green	E5
Pembroke Street	B8
Penley's Grove Street	D7-E7-E6
Percy's Lane	E4
Peters Way	A7-B7-B8
Piccadilly	D4-D3-E3-E4
Portland Street	C6
Pottery Lane	F8
Prices Lane	C2
Priory Street	B3-C3
Queen Annes Road	B6
Queen Street	B3
Railway Terrace	A3
Redness Street	F5-F6
Richardson Street	C1-D1
Rosslyn Street	A7
Rougier Street	C4
Russel Street	C1-C2
St Andrewgate	D5
St Aubyns Place	A1
St Benedict Road	C2
St Denys Road	E3-E4
St James Mount	A1
St Johns Street	D6-D7
St Leonards Place	D5-D6
St Lukes Grove	B8
St Marys	B6
St Maurices	D6-D5-E5
St Olaves Road	B7-B8
St Pauls Terrace	A3
St Peters Grove	B7
St Saviourgate	D4-D5-E5
Sandringham Street	E1
Saxon Place	E8-F8
Scarborough Terrace	C8
Scarcroft Hill	B1-B2
Scarcroft Road	A2-B2-C2-C1
Scott Street	C1-C2
Shambles	D4-D5
Shaws Terrace	B2-B3
Shipton Road	A8
Shipton Street	B8-C8
Skeldergate	C4-C3-D3
Skeldergate Bridge	D3
South Esplanade	D3

Southlands Road	C1
South Parade	B2-B3
Spen Lane	D5
Stanley Street	D8
Station Avenue	B4
Station Rise	B4
Station Road	B3-B4-C4-C5
Stonegate	C5-D5
Swann Street	C9
Swinegate	D5
Sycamore Place	B6
Sycamore Terrace	A5-B5-B6
Tanner Row	B4-C4
Telford Terrace	A1
The Avenue	A7
The Crescent	B3
The Mount	A1-A2-B2
The Stonebow	D4-E4-E5
Thorpe Street	C1-C2
Toft Green	B3-B4
Tower Street	D4-D3-E3
Townend Street	D7
Trent Holme Drive	A1
Trinity Lane	C3-C4
Union Terrace	C7
Upper Price Street	B2-C2
Victor Street	C3
Vine Street	C2-D2
Walmgate	D4-E4-E3-F3
Walpole Street	D8-E8
Water Lane	A8
Watson Street	A2-A3
Wellington Row	C4
Wellington Street	F2-F3
Wentworth Road	B1
Westminster Road	A7
Willis Street	F2-F3
Winterscale Street	E2
Wolsley Street	F2

AA Shop
5a and 6 Church Street
York, North Yorks YO1 2BG
Tel: 0904 652921   D5

•Index

Each placename entry in this index is identified by its county or region name. These are shown in italics. A list of the abbreviated forms used is given below.

To locate a placename in the atlas turn to the map page number indicated in bold type in the index and use the 4 figure grid reference.

e g Hythe *Kent.* .**29** TR1634 is found on page '29'. The two letters 'TR' refer to the National Grid. To pin point our example the first bold figure '**1**' is found along the bottom edge of the page. The following figure '6' indicates how many imaginary tenths to move east of line '1'. The next bold figure '**3**' is found along the left hand side of the page. The last figure '4' shows how many imaginary tenths to move north of line '3'. You will locate Hythe where these two lines intersect.

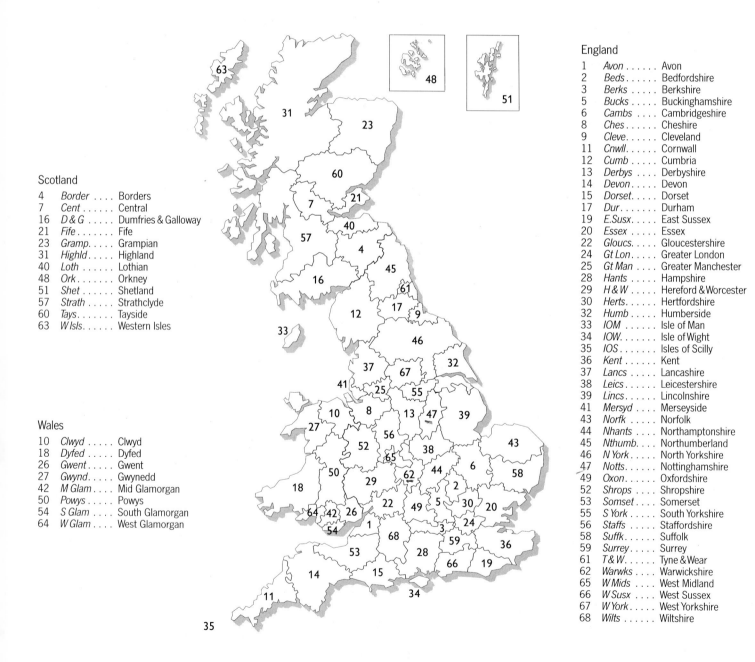

Scotland

4	*Border*	Borders
7	*Cent*	Central
16	*D & G*	Dumfries & Galloway
21	*Fife*	Fife
23	*Gramp.*	Grampian
31	*Highld*	Highland
40	*Loth*	Lothian
48	*Ork*	Orkney
51	*Shet*	Shetland
57	*Strath*	Strathclyde
60	*Tays.*	Tayside
63	*W Isls*	Western Isles

Wales

10	*Clwyd*	Clwyd
18	*Dyfed*	Dyfed
26	*Gwent*	Gwent
27	*Gwynd.*	Gwynedd
42	*M Glam*	Mid Glamorgan
50	*Powys*	Powys
54	*S Glam*	South Glamorgan
64	*W Glam*	West Glamorgan

England

1	*Avon*	Avon
2	*Beds*	Bedfordshire
3	*Berks*	Berkshire
5	*Bucks*	Buckinghamshire
6	*Cambs*	Cambridgeshire
8	*Ches*	Cheshire
9	*Cleve.*	Cleveland
11	*Cnwll.*	Cornwall
12	*Cumb*	Cumbria
13	*Derbys*	Derbyshire
14	*Devon*	Devon
15	*Dorset.*	Dorset
17	*Dur.*	Durham
19	*E.Susx.*	East Sussex
20	*Essex*	Essex
22	*Gloucs.*	Gloucestershire
24	*Gt Lon.*	Greater London
25	*Gt Man*	Greater Manchester
28	*Hants*	Hampshire
29	*H & W*	Hereford & Worcester
30	*Herts.*	Hertfordshire
32	*Humb*	Humberside
33	*IOM*	Isle of Man
34	*IOW.*	Isle of Wight
35	*IOS*	Isles of Scilly
36	*Kent*	Kent
37	*Lancs*	Lancashire
38	*Leics*	Leicestershire
39	*Lincs.*	Lincolnshire
41	*Mersyd*	Merseyside
43	*Norfk*	Norfolk
44	*Nhants*	Northamptonshire
45	*Nthumb.* . . .	Northumberland
46	*N York*	North Yorkshire
47	*Notts.*	Nottinghamshire
49	*Oxon.*	Oxfordshire
52	*Shrops*	Shropshire
53	*Somset*	Somerset
55	*S York*	South Yorkshire
56	*Staffs*	Staffordshire
58	*Suffk.*	Suffolk
59	*Surrey.*	Surrey
61	*T & W.*	Tyne & Wear
62	*Warwks*	Warwickshire
65	*W Mids*	West Midland
66	*W Susx*	West Sussex
67	*W York*	West Yorkshire
68	*Wilts*	Wiltshire

A'Chill Ambleside

A'Chill *Highld* 128 NG2705
Ab Kettleby *Leics* 63 SK7223
Ab Lench *H & W* 47 SP0151
Abbas Combe *Somset* 22 ST7022
Abberley *H & W* 47 SO7567
Abberley Common *H & W* 47 SO7467
Abberton *Essex* 41 TM0019
Abberton *H & W* 47 SO9953
Abberwick *Nthumb* 111 NU1313
Abbess Roding *Essex* 40 TL5711
Abbey *Devon* 9 ST1410
Abbey Dore *H & W* 46 SO3830
Abbey Green *Staffs* 72 SJ9757
Abbey Hill *Somset* 10 ST2718
Abbey St. Bathans *Border* 119 NT7661
Abbey Town *Cumb* 93 NY1750
Abbey Village *Lancs* 81 SD6422
Abbey Wood *Gt Lon* 27 TQ4779
Abbeycwmhir *Powys* 45 SO0571
Abbeydale *S York* 74 SK3281
Abbeylands *IOM* 153 SC4585
Abbeystead *Lancs* 81 SD5654
Abbot's Chair *Derbys* 74 SK0290
Abbot's Salford *Warwks* 48 SP0650
Abbotrule *Border* 110 NT6113
Abbots Bickington *Devon* 18 SS3813
Abbots Bromley *Staffs* 73 SK0724
Abbots Deuglie *Tays* 126 NO1111
Abbots Langley *Herts* 26 TL0901
Abbots Leigh *Avon* 34 ST5474
Abbots Morton *H & W* 48 SP0255
Abbots Ripton *Cambs* 52 TL2377
Abbots Worthy *Hants* 24 SU4932
Abbotsbury *Dorset* 10 SY5785
Abbotsford *Border* 109 NT5034
Abbotsham *Devon* 18 SS4226
Abbotskerswell *Devon* 7 SX8568
Abbotsleigh *Devon* 7 SX8048
Abbotsley *Cambs* 52 TL2256
Abbotstone *Hants* 24 SU5634
Abbotswood *Hants* 23 SU3623
Abbott Street *Dorset* 11 ST9800
Abbotts Ann *Hants* 23 SU3243
Abcott *Shrops* 46 SO3978
Abdon *Shrops* 59 SO5786
Abenhall *Gloucs* 35 SO6717
Aber *Gwynd* 69 SH6572
Aber Clydach *Powys* 33 SO1021
Aber-arad *Dyfed* 31 SN3140
Aber-banc *Dyfed* 31 SN3541
Aber-giar *Dyfed* 44 SN5040
Aber-Magwr *Dyfed* 43 SN6673
Aber-meurig *Dyfed* 44 SN5656
Aber-nant *M Glam* 33 SO0103
Aberaeron *Dyfed* 42 SN4562
Aberaman *M Glam* 33 SO0100
Aberangell *Powys* 57 SH8410
Aberarder *Highld* 140 NH6225
Aberargie *Tays* 126 NO1615
Aberarth *Dyfed* 42 SN4763
Aberavon *W Glam* 32 SS7489
Aberbargoed *M Glam* 33 SO1500
Aberbeeg *Gwent* 33 SO2002
Abercairny *Tays* 125 NN9222
Abercanaid *M Glam* 33 SO0503
Abercarn *Gwent* 33 ST2194
Abercastle *Dyfed* 30 SM8533
Abercegir *Powys* 57 SH8001
Aberchalder Lodge *Highld* 131 NH3403
Aberchirder *Gramp* 142 NJ6252
Abercraf *Powys* 33 SN8212
Abercregan *W Glam* 33 SS8496
Abercrombie *Fife* 127 NO5102
Abercwmboi *M Glam* 33 ST0299
Abercych *Dyfed* 31 SN2441
Abercynon *M Glam* 33 ST0794
Aberdalgie *Tays* 125 NO0720
Aberdare *Powys* 33 SO0002
Aberdaron *Gwynd* 56 SH1726
Aberdeen *Gramp* 135 NJ9306
Aberdesach *Gwynd* 68 SH4251
Aberdour *Fife* 117 NT1985
Aberdovey *Gwynd* 43 SN6196
Aberdulais *W Glam* 32 SS7799
Aberedw *Powys* 45 SO0847
Abereiddy *Dyfed* 30 SM7931
Abererch *Gwynd* 56 SH3936
Aberfan *M Glam* 33 SO0700
Aberfeldy *Tays* 125 NN8549
Aberffraw *Gwynd* 68 SH3569
Aberffrwd *Dyfed* 43 SN6878
Aberford *W York* 83 SE4337
Aberfoyle *Cent* 115 NN5200
Abergarw *M Glam* 33 SS9184
Abergarwed *W Glam* 33 SN8102
Abergavenny *Gwent* 34 SO2914
Abergele *Clwyd* 70 SH9477
Abergorlech *Dyfed* 44 SN5833
Abergwesyn *Powys* 45 SN8552
Abergwili *Dyfed* 31 SN4320
Abergwydol *Powys* 57 SH7903
Abergwynfi *W Glam* 33 SS8995
Abergynolwyn *Gwynd* 57 SH6806
Aberhosan *Powys* 43 SN8197
Aberkenfig *M Glam* 33 SS8984
Aberlady *Loth* 118 NT4679
Aberlemno *Tays* 127 NO5255
Aberllefenni *Gwynd* 57 SH7609
Aberllynfi *Powys* 45 SO1737
Aberlour *Gramp* 141 NJ2642
Abermorddu *Clwyd* 71 SJ3056
Abermule *Powys* 58 SO1694
Abernant *Dyfed* 31 SN3323
Abernethy *Tays* 126 NO1816
Abernyte *Tays* 126 NO2531
Aberporth *Dyfed* 42 SN2651
Aberriw *Powys* 58 SJ1801
Abersoch *Gwynd* 56 SH3127
Abersychan *Gwent* 34 SO2603
Aberthin *S Glam* 33 ST0074
Abertillery *Gwent* 33 SO2104
Abertridwr *M Glam* 33 ST1289
Abertridwr *Powys* 58 SJ0319
Abertysswg *M Glam* 33 SO1305
Aberuthven *Tays* 125 NN9815
Aberyscir *Powys* 45 SN9929
Aberystwyth *Dyfed* 43 SN5881
Abingdon *Oxon* 37 SU4997
Abinger *Surrey* 14 TQ1145
Abinger Hammer *Surrey* 14 TQ0947
Abington *Nhants* 50 SP7861
Abington *Strath* 108 NS9323
Abington Pigotts *Cambs* 39 TL3044
Ablington *Gloucs* 36 SP1007
Ablington *Wilts* 23 SU1546
Abney *Derbys* 74 SK1980
Above Church *Staffs* 73 SK0150
Aboyne *Gramp* 134 NO5298
Abram *Gt Man* 78 SD6001
Abriachan *Highld* 139 NH5535
Abridge *Essex* 27 TQ4696
Abson *Avon* 35 ST7074
Abthorpe *Nhants* 49 SP6446
Aby *Lincs* 77 TF4078
Acaster Malbis *N York* 83 SE5845
Acaster Selby *N York* 83 SE5741
Accott *Devon* 19 SS6432
Accrington *Lancs* 81 SD7628
Acha *Strath* 120 NM1854
Achahoish *Strath* 113 NR7877
Achalader *Tays* 126 NO1245
Achaleven *Strath* 122 NM9233
Achanalt *Highld* 139 NH2661
Achandunie *Highld* 146 NH6472
Achany *Highld* 146 NC5602
Acharacle *Highld* 121 NM6767
Acharn *Tays* 124 NN7543
Achavanich *Highld* 151 ND1842
Achduart *Highld* 145 NC0403
Achfary *Highld* 148 NC2939
Achiltibuie *Highld* 144 NC0208
Achinhoan *Strath* 105 NR7516
Achintee *Highld* 138 NG9441
Achlain *Highld* 131 NH2812
Achmelvich *Highld* 148 NC0524
Achmore *Highld* 138 NG8533
Achmore *W Isls* 154 NB3029
Achnacarnin *Highld* 148 NC0432
Achnacarry *Highld* 131 NN1787
Achnacloich *Highld* 129 NG5908
Achnaconeran *Highld* 139 NH4118
Achnacroish *Strath* 122 NM8541
Achnadrish Lodge *Strath* 121 NM4652
Achnafauld *Tays* 125 NN8736
Achnagarron *Highld* 146 NH6870
Achnaha *Highld* 128 NM4668
Achnahaird *Highld* 144 NC0013
Achnairn *Highld* 146 NC5512
Achnalea *Highld* 130 NM8561
Achnamara *Strath* 113 NR7887
Achnasheen *Highld* 138 NH1658
Achnashellach Station *Highld* 138 NH0048
Achnastank *Gramp* 141 NJ2733
Achosnich *Highld* 121 NM4467
Achranich *Highld* 122 NM7047
Achreamie *Highld* 150 ND0166
Achriabhach *Highld* 131 NN1468
Achriesgill *Highld* 148 NC2554
Achtoty *Highld* 149 NC6762
Achurch *Nhants* 51 TL0283
Achvaich *Highld* 146 NH7194
Ackenthwaite *Cumb* 87 SD5081
Acklam *Cleve* 97 NZ4817
Acklam *N York* 90 SE7861
Ackleton *Shrops* 60 SO7698
Acklington *Nthumb* 103 NU2301
Ackton *W York* 83 SE4121
Ackworth Moor Top *W York* 83 SE4316
Acle *Norfk* 67 TG4010
Acock's Green *W Mids* 61 SP1283
Acol *Kent* 29 TR3067
Acomb *N York* 83 SE5651
Acomb *Nthumb* 102 NY9366
Acombe *Somset* 9 ST1914
Aconbury *H & W* 46 SO5133
Acre *Lancs* 81 SD7924
Acrefair *Clwyd* 70 SJ2743
Acresford *Derbys* 61 SK2913
Acton *Ches* 71 SJ6352
Acton *Dorset* 11 SY9978
Acton *Gt Lon* 26 TQ2080
Acton *H & W* 47 SO8467
Acton *Shrops* 59 SO3185
Acton *Staffs* 72 SJ8241
Acton *Suffk* 54 TL8945
Acton Beauchamp *H & W* 47 SO6850
Acton Bridge *Ches* 71 SJ6075
Acton Burnell *Shrops* 59 SJ5302
Acton Green *H & W* 47 SO6950
Acton Park *Clwyd* 71 SJ3451
Acton Pigott *Shrops* 59 SJ5402
Acton Round *Shrops* 59 SO6395
Acton Scott *Shrops* 59 SO4589
Acton Trussell *Staffs* 72 SJ9318
Acton Turville *Avon* 35 ST8080
Adbaston *Staffs* 72 SJ7627
Adber *Dorset* 21 ST5920
Adbolton *Notts* 62 SK5938
Adderbury *Oxon* 49 SP4735
Adderley *Shrops* 72 SJ6640
Adderstone *Nthumb* 111 NU1330
Addiewell *Loth* 117 NS9962
Addingham *W York* 82 SE0749
Addington *Bucks* 49 SP7428
Addington *Gt Lon* 27 TQ3664
Addington *Kent* 28 TQ6559
Addiscombe *Gt Lon* 27 TQ3366
Addlestone *Surrey* 26 TQ0564
Addlestonemore *Surrey* 26 TQ0565
Addlethorpe *Lincs* 77 TF5468
Adeney *Shrops* 72 SJ6918
Adeyfield *Herts* 38 TL0708
Adfa *Powys* 58 SJ0601
Adforton *H & W* 46 SO4071
Adisham *Kent* 29 TR2253
Adlestrop *Gloucs* 48 SP2426
Adlingfleet *Humb* 84 SE8421
Adlington *Ches* 79 SJ9180
Adlington *Lancs* 81 SD6013
Admaston *Shrops* 59 SJ6313
Admaston *Staffs* 73 SK0423
Admington *Warwks* 48 SP2045
Adsborough *Somset* 20 ST2729
Adscombe *Somset* 20 ST1837
Adstock *Bucks* 49 SP7329
Adstone *Nhants* 49 SP5951
Adswood *Gt Man* 79 SJ8888
Adversane *W Susx* 14 TQ0723
Advie *Highld* 141 NJ1234
Adwalton *W York* 82 SE2328
Adwell *Oxon* 37 SU6999
Adwick Le Street *S York* 83 SE5308
Adwick upon Dearne *S York* 83 SE4701
Ae *D & G* 100 NX9889
Ae Bridgend *D & G* 100 NY0186
Affetside *Gt Man* 81 SD7513
Affleck *Gramp* 142 NJ5540
Affpuddle *Dorset* 11 SY8093
Affric Lodge *Highld* 138 NH1822
Afon-wen *Clwyd* 70 SJ1371
Afton *Devon* 7 SX8462
Afton *IOW* 12 SZ3486
Afton Bridgend *Strath* 107 NS6213
Agglethorpe *N York* 89 SE0885
Aigburth *Mersyd* 78 SJ3886
Aike *Humb* 84 TA0446
Aiketgate *Cumb* 94 NY4846
Aikhead *Cumb* 93 NY2349
Aikton *Cumb* 93 NY2753
Ailby *Lincs* 77 TF4376
Ailey *H & W* 46 SO3348
Ailsworth *Cambs* 64 TL1198
Ainderby Quernhow *N York* 89 SE3480
Ainderby Steeple *N York* 89 SE3392
Aingers Green *Essex* 41 TM1120
Ainsdale *Mersyd* 80 SD3112
Ainsdale-on-Sea *Mersyd* 80 SD2912
Ainstable *Cumb* 94 NY5246
Ainsworth *Gt Man* 79 SD7610
Ainthorpe *N York* 90 NZ7007
Aintree *Mersyd* 78 SJ3898
Aird *D & G* 98 NX0960
Aird *Strath* 113 NM7600
Aird *W Isls* 154 NB5635
Aird of Kinloch *Strath* 121 NM5228
Aird of Sleat *Highld* 129 NG5900
Airdeny *Strath* 122 NM9929
Airdrie *Strath* 116 NS7565
Airdriehill *Strath* 116 NS7867
Airds Bay *Strath* 122 NM9932
Airds of Kells *D & G* 99 NX6770
Airieland *D & G* 99 NX7556
Airmyn *Humb* 84 SE7224
Airntully *Tays* 125 NO0935
Airor *Highld* 129 NG7205
Airth *Cent* 116 NS9087
Airton *N York* 88 SD9059
Aisby *Lincs* 76 SK8692
Aisby *Lincs* 64 TF0138
Aisgill *Cumb* 88 SD7797
Aish *Devon* 7 SX6960
Aish *Devon* 7 SX8458
Aiskew *N York* 89 SE2788
Aislaby *Cleve* 89 NZ4012
Aislaby *N York* 90 NZ8608
Aislaby *N York* 90 SE7785
Aisthorpe *Lincs* 76 SK9480
Aith *Shet* 155 HU3455
Akeld *Nthumb* 111 NT9529
Akeley *Bucks* 49 SP7037
Akenham *Suffk* 54 TM1449
Albaston *Devon* 6 SX4270
Alberbury *Shrops* 59 SJ3614
Albert Street *Clwyd* 70 SJ2660
Albourne *W Susx* 15 TQ2516
Albourne Green *W Susx* 15 TQ2616
Albrighton *Shrops* 59 SJ4918
Albrighton *Shrops* 60 SJ8004
Alburgh *Norfk* 55 TM2687
Albury *Herts* 39 TL4324
Albury *Oxon* 37 SP6505
Albury *Surrey* 14 TQ0447
Albury End *Herts* 39 TL4223
Albury Heath *Surrey* 14 TQ0646
Alby Hill *Norfk* 67 TG1934
Alcaig *Highld* 139 NH5657
Alcaston *Shrops* 59 SO4587
Alcester *Warwks* 48 SP0857
Alcester Lane End *W Mids* 61 SP0780
Alciston *E Susx* 16 TQ5005
Alcombe *Wilts* 35 ST8169
Alconbury *Cambs* 52 TL1875
Alconbury Weston *Cambs* 52 TL1777
Aldborough *N York* 89 SE4066
Aldborough *Norfk* 66 TG1834
Aldbourne *Wilts* 36 SU2676
Aldbrough *Humb* 85 TA2438
Aldbury *Herts* 38 SP9612
Aldcliffe *Lancs* 87 SD4660
Aldclune *Tays* 132 NN8964
Aldeburgh *Suffk* 55 TM4656
Aldeby *Norfk* 67 TM4493
Aldenham *Herts* 26 TQ1498
Alder Moor *Staffs* 73 SK2226
Alderbury *Wilts* 23 SU1827
Aldercar *Derbys* 62 SK4447
Alderford *Norfk* 66 TG1218
Alderholt *Dorset* 12 SU1212
Alderley *Gloucs* 35 ST7690
Alderley Edge *Ches* 79 SJ8478
Aldermans Green *W Mids* 61 SP3683
Aldermaston *Berks* 24 SU5965
Alderminster *Warwks* 48 SP2348
Aldershot *Hants* 25 SU8650
Alderton *Gloucs* 47 SP0033
Alderton *Nhants* 49 SP7446
Alderton *Shrops* 59 SJ4924
Alderton *Suffk* 55 TM3441
Alderton *Wilts* 35 ST8482
Alderwasley *Derbys* 73 SK3053
Aldfield *N York* 89 SE2669
Aldford *Ches* 71 SJ4159
Aldgate *Leics* 63 SK9804
Aldham *Essex* 40 TL9126
Aldham *Suffk* 54 TM0545
Aldingbourne *W Susx* 14 SU9205
Aldingham *Cumb* 86 SD2870
Aldington *H & W* 48 SP0644
Aldington *Kent* 29 TR0736
Aldington Corner *Kent* 29 TR0636
Aldivalloch *Gramp* 141 NJ3526
Aldochlay *Strath* 115 NS3591
Aldon *Shrops* 46 SO4379
Aldoth *Cumb* 92 NY1448
Aldreth *Cambs* 53 TL4473
Aldridge *W Mids* 61 SK0500
Aldringham *Suffk* 55 TM4461
Aldro *N York* 90 SE8162
Aldsworth *Gloucs* 36 SP1509
Aldsworth *W Susx* 14 SU7608
Aldunie *Gramp* 141 NJ3626
Aldwark *Derbys* 74 SK2257
Aldwark *N York* 89 SE4663
Aldwick *W Susx* 14 SZ9198
Aldwincle *Nhants* 51 TL0081
Aldworth *Berks* 37 SU5579
Alexandria *Strath* 115 NS3979
Aley *Somset* 20 ST1838
Alfardisworthy *Devon* 18 SS2911
Alfington *Devon* 9 SY1197
Alfold *Surrey* 14 TQ0333
Alfold Bars *W Susx* 14 TQ0333
Alfold Crossways *Surrey* 14 TQ0335
Alford *Gramp* 142 NJ5715
Alford *Lincs* 77 TF4575
Alford *Somset* 21 ST6032
Alfreton *Derbys* 74 SK4155
Alfrick *H & W* 47 SO7453
Alfrick Pound *H & W* 47 SO7452
Alfriston *E Susx* 16 TQ5103
Algarkirk *Lincs* 64 TF2935
Alhampton *Somset* 21 ST6234
Alkborough *Humb* 84 SE8821
Alkerton *Gloucs* 35 SO7705
Alkerton *Oxon* 48 SP3743
Alkham *Kent* 29 TR2542
Alkington *Shrops* 71 SJ5339
Alkmonton *Derbys* 73 SK1838
All Cannings *Wilts* 23 SU0661
All Saints South Elmham *Suffk* 55 TM3482
All Stretton *Shrops* 59 SO4595
Allaleigh *Devon* 7 SX8053
Allanaquoich *Gramp* 133 NO1291
Allanbank *Strath* 116 NS8458
Allanton *Border* 119 NT8654
Allanton *Strath* 116 NS7454
Allanton *Strath* 116 NS8457
Allaston *Gloucs* 35 SO6304
Allbrook *Hants* 13 SU4521
Allen End *Warwks* 61 SP1696
Allen's Green *Herts* 39 TL4516
Allendale *Nthumb* 95 NY8355
Allenheads *Nthumb* 95 NY8645
Allensford *Dur* 95 NZ0750
Allensmore *H & W* 46 SO4635
Allenton *Derbys* 62 SK3732
Aller *Devon* 19 SS7625
Aller *Somset* 21 ST4029
Allerby *Cumb* 92 NY0839
Allercombe *Devon* 9 SY0494
Allerford *Somset* 20 SS9046
Allerston *N York* 90 SE8782
Allerthorpe *Humb* 84 SE7847
Allerton *Mersyd* 78 SJ3987
Allerton *W York* 82 SE1234
Allerton Bywater *W York* 83 SE4227
Allerton Mauleverer *N York* 89 SE4157
Allesley *W Mids* 61 SP3080
Allestree *Derbys* 62 SK3439
Allet Common *Cnwll* 3 SW7948
Allexton *Leics* 51 SK8100
Allgreave *Ches* 72 SJ9767
Allhallows *Kent* 28 TQ8377
Allhallows-on-Sea *Kent* 40 TQ8478
Alligin Shuas *Highld* 137 NG8357
Allimore Green *Staffs* 72 SJ8519
Allington *Dorset* 10 SY4693
Allington *Kent* 28 TQ7557
Allington *Lincs* 63 SK8540
Allington *Wilts* 35 ST8975
Allington *Wilts* 23 SU0663
Allington *Wilts* 23 SU2039
Allithwaite *Cumb* 87 SD3876
Alloa *Cent* 116 NS8892
Allonby *Cumb* 92 NY0842
Alloway *Strath* 106 NS3318
Allowenshay *Somset* 10 ST3913
Allscott *Shrops* 59 SJ6113
Allscott *Shrops* 60 SO7396
Alltami *Clwyd* 70 SJ2665
Alltchaorunn *Highld* 123 NN1951
Alltmawr *Powys* 45 SO0746
Alltwalis *Dyfed* 31 SN4431
Alltwen *W Glam* 32 SN7303
Alltyblaca *Dyfed* 44 SN5245
Allweston *Dorset* 11 ST6614
Allwood Green *Suffk* 54 TM0472
Almeley *H & W* 46 SO3351
Almeley Wooton *H & W* 46 SO3352
Almer *Dorset* 11 SY9199
Almholme *S York* 83 SE5808
Almington *Staffs* 72 SJ7034
Almodington *W Susx* 14 SZ8297
Almondbank *Tays* 125 NO0625
Almondbury *W York* 82 SE1614
Almondsbury *Avon* 34 ST6084
Alne *N York* 90 SE4965
Alnesbourn Priory *Suffk* 55 TM1940
Alness *Highld* 146 NH6569
Alnham *Nthumb* 111 NT9810
Alnmouth *Nthumb* 111 NU2410
Alnwick *Nthumb* 111 NU1813
Alperton *Gt Lon* 26 TQ1883
Alphamstone *Essex* 54 TL8735
Alpheton *Suffk* 54 TL8750
Alphington *Devon* 9 SX9190
Alpington *Norfk* 67 TG2901
Alport *Derbys* 74 SK2264
Alpraham *Ches* 71 SJ5859
Alresford *Essex* 41 TM0621
Alrewas *Staffs* 61 SK1614
Alsager *Ches* 72 SJ7955
Alsagers Bank *Staffs* 72 SJ7948
Alshot *Somset* 20 ST1935
Alsop en le Dale *Derbys* 73 SK1554
Alston *Cumb* 94 NY7146
Alston *Devon* 10 ST3002
Alston Sutton *Somset* 21 ST4151
Alstone *Gloucs* 47 SO9832
Alstone *Somset* 21 ST3146
Alstone Green *Staffs* 72 SJ8518
Alstonefield *Staffs* 73 SK1355
Alswear *Devon* 19 SS7222
Alt *Gt Man* 79 SD9403
Altandhu *Highld* 144 NB9812
Altarnun *Cnwll* 5 SX2281
Altass *Highld* 146 NC5000
Altcreich *Strath* 122 NM6938
Altgaltraig *Strath* 114 NS0473
Altham *Lancs* 81 SD7732
Althorne *Essex* 40 TQ9198
Althorpe *Humb* 84 SE8309
Altnabreac Station *Highld* 150 ND0045
Altnacraig *Strath* 122 NM8429
Altnaharra *Highld* 149 NC5635
Altofts *W York* 83 SE3823
Alton *Derbys* 74 SK3664
Alton *Hants* 24 SU7139
Alton *Staffs* 73 SK0741
Alton *Wilts* 23 SU1546
Alton Barnes *Wilts* 23 SU1062
Alton Pancras *Dorset* 11 ST7002
Alton Priors *Wilts* 23 SU1162
Altrincham *Gt Man* 79 SJ7687
Alva *Cent* 116 NS8897
Alvah *Gramp* 142 NJ6760
Alvanley *Ches* 71 SJ4974
Alvaston *Derbys* 62 SK3833
Alvechurch *H & W* 60 SP0272
Alvecote *Warwks* 61 SK2404
Alvediston *Wilts* 22 ST9723
Alveley *Shrops* 60 SO7584
Alverdiscott *Devon* 19 SS5225
Alverstoke *Hants* 13 SZ6098
Alverstone *IOW* 13 SZ5785
Alverthorpe *W York* 82 SE3121
Alverton *Notts* 63 SK7942
Alves *Gramp* 141 NJ1362
Alvescot *Oxon* 36 SP2704
Alveston *Avon* 35 ST6388
Alveston *Warwks* 48 SP2356
Alvingham *Lincs* 77 TF3691
Alvington *Gloucs* 34 SO6000
Alwalton *Cambs* 64 TL1396
Alwinton *Nthumb* 110 NT9106
Alwoodley *W York* 82 SE2840
Alwoodley Gates *W York* 82 SE3140
Alyth *Tays* 126 NO2448
Amber Hill *Lincs* 76 TF2346
Amber Row *Derbys* 74 SK3856
Ambergate *Derbys* 74 SK3451
Amberley *Gloucs* 35 SO8501
Amberley *W Susx* 14 TQ0213
Ambirstone *E Susx* 16 TQ5911
Amble *Nthumb* 103 NU2604
Amblecote *W Mids* 60 SO8985
Ambler Thorn *W York* 82 SE0929
Ambleside *Cumb* 87 NY3704

Ambleston
Atherton

Ambleston Dyfed 30 SN0025
Ambrosden Oxon 37 SP6019
Amcotts Humb 84 SE8514
America Cambs 53 TL4378
Amersham Bucks 26 SU9597
Amersham on the Hill Bucks 26 SU9798
Amerton Staffs 73 SJ9927
Amesbury Wilts 23 SU1541
Amington Staffs 61 SK2304
Amisfield Town D & G 100 NY0082
Amlwch Gwynd 68 SH4492
Ammanford Dyfed 32 SN6212
Amotherby N York 90 SE7473
Ampfield Hants 13 SU4023
Ampleforth N York 90 SE5878
Ampney Crucis Gloucs 36 SP0601
Ampney St. Mary Gloucs 36 SP0802
Ampney St. Peter Gloucs 36 SP0801
Amport Hants 23 SU3044
Ampthill Beds 38 TL0337
Ampton Suffk 54 TL8671
Amroth Dyfed 31 SN1608
Amwell Herts 39 TL1613
Anaheilt Highld 130 NM8162
Ancaster Lincs 63 SK9843
Anchor Shrops 58 SO1785
Ancroft Nthumb 111 NT9945
Ancrum Border 110 NT6224
Ancton W Susx 14 SU9800
Anderby Lincs 77 TF5275
Andersea Somset 21 ST3333
Andersfield Somset 20 ST2434
Anderson Dorset 11 SY8897
Anderton Ches 79 SJ6475
Anderton Cnwll 6 SX4351
Andover Hants 23 SU3645
Andoversford Gloucs 35 SP0219
Andreas IOM 153 SC4199
Anelog Gwynd 56 SH1527
Anerley Gt Lon 27 TQ3369
Anfield Mersyd 78 SJ3692
Angarrack Cnwll 2 SW5838
Angarrick Cnwll 3 SW7937
Angelbank Shrops 46 SO5776
Angersleigh Somset 20 ST1918
Angerton Cumb 93 NY2257
Angle Dyfed 30 SM8603
Angmering W Susx 14 TQ0604
Angram N York 88 SD8899
Angram N York 83 SE5248
Angrouse Cnwll 2 SW6619
Anick Nthumb 102 NY9465
Ankerville Highld 147 NH8174
Ankle Hill Leics 63 SK7518
Anlaby Humb 84 TA0328
Anmer Norfk 65 TF7429
Anmore Hants 13 SU6611
Anna Valley Hants 23 SU3543
Annan D & G 101 NY1966
Annaside Cumb 86 SD0986
Annat Highld 138 NG8954
Annat Strath 122 NN0322
Annathill Strath 116 NS7270
Annbank Strath 106 NS4023
Annesley Notts 75 SK5053
Annesley Woodhouse Notts 75 SK4953
Annfield Plain Dur 96 NZ1651
Anniesland Strath 115 NS5368
Annitsford T & W 103 NZ2674
Annscroft Shrops 59 SJ4507
Ansdell Lancs 80 SD3428
Ansford Somset 21 ST6433
Ansley Warwks 61 SP3091
Anslow Staffs 73 SK2125
Anslow Gate Staffs 73 SK1924
Anslow Lees Staffs 73 SK2024
Ansteadbrook Surrey 14 SU9332
Anstey Hants 24 SU7240
Anstey Herts 39 TL4033
Anstey Leics 62 SK5508
Anstruther Fife 127 NO5703
Anstruther Easter Fife 127 NO5704
Ansty W Susx 15 TQ2923
Ansty Warwks 61 SP4083
Ansty Wilts 22 ST9526
Ansty Cross Dorset 11 ST7603
Anthill Common Hants 13 SU6312
Anthony's Surrey 26 TQ0161
Anthorn Cumb 93 NY1958
Antingham Norfk 67 TG2533
Antony Cnwll 5 SX4054
Antrobus Ches 79 SJ6480
Antron Cnwll 2 SW6327
Anvil Corner Devon 18 SS3704
Anvil Green Kent 29 TR1049
Anwick Lincs 76 TF1150
Anwoth D & G 99 NX5856
Aperfield Gt Lon 27 TQ4158
Apes Dale H & W 60 SO9972
Apethorpe Nhants 51 TL0295
Apeton Staffs 72 SJ8518
Apley Lincs 76 TF1075
Apperknowle Derbys 74 SK3878
Apperley Gloucs 47 SO8628
Apperley Bridge W York 82 SE1937
Apperley Dene Nthumb 95 NZ0558
Appersett N York 88 SD8690
Appin Strath 122 NM9346
Appleby Humb 84 SE9514
Appleby Magna Leics 61 SK3109
Appleby Parva Leics 61 SK3008
Appleby Street Herts 39 TL3304
Appleby-in-Westmorland Cumb 94 NY6820
Applecross Highld 137 NG7144
Appledore Devon 18 SS4630
Appledore Devon 9 ST0614
Appledore Kent 17 TQ9529
Appledore Heath Kent 17 TQ9530
Appleford Oxon 37 SU5293
Applegarth Town D & G 100 NY1084
Applehaigh S York 83 SE3512
Appleshaw Hants 23 SU3048
Applethwaite Cumb 93 NY2625
Appleton Ches 78 SJ5186
Appleton Oxon 37 SP4401
Appleton Roebuck N York 83 SE5542
Appleton Wiske N York 89 NZ3804
Appleton-le-Moors N York 90 SE7387
Appleton-le-Street N York 90 SE7373
Appletreehall Border 109 NT5117
Appletreewick N York 88 SE0560
Appley Somset 20 ST0721
Appley Bridge Lancs 78 SD5209
Apse Heath IOW 13 SZ5683
Apsley End Beds 38 TL1232
Apsley Heath Warwks 61 SP0970
Apuldram W Susx 14 SU8403
Arbirlot Tays 127 NO6040
Arboll Highld 147 NH8781
Arborfield Berks 24 SU7567
Arborfield Cross Berks 24 SU7666
Arbory IOM 153 SC2470
Arbourthorne S York 74 SK3785
Arbroath Tays 127 NO6441
Arbuthnott Gramp 135 NO8074
Arcadia Kent 28 TQ8836
Archddu Dyfed 32 SN4401
Archdeacon Newton Dur 96 NZ2517
Archencarroch Strath 115 NS4182
Archiestown Gramp 141 NJ2244
Archirondel Jersey 152 JS2111
Arclid Green Ches 72 SJ7861
Ard a'Chapuill Strath 114 NS0179
Ardaily Strath 104 NR6450
Ardalanish Strath 121 NM3619
Ardanaiseig Hotel Strath 123 NN0824
Ardarroch Highld 137 NG8339
Ardarroch Strath 114 NS2494
Ardbeg Strath 104 NR4146
Ardbeg Strath 114 NS0766
Ardbeg Strath 114 NS1583
Ardcharnich Highld 145 NH1788
Ardchiavaig Strath 121 NM3818
Ardchonnel Strath 122 NM9812
Ardchullarie More Cent 124 NN5813
Arddleen Powys 58 SJ2616
Ardechive Highld 131 NN1490
Ardeer Strath 106 NS2740
Ardeley Herts 39 TL3027
Ardelve Highld 138 NG8627
Arden Strath 115 NS3684
Ardens Grafton Warwks 48 SP1154
Ardentinny Strath 114 NS1887
Ardeonaig Hotel Cent 124 NN6735
Ardersier Highld 140 NH7855
Ardessie Highld 145 NH0689
Ardfern Strath 122 NM8004
Ardgay Highld 146 NH5990
Ardgour Highld 130 NN0163
Ardgowan Strath 114 NS2073
Ardhallow Strath 114 NS1674
Ardhasig W Isls 154 NB1202
Ardheslaig Highld 137 NG7855
Ardindrean Highld 145 NH1588
Ardingly W Susx 15 TQ3429
Ardington Oxon 36 SU4388
Ardington Wick Oxon 36 SU4389
Ardlamont Strath 114 NR9865
Ardleigh Essex 41 TM0529
Ardleigh Heath Essex 41 TM0430
Ardler Tays 126 NO2642
Ardley Oxon 49 SP5427
Ardley End Essex 39 TL5214
Ardlui Strath 123 NN3115
Ardlussa Strath 113 NR6487
Ardmaddy Strath 123 NN0837
Ardmair Highld 145 NH1097
Ardmaleish Strath 114 NS0768
Ardminish Strath 104 NR6448
Ardmolich Highld 129 NM7172
Ardmore Highld 146 NH7086
Ardmore Strath 115 NS3178
Ardnadam Strath 114 NS1780
Ardnagrask Highld 139 NH5249
Ardnarff Highld 138 NG8935
Ardnastang Highld 130 NM8061
Ardno Strath 123 NN1508
Ardochy Lodge Hotel Highld 131 NH2002
Ardpatrick Strath 113 NR7660
Ardpeaton Strath 114 NS2185
Ardrishaig Strath 113 NR8585
Ardrossan Strath 106 NS2342
Ardshealach Highld 121 NM6867
Ardsley S York 83 SE3805
Ardsley East W York 82 SE3025
Ardslignish Highld 121 NM5661
Ardtalla Strath 112 NR4654
Ardtoe Highld 129 NM6270
Arduaine Strath 122 NM7910
Ardvasar Highld 129 NG6303
Ardvorlich Tays 124 NN6322
Ardvourlie W Isls 154 NB1810
Ardwell D & G 98 NX1045
Ardwick Gt Man 79 SJ8597
Areley Kings H & W 60 SO7970
Arevegaig Highld 129 NM6568
Arford Hants 14 SU8236
Argoed Gwent 33 ST1799
Argoed Shrops 59 SJ3220
Argoed Mill Powys 45 SN9963
Argos Hill E Susx 16 TQ5728
Aribruach W Isls 154 NB2417
Aridhglas Strath 120 NM3123
Arileod Strath 120 NM1655
Arinagour Strath 120 NM2257
Ariogan Strath 122 NM8627
Arisaig Highld 129 NM6586
Arisaig House Highld 129 NM6984
Arkendale N York 89 SE3861
Arkesden Essex 39 TL4834
Arkholme Lancs 87 SD5871
Arkleby Cumb 92 NY1439
Arkleton D & G 101 NY3791
Arkley Gt Lon 26 TQ2295
Arksey S York 83 SE5807
Arkwright Town Derbys 74 SK4270
Arle Gloucs 47 SO9223
Arlecdon Cumb 92 NY0419
Arlescote Warwks 48 SP3848
Arlesey Beds 39 TL1936
Arleston Shrops 60 SJ6609
Arley Ches 79 SJ6680
Arley Warwks 61 SP2890
Arlingham Gloucs 35 SO7010
Arlington Devon 19 SS6140
Arlington E Susx 16 TQ5407
Arlington Gloucs 36 SP1006
Arlington Beccott Devon 19 SS6241
Armadale Highld 150 NC7864
Armadale Loth 116 NS9368
Armaside Cumb 92 NY1527
Armathwaite Cumb 94 NY5046
Arminghall Norfk 67 TG2504
Armitage Staffs 73 SK0715
Armitage Bridge W York 82 SE1313
Armley W York 82 SE2833
Armshead Staffs 72 SJ9348
Armston Nhants 51 TL0685
Armthorpe S York 83 SE6204
Arnabost Strath 120 NM2159
Arnaby Cumb 86 SD1884
Arncliffe N York 88 SD9371
Arncliffe Cote N York 88 SD9470
Arncroach Fife 127 NO5105
Arndilly House Gramp 141 NJ2847
Arne Dorset 11 SY9788
Arnesby Leics 50 SP6192
Arnfield Derbys 79 SK0197
Arngask Tays 126 NO1410
Arnicle Strath 105 NR7138
Arnisdale Highld 130 NG8410
Arnish Highld 137 NG5948
Arniston Loth 118 NT3362
Arnol W Isls 154 NB3148
Arnold Humb 85 TA1241
Arnold Notts 62 SK5845
Arnprior Cent 116 NS6194
Arnside Cumb 87 SD4578
Aros Strath 121 NM5645
Arowry Clwyd 71 SJ4639
Arrad Foot Cumb 86 SD3080
Arram Humb 84 TA0344
Arrathorne N York 89 SE2093
Arreton IOW 13 SZ5386
Arrina Highld 137 NG7458
Arrington Cambs 52 TL3250
Arriundle Highld 130 NM8264
Arrochar Strath 123 NN2904
Arrow Warwks 48 SP0856
Arrowfield Top H & W 61 SP0374
Arscott Shrops 59 SJ4307
Artafallie Highld 140 NH6349
Arthington W York 82 SE2644
Arthingworth Nhants 50 SP7581
Arthog Gwynd 57 SH6414
Arthrath Gramp 143 NJ9636
Arthursdale W York 83 SE3737
Artrochie Gramp 143 NK0031
Arundel W Susx 14 TQ0106
Asby Cumb 92 NY0620
Ascog Strath 114 NS1062
Ascot Berks 25 SU9268
Ascott Warwks 48 SP3234
Ascott Earl Oxon 36 SP3018
Ascott-under-Wychwood Oxon 36 SP3018
Asenby N York 89 SE3975
Asfordby Leics 63 SK7019
Asfordby Hill Leics 63 SK7219
Asgarby Lincs 64 TF1145
Asgarby Lincs 77 TF3366
Ash Devon 19 SS5208
Ash Devon 7 SX8349
Ash Dorset 11 ST8610
Ash Kent 27 TQ6064
Ash Kent 29 TR2858
Ash Somset 20 ST2822
Ash Somset 21 ST4720
Ash Surrey 25 SU9051
Ash Green Surrey 25 SU9049
Ash Green Warwks 61 SP3384
Ash Magna Shrops 71 SJ5739
Ash Mill Devon 19 SS7823
Ash Parva Shrops 71 SJ5739
Ash Priors Somset 20 ST1529
Ash Street Suffk 54 TM0146
Ash Thomas Devon 9 ST0010
Ash Vale Surrey 25 SU8951
Ashampstead Berks 37 SU5676
Ashampstead Green Berks 37 SU5677
Ashbocking Suffk 54 TM1754
Ashbocking Green Suffk 54 TM1854
Ashbourne Derbys 73 SK1746
Ashbourne Green Derbys 73 SK1948
Ashbrittle Somset 20 ST0521
Ashburnham Place E Susx 16 TQ6814
Ashburton Devon 7 SX7570
Ashbury Devon 5 SX5098
Ashbury Oxon 36 SU2685
Ashby Humb 84 SE8908
Ashby by Partney Lincs 77 TF4266
Ashby cum Fenby Humb 77 TA2500
Ashby de la Launde Lincs 76 TF0555
Ashby Folville Leics 63 SK7012
Ashby Magna Leics 50 SP5690
Ashby Parva Leics 50 SP5288
Ashby Puerorum Lincs 77 TF3271
Ashby St. Ledgers Nhants 50 SP5768
Ashby St. Mary Norfk 67 TG3202
Ashby-de-la-Zouch Leics 62 SK3516
Ashchurch Gloucs 47 SO9233
Ashcombe Avon 21 ST3361
Ashcombe Devon 9 SX9179
Ashcott Somset 21 ST4336
Ashdon Essex 53 TL5842
Ashe Hants 24 SU5350
Asheldham Essex 41 TL9701
Ashen Essex 53 TL7442
Ashendon Bucks 37 SP7014
Asheridge Bucks 38 SP9304
Ashfield Cent 124 NN7803
Ashfield Hants 12 SU3619
Ashfield Suffk 55 TM2062
Ashfield Green Suffk 53 TL7655
Ashfield Green Suffk 55 TM2573
Ashfields Shrops 72 SJ7026
Ashfold Crossways W Susx 15 TQ2328
Ashford Devon 19 SS5335
Ashford Devon 7 SX6948
Ashford Kent 28 TR0142
Ashford Surrey 26 TQ0771
Ashford Bowdler Shrops 46 SO5170
Ashford Carbonel Shrops 46 SO5270
Ashford Hill Hants 24 SU5562
Ashford in the Water Derbys 74 SK1969
Ashgill Strath 116 NS7850
Ashill Devon 9 ST0811
Ashill Norfk 66 TF8804
Ashill Somset 10 ST3217
Ashingdon Essex 40 TQ8693
Ashington Nthumb 103 NZ2687
Ashington Somset 21 ST5621
Ashington W Susx 15 TQ1315
Ashkirk Border 109 NT4722
Ashlett Hants 13 SU4603
Ashleworth Gloucs 47 SO8125
Ashleworth Quay Gloucs 47 SO8125
Ashley Cambs 53 TL6961
Ashley Ches 79 SJ7784
Ashley Devon 19 SS6511
Ashley Gloucs 35 ST9394
Ashley Hants 23 SU3831
Ashley Hants 12 SZ2595
Ashley Kent 29 TR3048
Ashley Nhants 50 SP7990
Ashley Staffs 72 SJ7636
Ashley Wilts 22 ST8268
Ashley Green Bucks 38 SP9705
Ashley Heath Dorset 12 SU1204
Ashley Moor H & W 46 SO4767
Ashmansworth Hants 24 SU4157
Ashmansworthy Devon 18 SS3418
Ashmead Green Gloucs 35 ST7699
Ashmill Devon 5 SX3995
Ashmore Dorset 11 ST9117
Ashmore Green Berks 24 SU5069
Ashorne Warwks 48 SP3057
Ashover Derbys 74 SK3463
Ashover Hay Derbys 74 SK3460
Ashow Warwks 61 SP3170
Ashperton H & W 47 SO6441
Ashprington Devon 7 SX8157
Ashreigney Devon 19 SS6313
Ashridge Park Herts 38 SP9912
Ashtead Surrey 26 TQ1857
Ashton Cambs 64 TF1005
Ashton Ches 71 SJ5069
Ashton Cnwll 2 SW6028
Ashton Cnwll 5 SX3868
Ashton Devon 8 SX8584
Ashton H & W 46 SO5164
Ashton Hants 13 SU5419
Ashton Nhants 49 SP7649
Ashton Nhants 51 TL0588
Ashton Somset 21 ST4149
Ashton Common Wilts 22 ST8958
Ashton Hill Wilts 22 ST9057
Ashton Keynes Wilts 36 SU0494
Ashton under Hill H & W 47 SO9937
Ashton upon Mersey Gt Man 79 SJ7892
Ashton Watering Avon 21 ST5369
Ashton-in-Makerfield Gt Man 78 SJ5798
Ashton-under-Lyne Gt Man 79 SJ9399
Ashurst Hants 12 SU3310
Ashurst Kent 16 TQ5138
Ashurst W Susx 15 TQ1715
Ashurstwood W Susx 15 TQ4136
Ashwater Devon 5 SX3895
Ashwell Herts 39 TL2639
Ashwell Leics 63 SK8613
Ashwell End Herts 39 TL2540
Ashwellthorpe Norfk 66 TM1497
Ashwick Somset 21 ST6348
Ashwicken Norfk 65 TF7018
Ashwood Staffs 60 SO8688
Askam in Furness Cumb 86 SD2177
Aske Hall N York 89 NZ1703
Askern S York 83 SE5613
Askerswell Dorset 10 SY5292
Askett Bucks 38 SP8105
Askham Cumb 94 NY5123
Askham Notts 75 SK7374
Askham Bryan N York 83 SE5548
Askham Richard N York 83 SE5347
Asknish Strath 114 NR9391
Askrigg N York 88 SD9491
Askwith N York 82 SE1648
Aslackby Lincs 64 TF0830
Aslacton Norfk 54 TM1590
Aslockton Notts 63 SK7440
Asney Somset 21 ST4636
Aspall Suffk 54 TM1664
Aspatria Cumb 92 NY1441
Aspenden Herts 39 TL3528
Asperton Lincs 64 TF2637
Aspley Staffs 72 SJ8133
Aspley Guise Beds 38 SP9335
Aspley Heath Beds 38 SP9334
Aspull Gt Man 78 SD6108
Aspull Common Gt Man 79 SJ6498
Asselby Humb 84 SE7127
Asserby Lincs 77 TF4977
Asserby Turn Lincs 77 TF4777
Assington Suffk 54 TL9338
Assington Green Suffk 53 TL7751
Astbury Ches 72 SJ8461
Astcote Nhants 49 SP6753
Asterby Lincs 77 TF2679
Asterley Shrops 59 SJ3707
Asterton Shrops 59 SO3991
Asthall Oxon 36 SP2811
Asthall Leigh Oxon 36 SP3013
Astle Highld 146 NH7391
Astley Gt Man 79 SD7000
Astley H & W 47 SO7867
Astley Shrops 59 SJ5218
Astley W York 83 SE3828
Astley Warwks 61 SP3189
Astley Abbots Shrops 60 SO7096
Astley Bridge Gt Man 81 SD7111
Astley Cross H & W 47 SO8069
Astley Green Gt Man 79 SJ7099
Astley Town H & W 47 SO7968
Aston Berks 37 SU7884
Aston Ches 71 SJ5578
Aston Ches 71 SJ6146
Aston Clwyd 71 SJ3067
Aston Derbys 74 SK1783
Aston H & W 46 SO4662
Aston H & W 46 SO4671
Aston Herts 39 TL2722
Aston Oxon 36 SP3403
Aston S York 75 SK4685
Aston Shrops 59 SJ5328
Aston Shrops 59 SJ6109
Aston Shrops 60 SO8093
Aston Staffs 72 SJ7541
Aston Staffs 72 SJ8923
Aston Staffs 72 SJ9130
Aston W Mids 61 SP0888
Aston Abbotts Bucks 38 SP8420
Aston Botterell Shrops 59 SO6384
Aston Cantlow Warwks 48 SP1460
Aston Clinton Bucks 38 SP8812
Aston Crews H & W 47 SO6723
Aston Cross Gloucs 47 SO9433
Aston End Herts 39 TL2724
Aston Eyre Shrops 59 SO6594
Aston Fields H & W 47 SO9669
Aston Flamville Leics 50 SP4692
Aston Heath Ches 71 SJ5678
Aston Ingham H & W 47 SO6823
Aston juxta Mondrum Ches 72 SJ6456
Aston le Walls Nhants 49 SP4950
Aston Magna Gloucs 48 SP1935
Aston Munslow Shrops 59 SO5186
Aston on Clun Shrops 59 SO3981
Aston Pigott Shrops 59 SJ3305
Aston Rogers Shrops 59 SJ3406
Aston Rowant Oxon 37 SU7299
Aston Sandford Bucks 37 SP7507
Aston Somerville H & W 48 SP0438
Aston Subedge Gloucs 48 SP1441
Aston Tirrold Oxon 37 SU5586
Aston Upthorpe Oxon 37 SU5586
Aston-on-Trent Derbys 62 SK4129
Astonlane Shrops 59 SO6494
Astrop Nhants 49 SP5036
Astrope Herts 38 SP8914
Astwick Beds 39 TL2138
Astwith Derbys 75 SK4464
Astwood Bucks 38 SP9547
Astwood H & W 47 SO9365
Astwood Bank H & W 48 SP0462
Aswarby Lincs 64 TF0639
Aswardby Lincs 77 TF3770
Atch Lench H & W 48 SP0350
Atcham Shrops 59 SJ5409
Athelhampton Dorset 11 SY7694
Athelington Suffk 55 TM2171
Athelney Somset 21 ST3428
Athelstaneford Loth 118 NT5377
Atherfield Green IOW 13 SZ4679
Atherington Devon 19 SS5922
Atherington W Susx 14 TQ0000
Atherstone Somset 10 ST3816
Atherstone Warwks 61 SP3097
Atherstone on Stour Warwks 48 SP2051
Atherton Gt Man 79 SD6703

Atley Hill Barmpton

Atley Hill *N York* **89** NZ2802
Atlow *Derbys* **73** SK2248
Attadale *Highld* **138** NG9238
Attenborough *Notts* **62** SK5034
Atterby *Lincs* **76** SK9792
Attercliffe *S York* **74** SK3788
Atterley *Shrops* **59** SO6397
Atterton *Leics* **61** SP3598
Attleborough *Norfk* **66** TM0495
Attleborough *Warwks* **61** SP3790
Attlebridge *Norfk* **66** TG1216
Attleton Green *Suffk* **53** TL7454
Atwick *Humb* **85** TA1850
Atworth *Wilts* **22** ST8565
Auberrow *H & W* **46** SO4947
Aubourn *Lincs* **76** SK9262
Auchagallon *Strath* **105** NR8934
Auchedly *Gramp* **143** NJ8933
Auchenblae *Gramp* **135** NO7279
Auchenbowie *Cent* **116** NS7987
Auchencairn *D & G* **92** NX7951
Auchencairn *D & G* **100** NX9884
Auchencrow *Border* **119** NT8560
Auchendinny *Loth* **117** NT2561
Auchengray *Strath* **117** NS9954
Auchenhalrig *Gramp* **141** NJ3761
Auchenheath *Strath* **108** NS8043
Auchenhessnane *D & G* **100** NX8096
Auchenlochan *Strath* **114** NR9772
Auchenmade *Strath* **115** NS3548
Auchenmalg *D & G* **98** NX2352
Auchentibber *Strath* **116** NS6755
Auchentiber *Strath* **115** NS3647
Auchentroig *Cent* **115** NS5493
Auchindrean *Highld* **145** NH1980
Auchininna *Gramp* **142** NJ6546
Auchinleck *Strath* **107** NS5521
Auchinloch *Strath* **116** NS6570
Auchinstarry *Strath* **116** NS7176
Auchintore *Highld* **130** NN0972
Auchiries *Gramp* **143** NK0737
Auchlee *Gramp* **135** NO8996
Auchleven *Gramp* **142** NJ6224
Auchlochan *Strath* **107** NS7937
Auchlossan *Gramp* **134** NJ5601
Auchlyne *Cent* **124** NN5129
Auchmillan *Strath* **107** NS5129
Auchmithie *Tays* **127** NO6743
Auchmuirbridge *Fife* **126** NO2101
Auchnacree *Tays* **134** NO4663
Auchnagatt *Gramp* **143** NJ9241
Auchnotteroch *D & G* **98** NW9960
Auchroisk *Gramp* **141** NJ3351
Auchronie *Tays* **134** NO4480
Auchterarder *Tays* **125** NN9412
Auchteraw *Highld* **131** NH3507
Auchterblair *Highld* **140** NH9222
Auchtercairn *Highld* **144** NG8077
Auchterhouse *Tays* **126** NO3337
Auchterless *Gramp* **142** NJ7141
Auchtermuchty *Fife* **126** NO2311
Auchterneed *Highld* **139** NH4959
Auchtertool *Fife* **117** NT2190
Auchtertyre *Highld* **138** NG8427
Auchtoo *Cent* **124** NN5520
Auckengill *Highld* **151** ND3663
Auckley *S York* **75** SE6400
Audenshaw *Gt Man* **79** SJ9197
Audlem *Ches* **72** SJ6543
Audley *Staffs* **72** SJ7950
Audley End *Essex* **39** TL5337
Audley End *Essex* **54** TL8137
Audley End *Suffk* **54** TL8553
Audmore *Staffs* **72** SJ8321
Audnam *W Mids* **60** SO8986
Aughertree *Cumb* **93** NY2538
Aughton *Humb* **84** SE7038
Aughton *Lancs* **78** SD3905
Aughton *Lancs* **87** SD5567
Aughton *S York* **75** SK4586
Aughton *Wilts* **23** SU2356
Aughton Park *Lancs* **78** SD4006
Auldallan *Tays* **134** NO3158
Auldearn *Highld* **140** NH9255
Aulden *H & W* **46** SO4654
Auldgirth *D & G* **100** NX9186
Auldhame *Loth* **118** NT5984
Auldhouse *Strath* **116** NS6250
Ault a' chruinn *Highld* **138** NG9420
Ault Hucknall *Derbys* **75** SK4665
Aultbea *Highld* **144** NG8789
Aultgrishin *Highld* **144** NG7485
Aultguish Inn *Highld* **145** NH3570
Aultmore *Gramp* **142** NJ4053
Aultnagoire *Highld* **139** NH5423
Aultnamain Inn *Highld* **146** NH6681
Aunby *Lincs* **64** TF0214
Aunk *Devon* **9** ST0400
Aunsby *Lincs* **64** TF0438
Aust *Avon* **34** ST5788
Austendike *Lincs* **64** TF2821
Austerfield *Notts* **75** SK6694
Austerlands *Gt Man* **79** SD9505
Austhorpe *W York* **83** SE3733
Austonley *W York* **82** SE1107
Austrey *Warwks* **61** SK2906
Austwick *N York* **88** SD7668
Authorpe *Lincs* **77** TF3980
Authorpe Row *Lincs* **77** TF5373
Avebury *Wilts* **36** SU1069
Avebury Trusloe *Wilts* **36** SU0969
Aveley *Essex* **27** TQ5680
Avening *Gloucs* **35** ST8898
Averham *Notts* **75** SK7654
Aveton Gifford *Devon* **7** SX6947
Aviemore *Highld* **132** NH8913
Avington *Berks* **23** SU3767
Avoch *Highld* **140** NH7055
Avon *Dorset* **12** SZ1498
Avon Dassett *Warwks* **49** SP4150
Avonbridge *Cent* **116** NS9172
Avonmouth *Avon* **34** ST5178
Avonwick *Devon* **7** SX7158
Awbridge *Hants* **12** SU3224
Awkley *Avon* **34** ST5985
Awliscombe *Devon* **9** ST1301
Awre *Gloucs* **35** SO7008
Awsworth *Notts* **62** SK4844
Axborough *H & W* **60** SO8579
Axbridge *Somset* **21** ST4354
Axford *Hants* **24** SU6043
Axford *Wilts* **36** SU2370
Axminster *Devon* **10** SY2998
Axmouth *Devon* **10** SY2591
Axton *Clwyd* **70** SJ1080
Aycliffe *Dur* **96** NZ2822
Aylburton *Gloucs* **34** SO6101
Ayle *Cumb* **94** NY7149
Aylesbeare *Devon* **9** SY0392
Aylesbury *Bucks* **38** SP8213
Aylesby *Humb* **85** TA2007
Aylesford *Kent* **28** TQ7359
Aylesham *Kent* **29** TR2452
Aylestone *Leics* **50** SK5700
Aylestone Park *Leics* **50** SK5800
Aylmerton *Norfk* **66** TG1839
Aylsham *Norfk* **67** TG1926
Aylton *H & W* **47** SO6537
Aylworth *Gloucs* **36** SP1021
Aymestrey *H & W* **46** SO4265
Aynho *Nhants* **49** SP5133
Ayot Green *Herts* **39** TL2214
Ayot St. Lawrence *Herts* **39** TL1916
Ayot St. Peter *Herts* **39** TL2115
Ayr *Strath* **106** NS3321
Aysgarth *N York* **88** SE0088
Ayshford *Devon* **9** ST0415
Ayside *Cumb* **87** SD3983
Ayston *Leics* **51** SK8600
Aythorpe Roding *Essex* **40** TL5815
Ayton *Border* **119** NT9260
Azerley *N York* **89** SE2574

B

Babbacombe *Devon* **7** SX9265
Babbington *Notts* **62** SK4943
Babbinswood *Shrops* **59** SJ3329
Babbs Green *Herts* **39** TL3916
Babcary *Somset* **21** ST5628
Babel *Dyfed* **44** SN8235
Babel Green *Suffk* **53** TL7348
Babell *Clwyd* **70** SJ1573
Babeny *Devon* **7** SX6775
Babington *Somset* **22** ST7051
Bablock Hythe *Oxon* **36** SP4304
Babraham *Cambs* **53** TL5150
Babworth *Notts* **75** SK6880
Bachau *Gwynd* **68** SH4383
Bache *Shrops* **59** SO4681
Bacheldre *Powys* **58** SO2492
Bachelor Bump *E Susx* **17** TQ8412
Back o' th' Brook *Staffs* **73** SK0751
Back of Keppoch *Highld* **129** NM6587
Back Street *Suffk* **53** TL7458
Backaland *Ork* **155** HY5630
Backbarrow *Cumb* **87** SD3584
Backe *Dyfed* **31** SN2615
Backfolds *Gramp* **143** NK0252
Backford *Ches* **71** SJ3971
Backford Cross *Ches* **71** SJ3873
Backies *Highld* **147** NC8302
Backlass *Highld* **151** ND2053
Backwell *Avon* **21** ST4968
Backworth *T & W* **103** NZ3072
Bacon's End *W Mids* **61** SP1888
Baconsthorpe *Norfk* **66** TG1236
Bacton *H & W* **46** SO3732
Bacton *Norfk* **67** TG3433
Bacton *Suffk* **54** TM0567
Bacton Green *Suffk* **54** TM0365
Bacup *Lancs* **81** SD8622
Badachro *Highld* **137** NG7873
Badbury *Wilts* **36** SU1980
Badby *Nhants* **49** SP5658
Badcall *Highld* **148** NC1541
Badcall *Highld* **148** NC2455
Badcaul *Highld* **144** NH0291
Baddeley Edge *Staffs* **72** SJ9150
Baddeley Green *Staffs* **72** SJ9151
Baddesley Clinton *Warwks* **61** SP2070
Baddesley Ensor *Warwks* **61** SP2798
Baddidarroch *Highld* **145** NC0822
Badenscoth *Gramp* **142** NJ6938
Badenyon *Gramp* **141** NJ3319
Badgall *Cnwll* **5** SX2486
Badgeney *Cambs* **65** TL4397
Badger *Shrops* **60** SO7699
Badger's Cross *Cnwll* **2** SW4833
Badgers Mount *Kent* **27** TQ4962
Badgeworth *Gloucs* **35** SO9019
Badgworth *Somset* **21** ST3952
Badharlick *Cnwll* **5** SX2686
Badicaul *Highld* **137** NG7529
Badingham *Suffk* **55** TM3068
Badlesmere *Kent* **28** TR0153
Badlieu *Border* **108** NT0518
Badlipster *Highld* **151** ND2448
Badluachrach *Highld* **144** NG9994
Badninish *Highld* **147** NH7594
Badrallach *Highld* **145** NH0691
Badsey *H & W* **48** SP0743
Badshot Lea *Surrey* **25** SU8648
Badsworth *W York* **83** SE4614
Badwell Ash *Suffk* **54** TL9868
Badwell Green *Suffk* **54** TM0169
Bag Enderby *Lincs* **77** TF3571
Bagber *Dorset* **11** ST7513
Bagby *N York* **89** SE4680
Bagendon *Gloucs* **35** SP0106
Bagginswood *Shrops* **60** SO6881
Baggrow *Cumb* **93** NY1741
Bagham *Kent* **29** TR0753
Bagillt *Clwyd* **70** SJ2175
Baginton *Warwks* **61** SP3474
Baglan *W Glam* **32** SS7492
Bagley *Shrops* **59** SJ4027
Bagley *Somset* **21** ST4645
Bagley *W York* **82** SE2235
Bagmore *Hants* **24** SU6544
Bagnall *Staffs* **72** SJ9250
Bagnor *Berks* **24** SU4569
Bagot *Shrops* **46** SO5873
Bagshot *Surrey* **25** SU9063
Bagshot *Wilts* **23** SU3165
Bagstone *Avon* **35** ST6987
Bagthorpe *Notts* **75** SK4651
Bagworth *Leics* **62** SK4408
Bagwy Llydiart *H & W* **46** SO4426
Baildon *W York* **82** SE1539
Baildon Green *W York* **82** SE1439
Baile Mor *Strath* **120** NM2824
Bailey Green *Hants* **13** SU6627
Baileyhead *Cumb* **101** NY5179
Bailiff Bridge *W York* **82** SE1425
Baillieston *Strath* **116** NS6764
Bailrigg *Lancs* **87** SD4858
Bainbridge *N York* **88** SD9390
Bainshole *Gramp* **142** NJ6035
Bainton *Cambs* **64** TF0906
Bainton *Humb* **84** SE9652
Bainton *Oxon* **49** SP5827
Baintown *Fife* **126** NO3503
Bairnkine *Border* **110** NT6515
Baker Street *Essex* **40** TQ6381
Baker's End *Herts* **39** TL3917
Bakewell *Derbys* **74** SK2168
Bala *Gwynd* **58** SH9235
Balallan *W Isls* **154** NB2920
Balbeg *Highld* **139** NH4431
Balbeggie *Tays* **126** NO1629
Balblair *Highld* **139** NH5145
Balblair *Highld* **140** NH7066
Balby *S York* **75** SE5600
Balcary *D & G* **92** NX8149
Balchraggan *Highld* **139** NH5343
Balchrick *Highld* **148** NC1960
Balcombe *W Susx* **15** TQ3130
Balcombe Lane *W Susx* **15** TQ3132
Balcomie Links *Fife* **127** NO6209
Balcurvie *Fife* **118** NO3400
Baldersby *N York* **89** SE3578
Baldersby St. James *N York* **89** SE3676
Balderstone *Gt Man* **79** SD9010
Balderstone *Lancs* **81** SD6332
Balderton *Notts* **75** SK8151
Baldhu *Cnwll* **3** SW7743
Baldinnie *Fife* **127** NO4211
Baldinnies *Tays* **125** NO0216
Baldock *Herts* **39** TL2434
Baldovie *Tays* **127** NO4533
Baldrine *IOM* **153** SC4281
Baldslow *E Susx* **17** TQ8013
Baldwin *IOM* **153** SC3581
Baldwin's Gate *Staffs* **72** SJ7939
Baldwin's Hill *Surrey* **15** TQ3839
Baldwinholme *Cumb* **93** NY3351
Bale *Norfk* **66** TG0136
Baledgarno *Tays* **126** NO2730
Balemartine *Strath* **120** NL9841
Balerno *Loth* **117** NT1666
Balfarg *Fife* **126** NO2803
Balfield *Tays* **134** NO5468
Balfour *Ork* **155** HY4716
Balfron *Cent* **115** NS5489
Balgaveny *Gramp* **142** NJ6540
Balgavies *Tays* **127** NO5451
Balgonar *Fife* **117** NT0293
Balgowan *D & G* **98** NX1142
Balgowan *Highld* **132** NN6494
Balgown *Highld* **136** NG3868
Balgracie *D & G* **98** NW9860
Balgray *Tays* **126** NO4038
Balham *Gt Lon* **27** TQ2873
Balhary *Tays* **126** NO2646
Balholmie *Tays* **126** NO1436
Baligill *Highld* **150** NC8565
Balintore *Highld* **147** NH8675
Balintore *Tays* **133** NO2859
Balintraid *Highld* **146** NH7370
Balivanich *W Isls* **154** NF7755
Balk *N York* **89** SE4780
Balkeerie *Tays* **126** NO3244
Balkholme *Humb* **84** SE7828
Ball *Shrops* **59** SJ3026
Ball Green *Staffs* **72** SJ8952
Ball Haye Green *Staffs* **72** SJ9856
Ball Hill *Hants* **24** SU4163
Ball's Green *Gloucs* **35** ST8699
Ballabeg *IOM* **153** SC2570
Ballachgair *Strath* **105** NR7727
Ballachulish *Highld* **130** NN0858
Ballamodha *IOM* **153** SC2773
Ballantrae *Strath* **98** NX0882
Ballards Gore *Essex* **40** TQ9092
Ballards Green *Warwks* **61** SP2791
Ballasalla *IOM* **153** SC2870
Ballater *Gramp* **134** NO3695
Ballaugh *IOM* **153** SC3493
Ballchraggan *Highld* **147** NH7675
Ballechin *Tays* **125** NN9353
Ballencrieff *Loth* **118** NT4878
Ballevullin *Strath* **120** NL9546
Ballidon *Derbys* **73** SK2054
Balliekine *Strath* **105** NR8739
Balliemore *Strath* **114** NS1099
Balligmorrie *Strath* **106** NX2290
Ballimore *Cent* **124** NN5317
Ballimore *Strath* **114** NR9283
Ballindalloch *Gramp* **141** NJ1636
Ballindean *Tays* **126** NO2529
Ballingdon *Essex* **54** TL8640
Ballinger Common *Bucks* **38** SP9103
Ballingham *H & W* **46** SO5731
Ballingry *Fife* **117** NT1797
Ballinluig *Tays* **125** NN9752
Ballinshoe *Tays* **126** NO4153
Ballintuim *Tays* **126** NO1055
Balloch *Highld* **140** NH7247
Balloch *Strath* **106** NX3295
Balloch *Tays* **125** NN8419
Ballochroy *Strath* **113** NR7352
Ballogie *Gramp* **134** NO5795
Balls Cross *W Susx* **14** SU9826
Balls Green *E Susx* **16** TQ4936
Ballygown *Strath* **121** NM4343
Ballygrant *Strath* **112** NR3966
Ballyhaugh *Strath* **120** NM1758
Ballymenoch *Strath* **115** NS3086
Ballymichael *Strath* **105** NR9231
Balmacara *Highld* **137** NG8028
Balmaclellan *D & G* **99** NX6579
Balmae *D & G* **99** NX6844
Balmaha *Cent* **115** NS4290
Balmalcolm *Fife* **126** NO3208
Balmangan *D & G* **99** NX6445
Balmedie *Gramp* **143** NJ9618
Balmer Heath *Shrops* **59** SJ4434
Balmerino *Fife* **126** NO3524
Balmerlawn *Hants* **12** SU3003
Balmore *Strath* **115** NS5973
Balmuchy *Highld* **147** NH8678
Balmuir *Tays* **127** NO5648
Balmule *Fife* **117** NT2088
Balmullo *Fife* **127** NO4220
Balnaboth *Tays* **134** NO3166
Balnacoil Lodge *Highld* **147** NC8011
Balnacroft *Gramp* **133** NO2894
Balnafoich *Highld* **140** NH6835
Balnaguard *Tays* **125** NN9451
Balnahard *Strath* **121** NM4534
Balnahard *Strath* **112** NR4199
Balnain *Highld* **139** NH4430
Balnakeil *Highld* **149** NC3968
Balnapaling *Highld* **147** NH7969
Balquharn *Tays* **125** NO0235
Balquhidder *Cent* **124** NN5320
Balsall *W Mids* **61** SP2376
Balsall Common *W Mids* **61** SP2377
Balsall Heath *W Mids* **61** SP0784
Balsall Street *W Mids* **61** SP2276
Balscote *Oxon* **48** SP3942
Balsham *Cambs* **53** TL5850
Baltasound *Shet* **155** HP6208
Balterley *Staffs* **72** SJ7650
Balterley Green *Staffs* **72** SJ7650
Baltersan *D & G* **99** NX4261
Baltonsborough *Somset* **21** ST5434
Balvicar *Strath* **122** NM7616
Balvraid *Highld* **129** NG8416
Balvraid *Highld* **140** NH8231
Balwest *Cnwll* **2** SW5930
Bamber Bridge *Lancs* **81** SD5625
Bamber's Green *Essex* **40** TL5722
Bamburgh *Nthumb* **111** NU1734
Bamff *Tays* **126** NO2251
Bamford *Derbys* **74** SK2083
Bamford *Gt Man* **81** SD8612
Bampton *Cumb* **94** NY5118
Bampton *Devon* **20** SS9522
Bampton *Oxon* **36** SP3103
Bampton Grange *Cumb* **94** NY5218
Banavie *Highld* **130** NN1177
Banbury *Oxon* **49** SP4540
Banc-y-ffordd *Dyfed* **31** SN4037
Bancffosfelem *Dyfed* **32** SN4811
Banchory *Gramp* **135** NO6995
Banchory-Devenick *Gramp* **135** NJ9002
Bancycapel *Dyfed* **31** SN4214
Bancyfelin *Dyfed* **31** SN3218
Bandirran *Tays* **126** NO2030
Bandrake Head *Cumb* **86** SD3187
Banff *Gramp* **142** NJ6863
Bangor *Gwynd* **69** SH5772
Bangor's Green *Lancs* **78** SD3709
Bangor-is-y-coed *Clwyd* **71** SJ3845
Bangors *Cnwll* **18** SX2099
Banham *Norfk* **54** TM0687
Bank *Hants* **12** SU2807
Bank Ground *Cumb* **86** SD3196
Bank Newton *N York* **81** SD9053
Bank Street *H & W* **47** SO6362
Bank Top *Lancs* **78** SD5207
Bank Top *W York* **82** SE1024
Bankend *D & G* **100** NY0268
Bankend *Strath* **108** NS8033
Bankfoot *Tays* **125** NO0635
Bankglen *Strath* **107** NS5912
Bankhead *Gramp* **135** NJ9009
Bankhead *Strath* **106** NS3739
Banknock *Cent* **116** NS7779
Banks *Cumb* **101** NY5664
Banks *Lancs* **80** SD3920
Banks Green *H & W* **47** SO9967
Bankshill *D & G* **101** NY1982
Banningham *Norfk* **67** TG2129
Bannister Green *Essex* **40** TL6920
Bannockburn *Cent* **116** NS8190
Banstead *Surrey* **27** TQ2559
Bantham *Devon* **7** SX6643
Banton *Strath* **116** NS7480
Banwell *Avon* **21** ST3959
Bapchild *Kent* **28** TQ9263
Bapton *Wilts* **22** ST9938
Bar Hill *Cambs* **52** TL3863
Barassie *Strath* **106** NS3232
Barbaraville *Highld* **146** NH7472
Barber Booth *Derbys* **74** SK1184
Barber Green *Cumb* **87** SD3982
Barbieston *Strath* **107** NS4317
Barbon *Cumb* **87** SD6282
Barbridge *Ches* **71** SJ6156
Barbrook *Devon* **19** SS7147
Barby *Nhants* **50** SP5470
Barcaldine *Strath* **122** NM9641
Barcheston *Warwks* **48** SP2639
Barclose *Cumb* **101** NY4462
Barcombe *E Susx* **15** TQ4114
Barcombe Cross *E Susx* **15** TQ4115
Barcroft *W York* **82** SE0437
Barden *N York* **89** SE1493
Barden Park *Kent* **16** TQ5746
Bardfield End Green *Essex* **40** TL6231
Bardfield Saling *Essex* **40** TL6826
Bardney *Lincs* **76** TF1269
Bardon *Leics* **62** SK4412
Bardon Mill *Nthumb* **102** NY7764
Bardowie *Strath* **115** NS5873
Bardown *E Susx* **16** TQ6629
Bardrainney *Strath* **115** NS3373
Bardsea *Cumb* **86** SD3074
Bardsey *W York* **83** SE3643
Bardsley *Gt Man* **79** SD9201
Bardwell *Suffk* **54** TL9473
Bare *Lancs* **87** SD4564
Bareppa *Cnwll* **3** SW7729
Barewood *H & W* **46** SO3856
Barfad *D & G* **98** NX3266
Barford *Norfk* **66** TG1107
Barford *Warwks* **48** SP2760
Barford St. John *Oxon* **49** SP4433
Barford St. Martin *Wilts* **23** SU0531
Barford St. Michael *Oxon* **49** SP4332
Barfrestone *Kent* **29** TR2650
Bargate *Derbys* **62** SK3546
Bargeddie *Strath* **116** NS6964
Bargoed *M Glam* **33** ST1599
Bargrennan *D & G* **98** NX3577
Barham *Cambs* **52** TL1375
Barham *Kent* **29** TR2050
Barham *Suffk* **54** TM1451
Barholm *Lincs* **64** TF0810
Barkby *Leics* **63** SK6309
Barkby Thorpe *Leics* **63** SK6309
Barkers Green *Shrops* **59** SJ5228
Barkestone-le-Vale *Leics* **63** SK7734
Barkham *Berks* **25** SU7766
Barking *Gt Lon* **27** TQ4484
Barking *Suffk* **54** TM0753
Barking Tye *Suffk* **54** TM0652
Barkingside *Gt Lon* **27** TQ4489
Barkisland *W York* **82** SE0519
Barkla Shop *Cnwll* **3** SW7350
Barkston *Lincs* **63** SK9341
Barkston Ash *N York* **83** SE4936
Barkway *Herts* **39** TL3835
Barlanark *Strath* **116** NS6664
Barlaston *Staffs* **72** SJ8938
Barlavington *W Susx* **14** SU9716
Barlborough *Derbys* **75** SK4777
Barlby *N York* **83** SE6333
Barlestone *Leics* **62** SK4205
Barley *Herts* **39** TL4038
Barley *Lancs* **81** SD8240
Barley Hole *S York* **74** SK3697
Barleycroft End *Herts* **39** TL4327
Barleythorpe *Leics* **63** SK8409
Barling *Essex* **40** TQ9389
Barlings *Lincs* **76** TF0774
Barlochan *D & G* **92** NX8157
Barlow *Derbys* **74** SK3474
Barlow *N York* **83** SE6428
Barlow *T & W* **96** NZ1561
Barmby Moor *Humb* **84** SE7748
Barmby on the Marsh *Humb* **83** SE6928
Barmer *Norfk* **66** TF8133
Barming Heath *Kent* **28** TQ7255
Barmollack *Strath* **105** NR8043
Barmouth *Gwynd* **57** SH6116
Barmpton *Dur* **96** NZ3118

Barmston Berry Down Cross

Barmston *Humb* 91 TA1659
Barnaby Green *Suffk* 55 TM4780
Barnacabber *Strath* 114 NS1789
Barnacarry *Strath* 114 NS0094
Barnack *Cambs* 64 TF0705
Barnacle *Warwks* 61 SP3884
Barnard Castle *Dur* 95 NZ0516
Barnard Gate *Oxon* 36 SP4010
Barnardiston *Suffk* 53 TL7148
Barnbarroch *D & G* 92 NX8456
Barnburgh *S York* 83 SE4803
Barnby *Suffk* 55 TM4789
Barnby Dun *S York* 83 SE6109
Barnby in the Willows *Notts* 76 SK8552
Barnby Moor *Notts* 75 SK6684
Barncorkrie *D & G* 98 NX0935
Barnes *Gt Lon* 26 TQ2276
Barnes Street *Kent* 16 TQ6447
Barnet *Gt Lon* 26 TQ2496
Barnet Gate *Gt Lon* 26 TQ2195
Barnetby le Wold *Humb* 84 TA0509
Barney *Norfk* 66 TF9932
Barnham *Suffk* 54 TL8779
Barnham *W Susx* 14 SU9503
Barnham Broom *Norfk* 66 TG0807
Barnhead *Tays* 135 NO6657
Barnhill *Ches* 71 SJ4854
Barnhill *Gramp* 141 NJ1457
Barnhill *Tays* 127 NO4731
Barnhills *D & G* 98 NW9871
Barningham *Dur* 89 NZ0810
Barningham *Suffk* 54 TL9676
Barnoldby le Beck *Humb* 85 TA2303
Barnoldswick *Lancs* 81 SD8746
Barns Green *W Susx* 14 TQ1226
Barnsdale Bar *N York* 83 SE5014
Barnsley *Gloucs* 36 SP0704
Barnsley *S York* 83 SE3406
Barnsley *Shrops* 60 SO7592
Barnsole *Kent* 29 TR2756
Barnstaple *Devon* 19 SS5633
Barnston *Essex* 40 TL6419
Barnston *Mersyd* 78 SJ2783
Barnstone *Notts* 63 SK7335
Barnt Green *H & W* 60 SP0173
Barnton *Ches* 71 SJ6375
Barnton *Loth* 117 NT1874
Barnwell All Saints *Nhants* 51 TL0484
Barnwell St. Andrew *Nhants* 51 TL0584
Barnwood *Gloucs* 35 SO8518
Baron's Cross *H & W* 46 SO4758
Barons Wood *Devon* 8 SS7003
Baronwood *Cumb* 94 NY5143
Barr *Strath* 106 NX2794
Barrachan *D & G* 99 NX3649
Barrapoll *Strath* 120 NL9442
Barras *Cumb* 88 NY8312
Barrasford *Nthumb* 102 NY9173
Barrets Green *Ches* 71 SJ5859
Barrhead *Strath* 115 NS4958
Barrhill *Strath* 98 NX2382
Barrington *Cambs* 52 TL3849
Barrington *Somset* 10 ST3818
Barripper *Cnwll* 2 SW6338
Barrmill *Strath* 115 NS3651
Barrnacarry Bay *Strath* 122 NM8122
Barrock *Highld* 151 ND2570
Barrow *Gloucs* 47 SO8824
Barrow *Lancs* 81 SD7338
Barrow *Leics* 63 SK8815
Barrow *Shrops* 59 SJ6500
Barrow *Somset* 22 ST7231
Barrow *Suffk* 53 TL7663
Barrow Bridge *Gt Man* 81 SD6811
Barrow Burn *Nthumb* 110 NT8610
Barrow Gurney *Avon* 21 ST5268
Barrow Haven *Humb* 84 TA0622
Barrow Hill *Derbys* 74 SK4275
Barrow Nook *Lancs* 78 SD4402
Barrow Street *Wilts* 22 ST8330
Barrow upon Soar *Leics* 62 SK5717
Barrow upon Trent *Derbys* 62 SK3528
Barrow Vale *Avon* 21 ST6460
Barrow's Green *Ches* 78 SJ5287
Barrow's Green *Ches* 72 SJ6857
Barrow-in-Furness *Cumb* 86 SD2068
Barrow-upon-Humber *Humb* 84 TA0620
Barroway Drove *Norfk* 65 TF5703
Barrowby *Lincs* 63 SK8736
Barrowden *Leics* 51 SK9400
Barrowford *Lancs* 81 SD8539
Barry *S Glam* 20 ST1268
Barry *Tays* 127 NO5334
Barry Island *S Glam* 20 ST1166
Barsby *Leics* 63 SK6911
Barsham *Suffk* 55 TM3989
Barskimmings *Strath* 107 NS4825
Barston *W Mids* 61 SP2078
Bartestree *H & W* 46 SO5640
Barthol Chapel *Gramp* 143 NJ8133
Bartholomew Green *Essex* 40 TL7221
Barthomley *Ches* 72 SJ7652
Bartley *Hants* 12 SU3012
Bartley Green *W Mids* 60 SP0081
Bartlow *Cambs* 53 TL5845
Barton *Cambs* 52 TL4055
Barton *Ches* 71 SJ4454
Barton *Cumb* 94 NY4826
Barton *Devon* 7 SX9167
Barton *Gloucs* 48 SP0925
Barton *H & W* 46 SO2957
Barton *Lancs* 78 SD3509
Barton *Lancs* 80 SD5137
Barton *N York* 89 NZ2208
Barton *Oxon* 37 SP5507
Barton *Warwks* 48 SP1051
Barton Bendish *Norfk* 65 TF7105
Barton End *Gloucs* 35 ST8498
Barton Green *Staffs* 73 SK1717
Barton Hartshorn *Bucks* 49 SP6430
Barton in Fabis *Notts* 62 SK5132
Barton in the Beans *Leics* 62 SK3906
Barton Mills *Suffk* 53 TL7173
Barton on Sea *Hants* 12 SZ2393
Barton Seagrave *Nhants* 51 SP8877
Barton St. David *Somset* 21 ST5432
Barton Stacey *Hants* 24 SU4341
Barton Town *Devon* 19 SS6840
Barton Turf *Norfk* 67 TG3522
Barton upon Irwell *Gt Man* 79 SJ7697
Barton Waterside *Humb* 84 TA0222
Barton-le-Clay *Beds* 38 TL0830
Barton-le-Street *N York* 90 SE7274
Barton-le-Willows *N York* 90 SE7163
Barton-on-the-Heath *Warwks* 48 SP2532
Barton-Upon-Humber *Humb* 84 TA0221
Barton-under-Needwood *Staffs* 73 SK1818
Barugh *S York* 82 SE3108
Barugh Green *S York* 82 SE3107
Barvas *W Isls* 154 NB3649
Barway *Cambs* 53 TL5575
Barwell *Leics* 50 SP4496
Barwick *Devon* 8 SS5907
Barwick *Herts* 39 TL3819
Barwick *Somset* 10 ST5513
Barwick in Elmet *W York* 83 SE4037
Baschurch *Shrops* 59 SJ4221
Bascote *Warwks* 48 SP4063
Bascote Heath *Warwks* 48 SP3962
Base Green *Suffk* 54 TM0163
Basford Green *Staffs* 72 SJ9851
Bashall Eaves *Lancs* 81 SD6943
Bashall Town *Lancs* 81 SD7142
Bashley *Hants* 12 SZ2496
Basildon *Berks* 37 SU6078
Basildon *Essex* 40 TQ7189
Basingstoke *Hants* 24 SU6352
Baslow *Derbys* 74 SK2572
Bason Bridge *Somset* 21 ST3446
Bassaleg *Gwent* 34 ST2786
Bassendean *Border* 110 NT6245
Bassenthwaite *Cumb* 93 NY2332
Bassett *Hants* 13 SU4216
Bassingbourn *Cambs* 39 TL3343
Bassingfield *Notts* 62 SK6137
Bassingham *Lincs* 76 SK9060
Bassingthorpe *Leics* 63 SK9628
Bassus Green *Herts* 39 TL3025
Bastad *Kent* 27 TQ6055
Baston *Lincs* 64 TF1113
Bastwick *Norfk* 67 TG4217
Batch *Somset* 21 ST3255
Batchworth *Herts* 26 TQ0694
Batchworth Heath *Herts* 26 TQ0792
Batcombe *Somset* 22 ST6938
Bate Heath *Ches* 79 SJ6879
Batecombe *Dorset* 10 ST6103
Batford *Herts* 38 TL1415
Bath *Avon* 22 ST7464
Bath Side *Essex* 41 TM2532
Bathampton *Avon* 22 ST7766
Bathealton *Somset* 20 ST0823
Batheaston *Avon* 22 ST7767
Bathford *Avon* 22 ST7866
Bathgate *Loth* 117 NS9768
Bathley *Notts* 75 SK7759
Bathpool *Cnwll* 5 SX2874
Bathpool *Somset* 20 ST2526
Bathville *Loth* 116 NS9367
Bathway *Somset* 21 ST5952
Batley *W York* 82 SE2224
Batsford *Gloucs* 48 SP1833
Batson *Devon* 7 SX7339
Batt's Corner *Surrey* 25 SU8240
Battersby *N York* 90 NZ5907
Battersea *Gt Lon* 27 TQ2776
Battisborough Cross *Devon* 6 SX5948
Battisford *Suffk* 54 TM0554
Battisford Tye *Suffk* 54 TM0354
Battle *E Susx* 17 TQ7515
Battle *Powys* 45 SO0130
Battleborough *Somset* 21 ST3450
Battledown *Gloucs* 35 SO9621
Battledykes *Tays* 127 NO4555
Battlefield *Shrops* 59 SJ5117
Battlesbridge *Essex* 40 TQ7894
Battlesden *Beds* 38 SP9628
Battleton *Somset* 20 SS9127
Battlies Green *Suffk* 54 TL9064
Battramsley Cross *Hants* 12 SZ3198
Battye Ford *W York* 82 SE1920
Baughton *H & W* 47 SO8841
Baughurst *Hants* 24 SU5860
Baulds *Gramp* 134 NO6093
Baulking *Oxon* 36 SU3191
Baumber *Lincs* 76 TF2274
Baunton *H & W* 35 SP0104
Baveney Wood *Shrops* 60 SO6979
Baverstock *Wilts* 23 SU0332
Bawburgh *Norfk* 66 TG1508
Bawdeswell *Norfk* 66 TG0420
Bawdrip *Somset* 21 ST3439
Bawdsey *Suffk* 55 TM3440
Bawtry *Notts* 75 SK6493
Baxenden *Lancs* 81 SD7726
Baxter's Green *Suffk* 53 TL7557
Baxterley *Warwks* 61 SP2896
Baxton *Kent* 28 TQ8959
Bay Horse *Lancs* 80 SD4952
Bayble *W Isls* 154 NB5231
Baybridge *Hants* 13 SU5223
Baybridge *Nthumb* 95 NY9550
Baycliff *Cumb* 86 SD2872
Baydon *Wilts* 36 SU2878
Bayford *Herts* 39 TL3108
Bayford *Somset* 22 ST7229
Bayhead *W Isls* 154 NF7468
Bayley's Hill *Kent* 27 TQ5151
Baylham *Suffk* 54 TM1051
Baynard's Green *Oxon* 49 SP5429
Baysdale Abbey *N York* 90 NZ6206
Baysham *H & W* 46 SO5727
Bayston Hill *Shrops* 59 SJ4808
Baythorne End *Essex* 53 TL7242
Bayton *H & W* 60 SO6973
Bayton Common *H & W* 60 SO7173
Bayworth *Oxon* 37 SP4901
Beach *Avon* 35 ST7071
Beachampton *Bucks* 49 SP7736
Beachamwell *Norfk* 65 TF7505
Beachborough *Kent* 29 TR1638
Beachley *Gloucs* 34 ST5591
Beacon *Devon* 9 ST1805
Beacon End *Essex* 40 TL9524
Beacon Hill *E Susx* 16 TQ5030
Beacon Hill *Kent* 17 TQ8232
Beacon Hill *Notts* 75 SK8153
Beacon Hill *Surrey* 14 SU8736
Beacon's Bottom *Bucks* 37 SU7895
Beaconsfield *Bucks* 26 SU9490
Beacontree *Gt Lon* 27 TQ4786
Beadlam *N York* 90 SE6584
Beadlow *Beds* 38 TL1038
Beadnell *Nthumb* 111 NU2229
Beaford *Devon* 19 SS5515
Beal *N York* 83 SE5325
Beal *Nthumb* 111 NU0642
Bealbury *Cnwll* 5 SX3766
Bealsmill *Cnwll* 5 SX3576
Beam Hill *Staffs* 73 SK2325
Beamhurst *Staffs* 73 SK0536
Beaminster *Dorset* 10 ST4701
Beamish *Dur* 96 NZ2253
Beamsley *N York* 82 SE0752
Bean *Kent* 27 TQ5872
Beanacre *Wilts* 22 ST9066
Beanley *Nthumb* 111 NU0818
Beardon *Devon* 5 SX5184
Beardwood *Lancs* 81 SD6629
Beare *Devon* 9 SS9901
Beare Green *Surrey* 15 TQ1742
Bearley *Warwks* 48 SP1860
Bearley Cross *Warwks* 48 SP1761
Bearpark *Dur* 96 NZ2343
Bearsbridge *Nthumb* 94 NY7857
Bearsden *Strath* 115 NS5372
Bearsted *Kent* 28 TQ8055
Bearstone *Shrops* 72 SJ7239
Bearwood *W Mids* 60 SP0286
Beatley Heath *Herts* 27 TQ2599
Beattock *D & G* 108 NT0802
Beauchamp Roding *Essex* 40 TL5809
Beauchief *S York* 74 SK3381
Beaudesert *Warwks* 48 SP1565
Beaufort *Gwent* 33 SO1611
Beaulieu *Hants* 12 SU3802
Beauly *Highld* 139 NH5246
Beaumaris *Gwynd* 69 SH6076
Beaumont *Cumb* 93 NY3459
Beaumont *Essex* 41 TM1624
Beaumont *Jersey* 152 JS1109
Beaumont Hill *Dur* 96 NZ2918
Beausale *Warwks* 61 SP2470
Beauworth *Hants* 13 SU5726
Beaver *Kent* 28 TR0040
Beaver Green *Kent* 28 TR0041
Beaworthy *Devon* 18 SX4699
Beazley End *Essex* 40 TL7429
Bebington *Mersyd* 78 SJ3383
Bebside *Nthumb* 103 NZ2781
Beccles *Suffk* 55 TM4289
Becconsall *Lancs* 80 SD4523
Beck Foot *Cumb* 87 SD6196
Beck Hole *N York* 90 NZ8202
Beck Row *Suffk* 53 TL6977
Beck Side *Cumb* 86 SD2382
Beck Side *Cumb* 87 SD3780
Beckbury *Shrops* 60 SJ7601
Beckenham *Gt Lon* 27 TQ3769
Beckering *Lincs* 76 TF1280
Beckermet *Cumb* 86 NY0106
Beckett End *Norfk* 65 TL7798
Beckfoot *Cumb* 92 NY0949
Beckfoot *Cumb* 86 NY1600
Beckfoot *Cumb* 86 SD1989
Beckford *H & W* 47 SO9736
Beckhampton *Wilts* 23 SU0868
Beckingham *Lincs* 76 SK8753
Beckingham *Notts* 75 SK7789
Beckington *Somset* 22 ST8051
Beckjay *Shrops* 46 SO3977
Beckley *E Susx* 17 TQ8523
Beckley *Hants* 12 SZ2296
Beckley *Oxon* 37 SP5611
Becks *W York* 82 SE0345
Beckside *Cumb* 87 SD6187
Beckton *Gt Lon* 27 TQ4381
Beckwithshaw *N York* 82 SE2653
Becquet Vincent *Jersey* 152 JS1411
Bedale *N York* 89 SE2688
Bedburn *Dur* 95 NZ0931
Bedchester *Dorset* 11 ST8517
Beddau *M Glam* 33 ST0585
Beddgelert *Gwynd* 69 SH5948
Beddingham *E Susx* 16 TQ4407
Beddington *Gt Lon* 27 TQ3065
Beddington Corner *Gt Lon* 27 TQ2866
Bedfield *Suffk* 55 TM2166
Bedfield Little Green *Suffk* 55 TM2365
Bedford *Beds* 38 TL0449
Bedgebury Cross *Kent* 17 TQ7134
Bedham *W Susx* 14 TQ0122
Bedhampton *Hants* 13 SU7006
Bedingfield *Suffk* 54 TM1768
Bedingfield Green *Suffk* 54 TM1866
Bedingfield Street *Suffk* 54 TM1768
Bedlam *N York* 89 SE2661
Bedlam Lane *Kent* 28 TQ8845
Bedlington *T & W* 103 NZ2681
Bedlinog *M Glam* 33 SO0901
Bedminster *Avon* 34 ST5871
Bedminster Down *Avon* 34 ST5770
Bedmond *Herts* 38 TL0903
Bednall *Staffs* 72 SJ9517
Bedrule *Border* 110 NT6017
Bedstone *Shrops* 46 SO3676
Bedwas *M Glam* 33 ST1789
Bedwellty *Gwent* 33 SO1600
Bedworth *Warwks* 61 SP3687
Bedworth Woodlands *Warwks* 61 SP3487
Beeby *Leics* 63 SK6608
Beech *Hants* 24 SU6938
Beech *Staffs* 72 SJ8538
Beech Hill *Berks* 24 SU6964
Beechingstoke *Wilts* 23 SU0859
Beedon *Berks* 37 SU4878
Beedon Hill *Berks* 37 SU4877
Beeford *Humb* 85 TA1253
Beeley *Derbys* 74 SK2667
Beelsby *Humb* 85 TA2001
Beenham *Berks* 24 SU5868
Beer *Devon* 9 SY2289
Beer *Somset* 21 ST4031
Beer Hackett *Dorset* 10 ST6011
Beercrocombe *Somset* 21 ST3220
Beesands *Devon* 7 SX8140
Beesby *Lincs* 77 TF4680
Beeson *Devon* 7 SX8140
Beeston *Beds* 52 TL1648
Beeston *Ches* 71 SJ5358
Beeston *Norfk* 66 TF9015
Beeston *Notts* 62 SK5236
Beeston *W York* 82 SE2830
Beeston Regis *Norfk* 66 TG1642
Beeswing *D & G* 100 NX8969
Beetham *Cumb* 87 SD4979
Beetham *Somset* 10 ST2712
Beetley *Norfk* 66 TF9718
Began *S Glam* 34 ST2283
Begbroke *Oxon* 37 SP4614
Begdale *Cambs* 65 TF4506
Begelly *Dyfed* 31 SN1107
Beggar's Bush *Powys* 46 SO2664
Beggarinton Hill *W York* 82 SE2724
Beguildy *Powys* 45 SO1979
Beighton *Norfk* 67 TG3808
Beighton *S York* 75 SK4483
Beighton Hill *Derbys* 73 SK2951
Bein Inn *Tays* 126 NO1513
Beith *Strath* 115 NS3553
Bekesbourne *Kent* 29 TR1955
Bekesbourne Hill *Kent* 29 TR1856
Belaugh *Norfk* 67 TG2818
Belbroughton *H & W* 60 SO9277
Belchalwell *Dorset* 11 ST7909
Belchalwell Street *Dorset* 11 ST7909
Belchamp Otten *Essex* 54 TL8041
Belchamp St. Paul *Essex* 53 TL7942
Belchamp Walter *Essex* 54 TL8240
Belchford *Lincs* 77 TF2975
Belford *Nthumb* 111 NU1034
Belgrave *Leics* 62 SK5906
Belhelvie *Gramp* 143 NJ9417
Belhinnie *Gramp* 142 NJ4627
Bell Bar *Herts* 39 TL2505
Bell Busk *N York* 81 SD9056
Bell End *H & W* 60 SO9477
Bell Heath *H & W* 60 SO9477
Bell Hill *Hants* 13 SU7324
Bell o' th'Hill *Ches* 71 SJ5245
Bellabeg *Gramp* 134 NJ3513
Belladrum *Highld* 139 NH5142
Bellanoch *Strath* 113 NR7992
Bellasize *Humb* 84 SE8227
Bellaty *Tays* 133 NO2359
Belle Vue *Cumb* 92 NY1131
Belle Vue *Cumb* 93 NY3756
Belle Vue *W York* 83 SE3419
Belleau *Lincs* 77 TF4078
Bellerby *N York* 89 SE1192
Bellever *Devon* 8 SX6577
Bellfield *Strath* 108 NS8234
Bellfield *Strath* 108 NS9620
Bellimoor *H & W* 46 SO3840
Bellingdon *Bucks* 38 SP9405
Bellingham *Nthumb* 102 NY8383
Belloch *Strath* 105 NR6737
Bellochantuy *Strath* 104 NR6632
Bellows Cross *Dorset* 12 SU0613
Bells Cross *Suffk* 54 TM1552
Bells Yew Green *E Susx* 16 TQ6135
Bellshill *Nthumb* 111 NU1230
Bellshill *Strath* 116 NS7360
Bellside *Strath* 116 NS8058
Bellsquarry *Loth* 117 NT0465
Belluton *Avon* 21 ST6164
Belmesthorpe *Leics* 64 TF0410
Belmont *Gt Lon* 27 TQ2562
Belmont *Lancs* 81 SD6715
Belmont *Shet* 155 HP5600
Belmont *Strath* 106 NS3419
Belnacraig *Gramp* 141 NJ3716
Belowda *Cnwll* 4 SW9661
Belper *Derbys* 62 SK3447
Belper Lane End *Derbys* 74 SK3349
Belsay *Nthumb* 103 NZ0978
Belsay Castle *Nthumb* 103 NZ0878
Belses *Border* 110 NT5725
Belsford *Devon* 7 SX7659
Belsize *Herts* 26 TL0300
Belstead *Suffk* 54 TM1241
Belstone *Devon* 8 SX6293
Belthorn *Lancs* 81 SD7124
Beltinge *Kent* 29 TR1967
Beltingham *Nthumb* 102 NY7863
Beltoft *Humb* 84 SE8006
Belton *Humb* 84 SE7806
Belton *Leics* 62 SK4420
Belton *Leics* 63 SK8101
Belton *Lincs* 63 SK9339
Belton *Norfk* 67 TG4802
Beltring *Kent* 28 TQ6747
Belvedere *Gt Lon* 27 TQ4978
Belvoir *Leics* 63 SK8133
Bembridge *IOW* 13 SZ6488
Bemersley Green *Staffs* 72 SJ8854
Bemerton *Wilts* 23 SU1230
Bempton *Humb* 91 TA1972
Ben Rhydding *W York* 82 SE1347
Benacre *Suffk* 55 TM5184
Benbuie *D & G* 107 NX7196
Benderloch *Strath* 122 NM9038
Benenden *Kent* 17 TQ8033
Benfield *D & G* 99 NX3763
Benfieldside *Dur* 95 NZ0952
Bengates *Norfk* 67 TG3027
Bengeworth *H & W* 48 SP0443
Benhall Green *Suffk* 55 TM3961
Benhall Street *Suffk* 55 TM3561
Benholm *Gramp* 135 NO8069
Beningbrough *N York* 90 SE5257
Benington *Herts* 39 TL2923
Benington *Lincs* 77 TF3946
Benllech *Gwynd* 68 SH5182
Benmore *Strath* 114 NS1385
Bennacott *Cnwll* 5 SX2992
Bennan *Strath* 105 NR9921
Bennet Head *Cumb* 93 NY4423
Bennetland *Humb* 84 SE8228
Bennett End *Bucks* 37 SU7897
Bennington Sea End *Lincs* 65 TF4145
Benniworth *Lincs* 76 TF2081
Benny *Cnwll* 4 SX1192
Benover *Kent* 28 TQ7048
Benson *Oxon* 37 SU6291
Bentfield Green *Essex* 39 TL5025
Benthall *Shrops* 60 SJ6602
Bentham *Gloucs* 35 SO9116
Benthoul *Gramp* 135 NJ8003
Bentlawn *Shrops* 59 SJ3301
Bentley *Hants* 25 SU7844
Bentley *Humb* 84 TA0136
Bentley *S York* 83 SE5605
Bentley *Suffk* 54 TM1138
Bentley *Warwks* 61 SP2895
Bentley Heath *W Mids* 61 SP1675
Bentley Rise *S York* 83 SE5604
Benton *Devon* 19 SS6536
Bentpath *D & G* 101 NY3190
Bentwichen *Devon* 19 SS7333
Bentworth *Hants* 24 SU6640
Benvie *Tays* 126 NO3231
Benville *Dorset* 10 ST5303
Benwick *Cambs* 52 TL3490
Beoley *H & W* 48 SP0669
Beoraidbeg *Highld* 129 NM6793
Bepton *W Susx* 14 SU8618
Berden *Essex* 39 TL4629
Bere Alston *Devon* 6 SX4466
Bere Ferrers *Devon* 6 SX4563
Bere Regis *Dorset* 11 SY8494
Berea *Dyfed* 30 SM7930
Berepper *Cnwll* 2 SW6523
Bergh Apton *Norfk* 67 TG3001
Berhill *Somset* 21 ST4436
Berinsfield *Oxon* 37 SU5696
Berkeley *Gloucs* 35 ST6899
Berkeley Heath *Gloucs* 35 ST6999
Berkeley Road *Gloucs* 35 SO7200
Berkhamsted *Herts* 38 SP9907
Berkley *Somset* 22 ST8049
Berkswell *W Mids* 61 SP2479
Bermondsey *Gt Lon* 27 TQ3479
Bernera *Highld* 129 NG8020
Bernice *Strath* 114 NS1391
Bernisdale *Highld* 136 NG4050
Berrick Prior *Oxon* 37 SU6294
Berrick Salome *Oxon* 37 SU6293
Berriedale *Highld* 147 ND1222
Berrier *Cumb* 93 NY3929
Berrington *H & W* 46 SO5767
Berrington *Nthumb* 111 NU0043
Berrington *Shrops* 59 SJ5206
Berrington Green *H & W* 46 SO5766
Berrow *Somset* 20 ST2951
Berry Brow *W York* 82 SE1314
Berry Cross *Devon* 18 SS4714
Berry Down Cross *Devon* 19 SS5743

Berry Hill Blencarn

Berry Hill *Dyfed* 30 SN0640
Berry Hill *Glouc*s 34 SO5712
Berry Pomeroy *Devon* 7 SX8261
Berry's Green *Gt Lon* 27 TQ4359
Berryhillock *Gramp* 142 NJ5054
Berryhillock *Gramp* 142 NJ5060
Berrynarbor *Devon* 19 SS5646
Bersham *Clwyd* 71 SJ3049
Berthengam *Clwyd* 70 SJ1179
Berwick *E Susx* 16 TQ5105
Berwick Bassett *Wilts* 36 SU0973
Berwick Hill *Nthumb* 103 NZ1775
Berwick St. James *Wilts* 23 SU0739
Berwick St. John *Wilts* 22 ST9422
Berwick St. Leonard *Wilts* 22 ST9233
Berwick-upon-Tweed *Nthumb* 119 NT9953
Bescaby *Leics* 63 SK8126
Bescar *Cumb* 80 SD3913
Besford *H & W* 47 SO9144
Besford *Shrops* 59 SJ5525
Besom Hill *Gt Man* 79 SD9508
Bessacarr *S York* 75 SE6100
Bessels Leigh *Oxon* 37 SP4501
Besses o' th' Barn *Gt Man* 79 SD8005
Bessingby *Humb* 91 TA1566
Bessingham *Norfk* 66 TG1636
Bestbeech Hill *E Susx* 16 TQ6231
Besthorpe *Norfk* 66 TM0595
Besthorpe *Notts* 75 SK8264
Beswick *Humb* 84 TA0147
Betchworth *Surrey* 26 TQ2150
Bethania *Dyfed* 43 SN5763
Bethania *Gwynd* 57 SH7044
Bethel *Gwynd* 68 SH3970
Bethel *Gwynd* 68 SH5265
Bethel *Gwynd* 70 SH9839
Bethel *Powys* 58 SJ1021
Bethersden *Kent* 28 TQ9240
Bethesda *Dyfed* 31 SN0918
Bethesda *Gwynd* 69 SH6266
Bethlehem *Dyfed* 44 SN6825
Bethnal Green *Gt Lon* 27 TQ3482
Betley *Staffs* 72 SJ7548
Betsham *Kent* 27 TQ6071
Betteshanger *Kent* 29 TR3152
Bettisfield *Clwyd* 59 SJ4635
Betton *Shrops* 72 SJ6936
Betton Strange *Shrops* 59 SJ5009
Bettws *Gwent* 34 ST2890
Bettws Bledrws *Dyfed* 44 SN5952
Bettws Cedewain *Powys* 58 SO1296
Bettws Evan *Dyfed* 42 SN3047
Bettws-Newydd *Gwent* 34 SO3606
Bettyhill *Highld* 150 NC7061
Betws *Dyfed* 32 SN6311
Betws *M Glam* 33 SS9086
Betws Garmon *Gwynd* 69 SH5357
Betws Gwerfil Goch *Clwyd* 70 SJ0346
Betws-y-coed *Gwynd* 69 SH7956
Betws-yn-Rhos *Clwyd* 69 SH9073
Beulah *Dyfed* 42 SN2846
Beulah *Powys* 45 SN9251
Bevendean *E Susx* 15 TQ3306
Bevercotes *Notts* 75 SK6972
Beverley *Humb* 84 TA0339
Beverstone *Glouc*s 35 ST8694
Bevington *Glouc*s 35 ST6596
Bewaldeth *Cumb* 93 NY2034
Bewcastle *Cumb* 101 NY5674
Bewdley *H & W* 60 SO7875
Bewerley *N York* 89 SE1565
Bewholme *Humb* 85 TA1649
Bewlbridge *Kent* 16 TQ6834
Bexhill *E Susx* 17 TQ7407
Bexley *Gt Lon* 27 TQ4973
Bexley Heath *Gt Lon* 27 TQ4875
Bexleyhill *W Susx* 14 SU9125
Bexwell *Norfk* 65 TF6303
Beyton *Suffk* 54 TL9363
Beyton Green *Suffk* 54 TL9363
Bibstone *Avon* 35 ST6991
Bibury *Glouc*s 36 SP1106
Bicester *Oxon* 49 SP5823
Bickenhill *W Mids* 61 SP1882
Bicker *Lincs* 64 TF2237
Bicker Bar *Lincs* 64 TF2438
Bicker Gauntlet *Lincs* 64 TF2139
Bickershaw *Gt Man* 79 SD6201
Bickerstaffe *Lancs* 78 SD4404
Bickerton *Ches* 71 SJ5052
Bickerton *Devon* 7 SX8139
Bickerton *N York* 83 SE4550
Bickerton *Nthumb* 103 NT9900
Bickford *Staffs* 60 SJ8814
Bickington *Devon* 19 SS5332
Bickington *Devon* 7 SX8072
Bickleigh *Devon* 9 SS9407
Bickleigh *Devon* 6 SX5262
Bickleton *Devon* 19 SS5030
Bickley *Ches* 71 SJ5348
Bickley *Gt Lon* 27 TQ4268
Bickley *H & W* 47 SO6371
Bickley *N York* 91 SE9191
Bickley Moss *Ches* 71 SJ5448
Bicknacre *Essex* 40 TL7802
Bicknoller *Somset* 20 ST1139
Bicknor *Kent* 28 TQ8658
Bickton *Hants* 12 SU1412
Bicton *H & W* 46 SO4764
Bicton *Shrops* 59 SJ4415
Bicton *Shrops* 59 SO2983
Bidborough *Kent* 16 TQ5643
Bidden *Hants* 24 SU7049
Biddenden *Kent* 28 TQ8538
Biddenden Green *Kent* 28 TQ8842
Biddenham *Beds* 38 TL0250
Biddestone *Wilts* 35 ST8673
Biddisham *Somset* 21 ST3853
Biddlesden *Bucks* 49 SP6340
Biddlestone *Nthumb* 111 NT9508
Biddulph *Staffs* 72 SJ8858
Biddulph Moor *Staffs* 72 SJ9058
Bideford *Devon* 18 SS4526
Bidford-on-Avon *Warwks* 48 SP1052
Bidston *Mersyd* 78 SJ2890
Bielby *Humb* 84 SE7843
Bieldside *Gramp* 135 NJ8702
Bierley *IOW* 13 SZ5078
Bierton *Bucks* 38 SP8415
Big Balcraig *D & G* 99 NX3843
Big Carlae *D & G* 107 NX6597
Big Sand *Highld* 144 NG7578
Bigbury *Devon* 7 SX6646
Bigbury-on-Sea *Devon* 7 SX6544
Bigby *Lincs* 84 TA0507
Biggar *Cumb* 86 SD1966
Biggar *Strath* 108 NT0437
Biggin *Derbys* 74 SK1559
Biggin *Derbys* 73 SK2549
Biggin *N York* 83 SE5434
Biggin Hill *Gt Lon* 27 TQ4159
Biggleswade *Beds* 39 TL1944
Bigholms *D & G* 101 NY3180
Bighouse *Highld* 150 NC8964
Bighton *Hants* 24 SU6134
Bigland Hall *Cumb* 87 SD3583
Biglands *Cumb* 93 NY2553
Bignor *W Susx* 14 SU9814
Bigrigg *Cumb* 92 NY0013
Bilborough *Notts* 62 SK5241
Bilbrook *Somset* 20 ST0341
Bilbrook *Staffs* 60 SJ8703
Bilbrough *N York* 83 SE5346
Bilbster *Highld* 151 ND2853
Bildershaw *Dur* 96 NZ2024
Bildeston *Suffk* 54 TL9949
Billacott *Cnwll* 5 SX2690
Billericay *Essex* 40 TQ6794
Billesdon *Leics* 63 SK7202
Billesley *Warwks* 48 SP1456
Billingborough *Lincs* 64 TF1133
Billinge *Mersyd* 78 SD5200
Billingford *Norfk* 66 TG0120
Billingford *Norfk* 54 TM1678
Billingham *Cleve* 97 NZ4624
Billinghay *Lincs* 76 TF1554
Billingley *S York* 83 SE4304
Billingshurst *W Susx* 14 TQ0825
Billingsley *Shrops* 60 SO7085
Billington *Beds* 38 SP9422
Billington *Lancs* 81 SD7235
Billington *Staffs* 72 SJ8820
Billockby *Norfk* 67 TG4313
Billy Row *Dur* 96 NZ1637
Bilsborrow *Lancs* 80 SD5139
Bilsby *Lincs* 77 TF4776
Bilsham *W Susx* 14 SU9702
Bilsington *Kent* 17 TR0434
Bilsthorpe *Notts* 75 SK6460
Bilsthorpe Moor *Notts* 75 SK6560
Bilston *Loth* 117 NT2664
Bilston *W Mids* 60 SO9596
Bilstone *Leics* 62 SK3605
Bilting *Kent* 28 TR0549
Bilton *Humb* 85 TA1632
Bilton *N York* 83 SE4749
Bilton *Nthumb* 111 NU2210
Bilton *Warwks* 50 SP4873
Bilton Banks *Nthumb* 111 NU2010
Binbrook *Lincs* 76 TF2093
Binchester Blocks *Dur* 96 NZ2232
Bincombe *Dorset* 11 SY6884
Binegar *Somset* 21 ST6149
Bines Green *W Susx* 15 TQ1817
Binfield *Berks* 25 SU8471
Binfield Heath *Oxon* 37 SU7477
Bingfield *Nthumb* 102 NY9772
Bingham *Notts* 63 SK7039
Bingham's Melcombe *Dorset* 11 ST7702
Bingley *W York* 82 SE1039
Bings *Shrops* 59 SJ5318
Binham *Norfk* 66 TF9839
Binley *Hants* 24 SU4253
Binley *W Mids* 61 SP3778
Binnegar *Dorset* 11 SY8887
Binniehill *Cent* 116 NS8572
Binns Farm *Gramp* 141 NJ3164
Binscombe *Surrey* 25 SU9645
Binsey *Oxon* 37 SP4907
Binstead *Hants* 25 SU7740
Binstead *IOW* 13 SZ5892
Binsted *W Susx* 14 SU9806
Binton *Warwks* 48 SP1454
Bintree *Norfk* 66 TG0123
Binweston *Shrops* 59 SJ3004
Birch *Essex* 41 TL9419
Birch *Gt Man* 79 SD8507
Birch Close *Dorset* 11 ST8803
Birch Cross *Staffs* 73 SK1230
Birch Green *Essex* 40 TL9418
Birch Green *Herts* 39 TL2911
Birch Heath *Ches* 71 SJ5461
Birch Hill *Ches* 71 SJ5173
Birch Vale *Derbys* 74 SK0286
Birch Wood *Somset* 9 ST2414
Bircham Newton *Norfk* 65 TF7733
Bircham Tofts *Norfk* 65 TF7732
Birchanger *Essex* 39 TL5122
Birchencliffe *W York* 82 SE1218
Bircher *H & W* 46 SO4765
Birchfield *W Mids* 61 SP0790
Birchgrove *E Susx* 15 TQ4029
Birchgrove *S Glam* 33 ST1679
Birchgrove *W Glam* 32 SS7098
Birchington *Kent* 29 TR3069
Birchley Heath *Warwks* 61 SP2894
Birchmoor Green *Beds* 38 SP9534
Birchover *Derbys* 74 SK2362
Birchyfield *H & W* 47 SO6453
Bircotes *Notts* 75 SK6391
Bird End *W Mids* 60 SP0194
Bird Street *Suffk* 54 TM0052
Birdbrook *Essex* 53 TL7041
Birdforth *N York* 90 SE4875
Birdham *W Susx* 14 SU8200
Birdingbury *Warwks* 50 SP4368
Birdlip *Glouc*s 35 SO9214
Birdoswald *Cumb* 102 NY6166
Birds Edge *W York* 82 SE2007
Birds Green *Essex* 40 TL5808
Birdsall *N York* 90 SE8165
Birdsgreen *Shrops* 60 SO7785
Birdsmoorgate *Dorset* 10 ST3900
Birdwell *S York* 83 SE3401
Birdwood *Glouc*s 35 SO7418
Birgham *Border* 110 NT7939
Birichin *Highld* 147 NH7592
Birkacre *Lancs* 81 SD5714
Birkby *N York* 89 NZ3202
Birkdale *Mersyd* 80 SD3214
Birkenbog *Gramp* 142 NJ5365
Birkenhead *Mersyd* 78 SJ3288
Birkenhills *Gramp* 142 NJ7445
Birkenshaw *W York* 82 SE2028
Birkhall *Gramp* 134 NO3493
Birkhill *D & G* 109 NT2015
Birkhill *Tays* 126 NO3534
Birkholme *Lincs* 63 SK9623
Birkin *N York* 83 SE5326
Birks *W York* 82 SE2626
Birkshaw *Nthumb* 102 NY7765
Birley *H & W* 46 SO4553
Birley Carr *S York* 74 SK3392
Birling *Kent* 28 TQ6860
Birling *Nthumb* 111 NU2406
Birling Gap *E Susx* 16 TV5596
Birlingham *H & W* 47 SO9343
Birmingham *W Mids* 61 SP0786
Birnam *Tays* 125 NO0341
Birness *Gramp* 143 NJ9933
Birse *Gramp* 134 NO5697
Birsemore *Gramp* 134 NO5297
Birstall *Leics* 62 SK5909
Birstall *W York* 82 SE2225
Birstwith *N York* 89 SE2359
Birthorpe *Lincs* 64 TF1033
Birtley *H & W* 46 SO3669
Birtley *Nthumb* 102 NY8778
Birtley *T & W* 96 NZ2756
Birts Street *H & W* 47 SO7836
Bisbrooke *Leics* 51 SP8899
Biscathorpe *Lincs* 76 TF2284
Biscovey *Cnwll* 3 SX0552
Bish Mill *Devon* 19 SS7425
Bisham *Berks* 26 SU8485
Bishampton *H & W* 47 SO9951
Bishop Auckland *Dur* 96 NZ2028
Bishop Burton *Humb* 84 SE9839
Bishop Middleham *Dur* 96 NZ3231
Bishop Monkton *N York* 89 SE3266
Bishop Norton *Lincs* 76 SK9892
Bishop Sutton *Avon* 21 ST5859
Bishop Thornton *N York* 89 SE2563
Bishop Wilton *Humb* 84 SE7955
Bishop's Castle *Shrops* 59 SO3288
Bishop's Cleeve *Glouc*s 47 SO9627
Bishop's Frome *H & W* 47 SO6648
Bishop's Green *Essex* 40 TL6217
Bishop's Green *Hants* 24 SU5063
Bishop's Itchington *Warwks* 48 SP3857
Bishop's Norton *Glouc*s 47 SO8424
Bishop's Nympton *Devon* 19 SS7523
Bishop's Offley *Staffs* 72 SJ7729
Bishop's Stortford *Herts* 39 TL4821
Bishop's Sutton *Hants* 24 SU6032
Bishop's Tachbrook *Warwks* 48 SP3161
Bishop's Tawton *Devon* 19 SS5729
Bishop's Waltham *Hants* 13 SU5517
Bishop's Wood *Staffs* 60 SJ8309
Bishop's Caundle *Dorset* 11 ST6913
Bishopbridge *Lincs* 76 TF0391
Bishopbriggs *Strath* 116 NS6070
Bishops Cannings *Wilts* 23 SU0364
Bishops Gate *Surrey* 25 SU9871
Bishops Hull *Somset* 20 ST2024
Bishops Lydeard *Somset* 20 ST1729
Bishopsbourne *Kent* 29 TR1852
Bishopsteignton *Devon* 7 SX9073
Bishopstoke *Hants* 13 SU4619
Bishopston *W Glam* 32 SS5789
Bishopstone *Bucks* 38 SP8010
Bishopstone *E Susx* 16 TQ4701
Bishopstone *H & W* 46 SO4143
Bishopstone *Kent* 26 TQ2068
Bishopstone *Wilts* 23 SU0625
Bishopstone *Wilts* 36 SU2483
Bishopstrow *Wilts* 22 ST8943
Bishopswood *Somset* 10 ST2612
Bishopsworth *Avon* 21 ST5768
Bishopthorpe *N York* 83 SE5947
Bishopton *Dur* 96 NZ3621
Bishopton *Strath* 115 NS4371
Bishopton *Warwks* 48 SP1956
Bishton *Gwent* 34 ST3887
Bishton *Staffs* 73 SK0220
Bisley *Glouc*s 35 SO9005
Bisley *Surrey* 25 SU9559
Bisley Camp *Surrey* 25 SU9357
Bispham *Lancs* 80 SD3140
Bispham Green *Lancs* 80 SD4813
Bissoe *Cnwll* 3 SW7741
Bisterne *Hants* 12 SU1401
Bitchet Green *Kent* 27 TQ5654
Bitchfield *Lincs* 63 SK9828
Bittadon *Devon* 19 SS5441
Bittaford *Devon* 7 SX6656
Bittering *Norfk* 66 TF9417
Bitterley *Shrops* 46 SO5677
Bitterne *Hants* 13 SU4513
Bitteswell *Leics* 50 SP5385
Bitton *Avon* 35 ST6869
Bix *Oxon* 37 SU7284
Blaby *Leics* 50 SP5697
Black Bourton *Oxon* 36 SP2804
Black Callerton *T & W* 103 NZ1769
Black Car *Norfk* 66 TM0995
Black Corner *W Susx* 15 TQ2939
Black Corries *Highld* 123 NN2956
Black Crofts *Strath* 122 NM9234
Black Cross *Cnwll* 4 SW9060
Black Dog *Devon* 19 SS8009
Black Heddon *Nthumb* 103 NZ0775
Black Lane *Gt Man* 79 SD7708
Black Lane Ends *Lancs* 81 SD9243
Black Moor *W York* 82 SE2939
Black Notley *Essex* 40 TL7620
Black Street *Suffk* 55 TM5186
Black Tar *Dyfed* 30 SM9909
Black Torrington *Devon* 18 SS4605
Blackadder *Border* 119 NT8452
Blackawton *Devon* 7 SX8051
Blackbank *Warwks* 61 SP3586
Blackbeck *Cumb* 86 NY0207
Blackborough *Devon* 9 ST0909
Blackborough End *Norfk* 65 TF6615
Blackboys *E Susx* 16 TQ5220
Blackbrook *Derbys* 62 SK3347
Blackbrook *Staffs* 72 SJ7638
Blackbrook *Surrey* 15 TQ1846
Blackburn *Gramp* 135 NJ8212
Blackburn *Lancs* 81 SD6827
Blackburn *Loth* 117 NS9865
Blackcraig *Strath* 107 NS6308
Blackden Heath *Ches* 79 SJ7871
Blackdog *Gramp* 135 NJ9513
Blackdown *Devon* 5 SX5079
Blackdown *Dorset* 10 ST3903
Blackdyke *Cumb* 92 NY1452
Blackenall Heath *W Mids* 60 SK0002
Blacker *S York* 83 SE3309
Blacker Hill *S York* 83 SE3602
Blackfield *Hants* 13 SU4402
Blackford *Cumb* 101 NY3961
Blackford *Somset* 21 ST4147
Blackford *Somset* 21 ST6526
Blackford *Tays* 125 NN8908
Blackford Bridge *Gt Man* 79 SD8007
Blackfordby *Leics* 62 SK3217
Blackgang *IOW* 13 SZ4876
Blackhall Colliery *Dur* 97 NZ4539
Blackhaugh *Border* 109 NT4238
Blackheath *Gt Lon* 27 TQ3876
Blackheath *Suffk* 55 TM4274
Blackheath *Surrey* 14 TQ0346
Blackheath *W Mids* 60 SO9786
Blackhill *Dur* 95 NZ0851
Blackhill *Gramp* 143 NK0039
Blackhill *Gramp* 143 NK0755
Blackhorse *Devon* 9 SX9893
Blackhorse Hill *E Susx* 17 TQ7714
Blackjack *Lincs* 64 TF2639
Blackland *Somset* 19 SS8336
Blackland *Wilts* 22 SU0168
Blacklaw *D & G* 108 NT0408
Blackley *Gt Man* 79 SD8502
Blacklunans *Tays* 133 NO1460
Blackmarstone *H & W* 46 SO5038
Blackmill *M Glam* 33 SS9386
Blackmoor *Avon* 21 ST4661
Blackmoor *Hants* 14 SU7733
Blackmoorfoot *W York* 82 SE0913
Blackmore *Essex* 40 TL6001
Blackmore End *Essex* 40 TL7430
Blackmore End *Herts* 39 TL1716
Blackness *Loth* 117 NT0579
Blacknest *Berks* 25 SU9568
Blacknest *Hants* 25 SU7941
Blacko *Lancs* 81 SD8541
Blackpark *D & G* 100 NX9281
Blackpill *W Glam* 32 SS6190
Blackpool *Devon* 7 SX8547
Blackpool *Devon* 7 SX8174
Blackpool *Lancs* 80 SD3036
Blackpool Gate *Cumb* 101 NY5377
Blackridge *Loth* 116 NS8967
Blackrock *Cnwll* 2 SW6534
Blackrock *Gwent* 33 SO2112
Blackrock *Gwent* 34 ST5188
Blackrod *Gt Man* 78 SD6110
Blacksboat *Gramp* 141 NJ1838
Blackshaw *D & G* 100 NY0465
Blackshaw Head *W York* 82 SD9527
Blacksmith's Green *Suffk* 54 TM1465
Blacksnape *Lancs* 81 SD7121
Blackstone *W Susx* 15 TQ2316
Blackthorn *Oxon* 37 SP6219
Blackthorpe *Suffk* 54 TL9063
Blacktoft *Humb* 84 SE8324
Blacktop *Gramp* 135 NJ8604
Blackwall *Derbys* 73 SK2548
Blackwater *Cnwll* 3 SW7346
Blackwater *Hants* 25 SU8459
Blackwater *IOW* 13 SZ5086
Blackwater *Somset* 10 ST2615
Blackwaterfoot *Strath* 105 NR9028
Blackwell *Cumb* 93 NY4053
Blackwell *Derbys* 74 SK1272
Blackwell *Derbys* 75 SK4458
Blackwell *Dur* 89 NZ2713
Blackwell *H & W* 60 SO9972
Blackwell *Warwks* 48 SP2443
Blackwellsend Green *Glouc*s 47 SO7825
Blackwood *D & G* 100 NX9087
Blackwood *Gwent* 33 ST1797
Blackwood *Strath* 116 NS7844
Blackwood Hill *Staffs* 72 SJ9255
Blacon *Ches* 71 SJ3868
Bladbean *Kent* 29 TR1847
Bladnoch *D & G* 99 NX4254
Bladon *Oxon* 37 SP4514
Bladon *Somset* 21 ST4220
Blaen Dyryn *Powys* 45 SN9336
Blaen-y-Coed *Dyfed* 31 SN3427
Blaen-y-cwm *Gwent* 33 SO1311
Blaen-y-cwm *M Glam* 33 SS9298
Blaenannerch *Dyfed* 42 SN2448
Blaenau Ffestiniog *Gwynd* 57 SH7045
Blaenavon *Gwent* 34 SO2508
Blaenawey *Gwent* 34 SO2919
Blaenffos *Dyfed* 31 SN1937
Blaengarw *M Glam* 33 SS9092
Blaengeuffardd *Dyfed* 43 SN6480
Blaengwrach *W Glam* 33 SN8605
Blaengwynfi *W Glam* 33 SS8996
Blaenllechau *M Glam* 33 ST0097
Blaenpennal *Dyfed* 43 SN6264
Blaenplwyf *Dyfed* 43 SN5775
Blaenporth *Dyfed* 42 SN2648
Blaenrhondda *M Glam* 33 SS9299
Blaenwaun *Dyfed* 31 SN2327
Blaenycwm *Dyfed* 43 SN8275
Blagdon *Avon* 21 ST5059
Blagdon *Devon* 7 SX8561
Blagdon *Somset* 20 ST2118
Blagdon Hill *Somset* 9 ST2117
Blagill *Cumb* 94 NY7347
Blaguegate *Lancs* 78 SD4506
Blaich *Highld* 130 NN0376
Blain *Highld* 129 NM6769
Blaina *Gwent* 33 SO2008
Blair Atholl *Tays* 132 NN8665
Blair Drummond *Cent* 116 NS7399
Blairgowrie *Tays* 126 NO1745
Blairingone *Fife* 117 NS9896
Blairlogie *Cent* 116 NS8396
Blairmore *Highld* 148 NC1959
Blairmore *Strath* 114 NS1983
Blairnamarrow *Gramp* 141 NJ2015
Blairs Ferry *Strath* 114 NR9869
Blaisdon *Glouc*s 35 SO7017
Blake End *Essex* 40 TL7023
Blakebrook *H & W* 60 SO8276
Blakedown *H & W* 60 SO8878
Blakeley Lane *Staffs* 72 SJ9746
Blakemere *Ches* 71 SJ5571
Blakemere *H & W* 46 SO3641
Blakemore *Devon* 7 SX7660
Blakeney *Glouc*s 35 SO6707
Blakeney *Norfk* 66 TG0243
Blakenhall *Ches* 72 SJ7247
Blakenhall *W Mids* 60 SO9197
Blakeshall *H & W* 60 SO8381
Blakesley *Nhants* 49 SP6250
Blanchland *Nthumb* 95 NY9650
Bland Hill *N York* 82 SE2053
Blandford Camp *Dorset* 11 ST9107
Blandford Forum *Dorset* 11 ST8806
Blandford St. Mary *Dorset* 11 ST8805
Blankney *Lincs* 76 TF0660
Blantyre *Strath* 116 NS6957
Blar a' Chaorainn *Highld* 130 NN1066
Blargie *Highld* 132 NN6094
Blarmachfoldach *Highld* 130 NN0969
Blashford *Hants* 12 SU1506
Blaston *Leics* 51 SP8095
Blatherwycke *Nhants* 51 SP9795
Blawith *Cumb* 86 SD2888
Blawquhairn *D & G* 99 NX6282
Blaxhall *Suffk* 55 TM3656
Blaxton *S York* 75 SE6700
Blaydon *T & W* 103 NZ1863
Bleadney *Somset* 21 ST4845
Bleadon *Somset* 21 ST3456
Bleak Street *Somset* 22 ST7631
Blean *Kent* 29 TR1260
Bleasby *Lincs* 75 SK7149
Bleasby *Lincs* 76 TF1384
Bleasdale *Lancs* 81 SD5745
Bleatarn *Cumb* 94 NY7313
Bleathwood *H & W* 46 SO5570
Blebocraigs *Fife* 127 NO4214
Bleddfa *Powys* 45 SO2068
Bledington *Glouc*s 36 SP2422
Bledlow *Bucks* 37 SP7702
Bledlow Ridge *Bucks* 37 SU7997
Bleet *Wilts* 22 ST8958
Blegbie *Loth* 118 NT4861
Blencarn *Cumb* 94 NY6331

Blencogo Braehead

Blencogo *Cumb*	**93**	NY1947
Blendworth *Hants*	**13**	SU7113
Blennerhasset *Cumb*	**93**	NY1741
Bletchingdon *Oxon*	**37**	SP5018
Bletchingley *Surrey*	**27**	TQ3250
Bletchley *Bucks*	**38**	SP8633
Bletchley *Shrops*	**59**	SJ6233
Bletherston *Dyfed*	**31**	SN0721
Bletsoe *Beds*	**51**	TL0258
Blewbury *Oxon*	**37**	SU5385
Blickling *Norfk*	**66**	TG1728
Blidworth *Notts*	**75**	SK5956
Blidworth Bottoms *Notts*	**75**	SK5954
Blindburn *Nthumb*	**110**	NT8210
Blindcrake *Cumb*	**92**	NY1434
Blindley Heath *Surrey*	**15**	TQ3645
Blisland *Cnwll*	**4**	SX1073
Bliss Gate *H & W*	**60**	SO7472
Blissford *Hants*	**12**	SU1713
Blisworth *Nhants*	**49**	SP7253
Blithbury *Staffs*	**73**	SK0819
Blitterlees *Cumb*	**92**	NY1052
Blo Norton *Norfk*	**54**	TM0179
Blockley *Gloucs*	**48**	SP1634
Blofield *Norfk*	**67**	TG3309
Bloomfield *Border*	**110**	NT5824
Blore *Staffs*	**72**	SJ7234
Blore *Staffs*	**73**	SK1349
Blounts Green *Staffs*	**73**	SK0732
Blowick *Mersyd*	**80**	SD3516
Bloxham *Oxon*	**49**	SP4336
Bloxwith *W Mids*	**60**	SJ9902
Bloxworth *Dorset*	**11**	SY8894
Blubberhouses *N York*	**82**	SE1655
Blue Anchor *Cnwll*	**4**	SW9157
Blue Anchor *Somset*	**20**	ST0243
Blue Bell Hill *Kent*	**28**	TQ7462
Blue Point *IOM*	**153**	NX3902
Blundellsands *Mersyd*	**78**	SJ3099
Blundeston *Suffk*	**67**	TM5297
Blunham *Beds*	**52**	TL1551
Blunsdon St. Andrew *Wilts*	**36**	SU1389
Bluntington *H & W*	**60**	SO9074
Bluntisham *Cambs*	**52**	TL3674
Blunts *Cnwll*	**5**	SX3463
Blunts Green *Warwks*	**48**	SP1468
Blurton *Staffs*	**72**	SJ8941
Blyborough *Lincs*	**76**	SK9394
Blyford *Suffk*	**55**	TM4276
Blymhill *Staffs*	**60**	SJ8112
Blymhill Lawn *Staffs*	**60**	SJ8211
Blyth *Notts*	**75**	SK6287
Blyth *Nthumb*	**103**	NZ3181
Blyth Bridge *Border*	**117**	NT1345
Blythburgh *Suffk*	**55**	TM4475
Blythe *Border*	**110**	NT5849
Blythe Bridge *Staffs*	**72**	SJ9541
Blythe End *Warwks*	**61**	SP2190
Blyton *Lincs*	**76**	SK8594
Bo'Ness *Cent*	**117**	NT0081
Boar's Head *Gt Man*	**78**	SD5708
Boarhills *Fife*	**127**	NO5613
Boarhunt *Hants*	**13**	SU6008
Boarley *Kent*	**28**	TQ7659
Boars Hill *Oxon*	**37**	SP4902
Boarsgreave *Lancs*	**81**	SD8420
Boarshead *E Susx*	**16**	TQ5332
Boarstall *Bucks*	**37**	SP6214
Boasley Cross *Devon*	**5**	SX5093
Boat of Garten *Highld*	**140**	NH9319
Boath *Highld*	**146**	NH5774
Bobbing *Kent*	**28**	TQ8865
Bobbington *Staffs*	**60**	SO8090
Bobbingworth *Essex*	**39**	TL5305
Bocaddon *Cnwll*	**4**	SX1858
Bochym *Cnwll*	**2**	SW6920
Bocking *Essex*	**40**	TL7623
Bocking Churchstreet *Essex*	**40**	TL7525
Bockleton *H & W*	**46**	SO5961
Boconnoc *Cnwll*	**4**	SX1460
Boddam *Gramp*	**143**	NK1342
Boddam *Shet*	**155**	HU3915
Boddington *Gloucs*	**47**	SO8925
Bodedern *Gwynd*	**68**	SH3380
Bodelwyddan *Clwyd*	**70**	SJ0075
Bodenham *H & W*	**46**	SO5350
Bodenham *Wilts*	**23**	SU1626
Bodenham Moor *H & W*	**46**	SO5450
Bodewryd *Gwynd*	**68**	SH4090
Bodfari *Clwyd*	**70**	SJ0970
Bodffordd *Gwynd*	**68**	SH4277
Bodfuan *Gwynd*	**56**	SH3237
Bodham Street *Norfk*	**66**	TG1240
Bodiam *E Susx*	**17**	TQ7825
Bodicote *Oxon*	**49**	SP4538
Bodieve *Cnwll*	**4**	SW9973
Bodinnick *Cnwll*	**3**	SX1352
Bodle Street Green *E Susx*	**16**	TQ6514
Bodmin *Cnwll*	**4**	SX0667
Bodney *Norfk*	**66**	TL8298
Bodorgan *Gwynd*	**68**	SH3867
Bodrean *Cnwll*	**3**	SW8448
Bodsham Green *Kent*	**29**	TR1045
Bodwen *Cnwll*	**4**	SX0360
Bodymoor Heath *Warwks*	**61**	SP1996
Bogallan *Highld*	**140**	NH6350
Bogbrae *Gramp*	**143**	NK0335
Boghall *Loth*	**117**	NS9867
Boghall *Loth*	**117**	NT2465
Boghead *Strath*	**107**	NS7742
Boghead Farm *Gramp*	**141**	NJ3559
Boghole *Highld*	**140**	NH9655
Bogmoor *Gramp*	**141**	NJ3563
Bogmuir *Gramp*	**135**	NO6471
Bogniebrae *Gramp*	**142**	NJ5945
Bognor Regis *W Susx*	**14**	SZ9399
Bogroy *Highld*	**140**	NH9022
Bogue *D & G*	**99**	NX6481
Bohetherick *Devon*	**5**	SX4167
Bohortha *Cnwll*	**3**	SW8532
Bohuntine *Highld*	**133**	NN9983
Bojewyan *Cnwll*	**2**	SW3934
Bokiddick *Cnwll*	**4**	SX0562
Bolam *Dur*	**96**	NZ1922
Bolam *Nthumb*	**103**	NZ1082
Bolberry *Devon*	**7**	SX6939
Bold Heath *Mersyd*	**78**	SJ5389
Boldmere *W Mids*	**61**	SP1194
Boldon *T & W*	**96**	NZ3461
Boldon Colliery *T & W*	**96**	NZ3462
Boldre *Hants*	**12**	SZ3198
Boldron *Dur*	**95**	NZ0314
Bole *Notts*	**75**	SK7987
Bole Hill *Derbys*	**74**	SK3374
Bolehill *Derbys*	**73**	SK2955
Bolenowe *Cnwll*	**2**	SW6738
Bolfracks *Tays*	**125**	NN8248
Bolham *Devon*	**9**	SS9515
Bolham Water *Devon*	**9**	ST1612
Bolingey *Cnwll*	**3**	SW7653
Bollington *Ches*	**79**	SJ7286
Bollington *Ches*	**79**	SJ9377
Bollington Cross *Ches*	**79**	SJ9277
Bollow *Gloucs*	**35**	SO7413
Bolney *W Susx*	**15**	TQ2622
Bolnhurst *Beds*	**51**	TL0859
Bolshan *Tays*	**127**	NO6252
Bolsover *Derbys*	**75**	SK4770
Bolster Moor *W York*	**82**	SE0815
Bolsterstone *S York*	**74**	SK2696
Boltby *N York*	**90**	SE4886
Boltenstone *Gramp*	**134**	NJ4110
Bolter End *Bucks*	**37**	SU7992
Bolton *Cumb*	**94**	NY6323
Bolton *Gt Man*	**79**	SD7108
Bolton *Humb*	**84**	SE7752
Bolton *Loth*	**118**	NT5070
Bolton *Nthumb*	**111**	NU1013
Bolton Abbey *N York*	**82**	SE0754
Bolton Bridge *N York*	**82**	SE0653
Bolton by Bowland *Lancs*	**81**	SD7849
Bolton Hall *N York*	**88**	SE0789
Bolton Low Houses *Cumb*	**93**	NY2344
Bolton le Sands *Lancs*	**87**	SD4867
Bolton New Houses *Cumb*	**93**	NY2444
Bolton Percy *N York*	**83**	SE5341
Bolton Town End *Lancs*	**87**	SD4867
Bolton Upon Dearne *S York*	**83**	SE4502
Bolton-on-Swale *N York*	**89**	SE2599
Boltonfellend *Cumb*	**101**	NY4768
Boltongate *Cumb*	**93**	NY2340
Bolventor *Cnwll*	**4**	SX1876
Bomere Heath *Shrops*	**59**	SJ4719
Bonar Bridge *Highld*	**146**	NH6191
Bonawe *Strath*	**122**	NN0131
Bonawe Quarries *Strath*	**122**	NN0033
Bonby *Humb*	**84**	TA0015
Boncath *Dyfed*	**31**	SN2038
Bonchester Bridge *Border*	**110**	NT5812
Bonchurch *IOW*	**13**	SZ5778
Bond's Green *H & W*	**46**	SO3554
Bondleigh *Devon*	**8**	SS6505
Bonds *Lancs*	**80**	SD4944
Bone *Cnwll*	**2**	SW4632
Bonehill *Staffs*	**61**	SK1902
Boney Hay *Staffs*	**61**	SK0410
Bonhill *Strath*	**115**	NS3979
Boningale *Shrops*	**60**	SJ8202
Bonjedward *Border*	**110**	NT6522
Bonnington *Kent*	**17**	TR0535
Bonnington *Loth*	**117**	NT1269
Bonnington *Tays*	**127**	NO5739
Bonnybridge *Cent*	**116**	NS8279
Bonnykelly *Gramp*	**143**	NJ8653
Bonnyrigg *Loth*	**117**	NT3065
Bonnyton *Tays*	**126**	NO3338
Bonsall *Derbys*	**74**	SK2758
Bonshaw Tower *D & G*	**101**	NY2472
Bont *Gwent*	**34**	SO3819
Bont-Dolgadfan *Powys*	**57**	SH8800
Bontddu *Gwynd*	**57**	SH6718
Bonthorpe *Lincs*	**77**	TF4872
Bontnewydd *Dyfed*	**43**	SN6165
Bontnewydd *Gwynd*	**68**	SH4859
Bontuchel *Clwyd*	**70**	SJ0857
Bonvilston *S Glam*	**33**	ST0673
Bonwm *Clwyd*	**70**	SJ1042
Bonymaen *W Glam*	**32**	SS6795
Boode *Devon*	**19**	SS5037
Boohay *Devon*	**7**	SX8952
Booker *Bucks*	**37**	SU8391
Booley *Shrops*	**59**	SJ5625
Boon Hill *Staffs*	**72**	SJ8150
Boorley Green *Hants*	**13**	SU5014
Boosbeck *Cleve*	**97**	NZ6617
Boose's Green *Essex*	**40**	TL8431
Boot *Cnwll*	**5**	SX2697
Boot *Cumb*	**86**	NY1700
Booth *Humb*	**84**	SE7326
Booth *W York*	**82**	SE0427
Booth Green *Ches*	**79**	SJ9280
Booth Town *W York*	**82**	SE0926
Boothby Graffoe *Lincs*	**76**	SK9859
Boothby Pagnell *Lincs*	**63**	SK9730
Boothstown *Gt Man*	**79**	SD7200
Boothville *Nhants*	**50**	SP7864
Bootle *Cumb*	**86**	SD1088
Bootle *Mersyd*	**78**	SJ3495
Boots Green *Ches*	**79**	SJ7572
Booze *N York*	**88**	NZ0102
Boquhan *Cent*	**115**	NS5387
Boraston *Shrops*	**46**	SO6169
Bordeaux *Guern*	**152**	GN5512
Borden *Kent*	**28**	TQ8862
Borden *W Susx*	**14**	SU8324
Border *Cumb*	**92**	NY1654
Bordley *N York*	**88**	SD9465
Bordon *Hants*	**14**	SU8035
Bordon Camp *Hants*	**14**	SU7936
Boreham *Essex*	**40**	TL7609
Boreham *Wilts*	**22**	ST8944
Boreham Street *E Susx*	**16**	TQ6611
Borehamwood *Herts*	**26**	TQ1996
Boreland *D & G*	**100**	NY1691
Boreraig *Highld*	**136**	NG1853
Boreston *Devon*	**7**	SX7653
Boreton *Ches*	**59**	SJ5106
Borgie *Highld*	**149**	NC6759
Borgue *D & G*	**99**	NX6248
Borgue *Highld*	**151**	ND1326
Borley *Essex*	**54**	TL8443
Borley Green *Essex*	**54**	TL8442
Borley Green *Suffk*	**54**	TL9960
Borneskitaig *Highld*	**136**	NG3770
Borness *D & G*	**99**	NX6145
Borough Green *Kent*	**27**	TQ6157
Boroughbridge *N York*	**89**	SE3966
Borras Head *Clwyd*	**71**	SJ3653
Borrowash *Derbys*	**62**	SK4234
Borrowby *N York*	**97**	NZ7715
Borrowby *N York*	**89**	SE4289
Borrowdale *Cumb*	**93**	NY2514
Borrowstoun *Cent*	**117**	NS9980
Borstal *Kent*	**28**	TQ7366
Borth *Dyfed*	**43**	SN6090
Borth-y-Gest *Gwynd*	**57**	SH5637
Borthwick *Loth*	**118**	NT3659
Borthwickbrae *Border*	**109**	NT4113
Borthwickshiels *Border*	**109**	NT4315
Borve *Highld*	**136**	NG4448
Borve *W Isls*	**154**	NB4055
Borve *W Isls*	**154**	NF6501
Borwick *Lancs*	**87**	SD5272
Borwick Lodge *Cumb*	**87**	SD3499
Borwick Rails *Cumb*	**86**	SD1879
Bosavern *Cnwll*	**2**	SW3730
Bosbury *H & W*	**47**	SO6943
Boscarne *Cnwll*	**4**	SX0367
Boscastle *Cnwll*	**4**	SX0990
Boscombe *Dorset*	**12**	SZ1191
Boscombe *Wilts*	**23**	SU2038
Boscoppa *Cnwll*	**3**	SX0353
Bosham *W Susx*	**14**	SU8003
Bosham Hoe *W Susx*	**14**	SU8102
Bosherston *Dyfed*	**30**	SR9694
Boskednan *Cnwll*	**2**	SW4434
Boskennal *Cnwll*	**2**	SW4223
Bosley *Ches*	**72**	SJ9165
Bosoughan *Cnwll*	**4**	SW8760
Bossall *N York*	**90**	SE7160
Bossiney *Cnwll*	**4**	SX0688
Bossingham *Kent*	**29**	TR1548
Bossington *Somset*	**19**	SS8947
Bostock Green *Ches*	**79**	SJ6769
Boston *Lincs*	**64**	TF3343
Boston Spa *W York*	**83**	SE4245
Boswarthan *Cnwll*	**2**	SW4433
Boswinger *Cnwll*	**3**	SW9841
Botallack *Cnwll*	**2**	SW3732
Botany Bay *Gt Lon*	**27**	TQ2999
Botcheston *Leics*	**62**	SK4804
Botesdale *Suffk*	**54**	TM0475
Bothal *Nthumb*	**103**	NZ2386
Bothampstead *Berks*	**37**	SU5076
Bothamsall *Notts*	**75**	SK6773
Bothel *Cumb*	**93**	NY1838
Bothenhampton *Dorset*	**10**	SY4791
Bothwell *Strath*	**116**	NS7058
Botley *Bucks*	**26**	SP9802
Botley *Hants*	**13**	SU5113
Botley *Oxon*	**37**	SP4806
Botolph Claydon *Bucks*	**49**	SP7324
Botolph's Bridge *Kent*	**17**	TR1233
Botolphs *W Susx*	**15**	TQ1909
Bottesford *Humb*	**84**	SE8906
Bottesford *Leics*	**63**	SK8038
Bottisham *Cambs*	**53**	TL5460
Bottom o' th' Moor *Gt Man*	**81**	SD6511
Bottom of Hutton *Lancs*	**80**	SD4827
Bottomcraig *Fife*	**126**	NO3724
Bottoms *Cnwll*	**2**	SW3824
Bottoms *W York*	**81**	SD9321
Botts Green *Warwks*	**61**	SP2492
Botusfleming *Cnwll*	**5**	SX4061
Botwnnog *Gwynd*	**56**	SH2631
Bough Beech *Kent*	**16**	TQ4847
Boughrood *Powys*	**45**	SO1239
Boughspring *Gloucs*	**34**	ST5597
Boughton *Cambs*	**52**	TL1965
Boughton *Nhants*	**50**	SP7565
Boughton *Norfk*	**65**	TF7002
Boughton *Notts*	**75**	SK6768
Boughton Aluph *Kent*	**28**	TR0348
Boughton End *Beds*	**38**	SP9838
Boughton Green *Kent*	**28**	TQ7650
Boughton Lees *Kent*	**28**	TR0246
Boughton Malherbe *Kent*	**28**	TQ8849
Boughton Monchelsea *Kent*	**28**	TQ7749
Boughton Street *Kent*	**28**	TR0559
Boulby *Cleve*	**97**	NZ7618
Boulder Clough *W York*	**82**	SE0323
Bouldnor *IOW*	**12**	SZ3789
Bouldon *Shrops*	**59**	SO5485
Boulge *Suffk*	**55**	TM2552
Boulmer *Nthumb*	**111**	NU2614
Boulston *Dyfed*	**30**	SM9712
Boultham *Lincs*	**76**	SK9669
Bourn *Cambs*	**52**	TL3256
Bourne *Lincs*	**64**	TF0920
Bourne End *Beds*	**38**	SP9644
Bourne End *Beds*	**51**	TL0160
Bourne End *Bucks*	**26**	SU8987
Bourne End *Herts*	**38**	TL0206
Bournebridge *Essex*	**27**	TQ5094
Bournebrook *W Mids*	**61**	SP0483
Bournemouth *Dorset*	**12**	SZ0890
Bournes Green *Essex*	**40**	TQ9186
Bournes Green *Gloucs*	**35**	SO9104
Bournheath *H & W*	**60**	SO9574
Bournmoor *T & W*	**96**	NZ3150
Bournstream *Gloucs*	**35**	ST7494
Bournville *W Mids*	**61**	SP0481
Bourton *Avon*	**21**	ST3864
Bourton *Dorset*	**22**	ST7630
Bourton *Oxon*	**36**	SU2386
Bourton *Shrops*	**59**	SO5996
Bourton *Wilts*	**23**	SU0464
Bourton on Dunsmore *Warwks*	**50**	SP4370
Bourton-on-the- Hill *Gloucs*	**48**	SP1732
Bourton-on-the-Water *Gloucs*	**36**	SP1620
Bousd *Strath*	**120**	NM2563
Boustead Hill *Cumb*	**93**	NY2959
Bouth *Cumb*	**86**	SD3285
Bouthwaite *N York*	**89**	SE1271
Bouts *H & W*	**48**	SP0359
Bovain *Cent*	**124**	NN5430
Boveney *Berks*	**26**	SU9377
Boveridge *Dorset*	**12**	SU0514
Bovey Tracey *Devon*	**8**	SX8178
Bovingdon *Herts*	**38**	TL0103
Bovingdon Green *Bucks*	**37**	SU8386
Bovinger *Essex*	**39**	TL5205
Bovington Camp *Dorset*	**11**	SY8389
Bow *Cumb*	**93**	NY3356
Bow *Devon*	**8**	SS7201
Bow *Devon*	**7**	SX8156
Bow *Ork*	**155**	ND3693
Bow Brickhill *Bucks*	**38**	SP9034
Bow of Fife *Fife*	**126**	NO3212
Bow Street *Dyfed*	**43**	SN6285
Bow Street *Norfk*	**66**	TM0198
Bowbank *Dur*	**95**	NY9423
Bowbridge *Gloucs*	**35**	SO8505
Bowburn *Dur*	**96**	NZ3037
Bowcombe *IOW*	**13**	SZ4786
Bowd *Devon*	**9**	SY1090
Bowden *Border*	**109**	NT5530
Bowden *Devon*	**7**	SX8449
Bowden Hill *Wilts*	**22**	ST9367
Bowdon *Gt Man*	**79**	SJ7686
Bower *Highld*	**151**	ND2362
Bower Ashton *Avon*	**34**	ST5671
Bower Hinton *Somset*	**10**	ST4517
Bower House Tye *Suffk*	**54**	TL9840
Bower's Row *W York*	**83**	SE4028
Bowerchalke *Wilts*	**23**	SU0223
Bowerhill *Wilts*	**22**	ST9162
Bowermadden *Highld*	**151**	ND2464
Bowers *Staffs*	**72**	SJ8135
Bowers Gifford *Essex*	**40**	TQ7588
Bowershall *Fife*	**117**	NT0991
Bowes *Dur*	**95**	NY9913
Bowgreave *Lancs*	**80**	SD4943
Bowhill *Border*	**109**	NT4227
Bowhouse *D & G*	**100**	NY0165
Bowithick *Cnwll*	**4**	SX1882
Bowker's Green *Lancs*	**78**	SD4004
Bowland *Border*	**109**	NT4540
Bowland Bridge *Cumb*	**87**	SD4189
Bowlee *Gt Man*	**79**	SD8406
Bowley *H & W*	**46**	SO5452
Bowley Town *H & W*	**46**	SO5352
Bowlhead Green *Surrey*	**25**	SU9138
Bowling *Strath*	**115**	NS4373
Bowling *W York*	**82**	SE1731
Bowling Bank *Clwyd*	**71**	SJ3948
Bowling Green *H & W*	**47**	SO8251
Bowmanstead *Cumb*	**86**	SD3096
Bowmore *Strath*	**112**	NR3159
Bowness-on-Solway *Cumb*	**101**	NY2262
Bowness-on-Windermere *Cumb*	**87**	SD4097
Bowscale *Cumb*	**93**	NY3531
Bowsden *Nthumb*	**111**	NT9941
Bowthorpe *Norfk*	**66**	TG1709
Box *Gloucs*	**35**	SO8600
Box *Wilts*	**22**	ST8268
Box End *Beds*	**38**	TL0049
Box Hill *Surrey*	**26**	TQ1951
Box's Shop *Cnwll*	**18**	SS2101
Boxbush *Gloucs*	**35**	SO6720
Boxbush *Gloucs*	**35**	SO7413
Boxford *Berks*	**24**	SU4271
Boxford *Suffk*	**54**	TL9640
Boxgrove *W Susx*	**14**	SU9007
Boxholme *Lincs*	**76**	TF0653
Boxley *Kent*	**28**	TQ7758
Boxmoor *Herts*	**38**	TL0406
Boxted *Essex*	**41**	TL9933
Boxted *Suffk*	**54**	TL8251
Boxted Cross *Essex*	**41**	TM0032
Boxted Heath *Essex*	**41**	TM0031
Boxwell *Gloucs*	**35**	ST8192
Boxworth *Cambs*	**52**	TL3464
Boxworth End *Cambs*	**52**	TL3667
Boyden End *Suffk*	**53**	TL7355
Boyden Gate *Kent*	**29**	TR2265
Boylestone *Derbys*	**73**	SK1835
Boyndie *Gramp*	**142**	NJ6463
Boyndlie *Gramp*	**143**	NJ9162
Boynton *Humb*	**91**	TA1367
Boys Hill *Dorset*	**11**	ST6710
Boysack *Tays*	**127**	NO6249
Boythorpe *Derbys*	**74**	SK3869
Boyton *Cnwll*	**5**	SX3292
Boyton *Suffk*	**55**	TM3747
Boyton *Wilts*	**22**	ST9539
Boyton Cross *Essex*	**40**	TL6409
Boyton End *Suffk*	**53**	TL7244
Bozeat *Nhants*	**51**	SP9058
Braaid *IOM*	**153**	SC3276
Brabling Green *Suffk*	**55**	TM2964
Brabourne *Kent*	**29**	TR1041
Brabourne Lees *Kent*	**29**	TR0840
Brabstermire *Highld*	**151**	ND3169
Bracadale *Highld*	**136**	NG3538
Braceborough *Lincs*	**64**	TF0713
Bracebridge Heath *Lincs*	**76**	SK9867
Bracebridge Low Fields *Lincs*	**76**	SK9666
Braceby *Lincs*	**64**	TF0135
Bracewell *Lancs*	**81**	SD8648
Brackenfield *Derbys*	**74**	SK3759
Brackenhurst *Strath*	**116**	NS7468
Brackenthwaite *Cumb*	**93**	NY2946
Brackenthwaite *N York*	**82**	SE2851
Bracklesham *W Susx*	**14**	SZ8096
Brackletter *Highld*	**131**	NN1882
Brackley *Nhants*	**49**	SP5837
Brackley Hatch *Nhants*	**49**	SP6441
Bracknell *Berks*	**25**	SU8769
Braco *Tays*	**125**	NN8309
Bracobrae *Gramp*	**142**	NJ5053
Bracon *Humb*	**84**	SE7807
Bracon Ash *Norfk*	**66**	TM1899
Bracora *Highld*	**129**	NM7192
Bracorina *Highld*	**129**	NM7292
Bradaford *Devon*	**5**	SX3994
Bradbourne *Derbys*	**73**	SK2052
Bradbury *Dur*	**96**	NZ3128
Bradden *Nhants*	**49**	SP6448
Braddock *Cnwll*	**4**	SX1662
Bradeley *Staffs*	**72**	SJ8851
Bradenham *Bucks*	**37**	SU8297
Bradenstoke *Wilts*	**35**	SU0079
Bradfield *Berks*	**24**	SU6072
Bradfield *Devon*	**9**	ST0509
Bradfield *Essex*	**41**	TM1430
Bradfield *Norfk*	**67**	TG2733
Bradfield *S York*	**74**	SK2692
Bradfield Combust *Suffk*	**54**	TL8957
Bradfield Green *Ches*	**72**	SJ6859
Bradfield Heath *Essex*	**41**	TM1430
Bradfield St. Clare *Suffk*	**54**	TL9057
Bradfield St. George *Suffk*	**54**	TL9059
Bradford *Cnwll*	**4**	SX1175
Bradford *Devon*	**18**	SS4207
Bradford *Nthumb*	**111**	NU1532
Bradford *Nthumb*	**103**	NZ0679
Bradford *W York*	**82**	SE1632
Bradford Abbas *Dorset*	**10**	ST5813
Bradford Leigh *Wilts*	**22**	ST8362
Bradford Peverell *Dorset*	**11**	SY6593
Bradford-on-Avon *Wilts*	**22**	ST8261
Bradford-on-Tone *Somset*	**20**	ST1722
Brading *IOW*	**13**	SZ6087
Bradley *Ches*	**71**	SJ5377
Bradley *Clwyd*	**71**	SJ3253
Bradley *Derbys*	**73**	SK2246
Bradley *H & W*	**47**	SO9860
Bradley *Hants*	**24**	SU6341
Bradley *Humb*	**85**	TA2406
Bradley *N York*	**88**	SE0380
Bradley *Staffs*	**72**	SJ8717
Bradley *W Mids*	**60**	SO9595
Bradley *W York*	**82**	SE1720
Bradley Green *Ches*	**71**	SJ5045
Bradley Green *H & W*	**47**	SO9862
Bradley Green *Somset*	**20**	ST2538
Bradley Green *Warwks*	**61**	SK2800
Bradley in the Moors *Staffs*	**73**	SK0541
Bradley Stoke *Avon*	**34**	ST6181
Bradmore *Notts*	**62**	SK5830
Bradney *Somset*	**21**	ST3338
Bradninch *Devon*	**19**	SS6133
Bradninch *Devon*	**9**	SS9904
Bradnop *Staffs*	**73**	SK0155
Bradnor Green *H & W*	**46**	SO2957
Bradpole *Dorset*	**10**	SY4894
Bradshaw *Gt Man*	**81**	SD7312
Bradshaw *W York*	**82**	SE0514
Bradshaw *W York*	**82**	SE0729
Bradstone *Devon*	**5**	SX3880
Bradwall Green *Ches*	**72**	SJ7563
Bradwell *Bucks*	**38**	SP8340
Bradwell *Derbys*	**74**	SK1781
Bradwell *Devon*	**19**	SS5042
Bradwell *Essex*	**40**	TL8122
Bradwell *Norfk*	**67**	TG5003
Bradwell Waterside *Essex*	**41**	TL9907
Bradwell-on-Sea *Essex*	**41**	TM0006
Bradworthy *Devon*	**18**	SS3214
Brae *Highld*	**140**	NH6662
Brae *Shet*	**155**	HU3568
Brae Roy Lodge *Highld*	**131**	NN3391
Braeface *Cent*	**116**	NS7880
Braegrum *Tays*	**125**	NO0025
Braehead *D & G*	**99**	NX4152
Braehead *Strath*	**117**	NS9550
Braehead *Tays*	**127**	NO6952

C

Carreglefn *Gwynd* 68 SH3889
Carrhouse *Humb* 84 SE7706
Carrick *Strath* 114 NR9086
Carrick Castle *Strath* 114 NS1994
Carriden *Cent* 117 NT0181
Carrington *Gt Man* 79 SJ7492
Carrington *Lincs* 77 TF3155
Carrington *Loth* 117 NT3160
Carrismerry *Cnwll* 4 SX0158
Carrog *Clwyd* 70 SJ1043
Carrog *Gwynd* 69 SH7647
Carron *Cent* 116 NS8882
Carron *Gramp* 141 NJ2241
Carron Bridge *Cent* 116 NS7483
Carronbridge *D & G* 100 NX8698
Carronshore *Cent* 116 NS8983
Carrow Hill *Gwent* 34 ST4390
Carruth House *Strath* 115 NS3566
Carrutherstown *D & G* 100 NY1071
Carrville *Dur* 96 NZ3043
Carrycoats Hall *Nthumb* 102 NY9279
Carsaig *Strath* 121 NM5421
Carscreugh *D & G* 98 NX2260
Carse Gray *Tays* 127 NO4553
Carseriggan *D & G* 98 NX3167
Carsethorn *D & G* 92 NX9959
Carshalton *Gt Lon* 27 TQ2764
Carsington *Derbys* 73 SK2553
Carskey *Strath* 104 NR6508
Carsluith *D & G* 99 NX4854
Carsphairn *D & G* 107 NX5693
Carstairs *Strath* 116 NS9345
Carstairs Junction *Strath* 117 NS9545
Carswell Marsh *Oxon* 36 SU3299
Carter's Clay *Hants* 23 SU3024
Carters Green *Essex* 39 TL5110
Carterton *Oxon* 36 SP2806
Carterway Heads *Nthumb* 95 NZ0451
Carthew *Cnwll* 3 SX0056
Carthorpe *N York* 89 SE3083
Cartington *Nthumb* 103 NU0204
Cartland *Strath* 116 NS8646
Cartledge *Derbys* 74 SK3276
Cartmel *Cumb* 87 SD3878
Cartmel Fell *Cumb* 87 SD4188
Carway *Dyfed* 32 SN4606
Carwinley *Cumb* 101 NY4072
Cashe's Green *Gloucs* 35 SO8205
Cashmoor *Dorset* 11 ST9713
Cassington *Oxon* 37 SP4511
Cassop Colliery *Dur* 96 NZ3438
Castel *Guern* 152 GN5108
Castell *Gwynd* 69 SH7669
Castell-y-bwch *Gwent* 34 ST2792
Casterton *Lancs* 87 SD6279
Castle *Cnwll* 4 SX0958
Castle Acre *Norfk* 66 TF8115
Castle Ashby *Nhants* 51 SP8659
Castle Bolton *N York* 88 SE0391
Castle Bromwich *W Mids* 61 SP1489
Castle Bytham *Lincs* 63 SK9818
Castle Caereinion *Powys* 58 SJ1605
Castle Camps *Cambs* 53 TL6242
Castle Carrock *Cumb* 94 NY5455
Castle Cary *Somset* 21 ST6432
Castle Combe *Wilts* 35 ST8477
Castle Donington *Leics* 62 SK4427
Castle Douglas *D & G* 99 NX7662
Castle Eaton *Wilts* 36 SU1496
Castle Eden *Dur* 96 NZ4238
Castle End *Cambs* 64 TF1208
Castle Frome *H & W* 47 SO6645
Castle Gate *Cnwll* 2 SW4934
Castle Green *Cumb* 87 SD5392
Castle Green *Surrey* 25 SU9761
Castle Gresley *Derbys* 73 SK2717
Castle Hedingham *Essex* 53 TL7835
Castle Hill *Kent* 28 TQ6942
Castle Hill *Suffk* 54 TM1446
Castle Kennedy *D & G* 98 NX1159
Castle Lachlan *Strath* 114 NS0195
Castle Morris *Dyfed* 30 SM9031
Castle O'er *D & G* 101 NY2492
Castle Pulverbatch *Shrops* 59 SJ4202
Castle Rising *Norfk* 65 TF6624
Castle Street *W York* 82 SD9524
Castle Stuart *Highld* 140 NH7449
Castlebay *W Isls* 154 NL6698
Castlebythe *Dyfed* 30 SN0229
Castlecary *Strath* 116 NS7878
Castlecraig *Highld* 147 NH8269
Castlecroft *W Mids* 60 SO8797
Castleford *W York* 83 SE4225
Castlehill *Border* 109 NT2135
Castlehill *Highld* 151 ND1968
Castlemartin *Dyfed* 30 SR9198
Castlemorton *H & W* 47 SO7937
Castleside *Dur* 95 NZ0748
Castlethorpe *Bucks* 38 SP8044
Castlethorpe *Humb* 84 SE9807
Castleton *Border* 101 NY5189
Castleton *Derbys* 74 SK1582
Castleton *Gt Man* 79 SD8810
Castleton *Gwent* 34 ST2583
Castleton *N York* 90 NZ6807
Castletown *Dorset* 11 SY6874
Castletown *Highld* 151 ND1967
Castletown *IOM* 153 SC2667
Castletown *T & W* 96 NZ3658
Castley *N York* 82 SE2646
Caston *Norfk* 66 TL9597
Castor *Cambs* 64 TL1298
Caswell Bay *W Glam* 32 SS5987
Cat's Ash *Gwent* 34 ST3790
Catacol *Strath* 105 NR9149
Catbrook *Gwent* 34 SO5102
Catch *Clwyd* 70 SJ2070
Catchall *Cnwll* 2 SW4228
Catchem's Corner *W Mids* 61 SP2576
Catchgate *Dur* 96 NZ1652
Catcliffe *S York* 74 SK4288
Catcomb *Wilts* 35 SU0076
Catcott *Somset* 21 ST3939
Catcott Burtle *Somset* 21 ST4043
Caterham *Surrey* 27 TQ3455
Catfield *Norfk* 67 TG3821
Catfield Common *Norfk* 67 TG4021
Catfirth *Shet* 155 HU4354
Catford *Gt Lon* 27 TQ3773
Catforth *Lancs* 80 SD4735
Cathcart *Strath* 115 NS5860
Cathedine *Powys* 45 SO1425
Catherine Slack *W York* 82 SE0928
Catherine-de-Barnes *W Mids* 61 SP1780
Catherington *Hants* 13 SU6914
Catherston Leweston *Dorset* 10 SY3694
Catherton *Shrops* 47 SO6578
Cathpair *Border* 118 NT4646
Catisfield *Hants* 13 SU5506
Catley Lane Head *Gt Man* 81 SD8715
Catley Southfield *H & W* 47 SO6844
Catlodge *Highld* 132 NN6392
Catlow *Lancs* 81 SD8836
Catlowdy *Cumb* 101 NY4576
Catmere End *Essex* 39 TL4939
Catmore *Berks* 37 SU4580
Caton *Devon* 7 SX7872
Caton *Lancs* 87 SD5364
Caton Green *Lancs* 87 SD5565
Cator Court *Devon* 8 SX6877
Catrine *Strath* 107 NS5225
Catsfield *E Susx* 17 TQ7213
Catsfield Stream *E Susx* 17 TQ7113
Catsham *Somset* 21 ST5533
Catshill *H & W* 60 SO9573
Catstree *Shrops* 60 SO7496
Cattadale *Strath* 105 NR6710
Cattal *N York* 83 SE4454
Cattawade *Suffk* 41 TM1033
Catterall *Lancs* 80 SD4942
Catteralslane *Shrops* 71 SJ5640
Catterick *N York* 89 SE2397
Catterick Bridge *N York* 89 SE2299
Catterick Camp *N York* 89 SE1897
Catterlen *Cumb* 94 NY4833
Catterton *N York* 83 SE5145
Catteshall *Surrey* 25 SU9844
Catthorpe *Leics* 50 SP5578
Cattishall *Suffk* 54 TL8865
Cattistock *Dorset* 10 SY5999
Catton *Cumb* 95 NY8257
Catton *N York* 89 SE3678
Catton *Norfk* 67 TG2312
Catwick *Humb* 85 TA1345
Catworth *Cambs* 51 TL0873
Caudle Green *Gloucs* 35 SO9410
Caulcott *Beds* 38 TL0042
Caulcott *Oxon* 49 SP5024
Cauldcots *Tays* 127 NO6547
Cauldhame *Cent* 116 NS6493
Cauldmill *Border* 109 NT5315
Cauldon *Staffs* 73 SK0749
Cauldon Lowe *Staffs* 73 SK0747
Cauldwell *Derbys* 73 SK2517
Caulkerbush *D & G* 92 NX9257
Caulside *D & G* 101 NY4480
Caundle Marsh *Dorset* 11 ST6713
Caunsall *H & W* 60 SO8581
Caunton *Notts* 75 SK7460
Causeway *Hants* 13 SU7422
Causeway End *Cumb* 87 SD4885
Causeway End *D & G* 99 NX4260
Causeway End *Essex* 40 TL6819
Causewayend *Strath* 108 NT0336
Causewayhead *Cent* 116 NS8095
Causewayhead *Cumb* 92 NY1253
Causey Park *Nthumb* 103 NZ1794
Causeyend *Gramp* 143 NJ9419
Cavendish *Suffk* 54 TL8046
Cavenham *Suffk* 53 TL7670
Caversfield *Oxon* 49 SP5825
Caversham *Berks* 24 SU7274
Caverswall *Staffs* 72 SJ9542
Caverton Mill *Border* 110 NT7425
Cavil *Humb* 84 SE7730
Cawdor *Highld* 140 NH8450
Cawkwell *Lincs* 77 TF2879
Cawood *N York* 83 SE5737
Cawsand *Cnwll* 6 SX4350
Cawston *Norfk* 66 TG1323
Cawston *Warwks* 50 SP4773
Cawthorn *N York* 90 SE7788
Cawthorne *S York* 82 SE2808
Caxton *Cambs* 52 TL3058
Caxton End *Cambs* 52 TL2759
Caxton End *Cambs* 52 TL3157
Caxton Gibbet *Cambs* 52 TL2960
Caynham *Shrops* 46 SO5573
Caythorpe *Lincs* 76 SK9348
Caythorpe *Notts* 63 SK6845
Cayton *N York* 91 TA0583
Ceannacroc Lodge *Highld* 131 NH2211
Cecilford *Gwent* 34 SO5003
Cefn *Gwent* 34 ST2788
Cefn Berain *Clwyd* 70 SH9969
Cefn Byrle *Powys* 33 SN8311
Cefn Canel *Clwyd* 58 SJ2331
Cefn Coch *Powys* 58 SJ1026
Cefn Cribwr *M Glam* 33 SS8582
Cefn Cross *M Glam* 33 SS8682
Cefn Mably *M Glam* 34 ST2283
Cefn-brith *Clwyd* 70 SH9350
Cefn-bryn-brain *Dyfed* 32 SN7413
Cefn-coed-y-cymmer *M Glam* 33 SO0308
Cefn-ddwysarn *Gwynd* 70 SH9638
Cefn-Einion *Shrops* 58 SO2886
Cefn-mawr *Clwyd* 70 SJ2842
Cefn-y-bedd *Clwyd* 71 SJ3156
Cefn-y-pant *Dyfed* 31 SN1925
Cefneithin *Dyfed* 32 SN5513
Cefngorwydd *Powys* 45 SN9045
Cefnpennar *M Glam* 33 SO0300
Ceint *Gwynd* 68 SH4875
Cellan *Dyfed* 44 SN6149
Cellarhead *Staffs* 72 SJ9547
Cellerton *Cumb* 94 NY4925
Celynen *Gwent* 33 ST2195
Cemaes *Gwynd* 68 SH3793
Cemmaes *Powys* 57 SH8406
Cemmaes Road *Powys* 57 SH8104
Cenarth *Dyfed* 31 SN2641
Cerbyd *Dyfed* 30 SM8227
Ceres *Fife* 126 NO4011
Cerne Abbas *Dorset* 11 ST6601
Cerney Wick *Gloucs* 36 SU0796
Cerrigceinwen *Gwynd* 68 SH4274
Cerrigydrudion *Clwyd* 70 SH9548
Cess *Norfk* 67 TG4417
Ceunant *Gwynd* 69 SH5361
Chaceley *Gloucs* 47 SO8530
Chacewater *Cnwll* 3 SW7544
Chackmore *Bucks* 49 SP6835
Chacombe *Nhants* 49 SP4944
Chadbury *H & W* 47 SP0146
Chadderton *Gt Man* 79 SD9005
Chadderton Fold *Gt Man* 79 SD9006
Chaddesden *Derbys* 62 SK3836
Chaddesley Corbett *H & W* 60 SO8973
Chaddlehanger *Devon* 5 SX4678
Chaddleworth *Berks* 36 SU4178
Chadlington *Oxon* 36 SP3321
Chadshunt *Warwks* 48 SP3453
Chadwell *Leics* 63 SK7824
Chadwell *Shrops* 60 SJ7814
Chadwell End *Beds* 51 TL0865
Chadwell Heath *Gt Lon* 27 TQ4888
Chadwell St. Mary *Essex* 40 TQ6478
Chadwick *H & W* 47 SO8369
Chadwick End *W Mids* 61 SP2073
Chadwick Green *Mersyd* 78 SJ5299
Chaffcombe *Somset* 10 ST3510
Chafford Hundred *Essex* 40 TQ6079
Chagford *Devon* 8 SX7087
Chailey *E Susx* 15 TQ3919
Chainbridge *Cambs* 27 TL4200
Chainhurst *Kent* 28 TQ7248
Chalbury Common *Dorset* 12 SU0206
Chaldon *Surrey* 27 TQ3155
Chaldon Herring or East Chaldon *Dorset* 11 SY7983
Chale *IOW* 13 SZ4877
Chale Green *IOW* 13 SZ4879
Chalfont Common *Bucks* 26 TQ0092
Chalfont St. Giles *Bucks* 26 SU9893
Chalfont St. Peter *Bucks* 26 TQ0090
Chalford *Gloucs* 35 SO8802
Chalford *Oxon* 37 SP7200
Chalford *Wilts* 22 ST8650
Chalgrove *Beds* 38 TL0127
Chalgrove *Oxon* 37 SU6396
Chalk *Kent* 28 TQ6773
Chalk End *Essex* 40 TL6310
Chalkhouse Green *Berks* 37 SU7178
Chalkway *Somset* 10 ST3707
Chalkwell *Kent* 28 TQ8963
Challaborough *Devon* 7 SX6544
Challacombe *Devon* 19 SS6940
Challock Lees *Kent* 28 TR0050
Chalmington *Dorset* 10 ST5900
Chalton *Beds* 38 TL0326
Chalton *Beds* 52 TL1450
Chalton *Hants* 13 SU7315
Chalvey *Berks* 26 SU9679
Chalvington *E Susx* 16 TQ5109
Chambers Green *Kent* 28 TQ9243
Chandler's Cross *Herts* 26 TQ0698
Chandler's Ford *Hants* 13 SU4319
Chandlers Cross *H & W* 47 SO7738
Channel's End *Beds* 51 TL1056
Chantry *Somset* 22 ST7146
Chantry *Suffk* 54 TM1443
Chapel *Cumb* 93 NY2231
Chapel *Fife* 117 NT2593
Chapel Allerton *Somset* 21 ST4050
Chapel Allerton *W York* 82 SE3037
Chapel Amble *Cnwll* 4 SW9975
Chapel Brampton *Nhants* 50 SP7266
Chapel Chorlton *Staffs* 72 SJ8137
Chapel Cross *E Susx* 16 TQ6120
Chapel End *Beds* 38 TL0542
Chapel End *Beds* 51 TL1058
Chapel End *Cambs* 52 TL1282
Chapel End *Warwks* 61 SP3393
Chapel Field *Gt Man* 79 SD7906
Chapel Green *Warwks* 61 SP2785
Chapel Green *Warwks* 49 SP4660
Chapel Haddlesey *N York* 83 SE5826
Chapel Hill *Gramp* 143 NK0635
Chapel Hill *Gwent* 34 SO5399
Chapel Hill *Lincs* 76 TF2054
Chapel Hill *N York* 83 SE3446
Chapel Lawn *Shrops* 46 SO3176
Chapel Leigh *Somset* 20 ST1229
Chapel le Dale *N York* 88 SD7377
Chapel Milton *Derbys* 74 SK0581
Chapel of Garioch *Gramp* 142 NJ7124
Chapel Rossan *D & G* 98 NX1044
Chapel Row *Berks* 24 SU5769
Chapel Row *E Susx* 16 TQ6312
Chapel Row *Essex* 40 TL7900
Chapel St. Leonards *Lincs* 77 TF5672
Chapel Stile *Cumb* 86 NY3205
Chapel Town *Cnwll* 3 SW8855
Chapel-en-le-Frith *Derbys* 74 SK0580
Chapelbridge *Cambs* 64 TL2993
Chapelend Way *Essex* 53 TL7039
Chapelgate *Lincs* 65 TF4124
Chapelhall *Strath* 116 NS7862
Chapelknowe *D & G* 101 NY3173
Chapels *Cumb* 86 SD2383
Chapelton *Devon* 19 SS5726
Chapelton *Strath* 116 NS6848
Chapelton *Tays* 127 NO6247
Chapeltown *Gramp* 141 NJ2320
Chapeltown *Lancs* 81 SD7315
Chapeltown *S York* 74 SK3596
Chapmans Well *Devon* 5 SX3593
Chapmanslade *Wilts* 22 ST8247
Chapmore End *Herts* 39 TL3216
Chappel *Essex* 40 TL8928
Charaton *Cnwll* 5 SX3069
Chard *Somset* 10 ST3208
Chard Junction *Somset* 10 ST3404
Chardleigh Green *Somset* 10 ST3110
Chardstock *Devon* 10 ST3004
Charfield *Avon* 35 ST7292
Chargrove *Gloucs* 35 SO9219
Charing *Kent* 28 TQ9549
Charing Heath *Kent* 28 TQ9249
Charing Hill *Kent* 28 TQ9550
Charingworth *Gloucs* 48 SP1939
Charlbury *Oxon* 36 SP3519
Charlcombe *Avon* 22 ST7467
Charlcutt *Wilts* 35 ST9875
Charlecote *Warwks* 48 SP2656
Charles *Devon* 19 SS6832
Charles Tye *Suffk* 54 TM0252
Charleshill *Surrey* 25 SU8944
Charleston *Tays* 126 NO3845
Charlestown *Cnwll* 3 SX0351
Charlestown *Derbys* 74 SK0392
Charlestown *Dorset* 11 SY6579
Charlestown *Fife* 117 NT0683
Charlestown *Gramp* 135 NJ9300
Charlestown *Gt Man* 79 SD8100
Charlestown *Highld* 144 NG8174
Charlestown *Highld* 140 NH6448
Charlestown *Lincs* 63 SK9844
Charlestown *W York* 82 SD9726
Charlestown *W York* 82 SE1638
Charlesworth *Derbys* 79 SK0092
Charlinch *Somset* 20 ST2338
Charlton *Gt Lon* 27 TQ4178
Charlton *H & W* 60 SO8371
Charlton *H & W* 47 SP0045
Charlton *Hants* 23 SU3547
Charlton *Herts* 39 TL1728
Charlton *Nhants* 49 SP5335
Charlton *Nthumb* 102 NY8184
Charlton *Oxon* 36 SU4088
Charlton *Shrops* 59 SJ5911
Charlton *Somset* 20 ST2926
Charlton *Somset* 21 ST6343
Charlton *W Susx* 14 SU8812
Charlton *Wilts* 22 ST9022
Charlton *Wilts* 35 ST9588
Charlton *Wilts* 23 SU1156
Charlton *Wilts* 23 SU1723
Charlton Abbots *Gloucs* 48 SP0324
Charlton Adam *Somset* 21 ST5328
Charlton Hill *Shrops* 59 SJ5807
Charlton Horethorne *Somset* 22 ST6623
Charlton Kings *Gloucs* 35 SO9621
Charlton Mackrell *Somset* 21 ST5328
Charlton Marshall *Dorset* 11 ST9004
Charlton Musgrove *Somset* 22 ST7229
Charlton on the Hill *Dorset* 11 ST8903
Charlton-on-Otmoor *Oxon* 37 SP5616
Charlwood *Hants* 24 SU6731
Charlwood *Surrey* 15 TQ2441
Charminster *Dorset* 11 SY6792
Charmouth *Dorset* 10 SY3693
Charndon *Bucks* 49 SP6724
Charney Bassett *Oxon* 36 SU3894
Charnock Green *Lancs* 81 SD5516
Charnock Richard *Lancs* 81 SD5515
Charsfield *Suffk* 55 TM2556
Chart Corner *Kent* 28 TQ7950
Chart Hill *Kent* 28 TQ7949
Chart Sutton *Kent* 28 TQ8049
Charter Alley *Hants* 24 SU5958
Charterhall *Border* 110 NT7647
Charterhouse *Somset* 21 ST4955
Chartershall *Cent* 116 NS7990
Charterville Allotments *Oxon* 36 SP3110
Chartham *Kent* 29 TR1054
Chartham Hatch *Kent* 29 TR1056
Charton *Surrey* 26 TQ0869
Chartridge *Bucks* 38 SP9303
Chartway Street *Kent* 28 TQ8350
Charwelton *Nhants* 49 SP5356
Chase Terrace *Staffs* 61 SK0309
Chasetown *Staffs* 61 SK0408
Chastleton *Oxon* 48 SP2429
Chasty *Devon* 18 SS3402
Chatburn *Lancs* 81 SD7644
Chatcull *Staffs* 72 SJ7934
Chatham *Gwent* 33 ST2188
Chatham *Kent* 28 TQ7567
Chatham Green *Essex* 40 TL7115
Chathill *Nthumb* 111 NU1827
Chatley *H & W* 47 SO8561
Chattenden *Kent* 28 TQ7572
Chatter End *Essex* 39 TL4725
Chatteris *Cambs* 52 TL3985
Chatterton *Lancs* 81 SD7918
Chattisham *Suffk* 54 TM0942
Chatto *Border* 110 NT7717
Chatton *Nthumb* 111 NU0528
Chawleigh *Devon* 19 SS7112
Chawley *Oxon* 37 SP4604
Chawston *Beds* 52 TL1556
Chawton *Hants* 24 SU7037
Chaxhill *Gloucs* 35 SO7414
Chazey Heath *Oxon* 37 SU6977
Cheadle *Gt Man* 79 SJ8688
Cheadle *Staffs* 73 SK0043
Cheadle Heath *Gt Man* 79 SJ8789
Cheadle Hulme *Gt Man* 79 SJ8786
Cheam *Gt Lon* 26 TQ2463
Cheapside *Berks* 25 SU9469
Chearsley *Bucks* 37 SP7110
Chebsey *Staffs* 72 SJ8528
Checkendon *Oxon* 37 SU6683
Checkley *Ches* 72 SJ7346
Checkley *Staffs* 73 SK0237
Checkley Green *Ches* 72 SJ7245
Chedburgh *Suffk* 53 TL7957
Cheddar *Somset* 21 ST4553
Cheddington *Bucks* 38 SP9217
Cheddleton *Staffs* 72 SJ9752
Cheddleton Heath *Staffs* 72 SJ9853
Cheddon Fitzpaine *Somset* 20 ST2427
Chedglow *Wilts* 35 ST9493
Chedgrave *Norfk* 67 TM3699
Chedington *Dorset* 10 ST4805
Chediston *Suffk* 55 TM3577
Chediston Green *Suffk* 55 TM3578
Chedworth *Gloucs* 36 SP0512
Chedzoy *Somset* 21 ST3437
Cheesden *Gt Man* 81 SD8216
Cheeseman's Green *Kent* 28 TR0338
Cheetham Hill *Gt Man* 79 SD8401
Cheetwood *Gt Man* 79 SJ8399
Cheldon *Devon* 19 SS7313
Chelford *Ches* 79 SJ8174
Chellaston *Derbys* 62 SK3730
Chellington *Beds* 51 SP9555
Chelmarsh *Shrops* 60 SO7288
Chelmick *Shrops* 59 SO4791
Chelmondiston *Suffk* 55 TM2037
Chelmorton *Derbys* 74 SK1169
Chelmsford *Essex* 40 TL7007
Chelmsley Wood *W Mids* 61 SP1887
Chelsea *Gt Lon* 27 TQ2778
Chelsfield *Gt Lon* 27 TQ4864
Chelsham *Surrey* 27 TQ3758
Chelston *Somset* 20 ST1521
Chelsworth *Suffk* 54 TL9748
Cheltenham *Gloucs* 35 SO9422
Chelveston *Nhants* 51 SP9969
Chelvey *Avon* 21 ST4668
Chelwood *Avon* 21 ST6361
Chelwood Common *E Susx* 15 TQ4128
Chelwood Gate *E Susx* 15 TQ4130
Chelworth *Wilts* 35 ST9694
Chelworth Lower Green *Wilts* 36 SU0892
Chelworth Upper Green *Wilts* 36 SU0893
Cheney Longville *Shrops* 59 SO4284
Chenies *Bucks* 26 TQ0198
Chepstow *Gwent* 34 ST5393
Chequerbent *Gt Man* 79 SD6706
Chequers Corner *Norfk* 65 TF4908
Cherhill *Wilts* 36 SU0370
Cherington *Gloucs* 35 ST9098
Cherington *Warwks* 48 SP2936
Cheriton *Devon* 19 SS7346
Cheriton *Hants* 24 SU5828
Cheriton *Kent* 29 TR2037
Cheriton *W Glam* 32 SS4593
Cheriton Bishop *Devon* 8 SX7793
Cheriton Fitzpaine *Devon* 9 SS8606
Cheriton or Stackpole Elidor *Dyfed* 30 SR9897
Cherrington *Shrops* 72 SJ6619
Cherry Burton *Humb* 84 SE9841
Cherry Hinton *Cambs* 53 TL4856
Cherry Orchard *H & W* 47 SO8553
Cherry Willingham *Lincs* 76 TF0272
Chertsey *Surrey* 26 TQ0466
Cheselbourne *Dorset* 11 SY7699
Chesham *Bucks* 26 SP9601
Chesham *Gt Man* 81 SD8012
Chesham Bois *Bucks* 26 SU9699
Cheshunt *Herts* 27 TL3502
Chesley *Kent* 28 TQ8563
Cheslyn Hay *Staffs* 60 SJ9707
Chessetts Wood *Warwks* 61 SP1873
Chessington *Surrey* 26 TQ1863
Chester *Ches* 71 SJ4066
Chester Moor *Dur* 96 NZ2649
Chester-le-Street *T & W* 96 NZ2751
Chesterblade *Somset* 22 ST6641
Chesterfield *Derbys* 74 SK3871
Chesterfield *Staffs* 61 SK0905
Chesterhill *Loth* 118 NT3764
Chesters *Border* 110 NT6022
Chesters *Border* 110 NT6210

Chesterton Clydach

Chesterton *Cambs* 64 TL1295
Chesterton *Cambs* 53 TL4660
Chesterton *Gloucs* 35 SP0100
Chesterton *Oxon* 37 SP5621
Chesterton *Shrops* 60 SO7897
Chesterton *Staffs* 72 SJ8349
Chesterton Green *Warwks* 48 SP3558
Chesterwood *Nthumb* 102 NY8364
Chestfield *Kent* 29 TR1365
Chestnut Street *Kent* 28 TQ8763
Cheston *Devon* 7 SX6858
Cheswardine *Shrops* 72 SJ7130
Cheswell *Shrops* 72 SJ7116
Cheswick *Nthumb* 111 NU0346
Cheswick Green *W Mids* 61 SP1376
Chetnole *Dorset* 10 ST6008
Chettiscombe *Devon* 9 SS9614
Chettisham *Cambs* 53 TL5483
Chettle *Dorset* 11 ST9513
Chetton *Shrops* 60 SO6690
Chetwode *Bucks* 49 SP6429
Chetwynd *Shrops* 72 SJ7321
Chetwynd Aston *Shrops* 72 SJ7517
Cheveley *Cambs* 53 TL6861
Chevening *Kent* 27 TQ4857
Cheverton *IOW* 13 SZ4583
Chevington *Suffk* 53 TL7859
Chevington Drift *Nthumb* 103 NZ2598
Chevithorne *Devon* 9 SS9715
Chew Magna *Avon* 21 ST5763
Chew Moor *Gt Man* 79 SD6607
Chew Stoke *Avon* 21 ST5561
Chewton Keynsham *Avon* 21 ST6566
Chewton Mendip *Somset* 21 ST5953
Chichacott *Devon* 8 SX6096
Chicheley *Bucks* 38 SP9046
Chichester *W Susx* 14 SU8604
Chickerell *Dorset* 11 SY6480
Chickering *Suffk* 55 TM2176
Chicklade *Wilts* 22 ST9134
Chickward *H & W* 46 SO2853
Chidden *Hants* 13 SU6517
Chiddingfold *Surrey* 14 SU9635
Chiddingly *E Susx* 16 TQ5414
Chiddingstone *Kent* 16 TQ5045
Chiddingstone Causeway *Kent* 16 TQ5246
Chideock *Dorset* 10 SY4292
Chidham *W Susx* 14 SU7903
Chidswell *W York* 82 SE2623
Chieveley *Berks* 24 SU4774
Chignall Smealy *Essex* 40 TL6611
Chignall St. James *Essex* 40 TL6610
Chigwell *Essex* 27 TQ4494
Chigwell Row *Essex* 27 TQ4693
Chilbolton *Hants* 23 SU3940
Chilcomb *Hants* 24 SU5028
Chilcombe *Dorset* 10 SY5291
Chilcompton *Somset* 21 ST6451
Chilcote *Leics* 61 SK2811
Child Okeford *Dorset* 11 ST8312
Child's Ercall *Shrops* 72 SJ6625
Childer Thornton *Ches* 71 SJ3677
Childrey *Oxon* 36 SU3687
Childswickham *H & W* 48 SP0738
Childwall *Mersyd* 78 SJ4189
Childwick Bury *Herts* 38 TL1410
Childwick Green *Herts* 38 TL1410
Chilfrome *Dorset* 10 SY5898
Chilgrove *W Susx* 14 SU8314
Chilham *Kent* 29 TR0653
Chilhampton *Wilts* 23 SU0933
Chilla *Devon* 18 SS4402
Chillaton *Devon* 5 SX4381
Chillenden *Kent* 29 TR2753
Chillerton *IOW* 13 SZ4883
Chillesford *Suffk* 55 TM3852
Chillingham *Nthumb* 111 NU0525
Chillington *Devon* 7 SX7942
Chillington *Somset* 10 ST3811
Chilmark *Wilts* 22 ST9732
Chilmington Green *Kent* 28 TQ9840
Chilson *Oxon* 36 SP3119
Chilsworthy *Cnwll* 5 SX4172
Chilsworthy *Devon* 18 SS3206
Chiltern Green *Beds* 38 TL1319
Chilthorne Domer *Somset* 21 ST5219
Chilton *Bucks* 37 SP6811
Chilton *Devon* 9 SS8604
Chilton *Kent* 29 TR2743
Chilton *Oxon* 37 SU4885
Chilton *Suffk* 54 TL8842
Chilton Candover *Hants* 24 SU5940
Chilton Cantelo *Somset* 21 ST5722
Chilton Foliat *Wilts* 36 SU3170
Chilton Polden *Somset* 21 ST3740
Chilton Street *Suffk* 53 TL7546
Chilton Trinity *Somset* 20 ST2939
Chilwell *Notts* 62 SK5135
Chilworth *Hants* 13 SU4018
Chilworth *Surrey* 14 TQ0347
Chimney *Oxon* 36 SP3501
Chineham *Hants* 24 SU6555
Chingford *Gt Lon* 27 TQ3894
Chinley *Derbys* 74 SK0482
Chinnor *Oxon* 37 SP7501
Chipchase Castle *Nthumb* 102 NY8775
Chipnall *Shrops* 72 SJ7231
Chippenham *Cambs* 53 TL6669
Chippenham *Wilts* 35 ST9173
Chipperfield *Herts* 26 TL0401
Chipping *Herts* 39 TL3531
Chipping *Lancs* 81 SD6243
Chipping Campden *Gloucs* 48 SP1539
Chipping Hill *Essex* 40 TL8215
Chipping Norton *Oxon* 48 SP3127
Chipping Ongar *Essex* 39 TL5503
Chipping Sodbury *Avon* 35 ST7282
Chipping Warden *Nhants* 49 SP4948
Chipstable *Somset* 20 ST0427
Chipstead *Kent* 27 TQ5056
Chipstead *Surrey* 27 TQ2756
Chirbury *Shrops* 58 SO2698
Chirk *Clwyd* 58 SJ2837
Chirnside *Border* 119 NT8756
Chirnsidebridge *Border* 119 NT8556
Chirton *Wilts* 23 SU0757
Chisbury *Wilts* 23 SU2766
Chiselborough *Somset* 10 ST4614
Chiseldon *Wilts* 36 SU1880
Chisholme *Border* 109 NT4112
Chislehampton *Oxon* 37 SU5999
Chislehurst *Gt Lon* 27 TQ4470
Chislet *Kent* 29 TR2264
Chisley *W York* 82 SE0028
Chiswellgreen *Herts* 38 TL1304
Chiswick *Gt Lon* 26 TQ2078
Chiswick End *Cambs* 52 TL3745
Chisworth *Derbys* 79 SJ9991
Chitcombe *E Susx* 17 TQ8120
Chithurst *W Susx* 14 SU8423
Chittering *Cambs* 53 TL4969
Chitterne *Wilts* 22 ST9843
Chittlehamholt *Devon* 19 SS6520
Chittlehampton *Devon* 19 SS6325
Chittlehampton *Devon* 19 SS6511
Chittoe *Wilts* 22 ST9566
Chivelstone *Devon* 7 SX7838
Chivenor *Devon* 19 SS5034
Chlenry *D & G* 98 NX1260
Chobham *Surrey* 25 SU9762
Cholderton *Wilts* 23 SU2242
Cholesbury *Bucks* 38 SP9307
Chollerford *Nthumb* 102 NY9170
Chollerton *Nthumb* 102 NY9372
Cholsey *Oxon* 37 SU5886
Cholstrey *H & W* 46 SO4659
Chop Gate *N York* 90 SE5599
Choppington *T & W* 103 NZ2484
Chopwell *T & W* 95 NZ1158
Chorley *Ches* 71 SJ5751
Chorley *Lancs* 81 SD5817
Chorley *Shrops* 60 SO6983
Chorley *Staffs* 61 SK0710
Chorleywood *Herts* 26 TQ0396
Chorleywood West *Herts* 26 TQ0296
Chorlton *Ches* 72 SJ7250
Chorlton Lane *Ches* 71 SJ4547
Chorlton-cum-Hardy *Gt Man* 79 SJ8193
Choulton *Shrops* 59 SO3788
Chowley *Ches* 71 SJ4756
Chrishall *Essex* 39 TL4439
Chrisswell *Strath* 114 NS2274
Christchurch *Cambs* 65 TL4996
Christchurch *Dorset* 12 SZ1592
Christian Malford *Wilts* 35 ST9678
Christleton *Ches* 71 SJ4465
Christmas Common *Oxon* 37 SU7193
Christon *Avon* 21 ST3757
Christon Bank *Nthumb* 111 NU2123
Christow *Devon* 8 SX8385
Christskirk *Gramp* 142 NJ6027
Chuck Hatch *E Susx* 16 TQ4733
Chudleigh *Devon* 9 SX8679
Chudleigh Knighton *Devon* 8 SX8477
Chulmleigh *Devon* 19 SS6814
Chunal *Derbys* 74 SK0390
Church *Lancs* 81 SD7429
Church Ashton *Shrops* 72 SJ7317
Church Brampton *Nhants* 50 SP7165
Church Brough *Cumb* 95 NY7913
Church Broughton *Derbys* 73 SK2033
Church Crookham *Hants* 25 SU8051
Church Eaton *Staffs* 72 SJ8417
Church End *Beds* 38 SP9832
Church End *Beds* 38 SP9921
Church End *Beds* 38 TL0334
Church End *Beds* 51 TL0558
Church End *Beds* 51 TL1058
Church End *Beds* 39 TL1937
Church End *Cambs* 51 TL0873
Church End *Cambs* 52 TL2082
Church End *Cambs* 52 TL3278
Church End *Cambs* 53 TL4857
Church End *Essex* 40 TL6223
Church End *Essex* 40 TL7228
Church End *Essex* 40 TL7316
Church End *Gt Lon* 26 TQ2490
Church End *Hants* 24 SU6756
Church End *Herts* 38 TL1011
Church End *Herts* 39 TL2630
Church End *Herts* 39 TL4422
Church End *Lincs* 64 TF2234
Church End *Lincs* 77 TF4295
Church End *Warwks* 61 SP2490
Church End *Warwks* 61 SP2992
Church Enstone *Oxon* 48 SP3725
Church Fenton *N York* 83 SE5136
Church Green *Devon* 9 SY1796
Church Gresley *Derbys* 73 SK2918
Church Hanborough *Oxon* 36 SP4213
Church Hill *Ches* 72 SJ6465
Church Hill *Staffs* 60 SK0011
Church Houses *N York* 90 SE6697
Church Knowle *Dorset* 11 SY9481
Church Laneham *Notts* 75 SK8176
Church Langton *Leics* 50 SP7293
Church Lawford *Warwks* 50 SP4576
Church Lawton *Staffs* 72 SJ8255
Church Leigh *Staffs* 73 SK0235
Church Lench *H & W* 48 SP0251
Church Mayfield *Staffs* 73 SK1544
Church Minshull *Ches* 72 SJ6660
Church Norton *W Susx* 14 SZ8795
Church Preen *Shrops* 59 SO5498
Church Pulverbatch *Shrops* 59 SJ4303
Church Stoke *Powys* 58 SO2794
Church Stowe *Nhants* 49 SP6357
Church Street *Essex* 53 TL7943
Church Street *Kent* 28 TQ7174
Church Street *Suffk* 55 TM4883
Church Stretton *Shrops* 59 SO4593
Church Town *Humb* 84 SE7806
Church Village *M Glam* 33 ST0885
Church Warsop *Notts* 75 SK5668
Church Wilne *Derbys* 62 SK4431
Churcham *Gloucs* 35 SO7618
Churchbridge *Staffs* 60 SJ9808
Churchdown *Gloucs* 35 SO8819
Churchend *Essex* 41 TR0093
Churchfield *W Mids* 60 SP0192
Churchgate *Herts* 27 TL3402
Churchgate Street *Essex* 39 TL4811
Churchill *Avon* 21 ST4459
Churchill *Devon* 19 SS5940
Churchill *Devon* 10 ST2902
Churchill *H & W* 60 SO8879
Churchill *H & W* 47 SO9253
Churchill *Oxon* 48 SP2824
Churchinford *Devon* 9 ST2112
Churchover *Warwks* 50 SP5180
Churchstanton *Somset* 9 ST1914
Churchstow *Devon* 7 SX7145
Churchthorpe *Lincs* 77 TF3297
Churchtown *Derbys* 74 SK2662
Churchtown *Devon* 19 SS6744
Churchtown *Lancs* 80 SD3240
Churchtown *Lancs* 80 SD4843
Churchtown *Mersyd* 80 SD3618
Churnsike Lodge *Nthumb* 102 NY6677
Churston Ferrers *Devon* 7 SX9056
Churt *Surrey* 25 SU8538
Churton *Ches* 71 SJ4156
Churwell *W York* 82 SE2729
Chute Lodge *Wilts* 23 SU3051
Chwilog *Gwynd* 56 SH4338
Chyandour *Cnwll* 2 SW4731
Chyanvounder *Cnwll* 2 SW6522
Chyeowling *Cnwll* 3 SW7941
Chyvarloe *Cnwll* 2 SW6523
Cil *Powys* 58 SJ1701
Cilcain *Clwyd* 70 SJ1765
Cilcennin *Dyfed* 44 SN5260
Cilcewydd *Powys* 58 SJ2204
Cilfrew *W Glam* 32 SN7700
Cilfynydd *M Glam* 33 ST0891
Cilgerran *Dyfed* 31 SN1942
Cilgwyn *Dyfed* 44 SN7429
Ciliau-Aeron *Dyfed* 44 SN5057
Cilmaengwyn *W Glam* 32 SN7405
Cilmery *Powys* 45 SO0051
Cilrhedyn *Dyfed* 31 SN2834
Cilsan *Dyfed* 32 SN5922
Ciltalgarth *Gwynd* 57 SH8940
Cilycwm *Dyfed* 44 SN7539
Cimla *W Glam* 32 SS7696
Cinder Hill *W Mids* 60 SO9294
Cinderford *Gloucs* 35 SO6514
Cippenham *Bucks* 26 SU9480
Cirencester *Gloucs* 35 SP0201
Citadilla *N York* 89 SE2299
City *S Glam* 33 SS9878
City Dulas *Gwynd* 68 SH4687
Clabhach *Strath* 120 NM1858
Clachaig *Strath* 114 NS1181
Clachan *Highld* 137 NG5436
Clachan *S Glam* 113 NR7656
Clachan *Strath* 122 NM7819
Clachan *Strath* 122 NM8543
Clachan Mor *Strath* 120 NL9847
Clachan-a-Luib *W Isls* 154 NF8163
Clachan-Seil *Strath* 122 NM7718
Clachaneasy *D & G* 98 NX3574
Clachnaharry *Highld* 140 NH6446
Clachtoll *Highld* 148 NC0427
Clackavoid *Tays* 133 NO1463
Clackmannan *Cent* 116 NS9191
Clackmarass *Gramp* 141 NJ2458
Clacton-on-Sea *Essex* 41 TM1715
Cladich *Strath* 123 NN0921
Cladswell *H & W* 48 SP0558
Claggan *Highld* 122 NM7049
Claigan *Highld* 136 NG2354
Clandown *Avon* 22 ST6855
Clanfield *Hants* 13 SU6916
Clanfield *Oxon* 36 SP2801
Clannaborough *Devon* 8 SS7402
Clanville *Hants* 23 SU3148
Clanville *Somset* 21 ST6233
Claonaig *Strath* 113 NR8656
Clap Hill *Kent* 28 TR0537
Clapgate *Dorset* 11 SU0102
Clapgate *Herts* 39 TL4424
Clapham *Beds* 38 TL0352
Clapham *Devon* 9 SX8987
Clapham *Gt Lon* 27 TQ2975
Clapham *N York* 88 SD7469
Clapham *W Susx* 14 TQ0906
Clapham Folly *Beds* 38 TL0252
Clappersgate *Cumb* 87 NY3603
Clapton *Somset* 10 ST4106
Clapton *Somset* 21 ST6453
Clapton *Somset* 22 ST6852
Clapton-in-Gordano *Avon* 34 ST4773
Clapton-on-the-Hill *Gloucs* 36 SP1617
Clapworthy *Devon* 19 SS6724
Clarach *Dyfed* 43 SN6084
Claravale *T & W* 103 NZ1364
Clarbeston *Dyfed* 30 SN0521
Clarbeston Road *Dyfed* 30 SN0121
Clarborough *Notts* 75 SK7383
Clare *Suffk* 53 TL7745
Clarebrand *D & G* 99 NX7665
Claredon Park *Leics* 62 SK6002
Clarencefield *D & G* 100 NY0968
Clarewood *Nthumb* 103 NZ0169
Clarilaw *Border* 109 NT5218
Clark's Green *Surrey* 15 TQ1739
Clarken Green *Hants* 24 SU5651
Clarkston *Strath* 115 NS5757
Clashmore *Highld* 148 NC0331
Clashmore *Highld* 146 NH7489
Clashnessie *Highld* 148 NC0530
Clashnoir *Gramp* 141 NJ2222
Clathy *Tays* 125 NN9920
Clathymore *Tays* 125 NO0121
Clatt *Gramp* 142 NJ5326
Clatter *Powys* 58 SN9994
Clatterford End *Essex* 40 TL6113
Clatworthy *Somset* 20 ST0531
Claughton *Lancs* 80 SD5342
Claughton *Lancs* 87 SD5566
Claughton *Mersyd* 78 SJ3088
Clavelshay *Somset* 20 ST2531
Claverdon *Warwks* 48 SP1965
Claverham *Avon* 21 ST4566
Clavering *Essex* 39 TL4731
Claverley *Shrops* 60 SO7993
Claverton *Avon* 22 ST7864
Claverton Down *Avon* 22 ST7763
Clawdd-coch *S Glam* 33 ST0577
Clawdd-newydd *Clwyd* 70 SJ0852
Clawthorpe *Cumb* 87 SD5377
Clawton *Devon* 18 SX3599
Claxby *Lincs* 76 TF1194
Claxby *Lincs* 77 TF4571
Claxton *N York* 90 SE6959
Claxton *Norfk* 67 TG3303
Clay Common *Suffk* 55 TM4681
Clay Coton *Nhants* 50 SP5976
Clay Cross *Derbys* 74 SK3963
Clay End *Herts* 39 TL3024
Claybrooke Magna *Leics* 50 SP4988
Claydon *Oxon* 49 SP4549
Claydon *Suffk* 54 TM1349
Claygate *D & G* 101 NY3979
Claygate *Kent* 28 TQ7144
Claygate *Surrey* 26 TQ1563
Claygate Cross *Kent* 27 TQ6155
Clayhanger *Devon* 20 ST0222
Clayhanger *W Mids* 61 SK0404
Clayhidon *Devon* 9 ST1615
Clayhill *E Susx* 17 TQ8323
Clayhill *Hants* 12 SU3006
Clayhithe *Cambs* 53 TL5064
Clayock *Highld* 151 ND1659
Claypit Hill *Cambs* 52 TL3554
Claypits *Gloucs* 35 SO7606
Claypole *Lincs* 76 SK8449
Claythorpe *Lincs* 77 TF4178
Clayton *S York* 83 SE4507
Clayton *W Susx* 15 TQ2914
Clayton *W York* 82 SE1231
Clayton Green *Lancs* 81 SD5723
Clayton West *W York* 82 SE2510
Clayton-le-Moors *Lancs* 81 SD7530
Clayton-le-Woods *Lancs* 81 SD5622
Clayworth *Notts* 75 SK7387
Cleadale *Highld* 128 NM4789
Cleadon *T & W* 96 NZ3862
Clearbrook *Devon* 6 SX5265
Clearwell *Gloucs* 34 SO5608
Clearwell Meend *Gloucs* 34 SO5808
Cleasby *N York* 89 NZ2512
Cleat *Ork* 155 ND4584
Cleatlam *Dur* 95 NZ1118
Cleator *Cumb* 92 NY0113
Cleator Moor *Cumb* 92 NY0115
Cleckheaton *W York* 82 SE1825
Clee St. Margaret *Shrops* 59 SO5684
Cleedownton *Shrops* 59 SO5880
Cleehill *Shrops* 46 SO5975
Cleekhimin *Strath* 116 NS7658
Cleestanton *Shrops* 46 SO5779
Cleethorpes *Humb* 85 TA3008
Cleeton St. Mary *Shrops* 46 SO6178
Cleeve *Avon* 21 ST4666
Cleeve *Oxon* 37 SU6081
Cleeve Hill *Gloucs* 47 SO9827
Cleeve Prior *H & W* 48 SP0849
Cleghornie *Loth* 118 NT5983
Clehonger *H & W* 46 SO4637
Cleish *Tays* 117 NT0998
Cleland *Strath* 116 NS7958
Clement Street *Kent* 27 TQ5370
Clement's End *Beds* 38 TL0214
Clenamacrie *Strath* 122 NM9228
Clench Common *Wilts* 23 SU1765
Clenchwarton *Norfk* 65 TF5920
Clent *H & W* 60 SO9279
Clenterty *Gramp* 142 NJ7760
Cleobury Mortimer *Shrops* 60 SO6775
Cleobury North *Shrops* 59 SO6286
Cleongart *Strath* 105 NR6734
Clephanton *Highld* 140 NH8150
Clerkhill *D & G* 101 NY2697
Cleuch Head *Border* 110 NT5910
Cleuch-head *D & G* 108 NS8200
Clevancy *Wilts* 36 SU0575
Clevedon *Avon* 34 ST4171
Cleveleys *Lancs* 80 SD3143
Clevelode *H & W* 47 SO8347
Cleverton *Wilts* 35 ST9785
Clewer *Somset* 21 ST4351
Cley next the Sea *Norfk* 66 TG0444
Cliburn *Cumb* 94 NY5824
Cliddesden *Hants* 24 SU6349
Cliff *Warwks* 61 SP2197
Cliff End *E Susx* 17 TQ8813
Cliffe *Dur* 96 NZ2115
Cliffe *Kent* 28 TQ7376
Cliffe *Lancs* 81 SD7333
Cliffe *N York* 83 SE6631
Cliffe Woods *Kent* 28 TQ7373
Clifford *H & W* 46 SO2445
Clifford *W York* 83 SE4344
Clifford Chambers *Warwks* 48 SP1952
Clifford's Mesne *Gloucs* 47 SO7023
Cliffsend *Kent* 29 TR3464
Clifton *Avon* 34 ST5773
Clifton *Beds* 39 TL1639
Clifton *Cent* 123 NN3231
Clifton *Cumb* 94 NY5326
Clifton *Derbys* 73 SK1644
Clifton *Gt Man* 79 SD7703
Clifton *H & W* 47 SO8446
Clifton *Lancs* 80 SD4630
Clifton *N York* 83 SE5953
Clifton *Notts* 62 SK5434
Clifton *Nthumb* 103 NZ2082
Clifton *Oxon* 49 SP4931
Clifton *S York* 75 SK5296
Clifton *W York* 82 SE1622
Clifton *W York* 82 SE1948
Clifton Campville *Staffs* 61 SK2510
Clifton Hampden *Oxon* 37 SU5495
Clifton Reynes *Bucks* 38 SP9051
Clifton upon Dunsmore *Warwks* 50 SP5376
Clifton upon Teme *H & W* 47 SO7161
Cliftonville *Kent* 29 TR3771
Climping *W Susx* 14 SU9902
Clink *Somset* 22 ST7948
Clint *N York* 89 SE2659
Clint Green *Norfk* 66 TG0210
Clinterty *Gramp* 135 NJ8311
Clintmains *Border* 110 NT6132
Clipiau *Gwynd* 57 SH8410
Clippesby *Norfk* 67 TG4214
Clipsham *Leics* 63 SK9716
Clipston *Nhants* 50 SP7181
Clipston *Notts* 63 SK6334
Clipstone *Beds* 38 SP9426
Clitheroe *Lancs* 81 SD7441
Clive *Shrops* 59 SJ5124
Cloatley *Wilts* 35 ST9890
Clocaenog *Clwyd* 70 SJ0854
Clochan *Gramp* 142 NJ4060
Clochtow *Tays* 127 NO4852
Clock Face *Mersyd* 78 SJ5291
Cloddiau *Powys* 58 SJ2009
Clodock *H & W* 46 SO3227
Cloford *Somset* 22 ST7244
Clola *Gramp* 143 NK0043
Clophill *Beds* 38 TL0838
Clopton *Nhants* 51 TL0680
Clopton *Suffk* 55 TM2253
Clopton Corner *Suffk* 55 TM2254
Clopton Green *Suffk* 53 TL7655
Clopton Green *Suffk* 54 TL9759
Clos du Valle *Guern* 152 GN5412
Closeburn *D & G* 100 NX8992
Closeburnmill *D & G* 100 NX9094
Closeclark *IOM* 153 SC2775
Closworth *Somset* 10 ST5610
Clothall *Herts* 39 TL2731
Clotton *Ches* 71 SJ5264
Cloudesley Bush *Warwks* 50 SP4686
Clough *Gt Man* 79 SD9408
Clough Foot *W York* 81 SD9123
Clough Head *W York* 82 SE0918
Cloughton *N York* 91 TA0194
Cloughton Newlands *N York* 91 TA0096
Clousta *Shet* 155 HU3057
Clova *Tays* 134 NO3273
Clovelly *Devon* 18 SS3124
Clovenfords *Border* 109 NT4536
Clovulin *Highld* 130 NN0063
Clow Bridge *Lancs* 81 SD8228
Clowne *Derbys* 75 SK4875
Clows Top *H & W* 60 SO7172
Cloy *Clwyd* 71 SJ3943
Cluanie Inn *Highld* 130 NH0711
Cluanie Lodge *Highld* 130 NH0910
Clubworthy *Cnwll* 5 SX2792
Clugston *D & G* 98 NX3557
Clun *Shrops* 59 SO3080
Clunas *Highld* 140 NH8846
Clunbury *Shrops* 59 SO3780
Clune *Highld* 140 NH7925
Clunes *Highld* 131 NN1988
Clungunford *Shrops* 46 SO3978
Clunie *Gramp* 142 NJ6350
Clunie *Tays* 126 NO1043
Clunton *Shrops* 59 SO3381
Clutton *Avon* 21 ST6259
Clutton *Ches* 71 SJ4654
Clutton Hill *Avon* 21 ST6359
Clwt-y-bont *Gwynd* 69 SH5762
Clydach *Gwent* 34 SO2213

Clydach Corsley

Clydach *W Glam* 32 SN6800
Clydach Vale *M Glam* 33 SS9792
Clydebank *Strath* 115 NS4970
Clydey *Dyfed* 31 SN2535
Clyffe Pypard *Wilts* 36 SU0777
Clynder *Strath* 114 NS2484
Clynderwen *Dyfed* 31 SN1219
Clyne *W Glam* 32 SN8000
Clynnog-fawr *Gwynd* 68 SH4149
Clyro *Powys* 45 SO2143
Clyst Honiton *Devon* 9 SX9893
Clyst Hydon *Devon* 9 ST0301
Clyst St. George *Devon* 9 SX9888
Clyst St. Lawrence *Devon* 9 ST0200
Clyst St. Mary *Devon* 9 SX9791
Clyth *Highld* 151 ND2835
Cnwch Coch *Dyfed* 43 SN6774
Coad's Green *Cnwll* 5 SX2976
Coal Aston *Derbys* 74 SK3679
Coal Pool *W Mids* 60 SP0199
Coal Street *Suffk* 55 TM2371
Coalbrookdale *Shrops* 60 SJ6604
Coalbrookvale *Gwent* 33 SO1909
Coalburn *Strath* 108 NS8134
Coalburns *T & W* 96 NZ1260
Coalcleugh *Nthumb* 95 NY8045
Coaley *Gloucs* 35 SO7701
Coalfell *Cumb* 94 NY5959
Coalhill *Essex* 40 TQ7597
Coalmoor *Shrops* 60 SJ6607
Coalpit Heath *Avon* 35 ST6780
Coalport *Shrops* 60 SJ6902
Coalsnaughton *Cent* 116 NS9195
Coaltown of Balgonie *Fife* 117 NT2999
Coaltown of Wemyss *Fife* 118 NT3295
Coalville *Leics* 62 SK4214
Coanwood *Nthumb* 94 NY6859
Coat *Somset* 21 ST4520
Coatbridge *Strath* 116 NS7365
Coatdyke *Strath* 116 NS7465
Coate *Wilts* 23 SU0462
Coate *Wilts* 36 SU1882
Coates *Cambs* 64 TL3097
Coates *Gloucs* 35 SO9701
Coates *Lincs* 75 SK8181
Coates *Lincs* 76 SK9083
Coates *W Susx* 14 SU9917
Coatham *Cleve* 97 NZ5925
Coatham Mundeville *Dur* 96 NZ2820
Cobbaton *Devon* 19 SS6126
Coberley *Gloucs* 35 SO9616
Cobhall Common *H & W* 46 SO4535
Cobham *Kent* 28 TQ6768
Cobham *Surrey* 26 TQ1060
Coblers Green *Essex* 40 TL6819
Cobley *Dorset* 12 SU0220
Cobnash *H & W* 46 SO4560
Cobo *Guern* 152 GN4910
Cobridge *Staffs* 72 SJ8747
Coburby *Gramp* 143 NJ9164
Cock Alley *Derbys* 74 SK4170
Cock Bank *Clwyd* 71 SJ3545
Cock Bevington *Warwks* 48 SP0552
Cock Bridge *Gramp* 133 NJ2509
Cock Clarks *Essex* 40 TL8102
Cock End *Suffk* 53 TL7253
Cock Green *Essex* 40 TL6919
Cock Marling *E Susx* 17 TQ8718
Cock Street *Kent* 28 TQ7850
Cockayne *N York* 90 SE6198
Cockayne Hatley *Beds* 52 TL2649
Cockburnspath *Border* 119 NT7770
Cockenzie and Port Seton *Loth* 118 NT4075
Cocker Bar *Lancs* 80 SD5022
Cocker Brook *Lancs* 81 SD7425
Cockerdale *W York* 82 SE2329
Cockerham *Lancs* 80 SD4651
Cockermouth *Cumb* 92 NY1230
Cockernhoe Green *Herts* 38 TL1223
Cockett *W Glam* 32 SS6394
Cockfield *Dur* 96 NZ1224
Cockfield *Suffk* 54 TL9054
Cockfosters *Gt Lon* 27 TQ2796
Cocking *W Susx* 14 SU8717
Cocking Causeway *W Susx* 14 SU8819
Cockington *Devon* 7 SX8963
Cocklake *Somset* 21 ST4449
Cockley Beck *Cumb* 86 NY2501
Cockley Cley *Norfk* 66 TF7904
Cockpole Green *Berks* 37 SU7981
Cocks *Cnwll* 3 SW7652
Cockshutford *Shrops* 59 SO5885
Cockshutt *Shrops* 59 SJ4328
Cockthorpe *Norfk* 66 TF9842
Cockwells *Cnwll* 2 SW5234
Cockwood *Devon* 9 SX9780
Cockwood *Somset* 20 ST2242
Cockyard *Derbys* 74 SK0479
Cockyard *H & W* 46 SO4133
Coddenham *Suffk* 54 TM1354
Coddington *Ches* 71 SJ4555
Coddington *H & W* 47 SO7142
Coddington *Notts* 76 SK8354
Codford St. Mary *Wilts* 22 ST9739
Codford St. Peter *Wilts* 22 ST9639
Codicote *Herts* 39 TL2118
Codmore Hill *W Susx* 14 TQ0520
Codnor *Derbys* 74 SK4149
Codrington *Avon* 35 ST7278
Codsall *Staffs* 60 SJ8603
Codsall Wood *Staffs* 60 SJ8404
Coed Morgan *Gwent* 34 SO3511
Coed Talon *Clwyd* 70 SJ2659
Coed Ystumgwern *Gwynd* 57 SH5824
Coed-y-caerau *Gwent* 34 ST3891
Coed-y-paen *Gwent* 34 ST3398
Coed-yr-ynys *Powys* 33 SO1520
Coedana *Gwynd* 68 SH4382
Coedely *M Glam* 33 ST0285
Coedkernew *Gwent* 34 ST2783
Coedpoeth *Clwyd* 70 SJ2851
Coedway *Powys* 59 SJ3315
Coelbren *Powys* 33 SN8511
Coffinswell *Devon* 7 SX8968
Coffle End *Beds* 51 TL0159
Cofton Hackett *H & W* 60 SP0075
Cogan *S Glam* 33 ST1771
Cogenhoe *Nhants* 51 SP8260
Cogges *Oxon* 36 SP3609
Coggeshall *Essex* 40 TL8522
Coggin's Mill *E Susx* 16 TQ5927
Coignafearn *Highld* 140 NH7018
Coilacriech *Gramp* 134 NO3296
Coilantogle *Cent* 124 NN5907
Coillore *Highld* 136 NG3537
Coiltry *Highld* 131 NH3506
Coity *M Glam* 33 SS9281
Col *W Isls* 154 NB4739
Colaboll *Highld* 146 NC5610
Colan *Cnwll* 4 SW8661
Colaton Raleigh *Devon* 9 SY0787
Colbost *Highld* 136 NG2148
Colburn *N York* 89 SE1999
Colbury *Hants* 12 SU3410
Colby *Cumb* 94 NY6620
Colby *IOM* 153 SC2370
Colby *Norfk* 67 TG2231
Colchester *Essex* 41 TL9925
Cold Ash *Berks* 24 SU5169
Cold Ashby *Nhants* 50 SP6576
Cold Ashton *Avon* 35 ST7572
Cold Aston *Gloucs* 36 SP1219
Cold Blow *Dyfed* 31 SN1212
Cold Brayfield *Bucks* 38 SP9252
Cold Cotes *N York* 88 SD7171
Cold Green *H & W* 47 SO6842
Cold Hanworth *Lincs* 76 TF0383
Cold Harbour *Herts* 38 TL1415
Cold Harbour *Oxon* 37 SU6379
Cold Harbour *Wilts* 22 ST8645
Cold Hatton *Shrops* 59 SJ6221
Cold Hatton Heath *Shrops* 59 SJ6321
Cold Hesledon *Dur* 96 NZ4146
Cold Hiendley *W York* 83 SE3714
Cold Higham *Nhants* 49 SP6653
Cold Kirby *N York* 90 SE5384
Cold Newton *Leics* 63 SK7106
Cold Northcott *Cnwll* 5 SX2086
Cold Norton *Essex* 40 TL8500
Cold Overton *Leics* 63 SK8010
Cold Weston *Shrops* 59 SO5583
Coldbackie *Highld* 149 NC6160
Coldbeck *Cumb* 88 NY7204
Coldblow *Gt Lon* 27 TQ5073
Coldean *E Susx* 15 TQ3308
Coldeast *Devon* 7 SX8174
Colden *W York* 82 SD9628
Colden Common *Hants* 13 SU4822
Coldfair Green *Suffk* 55 TM4360
Coldham *Cambs* 65 TF4303
Coldharbour *Cnwll* 3 SW7548
Coldharbour *Gloucs* 34 SO5503
Coldharbour *Surrey* 15 TQ1443
Coldingham *Border* 119 NT9065
Coldmeece *Staffs* 72 SJ8532
Coldred *Kent* 29 TR2747
Coldridge *Devon* 8 SS6907
Coldstream *Border* 110 NT8439
Coldwaltham *W Susx* 14 TQ0216
Coldwell *H & W* 46 SO4235
Coldwells *Gramp* 143 NJ9538
Coldwells *Gramp* 143 NK1039
Cole *Somset* 22 ST6733
Cole End *Warwks* 61 SP2089
Cole Green *Herts* 39 TL2811
Cole Green *Herts* 39 TL4330
Cole Henley *Hants* 24 SU4651
Cole's Cross *Devon* 7 SX7746
Colebatch *Shrops* 59 SO3187
Colebrook *Devon* 9 ST0006
Colebrook *Devon* 6 SX5457
Colebrooke *Devon* 8 SX7699
Coleby *Humb* 84 SE8919
Coleby *Lincs* 76 SK9760
Coleford *Devon* 8 SS7701
Coleford *Gloucs* 34 SO5710
Coleford *Somset* 22 ST6848
Coleford Water *Somset* 20 ST1133
Colegate End *Norfk* 55 TM1987
Colehill *Dorset* 12 SU0201
Coleman Green *Herts* 39 TL1812
Coleman's Hatch *E Susx* 16 TQ4433
Colemere *Shrops* 59 SJ4332
Colemore *Hants* 24 SU7030
Colemore Green *Shrops* 60 SO7197
Colenden *Tays* 126 NO1029
Coleorton *Leics* 62 SK4017
Colerne *Wilts* 35 ST8271
Coles Cross *Dorset* 10 ST3902
Coles Green *Suffk* 54 TM1041
Colesbourne *Gloucs* 35 SP0013
Colesden *Beds* 52 TL1255
Coleshill *Bucks* 26 SU9495
Coleshill *Oxon* 36 SU2393
Coleshill *Warwks* 61 SP2089
Colestocks *Devon* 9 ST0900
Coleton *Devon* 7 SX9051
Coley *Avon* 21 ST5855
Colgate *W Susx* 15 TQ2332
Colgrain *Strath* 115 NS3280
Colinsburgh *Fife* 127 NO4703
Colinton *Loth* 117 NT2168
Colintraive *Strath* 114 NS0374
Colkirk *Norfk* 66 TF9126
Collace *Tays* 126 NO2032
Collafirth *Shet* 155 HU3482
Collaton *Devon* 7 SX7139
Collaton *Devon* 7 SX7952
Collaton St. Mary *Devon* 7 SX8660
College Green *Somset* 21 ST5736
College of Roseisle *Gramp* 141 NJ1466
College Town *Berks* 25 SU8560
Collessie *Fife* 126 NO2813
Colleton Mills *Devon* 19 SS6615
Collier Row *Gt Lon* 27 TQ5091
Collier Street *Kent* 28 TQ7145
Collier's End *Herts* 39 TL3720
Collier's Green *Kent* 17 TQ7822
Colliers Green *Kent* 28 TQ7538
Colliery Row *T & W* 96 NZ3249
Collieston *Gramp* 143 NK0328
Collin *D & G* 100 NY0276
Collingbourne Ducis *Wilts* 23 SU2453
Collingbourne Kingston *Wilts* 23 SU2355
Collingham *W York* 83 SE3945
Collington *H & W* 47 SO6460
Collingtree *Nhants* 49 SP7555
Collins Green *Ches* 78 SJ5594
Collins Green *H & W* 47 SO7457
Colliston *Tays* 127 NO6045
Colliton *Devon* 9 ST0804
Collyweston *Nhants* 63 SK9902
Colmonell *Strath* 98 NX1485
Colmworth *Beds* 51 TL1058
Coln Rogers *Gloucs* 36 SP0809
Coln St. Aldwyns *Gloucs* 36 SP1405
Coln St. Dennis *Gloucs* 36 SP0810
Colnbrook *Gt Lon* 26 TQ0277
Colne *Cambs* 52 TL3775
Colne *Lancs* 81 SD8939
Colne Bridge *W York* 82 SE1720
Colne Edge *Lancs* 81 SD8841
Colne Engaine *Essex* 40 TL8430
Colney *Norfk* 66 TG1807
Colney Heath *Herts* 39 TL2005
Colney Street *Herts* 26 TL1502
Colpy *Gramp* 142 NJ6432
Colquhar *Border* 109 NT3341
Colquite *Cnwll* 4 SX0570
Colscott *Devon* 18 SS3614
Colsterdale *N York* 89 SE1381
Colsterworth *Lincs* 63 SK9324
Colston Bassett *Notts* 63 SK7033
Colt Hill *Hants* 24 SU7551
Colt's Hill *Kent* 16 TQ6443
Coltfield *Gramp* 141 NJ1163
Coltishall *Norfk* 67 TG2719
Colton *Cumb* 86 SD3185
Colton *N York* 83 SE5444
Colton *Norfk* 66 TG1009
Colton *Staffs* 73 SK0420
Colton *W York* 83 SE3732
Columbjohn *Devon* 9 SX9699
Colva *Powys* 45 SO1952
Colvend *D & G* 92 NX8654
Colwall *H & W* 47 SO7542
Colwell *Nthumb* 102 NY9575
Colwich *Staffs* 73 SK0121
Colwick *Notts* 62 SK6140
Colwinston *S Glam* 33 SS9375
Colworth *W Susx* 14 SU9103
Colwyn Bay *Clwyd* 69 SH8578
Colyford *Devon* 10 SY2592
Colyton *Devon* 9 SY2494
Combe *Berks* 23 SU3760
Combe *Devon* 7 SX7238
Combe *Devon* 7 SX8448
Combe *H & W* 46 SO3463
Combe *Oxon* 36 SP4116
Combe Almer *Dorset* 11 SY9597
Combe Common *Surrey* 14 SU9436
Combe Fishacre *Devon* 7 SX8465
Combe Florey *Somset* 20 ST1531
Combe Hay *Avon* 22 ST7359
Combe Martin *Devon* 19 SS5846
Combe Moor *H & W* 46 SO3663
Combe Raleigh *Devon* 9 ST1502
Combe St. Nicholas *Somset* 10 ST3011
Combeinteignhead *Devon* 7 SX9071
Comberbach *Ches* 79 SJ6477
Comberford *Staffs* 61 SK1907
Comberton *Cambs* 52 TL3856
Comberton *H & W* 46 SO4968
Combridge *Staffs* 73 SK0937
Combrook *Warwks* 48 SP3051
Combs *Derbys* 74 SK0478
Combs *Suffk* 54 TM0456
Combs Ford *Suffk* 54 TM0457
Combwich *Somset* 20 ST2542
Comers *Gramp* 135 NJ6707
Comhampton *H & W* 47 SO8367
Commercial *Dyfed* 31 SN1416
Commercial End *Cambs* 53 TL5563
Commins Coch *Powys* 57 SH8402
Common Edge *Lancs* 80 SD3232
Common End *Cumb* 92 NY0022
Common Moor *Cnwll* 5 SX2469
Common Platt *Wilts* 36 SU1186
Common Side *Derbys* 74 SK3375
Common The *Wilts* 23 SU2432
Commondale *N York* 90 NZ6610
Commonside *Ches* 71 SJ5473
Commonside *Derbys* 73 SK2441
Commonwood *Clwyd* 71 SJ3753
Commonwood *Shrops* 59 SJ4828
Compass *Somset* 20 ST2934
Compstall *Gt Man* 79 SJ9690
Compstonend *D & G* 99 NX6652
Compton *Berks* 37 SU5280
Compton *Devon* 7 SX8664
Compton *Hants* 23 SU3529
Compton *Hants* 13 SU4625
Compton *Staffs* 60 SO8284
Compton *Surrey* 25 SU9546
Compton *W Susx* 14 SU7714
Compton *Wilts* 23 SU1351
Compton Abbas *Dorset* 22 ST8618
Compton Abdale *Gloucs* 36 SP0516
Compton Bassett *Wilts* 36 SU0372
Compton Beauchamp *Oxon* 36 SU2786
Compton Bishop *Somset* 21 ST3955
Compton Chamberlayne *Wilts* 23 SU0229
Compton Dando *Avon* 21 ST6464
Compton Dundon *Somset* 21 ST4932
Compton Durville *Somset* 10 ST4117
Compton Greenfield *Avon* 34 ST5681
Compton Martin *Avon* 21 ST5457
Compton Pauncefoot *Somset* 21 ST6426
Compton Valence *Dorset* 10 SY5993
Compton Verney *Warwks* 48 SP3152
Comrie *Fife* 117 NT0289
Comrie *Tays* 124 NN7722
Conaglen House *Highld* 130 NN0268
Conchra *Highld* 138 NG8827
Concraigie *Tays* 125 NO0944
Conderton *H & W* 47 SO9637
Condicote *Gloucs* 48 SP1528
Condorrat *Strath* 116 NS7373
Condover *Shrops* 59 SJ4905
Coney Hill *Gloucs* 35 SO8517
Coney Weston *Suffk* 54 TL9578
Coneyhurst Common *W Susx* 14 TQ1023
Coneysthorpe *N York* 90 SE7171
Conford *Hants* 14 SU8233
Congdon's Shop *Cnwll* 5 SX2878
Congerstone *Leics* 62 SK3605
Congham *Norfk* 65 TF7123
Conghurst *Kent* 17 TQ7628
Congl-y-wal *Gwynd* 57 SH7044
Congleton *Ches* 72 SJ8562
Congresbury *Avon* 21 ST4363
Congreve *Staffs* 60 SJ9013
Conheath *D & G* 100 NX9969
Conicavel *Gramp* 140 NH9853
Coningsby *Lincs* 76 TF2257
Conington *Cambs* 52 TL1885
Conington *Cambs* 52 TL3266
Conisbrough *S York* 75 SK5098
Conisholme *Lincs* 77 TF4095
Coniston *Cumb* 86 SD3097
Coniston *Humb* 85 TA1434
Coniston Cold *N York* 81 SD9054
Conistone *N York* 88 SD9867
Connah's Quay *Clwyd* 71 SJ2969
Connel *Strath* 122 NM9134
Connel Park *Strath* 107 NS6012
Connor Downs *Cnwll* 2 SW5939
Conon Bridge *Highld* 139 NH5455
Cononley *N York* 82 SD9846
Consall *Staffs* 72 SJ9848
Consett *Dur* 95 NZ1051
Constable Burton *N York* 89 SE1690
Constable Lee *Lancs* 81 SD8123
Constantine *Cnwll* 3 SW7329
Contin *Highld* 139 NH4556
Conwy *Gwynd* 69 SH7877
Conyer *Kent* 28 TQ9664
Conyer's Green *Suffk* 54 TL8867
Cooden *E Susx* 17 TQ7107
Cook's Green *Essex* 41 TM1818
Cookbury *Devon* 18 SS4006
Cookbury Wick *Devon* 18 SS3905
Cookham *Berks* 26 SU8985
Cookham Dean *Berks* 26 SU8685
Cookham Rise *Berks* 26 SU8885
Cookhill *Warwks* 48 SP0558
Cookley *H & W* 60 SO8480
Cookley *Suffk* 55 TM3475
Cookley Green *Oxon* 37 SU6990
Cookney *Gramp* 135 NO8693
Cooks Green *Suffk* 54 TL9753
Cooksbridge *E Susx* 15 TQ4013
Cooksey Green *H & W* 47 SO9069
Cookshill *Staffs* 72 SJ9443
Cooksland *Cnwll* 4 SX0867
Cooksmill Green *Essex* 40 TL6306
Cookson Green *Ches* 71 SJ5774
Cookson's Green *Dur* 96 NZ2933
Coolham *W Susx* 14 TQ1122
Cooling *Kent* 28 TQ7575
Cooling Street *Kent* 28 TQ7474
Coombe *Cnwll* 2 SW6242
Coombe *Cnwll* 3 SW8340
Coombe *Devon* 7 SX9373
Coombe *Devon* 9 SY1091
Coombe *Gloucs* 35 ST7694
Coombe *Hants* 13 SU6620
Coombe *Wilts* 23 SU1450
Coombe Bissett *Wilts* 23 SU1026
Coombe Cellars *Devon* 7 SX9072
Coombe Cross *Hants* 13 SU6620
Coombe End *Somset* 20 ST0329
Coombe Hill *Gloucs* 47 SO8826
Coombe Keynes *Dorset* 11 SY8484
Coombe Pafford *Devon* 7 SX9166
Coombe Street *Somset* 22 ST7631
Coombes *W Susx* 15 TQ1808
Coombeswood *W Mids* 60 SO9785
Cooper Street *Kent* 29 TR3060
Cooper Turning *Gt Man* 79 SD6308
Cooper's Corner *Kent* 16 TQ4849
Cooperhill *Gramp* 141 NH9953
Coopers Green *E Susx* 16 TQ4723
Coopersale Common *Essex* 27 TL4702
Coopersale Street *Essex* 27 TL4701
Cootham *W Susx* 14 TQ0714
Cop Street *Kent* 27 TQ2959
Copdock *Suffk* 54 TM1242
Copford Green *Essex* 40 TL9222
Copgrove *N York* 89 SE3463
Copister *Shet* 155 HU4879
Cople *Beds* 38 TL1048
Copley *Dur* 95 NZ0825
Copley *Gt Man* 79 SJ9798
Copley *W York* 82 SE0822
Coplow Dale *Derbys* 74 SK1679
Copmanthorpe *N York* 83 SE5646
Copmere End *Staffs* 72 SJ8029
Copp *Lancs* 80 SD4239
Coppathorne *Cnwll* 18 SS2000
Coppenhall *Staffs* 72 SJ9019
Coppenhall Moss *Ches* 72 SJ7058
Copperhouse *Cnwll* 2 SW5637
Coppers Green *Herts* 39 TL1909
Coppicegate *Shrops* 60 SO7379
Coppingford *Cambs* 52 TL1679
Coppins Corner *Kent* 28 TQ9448
Copplestone *Devon* 8 SS7702
Coppull *Lancs* 81 SD5614
Coppull Moor *Lancs* 81 SD5512
Copsale *W Susx* 15 TQ1724
Copster Green *Lancs* 81 SD6733
Copston Magna *Warwks* 50 SP4588
Copt Heath *W Mids* 61 SP1777
Copt Hewick *N York* 89 SE3471
Copthall Green *Essex* 27 TL4201
Copthorne *Cnwll* 5 SX2692
Copthorne *W Susx* 15 TQ3139
Copy's Green *Norfk* 66 TF9439
Copythorne *Hants* 12 SU3014
Coram Street *Suffk* 54 TM0042
Corbets Tay *Gt Lon* 27 TQ5685
Corbiere *Jersey* 152 JS0508
Corbridge *Nthumb* 103 NY9964
Corby *Nhants* 51 SP8988
Corby Glen *Lincs* 63 TF0024
Corby Hill *Cumb* 94 NY4857
Cordon *Strath* 105 NS0230
Cordwell *Derbys* 74 SK3176
Coreley *Shrops* 46 SO6173
Cores End *Bucks* 26 SU9087
Corfe *Somset* 20 ST2319
Corfe Castle *Dorset* 11 SY9681
Corfe Mullen *Dorset* 11 SY9798
Corfton *Shrops* 59 SO4985
Corgarff *Gramp* 133 NJ2708
Corhampton *Hants* 13 SU6120
Corks Pond *Kent* 28 TQ6540
Corley *Warwks* 61 SP3085
Corley Ash *Warwks* 61 SP2986
Corley Moor *Warwks* 61 SP2884
Cormuir *Tays* 134 NO3066
Cornard Tye *Suffk* 54 TL9041
Corndon *Devon* 8 SX6985
Corner Row *Lancs* 80 SD4134
Corney *Cumb* 86 SD1191
Cornforth *Dur* 96 NZ3134
Cornhill *Gramp* 142 NJ5858
Cornhill-on-Tweed *Nthumb* 110 NT8639
Cornholme *W York* 81 SD9126
Cornish Hall End *Essex* 53 TL6836
Cornoigmore *Strath* 120 NL9846
Cornriggs *Dur* 95 NY8441
Cornsay *Dur* 96 NZ1443
Cornsay Colliery *Dur* 96 NZ1643
Corntown *Highld* 139 NH5556
Corntown *M Glam* 33 SS9177
Cornwell *Oxon* 48 SP2727
Cornwood *Devon* 6 SX6059
Cornworthy *Devon* 7 SX8255
Corpach *Highld* 130 NN0976
Corpusty *Norfk* 66 TG1129
Corrachree *Gramp* 134 NJ4604
Corran *Cnwll* 3 SW9946
Corran *Highld* 130 NG8409
Corran *Highld* 130 NN0263
Corrany *IOM* 153 SC4589
Corrie *D & G* 101 NY2086
Corrie *Strath* 105 NS0242
Corriecravie *Strath* 105 NR9223
Corriegour Lodge Hotel *Highld* 131 NN2692
Corriemoille *Highld* 139 NH3663
Corrimony *Highld* 139 NH3730
Corringham *Essex* 40 TQ7083
Corringham *Lincs* 76 SK8691
Corris *Gwynd* 57 SH7508
Corris Uchaf *Gwynd* 57 SH7408
Corrow *Strath* 114 NN1800
Corry *Highld* 137 NG6424
Corrygills *Strath* 105 NS0335
Cors-y-Gedol *Gwynd* 57 SH6022
Corscombe *Devon* 8 SX6296
Corscombe *Dorset* 10 ST5105
Corse *Gloucs* 47 SO7826
Corse Lawn *Gloucs* 47 SO8330
Corsham *Wilts* 35 ST8770
Corsindae *Gramp* 135 NJ6808
Corsley *Wilts* 22 ST8246

Corsley Heath Crosshill

Corsley Heath *Wilts* 22 ST8245
Corsock *D & G* 99 NX7675
Corston *Avon* 22 ST6965
Corston *Wilts* 35 ST9283
Corstorphine *Loth* 117 NT1972
Cortachy *Tays* 134 NO3959
Corton *Suffk* 67 TM5497
Corton *Wilts* 22 ST9340
Corton Denham *Somset* 21 ST6322
Coruanan Lodge *Highld* 130 NN0668
Corvallie *IOM* 153 SC1968
Corwar *Strath* 98 NX2780
Corwen *Clwyd* 70 SJ0743
Coryates *Dorset* 10 SY6285
Coryton *Devon* 5 SX4583
Coryton *Essex* 40 TQ7382
Cosby *Leics* 50 SP5495
Coseley *W Mids* 60 SO9494
Cosford *Shrops* 60 SJ8005
Cosgrove *Nhants* 38 SP7942
Cosham *Hants* 13 SU6505
Cosheston *Dyfed* 30 SN0003
Coshieville *Tays* 124 NN7749
Cossall *Notts* 62 SK4842
Cossall Marsh *Notts* 62 SK4842
Cossington *Leics* 62 SK6013
Cossington *Somset* 21 ST3540
Costallack *Cnwll* 2 SW4525
Costessey *Norfk* 66 TG1711
Costock *Notts* 62 SK5726
Coston *Leics* 63 SK8422
Coston *Norfk* 66 TG0506
Cote *Oxon* 36 SP3502
Cote *Somset* 21 ST3444
Cotebrook *Ches* 71 SJ5765
Cotehill *Cumb* 93 NY4650
Cotes *Cumb* 87 SD4886
Cotes *Leics* 62 SK5520
Cotes *Staffs* 72 SJ8434
Cotes Heath *Staffs* 72 SJ8334
Cotesbach *Leics* 50 SP5382
Cotgrave *Notts* 63 SK6435
Cotham *Notts* 63 SK7947
Cothelstone *Somset* 20 ST1831
Cotherstone *Dur* 95 NZ0119
Cothill *Oxon* 37 SU4699
Cotleigh *Devon* 9 ST2002
Cotmanhay *Derbys* 62 SK4543
Coton *Cambs* 52 TL4058
Coton *Nhants* 50 SP6771
Coton *Shrops* 59 SJ5334
Coton *Staffs* 72 SJ8120
Coton *Staffs* 72 SJ9731
Coton *Staffs* 61 SK1804
Coton Clanford *Staffs* 72 SJ8723
Coton Hayes *Staffs* 72 SJ9832
Coton Hill *Shrops* 59 SJ4813
Coton in the Clay *Staffs* 73 SK1628
Coton in the Elms *Derbys* 73 SK2415
Coton Park *Derbys* 73 SK2617
Cott *Devon* 7 SX7861
Cottage End *Hants* 24 SU4143
Cottam *Humb* 91 SE9964
Cottam *Lancs* 80 SD5032
Cottam *Notts* 75 SK8179
Cottenham *Cambs* 53 TL4467
Cotterdale *N York* 88 SD8393
Cottered *Herts* 39 TL3129
Cotteridge *W Mids* 61 SP0480
Cotterstock *Nhants* 51 TL0490
Cottesbrooke *Nhants* 50 SP7173
Cottesmore *Leics* 63 SK9013
Cottingham *Humb* 84 TA0432
Cottingham *Nhants* 51 SP8490
Cottingley *W York* 82 SE1137
Cottisford *Oxon* 49 SP5831
Cottivett *Cnwll* 5 SX3662
Cotton *Suffk* 54 TM0666
Cotton End *Beds* 38 TL0845
Cotton Tree *Lancs* 81 SD9039
Cottown *Gramp* 142 NJ5026
Cottown *Gramp* 142 NJ7615
Cottown *Gramp* 143 NJ8140
Cottrell *S Glam* 33 ST0774
Cotts *Devon* 6 SX4365
Cotwall *Shrops* 59 SJ6017
Cotwalton *Staffs* 72 SJ9234
Couch's Mill *Cnwll* 4 SX1459
Coughton *H & W* 34 SO5921
Coughton *Warwks* 48 SP0860
Coulaghailtro *Strath* 113 NR7165
Coulags *Highld* 138 NG9645
Coulderton *Cumb* 86 NX9808
Coull *Gramp* 134 NJ5102
Coulport *Strath* 114 NS2187
Coulsdon *Gt Lon* 27 TQ2959
Coulston *Wilts* 22 ST9554
Coulter *Strath* 108 NT0234
Coultershaw Bridge *W Susx* 14 SU9719
Coultings *Somset* 20 ST2241
Coulton *N York* 90 SE6373
Coultra *Fife* 126 NO3523
Cound *Shrops* 59 SJ5505
Coundlane *Shrops* 59 SJ5705
Coundon *Dur* 96 NZ2329
Coundon Grange *Dur* 96 NZ2228
Countersett *N York* 88 SD9187
Countess *Wilts* 23 SU1542
Countess Cross *Essex* 40 TL8631
Countess Wear *Devon* 9 SX9489
Countesthorpe *Leics* 50 SP5895
Countisbury *Devon* 19 SS7449
Coup Green *Lancs* 81 SD5927
Coupar Angus *Tays* 126 NO2239
Coupland *Cumb* 94 NY7118
Coupland *Nthumb* 110 NT9330
Cour *Strath* 105 NR8248
Courance *D & G* 100 NY0590
Court Henry *Dyfed* 32 SN5522
Court-at-Street *Kent* 17 TR0935
Courteachan *Highld* 129 NM6897
Courteenhall *Nhants* 49 SP7653
Courtsend *Essex* 41 TR0293
Courtway *Somset* 20 ST2033
Cousland *Loth* 118 NT3768
Cousley Wood *E Susx* 16 TQ6533
Cove *Devon* 20 SS9619
Cove *Gramp* 135 NJ9501
Cove *Hants* 25 SU8555
Cove *Highld* 144 NG8191
Cove *Strath* 114 NS2282
Cove Bottom *Suffk* 55 TM4979
Covehithe *Suffk* 55 TM5282
Coven *Staffs* 60 SJ9106
Coven Lawn *Staffs* 60 SJ9005
Coveney *Cambs* 53 TL4882
Covenham St. Bartholomew *Lincs* 77 TF3394
Covenham St. Mary *Lincs* 77 TF3394
Coventry *W Mids* 61 SP3378
Coverack *Cnwll* 3 SW7818
Coverack Bridges *Cnwll* 2 SW6630
Coverham *N York* 89 SE1086
Covington *Cambs* 51 TL0570
Cow Green *Suffk* 54 TM0565
Cow Honeybourne *H & W* 48 SP1143
Cowan Bridge *Lancs* 87 SD6376
Cowbeech *E Susx* 16 TQ6114
Cowbit *Lincs* 64 TF2518
Cowbridge *S Glam* 33 SS9974
Cowdale *Derbys* 74 SK0771
Cowden *Kent* 16 TQ4640
Cowden Pound *Kent* 16 TQ4642
Cowden Station *Kent* 16 TQ4741
Cowdenbeath *Fife* 117 NT1691
Cowers Lane *Derbys* 73 SK3046
Cowes *IOW* 13 SZ4996
Cowesby *N York* 89 SE4689
Cowesfield Green *Wilts* 23 SU2523
Cowfold *W Susx* 15 TQ2122
Cowgill *Cumb* 88 SD7586
Cowhill *Avon* 34 ST6091
Cowie *Cent* 116 NS8389
Cowley *Derbys* 74 SK3376
Cowley *Devon* 9 SX9095
Cowley *Gloucs* 35 SO9614
Cowley *Gt Lon* 26 TQ0582
Cowley *Oxon* 37 SP5304
Cowley *Oxon* 49 SP6628
Cowling *Lancs* 81 SD5917
Cowling *N York* 82 SD9643
Cowling *N York* 89 SE2387
Cowlinge *Suffk* 53 TL7154
Cowmes *W York* 82 SE1815
Cowpe *Lancs* 81 SD8320
Cowpen *Nthumb* 103 NZ2981
Cowpen Bewley *Cleve* 97 NZ4824
Cowplain *Hants* 13 SU6810
Cowshill *Dur* 95 NY8540
Cowslip Green *Avon* 21 ST4861
Cowthorpe *N York* 83 SE4252
Cox Common *Suffk* 55 TM4082
Coxall *Shrops* 46 SO3774
Coxbank *Ches* 72 SJ6541
Coxbench *Derbys* 62 SK3743
Coxbridge *Somset* 21 ST5436
Coxford *Cnwll* 4 SX1696
Coxford *Norfk* 66 TF8529
Coxgreen *Staffs* 60 SO8086
Coxheath *Kent* 28 TQ7451
Coxhoe *Dur* 96 NZ3136
Coxley *Somset* 21 ST5343
Coxley *W York* 82 SE2717
Coxley Wick *Somset* 21 ST5243
Coxpark *Cnwll* 5 SX4072
Coxtie Green *Essex* 27 TQ5696
Coxwold *N York* 90 SE5377
Coychurch *M Glam* 33 SS9379
Coylton *Strath* 107 NS4219
Coylumbridge *Highld* 132 NH9111
Coytrahen *M Glam* 33 SS8885
Crab Orchard *Dorset* 12 SU0806
Crabbs Cross *H & W* 48 SP0465
Crabtree *W Susx* 15 TQ2125
Crabtree Green *Clwyd* 71 SJ3344
Crackenthorpe *Cumb* 94 NY6622
Crackington Haven *Cnwll* 4 SX1496
Crackley *Staffs* 72 SJ8350
Crackley *Warwks* 61 SP2973
Crackleybank *Shrops* 60 SJ7611
Crackpot *N York* 88 SD9796
Cracoe *N York* 88 SD9760
Craddock *Devon* 9 ST0812
Cradle End *Herts* 39 TL4521
Cradley *H & W* 47 SO7347
Cradoc *Powys* 45 SO0130
Crafthole *Cnwll* 5 SX3654
Crafton *Bucks* 38 SP8819
Crag Foot *Lancs* 87 SD4873
Cragg *W York* 82 SE0023
Cragg Hill *W York* 82 SE2437
Craggan *Highld* 141 NJ0226
Craghead *Dur* 96 NZ2150
Crai *Powys* 45 SN8924
Craibstone *Gramp* 142 NJ4959
Craibstone *Gramp* 135 NJ8710
Craichie *Tays* 127 NO5047
Craig *Tays* 127 NO6956
Craig Llangiwg *W Glam* 32 SN7204
Craig Penllyn *S Glam* 33 SS9777
Craig's End *Essex* 53 TL7137
Craig-y-Duke *W Glam* 32 SN7002
Craig-y-nos *Powys* 33 SN8415
Craigburn *Border* 117 NT2354
Craigcefnparc *W Glam* 32 SN6702
Craigcleuch *D & G* 101 NY3486
Craigdam *Gramp* 143 NJ8430
Craigdarroch *D & G* 107 NX7391
Craigdhu *Strath* 122 NM8205
Craigearn *Gramp* 142 NJ7214
Craigellachie *Gramp* 141 NJ2844
Craigend *Strath* 115 NS4670
Craigend *Tays* 126 NO1120
Craigendoran *Strath* 115 NS3181
Craigengillan *Strath* 107 NS4702
Craighlaw *D & G* 98 NX3061
Craigie *Strath* 107 NS4232
Craigie *Tays* 126 NO1143
Craigiefold *Gramp* 143 NJ9165
Craigley *D & G* 99 NX7658
Craiglockhart *Fife* 117 NT2271
Craiglug *Gramp* 141 NJ3355
Craigmillar *Loth* 117 NT3071
Craignant *Shrops* 58 SJ2535
Craigneston *D & G* 107 NX7587
Craigneuk *Strath* 116 NS7765
Craignure *Strath* 122 NM7236
Craigo *Tays* 135 NO6864
Craigrothie *Fife* 126 NO3810
Craigruie *Cent* 124 NN4920
Craigton *Gramp* 135 NJ8301
Craigton *Strath* 115 NS4954
Craigton *Tays* 127 NO5138
Craigton of Airlie *Tays* 126 NO3250
Craik *Border* 109 NT3408
Crail *Fife* 127 NO6107
Crailing *Border* 110 NT6824
Crakehall *N York* 89 SE2489
Crakehill *N York* 89 SE4273
Crakemarsh *Staffs* 73 SK0936
Crambe *N York* 90 SE7364
Cramlington *Nthumb* 103 NZ2676
Cramond *Loth* 117 NT1976
Cramond Bridge *Loth* 117 NT1775
Cranage *Ches* 79 SJ7568
Cranberry *Staffs* 72 SJ8235
Cranborne *Dorset* 12 SU0513
Cranbrook *Kent* 28 TQ7736
Cranbrook Common *Kent* 28 TQ7838
Crane Moor *S York* 82 SE3001
Crane's Corner *Norfk* 66 TF9113
Cranfield *Beds* 38 SP9542
Cranford *Devon* 18 SS3421
Cranford *Gt Lon* 26 TQ1076
Cranford St. Andrew *Nhants* 51 SP9277
Cranford St. John *Nhants* 51 SP9276
Cranham *Gloucs* 35 SO8913
Cranham *Gt Lon* 27 TQ5786
Cranhill *Warwks* 48 SP1253
Crank *Mersyd* 78 SJ5099
Cranleigh *Surrey* 14 TQ0539
Cranmer Green *Suffk* 54 TM0171
Cranmore *IOW* 13 SZ3990
Cranmore *Somset* 22 ST6643
Cranoe *Leics* 50 SP7695
Cransford *Suffk* 55 TM3164
Cranshaws *Border* 118 NT6861
Cranstal *IOM* 153 NX4602
Cranswick *Humb* 84 TA0252
Crantock *Cnwll* 4 SW7960
Cranwell *Lincs* 76 TF0349
Cranwich *Norfk* 65 TL7794
Cranworth *Norfk* 66 TF9804
Craobh Haven *Strath* 122 NM7907
Crapstone *Devon* 6 SX5067
Crarae *Strath* 114 NR9897
Crask Inn *Highld* 149 NC5224
Crask of Aigas *Highld* 139 NH4642
Craster *Nthumb* 111 NU2519
Craswall *H & W* 46 SO2735
Crateford *Staffs* 60 SJ9009
Cratfield *Suffk* 55 TM3175
Crathes *Gramp* 135 NO7596
Crathie *Gramp* 133 NO2695
Crathie *Highld* 132 NN5793
Crathorne *N York* 89 NZ4407
Craven Arms *Shrops* 59 SO4382
Crawcrook *T & W* 103 NZ1363
Crawford *Lancs* 78 SD4902
Crawford *Strath* 108 NS9520
Crawfordjohn *Strath* 108 NS8823
Crawick *D & G* 107 NS7811
Crawley *Hants* 24 SU4235
Crawley *Oxon* 36 SP3412
Crawley *W Susx* 15 TQ2636
Crawley Down *W Susx* 15 TQ3437
Crawley Side *Dur* 95 NY9940
Crawshawbooth *Lancs* 81 SD8125
Crawton *Gramp* 135 NO8779
Cray *N York* 88 SD9479
Cray's Pond *Oxon* 37 SU6380
Crayford *Gt Lon* 27 TQ5175
Crayke *N York* 90 SE5670
Craymere Beck *Norfk* 66 TG0631
Crays Hill *Essex* 40 TQ7192
Craythorne *Staffs* 73 SK2426
Craze Lowman *Devon* 9 SS9814
Crazies Hill *Oxon* 37 SU7980
Creacombe *Devon* 18 SS3219
Creagan Inn *Strath* 122 NM9744
Creagorry *W Isls* 154 NF7948
Creaguaineach Lodge *Highld* 131 NN3068
Creamore Bank *Shrops* 59 SJ5130
Creaton *Nhants* 50 SP7071
Creca *D & G* 101 NY2270
Credenhill *H & W* 46 SO4543
Crediton *Devon* 8 SS8300
Creebank *D & G* 98 NX3477
Creebridge *D & G* 99 NX4165
Creech Heathfield *Somset* 20 ST2727
Creech St. Michael *Somset* 20 ST2725
Creed *Cnwll* 3 SW9347
Creedy Park *Devon* 8 SS8301
Creekmouth *Gt Lon* 27 TQ4581
Creeting St. Mary *Suffk* 54 TM0956
Creeton *Lincs* 64 TF0120
Creetown *D & G* 99 NX4759
Creggans Inn *Strath* 123 NN0902
Cregneish *IOM* 153 SC1867
Cregrina *Powys* 45 SO1252
Creich *Fife* 126 NO3221
Creigiau *M Glam* 33 ST0781
Crelly *Cnwll* 2 SW6732
Cremyll *Cnwll* 6 SX4553
Cressage *Shrops* 59 SJ5904
Cressbrook *Derbys* 74 SK1673
Cresselly *Dyfed* 30 SN0606
Cressex *Bucks* 26 SU8492
Cressing *Essex* 40 TL7920
Cresswell *Dyfed* 30 SN0506
Cresswell *Nthumb* 103 NZ2993
Cresswell *Staffs* 72 SJ9739
Creswell *Derbys* 75 SK5274
Creswell Green *Staffs* 61 SK0710
Cretingham *Suffk* 55 TM2260
Cretshengan *Strath* 113 NR7166
Crew Green *Powys* 59 SJ3215
Crewe *Ches* 71 SJ4253
Crewe *Ches* 72 SJ7056
Crewe Green *Ches* 72 SJ7255
Crewkerne *Somset* 10 ST4409
Crews Hill *H & W* 35 SO6722
Crews Hill Station *Herts* 27 TL3000
Crewton *Derbys* 62 SK3733
Crianlarich *Strath* 123 NN3825
Cribbs Causeway *Avon* 34 ST5780
Cribyn *Dyfed* 44 SN5250
Criccieth *Gwynd* 56 SH4938
Crich *Derbys* 74 SK3454
Crich Carr *Derbys* 74 SK3354
Crich Common *Derbys* 74 SK3553
Crichton *Loth* 118 NT3862
Crick *Gwent* 34 ST4890
Crick *Nhants* 50 SP5872
Crickadarn *Powys* 45 SO0942
Cricket St. Thomas *Somset* 10 ST3708
Crickheath *Shrops* 59 SJ2922
Crickhowell *Powys* 33 SO2118
Cricklade *Wilts* 36 SU0993
Cricklewood *Gt Lon* 26 TQ2385
Cridling Stubbs *N York* 83 SE5221
Crieff *Tays* 125 NN8621
Criggan *Cnwll* 4 SX0160
Criggion *Powys* 59 SJ2915
Crigglestone *W York* 82 SE3116
Crimble *Gt Man* 81 SD8611
Crimond *Gramp* 143 NK0556
Crimonmogate *Gramp* 143 NK0358
Crimplesham *Norfk* 65 TF6503
Crimscote *Warwks* 48 SP2347
Crinan *Strath* 113 NR7894
Crindledyke *Strath* 116 NS8356
Cringleford *Norfk* 67 TG1905
Cringles *N York* 82 SE0448
Crinow *Dyfed* 31 SN1214
Cripp's Corner *E Susx* 17 TQ7721
Cripplesease *Cnwll* 2 SW5036
Cripplestyle *Dorset* 12 SU0812
Crizeley *H & W* 46 SO4532
Croachy *Highld* 140 NH6527
Croanford *Cnwll* 4 SX0371
Crochmare House *D & G* 100 NX8977
Crock Street *Somset* 10 ST3213
Crockenhill *Kent* 27 TQ5067
Crocker End *Oxon* 37 SU7086
Crocker's Ash *H & W* 34 SO5316
Crockerhill *W Susx* 14 SU9206
Crockernwell *Devon* 8 SX7592
Crockerton *Wilts* 22 ST8642
Crocketford *D & G* 100 NX8372
Crockey Hill *N York* 83 SE6246
Crockham Hill *Kent* 27 TQ4450
Crockhurst Street *Kent* 16 TQ6245
Crockleford Heath *Essex* 41 TM0426
Croes-lan *Dyfed* 42 SN3844
Croes-y-mwyalch *Gwent* 34 ST3092
Croes-y-pant *Gwent* 34 SO3104
Croeserw *W Glam* 33 SS8795
Croesgoch *Dyfed* 30 SM8330
Croesor *Gwynd* 57 SH6344
Croesyceiliog *Dyfed* 31 SN4016
Croesyceiliog *Gwent* 34 ST3096
Croft *Ches* 79 SJ6393
Croft *Devon* 5 SX5296
Croft *Leics* 50 SP5195
Croft *Lincs* 77 TF5061
Croft Michael *Cnwll* 2 SW6637
Croft-on-Tees *N York* 89 NZ2809
Croftamie *Cent* 115 NS4785
Crofton *Cumb* 93 NY3050
Crofton *Devon* 9 SX9680
Crofton *W York* 83 SE3817
Crofton *Wilts* 23 SU2562
Crofts *D & G* 99 NX7365
Crofts *Gramp* 141 NJ2850
Crofts of Dipple *Gramp* 141 NJ3259
Crofts of Savoch *Gramp* 143 NK0460
Crofty *W Glam* 32 SS5294
Crogen *Gwynd* 58 SJ0036
Croggan *Strath* 122 NM7027
Croglin *Cumb* 94 NY5747
Crogo *D & G* 99 NX7576
Croik *Highld* 146 NH4591
Cromarty *Highld* 140 NH7867
Crombie *Fife* 117 NT0584
Cromdale *Highld* 141 NJ0728
Cromer *Herts* 39 TL2928
Cromer *Norfk* 67 TG2242
Cromford *Derbys* 73 SK2956
Cromhall *Avon* 35 ST6990
Cromhall Common *Avon* 35 ST6989
Cromore *W Isls* 154 NB4021
Crompton Fold *Gt Man* 79 SD9409
Cromwell *Notts* 75 SK7961
Cronberry *Strath* 107 NS6022
Crondall *Hants* 25 SU7948
Cronton *Mersyd* 78 SJ4988
Crook *Cumb* 87 SD4695
Crook *Dur* 96 NZ1635
Crook Inn *Border* 108 NT1026
Crook of Devon *Tays* 117 NO0400
Crookdake *Cumb* 93 NY1943
Crooke *Gt Man* 78 SD5507
Crooked End *Gloucs* 35 SO6217
Crooked Holme *Cumb* 101 NY5161
Crooked Soley *Wilts* 36 SU3172
Crookedholm *Strath* 107 NS4537
Crookes *S York* 74 SK3287
Crookhall *Dur* 95 NZ1150
Crookham *Berks* 24 SU5464
Crookham *Nthumb* 110 NT9138
Crookham Village *Hants* 25 SU7952
Crooklands *Cumb* 87 SD5383
Cropper *Derbys* 73 SK2335
Cropredy *Oxon* 49 SP4646
Cropston *Leics* 62 SK5510
Cropthorne *H & W* 47 SO9945
Cropton *N York* 90 SE7589
Cropwell Bishop *Notts* 63 SK6835
Cropwell Butler *Notts* 63 SK6837
Crosbie *Strath* 114 NS2149
Crosby *Cumb* 92 NY0738
Crosby *Humb* 84 SE8912
Crosby *IOM* 153 SC3279
Crosby *Mersyd* 78 SJ3198
Crosby Garret *Cumb* 88 NY7209
Crosby on Eden *Cumb* 93 NY4459
Crosby Ravensworth *Cumb* 94 NY6214
Crosby Villa *Cumb* 92 NY0939
Croscombe *Somset* 21 ST5944
Crosemere *Shrops* 59 SJ4329
Cross *Somset* 21 ST4154
Cross Ash *Gwent* 34 SO4019
Cross Bush *W Susx* 14 TQ0306
Cross Coombe *Cnwll* 3 SW7251
Cross End *Beds* 51 TL0658
Cross End *Essex* 40 TL8534
Cross Flatts *W York* 82 SE1040
Cross Gates *W York* 83 SE3534
Cross Green *Devon* 5 SX3888
Cross Green *Staffs* 60 SJ9105
Cross Green *Suffk* 54 TL8353
Cross Green *Suffk* 54 TL8955
Cross Green *Suffk* 54 TL9852
Cross Hands *Dyfed* 31 SN0712
Cross Hands *Dyfed* 32 SN5612
Cross Hill *Derbys* 74 SK4148
Cross Hills *N York* 82 SE0145
Cross Houses *Shrops* 59 SJ5307
Cross Houses *Shrops* 60 SO6991
Cross Inn *Dyfed* 42 SN3957
Cross Inn *Dyfed* 43 SN5464
Cross Inn *M Glam* 33 ST0582
Cross in Hand *E Susx* 16 TQ5521
Cross Keys *Wilts* 35 ST8771
Cross Lane *IOW* 13 SZ5089
Cross Lane Head *Shrops* 60 SO7195
Cross Lanes *Clwyd* 71 SJ3746
Cross Lanes *Cnwll* 2 SW6921
Cross Lanes *Cnwll* 3 SW7642
Cross Lanes *N York* 90 SE5364
Cross Oak *Powys* 45 SO1023
Cross o' th' hands *Derbys* 73 SK2846
Cross of Jackston *Gramp* 142 NJ7432
Cross Roads *Powys* 45 SN9756
Cross Street *Suffk* 54 TM1876
Cross Town *Ches* 79 SJ7578
Cross Ways *Dorset* 11 SY7788
Cross-at-Hand *Kent* 28 TQ7846
Crossaig *Strath* 113 NR8351
Crossapoll *Strath* 120 NL9943
Crossbost *W Isls* 154 NB3924
Crosscanonby *Cumb* 92 NY0739
Crossdale Street *Norfk* 67 TG2239
Crossens *Mersyd* 80 SD3720
Crossford *Fife* 117 NT0786
Crossford *Strath* 116 NS8246
Crossgate *Cnwll* 5 SX3488
Crossgate *Lincs* 64 TF2426
Crossgate *Staffs* 72 SJ9437
Crossgatehall *Loth* 118 NT3669
Crossgates *Fife* 117 NT1488
Crossgates *Powys* 45 SO0864
Crossgates *Strath* 115 NS3744
Crossgill *Lancs* 87 SD5563
Crosshands *Dyfed* 31 SN1923
Crosshands *Strath* 107 NS4830
Crosshill *Fife* 117 NT1796

Crosshill Deepcut

Crosshill *Strath* 106 NS3206
Crosshouse *Strath* 106 NS3938
Crosskeys *Gwent* 34 ST2292
Crosskeys *Strath* 115 NS3385
Crosskirk *Highld* 150 ND0369
Crossland Edge *W York* 82 SE1012
Crossland Hill *W York* 82 SE1114
Crosslands *Cumb* 87 SD3489
Crosslanes *Shrops* 59 SJ3218
Crosslee *Border* 109 NT3018
Crosslee *Strath* 115 NS4066
Crossley *W York* 82 SE2021
Crossmichael *D & G* 99 NX7366
Crosspost *W Susx* 15 TQ2522
Crossroads *Gramp* 134 NJ5607
Crossroads *Gramp* 135 NO7594
Crosston *Tays* 127 NO5256
Crossway *Dyfed* 31 SN1542
Crossway *Gwent* 34 SO4419
Crossway *Powys* 45 SO0558
Crossway Green *Gwent* 34 ST5294
Crossway Green *H & W* 47 SO8468
Crosswell *Dyfed* 31 SN1236
Crosthwaite *Cumb* 87 SD4391
Croston *Lancs* 80 SD4818
Crostwick *Norfk* 67 TG2515
Crostwight *Norfk* 67 TG3429
Crouch *Kent* 28 TQ0558
Crouch End *Gt Lon* 27 TQ3088
Crouch Hill *Dorset* 11 ST7010
Croucheston *Wilts* 23 SU0625
Crough House Green *Kent* 16 TQ4346
Croughton *Nhants* 49 SP5433
Crovie *Gramp* 143 NJ8065
Crow *Hants* 12 SU1604
Crow Edge *S York* 82 SE1804
Crow End *Cambs* 52 TL3257
Crow Green *Essex* 27 TQ5796
Crow Hill *H & W* 47 SO6326
Crow's Green *Essex* 40 TL6926
Crow's Nest *Cnwll* 5 SX2669
Crowan *Cnwll* 2 SW6434
Crowborough *E Susx* 16 TQ5131
Crowborough Town *E Susx* 16 TQ5031
Crowcombe *Somset* 20 ST1436
Crowdecote *Derbys* 74 SK1065
Crowden *Derbys* 74 SK0699
Crowden *Devon* 18 SX4999
Crowdhill *Hants* 13 SU4920
Crowdleham *Kent* 27 TQ5659
Crowell *Oxon* 37 SU7499
Crowfield *Nhants* 49 SP6141
Crowfield *Suffk* 54 TM1457
Crowfield Green *Suffk* 54 TM1458
Crowgate Street *Norfk* 67 TG3121
Crowhill *Loth* 119 NT7374
Crowhole *Derbys* 74 SK3375
Crowhurst *E Susx* 17 TQ7512
Crowhurst *Surrey* 15 TQ3847
Crowhurst Lane End *Surrey* 15 TQ3747
Crowland *Lincs* 64 TF2410
Crowland *Suffk* 54 TM0170
Crowlas *Cnwll* 2 SW5133
Crowle *H & W* 47 SO9256
Crowle *Humb* 84 SE7712
Crowle Green *H & W* 47 SO9156
Crowmarsh Gifford *Oxon* 37 SU6189
Crown Corner *Suffk* 55 TM2570
Crownhill *Devon* 6 SX4858
Crownpits *Surrey* 25 SU9743
Crownthorpe *Norfk* 66 TG0803
Crowntown *Cnwll* 2 SW6330
Crows-an-Wra *Cnwll* 2 SW3927
Crowshill *Norfk* 66 TF9506
Crowsnest *Shrops* 59 SJ3601
Crowthorne *Berks* 25 SU8464
Crowton *Ches* 71 SJ5774
Croxall *Staffs* 61 SK1913
Croxby *Lincs* 76 TF1898
Croxdale *Dur* 96 NZ2636
Croxden *Staffs* 73 SK0639
Croxley Green *Herts* 26 TQ0795
Croxton *Cambs* 52 TL2460
Croxton *Humb* 85 TA0912
Croxton *Norfk* 66 TF9831
Croxton *Norfk* 54 TL8786
Croxton *Staffs* 72 SJ7832
Croxton Green *Ches* 71 SJ5552
Croxton Kerrial *Leics* 63 SK8329
Croxtonbank *Staffs* 72 SJ7832
Croy *Highld* 140 NH7949
Croy *Strath* 116 NS7275
Croyde *Devon* 18 SS4439
Croyde Bay *Devon* 18 SS4339
Croydon *Cambs* 52 TL3149
Croydon *Gt Lon* 27 TQ3265
Crubenmore *Highld* 132 NN6790
Cruckmeole *Shrops* 59 SJ4309
Cruckton *Shrops* 59 SJ4310
Cruden Bay *Gramp* 143 NK0836
Crudgington *Shrops* 59 SJ6318
Crudwell *Wilts* 35 ST9593
Crug *Powys* 45 SO1972
Crug-y-byddar *Powys* 58 SO1682
Crugmeer *Cnwll* 4 SW9076
Crugybar *Dyfed* 44 SN6537
Crumlin *Gwent* 33 ST2197
Crumplehorn *Cnwll* 5 SX2051
Crumpsall *Gt Man* 79 SD8402
Crumstane *Border* 119 NT8053
Crundale *Dyfed* 30 SM9718
Crundale *Kent* 29 TR0749
Crunwear *Dyfed* 31 SN1810
Cruwys Morchard *Devon* 19 SS8712
Crux Easton *Hants* 24 SU4256
Cruxton *Dorset* 10 SY6096
Crwbin *Dyfed* 32 SN4713
Cryers Hill *Bucks* 26 SU8796
Crymmych *Dyfed* 31 SN1834
Crynant *W Glam* 32 SN7904
Crystal Palace *Gt Lon* 27 TQ3371
Cuaig *Highld* 137 NG7057
Cubbington *Warwks* 48 SP3468
Cubert *Cnwll* 4 SW7857
Cubley *S York* 82 SE2401
Cublington *Bucks* 38 SP8422
Cublington *H & W* 46 SO4038
Cuckfield *W Susx* 15 TQ3025
Cucklington *Somset* 22 ST7527
Cuckney *Notts* 75 SK5671
Cuckold's Green *Kent* 28 TQ8276
Cuckoo Bridge *Lincs* 64 TF2020
Cuckoo's Corner *Hants* 24 SU7441
Cuckoo's Nest *Ches* 71 SJ3860
Cuddesdon *Oxon* 37 SP5903
Cuddington *Bucks* 37 SP7311
Cuddington *Ches* 71 SJ5971
Cuddington Heath *Ches* 71 SJ4746
Cuddy Hill *Lancs* 80 SD4937
Cudham *Gt Lon* 27 TQ4459
Cudliptown *Devon* 5 SX5279
Cudnell *Dorset* 12 SZ0696
Cudworth *S York* 83 SE3808
Cudworth *Somset* 10 ST3810
Cudworth Common *S York* 83 SE4007
Cuerden Green *Lancs* 81 SD5525
Cuerdley Cross *Ches* 78 SJ5486
Cufaude *Hants* 24 SU6557
Cuffley *Herts* 39 TL3003
Culbokie *Highld* 140 NH6059
Culbone *Somset* 19 SS8448
Culburnie *Highld* 139 NH4941
Culcabock *Highld* 140 NH6844
Culcharry *Highld* 140 NH8650
Culcheth *Ches* 79 SJ6694
Culdrain *Gramp* 142 NJ5134
Culford *Suffk* 54 TL8370
Culgaith *Cumb* 94 NY6029
Culham *Oxon* 37 SU5095
Culkein *Highld* 148 NC0333
Culkein Drumbeg *Highld* 148 NC1133
Culkerton *Gloucs* 35 ST9395
Cullen *Gramp* 142 NJ5167
Cullercoats *T & W* 103 NZ3570
Cullerlie *Gramp* 135 NJ7603
Cullicudden *Highld* 140 NH6463
Cullingworth *W York* 82 SE0636
Cullipool *Strath* 122 NM7413
Cullivoe *Shet* 155 HP5402
Culloden *Highld* 140 NH7246
Cullompton *Devon* 9 ST0207
Culm Davy *Devon* 9 ST1215
Culmalzie *D & G* 99 NX3753
Culmington *Shrops* 59 SO4982
Culmstock *Devon* 9 ST1013
Culnacraig *Highld* 145 NC0603
Culnaightrie *D & G* 92 NX7750
Culnaknock *Highld* 137 NG5162
Culpho *Suffk* 55 TM2149
Culrain *Highld* 146 NH5794
Culross *Fife* 117 NS9886
Culroy *Strath* 106 NS3114
Culsalmond *Gramp* 142 NJ6532
Culscadden *D & G* 99 NX4748
Culshabbin *D & G* 98 NX3051
Culswick *Shet* 155 HU2745
Cultercullen *Gramp* 143 NJ9223
Cults *Gramp* 135 NJ8903
Culverstone Green *Kent* 27 TQ6362
Culverthorpe *Lincs* 64 TF0240
Culworth *Nhants* 49 SP5446
Cum brwyno *Dyfed* 43 SN7180
Cumbernauld *Strath* 116 NS7674
Cumberworth *Lincs* 77 TF5073
Cumdivock *Cumb* 93 NY3448
Cuminestown *Gramp* 143 NJ8050
Cummersdale *Cumb* 93 NY3953
Cummertrees *D & G* 100 NY1366
Cummingston *Gramp* 141 NJ1368
Cumnor *Oxon* 37 SP4504
Cumrew *Cumb* 94 NY5550
Cumwhinton *Cumb* 93 NY4552
Cumwhitton *Cumb* 94 NY5052
Cundall *N York* 89 SE4272
Cunninghamhead *Strath* 106 NS3741
Cupar *Fife* 126 NO3714
Cupar Muir *Fife* 126 NO3613
Cupernham *Hants* 23 SU3622
Curbar *Derbys* 74 SK2574
Curbridge *Hants* 13 SU5211
Curbridge *Oxon* 36 SP3308
Curdridge *Hants* 13 SU5213
Curdworth *Warwks* 61 SP1792
Curland *Somset* 10 ST2717
Curridge *Berks* 24 SU4972
Currie *Loth* 117 NT1867
Curry Mallet *Somset* 21 ST3221
Curry Rivel *Somset* 21 ST3925
Curteis Corner *Kent* 28 TQ8539
Curtisden Green *Kent* 28 TQ7440
Curtisknowle *Devon* 7 SX7353
Cury *Cnwll* 2 SW6721
Cusgarne *Cnwll* 3 SW7540
Cushnie *Gramp* 134 NJ5211
Cushuish *Somset* 20 ST1930
Cusop *H & W* 46 SO2441
Cutcloy *D & G* 99 NX4534
Cutcombe *Somset* 20 SS9339
Cutgate *Gt Man* 81 SD8614
Cuthill *Highld* 147 NH7587
Cutiau *Gwynd* 57 SH6317
Cutler's Green *Essex* 40 TL5930
Cutmadoc *Cnwll* 4 SX0963
Cutmere *Cnwll* 5 SX3260
Cutnall Green *H & W* 47 SO8868
Cutsdean *Gloucs* 48 SP0830
Cutsyke *W York* 83 SE4224
Cutthorpe *Derbys* 74 SK3473
Cuxham *Oxon* 37 SU6695
Cuxton *Kent* 28 TQ7066
Cuxwold *Lincs* 85 TA1701
Cwm *Clwyd* 70 SJ0677
Cwm *Gwent* 33 SO1805
Cwm Capel *Dyfed* 32 SN4502
Cwm Irfon *Powys* 45 SN8549
Cwm Morgan *Dyfed* 31 SN2934
Cwm Penmachno *Gwynd* 69 SH7547
Cwm-bach *Dyfed* 31 SN4801
Cwm-Cewydd *Gwynd* 57 SH8713
Cwm-Crownon *Powys* 33 SO1419
Cwm-celyn *Gwent* 33 SO2008
Cwm-Llinau *Powys* 57 SH8408
Cwm-y-glo *Dyfed* 32 SN5513
Cwm-y-glo *Gwynd* 69 SH5562
Cwmafan *W Glam* 32 SS7791
Cwmaman *M Glam* 33 ST0099
Cwmann *Dyfed* 44 SN5847
Cwmavon *Gwent* 34 SO2706
Cwmbach *Dyfed* 31 SN2526
Cwmbach *M Glam* 33 SO0201
Cwmbach *Powys* 45 SO1639
Cwmbach Llechrhyd *Powys* 45 SO0254
Cwmbelan *Powys* 58 SN9481
Cwmbran *Gwent* 34 ST2994
Cwmcarn *Gwent* 34 ST2293
Cwmcarvan *Gwent* 34 SO4707
Cwmcoy *Dyfed* 31 SN2942
Cwmdare *M Glam* 33 SN9803
Cwmdu *Dyfed* 44 SN6330
Cwmdu *Powys* 45 SO1823
Cwmdu *W Glam* 32 SS6494
Cwmduad *Dyfed* 31 SN3731
Cwmdwr *Dyfed* 44 SN7132
Cwmergyr *Dyfed* 43 SN7982
Cwmfelin *M Glam* 33 SO0901
Cwmfelin *M Glam* 33 SS8589
Cwmfelin Boeth *Dyfed* 31 SN1919
Cwmfelin Mynach *Dyfed* 31 SN2224
Cwmfelinfach *Gwent* 33 ST1891
Cwmffrwd *Dyfed* 31 SN4217
Cwmgiedd *Powys* 32 SN7911
Cwmgorse *W Glam* 32 SN7010
Cwmgwili *Dyfed* 32 SN5710
Cwmgwrach *W Glam* 33 SN8604
Cwmhiraeth *Dyfed* 31 SN3437
Cwmisfael *Dyfed* 32 SN4915
Cwmllynfell *Dyfed* 32 SN7412
Cwmparc *M Glam* 33 SS9495
Cwmpengraig *Dyfed* 31 SN3536
Cwmpennar *M Glam* 33 SO0300
Cwmrhydyceirw *W Glam* 32 SS6699
Cwmsychpant *Dyfed* 44 SN4746
Cwmtillery *Gwent* 33 SO2105
Cwmyoy *Gwent* 46 SO2923
Cwmystwyth *Dyfed* 43 SN7874
Cwrt *Gwynd* 32 SN6800
Cwrt-newydd *Dyfed* 44 SN4947
Cwrt-y-gollen *Powys* 34 SO2317
Cyfronydd *Powys* 58 SJ1408
Cylibebyll *W Glam* 32 SN7404
Cymer *W Glam* 33 SS8695
Cymmer *M Glam* 33 ST0290
Cynghordy *Dyfed* 44 SN8040
Cynheidre *Dyfed* 32 SN4907
Cynonville *W Glam* 33 SS8395
Cynwyd *Clwyd* 70 SJ0541
Cynwyl Elfed *Dyfed* 31 SN3727

D

Daccombe *Devon* 7 SX9068
Dacre *Cumb* 93 NY4526
Dacre *N York* 89 SE1960
Dacre Banks *N York* 89 SE1962
Daddry Shield *Dur* 95 NY8937
Dadford *Bucks* 49 SP6638
Dadlington *Leics* 61 SP4097
Dafen *Dyfed* 32 SN5201
Daffy Green *Norfk* 66 TF9609
Dagenham *Gt Lon* 27 TQ5084
Daglingworth *Gloucs* 35 SO9905
Dagnall *Bucks* 38 SP9916
Dagworth *Suffk* 54 TM0361
Dailly *Strath* 106 NS2701
Dainton *Devon* 7 SX8566
Dairsie *Fife* 126 NO4117
Daisy Hill *Gt Man* 79 SD6504
Daisy Hill *W York* 82 SE2728
Dalavich *Strath* 122 NM9612
Dalbeattie *D & G* 100 NX8361
Dalblair *Strath* 107 NS6419
Dalbog *Tays* 134 NO5871
Dalbury *Derbys* 73 SK2634
Dalby *IOM* 153 SC2178
Dalby *Lincs* 77 TF4169
Dalby *N York* 90 SE6371
Dalcapon *Tays* 125 NN9754
Dalchalm *Highld* 147 NC9105
Dalchenna *Strath* 123 NN0706
Dalchreichart *Highld* 131 NH2812
Dalchruin *Tays* 124 NN7116
Dalcrue *Tays* 125 NO0427
Dalderby *Lincs* 77 TF2565
Dale *Cumb* 94 NY5443
Dale *Derbys* 62 SK4338
Dale *Dyfed* 30 SM8005
Dale Bottom *Cumb* 93 NY2921
Dale End *Derbys* 74 SK2161
Dale End *N York* 82 SD9645
Dale Hill *E Susx* 16 TQ7030
Dalehouse *N York* 97 NZ7717
Dalgarven *Strath* 115 NS2846
Dalgety Bay *Fife* 117 NT1683
Dalgig *Strath* 107 NS5512
Dalginross *Tays* 124 NN7721
Dalguise *Tays* 125 NN9847
Dalhalvaig *Highld* 150 NC8954
Dalham *Suffk* 53 TL7261
Daliburgh *W Isls* 154 NF7421
Dalkeith *Loth* 118 NT3367
Dallas *Gramp* 141 NJ1252
Dallinghoo *Suffk* 55 TM2655
Dallington *E Susx* 16 TQ6519
Dallow *N York* 89 SE1971
Dalmally *Strath* 123 NN1627
Dalmary *Cent* 115 NS5195
Dalmellington *Strath* 107 NS4705
Dalmeny *Loth* 117 NT1477
Dalmigavie *Highld* 140 NH7319
Dalmigavie Lodge *Highld* 140 NH7523
Dalmore *Highld* 140 NH6668
Dalnabreck *Highld* 129 NM7069
Dalnacardoch *Tays* 132 NN7270
Dalnahaitnach *Highld* 140 NH8519
Dalnaspidal *Tays* 132 NN6473
Dalnawillan Lodge *Highld* 150 ND0340
Daloist *Tays* 124 NN7857
Dalquhairn *Strath* 106 NX3296
Dalreavoch Lodge *Highld* 147 NC7508
Dalry *Strath* 115 NS2949
Dalrymple *Strath* 106 NS3514
Dalserf *Strath* 116 NS7950
Dalsmeran *Strath* 104 NR6413
Dalston *Cumb* 93 NY3650
Dalston *Gt Lon* 27 TQ3384
Dalswinton *D & G* 100 NX9385
Dalton *Cumb* 87 SD5476
Dalton *D & G* 100 NY1173
Dalton *Lancs* 78 SD4908
Dalton *N York* 89 NZ1108
Dalton *N York* 89 SE4376
Dalton *Nthumb* 103 NZ1172
Dalton *S York* 75 SK4594
Dalton in Furness *Cumb* 86 SD2274
Dalton Magna *S York* 75 SK4692
Dalton Parva *S York* 75 SK4593
Dalton Piercy *Cleve* 97 NZ4631
Dalton-le-Dale *Dur* 96 NZ4048
Dalton-on-Tees *N York* 89 NZ2907
Dalveen *D & G* 108 NS8806
Dalveich *Cent* 124 NN6124
Dalwhinnie *Highld* 132 NN6384
Dalwood *Devon* 9 ST2400
Dam Green *Norfk* 54 TM0485
Damask Green *Herts* 39 TL2529
Damerham *Hants* 12 SU1016
Damgate *Norfk* 67 TG4009
Dan's Castle *Dur* 95 NZ1139
Dan-y-Parc *Powys* 34 SO2217
Danaway *Kent* 28 TQ8663
Danbury *Essex* 40 TL7805
Danby *N York* 90 NZ7008
Danby Bottom *N York* 90 NZ6904
Danby Wiske *N York* 89 SE3398
Dandaleith *Gramp* 141 NJ2846
Danderhall *Loth* 117 NT3069
Dane End *Herts* 39 TL3321
Dane Hills *Leics* 62 SK5604
Dane Street *Kent* 28 TR0552
Danebridge *Ches* 72 SJ9665
Danegate *E Susx* 16 TQ5633
Danehill *E Susx* 15 TQ4027
Danemoor Green *Norfk* 66 TG0505
Danesford *Shrops* 60 SO7391
Danesmoor *Derbys* 74 SK4063
Daniel's Water *Kent* 28 TQ9541
Danshillock *Gramp* 142 NJ7157
Danskine *Loth* 118 NT5667
Danthorpe *Humb* 85 TA2532
Danzey Green *Warwks* 48 SP1269
Dapple Heath *Staffs* 73 SK0425
Darby Green *Hants* 25 SU8360
Darcy Lever *Gt Man* 79 SD7308
Daren-felen *Gwent* 34 SO2212
Darenth *Kent* 27 TQ5671
Daresbury *Ches* 78 SJ5882
Darfield *S York* 83 SE4104
Dargate *Kent* 29 TR0861
Darite *Cnwll* 5 SX2569
Darland *Clwyd* 71 SJ3757
Darland *Kent* 28 TQ7865
Darlaston *Staffs* 72 SJ8835
Darlaston *W Mids* 60 SO9796
Darlaston Green *W Mids* 60 SO9797
Darley *N York* 89 SE2059
Darley Abbey *Derbys* 62 SK3538
Darley Bridge *Derbys* 74 SK2661
Darley Dale *Derbys* 74 SK2663
Darley Green *Warwks* 61 SP1874
Darley Head *N York* 89 SE1959
Darleyhall *Herts* 38 TL1422
Darlingscott *Warwks* 48 SP2342
Darlington *Dur* 89 NZ2814
Darliston *Shrops* 59 SJ5733
Darlton *Notts* 75 SK7773
Darnford *Staffs* 61 SK1308
Darnick *Border* 109 NT5334
Darowen *Powys* 57 SH8201
Darra *Gramp* 142 NJ7447
Darracot *Cnwll* 18 SS2811
Darracott *Devon* 18 SS2317
Darracott *Devon* 18 SS4739
Darras Hall *T & W* 103 NZ1570
Darrington *W York* 83 SE4820
Darsham *Suffk* 55 TM4169
Dartford *Kent* 27 TQ5474
Dartington *Devon* 7 SX7862
Dartmeet *Devon* 7 SX6773
Dartmouth *Devon* 7 SX8751
Darton *S York* 82 SE3110
Darvel *Strath* 107 NS5637
Darwell Hole *E Susx* 16 TQ6919
Darwen *Lancs* 81 SD6922
Datchet *Berks* 26 SU9877
Datchworth *Herts* 39 TL2619
Datchworth Green *Herts* 39 TL2718
Daubhill *Gt Man* 79 SD7007
Dauntsey *Wilts* 35 ST9782
Dauntsey Green *Wilts* 35 ST9981
Dava *Highld* 141 NJ0038
Davenham *Ches* 79 SJ6571
Davenport *Gt Man* 79 SJ9088
Davenport Green *Ches* 79 SJ8379
Davenport Green *Gt Man* 79 SJ8086
Daventry *Nhants* 49 SP5762
David Street *Kent* 27 TQ6464
Davidson's Mains *Loth* 117 NT2175
Davidstow *Cnwll* 4 SX1587
Davington *D & G* 109 NT2302
Davington Hill *Kent* 28 TR0161
Daviot *Gramp* 142 NJ7428
Daviot *Highld* 140 NH7239
Daviot House *Highld* 140 NH7240
Davis's Town *E Susx* 16 TQ5217
Davoch of Grange *Gramp* 142 NJ4751
Daw End *W Mids* 61 SK0300
Daw's House *Cnwll* 5 SX3182
Dawesgreen *Surrey* 15 TQ2147
Dawley *Shrops* 60 SJ6808
Dawlish *Devon* 9 SX9576
Dawlish Warren *Devon* 9 SX9778
Dawn *Clwyd* 69 SH8672
Daws Green *Somset* 20 ST1921
Daws Heath *Essex* 40 TQ8188
Dawsmere *Lincs* 65 TF4430
Day Green *Ches* 72 SJ7757
Daybrook *Notts* 62 SK5744
Dayhills *Staffs* 72 SJ9532
Dayhouse Bank *H & W* 60 SO9678
Daylesford *Gloucs* 48 SP2425
Ddol *Clwyd* 70 SJ1471
Ddol-Cownwy *Powys* 58 SJ0117
Deal *Kent* 29 TR3752
Dean *Cumb* 92 NY0725
Dean *Devon* 19 SS6245
Dean *Devon* 19 SS7048
Dean *Devon* 7 SX7364
Dean *Dorset* 11 ST9715
Dean *Hants* 24 SU4431
Dean *Hants* 13 SU5619
Dean *Lancs* 81 SD8525
Dean *Oxon* 36 SP3422
Dean *Somset* 22 ST6743
Dean Bottom *Kent* 27 TQ5868
Dean Court *Oxon* 37 SP4705
Dean End *Dorset* 11 ST9717
Dean Head *S York* 74 SE2600
Dean Prior *Devon* 7 SX7363
Dean Row *Ches* 79 SJ8781
Dean Street *Kent* 28 TQ7453
Deanburnhaugh *Border* 109 NT3911
Deancombe *Devon* 7 SX7264
Deane *Gt Man* 79 SD6907
Deane *Hants* 24 SU5450
Deanhead *W York* 82 SE0415
Deanland *Dorset* 22 ST9918
Deanlane End *W Susx* 13 SU7412
Deanraw *Nthumb* 102 NY8162
Deanscales *Cumb* 92 NY0926
Deanshanger *Nhants* 49 SP7639
Deanshaugh *Gramp* 141 NJ3550
Deanston *Cent* 116 NN7101
Dearham *Cumb* 92 NY0736
Dearnley *Gt Man* 81 SD9215
Debach *Suffk* 55 TM2454
Debden *Essex* 53 TL5533
Debden *Essex* 27 TQ4496
Debden Green *Essex* 40 TL5831
Debenham *Suffk* 54 TM1763
Deblin's Green *H & W* 47 SO8148
Dechmont *Loth* 117 NT0370
Dechmont Road *Loth* 117 NT0269
Deddington *Oxon* 49 SP4631
Dedham *Essex* 41 TM0533
Dedham Heath *Essex* 41 TM0531
Dedworth *Berks* 26 SU9476
Deene *Nhants* 51 SP9492
Deenethorpe *Nhants* 51 SP9591
Deepcar *S York* 74 SK2897
Deepcut *Surrey* 25 SU9057

Duckend Green East Wellow

Duckend Green *Essex* 40 TL7223
Duckington *Ches* 71 SJ4851
Ducklington *Oxon* 36 SP3507
Duddingston *Loth* 117 NT2872
Duddington *Nhants* 51 SK9800
Duddlestone *Somset* 20 ST2321
Duddleswell *E Susx* 16 TQ4628
Duddlewick *Shrops* 59 SO6583
Duddo *Nthumb* 110 NT9342
Duddon *Ches* 71 SJ5164
Duddon Bridge *Cumb* 86 SD1988
Dudleston *Shrops* 71 SJ3438
Dudleston Heath *Shrops* 59 SJ3736
Dudley *T & W* 103 NZ2573
Dudley *W Mids* 60 SO9490
Dudley Hill *W York* 82 SE1830
Dudley Port *W Mids* 60 SO9691
Dudnill *Shrops* 47 SO6474
Dudsbury *Dorset* 12 SZ0798
Dudswell *Herts* 38 SP9609
Duffield *Derbys* 62 SK3443
Duffryn *M Glam* 33 SS8495
Dufftown *Gramp* 141 NJ3240
Duffus *Gramp* 141 NJ1668
Dufton *Cumb* 94 NY6825
Duggleby *N York* 90 SE8767
Duirinish *Highld* 137 NG7831
Duisdalemore *Highld* 129 NG7013
Duisky *Highld* 130 NN0076
Duke Street *Suffk* 54 TM0742
Dukestown *Gwent* 33 SO1410
Dukinfield *Gt Man* 79 SJ9397
Dulas *Gwynd* 68 SH4789
Dulcote *Somset* 21 ST5644
Dulford *Devon* 9 ST0706
Dull *Tays* 125 NN8049
Dullatur *Strath* 116 NS7476
Dullingham *Cambs* 53 TL6357
Dullingham Ley *Cambs* 53 TL6456
Dulnain Bridge *Highld* 141 NH9925
Duloe *Beds* 52 TL1560
Duloe *Cnwll* 5 SX2358
Dulverton *Somset* 20 SS9127
Dulwich *Gt Lon* 27 TQ3373
Dumbarton *Strath* 115 NS3975
Dumbleton *Gloucs* 47 SP0135
Dumcrieff *D & G* 108 NT1003
Dumfries *D & G* 100 NX9776
Dumgoyne *Cent* 115 NS5283
Dummer *Hants* 24 SU5846
Dumpton *Kent* 29 TR3966
Dun *Tays* 135 NO6659
Dunalastair *Tays* 132 NN7158
Dunan *Highld* 137 NG5828
Dunan *Strath* 114 NS1571
Dunan *Tays* 124 NN4757
Dunans *Strath* 114 NS0491
Dunaverty *Strath* 105 NR6807
Dunball *Somset* 21 ST3141
Dunbar *Loth* 118 NT6778
Dunbeath *Highld* 151 ND1629
Dunbeg *Strath* 122 NM8833
Dunblane *Cent* 116 NN7801
Dunbog *Fife* 126 NO2817
Dunbridge *Hants* 23 SU3226
Duncanston *Highld* 139 NH5856
Duncanstone *Gramp* 142 NJ5726
Dunchideock *Devon* 9 SX8787
Dunchurch *Warwks* 50 SP4871
Duncote *Nhants* 49 SP6750
Duncow *D & G* 100 NX9683
Duncrievie *Tays* 126 NO1309
Duncton *W Susx* 14 SU9617
Dundee *Tays* 126 NO4030
Dundon *Somset* 21 ST4832
Dundonald *Strath* 106 NS3634
Dundonnell *Highld* 145 NH0987
Dundraw *Cumb* 93 NY2149
Dundreggan *Highld* 131 NH3214
Dundrennan *D & G* 99 NX7447
Dundry *Avon* 21 ST5666
Dunecht *Gramp* 135 NJ7509
Dunfermline *Fife* 117 NT0987
Dunfield *Gloucs* 36 SU1497
Dunford Bridge *S York* 82 SE1502
Dungate *Kent* 28 TQ9159
Dungavel *Strath* 107 NS6537
Dunge *Wilts* 22 ST8954
Dunglass *Loth* 119 NT7671
Dungworth *S York* 74 SK2789
Dunham *Notts* 75 SK8074
Dunham Town *Gt Man* 79 SJ7387
Dunham Woodhouses *Gt Man* 79 SJ7287
Dunham-on-the-Hill *Ches* 71 SJ4772
Dunhampstead *H & W* 47 SO9160
Dunhampton *H & W* 47 SO8466
Dunholme *Lincs* 76 TF0279
Dunino *Fife* 127 NO5311
Dunipace *Cent* 116 NS8083
Dunk's Green *Kent* 27 TQ6152
Dunkeld *Tays* 125 NO0242
Dunkerton *Avon* 22 ST7159
Dunkeswell *Devon* 9 ST1407
Dunkeswick *W York* 82 SE3047
Dunkirk *Avon* 35 ST7885
Dunkirk *Ches* 71 SJ3872
Dunkirk *Kent* 29 TR0759
Dunkirk *Staffs* 72 SJ8152
Dunkirk *Wilts* 22 ST9962
Dunlappie *Tays* 134 NO5867
Dunley *H & W* 47 SO7869
Dunley *Hants* 24 SU4553
Dunlop *Strath* 115 NS4049
Dunmaglass *Highld* 140 NH5922
Dunmere *Cnwll* 4 SX0467
Dunmore *Cent* 116 NS8989
Dunmore *Strath* 113 NR7961
Dunn Street *Kent* 28 TQ7961
Dunnet *Highld* 151 ND2171
Dunnichen *Tays* 127 NO5048
Dunning *Tays* 125 NO0114
Dunnington *Humb* 85 TA1551
Dunnington *N York* 83 SE6652
Dunnington *Warwks* 48 SP0654
Dunnockshaw *Lancs* 81 SD8127
Dunoon *Strath* 114 NS1776
Dunphail *Gramp* 141 NJ0048
Dunragit *D & G* 98 NX1557
Duns *Border* 119 NT7853
Duns Tew *Oxon* 49 SP4528
Dunsa *Derbys* 74 SK2470
Dunsby *Lincs* 64 TF1026
Dunscar *Gt Man* 81 SD7113
Dunscore *D & G* 100 NX8684
Dunscroft *S York* 83 SE6409
Dunsdale *Cleve* 97 NZ6019
Dunsden Green *Oxon* 37 SU7377
Dunsdon *Devon* 18 SS3008
Dunsfold *Surrey* 14 TQ0035
Dunsford *Devon* 8 SX8189
Dunshelt *Fife* 126 NO2410
Dunshillock *Gramp* 143 NJ9848
Dunsill *Notts* 75 SK4661
Dunsley *N York* 90 NZ8511
Dunsley *Staffs* 60 SO8583
Dunsmore *Bucks* 38 SP8605
Dunsop Bridge *Lancs* 81 SD6649
Dunstable *Beds* 38 TL0122
Dunstall *Staffs* 73 SK1820
Dunstall Common *H & W* 47 SO8843
Dunstall Green *Suffk* 53 TL7460
Dunstan *Nthumb* 111 NU2419
Dunstan Steads *Nthumb* 111 NU2422
Dunster *Somset* 20 SS9943
Dunston *Lincs* 76 TF0662
Dunston *Norfk* 67 TG2202
Dunston *Staffs* 72 SJ9217
Dunston *T & W* 96 NZ2362
Dunston Heath *Staffs* 72 SJ9017
Dunstone *Devon* 6 SX5951
Dunstone *Devon* 7 SX7175
Dunsville *S York* 83 SE6407
Dunswell *Humb* 85 TA0735
Dunsyre *Strath* 117 NT0748
Dunterton *Devon* 5 SX3779
Dunthrop *Oxon* 48 SP3528
Duntisbourne Abbots *Gloucs* 35 SO9607
Duntisbourne Rouse *Gloucs* 35 SO9805
Duntish *Dorset* 11 ST6906
Duntocher *Strath* 115 NS4872
Dunton *Beds* 39 TL2344
Dunton *Bucks* 38 SP8224
Dunton *Norfk* 66 TF8830
Dunton Bassett *Leics* 50 SP5490
Dunton Green *Kent* 27 TQ5157
Dunton Wayletts *Essex* 40 TQ6590
Duntulm *Highld* 136 NG4174
Dunure *Strath* 106 NS2515
Dunvant *W Glam* 32 SS5993
Dunvegan *Highld* 136 NG2547
Dunwich *Suffk* 55 TM4770
Dunwood *Staffs* 72 SJ9455
Durdar *Cumb* 93 NY4051
Durgan *Cnwll* 3 SW7727
Durham *Dur* 96 NZ2742
Durisdeer *D & G* 108 NS8903
Durisdeermill *D & G* 108 NS8804
Durkar *W York* 82 SE3116
Durleigh *Somset* 20 ST2736
Durley *Hants* 13 SU5116
Durley *Wilts* 23 SU2364
Durley Street *Hants* 13 SU5217
Durlock *Kent* 29 TR2757
Durlock *Kent* 29 TR3164
Durlow Common *H & W* 47 SO6339
Durmgley *Tays* 127 NO4250
Durn *Gt Man* 82 SD9416
Durness *Highld* 149 NC4068
Duror *Highld* 122 NM9754
Durran *Highld* 151 ND1963
Durrington *W Susx* 14 TQ1105
Durrington *Wilts* 23 SU1544
Durris *Gramp* 135 NO7796
Dursley *Gloucs* 35 ST7598
Dursley Cross *Gloucs* 35 SO6920
Durston *Somset* 20 ST2928
Durweston *Dorset* 11 ST8508
Duston *Nhants* 49 SP7261
Duthil *Highld* 140 NH9324
Dutlas *Powys* 45 SO2177
Dutson *Cnwll* 5 SX3485
Dutton *Ches* 71 SJ5779
Duxford *Cambs* 53 TL4846
Duxford *Oxon* 36 SP3600
Dwygyfylchi *Gwynd* 69 SH7376
Dwyran *Gwynd* 68 SH4465
Dyce *Gramp* 135 NJ8812
Dye House *Nthumb* 95 NY9358
Dyer's End *Essex* 53 TL7238
Dyfatty *Dyfed* 32 SN4401
Dyffryn *M Glam* 33 SO0603
Dyffryn *S Glam* 33 ST0971
Dyffryn Ardudwy *Gwynd* 57 SH5823
Dyffryn Castell *Dyfed* 43 SN7782
Dyffryn Cellwen *W Glam* 33 SN8510
Dyke *Devon* 18 SS3123
Dyke *Gramp* 140 NH9858
Dyke *Lincs* 64 TF1022
Dykehead *Cent* 115 NS5997
Dykehead *Strath* 116 NS8759
Dykehead *Tays* 126 NO2453
Dykehead *Tays* 134 NO3859
Dykelands *Gramp* 135 NO7068
Dykends *Tays* 133 NO2557
Dykeside *Gramp* 142 NJ7243
Dylife *Powys* 43 SN8694
Dymchurch *Kent* 17 TR1029
Dymock *Gloucs* 47 SO7031
Dyrham *Avon* 35 ST7475
Dysart *Fife* 117 NT3093
Dyserth *Clwyd* 70 SJ0578

E

Eachway *H & W* 60 SO9876
Eachwick *Nthumb* 103 NZ1171
Eagland Hill *Lancs* 80 SD4345
Eagle *Lincs* 76 SK8766
Eagle Barnsdale *Lincs* 76 SK8865
Eagle Manor *Lincs* 76 SK8868
Eaglescliffe *Cleve* 96 NZ4215
Eaglesfield *Cumb* 92 NY0928
Eaglesfield *D & G* 101 NY2374
Eaglesham *Strath* 115 NS5751
Eagley *Gt Man* 81 SD7112
Eairy *IOM* 153 SC2977
Eakring *Notts* 75 SK6762
Ealand *Humb* 84 SE7811
Ealing *Gt Lon* 26 TQ1780
Eals *Nthumb* 94 NY6756
Eamont Bridge *Cumb* 94 NY5228
Earby *Lancs* 81 SD9046
Earcroft *Lancs* 81 SD6823
Eardington *Shrops* 60 SO7290
Eardisland *H & W* 46 SO4158
Eardisley *H & W* 46 SO3149
Eardiston *H & W* 47 SO6968
Eardiston *Shrops* 59 SJ3725
Earith *Cambs* 52 TL3875
Earl Shilton *Leics* 50 SP4697
Earl Soham *Suffk* 55 TM2363
Earl Sterndale *Derbys* 74 SK0966
Earl Stonham *Suffk* 54 TM1059
Earl's Croome *H & W* 47 SO8642
Earl's Down *E Susx* 16 TQ6419
Earl's Green *Suffk* 54 TM0366
Earle *Nthumb* 111 NT9826
Earlestown *Mersyd* 78 SJ5795
Earley *Berks* 24 SU7472
Earlham *Norfk* 67 TG1908
Earlish *Highld* 136 NG3861
Earls Barton *Nhants* 51 SP8563
Earls Colne *Essex* 40 TL8528
Earls Common *H & W* 47 SO9559
Earlsditton *Shrops* 47 SO6275
Earlsdon *W Mids* 61 SP3278
Earlsferry *Fife* 118 NO4800
Earlsfield *Gt Lon* 27 TQ2573
Earlsford *Gramp* 143 NJ8334
Earlsheaton *W York* 82 SE2621
Earlston *Border* 110 NT5738
Earlston *Strath* 106 NS4035
Earlswood *Surrey* 15 TQ2749
Earlswood *Warwks* 61 SP1174
Earlswood Common *Gwent* 34 ST4594
Earnley *W Susx* 14 SZ8196
Earnshaw Bridge *Lancs* 80 SD5222
Earsdon *Nthumb* 103 NZ1993
Earsdon *T & W* 103 NZ3272
Earsham *Norfk* 55 TM3288
Earswick *N York* 90 SE6157
Eartham *W Susx* 14 SU9309
Easby *N York* 90 NZ5708
Easebourne *W Susx* 14 SU9023
Easenhall *Warwks* 50 SP4679
Eashing *Surrey* 25 SU9443
Easington *Bucks* 37 SP6810
Easington *Cleve* 97 NZ7417
Easington *Dur* 96 NZ4143
Easington *Humb* 85 TA3919
Easington *Nthumb* 111 NU1234
Easington *Oxon* 37 SU6697
Easington Colliery *Dur* 96 NZ4344
Easington Lane *T & W* 96 NZ3646
Easingwold *N York* 90 SE5269
Easole Street *Kent* 29 TR2652
Eassie and Nevay *Tays* 126 NO3344
East Aberthaw *S Glam* 20 ST0366
East Allington *Devon* 7 SX7748
East Anstey *Devon* 19 SS8626
East Anton *Hants* 23 SU3747
East Appleton *N York* 89 SE2395
East Ashey *IOW* 13 SZ5888
East Ashling *W Susx* 14 SU8107
East Aston *Hants* 24 SU4445
East Ayton *N York* 91 SE9985
East Balsdon *Cnwll* 5 SX2898
East Bank *Gwent* 33 SO2105
East Barkwith *Lincs* 76 TF1681
East Barming *Kent* 28 TQ7254
East Barnby *N York* 90 NZ8212
East Barnet *Gt Lon* 27 TQ2795
East Barns *Loth* 119 NT7176
East Barsham *Norfk* 66 TF9133
East Beckham *Norfk* 66 TG1639
East Bedfont *Gt Lon* 26 TQ0873
East Bergholt *Suffk* 54 TM0734
East Bierley *W York* 82 SE1929
East Bilney *Norfk* 66 TF9519
East Blatchington *E Susx* 16 TQ4800
East Bloxworth *Dorset* 11 SY8894
East Boldon *T & W* 96 NZ3661
East Boldre *Hants* 12 SU3700
East Bolton *Nthumb* 111 NU1216
East Bower *Somset* 21 ST3237
East Bradenham *Norfk* 66 TF9308
East Brent *Somset* 21 ST3451
East Bridgford *Notts* 63 SK6943
East Briscoe *Dur* 95 NY9719
East Buckland *Devon* 19 SS6831
East Budleigh *Devon* 9 SY0684
East Burnham *Bucks* 26 SU9584
East Burton *Dorset* 11 SY8287
East Butsfield *Dur* 95 NZ1145
East Butterwick *Humb* 84 SE8306
East Calder *Loth* 117 NT0867
East Carleton *Norfk* 66 TG1701
East Carlton *Nhants* 51 SP8389
East Carlton *W York* 82 SE2143
East Challow *Oxon* 36 SU3888
East Charleton *Devon* 7 SX7642
East Chelborough *Dorset* 10 ST5505
East Chevington *Nthumb* 103 NZ2699
East Chiltington *E Susx* 15 TQ3715
East Chinnock *Somset* 10 ST4913
East Chisenbury *Wilts* 23 SU1452
East Cholderton *Hants* 23 SU2945
East Clandon *Surrey* 26 TQ0651
East Claydon *Bucks* 49 SP7325
East Clevedon *Avon* 34 ST4171
East Coker *Somset* 10 ST5412
East Combe *Somset* 20 ST1631
East Compton *Somset* 21 ST6141
East Cornworthy *Devon* 7 SX8455
East Cote *Cumb* 92 NY1255
East Cottingwith *Humb* 84 SE7042
East Cowes *IOW* 13 SZ5095
East Cowick *Humb* 83 SE6620
East Cowton *N York* 89 NZ3003
East Cramlington *Nthumb* 103 NZ2776
East Cranmore *Somset* 22 ST6743
East Creech *Dorset* 11 SY9382
East Curthwaite *Cumb* 93 NY3348
East Dean *E Susx* 16 TV5598
East Dean *H & W* 35 SO6520
East Dean *Hants* 23 SU2726
East Dean *W Susx* 14 SU9012
East Dereham *Norfk* 66 TF9913
East Down *Devon* 19 SS6041
East Drayton *Notts* 75 SK7775
East Dulwich *Gt Lon* 27 TQ3375
East Dundry *Avon* 21 ST5766
East Ella *Humb* 84 TA0529
East End *Avon* 34 ST4770
East End *Beds* 38 SP9642
East End *Beds* 51 TL1055
East End *Bucks* 38 SP9344
East End *Essex* 39 TL4210
East End *Hants* 24 SU4161
East End *Hants* 12 SZ3696
East End *Herts* 39 TL4527
East End *Humb* 85 TA1931
East End *Humb* 85 TA2927
East End *Kent* 17 TQ8335
East End *Kent* 28 TQ9673
East End *Oxon* 36 SP3915
East End *Somset* 22 ST6746
East Everleigh *Wilts* 23 SU2053
East Farleigh *Kent* 28 TQ7353
East Farndon *Nhants* 50 SP7184
East Ferry *Lincs* 75 SK8199
East Firsby *Lincs* 76 TF0085
East Fortune *Loth* 118 NT5479
East Garforth *W York* 83 SE4133
East Garston *Berks* 36 SU3576
East Ginge *Oxon* 37 SU4486
East Goscote *Leics* 63 SK6413
East Grafton *Wilts* 23 SU2560
East Grange *Gramp* 141 NJ0961
East Green *Suffk* 55 TM4065
East Grimstead *Wilts* 23 SU2227
East Grinstead *W Susx* 15 TQ3938
East Guldeford *E Susx* 17 TQ9321
East Haddon *Nhants* 50 SP6668
East Hagbourne *Oxon* 37 SU5288
East Halton *Humb* 85 TA1319
East Ham *Gt Lon* 27 TQ4283
East Hanney *Oxon* 36 SU4193
East Hanningfield *Essex* 40 TL7701
East Hardwick *W York* 83 SE4618
East Harling *Norfk* 54 TL9986
East Harlsey *N York* 89 SE4299
East Harnham *Wilts* 23 SU1428
East Harptree *Avon* 21 ST5655
East Hartburn *Cleve* 96 NZ4217
East Hartford *Nthumb* 103 NZ2679
East Harting *W Susx* 14 SU7919
East Hatch *Wilts* 22 ST9228
East Hatley *Cambs* 52 TL2850
East Hauxwell *N York* 89 SE1693
East Haven *Tays* 127 NO5836
East Heath *Berks* 25 SU7967
East Heckington *Lincs* 64 TF1944
East Hedleyhope *Dur* 96 NZ1540
East Helmsdale *Highld* 147 ND0315
East Hendred *Oxon* 37 SU4588
East Heslerton *N York* 91 SE9276
East Hewish *Avon* 21 ST4064
East Hoathly *E Susx* 16 TQ5216
East Holme *Dorset* 11 SY8986
East Holywell *T & W* 103 NZ3073
East Horndon *Essex* 40 TQ6389
East Horrington *Somset* 21 ST5846
East Horsley *Surrey* 26 TQ0952
East Horton *Nthumb* 111 NU0330
East Howe *Dorset* 12 SZ0795
East Huntington *N York* 83 SE6155
East Huntspill *Somset* 21 ST3445
East Hyde *Beds* 38 TL1217
East Ilkerton *Devon* 19 SS7147
East Ilsley *Berks* 37 SU4980
East Keal *Lincs* 77 TF3863
East Kennett *Wilts* 23 SU1167
East Keswick *W York* 83 SE3644
East Kilbride *Strath* 116 NS6354
East Kimber *Devon* 5 SX4998
East Kirkby *Lincs* 77 TF3362
East Knighton *Dorset* 11 SY8185
East Knowstone *Devon* 19 SS8423
East Knoyle *Wilts* 22 ST8830
East Kyloe *Nthumb* 111 NU0639
East Lambrook *Somset* 10 ST4318
East Langdon *Kent* 29 TR3346
East Langton *Leics* 50 SP7292
East Laroch *Highld* 130 NN0858
East Lavant *W Susx* 14 SU8608
East Lavington *W Susx* 14 SU9416
East Layton *N York* 89 NZ1609
East Leake *Notts* 62 SK5526
East Leigh *Devon* 8 SS6905
East Leigh *Devon* 7 SX6852
East Leigh *Devon* 7 SX7657
East Lexham *Norfk* 66 TF8517
East Linton *Loth* 118 NT5977
East Liss *Hants* 14 SU7827
East Lockinge *Oxon* 36 SU4287
East Lound *Humb* 75 SK7899
East Lulworth *Dorset* 11 SY8682
East Lutton *N York* 91 SE9469
East Lydford *Somset* 21 ST5731
East Malling *Kent* 28 TQ7056
East Malling Heath *Kent* 28 TQ6955
East Marden *W Susx* 14 SU8014
East Markham *Notts* 75 SK7373
East Martin *Hants* 12 SU0719
East Marton *N York* 81 SD9050
East Meon *Hants* 13 SU6822
East Mere *Devon* 9 SS9916
East Mersea *Essex* 41 TM0414
East Molesey *Surrey* 26 TQ1467
East Morden *Dorset* 11 SY9194
East Morton *D & G* 108 NS8800
East Morton *W York* 82 SE0942
East Ness *N York* 90 SE6978
East Newton *Humb* 85 TA2638
East Norton *Leics* 50 SK7800
East Oakley *Hants* 24 SU5749
East Ogwell *Devon* 7 SX8370
East Orchard *Dorset* 11 ST8317
East Ord *Nthumb* 119 NT9751
East Panson *Devon* 5 SX3692
East Parley *Dorset* 12 SZ1097
East Peckham *Kent* 28 TQ6648
East Pennar *Dyfed* 30 SM9602
East Pennard *Somset* 21 ST5937
East Perry *Cambs* 52 TL1566
East Portlemouth *Devon* 7 SX7538
East Prawle *Devon* 7 SX7836
East Preston *W Susx* 14 TQ0602
East Pulham *Dorset* 11 ST7209
East Putford *Devon* 18 SS3616
East Quantoxhead *Somset* 20 ST1343
East Rainham *Kent* 28 TQ8267
East Rainton *T & W* 96 NZ3347
East Ravendale *Lincs* 76 TF2399
East Raynham *Norfk* 66 TF8825
East Rigton *W York* 83 SE3743
East Rolstone *Avon* 21 ST3962
East Rounton *N York* 89 NZ4203
East Rudham *Norfk* 66 TF8228
East Runton *Norfk* 67 TG1942
East Ruston *Norfk* 67 TG3427
East Saltoun *Loth* 118 NT4767
East Scrafton *N York* 89 SE0884
East Sheen *Gt Lon* 26 TQ2075
East Shefford *Berks* 36 SU3874
East Sleekburn *Nthumb* 103 NZ2883
East Somerton *Norfk* 67 TG4719
East Stockwith *Lincs* 75 SK7894
East Stoke *Dorset* 11 SY8686
East Stoke *Notts* 75 SK7549
East Stour *Dorset* 22 ST8022
East Stourmouth *Kent* 29 TR2662
East Stowford *Devon* 19 SS6326
East Stratton *Hants* 24 SU5440
East Sutton *Kent* 28 TQ8349
East Taphouse *Cnwll* 4 SX1863
East Thirston *Nthumb* 89 NZ1900
East Tilbury *Essex* 28 TQ6877
East Tisted *Hants* 24 SU7032
East Torrington *Lincs* 76 TF1483
East Tuddenham *Norfk* 66 TG0711
East Tytherley *Hants* 23 SU2929
East Tytherton *Wilts* 35 ST9674
East Village *Devon* 8 SS8405
East Wall *Shrops* 59 SO5293
East Walton *Norfk* 65 TF7416
East Water *Somset* 21 ST5350
East Week *Devon* 8 SX6692
East Wellow *Hants* 12 SU3020

East Wemyss Ettiley Heath

East Wemyss Fife 118 NT3497
East Whitburn Loth 117 NS9665
East Wickham Gt Lon 27 TQ4677
East Williamston Dyfed 31 SN0904
East Winch Norfk 65 TF6916
East Winterslow Wilts 23 SU2434
East Wittering W Susx 14 SZ7997
East Witton N York 89 SE1486
East Woodburn Nthumb 102 NY9086
East Woodhay Hants 24 SU4061
East Woodlands Somset 22 ST7944
East Worldham Hants 24 SU7538
East Wretham Norfk 54 TL9190
East Youlstone Devon 18 SS2715
Eastbourne Dur 89 NZ3013
Eastbourne E Susx 16 TV6199
Eastbridge Suffk 55 TM4566
Eastbrook S Glam 33 ST1671
Eastburn W York 82 SE0144
Eastbury Berks 36 SU3477
Eastbury Herts 26 TQ1092
Eastby N York 82 SE0154
Eastchurch Kent 28 TQ9871
Eastcombe Gloucs 35 SO8904
Eastcote Gt Lon 26 TQ1088
Eastcote Nhants 49 SP6853
Eastcote W Mids 61 SP1979
Eastcott Cnwll 18 SS2515
Eastcott Wilts 23 SU0255
Eastcourt Wilts 35 ST9792
Eastcourt Wilts 23 SU2361
Eastdown Devon 7 SX8249
Eastend Essex 40 TQ9492
Eastend Strath 108 NS9537
Easter Balmoral Gramp 133 NO2694
Easter Compton Avon 34 ST5782
Easter Dalziel Highld 140 NH7550
Easter Howgate Loth 117 NT2463
Easter Kinkell Highld 139 NH5755
Easter Moniack Highld 139 NH5543
Easter Ord Gramp 135 NJ8304
Easter Pitkierie Fife 127 NO5606
Easter Skeld Shet 155 HU3144
Eastergate W Susx 14 SU9405
Easterhouse Strath 116 NS6865
Eastern Green W Mids 61 SP2879
Easterton Wilts 23 SU0254
Eastertown Somset 21 ST3454
Eastfield Cent 116 NS8964
Eastfield Strath 116 NS7475
Eastfiled N York 91 TA0484
Eastgate Dur 95 NY9538
Eastgate Lincs 64 TF1019
Eastgate Norfk 66 TG1423
Eastham Mersyd 78 SJ3680
Eastham Ferry Mersyd 78 SJ3681
Easthampstead Berks 25 SU8667
Easthampton H & W 46 SO4063
Easthope Shrops 59 SO5695
Easthorpe Essex 40 TL9121
Easthorpe Notts 75 SK7053
Eastington Devon 19 SS7408
Eastington Gloucs 36 SP1213
Eastlands D & G 100 NX8172
Eastleach Martin Gloucs 36 SP2004
Eastleach Turville Gloucs 36 SP1905
Eastleigh Devon 18 SS4827
Eastleigh Hants 13 SU4519
Eastling Kent 28 TQ9656
Eastly End Surrey 26 TQ0368
Eastmoor Norfk 65 TF7303
Eastney Hants 13 SZ6698
Eastnor H & W 47 SO7237
Eastoft Humb 84 SE8016
Easton Berks 24 SU4172
Easton Cambs 52 TL1371
Easton Cumb 93 NY2759
Easton Devon 8 SX7289
Easton Dorset 11 SY6971
Easton Hants 24 SU5132
Easton IOW 12 SZ3486
Easton Lincs 63 SK9326
Easton Norfk 66 TG1310
Easton Somset 21 ST5147
Easton Suffk 55 TM2858
Easton Wilts 35 ST8970
Easton Grey Wilts 35 ST8887
Easton Maudit Nhants 51 SP8858
Easton on the Hill Nhants 64 TF0104
Easton Royal Wilts 23 SU2060
Easton-in-Gordano Avon 34 ST5175
Eastpeek Devon 5 SX3494
Eastrea Cambs 64 TL2997
Eastriggs D & G 101 NY2466
Eastrington Humb 84 SE7929
Eastrop Wilts 36 SU2092
Eastry Kent 29 TR3054
Eastshaw W Susx 14 SU8724
Eastville Lincs 77 TF4056
Eastwell Leics 63 SK7728
Eastwick Herts 39 TL4311
Eastwood Essex 40 TQ8688
Eastwood Notts 62 SK4646
Eastwood W York 82 SD9726
Eastwood End Cambs 65 TL4292
Eathorpe Warwks 48 SP3969
Eaton Ches 71 SJ5763
Eaton Ches 72 SJ8765
Eaton Leics 63 SK7928
Eaton Norfk 67 TG2006
Eaton Notts 75 SK7077
Eaton Oxon 37 SP4403
Eaton Shrops 59 SO3789
Eaton Shrops 59 SO5089
Eaton Bishop H & W 46 SO4439
Eaton Bray Beds 38 SP9720
Eaton Constantine Shrops 59 SJ5906
Eaton Ford Beds 52 TL1759
Eaton Green Beds 38 SP9621
Eaton Hastings Oxon 36 SU2598
Eaton Mascott Shrops 59 SJ5305
Eaton Socon Beds 52 TL1759
Eaton upon Tern Shrops 72 SJ6523
Eaves Brow Ches 79 SJ6393
Eaves Green W Mids 61 SP2682
Ebberston N York 91 SE8982
Ebbesborne Wake Wilts 22 ST9924
Ebbw Vale Gwent 33 SO1609
Ebchester Dur 95 NZ1055
Ebdon Avon 21 ST3664
Ebford Devon 9 SX9887
Ebley Gloucs 35 SO8205
Ebnal Ches 71 SJ4948
Ebnall H & W 46 SO4758
Ebrington Gloucs 48 SP1840
Ebsworthy Town Devon 5 SX5090
Ecchinswell Hants 24 SU4959
Ecclaw Loth 119 NT7568
Ecclefechan D & G 101 NY1974
Eccles Border 110 NT7641
Eccles Gt Man 79 SJ7798
Eccles Kent 28 TQ7360
Eccles Green H & W 46 SO3748
Eccles Road Norfk 54 TM0189
Ecclesall S York 74 SK3284
Ecclesfield S York 74 SK3593
Eccleshall Staffs 72 SJ8329
Eccleshill W York 82 SE1736
Ecclesmachan Loth 117 NT0573
Eccleston Ches 71 SJ4162
Eccleston Lancs 80 SD5217
Eccleston Mersyd 78 SJ4895
Eccleston Green Lancs 80 SD5216
Echt Gramp 135 NJ7405
Eckford Border 110 NT7026
Eckington Derbys 75 SK4379
Eckington H & W 47 SO9241
Ecton Nhants 51 SP8263
Ecton Staffs 74 SK0958
Edale Derbys 74 SK1285
Edburton W Susx 15 TQ2311
Edderside Cumb 92 NY1045
Edderton Highld 146 NH7084
Eddington Kent 29 TR1867
Eddleston Border 117 NT2447
Eddlewood Strath 116 NS7153
Eden Mount Cumb 87 SD4077
Eden Park Gt Lon 27 TQ3667
Edenbridge Kent 16 TQ4446
Edenfield Lancs 81 SD8019
Edenhall Cumb 94 NY5632
Edenham Lincs 64 TF0621
Edensor Derbys 74 SK2469
Edentaggart Strath 115 NS3293
Edenthorpe S York 83 SE6206
Edern Gwynd 56 SH2739
Edgarley Somset 21 ST5238
Edgbaston W Mids 61 SP0684
Edgcombe Cnwll 2 SW7133
Edgcott Bucks 37 SP6722
Edgcott Devon 19 SS8438
Edge Gloucs 35 SO8409
Edge Shrops 59 SJ3908
Edge End Gloucs 34 SO5913
Edge Green Ches 71 SJ4851
Edgebolton Shrops 59 SJ5721
Edgefield Norfk 66 TG0934
Edgefield Green Norfk 66 TG0934
Edgefold Gt Man 79 SD7005
Edgehill Warwks 48 SP3747
Edgerley Shrops 59 SJ3518
Edgertown W York 82 SE1317
Edgeside Lancs 81 SD8322
Edgeworth Gloucs 35 SO9406
Edgeworthy Devon 19 SS8413
Edgiock H & W 48 SP0461
Edgmond Shrops 72 SJ7119
Edgmond Marsh Shrops 72 SJ7120
Edgton Shrops 59 SO3885
Edgware Gt Lon 26 TQ1991
Edgworth Lancs 81 SD7416
Edial Staffs 61 SK0808
Edinample Cent 124 NN6022
Edinbane Highld 136 NG3451
Edinburgh Loth 117 NT2573
Edingale Staffs 61 SK2111
Edingham D & G 100 NX8363
Edingley Notts 75 SK6655
Edingthorpe Norfk 67 TG3132
Edingthorpe Green Norfk 67 TG3031
Edington Border 119 NT8955
Edington Nthumb 103 NZ1582
Edington Somset 21 ST3839
Edington Wilts 22 ST9253
Edington Burtle Somset 21 ST3943
Edingworth Somset 21 ST3653
Edith Weston Leics 63 SK9205
Edithmead Somset 21 ST3249
Edlesborough Bucks 38 SP9719
Edlingham Nthumb 111 NU1109
Edlington Lincs 76 TF2371
Edmond Castle Cumb 94 NY4958
Edmondsham Dorset 12 SU0611
Edmondsley Dur 96 NZ2349
Edmondthorpe Leics 63 SK8517
Edmonton Cnwll 4 SW9672
Edmonton Gt Lon 27 TQ3492
Edmundbyers Dur 95 NZ0150
Ednam Border 110 NT7337
Ednaston Derbys 73 SK2341
Edradynate Tays 125 NN8751
Edrom Border 119 NT8255
Edstaston Shrops 59 SJ5132
Edstone Warwks 48 SP1861
Edvin Loach H & W 47 SO6658
Edwalton Notts 62 SK5935
Edwardstone Suffk 54 TL9442
Edwardsville M Glam 33 ST0896
Edwinsford Dyfed 44 SN6334
Edwinstowe Notts 75 SK6266
Edworth Beds 39 TL2241
Edwyn Ralph H & W 47 SO6457
Edzell Tays 134 NO6068
Efail Isaf M Glam 33 ST0884
Efail-fach W Glam 32 SS7895
Efail-rhyd Clwyd 58 SJ1626
Efailnewydd Gwynd 56 SH3535
Efailwen Dyfed 31 SN1325
Efenechtyd Clwyd 70 SJ1155
Effgill D & G 101 NY3092
Effingham Surrey 26 TQ1153
Efflinch Staffs 73 SK1816
Efford Devon 9 SS8901
Egbury Hants 24 SU4352
Egerton Gt Man 81 SD7014
Egerton Kent 28 TQ9147
Eggesford Devon 19 SS6811
Eggington Beds 38 SP9525
Egginton Derbys 73 SK2628
Egglescliffe Cleve 89 NZ4113
Eggleston Dur 95 NY9923
Egham Surrey 25 TQ0071
Egham Wick Surrey 25 SU9870
Eginswell Devon 7 SX8866
Egleton Leics 63 SK8707
Eglingham Nthumb 111 NU1019
Egloshayle Cnwll 4 SX0072
Egloskerry Cnwll 5 SX2786
Eglwys Cross Clwyd 71 SJ4740
Eglwys-Brewis S Glam 20 ST0068
Eglwysbach Gwynd 69 SH8070
Eglwysfach Dyfed 43 SN6996
Eglwyswrw Dyfed 31 SN1438
Egmanton Notts 75 SK7368
Egremont Cumb 86 NY0110
Egremont Mersyd 78 SJ3192
Egton N York 90 NZ8006
Egton Bridge N York 90 NZ8004
Eight Ash Green Essex 40 TL9425
Eight and Forty Humb 84 SE8529
Eilanreach Highld 129 NG8018
Elan Village Powys 45 SN9364
Elberton Avon 34 ST6088
Elbridge W Susx 14 SU9101
Elburton Devon 6 SX5353
Elcombe Wilts 36 SU1280
Elcot Berks 36 SU3969
Elder Street Essex 53 TL5734
Eldernell Cambs 64 TL3298
Eldersfield H & W 47 SO7931
Elderslie Strath 115 NS4463
Eldmire N York 89 SE4274
Eldon Dur 96 NZ2328
Eldwick W York 82 SE1240
Elfhill Gramp 135 NO8085
Elford Nthumb 111 NU1831
Elford Staffs 61 SK1810
Elgin Gramp 141 NJ2162
Elgol Highld 128 NG5213
Elham Kent 29 TR1744
Elie Fife 118 NO4900
Elilaw Nthumb 111 NT9708
Elim Gwynd 68 SH3584
Eling Hants 12 SU3612
Elishaw Nthumb 102 NY8595
Elkesley Notts 75 SK6975
Elkstone Gloucs 35 SO9612
Ella Gramp 142 NJ6459
Ellanbeich Strath 122 NM7417
Elland W York 82 SE1120
Elland Lower Edge W York 82 SE1221
Ellary Strath 113 NR7376
Ellastone Staffs 73 SK1143
Ellel Lancs 80 SD4856
Ellemford Border 119 NT7260
Ellen's Green Surrey 14 TQ0935
Ellenborough Cumb 92 NY0435
Ellenbrook Gt Man 79 SD7201
Ellenhall Staffs 72 SJ8426
Ellerbeck N York 89 SE4396
Ellerby N York 90 NZ7914
Ellerdine Heath Shrops 59 SJ6122
Ellerhayes Devon 9 SS9702
Elleric Strath 123 NN0448
Ellerker Humb 84 SE9229
Ellers N York 82 SE0043
Ellerton Humb 84 SE7039
Ellerton N York 89 SE2598
Ellerton Shrops 72 SJ7125
Ellesborough Bucks 38 SP8306
Ellesmere Shrops 59 SJ3934
Ellesmere Port Ches 71 SJ4076
Ellicombe Somset 20 SS9844
Ellingham Hants 12 SU1408
Ellingham Norfk 67 TM3592
Ellingham Nthumb 111 NU1725
Ellingstring N York 89 SE1783
Ellington Cambs 52 TL1671
Ellington Nthumb 103 NZ2791
Ellington Thorpe Cambs 52 TL1670
Elliots Green Somset 22 ST7945
Ellisfield Hants 24 SU6446
Ellishader Highld 137 NG5065
Ellistown Leics 62 SK4309
Ellon Gramp 143 NJ9530
Ellonby Cumb 93 NY4235
Ellough Suffk 55 TM4486
Elloughton Humb 84 SE9428
Ellwood Gloucs 34 SO5908
Elm Cambs 65 TF4707
Elm Green Essex 40 TL7705
Elm Grove Norfk 67 TG4803
Elm Park Gt Lon 27 TQ5385
Elmbridge H & W 47 SO9068
Elmdon Essex 39 TL4639
Elmdon W Mids 61 SP1783
Elmdon Heath W Mids 61 SP1680
Elmer W Susx 14 SU9800
Elmer's Green Lancs 78 SD5006
Elmers End Gt Lon 27 TQ3668
Elmesthorpe Leics 50 SP4696
Elmhurst Staffs 61 SK1112
Elmley Castle H & W 47 SO9841
Elmley Lovett H & W 47 SO8769
Elmore Gloucs 35 SO7815
Elmore Back Gloucs 35 SO7616
Elms Green H & W 47 SO7266
Elmscott Devon 18 SS2321
Elmsett Suffk 54 TM0546
Elmstead Heath Essex 41 TM0622
Elmstead Market Essex 41 TM0624
Elmstead Row Essex 41 TM0621
Elmsted Court Kent 29 TR1144
Elmstone Kent 29 TR2660
Elmstone Hardwicke Gloucs 47 SO9125
Elmswell Humb 91 SE9958
Elmswell Suffk 54 TL9964
Elmton Derbys 75 SK5073
Elphin Highld 145 NC2111
Elphinstone Loth 118 NT3970
Elrick Gramp 135 NJ8106
Elrig D & G 98 NX3248
Elrington Nthumb 102 NY8563
Elsdon Nthumb 102 NY9393
Elsecar S York 74 SK3899
Elsenham Essex 39 TL5326
Elsfield Oxon 37 SP5410
Elsham Humb 84 TA0312
Elsick House Gramp 135 NO8894
Elsing Norfk 66 TG0516
Elslack N York 81 SD9349
Elson Hants 13 SU6002
Elson Shrops 59 SJ3735
Elsrickle Strath 108 NT0643
Elstead Surrey 25 SU9043
Elsted W Susx 14 SU8119
Elsthorpe Lincs 64 TF0623
Elstob Dur 96 NZ3323
Elston Lancs 81 SD5932
Elston Notts 63 SK7647
Elston Wilts 23 SU0644
Elstone Devon 19 SS6716
Elstow Beds 38 TL0546
Elstree Herts 26 TQ1795
Elstronwick Humb 85 TA2232
Elswick Lancs 80 SD4238
Elswick T & W 103 NZ2263
Elsworth Cambs 52 TL3163
Elterwater Cumb 86 NY3204
Eltham Gt Lon 27 TQ4274
Eltisley Cambs 52 TL2759
Elton Cambs 51 TL0893
Elton Ches 71 SJ4575
Elton Cleve 96 NZ4017
Elton Derbys 74 SK2260
Elton Gloucs 35 SO7014
Elton Gt Man 81 SD7911
Elton H & W 46 SO4570
Elton Notts 63 SK7638
Elton Green Ches 71 SJ4574
Eltringham Nthumb 103 NZ0762
Elvaston Derbys 62 SK4032
Elveden Suffk 54 TL8280
Elvetham Hall Hants 25 SU7856
Elvingston Loth 118 NT4674
Elvington Kent 29 TR2750
Elvington N York 84 SE7047
Elwell Devon 19 SS6631
Elwick Cleve 97 NZ4532
Elwick Nthumb 111 NU1136
Elworth Ches 72 SJ7361
Elworthy Somset 20 ST0834
Ely Cambs 53 TL5480
Ely S Glam 33 ST1476
Emberton Bucks 38 SP8849
Embleton Cumb 92 NY1629
Embleton Dur 96 NZ4129
Embleton Nthumb 111 NU2322
Embo Highld 147 NH8192
Embo Street Highld 147 NH8091
Emborough Somset 21 ST6151
Embsay N York 82 SE0053
Emery Down Hants 12 SU2808
Emley W York 82 SE2413
Emley Moor W York 82 SE2313
Emmbrook Berks 25 SU8069
Emmer Green Berks 37 SU7276
Emmett Carr Derbys 75 SK4577
Emmington Oxon 37 SP7402
Emneth Cambs 65 TF4807
Emneth Hungate Norfk 65 TF5107
Empingham Leics 63 SK9508
Empshott Hants 24 SU7531
Empshott Green Hants 24 SU7431
Emsworth Hants 13 SU7406
Enborne Berks 24 SU4365
Enborne Row Hants 24 SU4463
Enchmarsh Shrops 59 SO5096
Encombe Dorset 11 SY9478
Enderby Leics 50 SP5399
Endmoor Cumb 87 SD5384
Endon Staffs 72 SJ9253
Endon Bank Staffs 72 SJ9253
Enfield Gt Lon 27 TQ3597
Enfield Lock Gt Lon 27 TQ3698
Enfield Wash Gt Lon 27 TQ3598
Enford Wilts 23 SU1351
Engine Common Avon 35 ST6984
England's Gate H & W 46 SO5451
Englefield Berks 24 SU6272
Englefield Green Surrey 25 SU9971
Englesea-brook Ches 72 SJ7551
English Bicknor Gloucs 34 SO5815
English Frankton Shrops 59 SJ4529
Englishcombe Avon 22 ST7162
Engollan Cnwll 4 SW8670
Enham-Alamein Hants 23 SU3649
Enmore Somset 20 ST2435
Enmore Green Dorset 22 ST8523
Ennerdale Bridge Cumb 92 NY0615
Enniscaven Cnwll 4 SW9659
Enochdhu Tays 133 NO0662
Ensay Strath 121 NM3648
Ensbury Dorset 12 SZ0896
Ensdon Shrops 59 SJ4017
Ensis Devon 19 SS5626
Enson Staffs 72 SJ9328
Enstone Oxon 48 SP3724
Enterkinfoot D & G 108 NS8504
Enterpen N York 89 NZ4605
Enville Staffs 60 SO8286
Enys Cnwll 3 SW7836
Epney Gloucs 35 SO7611
Epperstone Notts 75 SK6548
Epping Essex 27 TL4502
Epping Green Essex 39 TL4305
Epping Green Herts 39 TL2906
Epping Upland Essex 39 TL4404
Eppleby N York 89 NZ1713
Eppleworth Humb 84 TA0131
Epsom Surrey 26 TQ2160
Epwell Oxon 48 SP3540
Epworth Humb 84 SE7803
Epworth Turbary Humb 84 SE7603
Erbistock Clwyd 71 SJ3541
Erdington W Mids 61 SP1191
Ericstane D & G 108 NT0711
Eridge Green E Susx 16 TQ5535
Eridge Station E Susx 16 TQ5434
Erines Strath 113 NR8575
Erisey Cnwll 2 SW7117
Eriswell Suffk 53 TL7278
Erith Gt Lon 27 TQ5177
Erlestoke Wilts 22 ST9653
Ermington Devon 6 SX6353
Erpingham Norfk 67 TG1931
Erriottwood Kent 28 TQ9459
Errogie Highld 139 NH5622
Errol Tays 126 NO2422
Erskine Strath 115 NS4770
Ervie D & G 98 NX0067
Erwarton Suffk 55 TM2234
Eryholme N York 89 NZ3208
Eryrys Clwyd 70 SJ2057
Escalls Cnwll 2 SW3627
Escomb Dur 96 NZ1830
Escott Somset 20 ST0937
Escrick N York 83 SE6242
Esgair Dyfed 31 SN3728
Esgair Dyfed 43 SN5868
Esgairgeiliog Powys 57 SH7606
Esgyryn Gwynd 69 SH8078
Esh Dur 96 NZ1944
Esh Winning Dur 96 NZ1942
Esher Surrey 26 TQ1364
Esholt W York 82 SE1840
Eshott Nthumb 103 NZ2097
Eshton N York 81 SD9356
Eskadale Highld 139 NH4540
Eskbank Loth 118 NT3266
Eskdale Green Cumb 86 NY1400
Eskdalemuir D & G 101 NY2597
Eskett Cumb 92 NY0516
Eskham Lincs 77 TF3698
Eskholme S York 83 SE6317
Esperley Lane Ends Dur 96 NZ1324
Esprick Lancs 80 SD4036
Essendine Leics 64 TF0412
Essendon Herts 39 TL2708
Essich Highld 140 NH6439
Essington Staffs 60 SJ9603
Esslemont Gramp 143 NJ9229
Eston Cleve 97 NZ5418
Etal Nthumb 110 NT9339
Etchilhampton Wilts 23 SU0460
Etchingham E Susx 17 TQ7126
Etchinghill Kent 29 TR1639
Etchinghill Staffs 73 SK0218
Etchingwood E Susx 16 TQ5022
Etherdwick Humb 85 TA2337
Etling Green Norfk 66 TG0113
Etloe Gloucs 35 SO6806
Eton Berks 26 SU9677
Eton Wick Berks 26 SU9478
Etruria Staffs 72 SJ8647
Etteridge Highld 132 NN6892
Ettersgill Dur 95 NY8829
Ettiley Heath Ches 72 SJ7360

Fivelanes Galmisdale

Fivelanes *Cnwll* 5 SX2280
Fiveways *Warwks* 61 SP2370
Flack's Green *Essex* 40 TL7614
Flackwell Heath *Bucks* 26 SU8989
Fladbury *H & W* 47 SO9946
Fladdabister *Shet* 155 HU4332
Flagg *Derbys* 74 SK1368
Flamborough *Humb* 91 TA2270
Flamstead *Herts* 38 TL0714
Flansham *W Susx* 14 SU9601
Flanshaw *W York* 82 SE3020
Flappit Spring *W York* 82 SE0536
Flasby *N York* 82 SD9456
Flash *Staffs* 74 SK0266
Flashader *Highld* 136 NG3453
Flaunden *Herts* 26 TL0100
Flawborough *Notts* 63 SK7842
Flawith *N York* 90 SE4865
Flax Bourton *Avon* 21 ST5069
Flaxby *N York* 89 SE3957
Flaxley *Gloucs* 35 SO6815
Flaxmere *Ches* 71 SJ5572
Flaxpool *Somset* 20 ST1435
Flaxton *N York* 90 SE6762
Fleckney *Leics* 50 SP6493
Flecknoe *Warwks* 49 SP5163
Fledborough *Notts* 75 SK8072
Fleet *Dorset* 10 SY6380
Fleet *Hants* 13 SU7201
Fleet *Hants* 25 SU8053
Fleet *Lincs* 64 TF3823
Fleet Hargate *Lincs* 65 TF3925
Fleetend *Hants* 13 SU5006
Fleetwood *Lancs* 80 SD3348
Flemingston *S Glam* 20 ST0169
Flemington *Strath* 116 NS6559
Flempton *Suffk* 54 TL8169
Fletcher Green *Kent* 16 TQ5349
Fletchersbridge *Cnwll* 4 SX1065
Fletchertown *Cumb* 93 NY2042
Fletching *E Susx* 16 TQ4223
Flexbury *Cnwll* 18 SS2107
Flexford *Surrey* 25 SU9350
Flimby *Cumb* 92 NY0233
Flimwell *E Susx* 17 TQ7131
Flint *Clwyd* 70 SJ2472
Flint Mountain *Clwyd* 70 SJ2470
Flint's Green *W Mids* 61 SP2680
Flintham *Notts* 63 SK7445
Flinton *Humb* 85 TA2136
Flitcham *Norfk* 65 TF7326
Flitton *Beds* 38 TL0535
Flitwick *Beds* 38 TL0334
Flixborough *Humb* 84 SE8714
Flixborough Stather *Humb* 84 SE8614
Flixton *Gt Man* 79 SJ7494
Flixton *N York* 91 TA0479
Flixton *Suffk* 55 TM3186
Flockton *W York* 82 SE2314
Flockton Green *W York* 82 SE2515
Flodden *Nthumb* 110 NT9235
Flodigarry *Highld* 136 NG4671
Flookburgh *Cumb* 87 SD3675
Flordon *Norfk* 66 TM1897
Flore *Nhants* 49 SP6460
Flotterton *Nthumb* 103 NT9902
Flowers Green *E Susx* 16 TQ6311
Flowton *Suffk* 54 TM0846
Flushdyke *W York* 82 SE2820
Flushing *Cnwll* 3 SW8034
Fluxton *Devon* 9 SY0893
Flyford Flavell *H & W* 47 SO9755
Fobbing *Essex* 40 TQ7183
Fochabers *Gramp* 141 NJ3458
Fochriw *M Glam* 33 SO1005
Fockerby *Humb* 84 SE8519
Foddington *Somset* 21 ST5729
Foel *Powys* 58 SH9911
Foel y Dyffryn *M Glam* 33 SS8594
Foelgastell *Dyfed* 32 SN5414
Foffarty *Tays* 126 NO4145
Foggathorpe *Humb* 84 SE7537
Fogo *Border* 110 NT7649
Fogwatt *Gramp* 141 NJ2356
Foindle *Highld* 148 NC1948
Folda *Tays* 133 NO1963
Fole *Staffs* 73 SK0437
Foleshill *W Mids* 61 SP3582
Foliejon Park *Berks* 25 SU8974
Folke *Dorset* 11 ST6613
Folkestone *Kent* 29 TR2336
Folkingham *Lincs* 64 TF0733
Folkington *E Susx* 16 TQ5603
Folksworth *Cambs* 52 TL1489
Folkton *N York* 91 TA0579
Folla Rule *Gramp* 142 NJ7332
Follifoot *N York* 83 SE3452
Folly Gate *Devon* 8 SX5798
Folly Hill *Surrey* 25 SU8348
Fonmon *S Glam* 20 ST0467
Fonthill Bishop *Wilts* 22 ST9333
Fonthill Gifford *Wilts* 22 ST9231
Fontmell Magna *Dorset* 11 ST8616
Fontmell Parva *Dorset* 11 ST8214
Fontwell *W Susx* 14 SU9407
Foolow *Derbys* 74 SK1976
Foots Cray *Gt Lon* 27 TQ4770
Forbestown *Gramp* 134 NJ3513
Forcett *N York* 89 NZ1712
Ford *Bucks* 37 SP7709
Ford *Derbys* 74 SK4080
Ford *Devon* 18 SS4124
Ford *Devon* 6 SX6150
Ford *Devon* 7 SX7940
Ford *Gloucs* 48 SP0829
Ford *Nthumb* 110 NT9437
Ford *Shrops* 59 SJ4113
Ford *Somset* 20 ST0928
Ford *Somset* 21 ST5953
Ford *Staffs* 73 SK0653
Ford *Strath* 122 NM8603
Ford *W Susx* 14 SU9903
Ford *Wilts* 35 ST8475
Ford End *Essex* 40 TL6716
Ford Green *Lancs* 80 SD4746
Ford Heath *Shrops* 59 SJ4011
Ford Street *Somset* 20 ST1518
Ford's Green *Suffk* 54 TM0666
Forda *Devon* 8 SX5390
Fordcombe *Kent* 16 TQ5240
Fordell *Fife* 117 NT1588
Forden *Powys* 58 SJ2201
Forder *Devon* 8 SX6789
Forder Green *Devon* 7 SX7967
Fordham *Cambs* 53 TL6370
Fordham *Essex* 40 TL9228
Fordham *Norfk* 65 TL6199
Fordham Heath *Essex* 40 TL9426
Fordingbridge *Hants* 12 SU1414
Fordon *Humb* 91 TA0475
Fordoun *Gramp* 135 NO7475
Fordstreet *Essex* 40 TL9226
Fordton *Devon* 8 SX8399
Fordwells *Oxon* 36 SP3013
Fordwich *Kent* 29 TR1859
Fordyce *Gramp* 142 NJ5563
Forebridge *Staffs* 72 SJ9322
Foremark *Derbys* 62 SK3326
Forest *Guern* 152 GN4905
Forest *N York* 89 NZ2700
Forest Becks *Lancs* 81 SD7851
Forest Gate *Gt Lon* 27 TQ4085
Forest Green *Surrey* 14 TQ1241
Forest Hall *Cumb* 87 NY5401
Forest Head *Cumb* 94 NY5857
Forest Hill *Gt Lon* 27 TQ3672
Forest Hill *Oxon* 37 SP5807
Forest Lane Head *N York* 83 SE3356
Forest Lodge *Strath* 123 NN2742
Forest Mill *Cent* 117 NS9694
Forest Row *E Susx* 16 TQ4234
Forest Side *IOW* 13 SZ4889
Forest Town *Notts* 75 SK5662
Forest-in-Teesdale *Dur* 95 NY8630
Forestburn Gate *Nthumb* 103 NZ0696
Forestside *W Susx* 14 SU7612
Forfar *Tays* 127 NO4550
Forgandenny *Tays* 125 NO0818
Forge *Powys* 57 SN7699
Forge Hammer *Gwent* 34 ST2895
Forge Side *Gwent* 34 SO2408
Forgie *Gramp* 141 NJ3854
Forgieside *Gramp* 142 NJ4053
Forgorig *Border* 110 NT7748
Forhill *H & W* 61 SP0575
Formby *Mersyd* 78 SD3006
Forncett End *Norfk* 66 TM1493
Forncett St. Mary *Norfk* 66 TM1694
Forncett St. Peter *Norfk* 66 TM1693
Forneth *Tays* 126 NO1044
Fornham All Saints *Suffk* 54 TL8367
Fornham St. Martin *Suffk* 54 TL8567
Fornside *Cumb* 93 NY3220
Forres *Gramp* 141 NJ0358
Forsbrook *Staffs* 72 SJ9641
Forse *Highld* 151 ND2234
Forse House *Highld* 151 ND2135
Forshaw Heath *Warwks* 61 SP0873
Forsinain *Highld* 150 NC9148
Forsinard *Highld* 150 NC8942
Forston *Dorset* 11 SY6695
Fort Augustus *Highld* 131 NH3709
Fort George *Highld* 140 NH7656
Fort Hommet *Guern* 152 GN4810
Fort le Marchant *Guern* 152 GN5414
Fort William *Highld* 130 NN1074
Forteviot *Tays* 125 NO0517
Forth *Strath* 116 NS9453
Forthampton *Gloucs* 47 SO8532
Fortingall *Tays* 124 NN7347
Fortnighty *Highld* 140 NH9350
Forton *Hants* 24 SU4143
Forton *Lancs* 80 SD4851
Forton *Shrops* 59 SJ4316
Forton *Somset* 10 ST3307
Forton *Staffs* 72 SJ7521
Fortrose *Highld* 140 NH7256
Fortuneswell *Dorset* 11 SY6873
Forty Green *Bucks* 26 SU9291
Forty Hill *Gt Lon* 27 TQ3398
Forward Green *Suffk* 54 TM1059
Fosbury *Wilts* 23 SU3157
Foscot *Oxon* 36 SP2421
Foscote *Nhants* 49 SP6546
Fosdyke *Lincs* 64 TF3133
Fosdyke Bridge *Lincs* 64 TF3232
Foss *Tays* 132 NN7858
Foss-y-ffin *Dyfed* 42 SN4460
Fossebridge *Gloucs* 36 SP0711
Foster Street *Essex* 39 TL4809
Fosterhouses *S York* 83 SE6514
Foston *Derbys* 73 SK1931
Foston *Leics* 50 SP6094
Foston *Lincs* 63 SK8542
Foston *N York* 90 SE6965
Foston on the Wolds *Humb* 85 TA1055
Fotherby *Lincs* 77 TF3191
Fothergill *Cumb* 92 NY0234
Fotheringhay *Nhants* 51 TL0593
Fotrie *Gramp* 142 NJ6645
Foul End *Warwks* 61 SP2494
Foul Mile *E Susx* 16 TQ6215
Foulbridge *Cumb* 93 NY4248
Foulby *W York* 83 SE3917
Foulden *Border* 119 NT9256
Foulden *Norfk* 65 TL7699
Foulridge *Lancs* 81 SD8942
Foulsham *Norfk* 66 TG0324
Fountainhall *Border* 118 NT4249
Four Ashes *Staffs* 60 SJ9108
Four Ashes *Staffs* 60 SO8087
Four Ashes *Suffk* 54 TM0070
Four Ashes *W Mids* 61 SP1575
Four Cabots *Guern* 152 GN5107
Four Crosses *Powys* 58 SJ2618
Four Crosses *Staffs* 60 SJ9509
Four Elms *Kent* 16 TQ4648
Four Foot *Somset* 21 ST5833
Four Forks *Somset* 20 ST2336
Four Gates *Gt Man* 79 SD6407
Four Gotes *Cambs* 65 TF4516
Four Lane End *S York* 82 SE2702
Four Lane Ends *Ches* 71 SJ5561
Four Lanes *Cnwll* 2 SW6838
Four Marks *Hants* 24 SU6735
Four Mile Bridge *Gwynd* 68 SH2778
Four Oaks *E Susx* 17 TQ8524
Four Oaks *Gloucs* 47 SO6928
Four Oaks *W Mids* 61 SP1098
Four Oaks *W Mids* 61 SP2480
Four Points *Berks* 37 SU5579
Four Roads *Dyfed* 32 SN4409
Four Shire Stone *Warwks* 48 SP2232
Four Throws *Kent* 17 TQ7729
Four Wents *Kent* 27 TQ6251
Fourlanes End *Ches* 72 SJ8059
Fourpenny *Highld* 147 NH8094
Fourstones *Nthumb* 102 NY8867
Fovant *Wilts* 22 SU0028
Foveran *Gramp* 143 NJ9824
Fowey *Cnwll* 3 SX1251
Fowley Common *Ches* 79 SJ6795
Fowlhall *Kent* 28 TQ6946
Fowlis *Tays* 126 NO3233
Fowlis Wester *Tays* 125 NN9224
Fowlmere *Cambs* 53 TL4245
Fownhope *H & W* 46 SO5834
Fox Corner *Surrey* 25 SU9654
Fox Hatch *Essex* 27 TQ5798
Fox Street *Essex* 41 TM0227
Foxbar *Strath* 115 NS4561
Foxcombe *Devon* 5 SX4887
Foxcote *Gloucs* 35 SP0118
Foxcote *Somset* 22 ST7155
Foxdale *IOM* 153 SC2778
Foxearth *Essex* 54 TL8344
Foxendown *Kent* 27 TQ6466
Foxfield *Cumb* 86 SD2185
Foxham *Wilts* 35 ST9777
Foxhills *Hants* 12 SU3411
Foxhole *Cnwll* 3 SW9654
Foxhole *W Glam* 32 SS6694
Foxholes *N York* 91 TA0173
Foxhunt Green *E Susx* 16 TQ5417
Foxley *Nhants* 49 SP6451
Foxley *Norfk* 66 TG0422
Foxley *Wilts* 35 ST8986
Foxley Green *Wilts* 35 ST8985
Foxlydiate *H & W* 47 SP0167
Foxt *Staffs* 73 SK0348
Foxton *Cambs* 52 TL4148
Foxton *Dur* 96 NZ3624
Foxton *Leics* 50 SP7089
Foxton *N York* 89 SE4296
Foxup *N York* 88 SD8676
Foxwist Green *Ches* 71 SJ6268
Foxwood *Shrops* 47 SO6276
Foy *H & W* 46 SO5928
Foyers *Highld* 139 NH4921
Foynesfield *Highld* 140 NH8953
Fraddam *Cnwll* 2 SW5834
Fraddon *Cnwll* 4 SW9158
Fradley *Staffs* 61 SK1513
Fradswell *Staffs* 73 SJ9931
Fraisthorpe *Humb* 91 TA1561
Framfield *E Susx* 16 TQ4920
Framingham Earl *Norfk* 67 TG2702
Framingham Pigot *Norfk* 67 TG2703
Framlingham *Suffk* 55 TM2863
Frampton *Dorset* 10 SY6295
Frampton *Lincs* 64 TF3239
Frampton Cotterell *Avon* 35 ST6682
Frampton Mansell *Gloucs* 35 SO9202
Frampton on Severn *Gloucs* 35 SO7407
Frampton West End *Lincs* 64 TF3041
Framsden *Suffk* 55 TM1959
Framwellgate Moor *Dur* 96 NZ2644
Frances Green *Lancs* 81 SD6236
Franche *H & W* 60 SO8278
Frandley *Ches* 71 SJ6379
Frank's Bridge *Powys* 45 SO1156
Frankaborough *Devon* 5 SX3991
Frankby *Mersyd* 78 SJ2486
Frankfort *Norfk* 67 TG3024
Franklands Gate *H & W* 46 SO5346
Frankley *H & W* 60 SO9980
Frankton *Warwks* 50 SP4270
Frant *E Susx* 16 TQ5835
Fraserburgh *Gramp* 143 NJ9966
Frating *Essex* 41 TM0722
Frating Green *Essex* 41 TM0823
Fratton *Hants* 13 SU6500
Freathy *Cnwll* 5 SX3952
Freckenham *Suffk* 53 TL6672
Freckleton *Lancs* 80 SD4329
Freebirch *Derbys* 74 SK3072
Freeby *Leics* 63 SK8020
Freefolk *Hants* 24 SU4848
Freehay *Staffs* 73 SK0241
Freeland *Oxon* 36 SP4112
Freethorpe *Norfk* 67 TG4005
Freethorpe Common *Norfk* 67 TG4004
Freiston *Lincs* 64 TF3743
Fremington *Devon* 19 SS5132
Fremington *N York* 88 SE0499
French Street *Kent* 27 TQ4552
Frenchay *Avon* 35 ST6377
Frenchbeer *Devon* 8 SX6785
Frenich *Tays* 132 NN8258
Frensham *Surrey* 25 SU8441
Freshwater *IOW* 12 SZ3487
Freshwater Bay *IOW* 12 SZ3485
Fressingfield *Suffk* 55 TM2677
Freston *Suffk* 54 TM1638
Freswick *Highld* 151 ND3667
Fretherne *Gloucs* 35 SO7210
Frettenham *Norfk* 67 TG2417
Freuchie *Fife* 126 NO2806
Freystrop *Dyfed* 30 SM9511
Friar Waddon *Dorset* 11 SY6486
Friar's Gate *E Susx* 16 TQ4933
Friars' Hill *N York* 90 SE7485
Friday Bridge *Cambs* 65 TF4604
Friday Street *E Susx* 16 TQ6203
Friday Street *Suffk* 55 TM2459
Friday Street *Suffk* 55 TM3351
Friday Street *Suffk* 55 TM3760
Friday Street *Surrey* 14 TQ1245
Fridaythorpe *Humb* 90 SE8759
Friden *Derbys* 74 SK1660
Friendly *W York* 82 SE0524
Friern Barnet *Gt Lon* 27 TQ2892
Friesland Bay *Strath* 120 NM1954
Friesthorpe *Lincs* 76 TF0683
Frieston *Lincs* 63 SK9347
Frieth *Bucks* 37 SU7990
Friezeland *Notts* 75 SK4750
Frilford *Oxon* 37 SU4497
Frilsham *Berks* 24 SU5473
Frimley *Surrey* 25 SU8757
Frindsbury *Kent* 28 TQ7469
Fring *Norfk* 65 TF7334
Fringford *Oxon* 49 SP6029
Frinsted *Kent* 28 TQ8957
Frinton-on-Sea *Essex* 41 TM2320
Friockheim *Tays* 127 NO5949
Friog *Gwynd* 57 SH6112
Frisby on the Wreake *Leics* 63 SK6917
Friskney *Lincs* 77 TF4655
Friskney Eaudike *Lincs* 77 TF4755
Friston *E Susx* 16 TV5598
Friston *Suffk* 55 TM4160
Fritchley *Derbys* 74 SK3552
Frith Bank *Lincs* 77 TF3147
Frith Common *H & W* 47 SO6969
Fritham *Hants* 12 SU2314
Frithelstock *Devon* 18 SS4619
Frithelstock Stone *Devon* 18 SS4518
Frithend *Hants* 25 SU8039
Frithsden *Herts* 38 TL0009
Frithville *Lincs* 77 TF3150
Frittenden *Kent* 28 TQ8140
Frittiscombe *Devon* 7 SX8043
Fritton *Norfk* 67 TG4600
Fritton *Norfk* 67 TM2293
Fritwell *Oxon* 49 SP5229
Frizinghall *W York* 82 SE1435
Frizington *Cumb* 92 NY0316
Frocester *Gloucs* 35 SO7803
Frodesley *Shrops* 59 SJ5101
Frodsham *Ches* 71 SJ5177
Frog End *Cambs* 52 TL3946
Frog End *Cambs* 53 TL5358
Frog Pool *H & W* 47 SO8065
Frogden *Border* 110 NT7628
Froggatt *Derbys* 74 SK2476
Froghall *Staffs* 73 SK0247
Frogham *Hants* 12 SU1612
Frogham *Kent* 29 TR2550
Frogmore *Devon* 7 SX7742
Frognall *Lincs* 64 TF1610
Frogwell *Cnwll* 5 SX3468
Frolesworth *Leics* 50 SP5090
Frome *Somset* 22 ST7747
Frome St. Quintin *Dorset* 10 ST5902
Frome Whitfield *Dorset* 11 SY6991
Fromes Hill *H & W* 47 SO6846
Fron *Gwynd* 56 SH3539
Fron *Gwynd* 68 SH5054
Fron *Powys* 58 SJ2203
Fron *Powys* 58 SO1797
Fron Isaf *Clwyd* 70 SJ2740
Fron-goch *Gwynd* 70 SH9039
Froncysyllte *Clwyd* 70 SJ2640
Frostenden *Suffk* 55 TM4781
Frosterley *Dur* 95 NZ0237
Froxfield *Beds* 38 SP9733
Froxfield *Wilts* 23 SU2968
Froxfield Green *Hants* 13 SU7025
Fryern Hill *Hants* 13 SU4320
Fryerning *Essex* 40 TL6300
Fryton *N York* 90 SE6874
Fulbeck *Lincs* 76 SK9450
Fulbourn *Cambs* 53 TL5256
Fulbrook *Oxon* 36 SP2513
Fulflood *Hants* 24 SU4730
Fulford *N York* 83 SE6149
Fulford *Somset* 20 ST2029
Fulford *Staffs* 72 SJ9537
Fulham *Gt Lon* 27 TQ2576
Fulking *W Susx* 15 TQ2411
Full Sutton *Humb* 84 SE7455
Fullaford *Devon* 19 SS6838
Fullarton *Strath* 106 NS3238
Fuller Street *Essex* 40 TL7416
Fuller Street *Kent* 27 TQ5656
Fuller's End *Essex* 39 TL5325
Fuller's Moor *Ches* 71 SJ4954
Fullerton *Hants* 23 SU3739
Fulletby *Lincs* 77 TF2973
Fullready *Warwks* 48 SP2846
Fullwood *Strath* 115 NS4450
Fulmer *Bucks* 26 SU9985
Fulmodeston *Norfk* 66 TF9930
Fulneck *W York* 82 SE2232
Fulnetby *Lincs* 76 TF0979
Fulstone *W York* 82 SE1709
Fulstow *Lincs* 77 TF3297
Fulwell *Oxon* 36 SP3722
Fulwood *Lancs* 80 SD5431
Fulwood *Notts* 75 SK4757
Fulwood *S York* 74 SK3085
Fulwood *Somset* 20 ST2120
Fundenhall *Norfk* 66 TM1596
Funtington *W Susx* 14 SU8008
Funtley *Hants* 13 SU5608
Funtullich *Tays* 124 NN7526
Furley *Devon* 10 ST2604
Furnace *Dyfed* 32 SN5001
Furnace *Dyfed* 43 SN6895
Furnace *Strath* 114 NN0200
Furnace End *Warwks* 61 SP2491
Furner's Green *E Susx* 15 TQ4126
Furness Vale *Derbys* 79 SK0083
Furneux Pelham *Herts* 39 TL4327
Further Quarter *Kent* 28 TQ8939
Furtho *Nhants* 49 SP7743
Furze Platt *Berks* 26 SU8782
Furzehill *Devon* 19 SS7245
Furzehill *Dorset* 11 SU0101
Furzehills *Lincs* 77 TF2572
Furzeley Corner *Hants* 13 SU6510
Furzley *Hants* 12 SU2816
Fyfett *Somset* 9 ST2314
Fyfield *Essex* 40 TL5707
Fyfield *Hants* 23 SU2946
Fyfield *Oxon* 36 SU4298
Fyfield *Wilts* 23 SU1468
Fyfield *Wilts* 23 SU1760
Fyfield Bavant *Wilts* 22 SU0125
Fyfield Wick *Oxon* 36 SU4197
Fylingthorpe *N York* 91 NZ9404
Fyning *W Susx* 14 SU8123
Fyvie *Gramp* 142 NJ7637

G

Gabroc Hill *Strath* 115 NS4550
Gaddesby *Leics* 63 SK6813
Gaddesden Row *Herts* 38 TL0512
Gadfa *Gwynd* 68 SH4689
Gadgirth *Strath* 106 NS4022
Gadlas *Shrops* 59 SJ3737
Gaer *Powys* 33 SO1721
Gaer-llwyd *Gwent* 34 ST4496
Gaerwen *Gwynd* 68 SH4871
Gagingwell *Oxon* 48 SP4025
Gailes *Strath* 106 NS3235
Gailey *Staffs* 60 SJ9110
Gainford *Dur* 96 NZ1716
Gainsborough *Lincs* 75 SK8189
Gainsford End *Essex* 53 TL7235
Gairloch *Highld* 144 NG8076
Gairlochy *Highld* 131 NN1784
Gairneybridge *Tays* 117 NT1397
Gaisby *W York* 82 SE1536
Gaisgill *Cumb* 87 NY6305
Gaitsgill *Cumb* 93 NY3846
Galashiels *Border* 109 NT4936
Galby *Leics* 50 SK6900
Galcantray *Highld* 140 NH8148
Galgate *Lancs* 80 SD4855
Galhampton *Somset* 21 ST6329
Gallaberry *D & G* 100 NX9682
Gallanach *Strath* 120 NM2161
Gallanach *Strath* 122 NM8326
Gallantry Bank *Ches* 71 SJ5153
Gallatown *Fife* 117 NT2994
Galley Common *Warwks* 61 SP3091
Galleywood *Essex* 40 TL7003
Gallovie *Highld* 132 NN5589
Gallowfauld *Tays* 127 NO4342
Gallowhill *Tays* 126 NO1635
Gallows Green *H & W* 47 SO9362
Gallowstree Common *Oxon* 37 SU6980
Gallt-y-foel *Gwynd* 69 SH5862
Galltair *Highld* 129 NG8120
Gally Hill *Hants* 25 SU8051
Gallypot Street *E Susx* 16 TQ4735
Galmisdale *Highld* 128 NM4784

Galmpton

Gore

Galmpton *Devon* 7 SX6940
Galmpton *Devon* 7 SX8856
Galphay *N York* 89 SE2572
Galston *Strath* 107 NS5036
Galton *Dorset* 11 SY7785
Gamballs Green *Staffs* 74 SK0367
Gambles Green *Essex* 40 TL7614
Gamblesby *Cumb* 94 NY6039
Gamelsby *Cumb* 93 NY2552
Gamesley *Gt Man* 79 SK0194
Gamlingay *Cambs* 52 TL2452
Gamlingay Cinques *Cambs* 52 TL2352
Gamlingay Great Heath *Beds* 52 TL2151
Gammersgill *N York* 88 SE0582
Gamrie *Gramp* 143 NJ7962
Gamston *Notts* 75 SK7176
Gamston *Notts* 62 SK5937
Ganarew *H & W* 34 SO5216
Ganavan Bay *Strath* 122 NM8632
Gang *Cnwll* 5 SX3068
Ganllwyd *Gwynd* 57 SH7324
Gannachy *Tays* 134 NO5970
Ganstead *Humb* 85 TA1434
Ganthorpe *N York* 90 SE6870
Ganton *N York* 91 SE9977
Ganwick Corner *Herts* 27 TQ2599
Gappah *Devon* 9 SX8677
Garbity *Gramp* 141 NJ3152
Garboldisham *Norfk* 54 TM0081
Garchory *Gramp* 134 NJ3010
Garden City *Clwyd* 71 SJ3269
Garden Village *Derbys* 74 SK2698
Gardeners Green *Berks* 25 SU8266
Gardenstown *Gramp* 143 NJ8064
Garderhouse *Shet* 155 HU3347
Gardham *Humb* 84 SE9542
Gare Hill *Somset* 22 ST7840
Garelochhead *Strath* 114 NS2491
Garford *Oxon* 36 SU4296
Garforth *W York* 83 SE4033
Garforth Bridge *W York* 83 SE3932
Gargrave *N York* 81 SD9354
Gargunnock *Cent* 116 NS7094
Garizim *Gwynd* 69 SH6975
Garlic Street *Norfk* 55 TM2183
Garlieston *D & G* 99 NX4746
Garlinge *Kent* 29 TR3369
Garlinge Green *Kent* 29 TR1152
Garlogie *Gramp* 135 NJ7805
Garmond *Gramp* 143 NJ8052
Garmondsway *Dur* 96 NZ3434
Garmouth *Gramp* 141 NJ3364
Garmston *Shrops* 59 SJ6006
Garn *Gwynd* 56 SH2834
Garn-Dolbenmaen *Gwynd* 56 SH4943
Garnant *Dyfed* 32 SN6713
Garnett Bridge *Cumb* 87 SD5299
Garnkirk *Strath* 116 NS6768
Garnswllt *W Glam* 32 SN6209
Garrabost *W Isls* 154 NB5133
Garrallan *Strath* 107 NS5418
Garras *Cnwll* 2 SW7023
Garreg *Gwynd* 57 SH6141
Garrigill *Cumb* 94 NY7441
Garriston *N York* 89 SE1592
Garroch *D & G* 99 NX5981
Garrochtrie *D & G* 98 NX1138
Garrochty *Strath* 114 NS0953
Garros *Highld* 136 NG4962
Garrowby Hall *Humb* 90 SE7957
Garsdale *Cumb* 88 SD7489
Garsdale Head *Cumb* 88 SD7891
Garsdon *Wilts* 35 ST9687
Garshall Green *Staffs* 72 SJ9633
Garsington *Oxon* 37 SP5802
Garstang *Lancs* 80 SD4945
Garston *Herts* 26 TL1100
Garston *Mersyd* 78 SJ4084
Gartachossan *Strath* 112 NR3461
Gartcosh *Strath* 116 NS6967
Garth *Clwyd* 70 SJ2542
Garth *Gwent* 34 ST3492
Garth *IOM* 153 SC3177
Garth *M Glam* 33 SS8690
Garth *Powys* 45 SN9549
Garth *Powys* 46 SO2772
Garth Penrhyncoch *Dyfed* 43 SN6484
Garth Row *Cumb* 87 SD5297
Garthamlock *Strath* 116 NS6566
Garthbrengy *Powys* 45 SO0433
Gartheli *Dyfed* 44 SN5856
Garthmyl *Powys* 58 SO1999
Garthorpe *Humb* 84 SE8418
Garthorpe *Leics* 63 SK8320
Garths *Cumb* 87 SD5489
Gartly *Gramp* 142 NJ5232
Gartmore *Cent* 115 NS5297
Gartness *Cent* 115 NS5086
Gartness *Strath* 116 NS7864
Gartocharn *Strath* 115 NS4286
Garton *Humb* 85 TA2635
Garton End *Cambs* 64 TF1900
Garton-on-the-Wolds *Humb* 91 SE9759
Gartsherrie *Strath* 116 NS7265
Gartymore *Highld* 147 ND0114
Garvald *Loth* 118 NT5870
Garvan *Highld* 130 NM9777
Garvard *Strath* 112 NR3791
Garve *Highld* 139 NH3961
Garvestone *Norfk* 66 TG0207
Garvock *Strath* 114 NS2570
Garway *H & W* 34 SO4522
Garway Common *H & W* 34 SO4622
Garway Hill *H & W* 46 SO4425
Gasper *Wilts* 22 ST7633
Gass *Strath* 106 NS4105
Gastard *Wilts* 22 ST8868
Gasthorpe *Norfk* 54 TL9781
Gaston Green *Essex* 39 TL4917
Gatcombe *IOW* 13 SZ4985
Gate Burton *Lincs* 76 SK8382
Gate Helmsley *N York* 83 SE6955
Gatebeck *Cumb* 87 SD5485
Gateford *Notts* 75 SK5781
Gateforth *N York* 83 SE5628
Gatehead *Strath* 106 NS3936
Gatehouse *Nthumb* 102 NY7889
Gatehouse of Fleet *D & G* 99 NX5956
Gateley *Norfk* 66 TF9624
Gatenby *N York* 89 SE3287
Gates Heath *Ches* 71 SJ4760
Gatesgarth *Cumb* 93 NY1915
Gateshaw *Border* 110 NT7722
Gateshead *T & W* 96 NZ2562
Gateside *Fife* 126 NO1809
Gateside *Strath* 115 NS3653
Gateside *Strath* 115 NS4858
Gateside *Tays* 127 NO4344
Gateslack *D & G* 108 NS8902
Gathurst *Gt Man* 78 SD5407
Gatley *Gt Man* 79 SJ8488
Gatton *Surrey* 27 TQ2752
Gattonside *Border* 109 NT5435
Gaufron *Powys* 45 SN9968
Gauldry *Fife* 126 NO3723
Gauldswell *Tays* 126 NO2151
Gaulkthorn *Lancs* 81 SD7526
Gaultree *Norfk* 65 TF4907
Gaunt's Common *Dorset* 12 SU0205
Gaunt's End *Essex* 39 TL5525
Gaunton's Bank *Ches* 71 SJ5647
Gautby *Lincs* 76 TF1772
Gavinton *Border* 119 NT7652
Gawber *S York* 83 SE3207
Gawcott *Bucks* 49 SP6831
Gawsworth *Ches* 79 SJ8969
Gawthorpe *W York* 82 SE2721
Gawthrop *Cumb* 87 SD6987
Gawthwaite *Cumb* 86 SD2784
Gay Bowers *Essex* 40 TL7904
Gay Street *W Susx* 14 TQ0820
Gaydon *Warwks* 48 SP3653
Gayhurst *Bucks* 38 SP8446
Gayle *N York* 88 SD8688
Gayles *N York* 89 NZ1207
Gayton *Mersyd* 78 SJ2780
Gayton *Nhants* 49 SP7054
Gayton *Norfk* 65 TF7219
Gayton *Staffs* 72 SJ9828
Gayton le Marsh *Lincs* 77 TF4284
Gayton Thorpe *Norfk* 65 TF7418
Gaywood *Norfk* 65 TF6320
Gazeley *Suffk* 53 TL7264
Gear *Cnwll* 3 SW7224
Geary *Highld* 136 NG2661
Gedding *Suffk* 54 TL9457
Geddinge *Kent* 29 TR2346
Geddington *Nhants* 51 SP8983
Gedling *Notts* 62 SK6142
Gedney *Lincs* 65 TF4024
Gedney Broadgate *Lincs* 65 TF4022
Gedney Drove End *Lincs* 65 TF4629
Gedney Dyke *Lincs* 65 TF4126
Gedney Hill *Lincs* 64 TF3311
Gee Cross *Gt Man* 79 SJ9593
Geldeston *Norfk* 67 TM3991
Gelli *Gwent* 34 ST2792
Gelli *M Glam* 33 SS9794
Gelli Gynan *Clwyd* 70 SJ1854
Gellifor *Clwyd* 70 SJ1262
Gelligaer *M Glam* 33 ST1396
Gelligron *W Glam* 32 SN7104
Gellilydan *Gwynd* 57 SH6839
Gellinudd *W Glam* 32 SN7303
Gelly *Dyfed* 31 SN0819
Gellyburn *Tays* 125 NO0939
Gellywen *Dyfed* 31 SN2723
Gelston *D & G* 92 NX7758
Gelston *Lincs* 63 SK9145
Gembling *Humb* 91 TA1057
Gentleshaw *Staffs* 61 SK0511
George Green *Bucks* 26 SU9981
George Nympton *Devon* 19 SS7023
Georgefield *D & G* 101 NY2991
Georgeham *Devon* 18 SS4639
Georgia *Cnwll* 2 SW4836
Georth *Ork* 155 HY3625
Gerlan *Gwynd* 69 SH6366
Germansweek *Devon* 5 SX4394
Germoe *Cnwll* 2 SW5829
Gerrans *Cnwll* 3 SW8735
Gerrards Cross *Bucks* 26 TQ0088
Gerrick *Cleve* 90 NZ7012
Gestingthorpe *Essex* 54 TL8138
Geuffordd *Powys* 58 SJ2114
Gib Hill *Ches* 79 SJ6478
Gibraltar *Kent* 29 TR2038
Gibraltar *Lincs* 77 TF5558
Gibsmere *Notts* 75 SK7148
Giddeahall *Wilts* 35 ST8674
Giddy Green *Dorset* 11 SY8386
Gidea Park *Gt Lon* 27 TQ5290
Gidleigh *Devon* 8 SX6788
Giffnock *Strath* 115 NS5658
Gifford *Loth* 118 NT5368
Giffordtown *Fife* 126 NO2811
Giggleswick *N York* 88 SD8063
Gilberdyke *Humb* 84 SE8329
Gilbert Street *Hants* 24 SU6432
Gilbert's Cross *Staffs* 60 SO8187
Gilbert's End *H & W* 47 SO8342
Gilchriston *Loth* 118 NT4865
Gilcrux *Cumb* 92 NY1138
Gildersome *W York* 82 SE2429
Gildingwells *S York* 75 SK5585
Gilesgate Moor *Dur* 96 NZ2942
Gileston *S Glam* 20 ST0166
Gilfach *M Glam* 33 ST1598
Gilfach Goch *M Glam* 33 SS9790
Gilfachrheda *Dyfed* 42 SN4158
Gilgarran *Cumb* 92 NY0323
Gill *Cumb* 93 NY4429
Gill's Green *Kent* 17 TQ7532
Gillamoor *N York* 90 SE6889
Gillan *Cnwll* 3 SW7825
Gillesbie *D & G* 100 NY1691
Gilling *N York* 89 NZ1805
Gilling East *N York* 90 SE6176
Gillingham *Dorset* 22 ST8026
Gillingham *Kent* 28 TQ7768
Gillingham *Norfk* 67 TM4191
Gillock *Highld* 151 ND2159
Gillow Heath *Staffs* 72 SJ8858
Gills *Highld* 151 ND3272
Gilmanscleuch *Border* 109 NT3321
Gilmerton *Loth* 117 NT2868
Gilmerton *Tays* 125 NN8823
Gilmonby *Dur* 95 NY9912
Gilmorton *Leics* 50 SP5787
Gilsland *Nthumb* 102 NY6366
Gilson *Warwks* 61 SP1989
Gilstead *W York* 82 SE1239
Gilston *Herts* 39 TL4413
Gilston *Loth* 118 NT4456
Giltbrook *Notts* 62 SK4845
Gilwern *Gwent* 34 SO2414
Gimingham *Norfk* 67 TG2836
Ginclough *Ches* 79 SJ9576
Ginger Green *E Susx* 16 TQ6212
Gipping *Suffk* 54 TM0763
Gipsey Bridge *Lincs* 77 TF2849
Girdle Toll *Strath* 106 NS3440
Girlington *W York* 82 SE1334
Girlsta *Shet* 155 HU4250
Girsby *Cleve* 89 NZ3508
Girtford *Beds* 52 TL1649
Girthon *D & G* 99 NX6053
Girton *Cambs* 53 TL4262
Girton *Notts* 75 SK8265
Girvan *Strath* 106 NX1897
Gisburn *Lancs* 81 SD8248
Gisleham *Suffk* 55 TM5188
Gislingham *Suffk* 54 TM0771
Gissing *Norfk* 54 TM1485
Gittisham *Devon* 9 SY1398
Gladestry *Powys* 45 SO2355
Gladsmuir *Loth* 118 NT4573
Glais *W Glam* 32 SN7000
Glaisdale *N York* 90 NZ7705
Glamis *Tays* 126 NO3846
Glan-Duar *Dyfed* 44 SN5243
Glan-Mule *Powys* 58 SO1690
Glan-rhyd *W Glam* 32 SN7809
Glan-y-don *Clwyd* 70 SJ1679
Glan-y-llyn *M Glam* 33 ST1183
Glan-y-nant *Powys* 58 SN9384
Glan-yr-afon *Gwynd* 69 SH6080
Glan-yr-afon *Gwynd* 70 SH9140
Glan-yr-afon *Gwynd* 70 SJ0142
Glanaber *Gwynd* 69 SH6351
Glanafon *Dyfed* 30 SM9617
Glanaman *Dyfed* 32 SN6713
Glandford *Norfk* 66 TG0441
Glandwr *Dyfed* 31 SN1928
Glandyfi *Dyfed* 43 SN6996
Glangrwyne *Powys* 34 SO2416
Glanrhyd *Dyfed* 31 SN1442
Glanton *Nthumb* 111 NU0714
Glanton Pike *Nthumb* 111 NU0514
Glanvilles Wootton *Dorset* 11 ST6708
Glapthorn *Nhants* 51 TL0290
Glapwell *Derbys* 75 SK4766
Glasbury *Powys* 45 SO1739
Glascoed *Clwyd* 70 SH9973
Glascoed *Gwent* 34 SO3301
Glascote *Staffs* 61 SK2203
Glascwm *Powys* 45 SO1552
Glasfryn *Clwyd* 70 SH9250
Glasgow *Strath* 115 NS5865
Glasinfryn *Gwynd* 69 SH5868
Glasnacardoch Bay *Highld* 129 NM6795
Glasnakille *Highld* 128 NG5313
Glaspwll *Powys* 43 SN7397
Glass Houghton *W York* 83 SE4324
Glassenbury *Kent* 28 TQ7536
Glasserton *D & G* 99 NX4237
Glassford *Strath* 116 NS7247
Glasshouse *Gloucs* 35 SO7021
Glasshouse Hill *Gloucs* 35 SO7020
Glasshouses *N York* 89 SE1764
Glasson *Cumb* 101 NY2560
Glasson *Lancs* 80 SD4456
Glassonby *Cumb* 94 NY5738
Glasterlaw *Tays* 127 NO5951
Glaston *Leics* 51 SK8900
Glastonbury *Somset* 21 ST5038
Glatton *Cambs* 52 TL1586
Glazebrook *Ches* 79 SJ6992
Glazebury *Ches* 79 SJ6797
Glazeley *Shrops* 60 SO7088
Gleadsmoss *Ches* 79 SJ8168
Gleaston *Cumb* 86 SD2570
Gledhow *W York* 82 SE3137
Gledpark *D & G* 99 NX6250
Gledrid *Shrops* 59 SJ3036
Glemsford *Suffk* 54 TL8348
Glen *D & G* 99 NX5457
Glen Clunie Lodge *Gramp* 133 NO1383
Glen Maye *IOM* 153 SC2379
Glen Nevis House *Highld* 130 NN1272
Glen Parva *Leics* 50 SP5798
Glen Trool Lodge *D & G* 99 NX4080
Glenancross *Highld* 129 NM6691
Glenaros House *Strath* 121 NM5544
Glenbarr *Strath* 105 NR6736
Glenbeg *Highld* 121 NM5862
Glenboig *Strath* 116 NS7268
Glenborrodale *Highld* 121 NM6061
Glenbranter *Strath* 114 NS1197
Glenbreck *Border* 108 NT0521
Glenbrittle House *Highld* 128 NG4121
Glenbuck *Strath* 107 NS7429
Glencally *Tays* 134 NO3562
Glencaple *D & G* 100 NX9968
Glencarron Lodge *Highld* 138 NH0650
Glencarse *Tays* 126 NO1921
Glenceitlein *Highld* 123 NN1548
Glencoe *Highld* 130 NN1058
Glencothe *Border* 108 NT0829
Glencraig *Fife* 117 NT1894
Glencrosh *D & G* 107 NX7689
Glendale *Highld* 136 NG1749
Glendaruel *Strath* 114 NR9983
Glendevon *Tays* 125 NN9904
Glendoe Lodge *Highld* 131 NH4009
Glendoick *Tays* 126 NO2022
Glenduckie *Fife* 126 NO2818
Gleneagles *Tays* 125 NN9208
Glenegedale *Strath* 112 NR3351
Glenelg *Highld* 129 NG8119
Glenerney *Gramp* 141 NJ0146
Glenfarg *Tays* 126 NO1310
Glenfeshie Lodge *Highld* 132 NN8493
Glenfield *Leics* 62 SK5406
Glenfinnan *Highld* 130 NM9080
Glenfinntaig Lodge *Highld* 131 NN2286
Glenfoot *Tays* 126 NO1815
Glenfyne Lodge *Strath* 123 NN2215
Glengarnock *Strath* 115 NS3252
Glengolly *Highld* 151 ND1065
Glengorm Castle *Strath* 121 NM4457
Glengrasco *Highld* 136 NG4444
Glenholm *Border* 108 NT1033
Glenhoul *D & G* 107 NX6187
Glenkerry *Border* 109 NT2710
Glenkin *Strath* 114 NS1280
Glenkindie *Gramp* 142 NJ4314
Glenlee *D & G* 99 NX6080
Glenlivet *Gramp* 141 NJ1929
Glenlochar *D & G* 99 NX7364
Glenloig *Strath* 105 NR9435
Glenlomond *Tays* 126 NO1704
Glenluce *D & G* 98 NX1957
Glenmark *Tays* 134 NO4183
Glenmassen *Strath* 114 NS1088
Glenmavis *Strath* 116 NS7467
Glenmore *Highld* 136 NG4340
Glenmore Lodge *Highld* 133 NH9709
Glenquiech *Tays* 134 NO4261
Glenralloch *Strath* 113 NR8569
Glenridding *Cumb* 93 NY3817
Glenrothes *Fife* 117 NO2700
Glenshero Lodge *Highld* 132 NN5592
Glenstriven *Strath* 114 NS0878
Glentham *Lincs* 76 TF0090
Glentromie Lodge *Highld* 132 NN7897
Glentrool Village *D & G* 98 NX3578
Glentruim House *Highld* 132 NN6894
Glentworth *Lincs* 76 SK9488
Glenuig *Highld* 129 NM6677
Glenure *Strath* 123 NN0448
Glenurquhart *Highld* 140 NH7462
Glenvarragill *Highld* 136 NG4739
Glenwhilly *D & G* 98 NX1771
Glespin *Strath* 108 NS8127
Glewstone *H & W* 34 SO5521
Glinton *Cambs* 64 TF1505
Glooston *Leics* 50 SP7595
Glororum *Nthumb* 111 NU1633
Glossop *Derbys* 74 SK0393
Gloster Hill *Nthumb* 103 NU2504
Gloucester *Gloucs* 35 SO8318
Glover's Hill *Staffs* 73 SK0516
Glusburn *N York* 82 SE0045
Glutt Lodge *Highld* 150 ND0036
Gluvian *Cnwll* 4 SW9164
Glympton *Oxon* 36 SP4221
Glyn Ceiriog *Clwyd* 70 SJ2038
Glyn-Neath *W Glam* 33 SN8806
Glynarthen *Dyfed* 42 SN3148
Glyncorrwg *W Glam* 33 SS8798
Glynde *E Susx* 16 TQ4509
Glyndebourne *E Susx* 16 TQ4510
Glyndyfrdwy *Clwyd* 70 SJ1442
Glynn *Cnwll* 4 SX1165
Glyntaff *M Glam* 33 ST0889
Glyntawe *Powys* 33 SN8416
Glynteg *Dyfed* 31 SN3538
Gnosall *Staffs* 72 SJ8220
Gnosall Heath *Staffs* 72 SJ8220
Goadby *Leics* 50 SP7598
Goadby Marwood *Leics* 63 SK7726
Goat Lees *Kent* 28 TR0145
Goatacre *Wilts* 35 SU0276
Goatfield *Strath* 114 NN0100
Goatham Green *E Susx* 17 TQ8120
Goathill *Dorset* 11 ST6717
Goathland *N York* 90 NZ8301
Goathurst *Somset* 20 ST2534
Goathurst Common *Kent* 27 TQ4952
Gobowen *Shrops* 59 SJ3033
Godalming *Surrey* 25 SU9643
Godameavy *Devon* 6 SX5364
Goddard's Corner *Suffk* 55 TM2868
Goddard's Green *Kent* 17 TQ8134
Godford Cross *Devon* 9 ST1302
Godington *Bucks* 49 SP6427
Godley *Gt Man* 79 SJ9595
Godmanchester *Cambs* 52 TL2470
Godmanstone *Dorset* 11 SY6697
Godmersham *Kent* 28 TR0550
Godney *Somset* 21 ST4842
Godolphin Cross *Cnwll* 2 SW6031
Godre'r-graig *W Glam* 32 SN7506
Godshill *Hants* 12 SU1715
Godshill *IOW* 13 SZ5281
Godstone *Staffs* 73 SK0134
Godstone *Surrey* 27 TQ3551
Godsworthy *Devon* 5 SX5277
Godwinscroft *Hants* 12 SZ1996
Goetre *Gwent* 34 SO3206
Goff's Oak *Herts* 27 TL3202
Gofilon *Gwent* 34 SO2613
Gogar *Loth* 117 NT1672
Goginan *Dyfed* 43 SN6881
Golan *Gwynd* 57 SH5242
Golant *Cnwll* 3 SX1254
Golberdon *Cnwll* 5 SX3271
Golborne *Gt Man* 78 SJ6097
Golcar *W York* 82 SE0915
Gold Hill *Cambs* 65 TL5392
Gold Hill *Dorset* 11 ST8213
Goldcliff *Gwent* 34 ST3683
Golden Cross *E Susx* 16 TQ5312
Golden Green *Kent* 16 TQ6348
Golden Grove *Dyfed* 32 SN5919
Golden Hill *Dyfed* 30 SM9802
Golden Pot *Hants* 24 SU7143
Golden Valley *Derbys* 74 SK4251
Goldenhill *Staffs* 72 SJ8553
Golders Green *Gt Lon* 26 TQ2487
Goldfinch Bottom *Berks* 24 SU5063
Goldhanger *Essex* 40 TL9008
Golding *Shrops* 59 SJ5403
Goldington *Beds* 38 TL0750
Golds Green *W Mids* 60 SO9893
Goldsborough *N York* 90 NZ8314
Goldsborough *N York* 83 SE3856
Goldsithney *Cnwll* 2 SW5430
Goldstone *Kent* 29 TR2961
Goldstone *Shrops* 72 SJ7028
Goldsworth *Surrey* 25 SU9958
Goldthorpe *S York* 83 SE4604
Goldworthy *Devon* 18 SS3922
Golford *Kent* 28 TQ7936
Golford Green *Kent* 28 TQ7936
Gollanfield *Highld* 140 NH8053
Gollinglith Foot *N York* 89 SE1481
Golly *Clwyd* 71 SJ3358
Golsoncott *Somset* 20 ST0239
Golspie *Highld* 147 NC8300
Gomeldon *Wilts* 23 SU1835
Gomersal *W York* 82 SE2026
Gomshall *Surrey* 14 TQ0847
Gonalston *Notts* 63 SK6747
Gonerby Hill Foot *Lincs* 63 SK9037
Gonfirth *Shet* 155 HU3661
Good Easter *Essex* 40 TL6212
Gooderstone *Norfk* 65 TF7602
Goodleigh *Devon* 19 SS6034
Goodmanham *Humb* 84 SE8843
Goodnestone *Kent* 28 TR0461
Goodnestone *Kent* 29 TR2554
Goodrich *H & W* 34 SO5719
Goodrington *Devon* 7 SX8958
Goodshaw *Lancs* 81 SD8125
Goodshaw Fold *Lancs* 81 SD8026
Goodstone *Devon* 7 SX7872
Goodwick *Dyfed* 30 SM9438
Goodworth Clatford *Hants* 23 SU3642
Goodyers End *Warwks* 61 SP3385
Goole *Humb* 84 SE7423
Goolefields *Humb* 84 SE7520
Goom's Hill *H & W* 47 SP0154
Goonbell *Cnwll* 3 SW7249
Goonhavern *Cnwll* 3 SW7853
Goonvrea *Cnwll* 2 SW7149
Goose Green *Avon* 35 ST6774
Goose Green *Essex* 41 TM1327
Goose Green *Gt Man* 78 SD5603
Goose Green *Kent* 27 TQ6451
Goose Green *Kent* 28 TQ8437
Goose Green *W Susx* 14 TQ1118
Goose Pool *H & W* 46 SO4636
Goosecruives *Gramp* 135 NO7583
Gooseford *Devon* 8 SX6792
Gooseham *Cnwll* 18 SS2316
Goosehill Green *H & W* 47 SO9361
Goosemoor *Somset* 20 SS9635
Goosey *Oxon* 36 SU3591
Goosnargh *Lancs* 81 SD5536
Goostrey *Ches* 79 SJ7770
Gorddinog *Gwynd* 69 SH6773
Gordon *Border* 110 NT6443
Gordon Arms Hotel *Border* 109 NT3025
Gordonstown *Gramp* 142 NJ5656
Gordonstown *Gramp* 142 NJ7138
Gore *Powys* 46 SO2558

Gore Pit

Groes-faen

Gore Pit *Essex* **40** TL8719
Gore Street *Kent* **29** TR2765
Gorebridge *Loth* **118** NT3461
Gorefield *Cambs* **65** TF4112
Gores *Wilts* **23** SU1158
Gorey *Jersey* **152** SY2110
Goring *Oxon* **37** SU6080
Goring Heath *Oxon* **37** SU6579
Goring-by-Sea *W Susx* **14** TQ1102
Gorleston on Sea *Norfk* **67** TG5204
Gorrachie *Gramp* **142** NJ7358
Gorran *Cnwll* **3** SW9942
Gorran Haven *Cnwll* **3** SX0141
Gorran High Lanes *Cnwll* **3** SW9843
Gors *Dyfed* **43** SN6277
Gorse Hill *Wilts* **36** SU1586
Gorsedd *Clwyd* **70** SJ1576
Gorseinon *W Glam* **32** SS5998
Gorseybank *Derbys* **73** SK2953
Gorsgoch *Dyfed* **44** SN4850
Gorslas *Dyfed* **32** SN5713
Gorsley *Gloucs* **47** SO6925
Gorsley Common *Gloucs* **47** SO6825
Gorsley Green *Ches* **79** SJ8469
Gorst Hill *H & W* **60** SO7373
Gorstage *Ches* **71** SJ6172
Gorstan *Highld* **139** NH3862
Gorstello *Ches* **71** SJ3562
Gorsty Common *H & W* **46** SO4437
Gorsty Hill *Staffs* **73** SK1028
Gorten *Strath* **122** NM7432
Gorthleck *Highld* **139** NH5420
Gorton *Gt Man* **79** SJ8896
Gosbeck *Suffk* **54** TM1555
Gosberton *Lincs* **64** TF2331
Gosberton Clough *Lincs* **64** TF1929
Gosfield *Essex* **40** TL7829
Gosforth *Cumb* **86** NY0603
Gosforth *T & W* **103** NZ2368
Gosland Green *Ches* **71** SJ5758
Gosling Street *Somset* **21** ST5433
Gosmore *Herts* **39** TL1827
Gospel End *Staffs* **60** SO8993
Gospel Green *W Susx* **14** SU9431
Gosport *Hants* **13** SZ6099
Gossard Green *Beds* **38** SP9643
Goswick *Nthumb* **111** NU0644
Gotham *Notts* **62** SK5330
Gotherington *Gloucs* **47** SO9529
Gotton *Somset* **20** ST2428
Goudhurst *Kent* **28** TQ7237
Goulceby *Lincs* **77** TF2579
Gourdas *Gramp* **142** NJ7741
Gourdie *Tays* **126** NO3532
Gourdon *Gramp* **135** NO8270
Gourock *Strath* **114** NS2477
Govan *Strath* **115** NS5465
Goveton *Devon* **7** SX7546
Gowdall *Humb* **83** SE6222
Gower *Highld* **139** NH5058
Gowerton *W Glam* **32** SS5896
Gowkhall *Fife* **117** NT0589
Gowthorpe *Humb* **84** SE7654
Goxhill *Humb* **85** TA1021
Goxhill *Humb* **85** TA1844
Graby *Lincs* **64** TF0929
Grade *Cnwll* **2** SW7114
Gradeley Green *Ches* **71** SJ5851
Graffham *W Susx* **14** SU9217
Grafham *Cambs* **52** TL1669
Grafham *Surrey* **14** TQ0241
Grafton *H & W* **46** SO4936
Grafton *H & W* **46** SO5761
Grafton *H & W* **47** SO9837
Grafton *N York* **89** SE4163
Grafton *Oxon* **36** SP2600
Grafton *Shrops* **59** SJ4319
Grafton Flyford *H & W* **47** SO9655
Grafton Regis *Nhants* **49** SP7546
Grafton Underwood *Nhants* **51** SP9280
Grafty Green *Kent* **28** TQ8748
Graianrhyd *Clwyd* **70** SJ2156
Graig *Clwyd* **70** SJ0872
Graig *Gwynd* **69** SH8071
Graig-fechan *Clwyd* **70** SJ1454
Grain *Kent* **28** TQ8876
Grains Bar *Gt Man* **79** SD9608
Grainsby *Lincs* **77** TF2799
Grainthorpe *Lincs* **77** TF3896
Graizelound *Humb* **75** SK7698
Gramisdale *W Isls* **154** NF8155
Grampound *Cnwll* **3** SW9348
Grampound Road *Cnwll* **3** SW9150
Granborough *Bucks* **49** SP7625
Granby *Notts* **63** SK7536
Grand Chemins *Jersey* **152** JS1710
Grandborough *Warwks* **50** SP4966
Grandes Rocques *Guern* **152** GN5011
Grandtully *Tays* **125** NN9153
Grange *Cumb* **93** NY2517
Grange *Kent* **28** TQ7968
Grange *Mersyd* **78** SJ2286
Grange *Tays* **126** NO2625
Grange Crossroads *Gramp* **142** NJ4754
Grange Gate *Dorset* **11** SY9182
Grange Hall *Gramp* **141** NJ0660
Grange Hill *Gt Lon* **27** TQ4492
Grange Lindores *Fife* **126** NO2516
Grange Moor *W York* **82** SE2215
Grange Villa *Dur* **96** NZ2352
Grange-over-Sands *Cumb* **87** SD4077
Grangehall *Strath* **108** NS9642
Grangemill *Derbys* **74** SK2457
Grangemouth *Cent* **116** NS9281
Grangepans *Cent* **117** NT0181
Grangetown *Cleve* **97** NZ5420
Gransmoor *Humb* **91** TA1259
Gransmore Green *Essex* **40** TL6922
Granston *Dyfed* **30** SM8934
Grantchester *Cambs* **53** TL4355
Grantham *Lincs* **63** SK9135
Granton *Fife* **117** NT2376
Grantown-on-Spey *Highld* **141** NJ0328
Grantsfield *H & W* **46** SO5260
Grantshouse *Border* **119** NT8065
Grappenhall *Ches* **79** SJ6486
Grasby *Lincs* **85** TA0804
Grasmere *Cumb* **86** NY3307
Grass Green *Essex* **53** TL7338
Grasscroft *Gt Man* **82** SD9704
Grassendale *Mersyd* **78** SJ3985
Grassgarth *Cumb* **93** NY3444
Grassington *N York* **88** SE0063
Grassmoor *Derbys* **74** SK4067
Grassthorpe *Notts* **75** SK7967
Grateley *Hants* **23** SU2741
Gratwich *Staffs* **73** SK0231
Graveley *Cambs* **52** TL2563
Graveley *Herts* **39** TL2327
Gravelly Hill *W Mids* **61** SP1090
Gravelsbank *Shrops* **59** SJ3300
Graveney *Kent* **28** TR0562
Gravesend *Kent* **28** TQ6574
Gravir *W Isls* **154** NB3915
Grayingham *Lincs* **76** SK9396
Grayrigg *Cumb* **87** SD5796
Grays *Essex* **27** TQ6177
Grayshott *Hants* **14** SU8735
Grayson Green *Cumb* **92** NX9925
Grayswood *Surrey* **14** SU9134
Graythorpe *Cleve* **97** NZ5227
Grazeley *Berks* **24** SU6966
Greasbrough *S York* **74** SK4195
Greasby *Mersyd* **78** SJ2587
Greasley *Notts* **62** SK4846
Great Abington *Cambs* **53** TL5348
Great Addington *Nhants* **51** SP9675
Great Alne *Warwks* **48** SP1259
Great Altcar *Lancs* **78** SD3305
Great Amwell *Herts* **39** TL3712
Great Asby *Cumb* **94** NY6713
Great Ashfield *Suffk* **54** TL9967
Great Ayton *N York* **90** NZ5610
Great Baddow *Essex* **40** TL7304
Great Badminton *Avon* **35** ST8082
Great Bardfield *Essex* **40** TL6730
Great Barford *Beds* **52** TL1351
Great Barr *W Mids* **61** SP0495
Great Barrington *Gloucs* **36** SP2113
Great Barrow *Ches* **71** SJ4768
Great Barton *Suffk* **54** TL8967
Great Barugh *N York* **90** SE7479
Great Bavington *Nthumb* **102** NY9880
Great Bealings *Suffk* **55** TM2348
Great Bedwyn *Wilts* **23** SU2764
Great Bentley *Essex* **41** TM1021
Great Billing *Nhants* **51** SP8162
Great Bircham *Norfk* **65** TF7732
Great Blakenham *Suffk* **54** TM1150
Great Blencow *Cumb* **93** NY4532
Great Bolas *Shrops* **72** SJ6421
Great Bookham *Surrey* **26** TQ1354
Great Bosullow *Cnwll* **2** SW4133
Great Bourton *Oxon* **49** SP4545
Great Bowden *Leics* **50** SP7488
Great Bradley *Suffk* **53** TL6753
Great Braxted *Essex* **40** TL8614
Great Bricett *Suffk* **54** TM0350
Great Brickhill *Bucks* **38** SP9030
Great Bridge *W Mids* **60** SO9892
Great Bridgeford *Staffs* **72** SJ8827
Great Brington *Nhants* **50** SP6665
Great Bromley *Essex* **41** TM0826
Great Broughton *Cumb* **92** NY0731
Great Broughton *N York* **90** NZ5405
Great Budworth *Ches* **79** SJ6677
Great Burdon *Dur* **96** NZ3116
Great Burstead *Essex* **40** TQ6892
Great Busby *N York* **90** NZ5205
Great Canfield *Essex* **40** TL5918
Great Carlton *Lincs* **77** TF4085
Great Casterton *Leics* **63** TF0008
Great Chart *Kent* **28** TQ9841
Great Chatfield *Wilts* **22** ST8563
Great Chatwell *Staffs* **60** SJ7914
Great Chell *Staffs* **72** SJ8652
Great Chesterford *Essex* **39** TL5042
Great Cheverell *Wilts* **22** ST9854
Great Chishill *Cambs* **39** TL4238
Great Clacton *Essex* **41** TM1716
Great Cliffe *W York* **82** SE3015
Great Clifton *Cumb* **92** NY0429
Great Coates *Humb* **85** TA2309
Great Comberton *H & W* **47** SO9542
Great Comp *Kent* **27** TQ6356
Great Corby *Cumb* **93** NY4754
Great Cornard *Suffk* **54** TL8840
Great Cowden *Humb* **85** TA2342
Great Coxwell *Oxon* **36** SU2693
Great Cransley *Nhants* **51** SP8376
Great Cressingham *Norfk* **66** TF8501
Great Crosthwaite *Cumb* **93** NY2524
Great Cubley *Derbys* **73** SK1638
Great Dalby *Leics* **63** SK7414
Great Doddington *Nhants* **51** SP8864
Great Doward *H & W* **34** SO5416
Great Dunham *Norfk* **66** TF8714
Great Dunmow *Essex* **40** TL6222
Great Durnford *Wilts* **23** SU1338
Great Easton *Essex* **40** TL6025
Great Easton *Leics* **51** SP8492
Great Eccleston *Lancs* **80** SD4240
Great Ellingham *Norfk* **66** TM0196
Great Elm *Somset* **22** ST7449
Great Englebourne *Devon* **7** SX7756
Great Everdon *Nhants* **49** SP5957
Great Eversden *Cambs* **52** TL3653
Great Finborough *Suffk* **54** TM0158
Great Fransham *Norfk* **66** TF8913
Great Gaddesden *Herts* **38** TL0211
Great Gidding *Cambs* **52** TL1183
Great Givendale *Humb* **84** SE8153
Great Glemham *Suffk* **55** TM3361
Great Glen *Leics* **50** SP6597
Great Gonerby *Lincs* **63** SK8938
Great Gransden *Cambs* **52** TL2655
Great Green *Cambs* **39** TL2844
Great Green *Norfk* **55** TM2889
Great Green *Suffk* **54** TL9155
Great Green *Suffk* **54** TL9365
Great Habton *N York* **90** SE7576
Great Hale *Lincs* **64** TF1442
Great Hallingbury *Essex* **39** TL5119
Great Hanwood *Shrops* **59** SJ4409
Great Harrowden *Nhants* **51** SP8770
Great Harwood *Lancs* **81** SD7332
Great Haseley *Oxon* **37** SP6401
Great Hatfield *Humb* **85** TA1842
Great Haywood *Staffs* **73** SJ9922
Great Heck *N York* **83** SE5920
Great Henny *Essex* **54** TL8637
Great Hinton *Wilts* **22** ST9059
Great Hockham *Norfk* **66** TL9592
Great Holland *Essex* **41** TM2019
Great Horkesley *Essex* **41** TL9731
Great Hormead *Herts* **39** TL4029
Great Horton *W York* **82** SE1431
Great Horwood *Bucks* **49** SP7731
Great Houghton *Nhants* **50** SP7958
Great Houghton *S York* **83** SE4206
Great Hucklow *Derbys* **74** SK1777
Great Kelk *Humb* **91** TA1058
Great Kimble *Bucks* **38** SP8205
Great Kingshill *Bucks* **26** SU8797
Great Langdale *Cumb* **86** NY2906
Great Langton *N York* **89** SE2996
Great Leighs *Essex* **40** TL7217
Great Limber *Lincs* **85** TA1308
Great Linford *Bucks* **38** SP8542
Great Livermere *Suffk* **54** TL8871
Great Longstone *Derbys* **74** SK2071
Great Lumley *T & W* **96** NZ2949
Great Lyth *Shrops* **59** SJ4507
Great Malvern *H & W* **47** SO7746
Great Maplestead *Essex* **54** TL8034
Great Marton *Lancs* **80** SD3235
Great Massingham *Norfk* **66** TF7922
Great Melton *Norfk* **66** TG1206
Great Meols *Mersyd* **78** SJ2390
Great Milton *Oxon* **37** SP6202
Great Missenden *Bucks* **26** SP8901
Great Mitton *Lancs* **81** SD7138
Great Mongeham *Kent* **29** TR3551
Great Moulton *Norfk* **54** TM1690
Great Munden *Herts* **39** TL3524
Great Musgrave *Cumb* **94** NY7613
Great Ness *Shrops* **59** SJ3919
Great Nurcott *Somset* **20** SS9036
Great Oak *Gwent* **34** SO3810
Great Oakley *Essex* **41** TM1927
Great Oakley *Nhants* **51** SP8785
Great Offley *Herts* **38** TL1427
Great Ormside *Cumb* **94** NY7017
Great Orton *Cumb* **93** NY3254
Great Ouseburn *N York* **89** SE4461
Great Oxendon *Nhants* **50** SP7383
Great Oxney Green *Essex* **40** TL6606
Great Pattenden *Kent* **28** TQ7344
Great Paxton *Cambs* **52** TL2063
Great Plumpton *Lancs* **80** SD3833
Great Plumstead *Norfk* **67** TG3010
Great Ponton *Lincs* **63** SK9230
Great Potheridge *Devon* **19** SS5114
Great Preston *W York* **83** SE4029
Great Purston *Nhants* **49** SP5139
Great Raveley *Cambs* **52** TL2581
Great Rissington *Gloucs* **36** SP1917
Great Rollright *Oxon* **48** SP3231
Great Rudbaxton *Dyfed* **30** SM9620
Great Ryburgh *Norfk* **66** TF9527
Great Ryle *Nthumb* **111** NU0212
Great Ryton *Shrops* **59** SJ4803
Great Saling *Essex* **40** TL6925
Great Salkeld *Cumb* **94** NY5536
Great Sampford *Essex* **53** TL6435
Great Sankey *Ches* **78** SJ5688
Great Saredon *Staffs* **60** SJ9508
Great Saughall *Ches* **71** SJ3669
Great Saxham *Suffk* **53** TL7862
Great Shefford *Berks* **36** SU3875
Great Shelford *Cambs* **53** TL4651
Great Smeaton *N York* **89** NZ3404
Great Snoring *Norfk* **66** TF9434
Great Somerford *Wilts* **35** ST9682
Great Soudley *Shrops* **72** SJ7229
Great Stainton *Dur* **96** NZ3322
Great Stambridge *Essex* **40** TQ8991
Great Staughton *Cambs* **52** TL1264
Great Steeping *Lincs* **77** TF4364
Great Stonar *Kent* **29** TR3359
Great Strickland *Cumb* **94** NY5522
Great Stukeley *Cambs* **52** TL2274
Great Sturton *Lincs* **76** TF2176
Great Sutton *Ches* **71** SJ3775
Great Sutton *Shrops* **59** SO5183
Great Swinburne *Nthumb* **102** NY9375
Great Tew *Oxon* **48** SP4028
Great Tey *Essex* **40** TL8925
Great Torrington *Devon* **18** SS4919
Great Tosson *Nthumb* **103** NU0200
Great Totham *Essex* **40** TL8611
Great Totham *Essex* **40** TL8713
Great Tows *Lincs* **76** TF2290
Great Urswick *Cumb* **86** SD2674
Great Wakering *Essex* **40** TQ9487
Great Waldingfield *Suffk* **54** TL9144
Great Walsingham *Norfk* **66** TF9437
Great Waltham *Essex* **40** TL6913
Great Warley *Essex* **27** TQ5890
Great Washbourne *Gloucs* **47** SO9834
Great Weeke *Devon* **8** SX7187
Great Weldon *Nhants* **51** SP9289
Great Welnetham *Suffk* **54** TL8759
Great Wenham *Suffk* **54** TM0738
Great Whittington *Nthumb* **103** NZ0070
Great Wigborough *Essex* **41** TL9615
Great Wilbraham *Cambs* **53** TL5557
Great Wishford *Wilts* **23** SU0735
Great Witchingham *Norfk* **66** TG1020
Great Witcombe *Gloucs* **35** SO9114
Great Witley *H & W* **47** SO7566
Great Wolford *Warwks* **48** SP2534
Great Wratting *Essex* **53** TL6848
Great Wymondley *Herts* **39** TL2128
Great Wyrley *Staffs* **60** SJ9907
Great Wytheford *Shrops* **59** SJ5719
Great Yarmouth *Norfk* **67** TG5207
Great Yeldham *Essex* **53** TL7638
Greatfield *Wilts* **36** SU0785
Greatford *Lincs* **64** TF0811
Greatgate *Staffs* **73** SK0539
Greatham *Cleve* **97** NZ4927
Greatham *Hants* **14** SU7730
Greatham *W Susx* **14** TQ0415
Greatstone-on-Sea *Kent* **17** TR0822
Greatworth *Nhants* **49** SP5542
Grebby *Lincs* **77** TF4368
Green Bank *Cumb* **87** SD3780
Green Cross *Surrey* **14** SU8637
Green Down *Somset* **21** ST5753
Green End *Beds* **38** TL0147
Green End *Beds* **51** TL0864
Green End *Beds* **51** TL1063
Green End *Beds* **52** TL1252
Green End *Cambs* **52** TL2274
Green End *Cambs* **52** TL3856
Green End *Cambs* **53** TL4668
Green End *Cambs* **53** TL4861
Green End *Herts* **39** TL2630
Green End *Herts* **39** TL3222
Green End *Herts* **39** TL3333
Green End *Warwks* **61** SP2686
Green Hammerton *N York* **83** SE4556
Green Head *Cumb* **93** NY3649
Green Heath *Staffs* **60** SJ9913
Green Hill *Wilts* **36** SU0686
Green Hills *Cambs* **53** TL6072
Green Lane *Devon* **8** SX7877
Green Lane *H & W* **48** SP0664
Green Moor *S York* **74** SK2899
Green Oak *Humb* **84** SE8127
Green Ore *Somset* **21** ST5750
Green Quarter *Cumb* **87** NY4603
Green Street *E Susx* **17** TQ7611
Green Street *Gloucs* **35** SO8915
Green Street *H & W* **47** SO8749
Green Street *Herts* **39** TL4521
Green Street *Herts* **26** TQ1998
Green Street Green *Gt Lon* **27** TQ4563
Green Street Green *Kent* **27** TQ5870
Green Tye *Herts* **39** TL4418
Greenburn *Loth* **116** NS9360
Greencroft *Norfk* **66** TG0243
Greencroft Hall *Dur* **96** NZ1549
Greenend *Oxon* **36** SP3221
Greenfield *Beds* **38** TL0534
Greenfield *Clwyd* **70** SJ1977
Greenfield *Gt Man* **82** SD9904
Greenfield *Highld* **131** NH2000
Greenfield *Oxon* **37** SU7191
Greenfield *Strath* **114** NS2490
Greenford *Gt Lon* **26** TQ1482
Greengairs *Strath* **116** NS7870
Greengates *W York* **82** SE1937
Greengill *Cumb* **92** NY1037
Greenhalgh *Lancs* **80** SD4035
Greenham *Berks* **24** SU4865
Greenham *Somset* **20** ST0820
Greenhaugh *Nthumb* **102** NY7987
Greenhead *Nthumb* **102** NY6565
Greenheys *Gt Man* **79** SD7104
Greenhill *Cent* **116** NS8279
Greenhill *D & G* **100** NY1079
Greenhill *H & W* **47** SO7248
Greenhill *Kent* **29** TR1666
Greenhill *Strath* **108** NS9332
Greenhillocks *Derbys* **74** SK4049
Greenhithe *Kent* **27** TQ5875
Greenholm *Strath* **107** NS5437
Greenholme *Cumb* **87** NY5905
Greenhouse *Border* **109** NT5523
Greenhow Hill *N York* **89** SE1164
Greenland *Highld* **151** ND2367
Greenland *S York* **74** SK3988
Greenlands *Bucks* **37** SU7785
Greenlaw *Border* **110** NT7146
Greenlea *D & G* **100** NY0375
Greenloaning *Tays* **125** NN8307
Greenmoor Hill *Oxon* **37** SU6481
Greenmount *Gt Man* **81** SD7714
Greenock *Strath* **115** NS2876
Greenodd *Cumb* **86** SD3182
Greens Norton *Nhants* **49** SP6649
Greensgate *Norfk* **66** TG1015
Greenside *T & W* **96** NZ1362
Greenside *W York* **82** SE1716
Greenstead *Essex* **41** TM0125
Greenstead Green *Essex* **40** TL8227
Greensted *Essex* **39** TL5403
Greenstreet Green *Suffk* **54** TM0349
Greenway *Gloucs* **47** SO7033
Greenway *H & W* **60** SO7470
Greenway *S Glam* **33** ST0573
Greenway *Somset* **21** ST3124
Greenwich *Gt Lon* **27** TQ3877
Greet *Gloucs* **48** SP0230
Greete *Shrops* **46** SO5770
Greetham *Leics* **63** SK9214
Greetham *Lincs* **77** TF3070
Greetland *W York* **82** SE0821
Gregson Lane *Lancs* **81** SD5926
Greinton *Somset* **21** ST4136
Grenaby *IOM* **153** SC2672
Grendon *Nhants* **51** SP8760
Grendon *Warwks* **61** SP2799
Grendon Green *H & W* **46** SO5957
Grendon Underwood *Bucks* **37** SP6820
Grenofen *Devon* **6** SX4971
Grenoside *S York* **74** SK3393
Gresford *Clwyd* **71** SJ3454
Gresham *Norfk* **66** TG1638
Greshornish House Hotel *Highld* **136** NG3454
Gressenhall *Norfk* **66** TF9615
Gressenhall Green *Norfk* **66** TF9616
Gressingham *Lancs* **87** SD5769
Grestey Green *Ches* **72** SJ7053
Greta Bridge *Dur* **95** NZ0813
Gretna *D & G* **101** NY3167
Gretna Green *D & G* **101** NY3168
Gretton *Gloucs* **47** SP0030
Gretton *Nhants* **51** SP8994
Gretton *Shrops* **59** SO5195
Grewelthorpe *N York* **89** SE2376
Grey Friars *Suffk* **55** TM4770
Grey Green *Humb* **84** SE7807
Grey's Green *Oxon* **37** SU7182
Greygarth *N York* **89** SE1872
Greylake *Somset* **21** ST3833
Greyrigg *D & G* **100** NY0888
Greysouthern *Cumb* **92** NY0729
Greystoke *Cumb* **93** NY4430
Greystone *Tays* **127** NO5343
Greywell *Hants* **24** SU7151
Gribb *Dorset* **10** ST3703
Gribthorpe *Humb* **84** SE7635
Griff *Warwks* **61** SP3689
Griffithstown *Gwent* **34** ST2998
Griffydam *Leics* **62** SK4118
Griggs Green *Hants* **14** SU8231
Grimeford Village *Lancs* **81** SD6112
Grimesthorpe *S York* **74** SK3689
Grimethorpe *S York* **83** SE4109
Grimley *H & W* **47** SO8360
Grimmet *Strath* **106** NS3210
Grimoldby *Lincs* **77** TF3988
Grimpo *Shrops* **59** SJ3526
Grimsargh *Lancs* **81** SD5834
Grimsby *Humb* **85** TA2710
Grimscote *Nhants* **49** SP6553
Grimscott *Cnwll* **18** SS2606
Grimshader *W Isls* **154** NB4025
Grimshaw *Lancs* **81** SD7024
Grimshaw Green *Lancs* **80** SD4912
Grimsthorpe *Lincs* **64** TF0422
Grimston *Humb* **85** TA2735
Grimston *Leics* **63** SK6821
Grimston *Norfk* **65** TF7222
Grimston Hill *Notts* **75** SK6865
Grimstone *Dorset* **10** SY6394
Grimstone End *Suffk* **54** TL9368
Grinacombe Moor *Devon* **5** SX4191
Grindale *Humb* **91** TA1271
Grindle *Shrops* **60** SJ7503
Grindleford *Derbys* **74** SK2477
Grindleton *Lancs* **81** SD7545
Grindley Brook *Shrops* **71** SJ5242
Grindlow *Derbys* **74** SK1877
Grindon *Cleve* **96** NZ3925
Grindon *Nthumb* **110** NT9144
Grindon *Staffs* **73** SK0854
Grindon Hill *Nthumb* **102** NY8268
Grindonrigg *Nthumb* **110** NT9243
Gringley on the Hill *Notts* **75** SK7390
Grinsdale *Cumb* **93** NY3758
Grinshill *Shrops* **59** SJ5223
Grinton *N York* **88** SE0498
Grishipoll *Strath* **120** NM1859
Grisling Common *E Susx* **16** TQ4322
Gristhorpe *N York* **91** TA0981
Griston *Norfk* **66** TL9499
Gritley *Ork* **155** HY5504
Grittenham *Wilts* **36** SU0382
Grittleton *Wilts* **35** ST8580
Grizebeck *Cumb* **86** SD2384
Grizedale *Cumb* **86** SD3394
Groby *Leics* **62** SK5207
Groes *Clwyd* **70** SJ0064
Groes-faen *M Glam* **33** ST0680

Groes-Wen Harley

Groes-Wen *M Glam* 33 ST1286
Groesffordd *Gwynd* 56 SH2739
Groesffordd Marli *Clwyd* 70 SJ0073
Groesllwyd *Powys* 58 SJ2111
Groeslon *Gwynd* 68 SH4755
Groeslon *Gwynd* 68 SH5260
Grogport *Strath* 105 NR8144
Gromford *Suffk* 55 TM3858
Gronant *Clwyd* 70 SJ0983
Groombridge *E Susx* 16 TQ5337
Grosebay *W Isls* 154 NG1593
Grosmont *Gwent* 46 SO4024
Grosmont *N York* 90 NZ8305
Grossington *Gloucs* 35 SO7302
Groton *Suffk* 54 TL9641
Grotton *Gt Man* 79 SD9604
Grouville *Jersey* 152 JS1908
Grove *Bucks* 38 SP9122
Grove *Dorset* 11 SY6972
Grove *Dyfed* 30 SM9900
Grove *Kent* 29 TR2362
Grove *Notts* 75 SK7479
Grove *Oxon* 36 SU4090
Grove Green *Kent* 28 TQ7856
Grove Park *Gt Lon* 27 TQ4072
Grove Vale *W Mids* 61 SP0394
Grovenhurst *Kent* 28 TQ7140
Grovesend *Avon* 35 ST6589
Grovesend *W Glam* 32 SN5900
Grubb Street *Kent* 27 TQ5869
Gruids *Highld* 146 NC5603
Gruinard *Highld* 144 NG9489
Gruinart *Strath* 112 NR2966
Grula *Highld* 136 NG3826
Gruline *Strath* 121 NM5440
Grumbla *Cnwll* 2 SW4029
Grundisburgh *Suffk* 55 TM2251
Gruting *Shet* 155 HU2749
Gualachulain *Highld* 123 NN1145
Guanockgate *Lincs* 64 TF3710
Guardbridge *Fife* 127 NO4518
Guarlford *H & W* 47 SO8145
Guay *Tays* 125 NN9948
Guestling Green *E Susx* 17 TQ8513
Guestling Thorn *E Susx* 17 TQ8516
Guestwick *Norfk* 66 TG0626
Guide *Lancs* 81 SD7025
Guide Bridge *Gt Man* 79 SJ9297
Guilden Down *Shrops* 59 SO3082
Guilden Morden *Cambs* 39 TL2744
Guilden Sutton *Ches* 71 SJ4468
Guildford *Surrey* 25 SU9949
Guildstead *Kent* 28 TQ8262
Guildtown *Tays* 126 NO1331
Guilsborough *Nhants* 50 SP6772
Guilsfield *Powys* 58 SJ2211
Guilton *Kent* 29 TR2858
Guiltreehill *Strath* 106 NS3610
Guineaford *Devon* 19 SS5537
Guisborough *Cleve* 97 NZ6015
Guiseley *W York* 82 SE1942
Guist *Norfk* 66 TG0025
Guiting Power *Gloucs* 48 SP0924
Gullane *Loth* 118 NT4882
Gulling Green *Suffk* 54 TL8256
Gulval *Cnwll* 2 SW4831
Gulworthy *Devon* 6 SX4572
Gumfreston *Dyfed* 31 SN1001
Gumley *Leics* 50 SP6889
Gummow's Shop *Cnwll* 4 SW8657
Gun Green *Kent* 17 TQ7731
Gun Hill *E Susx* 16 TQ5614
Gun Hill *Warwks* 61 SP2889
Gunby *Humb* 84 SE7035
Gunby *Lincs* 63 SK9121
Gunby *Lincs* 77 TF4666
Gundleton *Hants* 24 SU6133
Gunn *Devon* 19 SS6333
Gunnerside *N York* 88 SD9598
Gunnerton *Nthumb* 102 NY9074
Gunness *Humb* 84 SE8411
Gunnislake *Devon* 6 SX4371
Gunnista *Shet* 155 HU5043
Gunthorpe *Cambs* 64 TF1802
Gunthorpe *Norfk* 66 TG0134
Gunthorpe *Notts* 63 SK6844
Gunton *Suffk* 67 TM5395
Gunville *IOW* 13 SZ4788
Gunwalloe *Cnwll* 2 SW6522
Gupworthy *Somset* 20 SS9734
Gurnard *IOW* 13 SZ4795
Gurnett *Ches* 79 SJ9271
Gurney Slade *Somset* 21 ST6249
Gurnos *W Glam* 32 SN7709
Gushmere *Kent* 28 TR0457
Gussage All Saints *Dorset* 11 SU0010
Gussage St. Michael *Dorset* 11 ST9811
Guston *Kent* 29 TR3244
Gutcher *Shet* 155 HU5499
Guthrie *Tays* 127 NO5650
Guy's Marsh *Dorset* 22 ST8420
Guyhirn *Cambs* 65 TF4003
Guyhirn Gull *Cambs* 65 TF3904
Guyzance *Nthumb* 103 NU2103
Gwaenysgor *Clwyd* 70 SJ0781
Gwalchmai *Gwynd* 68 SH3876
Gwastadnant *Gwynd* 69 SH6157
Gwaun-Cae-Gurwen *W Glam* 32 SN6911
Gwbert on Sea *Dyfed* 42 SN1650
Gwealavellan *Cnwll* 2 SW6041
Gwealeath *Cnwll* 2 SW6922
Gweek *Cnwll* 2 SW7026
Gwehelog *Gwent* 34 SO3804
Gwenddwr *Powys* 45 SO0643
Gwendreath *Cnwll* 3 SW7217
Gwennap *Cnwll* 3 SW7340
Gwenter *Cnwll* 3 SW7417
Gwernaffield *Clwyd* 70 SJ2065
Gwernesney *Gwent* 34 SO4101
Gwernogle *Dyfed* 44 SN5333
Gwernymynydd *Clwyd* 70 SJ2162
Gwersyllt *Clwyd* 71 SJ3153
Gwespyr *Clwyd* 70 SJ1183
Gwindra *Cnwll* 3 SW9552
Gwinear *Cnwll* 2 SW5937
Gwithian *Cnwll* 2 SW5841
Gwredog *Gwynd* 68 SH4085
Gwrhay *Gwent* 33 ST1899
Gwyddelwern *Clwyd* 70 SJ0746
Gwyddgrug *Dyfed* 44 SN4635
Gwynfryn *Clwyd* 70 SJ2552
Gwystre *Powys* 45 SO0665
Gwytherin *Clwyd* 69 SH8761
Gyfelia *Clwyd* 71 SJ3245
Gyrn-goch *Gwynd* 68 SH4048

H

Habberley *H & W* 60 SO8177
Habberley *Shrops* 59 SJ3903
Habergham *Lancs* 81 SD8033
Habertoft *Lincs* 77 TF5069
Habin *W Susx* 14 SU8022
Habrough *Humb* 85 TA1413
Hacconby *Lincs* 64 TF1025
Haceby *Lincs* 64 TF0236
Hacheston *Suffk* 55 TM3059
Hack Green *Ches* 72 SJ6448
Hackbridge *Gt Lon* 27 TQ2865
Hackenthorpe *S York* 74 SK4183
Hackford *Norfk* 66 TG0502
Hackforth *N York* 89 SE2492
Hackland *Ork* 155 HY3920
Hackleton *Nhants* 51 SP8055
Hacklinge *Kent* 29 TR3454
Hackman's Gate *H & W* 60 SO8978
Hackness *N York* 91 SE9790
Hackness *Somset* 21 ST3345
Hackney *Gt Lon* 27 TQ3484
Hackthorn *Lincs* 76 SK9982
Hackthorpe *Cumb* 94 NY5423
Hacton *Gt Lon* 27 TQ5585
Hadden *Border* 110 NT7836
Haddenham *Bucks* 37 SP7308
Haddenham *Cambs* 53 TL4675
Haddington *Lincs* 76 SK9162
Haddington *Loth* 118 NT5173
Haddiscoe *Norfk* 67 TM4497
Haddo *Gramp* 143 NJ8337
Haddon *Cambs* 64 TL1392
Hade Edge *W York* 82 SE1404
Hademore *Staffs* 61 SK1708
Hadfield *Derbys* 74 SK0296
Hadham Cross *Herts* 39 TL4218
Hadham Ford *Herts* 39 TL4321
Hadleigh *Essex* 40 TQ8187
Hadleigh *Suffk* 54 TM0242
Hadleigh Heath *Suffk* 54 TL9941
Hadley *H & W* 47 SO8564
Hadley *Shrops* 60 SJ6711
Hadley End *Staffs* 73 SK1320
Hadley Wood *Gt Lon* 27 TQ2698
Hadlow *Kent* 27 TQ6350
Hadlow Down *E Susx* 16 TQ5324
Hadnall *Shrops* 59 SJ5220
Hadstock *Essex* 53 TL5644
Hadzor *H & W* 47 SO9162
Haffenden Quarter *Kent* 28 TQ8840
Hafod-y-bwch *Clwyd* 71 SJ3147
Hafod-y-coed *Gwent* 34 SO2200
Hafodunos *Clwyd* 69 SH8666
Hafodyrynys *Gwent* 34 ST2298
Haggate *Lancs* 81 SD8735
Haggbeck *Cumb* 101 NY4773
Haggerston *Nthumb* 111 NU0443
Haggington Hill *Devon* 19 SS5547
Haggs *Cent* 116 NS7879
Hagley *H & W* 46 SO5641
Hagley *H & W* 60 SO9180
Hagnaby *Lincs* 77 TF3462
Hagworthingham *Lincs* 77 TF3469
Haigh *Gt Man* 78 SD6009
Haighton Green *Lancs* 81 SD5634
Hail Weston *Cambs* 52 TL1662
Haile *Cumb* 86 NY0308
Hailes *Gloucs* 48 SP0430
Hailey *Herts* 39 TL3710
Hailey *Oxon* 37 SU6485
Hailsham *E Susx* 16 TQ5909
Hainault *Gt Lon* 27 TQ4591
Haine *Kent* 29 TR3566
Hainford *Norfk* 67 TG2218
Hainton *Lincs* 76 TF1884
Hainworth *W York* 82 SE0638
Haisthorpe *Humb* 91 TA1264
Hakin *Dyfed* 30 SM8905
Halam *Notts* 75 SK6754
Halbeath *Fife* 117 NT1288
Halberton *Devon* 9 ST0112
Halcro *Highld* 151 ND2360
Hale *Ches* 78 SJ4782
Hale *Cumb* 87 SD5078
Hale *Gt Man* 79 SJ7786
Hale *Hants* 12 SU1818
Hale *Somset* 22 ST7427
Hale *Surrey* 25 SU8448
Hale Bank *Ches* 78 SJ4784
Hale Green *E Susx* 16 TQ5514
Hale Nook *Lancs* 80 SD3944
Hale Street *Kent* 28 TQ6749
Halebarns *Gt Man* 79 SJ7985
Hales *Norfk* 67 TM3797
Hales *Staffs* 72 SJ7134
Hales Green *Derbys* 73 SK1841
Hales Place *Kent* 29 TR1459
Halesgate *Lincs* 64 TF3226
Halesowen *W Mids* 60 SO9683
Halesworth *Suffk* 55 TM3877
Halewood *Mersyd* 78 SJ4585
Halewood Green *Mersyd* 78 SJ4486
Halford *Devon* 7 SX8174
Halford *Shrops* 59 SO4383
Halford *Warwks* 48 SP2645
Halfpenny *Cumb* 87 SD5387
Halfpenny Green *Staffs* 60 SO8291
Halfpenny Houses *N York* 89 SE2284
Halfway *Berks* 24 SU4068
Halfway *Dyfed* 44 SN6430
Halfway *Powys* 44 SN8232
Halfway *S York* 75 SK4381
Halfway Bridge *W Susx* 14 SU9321
Halfway House *Shrops* 59 SJ3411
Halfway Houses *Kent* 28 TQ9372
Halifax *W York* 82 SE0925
Halistra *Highld* 136 NG2459
Halket *Strath* 115 NS4252
Halkirk *Highld* 151 ND1359
Halkyn *Clwyd* 70 SJ2171
Hall *Strath* 115 NS4154
Hall Cliffe *W York* 82 SE2918
Hall Cross *Lancs* 80 SD4230
Hall Dunnerdale *Cumb* 86 SD2195
Hall End *Beds* 38 TL0045
Hall End *Beds* 38 TL0737
Hall End *W Mids* 60 SP0092
Hall Green *Ches* 72 SJ8356
Hall Green *W Mids* 61 SP1181
Hall's Green *Essex* 39 TL4108
Hall's Green *Herts* 39 TL2728
Hallam Fields *Derbys* 62 SK4739
Halland *E Susx* 16 TQ4916
Hallaton *Leics* 50 SP7896
Hallatrow *Avon* 21 ST6357
Hallbankgate *Cumb* 94 NY5859
Hallbeck *Cumb* 87 SD6288
Hallen *Avon* 34 ST5580
Hallfield Gate *Derbys* 74 SK3958
Hallgarth *Dur* 96 NZ3243
Hallin *Highld* 136 NG2558
Halling *Kent* 28 TQ7063
Hallington *Lincs* 77 TF3085
Hallington *Nthumb* 102 NY9875
Halliwell *Gt Man* 79 SD6910
Halloughton *Notts* 75 SK6951
Hallow *H & W* 47 SO8258
Hallow Heath *H & W* 47 SO8259
Hallrule *Border* 110 NT5914
Hallsands *Devon* 7 SX8138
Hallthwaites *Cumb* 86 SD1885
Halltoft End *Lincs* 64 TF3645
Hallworthy *Cnwll* 4 SX1787
Hallyne *Border* 109 NT1940
Halmer End *Staffs* 72 SJ7948
Halmond's Frome *H & W* 47 SO6747
Halnaker *W Susx* 14 SU9007
Halsall *Lancs* 78 SD3710
Halse *Nhants* 49 SP5640
Halse *Somset* 20 ST1428
Halsetown *Cnwll* 2 SW5038
Halsham *Humb* 85 TA2727
Halsinger *Devon* 19 SS5138
Halstead *Essex* 40 TL8130
Halstead *Kent* 27 TQ4861
Halstead *Leics* 63 SK7505
Halstock *Dorset* 10 ST5308
Halsway *Somset* 20 ST1337
Haltcliff Bridge *Cumb* 93 NY3636
Haltham *Lincs* 77 TF2463
Halton *Bucks* 38 SP8710
Halton *Ches* 78 SJ5481
Halton *Clwyd* 71 SJ3039
Halton *Lancs* 87 SD5064
Halton *Nthumb* 103 NY9967
Halton *W York* 83 SE3533
Halton East *N York* 82 SE0454
Halton Fenside *Lincs* 77 TF4263
Halton Gill *N York* 88 SD8776
Halton Green *Lancs* 87 SD5165
Halton Holegate *Lincs* 77 TF4165
Halton Lea Gate *Nthumb* 94 NY6458
Halton Quay *Cnwll* 5 SX4165
Halton Shields *Nthumb* 103 NZ0168
Halton West *N York* 81 SD8454
Haltwhistle *Nthumb* 102 NY7064
Halvergate *Norfk* 67 TG4106
Halwell *Devon* 7 SX7753
Halwill *Devon* 18 SX4299
Halwill Junction *Devon* 18 SS4400
Ham *Devon* 9 ST2301
Ham *Gloucs* 35 SO9721
Ham *Gloucs* 35 ST6898
Ham *Gt Lon* 26 TQ1772
Ham *Kent* 29 TR3254
Ham *Somset* 20 ST2825
Ham *Somset* 22 ST6748
Ham *Wilts* 23 SU3262
Ham Common *Dorset* 22 ST8125
Ham Green *Avon* 34 ST5375
Ham Green *H & W* 47 SO7544
Ham Green *H & W* 47 SP0163
Ham Green *Kent* 28 TQ8468
Ham Green *Kent* 17 TQ8926
Ham Hill *Kent* 28 TQ6960
Ham Street *Somset* 21 ST5534
Hamble *Hants* 13 SU4806
Hambleden *Bucks* 37 SU7886
Hambledon *Hants* 13 SU6414
Hambledon *Surrey* 25 SU9638
Hambleton *Lancs* 80 SD3742
Hambleton *N York* 83 SE5530
Hambleton Moss Side *Lancs* 80 SD3842
Hambridge *Somset* 21 ST3921
Hambridge *Somset* 21 ST5936
Hambrook *Avon* 35 ST6478
Hambrook *W Susx* 14 SU7806
Hamels *Herts* 39 TL3724
Hameringham *Lincs* 77 TF3167
Hamerton *Cambs* 52 TL1379
Hamilton *Strath* 116 NS7255
Hamlet *Dorset* 10 ST5908
Hamlins *E Susx* 16 TQ5908
Hammerpot *W Susx* 14 TQ0605
Hammersmith *Gt Lon* 26 TQ2378
Hammerwich *Staffs* 61 SK0707
Hammerwood *E Susx* 16 TQ4339
Hammond Street *Herts* 39 TL3304
Hammoon *Dorset* 11 ST8114
Hamnavoe *Shet* 155 HU4971
Hampden Park *E Susx* 16 TQ6002
Hampden Row *Bucks* 26 SP8501
Hamperden End *Essex* 40 TL5730
Hampnett *Gloucs* 36 SP0915
Hampole *S York* 83 SE5010
Hampreston *Dorset* 12 SZ0598
Hampsfield *Cumb* 87 SD4080
Hampson Green *Lancs* 80 SD4954
Hampstead *Gt Lon* 27 TQ2685
Hampstead Norrey's *Berks* 37 SU5276
Hampsthwaite *N York* 89 SE2559
Hampt *Cnwll* 5 SX3874
Hampton *Gt Lon* 26 TQ1369
Hampton *H & W* 48 SP0243
Hampton *Kent* 29 TR1568
Hampton *Shrops* 60 SO7486
Hampton *Wilts* 36 SU1892
Hampton Bishop *H & W* 46 SO5637
Hampton Green *Ches* 71 SJ5149
Hampton Heath *Ches* 71 SJ5049
Hampton in Arden *W Mids* 61 SP2080
Hampton Loade *Shrops* 60 SO7486
Hampton Lovett *H & W* 47 SO8865
Hampton Lucy *Warwks* 48 SP2557
Hampton on the Hill *Warwks* 48 SP2564
Hampton Poyle *Oxon* 37 SP5015
Hampton Wick *Gt Lon* 26 TQ1769
Hamptworth *Wilts* 12 SU2419
Hamrow *Norfk* 66 TF9124
Hamsey *E Susx* 15 TQ4012
Hamsey Green *Gt Lon* 27 TQ3559
Hamstall Ridware *Staffs* 73 SK1019
Hamstead *IOW* 13 SZ4091
Hamstead *W Mids* 61 SP0592
Hamstead Marshall *Berks* 24 SU4165
Hamsterley *Dur* 95 NZ1156
Hamsterley *Dur* 96 NZ1231
Hamstreet *Kent* 17 TR0033
Hamwood *Avon* 21 ST3756
Hamworthy *Dorset* 11 SY9991
Hanbury *H & W* 47 SO9664
Hanbury *Staffs* 73 SK1727
Hanby *Lincs* 64 TF0231
Hanchet End *Suffk* 53 TL6446
Hanchurch *Staffs* 72 SJ8441
Hand and Pen *Devon* 9 SY0495
Hand Green *Ches* 71 SJ5460
Handale *Cleve* 97 NZ7215
Handbridge *Ches* 71 SJ4065
Handcross *W Susx* 15 TQ2629
Handforth *Ches* 79 SJ8583
Handley *Ches* 71 SJ4657
Handley *Derbys* 74 SK3761
Handley Green *Essex* 40 TL6501
Handsacre *Staffs* 73 SK0915
Handsworth *S York* 74 SK4186
Handsworth *W Mids* 61 SP0489
Handy Cross *Bucks* 26 SU8590
Hanford *Dorset* 11 ST8411
Hanford *Staffs* 72 SJ8741
Hanging Langford *Wilts* 23 SU0337
Hangleton *E Susx* 15 TQ2607
Hangleton *W Susx* 14 TQ0803
Hanham *Avon* 35 ST6472
Hankelow *Ches* 72 SJ6645
Hankerton *Wilts* 35 ST9790
Hankham *E Susx* 16 TQ6105
Hanley *Staffs* 72 SJ8847
Hanley Castle *H & W* 47 SO8442
Hanley Child *H & W* 47 SO6565
Hanley Swan *H & W* 47 SO8142
Hanley William *H & W* 47 SO6766
Hanlith *N York* 88 SD8961
Hanmer *Clwyd* 71 SJ4539
Hannaford *Devon* 19 SS6029
Hannah *Lincs* 77 TF4979
Hannington *Hants* 24 SU5355
Hannington *Nhants* 51 SP8170
Hannington *Wilts* 36 SU1793
Hannington Wick *Wilts* 36 SU1795
Hanscombe End *Beds* 38 TL1133
Hanslope *Bucks* 38 SP8046
Hanthorpe *Lincs* 64 TF0823
Hanwell *Gt Lon* 26 TQ1579
Hanwell *Oxon* 49 SP4343
Hanworth *Gt Lon* 26 TQ1271
Hanworth *Norfk* 67 TG1935
Happendon *Strath* 108 NS8533
Happisburgh *Norfk* 67 TG3831
Happisburgh Common *Norfk* 67 TG3728
Hapsford *Ches* 71 SJ4774
Hapton *Lancs* 81 SD7931
Hapton *Norfk* 66 TM1796
Harberton *Devon* 7 SX7758
Harbertonford *Devon* 7 SX7856
Harbledown *Kent* 29 TR1357
Harborne *W Mids* 60 SP0284
Harborough Magna *Warwks* 50 SP4778
Harborough Parva *Warwks* 50 SP4878
Harbottle *Nthumb* 102 NT9304
Harbourneford *Devon* 7 SX7162
Harbours Hill *H & W* 47 SO9565
Harbridge *Hants* 12 SU1410
Harbridge Green *Hants* 12 SU1410
Harbury *Warwks* 48 SP3759
Harby *Leics* 63 SK7431
Harby *Notts* 76 SK8770
Harcombe *Devon* 9 SX8881
Harcombe *Devon* 9 SY1590
Harcombe Bottom *Devon* 10 SY3395
Harden *W Mids* 60 SK0100
Harden *W York* 82 SE0838
Hardenhuish *Wilts* 35 ST9174
Hardgate *D & G* 100 NX8167
Hardgate *Gramp* 135 NJ7901
Hardgate *N York* 89 SE2662
Hardgate *Strath* 115 NS5072
Hardham *W Susx* 14 TQ0317
Hardhorn *Lancs* 80 SD3537
Hardingham *Norfk* 66 TG0403
Hardings Wood *Staffs* 72 SJ8254
Hardingstone *Nhants* 49 SP7657
Hardington *Somset* 22 ST7452
Hardington Mandeville *Somset* 10 ST5111
Hardington Marsh *Somset* 10 ST5009
Hardington Moor *Somset* 10 ST5112
Hardisworthy *Devon* 18 SS2320
Hardley *Hants* 13 SU4205
Hardley Street *Norfk* 67 TG3701
Hardmead *Bucks* 38 SP9347
Hardraw *N York* 88 SD8691
Hardsough *Lancs* 81 SD7920
Hardstoft *Derbys* 75 SK4363
Hardway *Hants* 13 SU6001
Hardway *Somset* 22 ST7234
Hardwick *Bucks* 38 SP8019
Hardwick *Cambs* 52 TL3758
Hardwick *Lincs* 76 SK8675
Hardwick *Nhants* 51 SP8469
Hardwick *Norfk* 55 TM2289
Hardwick *Oxon* 36 SP3806
Hardwick *Oxon* 49 SP5729
Hardwick *S York* 75 SK4885
Hardwick *W Mids* 61 SP0798
Hardwick Green *H & W* 47 SO8133
Hardwicke *Gloucs* 35 SO7912
Hardwicke *Gloucs* 47 SO9027
Hardy's Green *Essex* 40 TL9320
Hare Croft *W York* 82 SE0835
Hare Green *Essex* 41 TM1025
Hare Hatch *Berks* 37 SU8077
Hare Street *Essex* 39 TL4209
Hare Street *Essex* 27 TL5300
Hare Street *Herts* 39 TL3929
Harebeating *E Susx* 16 TQ5910
Hareby *Lincs* 77 TF3365
Harefield *Gt Lon* 26 TQ0590
Harehill *Derbys* 73 SK1735
Harehills *W York* 82 SE3135
Harehope *Nthumb* 111 NU0920
Harelaw *Border* 109 NT5323
Harelaw *Dur* 96 NZ1652
Hareplain *Kent* 28 TQ8339
Harescough *Cumb* 94 NY6042
Harescombe *Gloucs* 35 SO8310
Haresfield *Gloucs* 35 SO8010
Harestock *Hants* 24 SU4631
Harewood *W York* 83 SE3245
Harewood End *H & W* 46 SO5227
Harford *Devon* 6 SX6359
Hargate *Norfk* 66 TM1191
Hargrave *Ches* 71 SJ4862
Hargrave *Nhants* 51 TL0370
Hargrave *Suffk* 53 TL7760
Hargrave Green *Suffk* 53 TL7759
Harker *Cumb* 101 NY3960
Harkstead *Suffk* 54 TM1834
Harlaston *Staffs* 61 SK2110
Harlaxton *Lincs* 63 SK8832
Harle Syke *Lancs* 81 SD8635
Harlech *Gwynd* 57 SH5831
Harlescott *Shrops* 59 SJ4916
Harlesden *Gt Lon* 26 TQ2183
Harlesthorpe *Derbys* 75 SK4976
Harleston *Devon* 7 SX7945
Harleston *Norfk* 55 TM2483
Harleston *Suffk* 54 TM0160
Harlestone *Nhants* 49 SP7064
Harley *S York* 74 SK3698

Harley Henry's Moat (Castell Hendre)

Harley *Shrops* **59** SJ5901
Harlington *Beds* **38** TL0330
Harlington *Gt Lon* **26** TQ0877
Harlington *S York* **83** SE4802
Harlosh *Highld* **136** NG2841
Harlow *Essex* **39** TL4611
Harlow Hill *Nthumb* **103** NZ0768
Harlthorpe *Humb* **84** SE7337
Harlton *Cambs* **52** TL3852
Harlyn Bay *Cnwll* **4** SW8775
Harman's Cross *Dorset* **11** SY9880
Harmby *N York* **89** SE1289
Harmer Green *Herts* **39** TL2515
Harmer Hill *Shrops* **59** SJ4822
Harmondsworth *Gt Lon* **26** TQ0577
Harmston *Lincs* **76** SK9662
Harnage *Shrops* **59** SJ5604
Harnham *Nthumb* **103** NZ0781
Harnhill *Gloucs* **36** SP0600
Harold Hill *Gt Lon* **27** TQ5392
Harold Wood *Gt Lon* **27** TQ5590
Haroldston West *Dyfed* **30** SM8615
Haroldswick *Shet* **155** HP6312
Harome *N York* **90** SE6481
Harpenden *Herts* **38** TL1314
Harpford *Devon* **9** SY0990
Harpham *Humb* **91** TA0861
Harpley *H & W* **47** SO6861
Harpley *Norfk* **65** TF7825
Harpole *Nhants* **49** SP6961
Harpsdale *Highld* **151** ND1355
Harpsden *Oxon* **37** SU7680
Harpswell *Lincs* **76** SK9389
Harpur Hill *Derbys* **74** SK0671
Harpurhey *Gt Man* **79** SD8501
Harraby *Cumb* **93** NY4154
Harracott *Devon* **19** SS5527
Harrapool *Highld* **129** NG6523
Harrietfield *Tays* **125** NN9829
Harrietsham *Kent* **28** TQ8652
Harringay *Gt Lon* **27** TQ3188
Harrington *Lincs* **77** TF3671
Harrington *Nhants* **50** SP7780
Harringworth *Nhants* **51** SP9197
Harriseahead *Staffs* **72** SJ8655
Harriston *Cumb* **92** NY1541
Harrogate *N York* **82** SE3054
Harrold *Beds* **51** SP9457
Harrop Dale *Gt Man* **82** SE0008
Harrow *Gt Lon* **26** TQ1588
Harrow Green *Suffk* **54** TL8654
Harrow on the Hill *Gt Lon* **26** TQ1587
Harrow Weald *Gt Lon* **26** TQ1591
Harrowbarrow *Cnwll* **5** SX4070
Harrowden *Beds* **38** TL0647
Harrowgate Village *Dur* **96** NZ2917
Harston *Cambs* **53** TL4250
Harston *Leics* **63** SK8331
Harswell *Humb* **84** SE8240
Hart *Cleve* **97** NZ4734
Hart Station *Cleve* **97** NZ4836
Hartburn *Nthumb* **103** NZ0885
Hartest *Suffk* **54** TL8352
Hartfield *E Susx* **16** TQ4735
Hartford *Cambs* **52** TL2572
Hartford *Ches* **71** SJ6372
Hartford *Somset* **20** SS9529
Hartford End *Essex* **40** TL6817
Hartfordbridge *Hants* **25** SU7757
Hartforth *N York* **89** NZ1606
Harthill *Ches* **71** SJ4955
Harthill *Loth* **116** NS9064
Harthill *S York* **75** SK4980
Hartington *Derbys* **74** SK1260
Hartland *Devon* **18** SS2524
Hartland Quay *Devon* **18** SS2224
Hartlebury *H & W* **60** SO8471
Hartlepool *Cleve* **97** NZ5032
Hartley *Cumb* **88** NY7808
Hartley *Kent* **27** TQ6066
Hartley *Kent* **17** TQ7634
Hartley *Nthumb* **103** NZ3475
Hartley Green *Kent* **27** TQ6067
Hartley Green *Staffs* **72** SJ9829
Hartley Wespall *Hants* **24** SU6958
Hartley Wintney *Hants* **24** SU7656
Hartlip *Kent* **28** TQ8464
Hartoft End *N York* **90** SE7493
Harton *N York* **90** SE7061
Harton *Shrops* **59** SO4888
Harton *T & W* **103** NZ3765
Hartpury *Gloucs* **47** SO7924
Hartshead *W York* **82** SE1822
Hartshead Moor Side *W York* **82** SE1625
Hartshill *Staffs* **72** SJ8546
Hartshill *Warwks* **61** SP3194
Hartshorne *Derbys* **62** SK3221
Hartside *Nthumb* **111** NT9716
Hartsop *Cumb* **93** NY4013
Hartswell *Somset* **20** ST0827
Hartwell *Nhants* **38** SP7850
Hartwith *N York* **89** SE2161
Hartwood *Strath* **116** NS8459
Hartwoodmyres *Border* **109** NT4324
Harvel *Kent* **28** TQ6563
Harvington *H & W* **60** SO8775
Harvington *H & W* **48** SP0549
Harwell *Notts* **75** SK6891
Harwell *Oxon* **37** SU4989
Harwich *Essex* **41** TM2531
Harwood *Gt Man* **79** SD7410
Harwood *Nthumb* **95** NY8233
Harwood *Nthumb* **103** NZ0189
Harwood Dale *N York* **91** SE9695
Harwood Lee *Gt Man* **81** SD7411
Harworth *Notts* **75** SK6191
Hasbury *W Mids* **60** SO9582
Hascombe *Surrey* **25** TQ0039
Haselbeach *Nhants* **50** SP7177
Haselbury Plucknett *Somset* **10** ST4710
Haseley *Warwks* **48** SP2367
Haseley Green *Warwks* **48** SP2369
Haseley Knob *Warwks* **61** SP2371
Haselor *Warwks* **48** SP1257
Hasfield *Gloucs* **47** SO8227
Hasguard *Dyfed* **30** SM8509
Haskayne *Lancs* **78** SD3508
Hasketon *Suffk* **55** TM2450
Hasland *Derbys* **74** SK3969
Hasland Green *Derbys* **74** SK3968
Haslemere *Surrey* **14** SU9032
Haslingden *Lancs* **81** SD7823
Haslingden Grane *Lancs* **81** SD7522
Haslingfield *Cambs* **52** TL4052
Haslington *Ches* **72** SJ7355
Hassall *Ches* **72** SJ7657
Hassall Green *Ches* **72** SJ7858
Hassell Street *Kent* **29** TR0946
Hassingham *Norfk* **67** TG3605
Hassness *Cumb* **93** NY1816
Hassocks *W Susx* **15** TQ3015
Hassop *Derbys* **74** SK2272
Haste Hill *Surrey* **14** SU9032
Haster *Highld* **151** ND3251
Hasthorpe *Lincs* **77** TF4869
Hastingleigh *Kent* **29** TR0945
Hastings *E Susx* **17** TQ8209
Hastings *Somset* **10** ST3116
Hastingwood *Essex* **39** TL4807
Hastoe *Herts* **38** SP9209
Haswell *Dur* **96** NZ3743
Haswell Plough *Dur* **96** NZ3742
Hatch *Beds* **52** TL1547
Hatch Beauchamp *Somset* **20** ST3020
Hatch End *Beds* **51** TL0760
Hatch End *Herts* **26** TQ1390
Hatchet Gate *Hants* **12** SU3701
Hatching Green *Herts* **38** TL1312
Hatchmere *Ches* **71** SJ5571
Hatcliffe *Humb* **76** TA2100
Hatfield *H & W* **46** SO5959
Hatfield *Herts* **39** TL2308
Hatfield *S York* **83** SE6609
Hatfield Broad Oak *Essex* **39** TL5416
Hatfield Heath *Essex* **39** TL5215
Hatfield Peverel *Essex* **40** TL7911
Hatfield Woodhouse *S York* **83** SE6708
Hatford *Oxon* **36** SU3395
Hatherden *Hants* **23** SU3450
Hatherleigh *Devon* **8** SS5404
Hathern *Leics* **62** SK5022
Hatherop *Gloucs* **36** SP1505
Hathersage *Derbys* **74** SK2381
Hathersage Booths *Derbys* **74** SK2480
Hatherton *Ches* **72** SJ6847
Hatherton *Staffs* **60** SJ9510
Hatley St. George *Cambs* **52** TL2751
Hatt *Cnwll* **5** SX4062
Hattingley *Hants* **24** SU6437
Hatton *Ches* **78** SJ5982
Hatton *Derbys* **73** SK2130
Hatton *Gramp* **143** NK0537
Hatton *Gt Lon* **26** TQ0975
Hatton *Lincs* **76** TF1776
Hatton *Shrops* **59** SO4790
Hatton *Tays* **127** NO4642
Hatton *Warwks* **48** SP2367
Hatton Heath *Ches* **71** SJ4561
Hatton of Fintray *Gramp* **143** NJ8316
Haugh *Lincs* **77** TF4175
Haugh *Strath* **107** NS4925
Haugh *W York* **81** SD9311
Haugh Head *Nthumb* **111** NU0026
Haugh of Glass *Gramp* **142** NJ4238
Haugh of Urr *D & G* **100** NX8066
Haugham *Lincs* **77** TF3381
Haughhead Inn *Strath* **116** NS6079
Haughley *Suffk* **54** TM0262
Haughley Green *Suffk* **54** TM0264
Haughton *Notts* **75** SK6872
Haughton *Powys* **59** SJ3018
Haughton *Shrops* **59** SJ3726
Haughton *Shrops* **59** SJ5516
Haughton *Shrops* **60** SJ7408
Haughton *Shrops* **60** SO6896
Haughton *Staffs* **72** SJ8620
Haughton Green *Gt Man* **79** SJ9393
Haughton le Skerne *Dur* **96** NZ3116
Haughton Moss *Ches* **71** SJ5756
Haultwick *Herts* **39** TL3323
Haunton *Staffs* **61** SK2310
Hautes Croix *Jersey* **152** JS1414
Hauxley *Nthumb* **103** NU2703
Hauxton *Cambs* **53** TL4452
Havannah *Ches* **72** SJ8664
Havant *Hants* **13** SU7106
Haven *H & W* **46** SO4054
Haven Bank *Lincs* **76** TF2352
Haven Side *Humb* **85** TA1827
Havenstreet *IOW* **13** SZ5690
Havercroft *W York* **83** SE3913
Haverfordwest *Dyfed* **30** SM9515
Haverhill *Suffk* **53** TL6745
Haverigg *Cumb* **86** SD1578
Havering-atte-Bower *Essex* **27** TQ5193
Haversham *Bucks* **38** SP8242
Haverthwaite *Cumb* **87** SD3483
Haverton Hill *Cleve* **97** NZ4822
Havyat *Avon* **21** ST4761
Havyatt *Somset* **21** ST5338
Hawarden *Clwyd* **71** SJ3165
Hawbridge *H & W* **47** SO9049
Hawbush Green *Essex* **40** TL7820
Hawcoat *Cumb* **86** SD2071
Hawe's Green *Norfk* **67** TM2399
Hawen *Dyfed* **42** SN3446
Hawes *N York* **88** SD8789
Hawford *H & W* **47** SO8460
Hawick *Border* **109** NT5014
Hawk Green *Gt Man* **79** SJ9687
Hawkchurch *Devon* **10** ST3400
Hawkedon *Suffk* **53** TL7953
Hawkenbury *Kent* **28** TQ8045
Hawkeridge *Wilts* **22** ST8653
Hawkerland *Devon* **9** SY0588
Hawkes End *W Mids* **61** SP2982
Hawkesbury *Avon* **35** ST7686
Hawkesbury *Warwks* **61** SP3784
Hawkesbury Upton *Avon* **35** ST7786
Hawkhill *Nthumb* **111** NU2212
Hawkhurst *Kent* **17** TQ7530
Hawkhurst Common *E Susx* **16** TQ5217
Hawkinge *Kent* **29** TR2139
Hawkley *Hants* **24** SU7429
Hawkridge *Devon* **19** SS8630
Hawksdale *Cumb* **93** NY3648
Hawkshaw *Gt Man* **81** SD7615
Hawkshead *Cumb* **87** SD3598
Hawkshead Hill *Cumb* **86** SD3398
Hawksland *Strath* **108** NS8439
Hawkspur Green *Essex* **40** TL6532
Hawkstone *Shrops* **59** SJ5830
Hawkswick *N York* **88** SD9570
Hawksworth *Notts* **63** SK7543
Hawksworth *W York* **82** SE1641
Hawkwell *Essex* **40** TQ8591
Hawley *Hants* **25** SU8657
Hawley *Kent* **27** TQ5471
Hawling *Gloucs* **36** SP0622
Hawnby *N York* **90** SE5489
Haworth *W York* **82** SE0337
Hawstead *Suffk* **54** TL8559
Hawstead Green *Suffk* **54** TL8658
Hawthorn *Dur* **96** NZ4145
Hawthorn *Hants* **24** SU6733
Hawthorn *M Glam* **33** ST0987
Hawthorn Hill *Berks* **25** SU8773
Hawthorn Hill *Lincs* **76** TF2155
Hawthorpe *Lincs* **64** TF0427
Hawton *Notts* **75** SK7851
Haxby *N York* **90** SE6058
Haxby Gates *N York* **83** SE6056
Haxey *Humb* **75** SK7799
Haxey Turbary *Humb* **84** SE7501
Haxted *Surrey* **16** TQ4245
Haxton *Wilts* **23** SU1449
Hay *Cnwll* **3** SW8651
Hay *Cnwll* **3** SW9243
Hay *Cnwll* **3** SW9552
Hay *Cnwll* **4** SW9770
Hay Green *Norfk* **65** TF5418
Hay Street *Herts* **39** TL3926
Hay-on-Wye *Powys* **45** SO2342
Haydock *Mersyd* **78** SJ5697
Haydon *Dorset* **11** ST6715
Haydon *Somset* **20** ST2523
Haydon Bridge *Nthumb* **102** NY8464
Haydon Wick *Wilts* **36** SU1387
Haye *Cnwll* **5** SX3570
Hayes *Gt Lon* **26** TQ0980
Hayes *Gt Lon* **27** TQ4066
Hayes End *Gt Lon* **26** TQ0882
Hayfield *Derbys* **74** SK0386
Hayfield *Strath* **123** NN0723
Haygate *Shrops* **59** SJ6410
Hayhillock *Tays* **127** NO5242
Hayle *Cnwll* **2** SW5537
Hayley Green *W Mids* **60** SO9582
Haymoor Green *Ches* **72** SJ6850
Hayne *Devon* **9** SS9515
Hayne *Devon* **8** SX7685
Haynes *Beds* **38** TL0740
Haynes West End *Beds* **38** TL0640
Hayscastle *Dyfed* **30** SM8925
Hayscastle Cross *Dyfed* **30** SM9125
Haysden *Kent* **16** TQ5745
Hayton *Cumb* **92** NY1041
Hayton *Cumb* **94** NY5157
Hayton *Humb* **84** SE8245
Hayton *Notts* **75** SK7284
Hayton's Bent *Shrops* **59** SO5280
Haytor Vale *Devon* **8** SX7777
Haytown *Devon* **18** SS3814
Haywards Heath *W Susx* **15** TQ3324
Haywood *H & W* **46** SO4834
Haywood *S York* **83** SE5812
Haywood Oaks *Notts* **75** SK6055
Hazards Green *E Susx* **16** TQ6812
Hazel Grove *Gt Man* **79** SJ9287
Hazel Street *Kent* **28** TQ6939
Hazel Stub *Suffk* **53** TL6544
Hazelbank *Strath* **116** NS8345
Hazelbury Bryan *Dorset* **11** ST7408
Hazeleigh *Essex* **40** TL8203
Hazeley *Hants* **24** SU7458
Hazelford *Notts* **75** SK7249
Hazelhurst *Gt Man* **79** SD9600
Hazelslade *Staffs* **60** SK0212
Hazelton Walls *Fife* **126** NO3322
Hazelwood *Derbys* **62** SK3245
Hazlemere *Bucks* **26** SU8895
Hazlerigg *T & W* **103** NZ2372
Hazles *Staffs* **73** SK0047
Hazleton *Gloucs* **36** SP0718
Heacham *Norfk* **65** TF6737
Headbourne Worthy *Hants* **24** SU4832
Headbrook *H & W* **46** SO2854
Headcorn *Kent* **28** TQ8344
Headingley *W York* **82** SE2836
Headington *Oxon* **37** SP5207
Headlam *Dur* **96** NZ1818
Headless Cross *H & W* **48** SP0365
Headlesscross *Strath* **116** NS9158
Headley *Hants* **24** SU5162
Headley *Hants* **14** SU8236
Headley *Surrey* **26** TQ2054
Headley Down *Hants* **14** SU8336
Headley Heath *H & W* **61** SP0676
Headon *Notts* **75** SK7476
Heads *Strath* **116** NS7247
Heads Nook *Cumb* **94** NY5054
Heage *Derbys* **74** SK3750
Healaugh *N York* **88** SE0199
Healaugh *N York* **83** SE5047
Heald Green *Gt Man* **79** SJ8485
Heale *Devon* **19** SS6446
Heale *Somset* **20** ST2420
Heale *Somset* **21** ST3825
Healey *Lancs* **81** SD8816
Healey *N York* **89** SE1780
Healey *Nthumb* **95** NZ0158
Healey *W York* **82** SE2719
Healeyfield *Dur* **95** NZ0648
Healing *Humb* **85** TA2110
Heamoor *Cnwll* **2** SW4631
Heanor *Derbys* **62** SK4346
Heanton Punchardon *Devon* **19** SS5035
Heapey *Lancs* **81** SD5920
Heapham *Lincs* **76** SK8788
Hearn *Hants* **14** SU8337
Hearts Delight *Kent* **28** TQ8862
Heasley Mill *Devon* **19** SS7332
Heast *Highld* **129** NG6417
Heath *Derbys* **75** SK4567
Heath *W York* **83** SE3520
Heath and Reach *Beds* **38** SP9228
Heath Common *W Susx* **14** TQ0915
Heath End *Bucks* **26** SU8898
Heath End *Hants* **24** SU4161
Heath End *Hants* **24** SU5862
Heath End *Leics* **62** SK3621
Heath End *Surrey* **25** SU8549
Heath End *Warwks* **48** SP2360
Heath Green *H & W* **61** SP0771
Heath Hayes *Staffs* **60** SK0110
Heath Hill *Shrops* **60** SJ7613
Heath House *Somset* **21** ST4146
Heath Town *W Mids* **60** SO9399
Heathall *D & G* **100** NX9979
Heathbrook *Shrops* **59** SJ6228
Heathcote *Derbys* **74** SK1460
Heathcote *Shrops* **72** SJ6528
Heathencote *Nhants* **49** SP7147
Heather *Leics* **62** SK3910
Heathfield *Devon* **8** SX8376
Heathfield *E Susx* **16** TQ5821
Heathfield *N York* **89** SE1367
Heathfield *Somset* **20** ST1626
Heathstock *Devon* **9** ST2402
Heathton *Shrops* **60** SO8192
Heatley *Gt Man* **79** SJ7088
Heatley *Staffs* **73** SK0626
Heaton *Gt Man* **79** SD6909
Heaton *Lancs* **87** SD4460
Heaton *Staffs* **72** SJ9562
Heaton *T & W* **103** NZ2666
Heaton *W York* **82** SE1335
Heaton Chapel *Gt Man* **79** SJ8891
Heaton Mersey *Gt Man* **79** SJ8690
Heaton Norris *Gt Man* **79** SJ8890
Heaton's Bridge *Lancs* **80** SD4011
Heaverham *Kent* **27** TQ5758
Heaviley *Gt Man* **79** SJ9088
Heavitree *Devon* **9** SX9492
Hebburn *T & W* **103** NZ3164
Hebden *N York* **88** SE0263
Hebden Bridge *W York* **82** SD9927
Hebden Green *Ches* **71** SJ6365
Hebing End *Herts* **39** TL3122
Hebron *Dyfed* **31** SN1827
Hebron *Nthumb* **103** NZ1989
Heckfield *Hants* **24** SU7160
Heckfield Green *Suffk* **54** TM1875
Heckfordbridge *Essex* **40** TL9421
Heckington *Lincs* **64** TF1444
Heckmondwike *W York* **82** SE1824
Heddington *Wilts* **22** ST9966
Heddon-on-the-Wall *Nthumb* **103** NZ1366
Hedenham *Norfk* **67** TM3193
Hedge End *Hants* **13** SU4912
Hedgerley *Bucks* **26** SU9687
Hedgerley Green *Bucks* **26** SU9787
Hedging *Somset* **20** ST3029
Hedley on the Hill *Nthumb* **95** NZ0759
Hednesford *Staffs* **60** SJ9912
Hedon *Humb* **85** TA1928
Hedsor *Bucks* **26** SU9086
Hegdon Hill *H & W* **46** SO5853
Heglibister *Shet* **155** HU3851
Heighington *Dur* **96** NZ2422
Heighington *Lincs* **76** TF0269
Heightington *H & W* **60** SO7671
Heiton *Border* **110** NT7130
Hele *Cnwll* **5** SX2198
Hele *Devon* **19** SS5347
Hele *Devon* **9** SS9902
Hele *Devon* **7** SX7470
Hele *Somset* **20** ST1824
Hele Lane *Devon* **19** SS7910
Helebridge *Cnwll* **18** SS2103
Helensburgh *Strath* **115** NS2982
Helenton *Strath* **106** NS3830
Helford *Cnwll* **3** SW7526
Helford Passage *Cnwll* **3** SW7626
Helhoughton *Norfk* **66** TF8626
Helions Bumpstead *Essex* **53** TL6541
Hell Corner *Berks* **23** SU3864
Hellaby *S York* **75** SK5092
Helland *Cnwll* **4** SX0771
Hellandbridge *Cnwll* **4** SX0671
Hellescott *Cnwll* **5** SX2888
Hellesdon *Norfk* **67** TG2010
Hellesvear *Cnwll* **2** SW5040
Hellidon *Nhants* **49** SP5158
Hellifield *N York* **81** SD8556
Hellingly *E Susx* **16** TQ5812
Hellington *Norfk* **67** TG3103
Helmdon *Nhants* **49** SP5943
Helme *W York* **82** SE0912
Helmingham *Suffk* **54** TM1857
Helmington Row *Dur* **96** NZ1835
Helmsdale *Highld* **147** ND0315
Helmshore *Lancs* **81** SD7821
Helmsley *N York* **90** SE6183
Helperby *N York* **89** SE4469
Helperthorpe *N York* **91** SE9570
Helpringham *Lincs* **64** TF1440
Helpston *Cambs* **64** TF1205
Helsby *Ches* **71** SJ4975
Helsey *Lincs* **77** TF5172
Helston *Cnwll* **2** SW6527
Helstone *Cnwll* **4** SX0881
Helton *Cumb* **94** NY5021
Helwith *N York* **88** NZ0702
Helwith Bridge *N York* **88** SD8069
Hemblington *Norfk* **67** TG3411
Hemel Hempstead *Herts* **38** TL0507
Hemerdon *Devon* **6** SX5657
Hemingbrough *N York* **83** SE6730
Hemingby *Lincs* **76** TF2374
Hemingfield *S York* **83** SE3801
Hemingford Abbots *Cambs* **52** TL2871
Hemingford Grey *Cambs* **52** TL2970
Hemingstone *Suffk* **54** TM1454
Hemington *Nhants* **51** TL0985
Hemington *Somset* **22** ST7253
Hemley *Suffk* **55** TM2842
Hemlington *Cleve* **90** NZ5014
Hemp Green *Suffk* **55** TM3769
Hempholme *Humb* **85** TA0850
Hempnall *Norfk* **67** TM2494
Hempnall Green *Norfk* **67** TM2493
Hempriggs *Gramp* **141** NJ1063
Hempstead *Essex* **53** TL6338
Hempstead *Gloucs* **35** SO8116
Hempstead *Kent* **28** TQ7964
Hempstead *Norfk* **66** TG1037
Hempstead *Norfk* **67** TG4028
Hempton *Norfk* **66** TF9129
Hempton *Oxon* **49** SP4431
Hemsby *Norfk* **67** TG4917
Hemswell *Lincs* **76** SK9290
Hemsworth *W York* **83** SE4213
Hemyock *Devon* **9** ST1313
Henbury *Avon* **34** ST5678
Henbury *Ches* **79** SJ8773
Hendersyde Park *Border* **110** NT7435
Hendham *Devon* **7** SX7450
Hendomen *Powys* **58** SO2197
Hendon *Gt Lon* **26** TQ2389
Hendra *Cnwll* **3** SW7237
Hendra *Cnwll* **4** SX0275
Hendre *M Glam* **33** SS9381
Hendy *Dyfed* **32** SN5803
Heneglwys *Gwynd* **68** SH4276
Henfield *W Susx* **15** TQ2115
Henford *Devon* **5** SX3794
Henghurst *Kent* **28** TQ9536
Hengoed *M Glam* **33** ST1494
Hengoed *Powys* **45** SO2253
Hengoed *Shrops* **58** SJ2833
Hengrave *Suffk* **54** TL8268
Henham *Essex* **39** TL5428
Henhurst *Kent* **28** TQ6669
Heniarth *Powys* **58** SJ1208
Henlade *Somset* **20** ST2623
Henley *Dorset* **11** ST6904
Henley *Gloucs* **35** SO9016
Henley *Shrops* **59** SO4588
Henley *Shrops* **46** SO5476
Henley *Somset* **21** ST4232
Henley *Suffk* **54** TM1551
Henley *W Susx* **14** SU8925
Henley Green *W Mids* **61** SP3681
Henley Park *Surrey* **25** SU9352
Henley Street *Kent* **28** TQ6667
Henley's Down *E Susx* **17** TQ7312
Henley-in-Arden *Warwks* **48** SP1566
Henley-on-Thames *Oxon* **37** SU7682
Henllan *Clwyd* **70** SJ0268
Henllan *Dyfed* **31** SN3540
Henllan Amgoed *Dyfed* **31** SN1819
Henllys *Gwent* **34** ST2691
Henlow *Beds* **39** TL1738
Hennock *Devon* **8** SX8381
Henny Street *Essex* **54** TL8738
Henry's Moat (Castell Hendre) *Dyfed* **30** SN0427

Hogsthorpe Hunt's Cross

Hogsthorpe *Lincs* 77 TF5372
Holbeach *Lincs* 64 TF3624
Holbeach Bank *Lincs* 64 TF3527
Holbeach Clough *Lincs* 64 TF3526
Holbeach Drove *Lincs* 64 TF3212
Holbeach Hurn *Lincs* 65 TF3926
Holbeach St. Johns *Lincs* 64 TF3518
Holbeach St. Mark's *Lincs* 64 TF3731
Holbeach St. Matthew *Lincs* 65 TF4132
Holbeck *Notts* 75 SK5473
Holbeck Woodhouse *Notts* 75 SK5472
Holberrow Green *H & W* 48 SP0259
Holbeton *Devon* 6 SX6150
Holborn *Gt Lon* 27 TQ3181
Holborough *Kent* 28 TQ7062
Holbrook *Derbys* 62 SK3644
Holbrook *S York* 75 SK4481
Holbrook *Suffk* 54 TM1636
Holbrook Moor *Derbys* 62 SK3645
Holburn *Nthumb* 111 NU0436
Holbury *Hants* 13 SU4303
Holcombe *Devon* 7 SX9574
Holcombe *Gt Man* 81 SD7816
Holcombe *Somset* 20 ST1129
Holcombe *Somset* 22 ST6749
Holcombe Brook *Gt Man* 81 SD7815
Holcombe Rogus *Devon* 20 ST0518
Holcot *Nhants* 50 SP7969
Holden *Lancs* 81 SD7749
Holden *Lancs* 81 SD8833
Holden Gate *W York* 81 SD8923
Holdenby *Nhants* 50 SP6967
Holder's Green *Essex* 40 TL6328
Holdgate *Shrops* 59 SO5689
Holdingham *Lincs* 76 TF0547
Holditch *Dorset* 10 ST3402
Holdsworth *W York* 82 SE0829
Hole *Devon* 18 SS4206
Hole Street *W Susx* 15 TQ1314
Hole-in-the-Wall *H & W* 46 SO6128
Holehouse *Derbys* 79 SK0092
Holemoor *Devon* 18 SS4205
Holford *Somset* 20 ST1541
Holgate *N York* 83 SE5851
Holker *Cumb* 87 SD3676
Holkham *Norfk* 66 TF8943
Hollacombe *Devon* 18 SS3702
Hollam *Somset* 20 SS9232
Holland Fen *Lincs* 76 TF2349
Holland Lees *Lancs* 78 SD5208
Holland-on-Sea *Essex* 41 TM1916
Hollandstoun *Ork* 155 HY7553
Hollesley *Suffk* 55 TM3544
Hollicombe *Devon* 7 SX8962
Hollies Hill *H & W* 60 SO9377
Hollin Green *Ches* 71 SJ5952
Hollingbourne *Kent* 28 TQ8455
Hollingdon *Bucks* 38 SP8727
Hollingthorpe *W York* 83 SE3831
Hollington *Derbys* 73 SK2239
Hollington *Staffs* 73 SK0538
Hollingworth *Gt Man* 79 SK0096
Hollinlane *Ches* 79 SJ8384
Hollins *Derbys* 74 SK3271
Hollins *Gt Man* 79 SD8107
Hollins *Staffs* 73 SJ9947
Hollins End *S York* 74 SK3883
Hollins Green *Ches* 79 SJ6990
Hollins Lane *Lancs* 80 SD4951
Hollinsclough *Staffs* 74 SK0666
Hollinswood *Shrops* 60 SJ7008
Hollinwood *Shrops* 59 SJ5136
Hollingrove *E Susx* 16 TQ6821
Hollocombe *Devon* 19 SS6311
Holloway *Derbys* 74 SK3256
Holloway *Gt Lon* 27 TQ3086
Holloway *Wilts* 22 ST8730
Hollowell *Nhants* 50 SP6971
Hollowmoor Heath *Ches* 71 SJ4868
Holly End *Norfk* 65 TF4906
Holly Green *H & W* 47 SO8641
Hollybush *Gwent* 33 SO1603
Hollybush *H & W* 47 SO7536
Hollybush *Strath* 106 NS3915
Hollyhurst *Ches* 71 SJ5744
Hollym *Humb* 85 TA3425
Hollywood *H & W* 61 SP0877
Holmbridge *W York* 82 SE1206
Holmbury St. Mary *Surrey* 14 TQ1143
Holmbush *Cnwll* 3 SX0352
Holmcroft *Staffs* 72 SJ9024
Holme *Cambs* 52 TL1987
Holme *Cumb* 87 SD5278
Holme *Humb* 84 SE9206
Holme *N York* 89 SE3582
Holme *Notts* 75 SK8059
Holme *W York* 82 SE1105
Holme Chapel *Lancs* 81 SD8728
Holme Green *N York* 83 SE5541
Holme Hale *Norfk* 66 TF8807
Holme Lacy *H & W* 46 SO5535
Holme Marsh *H & W* 46 SO3454
Holme next the Sea *Norfk* 65 TF7043
Holme on the Wolds *Humb* 84 SE9646
Holme Pierrepont *Notts* 62 SK6238
Holme St. Cuthbert *Cumb* 92 NY1047
Holme upon Spalding Moor *Humb* 84 SE8038
Holmer *H & W* 46 SO5042
Holmer Green *Bucks* 26 SU9097
Holmes Chapel *Ches* 72 SJ7667
Holmes Hill *E Susx* 16 TQ5312
Holmesfield *Derbys* 74 SK3277
Holmeswood *Lancs* 80 SD4316
Holmethorpe *Surrey* 27 TQ2851
Holmewood *Derbys* 75 SK4365
Holmfield *W York* 82 SE0828
Holmfirth *W York* 82 SE1408
Holmgate *Derbys* 74 SK3763
Holmhead *Strath* 107 NS5620
Holmpton *Humb* 85 TA3623
Holmrook *Cumb* 86 SD0799
Holmsey Green *Suffk* 53 TL6978
Holmshurst *E Susx* 16 TQ6425
Holmside *Dur* 96 NZ2149
Holmwood *Surrey* 15 TQ1647
Holmwrangle *Cumb* 94 NY5148
Holne *Devon* 7 SX7069
Holnest *Dorset* 11 ST6510
Holnicote *Somset* 20 SS9146
Holsworthy *Devon* 18 SS3403
Holsworthy Beacon *Devon* 18 SS3608
Holt *Clwyd* 71 SJ4053
Holt *Dorset* 12 SU0303
Holt *H & W* 47 SO8362
Holt *Norfk* 66 TG0838
Holt *Wilts* 22 ST8661
Holt End *H & W* 48 SP0769
Holt Fleet *H & W* 47 SO8263
Holt Green *Lancs* 78 SD3905
Holt Heath *Dorset* 12 SU0504
Holt Heath *H & W* 47 SO8163
Holt Street *Kent* 29 TR2551
Holtby *N York* 83 SE6754
Holton *Oxon* 37 SP6006
Holton *Somset* 22 ST6826
Holton *Suffk* 55 TM4077
Holton cum Beckering *Lincs* 76 TF1181
Holton Heath *Dorset* 11 SY9490
Holton Hill *E Susx* 16 TQ6625
Holton le Clay *Lincs* 85 TA2802
Holton le Moor *Lincs* 76 TF0897
Holton St. Mary *Suffk* 54 TM0536
Holtye *E Susx* 16 TQ4539
Holway *Clwyd* 70 SJ1876
Holwell *Dorset* 11 ST6911
Holwell *Herts* 39 TL1633
Holwell *Leics* 63 SK7323
Holwell *Oxon* 36 SP2309
Holwick *Dur* 95 NY9126
Holworth *Dorset* 11 SY7683
Holy Cross *H & W* 60 SO9278
Holy Island *Nthumb* 111 NU1241
Holybourne *Hants* 24 SU7340
Holyfield *Essex* 39 TL3803
Holyhead *Gwynd* 68 SH2482
Holymoorside *Derbys* 74 SK3369
Holyport *Berks* 26 SU8977
Holystone *Nthumb* 102 NT9502
Holytown *Strath* 116 NS7660
Holywell *Cambs* 52 TL3370
Holywell *Clwyd* 70 SJ1875
Holywell *Cnwll* 4 SW7659
Holywell *Dorset* 10 ST5904
Holywell Green *W York* 82 SE0819
Holywell Lake *Somset* 20 ST1020
Holywell Row *Suffk* 53 TL7177
Holywood *D & G* 100 NX9480
Hom Green *H & W* 34 SO5822
Homer *Shrops* 59 SJ6101
Homer Green *Mersyd* 78 SD3402
Homersfield *Suffk* 55 TM2885
Homescales *Cumb* 87 SD5587
Homington *Wilts* 23 SU1226
Honey Hill *Kent* 29 TR1161
Honey Tye *Suffk* 54 TL9535
Honeyborough *Dyfed* 30 SM9406
Honeybourne *H & W* 48 SP1144
Honeychurch *Devon* 8 SS6303
Honeystreet *Wilts* 23 SU1061
Honiley *Warwks* 61 SP2372
Honing *Norfk* 67 TG3227
Honingham *Norfk* 66 TG1011
Honington *Lincs* 63 SK9443
Honington *Suffk* 54 TL9174
Honington *Warwks* 48 SP2642
Honiton *Devon* 9 ST1600
Honley *W York* 82 SE1311
Honnington *Shrops* 72 SJ7215
Hoo *Kent* 27 TQ2964
Hoo *Kent* 28 TQ7872
Hoo End *Herts* 39 TL1820
Hoo Green *Ches* 79 SJ7182
Hoo Meavy *Devon* 6 SX5265
Hoobrook *H & W* 60 SO8374
Hood Green *S York* 82 SE3102
Hood Hill *S York* 74 SK3697
Hooe *Devon* 6 SX5052
Hooe *E Susx* 16 TQ6809
Hooe Common *E Susx* 16 TQ6910
Hoohill *Lancs* 80 SD3237
Hook *Cambs* 65 TL4293
Hook *Devon* 10 ST3005
Hook *Dyfed* 30 SM9711
Hook *Hants* 13 SU5105
Hook *Hants* 24 SU7254
Hook *Humb* 84 SE7625
Hook *Kent* 27 TQ6170
Hook *Surrey* 26 TQ1864
Hook *Wilts* 36 SU0784
Hook Bank *H & W* 47 SO8140
Hook Green *Kent* 16 TQ6535
Hook Norton *Oxon* 48 SP3533
Hook Street *Gloucs* 35 ST6799
Hook Street *Wilts* 36 SU0884
Hookagate *Shrops* 59 SJ4609
Hooke *Dorset* 10 ST5300
Hookgate *Staffs* 72 SJ7435
Hookway *Devon* 8 SX8598
Hookwood *Surrey* 15 TQ2643
Hooley *Surrey* 27 TQ2856
Hooley Bridge *Gt Man* 81 SD8511
Hooton *Ches* 71 SJ3678
Hooton Levitt *S York* 75 SK5291
Hooton Pagnell *S York* 83 SE4807
Hooton Roberts *S York* 75 SK4897
Hop Pole *Lincs* 64 TF1813
Hopcrofts Holt *Oxon* 49 SP4625
Hope *Clwyd* 71 SJ3058
Hope *Derbys* 74 SK1783
Hope *Devon* 7 SX6740
Hope *Powys* 58 SJ2507
Hope *Shrops* 59 SJ3401
Hope *Shrops* 46 SO5974
Hope *Staffs* 73 SK1254
Hope Bowdler *Shrops* 59 SO4792
Hope End Green *Essex* 40 TL5720
Hope Mansell *H & W* 35 SO6219
Hope under Dinmore *H & W* 46 SO5052
Hopehouse *Border* 109 NT2916
Hopeman *Gramp* 147 NJ1469
Hopesay *Shrops* 59 SO3983
Hopetown *W York* 83 SE3923
Hopperton *N York* 83 SE4256
Hopsford *Warwks* 50 SP4284
Hopstone *Shrops* 60 SO7894
Hopton *Derbys* 73 SK2653
Hopton *Shrops* 59 SJ3820
Hopton *Staffs* 72 SJ9426
Hopton *Suffk* 54 TL9979
Hopton Cangeford *Shrops* 59 SO5480
Hopton Castle *Shrops* 46 SO3678
Hopton on Sea *Norfk* 67 TM5299
Hopton Wafers *Shrops* 47 SO6376
Hoptonheath *Shrops* 46 SO3877
Hopwas *Staffs* 61 SK1804
Hopwood *Gt Man* 79 SD8609
Hopwood *H & W* 61 SP0375
Horam *E Susx* 16 TQ5717
Horbling *Lincs* 64 TF1135
Horbury *W York* 82 SE2918
Horcott *Gloucs* 36 SP1500
Horden *Dur* 96 NZ4440
Horderley *Shrops* 59 SO4086
Hordle *Hants* 12 SZ2795
Hordley *Shrops* 59 SJ3831
Horeb *Dyfed* 31 SN3942
Horeb *Dyfed* 32 SN4905
Horfield *Avon* 34 ST5976
Horham *Suffk* 55 TM2072
Horkesley Green *Essex* 41 TL9831
Horkesley Heath *Essex* 41 TL9829
Horkstow *Humb* 84 SE9817
Horley *Oxon* 49 SP4144
Horley *Surrey* 15 TQ2842
Horn Hill *Bucks* 26 TQ0192
Horn Street *Kent* 29 TR1836
Hornblotton Green *Somset* 21 ST5833
Hornby *Lancs* 87 SD5868
Hornby *N York* 89 NZ3605
Hornby *N York* 89 SE2293
Horncastle *Lincs* 77 TF2669
Hornchurch *Gt Lon* 27 TQ5387
Horndean *Border* 110 NT9049
Horndean *Hants* 13 SU7013
Horndon *Devon* 5 SX5280
Horndon on the Hill *Essex* 40 TQ6683
Horne *Surrey* 15 TQ3344
Horne Row *Essex* 40 TL7704
Horner *Somset* 20 SS9045
Horners Green *Suffk* 54 TL9641
Horney Common *E Susx* 16 TQ4525
Horning *Norfk* 67 TG3417
Horninghold *Leics* 51 SP8097
Horninglow *Staffs* 73 SK2425
Horningsea *Cambs* 53 TL4962
Horningsham *Wilts* 22 ST8141
Horningtoft *Norfk* 66 TF9323
Horningtops *Cnwll* 5 SX2760
Horns Cross *Devon* 18 SS3823
Horns Cross *E Susx* 17 TQ8222
Hornsby *Cumb* 94 NY5150
Hornsby *Somset* 10 ST3310
Hornsbygate *Cumb* 94 NY5250
Hornsea *Humb* 85 TA1947
Hornsey *Gt Lon* 27 TQ3089
Hornton *Oxon* 48 SP3945
Horpit *Wilts* 36 SU2183
Horra *Shet* 155 HU4693
Horrabridge *Devon* 6 SX5169
Horridge *Devon* 7 SX7674
Horringer *Suffk* 54 TL8261
Horringford *IOW* 13 SZ5485
Horrocks Fold *Gt Man* 81 SD7012
Horrocksford *Lancs* 81 SD7543
Horsacott *Devon* 19 SS5231
Horsebridge *Devon* 5 SX4075
Horsebridge *E Susx* 16 TQ5811
Horsebridge *Hants* 23 SU3430
Horsebridge *Shrops* 59 SJ3606
Horsebridge *Staffs* 72 SJ9553
Horsebrook *Staffs* 60 SJ8810
Horsecastle *Avon* 21 ST4265
Horsedown *Cnwll* 2 SW6134
Horsegate *Lincs* 64 TF1510
Horsehay *Shrops* 60 SJ6707
Horseheath *Cambs* 53 TL6147
Horsehouse *N York* 88 SE0480
Horsell *Surrey* 25 SU9959
Horseman's Green *Clwyd* 71 SJ4441
Horsenden *Bucks* 37 SP7902
Horsey *Norfk* 67 TG4622
Horsey *Somset* 21 ST3239
Horsey Corner *Norfk* 67 TG4523
Horsford *Norfk* 67 TG1916
Horsforth *W York* 82 SE2338
Horsham *H & W* 47 SO7358
Horsham *W Susx* 15 TQ1731
Horsham St. Faith *Norfk* 67 TG2115
Horsington *Lincs* 76 TF1968
Horsington *Somset* 22 ST7023
Horsley *Derbys* 62 SK3744
Horsley *Gloucs* 35 ST8497
Horsley *Nthumb* 102 NY8496
Horsley *Nthumb* 103 NZ0965
Horsley Cross *Essex* 41 TM1227
Horsley Woodhouse *Derbys* 62 SK3944
Horsley's Green *Bucks* 37 SU7894
Horsley-Gate *Derbys* 74 SK3076
Horsleycross Street *Essex* 41 TM1228
Horsleyhill *Border* 109 NT5319
Horsmonden *Kent* 28 TQ7040
Horspath *Oxon* 37 SP5705
Horstead *Norfk* 67 TG2619
Horsted Keynes *W Susx* 15 TQ3828
Horton *Avon* 35 ST7584
Horton *Berks* 26 TQ0175
Horton *Bucks* 38 SP9219
Horton *Dorset* 12 SU0307
Horton *Lancs* 81 SD8550
Horton *Nhants* 51 SP8154
Horton *Shrops* 59 SJ4929
Horton *Shrops* 60 SJ6814
Horton *Somset* 10 ST3214
Horton *Staffs* 72 SJ9457
Horton *W Glam* 32 SS4785
Horton *Wilts* 23 SU0463
Horton Cross *Somset* 10 ST3315
Horton Green *Ches* 71 SJ4549
Horton Heath *Hants* 13 SU4916
Horton in Ribblesdale *N York* 88 SD8071
Horton Kirby *Kent* 27 TQ5668
Horton-cum-Studley *Oxon* 37 SP5912
Horwich *Gt Man* 81 SD6311
Horwich End *Derbys* 79 SK0080
Horwood *Devon* 19 SS5027
Hoscar *Lancs* 80 SD4611
Hoscote *Border* 109 NT3911
Hose *Leics* 63 SK7329
Hosey Hill *Kent* 27 TQ4553
Hosh *Tays* 125 NN8523
Hoswick *Shet* 155 HU4123
Hotham *Humb* 84 SE8934
Hothfield *Kent* 28 TQ9644
Hoton *Leics* 62 SK5722
Hott *Nthumb* 102 NY7785
Hough *Ches* 72 SJ7151
Hough *Ches* 79 SJ8578
Hough End *W York* 82 SE2433
Hough Green *Ches* 78 SJ4886
Hough-on-the-Hill *Lincs* 63 SK9246
Hougham *Lincs* 63 SK8844
Houghton *Cambs* 52 TL2872
Houghton *Cumb* 93 NY4159
Houghton *Dyfed* 30 SM9807
Houghton *Hants* 23 SU3432
Houghton *Nthumb* 103 NZ1266
Houghton *W Susx* 14 TQ0111
Houghton Conquest *Beds* 38 TL0441
Houghton Green *Ches* 79 SJ6291
Houghton Green *E Susx* 17 TQ9222
Houghton le Side *Dur* 96 NZ2221
Houghton le Spring *T & W* 96 NZ3449
Houghton on the Hill *Leics* 63 SK6703
Houghton Regis *Beds* 38 TL0123
Houghton St. Giles *Norfk* 66 TF9235
Hound Green *Hants* 24 SU7359
Houndslow *Border* 110 NT6347
Houndsmoor *Somset* 20 ST1225
Houndwood *Border* 119 NT8463
Hounslow *Gt Lon* 26 TQ1375
Hounslow Green *Essex* 40 TL6518
Househill *Highld* 140 NH8855
Houses Hill *W York* 82 SE1916
Housieside *Gramp* 143 NJ8926
Houston *Strath* 115 NS4066
Houstry *Highld* 151 ND1534
Houton *Ork* 155 HY3104
Hove *E Susx* 15 TQ2804
Hove Edge *W York* 82 SE1324
Hoveringham *Notts* 63 SK6946
Hoveton *Norfk* 67 TG3018
Hovingham *N York* 90 SE6675
How *Cumb* 94 NY5056
How Caple *H & W* 46 SO6030
How End *Beds* 38 TL0340
Howbrook *S York* 74 SK3298
Howden *Humb* 84 SE7428
Howden-le-Wear *Dur* 96 NZ1633
Howe *Highld* 151 ND3061
Howe *N York* 89 SE3580
Howe *Norfk* 67 TM2799
Howe Bridge *Gt Man* 79 SD6602
Howe Green *Essex* 40 TL7403
Howe of Teuchar *Gramp* 143 NJ7946
Howe Street *Essex* 40 TL6914
Howe Street *Essex* 53 TL6934
Howegreen *Essex* 40 TL8301
Howell *Lincs* 76 TF1346
Howes *D & G* 101 NY1866
Howey *Powys* 45 SO0558
Howgate *Loth* 117 NT2457
Howgill *Lancs* 81 SD8246
Howick *Nthumb* 111 NU2517
Howle *Dur* 95 NZ0926
Howle *Shrops* 72 SJ6923
Howle Hill *H & W* 34 SO6020
Howlett End *Essex* 53 TL5834
Howley *Somset* 10 ST2609
Howmore *W Isls* 154 NF7536
Hownam *Border* 110 NT7719
Howrigg *Cumb* 93 NY3347
Howsham *Humb* 84 TA0404
Howsham *N York* 90 SE7362
Howt Green *Kent* 28 TQ8965
Howtel *Nthumb* 110 NT8934
Howton *Devon* 8 SX7487
Howton *H & W* 46 SO4129
Howtown *Cumb* 93 NY4419
Howwood *Strath* 115 NS3960
Hoxne *Suffk* 54 TM1777
Hoylake *Mersyd* 78 SJ2189
Hoyland Common *S York* 74 SE3600
Hoyland Nether *S York* 74 SE3700
Hoyland Swaine *S York* 82 SE2604
Hoyle *W Susx* 14 SU9018
Hoyle Mill *S York* 83 SE3506
Hubberholme *N York* 88 SD9278
Hubberston *Dyfed* 30 SM8906
Hubbert's Bridge *Lincs* 64 TF2643
Huby *N York* 82 SE2747
Huby *N York* 90 SE5665
Hucclecote *Gloucs* 35 SO8717
Hucking *Kent* 28 TQ8458
Hucknall *Notts* 75 SK5349
Huddersfield *W York* 82 SE1416
Huddington *H & W* 47 SO9457
Huddlesford *Staffs* 61 SK1509
Hudswell *N York* 89 NZ1400
Huggate *Humb* 84 SE8855
Hugglescote *Leics* 62 SK4212
Hugh Town *IOS* 2 SV9010
Hughenden Valley *Bucks* 26 SU8697
Hughley *Shrops* 59 SO5698
Huish *Devon* 19 SS5311
Huish *Wilts* 23 SU1463
Huish Champflower *Somset* 20 ST0529
Huish Episcopi *Somset* 21 ST4326
Hulberry *Kent* 27 TQ5265
Hulcote *Beds* 38 SP9438
Hulcott *Bucks* 38 SP8516
Hull *Humb* 85 TA0829
Hullaby *Devon* 7 SX6673
Hulland *Derbys* 73 SK2446
Hulland Ward *Derbys* 73 SK2546
Hullavington *Wilts* 35 ST8981
Hullbridge *Essex* 40 TQ8095
Hulme *Ches* 78 SJ6091
Hulme *Gt Man* 79 SJ8396
Hulme *Staffs* 72 SJ9345
Hulme End *Staffs* 74 SK1059
Hulme Walfield *Ches* 72 SJ8465
Hulse Heath *Ches* 79 SJ7283
Hulton Lane Ends *Gt Man* 79 SD6905
Hulver Street *Norfk* 66 TF9311
Hulver Street *Suffk* 55 TM4686
Hulverstone *IOW* 13 SZ3984
Humberston *Humb* 85 TA3105
Humberstone *Leics* 63 SK6305
Humberton *N York* 89 SE4168
Humbie *Loth* 118 NT4662
Humbleton *Humb* 85 TA2234
Humbleton *Nthumb* 111 NT9728
Humby *Lincs* 63 TF0032
Hume *Border* 110 NT7041
Humshaugh *Nthumb* 102 NY9171
Huna *Highld* 151 ND3573
Huncoat *Lancs* 81 SD7730
Huncote *Leics* 50 SP5197
Hundalee *Border* 110 NT6418
Hundall *Derbys* 74 SK3876
Hunderthwaite *Dur* 95 NY9821
Hundle Houses *Lincs* 77 TF2453
Hundleby *Lincs* 77 TF3966
Hundleton *Dyfed* 30 SM9600
Hundon *Suffk* 53 TL7348
Hundred Acres *Hants* 13 SU5911
Hundred End *Lancs* 80 SD4122
Hundred House *Powys* 45 SO1154
Hundred The *H & W* 46 SO5264
Hungarton *Leics* 63 SK6907
Hungate End *Bucks* 38 SP7946
Hunger Hill *Lancs* 80 SD5411
Hungerford *Berks* 23 SU3368
Hungerford *Hants* 12 SU1612
Hungerford *Somset* 20 ST0440
Hungerford Newtown *Berks* 36 SU3571
Hungerstone *H & W* 46 SO4435
Hungerton *Lincs* 63 SK8729
Hungryhatton *Shrops* 72 SJ6626
Hunmanby *N York* 91 TA0977
Hunningham *Warwks* 48 SP3767
Hunnington *H & W* 60 SO9681
Hunny Hill *IOW* 13 SZ4990
Hunsdon *Herts* 39 TL4114
Hunsingore *N York* 83 SE4253
Hunslet *W York* 82 SE3130
Hunsonby *Cumb* 94 NY5835
Hunstanton *Norfk* 65 TF6740
Hunstanworth *Dur* 95 NY9448
Hunston *Suffk* 54 TL9768
Hunston *W Susx* 14 SU8601
Hunston Green *Suffk* 54 TL9866
Hunstrete *Avon* 21 ST6462
Hunsworth *W York* 82 SE1827
Hunt End *H & W* 48 SP0364
Hunt's Corner *Norfk* 54 TM0588
Hunt's Cross *Mersyd* 78 SJ4385

Hunters Quay Kemback

Hunters Quay *Strath* 114 NS1879
Hunterston *Ches* 72 SJ6946
Huntham *Somset* 21 ST3426
Hunthill Lodge *Tays* 134 NO4771
Huntingdon *Cambs* 52 TL2471
Huntingdon *H & W* 46 SO2553
Huntingfield *Suffk* 55 TM3374
Huntingford *Dorset* 22 ST8030
Huntington *H & W* 46 SO4841
Huntington *Loth* 118 NT4874
Huntington *N York* 83 SE6156
Huntington *Staffs* 60 SJ9712
Huntley *Gloucs* 35 SO7219
Huntly *Gramp* 142 NJ5339
Hunton *Hants* 24 SU4840
Hunton *Kent* 28 TQ7149
Hunton *N York* 89 SE1892
Hunton Bridge *Herts* 26 TL0800
Hunts Green *Bucks* 38 SP8903
Hunts Green *Warwks* 61 SP1897
Huntscott *Somset* 20 SS9144
Huntsham *Devon* 20 ST0020
Huntshaw *Devon* 19 SS5023
Huntshaw Cross *Devon* 19 SS5222
Huntspill *Somset* 21 ST3145
Huntstile *Somset* 20 ST2633
Huntworth *Somset* 21 ST3134
Hunwick *Dur* 96 NZ1832
Hunworth *Norfk* 66 TG0635
Hurdcott *Wilts* 23 SU1733
Hurdsfield *Ches* 79 SJ9274
Hurley *Berks* 37 SU8283
Hurley *Warwks* 61 SP2495
Hurley Bottom *Berks* 37 SU8283
Hurley Common *Warwks* 61 SP2496
Hurlford *Strath* 107 NS4536
Hurlston Green *Lancs* 80 SD3911
Hurn *Dorset* 12 SZ1296
Hursley *Hants* 13 SU4225
Hurst *Berks* 25 SU7973
Hurst *Dorset* 11 SY7990
Hurst *N York* 88 NZ0402
Hurst *Somset* 10 ST4518
Hurst Green *E Susx* 17 TQ7327
Hurst Green *Lancs* 81 SD6838
Hurst Green *Surrey* 27 TQ3951
Hurst Hill *W Mids* 60 SO9393
Hurst Wickham *W Susx* 15 TQ2816
Hurstbourne Priors *Hants* 24 SU4346
Hurstbourne Tarrant *Hants* 23 SU3853
Hurstley *H & W* 46 SO3548
Hurstpierpoint *W Susx* 15 TQ2716
Hurstway Common *H & W* 46 SO2949
Hurstwood *Lancs* 81 SD8831
Hurtiso *Ork* 155 HY5001
Hurtmore *Surrey* 25 SU9445
Hurworth Burn *Dur* 96 NZ4033
Hurworth-on-Tees *Dur* 89 NZ3009
Hury *Dur* 95 NY9519
Husbands Bosworth *Leics* 50 SP6484
Husborne Crawley *Beds* 38 SP9635
Husthwaite *N York* 90 SE5175
Hut Green *N York* 83 SE5623
Hutcherleigh *Devon* 7 SX7850
Huthwaite *N York* 90 NZ4801
Huthwaite *Notts* 75 SK4659
Huttoft *Lincs* 77 TF5176
Hutton *Avon* 21 ST3558
Hutton *Border* 119 NT9053
Hutton *Cumb* 93 NY4326
Hutton *Essex* 40 TQ6395
Hutton *Humb* 84 TA0253
Hutton *Lancs* 80 SD4926
Hutton Bonville *N York* 89 NZ3300
Hutton Buscel *N York* 91 SE9784
Hutton Conyers *N York* 89 SE3273
Hutton Cranswick *Humb* 84 TA0252
Hutton End *Cumb* 93 NY4538
Hutton Hall *Cleve* 90 NZ6014
Hutton Hang *N York* 89 SE1788
Hutton Henry *Dur* 96 NZ4236
Hutton Lowcross *Cleve* 90 NZ5914
Hutton Magna *Dur* 89 NZ1212
Hutton Mulgrave *N York* 90 NZ8309
Hutton Roof *Cumb* 93 NY3734
Hutton Roof *Cumb* 87 SD5677
Hutton Rudby *N York* 89 NZ4606
Hutton Sessay *N York* 89 SE4776
Hutton Wandesley *N York* 83 SE5050
Hutton-le-Hole *N York* 90 SE7090
Huxham *Devon* 9 SX9497
Huxham Green *Somset* 21 ST5936
Huxley *Ches* 71 SJ5061
Huyton *Mersyd* 78 SJ4490
Hycemoor *Cumb* 86 SD0989
Hyde *Gloucs* 35 SO8801
Hyde *Gt Man* 79 SJ9494
Hyde *Hants* 12 SU1612
Hyde End *Berks* 24 SU7266
Hyde Heath *Bucks* 26 SP9300
Hyde Lea *Staffs* 72 SJ9120
Hyde Park Corner *Somset* 20 ST2832
Hydestile *Surrey* 25 SU9640
Hykeham Moor *Lincs* 76 SK9366
Hylands *Essex* 40 TL6704
Hynish *Strath* 120 NL9839
Hyssington *Powys* 59 SO3194
Hystfield *Gloucs* 35 ST6695
Hythe *Hants* 13 SU4207
Hythe *Kent* 29 TR1634
Hythe *Somset* 21 ST4452
Hythe End *Berks* 26 TQ0172
Hyton *Cumb* 86 SD0987

I

Ibberton *Dorset* 11 ST7807
Ible *Derbys* 74 SK2457
Ibsley *Hants* 12 SU1509
Ibstock *Leics* 62 SK4009
Ibstone *Bucks* 37 SU7593
Ibthorpe *Hants* 23 SU3753
Iburndale *N York* 90 NZ8707
Ibworth *Hants* 24 SU5654
Icelton *Avon* 21 ST3765
Ickburgh *Norfk* 66 TL8195
Ickenham *Gt Lon* 26 TQ0786
Ickford *Bucks* 37 SP6407
Ickham *Kent* 29 TR2258
Ickleford *Herts* 39 TL1831
Icklesham *E Susx* 17 TQ8716
Ickleton *Cambs* 39 TL4943
Icklingham *Suffk* 53 TL7772
Ickornshaw *N York* 82 SD9642
Ickwell Green *Beds* 52 TL1545
Icomb *Gloucs* 36 SP2122
Idbury *Oxon* 36 SP2319
Iddesleigh *Devon* 19 SS5708
Ide *Devon* 9 SX8990
Ide Hill *Kent* 27 TQ4851
Ideford *Devon* 9 SX8977
Iden *E Susx* 17 TQ9123
Iden Green *Kent* 28 TQ7437
Iden Green *Kent* 17 TQ8031
Idle *W York* 82 SE1737
Idless *Cnwll* 3 SW8147
Idlicote *Warwks* 48 SP2844
Idmiston *Wilts* 23 SU1937
Idridgehay *Derbys* 73 SK2849
Idrigill *Highld* 136 NG3863
Idstone *Oxon* 36 SU2584
Idvies *Tays* 127 NO5347
Iffley *Oxon* 37 SP5203
Ifield *W Susx* 15 TQ2537
Ifold *W Susx* 14 TQ0231
Iford *Dorset* 12 SZ1393
Iford *E Susx* 15 TQ4007
Ifton *Gwent* 34 ST4688
Ifton Heath *Shrops* 59 SJ3237
Ightham *Kent* 27 TQ5956
Ightfield *Shrops* 71 SJ5938
Iken *Suffk* 55 TM4155
Ilam *Staffs* 73 SK1350
Ilchester *Somset* 21 ST5222
Ilderton *Nthumb* 111 NU0121
Ilford *Gt Lon* 27 TQ4486
Ilford *Somset* 10 ST3617
Ilfracombe *Devon* 19 SS5247
Ilkeston *Derbys* 62 SK4641
Ilketshall St. Andrew *Suffk* 55 TM3887
Ilketshall St. Margaret *Suffk* 55 TM3485
Ilkley *W York* 82 SE1147
Illand *Cnwll* 5 SX2878
Illey *W Mids* 60 SO9881
Illidge Green *Ches* 72 SJ7963
Illingworth *W York* 82 SE0728
Illogan *Cnwll* 2 SW6743
Illston on the Hill *Leics* 50 SP7099
Ilmer *Bucks* 37 SP7605
Ilmington *Warwks* 48 SP2143
Ilminster *Somset* 10 ST3614
Ilsington *Dorset* 11 SY7592
Ilsington *Devon* 7 SX7875
Ilston *W Glam* 32 SS5590
Ilton *N York* 89 SE1978
Ilton *Somset* 10 ST3517
Imachar *Strath* 105 NR8640
Immingham *Humb* 85 TA1814
Immingham Dock *Humb* 85 TA1916
Impington *Cambs* 53 TL4463
Ince *Ches* 71 SJ4576
Ince Blundell *Mersyd* 78 SD3203
Ince-in-Makerfield *Gt Man* 78 SD5904
Inchbae Lodge Hotel *Highld* 146 NH4069
Inchbare *Tays* 134 NO6065
Inchberry *Gramp* 141 NJ3055
Inchinnan *Strath* 115 NS4868
Inchlaggan *Highld* 131 NH1701
Inchmichael *Tays* 126 NO2425
Inchnacardoch Hotel *Highld* 131 NH3810
Inchnadamph *Highld* 145 NC2521
Inchture *Tays* 126 NO2728
Inchvuilt *Highld* 139 NH2438
Inchyra *Tays* 126 NO1820
Indian Queens *Cnwll* 4 SW9159
Ingate Place *Suffk* 55 TM4288
Ingatestone *Essex* 40 TQ6499
Ingbirchworth *S York* 82 SE2205
Ingerthorpe *N York* 89 SE2866
Ingestre *Staffs* 72 SJ9724
Ingham *Lincs* 76 SK9483
Ingham *Norfk* 67 TG3926
Ingham *Suffk* 54 TL8570
Ingham Corner *Norfk* 67 TG3927
Ingleborough *Norfk* 65 TF4715
Ingleby *Derbys* 62 SK3426
Ingleby Arncliffe *N York* 89 NZ4400
Ingleby Barwick *Cleve* 89 NZ4414
Ingleby Cross *N York* 89 NZ4500
Ingleby Greenhow *N York* 90 NZ5706
Ingleigh Green *Devon* 8 SS6007
Inglesbatch *Avon* 22 ST7061
Inglesham *Wilts* 36 SU2098
Ingleston *D & G* 99 NX6048
Ingleston *D & G* 100 NX9865
Ingleton *Dur* 96 NZ1720
Ingleton *N York* 87 SD6972
Inglewhite *Lancs* 80 SD5439
Ingmire Hall *Cumb* 87 SD6391
Ingoe *Nthumb* 103 NZ0374
Ingoldisthorpe *Norfk* 65 TF6832
Ingoldmells *Lincs* 77 TF5668
Ingoldsby *Lincs* 64 TF0129
Ingon *Warwks* 48 SP2157
Ingram *Nthumb* 111 NU0115
Ingrave *Essex* 40 TQ6291
Ingrow *W York* 82 SE0539
Ings *Cumb* 87 SD4498
Ingst *Avon* 34 ST5887
Ingthorpe *Leics* 63 SK9908
Ingworth *Norfk* 67 TG1929
Injebreck *IOM* 153 SC3585
Inkberrow *H & W* 47 SP0157
Inkerman *Dur* 95 NZ1139
Inkhorn *Gramp* 143 NJ9239
Inkpen *Berks* 23 SU3664
Inkstack *Highld* 151 ND2570
Inmarsh *Wilts* 22 ST9460
Innellan *Strath* 114 NS1570
Innerleithen *Border* 109 NT3336
Innerleven *Fife* 118 NO3700
Innermessan *D & G* 98 NX0862
Innerwick *Loth* 119 NT7273
Innesmill *Gramp* 141 NJ2863
Insch *Gramp* 142 NJ6228
Insh *Highld* 132 NH8101
Inskip *Lancs* 80 SD4637
Inskip Moss Side *Lancs* 80 SD4539
Instow *Devon* 18 SS4730
Insworke *Cnwll* 6 SX4252
Intake *S York* 74 SK3884
Inver *Gramp* 133 NO2293
Inver *Highld* 147 NH8682
Inver *Tays* 125 NO0142
Inver-boyndie *Gramp* 142 NJ6664
Inverailort *Highld* 129 NM7681
Inverallign *Highld* 138 NG8457
Inverallochy *Gramp* 143 NK0365
Inveran *Highld* 146 NH5797
Inveraray *Strath* 123 NN0908
Inverarish *Highld* 137 NG5535
Inverarity *Tays* 127 NO4544
Inverarnan *Cent* 123 NN3118
Inveravon *Cent* 117 NS9579
Inverawe *Strath* 122 NN0231
Inverbervie *Gramp* 135 NO8272
Inverbroom *Highld* 145 NH1883
Inverchaolain *Strath* 114 NS0975
Invercreran House Hotel *Strath* 122 NN0146
Inverdruie *Highld* 132 NH8911
Inveresk *Loth* 118 NT3471
Inveresragan *Strath* 122 NM9835
Inverey *Gramp* 133 NO0889
Inverfarigaig *Highld* 139 NH5123
Inverfolia *Strath* 122 NM9544
Invergarry *Highld* 131 NH3001
Invergeldie *Tays* 124 NN7327
Invergloy *Highld* 131 NN2288
Invergordon *Highld* 140 NH7068
Invergowrie *Tays* 126 NO3430
Inverguseran *Highld* 129 NG7407
Inverhadden *Tays* 124 NN6757
Inverherive Hotel *Cent* 123 NN3626
Inverie *Highld* 129 NG7600
Inverinan *Strath* 122 NM9917
Inverinate *Highld* 138 NG9221
Inverkeilor *Tays* 127 NO6649
Inverkeithing *Fife* 117 NT1383
Inverkeithny *Gramp* 142 NJ6247
Inverkip *Strath* 114 NS2072
Inverkirkaig *Highld* 145 NC0719
Inverlael *Highld* 145 NH1885
Inverlair *Highld* 131 NN3479
Inverliever Lodge *Strath* 122 NM8905
Inverlochlarig *Cent* 124 NN4318
Inverlochy *Strath* 123 NN1927
Invermarkie *Gramp* 142 NJ4239
Invermoriston *Highld* 139 NH4216
Inverneg *Strath* 115 NS3497
Inverness *Highld* 140 NH6645
Invernoaden *Strath* 114 NS1297
Inveroran Hotel *Strath* 123 NN2741
Inverquharity *Tays* 134 NO4057
Inverquhomery *Gramp* 143 NK0146
Inverroy *Highld* 131 NN2581
Inversanda *Highld* 130 NM9459
Invershiel *Highld* 138 NG9319
Invershin *Highld* 146 NH5796
Invershore *Highld* 151 ND2435
Inversnaid Hotel *Cent* 123 NN3308
Inverugie *Gramp* 143 NK0948
Inveruglas *Strath* 123 NN3109
Inveruglass *Highld* 132 NH8000
Inverurie *Gramp* 142 NJ7721
Inwardleigh *Devon* 8 SX5699
Inworth *Essex* 40 TL8717
Iping *W Susx* 14 SU8522
Ipplepen *Devon* 7 SX8366
Ipsden *Oxon* 37 SU6285
Ipstones *Staffs* 73 SK0149
Ipswich *Suffk* 54 TM1644
Irby *Mersyd* 78 SJ2584
Irby in the Marsh *Lincs* 77 TF4663
Irby upon Humber *Humb* 85 TA1904
Irchester *Nhants* 51 SP9265
Ireby *Cumb* 93 NY2338
Ireby *Lancs* 87 SD6575
Ireland *Beds* 38 TL1341
Irelands Cross *Shrops* 72 SJ7341
Ireleth *Cumb* 86 SD2277
Ireshopeburn *Dur* 95 NY8638
Ireton Wood *Derbys* 73 SK2847
Irlam *Gt Man* 79 SJ7294
Irnham *Lincs* 64 TF0226
Iron Acton *Avon* 35 ST6783
Iron Bridge *Cambs* 65 TL4898
Iron Cross *Warwks* 48 SP0552
Ironbridge *Shrops* 60 SJ6703
Ironmacannie *D & G* 99 NX6675
Irons Bottom *Surrey* 15 TQ2446
Ironville *Derbys* 75 SK4351
Irstead *Norfk* 67 TG3620
Irthington *Cumb* 101 NY4961
Irthlingborough *Nhants* 51 SP9470
Irton *N York* 91 TA0184
Irvine *Strath* 106 NS3238
Isbister *Shet* 155 HU3790
Isfield *E Susx* 16 TQ4417
Isham *Nhants* 51 SP8873
Isington *Hants* 25 SU7842
Islandpool *H & W* 60 SO8780
Isle Abbotts *Somset* 21 ST3520
Isle Brewers *Somset* 21 ST3621
Isle of Whithorn *D & G* 99 NX4736
Isleham *Cambs* 53 TL6474
Isleornsay *Highld* 129 NG7012
Islesteps *D & G* 100 NX9672
Islet Village *Guern* 152 GN5212
Isley Walton *Leics* 62 SK4224
Islington *Gt Lon* 27 TQ3184
Islip *Nhants* 51 SP9879
Islip *Oxon* 37 SP5214
Islivig *W Isls* 154 NB0029
Isombridge *Shrops* 59 SJ6113
Istead Rise *Kent* 27 TQ6370
Itchen Abbas *Hants* 24 SU5333
Itchen Stoke *Hants* 24 SU5532
Itchingfield *W Susx* 15 TQ1328
Itchington *Avon* 35 ST6587
Itteringham *Norfk* 66 TG1430
Itton *Devon* 8 SX6899
Itton *Gwent* 34 ST4995
Ivegill *Cumb* 93 NY4143
Ivelet *N York* 88 SD9398
Iver *Bucks* 26 TQ0381
Iver Heath *Bucks* 26 TQ0283
Iveston *Dur* 96 NZ1350
Ivinghoe *Bucks* 38 SP9416
Ivinghoe Aston *Bucks* 38 SP9517
Ivington *H & W* 46 SO4756
Ivington Green *H & W* 46 SO4656
Ivy Cross *Dorset* 22 ST8623
Ivy Hatch *Kent* 27 TQ5854
Ivy Todd *Norfk* 66 TF8909
Ivybridge *Devon* 6 SX6356
Ivychurch *Kent* 17 TR0327
Iwade *Kent* 28 TQ9067
Iwerne Courtney or Shroton *Dorset* 11 ST8512
Iwerne Minster *Dorset* 11 ST8614
Ixworth *Suffk* 54 TL9370
Ixworth Thorpe *Suffk* 54 TL9173

J

Jack Green *Lancs* 81 SD5925
Jack Hill *N York* 82 SE1951
Jack-in-the-Green *Devon* 9 SY0195
Jacksdale *Notts* 75 SK4451
Jackson Bridge *W York* 82 SE1607
Jackton *Strath* 115 NS5952
Jacobs Well *Surrey* 25 TQ0053
Jacobstow *Cnwll* 5 SX1995
Jacobstowe *Devon* 8 SS5801
Jameston *Dyfed* 30 SS0598
Jamestown *Highld* 139 NH4756
Jamestown *Strath* 115 NS3981
Janets-town *Highld* 151 ND3551
Janetstown *Highld* 151 ND1932
Jardine Hall *D & G* 100 NY1088
Jarrow *T & W* 103 NZ3364
Jarvis Brook *E Susx* 16 TQ5329
Jasper's Green *Essex* 40 TL7226
Jawcraig *Cent* 116 NS8475
Jaywick *Essex* 41 TM1413
Jealott's Hill *Berks* 25 SU8673
Jeator Houses *N York* 89 SE4394
Jedburgh *Border* 110 NT6420
Jeffreston *Dyfed* 31 SN0906
Jemimaville *Highld* 140 NH7165
Jerbourg *Guern* 152 GN5305
Jerusalem *Lincs* 76 SK9170
Jesmond *T & W* 103 NZ2566
Jevington *E Susx* 16 TQ5601
Jingle Street *Gwent* 34 SO4710
Jockey End *Herts* 38 TL0413
Jodrell Bank *Ches* 79 SJ7970
John O'Groats *Highld* 151 ND3872
John's Cross *E Susx* 17 TQ7421
Johnby *Cumb* 93 NY4332
Johnshaven *Gramp* 135 NO7967
Johnson's Street *Norfk* 67 TG3717
Johnston *Dyfed* 30 SM9310
Johnston *Dyfed* 31 SN3919
Johnstone *Strath* 115 NS4263
Johnstonebridge *D & G* 100 NY1092
Johnstown *Clwyd* 71 SJ3046
Joppa *Dyfed* 43 SN5666
Joppa *Strath* 106 NS4119
Jordans *Bucks* 26 SU9791
Jordanston *Dyfed* 30 SM9132
Jordanthorpe *S York* 74 SK3580
Jubilee Corner *Kent* 28 TQ8447
Jump *S York* 83 SE3801
Jumper's Town *E Susx* 16 TQ4632
Juniper Green *Loth* 117 NT1968
Jurby *IOM* 153 SC3598

K

Kaber *Cumb* 88 NY7911
Kames *Strath* 114 NR9771
Kames *Strath* 107 NS6926
Kea *Cnwll* 3 SW8142
Keadby *Humb* 84 SE8311
Keal Cotes *Lincs* 77 TF3660
Kearby Town End *N York* 83 SE3447
Kearsley *Gt Man* 79 SD7504
Kearsney *Kent* 29 TR2844
Kearstwick *Cumb* 87 SD6079
Kearton *N York* 88 SD9998
Keasden *N York* 88 SD7266
Keason *Cnwll* 5 SX3168
Keaton *Devon* 7 SX6454
Keckwick *Ches* 78 SJ5783
Keddington *Lincs* 77 TF3488
Keddington Corner *Lincs* 77 TF3589
Kedington *Suffk* 53 TL7046
Kedleston *Derbys* 73 SK3040
Keelby *Lincs* 85 TA1610
Keele *Staffs* 72 SJ8045
Keele University *Staffs* 72 SJ8144
Keeley Green *Beds* 38 TL0046
Keelham *W York* 82 SE0732
Keeston *Dyfed* 30 SM9019
Keevil *Wilts* 22 ST9258
Kegworth *Leics* 62 SK4826
Kehelland *Cnwll* 2 SW6241
Keig *Gramp* 142 NJ6119
Keighley *W York* 82 SE0541
Keillour *Tays* 125 NN9725
Keiloch *Gramp* 133 NO1891
Keils *Strath* 113 NR5268
Keinton Mandeville *Somset* 21 ST5430
Keir Mill *D & G* 100 NX8593
Keirsleywell Row *Nthumb* 94 NY7751
Keisby *Lincs* 64 TF0328
Keisley *Cumb* 94 NY7124
Keiss *Highld* 151 ND3461
Keith *Gramp* 142 NJ4250
Keithick *Tays* 126 NO2038
Keithock *Tays* 134 NO6063
Keithtown *Gramp* 139 NH5256
Kelbrook *Lancs* 81 SD9044
Kelburn *Strath* 114 NS2156
Kelby *Lincs* 63 TF0041
Keld *Cumb* 94 NY5514
Keld *N York* 88 NY8900
Keld Head *N York* 90 SE7884
Keldholme *N York* 90 SE7086
Kelfield *Humb* 84 SE8201
Kelfield *N York* 83 SE5938
Kelham *Notts* 75 SK7755
Kelhead *D & G* 100 NY1469
Kellacott *Devon* 5 SX4088
Kellamergh *Lancs* 80 SD4029
Kellas *Gramp* 141 NJ1654
Kellas *Tays* 127 NO4535
Kellaton *Devon* 7 SX8039
Kelleth *Cumb* 87 NY6605
Kelling *Norfk* 66 TG0942
Kellington *N York* 83 SE5524
Kelloe *Dur* 96 NZ3436
Kells *Cumb* 92 NX9616
Kelly *Devon* 5 SX3981
Kelly Bray *Cnwll* 5 SX3671
Kelmarsh *Nhants* 50 SP7379
Kelmscot *Oxon* 36 SU2499
Kelsale *Suffk* 55 TM3865
Kelsall *Ches* 71 SJ5268
Kelshall *Herts* 39 TL3336
Kelsick *Cumb* 93 NY1950
Kelso *Border* 110 NT7234
Kelstedge *Derbys* 74 SK3363
Kelstern *Lincs* 77 TF2489
Kelsterton *Clwyd* 70 SJ2770
Kelston *Avon* 22 ST7067
Keltneyburn *Tays* 124 NN7749
Kelty *Fife* 117 NT1494
Kelvedon *Essex* 40 TL8619
Kelvedon Hatch *Essex* 27 TQ5698
Kelynack *Cnwll* 2 SW3729
Kemacott *Devon* 19 SS6647
Kemback *Fife* 126 NO4115

Kemberton Kirkby

Kemberton *Shrops* 60 SJ7204
Kemble *Wilts* 35 ST9897
Kemble Wick *Gloucs* 35 ST9895
Kemerton *H & W* 47 SO9536
Kemeys Commander *Gwent* 34 SO3404
Kemnay *Gramp* 142 NJ7316
Kemp Town *E Susx* 15 TQ3303
Kempe's Corner *Kent* 28 TR0346
Kempley *Gloucs* 47 SO6629
Kempley Green *Gloucs* 47 SO6728
Kemps Green *Warwks* 61 SP1470
Kempsey *H & W* 47 SO8549
Kempsford *Gloucs* 36 SU1696
Kempshott *Hants* 24 SU6050
Kempston *Beds* 38 TL0347
Kempston Hardwick *Beds* 38 TL0344
Kempton *Shrops* 59 SO3682
Kemsing *Kent* 27 TQ5558
Kemsley *Kent* 28 TQ9166
Kemsley Street *Kent* 28 TQ8062
Kenardington *Kent* 17 TQ9732
Kenchester *H & W* 46 SO4342
Kencot *Oxon* 36 SP2504
Kendal *Cumb* 87 SD5192
Kenderchurch *H & W* 46 SO4028
Kendleshire *Avon* 35 ST6679
Kenfig Hill *M Glam* 33 SS8382
Kenilworth *Warwks* 61 SP2871
Kenley *Gt Lon* 27 TQ3260
Kenley *Shrops* 59 SJ5500
Kenmore *Highld* 137 NG7557
Kenmore *Tays* 124 NN7745
Kenn *Avon* 21 ST4268
Kenn *Devon* 9 SX9285
Kennacraig *Strath* 113 NR8262
Kennards House *Cnwll* 5 SX2883
Kenneggy *Cnwll* 2 SW5628
Kennerleigh *Devon* 8 SS8107
Kennessee Green *Mersyd* 78 SD3801
Kennet *Cent* 116 NS9291
Kennethmont *Gramp* 142 NJ5428
Kennett *Cambs* 53 TL7068
Kennford *Devon* 9 SX9186
Kenninghall *Norfk* 54 TM0386
Kennington *Kent* 28 TR0245
Kennington *Oxon* 37 SP5201
Kennoway *Fife* 126 NO3502
Kenny *Somset* 10 ST3117
Kennyhill *Suffk* 53 TL6679
Kennythorpe *N York* 90 SE7865
Kenovay *Strath* 120 NL9946
Kensaleyre *Highld* 136 NG4151
Kensham Green *Kent* 17 TQ8229
Kensington *Gt Lon* 27 TQ2579
Kensworth *Beds* 38 TL0319
Kensworth Common *Beds* 38 TL0317
Kent End *Wilts* 36 SU0594
Kent Green *Ches* 72 SJ8458
Kent Street *E Susx* 17 TQ7816
Kent Street *Kent* 28 TQ6654
Kent's Green *Gloucs* 47 SO7423
Kent's Oak *Hants* 23 SU3224
Kentallen *Highld* 122 NN0057
Kentchurch *H & W* 46 SO4125
Kentford *Suffk* 53 TL7066
Kentisbeare *Devon* 9 ST0608
Kentisbury *Devon* 19 SS6243
Kentisbury Ford *Devon* 19 SS6242
Kentish Town *Gt Lon* 27 TQ2884
Kentmere *Cumb* 87 NY4504
Kenton *Devon* 9 SX9583
Kenton *Gt Lon* 26 TQ1788
Kenton *Suffk* 55 TM1965
Kenton *T & W* 103 NZ2267
Kenton Bank Foot *Nthumb* 103 NZ2069
Kentra *Highld* 129 NM6569
Kents Bank *Cumb* 87 SD3975
Kenwick *Shrops* 59 SJ4230
Kenwyn *Cnwll* 3 SW8145
Kenyon *Gt Man* 79 SJ6395
Keoldale *Highld* 149 NC3866
Keppoch *Highld* 138 NG8924
Kepwick *N York* 89 SE4690
Keresley *W Mids* 61 SP3282
Keresley Green *Warwks* 61 SP3283
Kergilliak *Cnwll* 3 SW7833
Kernborough *Devon* 7 SX7941
Kerne Bridge *H & W* 34 SO5818
Kerridge *Ches* 79 SJ9376
Kerridge-end *Ches* 79 SJ9475
Kerris *Cnwll* 2 SW4427
Kerry *Powys* 58 SO1490
Kerrycroy *Strath* 114 NS1061
Kersall *Notts* 75 SK7162
Kersbrook *Devon* 9 SY0683
Kerscott *Devon* 19 SS6329
Kersey *Suffk* 54 TM0044
Kersey Tye *Suffk* 54 TL9843
Kersey Upland *Suffk* 54 TL9942
Kershader *W Isls* 154 NB3320
Kershopefoot *D & G* 101 NY4782
Kersoe *H & W* 47 SO9940
Kerswell *Devon* 9 ST0806
Kerswell Green *H & W* 47 SO8646
Kerthen Wood *Cnwll* 2 SW5833
Kesgrave *Suffk* 55 TM2245
Kessingland *Suffk* 55 TM5286
Kessingland Beach *Suffk* 55 TM5385
Kestle *Cnwll* 3 SW9845
Kestle Mill *Cnwll* 4 SW8459
Keston *Gt Lon* 27 TQ4164
Keswick *Cumb* 93 NY2623
Keswick *Norfk* 67 TG2004
Ketsby *Lincs* 77 TF3676
Kettering *Nhants* 51 SP8678
Ketteringham *Norfk* 66 TG1603
Kettins *Tays* 126 NO2338
Kettle Green *Herts* 39 TL4118
Kettlebaston *Suffk* 54 TL9650
Kettlebridge *Fife* 126 NO3007
Kettlebrook *Staffs* 61 SK2103
Kettleburgh *Suffk* 55 TM2660
Kettleholm *D & G* 100 NY1577
Kettleshulme *Ches* 79 SJ9879
Kettlesing *N York* 82 SE2256
Kettlesing Bottom *N York* 89 SE2357
Kettlestoft *Ork* 155 HY6538
Kettlestone *Norfk* 66 TF9631
Kettlethorpe *Lincs* 76 SK8475
Kettlewell *N York* 88 SD9672
Ketton *Leics* 63 SK9704
Kew *Gt Lon* 26 TQ1876
Kexbrough *S York* 82 SE3009
Kexby *Lincs* 76 SK8785
Kexby *N York* 84 SE7050
Key Green *Ches* 72 SJ8963
Key Green *N York* 90 NZ8004
Key Street *Kent* 28 TQ8764
Key's Toft *Lincs* 77 TF4858
Keyham *Leics* 63 SK6706
Keyhaven *Hants* 12 SZ3091
Keyingham *Humb* 85 TA2425
Keymer *W Susx* 15 TQ3115
Keynsham *Avon* 21 ST6568
Keysoe *Beds* 51 TL0762
Keysoe Row *Beds* 51 TL0861
Keyston *Cambs* 51 TL0475
Keyworth *Notts* 62 SK6130
Kibbear *Somset* 20 ST2222
Kibblesworth *T & W* 96 NZ2456
Kibworth Beauchamp *Leics* 50 SP6893
Kibworth Harcourt *Leics* 50 SP6894
Kidbrooke *Gt Lon* 27 TQ4176
Kidburngill *Cumb* 92 NY0621
Kidd's Moor *Norfk* 66 TG1103
Kiddemore Green *Staffs* 60 SJ8509
Kidderminster *H & W* 60 SO8376
Kiddington *Oxon* 49 SP4123
Kidlington *Oxon* 37 SP4913
Kidmore End *Oxon* 37 SU6979
Kidsdale *D & G* 99 NX4336
Kidsgrove *Staffs* 72 SJ8454
Kidstones *N York* 88 SD9581
Kidwelly *Dyfed* 31 SN4006
Kiel Crofts *Strath* 122 NM9039
Kielder *Nthumb* 102 NY6293
Kiells *Strath* 112 NR4168
Kilbeg *Highld* 129 NG6506
Kilberry *Strath* 113 NR7164
Kilbirnie *Strath* 115 NS3154
Kilbride *Strath* 122 NM8525
Kilbride *Strath* 113 NR7279
Kilbride *Strath* 114 NS0367
Kilbride *W Isls* 154 NF7514
Kilburn *Derbys* 62 SK3845
Kilburn *Gt Lon* 26 TQ2483
Kilburn *N York* 90 SE5179
Kilby *Leics* 50 SP6295
Kilchamaig *Strath* 113 NR8060
Kilchattan *Strath* 112 NR3795
Kilchattan *Strath* 114 NS1054
Kilchenzie *Strath* 105 NR6724
Kilcheran *Strath* 122 NM8239
Kilchoan *Highld* 121 NM4863
Kilchrenan *Strath* 122 NN0322
Kilconquhar *Fife* 127 NO4802
Kilcot *Gloucs* 47 SO6925
Kilcoy *Highld* 139 NH5751
Kilcreggan *Strath* 114 NS2480
Kildale *N York* 90 NZ6009
Kildalloig *Strath* 105 NR7518
Kildary *Highld* 147 NH7674
Kildavanan *Strath* 114 NS0266
Kildonan *Highld* 147 NC9120
Kildonan *Strath* 105 NS0321
Kildonan Lodge *Highld* 147 NC9022
Kildonnan *Highld* 128 NM4885
Kildrochet House *D & G* 98 NX0856
Kildrummy *Gramp* 142 NJ4617
Kildwick *N York* 82 SE0046
Kilfinan *Strath* 114 NR9378
Kilfinnan *Highld* 131 NN2795
Kilgetty *Dyfed* 31 SN1207
Kilgrammie *Strath* 106 NS2502
Kilgwrrwg Common *Gwent* 34 ST4797
Kilham *Humb* 91 TA0664
Kilham *Nthumb* 110 NT8832
Kilkenneth *Strath* 120 NL9444
Kilkhampton *Cnwll* 18 SS2511
Killamarsh *Derbys* 75 SK4581
Killay *W Glam* 32 SS6092
Killearn *Cent* 115 NS5286
Killen *Highld* 140 NH6758
Killerby *Dur* 96 NZ1919
Killerton *Devon* 9 SS9700
Killichonan *Tays* 132 NN5458
Killiechronan *Strath* 121 NM5441
Killiecrankie *Tays* 132 NN9162
Killilan *Highld* 138 NG9430
Killin *Cent* 124 NN5733
Killinghall *N York* 89 SE2858
Killington *Cumb* 87 SD6188
Killington *Devon* 19 SS6646
Killingworth *T & W* 103 NZ2770
Killiow *Cnwll* 3 SW8042
Killivose *Cnwll* 3 SW8049
Killochyett *Border* 118 NT4545
Kilmacolm *Strath* 115 NS3567
Kilmahog *Cent* 124 NN6108
Kilmahumaig *Strath* 113 NR7893
Kilmaluag *Highld* 136 NG4374
Kilmany *Fife* 126 NO3821
Kilmarie *Highld* 129 NG5517
Kilmarnock *Strath* 107 NS4237
Kilmartin *Strath* 113 NR8398
Kilmaurs *Strath* 106 NS4141
Kilmelford *Strath* 122 NM8512
Kilmeny *Strath* 112 NR3965
Kilmersdon *Somset* 22 ST6952
Kilmeston *Hants* 13 SU5825
Kilmichael *Strath* 113 NR8593
Kilmichael of Inverlussa *Strath* 113 NR7786
Kilmington *Devon* 10 SY2797
Kilmington *Wilts* 22 ST7736
Kilmington Common *Wilts* 22 ST7735
Kilmington Street *Wilts* 22 ST7835
Kilmorack *Highld* 139 NH4944
Kilmore *Highld* 129 NG6507
Kilmory *Highld* 128 NM5270
Kilmory *Strath* 122 NM8825
Kilmory *Strath* 113 NR7074
Kilmuir *Highld* 136 NG2547
Kilmuir *Highld* 136 NG3770
Kilmuir *Highld* 140 NH6749
Kilmuir *Highld* 147 NH7573
Kilmun *Strath* 114 NS1781
Kiln Green *Berks* 37 SU8178
Kiln Pit Hill *Nthumb* 95 NZ0355
Kilnave *Strath* 112 NR2871
Kilncadzow *Strath* 116 NS8848
Kilndown *Kent* 16 TQ7035
Kilnhill *Cumb* 93 NY2132
Kilnhouses *Ches* 71 SJ6366
Kilnhurst *S York* 75 SK4597
Kilninver *Strath* 122 NM8221
Kilnsea *Humb* 85 TA4115
Kilnsey *N York* 88 SD9767
Kilnwick *Humb* 84 SE9949
Kilnwick Percy *Humb* 84 SE8249
Kiloran *Strath* 112 NR3996
Kilpeck *H & W* 46 SO4430
Kilpin *Humb* 84 SE7726
Kilpin Pike *Humb* 84 SE7626
Kilrie *Ches* 79 SJ7478
Kilsby *Nhants* 50 SP5671
Kilspindie *Tays* 126 NO2125
Kilstay *D & G* 98 NX1238
Kilsyth *Strath* 116 NS7178
Kiltarlity *Highld* 139 NH5041
Kilton *Cleve* 97 NZ7018
Kilton Thorpe *Cleve* 97 NZ6917
Kilvaxter *Highld* 136 NG3869
Kilve *Somset* 20 ST1442
Kilvington *Notts* 63 SK8042
Kilwinning *Strath* 106 NS3043
Kimberley *Norfk* 66 TG0603
Kimberley *Notts* 62 SK4944
Kimberworth *S York* 74 SK4093
Kimble Wick *Bucks* 38 SP8007
Kimblesworth *Dur* 96 NZ2547
Kimbolton *Cambs* 51 TL1067
Kimbolton *H & W* 46 SO5261
Kimcote *Leics* 50 SP5886
Kimmeridge *Dorset* 11 SY9179
Kimmerston *Nthumb* 111 NT9535
Kimpton *Hants* 23 SU2746
Kimpton *Herts* 39 TL1718
Kimworthy *Devon* 18 SS3112
Kinbrace *Highld* 150 NC8631
Kinbuck *Cent* 125 NN7905
Kincaple *Fife* 127 NO4618
Kincardine *Fife* 116 NS9387
Kincardine *Highld* 146 NH6089
Kincardine O'Neil *Tays* 134 NO5999
Kinclaven *Tays* 126 NO1538
Kincorth *Gramp* 135 NJ9403
Kincorth House *Gramp* 141 NJ0161
Kincraig *Highld* 132 NH8305
Kindallachan *Tays* 125 NN9949
Kinerarach *Strath* 113 NR6553
Kineton *Gloucs* 48 SP0926
Kineton *Warwks* 48 SP3350
Kinfauns *Tays* 126 NO1622
Kinfig *M Glam* 32 SS8081
King Sterndale *Derbys* 74 SK0972
King's Acre *H & W* 46 SO4841
King's Bromley *Staffs* 73 SK1216
King's Cliffe *Nhants* 51 TL0097
King's Coughton *Warwks* 48 SP0859
King's Heath *W Mids* 61 SP0781
King's Hill *Warwks* 61 SP3274
King's Lynn *Norfk* 65 TF6120
King's Mills *Guern* 152 GN4808
King's Moss *Lancs* 78 SD5000
King's Newton *Derbys* 62 SK3825
King's Norton *Leics* 50 SK6800
King's Norton *W Mids* 61 SP0579
King's Nympton *Devon* 19 SS6819
King's Pyon *H & W* 46 SO4450
King's Somborne *Hants* 23 SU3531
King's Stag *Dorset* 11 ST7210
King's Stanley *Gloucs* 35 SO8103
King's Sutton *Oxon* 49 SP4936
King's Walden *Herts* 39 TL1623
Kingarth *Strath* 114 NS0956
Kingcausie *Gramp* 135 NO8699
Kingcoed *Gwent* 34 SO4305
Kingerby *Lincs* 76 TF0592
Kingford *Devon* 18 SS2806
Kingham *Oxon* 48 SP2624
Kingholm Quay *D & G* 100 NX9773
Kinglassie *Loth* 117 NT2298
Kingoldrum *Tays* 126 NO3355
Kingoodie *Tays* 126 NO3329
Kings Bridge *W Glam* 32 SS5997
Kings Caple *H & W* 46 SO5528
Kings Green *Gloucs* 47 SO7734
Kings Hill *W Mids* 60 SO9896
Kings House Hotel *Highld* 123 NN2654
Kings Langley *Herts* 26 TL0702
Kings Meaburn *Cumb* 94 NY6221
Kings Muir *Border* 109 NT2539
Kings Newnham *Warwks* 50 SP4577
Kings Ripton *Cambs* 52 TL2676
Kings Weston *Avon* 34 ST5477
Kings Worthy *Hants* 24 SU4932
Kingsand *Cnwll* 6 SX4350
Kingsash *Bucks* 38 SP8805
Kingsbarns *Fife* 127 NO5912
Kingsbridge *Devon* 7 SX7344
Kingsbridge *Somset* 20 SS9837
Kingsburgh *Highld* 136 NG3955
Kingsbury *Gt Lon* 26 TQ1988
Kingsbury *Warwks* 61 SP2196
Kingsbury Episcopi *Somset* 21 ST4321
Kingsclere *Hants* 24 SU5258
Kingscote *Gloucs* 35 ST8196
Kingscott *Devon* 19 SS5318
Kingscross *Strath* 105 NS0428
Kingsdon *Somset* 21 ST5126
Kingsdown *Kent* 29 TR3748
Kingsdown *Wilts* 22 ST8167
Kingsdown *Wilts* 36 SU1688
Kingseat *Fife* 117 NT1290
Kingsey *Bucks* 37 SP7406
Kingsfold *W Susx* 15 TQ1636
Kingsford *H & W* 60 SO8181
Kingsford *Strath* 115 NS4447
Kingsgate *Kent* 29 TR3970
Kingshall Street *Suffk* 54 TL9161
Kingsheanton *Devon* 19 SS5537
Kingshouse Hotel *Cent* 124 NN5620
Kingshurst *W Mids* 61 SP1688
Kingside Hill *Cumb* 92 NY1551
Kingskerswell *Devon* 7 SX8767
Kingskettle *Fife* 126 NO3008
Kingsland *Dorset* 10 SY4597
Kingsland *H & W* 46 SO4461
Kingsley *Ches* 71 SJ5574
Kingsley *Hants* 25 SU7838
Kingsley *Staffs* 73 SK0146
Kingsley Green *W Susx* 14 SU8930
Kingsley Park *Nhants* 49 SP7762
Kingslow *Shrops* 60 SO7998
Kingsmead *Hants* 13 SU5813
Kingsmuir *Fife* 127 NO5308
Kingsmuir *Tays* 127 NO4849
Kingsnorth *Kent* 28 TR0039
Kingstanding *W Mids* 61 SP0794
Kingsteignton *Devon* 7 SX8773
Kingsthorne *H & W* 46 SO4931
Kingsthorpe *Nhants* 49 SP7563
Kingston *Cambs* 52 TL3455
Kingston *Cnwll* 5 SX3675
Kingston *Devon* 6 SX6347
Kingston *Dorset* 11 ST7509
Kingston *Dorset* 11 SY9579
Kingston *Gramp* 141 NJ3365
Kingston *Hants* 12 SU1401
Kingston *IOW* 13 SZ4781
Kingston *Kent* 29 TR1950
Kingston *Loth* 118 NT5482
Kingston *W Susx* 14 TQ0802
Kingston Bagpuize *Oxon* 36 SU4098
Kingston Blount *Oxon* 37 SU7399
Kingston by Sea *W Susx* 15 TQ2305
Kingston Deverill *Wilts* 22 ST8437
Kingston Lisle *Oxon* 36 SU3287
Kingston near Lewes *E Susx* 15 TQ3908
Kingston on Soar *Notts* 62 SK5027
Kingston Russell *Dorset* 10 SY5791
Kingston Seymour *Avon* 21 ST4066
Kingston St. Mary *Somset* 20 ST2229
Kingston Stert *Oxon* 37 SP7200
Kingston upon Thames *Gt Lon* 26 TQ1869
Kingstone *H & W* 46 SO4235
Kingstone *Oxon* 36 SU2685
Kingstone *Somset* 10 ST3713
Kingstone *Staffs* 73 SK0629
Kingstown *Cumb* 93 NY3959
Kingswear *Devon* 7 SX8851
Kingswells *Gramp* 135 NJ8606
Kingswinford *W Mids* 60 SO8888
Kingswood *Avon* 35 ST6473
Kingswood *Bucks* 37 SP6919
Kingswood *Gloucs* 35 ST7491
Kingswood *Kent* 28 TQ8350
Kingswood *Powys* 58 SJ2302
Kingswood *Somset* 20 ST1037
Kingswood *Surrey* 26 TQ2455
Kingswood *Warwks* 61 SP1871
Kingswood Brook *Warwks* 61 SP1970
Kingswood Common *H & W* 46 SO2954
Kingswood Common *Staffs* 60 SJ8302
Kingthorpe *Lincs* 76 TF1275
Kington *Avon* 35 ST6290
Kington *H & W* 46 SO2956
Kington *H & W* 47 SO9956
Kington Langley *Wilts* 35 ST9276
Kington Magna *Dorset* 22 ST7622
Kington St. Michael *Wilts* 35 ST9077
Kingussie *Highld* 132 NH7500
Kingweston *Somset* 21 ST5230
Kinharrachie *Gramp* 143 NJ9231
Kinharvie *D & G* 100 NX9266
Kinkell Bridge *Tays* 125 NN9316
Kinknockie *Gramp* 143 NK0041
Kinleith *Loth* 117 NT1866
Kinlet *Shrops* 60 SO7180
Kinloch *Highld* 149 NC3434
Kinloch *Highld* 149 NC5552
Kinloch *Highld* 128 NM4099
Kinloch *Tays* 126 NO1444
Kinloch *Tays* 126 NO2644
Kinloch Hourn *Highld* 130 NG9506
Kinloch Rannoch *Tays* 132 NN6658
Kinlochard *Cent* 124 NN4502
Kinlochbervie *Highld* 148 NC2256
Kinlocheil *Highld* 130 NM9779
Kinlochewe *Highld* 138 NH0261
Kinlochlaggan *Highld* 131 NN5289
Kinlochleven *Highld* 131 NN1861
Kinlochmoidart *Highld* 129 NM7072
Kinlochnanuagh *Highld* 129 NM7384
Kinloss *Gramp* 141 NJ0661
Kinmel Bay *Clwyd* 70 SH9880
Kinmount House *D & G* 100 NY1368
Kinmuck *Gramp* 143 NJ8119
Kinmundy *Gramp* 143 NJ8817
Kinnadie *Gramp* 143 NJ9743
Kinnaird *Tays* 133 NN9559
Kinnaird *Tays* 126 NO2428
Kinnaird Castle *Tays* 134 NO6357
Kinneddar *Gramp* 141 NJ2269
Kinneff *Gramp* 135 NO8574
Kinnelhead *D & G* 108 NT0201
Kinnell *Tays* 127 NO6150
Kinnerley *Shrops* 59 SJ3320
Kinnersley *H & W* 46 SO3449
Kinnersley *H & W* 47 SO8743
Kinnerton *Powys* 46 SO2463
Kinnerton *Shrops* 59 SO3796
Kinnerton Green *Clwyd* 71 SJ3361
Kinnesswood *Tays* 126 NO1702
Kinninvie *Dur* 95 NZ0521
Kinnordy *Tays* 126 NO3655
Kinoulton *Notts* 63 SK6730
Kinross *Tays* 126 NO1102
Kinrossie *Tays* 126 NO1832
Kinsbourne Green *Herts* 38 TL1016
Kinsey Heath *Ches* 72 SJ6642
Kinsham *H & W* 46 SO3665
Kinsham *H & W* 47 SO9335
Kinsley *W York* 83 SE4114
Kinson *Dorset* 12 SZ0796
Kintbury *Berks* 23 SU3866
Kintessack *Gramp* 141 NJ0060
Kintillo *Tays* 126 NO1317
Kinton *H & W* 46 SO4174
Kinton *Shrops* 59 SJ3719
Kintore *Gramp* 143 NJ7916
Kintour *Strath* 112 NR4551
Kintra *Strath* 120 NM3125
Kintraw *Strath* 122 NM8204
Kinveachy *Highld* 140 NH9018
Kinver *Staffs* 60 SO8483
Kiplin *N York* 89 SE2897
Kippax *W York* 83 SE4130
Kippen *Cent* 116 NS6494
Kippford or Scaur *D & G* 92 NX8354
Kipping's Cross *Kent* 16 TQ6440
Kirbister *Ork* 155 HY3607
Kirby Bedon *Norfk* 67 TG2705
Kirby Bellars *Leics* 63 SK7117
Kirby Cane *Norfk* 67 TM3794
Kirby Corner *W Mids* 61 SP2976
Kirby Cross *Essex* 41 TM2120
Kirby Fields *Leics* 62 SK5203
Kirby Grindalythe *N York* 91 SE9067
Kirby Hill *N York* 89 NZ1406
Kirby Hill *N York* 89 SE3968
Kirby Knowle *N York* 89 SE4687
Kirby le Soken *Essex* 41 TM2121
Kirby Misperton *N York* 90 SE7779
Kirby Muxloe *Leics* 62 SK5104
Kirby Row *Norfk* 67 TM3792
Kirby Sigston *N York* 89 SE4194
Kirby Underdale *Humb* 90 SE8058
Kirby Wiske *N York* 89 SE3784
Kirconnel *D & G* 100 NX9868
Kirdford *W Susx* 14 TQ0126
Kirk *Highld* 151 ND2859
Kirk Bramwith *S York* 83 SE6211
Kirk Deighton *N York* 83 SE3950
Kirk Ella *Humb* 84 TA0129
Kirk Hallam *Derbys* 62 SK4540
Kirk Hammerton *N York* 83 SE4655
Kirk Ireton *Derbys* 73 SK2650
Kirk Langley *Derbys* 73 SK2838
Kirk Merrington *Dur* 96 NZ2631
Kirk of Shotts *Strath* 116 NS8462
Kirk Sandall *S York* 83 SE6108
Kirk Smeaton *N York* 83 SE5216
Kirk Yetholm *Border* 110 NT8228
Kirkabister *Shet* 155 HU4938
Kirkandrews *D & G* 99 NX6048
Kirkandrews upon Eden *Cumb* 93 NY3558
Kirkbampton *Cumb* 93 NY3056
Kirkbean *D & G* 92 NX9759
Kirkbride *Cumb* 93 NY2256
Kirkbridge *N York* 89 SE2590
Kirkbuddo *Tays* 127 NO5043
Kirkburn *Border* 109 NT2938
Kirkburn *Humb* 84 SE9855
Kirkburton *W York* 82 SE1912
Kirkby *Lincs* 76 TF0592
Kirkby *Mersyd* 78 SJ4099
Kirkby *N York* 90 NZ5305

Kirkby Fleetham

Latcham

Kirkby Fleetham *N York* 89 SE2894
Kirkby Green *Lincs* 76 TF0857
Kirkby Hall *N York* 89 SE2795
Kirkby in Ashfield *Notts* 75 SK4856
Kirkby Lonsdale *Cumb* 87 SD6178
Kirkby la Thorpe *Lincs* 76 TF0946
Kirkby Malham *N York* 88 SD8960
Kirkby Mallory *Leics* 50 SK4500
Kirkby Malzeard *N York* 89 SE2374
Kirkby Mills *N York* 90 SE7085
Kirkby Overblow *N York* 83 SE3249
Kirkby on Bain *Lincs* 77 TF2462
Kirkby Stephen *Cumb* 88 NY7708
Kirkby Thore *Cumb* 94 NY6325
Kirkby Underwood *Lincs* 64 TF0727
Kirkby Wharf *N York* 83 SE5041
Kirkby Woodhouse *Notts* 75 SK4954
Kirkby-in-Furness *Cumb* 86 SD2282
Kirkbymoorside *N York* 90 SE6986
Kirkcaldy *Fife* 117 NT2892
Kirkcambeck *Cumb* 101 NY5368
Kirkchrist *D & G* 99 NX6751
Kirkcolm *D & G* 98 NX0268
Kirkconnel *D & G* 107 NS7311
Kirkconnell *D & G* 99 NX6760
Kirkcowan *D & G* 98 NX3260
Kirkcudbright *D & G* 99 NX6850
Kirkdale *Mersyd* 78 SJ3493
Kirkfieldbank *Strath* 108 NS8643
Kirkgunzeon *D & G* 100 NX8666
Kirkham *Lancs* 80 SD4232
Kirkham *N York* 90 SE7365
Kirkhamgate *W York* 82 SE2922
Kirkharle *Nthumb* 103 NZ0182
Kirkhaugh *Nthumb* 94 NY6949
Kirkheaton *Nthumb* 103 NZ0177
Kirkheaton *W York* 82 SE1818
Kirkhill *Highld* 139 NH5545
Kirkhope *Border* 109 NT3723
Kirkhope *Strath* 108 NS9606
Kirkhouse *Cumb* 94 NY5759
Kirkhouse Green *S York* 83 SE6213
Kirkibost *Highld* 129 NG5518
Kirkinch *Tays* 126 NO3044
Kirkinner *D & G* 99 NX4251
Kirkintilloch *Strath* 116 NS6573
Kirkland *Cumb* 92 NY0718
Kirkland *Cumb* 93 NY2648
Kirkland *Cumb* 94 NY6432
Kirkland *D & G* 107 NS7213
Kirkland *D & G* 99 NX4356
Kirkland *D & G* 100 NX8190
Kirkland *D & G* 100 NY0389
Kirkland Guards *Cumb* 93 NY1840
Kirkleatham *Cleve* 97 NZ5921
Kirklevington *Cleve* 89 NZ4309
Kirkley *Suffk* 67 TM5391
Kirklington *N York* 89 SE3181
Kirklington *Notts* 75 SK6757
Kirklinton *Cumb* 101 NY4367
Kirkliston *Loth* 117 NT1274
Kirkmabreck *D & G* 99 NX4856
Kirkmaiden *D & G* 98 NX1236
Kirkmichael *IOM* 153 SC3190
Kirkmichael *Strath* 106 NS3408
Kirkmichael *Tays* 133 NO0759
Kirkmuirhill *Strath* 107 NS7842
Kirknewton *Loth* 117 NT1166
Kirknewton *Nthumb* 110 NT9130
Kirkney *Gramp* 142 NJ5132
Kirkoswald *Cumb* 94 NY5541
Kirkoswald *Strath* 106 NS2407
Kirkpatrick *D & G* 100 NX9090
Kirkpatrick Durham *D & G* 100 NX7870
Kirkpatrick-Fleming *D & G* 101 NY2770
Kirksanton *Cumb* 86 SD1380
Kirkstall *W York* 82 SE2635
Kirkstead *Lincs* 76 TF1762
Kirkstile *D & G* 101 NY3690
Kirkstile *Gramp* 142 NJ5235
Kirkstone Pass Inn *Cumb* 87 NY4007
Kirkstyle *Highld* 151 ND3472
Kirkthorpe *W York* 83 SE3621
Kirkton *Border* 109 NT5413
Kirkton *D & G* 100 NX9781
Kirkton *Fife* 126 NO3625
Kirkton *Gramp* 142 NJ6425
Kirkton *Gramp* 143 NJ8243
Kirkton *Highld* 137 NG8227
Kirkton *Highld* 138 NG9141
Kirkton *Tays* 125 NN9618
Kirkton Manor *Border* 109 NT2238
Kirkton of Airlie *Tays* 126 NO3151
Kirkton of Auchterhouse *Tays* 126 NO3438
Kirkton of Barevan *Highld* 140 NH8347
Kirkton of Collace *Tays* 126 NO1931
Kirkton of Glenbuchat *Gramp* 141 NJ3715
Kirkton of Glenisla *Tays* 133 NO2160
Kirkton of Logie Buchan *Gramp* 143 NJ9829
Kirkton of Menmuir *Tays* 134 NO5364
Kirkton of Monikie *Tays* 127 NO5138
Kirkton of Rayne *Gramp* 142 NJ6930
Kirkton of Skene *Gramp* 135 NJ8007
Kirkton of Strathmartine *Tays* 126 NO3735
Kirkton of Tealing *Tays* 126 NO4038
Kirktown *Gramp* 143 NJ9965
Kirktown *Gramp* 143 NK0852
Kirktown of Bourtie *Gramp* 143 NJ8025
Kirktown of Fetteresso *Gramp* 135 NO8486
Kirktown of Mortlach *Gramp* 141 NJ3138
Kirktown of Slains *Gramp* 143 NK0329
Kirkwall *Ork* 155 HY4411
Kirkwhelpington *Nthumb* 103 NY9984
Kirmington *Humb* 85 TA1011
Kirmond le Mire *Lincs* 76 TF1892
Kirn *Strath* 114 NS1878
Kirriemuir *Tays* 126 NO3853
Kirstead Green *Norfk* 67 TM2997
Kirtlebridge *D & G* 101 NY2372
Kirtling *Cambs* 53 TL6857
Kirtling Green *Suffk* 53 TL6855
Kirtlington *Oxon* 37 SP4919
Kirtomy *Highld* 150 NC7463
Kirton *Gramp* 134 NJ6113
Kirton *Lincs* 64 TF3038
Kirton *Notts* 75 SK6969
Kirton *Suffk* 55 TM2740
Kirton End *Lincs* 64 TF2940
Kirton Holme *Lincs* 64 TF2642
Kirton in Lindsey *Lincs* 76 SK9398
Kirtonhill *Strath* 115 NS3875
Kirwaugh *D & G* 99 NX4054
Kishorn *Highld* 138 NG8440
Kislingbury *Nhants* 49 SP6959
Kite Green *Warwks* 48 SP1666
Kites Hardwick *Warwks* 50 SP4768
Kitleigh *Cnwll* 18 SX2499
Kitt Green *Gt Man* 78 SD5405
Kittisford *Somset* 20 ST0822
Kittle *W Glam* 32 SS5789
Kitts Green *W Mids* 61 SP1587
Kittybrewster *Gramp* 135 NJ9207
Kitwood *Hants* 24 SU6633
Kivernoll *H & W* 46 SO4632
Kiveton Park *S York* 75 SK4982
Knaith *Lincs* 75 SK8284
Knaith Park *Lincs* 76 SK8485
Knap Corner *Dorset* 22 ST8023
Knaphill *Surrey* 25 SU9658
Knaplock *Somset* 19 SS8633
Knapp *Somset* 20 ST3025
Knapp Hill *Hants* 13 SU4023
Knapthorpe *Notts* 75 SK7458
Knapton *N York* 83 SE5652
Knapton *N York* 90 SE8876
Knapton *Norfk* 67 TG3034
Knapton Green *H & W* 46 SO4452
Knapwell *Cambs* 52 TL3362
Knaresborough *N York* 89 SE3557
Knarsdale *Nthumb* 94 NY6754
Knaven *Gramp* 143 NJ8943
Knayton *N York* 89 SE4387
Knebworth *Herts* 39 TL2520
Knedlington *Humb* 84 SE7327
Kneesall *Notts* 75 SK7064
Kneesworth *Cambs* 39 TL3444
Kneeton *Notts* 63 SK7146
Knelston *W Glam* 32 SS4688
Knenhall *Staffs* 72 SJ9237
Knettishall *Suffk* 54 TL9780
Knightacott *Devon* 19 SS6539
Knightcote *Warwks* 48 SP4054
Knightley *Staffs* 72 SJ8125
Knightley Dale *Staffs* 72 SJ8123
Knighton *Devon* 6 SX5349
Knighton *Dorset* 10 ST6111
Knighton *Dorset* 12 SZ0497
Knighton *Leics* 62 SK6001
Knighton *Powys* 46 SO2872
Knighton *Somset* 20 ST1944
Knighton *Staffs* 72 SJ7240
Knighton *Staffs* 72 SJ7527
Knighton *Wilts* 36 SU2971
Knighton on Teme *H & W* 47 SO6369
Knightsmill *Cnwll* 4 SX0780
Knightwick *H & W* 47 SO7356
Knill *H & W* 46 SO2960
Knipton *Leics* 63 SK8231
Knitsley *Dur* 95 NZ1048
Kniveton *Derbys* 73 SK2050
Knock *Cumb* 94 NY6727
Knock *Gramp* 142 NJ5452
Knock *Highld* 129 NG6709
Knock *W Isls* 154 NB4931
Knock Castle *Strath* 114 NS1963
Knockally *Highld* 151 ND1429
Knockan *Highld* 145 NC2110
Knockandhu *Gramp* 141 NJ2023
Knockando *Gramp* 141 NJ1941
Knockbain *Highld* 139 NH5543
Knockbain *Highld* 140 NH6256
Knockdee *Highld* 151 ND1760
Knockdown *Wilts* 35 ST8388
Knockeen *Strath* 106 NX3195
Knockenkelly *Strath* 105 NS0427
Knockentiber *Strath* 106 NS4039
Knockespock House *Gramp* 142 NJ5423
Knockhall *Kent* 27 TQ5974
Knockholt *Kent* 27 TQ4658
Knockholt Pound *Kent* 27 TQ4859
Knockin *Shrops* 59 SJ3322
Knockinlaw *Strath* 107 NS4239
Knockmill *Kent* 27 TQ5761
Knocknain *D & G* 98 NW9764
Knocksheen *D & G* 99 NX5882
Knockvennie Smithy *D & G* 99 NX7571
Knodishall *Suffk* 55 TM4262
Knole *Somset* 21 ST4825
Knole Park *Avon* 34 ST5983
Knolls Green *Ches* 79 SJ8079
Knolton *Clwyd* 71 SJ3739
Knook *Wilts* 22 ST9341
Knossington *Leics* 63 SK8008
Knott End-on-Sea *Lancs* 80 SD3548
Knotting *Beds* 51 TL0063
Knotting Green *Beds* 51 TL0062
Knottingley *W York* 83 SE5023
Knotty Green *Bucks* 26 SU9392
Knowbury *Shrops* 46 SO5775
Knowe *D & G* 98 NX3171
Knowehead *D & G* 107 NX6090
Knoweside *Strath* 106 NS2512
Knowl Green *Essex* 53 TL7841
Knowl Hill *Berks* 37 SU8279
Knowle *Avon* 34 ST6070
Knowle *Devon* 18 SS4938
Knowle *Devon* 8 SS7801
Knowle *Devon* 9 ST0007
Knowle *Devon* 9 SY0582
Knowle *Shrops* 46 SO5973
Knowle *Somset* 20 SS9643
Knowle *W Mids* 61 SP1876
Knowle Cross *Devon* 9 SY0397
Knowle Green *Lancs* 81 SD6338
Knowle Hill *Surrey* 25 SU9966
Knowle St. Giles *Somset* 10 ST3411
Knowlton *Dorset* 12 SU0209
Knowlton *Kent* 29 TR2853
Knowsley *Mersyd* 78 SJ4395
Knowstone *Devon* 19 SS8323
Knox *N York* 89 SE2957
Knox Bridge *Kent* 28 TQ7840
Knucklas *Powys* 46 SO2574
Knuston *Nhants* 51 SP9266
Knutsford *Ches* 79 SJ7578
Knutton *Staffs* 72 SJ8347
Knypersley *Staffs* 72 SJ8856
Krumlin *W York* 82 SE0518
Kuggar *Cnwll* 3 SW7216
Kyle of Lochalsh *Highld* 137 NG7627
Kyleakin *Highld* 137 NG7526
Kylerhea *Highld* 129 NG7820
Kylesku *Highld* 148 NC2233
Kylesmorar *Highld* 129 NM8093
Kylestrome *Highld* 148 NC2234
Kyloe *Nthumb* 111 NU0540
Kynaston *H & W* 47 SO6435
Kynaston *Shrops* 59 SJ3520
Kynnersley *Shrops* 72 SJ6716
Kyre Green *H & W* 46 SO6162
Kyre Park *H & W* 47 SO6263
Kyrewood *H & W* 46 SO5967
Kyrle *Somset* 20 ST0522

L

L'Ancresse *Guern* 152 GN5413
L'Eree *Guern* 152 GN4508
L'Etacq *Jersey* 152 JS0514
La Beilleuse *Guern* 152 GN5206
La Fontenelle *Guern* 152 GN5513
La Fosse *Guern* 152 GN5205
La Greve *Guern* 152 GN5312
La Greve de Lecq *Jersey* 152 JS0815
La Hougue Bie *Jersey* 152 JS1810
La Houguette *Guern* 152 GN4607
La Passee *Guern* 152 GN5112
La Pulente *Jersey* 152 JS0608
La Rocque *Jersey* 152 JS2007
La Rousaillerie *Guern* 152 GN5209
La Villette *Guern* 152 GN5105
Labbacott *Devon* 18 SS4021
Laceby *Humb* 85 TA2106
Lacey Green *Bucks* 37 SP8200
Lach Dennis *Ches* 79 SJ7071
Lackenby *Cleve* 97 NZ5619
Lackford *Suffk* 53 TL7970
Lackford Green *Suffk* 53 TL7970
Lacock *Wilts* 22 ST9168
Ladbroke *Warwks* 49 SP4158
Ladderedge *Staffs* 72 SJ9654
Laddingford *Kent* 28 TQ6948
Lade Bank *Lincs* 77 TF3954
Ladock *Cnwll* 3 SW8950
Lady Hall *Cumb* 86 SD1986
Lady's Green *Suffk* 53 TL7559
Ladybank *Fife* 126 NO3009
Ladycross *Cnwll* 5 SX3188
Ladygill *Strath* 108 NS9428
Ladykirk *Border* 110 NT8847
Ladykirk Ho *Border* 110 NT8845
Ladywood *H & W* 47 SO8661
Ladywood *W Mids* 61 SP0586
Lag *D & G* 100 NX8786
Lagavulin *Strath* 104 NR4045
Lagg *Strath* 105 NR9521
Laggan *Highld* 131 NN2997
Laggan *Highld* 132 NN6194
Laggan *Strath* 98 NX0982
Laid *Highld* 149 NC4159
Laide *Highld* 144 NG9091
Laig *Highld* 128 NM4687
Laigh Church *Strath* 115 NS4647
Laigh Fenwick *Strath* 107 NS4542
Laigh Glenmuir *Strath* 107 NS6120
Laighstonehall *Strath* 116 NS7054
Laindon *Essex* 40 TQ6889
Lairg *Highld* 146 NC5806
Laisterdyke *W York* 82 SE1932
Laithes *Cumb* 93 NY4633
Lake *Devon* 19 SS5531
Lake *Dorset* 11 SY9990
Lake *IOW* 13 SZ5883
Lake *Wilts* 23 SU1339
Lake Side *Cumb* 87 SD3787
Lakenheath *Suffk* 53 TL7182
Laker's Green *Surrey* 14 TQ0335
Lakesend *Norfk* 65 TL5196
Lakley Lanes *Bucks* 38 SP8250
Laleham *Surrey* 26 TQ0568
Laleston *M Glam* 33 SS8779
Lamancha *Border* 117 NT2052
Lamanva *Cnwll* 3 SW7631
Lamarsh *Essex* 54 TL8835
Lamas *Norfk* 67 TG2423
Lamb Roe *Lancs* 81 SD7337
Lambden *Border* 110 NT7443
Lamberhurst *Kent* 28 TQ6736
Lamberhurst Down *Kent* 16 TQ6735
Lamberton *Border* 119 NT9658
Lambfair Green *Suffk* 53 TL7153
Lambley *Notts* 63 SK6345
Lambley *Nthumb* 94 NY6658
Lambourn *Berks* 36 SU3278
Lambourne End *Essex* 27 TQ4794
Lambs Green *W Susx* 15 TQ2136
Lambston *Dyfed* 30 SM9016
Lamerton *Devon* 5 SX4577
Lamesley *T & W* 96 NZ2557
Lamington *Strath* 108 NS9731
Lamlash *Strath* 105 NS0231
Lamonby *Cumb* 93 NY4036
Lamorick *Cnwll* 4 SX0364
Lamorna *Cnwll* 2 SW4424
Lamorran *Cnwll* 3 SW8741
Lampen *Cnwll* 4 SX1867
Lampeter *Dyfed* 44 SN5747
Lampeter Velfrey *Dyfed* 31 SN1514
Lamphey *Dyfed* 30 SN0100
Lamplugh *Cumb* 92 NY0820
Lamport *Nhants* 50 SP7574
Lamyatt *Somset* 21 ST6536
Lana *Devon* 18 SS3007
Lana *Devon* 5 SX3496
Lanark *Strath* 108 NS8843
Lanarth *Cnwll* 3 SW7621
Lancaster *Lancs* 87 SD4761
Lancaut *Gloucs* 34 ST5396
Lanchester *Dur* 96 NZ1647
Lancing *W Susx* 15 TQ1804
Land-hallow *Highld* 151 ND1833
Landbeach *Cambs* 53 TL4765
Landcross *Devon* 18 SS4523
Landerberry *Gramp* 135 NJ7404
Landewednack *Cnwll* 2 SW7012
Landford *Wilts* 12 SU2519
Landimore *W Glam* 32 SS4692
Landkey *Devon* 19 SS6031
Landkey Town *Devon* 19 SS5931
Landore *W Glam* 32 SS6695
Landrake *Cnwll* 5 SX3760
Lands End *Cnwll* 2 SW3425
Landscove *Devon* 7 SX7766
Landshipping *Dyfed* 30 SN0211
Landue *Cnwll* 5 SX3579
Landulph *Cnwll* 6 SX4361
Landwade *Cambs* 53 TL6268
Landywood *Staffs* 60 SJ9805
Lane *Cnwll* 4 SW8260
Lane Bottom *Lancs* 81 SD8735
Lane End *Bucks* 37 SU8091
Lane End *Ches* 79 SJ6890
Lane End *Cnwll* 4 SX0369
Lane End *Cumb* 86 SD1093
Lane End *Hants* 13 SU5525
Lane End *Kent* 27 TQ5671
Lane End *Lancs* 81 SD8747
Lane End *Wilts* 22 ST8145
Lane Ends *Derbys* 73 SK2334
Lane Ends *Dur* 96 NZ1833
Lane Ends *Lancs* 81 SD7930
Lane Ends *N York* 82 SD9743
Lane Green *Staffs* 60 SJ8703
Lane Head *Dur* 89 NZ1211
Lane Head *Gt Man* 79 SJ6296
Lane Head *W Mids* 35 SO9700
Lane Heads *Lancs* 80 SD4339
Lane Side *Lancs* 81 SD7922
Laneast *Cnwll* 5 SX2283
Laneham *Notts* 75 SK8076
Lanehead *Dur* 95 NY8441
Laneshaw Bridge *Lancs* 81 SD9240
Langaford *Devon* 18 SX4199
Langaller *Somset* 20 ST2626
Langar *Notts* 63 SK7234
Langbank *Strath* 115 NS3873
Langbar *N York* 82 SE0951
Langbaurgh *N York* 90 NZ5511
Langcliffe *N York* 88 SD8264
Langdale End *N York* 91 SE9391
Langdon *Cnwll* 5 SX3089
Langdon Beck *Dur* 95 NY8531
Langdown *Hants* 13 SU4206
Langdyke *Fife* 126 NO3304
Langenhoe *Essex* 41 TM0018
Langford *Avon* 21 ST4560
Langford *Beds* 39 TL1841
Langford *Devon* 9 ST0203
Langford *Essex* 40 TL8309
Langford *Notts* 75 SK8258
Langford *Oxon* 36 SP2402
Langford Budville *Somset* 20 ST1122
Langford End *Beds* 52 TL1753
Langham *Dorset* 22 ST7725
Langham *Essex* 41 TM0333
Langham *Leics* 63 SK8411
Langham *Norfk* 66 TG0141
Langham *Suffk* 54 TL9769
Langham Moor *Essex* 41 TM0131
Langham Wick *Essex* 41 TM0231
Langho *Lancs* 81 SD7034
Langholm *D & G* 101 NY3684
Langland *W Glam* 32 SS6087
Langley *Berks* 26 TQ0178
Langley *Ches* 79 SJ9471
Langley *Derbys* 62 SK4445
Langley *Essex* 39 TL4334
Langley *Gloucs* 47 SP0028
Langley *Gt Man* 79 SD8506
Langley *Hants* 13 SU4401
Langley *Herts* 39 TL2122
Langley *Kent* 28 TQ8052
Langley *Nthumb* 102 NY8261
Langley *Oxon* 36 SP2915
Langley *Somset* 20 ST0828
Langley *W Susx* 14 SU8029
Langley *Warwks* 48 SP1962
Langley Burrell *Wilts* 35 ST9375
Langley Castle *Nthumb* 102 NY8362
Langley Common *Derbys* 73 SK2937
Langley Green *Derbys* 73 SK2738
Langley Green *Essex* 40 TL8722
Langley Green *Warwks* 48 SP1962
Langley Marsh *Somset* 20 ST0729
Langley Mill *Derbys* 62 SK4446
Langley Moor *Dur* 96 NZ2540
Langley Park *Dur* 96 NZ2145
Langley Street *Norfk* 67 TG3601
Langleybury *Herts* 26 TL0700
Langney *E Susx* 16 TQ6302
Langold *Notts* 75 SK5886
Langore *Cnwll* 5 SX2986
Langport *Somset* 21 ST4226
Langrick *Lincs* 77 TF2648
Langridge *Avon* 35 ST7469
Langridge Ford *Devon* 19 SS5722
Langrigg *Cumb* 92 NY1645
Langrish *Hants* 13 SU7023
Langsett *S York* 74 SE2100
Langshaw *Border* 109 NT5139
Langside *Tays* 125 NN7913
Langstone *Gwent* 34 ST3789
Langstone *Hants* 13 SU7204
Langthorne *N York* 89 SE2491
Langthorpe *N York* 89 SE3867
Langthwaite *N York* 88 NZ0001
Langtoft *Humb* 91 TA0066
Langtoft *Lincs* 64 TF1212
Langton *Dur* 96 NZ1619
Langton *Lincs* 76 TF2368
Langton *Lincs* 77 TF3970
Langton *N York* 90 SE7966
Langton by Wragby *Lincs* 76 TF1476
Langton Green *Kent* 16 TQ5439
Langton Green *Suffk* 54 TM1474
Langton Herring *Dorset* 10 SY6182
Langtree *Devon* 18 SS4515
Langwathby *Cumb* 94 NY5733
Langwell House *Highld* 147 ND1122
Langwith *Derbys* 75 SK5370
Langworth *Lincs* 76 TF0676
Langworthy *Devon* 5 SX4894
Lanieth *Cnwll* 3 SW9752
Lanivet *Cnwll* 4 SX0464
Lank *Cnwll* 4 SX0875
Lanlivery *Cnwll* 4 SX0759
Lanner *Cnwll* 2 SW7139
Lanoy *Cnwll* 5 SX2977
Lanreath *Cnwll* 4 SX1857
Lansallos *Cnwll* 4 SX1751
Lanteglos *Cnwll* 4 SX0882
Lanteglos Highway *Cnwll* 3 SX1453
Lantilio-Crossenny *Gwent* 34 SO3914
Lanton *Border* 110 NT6221
Lanton *Nthumb* 110 NT9231
Lapford *Devon* 19 SS7308
Laphroaig *Strath* 104 NR3845
Lapley *Staffs* 60 SJ8712
Lapworth *Warwks* 61 SP1671
Larachbeg *Highld* 122 NM6948
Larbert *Cent* 116 NS8582
Larbreck *Lancs* 80 SD4040
Largie *Gramp* 142 NJ6131
Largiemore *Strath* 114 NR9486
Largoward *Fife* 127 NO4607
Largs *Strath* 114 NS2059
Largybeg *Strath* 105 NS0423
Largymore *Strath* 105 NS0424
Larkfield *Kent* 28 TQ7058
Larkfield *Strath* 114 NS2475
Larkhall *Strath* 116 NS7651
Larkhill *Wilts* 23 SU1244
Larling *Norfk* 54 TL9889
Lartington *Dur* 95 NZ0117
Lasborough *Gloucs* 35 ST8294
Lasham *Hants* 24 SU6742
Lashbrook *Devon* 18 SS4305
Lashenden *Kent* 28 TQ8440
Lask Edge *Staffs* 72 SJ9156
Lassodie *Fife* 117 NT1292
Lasswade *Loth* 117 NT3065
Lastingham *N York* 90 SE7290
Latcham *Somset* 21 ST4447

Llanmaes Lower Heysham

Llanmaes S Glam 20 SS9769
Llanmartin Gwent 34 ST3989
Llanmerewig Powys 58 SO1593
Llanmihangel S Glam 33 SS9871
Llanmiloe Dyfed 31 SN2408
Llanmorlais W Glam 32 SS5294
Llannefydd Clwyd 70 SH9870
Llannon Dyfed 32 SN5308
Llannor Gwynd 56 SH3537
Llanon Dyfed 42 SN5166
Llanover Gwent 34 SO3109
Llanpumsaint Dyfed 31 SN4229
Llanrhaeadr-ym-Mochnant Clwyd 58 SJ1226
Llanrhidian W Glam 32 SS4992
Llanrhos Gwynd 69 SH7980
Llanrhychwyn Gwynd 69 SH7761
Llanrhyddlad Gwynd 68 SH3389
Llanrhystud Dyfed 43 SN5369
Llanrian Dyfed 30 SM8231
Llanrothal H & W 34 SO4718
Llanrug Gwynd 69 SH5363
Llanrumney S Glam 34 ST2280
Llanrwst Gwynd 69 SH8061
Llansadurnen Dyfed 31 SN2810
Llansadwrn Dyfed 43 SN6931
Llansadwrn Gwynd 69 SH5575
Llansaint Dyfed 31 SN3808
Llansamlet W Glam 32 SS6897
Llansanffraid Glan Conwy Gwynd 69 SH8076
Llansannan Clwyd 70 SH9365
Llansannor S Glam 33 SS9977
Llansantffraed Powys 45 SO1223
Llansantffraed-Cwmdeuddwr Powys 45 SN9667
Llansantffraed-in-Elvel Powys 45 SO0954
Llansantffraid Dyfed 42 SN5167
Llansantffraid-ym-Mechain Powys 58 SJ2220
Llansawel Dyfed 44 SN6136
Llansilin Clwyd 58 SJ2128
Llansoy Gwent 34 SO4402
Llanspyddid Powys 45 SO0128
Llanstadwell Dyfed 30 SM9404
Llansteffan Dyfed 31 SN3511
Llanstephan Powys 45 SO1141
Llantarnam Gwent 34 ST3093
Llanteg Dyfed 31 SN1810
Llanthewy Skirrid Gwent 34 SO3416
Llanthony Gwent 46 SO2827
Llantilio Pertholey Gwent 34 SO3116
Llantrisant Gwent 34 ST3996
Llantrisant Gwynd 68 SH3584
Llantrisant M Glam 33 ST0483
Llantrithyd S Glam 33 ST0472
Llantwit Fardre M Glam 33 ST0886
Llantwit Major S Glam 20 SS9668
Llantysilio Clwyd 70 SJ1943
Llanuwchllyn Gwynd 57 SH8730
Llanvaches Gwent 34 ST4391
Llanvair Discoed Gwent 34 ST4492
Llanvapley Gwent 34 SO3614
Llanvetherine Gwent 34 SO3617
Llanveynoe H & W 46 SO3031
Llanvihangel Crucorney Gwent 34 SO3220
Llanvihangel Gobion Gwent 34 SO3409
Llanvihangel-Ystern-Llewern Gwent 34 SO4313
Llanwarne H & W 46 SO5027
Llanwddyn Powys 58 SJ0219
Llanwenarth Gwent 34 SO2714
Llanwenog Dyfed 44 SN4945
Llanwern Gwent 34 ST3688
Llanwinio Dyfed 31 SN2626
Llanwnda Dyfed 30 SM9339
Llanwnda Gwynd 68 SH4758
Llanwnen Dyfed 44 SN5347
Llanwnog Powys 58 SO0293
Llanwonno M Glam 33 ST0395
Llanwrda Dyfed 44 SN7131
Llanwrin Powys 57 SH7803
Llanwrthwl Powys 45 SN9763
Llanwrtyd Powys 45 SN8647
Llanwrtyd Wells Powys 45 SN8846
Llanwyddelan Powys 58 SJ0801
Llanyblodwel Shrops 58 SJ2323
Llanybri Dyfed 31 SN3312
Llanybydder Dyfed 44 SN5244
Llanycefn Dyfed 31 SN0923
Llanychaer Bridge Dyfed 30 SM9835
Llanycrwys Dyfed 44 SN6445
Llanymawddwy Gwynd 58 SH9019
Llanymynech Shrops 58 SJ2621
Llanynghenedl Gwynd 68 SH3181
Llanynis Powys 45 SN9950
Llanynys Clwyd 70 SJ1062
Llanyre Powys 45 SO0462
Llanystumdwy Gwynd 56 SH4738
Llanywern Powys 45 SO1028
Llawhaden Dyfed 31 SN0717
Llawnt Shrops 58 SJ2430
Llawryglyn Powys 58 SN9291
Llay Clwyd 71 SJ3355
Llechcynfarwy Gwynd 68 SH3880
Llechfaen Powys 45 SO0828
Llechryd Dyfed 31 SN2143
Lledrod Dyfed 43 SN6470
Llidiadnenog Dyfed 44 SN5437
Llidiardau Gwynd 57 SH8738
Llidiart-y-parc Clwyd 70 SJ1143
Llithfaen Gwynd 56 SH3542
Llong Clwyd 70 SJ2662
Llowes Powys 45 SO1941
Llwydcoed M Glam 33 SN9904
Llwydiarth Powys 58 SJ0315
Llwyn-drain Dyfed 31 SN2634
Llwyn-du Gwent 34 SO2816
Llwyn-on M Glam 33 SO0111
Llwyn-y-brain Dyfed 31 SN1914
Llwyn-y-Groes Dyfed 44 SN5956
Llwyncelyn Dyfed 42 SN4459
Llwyndafydd Dyfed 42 SN3755
Llwynderw Powys 58 SJ2104
Llwyndyrys Gwynd 56 SH3740
Llwyngwril Gwynd 57 SH5909
Llwynhendy Dyfed 32 SS5499
Llwynmawr Clwyd 58 SJ2237
Llwynypia M Glam 33 SS9993
Llyn-y-pandy Clwyd 70 SJ2065
Llynclys Shrops 58 SJ2824
Llynfaes Gwynd 68 SH4178
Llys-y-fran Dyfed 30 SN0424
Llysfaen Clwyd 69 SH8977
Llyswen Dyfed 44 SN4661
Llyswen Powys 45 SO1337
Llysworney S Glam 33 SS9673
Llywel Powys 45 SN8630
Load Brook S York 74 SK2788
Loan Cent 117 NS9675
Loanend Nthumb 119 NT9450
Loanhead Loth 117 NT2865
Loaningfoot D & G 92 NX9655
Loans Strath 106 NS3431
Lobb Devon 18 SS4737
Lobhillcross Devon 5 SX4686
Loch Katrine Pier Cent 124 NN4907
Loch Loyal Lodge Highld 149 NC6146
Loch Maree Hotel Highld 144 NG9170
Lochailort Highld 129 NM7682
Lochans D & G 98 NX0656
Locharbriggs D & G 100 NX9980
Lochavich Strath 122 NM9415
Lochawe Strath 123 NN1227
Lochboisdale W Isls 154 NF7919
Lochbuie Strath 121 NM6025
Lochcarron Highld 138 NG8939
Lochdon Strath 122 NM7233
Lochead Strath 113 NR7778
Lochearnhead Cent 124 NN5823
Lochee Tays 126 NO3731
Locheilside Station Highld 130 NM9978
Lochend Highld 140 NH5937
Locheport W Isls 154 NF8563
Lochfoot D & G 100 NX8973
Lochgair Strath 114 NR9290
Lochgelly Fife 117 NT1893
Lochgilphead Strath 113 NR8688
Lochgoilhead Strath 114 NN2001
Lochieheads Fife 126 NO2513
Lochill Gramp 141 NJ2964
Lochindorb Lodge Highld 140 NH9635
Lochinver Highld 145 NC0922
Lochluichart Highld 139 NH3363
Lochmaben D & G 100 NY0882
Lochmaddy W Isls 154 NF9169
Lochore Fife 117 NT1796
Lochranza Strath 105 NR9350
Lochside Gramp 135 NO7364
Lochside Highld 140 NH8152
Lochton Strath 98 NX2579
Lochty Fife 127 NO5208
Lochty Tays 134 NO5362
Lochuisge Highld 122 NM7955
Lochwinnoch Strath 115 NS3559
Lochwood D & G 100 NY0896
Lockengate Cnwll 4 SX0361
Lockerbie D & G 100 NY1381
Lockeridge Wilts 23 SU1467
Lockerley Hants 23 SU3025
Locking Avon 21 ST3659
Lockington Humb 84 SE9947
Lockington Leics 62 SK4627
Lockleywood Shrops 72 SJ6928
Locks Heath Hants 13 SU5107
Locksbottom Gt Lon 27 TQ4265
Locksgreen IOW 13 SZ4490
Lockton N York 90 SE8489
Loddington Leics 63 SK7902
Loddington Nhants 51 SP8178
Loddiswell Devon 7 SX7248
Loddon Norfk 67 TM3698
Lode Cambs 53 TL5362
Lode Heath W Mids 61 SP1580
Loders Dorset 10 SY4994
Lodge Green W Mids 61 SP2583
Lodsworth W Susx 14 SU9223
Lofthouse Gate W York 83 SE3324
Lofthouse N York 89 SE1073
Lofthouse W York 83 SE3325
Loftus Cleve 97 NZ7218
Logan Strath 107 NS5820
Loganbeck Cumb 86 SD1890
Loganlea Loth 117 NS9762
Loggerheads Staffs 72 SJ7336
Logie Fife 126 NO4020
Logie Gramp 141 NJ0150
Logie Tays 135 NO6963
Logie Coldstone Gramp 134 NJ4304
Logie Pert Tays 135 NO6664
Logierait Tays 125 NN9752
Login Dyfed 31 SN1623
Lolworth Cambs 52 TL3664
Lon-las W Glam 32 SS7097
Lonbain Highld 137 NG6852
Londesborough Humb 84 SE8645
London Gt Lon 27 TQ2879
London Apprentice Cnwll 3 SX0049
London Beach Kent 28 TQ8836
London Colney Herts 39 TL1803
Londonderry N York 89 SE3087
Londonthorpe Lincs 63 SK9537
Londubh Highld 144 NG8680
Long Ashton Avon 34 ST5570
Long Bank H & W 60 SO7674
Long Bennington Lincs 63 SK8344
Long Bredy Dorset 10 SY5690
Long Buckby Nhants 50 SP6367
Long Cause Devon 7 SX7961
Long Clawson Leics 63 SK7227
Long Common Hants 13 SU5014
Long Compton Staffs 72 SJ8522
Long Compton Warwks 48 SP2832
Long Crendon Bucks 37 SP6908
Long Crichel Dorset 11 ST9710
Long Ditton Surrey 26 TQ1766
Long Drax N York 83 SE6828
Long Duckmanton Derbys 75 SK4471
Long Eaton Derbys 62 SK4833
Long Green Ches 71 SJ4770
Long Green H & W 47 SO8433
Long Hedges Lincs 77 TF3547
Long Itchington Warwks 50 SP4165
Long Lane Shrops 59 SJ6315
Long Lawford Warwks 50 SP4776
Long Load Somset 21 ST4623
Long Marston Herts 38 SP8915
Long Marston N York 83 SE5051
Long Marston Warwks 48 SP1548
Long Marton Cumb 94 NY6624
Long Meadowend Shrops 59 SO4181
Long Melford Suffk 54 TL8645
Long Newnton Gloucs 35 ST9192
Long Newton Loth 118 NT5164
Long Preston N York 88 SD8358
Long Riston Humb 85 TA1242
Long Sight Gt Man 79 SD9206
Long Stratton Norfk 67 TM1992
Long Street Bucks 38 SP7947
Long Sutton Hants 24 SU7347
Long Sutton Lincs 65 TF4322
Long Sutton Somset 21 ST4725
Long Thurlow Suffk 54 TM0068
Long Waste Shrops 59 SJ6115
Long Whatton Leics 62 SK4723
Long Wittenham Oxon 37 SU5493
Longbenton T & W 103 NZ2668
Longborough Gloucs 48 SP1729
Longbridge W Mids 60 SP0177
Longbridge Warwks 48 SP2762
Longbridge Deverill Wilts 22 ST8640
Longburgh Cumb 93 NY3058
Longburton Dorset 11 ST6412
Longcliffe Derbys 73 SK2255
Longcombe Devon 7 SX8359
Longcot Oxon 36 SU2790
Longcroft Cumb 93 NY2158
Longcross Surrey 25 SU9865
Longden Shrops 59 SJ4406
Longden Common Shrops 59 SJ4305
Longdon H & W 47 SO8336
Longdon Staffs 61 SK0714
Longdon Green Staffs 61 SK0813
Longdon Heath H & W 47 SO8338
Longdon upon Tern Shrops 59 SJ6115
Longdown Devon 9 SX8691
Longdowns Cnwll 3 SW7434
Longfield Kent 27 TQ6069
Longford Derbys 73 SK2137
Longford Gloucs 35 SO8320
Longford Gt Lon 26 TQ0576
Longford Kent 27 TQ5156
Longford Shrops 72 SJ6434
Longford Shrops 72 SJ7218
Longford W Mids 61 SP3583
Longforgan Tays 126 NO2929
Longformacus Border 119 NT6957
Longframlington Nthumb 103 NU1300
Longham Dorset 12 SZ0698
Longham Norfk 66 TF9416
Longhirst Nthumb 103 NZ2289
Longhope Gloucs 35 SO6918
Longhorsley Nthumb 103 NZ1494
Longhoughton Nthumb 111 NU2415
Longlands Cumb 93 NY2636
Longlane Derbys 73 SK2437
Longlevens Gloucs 35 SO8519
Longley W York 82 SE0522
Longley W York 82 SE1406
Longley Green H & W 47 SO7350
Longleys Tays 126 NO2643
Longmanhill Gramp 142 NJ7362
Longmoor Camp Hants 14 SU7931
Longmorn Gramp 141 NJ2358
Longmoss Ches 79 SJ8974
Longnewton Border 110 NT5827
Longnewton Cleve 96 NZ3816
Longney Gloucs 35 SO7612
Longniddry Loth 118 NT4476
Longnor Shrops 59 SJ4800
Longnor Staffs 74 SK0864
Longparish Hants 24 SU4345
Longpark Cumb 101 NY4362
Longridge Lancs 81 SD6037
Longridge Loth 116 NS9462
Longridge Staffs 72 SJ9015
Longriggend Strath 116 NS8270
Longrock Cnwll 2 SW5031
Longsdon Staffs 72 SJ9654
Longshaw Common Gt Man 78 SD5302
Longside Gramp 143 NK0347
Longslow Shrops 72 SJ6535
Longstanton Cambs 52 TL3966
Longstock Hants 23 SU3537
Longstone Dyfed 31 SN1409
Longstowe Cambs 52 TL3054
Longstreet Wilts 23 SU1451
Longthorpe Cambs 64 TL1698
Longthwaite Cumb 93 NY4323
Longton Lancs 80 SD4825
Longton Staffs 72 SJ9143
Longtown Cumb 101 NY3768
Longtown H & W 46 SO3229
Longueville Jersey 152 JS1708
Longville in the Dale Shrops 59 SO5393
Longwick Bucks 38 SP7905
Longwitton Nthumb 103 NZ0788
Longwood D & G 99 NX7060
Longwood Shrops 59 SJ6007
Longwood House Hants 13 SU5324
Longworth Oxon 36 SU3899
Longyester Loth 118 NT5465
Lonmay Gramp 143 NK0159
Lonmore Highld 136 NG2646
Looe Cnwll 5 SX2553
Loose Kent 28 TQ7552
Loosebeare Devon 8 SS7105
Loosegate Lincs 64 TF3125
Loosley Row Bucks 37 SP8100
Lootcherbrae Gramp 142 NJ6053
Lopcombe Corner Wilts 23 SU2535
Lopen Somset 10 ST4214
Loppington Shrops 59 SJ4629
Lorbottle Nthumb 111 NU0306
Lordington W Susx 14 SU7809
Lordsbridge Norfk 65 TF5712
Lornty Tays 126 NO1746
Loscoe Derbys 62 SK4247
Loscombe Dorset 10 SY4997
Lossiemouth Gramp 141 NJ2370
Lostford Shrops 59 SJ6231
Lostock Gralam Ches 79 SJ6974
Lostock Green Ches 79 SJ6973
Lostock Hall Fold Gt Man 79 SD6509
Lostock Junction Gt Man 79 SD6708
Lostwithiel Cnwll 4 SX1059
Lothbeg Highld 147 NC9410
Lothersdale N York 82 SD9545
Lothmore Highld 147 NC9611
Loudwater Bucks 26 SU9090
Loughborough Leics 62 SK5319
Loughor W Glam 32 SS5698
Loughton Bucks 38 SP8337
Loughton Essex 27 TQ4296
Loughton Shrops 59 SO6182
Lound Lincs 64 TF0618
Lound Notts 75 SK6986
Lound Suffk 67 TM5099
Lounston Devon 7 SX7875
Lount Leics 62 SK3819
Louth Lincs 77 TF3287
Love Clough Lancs 81 SD8127
Lovedean Hants 13 SU6812
Lover Wilts 12 SU2120
Loversall S York 75 SK5798
Loves Green Essex 40 TL6404
Lovesome Hill N York 89 SE3699
Loveston Dyfed 31 SN0808
Lovington Somset 21 ST5930
Low Ackworth W York 83 SE4517
Low Angerton Nthumb 103 NZ0984
Low Barbeth D & G 98 NX0166
Low Barlings Lincs 76 TF0873
Low Bell End N York 90 SE7197
Low Bentham N York 87 SD6469
Low Biggins Cumb 87 SD6077
Low Borrowbridge Cumb 87 NY6101
Low Bradfield S York 74 SK2691
Low Bradley N York 82 SE0048
Low Braithwaite Cumb 93 NY4242
Low Burnham Humb 84 SE7802
Low Buston Nthumb 111 NU2207
Low Catton Humb 84 SE7053
Low Conisclife Dur 89 NZ2513
Low Dinsdale Dur 89 NZ3411
Low Eggborough N York 83 SE5623
Low Ellington N York 89 SE1983
Low Fell T & W 96 NZ2559
Low Gartachorrans Cent 115 NS4685
Low Gettbridge Cumb 94 NY5259
Low Grantley N York 89 SE2370
Low Green N York 89 SE2059
Low Habberley H & W 60 SO8077
Low Ham Somset 21 ST4329
Low Harrogate N York 82 SE2955
Low Hawsker N York 91 NZ9207
Low Hesket Cumb 93 NY4646
Low Hill H & W 60 SO8473
Low Hutton N York 90 SE7667
Low Knipe Cumb 94 NY5119
Low Laithe N York 89 SE1963
Low Langton Lincs 76 TF1576
Low Leighton Derbys 79 SK0085
Low Lorton Cumb 92 NY1525
Low Marnham Notts 75 SK8069
Low Middleton Nthumb 111 NU1035
Low Mill N York 90 SE6795
Low Moor Lancs 81 SD7341
Low Moor W York 82 SE1628
Low Moorsley T & W 96 NZ3446
Low Mowthorpe N York 91 SE8966
Low Newton Cumb 87 SD4082
Low Rogerscales Cumb 92 NY1426
Low Row Cumb 93 NY1944
Low Row Cumb 93 NY3536
Low Row Cumb 102 NY5863
Low Row N York 88 SD9797
Low Salchrie D & G 98 NX0365
Low Santon Humb 84 SE9412
Low Skeog D & G 99 NX4540
Low Street Essex 28 TQ6677
Low Street Norfk 67 TG3423
Low Tharston Norfk 66 TM1895
Low Toynton Lincs 77 TF2770
Low Valley S York 83 SE4003
Low Walworth Dur 96 NZ2417
Low Wood Cumb 87 SD3483
Low Worsall N York 89 NZ3909
Low Wray Cumb 87 NY3701
Lowbands H & W 47 SO7731
Lowca Cumb 92 NX9821
Lowdham Notts 63 SK6646
Lowe Shrops 59 SJ4930
Lowe Hill Staffs 73 SJ9955
Lower Aisholt Somset 20 ST2035
Lower Ansty Dorset 11 ST7603
Lower Apperley Gloucs 47 SO8527
Lower Arncott Oxon 37 SP6019
Lower Ashton Devon 8 SX8484
Lower Assendon Oxon 37 SU7484
Lower Ballam Lancs 80 SD3631
Lower Barewood H & W 46 SO3956
Lower Bartle Lancs 80 SD4933
Lower Bayston Shrops 59 SJ4908
Lower Beeding W Susx 15 TQ2127
Lower Benefield Nhants 51 SP9988
Lower Bentley H & W 47 SO9865
Lower Beobridge Shrops 60 SO7891
Lower Berry Hill Gloucs 34 SO5711
Lower Birchwood Derbys 75 SK4354
Lower Boddington Nhants 49 SP4852
Lower Boscaswell Cnwll 2 SW3734
Lower Bourne Surrey 25 SU8444
Lower Brailes Warwks 48 SP3139
Lower Breakish Highld 129 NG6723
Lower Bredbury Gt Man 79 SJ9191
Lower Broadheath H & W 47 SO8157
Lower Buckenhill H & W 46 SO6033
Lower Bullingham H & W 46 SO5138
Lower Burgate Hants 12 SU1515
Lower Burrowton Devon 9 SY0097
Lower Burton H & W 46 SO4256
Lower Caldecote Beds 52 TL1746
Lower Cam Gloucs 35 SO7400
Lower Canada Avon 21 ST3558
Lower Catesby Nhants 49 SP5159
Lower Chapel Powys 45 SO0235
Lower Chicksgrove Wilts 22 ST9729
Lower Chute Wilts 23 SU3153
Lower Clapton Gt Lon 27 TQ3485
Lower Clent H & W 60 SO9279
Lower Creedy Devon 8 SS8402
Lower Crossings Derbys 74 SK0480
Lower Cumberworth W York 82 SE2209
Lower Cwmtwrch Powys 32 SN7610
Lower Darwen Lancs 81 SD6825
Lower Dean Beds 51 TL0569
Lower Denby W York 82 SE2307
Lower Diabaig Highld 137 NG7960
Lower Dicker E Susx 16 TQ5511
Lower Dinchope Shrops 59 SO4584
Lower Down Shrops 59 SO3484
Lower Dunsforth N York 89 SE4464
Lower Egleton H & W 47 SO6245
Lower Elkstone Staffs 74 SK0658
Lower Ellastone Staffs 73 SK1142
Lower End Bucks 37 SP6809
Lower End Bucks 38 SP9238
Lower End Nhants 51 SP8861
Lower Everleigh Wilts 23 SU1854
Lower Exbury Hants 13 SZ4299
Lower Eythorne Kent 29 TR2849
Lower Failand Avon 34 ST5173
Lower Farringdon Hants 24 SU7035
Lower Feltham Gt Lon 26 TQ0971
Lower Fittleworth W Susx 14 TQ0118
Lower Frankton Shrops 59 SJ3732
Lower Freystrop Dyfed 30 SM9512
Lower Froyle Hants 24 SU7544
Lower Gabwell Devon 7 SX9169
Lower Gledfield Highld 146 NH5890
Lower Godney Somset 21 ST4742
Lower Gornal W Mids 60 SO9191
Lower Gravenhurst Beds 38 TL1035
Lower Green Essex 39 TL4334
Lower Green Gt Man 79 SJ7098
Lower Green Herts 39 TL1832
Lower Green Herts 39 TL4233
Lower Green Kent 16 TQ5640
Lower Green Kent 16 TQ6341
Lower Green Nhants 51 SP8159
Lower Green Norfk 66 TF9837
Lower Green Staffs 60 SJ9007
Lower Green Suffk 53 TL7465
Lower Hacheston Suffk 55 TM3156
Lower Halliford Surrey 26 TQ0866
Lower Halstock Leigh Dorset 10 ST5207
Lower Halstow Kent 28 TQ8567
Lower Hamworthy Dorset 11 SY9990
Lower Hardres Kent 29 TR1553
Lower Harpton H & W 46 SO2760
Lower Hartshay Derbys 74 SK3851
Lower Hartwell Bucks 38 SP7912
Lower Hatton Staffs 72 SJ8236
Lower Hawthwaite Cumb 86 SD2189
Lower Hergest H & W 46 SO2755
Lower Heyford Oxon 49 SP4824
Lower Heysham Lancs 87 SD4160

Lower Higham Market Bosworth

Lower Higham *Kent* 28 TQ7172
Lower Holbrook *Suffk* 54 TM1834
Lower Hordley *Shrops* 59 SJ3929
Lower Horncroft *W Susx* 14 TQ0017
Lower Howsell *H & W* 47 SO7848
Lower Irlam *Gt Man* 79 SJ7193
Lower Kilburn *Derbys* 62 SK3744
Lower Kilcott *Avon* 35 ST7889
Lower Killeyan *Strath* 104 NR2742
Lower Kingcombe *Dorset* 10 SY5599
Lower Kingswood *Surrey* 26 TQ2453
Lower Kinnerton *Ches* 71 SJ3462
Lower Langford *Avon* 21 ST4560
Lower Largo *Fife* 126 NO4102
Lower Leigh *Staffs* 73 SK0135
Lower Lemington *Gloucs* 48 SP2134
Lower Llanfadog *Powys* 45 SN9567
Lower Lovacott *Devon* 19 SS5227
Lower Loxhore *Devon* 19 SS6137
Lower Lydbrook *Gloucs* 34 SO5916
Lower Lye *H & W* 46 SO4066
Lower Machen *Gwent* 34 ST2288
Lower Maes-coed *H & W* 46 SO3430
Lower Mannington *Dorset* 12 SU0604
Lower Marston *Somset* 22 ST7644
Lower Meend *Gloucs* 34 SO5504
Lower Middleton Cheney *Nhants* 49 SP5041
Lower Milton *Somset* 21 ST5347
Lower Moor *W Mids* 47 SO9747
Lower Morton *Avon* 35 ST6491
Lower Nazeing *Essex* 39 TL3906
Lower Norton *Warwks* 48 SP2363
Lower Nyland *Dorset* 22 ST7521
Lower Penarth *S Glam* 20 ST1869
Lower Penn *Staffs* 60 SO8796
Lower Pennington *Hants* 12 SZ3193
Lower Penwortham *Lancs* 80 SD5327
Lower Peover *Ches* 79 SJ7474
Lower Place *Gt Man* 81 SD9011
Lower Pollicott *Bucks* 37 SP7013
Lower Pond Street *Essex* 39 TL4537
Lower Quinton *Warwks* 48 SP1847
Lower Rainham *Kent* 28 TQ8167
Lower Raydon *Suffk* 54 TM0338
Lower Roadwater *Somset* 20 ST0339
Lower Salter *Lancs* 87 SD6063
Lower Seagry *Wilts* 35 ST9580
Lower Sheering *Essex* 39 TL4914
Lower Shelton *Beds* 38 SP9942
Lower Shiplake *Oxon* 37 SU7679
Lower Shuckburgh *Warwks* 49 SP4862
Lower Slaughter *Gloucs* 36 SP1622
Lower Soothill *W York* 82 SE2523
Lower Soudley *Gloucs* 35 SO6609
Lower Standen *Kent* 29 TR2340
Lower Stanton St. Quintin *Wilts* 35 ST9180
Lower Stoke *Kent* 28 TQ8375
Lower Stone *Gloucs* 35 ST6794
Lower Stonnall *Staffs* 61 SK0803
Lower Stow Bedon *Norfk* 66 TL9694
Lower Street *Dorset* 11 SY8399
Lower Street *E Susx* 16 TQ7012
Lower Street *Norfk* 67 TG2635
Lower Street *Suffk* 53 TL7852
Lower Street *Suffk* 54 TM1052
Lower Stretton *Ches* 79 SJ6281
Lower Stroud *Dorset* 10 SY4598
Lower Sundon *Beds* 38 TL0526
Lower Swanwick *Hants* 13 SU4909
Lower Swell *Gloucs* 48 SP1725
Lower Tadmarton *Oxon* 48 SP4036
Lower Tale *Devon* 9 ST0601
Lower Tean *Staffs* 73 SK0138
Lower Thurlton *Norfk* 67 TM4299
Lower Town *Cnwll* 2 SW6528
Lower Town *Devon* 7 SX7172
Lower Town *Dyfed* 30 SM9637
Lower Town *H & W* 47 SO6342
Lower Tregantle *Cnwll* 5 SX3953
Lower Treluswell *Cnwll* 3 SW7735
Lower Tysoe *Warwks* 48 SP3445
Lower Ufford *Suffk* 55 TM2952
Lower Upcott *Devon* 9 SX8880
Lower Upham *Hants* 13 SU5219
Lower Upnor *Kent* 28 TQ7571
Lower Vexford *Somset* 20 ST1135
Lower Walton *Ches* 78 SJ6086
Lower Waterston *Dorset* 11 SY7395
Lower Weare *Somset* 21 ST4053
Lower Welson *H & W* 46 SO2950
Lower Westmancote *H & W* 47 SO9337
Lower Whatcombe *Dorset* 11 ST8401
Lower Whatley *Somset* 22 ST7447
Lower Whitley *Ches* 71 SJ6179
Lower Wick *Gloucs* 35 ST7096
Lower Wick *H & W* 47 SO8352
Lower Wield *Hants* 24 SU6340
Lower Wigginton *Herts* 38 SP9409
Lower Willingdon *E Susx* 16 TQ5803
Lower Winchendon *Bucks* 37 SP7312
Lower Woodend *Bucks* 37 SU8187
Lower Woodford *Wilts* 23 SU1235
Lower Wraxhall *Dorset* 10 ST5700
Lower Wyche *H & W* 47 SO7743
Lower Wyke *W York* 82 SE1525
Lowerhouse *Lancs* 81 SD8032
Lowesby *Leics* 63 SK7207
Lowestoft *Suffk* 67 TM5493
Loweswater *Cumb* 92 NY1421
Lowfield Heath *W Susx* 15 TQ2739
Lowgill *Cumb* 87 SD6297
Lowgill *Lancs* 87 SD6564
Lowick *Cumb* 86 SD2885
Lowick *Nhants* 51 SP9881
Lowick *Nthumb* 111 NU0139
Lowick Bridge *Cumb* 86 SD2986
Lowick Green *Cumb* 86 SD2985
Lowlands *Dur* 96 NZ1325
Lowlands *Gwent* 34 ST2996
Lowsonford *Warwks* 48 SP1868
Lowther *Cumb* 94 NY5323
Lowther Castle *Cumb* 94 NY5223
Lowtherton *D & G* 101 NY2466
Lowthorpe *Humb* 91 TA0860
Lowton *Devon* 8 SS6604
Lowton *Gt Man* 78 SJ6197
Lowton *Somset* 20 ST1918
Lowton Common *Gt Man* 79 SJ6397
Lowton St. Mary's *Gt Man* 79 SJ6397
Loxbeare *Devon* 9 SS9116
Loxhill *Surrey* 25 TQ0038
Loxhore *Devon* 19 SS6138
Loxhore Cott *Devon* 19 SS6138
Loxley *Warwks* 48 SP2553
Loxley Green *Staffs* 73 SK0630
Loxter *H & W* 47 SO7140
Loxton *Avon* 21 ST3755
Loxwood *W Susx* 14 TQ0331
Lubenham *Nhants* 50 SP7087
Lucas Green *Surrey* 25 SU9460
Lucasgate *Lincs* 77 TF4147
Luccombe *Somset* 20 SS9243
Luccombe Village *IOW* 13 SZ5879
Lucker *Nthumb* 111 NU1530
Luckett *Cnwll* 5 SX3873
Lucking Street *Essex* 54 TL8134
Luckington *Wilts* 35 ST8383
Lucklawhill *Fife* 127 NO4221
Lucknam *Wilts* 35 ST8272
Luckwell Bridge *Somset* 20 SS9038
Lucott *Somset* 19 SS8645
Lucton *H & W* 46 SO4364
Lucy Cross *N York* 89 NZ2112
Ludborough *Lincs* 77 TF2995
Ludbrook *Devon* 7 SX6654
Ludchurch *Dyfed* 31 SN1411
Luddenden *W York* 82 SE0426
Luddenden Foot *W York* 82 SE0325
Luddenham Court *Kent* 28 TQ9963
Luddesdown *Kent* 28 TQ6666
Luddington *Humb* 84 SE8316
Luddington *Warwks* 48 SP1652
Luddington in the Brook *Nhants* 51 TL1083
Ludford *Lincs* 76 TF1989
Ludford *Shrops* 46 SO5174
Ludgershall *Bucks* 37 SP6517
Ludgershall *Wilts* 23 SU2650
Ludgvan *Cnwll* 2 SW5033
Ludham *Norfk* 67 TG3818
Ludlow *Shrops* 46 SO5175
Ludney *Somset* 10 ST3812
Ludwell *Wilts* 22 ST9122
Ludworth *Dur* 96 NZ3641
Luffincott *Devon* 5 SX3394
Luffness *Loth* 118 NT4780
Lugar *Strath* 107 NS5921
Lugg Green *H & W* 46 SO4462
Luggate Burn *Loth* 118 NT5974
Luggiebank *Strath* 116 NS7672
Lugsdale *Ches* 78 SJ5285
Lugton *Strath* 115 NS4152
Lugwardine *H & W* 46 SO5540
Luib *Highld* 137 NG5627
Lulham *H & W* 46 SO4141
Lullington *Derbys* 61 SK2412
Lullington *E Susx* 16 TQ5202
Lullington *Somset* 22 ST7851
Lulsgate Bottom *Avon* 21 ST5165
Lulsley *H & W* 47 SO7455
Lulworth Camp *Dorset* 11 SY8381
Lumb *Lancs* 81 SD8324
Lumb *W York* 82 SE0221
Lumbutts *W York* 82 SD9523
Lumby *N York* 83 SE4830
Lumloch *Strath* 116 NS6370
Lumphanan *Gramp* 134 NJ5804
Lumphinnans *Fife* 117 NT1792
Lumsden *Gramp* 142 NJ4722
Lunan *Tays* 127 NO6851
Lunanhead *Tays* 127 NO4752
Luncarty *Tays* 125 NO0929
Lund *Humb* 84 SE9647
Lund *N York* 83 SE6532
Lundford Magna *Lincs* 76 TF1989
Lundie *Cent* 124 NN7304
Lundie *Tays* 126 NO2836
Lundin Links *Fife* 126 NO4002
Lundy Green *Norfk* 67 TM2392
Lunna *Shet* 155 HU4869
Lunsford *Kent* 28 TQ6959
Lunsford's Cross *E Susx* 17 TQ7210
Lunt *Mersyd* 78 SD3402
Luntley *H & W* 46 SO3955
Luppitt *Devon* 9 ST1606
Lupridge *Devon* 7 SX7153
Lupset *W York* 83 SE3119
Lupton *Cumb* 87 SD5581
Lurgashall *W Susx* 14 SU9326
Lurley *Devon* 9 SS9215
Lusby *Lincs* 77 TF3467
Luscombe *Devon* 7 SX7957
Luson *Devon* 6 SX6050
Luss *Strath* 115 NS3692
Lusta *Highld* 136 NG2656
Lustleigh *Devon* 8 SX7881
Luston *H & W* 46 SO4863
Luthermuir *Gramp* 135 NO6568
Luthrie *Fife* 126 NO3319
Lutley *W Mids* 60 SO9382
Luton *Beds* 38 TL0921
Luton *Devon* 9 ST0802
Luton *Devon* 9 SX9076
Luton *Kent* 28 TQ7766
Lutterworth *Leics* 50 SP5484
Lutton *Devon* 6 SX5959
Lutton *Dorset* 11 SY8980
Lutton *Lincs* 65 TF4325
Lutton *Nhants* 52 TL1187
Luxborough *Somset* 20 SS9738
Luxulyan *Cnwll* 4 SX0558
Luzley *Gt Man* 79 SD9600
Lybster *Highld* 151 ND2435
Lydbury North *Shrops* 59 SO3486
Lydcott *Devon* 19 SS6936
Lydd *Kent* 17 TR0420
Lydden *Kent* 29 TR2645
Lydden *Kent* 29 TR3567
Lyddington *Leics* 51 SP8797
Lyde Green *Hants* 24 SU7057
Lydeard St. Lawrence *Somset* 20 ST1332
Lydford *Devon* 5 SX5185
Lydford on Fosse *Somset* 21 ST5630
Lydgate *Gt Man* 82 SD9516
Lydgate *W York* 81 SD9225
Lydham *Shrops* 59 SO3391
Lydiard Green *Wilts* 36 SU0885
Lydiard Millicent *Wilts* 36 SU0986
Lydiard Tregoze *Wilts* 36 SU1085
Lydiate *Mersyd* 78 SD3604
Lydiate Ash *H & W* 60 SO9775
Lydlinch *Dorset* 11 ST7413
Lydney *Gloucs* 35 SO6303
Lydstep *Dyfed* 31 SS0898
Lye *W Mids* 60 SO9284
Lye Cross *Avon* 21 ST4962
Lye Green *Bucks* 38 SP9703
Lye Green *E Susx* 16 TQ5134
Lye Green *Warwks* 48 SP1965
Lye Head *H & W* 60 SO7573
Lye's Green *Wilts* 22 ST8146
Lyford *Oxon* 36 SU3994
Lymbridge Green *Kent* 29 TR1244
Lyme *Border* 109 NT2041
Lyme Regis *Dorset* 10 SY3492
Lyminge *Kent* 29 TR1641
Lymington *Hants* 12 SZ3295
Lyminster *W Susx* 14 TQ0204
Lymm *Ches* 79 SJ6887
Lympne *Kent* 17 TR1135
Lympsham *Somset* 21 ST3354
Lympstone *Devon* 9 SX9984
Lynbridge *Devon* 19 SS7248
Lynch *Somset* 20 SS9047
Lynch Green *Norfk* 66 TG1505
Lynchat *Highld* 132 NH7801
Lyndhurst *Hants* 12 SU3008
Lyndon *Leics* 63 SK9004
Lyndon Green *W Mids* 61 SP1485
Lyne *Surrey* 26 TQ0166
Lyne Down *H & W* 47 SO6431
Lyne Hill *Staffs* 60 SJ9212
Lyne of Skene *Gramp* 135 NJ7610
Lyneal *Shrops* 59 SJ4433
Lyneham *Devon* 8 SX8579
Lyneham *Oxon* 36 SP2720
Lyneham *Wilts* 35 SU0278
Lyneholmford *Cumb* 101 NY5172
Lynemouth *Nthumb* 103 NZ2991
Lyness *Ork* 155 ND3094
Lyng *Norfk* 66 TG0617
Lyng *Somset* 21 ST3329
Lynhales *H & W* 46 SO3255
Lynmouth *Devon* 19 SS7249
Lynn *Shrops* 72 SJ7815
Lynn of Shenval *Gramp* 141 NJ2129
Lynsted *Kent* 28 TQ9460
Lynstone *Cnwll* 18 SS2005
Lynton *Devon* 19 SS7249
Lyon's Gate *Dorset* 11 ST6505
Lyonshall *H & W* 46 SO3355
Lytchett Matravers *Dorset* 11 SY9495
Lytchett Minster *Dorset* 11 SY9693
Lyth *Highld* 151 ND2762
Lytham *Lancs* 80 SD3627
Lytham St. Anne's *Lancs* 80 SD3427
Lythbank *Shrops* 59 SJ4607
Lythe *N York* 90 NZ8413
Lythmore *Highld* 150 ND0566

M

Mabe Burnthouse *Cnwll* 3 SW7634
Mabie *D & G* 100 NX9570
Mablethorpe *Lincs* 77 TF5085
Macclesfield *Ches* 79 SJ9173
Macclesfield Forest *Ches* 79 SJ9772
Macduff *Gramp* 142 NJ7064
Macharioch *Strath* 105 NR7309
Machen *M Glam* 33 ST2189
Machire *Strath* 112 NR2164
Machrie Farm *Strath* 105 NR9033
Machrihanish *Strath* 104 NR6320
Machrins *Strath* 112 NR3693
Machynlleth *Powys* 57 SH7400
Machynys *Dyfed* 32 SS5198
Mackworth *Derbys* 62 SK3137
Macmerry *Loth* 118 NT4372
Maddaford *Devon* 8 SX5494
Madderty *Tays* 125 NN9522
Maddington *Wilts* 23 SU0744
Maddiston *Cent* 116 NS9476
Madehurst *W Susx* 14 SU9810
Madeley *Shrops* 60 SJ6904
Madeley *Staffs* 72 SJ7744
Madeley Heath *Staffs* 72 SJ7845
Madford *Devon* 9 ST1411
Madingley *Cambs* 52 TL3960
Madley *H & W* 46 SO4238
Madresfield *H & W* 47 SO8047
Madron *Cnwll* 2 SW4531
Maen-y-groes *Dyfed* 42 SN3858
Maenaddwyn *Gwynd* 68 SH4684
Maenan *Gwynd* 69 SH7965
Maenclochog *Dyfed* 31 SN0827
Maendy *S Glam* 33 ST0076
Maenporth *Cnwll* 3 SW7829
Maentwrog *Gwynd* 57 SH6640
Maer *Cnwll* 18 SS2008
Maer *Staffs* 72 SJ7938
Maerdy *M Glam* 33 SS9798
Maes-glas *Gwent* 34 ST2985
Maesbrook *Shrops* 59 SJ3021
Maesbury *Shrops* 59 SJ3026
Maesbury Marsh *Shrops* 59 SJ3125
Maesgwynne *Dyfed* 31 SN2024
Maeshafn *Clwyd* 70 SJ2061
Maesllyn *Dyfed* 42 SN3644
Maesmynis *Powys* 45 SO0146
Maesmynis *Powys* 45 SO0349
Maesteg *M Glam* 33 SS8590
Maesybont *Dyfed* 32 SN5616
Maesycwmmer *M Glam* 33 ST1594
Magdalen Laver *Essex* 39 TL5108
Maggieknockater *Gramp* 141 NJ3145
Maggots End *Essex* 39 TL4827
Magham Down *E Susx* 16 TQ6011
Maghull *Mersyd* 78 SD3703
Magor *Gwent* 34 ST4286
Maiden Bradley *Wilts* 22 ST8038
Maiden Head *Avon* 21 ST5666
Maiden Law *Dur* 96 NZ1749
Maiden Newton *Dorset* 10 SY5997
Maiden Wells *Dyfed* 30 SR9799
Maidencombe *Devon* 7 SX9268
Maidenhayne *Devon* 10 SY2795
Maidenhead *Berks* 26 SU8980
Maidens *Strath* 106 NS2107
Maidens Green *Berks* 25 SU8972
Maidenwell *Lincs* 77 TF3179
Maidford *Nhants* 49 SP6052
Maids Moreton *Bucks* 49 SP7035
Maidstone *Kent* 28 TQ7555
Maidwell *Nhants* 50 SP7476
Mains of Bainakettle *Gramp* 134 NO6274
Mains of Balhall *Tays* 134 NO5163
Mains of Dalvey *Highld* 141 NJ1132
Mains of Haulkerton *Gramp* 135 NO7172
Mainsforth *Dur* 96 NZ3131
Mainsriddle *D & G* 92 NX9456
Mainstone *Shrops* 58 SO2787
Maisemore *Gloucs* 35 SO8121
Major's Green *H & W* 61 SP1077
Makeney *Derbys* 62 SK3544
Malborough *Devon* 7 SX7139
Malcoff *Derbys* 74 SK0782
Malden *Surrey* 26 TQ2166
Malden Rushett *Gt Lon* 26 TQ1761
Maldon *Essex* 40 TL8506
Malham *N York* 88 SD9063
Mallaig *Highld* 129 NM6796
Mallaigvaig *Highld* 129 NM6897
Malleny Mills *Loth* 117 NT1665
Mallows Green *Essex* 39 TL4726
Malltraeth *Gwynd* 68 SH4068
Mallwyd *Gwynd* 57 SH8612
Malmesbury *Wilts* 35 ST9387
Malmsmead *Somset* 19 SS7947
Malpas *Ches* 71 SJ4847
Malpas *Cnwll* 3 SW8442
Malpas *Gwent* 34 ST3090
Maltby *Cleve* 89 NZ4613
Maltby *Lincs* 77 TF3183
Maltby *S York* 75 SK5392
Maltby le Marsh *Lincs* 77 TF4681
Malting Green *Essex* 41 TL9720
Maltman's Hill *Kent* 28 TQ9043
Malton *N York* 90 SE7871
Malvern Link *H & W* 47 SO7947
Malvern Wells *H & W* 47 SO7742
Malzie *D & G* 99 NX3754
Mamble *H & W* 60 SO6871
Mamhilad *Gwent* 34 SO3003
Manaccan *Cnwll* 3 SW7624
Manafon *Powys* 58 SJ1102
Manaton *Devon* 8 SX7581
Manby *Lincs* 77 TF3986
Mancetter *Warwks* 61 SP3296
Manchester *Gt Man* 79 SJ8497
Mancot *Clwyd* 71 SJ3167
Mandally *Highld* 131 NH2900
Manea *Cambs* 53 TL4789
Maney *W Mids* 61 SP1195
Manfield *N York* 89 NZ2113
Mangerton *Dorset* 10 SY4995
Mangotsfield *Avon* 35 ST6676
Mangrove Green *Herts* 38 TL1224
Manhay *Cnwll* 2 SW6930
Manish *W Isls* 154 NG1089
Mankinholes *W York* 82 SD9523
Manley *Ches* 71 SJ5071
Manmoel *Gwent* 33 SO1803
Mannel *Strath* 120 NL9840
Manning's Heath *W Susx* 15 TQ2028
Manningford Bohune *Wilts* 23 SU1357
Manningford Bruce *Wilts* 23 SU1358
Manningham *W York* 82 SE1435
Mannington *Dorset* 12 SU0605
Manningtree *Essex* 41 TM1031
Mannofield *Gramp* 135 NJ9104
Manor Park *Gt Lon* 27 TQ4285
Manorbier *Dyfed* 30 SS0697
Manorbier Newton *Dyfed* 30 SN0400
Manordeilo *Dyfed* 44 SN6726
Manorhill *Border* 110 NT6632
Manorowen *Dyfed* 30 SM9336
Mansell Gamage *H & W* 46 SO3944
Mansell Lacy *H & W* 46 SO4245
Mansergh *Cumb* 87 SD6082
Mansfield *Notts* 75 SK5361
Mansfield *Strath* 107 NS6214
Mansfield Woodhouse *Notts* 75 SK5363
Mansriggs *Cumb* 86 SD2980
Manston *Dorset* 11 ST8115
Manston *Kent* 29 TR3466
Manston *W York* 83 SE3634
Manswood *Dorset* 11 ST9708
Manthorpe *Lincs* 63 SK9137
Manthorpe *Lincs* 64 TF0715
Manton *Humb* 84 SE9302
Manton *Leics* 63 SK8704
Manton *Notts* 75 SK6078
Manton *Wilts* 23 SU1768
Manuden *Essex* 39 TL4926
Manwood Green *Essex* 39 TL5412
Maolachy *Strath* 122 NM8913
Maperton *Somset* 22 ST6726
Maple Cross *Herts* 26 TQ0393
Maplebeck *Notts* 75 SK7060
Mapledurham *Oxon* 37 SU6776
Mapledurwell *Hants* 24 SU6851
Maplehurst *W Susx* 15 TQ1824
Maplescombe *Kent* 27 TQ5664
Mapleton *Derbys* 73 SK1647
Mapleton *Kent* 16 TQ4649
Mapperley *Derbys* 62 SK4342
Mapperley Park *Notts* 62 SK5842
Mapperton *Dorset* 10 SY5099
Mappleborough Green *Warwks* 48 SP0866
Mappleton *Humb* 85 TA2243
Mappowder *Dorset* 11 ST7306
Marazanvose *Cnwll* 3 SW7950
Marazion *Cnwll* 2 SW5130
Marbury *Ches* 71 SJ5645
March *Cambs* 65 TL4196
March *Strath* 108 NS9914
Marcham *Oxon* 37 SU4596
Marchamley *Shrops* 59 SJ5929
Marchamley Wood *Shrops* 59 SJ5831
Marchington *Staffs* 73 SK1330
Marchington Woodlands *Staffs* 73 SK1128
Marchros *Gwynd* 56 SH3125
Marchwiel *Clwyd* 71 SJ3547
Marchwood *Hants* 12 SU3810
Marcross *S Glam* 20 SS9269
Marden *H & W* 46 SO5146
Marden *Kent* 28 TQ7444
Marden *Wilts* 23 SU0857
Marden Ash *Essex* 27 TL5502
Marden Beech *Kent* 28 TQ7442
Marden Thorn *Kent* 28 TQ7642
Mardens Hill *E Susx* 16 TQ5032
Mardleybury *Herts* 39 TL2618
Mardy *Gwent* 34 SO3015
Mare Green *Somset* 21 ST3326
Marefield *Leics* 63 SK7407
Mareham le Fen *Lincs* 77 TF2761
Mareham on the Hill *Lincs* 77 TF2867
Marehay *Derbys* 62 SK3947
Marehill *W Susx* 14 TQ0618
Maresfield *E Susx* 16 TQ4624
Marfleet *Humb* 85 TA1429
Marford *Clwyd* 71 SJ3556
Margam *W Glam* 32 SS7887
Margaret Marsh *Dorset* 22 ST8218
Margaretting *Essex* 40 TL6701
Margaretting Tye *Essex* 40 TL6800
Margate *Kent* 29 TR3571
Margnaheglish *Strath* 105 NS0332
Margrie *D & G* 99 NX5950
Margrove Park *Cleve* 97 NZ6515
Marham *Norfk* 65 TF7009
Marhamchurch *Cnwll* 18 SS2203
Marholm *Cambs* 64 TF1401
Marian-glas *Gwynd* 68 SH5084
Mariansleigh *Devon* 19 SS7422
Marine Town *Kent* 28 TQ9274
Marionburgh *Gramp* 135 NJ7006
Marishader *Highld* 136 NG4963
Maristow *Devon* 6 SX4764
Marjoriebanks *D & G* 100 NY0883
Mark *D & G* 98 NX1157
Mark *Somset* 21 ST3847
Mark Causeway *Somset* 21 ST3547
Mark Cross *E Susx* 16 TQ5010
Mark Cross *E Susx* 16 TQ5831
Mark's Corner *IOW* 13 SZ4692
Markbeech *Kent* 16 TQ4742
Markby *Lincs* 77 TF4878
Markeaton *Derbys* 62 SK3237
Market Bosworth *Leics* 62 SK4002

Market Deeping Midney

Market Deeping *Lincs* 64 TF1310
Market Drayton *Shrops* 72 SJ6734
Market Harborough *Leics* 50 SP7387
Market Lavington *Wilts* 22 SU0154
Market Overton *Leics* 63 SK8816
Market Rasen *Lincs* 76 TF1089
Market Stainton *Lincs* 76 TF2279
Market Street *Norfk* 67 TG2921
Market Weighton *Humb* 84 SE8741
Market Weston *Suffk* 54 TL9877
Markfield *Leics* 62 SK4809
Markham *Gwent* 33 SO1601
Markham Moor *Notts* 75 SK7173
Markinch *Fife* 126 NO2901
Markington *N York* 89 SE2865
Marks Tey *Essex* 40 TL9023
Marksbury *Avon* 22 ST6662
Markshall *Essex* 40 TL8425
Markwell *Cnwll* 5 SX3758
Markyate *Herts* 38 TL0616
Marl Bank *H & W* 47 SO7840
Marlborough *Wilts* 23 SU1868
Marlbrook *H & W* 36 SO5154
Marlbrook *H & W* 60 SO9774
Marlcliff *Warwks* 48 SP0950
Marldon *Devon* 7 SX8663
Marle Green *E Susx* 16 TQ5816
Marlesford *Suffk* 55 TM3258
Marley *Kent* 29 TR1850
Marley *Kent* 29 TR3353
Marley Green *Ches* 71 SJ5845
Marley Hill *T & W* 96 NZ2058
Marlingford *Norfk* 66 TG1309
Marloes *Dyfed* 30 SM7908
Marlow *Bucks* 26 SU8486
Marlow *H & W* 46 SO4076
Marlpit Hill *Kent* 16 TQ4347
Marlpits *E Susx* 16 TQ4528
Marlpits *E Susx* 16 TQ7013
Marlpool *Derbys* 62 SK4345
Marnhull *Dorset* 22 ST7818
Marple *Gt Man* 79 SJ9588
Marple Bridge *Gt Man* 79 SJ9688
Marr *S York* 83 SE5105
Marrick *N York* 88 SE0798
Marros *Dyfed* 31 SN2008
Marsden *T & W* 103 NZ3964
Marsden *W York* 82 SE0411
Marsden Height *Lancs* 81 SD8636
Marsett *N York* 88 SD9085
Marsh *Bucks* 38 SP8109
Marsh *Somset* 10 ST2510
Marsh *W York* 82 SE0235
Marsh Baldon *Oxon* 37 SU5699
Marsh Gibbon *Bucks* 37 SP6422
Marsh Green *Devon* 9 SY0493
Marsh Green *Kent* 16 TQ4344
Marsh Green *Shrops* 59 SJ6014
Marsh Green *Staffs* 72 SJ8858
Marsh Lane *Derbys* 74 SK4079
Marsh Lane *Gloucs* 34 SO5807
Marsh Street *Somset* 20 SS9944
Marsh The *Powys* 59 SO3197
Marshall's Heath *Herts* 39 TL1614
Marshalswick *Herts* 39 TL1608
Marsham *Norfk* 67 TG1923
Marshborough *Kent* 29 TR3057
Marshbrook *Shrops* 59 SO4489
Marshchapel *Lincs* 77 TF3599
Marshfield *Avon* 35 ST7873
Marshfield *Gwent* 34 ST2582
Marshgate *Cnwll* 4 SX1592
Marshland Green *Gt Man* 79 SJ6899
Marshland St James *Norfk* 65 TF5209
Marshside *Mersyd* 80 SD3619
Marshwood *Dorset* 10 SY3899
Marske *N York* 89 NZ1000
Marske-by-the-Sea *Cleve* 97 NZ6322
Marston *Ches* 79 SJ6775
Marston *H & W* 46 SO3557
Marston *Lincs* 63 SK8943
Marston *Oxon* 37 SP5208
Marston *Staffs* 60 SJ8313
Marston *Staffs* 72 SJ9227
Marston *Warwks* 61 SP2094
Marston *Wilts* 22 ST9656
Marston Green *W Mids* 61 SP1785
Marston Jabbet *Warwks* 61 SP3788
Marston Magna *Somset* 21 ST5922
Marston Meysey *Wilts* 36 SU1297
Marston Montgomery *Derbys* 73 SK1337
Marston Moretaine *Beds* 38 SP9941
Marston on Dove *Derbys* 73 SK2329
Marston St. Lawrence *Nhants* 49 SP5341
Marston Stannet *H & W* 46 SO5655
Marston Trussell *Nhants* 50 SP6985
Marstow *H & W* 34 SO5518
Marsworth *Bucks* 38 SP9114
Marten *Wilts* 23 SU2860
Marthall *Ches* 79 SJ7975
Martham *Norfk* 67 TG4518
Martin *Hants* 12 SU0619
Martin *Kent* 29 TR3447
Martin *Lincs* 76 TF1259
Martin *Lincs* 77 TF2466
Martin Dales *Lincs* 76 TF1762
Martin Drove End *Hants* 12 SU0520
Martin Hussingtree *H & W* 47 SO8860
Martindale *Cumb* 93 NY4319
Martinhoe *Devon* 19 SS6648
Martinscroft *Ches* 79 SJ6589
Martinstown *Dorset* 11 SY6489
Martlesham *Suffk* 55 TM2547
Martletwy *Dyfed* 30 SN0310
Martley *H & W* 47 SO7560
Martock *Somset* 21 ST4619
Marton *Ches* 71 SJ6267
Marton *Ches* 79 SJ8568
Marton *Cleve* 97 NZ5115
Marton *Humb* 85 TA1739
Marton *Lincs* 76 SK8381
Marton *N York* 89 SE4162
Marton *N York* 90 SE7383
Marton *Shrops* 58 SJ2802
Marton *Warwks* 48 SP4068
Marton-le-Moor *N York* 89 SE3770
Martyr Worthy *Hants* 24 SU5132
Martyr's Green *Surrey* 26 TQ0857
Marwick *Ork* 155 HY2324
Marwood *Devon* 19 SS5437
Mary Tavy *Devon* 5 SX5079
Marybank *Highld* 139 NH4853
Maryburgh *Highld* 139 NH5456
Maryculter *Gramp* 135 NO8599
Maryhill *Gramp* 143 NJ8245
Maryhill *Strath* 115 NS5669
Marykirk *Gramp* 135 NO6865
Maryland *Gwent* 34 SO5105
Marylebone *Gt Man* 78 SD5807
Marypark *Gramp* 141 NJ1938
Maryport *Cumb* 92 NY0336
Maryport *D & G* 98 NX1434
Marystow *Devon* 5 SX4382
Maryton *Tays* 127 NO6856
Marywell *Gramp* 135 NO9399
Marywell *Tays* 134 NO5895
Marywell *Tays* 127 NO6544
Masham *N York* 89 SE2280
Mashbury *Essex* 40 TL6511
Mason *T & W* 103 NZ2073
Masongill *N York* 87 SD6675
Mastin Moor *Derbys* 75 SK4575
Matching *Essex* 39 TL5212
Matching Green *Essex* 39 TL5311
Matching Tye *Essex* 39 TL5111
Matfen *Nthumb* 103 NZ0371
Matfield *Kent* 28 TQ6541
Mathern *Gwent* 34 ST5290
Mathon *H & W* 47 SO7346
Mathry *Dyfed* 30 SM8832
Matlaske *Norfk* 66 TG1534
Matlock *Derbys* 74 SK3059
Matlock Bank *Derbys* 74 SK3060
Matlock Bath *Derbys* 74 SK2958
Matlock Dale *Derbys* 74 SK2959
Matson *Gloucs* 35 SO8515
Matterdale End *Cumb* 93 NY3923
Mattersey *Notts* 75 SK6889
Mattersey Thorpe *Notts* 75 SK6889
Mattingley *Hants* 24 SU7357
Mattishall *Norfk* 66 TG0511
Mattishall Burgh *Norfk* 66 TG0512
Mauchline *Strath* 107 NS4927
Maud *Gramp* 143 NJ9148
Maufant *Jersey* 152 JS1811
Maugersbury *Gloucs* 48 SP2025
Maughold *IOM* 153 SC4991
Mauld *Highld* 139 NH4038
Maulden *Beds* 38 TL0538
Maulds Meaburn *Cumb* 94 NY6216
Maunby *N York* 89 SE3586
Maund Bryan *H & W* 46 SO5650
Maundown *Somset* 20 ST0628
Mautby *Norfk* 67 TG4812
Mavesyn Ridware *Staffs* 73 SK0816
Mavis Enderby *Lincs* 77 TF3666
Maw Green *Ches* 72 SJ7057
Maw Green *W Mids* 60 SP0196
Mawbray *Cumb* 92 NY0846
Mawdesley *Lancs* 80 SD4914
Mawdlam *M Glam* 32 SS8081
Mawgan *Cnwll* 2 SW7025
Mawgan Cross *Cnwll* 2 SW7024
Mawgan Porth *Cnwll* 4 SW8567
Mawla *Cnwll* 2 SW7045
Mawnan *Cnwll* 3 SW7827
Mawnan Smith *Cnwll* 3 SW7728
Mawthorpe *Lincs* 77 TF4672
Maxey *Cambs* 64 TF1208
Maxstoke *Warwks* 61 SP2386
Maxted Street *Kent* 29 TR1244
Maxton *Border* 110 NT6130
Maxton *Kent* 29 TR3041
Maxwell Town *D & G* 100 NX9676
Maxwellheugh *Border* 110 NT7333
Maxworthy *Cnwll* 5 SX2593
May Bank *Staffs* 72 SJ8547
May's Green *Oxon* 37 SU7480
May's Green *Surrey* 26 TQ0957
Mayals *W Glam* 32 SS6089
Maybole *Strath* 106 NS2909
Maybury *Surrey* 26 TQ0159
Mayes Green *Surrey* 14 TQ1239
Mayfield *E Susx* 16 TQ5826
Mayfield *Loth* 118 NT3565
Mayfield *Staffs* 73 SK1545
Mayford *Surrey* 25 SU9956
Mayland *Essex* 40 TL9201
Maynard's Green *E Susx* 16 TQ5818
Maypole *Gwent* 34 SO4716
Maypole *Kent* 29 TR2064
Maypole *W Mids* 61 SP0778
Maypole Green *Norfk* 67 TM4195
Maypole Green *Suffk* 54 TL9159
Maypole Green *Suffk* 55 TM2767
Mead *Devon* 18 SS2217
Meadgate *Avon* 22 ST6758
Meadle *Bucks* 38 SP8005
Meadowfield *Dur* 96 NZ2439
Meadowhall *S York* 74 SK3991
Meadowtown *Shrops* 59 SJ3001
Meadwell *Devon* 5 SX4081
Meal Bank *Cumb* 87 SD5495
Mealrigg *Cumb* 92 NY1345
Mealsgate *Cumb* 93 NY2042
Meamskirk *Strath* 115 NS5455
Meanwood *W York* 82 SE2837
Mearbeck *N York* 88 SD8160
Meare *Somset* 21 ST4541
Meare Green *Somset* 21 ST2922
Mears Ashby *Nhants* 51 SP8366
Measham *Leics* 62 SK3311
Meathop *Cumb* 87 SD4380
Meaux *Humb* 85 TA0839
Meavy *Devon* 6 SX5467
Medbourne *Leics* 51 SP8093
Meddon *Devon* 18 SS2717
Medlam *Lincs* 77 TF3156
Medlar *Lancs* 80 SD4135
Medmenham *Berks* 37 SU8084
Medomsley *Dur* 95 NZ1154
Medstead *Hants* 24 SU6537
Meer Common *H & W* 46 SO3652
Meer End *W Mids* 61 SP2474
Meerbrook *Staffs* 72 SJ9860
Meesden *Herts* 39 TL4332
Meeson *Shrops* 72 SJ6421
Meeth *Devon* 19 SS5408
Meeting Green *Suffk* 53 TL7455
Meeting House Hill *Norfk* 67 TG3028
Meidrim *Dyfed* 31 SN2920
Meifod *Powys* 58 SJ1513
Meigle *Tays* 126 NO2844
Meikle Carco *D & G* 107 NS7813
Meikle Earnock *Strath* 116 NS7053
Meikle Kilmory *Strath* 114 NS0560
Meikle Obney *Tays* 125 NO0337
Meikle Wartle *Gramp* 142 NJ7230
Meikleour *Tays* 126 NO1539
Meinciau *Dyfed* 32 SN4610
Meir *Staffs* 72 SJ9342
Meir Heath *Staffs* 72 SJ9240
Melbourn *Cambs* 39 TL3844
Melbourne *Derbys* 62 SK3825
Melbourne *Humb* 84 SE7543
Melbury *Devon* 18 SS3719
Melbury Abbas *Dorset* 22 ST8820
Melbury Bubb *Dorset* 10 ST5906
Melbury Osmond *Dorset* 10 ST5707
Melbury Sampford *Dorset* 10 ST5705
Melchbourne *Beds* 51 TL0265
Melcombe Bingham *Dorset* 11 ST7602
Meldon *Devon* 8 SX5692
Meldon *Nthumb* 103 NZ1183
Meldreth *Cambs* 52 TL3746
Meldrum *Cent* 116 NS7299
Meledor *Cnwll* 3 SW9254
Melfort *Strath* 122 NM8313
Melgund Castle *Tays* 127 NO5455
Meliden *Clwyd* 70 SJ0680
Melin Court *W Glam* 33 SN8201
Melin-byrhedyn *Powys* 57 SN8198
Melin-y-coed *Gwynd* 69 SH8160
Melin-y-ddol *Powys* 58 SJ0807
Melin-y-wig *Clwyd* 70 SJ0448
Melinau *Dyfed* 31 SN1613
Melkinthorpe *Cumb* 94 NY5525
Melkridge *Nthumb* 102 NY7364
Melksham *Wilts* 22 ST9063
Mell Green *Berks* 37 SU4577
Mellangoose *Cnwll* 2 SW6826
Melldalloch *Strath* 114 NR9374
Mellguards *Cumb* 93 NY4445
Melling *Lancs* 87 SD5970
Melling *Mersyd* 78 SD3800
Melling Mount *Mersyd* 78 SD4001
Mellis *Suffk* 54 TM0974
Mellon Charles *Highld* 144 NG8491
Mellon Udrigle *Highld* 144 NG8996
Mellor *Gt Man* 79 SJ9888
Mellor *Lancs* 81 SD6530
Mellor Brook *Lancs* 81 SD6431
Mells *Somset* 22 ST7248
Mells *Suffk* 55 TM4076
Melmerby *Cumb* 94 NY6137
Melmerby *N York* 88 SE0785
Melmerby *N York* 89 SE3376
Melness *Highld* 149 NC5861
Melon Green *Suffk* 54 TL8456
Melplash *Dorset* 10 SY4898
Melrose *Border* 109 NT5434
Melsetter *Ork* 155 ND2689
Melsonby *N York* 89 NZ1908
Meltham *S York* 82 SE1010
Meltham Mills *W York* 82 SE1110
Melton *Humb* 84 SE9726
Melton *Suffk* 55 TM2850
Melton Constable *Norfk* 66 TG0432
Melton Mowbray *Leics* 63 SK7518
Melton Ross *Humb* 84 TA0610
Meltonby *Humb* 84 SE7952
Melvaig *Highld* 144 NG7486
Melverley *Shrops* 59 SJ3316
Melverley Green *Shrops* 59 SJ3317
Melvich *Highld* 150 NC8764
Membury *Devon* 10 ST2803
Memsie *Gramp* 143 NJ9762
Menabilly *Cnwll* 3 SX0951
Menagissey *Cnwll* 2 SW7146
Menai Bridge *Gwynd* 69 SH5571
Mendham *Suffk* 55 TM2782
Mendlesham *Suffk* 54 TM1065
Mendlesham Green *Suffk* 54 TM0963
Menheniot *Cnwll* 5 SX2863
Menithwood *H & W* 47 SO7069
Mennock *D & G* 108 NS8107
Menston *W York* 82 SE1643
Menstrie *Cent* 116 NS8597
Menthorpe *N York* 84 SE7034
Mentmore *Bucks* 38 SP9019
Meoble *Highld* 129 NM7987
Meole Brace *Shrops* 59 SJ4810
Meonstoke *Hants* 13 SU6119
Meopham *Kent* 27 TQ6466
Meopham Green *Kent* 27 TQ6465
Meopham Station *Kent* 27 TQ6467
Mepal *Cambs* 53 TL4481
Meppershall *Beds* 38 TL1336
Mere *Ches* 79 SJ7281
Mere *Wilts* 22 ST8132
Mere Brow *Lancs* 80 SD4218
Mere Green *H & W* 47 SO9562
Mere Green *W Mids* 61 SP1198
Mere Heath *Ches* 79 SJ6670
Mereclough *Lancs* 81 SD8730
Meresborough *Kent* 28 TQ8264
Mereworth *Kent* 28 TQ6553
Meriden *W Mids* 61 SP2482
Merkadale *Highld* 136 NG3931
Merlin's Bridge *Dyfed* 30 SM9414
Merrifield *Devon* 7 SX8147
Merrington *Shrops* 59 SJ4720
Merrion *Dyfed* 30 SR9397
Merriott *Somset* 10 ST4412
Merrivale *Devon* 6 SX5475
Merrow *Surrey* 26 TQ0250
Merry Field Hill *Dorset* 12 SU0201
Merry Hill *Herts* 26 TQ1394
Merry Hill *W Mids* 60 SO9286
Merry Lees *Leics* 62 SK4705
Merryhill *W Mids* 60 SO8897
Merrymeet *Cnwll* 5 SX2766
Mersham *Kent* 28 TR0540
Merstham *Surrey* 27 TQ2853
Merston *W Susx* 14 SU8902
Merstone *IOW* 13 SZ5285
Merther *Cnwll* 3 SW8644
Merthyr *Dyfed* 31 SN3520
Merthyr Cynog *Powys* 45 SN9837
Merthyr Dyfan *S Glam* 20 ST1168
Merthyr Mawr *M Glam* 33 SS8877
Merthyr Tydfil *M Glam* 33 SO0406
Merthyr Vale *M Glam* 33 ST0799
Merton *Devon* 19 SS5212
Merton *Gt Lon* 27 TQ2570
Merton *Norfk* 66 TL9098
Merton *Oxon* 37 SP5717
Meshaw *Devon* 19 SS7619
Messing *Essex* 40 TL8918
Messingham *Humb* 84 SE8904
Metfield *Suffk* 55 TM2980
Metherell *Cnwll* 5 SX4069
Metherin *Cnwll* 4 SX1174
Metheringham *Lincs* 76 TF0661
Methil *Fife* 118 NT3799
Methleigh *Cnwll* 2 SW6226
Methley *W York* 83 SE3926
Methley Junction *W York* 83 SE3925
Methlick *Gramp* 143 NJ8537
Methven *Tays* 125 NO0225
Methwold *Norfk* 65 TL7394
Methwold Hythe *Norfk* 65 TL7194
Mettingham *Suffk* 55 TM3689
Metton *Norfk* 67 TG2037
Mevagissey *Cnwll* 3 SX0144
Mexborough *S York* 75 SE4700
Mey *Highld* 151 ND2872
Meyllteyrn *Gwynd* 56 SH2332
Meysey Hampton *Gloucs* 36 SP1100
Miavaig *W Isls* 154 NB0834
Michaelchurch *H & W* 46 SO5225
Michaelchurch Escley *H & W* 46 SO3134
Michaelchurch-on-Arrow *Powys* 46 SO2450
Michaelston-le-Pit *S Glam* 33 ST1572
Michaelston-y-Fedw *Gwent* 34 ST2484
Michaelstow *Cnwll* 4 SX0778
Michelcombe *Devon* 7 SX6969
Micheldever *Hants* 24 SU5139
Micheldever Station *Hants* 24 SU5143
Michelmersh *Hants* 23 SU3426
Mickfield *Suffk* 54 TM1361
Mickle Trafford *Ches* 71 SJ4469
Micklebring *S York* 75 SK5194
Mickleby *N York* 90 NZ8012
Micklefield *W York* 83 SE4432
Micklefield Green *Herts* 26 TQ0498
Mickleham *Surrey* 26 TQ1653
Mickleover *Derbys* 73 SK3033
Micklethwaite *Cumb* 93 NY2850
Micklethwaite *W York* 82 SE1041
Mickleton *Dur* 95 NY9623
Mickleton *Gloucs* 48 SP1643
Mickletown *W York* 83 SE4027
Mickley *Derbys* 74 SK3279
Mickley *N York* 89 SE2576
Mickley Green *Suffk* 54 TL8457
Mickley Square *Nthumb* 103 NZ0762
Mid Ardlaw *Gramp* 143 NJ9463
Mid Beltie *Gramp* 134 NJ6200
Mid Bockhampton *Hants* 12 SZ1796
Mid Calder *Loth* 117 NT0767
Mid Clyth *Highld* 151 ND2937
Mid Lavant *W Susx* 14 SU8508
Mid Mains *Highld* 139 NH4239
Mid Sannox *Strath* 105 NS0145
Mid Thorpe *Lincs* 77 TF2672
Mid Yell *Shet* 155 HU5190
Midbea *Ork* 155 HY4444
Middle Assendon *Oxon* 37 SU7385
Middle Aston *Oxon* 49 SP4726
Middle Barton *Oxon* 49 SP4325
Middle Chinnock *Somset* 10 ST4713
Middle Claydon *Bucks* 49 SP7225
Middle Duntisbourne *Gloucs* 35 SO9806
Middle Handley *Derbys* 74 SK4077
Middle Harling *Norfk* 54 TL9885
Middle Kames *Strath* 114 NR9189
Middle Littleton *H & W* 48 SP0847
Middle Madeley *Staffs* 72 SJ7745
Middle Maes-coed *H & W* 46 SO3333
Middle Mayfield *Staffs* 73 SK1444
Middle Mill *Dyfed* 30 SM8026
Middle Quarter *Kent* 28 TQ8938
Middle Rasen *Lincs* 76 TF0889
Middle Rocombe *Devon* 7 SX9069
Middle Salter *Lancs* 87 SD6062
Middle Stoford *Somset* 20 ST1821
Middle Stoke *Kent* 28 TQ8275
Middle Stoughton *Somset* 21 ST4249
Middle Street *Essex* 39 TL4005
Middle Street *Gloucs* 35 SO7704
Middle Taphouse *Cnwll* 4 SX1763
Middle Town *IOS* 2 SV8808
Middle Tysoe *Warwks* 48 SP3444
Middle Wallop *Hants* 23 SU2937
Middle Winterslow *Wilts* 23 SU2333
Middle Woodford *Wilts* 23 SU1136
Middle Yard *Gloucs* 35 SO8203
Middlebie *D & G* 101 NY2176
Middlebridge *Tays* 132 NN8866
Middlecliffe *S York* 83 SE4204
Middlecott *Devon* 8 SX7186
Middlegill *D & G* 108 NT0406
Middleham *N York* 89 SE1287
Middlehill *Cnwll* 5 SX2869
Middlehill *Wilts* 22 ST8168
Middlehope *Shrops* 59 SO4988
Middlemarsh *Dorset* 11 ST6707
Middlemore *Devon* 6 SX4973
Middlesbrough *Cleve* 97 NZ4919
Middlesceugh *Cumb* 93 NY4041
Middleshaw *Cumb* 87 SD5588
Middlesmoor *N York* 89 SE0973
Middlestone *Dur* 96 NZ2531
Middlestone Moor *Dur* 96 NZ2432
Middlestown *W York* 82 SE2617
Middlethird *Border* 110 NT6843
Middleton *Cleve* 97 NZ5233
Middleton *Cumb* 87 SD6285
Middleton *Derbys* 74 SK1963
Middleton *Derbys* 73 SK2755
Middleton *Essex* 54 TL8639
Middleton *Gt Man* 79 SD8705
Middleton *H & W* 46 SO5469
Middleton *Hants* 24 SU4244
Middleton *Lancs* 87 SD4258
Middleton *Loth* 118 NT3758
Middleton *N York* 90 SE7885
Middleton *Nhants* 51 SP8489
Middleton *Norfk* 65 TF6616
Middleton *Nthumb* 111 NU1035
Middleton *Nthumb* 103 NZ0584
Middleton *Shrops* 59 SJ3129
Middleton *Shrops* 46 SO5477
Middleton *Strath* 120 NL9443
Middleton *Strath* 115 NS3952
Middleton *Suffk* 55 TM4267
Middleton *Tays* 126 NO1206
Middleton *W Glam* 31 SS4287
Middleton *W York* 82 SE1249
Middleton *W York* 82 SE3028
Middleton *Warwks* 61 SP1798
Middleton Cheney *Nhants* 49 SP4941
Middleton Green *Staffs* 73 SJ9935
Middleton Hall *Nthumb* 111 NT9825
Middleton Moor *Suffk* 55 TM4167
Middleton One Row *Dur* 89 NZ3512
Middleton on the Hill *H & W* 46 SO5364
Middleton Priors *Shrops* 59 SO6290
Middleton Quernhow *N York* 89 SE3378
Middleton Scriven *Shrops* 60 SO6887
Middleton St. George *Dur* 89 NZ3412
Middleton Stoney *Oxon* 49 SP5323
Middleton Tyas *N York* 89 NZ2205
Middleton-in-Teesdale *Dur* 95 NY9425
Middleton-on-Leven *N York* 89 NZ4609
Middleton-on-Sea *W Susx* 14 SU9600
Middleton-on-the-Wolds *Humb* 84 SE9449
Middletown *Avon* 34 ST4571
Middletown *Cumb* 86 NX9908
Middletown *Powys* 59 SJ3012
Middlewich *Ches* 72 SJ7066
Middlewood *Cnwll* 5 SX2775
Middlewood *H & W* 46 SO2844
Middlewood Green *Suffk* 54 TM0961
Middleyard *Strath* 107 NS5132
Middlezoy *Somset* 21 ST3733
Middridge *Dur* 96 NZ2426
Midford *Avon* 22 ST7660
Midge Hall *Lancs* 80 SD5122
Midgeholme *Cumb* 94 NY6359
Midgham *Berks* 24 SU5567
Midgley *W York* 82 SE0226
Midgley *W York* 82 SE2714
Midhopestones *S York* 74 SK2399
Midhurst *W Susx* 14 SU8821
Midlem *Border* 109 NT5227
Midney *Somset* 21 ST4927

N

Newbiggin North Somercotes

Newbiggin *Dur* 96 NZ1447
Newbiggin *N York* 88 SD9591
Newbiggin *N York* 88 SE0086
Newbiggin-by-the-Sea *Nthumb* 103 NZ3087
Newbiggin-on-Lune *Cumb* 87 NY7005
Newbigging *Strath* 117 NT0145
Newbigging *Tays* 126 NO2841
Newbigging *Tays* 127 NO4237
Newbold *Derbys* 74 SK3672
Newbold *Leics* 62 SK4019
Newbold on Avon *Warwks* 50 SP4877
Newbold on Stour *Warwks* 48 SP2446
Newbold Pacey *Warwks* 48 SP2957
Newbold Revel *Warwks* 50 SP4580
Newbold Verdon *Leics* 62 SK4403
Newborough *Cambs* 64 TF2005
Newborough *Gwynd* 68 SH4265
Newborough *Staffs* 73 SK1325
Newbottle *Nhants* 49 SP5236
Newbottle *T & W* 96 NZ3351
Newbourne *Suffk* 55 TM2743
Newbridge *Clwyd* 70 SJ2841
Newbridge *Cnwll* 2 SW4231
Newbridge *Cnwll* 3 SW7944
Newbridge *D & G* 100 NX9479
Newbridge *Dyfed* 30 SM9431
Newbridge *Dyfed* 44 SN5059
Newbridge *Gwent* 33 ST2097
Newbridge *Hants* 12 SU2915
Newbridge *IOW* 13 SZ4187
Newbridge *Loth* 117 NT1272
Newbridge *Oxon* 36 SP4001
Newbridge Green *H & W* 47 SO8439
Newbridge on Wye *Powys* 45 SO0158
Newbridge-on-Usk *Gwent* 34 ST3894
Newbrough *Nthumb* 102 NY8767
Newbuildings *Devon* 8 SS7903
Newburgh *Fife* 126 NO2318
Newburgh *Gramp* 143 NJ9659
Newburgh *Gramp* 143 NJ9925
Newburgh *Lancs* 78 SD4810
Newburgh Priory *N York* 90 SE5476
Newburn *T & W* 103 NZ1665
Newbury *Berks* 24 SU4766
Newbury *Somset* 22 ST6949
Newbury *Wilts* 22 ST8241
Newby *Cumb* 94 NY5921
Newby *Lancs* 81 SD8146
Newby *N York* 90 NZ5012
Newby *N York* 88 SD7269
Newby *N York* 91 TA0190
Newby Bridge *Cumb* 87 SD3686
Newby Cross *Cumb* 93 NY3653
Newby East *Cumb* 93 NY4758
Newby Head *Cumb* 94 NY5821
Newby West *Cumb* 93 NY3753
Newby Wiske *N York* 89 SE3687
Newcastle *Gwent* 34 SO4417
Newcastle *Shrops* 58 SO2582
Newcastle Emlyn *Dyfed* 31 SN3040
Newcastle upon Tyne *T & W* 103 NZ2464
Newcastle-under-Lyme *Staffs* 72 SJ8445
Newcastleton *D & G* 101 NY4887
Newchapel *Dyfed* 31 SN2239
Newchapel *Staffs* 72 SJ8654
Newchapel *Surrey* 15 TQ3641
Newchurch *Gwent* 33 SO1710
Newchurch *Gwent* 34 ST4597
Newchurch *H & W* 46 SO3550
Newchurch *IOW* 13 SZ5685
Newchurch *Kent* 17 TR0531
Newchurch *Powys* 45 SO2150
Newchurch *Staffs* 73 SK1423
Newchurch in Pendle *Lancs* 81 SD8239
Newcraighall *Loth* 118 NT3272
Newdigate *Surrey* 15 TQ1942
Newell Green *Berks* 25 SU8770
Newenden *Kent* 17 TQ8327
Newent *Gloucs* 47 SO7225
Newfield *Dur* 96 NZ2033
Newfield *Dur* 96 NZ2452
Newfield *Highld* 147 NH7877
Newfound *Hants* 24 SU5851
Newgale *Dyfed* 30 SM8522
Newgate *Cambs* 52 TL3990
Newgate *Norfk* 66 TG0443
Newgate Street *Herts* 39 TL3005
Newhall *Ches* 71 SJ6145
Newhall *Derbys* 73 SK2820
Newham *Nthumb* 111 NU1728
Newhaven *Derbys* 74 SK1660
Newhaven *E Susx* 16 TQ4401
Newhey *Gt Man* 82 SD9411
Newholm *N York* 90 NZ8610
Newhouse *Strath* 116 NS7961
Newick *E Susx* 15 TQ4121
Newingreen *Kent* 29 TR1236
Newington *Kent* 28 TQ8564
Newington *Kent* 29 TR1837
Newington *Oxon* 37 SU6096
Newington *Shrops* 59 SO4283
Newington Bagpath *Gloucs* 35 ST8194
Newland *Cumb* 86 SD3079
Newland *Gloucs* 34 SO5509
Newland *H & W* 47 SO7948
Newland *Humb* 84 SE8029
Newland *Humb* 84 TA0631
Newland *N York* 83 SE6824
Newland *Oxon* 36 SP3609
Newland *Somset* 19 SS8238
Newlandrig *Loth* 118 NT3762
Newlands *Border* 101 NY5094
Newlands *Cumb* 93 NY3439
Newlands *Nthumb* 95 NZ0855
Newlands of Dundurcas *Gramp* 141 NJ2951
Newlyn *Cnwll* 2 SW4628
Newmachar *Gramp* 143 NJ8919
Newmains *Strath* 116 NS8256
Newman's End *Essex* 39 TL5112
Newman's Green *Suffk* 54 TL8843
Newmarket *Cumb* 93 NY3438
Newmarket *Suffk* 53 TL6463
Newmill *Border* 109 NT4510
Newmill *Gramp* 142 NJ4352
Newmill of Inshewan *Tays* 134 NO4260
Newmillerdam *W York* 83 SE3215
Newmills *Fife* 117 NT0186
Newmills *Gwent* 34 SO5107
Newmills *Loth* 117 NT1667
Newmiln *Tays* 126 NO1230
Newmilns *Strath* 107 NS5337
Newnes *Shrops* 59 SJ3834
Newney Green *Essex* 40 TL6507
Newnham *Gloucs* 35 SO6911
Newnham *H & W* 47 SO6469
Newnham *Hants* 24 SU7053
Newnham *Herts* 39 TL2437
Newnham *Kent* 28 TQ9557
Newnham *Nhants* 49 SP5859
Newnham Paddox *Warwks* 50 SP4983
Newport *Devon* 19 SS5632
Newport *Dorset* 11 SY8895
Newport *Dyfed* 30 SN0539
Newport *Essex* 39 TL5234
Newport *Gloucs* 35 ST7097
Newport *Gwent* 34 ST3188
Newport *Highld* 151 ND1324
Newport *Humb* 84 SE8530
Newport *IOW* 13 SZ5089
Newport *Norfk* 67 TG5017
Newport *Shrops* 72 SJ7419
Newport Pagnell *Bucks* 38 SP8743
Newport-on-Tay *Fife* 127 NO4228
Newpound Common *W Susx* 14 TQ0627
Newquay *Cnwll* 4 SW8161
Newsam Green *W York* 83 SE3630
Newsbank *Ches* 72 SJ8366
Newseat *Gramp* 142 NJ7032
Newsham *Lancs* 80 SD5136
Newsham *N York* 89 NZ1010
Newsham *N York* 89 SE3784
Newsham *Nthumb* 103 NZ3080
Newsholme *Humb* 84 SE7129
Newsholme *Lancs* 81 SD8451
Newstead *Border* 109 NT5634
Newstead *Notts* 75 SK5152
Newstead *Nthumb* 111 NU1527
Newstead *W York* 83 SE4014
Newtack *Gramp* 142 NJ4446
Newthorpe *N York* 83 SE4632
Newtimber Place *W Susx* 15 TQ2613
Newton *Beds* 39 TL2344
Newton *Border* 110 NT6020
Newton *Cambs* 65 TF4314
Newton *Cambs* 53 TL4349
Newton *Ches* 71 SJ4167
Newton *Ches* 71 SJ5059
Newton *Cumb* 86 SD2271
Newton *D & G* 100 NY1195
Newton *Derbys* 75 SK4459
Newton *Gramp* 141 NJ1663
Newton *Gramp* 141 NJ3362
Newton *H & W* 46 SO3432
Newton *H & W* 46 SO3769
Newton *H & W* 46 SO5153
Newton *Highld* 139 NH5850
Newton *Highld* 140 NH7448
Newton *Highld* 140 NH7866
Newton *Lancs* 80 SD3436
Newton *Lancs* 80 SD4430
Newton *Lancs* 87 SD5974
Newton *Lancs* 81 SD6950
Newton *Lincs* 64 TF0436
Newton *Loth* 117 NT0977
Newton *M Glam* 33 SS8377
Newton *N York* 90 SE8872
Newton *Nhants* 51 SP8883
Newton *Norfk* 66 TF8315
Newton *Notts* 63 SK6841
Newton *Nthumb* 110 NT9406
Newton *Nthumb* 103 NZ0364
Newton *Shrops* 59 SJ4234
Newton *Somset* 20 ST1038
Newton *Staffs* 73 SK0325
Newton *Strath* 114 NS0498
Newton *Strath* 116 NS6760
Newton *Strath* 108 NS9331
Newton *Suffk* 54 TL9240
Newton *W Mids* 61 SP0393
Newton *W York* 83 SE4527
Newton *Warwks* 50 SP5378
Newton *Wilts* 23 SU2322
Newton Abbot *Devon* 7 SX8571
Newton Arlosh *Cumb* 93 NY2055
Newton Aycliffe *Dur* 96 NZ2724
Newton Bewley *Cleve* 97 NZ4626
Newton Blossomville *Bucks* 38 SP9251
Newton Bromswold *Beds* 51 SP9966
Newton Burgoland *Leics* 62 SK3708
Newton by Toft *Lincs* 76 TF0487
Newton Ferrers *Cnwll* 5 SX3466
Newton Ferrers *Devon* 6 SX5548
Newton Ferry *W Isls* 154 NF8978
Newton Flotman *Norfk* 67 TM2198
Newton Green *Gwent* 34 ST5191
Newton Harcourt *Leics* 50 SP6497
Newton Heath *Gt Man* 79 SD8700
Newton Hill *W York* 83 SE3222
Newton Kyme *N York* 83 SE4644
Newton Longville *Bucks* 38 SP8431
Newton Mearns *Strath* 115 NS5355
Newton Morrell *N York* 89 NZ2309
Newton Mountain *Dyfed* 30 SM9808
Newton Mulgrave *N York* 97 NZ7815
Newton of Balcanquhal *Tays* 126 NO1610
Newton on Ouse *N York* 90 SE5159
Newton on Trent *Lincs* 76 SK8373
Newton on the Hill *Shrops* 59 SJ4823
Newton Poppleford *Devon* 9 SY0889
Newton Purcell *Oxon* 49 SP6230
Newton Regis *Warwks* 61 SK2707
Newton Reigny *Cumb* 93 NY4731
Newton Row *Highld* 151 ND3449
Newton Solney *Derbys* 73 SK2825
Newton St. Cyres *Devon* 9 SX8898
Newton St. Faith *Norfk* 67 TG2217
Newton St. Loe *Avon* 22 ST7064
Newton St. Petrock *Devon* 18 SS4112
Newton Stacey *Hants* 24 SU4140
Newton Stewart *D & G* 99 NX4065
Newton Toney *Wilts* 23 SU2140
Newton Tracey *Devon* 19 SS5226
Newton under Roseberry *Cleve* 90 NZ5713
Newton underwood *Nthumb* 103 NZ1486
Newton upon Derwent *Humb* 84 SE7149
Newton Valence *Hants* 24 SU7232
Newton-le-Willows *Mersyd* 78 SJ5995
Newton-le-Willows *N York* 89 SE2189
Newton-on-the-Moor *Nthumb* 111 NU1705
Newtongarry Croft *Gramp* 142 NJ5735
Newtongrange *Loth* 118 NT3364
Newtonhill *Gramp* 135 NO9193
Newtonloan *Loth* 118 NT3362
Newtonmill *Tays* 134 NO6064
Newtonmore *Highld* 132 NN7098
Newtown *Ches* 71 SJ5375
Newtown *Ches* 71 SJ6247
Newtown *Ches* 72 SJ9060
Newtown *Cnwll* 2 SW5729
Newtown *Cnwll* 3 SW7423
Newtown *Cnwll* 3 SX1052
Newtown *Cnwll* 5 SX2978
Newtown *Cumb* 92 NY1048
Newtown *Cumb* 101 NY5062
Newtown *Cumb* 94 NY5224
Newtown *D & G* 107 NS7710
Newtown *Derbys* 79 SJ9984
Newtown *Devon* 19 SS7625
Newtown *Dorset* 10 ST4802
Newtown *Dorset* 12 SZ0393
Newtown *Gloucs* 35 SO6702
Newtown *Gt Man* 78 SD5604
Newtown *Gwent* 33 SO1709
Newtown *H & W* 46 SO4757
Newtown *H & W* 46 SO5333
Newtown *H & W* 46 SO6145
Newtown *H & W* 47 SO7037
Newtown *H & W* 47 SO8755
Newtown *H & W* 60 SO9478
Newtown *Hants* 12 SU2710
Newtown *Hants* 24 SU4763
Newtown *Hants* 13 SU6013
Newtown *Highld* 131 NH3504
Newtown *IOW* 13 SZ4290
Newtown *Lancs* 80 SD5118
Newtown *M Glam* 33 ST0598
Newtown *Nthumb* 111 NT9631
Newtown *Nthumb* 103 NU0300
Newtown *Powys* 58 SO1091
Newtown *Shrops* 59 SJ4222
Newtown *Shrops* 59 SJ4731
Newtown *Staffs* 60 SJ9904
Newtown *Wilts* 22 ST9129
Newtown *Wilts* 23 SU2963
Newtown Linford *Leics* 62 SK5209
Newtown of Beltrees *Strath* 115 NS3758
Newtown St. Boswells *Border* 110 NT5732
Newtown Unthank *Leics* 62 SK4904
Newtyle *Tays* 126 NO2941
Newyears Green *Gt Lon* 26 TQ0788
Newyork *Strath* 122 NM9611
Nextend *H & W* 46 SO3357
Neyland *Dyfed* 30 SM9605
Niarbyl *IOM* 153 SC2177
Nibley *Avon* 35 ST6982
Nibley *Gloucs* 35 SO6606
Nibley Green *Gloucs* 35 ST7396
Nicholashayne *Devon* 9 ST1016
Nicholaston *W Glam* 32 SS5288
Nickies Hill *Cumb* 101 NY5367
Nidd *N York* 89 SE3060
Nigg *Gramp* 135 NJ9402
Nigg *Highld* 147 NH8071
Nightcott *Devon* 19 SS8925
Nine Elms *Wilts* 36 SU1085
Nine Wells *Dyfed* 30 SM7924
Ninebanks *Nthumb* 94 NY7853
Nineveh *H & W* 47 SO6265
Ninfield *E Susx* 16 TQ7012
Ningwood *IOW* 13 SZ3989
Nisbet *Border* 110 NT6725
Nisbet Hill *Border* 119 NT7950
Niton *IOW* 13 SZ5076
Nitshill *Strath* 115 NS5260
No Man's Heath *Ches* 71 SJ5148
No Man's Heath *Warwks* 61 SK2808
No Man's Land *Cnwll* 4 SW9470
No Man's Land *Cnwll* 5 SX2756
Noah's Ark *Kent* 27 TQ5557
Noak Bridge *Essex* 40 TQ6990
Noak Hill *Essex* 27 TQ5494
Noblethorpe *W York* 82 SE2805
Nobold *Shrops* 59 SJ4609
Nobottle *Nhants* 49 SP6763
Nocton *Lincs* 76 TF0564
Nogdam End *Norfk* 67 TG3900
Noke *Oxon* 37 SP5413
Nolton *Dyfed* 30 SM8618
Nolton Haven *Dyfed* 30 SM8618
Nomansland *Devon* 19 SS8313
Nomansland *Wilts* 12 SU2517
Noneley *Shrops* 59 SJ4828
Nonington *Kent* 29 TR2552
Nook *Cumb* 101 NY4679
Nook *Cumb* 87 SD5481
Norbiton Common *Gt Lon* 26 TQ2067
Norbreck *Lancs* 80 SD3140
Norbridge *H & W* 47 SO7144
Norbury *Ches* 71 SJ5547
Norbury *Derbys* 73 SK1241
Norbury *Gt Lon* 27 TQ3069
Norbury *Shrops* 59 SO3692
Norbury *Staffs* 72 SJ7823
Norbury Common *Ches* 71 SJ5548
Norbury Junction *Staffs* 72 SJ7923
Norchard *H & W* 47 SO8568
Norcott Brook *Ches* 78 SJ6080
Norcross *Lancs* 80 SD3341
Nordam *Humb* 84 SE8932
Nordelph *Norfk* 65 TF5501
Norden *Gt Man* 81 SD8614
Nordley *Shrops* 60 SO6996
Norham *Nthumb* 110 NT9047
Norland Town *W York* 82 SE0622
Norley *Ches* 71 SJ5772
Norleywood *Hants* 12 SZ3597
Norlington *E Susx* 16 TQ4413
Norman Cross *Cambs* 52 TL1690
Norman's Bay *E Susx* 16 TQ6805
Norman's Green *Devon* 9 ST0503
Normanby *Cleve* 97 NZ5418
Normanby *Humb* 84 SE8816
Normanby *Lincs* 76 SK9988
Normanby *N York* 90 SE7381
Normanby le Wold *Lincs* 76 TF1295
Normandy *Surrey* 25 SU9351
Normanton *Derbys* 62 SK3433
Normanton *Leics* 63 SK8140
Normanton *Leics* 63 SK9305
Normanton *Lincs* 63 SK9446
Normanton *Notts* 75 SK7054
Normanton *W York* 83 SE3822
Normanton *Wilts* 23 SU1340
Normanton le Heath *Leics* 62 SK3712
Normanton on Soar *Notts* 62 SK5122
Normanton on Trent *Notts* 75 SK7868
Normanton on the Wolds *Notts* 62 SK6232
Normoss *Lancs* 80 SD3437
Norney *Surrey* 25 SU9444
Norrington Common *Wilts* 22 ST8864
Norris Green *Cnwll* 5 SX4169
Norristhorpe *W York* 82 SE2123
North Anston *S York* 75 SK5184
North Aston *Oxon* 49 SP4828
North Baddesley *Hants* 13 SU3920
North Ballachulish *Highld* 130 NN0560
North Barrow *Somset* 21 ST6129
North Barsham *Norfk* 66 TF9135
North Benfleet *Essex* 40 TQ7588
North Bersted *W Susx* 14 SU9201
North Berwick *Loth* 118 NT5485
North Biddick *T & W* 96 NZ3153
North Bitchburn *Dur* 96 NZ1732
North Boarhunt *Hants* 13 SU6010
North Bockhampton *Hants* 12 SZ1797
North Bovey *Devon* 8 SX7484
North Bradley *Wilts* 22 ST8555
North Brentor *Devon* 5 SX4881
North Brewham *Somset* 22 ST7236
North Bridge *Surrey* 14 SU9636
North Brook End *Cambs* 39 TL2944
North Buckland *Devon* 18 SS4840
North Burlingham *Norfk* 67 TG3609
North Cadbury *Somset* 21 ST6327
North Carlton *Lincs* 76 SK9477
North Carlton *Notts* 75 SK5984
North Cave *Humb* 84 SE8932
North Cerney *Gloucs* 35 SP0107
North Charford *Hants* 12 SU1919
North Charlton *Nthumb* 111 NU1622
North Cheam *Gt Lon* 26 TQ2365
North Cheriton *Somset* 22 ST6925
North Chideock *Dorset* 10 SY4294
North Cliffe *Humb* 84 SE8736
North Clifton *Notts* 75 SK8272
North Close *Dur* 96 NZ2532
North Cockerington *Lincs* 77 TF3790
North Collingham *Notts* 76 SK8362
North Common *E Susx* 15 TQ3921
North Connel *Strath* 122 NM9034
North Cornelly *M Glam* 33 SS8181
North Corner *Cnwll* 3 SW7818
North Corry *Highld* 122 NM8353
North Cotes *Lincs* 77 TA3400
North Country *Cnwll* 2 SW6943
North Cove *Suffk* 55 TM4689
North Cowton *N York* 89 NZ2803
North Crawley *Bucks* 38 SP9244
North Cray *Gt Lon* 27 TQ4872
North Creake *Norfk* 66 TF8538
North Curry *Somset* 21 ST3125
North Dalton *Humb* 84 SE9351
North Deighton *N York* 83 SE3951
North Duffield *N York* 83 SE6837
North Duntulm *Highld* 136 NG4274
North Elham *Kent* 29 TR1844
North Elkington *Lincs* 77 TF2890
North Elmham *Norfk* 66 TF9820
North Elmsall *W York* 83 SE4712
North End *Avon* 21 ST4266
North End *Cumb* 93 NY3259
North End *Dorset* 22 ST8427
North End *Essex* 40 TL6618
North End *Hants* 12 SU1016
North End *Hants* 24 SU5828
North End *Hants* 13 SU6502
North End *Humb* 85 TA1022
North End *Humb* 85 TA1941
North End *Humb* 85 TA2831
North End *Humb* 85 TA3101
North End *Leics* 62 SK5715
North End *Lincs* 76 TF0499
North End *Lincs* 64 TF2341
North End *Lincs* 77 TF4289
North End *Mersyd* 78 SD3004
North End *Nhants* 51 SP9668
North End *Norfk* 66 TL9992
North End *W Susx* 14 SU9703
North End *W Susx* 14 TQ1109
North Erradale *Highld* 144 NG7480
North Evington *Leics* 62 SK6204
North Fambridge *Essex* 40 TQ8597
North Feorline *Strath* 105 NR9029
North Ferriby *Humb* 84 SE9826
North Frodingham *Humb* 85 TA1053
North Gorley *Hants* 12 SU1611
North Green *Norfk* 55 TM2288
North Green *Suffk* 55 TM3162
North Green *Suffk* 55 TM3966
North Grimston *N York* 90 SE8467
North Halling *Kent* 28 TQ7065
North Hayling *Hants* 13 SU7303
North Hazelrigg *Nthumb* 111 NU0533
North Heasley *Devon* 19 SS7333
North Heath *W Susx* 14 TQ0621
North Hele *Somset* 20 ST0323
North Hill *Cnwll* 5 SX2776
North Hillingdon *Gt Lon* 26 TQ0784
North Hinksey *Oxon* 37 SP4905
North Huish *Devon* 7 SX7156
North Hykeham *Lincs* 76 SK9465
North Kelsey *Humb* 84 TA0401
North Kessock *Highld* 140 NH6548
North Killingholme *Humb* 85 TA1417
North Kilvington *N York* 89 SE4285
North Kilworth *Leics* 50 SP6183
North Kingston *Hants* 12 SU1603
North Kyme *Lincs* 76 TF1552
North Landing *Humb* 91 TA2471
North Lee *Bucks* 38 SP8308
North Lees *N York* 89 SE2973
North Leigh *Kent* 29 TR1347
North Leigh *Oxon* 36 SP3813
North Leverton with Habblesthorpe *Notts* 75 SK7882
North Littleton *H & W* 48 SP0847
North Lopham *Norfk* 54 TM0382
North Luffenham *Leics* 63 SK9303
North Marden *W Susx* 14 SU8016
North Marston *Bucks* 37 SP7722
North Middleton *Loth* 118 NT3559
North Middleton *Nthumb* 111 NT9924
North Milmain *D & G* 98 NX0852
North Molton *Devon* 19 SS7329
North Moreton *Oxon* 37 SU5689
North Mundham *W Susx* 14 SU8702
North Muskham *Notts* 75 SK7958
North Newbald *Humb* 84 SE9136
North Newington *Oxon* 49 SP4240
North Newnton *Wilts* 23 SU1257
North Newton *Somset* 20 ST3031
North Nibley *Gloucs* 35 ST7495
North Oakley *Hants* 24 SU5354
North Ockendon *Gt Lon* 27 TQ5985
North Ormsby *Lincs* 77 TF2893
North Otterington *N York* 89 SE3689
North Owersby *Lincs* 76 TF0594
North Perrott *Somset* 10 ST4709
North Petherton *Somset* 20 ST2833
North Petherwin *Cnwll* 5 SX2789
North Pickenham *Norfk* 66 TF8606
North Piddle *H & W* 47 SO9654
North Pool *Devon* 7 SX7741
North Poorton *Dorset* 10 SY5298
North Poulner *Hants* 12 SU1606
North Quarme *Somset* 20 SS9236
North Queensferry *Fife* 117 NT1380
North Radworthy *Devon* 19 SS7534
North Rauceby *Lincs* 76 TF0246
North Reston *Lincs* 77 TF3883
North Rigton *N York* 82 SE2749
North Ripley *Hants* 12 SZ1699
North Rode *Ches* 72 SJ8866
North Row *Cumb* 93 NY2232
North Runcton *Norfk* 65 TF6416
North Scale *Cumb* 86 SD1869
North Scarle *Lincs* 76 SK8466
North Seaton *Nthumb* 103 NZ2986
North Seaton Colliery *Nthumb* 103 NZ2985
North Shian *Strath* 122 NM9143
North Shields *T & W* 103 NZ3568
North Shoebury *Essex* 40 TQ9286
North Shore *Lancs* 80 SD3037
North Side *Cambs* 64 TL2799
North Side *Cumb* 92 NX9929
North Skelton *Cleve* 97 NZ6718
North Skirlaugh *Humb* 85 TA1439
North Somercotes *Lincs* 77 TF4296

North Stainley Oskaig

North Stainley *N York* 89 SE2876
North Stainmore *Cumb* 95 NY8314
North Stifford *Essex* 40 TQ6080
North Stoke *Avon* 35 ST7069
North Stoke *Oxon* 37 SU6186
North Stoke *W Susx* 14 TQ0110
North Street *Berks* 24 SU6371
North Street *Cambs* 53 TL5868
North Street *Hants* 12 SU1518
North Street *Hants* 24 SU6433
North Street *Kent* 28 TQ8174
North Street *Kent* 28 TR0157
North Sunderland *Nthumb* 111 NU2131
North Tamerton *Cnwll* 5 SX3197
North Tawton *Devon* 8 SS6601
North Third *Cent* 116 NS7589
North Tidworth *Wilts* 23 SU2349
North Town *Berks* 26 SU8882
North Town *Devon* 19 SS5109
North Town *Somset* 21 ST5642
North Tuddenham *Norfk* 66 TG0314
North Walbottle *T & W* 103 NZ1767
North Walsham *Norfk* 67 TG2830
North Waltham *Hants* 24 SU5646
North Warnborough *Hants* 24 SU7351
North Weald Basset *Essex* 39 TL4904
North Wheatley *Notts* 75 SK7585
North Whilborough *Devon* 7 SX8766
North Wick *Avon* 21 ST5865
North Widcombe *Somset* 21 ST5758
North Willingham *Lincs* 76 TF1688
North Wingfield *Derbys* 74 SK4065
North Witham *Lincs* 63 SK9221
North Wootton *Dorset* 11 ST6514
North Wootton *Norfk* 65 TF6424
North Wootton *Somset* 21 ST5641
North Wraxall *Wilts* 35 ST8175
North Wroughton *Wilts* 36 SU1481
Northacre *Norfk* 66 TL9598
Northall *Bucks* 38 SP9520
Northall Green *Norfk* 66 TF9914
Northallerton *N York* 89 SE3694
Northam *Devon* 18 SS4529
Northam *Hants* 13 SU4312
Northampton *H & W* 47 SO8365
Northampton *Nhants* 49 SP7560
Northaw *Herts* 27 TL2702
Northay *Somset* 10 ST2811
Northborough *Cambs* 64 TF1507
Northbourne *Kent* 29 TR3352
Northbridge Street *E Susx* 17 TQ7324
Northbrook *Hants* 24 SU5139
Northbrook *Oxon* 37 SP4922
Northchapel *W Susx* 14 SU9529
Northchurch *Herts* 38 SP9708
Northcott *Devon* 9 ST0912
Northcott *Devon* 9 ST1209
Northcott *Devon* 5 SX3392
Northcourt *Oxon* 37 SU4998
Northdown *Kent* 29 TR3770
Northedge *Derbys* 74 SK3665
Northend *Bucks* 37 SU7392
Northend *Warwks* 48 SP3952
Northend Woods *Bucks* 26 SU9089
Northenden *Gt Man* 79 SJ8289
Northfield *Gramp* 135 NJ9008
Northfield *Humb* 84 TA0326
Northfield *W Mids* 60 SP0279
Northfields *Lincs* 64 TF0208
Northfleet *Kent* 27 TQ6374
Northiam *E Susx* 17 TQ8324
Northill *Beds* 52 TL1446
Northington *Gloucs* 35 SO7008
Northington *Hants* 24 SU5637
Northlands *Lincs* 77 TF3453
Northleach *Gloucs* 36 SP1114
Northleigh *Devon* 19 SS6034
Northleigh *Devon* 9 SY1995
Northlew *Devon* 19 SX5099
Northload Bridge *Somset* 21 ST4939
Northmooor *Somset* 20 SS9028
Northmoor *Oxon* 36 SP4202
Northmuir *Tays* 126 NO3854
Northney *Hants* 13 SU7303
Northolt *Gt Lon* 26 TQ1384
Northop *Clwyd* 70 SJ2468
Northop Hall *Clwyd* 70 SJ2667
Northorpe *Lincs* 76 SK8997
Northorpe *Lincs* 64 TF0917
Northorpe *Lincs* 64 TF2036
Northorpe *W York* 82 SE2221
Northover *Somset* 21 ST4838
Northover *Somset* 21 ST5223
Northowram *W York* 82 SE1126
Northport *Dorset* 11 SY9288
Northrepps *Norfk* 67 TG2439
Northway *Somset* 20 ST1329
Northway *W Glam* 32 SS5889
Northwich *Ches* 79 SJ6673
Northwick *Avon* 34 ST5686
Northwick *H & W* 47 SO8458
Northwick *Somset* 21 ST3548
Northwold *Norfk* 65 TL7597
Northwood *Derbys* 74 SK2664
Northwood *Gt Lon* 26 TQ0990
Northwood *IOW* 13 SZ4992
Northwood *Shrops* 59 SJ4633
Northwood *Staffs* 72 SJ8949
Northwood End *Beds* 38 TL0941
Northwood Green *Gloucs* 35 SO7216
Norton *Avon* 21 ST3463
Norton *Ches* 78 SJ5581
Norton *Cleve* 96 NZ4421
Norton *Cnwll* 4 SX0869
Norton *E Susx* 16 TQ4701
Norton *Gloucs* 47 SO8524
Norton *Gwent* 34 SO4420
Norton *H & W* 47 SO8751
Norton *H & W* 48 SP0447
Norton *Herts* 39 TL2334
Norton *IOW* 12 SZ3488
Norton *N York* 92 SE7971
Norton *Nhants* 49 SP5963
Norton *Notts* 75 SK5771
Norton *Powys* 46 SO3067
Norton *S York* 83 SE5415
Norton *S York* 74 SK3681
Norton *Shrops* 59 SJ5609
Norton *Shrops* 60 SJ7200
Norton *Shrops* 59 SO4681
Norton *Shrops* 59 SO6382
Norton *Suffk* 54 TL9565
Norton *W Glam* 32 SS6188
Norton *W Susx* 14 SU9206
Norton *Wilts* 35 ST8884
Norton Bavant *Wilts* 22 ST9043
Norton Bridge *Staffs* 72 SJ8630
Norton Canes *Staffs* 60 SK0107
Norton Canon *H & W* 46 SO3847
Norton Corner *Norfk* 66 TG0928
Norton Disney *Lincs* 76 SK8859
Norton Ferris *Wilts* 22 ST7936
Norton Fitzwarren *Somset* 20 ST1925
Norton Green *IOW* 12 SZ3488
Norton Green *Staffs* 60 SK0107
Norton Hawkfield *Avon* 21 ST5964
Norton Heath *Essex* 40 TL6004
Norton in Hales *Shrops* 72 SJ7038
Norton in the Moors *Staffs* 72 SJ8951
Norton Lindsey *Warwks* 48 SP2263
Norton Little Green *Suffk* 54 TL9766
Norton Malreward *Avon* 21 ST6064
Norton Mandeville *Essex* 40 TL5804
Norton St. Philip *Somset* 22 ST7755
Norton Subcourse *Norfk* 67 TM4198
Norton sub Hamdon *Somset* 10 ST4615
Norton Wood *H & W* 46 SO3648
Norton-Juxta-Twycross *Leics* 61 SK3207
Norton-le-Clay *N York* 89 SE4071
Norwell *Notts* 75 SK7761
Norwell Woodhouse *Notts* 75 SK7362
Norwich *Norfk* 67 TG2308
Norwick *Shet* 155 HP6414
Norwood *Cent* 116 NS8793
Norwood *Kent* 17 TR0530
Norwood *S York* 75 SK4681
Norwood End *Essex* 40 TL5608
Norwood Green *Gt Lon* 26 TQ1378
Norwood Green *W York* 82 SE1326
Norwood Hill *Surrey* 15 TQ2343
Norwoodside *Cambs* 65 TL4197
Noseley *Leics* 50 SP7398
Noss Mayo *Devon* 6 SX5547
Nosterfield *N York* 89 SE2780
Nosterfield End *Cambs* 53 TL6344
Nostie *Highld* 138 NG8527
Notgrove *Gloucs* 36 SP1020
Nottage *M Glam* 33 SS8177
Notter *Cnwll* 5 SX3960
Nottingham *Notts* 62 SK5739
Nottington *Dorset* 11 SY6682
Notton *W York* 83 SE3413
Notton *Wilts* 35 ST9169
Nottswood Hill *Gloucs* 35 SO7018
Nounsley *Essex* 40 TL7910
Noutard's Green *H & W* 47 SO8066
Nox *Shrops* 59 SJ4110
Nuffield *Oxon* 37 SU6687
Nun Monkton *N York* 90 SE5057
Nunburnholme *Humb* 84 SE8447
Nuncargate *Notts* 75 SK5054
Nunclose *Cumb* 94 NY4945
Nuneaton *Warwks* 61 SP3691
Nuneham Courtenay *Oxon* 37 SU5599
Nunhead *Gt Lon* 27 TQ3475
Nunkeeling *Humb* 85 TA1449
Nunnerie *Strath* 108 NS9612
Nunney *Somset* 22 ST7345
Nunney Catch *Somset* 22 ST7344
Nunnington *H & W* 46 SO5543
Nunnington *N York* 90 SE6679
Nunnykirk *Nthumb* 103 NZ0793
Nuns Moor *T & W* 103 NZ2266
Nunsthorpe *Humb* 85 TA2607
Nunthorpe *Cleve* 97 NZ5314
Nunthorpe *N York* 83 SE6050
Nunthorpe Village *Cleve* 90 NZ5413
Nunton *Wilts* 23 SU1526
Nunwick *N York* 89 SE3274
Nunwick *Nthumb* 102 NY8774
Nup End *Bucks* 38 SP8619
Nupdown *Avon* 35 ST6395
Nupend *Gloucs* 35 SO7806
Nuptow *Berks* 25 SU8873
Nursling *Hants* 12 SU3716
Nursted *Hants* 13 SU7521
Nursteed *Wilts* 23 SU0260
Nurton *Staffs* 60 SO8399
Nutbourne *W Susx* 14 SU7705
Nutbourne *W Susx* 14 TQ0718
Nutfield *Surrey* 27 TQ3050
Nuthall *Notts* 62 SK5243
Nuthampstead *Herts* 39 TL4034
Nuthurst *W Susx* 15 TQ1925
Nutley *E Susx* 16 TQ4427
Nutley *Hants* 24 SU6044
Nuttal Lane *Gt Man* 81 SD7915
Nutwell *S York* 83 SE6304
Nybster *Highld* 151 ND3663
Nyetimber *W Susx* 14 SZ8998
Nyewood *W Susx* 14 SU8021
Nymet Rowland *Devon* 19 SS7108
Nymet Tracey *Devon* 8 SS7200
Nympsfield *Gloucs* 35 SO8000
Nynehead *Somset* 20 ST1422
Nythe *Somset* 21 ST4234
Nyton *W Susx* 14 SU9305

O

Oad Street *Kent* 28 TQ8762
Oadby *Leics* 50 SK6200
Oak Cross *Devon* 8 SX5399
Oak Tree *Dur* 89 NZ3613
Oakall Green *H & W* 47 SO8161
Oakamoor *Staffs* 73 SK0444
Oakbank *Loth* 117 NT0766
Oakdale *Gwent* 33 ST1898
Oake *Somset* 20 ST1525
Oaken *Staffs* 60 SJ8602
Oakenclough *Lancs* 80 SD5447
Oakengates *Shrops* 60 SJ7010
Oakenholt *Clwyd* 70 SJ2571
Oakenshaw *Dur* 96 NZ1937
Oakenshaw *W York* 82 SE1727
Oaker Side *Derbys* 74 SK2760
Oakerthorpe *Derbys* 74 SK3854
Oakford *Devon* 20 SS9121
Oakford *Dyfed* 42 SN4558
Oakfordbridge *Devon* 20 SS9122
Oakgrove *Ches* 79 SJ9169
Oakham *Leics* 63 SK8608
Oakhanger *Ches* 72 SJ7754
Oakhanger *Hants* 14 SU7635
Oakhill *Somset* 21 ST6347
Oakhurst *Kent* 27 TQ5550
Oakington *Cambs* 52 TL4164
Oaklands *Powys* 45 SO0450
Oakle Street *Gloucs* 35 SO7517
Oakley *Beds* 51 TL0153
Oakley *Bucks* 37 SP6412
Oakley *Dorset* 11 SZ0198
Oakley *Hants* 24 SU5650
Oakley *Oxon* 37 SP7500
Oakley *Suffk* 54 TM1677
Oakley Green *Berks* 26 SU9276
Oakley Park *Powys* 58 SN9886
Oakridge *Gloucs* 35 SO9103
Oaks *Dur* 96 NZ1525
Oaks *Lancs* 81 SD6733
Oaks *Shrops* 59 SJ4204
Oaks Green *Derbys* 73 SK1533
Oaksey *Wilts* 35 ST9993
Oakshaw *Cumb* 101 NY5176
Oakshott *Hants* 13 SU7427
Oakthorpe *Leics* 61 SK3212
Oakwood *Nthumb* 102 NY9465
Oakwoodhill *Surrey* 15 TQ1337
Oakworth *W York* 82 SE0338
Oare *Kent* 28 TR0063
Oare *Somset* 19 SS7947
Oare *Wilts* 23 SU1563
Oasby *Lincs* 63 TF0039
Oath *Somset* 21 ST3827
Oathlaw *Tays* 127 NO4756
Oatlands Park *Surrey* 26 TQ0865
Oban *Strath* 122 NM8629
Obley *Shrops* 46 SO3377
Obney *Tays* 125 NO0237
Oborne *Dorset* 11 ST6518
Obthorpe *Lincs* 64 TF0914
Occlestone Green *Ches* 72 SJ6962
Occold *Suffk* 54 TM1570
Ochiltree *Strath* 107 NS5021
Ockbrook *Derbys* 62 SK4235
Ocker Hill *W Mids* 60 SO9793
Ockeridge *H & W* 47 SO7762
Ockham *Surrey* 26 TQ0756
Ockle *Highld* 129 NM5570
Ockley *Surrey* 15 TQ1440
Ocle Pychard *H & W* 46 SO5945
Octon *Humb* 91 TA0369
Odcombe *Somset* 10 ST5015
Odd Down *Avon* 22 ST7462
Oddingley *H & W* 47 SO9159
Oddington *Gloucs* 48 SP2225
Oddington *Oxon* 37 SP5515
Odell *Beds* 51 SP9657
Odham *Devon* 18 SS4703
Odiham *Hants* 24 SU7451
Odsal *W York* 82 SE1529
Odsey *Herts* 39 TL2938
Odstock *Wilts* 23 SU1426
Odstone *Leics* 62 SK3907
Offchurch *Warwks* 48 SP3565
Offenham *H & W* 48 SP0546
Offerton *T & W* 96 NZ3455
Offham *E Susx* 15 TQ4012
Offham *Kent* 28 TQ6557
Offham *W Susx* 14 TQ0208
Offleymarsh *Shrops* 72 SJ7829
Offord Cluny *Cambs* 52 TL2267
Offord Darcy *Cambs* 52 TL2266
Offton *Suffk* 54 TM0649
Offwell *Devon* 9 SY1999
Ogbourne Maizey *Wilts* 36 SU1871
Ogbourne St. Andrew *Wilts* 36 SU1872
Ogbourne St. George *Wilts* 36 SU2074
Ogden *W York* 82 SE0730
Ogle *Nthumb* 103 NZ1378
Oglet *Mersyd* 78 SJ4481
Ogmore *M Glam* 33 SS8876
Ogmore Vale *M Glam* 33 SS9390
Ogmore-by-Sea *M Glam* 33 SS8675
Ogwen Bank *Gwynd* 69 SH6265
Okeford Fitzpaine *Dorset* 11 ST8010
Okehampton *Devon* 8 SX5995
Olchard *Devon* 9 SX8777
Old *Nhants* 50 SP7872
Old Aberdeen *Gramp* 135 NJ9407
Old Alresford *Hants* 24 SU5834
Old Auchenbrack *D & G* 107 NX7597
Old Basford *Notts* 62 SK5543
Old Basing *Hants* 24 SU6652
Old Bewick *Nthumb* 111 NU0621
Old Bolingbroke *Lincs* 77 TF3565
Old Bracknell *Berks* 25 SU8668
Old Bramhope *W York* 82 SE2343
Old Brampton *Derbys* 74 SK3371
Old Bridge of Urr *D & G* 100 NX7767
Old Buckenham *Norfk* 66 TM0691
Old Burghclere *Hants* 24 SU4657
Old Byland *N York* 90 SE5585
Old Cassop *Dur* 96 NZ3339
Old Castle *M Glam* 33 SS9079
Old Church Stoke *Powys* 58 SO2894
Old Clee *Humb* 85 TA2808
Old Cleeve *Somset* 20 ST0441
Old Clipstone *Notts* 75 SK6064
Old Colwyn *Clwyd* 69 SH8678
Old Dailly *Strath* 106 NX2299
Old Dalby *Leics* 63 SK6723
Old Dam *Derbys* 74 SK1179
Old Deer *Gramp* 143 NJ9747
Old Ditch *Somset* 21 ST5049
Old Edington *S York* 75 SK5397
Old Eldon *Dur* 96 NZ2427
Old Ellerby *Humb* 85 TA1637
Old Felixstowe *Suffk* 55 TM3135
Old Fletton *Cambs* 64 TL1997
Old Forge *H & W* 34 SO5518
Old Furnace *H & W* 46 SO4923
Old Glossop *Derbys* 74 SK0494
Old Goole *Humb* 84 SE7422
Old Grimsby *IOS* 2 SV8915
Old Hall Green *Herts* 39 TL3722
Old Hall Street *Norfk* 67 TG3033
Old Harlow *Essex* 39 TL4711
Old Heath *Essex* 41 TM0122
Old Hunstanton *Norfk* 65 TF6842
Old Hutton *Cumb* 87 SD5688
Old Kea *Cnwll* 3 SW8441
Old Kilpatrick *Strath* 115 NS4672
Old Knebworth *Herts* 39 TL2320
Old Lakenham *Norfk* 67 TG2205
Old Langho *Lancs* 81 SD7035
Old Leake *Lincs* 77 TF4050
Old Malton *N York* 90 SE7972
Old Micklefield *W York* 83 SE4433
Old Milton *Hants* 12 SZ2394
Old Milverton *Warwks* 48 SP2967
Old Newton *Suffk* 54 TM0562
Old Quarrington *Dur* 96 NZ3237
Old Radford *Notts* 62 SK5540
Old Radnor *Powys* 46 SO2558
Old Rayne *Gramp* 142 NJ6728
Old Romney *Kent* 17 TR0325
Old Shoreham *W Susx* 15 TQ2006
Old Shoremore *Highld* 148 NC2058
Old Soar *Kent* 27 TQ6254
Old Sodbury *Avon* 35 ST7581
Old Somerby *Lincs* 63 SK9633
Old Stratford *Nhants* 49 SP7741
Old Sunnford *W Mids* 60 SO9083
Old Tebay *Cumb* 87 NY6105
Old Thirsk *N York* 89 SE4382
Old Town *Cumb* 93 NY4743
Old Town *Cumb* 87 SD5982
Old Town *E Susx* 16 TV5999
Old Town *IOS* 2 SV9110
Old Town *Nthumb* 102 NY8891
Old Town *W York* 82 SE0028
Old Trafford *Gt Man* 79 SJ8196
Old Tupton *Derbys* 74 SK3865
Old Warden *Beds* 38 TL1343
Old Weston *Cambs* 51 TL0977
Old Wick *Highld* 151 ND3649
Old Windsor *Berks* 25 SU9874
Old Wives Lees *Kent* 29 TR0754
Old Woking *Surrey* 26 TQ0157
Old Wolverton *Bucks* 38 SP8041
Oldany *Highld* 148 NC0932
Oldberrow *Warwks* 48 SP1265
Oldbury *Kent* 27 TQ5956
Oldbury *Shrops* 60 SO7192
Oldbury *W Mids* 60 SO9888
Oldbury *Warwks* 61 SP3194
Oldbury Naite *Avon* 35 ST6293
Oldbury on the Hill *Gloucs* 35 ST8188
Oldbury-on-Severn *Avon* 34 ST6092
Oldcastle *Gwent* 46 SO3224
Oldcastle Heath *Ches* 71 SJ4745
Oldcotes *Notts* 75 SK5888
Oldfield *H & W* 47 SO8464
Oldfield *W York* 82 SE0037
Oldford *Somset* 22 ST7850
Oldhall Green *Suffk* 54 TL8956
Oldham *Gt Man* 79 SD9204
Oldhamstocks *Loth* 119 NT7470
Oldhurst *Cambs* 52 TL3077
Oldland *Avon* 35 ST6771
Oldmeldrum *Gramp* 143 NJ8127
Oldmill *Cnwll* 5 SX3673
Oldmixon *Avon* 21 ST3358
Oldridge *Devon* 8 SX8296
Oldstead *N York* 90 SE5379
Oldwall *Cumb* 101 NY4761
Oldwalls *W Glam* 32 SS4891
Oldways End *Devon* 19 SS8724
Oldwhat *Gramp* 143 NJ8651
Oldwoods *Shrops* 59 SJ4520
Olive Green *Staffs* 73 SK1118
Oliver *Border* 108 NT0924
Oliver's Battery *Hants* 13 SU4527
Ollaberry *Shet* 155 HU3680
Ollach *Highld* 137 NG5137
Ollerton *Ches* 79 SJ7776
Ollerton *Notts* 75 SK6567
Ollerton *Shrops* 72 SJ6425
Olmarch *Dyfed* 44 SN6255
Olmstead Green *Cambs* 53 TL6341
Olney *Bucks* 38 SP8951
Olney *Nhants* 49 SP6643
Olrig House *Highld* 151 ND1866
Olton *W Mids* 61 SP1382
Olveston *Avon* 34 ST6086
Ombersley *H & W* 47 SO8463
Ompton *Notts* 75 SK6865
Onchan *IOM* 153 SC3978
One House *Suffk* 54 TM0159
Onecote *Staffs* 73 SK0455
Onen *Gwent* 34 SO4314
Ongar Street *H & W* 46 SO3967
Onibury *Shrops* 46 SO4579
Onich *Highld* 130 NN0261
Onllwyn *W Glam* 33 SN8410
Onneley *Staffs* 72 SJ7542
Onslow Village *Surrey* 25 SU9849
Onston *Ches* 71 SJ5873
Openwoodgate *Derbys* 62 SK3647
Opinan *Highld* 137 NG7472
Orbliston *Gramp* 141 NJ3057
Orbost *Highld* 136 NG2543
Orby *Lincs* 77 TF4967
Orchard Portman *Somset* 20 ST2421
Orcheston *Wilts* 23 SU0545
Orcop *H & W* 46 SO4726
Orcop Hill *H & W* 46 SO4727
Ord *Gramp* 142 NJ6258
Ord *Highld* 129 NG6113
Ordhead *Gramp* 135 NJ6610
Ordie *Gramp* 134 NJ4501
Ordiequish *Gramp* 141 NJ3357
Ordley *Nthumb* 95 NY9459
Ordsall *Notts* 75 SK7079
Ore *E Susx* 17 TQ8311
Oreleton Common *H & W* 46 SO4768
Oreton *Shrops* 59 SO6580
Orford *Ches* 78 SJ6190
Orford *Suffk* 55 TM4250
Organford *Dorset* 11 SY9392
Orgreave *Staffs* 73 SK1415
Orlestone *Kent* 17 TR0034
Orleton *H & W* 46 SO4967
Orleton *H & W* 47 SO7067
Orlingbury *Nhants* 51 SP8572
Ormathwaite *Cumb* 93 NY2625
Ormesby *Cleve* 97 NZ5317
Ormesby St. Margaret *Norfk* 67 TG4914
Ormesby St. Michael *Norfk* 67 TG4714
Ormiscaig *Highld* 144 NG8590
Ormiston *Loth* 118 NT4169
Ormsaigmore *Highld* 121 NM4763
Ormsary *Strath* 113 NR7472
Ormskirk *Lancs* 78 SD4108
Ornsby Hill *Dur* 96 NZ1648
Oronsay *Strath* 112 NR3588
Orphir *Ork* 155 HY3404
Orpington *Gt Lon* 27 TQ4666
Orrell *Gt Man* 78 SD5303
Orrell *Mersyd* 78 SJ3496
Orrell Post *Gt Man* 78 SD5305
Orrisdale *IOM* 153 SC3292
Orroland *D & G* 92 NX7746
Orsett *Essex* 40 TQ6482
Orslow *Staffs* 72 SJ8015
Orston *Notts* 63 SK7740
Orthwaite *Cumb* 93 NY2534
Ortner *Lancs* 80 SD5354
Orton *Cumb* 87 NY6208
Orton *Nhants* 51 SP8079
Orton *Staffs* 60 SO8795
Orton Longueville *Cambs* 64 TL1796
Orton Rigg *Cumb* 93 NY3352
Orton Waterville *Cambs* 64 TL1595
Orton-on-the-Hill *Leics* 61 SK3003
Orwell *Cambs* 52 TL3650
Osbaldeston *Lancs* 81 SD6431
Osbaldeston Green *Lancs* 81 SD6432
Osbaldwick *N York* 83 SE6251
Osbaston *Leics* 62 SK4204
Osbaston *Shrops* 59 SJ3222
Osborne *IOW* 13 SZ5194
Osbournby *Lincs* 64 TF0638
Oscroft *Ches* 71 SJ5067
Osgathorpe *Leics* 62 SK4319
Osgodby *Lincs* 76 TF0792
Osgodby *N York* 83 SE6433
Osgodby *N York* 91 TA0584
Oskaig *Highld* 137 NG5438

Oskamull
Penhale

Oskamull *Strath* 121 NM4540
Osmanthorpe *W York* 83 SE3333
Osmaston *Derbys* 73 SK1943
Osmington *Dorset* 11 SY7283
Osmington Mills *Dorset* 11 SY7381
Osmotherley *N York* 89 SE4596
Osney *Oxon* 37 SP4906
Ospringe *Kent* 28 TR0060
Ossett *W York* 82 SE2720
Ossington *Notts* 75 SK7564
Ostend *Essex* 40 TQ9397
Oswaldkirk *N York* 90 SE6278
Oswaldtwistle *Lancs* 81 SD7327
Oswestry *Shrops* 59 SJ2929
Otford *Kent* 27 TQ5359
Otham *Kent* 28 TQ7953
Otham Hole *Kent* 28 TQ8052
Othery *Somset* 21 ST3831
Otley *Suffk* 55 TM2055
Otley *W York* 82 SE2045
Otley Green *Suffk* 55 TM2156
Otter Ferry *Strath* 114 NR9384
Otterbourne *Hants* 13 SU4522
Otterburn *N York* 88 SD8857
Otterburn *Nthumb* 102 NY8893
Otterham *Cnwll* 4 SX1690
Otterham Quay *Kent* 28 TQ8366
Otterhampton *Somset* 20 ST2443
Ottershaw *Surrey* 26 TQ0263
Otterswick *Shet* 155 HU5285
Otterton *Devon* 9 SY0684
Otterwood *Hants* 13 SU4102
Ottery *Devon* 6 SX4475
Ottery St. Mary *Devon* 9 SY1095
Ottinge *Kent* 29 TR1642
Ottringham *Humb* 85 TA2624
Oughterby *Cumb* 93 NY2955
Oughtershaw *N York* 88 SD8780
Oughterside *Cumb* 92 NY1140
Oughtibridge *S York* 74 SK3093
Oughtrington *Ches* 79 SJ6987
Oulston *N York* 90 SE5474
Oulton *Cumb* 93 NY2450
Oulton *Norfk* 66 TG1328
Oulton *Staffs* 72 SJ7822
Oulton *Staffs* 72 SJ9035
Oulton *Suffk* 67 TM5294
Oulton *W York* 83 SE3628
Oulton Broad *Suffk* 67 TM5192
Oulton Street *Norfk* 66 TG1527
Oundle *Nhants* 51 TL0388
Ounsdale *Staffs* 60 SO8693
Ousby *Cumb* 94 NY6134
Ousden *Suffk* 53 TL7459
Ousefleet *Humb* 84 SE8323
Ouston *Dur* 96 NZ2554
Ouston *Nthumb* 103 NZ0770
Out Newton *Humb* 85 TA3821
Outchester *Nthumb* 111 NU1433
Outgate *Cumb* 87 SD3599
Outhgill *Cumb* 88 NY7801
Outhill *Warwks* 48 SP1066
Outlands *Staffs* 72 SJ7630
Outlane *W York* 82 SE0817
Outward Gate *Gt Man* 79 SD7805
Outwell *Norfk* 65 TF5103
Outwick *Hants* 12 SU1417
Outwood *Surrey* 15 TQ3145
Outwood *W York* 83 SE3323
Outwoods *Leics* 62 SK4018
Outwoods *Staffs* 72 SJ7817
Outwoods *Warwks* 61 SP2484
Ouzlewell Green *W York* 83 SE3326
Ovenden *W York* 82 SE0827
Over *Avon* 34 ST5882
Over *Cambs* 52 TL3770
Over *Ches* 71 SJ6365
Over *Gloucs* 35 SO8119
Over Burrows *Derbys* 73 SK2639
Over Compton *Dorset* 10 ST5816
Over End *Cambs* 51 TL0893
Over Green *Warwks* 61 SP1694
Over Haddon *Derbys* 74 SK2066
Over Kellet *Lancs* 87 SD5169
Over Kiddington *Oxon* 36 SP4021
Over Monnow *Gwent* 34 SO5012
Over Norton *Oxon* 48 SP3128
Over Silton *N York* 89 SE4493
Over Stenton *Fife* 117 NT2799
Over Stowey *Somset* 20 ST1838
Over Stratton *Somset* 10 ST4315
Over Tabley *Ches* 79 SJ7279
Over Wallop *Hants* 23 SU2838
Over Whitacre *Warwks* 61 SP2590
Over Woodhouse *Derbys* 75 SK4671
Over Worton *Oxon* 49 SP4329
Overbury *H & W* 47 SO9537
Overgreen *Derbys* 74 SK3273
Overleigh *Somset* 21 ST4835
Overley *Staffs* 73 SK1515
Overpool *Ches* 71 SJ3877
Overscaig Hotel *Highld* 149 NC4123
Overseal *Derbys* 73 SK2915
Oversland *Kent* 28 TR0557
Overstey Green *Warwks* 48 SP0957
Overstone *Nhants* 50 SP7966
Overstrand *Norfk* 67 TG2440
Overstreet *Wilts* 23 SU0637
Overthorpe *Nhants* 49 SP4840
Overton *Ches* 71 SJ5277
Overton *Clwyd* 71 SJ3741
Overton *Gramp* 143 NJ8714
Overton *Hants* 24 SU5149
Overton *Lancs* 87 SD4358
Overton *N York* 83 SE5555
Overton *Shrops* 46 SO5072
Overton *W Glam* 32 SS4685
Overton *W York* 82 SE2516
Overton Bridge *Clwyd* 71 SJ3542
Overton Green *Ches* 72 SJ8060
Overtown *Lancs* 87 SD6275
Overtown *Strath* 116 NS8053
Overtown *W York* 83 SE3516
Overtown *Wilts* 36 SU1579
Overy *Oxon* 37 SU5893
Overy Staithe *Norfk* 66 TF8444
Oving *Bucks* 37 SP7821
Oving *W Susx* 14 SU9004
Ovingdean *E Susx* 15 TQ3503
Ovingham *Nthumb* 103 NZ0863
Ovington *Dur* 89 NZ1314
Ovington *Essex* 53 TL7642
Ovington *Hants* 24 SU5631
Ovington *Norfk* 66 TF9202
Ovington *Nthumb* 103 NZ0663
Ower *Hants* 12 SU3215
Ower *Hants* 13 SU4702
Owermoigne *Dorset* 11 SY7685
Owl's Green *Suffk* 55 TM2869
Owlbury *Shrops* 59 SO3191
Owlerton *S York* 74 SK3389
Owlpen *Gloucs* 35 ST7998
Owlsmoor *Berks* 25 SU8462
Owlswick *Bucks* 37 SP7806
Owmby *Lincs* 85 TA0704
Owmby *Lincs* 76 TF0087
Owslebury *Hants* 13 SU5123
Owston *Leics* 63 SK7707
Owston *S York* 83 SE5511
Owston Ferry *Humb* 75 SE8000
Owstwick *Humb* 85 TA2732
Owthorne *Humb* 85 TA3328
Owthorpe *Notts* 63 SK6733
Oxborough *Norfk* 65 TF7401
Oxbridge *Dorset* 10 SY4797
Oxcombe *Lincs* 77 TF3177
Oxcroft *Derbys* 75 SK4873
Oxen End *Essex* 40 TL6629
Oxen Park *Cumb* 86 SD3187
Oxenholme *Cumb* 87 SD5290
Oxenhope *W York* 82 SE0334
Oxenpill *Somset* 21 ST4441
Oxenton *Gloucs* 47 SO9531
Oxenwood *Wilts* 23 SU3058
Oxford *Oxon* 37 SP5106
Oxhey *Herts* 26 TQ1295
Oxhill *Dur* 96 NZ1852
Oxhill *Warwks* 48 SP3146
Oxley *W Mids* 60 SJ9001
Oxley Green *Essex* 40 TL9014
Oxley's Green *E Susx* 16 TQ6921
Oxlode *Cambs* 53 TL4886
Oxnam *Border* 110 NT6918
Oxnead *Norfk* 67 TG2224
Oxshott *Surrey* 26 TQ1460
Oxshott Heath *Surrey* 26 TQ1361
Oxspring *S York* 82 SE2601
Oxted *Surrey* 27 TQ3852
Oxton *Border* 118 NT4953
Oxton *N York* 83 SE5043
Oxton *Notts* 75 SK6351
Oxwich *W Glam* 32 SS4986
Oxwich Green *W Glam* 32 SS4985
Oxwick *Norfk* 66 TF9125
Oykel Bridge Hotel *Highld* 145 NC3801
Oyne *Gramp* 142 NJ6725
Oystermouth *W Glam* 32 SS6187
Ozleworth *Gloucs* 35 ST7993

P

Packers hill *Dorset* 11 ST7110
Packington *Leics* 62 SK3614
Packmoor *Staffs* 72 SJ8654
Packmores *Warwks* 48 SP2866
Padanaram *Tays* 127 NO4251
Padbury *Bucks* 49 SP7230
Paddington *Ches* 79 SJ6389
Paddington *Gt Lon* 27 TQ2681
Paddlesworth *Kent* 28 TQ6862
Paddlesworth *Kent* 29 TR1939
Paddock Wood *Kent* 28 TQ6744
Paddolgreen *Shrops* 59 SJ5032
Padeswood *Clwyd* 70 SJ2762
Padfield *Derbys* 74 SK0296
Padgate *Ches* 79 SJ6389
Padhams Green *Essex* 40 TQ6497
Padiham *Lancs* 81 SD7933
Padside *N York* 89 SE1659
Padstow *Cnwll* 4 SW9175
Padworth *Berks* 24 SU6166
Page Bank *Dur* 96 NZ2335
Pagham *W Susx* 14 SZ8897
Paglesham *Essex* 40 TQ9293
Paignton *Devon* 7 SX8860
Pailton *Warwks* 50 SP4781
Paine's Cross *E Susx* 16 TQ6223
Painleyhill *Staffs* 73 SK0333
Painscastle *Powys* 45 SO1646
Painshawfield *Nthumb* 103 NZ0560
Painsthorpe *Humb* 90 SE8158
Painswick *Gloucs* 35 SO8609
Painter's Forstal *Kent* 28 TQ9958
Paisley *Strath* 115 NS4864
Pakefield *Suffk* 55 TM5390
Pakenham *Suffk* 54 TL9267
Pale *Gwynd* 58 SH9836
Pale Green *Essex* 53 TL6542
Palestine *Hants* 23 SU2640
Paley Street *Berks* 26 SU8776
Palfrey *W Mids* 60 SP0196
Palgrave *Suffk* 54 TM1178
Pallington *Dorset* 11 SY7891
Palmers Green *Gt Lon* 27 TQ3192
Palmersbridge *Cnwll* 5 SX1977
Palmerston *Strath* 107 NS5019
Palmerstown *S Glam* 20 ST1369
Palnackie *D & G* 92 NX8157
Palnure *D & G* 99 NX4563
Palterton *Derbys* 75 SK4768
Pamber End *Hants* 24 SU6158
Pamber Green *Hants* 24 SU6159
Pamber Heath *Hants* 24 SU6162
Pamington *Gloucs* 47 SO9433
Pamphill *Dorset* 11 ST9900
Pampisford *Cambs* 53 TL4948
Panborough *Somset* 21 ST4745
Panbride *Tays* 127 NO5635
Pancrasweek *Devon* 18 SS2905
Pancross *S Glam* 20 ST0469
Pandy *Clwyd* 58 SJ1935
Pandy *Gwent* 34 SO3322
Pandy *Gwynd* 57 SH6202
Pandy *Gwynd* 57 SH8729
Pandy *Powys* 58 SH9004
Pandy Tudur *Clwyd* 69 SH8564
Pandy'r Capel *Clwyd* 70 SJ0850
Panfield *Essex* 40 TL7325
Pangbourne *Berks* 37 SU6376
Pangdean *W Susx* 15 TQ2911
Panks Bridge *H & W* 47 SO6248
Pannal *N York* 82 SE3051
Pannal Ash *N York* 82 SE2953
Pannanich Wells Hotel *Gramp* 134 NO4097
Pant *Shrops* 58 SJ2722
Pant Mawr *Powys* 43 SN8482
Pant-Gwyn *Dyfed* 44 SN5925
Pant-glas *Gwynd* 68 SH4747
Pant-pastynog *Clwyd* 70 SJ0461
Pant-y-dwr *Powys* 45 SN9874
Pant-y-ffridd *Powys* 58 SJ1502
Pant-y-gog *M Glam* 33 SS9090
Pant-y-mwyn *Clwyd* 70 SJ1964
Pantasaph *Clwyd* 70 SJ1675
Pantersbridge *Cnwll* 4 SX1667
Pantglas *Powys* 43 SN7797
Panton *Lincs* 76 TF1778
Pantperthog *Gwynd* 57 SH7404
Pantyffynnon *Dyfed* 32 SN6210
Pantygasseg *Gwent* 34 ST2599
Pantymenyn *Dyfed* 31 SN1426
Panxworth *Norfk* 67 TG3513
Papcastle *Cumb* 92 NY1031
Papigoe *Highld* 151 ND3851
Papple *Loth* 118 NT5972
Papplewick *Notts* 75 SK5451
Papworth Everard *Cambs* 52 TL2862
Papworth St. Agnes *Cambs* 52 TL2664
Par *Cnwll* 3 SX0753
Paramour Street *Kent* 29 TR2961
Parbold *Lancs* 80 SD4911
Parbrook *Somset* 21 ST5736
Parbrook *W Susx* 14 TQ0825
Parc *Gwynd* 57 SH8834
Parc Seymour *Gwent* 34 ST4091
Parcllyn *Dyfed* 42 SN2451
Pardshaw *Cumb* 92 NY0924
Parham *Suffk* 55 TM3060
Park *D & G* 100 NX9091
Park *Gramp* 135 NO7898
Park *Nthumb* 102 NY6861
Park Bottom *Cnwll* 2 SW6642
Park Bridge *Gt Man* 79 SD9402
Park Corner *Berks* 26 SU8582
Park Corner *E Susx* 16 TQ5336
Park Corner *Oxon* 37 SU6988
Park End *Beds* 38 SP9952
Park End *Nthumb* 102 NY8675
Park End *Staffs* 72 SJ7851
Park Gate *H & W* 60 SO9371
Park Gate *Hants* 13 SU5108
Park Gate *W York* 82 SE1841
Park Green *Essex* 39 TL4628
Park Green *Suffk* 54 TM1364
Park Head *Cumb* 94 NY5841
Park Head *Derbys* 74 SK3654
Park Head *W York* 82 SE2007
Park Hill *Gloucs* 34 ST5799
Park Royal *Gt Lon* 26 TQ1982
Park Street *W Susx* 14 TQ1131
Parkend *Gloucs* 34 SO6108
Parkers Green *Kent* 16 TQ6148
Parkeston *Essex* 41 TM2332
Parkeston Quay *Essex* 41 TM2332
Parkfield *Bucks* 37 SP8002
Parkfield *Cnwll* 5 SX3167
Parkgate *Ches* 70 SJ2878
Parkgate *Ches* 79 SJ7873
Parkgate *Cumb* 93 NY2146
Parkgate *D & G* 100 NY0288
Parkgate *E Susx* 17 TQ7214
Parkgate *Essex* 40 TL6829
Parkgate *Kent* 27 TQ5064
Parkgate *Kent* 17 TQ8534
Parkgate *Surrey* 15 TQ2043
Parkhall *Strath* 115 NS4871
Parkham *Devon* 18 SS3921
Parkham Ash *Devon* 18 SS3620
Parkhill *Notts* 75 SK6952
Parkhill House *Gramp* 143 NJ8914
Parkhouse *Gwent* 34 SO5003
Parkmill *W Glam* 32 SS5489
Parkside *Clwyd* 71 SJ3855
Parkside *Dur* 96 NZ4248
Parkstone *Dorset* 12 SZ0391
Parley Green *Dorset* 12 SZ1097
Parlington *W York* 83 SE4235
Parmoor *Bucks* 37 SU7989
Parndon *Essex* 39 TL4308
Parr Bridge *Gt Man* 79 SD7001
Parracombe *Devon* 19 SS6745
Parrah Green *Ches* 72 SJ7145
Parrog *Dyfed* 30 SN0539
Parson Drove *Cambs* 64 TF3708
Parson's Cross *S York* 74 SK3492
Parson's Heath *Essex* 41 TM0226
Parson's Hill *Derbys* 73 SK2926
Parsonby *Cumb* 92 NY1438
Partick *Strath* 115 NS5467
Partington *Gt Man* 79 SJ7191
Partney *Lincs* 77 TF4068
Parton *Cumb* 92 NX9820
Parton *D & G* 99 NX6970
Partridge Green *W Susx* 15 TQ1919
Partrishow *Powys* 34 SO2722
Parwich *Derbys* 73 SK1854
Paslow Wood Common *Essex* 27 TL5802
Passenham *Nhants* 38 SP7839
Passfield *Hants* 14 SU8234
Passingford Bridge *Essex* 27 TQ5097
Paston *Cambs* 64 TF1802
Paston *Norfk* 67 TG3234
Pasturefields *Staffs* 73 SJ9924
Patchacott *Devon* 5 SX4798
Patcham *E Susx* 15 TQ3008
Patchetts Green *Herts* 26 TQ1497
Patching *W Susx* 14 TQ0806
Patchole *Devon* 19 SS6142
Patchway *Avon* 34 ST6082
Pateley Bridge *N York* 89 SE1565
Paternoster Heath *Essex* 40 TL9115
Pateshall *H & W* 46 SO5262
Path of Condie *Tays* 125 NO0711
Pathe *Somset* 21 ST3730
Pathhead *Fife* 117 NT2992
Pathhead *Gramp* 135 NO7263
Pathhead *Loth* 118 NT3964
Pathhead *Strath* 107 NS6114
Pathlow *Warwks* 48 SP1758
Patmore Heath *Herts* 39 TL4425
Patna *Strath* 106 NS4110
Patney *Wilts* 23 SU0758
Patrick *IOM* 153 SC2482
Patrick Brompton *N York* 89 SE2190
Patricroft *Gt Man* 79 SJ7597
Patrington *Humb* 85 TA3122
Patrixbourne *Kent* 29 TR1855
Patterdale *Cumb* 93 NY3915
Pattingham *Staffs* 60 SO8299
Pattishall *Nhants* 49 SP6754
Pattiswick Green *Essex* 40 TL8124
Patton *Shrops* 59 SO5895
Paul *Cnwll* 2 SW4627
Paul's Dene *Wilts* 23 SU1432
Paulerspury *Bucks* 49 SP7145
Paull *Humb* 85 TA1626
Paulton *Avon* 21 ST6556
Paunton *H & W* 47 SO6650
Pauperhaugh *Nthumb* 103 NZ1099
Pave Lane *Shrops* 72 SJ7616
Pavenham *Beds* 51 SP9955
Pawlett *Somset* 20 ST2942
Pawston *Nthumb* 110 NT8532
Paxford *Gloucs* 48 SP1837
Paxton *Border* 119 NT9353
Payden Street *Kent* 28 TQ9254
Payhembury *Devon* 9 ST0901
Paythorne *Lancs* 81 SD8251
Paytoe *H & W* 46 SO4171
Peacehaven *E Susx* 15 TQ4101
Peak Dale *Derbys* 74 SK0976
Peak Forest *Derbys* 74 SK1179
Peak Hill *Lincs* 64 TF2615
Peakirk *Cambs* 64 TF1606
Pean *Kent* 29 TR1837
Peanmeanach *Highld* 129 NM7180
Pearsie *Tays* 134 NO3659
Pearson's Green *Kent* 28 TQ6943
Pease Pottage *W Susx* 15 TQ2633
Peasedown St. John *Avon* 22 ST7057
Peasehill *Derbys* 74 SK4049
Peaseland Green *Norfk* 66 TG0516
Peasemore *Berks* 37 SU4577
Peasenhall *Suffk* 55 TM3569
Peaslake *Surrey* 14 TQ0844
Peasley Cross *Mersyd* 78 SJ5294
Peasmarsh *E Susx* 17 TQ8822
Peasmarsh *Somset* 10 ST3312
Peasmarsh *Surrey* 25 SU9946
Peat Inn *Fife* 127 NO4509
Peathill *Gramp* 143 NJ9366
Peatling Magna *Leics* 50 SP5992
Peatling Parva *Leics* 50 SP5889
Peaton *Shrops* 59 SO5385
Pebmarsh *Essex* 40 TL8533
Pebworth *H & W* 48 SP1347
Pecket Well *W York* 82 SD9929
Peckforton *Ches* 71 SJ5356
Peckham *Gt Lon* 27 TQ3476
Peckleton *Leics* 62 SK4701
Pedair-ffordd *Powys* 58 SJ1124
Pedlinge *Kent* 17 TR1335
Pedmore *W Mids* 60 SO9182
Pedwell *Somset* 21 ST4236
Peebles *Border* 109 NT2540
Peel *IOM* 153 SC2483
Peel *Lancs* 80 SD3531
Peel Common *Hants* 13 SU5703
Peening Quarter *Kent* 17 TQ8828
Pegsdon *Beds* 38 TL1130
Pegswood *Nthumb* 103 NZ2287
Pegwell *Kent* 29 TR3664
Peinchorran *Highld* 137 NG5233
Peinlich *Highld* 136 NG4158
Pelaw *T & W* 96 NZ3061
Pelcomb *Dyfed* 30 SM9218
Pelcomb Bridge *Dyfed* 30 SM9317
Peldon *Essex* 41 TL9816
Pell Green *E Susx* 16 TQ6432
Pelsall *W Mids* 60 SK0203
Pelsall Wood *W Mids* 60 SK0204
Pelton *Dur* 96 NZ2553
Pelton Fell *Dur* 96 NZ2551
Pelutho *Cumb* 92 NY1249
Pelynt *Cnwll* 5 SX2055
Pemberton *Dyfed* 32 SN5300
Pemberton *Gt Man* 78 SD5503
Pembles Cross *Kent* 28 TQ8947
Pembrey *Dyfed* 31 SN4301
Pembridge *H & W* 46 SO3958
Pembroke *Dyfed* 30 SM9801
Pembroke Dock *Dyfed* 30 SM9603
Pembury *Kent* 16 TQ6240
Pen Rhiwfawr *W Glam* 32 SN7410
Pen-bont Rhydybeddau *Dyfed* 43 SN6783
Pen-ffordd *Dyfed* 31 SN0722
Pen-groes-oped *Gwent* 34 SO3106
Pen-llyn *Gwynd* 68 SH3582
Pen-lon *Gwynd* 68 SH4365
Pen-rhiw *Dyfed* 31 SN2440
Pen-twyn *Gwent* 33 SO2000
Pen-twyn *Gwent* 34 SO2603
Pen-twyn *Gwent* 34 SO5209
Pen-y-Bont-Fawr *Powys* 58 SJ0824
Pen-y-bont *Clwyd* 58 SJ2123
Pen-y-bryn *Dyfed* 31 SN1742
Pen-y-bryn *M Glam* 33 SS8384
Pen-y-cae *Powys* 33 SN8413
Pen-y-cae-mawr *Gwent* 34 ST4195
Pen-y-cefn *Clwyd* 70 SJ1175
Pen-y-clawdd *Gwent* 34 SO4507
Pen-y-coedcae *M Glam* 33 ST0587
Pen-y-cwn *Dyfed* 30 SM8523
Pen-y-darren *M Glam* 33 SO0506
Pen-y-fai *M Glam* 33 SS8981
Pen-y-felin *Clwyd* 70 SJ1569
Pen-y-Gwryd Hotel *Gwynd* 69 SH6655
Pen-y-garn *Dyfed* 43 SN6285
Pen-y-genffordd *Powys* 45 SO1729
Pen-y-graig *Gwynd* 56 SH2033
Pen-y-lan *S Glam* 33 SS9976
Pen-y-pass *Gwynd* 69 SH6455
Pen-y-stryt *Clwyd* 70 SJ1952
Pen-yr-Heol *Gwent* 34 SO4311
Pen-yr-Heolgerrig *M Glam* 33 SO0306
Penair *Cnwll* 3 SW8445
Penallt *Gwent* 34 SO5210
Penally *Dyfed* 31 SS1199
Penalt *H & W* 46 SO5629
Penare *Cnwll* 3 SW9940
Penarth *S Glam* 33 ST1871
Penbryn *Dyfed* 42 SN2951
Pencader *Dyfed* 31 SN4436
Pencaitland *Loth* 118 NT4468
Pencalenick *Cnwll* 3 SW8545
Pencarnisiog *Gwynd* 68 SH3573
Pencarreg *Dyfed* 44 SN5445
Pencarrow *Cnwll* 4 SX1082
Pencelli *Powys* 45 SO0925
Penclawdd *W Glam* 32 SS5495
Pencoed *M Glam* 33 SS9581
Pencombe *H & W* 46 SO5952
Pencoyd *H & W* 46 SO5126
Pencraig *H & W* 34 SO5620
Pencraig *Powys* 58 SJ0426
Pendeen *Cnwll* 2 SW3834
Penderyn *M Glam* 33 SN9408
Pendine *Dyfed* 31 SN2208
Pendlebury *Gt Man* 79 SD7802
Pendleton *Lancs* 81 SD7539
Pendock *H & W* 47 SO7832
Pendoggett *Cnwll* 4 SX0279
Pendomer *Somset* 10 ST5210
Pendoylan *S Glam* 33 ST0576
Pendre *M Glam* 33 SS9181
Penegoes *Powys* 57 SH7600
Penelewey *Cnwll* 3 SW8140
Pengam *Gwent* 33 ST1597
Pengam *S Glam* 33 ST2177
Penge *Gt Lon* 27 TQ3570
Pengelly *Cnwll* 3 SW8551
Pengelly *Cnwll* 4 SX0783
Pengorffwysfa *Gwynd* 68 SH4692
Pengover Green *Cnwll* 5 SX2765
Pengrugla *Cnwll* 3 SW9947
Pengwern *Clwyd* 70 SJ0276
Penhale *Cnwll* 2 SW6918
Penhale *Cnwll* 4 SW9057
Penhale *Cnwll* 4 SX0860
Penhale *Cnwll* 5 SX4153

293

Pontamman Radcliffe on Trent

Pontamman	*Dyfed*	32	SN6312
Pontantwn	*Dyfed*	32	SN4412
Pontardawe	*W Glam*	32	SN7204
Pontarddulais	*W Glam*	32	SN5903
Pontarsais	*Dyfed*	31	SN4428
Pontblyddyn	*Clwyd*	70	SJ2760
Pontdolgoch	*Powys*	58	SO0193
Pontefract	*W York*	83	SE4521
Ponteland	*Nthumb*	103	NZ1672
Ponterwyd	*Dyfed*	43	SN7481
Pontesbury Hill	*Shrops*	59	SJ3905
Pontesford	*Shrops*	59	SJ4106
Pontfadog	*Clwyd*	70	SJ2338
Pontfaen	*Dyfed*	30	SN0234
Pontgarreg	*Dyfed*	42	SN3353
Ponthenry	*Dyfed*	32	SN4709
Ponthir	*Gwent*	34	ST3292
Ponthirwaun	*Dyfed*	42	SN2645
Pontllanfraith	*Gwent*	33	ST1895
Pontlliw	*W Glam*	57	SN6199
Pontlottyn	*M Glam*	33	SO1106
Pontlyfni	*Gwynd*	68	SH4352
Pontnewydd	*Gwent*	34	ST2896
Pontnewynydd	*Gwent*	34	SO2701
Pontop	*Dur*	96	NZ1453
Pontrhydfendigaid	*Dyfed*	43	SN7366
Pontrhydygroes	*Dyfed*	43	SN7472
Pontrhydyrun	*Gwent*	34	ST2997
Pontrilas	*H & W*	46	SO3927
Ponts Green	*E Susx*	16	TQ6715
Pontshaen	*Dyfed*	42	SN4446
Pontshill	*H & W*	35	SO6421
Pontsticill	*M Glam*	33	SO0511
Pontwelly	*Dyfed*	31	SN4140
Pontyates	*Dyfed*	32	SN4708
Pontyberem	*Dyfed*	32	SN5010
Pontybodkin	*Clwyd*	70	SJ2759
Pontyclun	*M Glam*	33	ST0381
Pontycymer	*M Glam*	33	SS9091
Pontyglasier	*Dyfed*	31	SN1436
Pontygwaith	*M Glam*	33	ST0094
Pontygynon	*Dyfed*	31	SN1237
Pontymoel	*Gwent*	34	SO2900
Pontypool	*Gwent*	34	SO2800
Pontypool Road	*Gwent*	34	ST3099
Pontypridd	*M Glam*	33	ST0789
Pontywaun	*Gwent*	34	ST2292
Pooksgreen	*Hants*	12	SU3710
Pool	*Cnwll*	2	SW6641
Pool	*IOS*	2	SV8714
Pool	*W York*	82	SE2445
Pool Head	*H & W*	46	SO5550
Pool o'Muckhart	*Cent*	117	NO0000
Pool Quay	*Powys*	58	SJ2511
Pool Street	*Essex*	53	TL7636
Poole	*Dorset*	11	SZ0090
Poole Keynes	*Wilts*	35	ST9995
Poolewe	*Highld*	144	NG8580
Pooley Bridge	*Cumb*	93	NY4724
Pooley Street	*Norfk*	54	TM0581
Poolfold	*Staffs*	72	SJ8959
Poolhill	*Gloucs*	47	SO7229
Pooting's	*Kent*	16	TQ4549
Popham	*Hants*	24	SU5543
Poplar	*Gt Lon*	27	TQ3780
Poplar Street	*Suffk*	55	TM4465
Porchbrook	*H & W*	60	SO7270
Porchfield	*IOW*	13	SZ4491
Poringland	*Norfk*	67	TG2701
Porkellis	*Cnwll*	2	SW6933
Porlock	*Somset*	19	SS8846
Porlock Weir	*Somset*	19	SS8647
Port Appin	*Strath*	122	NM9045
Port Askaig	*Strath*	112	NR4369
Port Bannatyne	*Strath*	114	NS0767
Port Carlisle	*Cumb*	101	NY2461
Port Charlotte	*Strath*	112	NR2558
Port Clarence	*Cleve*	97	NZ5021
Port Dinorwic	*Gwynd*	68	SH5267
Port Dolgarrog	*Gwynd*	69	SH7766
Port Driseach	*Strath*	114	NR9873
Port Einon	*W Glam*	32	SS4685
Port Ellen	*Strath*	104	NR3645
Port Elphinstone	*Gramp*	142	NJ7720
Port Erin	*IOM*	153	SC1969
Port Gaverne	*Cnwll*	4	SX0080
Port Glasgow	*Strath*	115	NS3274
Port Henderson	*Highld*	137	NG7573
Port Isaac	*Cnwll*	4	SW9980
Port Logan	*D & G*	98	NX0940
Port Mor	*Highld*	128	NM4279
Port Mulgrave	*N York*	97	NZ7917
Port Na Craig	*Tays*	125	NN9357
Port of Menteith	*Cent*	115	NN5801
Port of Ness	*W Isls*	154	NB5363
Port Quin	*Cnwll*	4	SW9780
Port Ramsay	*Strath*	122	NM8845
Port Soderick	*IOM*	153	SC3472
Port St. Mary	*IOM*	153	SC2067
Port Sunlight	*Mersyd*	78	SJ3384
Port Talbot	*W Glam*	32	SS7689
Port Tennant	*W Glam*	32	SS6893
Port Wemyss	*Strath*	112	NR1651
Port William	*D & G*	98	NX3343
Port-an-Eorna	*Highld*	137	NG7732
Portachoillan	*Strath*	113	NR7557
Portavadie	*Strath*	114	NR9369
Portbury	*Avon*	34	ST5075
Portchester	*Hants*	13	SU6105
Portencalzie	*D & G*	98	NX0171
Portencross	*Strath*	114	NS1748
Portesham	*Dorset*	10	SY6085
Portessie	*Gramp*	142	NJ4366
Portfield Gate	*Dyfed*	30	SM9215
Portgate	*Devon*	5	SX4285
Portgordon	*Gramp*	142	NJ3964
Portgower	*Highld*	147	ND0013
Porth	*Cnwll*	4	SW8362
Porth	*M Glam*	33	ST0291
Porth Dinllaen	*Gwynd*	56	SH2740
Porth Navas	*Cnwll*	3	SW7527
Porth-y-Waen	*Shrops*	58	SJ2623
Porthallow	*Cnwll*	3	SW7923
Porthallow	*Cnwll*	5	SX2251
Porthcawl	*M Glam*	33	SS8177
Porthcothan	*Cnwll*	4	SW8672
Porthcurno	*Cnwll*	2	SW3822
Porthgain	*Dyfed*	30	SM8132
Porthgwarra	*Cnwll*	2	SW3721
Porthill	*Staffs*	72	SJ8448
Porthkea	*Cnwll*	3	SW8242
Porthkerry	*S Glam*	20	ST0866
Porthleven	*Cnwll*	2	SW6225
Porthmadog	*Gwynd*	57	SH5638
Porthmeor	*Cnwll*	2	SW4337
Portholland	*Cnwll*	3	SW9541
Porthoustock	*Cnwll*	3	SW8021
Porthpean	*Cnwll*	3	SX0250
Porthtowan	*Cnwll*	2	SW6947
Porthyrhyd	*Dyfed*	32	SN5215
Portincaple	*Strath*	114	NS2393
Portinfer	*Jersey*	152	JS0615
Portington	*Humb*	84	SE7831
Portinnisherrich	*Strath*	122	NM9711
Portinscale	*Cumb*	93	NY2523
Portishead	*Avon*	34	ST4675
Portknockie	*Gramp*	142	NJ4868
Portlethen	*Gramp*	135	NO9196
Portling	*D & G*	92	NX8753
Portloe	*Cnwll*	3	SW9339
Portlooe	*Cnwll*	5	SX2452
Portmahomack	*Highld*	147	NH9184
Portmellon	*Cnwll*	3	SX0144
Portmore	*Hants*	12	SZ3397
Portnacroish	*Strath*	122	NM9247
Portnaguiran	*W Isls*	154	NB5537
Portnahaven	*Strath*	112	NR1652
Portnalong	*Highld*	136	NG3434
Portobello	*Loth*	117	NT3073
Portobello	*T & W*	96	NZ2856
Portobello	*W Mids*	60	SO9598
Porton	*Wilts*	23	SU1836
Portontown	*Devon*	5	SX4176
Portpatrick	*D & G*	98	NW9954
Portreath	*Cnwll*	2	SW6545
Portreath	*Cnwll*	4	SW9679
Portree	*Highld*	136	NG4843
Portrye	*Strath*	114	NS1757
Portscatho	*Cnwll*	3	SW8735
Portsea	*Hants*	13	SU6300
Portskerra	*Highld*	150	NC8765
Portskewett	*Gwent*	34	ST4988
Portslade	*E Susx*	15	TQ2506
Portslade-by-Sea	*E Susx*	15	TQ2605
Portslogan	*D & G*	98	NW9858
Portsmouth	*Hants*	13	SU6400
Portsmouth	*W York*	81	SD9026
Portsoy	*Gramp*	142	NJ5866
Portswood	*Hants*	13	SU4214
Portuairk	*Highld*	128	NM4368
Portway	*H & W*	46	SO4844
Portway	*H & W*	46	SO4935
Portway	*W Mids*	60	SO9787
Portwrinkle	*Cnwll*	5	SX3553
Portyerrock	*D & G*	99	NX4738
Posbury	*Devon*	8	SX8197
Posenhall	*Shrops*	59	SJ6501
Poslingford	*Suffk*	53	TL7648
Posso	*Border*	109	NT2033
Post Green	*Dorset*	11	SY9593
Postbridge	*Devon*	8	SX6579
Postcombe	*Oxon*	37	SP7000
Postling	*Kent*	29	TR1439
Postwick	*Norfk*	67	TG2907
Pothole	*Cnwll*	3	SW9750
Potsgrove	*Beds*	38	SP9530
Pott Row	*Norfk*	65	TF7022
Pott Shrigley	*Ches*	79	SJ9479
Pott's Green	*Essex*	40	TL9122
Potten End	*Herts*	38	TL0109
Potten Street	*Kent*	29	TR2567
Potter Brompton	*N York*	91	SE9777
Potter Heigham	*Norfk*	67	TG4119
Potter Row	*Bucks*	26	SP9002
Potter Somersal	*Derbys*	73	SK1335
Potter's Cross	*Staffs*	60	SO8484
Potter's Forstal	*Kent*	28	TQ8946
Potter's Green	*E Susx*	16	TQ5023
Potter's Green	*Herts*	39	TL3520
Pottergate Street	*Norfk*	66	TM1591
Potterhanworth	*Lincs*	76	TF0566
Potterhanworth Booths	*Lincs*	76	TF0767
Potterne	*Wilts*	22	ST9958
Potterne Wick	*Wilts*	22	ST9957
Potters Bar	*Herts*	26	TL2401
Potters Brook	*Lancs*	80	SD4852
Potters Crouch	*Herts*	38	TL1105
Potters Green	*W Mids*	61	SP3782
Potters Marston	*Leics*	50	SP4996
Pottersheath	*Herts*	39	TL2318
Potterspury	*Nhants*	49	SP7543
Potterton	*W York*	83	SE4038
Potthorpe	*Norfk*	66	TF9422
Pottle Street	*Wilts*	22	ST8140
Potto	*N York*	89	NZ4703
Potton	*Beds*	52	TL2249
Poughill	*Cnwll*	18	SS2207
Poughill	*Devon*	19	SS8508
Poulner	*Hants*	12	SU1606
Poulshot	*Wilts*	22	ST9659
Poulston	*Devon*	7	SX7754
Poulton	*Gloucs*	36	SP0901
Poulton	*Mersyd*	78	SJ3091
Poulton Priory	*Gloucs*	36	SP0900
Poulton-le-Fylde	*Lancs*	80	SD3439
Pound Bank	*H & W*	60	SO7374
Pound Green	*E Susx*	16	TQ5123
Pound Green	*H & W*	60	SO7579
Pound Green	*Suffk*	53	TL7153
Pound Hill	*W Susx*	15	TQ2937
Pound Street	*Hants*	24	SU4561
Poundffald	*W Glam*	32	SS5694
Poundgates	*E Susx*	16	TQ4928
Poundon	*Bucks*	49	SP6425
Poundsbridge	*Kent*	16	TQ5341
Poundsgate	*Devon*	7	SX7072
Poundstock	*Cnwll*	18	SX2099
Pounsley	*E Susx*	16	TQ5221
Pouton	*D & G*	99	NX4645
Povey Cross	*Surrey*	15	TQ2642
Pow Green	*H & W*	47	SO7144
Powburn	*Nthumb*	111	NU0616
Powderham	*Devon*	9	SX9684
Powerstock	*Dorset*	10	SY5196
Powfoot	*D & G*	100	NY1465
Powhill	*Cumb*	93	NY2355
Powick	*H & W*	47	SO8351
Powmill	*Tays*	117	NT0297
Poxwell	*Dorset*	11	SY7384
Poyle	*Gt Lon*	26	TQ0376
Poynings	*W Susx*	15	TQ2611
Poynter's Lane End	*Cnwll*	2	SW6743
Poyntington	*Dorset*	21	ST6520
Poynton	*Ches*	79	SJ9283
Poynton	*Shrops*	59	SJ5617
Poynton Green	*Shrops*	59	SJ5618
Poys Street	*Suffk*	55	TM3570
Poyston Cross	*Dyfed*	30	SM9819
Poystreet Green	*Suffk*	54	TL9758
Praa Sands	*Cnwll*	2	SW5828
Pratt's Bottom	*Gt Lon*	27	TQ4762
Praze-an-Beeble	*Cnwll*	2	SW6335
Predannack Wollas	*Cnwll*	2	SW6616
Prees	*Shrops*	59	SJ5533
Prees Green	*Shrops*	59	SJ5531
Prees Heath	*Shrops*	71	SJ5538
Prees Higher Heath	*Shrops*	59	SJ5635
Prees Lower Heath	*Shrops*	59	SJ5732
Preesall	*Lancs*	80	SD3647
Pren-gwyn	*Dyfed*	42	SN4244
Prendwick	*Nthumb*	111	NU0012
Prenteg	*Gwynd*	57	SH5841
Prenton	*Mersyd*	78	SJ3086
Prescot	*Mersyd*	78	SJ4692
Prescott	*Devon*	9	ST0814
Prescott	*Shrops*	59	SJ4220
Prescott	*Shrops*	60	SO6681
Presnerb	*Tays*	133	NO1866
Pressen	*Nthumb*	110	NT8335
Prestatyn	*Clwyd*	70	SJ0682
Prestbury	*Ches*	79	SJ8976
Prestbury	*Gloucs*	47	SO9723
Presteigne	*Powys*	46	SO3164
Prestleigh	*Somset*	21	ST6340
Prestolee	*Gt Man*	79	SD7505
Preston	*Border*	119	NT7957
Preston	*Devon*	7	SX7451
Preston	*Devon*	7	SX8574
Preston	*Devon*	7	SX8962
Preston	*Dorset*	11	SY7083
Preston	*E Susx*	15	TQ3106
Preston	*Gloucs*	47	SO6834
Preston	*Gloucs*	36	SP0400
Preston	*Herts*	39	TL1824
Preston	*Humb*	85	TA1830
Preston	*Kent*	28	TR0260
Preston	*Kent*	29	TR2460
Preston	*Lancs*	80	SD5329
Preston	*Leics*	63	SK8602
Preston	*Loth*	118	NT5977
Preston	*Nthumb*	111	NU1825
Preston	*Shrops*	59	SJ5211
Preston	*Somset*	20	ST0935
Preston	*Suffk*	54	TL9450
Preston	*Wilts*	36	SU2774
Preston Bagot	*Warwks*	48	SP1765
Preston Bissett	*Bucks*	49	SP6529
Preston Bowyer	*Somset*	20	ST1326
Preston Brockhurst	*Shrops*	59	SJ5324
Preston Brook	*Ches*	78	SJ5680
Preston Candover	*Hants*	24	SU6041
Preston Capes	*Nhants*	49	SP5754
Preston Crowmarsh	*Oxon*	37	SU6190
Preston Deanery	*Nhants*	50	SP7855
Preston Green	*Warwks*	48	SP1665
Preston Gubbals	*Shrops*	59	SJ4919
Preston Montford	*Shrops*	59	SJ4314
Preston on Stour	*Warwks*	48	SP2049
Preston on the Hill	*Ches*	78	SJ5780
Preston on Wye	*H & W*	46	SO3842
Preston Patrick	*Cumb*	87	SD5483
Preston Plucknett	*Somset*	10	ST5316
Preston Street	*Kent*	29	TR2561
Preston upon the Weald Moors	*Shrops*	72	SJ6815
Preston Wynne	*H & W*	46	SO5546
Preston-under-Scar	*N York*	88	SE0691
Prestonpans	*Loth*	118	NT3874
Prestwich	*Gt Man*	79	SD8104
Prestwick	*Nthumb*	103	NZ1872
Prestwick	*Strath*	106	NS3525
Prestwood	*Bucks*	26	SP8700
Prestwood	*Staffs*	60	SO8786
Price Town	*M Glam*	33	SS9391
Prickwillow	*Cambs*	53	TL5982
Priddy	*Somset*	21	ST5250
Priest Hutton	*Lancs*	87	SD5273
Priestacott	*Devon*	18	SS4206
Priestcliffe	*Derbys*	74	SK1471
Priestcliffe Ditch	*Derbys*	74	SK1371
Priestend	*Bucks*	37	SP6905
Priestley Green	*W York*	82	SE1326
Priestweston	*Shrops*	59	SO2997
Priestwood Green	*Kent*	28	TQ6564
Primethorpe	*Leics*	50	SP5293
Primrose Green	*Norfk*	66	TG0716
Primrose Hill	*Cambs*	52	TL3889
Primrose Hill	*Derbys*	75	SK4358
Primrose Hill	*Lancs*	78	SD3809
Primrose Hill	*W Mids*	60	SO9487
Primrosehill	*Border*	119	NT7857
Primsidemill	*Border*	110	NT8126
Princes Gate	*Dyfed*	31	SN1312
Princes Risborough	*Bucks*	38	SP8003
Princethorpe	*Warwks*	61	SP4070
Princetown	*Devon*	6	SX5873
Prinsted	*W Susx*	14	SU7605
Prior Rigg	*Cumb*	101	NY4568
Priors Halton	*Shrops*	46	SO4975
Priors Hardwick	*Warwks*	49	SP4756
Priors Marston	*Warwks*	49	SP4957
Priors Norton	*Gloucs*	47	SO8624
Priory Wood	*H & W*	46	SO2645
Prisk	*S Glam*	33	ST0176
Priston	*Avon*	22	ST6960
Pristow Green	*Norfk*	54	TM1388
Prittlewell	*Essex*	40	TQ8687
Privett	*Hants*	13	SU6727
Probus	*Cnwll*	3	SW8947
Prospect	*Cumb*	92	NY1140
Prospidnick	*Cnwll*	2	SW6431
Protstonhill	*Gramp*	143	NJ8163
Providence	*Avon*	34	ST5370
Prudhoe	*Nthumb*	103	NZ0962
Prussia Cove	*Cnwll*	2	SW5528
Ptarmigan Lodge	*Cent*	115	NN3500
Publow	*Avon*	21	ST6264
Puckeridge	*Herts*	39	TL3823
Puckington	*Somset*	10	ST3718
Pucklechurch	*Avon*	35	ST6976
Puckrup	*Gloucs*	47	SO8836
Puddinglake	*Ches*	79	SJ7269
Puddington	*Ches*	71	SJ3273
Puddington	*Devon*	19	SS8310
Puddledock	*Norfk*	66	TM0592
Puddletown	*Dorset*	11	SY7594
Pudsey	*W York*	82	SE2232
Pulborough	*W Susx*	14	TQ0418
Puleston	*Shrops*	72	SJ7322
Pulford	*Ches*	71	SJ3758
Pulham	*Dorset*	11	ST7008
Pulham Market	*Norfk*	55	TM1986
Pulham St. Mary	*Norfk*	55	TM2085
Pullens Green	*Avon*	34	ST6192
Pulley	*Shrops*	59	SJ4809
Pulloxhill	*Beds*	38	TL0634
Pumpherston	*Loth*	117	NT0669
Pumsaint	*Dyfed*	44	SN6540
Puncheston	*Dyfed*	30	SN0129
Puncknowle	*Dorset*	10	SY5388
Punnett's Town	*E Susx*	16	TQ6220
Purbrook	*Hants*	13	SU6707
Purbrook Park	*Hants*	13	SU6707
Purfleet	*Essex*	27	TQ5578
Puriton	*Somset*	21	ST3241
Purleigh	*Essex*	40	TL8402
Purley	*Berks*	37.	SU6675
Purley	*Gt Lon*	27	TQ3161
Purlogue	*Shrops*	46	SO2877
Purlpit	*Wilts*	22	ST8766
Purls Bridge	*Cambs*	53	TL4786
Purse Caundle	*Dorset*	11	ST6917
Purshall Green	*H & W*	60	SO8971
Purslow	*Shrops*	59	SO3680
Purston Jaglin	*W York*	83	SE4319
Purtington	*Somset*	10	ST3908
Purton	*Gloucs*	35	SO6904
Purton	*Gloucs*	35	SO6705
Purton	*Wilts*	36	SU0987
Purton Stoke	*Wilts*	36	SU0990
Pury End	*Nhants*	49	SP7145
Pusey	*Oxon*	36	SU3596
Putley	*H & W*	47	SO6337
Putley Green	*H & W*	47	SO6437
Putloe	*Gloucs*	35	SO7709
Putney	*Gt Lon*	26	TQ2374
Putron Village	*Guern*	152	GN5306
Putsborough	*Devon*	18	SS4440
Puttenham	*Herts*	38	SP8814
Puttenham	*Surrey*	25	SU9247
Puttock End	*Essex*	54	TL8040
Puttock's End	*Essex*	40	TL5719
Putton	*Dorset*	11	SY6480
Puxley	*Nhants*	49	SP7542
Puxton	*Avon*	21	ST4063
Pwll	*Dyfed*	32	SN4801
Pwll Trap	*Dyfed*	31	SN2616
Pwll-du	*Gwent*	34	SO2411
Pwll-y-glaw	*W Glam*	32	SS7993
Pwllcrochan	*Dyfed*	30	SM9202
Pwllglas	*Clwyd*	70	SJ1154
Pwllgloyw	*Powys*	45	SO0333
Pwllheli	*Gwynd*	56	SH3735
Pwllmeyric	*Gwent*	34	ST5292
Pydew	*Gwynd*	69	SH8079
Pye Bridge	*Derbys*	75	SK4452
Pye Corner	*Gwent*	34	ST3485
Pye Corner	*Herts*	39	TL4412
Pye Green	*Staffs*	60	SJ9813
Pyecombe	*W Susx*	15	TQ2813
Pyle	*M Glam*	33	SS8282
Pyleigh	*Somset*	20	ST1330
Pylle	*Somset*	21	ST6038
Pymore	*Cambs*	53	TL4986
Pymore	*Dorset*	10	SY4694
Pyrford	*Surrey*	26	TQ0358
Pyrton	*Oxon*	37	SU6896
Pytchley	*Nhants*	51	SP8574
Pyworthy	*Devon*	18	SS3102

Q

Quabbs	*Shrops*	58	SO2180
Quadring	*Lincs*	64	TF2233
Quadring Eaudike	*Lincs*	64	TF2433
Quainton	*Bucks*	37	SP7420
Quaker's Yard	*M Glam*	33	ST0995
Quaking Houses	*Dur*	96	NZ1850
Quarley	*Hants*	23	SU2743
Quarndon	*Derbys*	62	SK3340
Quarr Hill	*IOW*	13	SZ5792
Quarrier's Homes	*Strath*	115	NS3666
Quarrington	*Lincs*	64	TF0544
Quarrington Hill	*Dur*	96	NZ3337
Quarry Bank	*W Mids*	60	SO9386
Quarrybank	*Ches*	71	SJ5465
Quarrywood	*Gramp*	141	NJ1763
Quarter	*Strath*	116	NS7251
Quatford	*Shrops*	60	SO7391
Quatt	*Shrops*	60	SO7588
Quebec	*Dur*	96	NZ1743
Quedgeley	*Gloucs*	35	SO8014
Queen Adelaide	*Cambs*	53	TL5681
Queen Camel	*Somset*	21	ST5924
Queen Charlton	*Avon*	21	ST6367
Queen Dart	*Devon*	19	SS8316
Queen Oak	*Dorset*	22	ST7831
Queen Street	*Kent*	28	TQ6845
Queen Street	*Wilts*	35	SU0287
Queen's Bower	*IOW*	13	SZ5684
Queen's Head	*Shrops*	59	SJ3327
Queen's Park	*Beds*	38	TL0349
Queen's Park	*Nhants*	49	SP7562
Queenborough	*Kent*	28	TQ9172
Queenhill	*H & W*	47	SO8537
Queensbury	*W York*	82	SE1030
Queensferry	*Clwyd*	71	SJ3168
Queenslie	*Strath*	116	NS6565
Queenzieburn	*Strath*	116	NS6977
Quendon	*Essex*	39	TL5130
Queniborough	*Leics*	63	SK6412
Quenington	*Gloucs*	36	SP1404
Quernmore	*Lancs*	87	SD5160
Quernmore Park Hall	*Lancs*	87	SD5162
Queslett	*W Mids*	61	SP0695
Quethiock	*Cnwll*	5	SX3164
Quick's Green	*Berks*	37	SU5876
Quidenham	*Norfk*	54	TM0287
Quidhampton	*Hants*	24	SU5150
Quidhampton	*Wilts*	23	SU1030
Quina Brook	*Shrops*	59	SJ5232
Quinberry End	*Nhants*	49	SP6250
Quinton	*Nhants*	49	SP7754
Quinton	*W Mids*	60	SO9984
Quinton Green	*Nhants*	50	SP7853
Quintrell Downs	*Cnwll*	4	SW8460
Quither	*Devon*	5	SX4481
Quixhill	*Staffs*	73	SK1041
Quixwood	*Border*	119	NT7863
Quoditch	*Devon*	5	SX4097
Quorndon	*Leics*	62	SK5616
Quothquan	*Strath*	108	NS9939
Quoyburray	*Ork*	155	HY5005
Quoyloo	*Ork*	155	HY2420

R

RAF College (Cranwell)	*Lincs*	76	TF0049
Rabbit's Cross	*Kent*	28	TQ7847
Rableyheath	*Herts*	39	TL2319
Raby	*Cumb*	93	NY1951
Raby	*Mersyd*	71	SJ3179
Rachan Mill	*Border*	108	NT1134
Rachub	*Gwynd*	69	SH6267
Rackenford	*Devon*	19	SS8518
Rackham	*W Susx*	14	TQ0413
Rackheath	*Norfk*	67	TG2814
Rackwick	*Ork*	155	ND2099
Radbourne	*Derbys*	73	SK2836
Radcliffe	*Gt Man*	79	SD7806
Radcliffe	*Nthumb*	103	NU2602
Radcliffe on Trent	*Notts*	63	SK6439

Roag St Ewe

Roag *Highld* 136 NG2744
Roan of Craigoch *Strath* 106 NS2904
Roast Green *Essex* 39 TL4632
Roath *S Glam* 33 ST1977
Roberton *Border* 109 NT4214
Roberton *Strath* 108 NS9428
Robertsbridge *E Susx* 17 TQ7423
Roberttown *W York* 82 SE1922
Robeston Wathen *Dyfed* 31 SN0815
Robgill Tower *D & G* 101 NY2471
Robin Hill *Staffs* 72 SJ9057
Robin Hood *Lancs* 80 SD5211
Robin Hood *W York* 83 SE3227
Robin Hood's Bay *N York* 91 NZ9505
Robinhood End *Essex* 53 TL7036
Roborough *Devon* 19 SS5717
Roby *Mersyd* 78 SJ4390
Roby Mill *Lancs* 78 SD5107
Rocester *Staffs* 73 SK1039
Roch *Dyfed* 30 SM8821
Roch Gate *Dyfed* 30 SM8720
Rochdale *Gt Man* 81 SD8913
Roche *Cnwll* 4 SW9860
Rochester *Kent* 28 TQ7468
Rochester *Nthumb* 102 NY8298
Rochford *Essex* 40 TQ8790
Rochford *H & W* 47 SO6268
Rochville *Strath* 114 NS2390
Rock *Cnwll* 4 SW9375
Rock *H & W* 60 SO7371
Rock *Nthumb* 111 NU2020
Rock *W Glam* 32 SS7893
Rock *W Susx* 14 TQ1213
Rock Ferry *Mersyd* 78 SJ3386
Rock Hill *H & W* 47 SO9569
Rockbeare *Devon* 9 SY0194
Rockbourne *Hants* 12 SU1118
Rockcliffe *Cumb* 101 NY3561
Rockcliffe *D & G* 92 NX8454
Rockcliffe Cross *Cumb* 101 NY3463
Rockesta *Cnwll* 2 SW3722
Rockfield *Gwent* 34 SO4814
Rockfield *Highld* 147 NH9282
Rockford *Devon* 19 SS7547
Rockford *Hants* 12 SU1607
Rockgreen *Shrops* 46 SO5275
Rockhampton *Gloucs* 35 ST6593
Rockhead *Cnwll* 4 SX0784
Rockhill *Shrops* 46 SO2978
Rockingham *Nhants* 51 SP8691
Rockland All Saints *Norfk* 66 TL9996
Rockland St. Mary *Norfk* 67 TG3104
Rockland St. Peter *Norfk* 66 TL9897
Rockley *Notts* 75 SK7174
Rockley *Wilts* 36 SU1571
Rockliffe *Lancs* 81 SD8722
Rockwell End *Bucks* 37 SU7988
Rockwell Green *Somset* 20 ST1220
Rodborough *Gloucs* 35 SO8404
Rodbourne *Wilts* 36 SU1485
Rodbourne *Wilts* 35 ST9383
Rodd *H & W* 46 SO3262
Rodden *Dorset* 10 SY6184
Roddam *Nthumb* 111 NU0220
Roddymoor *Dur* 96 NZ1536
Rode *Somset* 22 ST8053
Rode Heath *Ches* 72 SJ8056
Rode Heath *Ches* 72 SJ8767
Rodel *W Isls* 154 NG0483
Roden *Shrops* 59 SJ5716
Rodhuish *Somset* 20 ST0139
Rodington *Shrops* 59 SJ5814
Rodington Heath *Shrops* 59 SJ5814
Rodley *Gloucs* 35 SO7411
Rodley *W York* 82 SE2236
Rodmarton *Gloucs* 35 ST9498
Rodmell *E Susx* 15 TQ4106
Rodmersham *Kent* 28 TQ9261
Rodmersham Green *Kent* 28 TQ9161
Rodney Stoke *Somset* 21 ST4849
Rodono Hotel *Border* 109 NT2321
Rodsley *Derbys* 73 SK2040
Rodway *Somset* 20 ST2540
Roe Cross *Gt Man* 79 SJ9896
Roe Green *Gt Man* 79 SD7501
Roe Green *Herts* 39 TL2107
Roe Green *Herts* 39 TL3133
Roecliffe *N York* 89 SE3765
Roehampton *Gt Lon* 26 TQ2273
Roffey *W Susx* 15 TQ1932
Rogart *Highld* 146 NC7202
Rogate *W Susx* 14 SU8023
Roger Ground *Cumb* 87 SD3597
Rogerstone *Gwent* 34 ST2787
Rogiet *Gwent* 34 ST4587
Roke *Oxon* 37 SU6293
Roker *T & W* 96 NZ4058
Rollesby *Norfk* 67 TG4416
Rolleston *Leics* 50 SK7300
Rolleston *Notts* 75 SK7452
Rolleston *Staffs* 73 SK2327
Rolston *Humb* 85 TA2144
Rolstone *Avon* 21 ST3962
Rolvenden *Kent* 17 TQ8431
Rolvenden Layne *Kent* 17 TQ8530
Romaldkirk *Dur* 95 NY9922
Romanby *N York* 89 SE3693
Romanno Bridge *Border* 117 NT1647
Romansleigh *Devon* 19 SS7220
Romden Castle *Kent* 28 TQ8941
Romesdal *Highld* 136 NG4053
Romford *Dorset* 12 SU0709
Romford *Gt Lon* 27 TQ5188
Romiley *Gt Man* 79 SJ9490
Romney Street *Kent* 27 TQ5561
Romsey *Hants* 12 SU3521
Romsley *H & W* 60 SO9680
Romsley *Shrops* 60 SO7883
Ronachan *Strath* 113 NR7454
Rookhope *Dur* 95 NY9342
Rookley *IOW* 13 SZ5084
Rookley Green *IOW* 13 SZ5083
Rooks Bridge *Somset* 21 ST3652
Rooks Nest *Somset* 20 ST0933
Rookwith *N York* 89 SE2086
Roos *Humb* 85 TA2830
Roose *Cumb* 86 SD2269
Roosebeck *Cumb* 86 SD2567
Roothams Green *Beds* 51 TL0957
Ropley *Hants* 24 SU6431
Ropley Dean *Hants* 24 SU6232
Ropley Soke *Hants* 24 SU6533
Ropsley *Lincs* 63 SK9933
Rora *Gramp* 143 NK0650
Rorrington *Shrops* 59 SJ3000
Rosarie *Gramp* 141 NJ3850
Roscroggan *Cnwll* 2 SW6542
Rose *Cnwll* 3 SW7754
Rose Ash *Devon* 19 SS7921
Rose Green *Essex* 40 TL9028
Rose Green *Suffk* 54 TL9337
Rose Green *Suffk* 54 TL9744
Rose Green *W Susx* 14 SZ9099
Rose Hill *E Susx* 16 TQ4516
Rose Hill *Lancs* 81 SD8231
Rose Lands *E Susx* 16 TQ6200
Roseacre *Lancs* 80 SD4336
Rosebank *Strath* 116 NS8049
Rosebush *Dyfed* 31 SN0729
Rosecare *Cnwll* 4 SX1695
Rosecliston *Cnwll* 4 SW8159
Rosedale Abbey *N York* 90 SE7296
Roseden *Nthumb* 111 NU0321
Rosehall *Highld* 146 NC4702
Rosehearty *Gramp* 143 NJ9267
Rosehill *Shrops* 59 SJ4715
Roseisle *Gramp* 141 NJ1466
Rosemarket *Dyfed* 30 SM9508
Rosemarkie *Highld* 140 NH7357
Rosemary Lane *Devon* 9 ST1514
Rosemount *Tays* 126 NO1843
Rosenannon *Cnwll* 4 SW9566
Rosenithon *Cnwll* 3 SW8021
Roser's Cross *E Susx* 16 TQ5420
Rosevean *Cnwll* 4 SX0258
Rosevine *Cnwll* 3 SW8736
Rosewarne *Cnwll* 2 SW6036
Rosewell *Loth* 117 NT2862
Roseworth *Cleve* 96 NZ4221
Roseworthy *Cnwll* 2 SW6139
Rosgill *Cumb* 94 NY5316
Roshven *Highld* 129 NM7078
Roskhill *Highld* 136 NG2744
Roskorwell *Cnwll* 3 SW7923
Roskrow *Cnwll* 3 SW7635
Rosley *Cumb* 93 NY3245
Roslin *Loth* 117 NT2763
Rosliston *Derbys* 73 SK2416
Rosneath *Strath* 114 NS2583
Ross *D & G* 99 NX6444
Ross *Nthumb* 111 NU1337
Ross-on-Wye *H & W* 46 SO5923
Rossett *Clwyd* 71 SJ3657
Rossett Green *N York* 82 SE2952
Rossington *Notts* 75 SK6298
Rosskeen *Highld* 146 NH6869
Rossland *Strath* 115 NS4370
Roster *Highld* 151 ND2639
Rostherne *Ches* 79 SJ7483
Rosthwaite *Cumb* 93 NY2514
Roston *Derbys* 73 SK1340
Rosudgeon *Cnwll* 2 SW5529
Rosyth *Loth* 117 NT1082
Rothbury *Nthumb* 103 NU0501
Rotherby *Leics* 63 SK6716
Rotherfield *E Susx* 16 TQ5529
Rotherfield Greys *Oxon* 37 SU7282
Rotherfield Peppard *Oxon* 37 SU7182
Rotherham *S York* 75 SK4392
Rothersthorpe *Nhants* 49 SP7156
Rotherwick *Hants* 24 SU7156
Rothes *Gramp* 141 NJ2749
Rothesay *Strath* 114 NS0864
Rothiebrisbane *Gramp* 142 NJ7437
Rothiemay *Gramp* 142 NJ5548
Rothienorman *Gramp* 142 NJ7235
Rothley *Leics* 62 SK5812
Rothley *Nthumb* 103 NZ0488
Rothmaise *Gramp* 142 NJ6832
Rothwell *Lincs* 76 TF1499
Rothwell *Nhants* 51 SP8181
Rothwell *W York* 83 SE3428
Rothwell Haigh *W York* 83 SE3328
Rotsea *Humb* 84 TA0651
Rottal Lodge *Tays* 134 NO3769
Rottingdean *E Susx* 15 TQ3602
Rottington *Cumb* 92 NX9613
Roucan *D & G* 100 NY0277
Roud *IOW* 13 SZ5180
Rough Close *Staffs* 72 SJ9239
Rough Common *Kent* 29 TR1259
Rougham *Norfk* 66 TF8320
Rougham Green *Suffk* 54 TL9061
Roughlee *Lancs* 81 SD8440
Roughley *W Mids* 61 SP1399
Roughpark *Gramp* 134 NJ3412
Roughton *Lincs* 77 TF2464
Roughton *Norfk* 67 TG2136
Roughton *Shrops* 60 SO7594
Roughway *Kent* 27 TQ6153
Round Bush *Herts* 26 TQ1498
Round Green *Beds* 38 TL1022
Round Street *Kent* 28 TQ6568
Roundbush *Essex* 40 TL8501
Roundbush Green *Essex* 40 TL5814
Roundham *Somset* 10 ST4209
Roundhay *W York* 83 SE3337
Rounds Green *W Mids* 60 SO9889
Roundstreet Common *W Susx* 14 TQ0528
Roundway *Wilts* 22 SU0163
Roundyhill *Tays* 126 NO3750
Rous Lench *H & W* 47 SP0153
Rousdon *Devon* 10 SY2991
Rousham *Oxon* 49 SP4724
Rout's Green *Bucks* 37 SU7898
Routenbeck *Cumb* 93 NY1930
Routenburn *Strath* 114 NS1961
Routh *Humb* 85 TA0942
Row *Cnwll* 4 SX0976
Row *Cumb* 94 NY6234
Row *Cumb* 87 SD4589
Row Ash *Hants* 13 SU5413
Row Green *Essex* 40 TL7420
Rowanburn *D & G* 101 NY4177
Rowardennan Hotel *Cent* 115 NS3698
Rowarth *Derbys* 79 SK0189
Rowberrow *Somset* 21 ST4558
Rowborough *IOW* 13 SZ4684
Rowde *Wilts* 22 ST9762
Rowden *Devon* 8 SX6499
Rowen *Gwynd* 69 SH7671
Rowfield *Derbys* 73 SK1948
Rowfoot *Nthumb* 102 NY6860
Rowford *Somset* 20 ST2327
Rowhedge *Essex* 41 TM0221
Rowhook *W Susx* 14 TQ1234
Rowington *Warwks* 48 SP2069
Rowland *Derbys* 74 SK2172
Rowland's Castle *Hants* 13 SU7310
Rowland's Gill *T & W* 96 NZ1658
Rowledge *Surrey* 25 SU8243
Rowley *Dur* 95 NZ0848
Rowley *Humb* 84 SE9732
Rowley *Shrops* 59 SJ3006
Rowley Green *W Mids* 61 SP3483
Rowley Hill *W York* 82 SE1914
Rowley Regis *W Mids* 60 SO9787
Rowlstone *H & W* 46 SO3727
Rowly *Surrey* 14 TQ0440
Rowner *Hants* 13 SU5801
Rowney Green *H & W* 61 SP0471
Rownhams *Hants* 12 SU3817
Rows of Trees *Ches* 79 SJ8379
Rowsham *Bucks* 38 SP8417
Rowsley *Derbys* 74 SK2565
Rowstock *Oxon* 37 SU4789
Rowston *Lincs* 76 TF0856
Rowthorne *Derbys* 75 SK4764
Rowton *Ches* 71 SJ4564
Rowton *Shrops* 59 SJ3612
Rowton *Shrops* 59 SJ6119
Rowton *Shrops* 59 SO4180
Rowtown *Surrey* 26 TQ0363
Roxburgh *Border* 110 NT6930
Roxby *Humb* 84 SE9116
Roxby *N York* 97 NZ7616
Roxton *Beds* 52 TL1554
Roxwell *Essex* 40 TL6408
Roy Bridge *Highld* 131 NN2681
Royal Oak *Dur* 96 NZ2023
Royal Oak *Lancs* 78 SD4103
Royal's Green *Ches* 71 SJ6242
Roydhouse *W York* 82 SE2112
Roydon *Essex* 39 TL4010
Roydon *Norfk* 65 TF7023
Roydon *Norfk* 54 TM1080
Roydon Hamlet *Essex* 39 TL4107
Royston *Herts* 39 TL3540
Royston *S York* 83 SE3611
Royton *Gt Man* 79 SD9107
Rozel *Jersey* 152 JS1914
Ruabon *Clwyd* 71 SJ3043
Ruaig *Strath* 120 NM0747
Ruan High Lanes *Cnwll* 3 SW9039
Ruan Lanihorne *Cnwll* 3 SW8942
Ruan Major *Cnwll* 2 SW7016
Ruan Minor *Cnwll* 2 SW7115
Ruardean *Gloucs* 35 SO6217
Ruardean Hill *Gloucs* 35 SO6317
Ruardean Woodside *Gloucs* 35 SO6216
Rubery *H & W* 60 SO9977
Ruckcroft *Cumb* 94 NY5344
Ruckhall Common *H & W* 46 SO4539
Ruckinge *Kent* 17 TR0233
Ruckland *Lincs* 77 TF3378
Ruckley *Shrops* 59 SJ5300
Rudby *N York* 89 NZ4706
Rudchester *Nthumb* 103 NZ1167
Ruddington *Notts* 62 SK5732
Ruddle *Gloucs* 35 SO6811
Ruddlemoor *Cnwll* 3 SX0054
Rudford *Gloucs* 35 SO7721
Rudge *Somset* 22 ST8251
Rudgeway *Avon* 35 ST6386
Rudgwick *W Susx* 14 TQ0834
Rudhall *H & W* 47 SO6225
Rudheath *Ches* 79 SJ6772
Rudheath *Ches* 79 SJ7471
Rudley Green *Essex* 40 TL8303
Rudloe *Wilts* 35 ST8470
Rudry *M Glam* 33 ST2086
Rudston *Humb* 91 TA0967
Rudyard *Staffs* 72 SJ9557
Ruecastle *Border* 110 NT6120
Rufford *Lancs* 80 SD4615
Rufforth *N York* 83 SE5251
Rug *Clwyd* 70 SJ0543
Rugby *Warwks* 50 SP5075
Rugeley *Staffs* 73 SK0418
Ruggaton *Devon* 19 SS5545
Ruishton *Somset* 20 ST2625
Ruislip *Gt Lon* 26 TQ0987
Ruletown Head *Border* 110 NT6113
Rumbach *Gramp* 141 NJ3852
Rumbling Bridge *Tays* 117 NT0199
Rumburgh *Suffk* 55 TM3481
Rumby Hill *Dur* 96 NZ1634
Rumford *Cent* 116 NS9377
Rumford *Cnwll* 4 SW8970
Rumney *S Glam* 33 ST2178
Rumwell *Somset* 20 ST1923
Runcorn *Ches* 78 SJ5182
Runcton *W Susx* 14 SU8802
Runcton Holme *Norfk* 65 TF6109
Runfold *Surrey* 25 SU8647
Runhall *Norfk* 66 TG0507
Runham *Norfk* 67 TG4610
Runham *Norfk* 67 TG5108
Running Waters *Dur* 96 NZ3240
Runnington *Somset* 20 ST1221
Runsell Green *Essex* 40 TL7905
Runshaw Moor *Lancs* 80 SD5319
Runswick *N York* 97 NZ8016
Runtaleave *Tays* 133 NO2867
Runwell *Essex* 40 TQ7594
Ruscombe *Berks* 37 SU7976
Rush Green *Ches* 79 SJ6987
Rush Green *Essex* 41 TM1515
Rush Green *Gt Lon* 27 TQ5187
Rush Green *Herts* 39 TL2123
Rush Green *Herts* 39 TL3325
Rushall *H & W* 47 SO6435
Rushall *Norfk* 55 TM1982
Rushall *W Mids* 60 SK0200
Rushall *Wilts* 23 SU1255
Rushbrooke *Suffk* 54 TL8961
Rushbury *Shrops* 59 SO5191
Rushden *Herts* 39 TL3031
Rushden *Nhants* 51 SP9566
Rushenden *Kent* 28 TQ9071
Rusher's Cross *E Susx* 16 TQ6028
Rushett Common *Surrey* 14 TQ0242
Rushford *Devon* 5 SX4576
Rushford *Norfk* 54 TL9281
Rushlake Green *E Susx* 16 TQ6218
Rushmere *Suffk* 55 TM4986
Rushmere St. Andrew *Suffk* 55 TM1946
Rushmoor *Surrey* 25 SU8740
Rushock *H & W* 46 SO3058
Rushock *H & W* 60 SO8871
Rusholme *Gt Man* 79 SJ8594
Rushton *Ches* 71 SJ5863
Rushton *Nhants* 51 SP8482
Rushton *Shrops* 59 SJ6008
Rushton Spencer *Staffs* 72 SJ9362
Rushwick *H & W* 47 SO8254
Rushyford *Dur* 96 NZ2828
Ruskie *Cent* 116 NN6200
Ruskington *Lincs* 76 TF0851
Rusland *Cumb* 87 SD3488
Rusper *W Susx* 15 TQ2037
Ruspidge *Gloucs* 35 SO6611
Russ Hill *Surrey* 15 TQ2240
Russel's Green *Suffk* 55 TM2572
Russell Green *Essex* 40 TL7413
Russell's Green *E Susx* 16 TQ7011
Russell's Water *Oxon* 37 SU7089
Rusthall *Kent* 16 TQ5639
Rustington *W Susx* 14 TQ0402
Ruston *N York* 91 SE9583
Ruston Parva *Humb* 91 TA0661
Ruswarp *N York* 90 NZ8809
Ruthall *Shrops* 59 SO5990
Rutherford *Border* 110 NT6430
Rutherglen *Strath* 116 NS6161
Ruthernbridge *Cnwll* 4 SX0166
Ruthin *Clwyd* 70 SJ1258
Ruthrieston *Gramp* 135 NJ9204
Ruthven *Gramp* 142 NJ5046
Ruthven *Highld* 140 NH8132
Ruthven *Highld* 132 NN7699
Ruthven *Tays* 126 NO2848
Ruthven House *Tays* 126 NO3047
Ruthvoes *Cnwll* 4 SW9260
Ruthwaite *Cumb* 93 NY2336
Ruthwell *D & G* 100 NY0967
Ruxley Corner *Gt Lon* 27 TQ4770
Ruxton Green *H & W* 34 SO5419
Ruyton-XI-Towns *Shrops* 59 SJ3922
Ryal *Nthumb* 103 NZ0174
Ryall *Dorset* 10 SY4095
Ryall *H & W* 47 SO8640
Ryarsh *Kent* 28 TQ6660
Rycote *Oxon* 37 SP6705
Rydal *Cumb* 87 NY3606
Ryde *IOW* 13 SZ5992
Rye *E Susx* 17 TQ9220
Rye Cross *H & W* 47 SO7735
Rye Foreign *E Susx* 17 TQ8922
Rye Harbour *E Susx* 17 TQ9319
Rye Street *H & W* 47 SO7835
Ryebank *Shrops* 59 SJ5131
Ryeford *H & W* 35 SO6322
Ryeish Green *Nhants* 24 SU7267
Ryhall *Leics* 64 TF0310
Ryhill *W York* 83 SE3814
Ryhope *T & W* 96 NZ4152
Rylah *Derbys* 75 SK4667
Ryland *Lincs* 76 TF0179
Rylands *Notts* 62 SK5335
Rylstone *N York* 88 SD9658
Ryme Intrinseca *Dorset* 10 ST5810
Ryther *N York* 83 SE5539
Ryton *N York* 90 SE7975
Ryton *Shrops* 60 SJ7602
Ryton *T & W* 103 NZ1564
Ryton *Warwks* 61 SP4086
Ryton Woodside *T & W* 96 NZ1462
Ryton-on-Dunsmore *Warwks* 61 SP3874

S

Sabden *Lancs* 81 SD7837
Sabine's Green *Essex* 27 TQ5496
Sacombe *Herts* 39 TL3319
Sacombe Green *Herts* 39 TL3419
Sacriston *T & W* 96 NZ2447
Sadberge *Dur* 96 NZ3416
Saddell *Strath* 105 NR7832
Saddington *Leics* 50 SP6691
Saddle Bow *Norfk* 65 TF6015
Saddlescombe *W Susx* 15 TQ2711
Sadgill *Cumb* 87 NY4805
Saffron Walden *Essex* 39 TL5438
Sageston *Dyfed* 30 SN0503
Saham Hills *Norfk* 66 TF9003
Saham Toney *Norfk* 66 TF8901
Saighton *Ches* 71 SJ4462
Saintbury *Gloucs* 48 SP1139
St Abbs *Border* 119 NT9167
St Agnes *Cnwll* 2 SW7150
St Agnes *Loth* 118 NT6763
St Albans *Herts* 38 TL1407
St Allen *Cnwll* 3 SW8250
St Andrew *Guern* 152 GN5007
St Andrew's Major *S Glam* 33 ST1371
St Andrews *Fife* 127 NO5116
St Andrews Well *Dorset* 10 SY4793
St Ann's *D & G* 100 NY0793
St Ann's Chapel *Cnwll* 5 SX4170
St Ann's Chapel *Devon* 7 SX6647
St Anne's *Lancs* 80 SD3228
St Anthony *Cnwll* 3 SW7825
St Anthony's Hill *E Susx* 16 TQ6201
St Arvans *Gwent* 34 ST5296
St Asaph *Clwyd* 70 SJ0374
St Athan *S Glam* 20 ST0167
St Aubin *Jersey* 152 JS1008
St Austell *Cnwll* 3 SX0152
St Bees *Cumb* 86 NX9711
St Blazey *Cnwll* 3 SX0654
St Blazey Gate *Cnwll* 3 SX0653
St Boswells *Border* 110 NT5930
St Brelade *Jersey* 152 JS0809
St Brelades Bay *Jersey* 152 JS0808
St Breock *Cnwll* 4 SW9771
St Breward *Cnwll* 4 SX0977
St Briavels *Gloucs* 34 SO5604
St Bride's Major *M Glam* 33 SS8974
St Brides *Dyfed* 30 SM8010
St Brides Netherwent *Gwent* 34 ST4289
St Brides super-Ely *S Glam* 33 ST0977
St Brides Wentlooge *Gwent* 34 ST2982
St Budeaux *Devon* 6 SX4558
St Buryan *Cnwll* 2 SW4025
St Cadoc *Cnwll* 4 SW8875
St Catherine *Avon* 35 ST7769
St Catherines *Strath* 123 NN1207
St Chloe *Gloucs* 35 SO8401
St Clears *Dyfed* 31 SN2816
St Cleer *Cnwll* 5 SX2468
St Clement *Cnwll* 3 SW8543
St Clement *Jersey* 152 JS1807
St Clether *Cnwll* 5 SX2084
St Colmac *Strath* 114 NS0467
St Columb Major *Cnwll* 4 SW9163
St Columb Minor *Cnwll* 4 SW8362
St Columb Road *Cnwll* 4 SW9159
St Combs *Gramp* 143 NK0563
St Cross South Elmham *Suffk* 55 TM2984
St Cyrus *Gramp* 135 NO7464
St David's *Tays* 125 NN9420
St Davids *Dyfed* 30 SM7525
St Day *Cnwll* 3 SW7242
St Decumans *Somset* 20 ST0642
St Dennis *Cnwll* 4 SW9557
St Devereux *H & W* 46 SO4431
St Dogmaels *Dyfed* 42 SN1645
St Dogwells *Dyfed* 30 SM9727
St Dominick *Cnwll* 5 SX4067
St Donats *S Glam* 20 SS9368
St Edith's Marsh *Wilts* 22 ST9764
St Endellion *Cnwll* 4 SW9978
St Enoder *Cnwll* 3 SW8956
St Erme *Cnwll* 3 SW8449
St Erney *Cnwll* 5 SX3759
St Erth *Cnwll* 2 SW5535
St Erth Praze *Cnwll* 2 SW5735
St Ervan *Cnwll* 4 SW8970
St Ewe *Cnwll* 3 SW9746

St Fagans Seaton Burn

St Fagans *S Glam*	**33**	ST1277
St Fergus *Gramp*	**143**	NK0952
St Fillans *Tays*	**124**	NN6924
St Florence *Dyfed*	**31**	SN0801
St Gennys *Cnwll*	**4**	SX1497
St George *Clwyd*	**70**	SH9775
St George's *S Glam*	**33**	ST1076
St George's Hill *Surrey*	**26**	TQ0862
St Georges *Avon*	**21**	ST3762
St Germans *Cnwll*	**5**	SX3657
St Giles in the Wood *Devon*	**19**	SS5319
St Giles-on-the-Heath *Cnwll*	**5**	SX3690
St Harmon *Powys*	**45**	SN9872
St Helen Auckland *Dur*	**96**	NZ1826
St Helena *Norfk*	**66**	TG1816
St Helens *Cumb*	**92**	NY0232
St Helens *E Susx*	**17**	TQ8212
St Helens *IOW*	**13**	SZ6289
St Helens *Mersyd*	**78**	SJ5195
St Helier *Gt Lon*	**27**	TQ2567
St Helier *Jersey*	**152**	JS1508
St Hilary *Cnwll*	**2**	SW5431
St Hilary *S Glam*	**33**	ST0173
St Hill *Devon*	**9**	ST0908
St Hill *W Susx*	**15**	TQ3835
St Ibbs *Herts*	**39**	TL1926
St Illtyd *Gwent*	**34**	SO2202
St Ishmaels *Dyfed*	**30**	SM8307
St Issey *Cnwll*	**4**	SW9271
St Ive *Cnwll*	**5**	SX3167
St Ives *Cambs*	**52**	TL3171
St Ives *Cnwll*	**2**	SW5140
St Ives *Dorset*	**12**	SU1204
St Jame's End *Nhants*	**49**	SP7460
St James *Norfk*	**67**	TG2720
St James South Elmham *Suffk*	**55**	TM3281
St John *Cnwll*	**5**	SX4053
St John *Jersey*	**152**	JS1215
St John's *IOM*	**153**	SC2781
St John's Chapel *Devon*	**19**	SS5329
St John's Chapel *Dur*	**95**	NY8837
St John's Fen End *Norfk*	**65**	TF5312
St John's Highway *Norfk*	**65**	TF5214
St John's Kirk *Strath*	**108**	NS9836
St John's Town of Dalry *D & G*	**99**	NX6281
St John's Wood *Gt Lon*	**27**	TQ2683
St Johns *Dur*	**95**	NZ0633
St Johns *H & W*	**47**	SO8454
St Johns *Kent*	**27**	TQ5356
St Johns *Surrey*	**25**	SU9857
St Jude's *IOM*	**153**	SC3996
St Just *Cnwll*	**2**	SW3731
St Just *Cnwll*	**3**	SW8435
St Just Lane *Cnwll*	**3**	SW8535
St Katherines *Gramp*	**142**	NJ7834
St Keverne *Cnwll*	**3**	SW7921
St Kew *Cnwll*	**4**	SX0276
St Kew Highway *Cnwll*	**4**	SX0375
St Keyne *Cnwll*	**5**	SX2461
St Laurence *Kent*	**29**	TR3665
St Lawrence *Cnwll*	**4**	SX0466
St Lawrence *Essex*	**41**	TL9604
St Lawrence *IOW*	**13**	SZ5376
St Lawrence *Jersey*	**152**	JS1211
St Leonards *Bucks*	**38**	SP9007
St Leonards *Dorset*	**12**	SU1103
St Leonards *E Susx*	**17**	TQ8009
St Leonards Street *Kent*	**28**	TQ6756
St Levan *Cnwll*	**2**	SW3822
St Lythans *S Glam*	**33**	ST1072
St Mabyn *Cnwll*	**4**	SX0473
St Madoes *Tays*	**126**	NO1921
St Margaret South Elmham *Suffk*	**55**	TM3183
St Margaret's at Cliffe *Kent*	**29**	TR3544
St Margarets *H & W*	**46**	SO3533
St Margarets *Herts*	**39**	TL3811
St Margarets Hope *Ork*	**155**	ND4493
St Marks *IOM*	**153**	SC2974
St Martin *Cnwll*	**5**	SX2555
St Martin *Guern*	**152**	GN5206
St Martin *Jersey*	**152**	JS1912
St Martin's *Tays*	**126**	NO1530
St Martin's Green *Cnwll*	**3**	SW7323
St Martin's Moor *Shrops*	**59**	SJ3135
St Martins *Shrops*	**59**	SJ3236
St Mary *Jersey*	**152**	JS1014
St Mary Bourne *Hants*	**24**	SU4250
St Mary Church *S Glam*	**33**	ST0071
St Mary Cray *Gt Lon*	**27**	TQ4768
St Mary Hill *S Glam*	**33**	SS9678
St Mary in the Marsh *Kent*	**17**	TR0627
St Mary's *Ork*	**155**	HY4701
St Mary's Bay *Kent*	**17**	TR0827
St Mary's Grove *Avon*	**21**	ST4669
St Mary's Hoo *Kent*	**28**	TQ8076
St Marychurch *Devon*	**7**	SX9166
St Marylebone *Gt Lon*	**27**	TQ2782
St Maughans *Gwent*	**34**	SO4617
St Maughans Green *Gwent*	**34**	SO4717
St Mawes *Cnwll*	**3**	SW8433
St Mawgan *Cnwll*	**4**	SW8765
St Mellion *Cnwll*	**5**	SX3965
St Mellons *S Glam*	**34**	ST2281
St Merryn *Cnwll*	**4**	SW8874
St Mewan *Cnwll*	**3**	SW9951
St Michael Caerhays *Cnwll*	**3**	SW9642
St Michael Church *Somset*	**20**	ST3030
St Michael Penkevil *Cnwll*	**3**	SW8541
St Michael South Elmham *Suffk*	**55**	TM3483
St Michael's on Wyre *Lancs*	**80**	SD4641
St Michaels *H & W*	**46**	SO5865
St Michaels *Kent*	**17**	TQ8835
St Minver *Cnwll*	**4**	SW9677
St Monans *Fife*	**127**	NO5201
St Neot *Cnwll*	**4**	SX1868
St Neots *Cambs*	**52**	TL1860
St Newlyn East *Cnwll*	**3**	SW8256
St Nicholas *Dyfed*	**30**	SM9035
St Nicholas *S Glam*	**33**	ST0974
St Nicholas at Wade *Kent*	**29**	TR2666
St Ninians *Cent*	**116**	NS7991
St Olaves *Norfk*	**67**	TM4599
St Osyth *Essex*	**41**	TM1215
St Ouen *Jersey*	**152**	JS0713
St Owens Cross *H & W*	**46**	SO5324
St Paul's Walden *Herts*	**39**	TL1922
St Pauls Cray *Gt Lon*	**27**	TQ4768
St Peter *Jersey*	**152**	JS0911
St Peter Port *Guern*	**152**	GN5308
St Peter's *Guern*	**152**	GN4706
St Peter's *Kent*	**29**	TR3868
St Peter's Hill *Cambs*	**52**	TL2372
St Petrox *Dyfed*	**30**	SR9797
St Pinnock *Cnwll*	**5**	SX2063
St Quivox *Strath*	**106**	NS3723
St Ruan *Cnwll*	**2**	SW7115
St Sampson *Guern*	**152**	GN5411
St Saviour *Guern*	**152**	GN4807
St Saviour *Jersey*	**152**	JS0000
St Stephen *Cnwll*	**3**	SW9453
St Stephen's Coombe *Cnwll*	**3**	SW9451
St Stephens *Cnwll*	**5**	SX3285
St Stephens *Cnwll*	**5**	SX4158
St Teath *Cnwll*	**4**	SX0680
St Tudy *Cnwll*	**4**	SX0676
St Twynnells *Dyfed*	**30**	SR9597
St Veep *Cnwll*	**3**	SX1455
St Vigeans *Tays*	**127**	NO6443
St Wenn *Cnwll*	**4**	SW9664
St Weonards *H & W*	**46**	SO4924
Salachail *Strath*	**123**	NN0551
Salcombe *Devon*	**7**	SX7439
Salcombe Regis *Devon*	**9**	SY1588
Salcott *Essex*	**40**	TL9413
Sale *Gt Man*	**79**	SJ7991
Sale Green *H & W*	**47**	SO9358
Saleby *Lincs*	**77**	TF4578
Salehurst *E Susx*	**17**	TQ7524
Salem *Dyfed*	**44**	SN6226
Salem *Dyfed*	**43**	SN6684
Salem *Gwynd*	**69**	SH5456
Salen *Highld*	**121**	NM6864
Salen *Strath*	**121**	NM5743
Salesbury *Lancs*	**81**	SD6832
Salford *Beds*	**38**	SP9339
Salford *Gt Man*	**79**	SJ8197
Salford *Oxon*	**48**	SP2828
Salford Priors *Warwks*	**48**	SP0751
Salfords *Surrey*	**15**	TQ2846
Salhouse *Norfk*	**67**	TG3114
Saline *Fife*	**117**	NT0292
Salisbury *Wilts*	**23**	SU1429
Salkeld Dykes *Cumb*	**94**	NY5437
Sallachy *Highld*	**146**	NC5408
Salle *Norfk*	**66**	TG1024
Salmonby *Lincs*	**77**	TF3273
Salperton *Gloucs*	**36**	SP0720
Salph End *Beds*	**38**	TL0852
Salsburgh *Strath*	**116**	NS8262
Salt *Staffs*	**72**	SJ9527
Salt Cotes *Cumb*	**93**	NY1853
Salta *Cumb*	**92**	NY0845
Saltaire *W York*	**82**	SE1438
Saltash *Cnwll*	**6**	SX4258
Saltburn *Highld*	**146**	NH7270
Saltburn-by-the-Sea *Cleve*	**97**	NZ6621
Saltby *Leics*	**63**	SK8526
Saltcoats *Cumb*	**86**	SD0797
Saltcoats *Lancs*	**80**	SD3728
Saltcoats *Strath*	**106**	NS2441
Saltdean *E Susx*	**15**	TQ3802
Salterbeck *Cumb*	**92**	NX9926
Salterforth *Lancs*	**81**	SD8845
Salterswall *Ches*	**71**	SJ6266
Salterton *Wilts*	**23**	SU1236
Saltfleet *Lincs*	**77**	TF4593
Saltfleetby All Saints *Lincs*	**77**	TF4590
Saltfleetby St. Clements *Lincs*	**77**	TF4691
Saltfleetby St. Peter *Lincs*	**77**	TF4489
Saltford *Avon*	**22**	ST6867
Salthouse *Norfk*	**66**	TG0743
Saltley *W Mids*	**61**	SP1088
Saltmarsh *Gwent*	**34**	ST3482
Saltmarshe *Humb*	**84**	SE7824
Saltney *Ches*	**71**	SJ3865
Salton *N York*	**90**	SE7179
Saltrens *Devon*	**18**	SS4522
Saltwick *Nthumb*	**103**	NZ1780
Saltwood *Kent*	**29**	TR1535
Salvington *W Susx*	**14**	TQ1205
Salwarpe *H & W*	**47**	SO8762
Salwayash *Dorset*	**10**	SY4596
Sambourne *Warwks*	**48**	SP0662
Sambrook *Shrops*	**72**	SJ7124
Samlesbury *Lancs*	**81**	SD5930
Samlesbury Bottoms *Lancs*	**81**	SD6228
Sampford Arundel *Somset*	**20**	ST1118
Sampford Brett *Somset*	**20**	ST0741
Sampford Courtenay *Devon*	**8**	SS6301
Sampford Moor *Somset*	**20**	ST1118
Sampford Peverell *Devon*	**9**	ST0314
Sampford Spiney *Devon*	**6**	SX5372
Samson's Corner *Essex*	**41**	TM0818
Samsonlane *Ork*	**155**	HY6526
Samuelston *Loth*	**118**	NT4870
Sanaigmore *Strath*	**112**	NR2370
Sancreed *Cnwll*	**2**	SW4129
Sancton *Humb*	**84**	SE8939
Sand *Somset*	**21**	ST4346
Sand Cross *E Susx*	**16**	TQ5820
Sand Hills *W York*	**83**	SE3739
Sand Hole *Humb*	**84**	SE8137
Sand Hutton *N York*	**90**	SE6958
Sand Side *Cumb*	**86**	SD2282
Sandaig *Highld*	**129**	NG7102
Sandal Magna *W York*	**83**	SE3417
Sandale *Cumb*	**93**	NY2440
Sandavore *Highld*	**128**	NM4785
Sandbach *Ches*	**72**	SJ7560
Sandbank *Strath*	**114**	NS1680
Sandbanks *Dorset*	**12**	SZ0487
Sandend *Gramp*	**142**	NJ5566
Sanderstead *Gt Lon*	**27**	TQ3461
Sandford *Avon*	**21**	ST4259
Sandford *Cumb*	**94**	NY7316
Sandford *Devon*	**8**	SS8202
Sandford *Dorset*	**11**	SY9289
Sandford *Hants*	**12**	SU1601
Sandford *IOW*	**13**	SZ5381
Sandford *Shrops*	**59**	SJ3423
Sandford *Shrops*	**59**	SJ5833
Sandford *Strath*	**107**	NS7143
Sandford Orcas *Dorset*	**21**	ST6220
Sandford St. Martin *Oxon*	**49**	SP4226
Sandford-on-Thames *Oxon*	**37**	SP5301
Sandgate *Kent*	**29**	TR2035
Sandhaven *Gramp*	**143**	NJ9667
Sandhead *D & G*	**98**	NX0949
Sandhill *S York*	**83**	SK4496
Sandhills *Dorset*	**10**	ST5800
Sandhills *Dorset*	**11**	ST6810
Sandhills *Oxon*	**37**	SP5507
Sandhills *Staffs*	**61**	SK0604
Sandhills *Surrey*	**14**	SU9337
Sandhoe *Nthumb*	**102**	NY9666
Sandhole *Strath*	**114**	NS0098
Sandholme *Humb*	**84**	SE8230
Sandholme *Lincs*	**64**	TF3337
Sandhurst *Berks*	**25**	SU8361
Sandhurst *Gloucs*	**47**	SO8223
Sandhurst *Kent*	**17**	TQ8028
Sandhurst Cross *Kent*	**17**	TQ7827
Sandhutton *N York*	**89**	SE3881
Sandiacre *Derbys*	**62**	SK4736
Sandilands *Lincs*	**77**	TF5280
Sandiway *Ches*	**71**	SJ6070
Sandleheath *Hants*	**12**	SU1215
Sandley *Dorset*	**22**	ST7724
Sandling *Kent*	**28**	TQ7557
Sandlow Green *Ches*	**72**	SJ7865
Sandness *Shet*	**155**	HU1957
Sandon *Essex*	**40**	TL7404
Sandon *Herts*	**39**	TL3234
Sandon *Staffs*	**72**	SJ9429
Sandon Bank *Staffs*	**72**	SJ9428
Sandown *IOW*	**13**	SZ5984
Sandplace *Cnwll*	**5**	SX2557
Sandridge *Herts*	**39**	TL1710
Sandridge *Wilts*	**22**	ST9465
Sandringham *Norfk*	**65**	TF6928
Sands *Bucks*	**26**	SU8493
Sandsend *N York*	**90**	NZ8612
Sandtoft *Humb*	**84**	SE7408
Sandwich *Kent*	**29**	TR3358
Sandwick *Cumb*	**93**	NY4219
Sandwick *Shet*	**155**	HU4323
Sandwith *Cumb*	**92**	NX9614
Sandwith Newtown *Cumb*	**92**	NX9614
Sandy *Beds*	**52**	TL1649
Sandy Bank *Lincs*	**77**	TF2655
Sandy Cross *H & W*	**47**	SO6757
Sandy Haven *Dyfed*	**30**	SM8507
Sandy Lane *Clwyd*	**71**	SJ4040
Sandy Lane *W York*	**82**	SE1135
Sandy Lane *Wilts*	**22**	ST9668
Sandy Park *Devon*	**8**	SX7189
Sandycroft *Clwyd*	**71**	SJ3366
Sandyford *D & G*	**101**	NY2093
Sandygate *Devon*	**7**	SX8674
Sandygate *IOM*	**153**	SC3797
Sandyhills *D & G*	**92**	NX8855
Sandylands *Lancs*	**87**	SD4263
Sandylane *Staffs*	**72**	SJ7035
Sandylane *W Glam*	**32**	SS5589
Sandyway *H & W*	**46**	SO4925
Sangobeg *Highld*	**149**	NC4266
Sangomore *Highld*	**149**	NC4067
Sankey Bridges *Ches*	**78**	SJ5887
Sankyn's Green *H & W*	**47**	SO7965
Sanna Bay *Highld*	**128**	NM4469
Sanquhar *D & G*	**107**	NS7809
Santon *Cumb*	**86**	NY1001
Santon *IOM*	**153**	SC3171
Santon Bridge *Cumb*	**86**	NY1101
Santon Downham *Suffk*	**54**	TL8187
Sapcote *Leics*	**50**	SP4893
Sapey Common *H & W*	**47**	SO7064
Sapiston *Suffk*	**54**	TL9175
Sapley *Cambs*	**52**	TL2474
Sapperton *Derbys*	**73**	SK1834
Sapperton *Gloucs*	**35**	SO9403
Sapperton *Lincs*	**64**	TF0133
Saracen's Head *Lincs*	**64**	TF3427
Sarclet *Highld*	**151**	ND3443
Sarisbury *Hants*	**13**	SU5008
Sarn *Gwynd*	**56**	SH2432
Sarn *M Glam*	**33**	SS9083
Sarn *Powys*	**58**	SN9597
Sarn *Powys*	**58**	SO2090
Sarn-bach *Gwynd*	**56**	SH3026
Sarn-wen *Powys*	**58**	SJ2718
Sarnau *Dyfed*	**42**	SN3150
Sarnau *Dyfed*	**31**	SN3318
Sarnau *Gwynd*	**70**	SH9639
Sarnau *Powys*	**58**	SJ2315
Sarnau *Powys*	**45**	SO0232
Sarnesfield *H & W*	**46**	SO3750
Saron *Dyfed*	**31**	SN3737
Saron *Dyfed*	**32**	SN6012
Saron *Gwynd*	**69**	SH5365
Sarratt *Herts*	**26**	TQ0499
Sarre *Kent*	**29**	TR2565
Sarsden *Oxon*	**36**	SP2822
Sarson *Hants*	**23**	SU3044
Sartfield *IOM*	**153**	SC3599
Satley *Dur*	**95**	NZ1143
Satmar *Kent*	**29**	TR2539
Satron *N York*	**88**	SD9397
Satterleigh *Devon*	**19**	SS6622
Satterthwaite *Cumb*	**86**	SD3392
Satwell *Oxon*	**37**	SU7083
Sauchen *Gramp*	**135**	NJ7011
Saucher *Tays*	**126**	NO1933
Sauchieburn *Gramp*	**135**	NO6669
Saul *Gloucs*	**35**	SO7409
Saundby *Notts*	**75**	SK7888
Saundersfoot *Dyfed*	**31**	SN1304
Saunderton *Bucks*	**37**	SP7901
Saunton *Devon*	**18**	SS4637
Sausthorpe *Lincs*	**77**	TF3868
Saveock Water *Cnwll*	**3**	SW7645
Saverley Green *Staffs*	**72**	SJ9638
Savile Town *W York*	**82**	SE2420
Sawbridge *Warwks*	**50**	SP5065
Sawbridgeworth *Herts*	**39**	TL4814
Sawdon *N York*	**91**	SE9485
Sawley *Derbys*	**62**	SK4631
Sawley *Lancs*	**81**	SD7746
Sawley *N York*	**89**	SE2467
Sawston *Cambs*	**53**	TL4849
Sawtry *Cambs*	**52**	TL1683
Saxby *Leics*	**63**	SK8219
Saxby *Lincs*	**76**	TF0086
Saxby *W Susx*	**14**	SU9604
Saxby All Saints *Humb*	**84**	SE9816
Saxelbye *Leics*	**63**	SK6921
Saxham Street *Suffk*	**54**	TM0861
Saxilby *Lincs*	**76**	SK8975
Saxlingham *Norfk*	**66**	TG0239
Saxlingham Green *Norfk*	**67**	TM2396
Saxlingham Nethergate *Norfk*	**67**	TM2297
Saxlingham Thorpe *Norfk*	**67**	TM2197
Saxmundham *Suffk*	**55**	TM3863
Saxon Street *Cambs*	**53**	TL6759
Saxondale *Notts*	**63**	SK6839
Saxtead *Suffk*	**55**	TM2665
Saxtead Green *Suffk*	**55**	TM2564
Saxtead Little Green *Suffk*	**55**	TM2466
Saxthorpe *Norfk*	**66**	TG1130
Saxton *N York*	**83**	SE4736
Sayers Common *W Susx*	**15**	TQ2618
Scackleton *N York*	**90**	SE6472
Scaftworth *Notts*	**75**	SK6691
Scagglethorpe *N York*	**90**	SE8372
Scalasaig *Strath*	**112**	NR3993
Scalby *Humb*	**84**	SE8429
Scalby *N York*	**91**	TA0090
Scald End *Beds*	**51**	TL0457
Scaldwell *Nhants*	**50**	SP7672
Scale Houses *Cumb*	**94**	NY5845
Scaleby *Cumb*	**101**	NY4463
Scalebyhill *Cumb*	**101**	NY4463
Scales *Cumb*	**93**	NY3426
Scales *Cumb*	**86**	SD2772
Scales *Lancs*	**80**	SD4531
Scalesceugh *Cumb*	**93**	NY4449
Scalford *Leics*	**63**	SK7624
Scaling *N York*	**90**	NZ7413
Scaling Dam *N York*	**90**	NZ7412
Scalloway *Shet*	**155**	HU4039
Scamblesby *Lincs*	**77**	TF2778
Scammonden *W York*	**82**	SE0515
Scamodale *Highld*	**129**	NM8373
Scampston *N York*	**90**	SE8575
Scampton *Lincs*	**76**	SK9579
Scaniport *Highld*	**140**	NH6239
Scapegoat Hill *W York*	**82**	SE0916
Scarborough *N York*	**91**	TA0488
Scarcewater *Cnwll*	**3**	SW9154
Scarcliffe *Derbys*	**75**	SK4968
Scarcroft *W York*	**83**	SE3541
Scarcroft Hill *W York*	**83**	SE3741
Scarfskerry *Highld*	**151**	ND2674
Scargill *Dur*	**88**	NZ0510
Scarinish *Strath*	**120**	NM0444
Scarisbrick *Lancs*	**80**	SD3713
Scarness *Cumb*	**93**	NY2230
Scarning *Norfk*	**66**	TF9512
Scarrington *Notts*	**63**	SK7341
Scarth Hill *Lancs*	**78**	SD4206
Scarthingwell *N York*	**83**	SE4937
Scartho *Humb*	**85**	TA2606
Scawby *Humb*	**84**	SE9605
Scawsby *S York*	**83**	SE5305
Scawthorpe *S York*	**83**	SE5506
Scawton *N York*	**90**	SE5483
Scayne's Hill *W Susx*	**15**	TQ3623
Scethrog *Powys*	**45**	SO1025
Scholar Green *Staffs*	**72**	SJ8357
Scholes *Gt Man*	**78**	SD5905
Scholes *S York*	**74**	SK3895
Scholes *W York*	**82**	SE1507
Scholes *W York*	**82**	SE1625
Scholes *W York*	**83**	SE3736
Scholey Hill *W York*	**83**	SE3825
School Aycliffe *Dur*	**96**	NZ2523
School Green *Ches*	**72**	SJ6464
School Green *W York*	**82**	SE1132
School House *Dorset*	**10**	ST3602
Schoolgreen *Berks*	**24**	SU7367
Scissett *W York*	**82**	SE2410
Scleddau *Dyfed*	**30**	SM9434
Sco Ruston *Norfk*	**67**	TG2821
Scofton *Notts*	**75**	SK6280
Scole *Norfk*	**54**	TM1579
Sconser *Highld*	**137**	NG5132
Scoonie *Fife*	**126**	NO3801
Scopwick *Lincs*	**76**	TF0757
Scoraig *Highld*	**144**	NH0096
Scorborough *Humb*	**84**	TA0145
Scorrier *Cnwll*	**3**	SW7244
Scorriton *Devon*	**7**	SX7068
Scorton *Lancs*	**80**	SD5048
Scorton *N York*	**89**	NZ2500
Scot Hay *Staffs*	**72**	SJ7947
Scot Lane End *Gt Man*	**79**	SD6209
Scot's Gap *Nthumb*	**103**	NZ0386
Scotby *Cumb*	**93**	NY4455
Scotch Corner *N York*	**89**	NZ2105
Scotforth *Lancs*	**87**	SD4859
Scothern *Lincs*	**76**	TF0377
Scotland *Lincs*	**63**	TF0030
Scotland *W York*	**82**	SE2340
Scotland Gate *T & W*	**103**	NZ2584
Scotlandwell *Tays*	**126**	NO1801
Scotscalder Station *Highld*	**151**	ND0956
Scotscraig *Fife*	**127**	NO4428
Scotsdike *Cumb*	**101**	NY3872
Scotsmill *Gramp*	**142**	NJ5618
Scotstoun *Strath*	**115**	NS5267
Scotswood *T & W*	**103**	NZ2063
Scotter *Lincs*	**76**	SE8800
Scotterthorpe *Lincs*	**84**	SE8701
Scottlethorpe *Lincs*	**64**	TF0520
Scotton *Lincs*	**76**	SK8899
Scotton *N York*	**89**	SE1895
Scotton *N York*	**89**	SE3259
Scottow *Norfk*	**67**	TG2823
Scoulton *Norfk*	**66**	TF9800
Scounslow Green *Staffs*	**73**	SK0929
Scourie *Highld*	**148**	NC1544
Scouriemore *Highld*	**148**	NC1443
Scousburgh *Shet*	**155**	HU3717
Scouthead *Gt Man*	**79**	SD9605
Scrabster *Highld*	**151**	ND1070
Scraesburgh *Border*	**110**	NT6718
Scrafield *Lincs*	**77**	TF3068
Scrainwood *Nthumb*	**111**	NT9808
Scrane End *Lincs*	**64**	TF3841
Scraptoft *Leics*	**63**	SK6405
Scratby *Norfk*	**67**	TG5015
Scrayingham *N York*	**90**	SE7359
Scrays *E Susx*	**17**	TQ7619
Scredington *Lincs*	**64**	TF0940
Screel *D & G*	**92**	NX8053
Scremby *Lincs*	**77**	TF4467
Scremerston *Nthumb*	**111**	NU0148
Screveton *Notts*	**63**	SK7343
Scrivelsby *Lincs*	**77**	TF2766
Scriven *N York*	**89**	SE3458
Scrooby *Notts*	**75**	SK6590
Scropton *Derbys*	**73**	SK1930
Scrub Hill *Lincs*	**76**	TF2355
Scruschloch *Tays*	**133**	NO2357
Scruton *N York*	**89**	SE2992
Scuggate *Cumb*	**101**	NY4474
Sculthorpe *Norfk*	**66**	TF8930
Scunthorpe *Humb*	**84**	SE8910
Scurlage *W Glam*	**32**	SS4687
Sea *Somset*	**10**	ST3412
Sea Palling *Norfk*	**67**	TG4226
Seaborough *Dorset*	**10**	ST4206
Seabridge *Staffs*	**72**	SJ8343
Seabrook *Kent*	**29**	TR1835
Seaburn *T & W*	**96**	NZ4059
Seacombe *Mersyd*	**78**	SJ3290
Seacroft *Lincs*	**77**	TF5661
Seacroft *W York*	**83**	SE3635
Seafield *Highld*	**136**	NG4743
Seafield *Loth*	**117**	NT0066
Seaford *E Susx*	**16**	TV4899
Seaforth *Mersyd*	**78**	SJ3297
Seagrave *Leics*	**62**	SK6117
Seagry Heath *Wilts*	**35**	ST9581
Seaham *Dur*	**96**	NZ4149
Seahouses *Nthumb*	**111**	NU2231
Seal *Kent*	**27**	TQ5556
Seale *Surrey*	**25**	SU8947
Seamer *N York*	**90**	NZ4910
Seamer *N York*	**91**	TA0183
Seamill *Strath*	**114**	NS2047
Searby *Lincs*	**85**	TA0705
Seasalter *Kent*	**29**	TR0864
Seascale *Cumb*	**86**	NY0301
Seathwaite *Cumb*	**93**	NY2312
Seathwaite *Cumb*	**86**	SD2295
Seatle *Cumb*	**87**	SD3783
Seatoller *Cumb*	**93**	NY2413
Seaton *Cnwll*	**5**	SX3054
Seaton *Cumb*	**92**	NY0130
Seaton *Devon*	**9**	SY2490
Seaton *Dur*	**96**	NZ3949
Seaton *Humb*	**85**	TA1646
Seaton *Kent*	**29**	TR2258
Seaton *Leics*	**51**	SP9098
Seaton *Nthumb*	**103**	NZ3276
Seaton Burn *T & W*	**103**	NZ2373

Seaton Carew Sindlesham

Seaton Carew *Cleve* 97 NZ5229
Seaton Delaval *Nthumb* 103 NZ3075
Seaton Ross *Humb* 84 SE7840
Seaton Sluice *Nthumb* 103 NZ3376
Seatown *Dorset* 10 SY4291
Seave Green *N York* 90 NZ5500
Seaview *IOW* 13 SZ6291
Seaville *Cumb* 92 NY1553
Seavington St. Mary *Somset* 10 ST4014
Seavington St. Michael *Somset* 10 ST4015
Sebastopol *Gwent* 34 ST2998
Sebergham *Cumb* 93 NY3641
Seckington *Warwks* 61 SK2507
Sedbergh *Cumb* 87 SD6591
Sedbury *Gloucs* 34 ST5493
Sedbusk *N York* 88 SD8891
Sedgeberrow *H & W* 48 SP0238
Sedgebrook *Lincs* 63 SK8537
Sedgefield *Dur* 96 NZ3528
Sedgeford *Norfk* 65 TF7036
Sedgehill *Wilts* 22 ST8627
Sedgley *W Mids* 60 SO9193
Sedgley Park *Gt Man* 79 SD8202
Sedgwick *Cumb* 87 SD5186
Sedlescombe *E Susx* 17 TQ7818
Sedrup *Bucks* 38 SP8011
Seed *Kent* 28 TQ9456
Seend *Wilts* 22 ST9460
Seend Cleeve *Wilts* 22 ST9360
Seer Green *Bucks* 26 SU9692
Seething *Norfk* 67 TM3197
Sefton *Mersyd* 78 SD3501
Sefton Town *Mersyd* 78 SD3400
Seghill *Nthumb* 103 NZ2874
Seighford *Staffs* 72 SJ8825
Seion *Gwynd* 69 SH5466
Seisdon *Staffs* 60 SO8495
Selattyn *Shrops* 58 SJ2633
Selborne *Hants* 24 SU7433
Selby *N York* 83 SE6132
Selham *W Susx* 14 SU9320
Selhurst *Gt Lon* 27 TQ3267
Selkirk *Border* 109 NT4728
Sellack *H & W* 46 SO5627
Sellafirth *Shet* 155 HU5198
Sellan *Cnwll* 2 SW4230
Sellick's Green *Somset* 20 ST2119
Sellindge *Kent* 29 TR0938
Selling *Kent* 28 TR0456
Sells Green *Wilts* 22 ST9462
Selly Oak *W Mids* 61 SP0482
Selmeston *E Susx* 16 TQ5007
Selsdon *Gt Lon* 27 TQ3562
Selsey *W Susx* 14 SZ8593
Selsfield Common *Gwynd* 15 TQ3434
Selside *Cumb* 87 SD5399
Selside *N York* 88 SD7875
Selstead *Kent* 29 TR2144
Selston *Notts* 75 SK4553
Selworthy *Somset* 20 SS9246
Semer *Suffk* 54 TL9946
Semington *Wilts* 22 ST8960
Semley *Wilts* 22 ST8926
Send *Surrey* 26 TQ0155
Send Marsh *Surrey* 26 TQ0355
Senghenydd *M Glam* 33 ST1190
Sennen *Cnwll* 2 SW3525
Sennen Cove *Cnwll* 2 SW3526
Sennybridge *Powys* 45 SN9228
Serlby *Notts* 75 SK6389
Sessay *N York* 89 SE4575
Setchey *Norfk* 65 TF6313
Setley *Hants* 12 SU3000
Seton Mains *Loth* 118 NT4275
Settle *N York* 88 SD8163
Settlingstones *Nthumb* 102 NY8468
Settrington *N York* 90 SE8370
Seven Ash *Somset* 20 ST1533
Seven Kings *Gt Lon* 27 TQ4587
Seven Sisters *W Glam* 33 SN8208
Seven Springs *Gloucs* 35 SO9617
Seven Star Green *Essex* 40 TL9325
Seven Wells *Gloucs* 48 SP1134
Sevenhampton *Gloucs* 36 SP0321
Sevenhampton *Wilts* 36 SU2090
Sevenoaks *Kent* 27 TQ5255
Sevenoaks Weald *Kent* 27 TQ5250
Severn Beach *Avon* 34 ST5484
Severn Stoke *H & W* 47 SO8644
Sevicks End *Beds* 51 TL0954
Sevington *Kent* 28 TR0340
Sewards End *Essex* 53 TL5738
Sewardstonebury *Gt Lon* 27 TQ3995
Sewell *Beds* 38 SP9922
Sewerby *Humb* 91 TA1968
Seworgan *Cnwll* 2 SW7030
Sewstern *Leics* 63 SK8821
Sexhow *N York* 89 NZ4706
Sezincote *Gloucs* 48 SP1731
Shabbington *Bucks* 37 SP6606
Shackerstone *Leics* 62 SK3706
Shacklecross *Derbys* 62 SK4234
Shackleford *Surrey* 25 SU9345
Shade *W York* 81 SD9323
Shader *W Isls* 154 NB3854
Shadforth *Dur* 96 NZ3440
Shadingfield *Suffk* 55 TM4384
Shadoxhurst *Kent* 28 TQ9737
Shadwell *Norfk* 54 TL9383
Shadwell *W York* 83 SE3439
Shaftenhoe End *Herts* 39 TL4037
Shaftesbury *Dorset* 22 ST8623
Shaftholme *S York* 83 SE5708
Shafton *S York* 83 SE3911
Shafton Two Gates *S York* 83 SE3910
Shalbourne *Wilts* 23 SU3163
Shalcombe *IOW* 13 SZ3985
Shalden *Hants* 24 SU6941
Shalden Green *Hants* 24 SU7043
Shaldon *Devon* 7 SX9372
Shalfleet *IOW* 13 SZ4189
Shalford *Essex* 40 TL7229
Shalford *Surrey* 25 TQ0047
Shalford Green *Essex* 40 TL7127
Shallowford *Staffs* 72 SJ8729
Shalmsford Street *Kent* 29 TR0954
Shalstone *Bucks* 49 SP6436
Shamley Green *Surrey* 14 TQ0343
Shandford *Tays* 134 NO4962
Shandon *Strath* 114 NS2586
Shandwick *Highld* 147 NH8575
Shangton *Leics* 50 SP7196
Shankhouse *Nthumb* 103 NZ2778
Shanklin *IOW* 13 SZ5881
Shap *Cumb* 94 NY5615
Shapwick *Dorset* 11 ST9301
Shapwick *Somset* 21 ST4138
Shard End *W Mids* 61 SP1588
Shardlow *Derbys* 62 SK4330
Shareshill *Staffs* 60 SJ9406
Sharlston *W York* 83 SE3918
Sharlston Common *W York* 83 SE3919
Sharman's Cross *W Mids* 61 SP1279
Sharnal Street *Kent* 28 TQ7974
Sharnbrook *Beds* 51 SP9959
Sharneyford *Lancs* 81 SD8824
Sharnford *Leics* 50 SP4891
Sharnhill Green *Dorset* 11 ST7105
Sharoe Green *Lancs* 80 SD5333
Sharow *N York* 89 SE3371
Sharp Green *Norfk* 67 TG3820
Sharpenhoe *Beds* 38 TL0630
Sharperton *Nthumb* 102 NT9503
Sharpness *Gloucs* 35 SO6702
Sharpthorne *W Susx* 15 TQ3732
Sharptor *Cnwll* 5 SX2573
Sharpway Gate *H & W* 47 SO9565
Sharrington *Norfk* 66 TG0337
Shatterford *H & W* 60 SO7981
Shatterling *Kent* 29 TR2658
Shaugh Prior *Devon* 6 SX5463
Shave Cross *Dorset* 10 SY4198
Shavington *Ches* 72 SJ6951
Shaw *Berks* 24 SU4768
Shaw *Gt Man* 79 SD9308
Shaw *W York* 82 SE0235
Shaw *Wilts* 22 ST8965
Shaw *Wilts* 36 SU1185
Shaw Common *Gloucs* 47 SO6826
Shaw Green *Herts* 39 TL3032
Shaw Green *Lancs* 80 SD5218
Shaw Green *N York* 82 SE2652
Shaw Hill *Lancs* 81 SD5720
Shaw Mills *N York* 89 SE2562
Shawbost *W Isls* 154 NB2646
Shawbury *Shrops* 59 SJ5521
Shawclough *Gt Man* 81 SD8914
Shawdon Hill *Nthumb* 111 NU0813
Shawell *Leics* 50 SP5480
Shawford *Hants* 13 SU4625
Shawforth *Lancs* 81 SD8920
Shawhead *D & G* 100 NX8675
Shear Cross *Wilts* 22 ST8642
Shearington *D & G* 100 NY0266
Shearsby *Leics* 50 SP6290
Shearston *Somset* 20 ST2830
Shebbear *Devon* 18 SS4409
Shebdon *Staffs* 72 SJ7625
Shebster *Highld* 150 ND0164
Shedfield *Hants* 13 SU5613
Sheen *Derbys* 74 SK1161
Sheep Hill *Dur* 96 NZ1757
Sheep-ridge *W York* 82 SE1519
Sheepbridge *Derbys* 74 SK3674
Sheepscar *W York* 82 SE3134
Sheepscombe *Gloucs* 35 SO8910
Sheepstor *Devon* 6 SX5667
Sheepwash *Devon* 18 SS4806
Sheepwash *Nthumb* 103 NZ2585
Sheepway *Avon* 34 ST4976
Sheepy Magna *Leics* 61 SK3201
Sheepy Parva *Leics* 62 SK3301
Sheering *Essex* 39 TL5014
Sheerness *Kent* 28 TQ9174
Sheerwater *Surrey* 26 TQ0461
Sheet *Hants* 13 SU7524
Sheffield *Cnwll* 2 SW4526
Sheffield *S York* 74 SK3587
Sheffield Bottom *Berks* 24 SU6469
Sheffield Green *E Susx* 15 TQ4125
Shefford *Beds* 38 TL1439
Shegra *Highld* 148 NC1860
Sheinton *Shrops* 59 SJ6003
Shelderton *Shrops* 46 SO4077
Sheldon *Derbys* 74 SK1768
Sheldon *Devon* 9 ST1208
Sheldon *W Mids* 61 SP1584
Sheldwich *Kent* 28 TR0156
Sheldwich Lees *Kent* 28 TR0156
Shelf *W York* 82 SE1228
Shelfanger *Norfk* 54 TM1083
Shelfield *W Mids* 61 SK0302
Shelfield *Warwks* 48 SP1263
Shelfield Green *Warwks* 48 SP1261
Shelford *Notts* 63 SK6642
Shelford *Warwks* 50 SP4288
Shellacres *Border* 110 NT8943
Shelley *Essex* 39 TL5505
Shelley *Suffk* 54 TM0238
Shelley *W York* 82 SE2011
Shelley Far Bank *W York* 82 SE2010
Shellingford *Oxon* 36 SU3193
Shellow Bowells *Essex* 40 TL6007
Shelsley Beauchamp *H & W* 47 SO7363
Shelsley Walsh *H & W* 47 SO7263
Shelton *Beds* 51 TL0368
Shelton *Norfk* 67 TM2291
Shelton *Notts* 63 SK7844
Shelton *Shrops* 59 SJ4613
Shelton Green *Norfk* 55 TM2390
Shelton Lock *Derbys* 62 SK3730
Shelton Under Harley *Staffs* 72 SJ8139
Shelve *Shrops* 59 SO3399
Shelwick *H & W* 46 SO5242
Shenfield *Essex* 40 TQ6095
Shenington *Oxon* 48 SP3742
Shenley *Herts* 26 TL1800
Shenley Brook End *Bucks* 38 SP8335
Shenley Church End *Bucks* 38 SP8336
Shenleybury *Herts* 26 TL1801
Shenmore *H & W* 46 SO3937
Shennanton *D & G* 98 NX3363
Shenstone *H & W* 60 SO8673
Shenstone *Staffs* 61 SK1004
Shenstone Woodend *Staffs* 61 SK1101
Shenton *Leics* 61 SK3800
Shepeau Stow *Lincs* 64 TF3012
Shephall *Herts* 39 TL2623
Shepherd's Bush *Gt Lon* 26 TQ2380
Shepherd's Green *Oxon* 37 SU7183
Shepherds *Cnwll* 3 SW8154
Shepherds Patch *Gloucs* 35 SO7304
Shepherdswell *Kent* 29 TR2647
Shepley *W York* 82 SE1909
Shepperdine *Avon* 35 ST6295
Shepperton *Surrey* 26 TQ0766
Shepperton Green *Surrey* 26 TQ0767
Shepreth *Cambs* 52 TL3947
Shepshed *Leics* 62 SK4819
Shepton Beauchamp *Somset* 10 ST4017
Shepton Mallet *Somset* 21 ST6143
Shepton Montague *Somset* 22 ST6831
Shepway *Kent* 28 TQ7753
Sheraton *Dur* 96 NZ4435
Sherborne *Dorset* 10 ST6316
Sherborne *Gloucs* 36 SP1614
Sherborne *Somset* 21 ST5855
Sherborne Causeway *Dorset* 22 ST8323
Sherborne St. John *Hants* 24 SU6255
Sherbourne *Warwks* 48 SP2661
Sherburn *Dur* 96 NZ3142
Sherburn *N York* 91 SE9576
Sherburn Hill *Dur* 96 NZ3342
Sherburn in Elmet *N York* 83 SE4933
Shere *Surrey* 14 TQ0747
Shereford *Norfk* 66 TF8829
Sherfield English *Hants* 23 SU2922
Sherfield on Loddon *Hants* 24 SU6858
Sherfin *Lancs* 81 SD7925
Sherford *Devon* 7 SX7844
Sherford *Dorset* 11 SY9193
Sheriff Hutton *N York* 90 SE6566
Sheriffhales *Shrops* 60 SJ7512
Sheringham *Norfk* 66 TG1543
Sherington *Bucks* 38 SP8846
Shermanbury *W Susx* 15 TQ2019
Shernborne *Norfk* 65 TF7132
Sherril *Devon* 7 SX6874
Sherrington *Wilts* 22 ST9639
Sherston *Wilts* 35 ST8586
Sherwood *Notts* 62 SK5643
Shettleston *Strath* 116 NS6464
Shevington *Gt Man* 78 SD5408
Shevington Moor *Gt Man* 78 SD5410
Shevington Vale *Gt Man* 78 SD5309
Sheviock *Cnwll* 5 SX3755
Shibden Head *W York* 82 SE0928
Shide *IOW* 13 SZ5088
Shidlaw *Nthumb* 110 NT8037
Shiel Bridge *Highld* 138 NG9318
Shieldaig *Highld* 137 NG8154
Shieldhill *Cent* 116 NS8976
Shieldhill *D & G* 100 NY0385
Shieldhill House Hotel *Strath* 108 NT0040
Shields *Strath* 116 NS7755
Shielfoot *Highld* 129 NM6670
Shielhill *Strath* 114 NS2472
Shielhill *Tays* 134 NO4257
Shifford *Oxon* 36 SP3701
Shifnal *Shrops* 60 SJ7407
Shilbottle *Nthumb* 111 NU1908
Shildon *Dur* 96 NZ2226
Shillingford *Devon* 20 SS9824
Shillingford *Oxon* 37 SU5992
Shillingford Abbot *Devon* 9 SX9088
Shillingford St. George *Devon* 9 SX9087
Shillingstone *Dorset* 11 ST8211
Shillington *Beds* 38 TL1234
Shillmoor *Nthumb* 110 NT8807
Shilton *Oxon* 36 SP2608
Shilton *Warwks* 61 SP4084
Shilvinghampton *Dorset* 10 SY6284
Shimpling *Norfk* 54 TM1583
Shimpling *Suffk* 54 TL8651
Shimpling Street *Suffk* 54 TL8753
Shincliffe *Dur* 96 NZ2940
Shiney Row *T & W* 96 NZ3252
Shinfield *Berks* 24 SU7368
Shingay *Cambs* 52 TL3046
Shingle Street *Suffk* 55 TM3642
Shinnersbridge *Devon* 7 SX7862
Shinness *Highld* 146 NC5215
Shipbourne *Kent* 27 TQ5952
Shipbrookhill *Ches* 79 SJ6771
Shipdham *Norfk* 66 TF9507
Shipham *Somset* 21 ST4457
Shiphay *Devon* 7 SX8965
Shiplake *Oxon* 37 SU7678
Shiplake Row *Oxon* 37 SU7478
Shipley *Shrops* 60 SO8095
Shipley *W Susx* 15 TQ1421
Shipley *W York* 82 SE1537
Shipley Bridge *Surrey* 15 TQ3040
Shipley Hatch *Kent* 28 TR0038
Shipmeadow *Suffk* 55 TM3790
Shippea Hill Halt *Cambs* 53 TL6484
Shippon *Oxon* 37 SU4898
Shipston on Stour *Warwks* 48 SP2540
Shipton *Bucks* 49 SP7727
Shipton *Gloucs* 36 SP0318
Shipton *N York* 90 SE5558
Shipton *Shrops* 59 SO5692
Shipton Bellinger *Hants* 23 SU2345
Shipton Gorge *Dorset* 10 SY4991
Shipton Green *W Susx* 14 SZ8099
Shipton Moyne *Gloucs* 35 ST8989
Shipton-on-Cherwell *Oxon* 37 SP4716
Shipton-under-Wychwood *Oxon* 36 SP2817
Shiptonthorpe *Humb* 84 SE8543
Shirburn *Oxon* 37 SU6995
Shirdley Hill *Lancs* 80 SD3612
Shire *Cumb* 94 NY6135
Shire Oak *W Mids* 61 SK0504
Shirebrook *Notts* 75 SK5267
Shiregreen *S York* 74 SK3691
Shirehampton *Avon* 34 ST5376
Shiremoor *T & W* 103 NZ3171
Shirenewton *Gwent* 34 ST4793
Shireoaks *Notts* 75 SK5580
Shirkoak *Kent* 17 TQ9435
Shirl Heath *H & W* 46 SO4359
Shirland *Derbys* 74 SK4058
Shirlett *Shrops* 59 SO6497
Shirley *Derbys* 73 SK2141
Shirley *Gt Lon* 27 TQ3565
Shirley *Hants* 13 SU4014
Shirley *W Mids* 61 SP1278
Shirrell Heath *Hants* 13 SU5714
Shirven *Strath* 113 NR8784
Shirwell *Devon* 19 SS6037
Shirwell Cross *Devon* 19 SS5936
Shittlehope *Dur* 95 NZ0039
Shobdon *H & W* 46 SO4062
Shobley *Hants* 12 SU1806
Shobrooke *Devon* 9 SS8601
Shoby *Leics* 63 SK6820
Shocklach Green *Ches* 71 SJ4349
Shoeburyness *Essex* 40 TQ9385
Sholden *Kent* 29 TR3552
Sholing *Hants* 13 SU4511
Shoose *Cumb* 92 NY0127
Shoot Hill *Shrops* 59 SJ4112
Shop *Cnwll* 18 SS2214
Shop *Cnwll* 4 SW8773
Shop Street *Suffk* 55 TM2268
Shopwyke *W Susx* 14 SU8805
Shore *Gt Man* 81 SD9216
Shoreditch *Gt Lon* 27 TQ3382
Shoreditch *Somset* 20 ST2422
Shoreham *Kent* 27 TQ5161
Shoreham-by-Sea *W Susx* 15 TQ2105
Shoreswood *Nthumb* 110 NT9446
Shorley *Hants* 13 SU5726
Shorncote *Gloucs* 35 SU0296
Shorne *Kent* 28 TQ6971
Shorne Ridgeway *Kent* 28 TQ6970
Short Heath *W Mids* 60 SJ9700
Short Heath *W Mids* 61 SP0992
Shorta Cross *Cnwll* 5 SX2857
Shortbridge *E Susx* 16 TQ4521
Shortfield Common *Surrey* 25 SU8442
Shortgate *E Susx* 16 TQ4915
Shortlanesend *Cnwll* 3 SW8047
Shorwell *IOW* 13 SZ4583
Shoscombe *Avon* 22 ST7156
Shotesham *Norfk* 67 TM2499
Shotgate *Essex* 40 TQ7592
Shotley *Suffk* 55 TM2335
Shotley Bridge *Nthumb* 95 NZ0953
Shotley Gate *Suffk* 41 TM2433
Shotley Street *Suffk* 55 TM2335
Shotleyfield *Nthumb* 95 NZ0553
Shottenden *Kent* 28 TR0454
Shottermill *Surrey* 14 SU8832
Shottery *Warwks* 48 SP1854
Shotteswell *Warwks* 49 SP4245
Shottisham *Suffk* 55 TM3244
Shottle *Derbys* 74 SK3149
Shottlegate *Derbys* 62 SK3147
Shotton *Clwyd* 71 SJ3168
Shotton *Dur* 96 NZ3625
Shotton *Dur* 96 NZ4139
Shotton *Nthumb* 110 NT8430
Shotton *Nthumb* 103 NZ2277
Shotton Colliery *Dur* 96 NZ3941
Shotwick *Ches* 71 SJ3371
Shougle *Gramp* 141 NJ2155
Shouldham *Norfk* 65 TF6709
Shouldham Thorpe *Norfk* 65 TF6607
Shoulton *H & W* 47 SO8159
Shover's Green *E Susx* 16 TQ6530
Shraleybrook *Staffs* 72 SJ7849
Shrawardine *Shrops* 59 SJ3915
Shrawley *H & W* 47 SO8065
Shreding Green *Bucks* 26 TQ0280
Shrewley *Warwks* 48 SP2167
Shrewsbury *Shrops* 59 SJ4912
Shrewton *Wilts* 23 SU0743
Shripney *W Susx* 14 SU9302
Shrivenham *Oxon* 36 SU2389
Shropham *Norfk* 66 TL9893
Shrub End *Essex* 41 TL9723
Shucknall *H & W* 46 SO5842
Shudy Camps *Cambs* 53 TL6244
Shurdington *Gloucs* 35 SO9218
Shurlock Row *Berks* 25 SU8374
Shurnock *H & W* 48 SP0360
Shurrery *Highld* 150 ND0458
Shurrery Lodge *Highld* 150 ND0456
Shurton *Somset* 20 ST2044
Shustoke *Warwks* 61 SP2290
Shut End *W Mids* 60 SO9089
Shut Heath *Staffs* 72 SJ8621
Shute *Devon* 9 SS8900
Shute *Devon* 10 SY2597
Shutford *Oxon* 48 SP3840
Shuthonger *Gloucs* 47 SO8935
Shutlanger *Nhants* 49 SP7249
Shutt Green *Staffs* 60 SJ8709
Shutterton *Devon* 9 SX9679
Shuttington *Warwks* 61 SK2505
Shuttlewood *Derbys* 75 SK4673
Shuttlewood Common *Derbys* 75 SK4773
Shuttleworth *Lancs* 81 SD8017
Sibbertoft *Nhants* 50 SP6882
Sibdon Carwood *Shrops* 59 SO4183
Sibford Ferris *Oxon* 48 SP3537
Sibford Gower *Oxon* 48 SP3537
Sible Hedingham *Essex* 53 TL7734
Sibley's Green *Essex* 40 TL6128
Siblyback *Cnwll* 5 SX2372
Sibsey *Lincs* 77 TF3550
Sibsey Fenside *Lincs* 77 TF3452
Sibson *Cambs* 51 TL0997
Sibson *Leics* 61 SK3500
Sibster *Highld* 151 ND3253
Sibthorpe *Notts* 75 SK7273
Sibthorpe *Notts* 63 SK7645
Sibton *Suffk* 55 TM3669
Sicklesmere *Suffk* 54 TL8760
Sicklinghall *N York* 83 SE3648
Sid Cop *S York* 83 SE3809
Sidbrook *Somset* 20 ST2527
Sidbury *Devon* 9 SY1391
Sidbury *Shrops* 60 SO6885
Sidcot *Somset* 21 ST4257
Sidcup *Gt Lon* 27 TQ4672
Siddick *Cumb* 92 NY0031
Siddington *Ches* 79 SJ8470
Siddington *Gloucs* 36 SU0399
Sidemoor *H & W* 60 SO9571
Sidestrand *Norfk* 67 TG2539
Sidford *Devon* 9 SY1390
Sidlesham *W Susx* 14 SZ8599
Sidlesham Common *W Susx* 14 SZ8599
Sidley *E Susx* 17 TQ7408
Sidmouth *Devon* 9 SY1287
Siefton *Shrops* 59 SO4883
Sigford *Devon* 7 SX7773
Sigglesthorne *Humb* 85 TA1545
Sigingstone *S Glam* 33 SS9771
Signet *Oxon* 36 SP2410
Silchester *Hants* 24 SU6261
Sileby *Leics* 62 SK6015
Silecroft *Cumb* 86 SD1381
Silfield *Norfk* 66 TM1299
Silian *Dyfed* 44 SN5751
Silk Willoughby *Lincs* 64 TF0542
Silkstead *Hants* 13 SU4424
Silkstone *S York* 82 SE2805
Silkstone Common *S York* 82 SE2904
Silksworth *T & W* 96 NZ3752
Silloth *Cumb* 92 NY1153
Silpho *N York* 91 SE9692
Silsden *W York* 82 SE0446
Silsoe *Beds* 38 TL0835
Silton *Dorset* 22 ST7829
Silver End *Beds* 38 TL1042
Silver End *Essex* 40 TL8119
Silver Street *H & W* 61 SP0776
Silver Street *Kent* 28 TQ8760
Silver Street *Somset* 21 ST5432
Silverburn *Loth* 117 NT2060
Silverdale *Lancs* 87 SD4674
Silverdale *Staffs* 72 SJ8146
Silverdale Green *Lancs* 87 SD4674
Silverford *Gramp* 142 NJ7763
Silvergate *Norfk* 66 TG1727
Silverlace Green *Suffk* 55 TM3160
Silverley's Green *Suffk* 55 TM2976
Silverstone *Nhants* 49 SP6743
Silverton *Devon* 9 SS9502
Silverwell *Cnwll* 3 SW7448
Silvington *Shrops* 47 SO6279
Simmondley *Derbys* 74 SK0293
Simonburn *Nthumb* 102 NY8773
Simons Burrow *Devon* 9 ST1416
Simonsbath *Somset* 19 SS7739
Simonstone *Lancs* 81 SD7734
Simonstone *N York* 88 SD8791
Simpson *Bucks* 38 SP8836
Simpson Cross *Dyfed* 30 SM8919
Sinclair's Hill *Border* 119 NT8150
Sinclairston *Strath* 107 NS4716
Sinderby *N York* 89 SE3482
Sinderhope *Nthumb* 95 NY8451
Sinderland Green *Gt Man* 79 SJ7389
Sindlesham *Berks* 25 SU7769

Single Street Southwell

Single Street *Gt Lon* 27 TQ4359
Singleborough *Bucks* 49 SP7631
Singleton *Lancs* 80 SD3838
Singleton *W Susx* 14 SU8713
Singlewell *Kent* 28 TQ6570
Sinkhurst Green *Kent* 28 TQ8142
Sinnarhard *Gramp* 134 NJ4713
Sinnington *N York* 90 SE7485
Sinton *H & W* 47 SO8160
Sinton Green *H & W* 47 SO8160
Sipson *Gt Lon* 26 TQ0777
Sirhowy *Gwent* 33 SO1410
Sissinghurst *Kent* 28 TQ7937
Siston *Avon* 35 ST6875
Sitcott *Devon* 5 SX3691
Sithney *Cnwll* 2 SW6328
Sithney Common *Cnwll* 2 SW6428
Sithney Green *Cnwll* 2 SW6429
Sittingbourne *Kent* 28 TQ9063
Six Ashes *Staffs* 60 SO7988
Six Bells *Gwent* 34 SO2202
Six Mile Bottom *Cambs* 53 TL5756
Six Mile Cottages *Kent* 29 TR1344
Six Rues *Jersey* 152 JS1113
Sixhills *Lincs* 76 TF1787
Sixpenny Handley *Dorset* 11 ST9917
Sizewell *Suffk* 55 TM4762
Skaill *Ork* 155 HY5806
Skares *Strath* 107 NS5317
Skateraw *Loth* 119 NT7375
Skeabost *Highld* 136 NG4148
Skeeby *N York* 89 NZ1902
Skeffington *Leics* 63 SK7402
Skeffling *Humb* 85 TA3719
Skegby *Notts* 75 SK4961
Skegby *Notts* 75 SK7869
Skegness *Lincs* 77 TF5663
Skelbo *Highld* 147 NH7895
Skelbo Street *Highld* 147 NH7994
Skelbrooke *S York* 83 SE5012
Skeldyke *Lincs* 64 TF3337
Skellingthorpe *Lincs* 76 SK9272
Skellorm Green *Ches* 79 SJ9281
Skellow *S York* 83 SE5310
Skelmanthorpe *W York* 82 SE2310
Skelmersdale *Lancs* 78 SD4606
Skelmorlie *Strath* 114 NS1967
Skelpick *Highld* 150 NC7256
Skelston *D & G* 100 NX8285
Skelton *Cleve* 97 NZ6618
Skelton *Cumb* 93 NY4335
Skelton *Humb* 84 SE7625
Skelton *N York* 89 NZ0900
Skelton *N York* 89 SE3668
Skelton *N York* 83 SE5756
Skelwith Bridge *Cumb* 87 NY3403
Skendleby *Lincs* 77 TF4369
Skene House *Gramp* 135 NJ7610
Skenfrith *Gwent* 34 SO4520
Skerne *Humb* 84 TA0455
Skerray *Highld* 149 NC6563
Skerricha *Highld* 148 NC2350
Skerton *Lancs* 87 SD4763
Sketchley *Leics* 50 SP4292
Sketty *W Glam* 32 SS6292
Skewen *W Glam* 32 SS7296
Skewsby *N York* 90 SE6270
Skeyton *Norfk* 67 TG2425
Skeyton Corner *Norfk* 67 TG2527
Skiall *Highld* 150 ND0267
Skidbrooke *Lincs* 77 TF4393
Skidbrooke North End *Lincs* 77 TF4395
Skidby *Humb* 84 TA0133
Skigersta *W Isls* 154 NB5461
Skilgate *Somset* 20 SS9827
Skillington *Lincs* 63 SK8925
Skinburness *Cumb* 92 NY1256
Skinflats *Cent* 116 NS9082
Skinidin *Highld* 136 NG2247
Skinners Green *Berks* 24 SU4465
Skinningrove *Cleve* 97 NZ7119
Skipness *Strath* 114 NR9057
Skipper's Bridge *Cumb* 101 NY3783
Skiprigg *Cumb* 93 NY3945
Skipsea *Humb* 85 TA1654
Skipsea Brough *Humb* 85 TA1454
Skipton *N York* 82 SD9851
Skipton-on-Swale *N York* 89 SE3679
Skipwith *N York* 83 SE6638
Skirling *Border* 108 NT0739
Skirmett *Bucks* 37 SU7790
Skirpenbeck *Humb* 84 SE7456
Skirwith *Cumb* 94 NY6132
Skirwith *N York* 87 SD7073
Skirza *Highld* 151 ND3868
Skitby *Cumb* 101 NY4465
Skittle Green *Bucks* 37 SP7703
Skulamus *Highld* 129 NG6622
Skullomie *Highld* 149 NC6161
Skyborry Green *Shrops* 46 SO2674
Skye Green *Essex* 40 TL8722
Skye of Curr *Highld* 141 NH9924
Skyreholme *N York* 88 SE0660
Slack *Derbys* 74 SK3362
Slack *W York* 82 SD9728
Slack Head *Cumb* 87 SD4978
Slack Side *W York* 82 SE1430
Slackcote *Gt Man* 82 SD9709
Slackholme End *Lincs* 77 TF5370
Slacks of Cairnbanno *Gramp* 143 NJ8445
Slad *Gloucs* 35 SO8707
Slade *Devon* 19 SS5046
Slade *Devon* 9 ST1108
Slade *Somset* 19 SS8327
Slade End *Oxon* 37 SU5990
Slade Green *Kent* 27 TQ5276
Slade Heath *Staffs* 60 SJ9106
Slade Hooton *S York* 75 SK5288
Sladen *Derbys* 74 SK0771
Slades Green *H & W* 47 SO8134
Sladesbridge *Cnwll* 4 SX0171
Slaggan *Highld* 144 NG8494
Slaggyford *Nthumb* 94 NY6752
Slagnaw *D & G* 99 NX7458
Slaid Hill *W York* 83 SE3240
Slaidburn *Lancs* 81 SD7152
Slaithwaite *W York* 82 SE0813
Slaley *Derbys* 74 SK2757
Slaley *Nthumb* 95 NY9657
Slamannan *Cent* 116 NS8572
Slapton *Bucks* 38 SP9320
Slapton *Devon* 7 SX8245
Slapton *Nhants* 49 SP6446
Slattocks *Gt Man* 79 SD8808
Slaugham *W Susx* 15 TQ2528
Slaughterford *Wilts* 35 ST8473
Slawston *Leics* 50 SP7894
Sleaford *Hants* 25 SU8038
Sleaford *Lincs* 64 TF0645
Sleagill *Cumb* 94 NY5919
Sleap *Shrops* 59 SJ4826
Sleapford *Shrops* 59 SJ6315
Sleasdairidh *Highld* 146 NH6496
Sledge Green *H & W* 47 SO8134
Sledmere *Humb* 91 SE9364
Sleight *Dorset* 11 SY9898
Sleightholme *Dur* 88 NY9510
Sleights *N York* 90 NZ8607
Slepe *Dorset* 11 SY9293
Slerra *Devon* 18 SS3124
Slickly *Highld* 151 ND2966
Sliddery *Strath* 105 NR9323
Sligachan *Highld* 136 NG4829
Sligrachan *Strath* 114 NS1791
Slimbridge *Gloucs* 35 SO7303
Slindon *Staffs* 72 SJ8232
Slindon *W Susx* 14 SU9608
Slinfold *W Susx* 14 TQ1131
Sling *Gwynd* 69 SH6066
Slingsby *N York* 90 SE6974
Slip End *Beds* 38 TL0718
Slip End *Herts* 39 TL2837
Slipton *Nhants* 51 SP9579
Slitting Mill *Staffs* 73 SK0217
Slockavullin *Strath* 113 NR8297
Slogarie *D & G* 99 NX6568
Sloley *Norfk* 67 TG2923
Sloncombe *Devon* 8 SX7386
Sloothby *Lincs* 77 TF4970
Slough *Berks* 26 SU9879
Slough Green *Somset* 20 ST2719
Slough Green *W Susx* 15 TQ2826
Slumbay *Highld* 138 NG8938
Slyfield Green *Surrey* 25 SU9952
Slyne *Lancs* 87 SD4765
Smailholm *Border* 110 NT6436
Small Dole *W Susx* 15 TQ2112
Small Heath *W Mids* 61 SP1085
Small Hythe *Kent* 17 TQ8930
Small Wood Hey *Lancs* 80 SD3948
Smallbridge *Gt Man* 81 SD9115
Smallbrook *Devon* 9 SX8698
Smallbrook *Gloucs* 34 SO5900
Smallburgh *Norfk* 67 TG3324
Smalldale *Derbys* 74 SK0977
Smalldale *Derbys* 74 SK1781
Smalley *Derbys* 62 SK4044
Smalley Common *Derbys* 62 SK4042
Smalley Green *Derbys* 62 SK4043
Smallfield *Surrey* 15 TQ3143
Smallridge *Devon* 10 ST3001
Smallthorne *Staffs* 72 SJ8850
Smallwood *Ches* 72 SJ8060
Smallworth *Norfk* 54 TM0080
Smannell *Hants* 23 SU3749
Smardale *Cumb* 88 NY7308
Smarden *Kent* 28 TQ8742
Smarden Bell *Kent* 28 TQ8742
Smart's Hill *Kent* 16 TQ5242
Smeafield *Nthumb* 111 NU0937
Smeale *IOM* 153 NX4102
Smearisary *Highld* 129 NM6476
Smeatharpe *Devon* 9 ST1910
Smeeth *Kent* 29 TR0739
Smeeton Westerby *Leics* 50 SP6892
Smelthouses *N York* 89 SE1964
Smerral *Highld* 151 ND1733
Smestow *Staffs* 60 SO8591
Smethwick *W Mids* 60 SP0287
Smethwick Green *Ches* 72 SJ8063
Smisby *Derbys* 62 SK3418
Smith End Green *H & W* 47 SO7752
Smith Green *Lancs* 80 SD4955
Smith's End *Herts* 39 TL4037
Smith's Green *Essex* 40 TL5721
Smith's Green *Essex* 53 TL6640
Smitheclose *IOW* 13 SZ5391
Smithfield *Cumb* 101 NY4465
Smithies *S York* 83 SE3508
Smithincott *Devon* 9 ST0611
Smithstown *Highld* 144 NG7977
Smithton *Highld* 140 NH7145
Smithy Green *Ches* 79 SJ7474
Smithy Green *Gt Man* 79 SJ8785
Smithy Houses *Derbys* 62 SK3846
Smockington *Leics* 50 SP4589
Smoo *Highld* 149 NC4167
Smythe's Green *Essex* 41 TL9218
Snade *D & G* 100 NX8485
Snailbeach *Shrops* 59 SJ3702
Snailwell *Cambs* 53 TL6467
Snainton *N York* 91 SE9282
Snaith *Humb* 83 SE6422
Snake Pass Inn *Derbys* 74 SK1190
Snape *N York* 89 SE2684
Snape *Suffk* 55 TM3959
Snape Green *Mersyd* 80 SD3813
Snape Street *Suffk* 55 TM3958
Snarestone *Leics* 62 SK3409
Snarford *Lincs* 76 TF0482
Snargate *Kent* 17 TQ9928
Snave *Kent* 17 TR0129
Sneachill *H & W* 47 SO9053
Snead *Powys* 59 SO3192
Sneath Common *Norfk* 54 TM1689
Sneaton *N York* 91 NZ8907
Sneatonthorpe *N York* 91 NZ9006
Snelland *Lincs* 76 TF0780
Snelston *Derbys* 73 SK1543
Snetterton *Norfk* 66 TL9991
Snettisham *Norfk* 65 TF6834
Snibston *Leics* 62 SK4114
Snig's End *Gloucs* 47 SO7828
Snitter *Nthumb* 103 NU0203
Snitterby *Lincs* 76 SK9894
Snitterfield *Warwks* 48 SP2159
Snitterton *Derbys* 74 SK2760
Snittlegarth *Cumb* 93 NY2138
Snitton *Shrops* 46 SO5575
Snoadhill *Kent* 28 TQ9442
Snodhill *H & W* 46 SO3240
Snodland *Kent* 28 TQ7061
Snoll Hatch *Kent* 28 TQ6648
Snow End *Herts* 39 TL4032
Snow Street *Norfk* 54 TM0981
Snowden Hill *S York* 74 SE2600
Snowshill *Gloucs* 48 SP0933
Soake *Hants* 13 SU6611
Soar *M Glam* 33 ST0983
Soar *Powys* 45 SN9731
Soberton *Hants* 13 SU6116
Soberton Heath *Hants* 13 SU6014
Sockbridge *Cumb* 94 NY4926
Sockburn *Nthumb* 89 NZ3406
Sodylt Bank *Shrops* 71 SJ3439
Soham *Cambs* 53 TL5973
Soham Cotes *Cambs* 53 TL5775
Solbury *Dyfed* 30 SM8912
Soldon *Devon* 18 SS3210
Soldon Cross *Devon* 18 SS3210
Soldridge *Hants* 24 SU6535
Sole Street *Kent* 28 TQ6567
Sole Street *Kent* 29 TR0949
Solihull *W Mids* 61 SP1679
Sollas *W Isls* 154 NF8074
Sollers Dilwyn *H & W* 46 SO4255
Sollers Hope *H & W* 46 SO6132
Sollom *Lancs* 80 SD4518
Solva *Dyfed* 30 SM8024
Solwaybank *D & G* 101 NY3077
Somerby *Leics* 63 SK7710
Somerby *Lincs* 84 TA0606
Somercotes *Derbys* 74 SK4253
Somerford Keynes *Gloucs* 35 SU0195
Somerley *W Susx* 14 SZ8198
Somerleyton *Suffk* 67 TM4897
Somersal Herbert *Derbys* 73 SK1335
Somersby *Lincs* 77 TF3472
Somersham *Cambs* 52 TL3678
Somersham *Suffk* 54 TM0848
Somerton *Oxon* 49 SP4928
Somerton *Somset* 21 ST4928
Somerton *Suffk* 54 TL8153
Somerwood *Shrops* 59 SJ5614
Sompting *W Susx* 15 TQ1505
Sonning *Berks* 37 SU7575
Sonning Common *Oxon* 37 SU7180
Sonning Eye *Oxon* 37 SU7476
Sontley *Clwyd* 71 SJ3347
Sopley *Hants* 12 SZ1596
Sopworth *Wilts* 35 ST8286
Sorbie *D & G* 99 NX4346
Sordale *Highld* 151 ND1462
Sorisdale *Strath* 120 NM2763
Sorn *Strath* 107 NS5526
Sortat *Highld* 151 ND2863
Sosgill *Cumb* 92 NY1024
Sotby *Lincs* 76 TF2078
Sots Hole *Lincs* 76 TF1264
Sotterly *Suffk* 55 TM4484
Sotwell *Oxon* 37 SU5890
Soughton *Clwyd* 70 SJ2466
Soulbury *Bucks* 38 SP8826
Soulby *Cumb* 93 NY4625
Soulby *Cumb* 88 NY7411
Souldern *Oxon* 49 SP5231
Souldrop *Beds* 51 SP9861
Sound Muir *Gramp* 141 NJ3652
Soundwell *Avon* 35 ST6575
Sourton *Devon* 8 SX5390
Soutergate *Cumb* 86 SD2281
South Acre *Norfk* 66 TF8114
South Alkham *Kent* 29 TR2441
South Allington *Devon* 7 SX7938
South Alloa *Cent* 116 NS8791
South Ambersham *W Susx* 14 SU9120
South Anston *S York* 75 SK5183
South Ascot *Berks* 25 SU9268
South Ashford *Kent* 28 TR0041
South Baddesley *Hants* 12 SZ3596
South Bank *Cleve* 97 NZ5320
South Bank *N York* 83 SE5950
South Barrow *Somset* 21 ST6028
South Beddington *Gt Lon* 27 TQ2863
South Beer *Cnwll* 5 SX3091
South Benfleet *Essex* 40 TQ7787
South Bersted *W Susx* 14 SU9300
South Bockhampton *Dorset* 12 SZ1795
South Bowood *Dorset* 10 SY4498
South Bramwith *S York* 83 SE6211
South Brent *Devon* 7 SX6960
South Brewham *Somset* 22 ST7236
South Broomhill *Nthumb* 103 NZ2499
South Burlingham *Norfk* 67 TG3807
South Cadbury *Somset* 21 ST6325
South Cairn *D & G* 98 NW9769
South Carlton *Lincs* 76 SK9476
South Carlton *Notts* 75 SK5883
South Cave *Humb* 84 SE9230
South Cerney *Gloucs* 36 SU0497
South Charlton *Nthumb* 111 NU1620
South Cheriton *Somset* 22 ST6924
South Church *Dur* 96 NZ2128
South Cleatlam *Dur* 96 NZ1218
South Cliffe *Humb* 84 SE8735
South Clifton *Notts* 75 SK8270
South Collingham *Notts* 75 SK8261
South Cornelly *M Glam* 33 SS8280
South Cove *Suffk* 55 TM4981
South Creake *Norfk* 66 TF8536
South Crosland *W York* 82 SE1112
South Croxton *Leics* 63 SK6810
South Dalton *Humb* 84 SE9645
South Duffield *N York* 83 SE6833
South Elkington *Lincs* 77 TF2988
South Elmsall *W York* 83 SE4711
South End *H & W* 47 SO7444
South End *Hants* 12 SU1015
South End *Humb* 85 TA1120
South End *Humb* 85 TA3918
South End *Norfk* 54 TL9990
South Erradale *Highld* 137 NG7471
South Fambridge *Essex* 40 TQ8694
South Fawley *Berks* 36 SU3880
South Feorline *Strath* 105 NR9028
South Ferriby *Humb* 84 SE9820
South Field *Humb* 84 TA0225
South Godstone *Surrey* 15 TQ3648
South Gorley *Hants* 12 SU1610
South Gosworth *T & W* 103 NZ2467
South Green *Essex* 41 TM0319
South Green *Essex* 40 TQ6893
South Green *Kent* 28 TQ8560
South Green *Norfk* 66 TG0510
South Green *Suffk* 54 TM1775
South Hanningfield *Essex* 40 TQ7497
South Harting *W Susx* 14 SU7819
South Hayling *Hants* 13 SZ7299
South Hazelrigg *Nthumb* 111 NU0532
South Heath *Bucks* 26 SP9101
South Heighton *E Susx* 16 TQ4402
South Hetton *Cleve* 96 NZ3845
South Hiendley *W York* 83 SE3912
South Hill *Cnwll* 5 SX3272
South Hill *Somset* 21 ST4726
South Hinksey *Oxon* 37 SP5104
South Hole *Devon* 18 SS2220
South Holmwood *Surrey* 15 TQ1744
South Hornchurch *Gt Lon* 27 TQ5183
South Huish *Devon* 7 SX6941
South Hykeham *Lincs* 76 SK9364
South Hylton *T & W* 96 NZ3556
South Kelsey *Lincs* 76 TF0498
South Kessock *Highld* 140 NH6547
South Killingholme *Humb* 85 TA1416
South Kilvington *N York* 89 SE4284
South Kilworth *Nhants* 50 SP6081
South Kirkby *W York* 83 SE4410
South Knighton *Devon* 7 SX8172
South Kyme *Lincs* 76 TF1749
South Lambeth *Gt Lon* 27 TQ3077
South Lawn *Oxon* 36 SP2814
South Leigh *Oxon* 36 SP3909
South Leverton *Notts* 75 SK7881
South Littleton *H & W* 48 SP0746
South Lopham *Norfk* 54 TM0481
South Luffenham *Leics* 63 SK9301
South Mains *D & G* 107 NS7807
South Malling *E Susx* 16 TQ4210
South Marston *Wilts* 36 SU1987
South Merstham *Surrey* 27 TQ2952
South Middleton *Nthumb* 111 NT9923
South Milford *N York* 83 SE4931
South Milton *Devon* 7 SX7042
South Mimms *Herts* 26 TL2201
South Molton *Devon* 19 SS7125
South Moor *Dur* 96 NZ1951
South Moreton *Oxon* 37 SU5688
South Mundham *W Susx* 14 SU8700
South Muskham *Notts* 75 SK7957
South Newbald *Humb* 84 SE9035
South Newington *Oxon* 48 SP4033
South Newton *Wilts* 23 SU0834
South Normanton *Derbys* 75 SK4456
South Norwood *Gt Lon* 27 TQ3368
South Nutfield *Surrey* 15 TQ3049
South Ockendon *Essex* 27 TQ5983
South Ormsby *Lincs* 77 TF3675
South Ossett *W York* 82 SE2819
South Otterington *N York* 89 SE3787
South Owersby *Lincs* 76 TF0693
South Park *Surrey* 15 TQ2448
South Perrott *Dorset* 10 ST4706
South Petherton *Somset* 10 ST4316
South Petherwin *Cnwll* 5 SX3181
South Pickenham *Norfk* 66 TF8504
South Pill *Cnwll* 6 SX4259
South Pool *Devon* 7 SX7740
South Poorton *Dorset* 10 SY5297
South Quarme *Somset* 20 SS9236
South Queensferry *Loth* 117 NT1378
South Radworthy *Devon* 19 SS7432
South Rauceby *Lincs* 64 TF0245
South Raynham *Norfk* 66 TF8723
South Reddish *Gt Man* 79 SJ8891
South Reston *Lincs* 77 TF4083
South Runcton *Norfk* 65 TF6308
South Scarle *Notts* 76 SK8463
South Shian *Strath* 122 NM9042
South Shields *T & W* 103 NZ3666
South Shore *Lancs* 80 SD3033
South Skirlaugh *Humb* 85 TA1438
South Somercotes *Lincs* 77 TF4193
South Stainley *N York* 89 SE3063
South Stifford *Essex* 27 TQ5978
South Stoke *Avon* 22 ST7461
South Stoke *Oxon* 37 SU5983
South Stoke *W Susx* 14 TQ0209
South Stour *Kent* 28 TR0338
South Street *E Susx* 15 TQ3918
South Street *Kent* 27 TQ6363
South Street *Kent* 28 TR0557
South Street *Kent* 29 TR1265
South Tarbrax *Strath* 117 NT0353
South Tawton *Devon* 8 SX6594
South Thoresby *Lincs* 77 TF4076
South Tidworth *Hants* 23 SU2347
South Town *Hants* 24 SU6536
South Walsham *Norfk* 67 TG3613
South Warnborough *Hants* 24 SU7247
South Weald *Essex* 27 TQ5694
South Weston *Oxon* 37 SU7098
South Wheatley *Cnwll* 5 SX2492
South Widcombe *Somset* 21 ST5856
South Wigston *Leics* 50 SP5897
South Willesborough *Kent* 28 TR0240
South Willingham *Lincs* 76 TF1983
South Wingate *Dur* 96 NZ4134
South Wingfield *Derbys* 74 SK3755
South Witham *Lincs* 63 SK9219
South Wonston *Hants* 24 SU4636
South Woodham Ferrers *Essex* 40 TQ8097
South Wootton *Norfk* 65 TF6422
South Wraxall *Wilts* 22 ST8364
South Zeal *Devon* 8 SX6593
Southall *Gt Lon* 26 TQ1279
Southam *Gloucs* 47 SO9725
Southam *Warwks* 49 SP4161
Southampton *Hants* 13 SU4112
Southborough *Gt Lon* 27 TQ4267
Southborough *Kent* 16 TQ5842
Southbourne *Dorset* 12 SZ1491
Southbourne *W Susx* 14 SU7705
Southbrook *Dorset* 11 SY8494
Southburgh *Norfk* 66 TG0005
Southburn *Humb* 84 SE9854
Southchurch *Essex* 40 TQ9086
Southcott *Cnwll* 5 SX1995
Southcott *Devon* 18 SS4416
Southcott *Devon* 8 SX5495
Southcott *Devon* 8 SX7580
Southcott *Wilts* 23 SU1659
Southcourt *Bucks* 38 SP8112
Southease *E Susx* 16 TQ4205
Southend *Strath* 105 NR6908
Southend *Wilts* 36 SU1973
Southend-on-Sea *Essex* 40 TQ8885
Southernby *Cumb* 93 NY3639
Southernden *Kent* 28 TQ8645
Southerndown *M Glam* 33 SS8873
Southerness *D & G* 92 NX9754
Southery *Norfk* 65 TL6194
Southfield *Cent* 116 NS8472
Southfleet *Kent* 27 TQ6171
Southford *IOW* 13 SZ5179
Southgate *Gt Lon* 27 TQ2994
Southgate *Norfk* 65 TF6833
Southgate *Norfk* 66 TF8635
Southgate *Norfk* 66 TG1324
Southgate *W Glam* 32 SS5587
Southill *Beds* 39 TL1542
Southington *Hants* 24 SU5049
Southleigh *Devon* 9 SY2093
Southminster *Essex* 40 TQ9599
Southmoor *Oxon* 36 SU3998
Southmuir *Tays* 126 NO3852
Southoe *Cambs* 52 TL1864
Southolt *Suffk* 55 TM1968
Southorpe *Cambs* 64 TF0803
Southover *Dorset* 10 SY6294
Southover *E Susx* 16 TQ6525
Southowram *W York* 82 SE1123
Southport *Mersyd* 80 SD3317
Southrepps *Norfk* 67 TG2536
Southrey *Lincs* 76 TF1366
Southrop *Gloucs* 36 SP1903
Southrope *Hants* 24 SU6644
Southsea *Clwyd* 71 SJ3051
Southsea *Hants* 13 SZ6599
Southside *Dur* 95 NZ1026
Southtown *Norfk* 67 TG5106
Southtown *Somset* 10 ST3216
Southwaite *Cumb* 93 NY4445
Southwark *Gt Lon* 27 TQ3279
Southwater *W Susx* 15 TQ1526
Southwater Street *W Susx* 15 TQ1427
Southway *Somset* 21 ST5242
Southwell *Dorset* 11 SY6870

Southwell

Stoke by Clare

Southwell Notts 75 SK6953
Southwick Hants 13 SU6208
Southwick Nhants 51 TL0292
Southwick Somset 21 ST3646
Southwick T & W 96 NZ3758
Southwick W Susx 15 TQ2405
Southwick Wilts 22 ST8355
Southwold Suffk 55 TM5076
Southwood Norfk 67 TG3905
Southwood Somset 21 ST5533
Sowe Common W Mids 61 SP3782
Sower Carr Lancs 80 SD3743
Sowerby N York 89 SE4380
Sowerby W York 82 SE0423
Sowerby Bridge W York 82 SE0523
Sowerby Row Cumb 93 NY3940
Sowerhill Somset 19 SS8924
Sowhill Gwent 34 SO2700
Sowley Green Suffk 53 TL7050
Sowood W York 82 SE0818
Sowton Devon 6 SX5065
Sowton Devon 9 SX9792
Soyland Town W York 82 SE0320
Spa Common Norfk 67 TG2930
Spain's End Essex 53 TL6637
Spalding Lincs 64 TF2422
Spaldington Humb 84 SE7633
Spaldwick Cambs 52 TL1372
Spalford Notts 76 SK8369
Spanish Green Hants 24 SU6958
Sparham Norfk 66 TG0719
Sparhamill Norfk 66 TG0818
Spark Bridge Cumb 86 SD3084
Sparket Cumb 93 NY4325
Sparkford Somset 21 ST6025
Sparkhill W Mids 61 SP1083
Sparkwell Devon 6 SX5857
Sparrow Green Norfk 66 TF9414
Sparrowpit Derbys 74 SK0880
Sparrows Green E Susx 16 TQ6332
Sparsholt Hants 24 SU4331
Sparsholt Oxon 36 SU3487
Spartylea Cumb 95 NY8548
Spath Staffs 73 SK0835
Spaunton N York 90 SE7289
Spaxton Somset 20 ST2237
Spean Bridge Highld 131 NN2281
Spear Hill W Susx 15 TQ1317
Spearywell Hants 23 SU3127
Speen Berks 24 SU4567
Speen Bucks 26 SU8499
Speeton N York 91 TA1574
Speke Mersyd 78 SJ4383
Speldhurst Kent 16 TQ5541
Spellbrook Herts 39 TL4817
Spelmonden Kent 28 TQ7037
Spelsbury Oxon 36 SP3421
Spen W York 82 SE1925
Spen Green Ches 72 SJ8160
Spencers Wood Berks 24 SU7166
Spennithorne N York 89 SE1388
Spennymoor Dur 96 NZ2533
Spernall Warwks 48 SP0862
Spestos Devon 8 SX7298
Spetchley H & W 47 SO8953
Spettisbury Dorset 11 ST9102
Spexhall Suffk 55 TM3780
Spey Bay Gramp 141 NJ3565
Speybridge Highld 141 NJ0326
Speyview Gramp 141 NJ2541
Spilsby Lincs 77 TF4066
Spindlestone Nthumb 111 NU1533
Spinkhill Derbys 75 SK4578
Spinningdale Highld 146 NH6789
Spirthill Wilts 35 ST9976
Spital Berks 26 SU9675
Spital Mersyd 78 SJ3482
Spital Hill Notts 75 SK6193
Spital in the Street Lincs 76 SK9690
Spithurst E Susx 16 TQ4217
Spittal Dyfed 30 SM9723
Spittal Highld 151 ND1654
Spittal Humb 84 SE7652
Spittal Loth 118 NT4677
Spittal Nthumb 119 NU0051
Spittal of Glenmuick Gramp 134 NO3085
Spittal of Glenshee Tays 133 NO1070
Spittal-on-Rule Border 110 NT5819
Spittalfield Tays 126 NO1040
Spixworth Norfk 67 TG2415
Splatt Cnwll 4 SW9476
Splatt Cnwll 5 SX2288
Splatt Devon 8 SS6005
Splayne's Green E Susx 16 TQ4224
Splottlands S Glam 33 ST2077
Spodegreen Ches 79 SJ7385
Spofforth N York 83 SE3651
Spon Green Clwyd 70 SJ2863
Spondon Derbys 62 SK4036
Spooner Row Norfk 66 TM0997
Sporle Norfk 66 TF8411
Spott Loth 118 NT6775
Spottiswoode Border 110 NT6049
Spratton Nhants 50 SP7169
Spreakley Surrey 25 SU8341
Spreyton Devon 8 SX6996
Spriddlestone Devon 6 SX5351
Spridlington Lincs 76 TF0084
Spring Vale S York 82 SE2502
Springburn Strath 116 NS6068
Springfield D & G 101 NY3268
Springfield Essex 40 TL7208
Springfield Fife 126 NO3411
Springhill Staffs 60 SJ9704
Springhill Staffs 61 SK0705
Springholm D & G 100 NX8070
Springkell D & G 101 NY2575
Springside Strath 106 NS3738
Springthorpe Lincs 76 SK8789
Springwell T & W 96 NZ2858
Sproatley Humb 85 TA1934
Sproston Green Ches 72 SJ7366
Sprotbrough S York 83 SE5301
Sproughton Suffk 54 TM1244
Sprouston Border 110 NT7535
Sprowston Norfk 67 TG2512
Sproxton Leics 63 SK8524
Sproxton N York 90 SE6181
Sprytown Devon 5 SX4185
Spunhill Shrops 59 SJ4133
Spurstow Ches 71 SJ5657
Spyway Dorset 10 SY5293
Squirrel's Heath Gt Lon 27 TQ5389
St-y-Nyll S Glam 33 ST0977
Stableford Shrops 60 SO7598
Stableford Staffs 72 SJ8138
Stacey Bank Derbys 74 SK2890
Stackhouse N York 88 SD8165
Stackpole Dyfed 30 SR9896
Stacksford Norfk 54 TM0590
Stacksteads Lancs 81 SD8521
Stadbury Devon 7 SX6846
Staddiscombe Devon 6 SX5151
Staddlethorpe Humb 84 SE8328
Stadhampton Oxon 37 SU6098
Staffield Cumb 94 NY5442
Staffin Highld 136 NG4967
Stafford Staffs 72 SJ9223
Stag Green Cumb 86 SD1679
Stagsden Beds 38 SP9848
Stainburn Cumb 92 NY0129
Stainburn N York 82 SE2548
Stainby Lincs 63 SK9022
Staincross S York 83 SE3210
Staindrop Dur 96 NZ1220
Staines Surrey 26 TQ0371
Stainfield Lincs 64 TF0824
Stainfield Lincs 76 TF1172
Stainforth N York 88 SD8267
Stainforth S York 83 SE6411
Staining Lancs 80 SD3436
Stainland W York 82 SE0719
Stainsacre N York 91 NZ9108
Stainton Cleve 97 NZ4714
Stainton Cumb 93 NY3857
Stainton Cumb 94 NY4828
Stainton Cumb 87 SD5285
Stainton Dur 95 NZ0718
Stainton N York 89 SE1096
Stainton S York 75 SK5593
Stainton by Langworth Lincs 76 TF0677
Stainton le Vale Lincs 76 TF1794
Stainton with Adgarley Cumb 86 SD2472
Staintondale N York 91 SE9998
Stair Cumb 93 NY2321
Stair Strath 107 NS4423
Stair Haven D & G 98 NX2153
Stairfoot S York 83 SE3705
Staithes N York 97 NZ7818
Stake Pool Lancs 80 SD4147
Stakeford Nthumb 103 NZ2685
Stakes Hants 13 SU6808
Stalbridge Dorset 11 ST7317
Stalbridge Weston Dorset 11 ST7116
Stalham Norfk 67 TG3725
Stalham Green Norfk 67 TG3824
Stalisfield Green Kent 28 TQ9552
Stallen Dorset 10 ST6016
Stalling Busk N York 88 SD9186
Stallingborough Humb 85 TA1911
Stallington Staffs 72 SJ9439
Stalmine Lancs 80 SD3745
Stalmine Moss Side Lancs 80 SD3845
Stalybridge Gt Man 79 SJ9698
Stambourne Essex 53 TL7238
Stambourne Green Essex 53 TL6938
Stamford Lincs 64 TF0307
Stamford Nthumb 111 NU2219
Stamford Bridge Ches 71 SJ4667
Stamford Bridge Humb 84 SE7155
Stamford Hill Gt Lon 27 TQ3387
Stamfordham Nthumb 103 NZ0771
Stamton Lees Derbys 74 SK2562
Stanah Lancs 80 SD3542
Stanborough Herts 39 TL2211
Stanbridge Beds 38 SP9624
Stanbridge Dorset 11 SU0004
Stanbury W York 82 SE0137
Stand Gt Man 79 SD7905
Stand Strath 116 NS7668
Standburn Cent 116 NS9274
Standeford Staffs 60 SJ9107
Standen Kent 28 TQ8540
Standen Street Kent 17 TQ8030
Standerwick Somset 22 ST8150
Standford Hants 14 SU8134
Standingstone Cumb 92 NY0533
Standish Gt Man 78 SD5610
Standish Lower Ground Gt Man 78 SD5507
Standlake Oxon 36 SP3903
Standon Hants 13 SU4226
Standon Herts 39 TL3922
Standon Staffs 72 SJ8135
Standon Green End Herts 39 TL3620
Standwell Green Suffk 54 TM1369
Stane Strath 116 NS8859
Stanfield Norfk 66 TF9320
Stanford Beds 39 TL1640
Stanford Kent 29 TR1238
Stanford Shrops 59 SJ3313
Stanford Bishop H & W 47 SO6851
Stanford Bridge H & W 47 SO7265
Stanford Bridge Shrops 72 SJ7024
Stanford Dingley Berks 24 SU5771
Stanford in the Vale Oxon 36 SU3493
Stanford le Hope Essex 40 TQ6882
Stanford on Avon Nhants 50 SP5978
Stanford on Soar Notts 62 SK5421
Stanford on Teme H & W 47 SO7065
Stanford Rivers Essex 27 TL5301
Stanfree Derbys 75 SK4773
Stanghow Cleve 97 NZ6715
Stanground Cambs 64 TL2097
Stanhill Lancs 81 SD7227
Stanhoe Norfk 66 TF8036
Stanhope Border 108 NT1229
Stanhope Dur 95 NY9939
Stanhope Bretby Derbys 73 SK2921
Stanion Nhants 51 SP9186
Stanley Derbys 62 SK4140
Stanley Dur 96 NZ1953
Stanley Notts 75 SK4662
Stanley Shrops 60 SO7483
Stanley Staffs 72 SJ9352
Stanley Tays 126 NO1033
Stanley W York 83 SE3422
Stanley Common Derbys 62 SK4042
Stanley Crook Dur 96 NZ1637
Stanley Gate Lancs 78 SD4405
Stanley Moor Staffs 72 SJ9251
Stanley Pontlarge Gloucs 47 SP0030
Stanmer E Susx 15 TQ3309
Stanmore Berks 37 SU4778
Stanmore Gt Lon 26 TQ1692
Stanmore Hants 24 SU4628
Stannersburn Nthumb 102 NY7286
Stanningley W York 82 SE2234
Stannington Nthumb 103 NZ2179
Stannington S York 74 SK2987
Stansbatch H & W 46 SO3461
Stansfield Suffk 53 TL7852
Stanshope Staffs 73 SK1253
Stanstead Suffk 54 TL8449
Stanstead Abbots Herts 39 TL3811
Stanstead Street Suffk 54 TL8448
Stansted Kent 27 TQ6062
Stansted Mountfitchet Essex 39 TL5125
Stanton Derbys 73 SK2718
Stanton Devon 7 SX7050
Stanton Gloucs 48 SP0634
Stanton Gwent 34 SO3021
Stanton Nthumb 103 NZ1390
Stanton Staffs 73 SK1245
Stanton Suffk 54 TL9673
Stanton Butts Cambs 52 TL2372
Stanton by Bridge Derbys 62 SK3726
Stanton by Dale Derbys 62 SK4637
Stanton Drew Avon 21 ST5963
Stanton Fitzwarren Wilts 36 SU1790
Stanton Harcourt Oxon 36 SP4105
Stanton Hill Notts 75 SK4760
Stanton in Peak Derbys 74 SK2364
Stanton Lacy Shrops 46 SO4978
Stanton Long Shrops 59 SO5791
Stanton on the Wolds Notts 63 SK6330
Stanton Prior Avon 22 ST6762
Stanton St. Bernard Wilts 23 SU0961
Stanton St. John Oxon 37 SP5709
Stanton St. Quintin Wilts 35 ST9079
Stanton Street Suffk 54 TL9566
Stanton under Bardon Leics 62 SK4610
Stanton upon Hine Heath Shrops 59 SJ5624
Stanton Wick Avon 21 ST6162
Stantway Gloucs 35 SO7313
Stanwardine in the Field Shrops 59 SJ4124
Stanwardine in the Wood Shrops 59 SJ4227
Stanway Essex 40 TL9424
Stanway Gloucs 48 SP0632
Stanway Green Essex 40 TL9523
Stanway Green Suffk 55 TM2470
Stanwell Surrey 26 TQ0574
Stanwell Moor Surrey 26 TQ0474
Stanwick Nhants 51 SP9771
Stanwix Cumb 93 NY4057
Stape N York 90 SE7994
Stapehill Dorset 12 SU0500
Stapeley Ches 72 SJ6749
Stapenhill Staffs 73 SK2521
Staple Kent 29 TR2756
Staple Somset 20 ST1141
Staple Cross Devon 20 ST0320
Staple Cross E Susx 17 TQ7822
Staple Fitzpaine Somset 10 ST2618
Staple Hill H & W 60 SO9773
Staplefield W Susx 15 TQ2728
Stapleford Cambs 53 TL4751
Stapleford Herts 39 TL3117
Stapleford Leics 63 SK8018
Stapleford Lincs 76 SK8857
Stapleford Notts 62 SK4837
Stapleford Wilts 23 SU0737
Stapleford Abbotts Essex 27 TQ5194
Stapleford Tawney Essex 27 TQ5099
Staplegrove Somset 20 ST2126
Staplehay Somset 20 ST2121
Staplehurst Kent 28 TQ7843
Staplers IOW 13 SZ5189
Staplestreet Kent 29 TR0660
Staplet Cumb 101 NY5071
Stapleton H & W 46 SO3265
Stapleton Leics 50 SP4398
Stapleton N York 89 NZ2612
Stapleton Shrops 59 SJ4704
Stapleton Somset 21 ST4621
Stapley Somset 9 ST1913
Staploe Beds 52 TL1560
Staplow H & W 47 SO6941
Star Dyfed 31 SN2434
Star Fife 126 NO3103
Star Somset 21 ST4358
Starbeck N York 83 SE3255
Starbotton N York 88 SD9574
Starcross Devon 9 SX9781
Stareton Warwks 61 SP3371
Starkholmes Derbys 74 SK3058
Starklin H & W 60 SO8574
Starling Gt Man 79 SD7710
Starlings Green Essex 39 TL4631
Starr's Green E Susx 17 TQ7615
Starston Norfk 55 TM2384
Start Devon 7 SX8044
Startforth Dur 95 NZ0415
Startley Wilts 35 ST9482
Statenborough Kent 29 TR3155
Statham Ches 79 SJ6787
Stathe Somset 21 ST3728
Stathern Leics 63 SK7731
Station Town Dur 96 NZ4036
Staughton Green Cambs 52 TL1365
Staughton Highway Cambs 52 TL1364
Staunton Gloucs 34 SO5512
Staunton Gloucs 47 SO7829
Staunton Green H & W 46 SO3661
Staunton in the Vale Notts 63 SK8043
Staunton on Arrow H & W 46 SO3660
Staunton on Wye H & W 46 SO3644
Staveley Cumb 87 SD3786
Staveley Cumb 87 SD4698
Staveley Derbys 75 SK4374
Staveley N York 89 SE3662
Staverton Devon 7 SX7964
Staverton Gloucs 47 SO8923
Staverton Nhants 49 SP5361
Staverton Wilts 22 ST8560
Staverton Bridge Gloucs 35 SO8722
Stawell Somset 21 ST3738
Stawley Somset 20 ST0622
Staxigoe Highld 151 ND3852
Staxton N York 91 TA0179
Staylittle Dyfed 43 SN6489
Staylittle Powys 43 SN8891
Staynall Lancs 80 SD3643
Staythorpe Notts 75 SK7554
Stead W York 82 SE1446
Stean N York 89 SE0973
Steane Nhants 49 SP5538
Stearsby N York 90 SE6171
Steart Somset 20 ST2745
Stebbing Essex 40 TL6624
Stebbing Green Essex 40 TL6823
Stebbing Park Essex 40 TL6524
Stechford W Mids 61 SP1287
Stede Quarter Kent 28 TQ8738
Stedham W Susx 14 SU8622
Steel Nthumb 95 NY9458
Steel Cross E Susx 16 TQ5331
Steel Heath Shrops 59 SJ5436
Steele Road Border 101 NY5293
Steen's Bridge H & W 46 SO5357
Steep Hants 13 SU7425
Steep Lane W York 82 SE0223
Steephill IOW 13 SZ5477
Steeple Dorset 11 SY9080
Steeple Essex 40 TL9303
Steeple Ashton Wilts 22 ST9056
Steeple Aston Oxon 49 SP4725
Steeple Barton Oxon 49 SP4424
Steeple Bumpstead Essex 53 TL6841
Steeple Claydon Bucks 49 SP7026
Steeple Gidding Cambs 52 TL1381
Steeple Langford Wilts 23 SU0337
Steeple Morden Cambs 39 TL2842
Steeton W York 82 SE0344
Stein Highld 136 NG2656
Stella T & W 103 NZ1763
Stelling Minnis Kent 29 TR1447
Stembridge Somset 21 ST4220
Stenalees Cnwll 3 SX0156
Stenhouse D & G 100 NX8093
Stenhousemuir Cent 116 NS8783
Stenigot Lincs 77 TF2480
Stenscholl Highld 136 NG4767
Stenton Loth 118 NT6274
Stepaside Dyfed 31 SN1407
Stepney Gt Lon 27 TQ3681
Stepping Hill Gt Man 79 SJ9187
Steppingley Beds 38 TL0035
Stepps Strath 116 NS6568
Sternfield Suffk 55 TM3861
Sterridge Devon 19 SS5545
Stert Wilts 23 SU0259
Stetchworth Cambs 53 TL6459
Steven's Crouch E Susx 17 TQ7115
Stevenage Herts 39 TL2325
Stevenston Strath 106 NS2742
Steventon Hants 24 SU5447
Steventon Oxon 37 SU4691
Steventon End Essex 53 TL5942
Stevington Beds 51 SP9853
Stewartby Beds 38 TL0142
Stewarton Strath 115 NS4245
Stewkley Bucks 38 SP8526
Stewley Somset 10 ST3118
Stewton Lincs 77 TF3587
Steyne Cross IOW 13 SZ6487
Steyning W Susx 15 TQ1711
Steynton Dyfed 30 SM9107
Stibb Cnwll 18 SS2210
Stibb Cross Devon 18 SS4314
Stibb Green Wilts 23 SU2262
Stibbard Norfk 66 TF9828
Stibbington Cambs 51 TL0898
Stichill Border 110 NT7138
Sticker Cnwll 3 SW9750
Stickford Lincs 77 TF3560
Sticklepath Devon 8 SX6494
Sticklepath Somset 20 ST0436
Stickling Green Essex 39 TL4732
Stickney Lincs 77 TF3457
Stidd Lancs 81 SD6536
Stiff Green Kent 28 TQ8761
Stiffkey Norfk 66 TF9742
Stifford's Bridge H & W 47 SO7348
Stile Bridge Kent 28 TQ7547
Stileway Somset 21 ST4641
Stilligarry W Isls 154 NF7638
Stillingfleet N York 83 SE5940
Stillington Cleve 96 NZ3723
Stillington N York 90 SE5867
Stilton Cambs 52 TL1689
Stinchcombe Gloucs 35 ST7298
Stinsford Dorset 11 SY7091
Stiperstones Shrops 59 SJ3600
Stirchley Shrops 60 SJ6907
Stirchley W Mids 61 SP0581
Stirling Cent 116 NS7993
Stirling Gramp 143 NK1242
Stirtloe Cambs 52 TL1966
Stirton N York 82 SD9752
Stisted Essex 40 TL8024
Stitchcombe Wilts 36 SU2369
Stithians Cnwll 3 SW7336
Stivichall W Mids 61 SP3376
Stixwould Lincs 76 TF1765
Stoak Ches 71 SJ4273
Stobo Border 109 NT1837
Stoborough Dorset 11 SY9286
Stoborough Green Dorset 11 SY9285
Stobs Castle Border 109 NT5008
Stobswood Nthumb 103 NZ2195
Stock Avon 21 ST4561
Stock Essex 40 TQ6998
Stock Green H & W 47 SO9859
Stock Wood H & W 47 SP0058
Stockbridge Hants 23 SU3535
Stockbriggs Strath 107 NS7936
Stockbury Kent 28 TQ8461
Stockcross Berks 24 SU4368
Stockdale Cnwll 3 SW7837
Stockdalewath Cumb 93 NY3845
Stocker's Hill Kent 28 TQ9650
Stockerston Leics 51 SP8397
Stocking H & W 47 SO6230
Stocking Green Bucks 38 SP8047
Stocking Pelham Herts 39 TL4529
Stockingford Warwks 61 SP3391
Stockland Devon 9 ST2404
Stockland Bristol Somset 20 ST2443
Stockland Green Kent 16 TQ5642
Stockleigh English Devon 8 SS8506
Stockleigh Pomeroy Devon 9 SS8703
Stockley Wilts 22 ST9967
Stockley Hill H & W 46 SO3738
Stocklinch Somset 10 ST3817
Stockmoor H & W 46 SO3954
Stockport Gt Man 79 SJ8990
Stocksbridge S York 74 SK2698
Stocksfield Nthumb 103 NZ0561
Stockstreet Essex 40 TL8222
Stockton H & W 46 SO5261
Stockton Norfk 67 TM3894
Stockton Shrops 58 SJ2601
Stockton Shrops 72 SJ7716
Stockton Shrops 60 SO7299
Stockton Warwks 49 SP4363
Stockton Wilts 22 ST9838
Stockton Brook Staffs 72 SJ9151
Stockton Heath Ches 78 SJ6185
Stockton on Teme H & W 47 SO7167
Stockton on the Forest N York 83 SE6556
Stockton-on-Tees Cleve 96 NZ4419
Stockwell Gloucs 35 SO9414
Stockwell End W Mids 60 SJ8900
Stockwell Heath Staffs 73 SK0521
Stockwood Avon 21 ST6368
Stockwood Dorset 10 ST5906
Stodday Lancs 87 SD4658
Stodmarsh Kent 29 TR2260
Stody Norfk 66 TG0535
Stoer Highld 148 NC0328
Stoford Somset 10 ST5613
Stoford Wilts 23 SU0835
Stogumber Somset 20 ST0937
Stogursey Somset 20 ST2042
Stoke Devon 18 SS2324
Stoke Hants 24 SU4051
Stoke Hants 13 SU7202
Stoke Kent 28 TQ8274
Stoke W Mids 61 SP3778
Stoke Abbott Dorset 10 ST4500
Stoke Albany Nhants 51 SP8088
Stoke Ash Suffk 54 TM1170
Stoke Bardolph Notts 63 SK6441
Stoke Bliss H & W 47 SO6563
Stoke Bruerne Nhants 49 SP7449
Stoke by Clare Suffk 53 TL7443

Stoke Canon Swanton Morley

Stoke Canon Devon 9 SX9398
Stoke Charity Hants 24 SU4839
Stoke Climsland Cnwll 5 SX3674
Stoke Cross H & W 47 SO6250
Stoke D'Abernon Surrey 26 TQ1258
Stoke Doyle Nhants 51 TL0286
Stoke Dry Leics 51 SP8596
Stoke End Warwks 61 SP1797
Stoke Farthing Wilts 23 SU0525
Stoke Ferry Norfk 65 TF7000
Stoke Fleming Devon 7 SX8648
Stoke Gabriel Devon 7 SX8557
Stoke Gifford Avon 35 ST6279
Stoke Golding Leics 61 SP3997
Stoke Goldington Bucks 38 SP8348
Stoke Green Bucks 26 SU9882
Stoke Hammond Bucks 38 SP8829
Stoke Heath H & W 47 SO9468
Stoke Heath Shrops 72 SJ6529
Stoke Heath W Mids 61 SP3681
Stoke Holy Cross Norfk 67 TG2301
Stoke Lacy H & W 47 SO6249
Stoke Lyne Oxon 49 SP5628
Stoke Mandeville Bucks 38 SP8310
Stoke Newington Gt Lon 27 TQ3386
Stoke Orchard Gloucs 47 SO9128
Stoke Poges Bucks 26 SU9783
Stoke Pound H & W 47 SO9667
Stoke Prior H & W 46 SO5256
Stoke Prior H & W 47 SO9467
Stoke Rivers Devon 19 SS6335
Stoke Rochford Lincs 63 SK9127
Stoke Row Oxon 37 SU6884
Stoke St. Gregory Somset 21 ST3427
Stoke St. Mary Somset 20 ST2622
Stoke St. Michael Somset 22 ST6646
Stoke St. Milborough Shrops 59 SO5682
Stoke sub Hamdon Somset 10 ST4717
Stoke Talmage Oxon 37 SU6799
Stoke Trister Somset 22 ST7428
Stoke upon Tern Shrops 59 SJ6328
Stoke Wake Dorset 11 ST7606
Stoke Wharf H & W 47 SO9567
Stoke-by-Nayland Suffk 54 TL9836
Stoke-on-Trent Staffs 72 SJ8747
Stoke-upon-Trent Staffs 72 SJ8745
Stokeford Dorset 11 SY8687
Stokeham Notts 75 SK7876
Stokeinteignhead Devon 7 SX9170
Stokenchurch Bucks 37 SU7696
Stokenham Devon 7 SX8042
Stokesay Shrops 59 SO4381
Stokesby Norfk 67 TG4310
Stokesley N York 90 NZ5208
Stolford Somset 20 ST0332
Stolford Somset 20 ST2345
Ston Easton Somset 21 ST6253
Stondon Massey Essex 27 TL5800
Stone Bucks 37 SP7812
Stone Gloucs 35 ST6895
Stone H & W 60 SO8675
Stone Kent 27 TQ5774
Stone Kent 17 TQ9427
Stone S York 75 SK5589
Stone Somset 21 ST5834
Stone Staffs 72 SJ9034
Stone Allerton Somset 21 ST3951
Stone Bridge Corner Cambs 64 TF2700
Stone Chair W York 82 SE1227
Stone Cross E Susx 16 TQ5128
Stone Cross E Susx 16 TQ6104
Stone Cross E Susx 16 TQ6431
Stone Cross Kent 16 TQ5239
Stone Cross Kent 28 TR0236
Stone Cross Kent 29 TR3257
Stone Hill S York 83 SE6809
Stone House Cumb 88 SD7685
Stone Rows Leics 61 SK3214
Stone Street Kent 27 TQ5754
Stone Street Suffk 54 TL9639
Stone Street Suffk 54 TM0143
Stone Street Suffk 55 TM3882
Stone-edge-Batch Avon 34 ST4671
Stonea Cambs 65 TL4593
Stonebridge Avon 21 ST3859
Stonebridge Norfk 54 TL9290
Stonebridge W Mids 61 SP2182
Stonebroom Derbys 74 SK4059
Stonebury Herts 39 TL3828
Stonechrubie Highld 145 NC2419
Stonecross Green Suffk 54 TL8257
Stonecrouch Kent 16 TQ7033
Stoneferry Humb 85 TA1031
Stonefield Castle Hotel Strath 113 NR8671
Stonegarthside Cumb 101 NY4780
Stonegate E Susx 16 TQ6628
Stonegate N York 90 NZ7708
Stonegrave N York 90 SE6577
Stonehall H & W 47 SO8848
Stonehaugh Nthumb 102 NY7976
Stonehaven Gramp 135 NO8786
Stonehill Green Gt Lon 27 TQ5070
Stonehouse Ches 71 SJ5070
Stonehouse D & G 100 NX8268
Stonehouse Devon 6 SX4654
Stonehouse Gloucs 35 SO8005
Stonehouse Nthumb 94 NY6958
Stonehouse Strath 116 NS7546
Stoneleigh Warwks 61 SP3372
Stoneley Green Ches 71 SJ6151
Stonely Cambs 52 TL1167
Stoner Hill Hants 13 SU7225
Stones Green Essex 41 TM1626
Stonesby Leics 63 SK8224
Stonesfield Oxon 36 SP3917
Stonethwaite Cumb 93 NY2613
Stonetree Green Kent 29 TR0637
Stonewells Gramp 141 NJ2865
Stonewood Kent 27 TQ5972
Stoney Cross Hants 12 SU2611
Stoney Middleton Derbys 74 SK2375
Stoney Stanton Leics 50 SP4994
Stoney Stoke Somset 22 ST7032
Stoney Stratton Somset 21 ST6539
Stoney Stretton Shrops 59 SJ3809
Stoneybridge H & W 60 SO9476
Stoneybridge W Isls 154 NF7532
Stoneyburn Loth 117 NS9862
Stoneygate Leics 62 SK6002
Stoneyhills Essex 40 TQ9597
Stoneykirk D & G 98 NX0853
Stoneywood Cent 116 NS7982
Stoneywood Gramp 135 NJ8811
Stonham Aspal Suffk 54 TM1359
Stonnall Staffs 61 SK0603
Stonor Oxon 37 SU7388
Stonton Wyville Leics 50 SP7395
Stony Cross H & W 46 SO5466
Stony Cross H & W 47 SO7247
Stony Houghton Derbys 75 SK4966
Stony Stratford Bucks 38 SP7840
Stonyford Hants 12 SU3215
Stonywell Staffs 61 SK0712
Stoodleigh Devon 19 SS6532
Stoodleigh Devon 20 SS9218
Stopham W Susx 14 TQ0219
Stopsley Beds 38 TL1023
Stoptide Cnwll 4 SW9475
Storeton Mersyd 78 SJ3084
Storeyard Green H & W 47 SO7144
Stormy Corner Lancs 78 SD4707
Stornoway W Isls 154 NB4232
Storrington W Susx 14 TQ0814
Storth Cumb 87 SD4779
Storwood Humb 84 SE7144
Stotfold Beds 39 TL2136
Stottesdon Shrops 60 SO6782
Stoughton Leics 63 SK6402
Stoughton Surrey 25 SU9851
Stoughton W Susx 14 SU8011
Stoul Highld 129 NM7594
Stoulton H & W 47 SO9049
Stour Provost Dorset 22 ST7921
Stour Row Dorset 22 ST8221
Stourbridge W Mids 60 SO8983
Stourpaine Dorset 11 ST8609
Stourport-on-Severn H & W 60 SO8171
Stourton Staffs 60 SO8684
Stourton W York 83 SE3230
Stourton Warwks 48 SP2936
Stourton Wilts 22 ST7734
Stourton Caundle Dorset 11 ST7115
Stout Somset 21 ST4331
Stove Shet 155 HU4224
Stoven Suffk 55 TM4481
Stow Border 118 NT4544
Stow Lincs 76 SK8882
Stow Bardolph Norfk 65 TF6206
Stow Bedon Norfk 66 TL9596
Stow cum Quy Cambs 53 TL5260
Stow Longa Cambs 51 TL1070
Stow Maries Essex 40 TQ8399
Stow-on-the-Wold Gloucs 48 SP1925
Stowbridge Norfk 65 TF6007
Stowe Gloucs 34 SO5606
Stowe Shrops 46 SO3173
Stowe Staffs 61 SK1210
Stowe by Chartley Staffs 73 SK0026
Stowehill Nhants 49 SP6458
Stowell Somset 22 ST6822
Stowey Somset 21 ST5959
Stowford Devon 19 SS6541
Stowford Devon 5 SX4387
Stowford Devon 9 SY1189
Stowlangtoft Suffk 54 TL9568
Stowmarket Suffk 54 TM0458
Stowting Kent 29 TR1242
Stowting Common Kent 29 TR1243
Stowupland Suffk 54 TM0760
Straanruie Highld 141 NH9916
Strachan Gramp 135 NO6792
Strachur Strath 114 NN0901
Stradbroke Suffk 55 TM2373
Stradbrook Wilts 22 ST9152
Stradishall Suffk 53 TL7552
Stradsett Norfk 65 TF6605
Stragglethorpe Notts 63 SK6537
Straight Soley Wilts 36 SU3172
Straiton Loth 117 NT2766
Straiton Strath 106 NS3804
Straloch Gramp 143 NJ8620
Straloch Tays 133 NO0463
Stramshall Staffs 73 SK0735
Strang IOM 153 SC3578
Strangford H & W 46 SO5827
Stranraer D & G 98 NX0560
Strata Florida Dyfed 43 SN7465
Stratfield Mortimer Berks 24 SU6664
Stratfield Saye Hants 24 SU6861
Stratfield Turgis Hants 24 SU6959
Stratford Beds 52 TL1748
Stratford Gt Lon 27 TQ3884
Stratford St. Andrew Suffk 55 TM3560
Stratford St. Mary Suffk 54 TM0434
Stratford sub Castle Wilts 23 SU1332
Stratford Tony Wilts 23 SU0926
Stratford-upon-Avon Warwks 48 SP2055
Strath Highld 151 ND2652
Strath Highld 144 NG7978
Strathan Highld 145 NC0821
Strathan Highld 149 NC5764
Strathan Highld 130 NM9791
Strathaven Strath 116 NS7044
Strathblane Cent 115 NS5679
Strathcarron Sta Highld 138 NG9442
Strathcoil Strath 122 NM6830
Strathdon Gramp 134 NJ3512
Strathkanaird Highld 145 NC1501
Strathkinness Fife 127 NO4516
Strathmashie House Tays 132 NN5891
Strathmiglo Fife 126 NO2109
Strathpeffer Highld 139 NH4858
Strathtay Tays 125 NN9153
Strathwhillan Strath 105 NS0235
Strathy Highld 150 NC8464
Strathy Inn Highld 150 NC8365
Strathyre Cent 124 NN5617
Stratton Cnwll 18 SS2306
Stratton Dorset 11 SY6593
Stratton Gloucs 35 SP0103
Stratton Audley Oxon 49 SP6025
Stratton St. Margaret Wilts 36 SU1786
Stratton St. Michael Norfk 67 TM2093
Stratton Strawless Norfk 67 TG2220
Stratton-on-the-Fosse Somset 22 ST6560
Stravithie Fife 127 NO5313
Stream Somset 20 ST0639
Streat E Susx 15 TQ3515
Streatham Gt Lon 27 TQ3071
Streatley Beds 38 TL0728
Streatley Berks 37 SU5980
Street Devon 9 SY1888
Street Lancs 80 SD5252
Street N York 90 NZ7304
Street Somset 21 ST4836
Street Ashton Warwks 50 SP4582
Street Dinas Shrops 71 SJ3338
Street End E Susx 16 TQ6023
Street End Kent 29 TR1453
Street End W Susx 14 SZ8599
Street Gate T & W 96 NZ2159
Street Houses Cleve 97 NZ7419
Street Houses N York 83 SE5245
Street Lane Derbys 74 SK3848
Street on the Fosse Somset 21 ST6239
Streethay Staffs 61 SK1410
Streetlam N York 89 SE3098
Streetly W Mids 61 SP0898
Strefford Shrops 59 SO4485
Strelitz Tays 126 NO1836
Strelley Notts 62 SK5141
Strensall N York 90 SE6360
Strensham H & W 47 SO9140
Stretcholt Somset 20 ST2943
Strete Devon 7 SX8446
Stretford Gt Man 79 SJ7994
Stretford H & W 46 SO4455
Stretford H & W 46 SO5257
Strethall Essex 39 TL4839
Stretham Cambs 53 TL5174
Strettington W Susx 14 SU8907
Stretton Ches 71 SJ4452
Stretton Ches 79 SJ6282
Stretton Derbys 74 SK3961
Stretton Leics 63 SK9415
Stretton Staffs 60 SJ8811
Stretton Staffs 73 SK2526
Stretton en le Field Leics 61 SK3011
Stretton Grandison H & W 47 SO6344
Stretton Heath Shrops 59 SJ3610
Stretton on Fosse Warwks 48 SP2238
Stretton Sugwas H & W 46 SO4642
Stretton under Fosse Warwks 50 SP4581
Stretton Westwood Shrops 59 SO5998
Stretton-on-Dunsmore Warwks 61 SP4072
Strichen Gramp 143 NJ9455
Strines Gt Man 79 SJ9786
Stringston Somset 20 ST1742
Strixton Nhants 51 SP9061
Stroat Gloucs 34 ST5797
Stromeferry Highld 138 NG8634
Stromness Ork 155 HY2508
Stronachlachar Cent 123 NN4010
Stronafian Strath 114 NS0281
Strone Highld 131 NN1481
Strone Strath 114 NS1980
Stronenaba Highld 131 NN2084
Stronmilchan Strath 123 NN1528
Strontian Highld 130 NM8161
Strood Kent 28 TQ7268
Strood Kent 17 TQ8532
Strood Green Surrey 15 TQ2048
Strood Green W Susx 14 TQ0224
Strood Green W Susx 15 TQ1332
Stroud Gloucs 35 SO8505
Stroud Hants 13 SU7223
Stroud Green Essex 40 TQ8590
Stroud Green Gloucs 35 SO8007
Stroude Surrey 25 TQ0068
Stroxton Lincs 63 SK9030
Struan Highld 136 NG3438
Struan Tays 132 NN8065
Strubby Lincs 77 TF4582
Strumpshaw Norfk 67 TG3407
Strutherhill Strath 116 NS7649
Struthers Fife 126 NO3709
Struy Highld 139 NH4040
Stryt-issa Clwyd 70 SJ2845
Stuartfield Gramp 143 NJ9745
Stubbers Green W Mids 61 SK0401
Stubbington Hants 13 SU5503
Stubbins Gt Man 81 SD7918
Stubbs Green Norfk 67 TM2598
Stubhampton Dorset 11 ST9113
Stubshaw Cross Gt Man 78 SJ5899
Stubton Lincs 76 SK8748
Stuchbury Nhants 49 SP5643
Stuckeridge Devon 20 SS9221
Stuckton Hants 12 SU1613
Stud Green Berks 26 SU8877
Studfold N York 88 SD8169
Studham Beds 38 TL0215
Studholme Cumb 93 NY2556
Studland Dorset 12 SZ0382
Studley Warwks 48 SP0764
Studley Wilts 35 ST9671
Studley Common H & W 48 SP0664
Studley Roger N York 89 SE2970
Studley Royal N York 89 SE2770
Stump Cross Cambs 39 TL5044
Stuntney Cambs 53 TL5578
Stunts Green E Susx 16 TQ6213
Sturbridge Staffs 72 SJ8330
Sturgate Lincs 76 SK8888
Sturmer Essex 53 TL6943
Sturminster Common Dorset 11 ST7812
Sturminster Marshall Dorset 11 ST9500
Sturminster Newton Dorset 11 ST7814
Sturry Kent 29 TR1760
Sturton Humb 84 SE9604
Sturton by Stow Lincs 76 SK8980
Sturton le Steeple Notts 75 SK7883
Stuston Suffk 54 TM1377
Stutton N York 83 SE4841
Stutton Suffk 54 TM1534
Styal Ches 79 SJ8383
Stynie Gramp 141 NJ3360
Styrrup Notts 75 SK6090
Succoth Strath 123 NN2905
Suckley H & W 47 SO7251
Suckley Green H & W 47 SO7253
Sudborough Nhants 51 SP9682
Sudbourne Suffk 55 TM4153
Sudbrook Gwent 34 ST5087
Sudbrook Lincs 63 SK9744
Sudbrooke Lincs 76 TF0376
Sudbury Derbys 73 SK1631
Sudbury Gt Lon 26 TQ1685
Sudbury Suffk 54 TL8741
Sudden Gt Man 81 SD8812
Suddie Highld 140 NH6554
Suddington H & W 47 SO8463
Sudgrove Gloucs 35 SO9308
Suffield N York 91 SE9890
Suffield Norfk 67 TG2232
Sugdon Shrops 59 SJ6015
Sugnall Staffs 72 SJ7931
Sugwas Pool H & W 46 SO4541
Suisnish Highld 129 NG5816
Sulby IOM 153 SC3894
Sulgrave Nhants 49 SP5544
Sulham Berks 24 SU6474
Sulhamstead Berks 24 SU6368
Sulhamstead Abbots Berks 24 SU6467
Sulhamstead Bannister Berks 24 SU6368
Sullington W Susx 14 TQ0913
Sullom Shet 155 HU3573
Sullom Voe Shet 155 HU4075
Sully S Glam 20 ST1568
Summer Heath Bucks 37 SU7490
Summer Hill Clwyd 71 SJ3153
Summerbridge N York 89 SE2062
Summercourt Cnwll 3 SW8856
Summerfield H & W 60 SO8473
Summerfield Norfk 65 TF7538
Summerhouse Dur 96 NZ2019
Summerlands Cumb 87 SD5386
Summerley Derbys 74 SK3778
Summersdale W Susx 14 SU8606
Summerseat Gt Man 81 SD7914
Summertown Oxon 37 SP5009
Summit Gt Man 79 SD9109
Summit Gt Man 81 SD9418
Sunbiggin Cumb 87 NY6608
Sunbury Surrey 26 TQ1168
Sundaywell D & G 100 NX8284
Sunderland Cumb 93 NY1735
Sunderland Lancs 80 SD4255
Sunderland Strath 112 NR2464
Sunderland T & W 96 NZ3957
Sunderland Bridge Dur 96 NZ2637
Sundhope Border 109 NT3325
Sundon Park Beds 38 TL0525
Sundridge Kent 27 TQ4855
Sunk Island Humb 85 TA2619
Sunningdale Berks 25 SU9567
Sunninghill Surrey 25 SU9367
Sunningwell Oxon 37 SP4900
Sunniside Dur 96 NZ1438
Sunniside T & W 96 NZ2059
Sunny Bank Lancs 81 SD7720
Sunny Brow Dur 96 NZ1934
Sunnyhill Derbys 62 SK3432
Sunnyhurst Lancs 81 SD6722
Sunnylaw Cent 116 NS7998
Sunnymead Oxon 37 SP5009
Sunton Wilts 23 SU2454
Sunwick Border 119 NT9052
Surbiton Gt Lon 26 TQ1867
Surfleet Lincs 64 TF2528
Surfleet Seas End Lincs 64 TF2628
Surlingham Norfk 67 TG3106
Surrex Essex 40 TL8722
Sustead Norfk 66 TG1837
Susworth Lincs 84 SE8302
Sutcombe Devon 18 SS3411
Sutcombemill Devon 18 SS3411
Suton Norfk 66 TM0999
Sutterby Lincs 77 TF3872
Sutterton Lincs 64 TF2835
Sutton Beds 52 TL2247
Sutton Cambs 51 TL0998
Sutton Cambs 53 TL4479
Sutton Devon 8 SS7202
Sutton Devon 7 SX7042
Sutton Dyfed 30 SM9115
Sutton E Susx 16 TV4999
Sutton Gt Lon 27 TQ2564
Sutton Kent 29 TR3349
Sutton Mersyd 78 SJ5393
Sutton N York 83 SE4925
Sutton Norfk 67 TG3823
Sutton Notts 75 SK6784
Sutton Notts 63 SK7637
Sutton Oxon 36 SP4106
Sutton S York 83 SE5512
Sutton Shrops 59 SJ3527
Sutton Shrops 59 SJ5010
Sutton Shrops 72 SJ6631
Sutton Shrops 60 SO7386
Sutton Staffs 72 SJ7622
Sutton Suffk 55 TM3046
Sutton W Susx 14 SU9715
Sutton at Hone Kent 27 TQ5569
Sutton Bassett Nhants 50 SP7790
Sutton Benger Wilts 35 ST9478
Sutton Bingham Somset 10 ST5410
Sutton Bonington Notts 62 SK5024
Sutton Bridge Lincs 65 TF4721
Sutton Cheney Leics 50 SK4100
Sutton Coldfield W Mids 61 SP1295
Sutton Courtenay Oxon 37 SU5094
Sutton Crosses Lincs 65 TF4321
Sutton Grange N York 89 SE2873
Sutton Green Clwyd 71 SJ4048
Sutton Green Oxon 36 SP4107
Sutton Green Surrey 25 TQ0054
Sutton Howgrave N York 89 SE3179
Sutton in Ashfield Notts 75 SK4958
Sutton in the Elms Leics 50 SP5193
Sutton Lane Ends Ches 79 SJ9270
Sutton le Marsh Lincs 77 TF5280
Sutton Maddock Shrops 60 SJ7201
Sutton Mallet Somset 21 ST3736
Sutton Mandeville Wilts 22 ST9828
Sutton Manor Mersyd 78 SJ5190
Sutton Marsh H & W 46 SO5544
Sutton Montis Somset 21 ST6224
Sutton on Sea Lincs 77 TF5281
Sutton on Trent Notts 75 SK7965
Sutton on the Hill Derbys 73 SK2333
Sutton Poyntz Dorset 11 SY7083
Sutton Scansdale Derbys 75 SK4468
Sutton Scotney Hants 24 SU4639
Sutton St. Edmund Lincs 64 TF3613
Sutton St. James Lincs 65 TF3918
Sutton St. Nicholas H & W 46 SO5245
Sutton Street Kent 28 TQ8055
Sutton upon Derwent Humb 84 SE7047
Sutton Valence Kent 28 TQ8149
Sutton Veny Wilts 22 ST9041
Sutton Waldron Dorset 11 ST8615
Sutton Weaver Ches 71 SJ5479
Sutton Wick Avon 21 ST5759
Sutton Wick Oxon 37 SU4894
Sutton-in-Craven N York 82 SE0043
Sutton-on-Hull Humb 85 TA1232
Sutton-on-the-Forest N York 90 SE5864
Sutton-under-Brailes Warwks 48 SP3037
Sutton-under-Whitestonecliffe N York 90 SE4882
Swaby Lincs 77 TF3877
Swadlincote Derbys 73 SK2919
Swaffham Norfk 66 TF8108
Swaffham Bulbeck Cambs 53 TL5562
Swaffham Prior Cambs 53 TL5764
Swafield Norfk 67 TG2832
Swainby N York 89 NZ4701
Swainshill H & W 46 SO4641
Swainsthorpe Norfk 67 TG2101
Swainswick Avon 22 ST7668
Swalcliffe Oxon 48 SP3737
Swalecliffe Kent 29 TR1367
Swallow Lincs 85 TA1703
Swallow Beck Lincs 76 SK9567
Swallow Nest S York 75 SK4585
Swallowcliffe Wilts 22 ST9627
Swallowfield Berks 24 SU7264
Swallows Cross Essex 40 TQ6198
Swampton Hants 24 SU4150
Swan Green Ches 79 SJ7373
Swan Street Essex 40 TL8927
Swan Village W Mids 60 SO9892
Swanage Dorset 12 SZ0378
Swanbourne Bucks 38 SP8026
Swanbridge S Glam 20 ST1667
Swancote Shrops 60 SO7494
Swanland Humb 84 SE9928
Swanley Kent 27 TQ5168
Swanley Village Kent 27 TQ5369
Swanmore Hants 13 SU5716
Swannington Leics 62 SK4116
Swannington Norfk 66 TG1319
Swanpool Garden Suberb Lincs 76 SK9569
Swanscombe Kent 27 TQ6074
Swansea W Glam 32 SS6592
Swanton Abbot Norfk 67 TG2625
Swanton Morley Norfk 66 TG0117

Swanton Novers Thornliebank

Swanton Novers Norfk 66 TG0231
Swanton Street Kent 28 TQ8759
Swanwick Derbys 74 SK4053
Swanwick Hants 13 SU5109
Swarby Lincs 64 TF0440
Swardeston Norfk 67 TG2002
Swarkestone Derbys 62 SK3728
Swarland Nthumb 103 NU1602
Swarland Estate Nthumb 103 NU1603
Swarraton Hants 24 SU5636
Swartha W York 82 SE0546
Swarthmoor Cumb 86 SD2777
Swaton Lincs 64 TF1337
Swavesey Cambs 52 TL3668
Sway Hants 12 SZ2798
Swayfield Lincs 63 SK9922
Swaythling Hants 13 SU4416
Sweet Green H & W 47 SO6462
Sweetham Devon 9 SX8899
Sweethaws E Susx 16 TQ5028
Sweetlands Corner Kent 28 TQ7845
Sweets Cnwll 4 SX1595
Sweetshouse Cnwll 4 SX0861
Swefling Suffk 55 TM3463
Swepstone Leics 62 SK3610
Swerford Oxon 48 SP3731
Swettenham Ches 72 SJ8067
Swffryd Gwent 33 ST2198
Swift's Green Kent 28 TQ8744
Swiftsden E Susx 17 TQ7328
Swilland Suffk 54 TM1852
Swillbrook Lancs 80 SD4834
Swillington W York 83 SE3830
Swimbridge Devon 19 SS6230
Swimbridge Newland Devon 19 SS6030
Swinbrook Oxon 36 SP2812
Swincliffe N York 89 SE2458
Swincliffe W York 82 SE2027
Swincombe Devon 19 SS6941
Swinden N York 81 SD8554
Swinderby Lincs 76 SK8663
Swindon Gloucs 47 SO9325
Swindon Nthumb 102 NY9799
Swindon Staffs 60 SO8690
Swindon Wilts 36 SU1484
Swine Humb 85 TA1335
Swinefleet Humb 84 SE7621
Swineford Avon 35 ST6969
Swineshead Beds 51 TL0565
Swineshead Lincs 64 TF2340
Swineshead Bridge Lincs 64 TF2242
Swiney Highld 151 ND2335
Swinford Leics 50 SP5679
Swinford Oxon 37 SP4408
Swingfield Minnis Kent 29 TR2142
Swingfield Street Kent 29 TR2343
Swingleton Green Suffk 54 TL9647
Swinhill Strath 116 NS7748
Swinhoe Nthumb 111 NU2128
Swinhope Lincs 76 TF2196
Swinithwaite N York 88 SE0489
Swinmore Common H & W 47 SO6741
Swinscoe Staffs 73 SK1247
Swinside Cumb 93 NY2421
Swinstead Lincs 64 TF0122
Swinthorpe Lincs 76 TF0680
Swinton Border 110 NT8347
Swinton Gt Man 79 SD7701
Swinton N York 89 SE2179
Swinton N York 90 SE7573
Swinton S York 75 SK4599
Swithland Leics 62 SK5512
Swordale Highld 139 NH5765
Swordland Highld 129 NM7891
Swordly Highld 150 NC7463
Sworton Heath Ches 79 SJ6884
Swyddffynnon Dyfed 43 SN6966
Swynnerton Staffs 72 SJ8535
Swyre Dorset 10 SY5288
Sycharth Clwyd 58 SJ2025
Sychnant Powys 45 SN9777
Sychtyn Powys 58 SH9907
Sydallt Clwyd 71 SJ3055
Syde Gloucs 35 SO9511
Sydenham Gt Lon 27 TQ3671
Sydenham Oxon 37 SP7301
Sydenham Damerel Devon 5 SX4176
Sydenhurst Surrey 14 SU9534
Syderstone Norfk 66 TF8332
Sydling St. Nicholas Dorset 10 SY6399
Sydmonton Hants 24 SU4857
Sydnal Lane Shrops 60 SJ8005
Syerston Notts 63 SK7447
Syke Gt Man 81 SD8915
Sykehouse S York 83 SE6316
Syleham Suffk 55 TM2078
Sylen Dyfed 32 SN5106
Symbister Shet 155 HU5462
Symington Strath 106 NS3831
Symington Strath 108 NS9935
Symonds Yat H & W 34 SO5515
Symondsbury Dorset 10 SY4493
Sympson Green W York 82 SE1838
Synderford Dorset 10 ST3803
Synod Inn Dyfed 42 SN4054
Syre Highld 149 NC6943
Syreford Gloucs 35 SP0220
Syresham Nhants 49 SP6241
Syston Leics 62 SK6211
Syston Lincs 63 SK9240
Sytchampton H & W 47 SO8466
Sywell Nhants 51 SP8267

T

Tabley Hill Ches 79 SJ7379
Tackley Oxon 37 SP4719
Tacolneston Norfk 66 TM1495
Tadcaster N York 83 SE4843
Taddington Derbys 74 SK1371
Taddington Gloucs 48 SP0831
Taddiport Devon 18 SS4818
Tadley Hants 24 SU6061
Tadlow Cambs 52 TL2847
Tadmarton Oxon 48 SP3937
Tadwick Avon 35 ST7470
Tadworth Surrey 26 TQ2257
Tafarn-y-bwlch Dyfed 31 SN0834
Tafarn-y-Gelyn Clwyd 70 SJ1961
Tafarnaubach M Glam 33 SO1210
Taff's Well M Glam 33 ST1283
Tafolwern Powys 57 SH8902
Tai'r Bull Powys 45 SN9925
Taibach W Glam 32 SS7788
Tain Highld 151 ND2266
Tain Highld 147 NH7781
Takeley Essex 40 TL5621
Takeley Street Essex 39 TL5421
Tal-y-Bont Gwynd 69 SH7668
Tal-y-bont Gwynd 57 SH5921
Tal-y-bont Gwynd 69 SH6070
Tal-y-cafn Gwynd 69 SH7871
Tal-y-coed Gwent 34 SO4115
Tal-y-garn M Glam 33 ST0379
Tal-y-llyn Gwynd 57 SH7109
Tal-y-Waun Gwent 34 SO2604
Talachddu Powys 45 SO0833
Talacre Clwyd 70 SJ1183
Talaton Devon 9 SY0699
Talbenny Dyfed 30 SM8411
Talbot Green M Glam 33 ST0382
Talbot Village Dorset 12 SZ0793
Talerddig Powys 58 SH9300
Talgarreg Dyfed 42 SN4251
Talgarth Gwynd 57 SN6899
Talgarth Powys 45 SO1533
Taliesin Dyfed 43 SN6591
Talisker Highld 136 NG3230
Talke Staffs 72 SJ8253
Talke Pits Staffs 72 SJ8353
Talkin Cumb 94 NY5557
Talla Linnfoots Border 108 NT1320
Talladale Highld 144 NG9170
Tallaminnock Strath 106 NX4098
Tallarn Green Clwyd 71 SJ4444
Tallentire Cumb 92 NY1035
Talley Dyfed 44 SN6332
Tallington Lincs 64 TF0908
Tallwrn Clwyd 71 SJ2947
Talmine Highld 149 NC5863
Talog Dyfed 31 SN3325
Talsarn Dyfed 44 SN5456
Talsarnau Gwynd 57 SH6135
Talskiddy Cnwll 4 SW9165
Talwrn Clwyd 71 SJ3847
Talwrn Gwynd 68 SH4877
Talybont Dyfed 43 SN6589
Talybont-on-Usk Powys 33 SO1122
Talysarn Gwynd 68 SH4952
Talywern Powys 57 SH8200
Tamer Lane End Gt Man 79 SD6401
Tamerton Foliot Devon 6 SX4761
Tamworth Staffs 61 SK2003
Tamworth Green Lincs 64 TF3842
Tan Hill N York 88 NY8906
Tan Office Green Suffk 53 TL7858
Tan-y-Bwlch Gwynd 57 SH6540
Tan-y-fron Clwyd 70 SH9564
Tan-y-fron Clwyd 71 SJ2952
Tan-y-groes Dyfed 42 SN2849
Tancred N York 89 SE4558
Tancredston Dyfed 30 SM8826
Tandlemuir Strath 115 NS3361
Tandridge Surrey 27 TQ3750
Tanfield Dur 96 NZ1855
Tanfield Lea Dur 96 NZ1854
Tangiers Dyfed 30 SM9518
Tangley Hants 23 SU3252
Tangmere W Susx 14 SU9006
Tankerness Ork 155 HY5109
Tankersley S York 74 SK3499
Tankerton Kent 29 TR1166
Tannach Highld 151 ND3247
Tannachie Grampn 135 NO7884
Tannadice Tays 134 NO4758
Tanner Green H & W 61 SP0874
Tannington Suffk 55 TM2467
Tannochside Strath 116 NS7061
Tansley Derbys 74 SK3259
Tansor Nhants 51 TL0590
Tantobie Dur 96 NZ1754
Tanton N York 90 NZ5210
Tanworth in Arden Warwks 61 SP1170
Tanygrisiau Gwynd 57 SH6945
Taplow Bucks 26 SU9182
Tarbert Strath 113 NR6551
Tarbert Strath 113 NR8668
Tarbert W Isls 154 NB1500
Tarbet Highld 148 NC1649
Tarbet Highld 129 NM7992
Tarbet Strath 123 NN3104
Tarbock Green Mersyd 78 SJ4687
Tarbolton Strath 107 NS4327
Tarbrax Strath 117 NT0255
Tardebigge H & W 47 SO9969
Tardy Gate Lancs 80 SD5425
Tarfside Tays 134 NO4879
Tarland Grampn 134 NJ4804
Tarleton Lancs 80 SD4520
Tarlscough Lancs 80 SD4314
Tarlton Gloucs 35 ST9599
Tarnock Somset 21 ST3752
Tarns Cumb 92 NY1248
Tarnside Cumb 87 SD4390
Tarporley Ches 71 SJ5562
Tarr Somset 19 SS8632
Tarr Somset 20 ST1030
Tarrant Crawford Dorset 11 ST9203
Tarrant Gunville Dorset 11 ST9213
Tarrant Hinton Dorset 11 ST9311
Tarrant Keynston Dorset 11 ST9204
Tarrant Launceston Dorset 11 ST9409
Tarrant Monkton Dorset 11 ST9408
Tarrant Rawston Dorset 11 ST9306
Tarrant Rushton Dorset 11 ST9305
Tarring Neville E Susx 16 TQ4403
Tarrington H & W 46 SO6140
Tarskavaig Highld 129 NG5810
Tarves Grampn 143 NJ8631
Tarvie Tays 133 NO0164
Tarvin Ches 71 SJ4966
Tarvin Sands Ches 71 SJ4967
Tasburgh Norfk 67 TM1996
Tasley Shrops 60 SO6894
Taston Oxon 36 SP3521
Tatenhill Staffs 73 SK2021
Tathall End Bucks 38 SP8246
Tatham Lancs 87 SD6069
Tathwell Lincs 77 TF3182
Tatsfield Surrey 27 TQ4156
Tattenhall Ches 71 SJ4858
Tatterford Norfk 66 TF8628
Tattersett Norfk 66 TF8429
Tattershall Lincs 76 TF2157
Tattershall Bridge Lincs 76 TF1956
Tattershall Thorpe Lincs 76 TF2159
Tattingstone Suffk 54 TM1337
Tattingstone White Horse Suffk 54 TM1338
Tatworth Somset 10 ST3205
Tauchers Grampn 141 NJ3749
Taunton Somset 20 ST2224
Taverham Norfk 66 TG1613
Taverners Green Essex 40 TL5618
Tavernspite Dyfed 31 SN1812
Tavistock Devon 6 SX4874
Taw green Devon 8 SX6597
Tawstock Devon 19 SS5529
Taxal Derbys 79 SK0079
Taychreggan Hotel Strath 123 NN0421
Tayinloan Strath 105 NR7046
Taynton Gloucs 35 SO7222
Taynton Oxon 36 SP2313
Taynuilt Strath 122 NN0031
Tayport Fife 127 NO4628
Tayvallich Strath 113 NR7487
Tealby Lincs 76 TF1590
Teangue Highld 129 NG6609
Teanord Highld 140 NH5964
Tebay Cumb 87 NY6104
Tebworth Beds 38 SP9926
Tedburn St. Mary Devon 8 SX8194
Teddington Gloucs 47 SO9633
Teddington Gt Lon 26 TQ1670
Tedstone Delamere H & W 47 SO6958
Tedstone Wafer H & W 47 SO6759
Teesport Cleve 97 NZ5423
Teeton Nhants 50 SP6970
Teffont Evias Wilts 22 ST9931
Teffont Magna Wilts 22 ST9932
Tegryn Dyfed 31 SN2233
Teigh Leics 63 SK8615
Teigncombe Devon 8 SX6787
Teigngrace Devon 7 SX8574
Teignmouth Devon 7 SX9473
Teindside Border 109 NT4408
Telford Shrops 60 SJ6911
Tellisford Somset 22 ST8055
Telscombe E Susx 15 TQ4003
Telscombe Cliffs E Susx 15 TQ4001
Tempar Tays 124 NN6857
Templand D & G 100 NY0886
Temple Cnwll 4 SX1473
Temple Loth 117 NT3158
Temple Strath 115 NS5469
Temple Balsall W Mids 61 SP2076
Temple Bar Dyfed 44 SN5354
Temple Cloud Avon 21 ST6257
Temple End Suffk 53 TL6650
Temple Ewell Kent 29 TR2844
Temple Grafton Warwks 48 SP1255
Temple Guiting Gloucs 48 SP0928
Temple Hirst N York 83 SE6024
Temple Normanton Derbys 74 SK4167
Temple Pier Highld 139 NH5330
Temple Sowerby Cumb 94 NY6127
Templecombe Somset 22 ST7022
Templeton Devon 19 SS8813
Templeton Dyfed 31 SN1111
Templetown Dur 95 NZ1050
Tempsford Beds 52 TL1653
Ten Mile Bank Norfk 65 TL5996
Tenbury Wells H & W 46 SO5968
Tenby Dyfed 31 SN1300
Tendring Essex 41 TM1424
Tendring Green Essex 41 TM1325
Tendring Heath Essex 41 TM1326
Tenpenny Heath Essex 41 TM0820
Tenterden Kent 17 TQ8833
Terling Essex 40 TL7715
Tern Shrops 59 SJ6216
Ternhill Shrops 59 SJ6332
Terregles D & G 100 NX9377
Terrington N York 90 SE6770
Terrington St. Clement Norfk 65 TF5520
Terrington St. John Norfk 65 TF5314
Terry's Green Warwks 61 SP1073
Teston Kent 28 TQ7053
Testwood Hants 12 SU3514
Tetbury Gloucs 35 ST8993
Tetbury Upton Gloucs 35 ST8895
Tetchill Shrops 59 SJ3932
Tetcott Devon 5 SX3396
Tetford Lincs 77 TF3374
Tetney Lincs 77 TA3100
Tetney Lock Lincs 85 TA3402
Tetsworth Oxon 37 SP6801
Tettenhall W Mids 60 SJ8800
Tettenhall Wood W Mids 60 SO8899
Tetworth Cambs 52 TL2253
Teversal Notts 75 SK4861
Teversham Cambs 53 TL4958
Teviothead Border 109 NT4005
Tewel Grampn 135 NO8085
Tewin Herts 39 TL2714
Tewkesbury Gloucs 47 SO8932
Teynham Kent 28 TQ9662
Thackley W York 82 SE1738
Thackthwaite Cumb 92 NY1423
Thackthwaite Cumb 93 NY4225
Thakeham W Susx 14 TQ1017
Thame Oxon 37 SP7005
Thames Ditton Surrey 26 TQ1567
Thamesmead Gt Lon 27 TQ4780
Thanington Kent 29 TR1356
Thankerton Strath 108 NS9738
Tharston Norfk 66 TM1894
Thatcham Berks 24 SU5167
Thatto Heath Mersyd 78 SJ5093
Thaxted Essex 40 TL6131
The Bank Ches 72 SJ8457
The Bank Shrops 59 SO6199
The Beeches Gloucs 36 SP0302
The Biggins Cambs 53 TL4788
The Blythe Staffs 73 SK0428
The Bourne H & W 47 SO9856
The Braes Highld 137 NG5234
The Bratch Staffs 60 SO8693
The Broad H & W 46 SO4961
The Brunt Loth 118 NT6873
The Bungalow IOM 153 SC3986
The Bush Kent 28 TQ6649
The Butts Gloucs 35 SO8916
The Chequer Clwyd 71 SJ4840
The City Beds 52 TL1159
The City Bucks 37 SU7896
The Common Oxon 48 SP2927
The Common Wilts 35 SU0285
The Corner Kent 28 TQ7041
The Corner Shrops 59 SO4387
The Den Strath 115 NS3251
The Flatt Cumb 101 NY5678
The Forge H & W 46 SO3459
The Forstal Kent 28 TQ8946
The Forstal Kent 28 TR0438
The Fouralls Shrops 72 SJ6831
The Green Cumb 86 SD1884
The Green Essex 40 TL7719
The Grove H & W 47 SO8741
The Haven W Susx 14 TQ0830
The Haw Gloucs 47 SO8427
The Hill Cumb 86 SD1783
The Hirsel Border 110 NT8240
The Holt Berks 37 SU8078
The Horns Kent 17 TQ7429
The Leacon Kent 17 TQ9833
The Lee Bucks 38 SP9004
The Lhen IOM 153 NX3801
The Marsh Ches 72 SJ8462
The Middles Dur 96 NZ2051
The Moor Kent 17 TQ7529
The Mumbles W Glam 32 SS6187
The Mythe Gloucs 47 SO8934
The Narth Gwent 34 SO5206
The Neuk Grampn 135 NO7397
The Quarry Gloucs 35 ST7499
The Quarter Kent 28 TQ8844
The Reddings Gloucs 35 SO9121
The Rookery Staffs 72 SJ8555
The Ross Tays 124 NN7621
The Rowe Staffs 72 SJ8238
The Sands Surrey 25 SU8846
The Shoe Wilts 35 ST8074
The Smithies Shrops 60 SO6897
The Spike Cambs 53 TL4848
The Spring Warwks 61 SP2873
The Square Gwent 34 ST2796
The Stair Kent 16 TQ6047
The Stocks Kent 17 TQ9127
The Straits Hants 25 SU7839
The Strand Wilts 22 ST9259
The Thrift Herts 39 TL3139
The Towans Cnwll 2 SW5538
The Vauld H & W 46 SO5349
The Wyke Shrops 60 SJ7206
Theakston N York 89 SE3085
Thealby Humb 84 SE8917
Theale Berks 24 SU6471
Theale Somset 21 ST4646
Thearne Humb 85 TA0736
Theberton Suffk 55 TM4365
Thedden Grange Hants 24 SU6839
Theddingworth Leics 50 SP6685
Theddlethorpe All Saints Lincs 77 TF4688
Theddlethorpe St. Helen Lincs 77 TF4788
Thelnetham Suffk 54 TM0178
Thelveton Norfk 54 TM1681
Thelwall Ches 79 SJ6587
Themelthorpe Norfk 66 TG0524
Thenford Nhants 49 SP5241
Theobald's Green Wilts 23 SU0268
Therfield Herts 39 TL3337
Thetford Norfk 54 TL8783
Thethwaite Cumb 93 NY3744
Theydon Bois Essex 27 TQ4499
Thicket Prior Humb 83 SE6943
Thickwood Wilts 35 ST8272
Thimbleby Lincs 77 TF2470
Thimbleby N York 89 SE4495
Thingwall Mersyd 78 SJ2784
Thirkleby N York 89 SE4778
Thirlby N York 90 SE4883
Thirlestane Border 118 NT5647
Thirlspot Cumb 93 NY3118
Thirn N York 89 SE2185
Thirsk N York 89 SE4281
Thirtleby Humb 85 TA1634
Thistleton Lancs 80 SD4037
Thistleton Leics 63 SK9118
Thistley Green Suffk 53 TL6676
Thixendale N York 90 SE8460
Thockrington Nthumb 102 NY9578
Tholomas Drove Cambs 65 TF4006
Tholthorpe N York 89 SE4766
Thomas Chapel Dyfed 31 SN1008
Thomas Close Cumb 93 NY4340
Thomastown Grampn 142 NJ5736
Thompson Norfk 66 TL9296
Thomshill Grampn 141 NJ2157
Thong Kent 28 TQ6770
Thoralby N York 88 SE0086
Thoresby Notts 75 SK6371
Thoresthorpe Lincs 77 TF4577
Thoresway Lincs 76 TF1696
Thorganby Lincs 76 TF2097
Thorganby N York 83 SE6841
Thorgill N York 90 SE7096
Thorington Suffk 55 TM4174
Thorington Street Suffk 54 TM0035
Thorlby N York 82 SD9653
Thorley Herts 39 TL4718
Thorley IOW 12 SZ3689
Thorley Houses Herts 39 TL4620
Thorley Street IOW 12 SZ3788
Thormanby N York 90 SE4974
Thorn's Flush Surrey 14 TQ0440
Thornaby-on-Tees Cleve 97 NZ4518
Thornage Norfk 66 TG0536
Thornborough Bucks 49 SP7433
Thornborough N York 89 SE2979
Thornbury Avon 35 ST6390
Thornbury Devon 18 SS4008
Thornbury H & W 47 SO6259
Thornbury W York 82 SE1933
Thornby Cumb 93 NY2851
Thornby Nhants 50 SP6775
Thorncliff Staffs 73 SK0158
Thorncombe Dorset 10 ST3703
Thorncombe Street Surrey 25 SU9941
Thorncott Green Beds 52 TL1547
Thorncross IOW 13 SZ4381
Thorndon Suffk 54 TM1469
Thorndon Cross Devon 8 SX5394
Thorne S York 83 SE6812
Thorne Somset 10 ST5217
Thorne St. Margaret Somset 20 ST1020
Thornecroft Devon 7 SX7767
Thornehillhead Devon 18 SS4116
Thorner W York 83 SE3740
Thornes Staffs 61 SK0703
Thornes W York 83 SE3219
Thorney Bucks 26 TQ0379
Thorney Cambs 64 TF2804
Thorney Notts 76 SK8572
Thorney Somset 21 ST4223
Thorney Hill Hants 12 SZ2099
Thorney Toll Cambs 64 TF3404
Thornfalcon Somset 20 ST2823
Thornford Dorset 10 ST6012
Thorngrafton Nthumb 102 NY7865
Thorngrove Somset 21 ST3632
Thorngumbald Humb 85 TA2026
Thornham Norfk 65 TF7343
Thornham Magna Suffk 54 TM1070
Thornham Parva Suffk 54 TM1072
Thornhaugh Cambs 64 TF0600
Thornhill Cent 116 NN6600
Thornhill D & G 100 NX8795
Thornhill Derbys 74 SK1983
Thornhill Hants 13 SU4612
Thornhill M Glam 33 ST1584
Thornhill W York 82 SE2518
Thornhill Lees W York 82 SE2419
Thornhills W York 82 SE1523
Thornholme Humb 91 TA1164
Thornicombe Dorset 11 ST8703
Thornington Nthumb 110 NT8833
Thornley Dur 95 NZ1137
Thornley Dur 96 NZ3639
Thornley Gate Cumb 95 NY8356
Thornliebank Strath 115 NS5559

Thorns Townwell

Thorns Suffk 53 TL7455
Thorns Green Gt Man 79 SJ7884
Thornsett Derbys 79 SK0086
Thornthwaite Cumb 93 NY2225
Thornthwaite N York 89 SE1758
Thornton Bucks 49 SP7435
Thornton Cleve 89 NZ4713
Thornton Dyfed 30 SM9007
Thornton Fife 117 NT2897
Thornton Humb 84 SE7645
Thornton Lancs 80 SD3342
Thornton Leics 62 SK4607
Thornton Lincs 77 TF2467
Thornton Mersyd 78 SD3301
Thornton Nthumb 111 NT9547
Thornton Tays 126 NO3946
Thornton W York 82 SE0932
Thornton Curtis Humb 85 TA0817
Thornton Dale N York 90 SE8383
Thornton Green Ches 71 SJ4473
Thornton Heath Gt Lon 27 TQ3168
Thornton Hough Mersyd 78 SJ3080
Thornton in Lonsdale N York 87 SD6873
Thornton le Moor Lincs 76 TF0496
Thornton Rust N York 88 SD9689
Thornton Steward N York 89 SE1787
Thornton Watlass N York 89 SE2385
Thornton-in-Craven N York 81 SD9048
Thornton-le-Beans N York 89 SE3990
Thornton-le-Clay N York 90 SE6865
Thornton-le-Moor N York 89 SE3988
Thornton-le-Moors Ches 71 SJ4474
Thornton-le-Street N York 89 SE4186
Thorntonhall Strath 115 NS5955
Thorntonloch Loth 119 NT7574
Thornwood Common Essex 39 TL4604
Thornydykes Border 110 NT6148
Thornythwaite Cumb 93 NY3922
Thoroton Notts 63 SK7642
Thorp Arch W York 83 SE4345
Thorpe Derbys 73 SK1550
Thorpe Humb 84 SE9946
Thorpe Lincs 77 TF4981
Thorpe N York 88 SE0161
Thorpe Norfk 67 TM4398
Thorpe Notts 75 SK7649
Thorpe Surrey 26 TQ0168
Thorpe Abbotts Norfk 55 TM1979
Thorpe Acre Leics 62 SK5119
Thorpe Arnold Leics 63 SK7720
Thorpe Audlin W York 83 SE4715
Thorpe Bassett N York 90 SE8673
Thorpe Bay Essex 40 TQ9185
Thorpe by Water Leics 51 SP8996
Thorpe Common S York 74 SK3895
Thorpe Constantine Staffs 61 SK2508
Thorpe End Norfk 67 TG2810
Thorpe Green Essex 41 TM1623
Thorpe Green Lancs 81 SD5923
Thorpe Green Suffk 54 TL9354
Thorpe Hesley S York 74 SK3796
Thorpe in Balne S York 83 SE5910
Thorpe in the Fallows Lincs 76 SK9180
Thorpe Langton Leics 50 SP7492
Thorpe Larches Dur 96 NZ3826
Thorpe Lea Surrey 26 TQ0170
Thorpe le Street Humb 84 SE8343
Thorpe Malsor Nhants 51 SP8378
Thorpe Mandeville Nhants 49 SP5244
Thorpe Market Norfk 67 TG2436
Thorpe Morieux Suffk 54 TL9453
Thorpe on the Hill Lincs 76 SK9065
Thorpe on the Hill W York 82 SE3126
Thorpe Salvin S York 75 SK5281
Thorpe Satchville Leics 63 SK7311
Thorpe St. Andrew Norfk 67 TG2508
Thorpe St. Peter Lincs 77 TF4860
Thorpe Thewles Cleve 96 NZ3923
Thorpe Tilney Lincs 76 TF1257
Thorpe Underwood N York 89 SE4659
Thorpe Underwood Nhants 50 SP7981
Thorpe Waterville Nhants 51 TL0281
Thorpe Willoughby N York 83 SE5731
Thorpe-le-Soken Essex 41 TM1722
Thorpeness Suffk 55 TM4759
Thorpland Norfk 65 TF6108
Thorrington Essex 41 TM0919
Thorverton Devon 9 SS9202
Thrales End Beds 38 TL1116
Thrandeston Suffk 54 TM1176
Thrapston Nhants 51 SP9978
Threapland Cumb 92 NY1539
Threapland N York 88 SD9860
Threapwood Ches 71 SJ4344
Threapwood Staffs 73 SK0342
Threapwood Head Staffs 73 SK0342
Threave Strath 106 NS3306
Three Ashes H & W 34 SO5122
Three Bridges W Susx 15 TQ2837
Three Burrows Cnwll 3 SW7446
Three Chimneys Kent 28 TQ8238
Three Cocks Powys 45 SO1737
Three Crosses W Glam 32 SS5794
Three Cups Corner E Susx 16 TQ6320
Three Gates H & W 47 SO6862
Three Hammers Cnwll 5 SX2287
Three Holes Norfk 65 TF5000
Three Lane Ends Gt Man 79 SD8309
Three Leg Cross E Susx 16 TQ6831
Three Legged Cross Dorset 12 SU0805
Three Mile Cross Berks 24 SU7167
Three Mile Stone Cnwll 3 SW7745
Three Miletown Loth 117 NT0675
Three Oaks E Susx 17 TQ8314
Threehammer Common Norfk 67 TG3419
Threekingham Lincs 64 TF0836
Threepwood Border 109 NT5143
Threlkeld Cumb 93 NY3125
Threshfield N York 88 SD9863
Thrigby Norfk 67 TG4612
Thringarth Dur 95 NY9322
Thringstone Leics 62 SK4217
Thrintoft N York 89 SE3192
Thriplow Cambs 53 TL4346
Throapham S York 75 SK5387
Throckenhalt Lincs 64 TF3509
Throcking Herts 39 TL3330
Throckley T & W 103 NZ1566
Throckmorton H & W 47 SO9850
Throop Dorset 11 SY8292
Throop Dorset 12 SZ1195
Throphill Nthumb 103 NZ1285
Thropton Nthumb 103 NU0202
Througham Gloucs 35 SO9108
Throughgate D & G 100 NX8784
Throwleigh Devon 8 SX6690
Throwley Kent 28 TQ9955
Throwley Forstal Kent 28 TQ9854
Thrumpton Notts 62 SK5031
Thrumpton Notts 75 SK7080
Thrumster Highld 151 ND3345
Thrunscoe Humb 85 TA3107
Thrup Oxon 36 SU2999
Thrupp Gloucs 35 SO8603
Thrupp Oxon 37 SP4716
Thrushelton Devon 5 SX4487
Thrushesbush Essex 39 TL4909
Thrussington Leics 63 SK6515
Thruxton H & W 46 SO4334
Thruxton Hants 23 SU2945
Thrybergh S York 75 SK4695
Thulston Derbys 62 SK4031
Thundersley Essex 40 TQ7988
Thurcaston Leics 62 SK5610
Thurcroft S York 75 SK4988
Thurdistoft Highld 151 ND2167
Thurdon Cnwll 18 SS2810
Thurgarton Norfk 66 TG1834
Thurgarton Notts 75 SK6949
Thurgoland S York 82 SE2901
Thurlaston Leics 50 SP5099
Thurlaston Warwks 50 SP4670
Thurlbear Somset 20 ST2621
Thurlby Lincs 76 SK9061
Thurlby Lincs 64 TF0916
Thurlby Lincs 77 TF4776
Thurleigh Beds 51 TL0558
Thurlestone Devon 7 SX6742
Thurlow Suffk 53 TL6750
Thurloxton Somset 20 ST2730
Thurlstone S York 82 SE2303
Thurlton Norfk 67 TM4198
Thurlwood Ches 72 SJ8057
Thurmaston Leics 62 SK6109
Thurnby Leics 63 SK6403
Thurne Norfk 67 TG4015
Thurnham Kent 28 TQ8057
Thurning Nhants 51 TL0882
Thurning Norfk 66 TG0729
Thurnscoe S York 83 SE4505
Thursby Cumb 93 NY3250
Thursden Lancs 81 SD9034
Thursford Norfk 66 TF9833
Thursley Surrey 25 SU9039
Thurso Highld 151 ND1168
Thurstaston Mersyd 78 SJ2484
Thurston Suffk 54 TL9265
Thurston Clough Gt Man 82 SD9707
Thurston Planch Suffk 54 TL9364
Thurstonfield Cumb 93 NY3156
Thurstonland W York 82 SE1610
Thurton Norfk 67 TG3200
Thurvaston Derbys 73 SK2437
Thuxton Norfk 66 TG0307
Thwaite N York 88 SD8998
Thwaite Suffk 54 TM1168
Thwaite Head Cumb 87 SD3490
Thwaite St. Mary Norfk 67 TM3395
Thwaites W York 82 SE0741
Thwaites Brow W York 82 SE0740
Thwing Humb 91 TA0470
Tibbermore Tays 125 NO0423
Tibbers D & G 100 NX8696
Tibberton Gloucs 35 SO7521
Tibberton H & W 47 SO9057
Tibberton Shrops 72 SJ6820
Tibbie Shiels Inn Border 109 NT2420
Tibenham Norfk 54 TM1389
Tibshelf Derbys 75 SK4461
Tibthorpe Humb 84 SE9555
Ticehurst E Susx 16 TQ6830
Tichborne Hants 24 SU5730
Tickencote Leics 63 SK9809
Tickenham Avon 34 ST4571
Tickford End Bucks 38 SP8843
Tickhill S York 75 SK5993
Ticklerton Shrops 59 SO4890
Ticknall Derbys 62 SK3523
Tickton Humb 84 TA0541
Tidbury Green W Mids 61 SP1075
Tidcombe Wilts 23 SU2858
Tiddington Oxon 37 SP6404
Tiddington Warwks 48 SP2255
Tidebrook E Susx 16 TQ6130
Tideford Cnwll 5 SX3559
Tideford Cross Cnwll 5 SX3461
Tidenham Gloucs 34 ST5595
Tideswell Derbys 74 SK1575
Tidmarsh Berks 24 SU6374
Tidmington Warwks 48 SP2538
Tidpit Hants 12 SU0718
Tiers Cross Dyfed 30 SM9010
Tiffield Nhants 49 SP7051
Tifty Gramp 142 NJ7740
Tigerton Tays 134 NO5364
Tigharry W Isls 154 NF7172
Tighnabruaich Strath 114 NR9873
Tigley Devon 7 SX7660
Tilbrook Cambs 51 TL0869
Tilbury Essex 27 TQ6476
Tilbury Green Essex 53 TL7441
Tile Cross W Mids 61 SP1687
Tile Hill W Mids 61 SP2777
Tilehouse Green W Mids 61 SP1776
Tilehurst Berks 24 SU6673
Tilford Surrey 25 SU8743
Tilgate W Susx 15 TQ2734
Tilgate Forest Row W Susx 15 TQ2632
Tilham Street Somset 21 ST5535
Tillers Green Gloucs 47 SO6932
Tillicoultry Cent 116 NS9197
Tillingham Essex 41 TL9904
Tillington H & W 46 SO4644
Tillington W Susx 14 SU9621
Tillington Common H & W 46 SO4545
Tilly Essex 40 TL5926
Tillybirloch Gramp 135 NJ6807
Tillycairn Gramp 134 NO4697
Tillyfourie Gramp 135 NJ6412
Tillygreig Gramp 143 NJ8822
Tillyrie Tays 126 NO1006
Tilmanstone Kent 29 TR3051
Tiln Notts 75 SK7084
Tilney All Saints Norfk 65 TF5618
Tilney High End Norfk 65 TF5617
Tilney St. Lawrence Norfk 65 TF5414
Tilshead Wilts 23 SU0347
Tilstock Shrops 59 SJ5437
Tilston Ches 71 SJ4650
Tilstone Bank Ches 71 SJ5659
Tilstone Fearnall Ches 71 SJ5660
Tilsworth Beds 38 SP9824
Tilton on the Hill Leics 63 SK7405
Tiltups End Gloucs 35 ST8497
Timberland Lincs 76 TF1258
Timbersbrook Ches 72 SJ8962
Timberscombe Somset 20 SS9542
Timble N York 82 SE1853
Timewell Devon 20 SS9625
Timpanheck D & G 101 NY3274
Timperley Gt Man 79 SJ7888
Timsbury Avon 22 ST6758
Timsbury Hants 23 SU3424
Timsgarry W Isls 154 NB0534
Timworth Suffk 54 TL8669
Timworth Green Suffk 54 TL8669
Tincleton Dorset 11 SY7692
Tindale Cumb 94 NY6159
Tindale Crescent Dur 96 NZ1927
Tingewick Bucks 49 SP6532
Tingley W York 82 SE2826
Tingrith Beds 38 TL0032
Tinhay Devon 5 SX3985
Tinker's Hill Hants 24 SU4047
Tinkersley Derbys 74 SK2664
Tinsley S York 74 SK4090
Tinsley Green W Susx 15 TQ2839
Tintagel Cnwll 4 SX0588
Tintern Parva Gwent 34 SO5200
Tintinhull Somset 21 ST4919
Tintwistle Derbys 79 SK0197
Tinwald D & G 100 NY0081
Tinwell Leics 63 TF0006
Tipp's End Norfk 65 TL5095
Tippacott Devon 19 SS7647
Tiptoe Hants 12 SZ2597
Tipton W Mids 60 SO9492
Tipton Green W Mids 60 SO9592
Tipton St. John Devon 9 SY0991
Tiptree Essex 40 TL8916
Tiptree Heath Essex 40 TL8815
Tir-y-fron Clwyd 70 SJ2859
Tirabad Powys 45 SN8741
Tiretigan Strath 113 NR7162
Tirley Gloucs 47 SO8328
Tirphil M Glam 33 SO1303
Tirril Cumb 94 NY5026
Tisbury Wilts 22 ST9429
Tisman's Common W Susx 14 TQ0632
Tissington Derbys 73 SK1752
Titchberry Devon 18 SS2427
Titchfield Hants 13 SU5405
Titchfield Common Hants 13 SU5206
Titchmarsh Nhants 51 TL0279
Titchwell Norfk 65 TF7643
Tithby Notts 63 SK6937
Titley H & W 46 SO3360
Titmore Green Herts 39 TL2126
Titsey Surrey 27 TQ4054
Tittensor Staffs 72 SJ8738
Tittleshall Norfk 66 TF8921
Titton H & W 60 SO8370
Tiverton Ches 71 SJ5560
Tiverton Devon 9 SS9512
Tivetshall St. Margaret Norfk 54 TM1787
Tivetshall St. Mary Norfk 54 TM1686
Tivington Somset 20 SS9345
Tivy Dale S York 82 SE2707
Tixall Staffs 72 SJ9722
Tixover Leics 51 SK9700
Toab Shet 155 HU3811
Toadhole Derbys 74 SK3856
Toadmoor Derbys 74 SK3451
Tobermory Strath 121 NM5055
Toberonochy Strath 122 NM7408
Tocher Gramp 142 NJ6932
Tochieneal Gramp 142 NJ5165
Tockenham Wilts 36 SU0379
Tockenham Wick Wilts 36 SU0381
Tocketts Cleve 97 NZ6217
Tockington Avon 34 ST6086
Tockwith N York 83 SE4652
Todber Dorset 22 ST7919
Todburn Nthumb 103 NZ1295
Toddington Beds 38 TL0128
Toddington Gloucs 48 SP0333
Todds Green Herts 39 TL2226
Todenham Gloucs 48 SP2335
Todhills Cumb 101 NY3762
Todhills Dur 96 NZ2133
Todhills Tays 127 NO4239
Todmorden W York 81 SD9324
Todwick S York 75 SK4984
Toft Cambs 52 TL3656
Toft Ches 79 SJ7576
Toft Lincs 64 TF0717
Toft Shet 155 HU4376
Toft Warwks 50 SP4770
Toft Hill Dur 96 NZ1528
Toft Monks Norfk 67 TM4294
Toft next Newton Lincs 76 TF0388
Toftrees Norfk 66 TF8927
Tofts Highld 151 ND3668
Toftwood Norfk 66 TF9811
Togston Nthumb 103 NU2402
Tokavaig Highld 129 NG6011
Tokers Green Oxon 37 SU7077
Toldavas Cnwll 2 SW4226
Toldish Cnwll 4 SW9259
Toll Bar S York 83 SE5507
Tolland Somset 20 ST1032
Tollard Farnham Dorset 11 ST9515
Tollard Royal Wilts 11 ST9417
Tollbar End W Mids 61 SP3675
Toller Fratrum Dorset 10 SY5797
Toller Porcorum Dorset 10 SY5698
Toller Whelme Dorset 10 ST5101
Tollerton N York 90 SE5164
Tollerton Notts 62 SK6134
Tollesbury Essex 40 TL9510
Tolleshunt D'Arcy Essex 40 TL9211
Tolleshunt Knights Essex 40 TL9114
Tolleshunt Major Essex 40 TL9011
Tolpuddle Dorset 11 SY7994
Tolsta W Isls 154 NB5347
Tolvan Cnwll 2 SW7028
Tolver Cnwll 2 SW4832
Tolworth Gt Lon 26 TQ1966
Tomaknock Tays 125 NN8721
Tomatin Highld 140 NH8028
Tomchrasky Highld 131 NH2512
Tomdoun Highld 131 NH1500
Tomich Highld 146 NC6005
Tomich Highld 139 NH3027
Tomich Highld 139 NH5348
Tomich Highld 146 NH6971
Tomintoul Gramp 141 NJ1619
Tomintoul Gramp 133 NO1490
Tomlow Warwks 49 SP4563
Tomnacross Highld 139 NH5141
Tomnavoulin Gramp 141 NJ2126
Tompkin Staffs 72 SJ9451
Ton Gwent 34 SO3301
Ton Gwent 34 ST3695
Ton-teg M Glam 33 ST0986
Tonbridge Kent 16 TQ5846
Tondu M Glam 33 SS8984
Tonedale Somset 20 ST1321
Tong Kent 28 TQ9556
Tong Shrops 60 SJ7907
Tong W York 82 SE2230
Tong Green Kent 28 TQ9853
Tong Norton Shrops 60 SJ7908
Tong Street W York 82 SE1930
Tonge Leics 62 SK4223
Tongham Surrey 25 SU8848
Tongland D & G 99 NX6954
Tongue Highld 149 NC5956
Tongue End Lincs 64 TF1518
Tongwynlais S Glam 33 ST1382
Tonna W Glam 32 SS7798
Tonwell Herts 39 TL3316
Tonypandy M Glam 33 SS9991
Tonyrefail M Glam 33 ST0188
Toot Baldon Oxon 37 SP5600
Toot Hill Essex 27 TL5102
Toot Hill Hants 12 SU3818
Toothill Wilts 36 SU1183
Tooting Gt Lon 27 TQ2771
Tooting Bec Gt Lon 27 TQ2872
Top of Hebers Gt Man 79 SD8607
Top-y-rhos Clwyd 70 SJ2558
Topcliffe N York 89 SE3976
Topcroft Norfk 67 TM2693
Topcroft Street Norfk 67 TM2691
Topham S York 83 SE6217
Toppesfield Essex 53 TL7437
Toppings Gt Man 81 SD7213
Toprow Norfk 66 TM1698
Topsham Devon 9 SX9688
Torbeg Strath 105 NR8929
Torboll Highld 147 NH7599
Torbreck Highld 140 NH6441
Torbryan Devon 7 SX8266
Torcastle Highld 131 NN1378
Torcross Devon 7 SX8241
Tore Highld 140 NH6052
Torfrey Cnwll 3 SX1154
Torksey Lincs 76 SK8378
Tormarton Avon 35 ST7678
Tormitchell Strath 106 NX2394
Tormore Strath 105 NR8932
Tornagrain Highld 140 NH7650
Tornaveen Gramp 134 NJ6106
Tornness Highld 139 NH5826
Tornewton Devon 7 SX8167
Toronto Nthumb 96 NZ1930
Torosay Castle Strath 122 NM7335
Torpenhow Cumb 93 NY2039
Torphichen Loth 117 NS9672
Torphins Gramp 134 NJ6202
Torpoint Cnwll 6 SX4355
Torquay Devon 7 SX9164
Torquhan Border 118 NT4448
Torr Devon 6 SX5851
Torran Highld 137 NG5949
Torrance Strath 116 NS6173
Torranyard Strath 115 NS3544
Torridon Highld 138 NG9055
Torridon House Highld 138 NG8657
Torrin Highld 129 NG5721
Torrisdale Highld 149 NC6761
Torrisdale Square Strath 105 NR7936
Torrish Highld 147 NC9718
Torrisholme Lancs 87 SD4563
Torrobull Highld 146 NC5904
Torry Gramp 135 NJ9405
Torryburn Fife 117 NT0286
Torrylin Strath 105 NR9521
Tortan H & W 60 SO8472
Torteval Guern 152 GN4505
Torthorwald D & G 100 NY0378
Tortington W Susx 14 TQ0004
Tortworth Avon 35 ST7093
Torvaig Highld 136 NG4944
Torver Cumb 86 SD2894
Torwood Cent 116 NS8385
Torwoodlee Border 109 NT4738
Torworth Notts 75 SK6586
Toscaig Highld 137 NG7138
Toseland Cambs 52 TL2462
Tosside Lancs 81 SD7656
Tostock Suffk 54 TL9563
Totaig Highld 136 NG2050
Tote Highld 136 NG4149
Tote Hill W Susx 14 SU8624
Tothill Lincs 77 TF4181
Totland IOW 12 SZ3287
Totley S York 74 SK3079
Totley Brook S York 74 SK3180
Totnes Devon 7 SX8060
Toton Notts 62 SK5034
Totronald Strath 120 NM1656
Totscore Highld 136 NG3866
Tottenham Gt Lon 27 TQ3390
Tottenhill Norfk 65 TF6411
Totteridge Gt Lon 26 TQ2494
Totternhoe Beds 38 SP9821
Tottington Gt Man 81 SD7712
Tottleworth Lancs 81 SD7331
Totton Hants 12 SU3613
Touchen End Berks 26 SU8776
Toulston N York 83 SE4543
Toulton Somset 20 ST1931
Toulvaddie Highld 147 NH8880
Toux Gramp 142 NJ5459
Tovil Kent 28 TQ7554
Tow Law Dur 95 NZ1138
Towan Cnwll 4 SW8774
Towan Cnwll 3 SX0148
Toward Strath 114 NS1368
Toward Quay Strath 114 NS1167
Towcester Nhants 49 SP6948
Towednack Cnwll 2 SW4838
Towersey Oxon 37 SP7305
Towie Gramp 134 NJ4312
Town End Cambs 65 TL4195
Town End Cumb 87 NY3406
Town End Cumb 94 NY6325
Town End Cumb 87 SD3687
Town End Cumb 87 SD4483
Town End Lincs 63 SK9943
Town Green Lancs 78 SD4005
Town Green Norfk 67 TG3612
Town Head Cumb 87 NY4103
Town Head N York 88 SD8258
Town Head N York 82 SE1748
Town Kelloe Dur 96 NZ3536
Town Lane Gt Man 79 SJ6999
Town Littleworth E Susx 15 TQ4117
Town Moor T & W 103 NZ2465
Town of Lowdon Mersyd 78 SJ6196
Town Row E Susx 16 TQ5630
Town Street Suffk 53 TL7785
Town Yetholm Border 110 NT8128
Towngate Cumb 94 NY5246
Towngate Lincs 64 TF1310
Townhead Cumb 92 NY0735
Townhead Cumb 94 NY6334
Townhead D & G 100 NY0088
Townhead S York 82 SE1602
Townhead of Greenlaw D & G 99 NX7464
Townhill Loth 117 NT1089
Townlake Devon 5 SX4074
Towns End Hants 24 SU5659
Townsend Somset 10 ST3614
Townshend Cnwll 2 SW5932
Townwell Avon 35 ST7090

Towthorpe
Tytherington

Towthorpe *Humb* **91** SE8962
Towthorpe *N York* **90** SE6258
Towton *N York* **83** SE4839
Towyn *Clwyd* **70** SH9779
Toxteth *Mersyd* **78** SJ3588
Toy's Hill *Kent* **27** TQ4651
Toynton All Saints *Lincs* **77** TF3963
Toynton Fen Side *Lincs* **77** TF3961
Toynton St. Peter *Lincs* **77** TF4063
Trabboch *Strath* **107** NS4421
Trabbochburn *Strath* **107** NS4621
Traboe *Cnwll* **3** SW7421
Tracebridge *Somset* **20** ST0621
Tradespark *Highld* **140** NH8656
Traethsaith *Dyfed* **42** SN2851
Trafford Park *Gt Man* **79** SJ7896
Trallong *Powys* **45** SN9629
Tranent *Loth* **118** NT4072
Tranmere *Mersyd* **78** SJ3187
Trannack *Cnwll* **2** SW5633
Trantelbeg *Highld* **150** NC8952
Trantlemore *Highld* **150** NC8953
Tranwell *Nthumb* **103** NZ1883
Trap *Dyfed* **32** SN6518
Trap's Green *Warwks* **48** SP1069
Trapshill *Berks* **23** SU3763
Traquair *Border* **109** NT3334
Trash Green *Berks* **24** SU6569
Traveller's Rest *Devon* **19** SS6127
Trawden *Lancs* **81** SD9138
Trawscoed *Dyfed* **43** SN6672
Trawsfynydd *Gwynd* **57** SH7035
Tre Aubrey *S Glam* **33** ST0372
Tre'r-ddol *Dyfed* **43** SN6692
Tre-Gibbon *M Glam* **33** SN9905
Tre-gagle *Gwent* **34** SO5207
Tre-groes *Dyfed* **42** SN4044
Tre-Mostyn *Clwyd* **70** SJ1479
Tre-Vaughan *Dyfed* **31** SN3921
Tre-wyn *Gwent* **34** SO3222
Trealaw *M Glam* **33** ST0092
Treales *Lancs* **80** SD4332
Treamble *Cnwll* **3** SW7856
Trearddur Bay *Gwynd* **68** SH2579
Treaslane *Highld* **136** NG3953
Treator *Cnwll* **4** SW9075
Trebanog *M Glam* **33** ST0190
Trebanos *W Glam* **32** SN7103
Trebartha *Cnwll* **5** SX2677
Trebarvah *Cnwll* **2** SW7130
Trebarwith *Cnwll* **4** SX0586
Trebeath *Cnwll* **5** SX2587
Trebehor *Cnwll* **2** SW3724
Trebelzue *Cnwll* **4** SW8464
Trebetherick *Cnwll* **4** SW9378
Trebudannon *Cnwll* **4** SW8961
Trebullett *Cnwll* **5** SX3278
Treburgett *Cnwll* **4** SX0579
Treburick *Cnwll* **4** SW8971
Treburley *Cnwll* **5** SX3577
Treburrick *Cnwll* **4** SW8670
Trebyan *Cnwll* **4** SX0763
Trecastle *Powys* **45** SN8829
Trecogo *Cnwll* **5** SX3080
Trecott *Devon* **8** SS6300
Trecwn *Dyfed* **30** SM9632
Trecynon *M Glam* **33** SN9903
Tredaule *Cnwll* **5** SX2381
Tredavoe *Cnwll* **2** SW4528
Tredegar *Gwent* **33** SO1408
Tredethy *Cnwll* **4** SX0672
Tredington *Gloucs* **47** SO9029
Tredington *Warwks* **48** SP2543
Tredinnick *Cnwll* **4** SW9270
Tredinnick *Cnwll* **4** SX0459
Tredinnick *Cnwll* **4** SX1666
Tredinnick *Cnwll* **5** SX2357
Tredinnick *Cnwll* **5** SX2957
Tredomen *Powys* **45** SO1231
Tredrissi *Dyfed* **31** SN0742
Tredrizzick *Cnwll* **4** SW9577
Tredunhock *Gwent* **34** ST3794
Tredustan *Powys* **45** SO1332
Treen *Cnwll* **2** SW3923
Treesmill *Cnwll* **3** SX0855
Treeton *S York* **75** SK4387
Trefacca *Powys* **45** SO1431
Trefasser *Dyfed* **30** SM8938
Trefdraeth *Gwynd* **68** SH4170
Trefeglwys *Powys* **58** SN9690
Trefenter *Dyfed* **43** SN6068
Treffgarne *Dyfed* **30** SM9523
Treffgarne Owen *Dyfed* **30** SM8625
Trefforest *M Glam* **33** ST0888
Treffynnon *Dyfed* **30** SM8528
Trefil *Gwent* **33** SO1212
Trefilan *Dyfed* **44** SN5456
Treflach Wood *Shrops* **58** SJ2625
Trefnannau *Powys* **58** SJ2316
Trefnant *Clwyd* **70** SJ0570
Trefonen *Shrops* **58** SJ2526
Trefor *Gwynd* **68** SH3780
Treforda *Cnwll* **4** SX0988
Trefrew *Cnwll* **4** SX1084
Trefriw *Gwynd* **69** SH7863
Tregadillett *Cnwll* **5** SX2983
Tregaian *Gwynd* **68** SH4580
Tregare *Gwent* **34** SO4110
Tregarne *Cnwll* **3** SW7823
Tregaron *Dyfed* **44** SN6759
Tregarth *Gwynd* **69** SH6067
Tregaswith *Cnwll* **4** SW8962
Tregatta *Cnwll* **4** SX0587
Tregawne *Cnwll* **4** SX0066
Tregear *Cnwll* **3** SW8650
Tregeare *Cnwll* **5** SX2486
Tregeiriog *Clwyd* **58** SJ1733
Tregele *Gwynd* **68** SH3592
Tregellist *Cnwll* **4** SX0177
Tregenna *Cnwll* **3** SW8743
Tregenna *Cnwll* **4** SX0973
Tregeseal *Cnwll* **2** SW3731
Tregew *Cnwll* **3** SW8034
Tregidden *Cnwll* **3** SW7523
Tregiddle *Cnwll* **2** SW6723
Tregidgeo *Cnwll* **3** SW9647
Tregiskey *Cnwll* **3** SX0146
Treglemais *Dyfed* **30** SM8229
Tregole *Cnwll* **5** SX1998
Tregolls *Cnwll* **3** SW7335
Tregonce *Cnwll* **4** SW9373
Tregonetha *Cnwll* **4** SW9563
Tregony *Cnwll* **3** SW9244
Tregoodwell *Cnwll* **4** SX1183
Tregoose *Cnwll* **2** SW6823
Tregoss *Cnwll* **4** SW9660
Tregowris *Cnwll* **3** SW7722
Tregoyd *Powys* **45** SO1937
Tregrehan Mills *Cnwll* **3** SX0453
Tregullon *Cnwll* **4** SX0664
Tregunna *Cnwll* **4** SW9673
Tregunnon *Cnwll* **5** SX2283
Tregurrian *Cnwll* **4** SW8565
Tregustick *Cnwll* **4** SW9866
Tregynon *Powys* **58** SO0998
Trehafod *M Glam* **33** ST0490
Trehan *Cnwll* **5** SX4058
Treharris *M Glam* **33** ST0996
Treharrock *Cnwll* **4** SX0178
Trehemborne *Cnwll* **4** SW8773
Treherbert *Dyfed* **44** SN5847
Treherbert *M Glam* **33** SS9498
Treheveras *Cnwll* **3** SW8046
Trehunist *Cnwll* **5** SX3263
Trekelland *Cnwll* **5** SX3480
Trekenner *Cnwll* **5** SX3478
Treknow *Cnwll* **4** SX0586
Trelan *Cnwll* **3** SW7418
Trelash *Cnwll* **4** SX1890
Trelassick *Cnwll* **3** SW8752
Trelawne *Cnwll* **5** SX2154
Trelawnyd *Clwyd* **70** SJ0979
Treleague *Cnwll* **3** SW7821
Treleaver *Cnwll* **3** SW7716
Trelech *Dyfed* **31** SN2830
Trelech a'r Betws *Dyfed* **31** SN3026
Treleddyd-fawr *Dyfed* **30** SM7528
Trelew *Cnwll* **3** SW8135
Trelewis *M Glam* **33** ST1096
Treligga *Cnwll* **4** SX0484
Trelights *Cnwll* **4** SW9979
Trelill *Cnwll* **4** SX0478
Trelinnoe *Cnwll* **5** SX3181
Trelion *Cnwll* **3** SW9252
Trelissick *Cnwll* **3** SW8339
Trelleck *Gwent* **34** SO5005
Trelleck Grange *Gwent* **34** SO4901
Trelogan *Clwyd* **70** SJ1180
Trelonk *Cnwll* **3** SW8941
Trelow *Cnwll* **4** SW9269
Trelowarren *Cnwll* **2** SW7124
Trelowia *Cnwll* **5** SX2956
Treluggan *Cnwll* **3** SW8838
Trelystan *Powys* **58** SJ2503
Tremadog *Gwynd* **57** SH5640
Tremail *Cnwll* **4** SX1686
Tremaine *Cnwll* **5** SX2389
Tremar *Cnwll* **5** SX2568
Trematon *Cnwll* **5** SX3959
Trembraze *Cnwll* **5** SX2565
Tremeirchion *Clwyd* **70** SJ0873
Tremethick Cross *Cnwll* **2** SW4430
Tremollett *Cnwll* **5** SX2975
Tremore *Cnwll* **4** SX0164
Trenance *Cnwll* **3** SW8022
Trenance *Cnwll* **4** SW8568
Trenance *Cnwll* **4** SW9270
Trenarren *Cnwll* **3** SX0348
Trenault *Cnwll* **5** SX2683
Trench *Shrops* **60** SJ6912
Trench Green *Oxon* **37** SU6877
Trencreek *Cnwll* **4** SW8260
Trencreek *Cnwll* **4** SX1896
Trendeal *Cnwll* **3** SW8952
Trendrine *Cnwll* **2** SW4739
Treneague *Cnwll* **4** SW9871
Trenear *Cnwll* **2** SW6731
Treneglos *Cnwll* **5** SX2088
Trenerth *Cnwll* **2** SW6035
Trenewan *Cnwll* **4** SX1753
Trenewth *Cnwll* **4** SX0778
Trengothal *Cnwll* **2** SW3724
Trengune *Cnwll* **4** SX1893
Treninnick *Cnwll* **4** SW8160
Trenowah *Cnwll* **4** SW7959
Trenoweth *Cnwll* **3** SW7533
Trent *Dorset* **10** ST5918
Trent Port *Lincs* **76** SK8381
Trent Vale *Staffs* **72** SJ8643
Trentham *Staffs* **72** SJ8740
Trentishoe *Devon* **19** SS6448
Trentlock *Derbys* **62** SK4831
Treoes *S Glam* **33** SS9478
Treorchy *M Glam* **33** SS9597
Trequite *Cnwll* **4** SX0377
Trerhyngyll *S Glam* **33** ST0077
Trerulefoot *Cnwll* **5** SX3358
Tresahor *Cnwll* **3** SW7431
Tresawle *Cnwll* **3** SW8846
Trescott *Staffs* **60** SO8597
Trescowe *Cnwll* **2** SW5731
Tresean *Cnwll* **4** SW7858
Tresham *Avon* **35** ST7991
Tresillian *Cnwll* **3** SW8646
Tresinney *Cnwll* **4** SX1081
Treskinnick Cross *Cnwll* **5** SX2098
Treslea *Cnwll* **4** SX1368
Tresmeer *Cnwll* **5** SX2387
Tresparrett *Cnwll* **4** SX1491
Tressait *Tays* **132** NN8160
Tresta *Shet* **155** HU3650
Tresta *Shet* **155** HU6090
Treswell *Notts* **75** SK7879
Treswithian *Cnwll* **2** SW6241
Trethawle *Cnwll* **5** SX2662
Trethevey *Cnwll* **4** SX0789
Trethewey *Cnwll* **2** SW3823
Trethomas *M Glam* **33** ST1888
Trethosa *Cnwll* **3** SW9454
Trethurgy *Cnwll* **3** SX0355
Tretio *Dyfed* **30** SM7829
Tretire *H & W* **46** SO5123
Tretower *Powys* **33** SO1821
Treuddyn *Clwyd* **70** SJ2557
Trevadlock *Cnwll* **5** SX2679
Trevague *Cnwll* **5** SX2379
Trevalga *Cnwll* **4** SX0890
Trevalyn *Clwyd* **71** SJ3856
Trevanger *Cnwll* **4** SW9677
Trevanson *Cnwll* **4** SW9773
Trevarrack *Cnwll* **2** SW4731
Trevarren *Cnwll* **4** SW9160
Trevarrian *Cnwll* **4** SW8566
Trevarrick *Cnwll* **3** SW9843
Trevarth *Cnwll* **3** SW7240
Trevaughan *Dyfed* **31** SN2015
Treveal *Cnwll* **2** SW4740
Treveal *Cnwll* **4** SW7858
Treveale *Cnwll* **3** SW8751
Treveighan *Cnwll* **4** SX0779
Trevellas Downs *Cnwll* **3** SW7452
Trevelmond *Cnwll* **5** SX2063
Trevempor *Cnwll* **4** SW8159
Treveneague *Cnwll* **2** SW5432
Treveor *Cnwll* **3** SW9841
Treverbyn *Cnwll* **3** SW8849
Treverbyn *Cnwll* **4** SX0157
Treverva *Cnwll* **3** SW7531
Trevescan *Cnwll* **2** SW3524
Trevethin *Gwent* **34** SO2801
Trevia *Cnwll* **4** SX0983
Trevigro *Cnwll* **5** SX3369
Trevilla *Cnwll* **3** SW8239
Trevilledor *Cnwll* **4** SW8867
Trevilson *Cnwll* **3** SW8455
Trevine *Dyfed* **30** SM8432
Treviscoe *Cnwll* **3** SW9455
Treviskey *Cnwll* **3** SW9340
Trevissick *Cnwll* **3** SX0248
Trevithal *Cnwll* **2** SW4626
Trevithick *Cnwll* **4** SW8862
Trevithick *Cnwll* **3** SW9645
Trevivian *Cnwll* **4** SX1785
Trevoll *Cnwll* **4** SW8358
Trevone *Cnwll* **4** SW8975
Trevor *Clwyd* **70** SJ2742
Trevor *Gwynd* **56** SH3746
Trevorgans *Cnwll* **2** SW4025
Trevorrick *Cnwll* **4** SW8672
Trevorrick *Cnwll* **4** SW9273
Trevose *Cnwll* **4** SW8675
Trew *Cnwll* **2** SW6129
Trewalder *Cnwll* **4** SX0782
Trewalkin *Powys* **45** SO1531
Trewarlett *Cnwll* **5** SX3380
Trewarmett *Cnwll* **4** SX0686
Trewarthenick *Cnwll* **3** SW9044
Trewassa *Cnwll* **4** SX1486
Trewaves *Cnwll* **2** SW5926
Treween *Cnwll* **5** SX2182
Trewellard *Cnwll* **2** SW3733
Trewen *Cnwll* **4** SX0577
Trewennack *Cnwll* **2** SW6728
Trewent *Dyfed* **30** SS0197
Trewern *Powys* **58** SJ2811
Trewetha *Cnwll* **4** SX0080
Trewethern *Cnwll* **4** SX0076
Trewidland *Cnwll* **5** SX2559
Trewillis *Cnwll* **3** SW7717
Trewince *Cnwll* **3** SW8633
Trewint *Cnwll* **4** SX1072
Trewint *Cnwll* **5** SX2180
Trewint *Cnwll* **5** SX2963
Trewirgie *Cnwll* **3** SW8845
Trewithian *Cnwll* **3** SW8737
Trewoodloe *Cnwll* **5** SX3271
Trewoofe *Cnwll* **2** SW4425
Trewoon *Cnwll* **2** SW6819
Trewoon *Cnwll* **3** SW9952
Treworgan *Cnwll* **3** SW8349
Treworlas *Cnwll* **3** SW8938
Treworld *Cnwll* **4** SX1190
Treworthal *Cnwll* **3** SW8839
Treyarnon *Cnwll* **4** SW8673
Treyford *W Susx* **14** SU8218
Triangle *W York* **82** SE0422
Trickett's Cross *Dorset* **12** SU0800
Triermain *Cumb* **102** NY5966
Triffleton *Dyfed* **30** SM9724
Trillacott *Cnwll* **5** SX2689
Trimdon *Dur* **96** NZ3634
Trimdon Colliery *Dur* **96** NZ3735
Trimdon Grange *Dur* **96** NZ3635
Trimingham *Norfk* **67** TG2838
Trimley *Suffk* **55** TM2737
Trimley Heath *Suffk* **55** TM2738
Trimley Lower Street *Suffk* **55** TM2636
Trimpley *H & W* **60** SO7978
Trimsaran *Dyfed* **32** SN4504
Trimstone *Devon* **19** SS5043
Trinafour *Tays* **132** NN7264
Trinant *Gwent* **33** ST2099
Tring *Herts* **38** SP9211
Tring Wharf *Herts* **38** SP9212
Tringford *Herts* **38** SP9113
Trinity *Jersey* **152** JS1614
Trinity *Tays* **134** NO6061
Trinity Gask *Tays* **125** NN9718
Triscombe *Somset* **20** SS9237
Triscombe *Somset* **20** ST1535
Trislaig *Highld* **130** NN0874
Trispen *Cnwll* **3** SW8450
Tritlington *Nthumb* **103** NZ2092
Troan *Cnwll* **4** SW8957
Trochry *Tays* **125** NN9740
Troedrhiwfuwch *M Glam* **33** SO1204
Troedyraur *Dyfed* **42** SN3245
Troedyrhiw *M Glam* **33** SO0702
Trofarth *Clwyd* **69** SH8571
Trois Bois *Jersey* **152** JS1212
Troon *Cnwll* **2** SW6638
Troon *Strath* **106** NS3230
Trossachs Hotel *Cent* **124** NN5107
Troston *Suffk* **54** TL8972
Troswell *Cnwll* **5** SX2592
Trots Hill *H & W* **47** SO8855
Trottiscliffe *Kent* **27** TQ6460
Trotton *W Susx* **14** SU8322
Trough Gate *Lancs* **81** SD8821
Troughend *Nthumb* **102** NY8692
Troutbeck *Cumb* **93** NY3825
Troutbeck *Cumb* **87** NY4002
Troutbeck Bridge *Cumb* **87** NY4000
Troway *Derbys* **74** SK3879
Trowbridge *Wilts* **22** ST8558
Trowell *Notts* **62** SK4839
Trowle Common *Wilts* **22** ST8458
Trowse Newton *Norfk* **67** TG2406
Troy *W York* **82** SE2439
Trudoxhill *Somset* **22** ST7443
Trull *Somset* **20** ST2122
Trumfleet *S York* **83** SE6011
Trumpan *Highld* **136** NG2261
Trumpet *H & W* **47** SO6539
Trumpington *Cambs* **53** TL4454
Trumpsgreen *Surrey* **25** SU9967
Trunch *Norfk* **67** TG2834
Trunnah *Lancs* **80** SD3442
Truro *Cnwll* **3** SW8244
Truscott *Cnwll* **5** SX2985
Trusham *Devon* **8** SX8582
Trusley *Derbys* **73** SK2535
Trysull *Staffs* **60** SO8594
Tubney *Oxon* **36** SU4399
Tuckenhay *Devon* **7** SX8156
Tuckhill *Shrops* **60** SO7888
Tuckingmill *Cnwll* **2** SW6540
Tuckingmill *Wilts* **22** ST9329
Tuckton *Dorset* **12** SZ1492
Tucoyse *Cnwll* **3** SW9645
Tuddenham *Suffk* **53** TL7371
Tuddenham *Suffk* **55** TM1948
Tudeley *Kent* **16** TQ6245
Tudhoe *Dur* **96** NZ2535
Tudweiloig *Gwynd* **56** SH2436
Tuesley *Surrey* **25** SU9642
Tuffley *Gloucs* **35** SO8314
Tufton *Dyfed* **30** SN0428
Tufton *Hants* **24** SU4546
Tugby *Leics* **63** SK7601
Tugford *Shrops* **59** SO5587
Tughall *Nthumb* **111** NU2126
Tullibody *Cent* **116** NS8595
Tullich *Highld* **140** NH6328
Tullich *Highld* **147** NH8576
Tullich *Strath* **123** NN0815
Tulliemet *Tays* **125** NO0052
Tulloch *Cent* **124** NN5120
Tulloch *Gramp* **143** NJ8031
Tulloch Station *Highld* **131** NN3580
Tullochgorm *Strath* **114** NR9695
Tullybeagles Lodge *Tays* **125** NO0136
Tullynessle *Gramp* **142** NJ5519
Tumble *Dyfed* **32** SN5411
Tumbler's Green *Essex* **40** TL8025
Tumby *Lincs* **76** TF2359
Tumby Woodside *Lincs* **77** TF2757
Tummel Bridge *Tays* **132** NN7659
Tunbridge Wells *Kent* **16** TQ5839
Tundergarth *D & G* **101** NY1780
Tungate *Norfk* **67** TG2629
Tunstall *Humb* **85** TA3031
Tunstall *Kent* **28** TQ8961
Tunstall *Lancs* **87** SD6073
Tunstall *N York* **89** SE2196
Tunstall *Norfk* **67** TG4107
Tunstall *Staffs* **72** SJ7727
Tunstall *Staffs* **72** SJ8651
Tunstall *Suffk* **55** TM3655
Tunstall *T & W* **96** NZ3953
Tunstead *Derbys* **74** SK1074
Tunstead *Norfk* **67** TG3022
Tunstead Milton *Derbys* **79** SK0180
Tunworth *Hants* **24** SU6748
Tupsley *H & W* **46** SO5340
Tur Langton *Leics* **50** SP7194
Turgis Green *Hants* **24** SU6959
Turkdean *Gloucs* **36** SP1017
Turleigh *Wilts* **22** ST8060
Turleygreen *Shrops* **60** SO7685
Turn *Lancs* **81** SD8118
Turnastone *H & W* **46** SO3536
Turnberry *Strath* **106** NS2005
Turnchapel *Devon* **6** SX4953
Turnditch *Derbys* **73** SK2946
Turner Green *Lancs* **81** SD6030
Turner's Green *E Susx* **16** TQ6319
Turner's Green *Warwks* **48** SP1969
Turner's Hill *W Susx* **15** TQ3435
Turners Puddle *Dorset* **11** SY8393
Turnworth *Dorset* **11** ST8207
Turriff *Gramp* **142** NJ7250
Turton Bottoms *Gt Man* **81** SD7315
Turvey *Beds* **38** SP9452
Turville *Bucks* **37** SU7691
Turville Heath *Bucks* **37** SU7490
Turweston *Bucks* **49** SP6037
Tushielaw Inn *Border* **109** NT3017
Tushingham cum Grindley *Ches* **71** SJ5246
Tutbury *Staffs* **73** SK2128
Tutnall *H & W* **60** SO9970
Tutshill *Gloucs* **34** ST5494
Tuttington *Norfk* **67** TG2227
Tutwell *Cnwll* **5** SX3875
Tuxford *Notts* **75** SK7471
Twatt *Ork* **155** HY2724
Twatt *Shet* **155** HU3253
Twechar *Strath* **116** NS6975
Tweedmouth *Nthumb* **119** NT9952
Tweedsmuir *Border* **108** NT1024
Twelve Oaks *E Susx* **16** TQ6820
Twelveheads *Cnwll* **3** SW7542
Twemlow Green *Ches* **79** SJ7868
Twenty *Lincs* **64** TF1520
Twerton *Avon* **22** ST7264
Twickenham *Gt Lon* **26** TQ1673
Twigworth *Gloucs* **35** SO8422
Twineham *W Susx* **15** TQ2519
Twineham Green *W Susx* **15** TQ2520
Twinhoe *Avon* **22** ST7559
Twinstead *Essex* **54** TL8636
Twiss Green *Ches* **79** SJ6595
Twitchen *Devon* **19** SS7930
Twitchen *Shrops* **46** SO3779
Twitham *Kent* **29** TR2656
Two Bridges *Devon* **6** SX6174
Two Dales *Derbys* **74** SK2763
Two Gates *Staffs* **61** SK2101
Two Mile Oak Cross *Devon* **7** SX8468
Two Pots *Devon* **19** SS5344
Two Waters *Herts* **38** TL0505
Twycross *Leics* **62** SK3304
Twyford *Berks* **37** SU7976
Twyford *Bucks* **49** SP6626
Twyford *Derbys* **62** SK3228
Twyford *Hants* **13** SU4824
Twyford *Leics* **63** SK7210
Twyford *Lincs* **63** SK9323
Twyford *Norfk* **66** TG0123
Twyford Common *H & W* **46** SO5135
Twyn-carno *M Glam* **33** SO1108
Twyn-y-Sheriff *Gwent* **34** SO4005
Twyn-yr-Odyn *S Glam* **33** ST1173
Twynholm *D & G* **99** NX6654
Twyning *Gloucs* **47** SO8936
Twyning Green *Gloucs* **47** SO9036
Twynllanan *Dyfed* **44** SN7524
Twywell *Nhants* **51** SP9578
Ty'n-dwr *Clwyd* **70** SJ2341
Ty'n-y-coedcae *M Glam* **33** ST1988
Ty'n-y-groes *Gwynd* **69** SH7771
Ty-croes *Dyfed* **32** SN6010
Ty-nant *Clwyd* **70** SH9944
Ty-nant *Gwynd* **58** SH9026
Tyberton *H & W* **46** SO3839
Tyburn *W Mids* **61** SP1391
Tycrwyn *Powys* **58** SJ1018
Tydd Gote *Lincs* **65** TF4518
Tydd St. Giles *Cambs* **65** TF4216
Tydd St. Mary *Lincs* **65** TF4418
Tye *Hants* **13** SU7302
Tye Green *Essex* **39** TL5424
Tye Green *Essex* **53** TL5935
Tye Green *Essex* **40** TL7821
Tyersal *W York* **82** SE1932
Tyldesley *Gt Man* **79** SD6802
Tyler Hill *Kent* **29** TR1461
Tyler's Green *Essex* **39** TL5005
Tylers Green *Bucks* **26** SU9093
Tylers Green *Surrey* **27** TQ3552
Tylorstown *M Glam* **33** ST0095
Tylwch *Powys* **58** SN9780
Tyn-y-nant *M Glam* **33** ST0685
Tyndrum *Cent* **123** NN3230
Tyneham *Dorset* **11** SY8880
Tynemouth *T & W* **103** NZ3669
Tynewydd *M Glam* **33** SS9398
Tyninghame *Loth* **118** NT6179
Tynron *D & G* **100** NX8093
Tynygongl *Gwynd* **68** SH5082
Tynygraig *Dyfed* **43** SN6969
Tyringham *Bucks* **38** SP8547
Tyseley *W Mids* **61** SP1184
Tythegston *M Glam* **33** SS8578
Tytherington *Avon* **35** ST6688
Tytherington *Ches* **79** SJ9175
Tytherington *Somset* **22** ST7644
Tytherington *Wilts* **22** ST9141

Tytherleigh Walgherton

Tytherleigh *Devon* 10 ST3103
Tywardreath *Cnwll* 3 SX0854
Tywardreath Highway *Cnwll* 3 SX0755
Tywyn *Gwynd* 57 SH5800
Tywyn *Gwynd* 69 SH7878

U

Ubbeston Green *Suffk* 55 TM3271
Ubley *Avon* 21 ST5258
Uckerby *N York* 89 NZ2402
Uckfield *E Susx* 16 TQ4721
Uckinghall *H & W* 47 SO8637
Uckington *Gloucs* 47 SO9124
Uckington *Shrops* 59 SJ5709
Uddingston *Strath* 116 NS6960
Uddington *Strath* 108 NS8633
Udimore *E Susx* 17 TQ8719
Udny Green *Gramp* 143 NJ8726
Udny Station *Gramp* 143 NJ9024
Uffcott *Wilts* 36 SU1277
Uffculme *Devon* 9 ST0612
Uffington *Oxon* 36 SU3089
Uffington *Shrops* 59 SJ5313
Ufford *Cambs* 64 TF0903
Ufford *Suffk* 55 TM2952
Ufton *Warwks* 48 SP3762
Ufton Nervet *Berks* 24 SU6367
Ugadale *Strath* 105 NR7828
Ugborough *Devon* 7 SX6755
Uggeshall *Suffk* 55 TM4480
Ugglebarnby *N York* 90 NZ8707
Ughill *Derbys* 74 SK2590
Ugley *Essex* 39 TL5228
Ugley Green *Essex* 39 TL5227
Ugthorpe *N York* 90 NZ7911
Uig *Highld* 136 NG1952
Uig *Highld* 136 NG3963
Uig *Strath* 120 NM1654
Uig *W Isls* 154 NB0533
Uigshader *Highld* 136 NG4346
Uisken *Strath* 121 NM3919
Ulbster *Highld* 151 ND3241
Ulcat Row *Cumb* 93 NY4022
Ulceby *Humb* 85 TA1014
Ulceby *Lincs* 77 TF4272
Ulceby Skitter *Humb* 85 TA1215
Ulcombe *Kent* 28 TQ8448
Uldale *Cumb* 93 NY2437
Uley *Gloucs* 35 ST7898
Ulgham *Nthumb* 103 NZ2392
Ullapool *Highld* 145 NH1294
Ullceby Cross *Lincs* 77 TF4173
Ullenhall *Warwks* 48 SP1267
Ullenwood *Gloucs* 35 SO9416
Ulleskelf *N York* 83 SE5239
Ullesthorpe *Leics* 50 SP5087
Ulley *S York* 75 SK4687
Ullingswick *H & W* 46 SO5949
Ullinish Lodge Hotel *Highld* 136 NG3237
Ullock *Cumb* 92 NY0724
Ulpha *Cumb* 86 SD1993
Ulpha *Cumb* 87 SD4581
Ulrome *Humb* 85 TA1656
Ulsta *Shet* 155 HU4680
Ulting Wick *Essex* 40 TL8009
Ulverley Green *W Mids* 61 SP1382
Ulverston *Cumb* 86 SD2878
Ulwell *Dorset* 12 SZ0280
Umachan *Highld* 137 NG6050
Umberleigh *Devon* 19 SS6023
Unapool *Highld* 148 NC2333
Under Burnmouth *D & G* 101 NY4783
Under River *Kent* 27 TQ5552
Underbarrow *Cumb* 87 SD4692
Undercliffe *W York* 82 SE1834
Underdale *Shrops* 59 SJ5013
Underley Hall *Cumb* 87 SD6179
Underling Green *Kent* 28 TQ7546
Underwood *Notts* 75 SK4750
Undley *Suffk* 53 TL6981
Undy *Gwent* 34 ST4386
Union Mills *IOM* 153 SC3577
Union Street *E Susx* 16 TQ7031
Unstone *Derbys* 74 SK3777
Unstone Green *Derbys* 74 SK3776
Unsworth *Gt Man* 79 SD8207
Unthank *Cumb* 93 NY3948
Unthank *Cumb* 93 NY4536
Unthank *Cumb* 94 NY6040
Unthank *Derbys* 74 SK3075
Unthank *Nthumb* 111 NT9848
Unthank End *Cumb* 93 NY4535
Up Cerne *Dorset* 11 ST6502
Up Exe *Devon* 9 SS9402
Up Holland *Lancs* 78 SD5205
Up Marden *W Susx* 14 SU7913
Up Mudford *Somset* 10 ST5718
Up Nately *Hants* 24 SU6951
Up Somborne *Hants* 23 SU3932
Up Sydling *Dorset* 10 ST6201
Upavon *Wilts* 23 SU1354
Upchurch *Kent* 28 TQ8467
Upcott *Devon* 19 SS5838
Upcott *Devon* 19 SS7529
Upcott *H & W* 46 SO3250
Upcott *Somset* 20 SS9025
Updown Hill *Surrey* 25 SU9363
Upend *Cambs* 53 TL7058
Upgate *Norfk* 66 TG1318
Upgate Street *Norfk* 66 TM0992
Upgate Street *Norfk* 67 TM2891
Uphall *Dorset* 10 ST5502
Uphall *Loth* 117 NT0671
Upham *Devon* 19 SS8808
Upham *Hants* 13 SU5320
Uphampton *H & W* 46 SO3963
Uphampton *H & W* 47 SO8364
Uphill *Avon* 21 ST3158
Uplawmoor *Strath* 115 NS4355
Upleadon *Gloucs* 47 SO7527
Upleatham *Cleve* 97 NZ6319
Uplees *Kent* 28 TR0064
Uploders *Dorset* 10 SY5093
Uplowman *Devon* 9 ST0115
Uplyme *Devon* 10 SY3293
Upminster *Gt Lon* 27 TQ5686
Upottery *Devon* 9 ST2007
Uppaton *Devon* 5 SX4380
Upper Affcot *Shrops* 59 SO4486
Upper Ardchronie *Highld* 146 NH6188
Upper Arley *H & W* 60 SO7680
Upper Arncott *Oxon* 37 SP6117
Upper Astrop *Nhants* 49 SP5137
Upper Basildon *Berks* 37 SU5976
Upper Batley *W York* 82 SE2325
Upper Beeding *W Susx* 15 TQ1910
Upper Benefield *Nhants* 51 SP9789
Upper Bentley *H & W* 47 SO9966
Upper Bighouse *Highld* 150 NC8856
Upper Birchwood *Derbys* 75 SK4355
Upper Boat *M Glam* 33 ST1086
Upper Boddington *Nhants* 49 SP4852
Upper Borth *Dyfed* 43 SN6088
Upper Brailes *Warwks* 48 SP3039
Upper Breakish *Highld* 129 NG6823
Upper Breinton *H & W* 46 SO4640
Upper Broadheath *H & W* 47 SO8056
Upper Broughton *Notts* 63 SK6826
Upper Bucklebury *Berks* 24 SU5468
Upper Burgate *Hants* 12 SU1516
Upper Bush *Kent* 28 TQ6966
Upper Cairn *D & G* 107 NS6912
Upper Caldecote *Beds* 52 TL1645
Upper Canada *Avon* 21 ST3658
Upper Canterton *Hants* 12 SU2612
Upper Catesby *Nhants* 49 SP5259
Upper Catshill *H & W* 60 SO9674
Upper Chapel *Powys* 45 SO0040
Upper Cheddon *Somset* 20 ST2328
Upper Chicksgrove *Wilts* 22 ST9529
Upper Chute *Wilts* 23 SU2953
Upper Clapton *Gt Lon* 27 TQ3487
Upper Clatford *Hants* 23 SU3543
Upper Clynnog *Gwynd* 56 SH4646
Upper Coberley *Gloucs* 35 SO9816
Upper Cokeham *W Susx* 15 TQ1605
Upper Cotton *Staffs* 73 SK0547
Upper Cound *Shrops* 59 SJ5505
Upper Cudworth *S York* 83 SE3909
Upper Cumberworth *W York* 82 SE2008
Upper Cwmtwrch *Powys* 32 SN7511
Upper Dallachy *Gramp* 141 NJ3662
Upper Deal *Kent* 29 TR3651
Upper Dean *Beds* 51 TL0467
Upper Denby *W York* 82 SE2207
Upper Denton *Cumb* 102 NY6165
Upper Dicker *E Susx* 16 TQ5509
Upper Dinchope *Shrops* 59 SO4583
Upper Dovercourt *Essex* 41 TM2330
Upper Drumbane *Cent* 124 NN6606
Upper Dunsforth *N York* 89 SE4463
Upper Eashing *Surrey* 25 SU9543
Upper Egleton *H & W* 47 SO6344
Upper Elkstone *Staffs* 74 SK0558
Upper Ellastone *Staffs* 73 SK1043
Upper End *Derbys* 74 SK0875
Upper Enham *Hants* 23 SU3650
Upper Ethrie *Highld* 140 NH7662
Upper Farmcote *Shrops* 60 SO7791
Upper Farringdon *Hants* 24 SU7135
Upper Framilode *Gloucs* 35 SO7510
Upper Froyle *Hants* 24 SU7543
Upper Godney *Somset* 21 ST4842
Upper Gravenhurst *Beds* 38 TL1136
Upper Green *Berks* 23 SU3763
Upper Green *Essex* 53 TL5935
Upper Green *Gwent* 34 SO3818
Upper Green *Suffk* 53 TL7464
Upper Grove Common *H & W* 46 SO5526
Upper Hackney *Derbys* 74 SK2861
Upper Hale *Surrey* 25 SU8349
Upper Halliford *Surrey* 26 TQ0968
Upper Halling *Kent* 28 TQ6964
Upper Hambleton *Leics* 63 SK9007
Upper Harbledown *Kent* 29 TR1158
Upper Hardres Court *Kent* 29 TR1550
Upper Hardwick *H & W* 46 SO4057
Upper Hartfield *E Susx* 16 TQ4634
Upper Hartshay *Derbys* 74 SK3850
Upper Hatherley *Gloucs* 35 SO9220
Upper Hatton *Staffs* 72 SJ8237
Upper Haugh *S York* 74 SK4297
Upper Hayton *Shrops* 59 SO5181
Upper Heaton *W York* 82 SE1719
Upper Helmsley *N York* 83 SE6956
Upper Hergest *H & W* 46 SO2654
Upper Heyford *Nhants* 49 SP6659
Upper Heyford *Oxon* 49 SP4925
Upper Hill *H & W* 46 SO4753
Upper Hockenden *Kent* 27 TQ5069
Upper Hopton *W York* 82 SE1918
Upper Howsell *H & W* 47 SO7848
Upper Hulme *Staffs* 73 SK0160
Upper Ifold *Surrey* 14 TQ0033
Upper Inglesham *Wilts* 36 SU2096
Upper Keith *Loth* 118 NT4562
Upper Kilcott *Avon* 35 ST7988
Upper Killay *W Glam* 32 SS5892
Upper Kinchrackine *Strath* 123 NN1627
Upper Lambourn *Berks* 36 SU3080
Upper Landywood *Staffs* 60 SJ9805
Upper Langford *Avon* 21 ST4659
Upper Langwith *Derbys* 75 SK5169
Upper Largo *Fife* 127 NO4203
Upper Leigh *Staffs* 73 SK0136
Upper Ley *Gloucs* 35 SO7217
Upper Littleton *Avon* 21 ST5564
Upper Lochton *Gramp* 135 NO6997
Upper Longdon *Staffs* 61 SK0614
Upper Ludstone *Shrops* 60 SO8095
Upper Lybster *Highld* 151 ND2537
Upper Lydbrook *Gloucs* 34 SO6015
Upper Lyde *H & W* 46 SO4944
Upper Lye *H & W* 46 SO3965
Upper Maes-coed *H & W* 46 SO3334
Upper Midhope *Derbys* 74 SK2199
Upper Milton *H & W* 60 SO8172
Upper Minety *Wilts* 35 SU0091
Upper Moor *H & W* 47 SO9747
Upper Moor Side *W York* 82 SE2430
Upper Mulben *Gramp* 141 NJ3551
Upper Nesbet *Border* 110 NT6727
Upper Netchwood *Shrops* 59 SO6092
Upper Nobut *Staffs* 73 SK0335
Upper Norwood *W Susx* 14 SU9317
Upper Padley *Derbys* 74 SK2478
Upper Pennington *Hants* 12 SZ3095
Upper Pickwick *Wilts* 35 ST8571
Upper Pollicott *Bucks* 37 SP7013
Upper Pond Street *Essex* 39 TL4636
Upper Poppleton *N York* 83 SE5553
Upper Pulley *Shrops* 59 SJ4808
Upper Quinton *Warwks* 48 SP1846
Upper Ratley *Hants* 23 SU3223
Upper Rochford *H & W* 47 SO6367
Upper Ruscoe *D & G* 99 NX5661
Upper Sapey *H & W* 47 SO6863
Upper Seagry *Wilts* 35 ST9480
Upper Shelton *Beds* 38 SP9843
Upper Sheringham *Norfk* 66 TG1441
Upper Shuckburgh *Warwks* 49 SP5061
Upper Slaughter *Gloucs* 48 SP1523
Upper Soudley *Gloucs* 35 SO6510
Upper Spond *H & W* 46 SO3152
Upper Standen *Kent* 29 TR2139
Upper Staploe *Beds* 52 TL1459
Upper Stepford *D & G* 100 NX8681
Upper Stoke *Norfk* 67 TG2502
Upper Stondon *Beds* 38 TL1435
Upper Stowe *Nhants* 49 SP6456
Upper Street *Hants* 12 SU1518
Upper Street *Norfk* 67 TG3217
Upper Street *Norfk* 67 TG3616
Upper Street *Norfk* 54 TM1779
Upper Street *Suffk* 53 TL7851
Upper Street *Suffk* 54 TM1050
Upper Street *Suffk* 54 TM1434
Upper Sundon *Beds* 38 TL0428
Upper Swell *Gloucs* 48 SP1726
Upper Tankersley *S York* 74 SK3499
Upper Tasburgh *Norfk* 67 TM2095
Upper Tean *Staffs* 73 SK0139
Upper Threapwood *Ches* 71 SJ4345
Upper Town *Avon* 21 ST5265
Upper Town *Derbys* 73 SK2351
Upper Town *Derbys* 74 SK2361
Upper Town *Dur* 95 NZ0737
Upper Town *H & W* 46 SO5848
Upper Town *Suffk* 54 TL9267
Upper Tysoe *Warwks* 48 SP3343
Upper Ufford *Suffk* 55 TM2952
Upper Upham *Wilts* 36 SU2277
Upper Upnor *Kent* 28 TQ7570
Upper Victoria *Tays* 127 NO5336
Upper Vobster *Somset* 22 ST7049
Upper Wardington *Oxon* 49 SP4945
Upper Weald *Bucks* 38 SP8037
Upper Weedon *Nhants* 49 SP6258
Upper Wellingham *E Susx* 16 TQ4313
Upper Weston *Avon* 22 ST7267
Upper Weybread *Suffk* 55 TM2379
Upper Wick *H & W* 47 SO8252
Upper Wield *Hants* 24 SU6238
Upper Winchendon *Bucks* 37 SP7414
Upper Witton *W Mids* 61 SP0891
Upper Woodford *Wilts* 23 SU1237
Upper Wootton *Hants* 24 SU5754
Upper Wraxall *Wilts* 35 ST8074
Upper Wyche *H & W* 47 SO7643
Upperby *Cumb* 93 NY4153
Upperglen *Highld* 136 NG3151
Uppermill *Gt Man* 82 SD9905
Upperthong *W York* 82 SE1208
Upperthorpe *Derbys* 75 SK4580
Upperton *W Susx* 14 SU9522
Uppertown *Derbys* 74 SK3264
Uppertown *Highld* 151 ND3576
Upperup *Gloucs* 36 SU0496
Upperwood *Derbys* 73 SK2956
Uppincott *Devon* 9 SS9006
Uppingham *Leics* 51 SP8699
Uppington *Dorset* 12 SU0206
Uppington *Shrops* 59 SJ5909
Upsall *N York* 89 SE4586
Upsettlington *Border* 110 NT8846
Upshire *Essex* 27 TL4101
Upstreet *Kent* 29 TR2263
Upthorpe *Suffk* 54 TL9772
Upton *Berks* 26 SU9779
Upton *Bucks* 37 SP7711
Upton *Cambs* 64 TF1000
Upton *Cambs* 52 TL1778
Upton *Ches* 71 SJ4069
Upton *Ches* 78 SJ5087
Upton *Cnwll* 18 SS2004
Upton *Cnwll* 5 SX2772
Upton *Cumb* 93 NY3139
Upton *Devon* 9 ST0902
Upton *Devon* 7 SX7043
Upton *Dorset* 11 SY7483
Upton *Dorset* 11 SY9893
Upton *Dyfed* 30 SN0204
Upton *Hants* 23 SU3555
Upton *Hants* 12 SU3716
Upton *Humb* 85 TA1454
Upton *Leics* 61 SP3699
Upton *Lincs* 76 SK8686
Upton *Mersyd* 78 SJ2788
Upton *Nhants* 49 SP7159
Upton *Norfk* 67 TG3912
Upton *Notts* 75 SK7354
Upton *Notts* 75 SK7476
Upton *Oxon* 36 SP2312
Upton *Oxon* 37 SU5187
Upton *Somset* 20 SS9928
Upton *Somset* 21 ST4526
Upton *W York* 83 SE4713
Upton *Warwks* 48 SP1257
Upton Cheyney *Avon* 35 ST6970
Upton Cressett *Shrops* 59 SO6592
Upton Crews *H & W* 47 SO6527
Upton Cross *Cnwll* 5 SX2872
Upton End *Beds* 38 TL1234
Upton Grey *Hants* 24 SU6948
Upton Heath *Ches* 71 SJ4169
Upton Hellions *Devon* 8 SS8403
Upton Lovell *Wilts* 22 ST9440
Upton Magna *Shrops* 59 SJ5512
Upton Noble *Somset* 22 ST7139
Upton Pyne *Devon* 9 SX9198
Upton Scudamore *Wilts* 22 ST8647
Upton Snodsbury *H & W* 47 SO9454
Upton St. Leonards *Gloucs* 35 SO8615
Upton Towans *Cnwll* 2 SW5740
Upton upon Severn *H & W* 47 SO8540
Upton Warren *H & W* 47 SO9267
Upwaltham *W Susx* 14 SU9413
Upware *Cambs* 53 TL5470
Upwell *Norfk* 65 TF4902
Upwey *Dorset* 11 SY6685
Upwick Green *Herts* 39 TL4524
Upwood *Cambs* 52 TL2582
Urchfont *Wilts* 23 SU0357
Urdimarsh *H & W* 46 SO5248
Ure Bank *N York* 89 SE3172
Urlay Nook *Cleve* 89 NZ4014
Urmston *Gt Man* 79 SJ7694
Urquhart *Gramp* 141 NJ2862
Urra *N York* 90 NZ5601
Urray *Highld* 139 NH5052
Usan *Tays* 127 NO7254
Ushaw Moor *Dur* 96 NZ2242
Usk *Gwent* 34 SO3700
Usselby *Lincs* 76 TF0993
Usworth *T & W* 96 NZ3057
Utley *W York* 82 SE0542
Uton *Devon* 8 SX8298
Utterby *Lincs* 77 TF3093
Uttoxeter *Staffs* 73 SK0933
Uwchmynydd *Gwynd* 56 SH1525
Uxbridge *Gt Lon* 26 TQ0584
Uyeasound *Shet* 155 HP5901
Uzmaston *Dyfed* 30 SM9714

V

Vale *Guern* 152 GN5312
Valley *Gwynd* 68 SH2979
Valley End *Surrey* 25 SU9564
Valley Truckle *Cnwll* 4 SX0982
Valtos *Highld* 137 NG5163
Valtos *W Isls* 154 NB0936
Van *M Glam* 33 ST1686
Vange *Essex* 40 TQ7186
Varteg *Gwent* 34 SO2606
Vatsetter *Shet* 155 HU5389
Vatten *Highld* 136 NG2843
Vaynor *M Glam* 33 SO0410
Velindre *Powys* 45 SO1836
Vellow *Somset* 20 ST0938
Velly *Devon* 18 SS2924
Venn *Devon* 7 SX8549
Venn Ottery *Devon* 9 SY0891
Venngreen *Devon* 18 SS3711
Vennington *Shrops* 59 SJ3309
Venny Tedburn *Devon* 8 SX8297
Venterdon *Cnwll* 5 SX3675
Ventnor *IOW* 13 SZ5677
Venton *Devon* 6 SX5956
Vernham Dean *Hants* 23 SU3356
Vernham Street *Hants* 23 SU3457
Vernolds Common *Shrops* 59 SO4780
Verwood *Dorset* 12 SU0809
Veryan *Cnwll* 3 SW9139
Veryan Green *Cnwll* 3 SW9140
Vickerstown *Cumb* 86 SD1868
Victoria *Cnwll* 4 SW9861
Victoria *Gwent* 33 SO1707
Victoria *S York* 82 SE1705
Vidlin *Shet* 155 HU4765
Viewfield *Gramp* 141 NJ2864
Viewpark *Strath* 116 NS7061
Vigo *Kent* 27 TQ6361
Ville la Bas *Jersey* 152 JS0515
Villiaze *Guern* 152 GN4906
Vine's Cross *E Susx* 16 TQ5917
Vinehall Street *E Susx* 17 TQ7520
Virginia Water *Surrey* 25 TQ0067
Virginstow *Devon* 5 SX3792
Virley *Essex* 40 TL9414
Vobster *Somset* 22 ST7048
Voe *Shet* 155 HU4062
Vowchurch *H & W* 46 SO3636
Vulcan Village *Ches* 78 SJ5894

W

Wackerfield *Dur* 96 NZ1522
Wacton *Norfk* 66 TM1791
Wadborough *H & W* 47 SO9047
Waddesdon *Bucks* 37 SP7416
Waddeton *Devon* 7 SX8756
Waddicar *Mersyd* 78 SJ3999
Waddingham *Lincs* 76 SK9896
Waddington *Lancs* 81 SD7343
Waddington *Lincs* 76 SK9764
Waddon *Dorset* 10 SY6285
Wadebridge *Cnwll* 4 SW9972
Wadeford *Somset* 10 ST3110
Wadenhoe *Nhants* 51 TL0183
Wadesmill *Herts* 39 TL3617
Wadhurst *E Susx* 16 TQ6431
Wadshelf *Derbys* 74 SK3170
Wadswick *Wilts* 22 ST8467
Wadworth *S York* 75 SK5696
Waen *Clwyd* 70 SH9962
Waen *Clwyd* 70 SJ1065
Waen *Powys* 58 SJ2319
Waen Fach *Powys* 58 SJ2017
Waen-pentir *Gwynd* 69 SH5766
Waen-wen *Gwynd* 69 SH5768
Wagbeach *Shrops* 59 SJ3602
Wainfelin *Gwent* 34 SO2701
Wainfleet All Saints *Lincs* 77 TF4959
Wainfleet Bank *Lincs* 77 TF4759
Wainford *Norfk* 55 TM3490
Wainhouse Corner *Cnwll* 4 SX1895
Wains Hill *Avon* 34 ST3970
Wainscott *Kent* 28 TQ7470
Wainstalls *W York* 82 SE0428
Waitby *Cumb* 88 NY7508
Waithe *Lincs* 77 TA2800
Wake Green *W Mids* 61 SP0982
Wakefield *W York* 83 SE3320
Wakerley *Nhants* 51 SP9599
Wakes Colne *Essex* 40 TL8928
Wal-wen *Clwyd* 70 SJ2076
Walberswick *Suffk* 55 TM4974
Walberton *W Susx* 14 SU9705
Walbottle *T & W* 103 NZ1666
Walbutt *D & G* 99 NX7468
Walby *Cumb* 101 NY4460
Walcombe *Somset* 21 ST5546
Walcot *Humb* 84 SE8720
Walcot *Lincs* 64 TF0635
Walcot *Lincs* 76 TF1356
Walcot *Shrops* 59 SJ5912
Walcot *Shrops* 59 SO3485
Walcot *Warwks* 48 SP1358
Walcot *Wilts* 36 SU1684
Walcot Green *Norfk* 54 TM1280
Walcote *Leics* 50 SP5683
Walcott *Norfk* 67 TG3532
Walden *N York* 88 SE0082
Walden Head *N York* 88 SD9880
Walden Stubbs *N York* 83 SE5516
Walderslade *Kent* 28 TQ7663
Walderton *W Susx* 14 SU7910
Walditch *Dorset* 10 SY4892
Waldley *Derbys* 73 SK1236
Waldridge *Dur* 96 NZ2549
Waldringfield *Suffk* 55 TM2845
Waldron *E Susx* 16 TQ5419
Wales *S York* 75 SK4882
Wales *Somset* 21 ST5824
Walesby *Lincs* 76 TF1392
Walesby *Notts* 75 SK6870
Walford *H & W* 46 SO3872
Walford *H & W* 34 SO5820
Walford *Shrops* 59 SJ4320
Walford *Staffs* 72 SJ8133
Walford Heath *Shrops* 59 SJ4419
Walgherton *Ches* 72 SJ6948

Walgrave West Bradenham

Walgrave *Nhants*	**51**	SP8071
Walhampton *Hants*	**12**	SZ3396
Walk Mill *Lancs*	**81**	SD8729
Walkden *Gt Man*	**79**	SD7302
Walker *T & W*	**103**	NZ2864
Walker Fold *Lancs*	**81**	SD6741
Walker's Green *H & W*	**46**	SO5247
Walker's Heath *W Mids*	**61**	SP0578
Walkerburn *Border*	**109**	NT3637
Walkeringham *Notts*	**75**	SK7792
Walkerith *Notts*	**75**	SK7892
Walkern *Herts*	**39**	TL2826
Walkerton *Fife*	**126**	NO2301
Walkhampton *Devon*	**6**	SX5369
Walkington *Humb*	**84**	SE9936
Walkley *S York*	**74**	SK3388
Walkwood *H & W*	**48**	SP0364
Wall *Border*	**109**	NT4622
Wall *Cnwll*	**2**	SW6036
Wall *Nthumb*	**102**	NY9168
Wall *Staffs*	**61**	SK1006
Wall End *Cumb*	**86**	SD2383
Wall End *H & W*	**46**	SO4457
Wall Heath *W Mids*	**60**	SO8889
Wall under Haywood *Shrops*	**59**	SO5092
Wallacetown *Strath*	**106**	NS2703
Wallacetown *Strath*	**106**	NS3422
Wallands Park *E Susx*	**15**	TQ4010
Wallasey *Mersyd*	**78**	SJ2992
Wallend *Kent*	**28**	TQ8775
Waller's Green *H & W*	**47**	SO6739
Wallfield *Fife*	**126**	NO1909
Wallhead *Cumb*	**101**	NY4660
Wallingford *Oxon*	**37**	SU6089
Wallington *Gt Lon*	**27**	TQ2864
Wallington *Hants*	**13**	SU5806
Wallington *Herts*	**39**	TL2933
Wallington Heath *W Mids*	**60**	SJ9903
Wallis *Dyfed*	**30**	SN0125
Wallisdown *Dorset*	**12**	SZ0694
Walliswood *W Susx*	**14**	TQ1138
Walls *Shet*	**155**	HU2449
Wallsend *T & W*	**103**	NZ2966
Wallthwaite *Cumb*	**93**	NY3526
Wallyford *Loth*	**118**	NT3671
Walmer *Kent*	**29**	TR3750
Walmer Bridge *Lancs*	**80**	SD4724
Walmersley *Gt Man*	**81**	SD8013
Walmestone *Kent*	**29**	TR2559
Walmley *W Mids*	**61**	SP1393
Walmley Ash *W Mids*	**61**	SP1492
Walmsgate *Lincs*	**77**	TF3677
Walpole *Somset*	**20**	ST3042
Walpole *Suffk*	**55**	TM3674
Walpole Cross Keys *Norfk*	**65**	TF5119
Walpole Highway *Norfk*	**65**	TF5114
Walpole St. Andrew *Norfk*	**65**	TF5017
Walpole St. Peter *Norfk*	**65**	TF5016
Walrow *Somset*	**21**	ST3447
Walsall *W Mids*	**60**	SP0198
Walsall Wood *W Mids*	**61**	SK0403
Walsden *W York*	**81**	SD9321
Walsgrave on Sowe *W Mids*	**61**	SP3881
Walshall Green *Herts*	**39**	TL4430
Walsham le Willows *Suffk*	**54**	TM0071
Walshaw *Gt Man*	**81**	SD7711
Walshaw *W York*	**82**	SD9731
Walshford *N York*	**83**	SE4153
Walsoken *Norfk*	**65**	TF4710
Walston *Strath*	**117**	NT0545
Walsworth *Herts*	**39**	TL1930
Walter Ash *Bucks*	**37**	SU8398
Walters Green *Kent*	**16**	TQ5140
Walterston *S Glam*	**33**	ST0671
Walterstone *H & W*	**46**	SO3425
Waltham *Humb*	**85**	TA2603
Waltham *Kent*	**29**	TR1048
Waltham Abbey *Essex*	**27**	TL3800
Waltham Chase *Hants*	**13**	SU5614
Waltham Cross *Herts*	**27**	TL3600
Waltham on the Wolds *Leics*	**63**	SK8024
Waltham St. Lawrence *Berks*	**37**	SU8276
Waltham's Cross *Essex*	**40**	TL6930
Walthamstow *Gt Lon*	**27**	TQ3689
Walton *Bucks*	**38**	SP8936
Walton *Cambs*	**64**	TF1702
Walton *Cumb*	**101**	NY5264
Walton *Derbys*	**74**	SK3568
Walton *Leics*	**50**	SP5987
Walton *Powys*	**46**	SO2559
Walton *Shrops*	**59**	SJ5818
Walton *Shrops*	**46**	SO4679
Walton *Somset*	**21**	ST4636
Walton *Staffs*	**72**	SJ8528
Walton *Staffs*	**72**	SJ8932
Walton *Suffk*	**55**	TM2935
Walton *W Susx*	**14**	SU8104
Walton *W York*	**83**	SE3516
Walton *W York*	**83**	SE4447
Walton *Warwks*	**48**	SP2853
Walton Cardiff *Gloucs*	**47**	SO9032
Walton East *Dyfed*	**30**	SN0223
Walton Elm *Dorset*	**11**	ST7717
Walton Grounds *Nhants*	**49**	SP5135
Walton Lower Street *Suffk*	**55**	TM2834
Walton on the Hill *Surrey*	**26**	TQ2255
Walton on the Naze *Essex*	**41**	TM2522
Walton on the Wolds *Leics*	**62**	SK5919
Walton Park *Avon*	**34**	ST4172
Walton West *Dyfed*	**30**	SM8612
Walton-in-Gordano *Avon*	**34**	ST4273
Walton-le-Dale *Lancs*	**81**	SD5628
Walton-on-Thames *Surrey*	**26**	TQ1066
Walton-on-Trent *Derbys*	**73**	SK2118
Walton-on-the-Hill *Staffs*	**72**	SJ9520
Walwen *Clwyd*	**70**	SJ1179
Walwen *Clwyd*	**70**	SJ1771
Walwick *Nthumb*	**102**	NY9070
Walworth *Dur*	**96**	NZ2318
Walworth Gate *Dur*	**96**	NZ2320
Walwyn's Castle *Dyfed*	**30**	SM8711
Wambrook *Somset*	**10**	ST2907
Wamphray *D & G*	**100**	NY1295
Wampool *Cumb*	**93**	NY2454
Wanborough *Surrey*	**25**	SU9348
Wanborough *Wilts*	**36**	SU2082
Wandel *Strath*	**108**	NS9427
Wandon End *Herts*	**38**	TL1322
Wandsworth *Gt Lon*	**27**	TQ2574
Wangford *Suffk*	**55**	TM4679
Wanlip *Leics*	**62**	SK5910
Wanlockhead *D & G*	**108**	NS8712
Wannock *E Susx*	**16**	TQ5703
Wansford *Cambs*	**64**	TL0799
Wansford *Humb*	**84**	TA0656
Wanshurst Green *Kent*	**28**	TQ7645
Wanstead *Gt Lon*	**27**	TQ4088
Wanstrow *Somset*	**22**	ST7141
Wanswell *Gloucs*	**35**	SO6801
Wantage *Oxon*	**36**	SU3988
Wants Green *H & W*	**47**	SO7557
Wapley *Avon*	**35**	ST7179
Wappenbury *Warwks*	**48**	SP3769
Wappenham *Nhants*	**49**	SP6245
Warbister *Ork*	**155**	HY3932
Warbleton *E Susx*	**16**	TQ6018
Warborough *Oxon*	**37**	SU5993
Warboys *Cambs*	**52**	TL3080
Warbreck *Lancs*	**80**	SD3238
Warbstow *Cnwll*	**5**	SX2090
Warburton *Gt Man*	**79**	SJ7089
Warcop *Cumb*	**94**	NY7415
Ward End *W Mids*	**61**	SP1188
Ward Green *Suffk*	**54**	TM0464
Warden *Kent*	**28**	TR0271
Warden *Nthumb*	**102**	NY9166
Warden Law *T & W*	**96**	NZ3649
Warden Street *Beds*	**38**	TL1244
Wardhedges *Beds*	**38**	TL0635
Wardington *Oxon*	**49**	SP4846
Wardle *Ches*	**71**	SJ6156
Wardle *Gt Man*	**81**	SD9116
Wardley *Gt Man*	**79**	SD7602
Wardley *Leics*	**51**	SK8300
Wardlow *Derbys*	**74**	SK1874
Wardsend *Ches*	**79**	SJ9382
Wardy Hill *Cambs*	**53**	TL4782
Ware *Herts*	**39**	TL3514
Ware Street *Kent*	**28**	TQ7956
Wareham *Dorset*	**11**	SY9287
Warehorne *Kent*	**17**	TQ9832
Waren Mill *Nthumb*	**111**	NU1434
Warenford *Nthumb*	**111**	NU1328
Warenton *Nthumb*	**111**	NU1030
Wareside *Herts*	**39**	TL3915
Waresley *Cambs*	**52**	TL2554
Waresley *H & W*	**60**	SO8470
Warfield *Berks*	**25**	SU8872
Warfleet *Devon*	**7**	SX8750
Wargate *Lincs*	**64**	TF2330
Wargrave *Berks*	**37**	SU7978
Warham *H & W*	**46**	SO4838
Warham All Saints *Norfk*	**66**	TF9541
Warham St. Mary *Norfk*	**66**	TF9441
Wark *Nthumb*	**110**	NT8238
Wark *Nthumb*	**102**	NY8577
Warkleigh *Devon*	**19**	SS6422
Warkton *Nhants*	**51**	SP8979
Warkworth *Nhants*	**49**	SP4840
Warkworth *Nthumb*	**111**	NU2406
Warlaby *N York*	**89**	SE3491
Warland *W York*	**82**	SD9420
Warleggan *Cnwll*	**4**	SX1569
Warleigh *Avon*	**22**	ST7964
Warley Town *W York*	**82**	SE0524
Warlingham *Surrey*	**27**	TQ3658
Warmanbie *D & G*	**101**	NY1969
Warmbrook *Derbys*	**73**	SK2853
Warmfield *W York*	**83**	SE3720
Warmingham *Ches*	**72**	SJ7061
Warmington *Nhants*	**51**	TL0790
Warmington *Warwks*	**49**	SP4147
Warminster *Wilts*	**22**	ST8745
Warmley *Avon*	**35**	ST6673
Warmsworth *S York*	**75**	SE5400
Warmwell *Dorset*	**11**	SY7585
Warndon *H & W*	**47**	SO8856
Warnford *Hants*	**13**	SU6223
Warnham *W Susx*	**15**	TQ1533
Warnham Court *W Susx*	**15**	TQ1533
Warningcamp *W Susx*	**14**	TQ0307
Warninglid *W Susx*	**15**	TQ2426
Warren *Ches*	**79**	SJ8870
Warren *Dyfed*	**30**	SR9397
Warren Row *Berks*	**37**	SU8180
Warren Street *Kent*	**28**	TQ9252
Warren's Green *Herts*	**39**	TL2628
Warrenhill *Strath*	**108**	NS9438
Warrington *Bucks*	**51**	SP8953
Warrington *Ches*	**78**	SJ6088
Warriston *Loth*	**117**	NT2575
Warsash *Hants*	**13**	SU4906
Warslow *Staffs*	**74**	SK0858
Warsop *Notts*	**75**	SK5667
Warter *Humb*	**84**	SE8750
Warter Priory *Humb*	**84**	SE8449
Warthermaske *N York*	**89**	SE2078
Warthill *N York*	**83**	SE6755
Wartling *E Susx*	**16**	TQ6509
Wartnaby *Leics*	**63**	SK7123
Warton *Lancs*	**80**	SD4128
Warton *Lancs*	**87**	SD4972
Warton *Nthumb*	**103**	NU0002
Warton *Warwks*	**61**	SK2803
Warwick *Cumb*	**93**	NY4656
Warwick *Warwks*	**48**	SP2865
Warwick Bridge *Cumb*	**93**	NY4756
Warwicksland *Cumb*	**101**	NY4577
Wasdale Head *Cumb*	**86**	NY1808
Wash *Derbys*	**74**	SK0682
Wash *Devon*	**7**	SX7665
Washaway *Cnwll*	**4**	SX0369
Washbourne *Devon*	**7**	SX7954
Washbrook *Somset*	**21**	ST4250
Washbrook *Suffk*	**54**	TM1142
Washfield *Devon*	**9**	SS9315
Washfold *N York*	**88**	NZ0502
Washford *Somset*	**20**	ST0541
Washford Pyne *Devon*	**19**	SS8111
Washingborough *Lincs*	**76**	TF0170
Washington *T & W*	**96**	NZ3155
Washington *W Susx*	**14**	TQ1112
Washwood Heath *W Mids*	**61**	SP1088
Wasing *Berks*	**24**	SU5764
Waskerley *Dur*	**95**	NZ0445
Wasperton *Warwks*	**48**	SP2658
Wasps Nest *Lincs*	**76**	TF0764
Wass *N York*	**90**	SE5579
Watchet *Somset*	**20**	ST0743
Watchfield *Oxon*	**36**	SU2490
Watchfield *Somset*	**21**	ST3446
Watchgate *Cumb*	**87**	SD5398
Watchill *Cumb*	**93**	NY1842
Watcombe *Devon*	**7**	SX9267
Watendlath *Cumb*	**93**	NY2716
Water *Devon*	**8**	SX7580
Water *Lancs*	**81**	SD8425
Water Eaton *Oxon*	**37**	SP5112
Water Eaton *Staffs*	**60**	SJ9011
Water End *Beds*	**38**	TL0637
Water End *Beds*	**38**	TL1047
Water End *Beds*	**38**	TL1051
Water End *Essex*	**53**	TL5840
Water End *Herts*	**38**	TL0310
Water End *Herts*	**39**	TL2304
Water End *Humb*	**84**	SE7938
Water Fryston *W York*	**83**	SE4726
Water Newton *Cambs*	**51**	TL1097
Water Orton *Warwks*	**61**	SP1790
Water Stratford *Bucks*	**49**	SP6534
Water Street *M Glam*	**32**	SS8083
Water Yeat *Cumb*	**86**	SD2889
Water's Nook *Gt Man*	**79**	SD6605
Waterbeach *Cambs*	**53**	TL4965
Waterbeach *W Susx*	**14**	SU8908
Waterbeck *D & G*	**101**	NY2477
Watercombe *Dorset*	**11**	SY7585
Waterden *Norfk*	**66**	TF8836
Waterend *Cumb*	**92**	NY1122
Waterfall *Staffs*	**73**	SK0851
Waterfoot *Lancs*	**81**	SD8321
Waterfoot *Strath*	**115**	NS5655
Waterford *Herts*	**39**	TL3114
Watergate *Cnwll*	**4**	SX1181
Waterhead *Cumb*	**87**	NY3703
Waterhead *Strath*	**107**	NS5411
Waterheads *Border*	**117**	NT2451
Waterhouses *Dur*	**96**	NZ1841
Waterhouses *Staffs*	**73**	SK0850
Wateringbury *Kent*	**28**	TQ6853
Waterlane *Gloucs*	**35**	SO9204
Waterloo *Cnwll*	**4**	SX1072
Waterloo *Derbys*	**74**	SK4163
Waterloo *Dorset*	**11**	SZ0193
Waterloo *Dyfed*	**30**	SM9803
Waterloo *H & W*	**46**	SO3447
Waterloo *Highld*	**129**	NG6623
Waterloo *Mersyd*	**78**	SJ3298
Waterloo *Norfk*	**67**	TG2219
Waterloo *Strath*	**116**	NS8154
Waterloo *Tays*	**125**	NO0537
Waterloo Cross *Devon*	**9**	ST0514
Waterloo Port *Gwynd*	**68**	SH4964
Waterlooville *Hants*	**13**	SU6809
Watermillock *Cumb*	**93**	NY4422
Waterperry *Oxon*	**37**	SP6206
Waterrow *Somset*	**20**	ST0525
Waters Upton *Shrops*	**59**	SJ6319
Watersfield *W Susx*	**14**	TQ0115
Waterside *Bucks*	**26**	SP9600
Waterside *Cumb*	**93**	NY2245
Waterside *Lancs*	**81**	SD7123
Waterside *S York*	**83**	SE6714
Waterside *Strath*	**107**	NS4308
Waterside *Strath*	**107**	NS4843
Waterside *Strath*	**116**	NS6773
Waterstock *Oxon*	**37**	SP6305
Waterston *Dyfed*	**30**	SM9305
Watford *Herts*	**26**	TQ1196
Watford *Nhants*	**50**	SP6069
Wath *N York*	**89**	SE1467
Wath *N York*	**89**	SE3277
Wath upon Dearne *S York*	**75**	SE4300
Watlington *Norfk*	**65**	TF6111
Watlington *Oxon*	**37**	SU6894
Watnall *Notts*	**62**	SK5046
Watten *Highld*	**151**	ND2454
Wattisfield *Suffk*	**54**	TM0074
Wattisham *Suffk*	**54**	TM0151
Watton *Dorset*	**10**	SY4591
Watton *Humb*	**84**	TA0150
Watton *Norfk*	**66**	TF9100
Watton Green *Norfk*	**66**	TF9201
Watton-at-Stone *Herts*	**39**	TL3019
Wattons Green *Essex*	**27**	TQ5295
Wattstown *M Glam*	**33**	ST0193
Wattsville *Gwent*	**33**	ST2091
Wauldby *Humb*	**84**	SE9629
Waulkmill *Gramp*	**135**	NO6492
Waunarlwydd *W Glam*	**32**	SS6095
Waunfawr *Dyfed*	**43**	SN6081
Waunfawr *Gwynd*	**68**	SH5259
Waungron *W Glam*	**32**	SN5901
Waunlwyd *Gwent*	**33**	SO1806
Wavendon *Bucks*	**38**	SP9137
Waverbridge *Cumb*	**93**	NY2249
Waverton *Ches*	**71**	SJ4663
Waverton *Cumb*	**93**	NY2247
Wawne *Humb*	**85**	TA0936
Waxham *Norfk*	**67**	TG4426
Waxholme *Humb*	**85**	TA3229
Way *Kent*	**29**	TR3265
Way Village *Devon*	**19**	SS8810
Way Wick *Avon*	**21**	ST3862
Waye *Devon*	**7**	SX7771
Wayford *Somset*	**10**	ST4006
Waytown *Dorset*	**10**	SY4797
Weacombe *Somset*	**20**	ST1140
Weald *Cambs*	**52**	TL2259
Weald *Oxon*	**36**	SP3002
Wealdstone *Gt Lon*	**26**	TQ1589
Wear Head *Dur*	**95**	NY8539
Weardley *W York*	**82**	SE2944
Weare *Somset*	**21**	ST4152
Weare Giffard *Devon*	**18**	SS4721
Wearne *Somset*	**21**	ST4228
Weasdale *Cumb*	**87**	NY6903
Weasenham All Saints *Norfk*	**66**	TF8421
Weasenham St. Peter *Norfk*	**66**	TF8522
Weasle *Gt Man*	**79**	SJ8098
Weatheroak Hill *H & W*	**61**	SP0674
Weaverham *Ches*	**71**	SJ6174
Weaverslake *Staffs*	**73**	SK1319
Weaverthorpe *N York*	**91**	SE9670
Webb's Heath *Avon*	**35**	ST6873
Webbington *Somset*	**21**	ST3855
Webheath *H & W*	**48**	SP0266
Webton *H & W*	**46**	SO4136
Wedderlairs *Gramp*	**143**	NJ8532
Wedding Hall Fold *N York*	**82**	SD9445
Weddington *Kent*	**29**	TR2959
Weddington *Warwks*	**61**	SP3693
Wedhampton *Wilts*	**23**	SU0557
Wedmore *Somset*	**21**	ST4347
Wednesbury *W Mids*	**60**	SO9895
Wednesfield *W Mids*	**60**	SJ9400
Weecar *Notts*	**75**	SK8266
Weedon *Bucks*	**38**	SP8118
Weedon Lois *Nhants*	**49**	SP6046
Weeford *Staffs*	**61**	SK1403
Week *Devon*	**19**	SS5727
Week *Devon*	**19**	SS7316
Week *Devon*	**7**	SX7862
Week *Somset*	**20**	SS9133
Week St. Mary *Cnwll*	**5**	SX2397
Weeke *Devon*	**8**	SS7606
Weeke *Hants*	**24**	SU4630
Weekley *Nhants*	**51**	SP8881
Weel *Humb*	**84**	TA0639
Weeley *Essex*	**41**	TM1422
Weeley Heath *Essex*	**41**	TM1520
Weem *Tays*	**125**	NN8449
Weeping Cross *Staffs*	**72**	SJ9421
Weethley Hamlet *Warwks*	**48**	SP0555
Weeting *Norfk*	**53**	TL7788
Weeton *Humb*	**85**	TA3520
Weeton *Lancs*	**80**	SD3834
Weeton *W York*	**82**	SE2847
Weetwood *W York*	**82**	SE2737
Weir *Lancs*	**81**	SD8625
Weir Quay *Devon*	**6**	SX4365
Weirbrook *Shrops*	**59**	SJ3424
Welbeck Abbey *Notts*	**75**	SK5574
Welborne *Norfk*	**66**	TG0610
Welbourn *Lincs*	**76**	SK9654
Welburn *N York*	**90**	SE7267
Welbury *N York*	**89**	NZ3902
Welby *Lincs*	**63**	SK9738
Welches Dam *Cambs*	**53**	TL4686
Welcombe *Devon*	**18**	SS2318
Welford *Berks*	**24**	SU4073
Welford *Nhants*	**50**	SP6480
Welford-on-Avon *Warwks*	**48**	SP1452
Welham *Leics*	**50**	SP7692
Welham *Notts*	**75**	SK7281
Welham Green *Herts*	**39**	TL2305
Well *Hants*	**24**	SU7646
Well *Lincs*	**77**	TF4473
Well *N York*	**89**	SE2681
Well End *Bucks*	**26**	SU8888
Well End *Herts*	**26**	TQ2098
Well Fold *W York*	**82**	SE2024
Well Head *Herts*	**39**	TL1727
Well Hill *Kent*	**27**	TQ4963
Welland *H & W*	**47**	SO7940
Welland Stone *H & W*	**47**	SO8138
Wellbank *Tays*	**127**	NO4737
Wellbury *Herts*	**38**	TL1329
Wellesbourne *Warwks*	**48**	SP2855
Wellesbourne Mountford *Warwks*	**48**	SP2755
Wellhouse *Berks*	**24**	SU5272
Welling *Gt Lon*	**27**	TQ4675
Wellingborough *Nhants*	**51**	SP8967
Wellingham *Norfk*	**66**	TF8722
Wellingore *Lincs*	**76**	SK9856
Wellington *Cumb*	**86**	NY0704
Wellington *H & W*	**46**	SO4948
Wellington *Shrops*	**59**	SJ6511
Wellington *Somset*	**20**	ST1320
Wellington Heath *H & W*	**47**	SO7140
Wellington Marsh *H & W*	**46**	SO4946
Wellow *Avon*	**22**	ST7458
Wellow *IOW*	**12**	SZ3888
Wellow *Notts*	**75**	SK6766
Wellpond Green *Herts*	**39**	TL4122
Wells *Somset*	**21**	ST5445
Wells Green *Ches*	**72**	SJ6853
Wells Head *W York*	**82**	SE0833
Wells-Next-The-Sea *Norfk*	**66**	TF9143
Wellsborough *Leics*	**62**	SK3602
Wellstye Green *Essex*	**40**	TL6318
Welltree *Tays*	**125**	NN9622
Wellwood *Fife*	**117**	NT0988
Welney *Norfk*	**65**	TL5293
Welsh End *Shrops*	**59**	SJ5135
Welsh Frankton *Shrops*	**59**	SJ3533
Welsh Hook *Dyfed*	**30**	SM9327
Welsh Newton *H & W*	**34**	SO5017
Welsh St. Donats *S Glam*	**33**	ST0276
Welshampton *Shrops*	**59**	SJ4335
Welshpool *Powys*	**58**	SJ2207
Welton *Cumb*	**93**	NY3544
Welton *Humb*	**84**	SE9627
Welton *Lincs*	**76**	TF0179
Welton *Nhants*	**50**	SP5865
Welton le Marsh *Lincs*	**77**	TF4768
Welton le Wold *Lincs*	**77**	TF2787
Welwick *Humb*	**85**	TA3421
Welwyn *Herts*	**39**	TL2316
Welwyn Garden City *Herts*	**39**	TL2312
Wem *Shrops*	**59**	SJ5128
Wembdon *Somset*	**20**	ST2837
Wembley *Gt Lon*	**26**	TQ1885
Wembury *Devon*	**6**	SX5248
Wembworthy *Devon*	**19**	SS6609
Wemyss Bay *Strath*	**114**	NS1969
Wenallt *Dyfed*	**43**	SN6771
Wendens Ambo *Essex*	**39**	TL5136
Wendlebury *Oxon*	**37**	SP5619
Wendling *Norfk*	**66**	TF9312
Wendover *Bucks*	**38**	SP8607
Wendron *Cnwll*	**2**	SW6731
Wendy *Cambs*	**52**	TL3247
Wenfordbridge *Cnwll*	**4**	SX0875
Wenhaston *Suffk*	**55**	TM4275
Wennington *Cambs*	**52**	TL2379
Wennington *Gt Lon*	**27**	TQ5381
Wennington *Lancs*	**87**	SD6170
Wensley *Derbys*	**74**	SK2661
Wensley *N York*	**89**	SE0989
Wentbridge *W York*	**83**	SE4817
Wentnor *Shrops*	**59**	SO3892
Wentworth *Cambs*	**53**	TL4878
Wentworth *S York*	**74**	SK3898
Wentworth Castle *S York*	**83**	SE3202
Wenvoe *S Glam*	**33**	ST1272
Weobley *H & W*	**46**	SO4051
Weobley Marsh *H & W*	**46**	SO4151
Wepham *W Susx*	**14**	TQ0408
Wereham *Norfk*	**65**	TF6801
Wergs *Staffs*	**60**	SJ8700
Wern *Powys*	**58**	SH9612
Wern *Powys*	**58**	SJ2513
Wern *Powys*	**33**	SO1217
Wern *Shrops*	**58**	SJ2734
Wern-y-gaer *Clwyd*	**70**	SJ2068
Werneth Low *Gt Man*	**79**	SJ9592
Wernffrwd *W Glam*	**32**	SS5194
Werrington *Cambs*	**64**	TF1603
Werrington *Cnwll*	**5**	SX3287
Werrington *Staffs*	**72**	SJ9447
Wervin *Ches*	**71**	SJ4271
Wesham *Lancs*	**80**	SD4133
Wessington *Derbys*	**74**	SK3757
West Aberthaw *S Glam*	**20**	ST0266
West Acre *Norfk*	**65**	TF7815
West Allerdean *Nthumb*	**111**	NT9646
West Alvington *Devon*	**7**	SX7243
West Amesbury *Wilts*	**23**	SU1341
West Anstey *Devon*	**19**	SS8527
West Appleton *N York*	**89**	SE2294
West Ashby *Lincs*	**77**	TF2672
West Ashling *W Susx*	**14**	SU8107
West Ashton *Wilts*	**22**	ST8755
West Auckland *Dur*	**96**	NZ1826
West Ayton *N York*	**91**	SE9884
West Bagborough *Somset*	**20**	ST1733
West Balsdon *Cnwll*	**5**	SX2798
West Bank *Ches*	**78**	SJ5183
West Bank *Gwent*	**33**	SO2105
West Barkwith *Lincs*	**76**	TF1580
West Barnby *N York*	**90**	NZ8212
West Barnham *W Susx*	**14**	SU9505
West Barns *Loth*	**118**	NT6578
West Barsham *Norfk*	**66**	TF9033
West Bay *Dorset*	**10**	SY4690
West Beckham *Norfk*	**66**	TG1439
West Bedfont *Surrey*	**26**	TQ0674
West Bergholt *Essex*	**40**	TL9527
West Bexington *Dorset*	**10**	SY5386
West Bilney *Norfk*	**65**	TF7115
West Blatchington *E Susx*	**15**	TQ2707
West Boldon *T & W*	**96**	NZ3561
West Bourton *Dorset*	**22**	ST7629
West Bowling *W York*	**82**	SE1630
West Brabourne *Kent*	**29**	TR0842
West Bradenham *Norfk*	**66**	TF9108

West Bradford Whinny Hill

West Bradford *Lancs* 81 SD7444
West Bradley *Somset* 21 ST5536
West Bretton *W York* 82 SE2813
West Bridgford *Notts* 62 SK5836
West Briscoe *Dur* 95 NY9619
West Bromwich *W Mids* 60 SP0091
West Buccleigh Hotel *Border* 109 NT3214
West Buckland *Devon* 19 SS6531
West Buckland *Somset* 20 ST1720
West Burton *N York* 88 SE0186
West Burton *W Susx* 14 SU9914
West Butsfield *Dur* 95 NZ1044
West Butterwick *Humb* 84 SE8305
West Byfleet *Surrey* 26 TQ0461
West Cairngaan *D & G* 98 NX1231
West Caister *Norfk* 67 TG5011
West Calder *Loth* 117 NT0163
West Camel *Somset* 21 ST5724
West Chaldon *Dorset* 11 SY7782
West Challow *Oxon* 36 SU3688
West Charleton *Devon* 7 SX7542
West Chelborough *Dorset* 10 ST5405
West Chevington *Nthumb* 103 NZ2297
West Chiltington *W Susx* 14 TQ0818
West Chinnock *Somset* 10 ST4613
West Chisenbury *Wilts* 23 SU1352
West Clandon *Surrey* 26 TQ0552
West Cliffe *Kent* 29 TR3444
West Coker *Somset* 10 ST5113
West Combe *Devon* 7 SX7662
West Compton *Dorset* 10 SY5694
West Compton *Somset* 21 ST5942
West Cottingwith *N York* 83 SE6942
West Cowick *Humb* 83 SE6421
West Cross *W Glam* 32 SS6189
West Curry *Cnwll* 5 SX2893
West Curthwaite *Cumb* 93 NY3249
West Dean *W Susx* 14 SU8612
West Dean *Wilts* 23 SU2526
West Deeping *Lincs* 64 TF1008
West Derby *Mersyd* 78 SJ3993
West Dereham *Norfk* 65 TF6500
West Down *Devon* 19 SS5142
West Drayton *Gt Lon* 26 TQ0579
West Drayton *Notts* 75 SK7074
West Dunnet *Highld* 151 ND2171
West Ella *Humb* 84 TA0029
West End *Avon* 21 ST4569
West End *Avon* 35 ST7188
West End *Beds* 51 SP9853
West End *Berks* 37 SU8275
West End *Cambs* 52 TL3168
West End *Cumb* 93 NY3258
West End *Gwent* 33 ST2195
West End *Hants* 13 SU4614
West End *Hants* 24 SU6335
West End *Herts* 39 TL2608
West End *Herts* 39 TL3306
West End *Humb* 84 SE9130
West End *Humb* 85 TA1830
West End *Humb* 85 TA2627
West End *Lancs* 81 SD7328
West End *Lincs* 77 TF3598
West End *N York* 89 SE1457
West End *N York* 83 SE5140
West End *Norfk* 66 TF9009
West End *Norfk* 67 TG5011
West End *Oxon* 37 SU5886
West End *Somset* 22 ST6734
West End *Surrey* 25 SU9461
West End *Surrey* 26 TQ1263
West End *W Susx* 15 TQ2016
West End *W York* 82 SE2238
West End *Wilts* 22 ST9124
West End *Wilts* 35 ST9777
West End *Wilts* 22 ST9824
West End Green *Hants* 24 SU6661
West Ewell *Surrey* 26 TQ2063
West Farleigh *Kent* 28 TQ7152
West Farndon *Nhants* 49 SP5251
West Felton *Shrops* 59 SJ3425
West Firle *E Susx* 16 TQ4707
West Firsby *Lincs* 76 SK9784
West Flotmanby *N York* 91 TA0779
West Garforth *W York* 83 SE3932
West Ginge *Oxon* 37 SU4486
West Grafton *Wilts* 23 SU2460
West Green *Hants* 24 SU7456
West Grimstead *Wilts* 23 SU2026
West Grinstead *W Susx* 15 TQ1720
West Haddlesey *N York* 83 SE5626
West Haddon *Nhants* 50 SP6371
West Hagbourne *Oxon* 37 SU5187
West Hagley *H & W* 60 SO9080
West Hallam *Derbys* 62 SK4341
West Hallam Common *Derbys* 62 SK4241
West Halton *Humb* 84 SE9020
West Ham *Gt Lon* 27 TQ3983
West Handley *Derbys* 74 SK3977
West Hanney *Oxon* 36 SU4092
West Hanningfield *Essex* 40 TQ7399
West Harnham *Wilts* 23 SU1329
West Harptree *Avon* 21 ST5556
West Harting *W Susx* 14 SU7820
West Hatch *Somset* 20 ST2821
West Hatch *Wilts* 22 ST9227
West Haven *Tays* 127 NO5735
West Head *Norfk* 65 TF5705
West Heath *Hants* 24 SU5858
West Heath *W Mids* 60 SP0277
West Helmsdale *Highld* 147 ND0115
West Hendred *Oxon* 37 SU4488
West Heslerton *N York* 91 SE9176
West Hewish *Avon* 21 ST3963
West Hill *Devon* 9 SY0794
West Hoathly *W Susx* 15 TQ3632
West Holme *Dorset* 11 SY8885
West Holywell *T & W* 103 NZ3072
West Horndon *Essex* 40 TQ6288
West Horrington *Somset* 21 ST5747
West Horsley *Surrey* 26 TQ0752
West Horton *Nthumb* 111 NU0230
West Hougham *Kent* 29 TR2640
West Howe *Dorset* 12 SZ0595
West Howetown *Somset* 20 SS9134
West Huntingtower *Tays* 125 NO0724
West Huntspill *Somset* 20 ST3044
West Hyde *Beds* 38 TL1117
West Hyde *Herts* 26 TQ0391
West Hythe *Kent* 17 TR1234
West Ilkerton *Devon* 19 SS7046
West Ilsley *Berks* 37 SU4782
West Itchenor *W Susx* 14 SU7901
West Keal *Lincs* 77 TF3663
West Kennet *Wilts* 23 SU1168
West Kilbride *Strath* 114 NS2048
West Kingsdown *Kent* 27 TQ5763
West Kington *Wilts* 35 ST8077
West Kirby *Mersyd* 78 SJ2186
West Knapton *N York* 90 SE8775
West Knighton *Dorset* 11 SY7387
West Knoyle *Wilts* 22 ST8632
West Lambrook *Somset* 10 ST4118
West Langdon *Kent* 29 TR3247
West Laroch *Highld* 130 NN0758
West Lavington *W Susx* 14 SU8920
West Lavington *Wilts* 22 SU0052
West Layton *N York* 89 NZ1410
West Leake *Notts* 62 SK5226
West Learmouth *Nthumb* 110 NT8437
West Lees *N York* 89 NZ4702
West Leigh *Devon* 8 SS6805
West Leigh *Devon* 7 SX7557
West Leigh *Somset* 20 ST1230
West Lexham *Norfk* 66 TF8417
West Lilling *N York* 90 SE6465
West Linton *Border* 117 NT1551
West Littleton *Avon* 35 ST7675
West Lockinge *Oxon* 36 SU4187
West Lulworth *Dorset* 11 SY8280
West Lutton *N York* 91 SE9369
West Lydford *Somset* 21 ST5631
West Lyn *Devon* 19 SS7248
West Lyng *Somset* 21 ST3128
West Lynn *Norfk* 65 TF6120
West Malling *Kent* 28 TQ6757
West Malvern *H & W* 47 SO7646
West Marden *W Susx* 14 SU7713
West Markham *Notts* 75 SK7272
West Marsh *Humb* 85 TA2509
West Marton *N York* 81 SD8950
West Melbury *Dorset* 22 ST8720
West Melton *S York* 83 SE4201
West Meon *Hants* 13 SU6423
West Meon Hut *Hants* 13 SU6526
West Meon Woodlands *Hants* 13 SU6426
West Mersea *Essex* 41 TM0112
West Milton *Dorset* 10 SY5096
West Minster *Kent* 28 TQ9073
West Monkton *Somset* 20 ST2628
West Moor *T & W* 103 NZ2770
West Moors *Dorset* 12 SU0802
West Morden *Dorset* 11 SY9095
West Morton *W York* 82 SE0942
West Mudford *Somset* 21 ST5620
West Ness *N York* 90 SE6879
West Newbiggin *Dur* 96 NZ3518
West Newton *Humb* 85 TA2037
West Newton *Norfk* 65 TF6928
West Newton *Somset* 20 ST2829
West Norwood *Gt Lon* 27 TQ3171
West Ogwell *Devon* 7 SX8270
West Orchard *Dorset* 11 ST8216
West Overton *Wilts* 23 SU1267
West Panson *Devon* 5 SX3491
West Parley *Dorset* 12 SZ0896
West Peckham *Kent* 27 TQ6452
West Pelton *Dur* 96 NZ2353
West Pennard *Somset* 21 ST5438
West Pentire *Cnwll* 4 SW7760
West Perry *Cambs* 52 TL1466
West Prawle *Devon* 7 SX7637
West Preston *W Susx* 14 TQ0602
West Pulham *Dorset* 11 ST7008
West Putford *Devon* 18 SS3616
West Quantoxhead *Somset* 20 ST1141
West Raddon *Devon* 9 SS8902
West Rainton *T & W* 96 NZ3246
West Rasen *Lincs* 76 TF0689
West Ravendale *Humb* 76 TF2299
West Raynham *Norfk* 66 TF8725
West Retford *Notts* 75 SK6981
West Rounton *N York* 89 NZ4103
West Row *Suffk* 53 TL6775
West Rudham *Norfk* 66 TF8127
West Runton *Norfk* 66 TG1842
West Saltoun *Loth* 118 NT4667
West Sandford *Devon* 8 SS8102
West Sandwick *Shet* 155 HU4588
West Scrafton *N York* 88 SE0783
West Sleekburn *Nthumb* 103 NZ2884
West Somerton *Norfk* 67 TG4620
West Stafford *Dorset* 11 SY7289
West Stockwith *Notts* 75 SK7895
West Stoke *W Susx* 14 SU8208
West Stonesdale *N York* 88 NY8801
West Stoughton *Somset* 21 ST4148
West Stour *Dorset* 22 ST7822
West Stourmouth *Kent* 29 TR2562
West Stow *Suffk* 54 TL8171
West Stowell *Wilts* 23 SU1361
West Stratton *Hants* 24 SU5240
West Street *Kent* 28 TQ7376
West Street *Kent* 28 TQ9054
West Street *Kent* 29 TR3254
West Street *Suffk* 54 TL9871
West Tanfield *N York* 89 SE2678
West Taphouse *Cnwll* 4 SX1463
West Tarbert *Strath* 113 NR8467
West Tarring *W Susx* 14 TQ1103
West Thorney *W Susx* 14 SU7602
West Thorpe *Notts* 62 SK6225
West Thurrock *Essex* 27 TQ5877
West Tilbury *Essex* 40 TQ6678
West Tisted *Hants* 24 SU6529
West Torrington *Lincs* 76 TF1381
West Town *Avon* 21 ST4868
West Town *Avon* 21 ST5160
West Town *H & W* 46 SO4361
West Town *Hants* 13 SZ7199
West Town *Somset* 21 ST5335
West Town *Somset* 22 ST7042
West Tytherley *Hants* 23 SU2729
West Tytherton *Wilts* 35 ST9474
West Walton *Norfk* 65 TF4613
West Walton Highway *Norfk* 65 TF4913
West Weetwood *Nthumb* 111 NU0028
West Wellow *Hants* 12 SU2819
West Wembury *Devon* 6 SX5249
West Wemyss *Fife* 118 NT3294
West Wick *Avon* 21 ST3761
West Wickham *Cambs* 53 TL6149
West Wickham *Gt Lon* 27 TQ3766
West Williamston *Dyfed* 30 SN0305
West Winch *Norfk* 65 TF6316
West Winterslow *Wilts* 23 SU2331
West Wittering *W Susx* 14 SZ7898
West Witton *N York* 88 SE0588
West Woodburn *Nthumb* 102 NY8987
West Woodhay *Berks* 23 SU3963
West Woodlands *Somset* 22 ST7743
West Woodside *Cumb* 93 NY3049
West Worldham *Hants* 24 SU7436
West Worthing *W Susx* 15 TQ1302
West Wratting *Essex* 53 TL6052
West Wycombe *Bucks* 37 SU8294
West Wylam *Nthumb* 103 NZ1063
West Yatton *Wilts* 35 ST8575
West Yoke *Kent* 27 TQ6065
West Youlstone *Cnwll* 18 SS2615
Westbere *Kent* 29 TR1961
Westborough *Lincs* 63 SK8544
Westbourne *W Susx* 13 SU7507
Westbrook *Berks* 24 SU4272
Westbrook *Kent* 29 TR3470
Westbrook *Wilts* 22 ST9565
Westbury *Bucks* 49 SP6235
Westbury *Shrops* 59 SJ3509
Westbury *Wilts* 22 ST8751
Westbury Leigh *Wilts* 22 ST8649
Westbury on Severn *Gloucs* 35 SO7114
Westbury-on-Trym *Avon* 34 ST5777
Westbury-sub-Mendip *Somset* 21 ST5049
Westby *Lancs* 80 SD3831
Westcliff-on-Sea *Essex* 40 TQ8685
Westcombe *Somset* 22 ST6739
Westcote *Gloucs* 36 SP2120
Westcott *Bucks* 37 SP7116
Westcott *Devon* 9 ST0204
Westcott *Somset* 19 SS8720
Westcott *Surrey* 15 TQ1448
Westcott Barton *Oxon* 49 SP4325
Westcourt *Wilts* 23 SU2261
Westdean *E Susx* 16 TV5299
Westdown Camp *Wilts* 23 SU0447
Westdowns *Cnwll* 4 SX0582
Wested *Kent* 27 TQ5166
Westend *Gloucs* 35 SO7807
Westend Town *Nthumb* 102 NY7865
Westenhanger *Kent* 29 TR1237
Wester Drumashie *Highld* 140 NH6032
Wester Essenside *Border* 109 NT4320
Wester Ochiltree *Loth* 117 NT0374
Wester Pitkierie *Fife* 127 NO5505
Westerdale *Highld* 151 ND1251
Westerdale *N York* 90 NZ6605
Westerfield *Suffk* 54 TM1747
Westergate *W Susx* 14 SU9305
Westerham *Kent* 27 TQ4454
Westerhope *T & W* 103 NZ1966
Westerland *Devon* 7 SX8662
Westerleigh *Avon* 35 ST6979
Westerton *Tays* 127 NO6754
Westfield *Avon* 22 ST6753
Westfield *D & G* 92 NX9926
Westfield *E Susx* 17 TQ8115
Westfield *Loth* 116 NS9472
Westfield *Norfk* 66 TF9909
Westfield Sole *Kent* 28 TQ7761
Westfields *Dorset* 11 ST7206
Westfields *H & W* 46 SO4941
Westfields of Rattray *Tays* 126 NO1746
Westford *Somset* 20 ST1220
Westgate *Dur* 95 NY9038
Westgate *Humb* 84 SE7707
Westgate *Norfk* 66 TF9740
Westgate Hill *W York* 82 SE2029
Westgate on Sea *Kent* 29 TR3270
Westgate Street *Norfk* 67 TG1921
Westhall *Suffk* 55 TM4280
Westham *Dorset* 11 SY6679
Westham *E Susx* 16 TQ6404
Westham *Somset* 21 ST4046
Westhampnett *W Susx* 14 SU8806
Westhay *Somset* 21 ST4342
Westhead *Lancs* 78 SD4407
Westhide *H & W* 46 SO5843
Westhill *Gramp* 135 NJ8307
Westholme *Somset* 21 ST5741
Westhope *H & W* 46 SO4651
Westhope *Shrops* 59 SO4786
Westhorp *Nhants* 49 SP5152
Westhorpe *Lincs* 64 TF2231
Westhorpe *Suffk* 54 TM0468
Westhoughton *Gt Man* 79 SD6506
Westhouse *N York* 87 SD6773
Westhouses *Derbys* 74 SK4157
Westhumble *Surrey* 26 TQ1651
Westlake *Devon* 6 SX6253
Westland Green *Herts* 39 TL4222
Westleigh *Devon* 18 SS4728
Westleigh *Devon* 9 ST0617
Westleton *Suffk* 55 TM4369
Westley *Shrops* 59 SJ3607
Westley *Suffk* 54 TL8264
Westley Waterless *Cambs* 53 TL6156
Westlington *Bucks* 37 SP7610
Westlinton *Cumb* 101 NY3964
Westmarsh *Kent* 29 TR2761
Westmeston *E Susx* 15 TQ3313
Westmill *Herts* 39 TL3627
Westmuir *Tays* 126 NO3652
Westnewton *Cumb* 92 NY1344
Westnewton *T & W* 103 NZ3765
Weston *Avon* 22 ST7366
Weston *Berks* 36 SU3973
Weston *Ches* 78 SJ5080
Weston *Ches* 72 SJ7352
Weston *Devon* 9 ST1400
Weston *Devon* 9 SY1688
Weston *Dorset* 11 SY6871
Weston *H & W* 46 SO3656
Weston *Hants* 13 SU7221
Weston *Herts* 39 TL2530
Weston *Lincs* 64 TF2924
Weston *Nhants* 49 SP5846
Weston *Notts* 75 SK7767
Weston *Shrops* 59 SJ2927
Weston *Shrops* 59 SJ5629
Weston *Shrops* 46 SO3273
Weston *Staffs* 72 SJ9726
Weston *W York* 82 SE1747
Weston Beggard *H & W* 46 SO5841
Weston by Welland *Nhants* 50 SP7791
Weston Colley *Hants* 24 SU5039
Weston Colville *Cambs* 53 TL6153
Weston Corbett *Hants* 24 SU6846
Weston Coyney *Staffs* 72 SJ9343
Weston Favell *Nhants* 50 SP7962
Weston Green *Cambs* 53 TL6252
Weston Heath *Shrops* 60 SJ7713
Weston Hills *Lincs* 64 TF2720
Weston in Arden *Warwks* 61 SP3886
Weston Jones *Staffs* 72 SJ7624
Weston Longville *Norfk* 66 TG1115
Weston Lullingfields *Shrops* 59 SJ4224
Weston Patrick *Hants* 24 SU6946
Weston Rhyn *Shrops* 58 SJ2835
Weston Subedge *Gloucs* 48 SP1241
Weston Turville *Bucks* 38 SP8510
Weston Underwood *Bucks* 38 SP8650
Weston Underwood *Derbys* 73 SK2942
Weston under Penyard *H & W* 35 SO6322
Weston under Wetherley *Warwks* 48 SP3669
Weston-in-Gordano *Avon* 34 ST4474
Weston-on-Trent *Derbys* 62 SK4027
Weston-on-the-Green *Oxon* 37 SP5318
Weston-Super-Mare *Avon* 21 ST3260
Weston-under-Lizard *Staffs* 60 SJ8010
Westonbirt *Gloucs* 35 ST8589
Westoning *Beds* 38 TL0332
Westoning Woodend *Beds* 38 TL0232
Westonzoyland *Somset* 21 ST3534
Westover *Hants* 23 SU3640
Westow *N York* 90 SE7565
Westpeek *Devon* 5 SX3493
Westport *Somset* 21 ST3820
Westport *Strath* 104 NR6526
Westquarter *Cent* 116 NS9178
Westra *S Glam* 33 ST1470
Westridge Green *Berks* 37 SU5679
Westrigg *Loth* 116 NS9067
Westrop *Wilts* 36 SU2093
Westruther *Border* 110 NT6349
Westry *Cambs* 65 TL4098
Westthorpe *Derbys* 75 SK4579
Westward *Cumb* 93 NY2744
Westward Ho *Devon* 18 SS4329
Westwell *Kent* 28 TQ9947
Westwell *Oxon* 36 SP2209
Westwell Leacon *Kent* 28 TQ9647
Westwick *Cambs* 53 TL4265
Westwick *Dur* 95 NZ0715
Westwick *Norfk* 67 TG2726
Westwood *Devon* 9 SY0199
Westwood *Kent* 27 TQ6070
Westwood *Kent* 29 TR3667
Westwood *Notts* 75 SK4551
Westwood *Wilts* 22 ST8059
Westwood Heath *W Mids* 61 SP2776
Westwoodside *Humb* 75 SE7400
Wetham Green *Kent* 28 TQ8468
Wetheral *Cumb* 93 NY4654
Wetherby *W York* 83 SE4048
Wetherden *Suffk* 54 TM0062
Wetheringsett *Suffk* 54 TM1266
Wethersfield *Essex* 40 TL7131
Wetherup Street *Suffk* 54 TM1464
Wetley Rocks *Staffs* 72 SJ9649
Wettenhall *Ches* 71 SJ6261
Wetton *Staffs* 73 SK1055
Wetwang *Humb* 91 SE9359
Wetwood *Staffs* 72 SJ7733
Wexcombe *Wilts* 23 SU2758
Wexham *Bucks* 26 SU9882
Wexham Street *Bucks* 26 SU9883
Weybourne *Norfk* 66 TG1142
Weybread *Suffk* 55 TM2480
Weybread Street *Suffk* 55 TM2479
Weybridge *Surrey* 26 TQ0764
Weydale *Highld* 151 ND1564
Weyhill *Hants* 23 SU3146
Weymouth *Dorset* 11 SY6779
Whaddon *Bucks* 38 SP8034
Whaddon *Cambs* 52 TL3546
Whaddon *Gloucs* 35 SO8313
Whaddon *Wilts* 22 ST8861
Whaddon *Wilts* 23 SU1926
Whale *Cumb* 94 NY5221
Whaley *Derbys* 75 SK5171
Whaley Bridge *Derbys* 79 SK0180
Whaligoe *Highld* 151 ND3140
Whalley *Lancs* 81 SD7336
Whalley Banks *Lancs* 81 SD7335
Whalton *Nthumb* 96 NZ1318
Whamley *Nthumb* 102 NY8766
Whaplode *Lincs* 64 TF3224
Whaplode Drove *Lincs* 64 TF3213
Wharf *Warwks* 49 SP4352
Wharfe *N York* 88 SD7869
Wharles *Lancs* 80 SD4435
Wharley End *Beds* 38 SP9442
Wharncliffe Side *S York* 74 SK2994
Wharram-le-Street *N York* 90 SE8665
Wharton *Ches* 72 SJ6666
Wharton *H & W* 46 SO5055
Whashton Green *N York* 89 NZ1405
Whasset *Cumb* 87 SD5080
Whaston *N York* 89 NZ1506
Whatcote *Warwks* 48 SP2944
Whateley *Warwks* 61 SP2299
Whatfield *Suffk* 54 TM0246
Whatley *Somset* 10 ST3607
Whatley *Somset* 22 ST7347
Whatley's End *Avon* 35 ST6581
Whatlington *E Susx* 17 TQ7618
Whatsole Street *Kent* 29 TR1144
Whatstandwell *Derbys* 74 SK3354
Whatton *Notts* 63 SK7439
Whauphill *D & G* 99 NX4049
Whaw *N York* 88 NY9804
Wheal Rose *Cnwll* 2 SW7144
Wheatacre *Norfk* 67 TM4694
Wheatfield *Oxon* 37 SU6899
Wheathampstead *Herts* 39 TL1714
Wheathill *Shrops* 59 SO6282
Wheathill *Somset* 21 ST5830
Wheatley *Hants* 25 SU7840
Wheatley *Oxon* 37 SP5905
Wheatley *W York* 82 SE0726
Wheatley Hill *Dur* 96 NZ3738
Wheatley Hills *S York* 83 SE5904
Wheatley Lane *Lancs* 81 SD8337
Wheaton Aston *Staffs* 60 SJ8512
Wheatsheaf *Clwyd* 71 SJ3253
Wheddon Cross *Somset* 20 SS9238
Wheel Inn *Cnwll* 2 SW6921
Wheelbarrow Town *Kent* 29 TR1445
Wheeler's Green *Oxon* 24 SU7672
Wheeler's Street *Kent* 28 TQ8444
Wheelerend Common *Bucks* 37 SU8093
Wheelerstreet *Surrey* 25 SU9440
Wheelock *Ches* 72 SJ7559
Wheelock Heath *Ches* 72 SJ7557
Wheelton *Lancs* 81 SD6021
Wheldale *W York* 83 SE4526
Wheldrake *N York* 83 SE6844
Whelpley Hill *Bucks* 38 SP9904
Whelpo *Cumb* 93 NY3139
Whelston *Clwyd* 70 SJ2076
Whempstead *Herts* 39 TL3221
Whenby *N York* 90 SE6369
Whepstead *Suffk* 54 TL8358
Wherstead *Suffk* 54 TM1540
Wherwell *Hants* 23 SU3841
Wheston *Derbys* 74 SK1376
Whetsted *Kent* 28 TQ6646
Whetstone *Gt Lon* 27 TQ2693
Whetstone *Leics* 50 SP5597
Wheyrigg *Cumb* 93 NY1948
Whicham *Cumb* 86 SD1382
Whichford *Warwks* 48 SP3134
Whickham *T & W* 96 NZ2061
Whiddon *Devon* 18 SX4799
Whiddon Down *Devon* 8 SX6992
Whight's Corner *Suffk* 54 TM1242
Whigstreet *Tays* 127 NO4844
Whiligh *E Susx* 16 TQ6431
Whilton *Nhants* 49 SP6364
Whimble *Devon* 18 SS3503
Whimple *Devon* 9 SY0497
Whimpwell Green *Norfk* 67 TG3829
Whin Lane End *Lancs* 80 SD3941
Whinburgh *Norfk* 66 TG0009
Whinnie Liggate *D & G* 99 NX7252
Whinnow *Cumb* 93 NY3051
Whinny Hill *Cleve* 96 NZ3818

Whinnyfold

Witby Mills

Whinnyfold *Gramp* 143 NK0733
Whippingham *IOW* 13 SZ5193
Whipsnade *Beds* 38 TL0117
Whipton *Devon* 9 SX9493
Whisby *Lincs* 76 SK9067
Whissendine *Leics* 63 SK8214
Whissonsett *Norfk* 66 TF9123
Whistlefield Inn *Strath* 114 NS1492
Whistley Green *Berks* 25 SU7974
Whiston *Mersyd* 78 SJ4791
Whiston *Nhants* 51 SP8460
Whiston *S York* 75 SK4489
Whiston *Staffs* 60 SJ8914
Whiston *Staffs* 73 SK0347
Whiston Cross *Shrops* 60 SJ7903
Whiston Eaves *Staffs* 73 SK0446
Whiston Lane End *Mersyd* 78 SJ4690
Whitacre Fields *Warwks* 61 SP2592
Whitbeck *Cumb* 86 SD1184
Whitbourne *H & W* 47 SO7257
Whitburn *Loth* 116 NS9464
Whitburn *T & W* 96 NZ4062
Whitby *Ches* 71 SJ3975
Whitby *N York* 91 NZ8910
Whitbyheath *Ches* 71 SJ3974
Whitchurch *Avon* 21 ST6167
Whitchurch *Bucks* 38 SP8020
Whitchurch *Devon* 6 SX4972
Whitchurch *Dyfed* 30 SM8025
Whitchurch *H & W* 34 SO5517
Whitchurch *Hants* 24 SU4648
Whitchurch *Oxon* 37 SU6377
Whitchurch *S Glam* 33 ST1579
Whitchurch *Shrops* 71 SJ5341
Whitchurch Canonicorum *Dorset* 10 SY3995
Whitchurch Hill *Oxon* 37 SU6378
Whitcombe *Dorset* 11 SY7188
Whitcot *Shrops* 59 SO3791
Whitcott Keysett *Shrops* 58 SO2782
White Ball *Somset* 20 ST1019
White Chapel *H & W* 48 SP0740
White Chapel *Lancs* 81 SD5541
White Colne *Essex* 40 TL8729
White Coppice *Lancs* 81 SD6118
White Cross *Cnwll* 2 SW6821
White End *H & W* 47 SO7834
White Lackington *Dorset* 11 SY7198
White Ladies Aston *H & W* 47 SO9252
White Notley *Essex* 40 TL7818
White Ox Mead *Avon* 22 ST7258
White Pit *Lincs* 77 TF3777
White Roding *Essex* 40 TL5613
White Stake *Lancs* 80 SD5125
White Stone *H & W* 46 SO5642
White Waltham *Berks* 26 SU8577
White-le-Head *Dur* 96 NZ1654
Whiteacre *Kent* 29 TR1148
Whiteacre Heath *Warwks* 61 SP2292
Whiteash Green *Essex* 40 TL7930
Whitebirk *Lancs* 81 SD7028
Whitebridge *Highld* 139 NH4815
Whitebrook *Gwent* 34 SO5306
Whitecairns *Gramp* 143 NJ9218
Whitechapel *Gt Lon* 27 TQ3381
Whitechurch *Dyfed* 31 SN1536
Whitecliffe *Gloucs* 34 SO5609
Whitecraig *Loth* 118 NT3470
Whitecroft *Gloucs* 35 SO6206
Whitecrook *D & G* 98 NX1656
Whitecross *Cnwll* 2 SW5234
Whitecross *Cnwll* 4 SW9672
Whiteface *Highld* 146 NH7088
Whitefarland *Strath* 105 NR8642
Whitefield *Devon* 19 SS7035
Whitefield *Gt Man* 79 SD8006
Whitefield Lane End *Mersyd* 78 SJ4589
Whiteford *Gramp* 142 NJ7126
Whitegate *Ches* 71 SJ6269
Whitehall *Hants* 24 SU7452
Whitehall *Ork* 155 HY6528
Whitehall *W Susx* 15 TQ1321
Whitehaven *Cumb* 92 NX9718
Whitehill *Hants* 14 SU7934
Whitehill *Kent* 28 TR0059
Whitehills *Gramp* 142 NJ6565
Whitehouse *Gramp* 142 NJ6114
Whitehouse *Strath* 113 NR8161
Whitehouse Common *W Mids* 61 SP1397
Whitekirk *Loth* 118 NT5981
Whitelackington *Somset* 10 ST3815
Whiteley *Hants* 13 SU5209
Whiteley Bank *IOW* 13 SZ5581
Whiteley Green *Ches* 79 SJ9278
Whiteley Village *Surrey* 26 TQ0962
Whitemans Green *W Susx* 15 TQ3025
Whitemire *Gramp* 140 NH9854
Whitemoor *Cnwll* 4 SW9757
Whitemoor *Derbys* 62 SK3647
Whitemoor *Notts* 62 SK5441
Whitemoor *Staffs* 72 SJ8861
Whitenap *Hants* 12 SU3620
Whiteness *Shet* 155 HU3844
Whiteoak Green *Oxon* 36 SP3414
Whiteparish *Wilts* 23 SU2423
Whiterashes *Gramp* 143 NJ8523
Whiterow *Gramp* 141 NJ0257
Whiterow *Highld* 151 ND3648
Whiteshill *Gloucs* 35 SO8406
Whitesmith *E Susx* 16 TQ5213
Whitestaunton *Somset* 10 ST2810
Whitestone *Devon* 9 SX8694
Whitestone Cross *Devon* 9 SX8993
Whitestreet Green *Suffk* 54 TL9739
Whitewall Corner *N York* 90 SE7969
Whiteway *Avon* 22 ST7264
Whitewell *Lancs* 81 SD6646
Whiteworks *Devon* 6 SX6171
Whitfield *Avon* 35 ST6791
Whitfield *Kent* 29 TR3045
Whitfield *Nhants* 49 SP6039
Whitfield *Nthumb* 94 NY7758
Whitfield Hall *Nthumb* 94 NY7756
Whitford *Clwyd* 70 SJ1478
Whitford *Devon* 10 SY2595
Whitgift *Humb* 84 SE8122
Whitgreave *Staffs* 72 SJ9028
Whithorn *D & G* 99 NX4440
Whiting Bay *Strath* 105 NS0425
Whitington *Norfk* 65 TL7199
Whitkirk *W York* 83 SE3633
Whitland *Dyfed* 31 SN1916
Whitlaw *Border* 109 NT5012
Whitletts *Strath* 106 NS3623
Whitley *Berks* 24 SU7270
Whitley *N York* 83 SE5620
Whitley *S York* 74 SK3494
Whitley *Wilts* 22 ST8866
Whitley Bay *T & W* 103 NZ3571
Whitley Chapel *Nthumb* 95 NY9257
Whitley Heath *Staffs* 72 SJ8126
Whitley Lower *W York* 82 SE2217
Whitley Row *Kent* 27 TQ4952
Whitlock's End *W Mids* 61 SP1076
Whitlow *S York* 74 SK3182
Whitminster *Gloucs* 35 SO7708
Whitmore *Dorset* 12 SU0609
Whitmore *Staffs* 72 SJ8140
Whitnage *Devon* 9 ST0215
Whitnash *Warwks* 48 SP3263
Whitney *H & W* 46 SO2747
Whitrigg *Cumb* 93 NY2038
Whitrigg *Cumb* 93 NY2257
Whitrigglees *Cumb* 93 NY2457
Whitsbury *Hants* 12 SU1219
Whitsford *Devon* 19 SS6633
Whitsome *Border* 119 NT8650
Whitson *Gwent* 34 ST3883
Whitstable *Kent* 29 TR1066
Whitstone *Cnwll* 5 SX2698
Whittingehame *Loth* 118 NT6073
Whittingham *Nthumb* 111 NU0611
Whittingslow *Shrops* 59 SO4388
Whittington *Derbys* 74 SK3875
Whittington *Gloucs* 35 SP0120
Whittington *H & W* 47 SO8753
Whittington *Lancs* 87 SD6075
Whittington *Shrops* 59 SJ3231
Whittington *Staffs* 61 SK1508
Whittington *Staffs* 60 SO8682
Whittington *Warwks* 61 SP2999
Whittle-le-Woods *Lancs* 81 SD5821
Whittlebury *Nhants* 49 SP6943
Whittlesey *Cambs* 64 TL2697
Whittlesford *Cambs* 53 TL4748
Whittlestone Head *Lancs* 81 SD7119
Whitton *Cleve* 96 NZ3822
Whitton *Humb* 84 SE9024
Whitton *Powys* 46 SO2767
Whitton *Shrops* 46 SO5772
Whitton *Suffk* 54 TM1447
Whittonditch *Wilts* 36 SU2872
Whittonstall *Nthumb* 95 NZ0757
Whitway *Hants* 24 SU4559
Whitwell *Derbys* 75 SK5276
Whitwell *Herts* 39 TL1820
Whitwell *IOW* 13 SZ5277
Whitwell *Leics* 63 SK9208
Whitwell *N York* 89 SE2899
Whitwell Street *Norfk* 66 TG1022
Whitwell-on-the-Hill *N York* 90 SE7265
Whitwick *Leics* 62 SK4315
Whitwood *W York* 83 SE4024
Whitworth *Lancs* 81 SD8818
Whixall *Shrops* 59 SJ5134
Whixley *N York* 89 SE4458
Whorlton *Dur* 95 NZ1014
Whorlton *N York* 90 NZ4802
Whyle *H & W* 46 SO5561
Whyteleafe *Surrey* 27 TQ3358
Wibdon *Gloucs* 34 ST5797
Wibsey *W York* 82 SE1430
Wibtoft *Warwks* 50 SP4887
Wichenford *H & W* 47 SO7860
Wichling *Kent* 28 TQ9256
Wick *Avon* 35 ST7072
Wick *Devon* 9 ST1704
Wick *Dorset* 12 SZ1591
Wick *H & W* 47 SO9645
Wick *Highld* 151 ND3650
Wick *M Glam* 33 SS9271
Wick *Somset* 20 ST2144
Wick *Somset* 21 ST4026
Wick *W Susx* 14 TQ0203
Wick *Wilts* 12 SU1621
Wick End *Beds* 38 SP9850
Wick Rissington *Gloucs* 36 SP1821
Wick St. Lawrence *Avon* 21 ST3665
Wicken *Cambs* 53 TL5770
Wicken *Nhants* 49 SP7439
Wicken Bonhunt *Essex* 39 TL4933
Wickenby *Lincs* 76 TF0982
Wicker Street Green *Suffk* 54 TL9742
Wickersley *S York* 75 SK4791
Wickford *Essex* 40 TQ7493
Wickham *Berks* 36 SU3971
Wickham *Hants* 13 SU5711
Wickham Bishops *Essex* 40 TL8412
Wickham Green *Berks* 24 SU4072
Wickham Green *Suffk* 54 TM0969
Wickham Heath *Berks* 24 SU4169
Wickham Market *Suffk* 55 TM3055
Wickham Skeith *Suffk* 54 TM0969
Wickham St. Paul *Essex* 54 TL8336
Wickham Street *Suffk* 53 TL7654
Wickham Street *Suffk* 54 TM0869
Wickhambreaux *Kent* 29 TR2158
Wickhambrook *Suffk* 53 TL7554
Wickhamford *H & W* 48 SP0641
Wickhampton *Norfk* 67 TG4205
Wicklewood *Norfk* 66 TG0702
Wickmere *Norfk* 66 TG1733
Wickstreet *E Susx* 16 TQ5308
Wickwar *Avon* 35 ST7288
Widdington *Essex* 39 TL5331
Widdop *Lancs* 81 SD9233
Widdrington *T & W* 103 NZ2595
Widdrington Station *T & W* 103 NZ2494
Wide Open *T & W* 103 NZ2472
Widecombe in the Moor *Devon* 8 SX7176
Widegates *Cnwll* 5 SX2858
Widemouth Bay *Cnwll* 18 SS2002
Widford *Essex* 40 TL6904
Widford *Herts* 39 TL4216
Widford *Oxon* 36 SP2712
Widham *Wilts* 36 SU0988
Widmer End *Bucks* 26 SU8896
Widmerpool *Notts* 63 SK6327
Widmore *Gt Lon* 27 TQ4268
Widnes *Ches* 78 SJ5184
Wigan *Gt Man* 78 SD5805
Wigborough *Somset* 10 ST4415
Wiggaton *Devon* 9 SY1093
Wiggenhall St. Germans *Norfk* 65 TF5914
Wiggenhall St. Mary Magdalen *Norfk* 65 TF5911
Wiggenhall St. Mary the Virgin *Norfk* 65 TF5813
Wiggens Green *Essex* 53 TL6642
Wiggenstall *Staffs* 74 SK0960
Wiggington *Shrops* 59 SJ3335
Wigginton *Herts* 38 SP9310
Wigginton *N York* 90 SE6058
Wigginton *Oxon* 48 SP3833
Wigginton *Staffs* 61 SK2006
Wigglesworth *N York* 81 SD8156
Wiggold *Gloucs* 36 SP0404
Wiggonby *Cumb* 93 NY2952
Wiggonholt *W Susx* 14 TQ0616
Wighill *N York* 83 SE4746
Wighton *Norfk* 66 TF9439
Wigley *Hants* 12 SU3217
Wigmore *H & W* 46 SO4169
Wigmore *Kent* 28 TQ7964
Wigsley *Notts* 76 SK8570
Wigsthorpe *Nhants* 51 TL0482
Wigston *Leics* 50 SP6198
Wigston Fields *Leics* 50 SK6000
Wigston Parva *Leics* 50 SP4689
Wigthorpe *Notts* 75 SK5983
Wigtoft *Lincs* 64 TF2636
Wigton *Cumb* 93 NY2548
Wigtown *D & G* 99 NX4355
Wigtwizzle *S York* 74 SK2495
Wike *W York* 83 SE3342
Wilbarston *Nhants* 51 SP8188
Wilberfoss *Humb* 84 SE7350
Wilburton *Cambs* 53 TL4775
Wilby *Nhants* 51 SP8666
Wilby *Norfk* 54 TM0389
Wilby *Suffk* 55 TM2472
Wilcot *Wilts* 23 SU1360
Wilcrick *Gwent* 34 ST4088
Wilday Green *Derbys* 74 SK3274
Wildboarclough *Ches* 79 SJ9868
Wilden *Beds* 51 TL0955
Wilden *H & W* 60 SO8272
Wildhern *Hants* 23 SU3550
Wildhill *Herts* 39 TL2606
Wildmanbridge *Strath* 116 NS8253
Wildmoor *H & W* 60 SO9575
Wildsworth *Lincs* 75 SK8097
Wilford *Notts* 62 SK5637
Wilkesley *Ches* 71 SJ6241
Wilkhaven *Highld* 147 NH9486
Wilkieston *Fife* 117 NT1268
Wilkin's Green *Herts* 39 TL1907
Wilksby *Lincs* 77 TF2862
Willand *Devon* 9 ST0310
Willards Hill *E Susx* 17 TQ7124
Willaston *Ches* 71 SJ3377
Willaston *Ches* 72 SJ6852
Willcott *Shrops* 59 SJ3718
Willen *Bucks* 38 SP8741
Willenhall *W Mids* 60 SO9798
Willenhall *W Mids* 61 SP3676
Willerby *Humb* 84 TA0230
Willerby *N York* 91 TA0079
Willersey *Gloucs* 48 SP1039
Willersley *H & W* 46 SO3147
Willesborough *Kent* 28 TR0441
Willesborough Lees *Kent* 28 TR0342
Willesden *Gt Lon* 26 TQ2284
Willesleigh *Devon* 19 SS6033
Willesley *Wilts* 35 ST8588
Willett *Somset* 20 ST1033
Willey *Shrops* 60 SO6799
Willey *Warwks* 50 SP4984
Willey Green *Surrey* 25 SU9351
Williamscot *Oxon* 49 SP4845
Williamstown *M Glam* 33 ST0090
Willian *Herts* 39 TL2230
Willingale *Essex* 40 TL5907
Willingdon *E Susx* 16 TQ5902
Willingham *Cambs* 52 TL4070
Willingham *Lincs* 76 SK8784
Willingham Green *Cambs* 53 TL6254
Willington *Beds* 52 TL1150
Willington *Derbys* 73 SK2928
Willington *Dur* 96 NZ1935
Willington *Kent* 28 TQ7853
Willington *Warwks* 48 SP2639
Willington Corner *Ches* 71 SJ5266
Willington Quay *T & W* 103 NZ3267
Willitoft *Humb* 84 SE7434
Williton *Somset* 20 ST0840
Willoughbridge *Staffs* 72 SJ7440
Willoughby *Lincs* 64 TF0537
Willoughby *Lincs* 77 TF4771
Willoughby *Warwks* 50 SP5167
Willoughby Hills *Lincs* 64 TF3545
Willoughby Waterleys *Leics* 50 SP5792
Willoughby-on-the-Wolds *Notts* 63 SK6325
Willoughton *Lincs* 76 SK9293
Willow Green *Ches* 71 SJ6076
Willows Green *Essex* 40 TL7219
Willsbridge *Avon* 35 ST6670
Willsworthy *Devon* 8 SX5381
Willtown *Somset* 21 ST3924
Wilmcote *Warwks* 48 SP1658
Wilmington *Avon* 22 ST6962
Wilmington *Devon* 9 SY2199
Wilmington *E Susx* 16 TQ5404
Wilmington *Kent* 27 TQ5372
Wilmslow *Ches* 79 SJ8481
Wilnecote *Staffs* 61 SK2200
Wilpshire *Lancs* 81 SD6832
Wilsden *W York* 82 SE0936
Wilsford *Lincs* 63 TF0042
Wilsford *Wilts* 23 SU1057
Wilsford *Wilts* 23 SU1339
Wilsham *Devon* 19 SS7548
Wilshaw *W York* 82 SE1109
Wilsill *N York* 89 SE1864
Wilsley Green *Kent* 28 TQ7736
Wilsley Pound *Kent* 28 TQ7837
Wilson *H & W* 46 SO5523
Wilson *Leics* 62 SK4024
Wilsontown *Strath* 116 NS9455
Wilstead *Beds* 38 TL0643
Wilsthorpe *Lincs* 64 TF0913
Wilstone *Herts* 38 SP9014
Wilstone Green *Herts* 38 SP9013
Wilton *Cleve* 97 NZ5819
Wilton *Cumb* 86 NY0311
Wilton *H & W* 46 SO5824
Wilton *N York* 90 SE8582
Wilton *Wilts* 23 SU0931
Wilton *Wilts* 23 SU2661
Wilton Dean *Border* 109 NT4914
Wimbish *Essex* 53 TL5936
Wimbish Green *Essex* 53 TL6035
Wimblebury *Staffs* 60 SK0111
Wimbledon *Gt Lon* 26 TQ2370
Wimblington *Cambs* 65 TL4192
Wimborne Minster *Dorset* 11 SZ0199
Wimborne St. Giles *Dorset* 12 SU0311
Wimbotsham *Norfk* 65 TF6205
Wimpstone *Warwks* 48 SP2148
Wincanton *Somset* 22 ST7128
Winceby *Lincs* 77 TF3268
Wincham *Ches* 79 SJ6775
Winchburgh *Loth* 117 NT0975
Winchcombe *Gloucs* 48 SP0228
Winchelsea *E Susx* 17 TQ9017
Winchelsea Beach *E Susx* 17 TQ9116
Winchester *Hants* 24 SU4829
Winchet Hill *Kent* 28 TQ7340
Winchfield *Hants* 24 SU7654
Winchmore Hill *Bucks* 26 SU9395
Winchmore Hill *Gt Lon* 27 TQ3194
Wincle *Ches* 72 SJ9566
Wincobank *S York* 74 SK3891
Winder *Cumb* 92 NY0417
Windermere *Cumb* 87 SD4098
Winderton *Warwks* 48 SP3240
Windhill *Highld* 139 NH5348
Windlehurst *Gt Man* 79 SJ9586
Windlesham *Surrey* 25 SU9364
Windmill *Cnwll* 4 SW8974
Windmill *Derbys* 74 SK1677
Windmill Hill *E Susx* 16 TQ6412
Windmill Hill *Somset* 10 ST3116
Windrush *Gloucs* 36 SP1913
Windsole *Gramp* 142 NJ5560
Windsor *Berks* 26 SU9576
Windsor Green *Suffk* 54 TL8954
Windsoredge *Gloucs* 35 SO8400
Windy Arbour *Warwks* 61 SP2971
Windy Hill *Clwyd* 71 SJ3054
Windygates *Fife* 118 NO3500
Windyharbour *Ches* 79 SJ8270
Wineham *W Susx* 15 TQ2320
Winestead *Humb* 85 TA2924
Winewall *Lancs* 81 SD9140
Winfarthing *Norfk* 54 TM1085
Winford *Avon* 21 ST5464
Winford *IOW* 13 SZ5584
Winforton *H & W* 46 SO2946
Winfrith Newburgh *Dorset* 11 SY8084
Wing *Bucks* 38 SP8822
Wing *Leics* 63 SK8903
Wingate *Dur* 96 NZ4036
Wingates *Gt Man* 79 SD6507
Wingates *Nthumb* 103 NZ0995
Wingerworth *Derbys* 74 SK3867
Wingfield *Beds* 38 TL0026
Wingfield *Suffk* 55 TM2277
Wingfield *Wilts* 22 ST8256
Wingfield Green *Suffk* 55 TM2177
Wingham *Kent* 29 TR2457
Wingham Well *Kent* 29 TR2356
Wingmore *Kent* 29 TR1946
Wingrave *Bucks* 38 SP8719
Winkburn *Notts* 75 SK7058
Winkfield *Berks* 25 SU9072
Winkfield Row *Berks* 25 SU8971
Winkfield Street *Berks* 25 SU8972
Winkhill *Staffs* 73 SK0651
Winkhurst Green *Kent* 16 TQ4949
Winkleigh *Devon* 19 SS6308
Winksley *N York* 89 SE2571
Winkton *Dorset* 12 SZ1696
Winlaton *T & W* 96 NZ1762
Winlaton Mill *T & W* 96 NZ1860
Winless *Highld* 151 ND3054
Winllan *Powys* 58 SJ2221
Winmarleigh *Lancs* 80 SD4647
Winnall *H & W* 47 SO8167
Winnall *Hants* 24 SU4829
Winnersh *Berks* 25 SU7870
Winnington *Ches* 79 SJ6474
Winscales *Cumb* 92 NY0226
Winscombe *Avon* 21 ST4257
Winsford *Ches* 72 SJ6566
Winsford *Somset* 20 SS9034
Winsham *Devon* 19 SS5038
Winsham *Somset* 10 ST3706
Winshill *Staffs* 73 SK2623
Winshwen *W Glam* 32 SS6896
Winskill *Cumb* 94 NY5834
Winslade *Hants* 24 SU6548
Winsley *Wilts* 22 ST7960
Winslow *Bucks* 49 SP7727
Winslow *Oxon* 36 SU2685
Winson *Gloucs* 36 SP0808
Winsor *Hants* 12 SU3114
Winster *Cumb* 87 SD4193
Winster *Derbys* 74 SK2460
Winston *Dur* 96 NZ1416
Winston *Suffk* 54 TM1861
Winston Green *Suffk* 54 TM1761
Winstone *Gloucs* 35 SO9509
Winswell *Devon* 18 SS4913
Winterborne Came *Dorset* 11 SY7088
Winterborne Clenston *Dorset* 11 ST8303
Winterborne Herringston *Dorset* 11 SY6888
Winterborne Houghton *Dorset* 11 ST8204
Winterborne Kingston *Dorset* 11 SY8697
Winterborne Monkton *Dorset* 11 SY6787
Winterborne Stickland *Dorset* 11 ST8304
Winterborne Tomson *Dorset* 11 SY8897
Winterborne Whitechurch *Dorset* 11 ST8300
Winterborne Zelston *Dorset* 11 SY8997
Winterbourne *Avon* 35 ST6480
Winterbourne *Berks* 24 SU4572
Winterbourne Abbas *Dorset* 10 SY6190
Winterbourne Bassett *Wilts* 36 SU0974
Winterbourne Dauntsey *Wilts* 23 SU1734
Winterbourne Earls *Wilts* 23 SU1734
Winterbourne Gunner *Wilts* 23 SU1735
Winterbourne Monkton *Wilts* 36 SU0971
Winterbourne Steepleton *Dorset* 10 SY6289
Winterbourne Stoke *Wilts* 23 SU0741
Winterbrook *Oxon* 37 SU6088
Winterburn *N York* 88 SD9358
Winteringham *Humb* 84 SE9221
Winterley *Ches* 72 SJ7457
Wintersett *W York* 83 SE3815
Winterslow *Wilts* 23 SU2332
Winterton *Humb* 84 SE9218
Winterton-on-Sea *Norfk* 67 TG4919
Winthorpe *Lincs* 77 TF5665
Winthorpe *Notts* 75 SK8156
Winton *Cumb* 88 NY7810
Winton *Dorset* 12 SZ0893
Winton *E Susx* 16 TQ5103
Winton *N York* 89 SE4196
Wintringham *N York* 90 SE8873
Winwick *Cambs* 51 TL1080
Winwick *Ches* 78 SJ6092
Winwick *Nhants* 50 SP6273
Wirksworth *Derbys* 73 SK2854
Wirswall *Ches* 71 SJ5444
Wisbech *Cambs* 65 TF4609
Wisbech St. Mary *Cambs* 65 TF4208
Wisborough Green *W Susx* 14 TQ0525
Wiseman's Bridge *Dyfed* 31 SN1406
Wiseton *Notts* 75 SK7189
Wishanger *Gloucs* 35 SO9109
Wishaw *Strath* 116 NS7955
Wishaw *Warwks* 61 SP1794
Wisley *Surrey* 26 TQ0659
Wispington *Lincs* 76 TF2071
Wissenden *Kent* 28 TQ9041
Wissett *Suffk* 55 TM3679
Wissington *Suffk* 40 TL9533
Wistanstow *Shrops* 59 SO4385
Wistanswick *Shrops* 72 SJ6629
Wistaston *Ches* 72 SJ6853
Wistaston Green *Ches* 72 SJ6854
Wisterfield *Ches* 79 SJ8371
Wiston *Dyfed* 30 SN0218
Wiston *Strath* 108 NS9532
Wiston *W Susx* 15 TQ1512
Wistow *Cambs* 52 TL2780
Wistow *N York* 83 SE5935
Wiswell *Lancs* 81 SD7437
Witby Mills *Avon* 22 ST6657

Witcham Wyville

Witcham *Cambs* 53 TL4680
Witchampton *Dorset* 11 ST9806
Witchford *Cambs* 53 TL5078
Witcombe *Somset* 21 ST4721
Witham *Essex* 40 TL8214
Witham Friary *Somset* 22 ST7441
Witham on the Hill *Lincs* 64 TF0516
Withcall *Lincs* 77 TF2883
Withdean *E Susx* 15 TQ3007
Witherenden Hill *E Susx* 16 TQ6426
Witheridge *Devon* 19 SS8014
Witherley *Leics* 61 SP3297
Withern *Lincs* 77 TF4282
Withernsea *Humb* 85 TA3427
Withernwick *Humb* 85 TA1940
Withersdale Street *Suffk* 55 TM2680
Withersfield *Essex* 53 TL6548
Witherslack *Cumb* 87 SD4384
Witherslack Hall *Cumb* 87 SD4385
Withiel *Cnwll* 4 SW9965
Withiel Florey *Somset* 20 SS9833
Withielgoose *Cnwll* 4 SX0065
Withington *Ches* 79 SJ8169
Withington *Gloucs* 35 SP0215
Withington *Gt Man* 79 SJ8492
Withington *H & W* 46 SO5643
Withington *Shrops* 59 SJ5713
Withington *Staffs* 73 SK0335
Withington Green *Ches* 79 SJ8071
Withleigh *Devon* 9 SS9012
Withnell *Lancs* 81 SD6322
Withybed Green *H & W* 60 SP0172
Withybrook *Warwks* 50 SP4383
Withycombe *Somset* 20 ST0141
Withyditch *Avon* 22 ST6959
Withyham *E Susx* 16 TQ4935
Withypool *Devon* 19 SS8435
Witley *Surrey* 25 SU9439
Witnesham *Suffk* 54 TM1751
Witney *Oxon* 36 SP3510
Wittering *Cambs* 64 TF0502
Wittersham *Kent* 17 TQ9027
Witton *H & W* 47 SO8962
Witton *Norfk* 67 TG3109
Witton *Norfk* 67 TG3331
Witton Gilbert *Dur* 96 NZ2345
Witton Green *Norfk* 67 TG4102
Witton le Wear *Dur* 96 NZ1431
Witton Park *Dur* 96 NZ1730
Wiveliscombe *Somset* 20 ST0827
Wivelrod *Hants* 24 SU6738
Wivelsfield *E Susx* 15 TQ3420
Wivelsfield Green *E Susx* 15 TQ3519
Wivelsfield Station *W Susx* 15 TQ3219
Wivenhoe *Essex* 41 TM0321
Wivenhoe Cross *Essex* 41 TM0423
Wiveton *Norfk* 66 TG0442
Wix *Essex* 41 TM1628
Wix Green *Essex* 41 TM1728
Wixford *Warwks* 48 SP0854
Wixhill *Shrops* 59 SJ5528
Wixoe *Essex* 53 TL7143
Woburn *Beds* 38 SP9433
Woburn Sands *Bucks* 38 SP9235
Wokefield Park *Berks* 24 SU6765
Woking *Surrey* 25 TQ0058
Wokingham *Berks* 25 SU8168
Wolborough *Devon* 7 SX8570
Wold Newton *Humb* 91 TA0473
Wold Newton *Humb* 77 TF2496
Woldingham *Surrey* 27 TQ3755
Wolf Hills *Nthumb* 94 NY7258
Wolf's Castle *Dyfed* 30 SM9526
Wolfclyde *Strath* 108 NT0236
Wolferlow *H & W* 47 SO6661
Wolferton *Norfk* 65 TF6528
Wolfhampcote *Warwks* 50 SP5265
Wolfhill *Tays* 126 NO1533
Wolfsdale *Dyfed* 30 SM9321
Wollaston *Nhants* 51 SP9062
Wollaston *Shrops* 59 SJ3212
Wollaton *Notts* 62 SK5239
Wollerton *Shrops* 59 SJ6130
Wollescote *W Mids* 60 SO9283
Wolseley *Staffs* 73 SK0220
Wolsingham *Dur* 95 NZ0737
Wolstanton *Staffs* 72 SJ8548
Wolstenholme *Gt Man* 81 SD8414
Wolston *Warwks* 50 SP4175
Wolsty *Cumb* 92 NY1050
Wolvercote *Oxon* 37 SP4910
Wolverhampton *W Mids* 60 SO9198
Wolverley *H & W* 60 SO8379
Wolverley *Shrops* 59 SJ4731
Wolverton *Bucks* 38 SP8141
Wolverton *Hants* 24 SU5558
Wolverton *Kent* 29 TR2642
Wolverton *Warwks* 48 SP2062
Wolverton *Wilts* 22 ST7831
Wolverton Common *Hants* 24 SU5659
Wolvesnewton *Gwent* 34 ST4599
Wolvey *Warwks* 50 SP4387
Wolvey Heath *Warwks* 50 SP4388
Wolviston *Cleve* 97 NZ4525
Wombleton *N York* 90 SE6683
Wombourne *Staffs* 60 SO8793
Wombwell *S York* 83 SE4002
Womenswold *Kent* 29 TR2250
Womersley *N York* 83 SE5319
Wonastow *Gwent* 34 SO4810
Wonersh *Surrey* 14 TQ0145
Wonford *Devon* 9 SX9491
Wonson *Devon* 8 SX6789
Wonston *Hants* 24 SU4739
Wooburn *Bucks* 26 SU9087
Wooburn Green *Bucks* 26 SU9188
Wooburn Moor *Bucks* 26 SU9189
Wood Bevington *Warwks* 48 SP0554
Wood Burcot *Nhants* 49 SP6946
Wood Dalling *Norfk* 66 TG0827
Wood Eaton *Staffs* 72 SJ8417
Wood End *Beds* 38 TL0046
Wood End *Beds* 51 TL0866
Wood End *Cambs* 52 TL3675
Wood End *Gt Lon* 26 TQ1385
Wood End *Herts* 39 TL3225
Wood End *W Mids* 60 SJ9400
Wood End *Warwks* 61 SP1171
Wood End *Warwks* 61 SP2498
Wood End *Warwks* 61 SP2987
Wood Enderby *Lincs* 77 TF2764
Wood Green *Gt Lon* 27 TQ3090
Wood Hayes *W Mids* 60 SJ9402
Wood Lane *Shrops* 59 SJ4132
Wood Lane *Staffs* 72 SJ8149
Wood Norton *Norfk* 66 TG0127
Wood Row *W York* 83 SE3827
Wood Street *Norfk* 67 TG3722
Wood Street *Surrey* 25 SU9550
Wood Top *Lancs* 81 SD5643
Wood Walton *Cambs* 52 TL2180
Wood's Corner *E Susx* 16 TQ6619
Wood's Green *E Susx* 16 TQ6333
Woodale *N York* 88 SE0279
Woodall *S York* 75 SK4880
Woodbastwick *Norfk* 67 TG3315
Woodbeck *Notts* 75 SK7777
Woodborough *Notts* 63 SK6347
Woodborough *Wilts* 23 SU1159
Woodbridge *Dorset* 22 ST8518
Woodbridge *Suffk* 55 TM2649
Woodbury *Devon* 9 SY0087
Woodbury Salterton *Devon* 9 SY0189
Woodchester *Gloucs* 35 SO8302
Woodchurch *Kent* 17 TQ9434
Woodchurch *Mersyd* 78 SJ2786
Woodcombe *Somset* 20 SS9546
Woodcote *Oxon* 37 SU6482
Woodcote *Shrops* 72 SJ7615
Woodcote Green *H & W* 60 SO9172
Woodcott *Hants* 24 SU4354
Woodcroft *Gloucs* 34 ST5495
Woodcutts *Dorset* 11 ST9717
Woodditton *Cambs* 53 TL6559
Woodeaton *Oxon* 37 SP5312
Woodend *Highld* 130 NM7861
Woodend *Loth* 116 NS9269
Woodend *Nhants* 49 SP6149
Woodend *Staffs* 73 SK1726
Woodend *W Susx* 14 SU8108
Woodend Green *Essex* 39 TL5528
Woodfalls *Wilts* 12 SU1920
Woodford *Devon* 7 SX7950
Woodford *Gloucs* 35 ST6995
Woodford *Gt Man* 79 SJ8882
Woodford *Nhants* 51 SP9676
Woodford Bridge *Gt Lon* 27 TQ4291
Woodford Halse *Nhants* 49 SP5452
Woodford Wells *Gt Lon* 27 TQ4092
Woodgate *Devon* 9 ST1015
Woodgate *H & W* 47 SO9666
Woodgate *Norfk* 66 TF8915
Woodgate *Norfk* 66 TG0215
Woodgate *W Mids* 60 SO9982
Woodgate *W Susx* 14 SU9304
Woodgreen *Hants* 12 SU1717
Woodgreen *Oxon* 36 SP3610
Woodhall *N York* 88 SD9790
Woodhall Hill *W York* 82 SE2035
Woodhall Spa *Lincs* 76 TF1963
Woodham *Bucks* 37 SP7018
Woodham *Dur* 96 NZ2826
Woodham *Lincs* 76 TF2267
Woodham Ferrers *Essex* 40 TQ7999
Woodham Mortimer *Essex* 40 TL8104
Woodham Walter *Essex* 40 TL8007
Woodhaven *Fife* 126 NO4126
Woodhead *Gramp* 142 NJ7838
Woodhill *Somset* 21 ST3527
Woodhorn *Nthumb* 103 NZ2988
Woodhorn Demesne *Nthumb* 103 NZ3088
Woodhouse *Leics* 62 SK5314
Woodhouse *S York* 74 SK4284
Woodhouse *W York* 82 SE2935
Woodhouse *W York* 83 SE3821
Woodhouse Eaves *Leics* 62 SK5214
Woodhouse Green *Staffs* 72 SJ9162
Woodhouse Mill *S York* 75 SK4385
Woodhouselee *Loth* 117 NT2364
Woodhouselees *D & G* 101 NY3975
Woodhouses *Cumb* 93 NY3252
Woodhouses *Gt Man* 79 SD9100
Woodhouses *Staffs* 61 SK0709
Woodhouses *Staffs* 73 SK1518
Woodhuish *Devon* 7 SX9152
Woodhurst *Cambs* 52 TL3176
Woodingdean *E Susx* 15 TQ3505
Woodkirk *W York* 82 SE2725
Woodland *Devon* 7 SX7968
Woodland *Dur* 95 NZ0726
Woodland *Gramp* 143 NJ8723
Woodland *Kent* 29 TR1441
Woodland *Strath* 106 NX1795
Woodland Head *Devon* 8 SX7796
Woodland Street *Somset* 21 ST5337
Woodland View *S York* 74 SK3188
Woodlands *Dorset* 12 SU0509
Woodlands *Gramp* 135 NO7895
Woodlands *Hants* 12 SU3211
Woodlands *Kent* 27 TQ5660
Woodlands *N York* 83 SE3254
Woodlands *S York* 83 SE5308
Woodlands Park *Berks* 26 SU8678
Woodlands St. Mary *Berks* 36 SU3375
Woodleigh *Devon* 7 SX7349
Woodlesford *W York* 83 SE3629
Woodley *Berks* 25 SU7773
Woodley *Gt Man* 79 SJ9392
Woodley Green *Berks* 26 SU8480
Woodmancote *Gloucs* 47 SO9727
Woodmancote *Gloucs* 35 SP0008
Woodmancote *Gloucs* 35 ST7597
Woodmancote *H & W* 47 SO9142
Woodmancote *W Susx* 14 SU7707
Woodmancote *W Susx* 15 TQ2314
Woodmancott *Hants* 24 SU5642
Woodmansey *Humb* 84 TA0538
Woodmansgreen *W Susx* 14 SU8627
Woodmansterne *Surrey* 27 TQ2759
Woodmarsh *Wilts* 22 ST8555
Woodmill *Staffs* 73 SK1320
Woodminton *Wilts* 22 SU0022
Woodnesborough *Kent* 29 TR3157
Woodnewton *Nhants* 51 TL0394
Woodnook *Notts* 75 SK4752
Woodplumpton *Lancs* 80 SD4934
Woodrising *Norfk* 66 TF9803
Woodrow *H & W* 60 SO8974
Woodseaves *Shrops* 72 SJ6831
Woodseaves *Staffs* 72 SJ7925
Woodsend *Wilts* 36 SU2176
Woodsetts *S York* 75 SK5483
Woodsford *Dorset* 11 SY7590
Woodside *Berks* 25 SU9371
Woodside *Cumb* 92 NY0434
Woodside *Essex* 39 TL4704
Woodside *Fife* 127 NO4207
Woodside *Gt Lon* 27 TQ3467
Woodside *Hants* 12 SZ3294
Woodside *Herts* 39 TL2406
Woodside *Tays* 126 NO2037
Woodside Green *Kent* 28 TQ9053
Woodstock *Dyfed* 30 SN0325
Woodstock *Oxon* 37 SP4416
Woodston *Cambs* 64 TL1897
Woodthorpe *Derbys* 75 SK4574
Woodthorpe *Leics* 62 SK5417
Woodthorpe *Lincs* 77 TF4380
Woodton *Norfk* 67 TM2994
Woodtown *Devon* 18 SS4123
Woodvale *Mersyd* 78 SD3010
Woodville *Derbys* 62 SK3118
Woodwall Green *Staffs* 72 SJ7831
Woody Bay *Devon* 19 SS6748
Woodyates *Dorset* 12 SU0219
Woofferton *Shrops* 46 SO5268
Wookey *Somset* 21 ST5145
Wookey Hole *Somset* 21 ST5347
Wool *Dorset* 11 SY8486
Woolacombe *Devon* 18 SS4643
Woolage Green *Kent* 29 TR2349
Woolaston *Gloucs* 34 ST5899
Woolaston Common *Gloucs* 34 SO5801
Woolavington *Somset* 21 ST3441
Woolbeding *W Susx* 14 SU8722
Woolcotts *Somset* 20 SS9631
Wooldale *W York* 82 SE1508
Wooler *Nthumb* 111 NT9927
Wooley Bridge *Derbys* 79 SK0194
Woolfardisworthy *Devon* 18 SS3321
Woolfardisworthy *Devon* 19 SS8208
Woolfold *Gt Man* 81 SD7811
Woolfords *Strath* 117 NT0056
Woolhampton *Berks* 24 SU5766
Woolhanger *Devon* 19 SS6945
Woolhope *H & W* 46 SO6135
Woolland *Dorset* 11 ST7707
Woollard *Avon* 21 ST6364
Woollensbrook *Herts* 39 TL3609
Woolley *Avon* 22 ST7468
Woolley *Cambs* 52 TL1574
Woolley *Cnwll* 18 SS2516
Woolley *Derbys* 74 SK3760
Woolley *W York* 83 SE3212
Woolmer Green *Herts* 39 TL2518
Woolmere Green *H & W* 47 SO9663
Woolmerston *Somset* 20 ST2833
Woolminstone *Somset* 10 ST4108
Woolpack *Kent* 28 TQ8537
Woolpit *Suffk* 54 TL9762
Woolpit Green *Suffk* 54 TL9761
Woolscott *Warwks* 50 SP5068
Woolsgrove *Devon* 8 SS7902
Woolsington *T & W* 103 NZ1870
Woolstaston *Shrops* 59 SO4598
Woolsthorpe *Lincs* 63 SK8333
Woolsthorpe *Lincs* 63 SK9224
Woolston *Ches* 79 SJ6489
Woolston *Devon* 7 SX7141
Woolston *Devon* 7 SX7150
Woolston *Hants* 13 SU4310
Woolston *Shrops* 59 SJ3224
Woolston *Shrops* 59 SO4287
Woolston *Somset* 20 ST0939
Woolston *Somset* 21 ST6527
Woolston Green *Devon* 7 SX7766
Woolstone *Bucks* 38 SP8738
Woolstone *Gloucs* 47 SO9630
Woolstone *Oxon* 36 SU2987
Woolton *Mersyd* 78 SJ4286
Woolton Hill *Hants* 24 SU4361
Woolverstone *Suffk* 54 TM1738
Woolverton *Somset* 22 ST7953
Woolwich *Gt Lon* 27 TQ4478
Woonton *H & W* 46 SO3552
Wooperton *Nthumb* 111 NU0420
Woore *Shrops* 72 SJ7342
Wootten Breadmead *Beds* 38 TL0243
Wootten Green *Suffk* 55 TM2372
Wootton *Beds* 38 TL0044
Wootton *H & W* 46 SO3252
Wootton *Hants* 12 SZ2498
Wootton *Humb* 85 TA0815
Wootton *IOW* 13 SZ5392
Wootton *Kent* 29 TR2246
Wootton *Nhants* 49 SP7656
Wootton *Oxon* 37 SP4419
Wootton *Oxon* 37 SP4701
Wootton *Shrops* 59 SJ3327
Wootton *Staffs* 72 SJ8227
Wootton *Staffs* 73 SK1044
Wootton Bassett *Wilts* 36 SU0682
Wootton Bridge *IOW* 13 SZ5492
Wootton Common *IOW* 13 SZ5391
Wootton Courtenay *Somset* 20 SS9343
Wootton Fitzpaine *Dorset* 10 SY3695
Wootton Rivers *Wilts* 23 SU1962
Wootton St. Lawrence *Hants* 24 SU5953
Wootton Wawen *Warwks* 48 SP1563
Worbarrow *Dorset* 11 SY8779
Worcester *H & W* 47 SO8554
Worcester Park *Gt Lon* 26 TQ2165
Wordsley *W Mids* 60 SO8987
Worfield *Shrops* 60 SO7595
Worgret *Dorset* 11 SY9087
Workington *Cumb* 92 NY0028
Worksop *Notts* 75 SK5879
Worlaby *Humb* 84 TA0113
Worlaby *Lincs* 77 TF3476
World's End *Berks* 37 SU4877
Worlds End *Bucks* 38 SP8509
Worlds End *Hants* 13 SU6311
Worlds End *W Susx* 15 TQ3220
Worle *Avon* 21 ST3562
Worleston *Ches* 72 SJ6556
Worlingham *Suffk* 55 TM4489
Worlington *Devon* 19 SS7713
Worlington *Suffk* 53 TL6973
Worlingworth *Suffk* 55 TM2368
Wormald Green *N York* 89 SE3065
Wormbridge *H & W* 46 SO4230
Wormegay *Norfk* 65 TF6611
Wormelow Tump *H & W* 46 SO4930
Wormhill *Derbys* 74 SK1274
Wormhill *H & W* 46 SO4239
Wormingford *Essex* 40 TL9332
Worminghall *Bucks* 37 SP6308
Wormington *Gloucs* 48 SP0336
Worminster *Somset* 21 ST5743
Wormiston *Border* 117 NT2345
Wormit *Tays* 126 NO4026
Wormleighton *Warwks* 49 SP4553
Wormley *Herts* 39 TL3605
Wormley *Surrey* 25 SU9438
Wormley Hill *S York* 83 SE6616
Wormleybury *Herts* 39 TL3506
Wormshill *Kent* 28 TQ8857
Wormsley *H & W* 46 SO4247
Worplesdon *Surrey* 25 SU9753
Worrall *S York* 74 SK3092
Worrall Hill *Gloucs* 34 SO6014
Worsbrough *S York* 83 SE3602
Worsbrough Bridge *S York* 83 SE3503
Worsbrough Dale *S York* 83 SE3604
Worsley *Gt Man* 79 SD7500
Worsley Mesnes *Gt Man* 78 SD5703
Worstead *Norfk* 67 TG3025
Worsthorne *Lancs* 81 SD8732
Worston *Devon* 6 SX5953
Worston *Lancs* 81 SD7742
Worth *Kent* 29 TR3355
Worth *Somset* 21 ST5144
Worth *W Susx* 15 TQ3036
Worth Abbey *Surrey* 15 TQ3134
Worth Matravers *Dorset* 11 SY9777
Wortham *Suffk* 54 TM0877
Worthen *Shrops* 59 SJ3204
Worthenbury *Clwyd* 71 SJ4146
Worthing *Norfk* 66 TF9919
Worthing *W Susx* 15 TQ1403
Worthington *Leics* 62 SK4020
Worthybrook *Gwent* 34 SO4711
Worting *Hants* 24 SU5952
Wortley *S York* 74 SK3099
Wortley *W York* 82 SE2732
Worton *N York* 88 SD9589
Worton *Wilts* 22 ST9757
Wortwell *Norfk* 55 TM2784
Wotherton *Shrops* 58 SJ2800
Wothorpe *Cambs* 64 TF0205
Wotter *Devon* 6 SX5661
Wotton *Surrey* 14 TQ1247
Wotton Underwood *Bucks* 37 SP6815
Wotton-under-Edge *Gloucs* 35 ST7593
Woughton on the Green *Bucks* 38 SP8737
Wouldham *Kent* 28 TQ7164
Woundale *Shrops* 60 SO7793
Wrabness *Essex* 41 TM1731
Wrafton *Devon* 18 SS4935
Wragby *Lincs* 76 TF1378
Wragby *W York* 83 SE4116
Wramplingham *Norfk* 66 TG1106
Wrangaton *Devon* 7 SX6758
Wrangbrook *W York* 83 SE4913
Wrangle *Lincs* 77 TF4250
Wrangle Common *Lincs* 77 TF4253
Wrangle Lowgate *Lincs* 77 TF4451
Wrangway *Somset* 20 ST1218
Wrantage *Somset* 20 ST3022
Wrawby *Humb* 84 TA0108
Wraxall *Avon* 34 ST4971
Wraxall *Somset* 21 ST6036
Wray *Lancs* 87 SD6067
Wray Castle *Cumb* 87 NY3700
Wraysbury *Berks* 25 TQ0074
Wrayton *Lancs* 87 SD6172
Wrea Green *Lancs* 80 SD3931
Wreaks End *Cumb* 86 SD2286
Wreay *Cumb* 93 NY4348
Wreay *Cumb* 93 NY4423
Wrecclesham *Surrey* 25 SU8244
Wrekenton *T & W* 96 NZ2759
Wrelton *N York* 90 SE7686
Wrenbury *Ches* 71 SJ5947
Wrench Green *N York* 91 SE9689
Wreningham *Norfk* 66 TM1698
Wrentham *Suffk* 55 TM4982
Wrenthorpe *W York* 82 SE3122
Wrentnall *Shrops* 59 SJ4203
Wressle *Humb* 84 SE7131
Wressle *Humb* 84 SE9709
Wrestlingworth *Beds* 52 TL2547
Wretton *Norfk* 65 TF6900
Wrexham *Clwyd* 71 SJ3350
Wribbenhall *H & W* 60 SO7975
Wrickton *Shrops* 59 SO6486
Wright's Green *Essex* 39 TL5017
Wrightington Bar *Lancs* 80 SD5313
Wrinehill *Staffs* 72 SJ7547
Wrington *Avon* 21 ST4762
Wringworthy *Cnwll* 5 SX2658
Writhlington *Somset* 22 ST6954
Writtle *Essex* 40 TL6706
Wrockwardine *Shrops* 59 SJ6212
Wroot *Humb* 84 SE7103
Wrose *W York* 82 SE1636
Wrotham *Kent* 27 TQ6158
Wrotham Heath *Kent* 27 TQ6357
Wrottesley *Staffs* 60 SJ8200
Wroughton *Wilts* 36 SU1480
Wroxall *IOW* 13 SZ5579
Wroxall *Warwks* 61 SP2271
Wroxeter *Shrops* 59 SJ5608
Wroxham *Norfk* 67 TG3017
Wroxton *Oxon* 49 SP4141
Wyaston *Derbys* 73 SK1842
Wyatt's Green *Essex* 40 TQ5999
Wyberton *Lincs* 64 TF3240
Wyboston *Beds* 52 TL1656
Wybunbury *Ches* 72 SJ6949
Wych *Dorset* 10 SY4791
Wych Cross *E Susx* 15 TQ4131
Wychbold *H & W* 47 SO9266
Wychnor *Staffs* 73 SK1715
Wyck *Hants* 24 SU7539
Wycliffe *Dur* 95 NZ1114
Wycoller *Lancs* 81 SD9339
Wycomb *Leics* 63 SK7724
Wycombe Marsh *Bucks* 26 SU8892
Wyddial *Herts* 39 TL3731
Wye *Kent* 28 TR0546
Wyesham *Gwent* 34 SO5211
Wyfordby *Leics* 63 SK7918
Wyke *Devon* 9 SX8799
Wyke *Devon* 10 SY2996
Wyke *Dorset* 22 ST7926
Wyke *Shrops* 59 SJ6402
Wyke *Surrey* 25 SU9251
Wyke *W York* 82 SE1526
Wyke Champflower *Somset* 22 ST6634
Wyke Regis *Dorset* 11 SY6677
Wykeham *N York* 90 SE8175
Wykeham *N York* 91 SE9683
Wyken *Shrops* 60 SO7695
Wyken *W Mids* 61 SP3780
Wykey *Shrops* 59 SJ3824
Wykin *Leics* 61 SP4095
Wylam *Nthumb* 103 NZ1164
Wylde Green *W Mids* 61 SP1294
Wylye *Wilts* 22 SU0037
Wymeswold *Leics* 62 SK6023
Wymington *Beds* 51 SP9564
Wymondham *Leics* 63 SK8418
Wymondham *Norfk* 66 TG1001
Wyndham *M Glam* 33 SS9392
Wynds Point *H & W* 47 SO7640
Wynford Eagle *Dorset* 10 SY5896
Wyre Piddle *H & W* 47 SO9647
Wysall *Notts* 62 SK6027
Wyson *H & W* 46 SO5267
Wythall *H & W* 61 SP0774
Wytham *Oxon* 37 SP4708
Wythburn *Cumb* 93 NY3214
Wythenshawe *Gt Man* 79 SJ8386
Wythop Mill *Cumb* 92 NY1729
Wyton *Cambs* 52 TL2772
Wyton *Humb* 85 TA1733
Wyverstone *Suffk* 54 TM0468
Wyverstone Street *Suffk* 54 TM0367
Wyville *Lincs* 63 SK8729

DON'T GET CAUGHT IN A TRAFFIC JAM...

find out where the hold-ups are before you start your journey

Ring the AA's famous ROADWATCH service for the very latest reports on traffic conditions throughout Britain.

Dial 0336-401 followed by the 3 digits for the appropriate area. (See maps below).

NATIONAL TRAFFIC ROADWORKS AND WEATHER

Wherever you are driving call the AA's ROADWATCH service for the latest traffic reports.

AA Roadwatch

LONDON AND SOUTH-EAST TRAFFIC, ROADWORKS AND WEATHER

If you are driving in the London and South-eastern areas phone before you go and save yourself time and frustration.

For a report on the M25 ORBITAL dial **0336-401 127**

National Motorway Network report dial **0336-401 110**

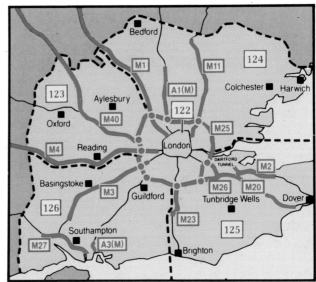

CONTINENTAL ROADWATCH
Regularly updated 24 hours a day.

Road conditions to and from Ferry Ports
Ferry news and adverse Continental weather   **0336-401 904**

For copies of the full AA Directory of Recorded Information please call 0256 491648

Calls are charged at 36p per minute cheap rate, 48p per minute at all other times